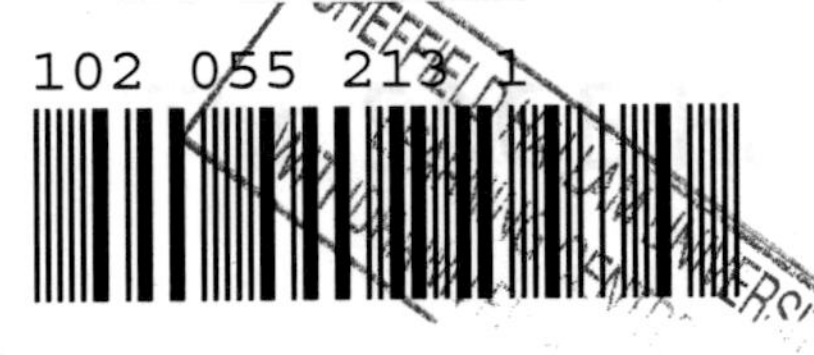

dbook of

Architectural Theory

The SAGE Handbook of
Architectural Theory

Edited by
C. Greig Crysler,
Stephen Cairns
and Hilde Heynen

Los Angeles | London | New Delhi
Singapore | Washington DC

First published 2012

This paperback edition first printed 2013

SAGE Publications Ltd
1 Oliver's Yard
55 City Road
London EC1Y 1SP

SAGE Publications Inc.
2455 Teller Road
Thousand Oaks, California 91320

SAGE Publications India Pvt Ltd
B 1/I 1 Mohan Cooperative Industrial Area
Mathura Road, Post Bag 7
New Delhi 110 044

SAGE Publications Asia-Pacific Pte Ltd
3 Church Street
#10-04 Samsung Hub
Singapore 049483

Library of Congress Control Number: 2010942920

British Library Cataloguing in Publication data

A catalogue record for this book is available from the British Library

ISBN 978-1-4129-4613-1
ISBN 978-1-4462-8263-2 (pbk)

Typeset by Cenveo Publisher Services
Printed and bound by CPI Group (UK) Ltd, Croydon, CR0 4YY
Printed on paper from sustainable resources

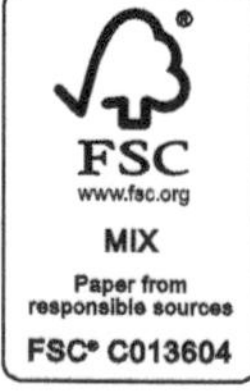

Contents

List of Contributors

Stefan Al is Director of the Urban Design Programme at the University of Hong Kong. He has edited the book *Factory Towns of South China*, and is currently writing a book on the Las Vegas Strip. As a practicing architect he worked on the 612-meter high Canton Tower. Al holds a M.Sc. in Architecture from Delft University of Technology, an M.Arch. from the Bartlett UCL, and a Ph.D. in City and Regional Planning from UC Berkeley.

M. Christine Boyer is the William R. Kenan Jr. Professor of Architecture and Urbanism, at the School of Architecture, Princeton University. She is the author of *Le Corbusier, Homme de Lettres* (Princeton Architecture Press, 2011), *CyberCities: Visual Perception in the Age of Electronic Communication* (Princeton Architectural Press, 1996), *The City of Collective Memory: Its Historical Imagery and Architectural Entertainments* (MIT Press, 1994), *Manhattan Manners: Architecture and Style 1850–1890* (Rizzoli, 1985) and *Dreaming the Rational City: the Myth of City Planning 1890–1945* (MIT Press, 1983). In addition, she has written many articles and lectured widely on the topic of urbanism in the 19th and 20th centuries. M. Christine Boyer received her Ph.D. and Master of City Planning from Massachusetts Institute of Technology. She also holds a Master of Science in Computer and Information Science from the Moore School of Electrical Engineering at the University of Pennsylvania.

Robert Brown is Professor of Architecture and Head of Architecture at Plymouth University, UK. He has over 20 years of experience in professional practice, having worked in urban regeneration and community development in the UK, USA, Africa and India. Recent publications include articles in *Traditional Settlements and Dwellings Review* (2011) and *Open House International* (2011), and with Daniel Maudlin he is editor of the forthcoming special issue of the *Journal of Architecture* 'Intentionally Incomplete'.

Stephen Cairns is Professor of Architecture and Urbanism at the University of Edinburgh. He is also the Scientific Co-ordinator of the Future Cities Laboratory, a research initiative of ETH Zurich and the National Research Foundation of Singapore focused on urban sustainability in a global frame.

Jiat-Hwee Chang, Ph.D. (UC Berkeley), is Assistant Professor at the Department of Architecture, National University of Singapore. He has researched and published on colonial and postcolonial architectural history, socio-technical dimensions of sustainable architecture and design culture in Asia. He is the co-editor of *Non West Modernist Past* (World Scientific, 2011) and a special issue of *Singapore Journal of Tropical Geography* on "tropical spatialities" (2011).

C. Greig Crysler is an Associate Professor in the Department of Architecture at the College of Environmental Design at UC Berkeley, where he teaches courses in design theory and criticism. His research interests include architecture and activism; globalization and the built environment; and the changing relationship between museums, memorials and citizenship. His first book, *Writing Spaces: Discourses of Architecture, Urbanism and the Built Environment, 1960–2000*, was published by Routledge in 2003.

Dana Cuff is a professor, author, and practitioner in architecture at the University of California, Los Angeles where she is also the founding Director of cityLAB, a think tank that explores design innovations in the emerging metropolis (www.cityLAB.aud.ucla.edu). Since receiving her Ph.D. in architecture from Berkeley, Cuff has published and lectured widely about modern American urbanism, the architectural profession, affordable housing and spatially embedded computing.

Fernando Diez is Professor at Universidad de Palermo, Buenos Aires. He graduated as an architect from Belgrano University (1979), and as Doctor in Architecture UFRGS, Brazil (2005). He is the Editorial Director of the journal *Summa+*. He is member of the Argentine Academy of Environmental Sciences, adviser for the National University Accreditation Council and government and public institutions. He is author of several books, among them *Crisis de Autenticidad* (2008), and is contributor on environmental issues to the op-ed section of *La Nación* newspaper in Buenos Aires.

Peter Droege, Professor and Chair of Sustainable Spatial Development, University of Liechtenstein taught at MIT, Tokyo and Sydney. A key member of many international policy and research bodies, he has edited and authored *Intelligent Environments* (Elsevier, 1998), *The Renewable City* (Wiley, 2006), *Urban Energy Transition* (Elsevier, 2008), *100 Percent Renewable – Energy Autonomy in Action* (Earthscan, 2009) and *Climate Design* (ORO Editions, 2010). He is founding chair of the Liechtenstein Congress for Sustainable Development and Responsible Investing.

Ole W. Fischer is an architect, theoretician, historian and curator. Currently he serves as Assistant Professor for history theory at the University of Utah. Previously he has conducted research and taught at ETH Zurich, Harvard GSD, MIT and RISD. He is co-editor of *Precisions – Architecture between Sciences and the Arts* (Jovis, 2008), as well as *Sehnsucht – a Book of Architectural Longings* (Springer, 2010) and wrote the forthcoming *Nietzsches Schatten* (Gebr. Mann, 2011).

Todd Gannon is a registered architect and writer based in Los Angeles. He teaches history, theory and design studio at the Southern California Institute of Architecture, where he also coordinates the Cultural Studies curriculum. His published books include *The Light Construction Reader* and monographs on the work of Morphosis, Bernard Tschumi, UN Studio, Steven Holl, Mack Scogin/Merrill Elam, Zaha Hadid and Peter Eisenman.

Arie Graafland is Antoni van Leeuwenhoek Professor in Architectural Theory at the Tu-Delft. He has been visiting professor in Tokyo and Budapest and is Head of the Delft School of Design. He has lectured internationally and published extensively in the areas of architecture and urban theory. He is the author of books such as *Architectural Bodies* (1996) and *The Socius of Architecture* (2000). He is the editor of The Delft School of Design Series on Architecture and Urbanism with 010 Publishers. Together with Harry Kerssen he is principal of Kerssen Graafland Architects in Amsterdam.

Simon Guy is Professor of Architecture, Director of the Manchester Architecture Research Centre and Head of the School of Environment and Development at the University of Manchester, UK. His research explores the co-evolution of design and development strategies and socio-technical-ecological processes that mediate urban futures. His work engages with interdisciplinary approaches to sustainable urbanism, engaging with changing forms of architectural knowledge and practice and specifically with debates about buildings, networks and cities across diverse geographies.

Jonathan Hale is an architect, Associate Professor and Reader in Architectural Theory at the University of Nottingham, UK. His research interests include: architectural theory and criticism; phenomenology and the philosophy of technology; the relationship between architecture and the body; museums and architectural exhibitions. He has published books, chapters in books, refereed articles and conference papers in these areas and has obtained grants from the EPSRC, the Leverhulme Trust, British Academy, and the Arts Council. He is founder and Steering Group member of the international subject network: Architectural Humanities Research Association (http://www.ahra-architecture.org.uk/AHRA).

N. Katherine Hayles is Professor in the Literature Program at Duke University. Her interests include digital humanities; electronic literature; literature, science and technology; science fiction; and critical theory. She is the author of numerous books, including *How We Became Posthuman: Virtual Bodies in Cybernetics, Literature and Informatics* (1999), for which she won the Rene Wellek Prize. Her most recent publications are *Electronic Literature: New Horizons for the Literary* (2008), a primer of electronic literature; *My Mother Was a Computer: Digital Subjects and Literary Texts* (2005); *Nanoculture: Implications of the New Technoscience* (ed.) (2004).

Hilde Heynen is Professor of Architectural Theory and Head of the Department of Architecture, Urbanism and Planning at the University of Leuven, Belgium. Her books include *Architecture and Modernity. A Critique* (1999), *Back from Utopia: The Challenge of the Modern Movement* (co-edited with Hubert-Jan Henket, 2002) and *Negotiating Domesticity: Spatial Productions of Gender in Modern Architecture* (co-edited with Gulsum Baydar, 2005). She regularly publishes in journals such as *Home Cultures*, *The Journal of Architecture* and *Technology and Culture*.

Christopher Hight is an Associate Professor and Director of Undergraduate Studies at the Rice University School of Architecture, where he is pursuing design and research on architecture's potential at the nexus of social, natural and subjective ecologies within the built environment. A Fulbright Scholar, he obtained a masters degree in histories and theories of architecture from the Architectural Association, and a Ph.D. from the London Consortium at the University of London.

Jyoti Hosagrahar teaches at Columbia University, New York and is Director of Sustainable Urbanism International at Columbia University, and Bangalore, India. Since 2006 she has served as an expert for UNESCO in the areas of historic cities, urban sustainability, as well as culture and development. She is author of *Indigenous Modernities: Negotiating Architecture* *and Urbanism* (Architext Series, Routledge, 2005) and has led SUI in designing innovative strategies to integrate heritage preservation with social development in India.

Richard Ingersoll has taught sixteenth-century Italian architecture and surveys of Italian urbanism at Rice University, the ETH Zurich, Università di Ferrara, and Syracuse University's Florence programme. Ingersoll was the editor of *Design Book Review* and art director for the film *Esther.* His recent books include *Sprawltown* and *Global Architecture 1900–2000,* vol. I. His articles appear regularly in *Arquitectura Viva, Il Giornale di Architettura, Harvard Design Magazine, Architecture*, and *Bauwelt*.

Sandra Kaji-O'Grady is Professor of Architecture in the Faculty of Architecture, Design and Planning at the University of Sydney. Her research interests are in the cross-fertilization between architecture, science and art in the 1960s and 1970s. Kaji-O'Grady draws out the relationships between emerging sciences such as computerisation and robotics, the development of performance art and installation, and the architecture of the 1970s. She situates these exchanges in their historical and cultural contexts and alongside theoretical debates in and out of architecture. As a critic, she is concerned to assess the consequences of individual buildings for the discipline. Additionally, she researches notation and colour through her own art practice and is interested in supervising higher degree research by project.

Shiloh Krupar is an Assistant Professor in the Culture and Politics Program at Georgetown University's School of Foreign Service. She holds a Ph.D. in cultural geography from the University of California at Berkeley, and an M.A. in East Asian studies from Stanford University. Her research and teaching interests, which lie at the intersection of geography, architecture, and performance, have focused on the relations between spectacle and waste through case studies that range from exhibitions in postsocialist urban China to decommissioned military sites in the US West. The latter will be featured in her book *Hot Spotter's Manifesto* with the University of Minnesota Press. Krupar also has several articles published in major peer-reviewed journals, including *Society and Space*, *Public Culture* and *Radical History Review*.

Abidin Kusno is Associate Professor at the Institute of Asian Research at the University of British Columbia where he holds a Canada Research Chair in Asian Urbanism and Culture (Tier II). He is the author of *The Appearances of Memory: Mnemonic Practices of Architecture and Urban Form in Indonesia* (Duke University Press, 2010) and *Behind the Postcolonial: Architecture, Urban Space and Political Cultures in Indonesia* (Routledge, 2000).

Iain Low is Professor at the University of Cape Town where he convenes post-graduate programmes in architecture. He has worked in rural schools for a self-reliance project in Lesotho, and has designed an award winning installation for Iziko SA Museum's San Rock Art collection in Cape Town. His research area is space and transformation, specializing in the post-apartheid city, with particular focus on agency in re-writing architectural type. He is editor of the *Digest of South African Architecture*.

Duanfang Lu is Senior Lecturer in the Faculty of Architecture, Design and Planning at the University of Sydney, Australia. She has published widely on modern Chinese architectural and planning history. Her recent publications include *Remaking Chinese Urban Form* (2006, 2011) and *Third World Modernism* (2010). She serves on editorial boards of the journals *Architectural Theory Review* and *Traditional Dwellings and Settlements Review*.

John Macarthur is Dean and Head of the School of Architecture at the University of Queensland, Australia, where he directs the research group ATCH (architecture, theory, criticism, and history). He writes on the cultural history and aesthetics of architecture and his particular interest has been the picturesque and its relation to modern architecture, urbanism and visual culture.

Daniel Maudlin is Associate Professor of Architectural History and Theory, School of Architecture, Design and Environment, University of Plymouth, UK. He has published widely on architecture, everyday life and material culture, including papers in *Journal of Architectural Education*, *Design History*, *Architectural History*, *Architectural Heritage*, *Buildings and Landscapes*, *Vernacular Architecture* and *Traditional Dwellings and Settlements Review*. His book *The Highland House Transformed: Architecture and Identity on the Edge of Empire* was *Scotsman* Book of the Year, 2009.

Brian McGrath is an architect and founder of urban–interface, a design studio working at the intersection of urbanism, ecology and media. He is the Research Chair in Urban Design at Parsons The New School for Design and the Director of the Urban Design Research Group at the Baltimore Ecosystem Study. McGrath has served as a Fulbright Senior Scholar in Thailand and as a Fellow at the India China Institute.

Ana Miljački is an Assistant Professor of Architecture at Massachusetts Institute of Technology. She has previously taught studios and seminars at Columbia University, City College in New York and Harvard University Graduate School of Design. She holds a Ph.D. (2007) in history and theory of architecture from Harvard University, an M.Arch. from Rice University and a B.A. from Bennington College. Her research interests range from the role of architecture and architects in the Cold War era Eastern Europe, through the theories of postmodernism in late socialism to politics of contemporary architectural production.

Deborah Natsios is co-director with John Young of Cryptome, an open source of online documents that expose the repercussions of security practices on civil liberties. She has taught in architecture and urban design programmes at Columbia University and Parsons the New School for Design, among others. She is a principal of Natsios Young Architects in New York City.

Jorge Otero-Pailos is an architect, artist and theorist specialized in experimental forms of preservation. He is Associate Professor of Historic Preservation in Columbia University's Graduate School of Architecture, Planning and Preservation. His research and work rethinks preservation as a powerful countercultural practice that creates alternative futures for our world heritage. His installations have been exhibited at the Venice Art Biennial (2009), and the Manifesta European Contemporary Art Biennial (2008). He is the Founder and Editor of the journal *Future Anterior*, and the author of *Architecture's Historical Turn: Phenomenology and the Rise of the Postmodern* (University of Minnesota Press, 2010).

Antoine Picon is Professor of the History of Architecture and Technology at Harvard Graduate School of Design where he also co-chairs the doctoral programmes. He holds simultaneously a research position at the École Nationale des Ponts et Chaussées. He has published numerous books and articles mostly dealing with the complementary histories of architecture and technology, among which are: *French Architects and Engineers in the Age of Enlightenment, Claude Perrault (1613–1688), L'Invention de L'ingénieur moderne, La ville territoire des* *cyborgs*, and *Les Saint-Simoniens: Raison, Imaginaire, et Utopie*. Published in 2010, Picon's most recent book, *Digital Culture in Architecture* proposes a comprehensive interpretation of the changes brought by the computer to the design professions.

Mrinalini Rajagopalan is Assistant Professor in the Department of the History of Art and Architecture at the University of Pittsburgh. Her recent publications include: 'A Medieval Monument and its Modern Myths of Iconoclasm' in, *Reuse Value: Spolia and Appropriation in Art and Architecture, from Constantine to Sherrie Levine,* edited by Dale Kinney and Richard Brilliant (Ashgate, 2011) and 'From Loot to Trophy: The Vexed History of Architectural Heritage in Imperial India' (*Newsletter of the International Institute of Asian Studies*, No. 57, Spring 2011, Leiden University Press).

Vyjayanthi Rao is Assistant Professor of Anthropology at The New School for Social Research. She works on cities after globalization, specifically on the intersections of urban planning, design, art, violence and speculation in the articulation of the contemporary global city. She is the author of numerous articles on these topics and is completing a book manuscript titled *The Speculative City*.

Jane Rendell is a writer and architectural historian/theorist/designer whose work explores interdisciplinary intersections between architecture, art, feminism and psychoanalysis. Her authored books include *Site-Writing* (2010), *Art and Architecture* (2006), and *The Pursuit of Pleasure* (2002), and she is co-editor of *Pattern* (2007), *Critical Architecture* (2007), *Spatial Imagination* (2005), *The Unknown City* (2001), *Intersections* (2000), *Gender, Space, Architecture* (1999) and *Strangely Familiar* (1995). She is Professor of Architecture and Art, and Vice Dean of Research at the Bartlett, UCL.

David Salomon has taught architectural theory, history and design at Cornell University, the University of Pennsylvania and Syracuse University. He is the co-author of the *Architecture of Patterns* (Norton, 2010). His essays have appeared in the journals *Log*, *Grey Room*, *Harvard Design Magazine*, *The Cornell Journal of Architecture* and the *Journal of Architectural Education*. He received his Ph.D. from the Critical Studies in Architectural Culture programme at UCLA.

Grahame Shane, A.A. Dip., M.Arch. (Cornell UD), Ph.D. in Architectural and Urban History with Colin Rowe. Since 1985 he has taught at Columbia University. He also teaches at the Cooper Union, New York, University College, London, the Milan Polytechnic and Venice IAUV. He published *Recombinant Urbanism* (2005) and *Urban Design Since 1945; a Global Perspective* (2011). He co-edited the *AD* Special Issue *Sensing the Twenty-First Century City; Upclose and Remote* (2005) with Brian McGrath.

Kelly Shannon received her Ph.D., which focused on landscape urbanism and cases in Vietnam, from the University of Leuven, Belgium, where she is now teaching. Her recent design research is focused on the interplays of water and urbanism in Asian cities. Publications include: *The Contemporary Landscape of Infrastructure* (NAi, 2010), *Human Settlements: Formulations and (re) Calibrations* (ed., Sun Academia, 2010), *Reclaiming (the Urbanism of) Mumbai* (ed., Sun Academia, 2009), *Water Urbanisms* (Sun, 2008).

AbdouMaliq Simone is an urbanist with particular interest in emerging forms of social and economic intersection across diverse trajectories of change for cities in the Global South.

Simone is presently Professor of Sociology at Goldsmiths College, University of London and Visiting Professor of Urban Studies at the African Centre for Cities, University of Cape Town. Key publications include *In Whose Image: Political Islam and Urban Practices in Sudan* (University of Chicago Press, 1994), *For the City Yet to Come: Urban Change in Four African Cities* (Duke University Press, 2004) and *City Life from Jakarta to Dakar: Movements at the Crossroads* (Routledge, 2009).

Heidi Sohn is Assistant Professor of Architecture Theory at the Delft School of Design, Faculty of Architecture, TU-Delft. She is founder and programme director of the Urban Asymmetries research and design project, and academic coordinator of the Future Cities graduate programme of the DSD. She is a trained architect and holds an M.Sc. degree in urban planning. She received her Ph.D. in architecture theory from the Faculty of Architecture of the TU-Delft in 2006. She has lectured and published extensively.

Naomi Stead is a Research Fellow in the ATCH (Architecture | Theory | Criticism | History) Research Centre in the School of Architecture at the University of Queensland, Australia. She is a co-editor of *Architectural Theory Review*. Her research interests lie within the architectural humanities and the cultural studies of architecture, in both its production and reception. Current projects examine architectural criticism, experimental writing practices in architecture, and intersections between architecture and the other arts.

Paolo Tombesi is the Chair of Construction, Faculty of Architecture, Building and Planning at the University of Melbourne, Australia. He also was visiting professor at the University of Reading, UK and at the Polytechnic of Turin, Italy. His primary area of research is the relationship between the intellectual dimension of building and the socio-technical aspect of building procurement. His current work draws on microeconomics and political economy as well as labour and industrial theory to examine the relationship between design, built quality, technological innovation and construction markets.

Bart Verschaffel (1956) studied philosophy at the University of Louvain and since 2004 is full Professor in the Department of Architecture and Urban Planning at Ghent University Belgium. He has numerous publications in the fields of architectural theory, aesthetics and art criticism and philosophy of culture. His monograph publications include: *Architecture is (as) a Gesture?* (2001); *à propos de Balthus* (2004); *Essais sur les genres en peinture. Nature morte, portrait, paysage* (2007); *Van Hermes en Hestia. Over architectuur* (2010); *De zaak van de kunst. Over kennis, kritiek, en schoonheid* (2011).

Paola Viganò is full Professor of Urbanism at Università IUAV of Venezia and coordinator of the Ph.D. program in urbanism. Guest professor in several european schools of architecture, she is the author of *I territori dell'urbanistica – Il progetto come produttore di conoscenza* (Officina, Roma 2010). In 1990 she founded Studio, together with Bernardo Secchi, one of the 10 teams selected for the "Grand Paris project" in 2009. In 2010 she was nominated for the *Grand Prix d'Urbanisme*.

Paul Walker is Associate Professor of Architecture at the University of Melbourne. His publications include: *Looking for the Local: Architecture and the New Zealand Modern*, with Justine Clark (Victoria University Press, 2000); and chapters in Mark Crinson and Claire Zimmerman, eds, *Neo-Avant-garde and Postmodern* (Yale University Press, 2010); and Peter Scriver and Vikramaditya Prakash, eds, *Colonial Modernities* (Routledge, 2007).

Ines Weizman is an architect and theorist based in London. She teaches at London Metropolitan University and the Architectural Association School of Architecture. In recent years, following the subject of her Ph.D. thesis she researched and published on the political and ideological spectacles enacted by Soviet-era architecture, particularly on the urban historiography of what was East Germany. This was also an attempt in understanding figures and practices of dissidence in architecture.

Delia Duong Ba Wendel is a Harvard University Ph.D. candidate who researches post-conflict and post-disaster rebuilding strategies, focusing on the relations between spatial and socio-political repair. This research is dually informed by postgraduate degrees in cultural geography and architectural history. Wendel was trained as an architect, spent several years in practice, researched for UN-HABITAT, and taught at the University of Edinburgh. She is the co-editor of a forthcoming Graham Foundation funded publication, the *Design Politics Reader*.

Gwendolyn Wright is Professor of Architecture at Columbia University. Her work has focused principally on American architecture and urbanism from the late-nineteenth century to the present day. She has also written extensively about transnational exchanges, especially colonial and more recent neo-colonial aspects of both modernism and historic preservation. Her newest book is *USA*, part of the Modern Architectures in History series from Reaktion Books.

Preface and Acknowledgments

The firmly bound pages of this Handbook belie the dispersed sites and different media of its production. This is perhaps the case with all books involving multiple authors. Yet the Handbook format, seeking as it does an all-embracing coverage of the state of a disciplinary field, exaggerates (and exploits) the spatially dispersed and mediated nature of the contemporary academy.

Our editorial meetings have almost all been mediated electronically. The Handbook's incubation period (2006–2010) has been such that we have both witnessed and experienced the extraordinarily rapid development of electronic communication and collaboration technologies. Conference telephone calls, e-mail, a Yahoo chat room, Skype, and Google Documents have collectively provided the shifting electronic medium of this collection. This electronic space has, of course, intersected with numerous places too – conference halls, offices, studies, public libraries, cafés, art galleries, and airport departure lounges. The most architecturally striking of these were Diller Scofidio + Renfro's Institute of Contemporary Art (ICA) building (2001–2006), and Carrère and Hastings' New York Public Library (1897–1911). The café and galleries of the Boston ICA served as a stimulating site for a day-long meeting of the three editors, while the outlines of the two introductions were drafted in the reading rooms of the New York Public Library. Both buildings, and their speedy wi-fi connections, have been instrumental in the assembly of this Handbook.

The editorial work of the Handbook has involved a number of structured workshops. The first was generously hosted and funded by Arie Graafland at the Delft School of Design (DSD), TU Delft, in May 2007. This was a significant two-day event that allowed the wider editorial collective to meet and reflect upon the emerging shape of the collection. Many of the section and project editors worked together for the first time at this event. We are especially grateful to Arie and his team at the DSD for helping to build the project's momentum in this way. Further two-day workshops were held at the Radcliffe Institute, Harvard University, in January and June 2008. Draft material for the Handbook was discussed among a large group including many of the section editors at both events. We thank the Radcliffe Institute for providing Hilde Heynen with a fellowship that greatly facilitated the coordination of editorial activities in 2007–2008 and for the material support in organizing these workshops. We would also like to thank all of those section and project editors who participated in these events, some of whom travelled great distances. We are grateful to the various home institutions of these participants who supported their attendance.

In addition to these larger, structured meetings, the three Handbook editors have met at various locations and times. The offices of our publisher in London were often the venue for such meetings, starting in February 2006, when we first set out what would become the structure of the Handbook, and continuing until June 2010, when the last arrangements for the delivery of the manuscript were made. We met twice in New York, either using offices provided by the Parsons New School of Design (September 2008) or the New York Public Library (November 2009). Intermittently some of us met in Leuven (September 2006), San Francisco (February 2008), Edinburgh (August 2009), and Guimarães (June 2010).

For the latter opportunity we thank Alona Nitzan-Shiftan and Carmen Popescu who chaired a session on 'The spatial turn' at the EAHN conference in Guimarães, and provided us with the opportunity to talk about the Handbook. We also benefited from the invitation to speak at the EAAE workshop on architectural theory in Hasselt (2006), where the structure and wider themes of the Handbook were aired. Hilde Heynen was hosted by Ralph Lerner at the Department of Architecture of the University of Hong Kong and its Study Center in Shanghai (April 2009), where she presented some of the material brought together in the volume.

The Handbook benefited enormously from the input of eleven anonymous readers who reviewed our original proposal. Each offered careful, insightful, and sustained responses to the proposal. Each one, perhaps knowing better than we as to what then lay ahead of us, were supportive and encouraging. Sibel Bozdogan made important contributions to the initial framing and conception of the Handbook, and contributed to editorial workshops at the Radcliffe Institute. Sarah Whiting was a valuable respondent to the original proposal, helping us better understand the possibilities and nuances of the thematic structure that we had proposed. We are grateful to Jane M. Jacobs, Katerina Ruedi, and André Loeckx for their insights and comments upon key aspects of the text.

In the course of the past five years, we have discussed aspects of the Handbook with a lot of people – colleagues, doctoral students, fellow participants in conferences – who offered us enthusiastic support and helpful suggestions. Without that extensive network we would not have succeeded in finding and building such effective working relationships with the various authors that now figure in this book. Armeet Panesar took some excellent photographs for the Handbook, not all of which were able to be included. Chris French helped with sourcing visual materials for the cover.

We appreciated very much the calm, supportive, and enabling work of the team at SAGE Publications. Much of our initial interest in this project – and our recognition of its potential to instigate, and in some ways change the terms of debate in architectural theory – was due in no small measure to our contact with Robert Rojek, the commissioning editor and publisher at SAGE who initiated this volume. For his wise guidance, generous support, and for the risk he took in commissioning a project operating in largely uncharted waters for SAGE, we thank him. Sarah-Jayne Boyd, the assistant editor at SAGE who worked closely with us from the early stages to completion, remained supportive and (heroically) patient throughout, providing consistently sound and thoughtful advice in relation to the many practical issues we encountered along the way. Completing a project of this scale would not have been possible without the intellectual and technical infrastructure provided by SAGE.

Finally, we thank the section editors, project editors, and contributors for the seriousness with which they engaged with the wider aspirations of the Handbook project, and the sustained intellectual energy they invested in it. We appreciate, too, their patience as we completed the final stage of the work.

C. Greig Crysler (Berkeley)
Stephen Cairns (Edinburgh)
Hilde Heynen (Leuven)

Introduction – 1: Architectural Theory in an Expanded Field

C. Greig Crysler, Stephen Cairns
and Hilde Heynen

REVISITING PARC DE LA VILLETTE

On a midsummer's afternoon in Paris' Parc de la Villette locals and tourists mingle amongst the famous red follies that dot the park. Children paddle in a shallow pool that surrounds one of the follies. Family groups and friends gather at tented cafés and bars that have sprouted up alongside one another. Strolling couples take in the sun, cyclists weave along the banks of the canal, while the distant din of an impromptu football match thickens the atmosphere. It is an evidently multicultural scene. Many women are dressed in strongly coloured and patterned fabrics of distant places, others wear hijabs. Some men wear kaftans, while many teens and children wear football strips bearing the names of global stars of the game such as Zidane, Ronaldo and Drogba. Security men

Figure 0.1 (Below) Temporary café next to a Folly at Parc de la Villette, Paris. (Stephen Cairns)

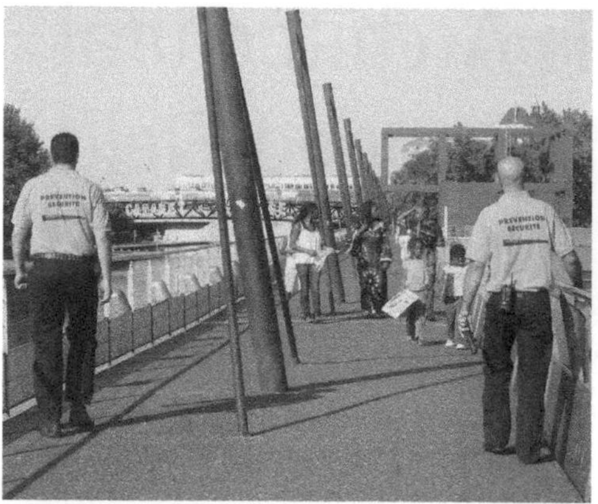

Figure 0.2 (Above) Security guards on elevated walkway at Parc de la Villette, Paris. (Stephen Cairns)

walk their beats in pairs on the elevated decks that cut across the park. They wear black combat trousers and orange T-shirts branded with 'Prevention Securité' on the back. Walkie-talkies and bundles of keys hang from their belts. One of the routine jobs on their beat is to rattle the door handles of each of the 35 follies. They are checking that the follies are locked. Most are empty. Some have begun to appear a little dilapidated and worn. Once solidly red, some follies are now a patchwork of stained and faded panels and brighter replacements. At some, one can even stare through rusted panels to the structure within. But they are now also 'worn in'. Once stark markers set out on a grid across the park, the follies are nowadays embedded, albeit ambiguously, in a mature landscape of trees, shrubs and human activity.

These follies began their lives as trademark elements of the original Parc de la Villette landscape, as designed by architect Bernard Tschumi. Tschumi won the commission to design Parc de la Villette in an international competition launched in 1982 by the then French Minister of Culture, Jack Lang. The forward-looking competition brief had little in the way of functional requirements, emphasizing instead the values of urbanism, pleasure and experimentation, calling for nothing less than an urban park for the twenty-first century. The seemingly open brief was underpinned by ambitious cultural and urban planning policy aspirations. To be sited on 55 hectares of semi-derelict land in the northeast corner of Paris, and framed by a new Science Museum and Music Centre, the Parc de la Villette was to reanimate what had been a relatively marginalized area of the city, open up the city to the suburbs beyond, and sustain Paris' place as a global centre of cultural innovation.

Tschumi's winning design proposal was significant not simply because of its intrinsic architectural qualities. It gained notoriety for the way it was self-consciously animated by 'theory'. Parc de la Villette was widely regarded as a built manifestation of Tschumi's ongoing critique of the foundational principles of architectural modernism, specifically the assumptions about the determinate role of function, structure and economy-of-means on built form. Parc de la Villette was not simply theorized after the event of its design and making, it was conceived in and through a specific articulation of design thinking that linked architecture to debates in literary theory and philosophy. This mobilization of theory in the design – enhanced by Tschumi's invitation to Jacques Derrida and Peter Eisenman to collaborate on an aspect of it[1] – triggered a scramble amongst critics, commentators and academics in the discipline to acquire the novel vocabularies required to appropriately engage. Suddenly, it seemed, architecture was pursuing theory in various postmodernist, post-structuralist and deconstructivist guises.

The Parc de la Villette project was by no means a unique nor even inaugural activation of theory in architecture, as we will see. Nor should it be seen as some emblematic monument of architectural theory. But it did demonstrate a self-conscious engagement with a particular kind of theory that, as Jonathan Culler usefully notes, is essentially a 'nickname' for eclectic styles of scholarship that challenge and reorient thinking across diverse disciplinary lines. The coherence that is attributed to writings in this mode resides, Culler suggests, in 'their analyses of language, mind, history, or culture [that] offer novel and persuasive accounts of signification, make strange the familiar and perhaps persuade readers to conceive of their own thinking and the institutions to which it relates in new ways' (Culler 1994, 13). In the 1980s this set of developments gave rise to new textbooks and special issue journals, as well as prestigious exhibitions. Titles such as *What is Deconstruction?* (Norris and Benjamin 1988), *Deconstruction in Architecture* (Papadakis 1988) and *Deconstructivist Architecture* (Johnson and Wigley 1988), mark architecture's engagement with this extra- and interdisciplinary body of work. Theory was in the air and the Parc de la Villette project seemed to encapsulate it. This particular kind of theory mobilized not only a critique of architectures already made, but also saw this critique as grounds for an enrichment of the architectural design process itself. This involved the (re)invention of a host of metaphorical and literal design operations – montage, collage, automatic drawing, excavation, layering, fragmenting, juxtaposing, tracing – that coalesced in an 'auto-generative' design process in which the conventional agencies of client, user and architect came to be scrambled.[2]

Just as Parc de la Villette has found a place in the fabric and everyday life of Paris, so too has it found a place in the discipline's history of itself. Parc de la Villette is today part of the architectural canon. With its architectural fabric now worn in, there is also an unavoidable sense that Parc de la Villette's theory has worn thin. Tschumi explicitly sought to unhinge the conventional expectation that form should, as Sullivan's cliché has it, 'follow' function. He did so by activating the ambiguities of chance and play, and the follies (which were loosely functional, sculptural, pavilion-like structures) played a key part in articulating this commitment. As such, the image of security guards rattling the locks of an empty pavilion, while an animated crowd is served beer and wine from a tent pitched in its shadow, is striking in its irony. Is it that the Parc, as critics at the time chimed, replaced functionalism with an intensified formalism? Is it that the Parc's design, informed as it was by theory, was too clever for its own good? Or is it that the informal, performative and lived will always outflank a leaden-footed practice such as architecture, however radically it might be conceived?[3] Despite this, the Parc has evidently been creatively and successfully programmed by the management teams of the Parc and the adjacent Science Museum and Music Centre. A myriad of local volunteer organizations have acquired spaces for daily and weekly events such as exhibitions, dance and theatrical performances, and gardening classes. These user groups have exploited the indeterminacy of the design. They have stitched themselves into the fabric of the Parc in multiple ways, sometimes as sustained and sanctioned user groups, and other times through fleeting and unpredictable appropriations.

With its vibrant activity co-existing with often-fallow follies, Parc de la Villette encapsulates the hope and ambiguity of architecture's earlier engagement with post-structuralist theory. For example, it still captures something of the adventurous and open potential of critical attitudes to entrenched disciplinary truths such as functionalism, formulas of composition and essentialisms of place. As a marker of a disciplinary turning point, Parc de la Villette also reminds us of the ways in which connections with theoretical debates in other disciplines enabled architecture to see itself anew through emerging critiques of logocentrism, phallogocentrism and eurocentrism. The debates that followed provided openings for restructuring not only the Enlightenment intellectual legacy embedded in architecture, but also genuine practical alternatives for how architecture might comport itself in the world. These included new ways of conceptualizing and producing architecture, new modes of pedagogy, new logics of office organization, new commitments to a more inclusive, universally accessible architectural profession.

For all these gains, architecture's engagement with post-structuralist theory also meant that more established conceptions of architectural theory were increasingly seen as unsatisfactory. The problematizing of such more conventional approaches saw many of them marginalized or merely rendered unfashionable. This certainly happened to established traditions of theory building in architecture that could be defined in terms of a Popperian 'scientific method' (Popper 2002 [1963], 333). Within architecture, a wide range of architectural theory followed this template, including building sciences, the 'first generation' of design methodologists (Alexander 1964; Broadbent and Ward 1969), instrumentally inflected approaches to design based on post-occupancy evaluation (Proshansky et al. 1970), amongst others. Theoretical approaches defined in terms of a Husserlian 'phenomenological method' (Husserl 1931) that garnered significant followings in architecture were suspiciously cast as essentialist (Norberg-Schulz 1965; Perez-Gomez 1985; see also Chapter 7 in this volume). Studies of vernacular built forms and environments, supported by Levi-Straussian structuralism (van Eyck 1961 and 1967; Bourdieu 1970; Blier 1995 ; Hertzberger 2005), were seen as tainted by their latent humanism. The discipline's ancient investment in theories of aesthetic formalism, wherein various systems of proportion and composition authorized the proper arrangement of architectural forms and spaces (Boudon 1971; Ching 1979; Le Corbusier 2000 [1955]; Papadakis and Aslet 1988), were also questioned. As was the renewed interest in European urban history, urban morphology and architectural type that had, since the 1960s, begun to coalesce under the heading of 'neo-rationalism' (Krier 1988; Muratori 1967; Rossi 1982 [1966]; Panerai et al. 2004 [1977]). And finally, in the wake of post-structuralist theory, architecture's intermittent engagement with critical theoretical traditions, such as Marxism (Tafuri 1980 [1968]; Tzonis 1972), was in some quarters thought too cheerless and too normative.

ENDS OF THEORY?

Many of the tensions between scientific, phenomenological and post-structuralist definitions of theory have been rehearsed, elaborated and reconsidered in one way or another, within a wider debate on the 'ends of theory' (Callus and Herbrechter 2004; Rabate 2002; Cunningham 2002; Butler et al. 2000; Payne and Schad 2004; Jameson 2004 in a special issue of *Critical Inquiry* on the theme). The seeds of this debate were, of course, already present in the unstable constellation of approaches, tendencies and tactics that were gathered under the heading of post-structuralism. In this respect, post-structuralist 'theory' was itself a thoroughgoing attack on the idea of theory – a tension that is nicely captured in a pair of essays by American literary critics J. Hillis Miller on 'the triumph of theory' (1987), and Paul de Man on the 'resistance to theory' (1982). Some strands of this debate might be characterized as a blatant reassertion of the 'grand narratives' of progress, universal justice or equality, in the name of an effective politics of globalization (Eagleton 2003). Other strands have taken the form of discipline- or medium-specific resistances (especially in those fields that are focused on creative practice, such as film studies, fine art and performance studies) subsumed within the language of critique or the language metaphor *per se* (Culler 2000). Often motivated by materialist or pragmatist attitudes, still further strands in this debate sought to 'reconstruct' disciplinary paradigms that were regarded as suffering the destructive effects of theory (see, for example, Bordwell and Carroll 1996).

Manfredo Tafuri's neo-Marxist critique of architecture and capitalism was an important site for the development of a discipline-specific 'resistance to theory'. In his *Architecture and Utopia* (1976 [1973]), Tafuri characterized semiology and structuralism as a 'delicate ideological veil' (Tafuri 1976, 150), and its application to architecture as disguising the deeper penetration of capital and economic logics into the processes of architectural production. Tropes that came to be so important in architectural theory – such as indeterminacy, open-endedness and ambiguity – were diagnosed in nascent form in the semiological project and critiqued by Tafuri as serving to dissolve the medium or materiality of architecture. While this served, in turn, to buttress architects' sense of their own agency and creative freedom, it did so at the cost of disguising architecture's growing sense of impotence in the world. That is, while 'architecture seeks its own meaning' through semiology, the discipline is, argues Tafuri, 'tormented by the sense of having lost its meaning altogther' (Tafuri 1976, 161). This line of argument was pointedly elaborated in his essay 'L'Architecture dans le Boudoir' (1974) where the theme of an illusory and destructive interiorization through theory was articulated through analysis of the work of specific avant-garde architects (the New York Five, Aldo Rossi, James Stirling). Tafuri's critique of the avant-garde's subsequent embrace of post-structuralist theory is articulated more fully in a set of essays and interviews in a special issue of *Casabella* (Gregotti 1995). Other authors have revisited this critical approach by attempting to reconcile its emphasis on architectural history with some of the themes that theory has activated, such as the everyday, gender and postcolonialism (see, for example, Borden and Rendell 2000; Heynen and Loeckx 1998).

The more recent end-of-theory atmosphere has found concrete expression in architecture under the name of the 'post-critical' (Baird 2004; Chapter 2 of this volume). Robert Somol and Sarah Whiting published in 2002 an article on 'Projective architecture' that came to be understood as an appeal for a 'post-critical' architecture (although the authors themselves were careful not to use that characterization). In the aftermath of this publication, many more voices were raised that pleaded for a more modest understanding of architecture's capacities to critically reflect on the world, given that architecture is, out of necessity, mostly complicit with the flows of capital that increasingly structure that world.. This formulation was, in a way, a foregrounding of the disciplinary medium – bricks, mortar, glass, concrete and capital – and practice at the expense of the philosophical reflection that animated earlier theoretical paradigms. Other commentators (Allen 2004, Speaks 2001, 2002 (a), (b), (c); Martin 2005) rhetorically elaborated this view, suggesting that (as it coincided with an upturn in the economy and an increase in availability of work for architects) the pragmatic embrace of the market economy served as motivation, intellectual licence and ethical horizon for architectural practice.

The displacements, deconstructions and disruptions of long-held and relatively stable disciplinary norms served to proliferate what Jean-François Lyotard famously called 'little narratives'. Architectural theory, as we have seen, inventively took up the possibilities of this new, fragmented discursive terrain. But it also seemed, in retrospect, especially susceptible to the consumptive mode that it inspired, in which novel theoretical vocabularies were adopted, briefly entertained, or (worse) 'applied' to built form, then abandoned as outdated only to be replaced by new paradigms. We hope that this Handbook will make a contribution to the longer, slower and oscillating history of architectural theory. The Handbook does not propose a fresh set of 'posts-', turns or paradigms that break with all that precedes it. Nor does it promote a return to the universalist aspirations of scientific theory in its various guises, or the essentialisms of experience. It builds upon the irrefutable theoretical energy that the Parc de la Villette embodied, but does so by putting the critical sensitivities, the pluralist sensibility, the self-reflexivity and speculative ambition that post-structuralism inculcated in the discipline into contact with a wider set of world conditions.

Understanding the architectural afterlife of Parc de la Villette today is not well served by the theoretical vocabulary by which it was conceived. The eventual effectiveness of the Parc as built, inhabited and appropriated reality was, in many respects, unforeseen. This is, of course, an inevitable fact of all architectures. The circumstantial eventfulness that gathers to them, the life (and death) that flows and ebbs through them, inevitably complicates and usually exceeds any inaugurating motivations or principles (see Ockman 2000; Till 2009). A theoretical framework that is sensitive to this play between the principle of a building (what it is as a design) and the circumstance of a building (what it comes to be) must be couched in more expansive terms. This is not merely to claim that architectural theory can somehow incorporate circumstance in the name of 'the political', 'the technical' or 'the social'. It is to suggest that architectural theory can sensitize the discipline to the myriad of relationships – proximities, interconnections, entanglements, distances, contiguities, framings and short-circuitings – that buildings establish between themselves and the forms of life that pulse through and within them. An architectural theory conceived along these relational lines draws us both outwards from the building to the wider network, ecology or milieu within which it sits, and inwards to the material fabric of the building itself. It also ensures that these outward and inward trajectories are not mutually exclusive, but have the capacity to be short-circuited, and related intimately. This expanded field suggests that architectural theory is porous and open to the circumstances of the world.[4]

INSTITUTIONAL CONTEXTS

Worldly theory is bound up with modes of production and dissemination. As with the other humanities, the privileged medium for architectural theory has, until the very recent past, been printed text – monographs, edited collections, anthologies, journal articles and conference proceedings (as can be gathered from the bibliographies of each section in this Handbook). A number of important journals appeared in the 1980s and 1990s that came to be crucial vehicles for the development of architectural theory. Journals such as *Oppositions* and *Assemblage* in the USA, *AA Files* in the UK, *Archis* in the Netherlands, *Lotus International* in Italy all supported, in varying ways, the rapid development and dissemination of interdisciplinary themes and styles of debate. Unlike journals in the sciences, these periodicals were very much identified with their editors or with their editorial boards, being known for taking up specific positions and critically aligning themselves with certain paradigms (Crysler 2003). In the last decade or so, pressure has been rising to give more prominence to peer-reviewed journals, which are supposedly more open and neutral. Hence we have seen the emergence of journals like *Architectural Theory Review*, which is entirely devoted to the exchange of information and ideas on areas of architectural interest. Scholars in architectural theory have also experimented with web-based publications. The best known is the *Haecceity* platform (www.haecceityinc.com), which aims at supporting critical architectural theory by addressing the status of architecture 'at the end of metaphysics'. Some would argue that web publications are the future of our discipline, but thus far printed materials still have greater reach and influence than those limited to cyberspace – as the bibliographical sections in this Handbook show.

These references already indicate that architectural theory's dominant language is currently English. Although its past and present references are steeped in Italian, French and German, architectural theorists who solely use one of these languages are unlikely to gain international prominence today. International exchange and communication mainly happens in English, and the best known academic centres of architectural theory are located within the Anglo-Saxon cultural sphere – London, the American East and West Coasts, one or two centres in Australia. Paris, Venice and Berlin, like Barcelona and Rotterdam, are on the map, but they do not have the same force of gravity. Other parts of the world – the whole of Asia, Africa and Latin America – do not really play along. Some centers operate within regional or national debates, while others lack the resources needed to produce publications for an anglophonic debate that is increasingly dominated by large multinational presses. This situation, of course, is consistent with the overall cultural hegemony of Western-based institutions. It is a hegemony that one can (and should) deplore and criticize, but at the same time one has to recognize that this hegemony is structurally part of the way our academic institutions function.

Confronting the 'spaces of theory' through the production of this Handbook proved to be a sobering experience. Given our interdisciplinary and cross-cultural ambitions, we were keen to offer the Handbook as a platform for voices of intellectuals who were based outside established academic centres in Europe, North America or Australasia. This aspiration proved more difficult to fulfil than we had anticipated. This volume does feature the work of authors who come from Latin America, South and East Asia, Southeast Asia and Africa, and they tackle a diverse range of issues that are as cosmopolitan and engaged with global debates in the discipline as any other contributor. But is one's place of origin especially significant in the global academy today? Most contributors to this volume undertook doctoral studies and developed academic careers in the West. Most are based at academic institutions in the West. Clearly, global cities such as Singapore, Johannesburg and Shanghai, for example, host significant sites of scholarship in the field, and their emergence suggests that the academic world is expanding geographically. But this begs the question: does an expansion of geographical horizons imply an equivalent diversification of intellectual horizons? That is, does the academy – in the name of academic freedom and disinterested inquiry – recognize, support or even catalyse new forms of knowledge and styles of thinking that might emerge outside established centres? Or does the academy today seek to expand and entrench a newly commodified global format for the production and consumption of knowledge?

In their book *Academic Capitalism and the New Economy*, Sheila Slaughter and Gary Rhoades (2004) outline a political economy of knowledge production in the contemporary academy.[5] They document the ways in which the academy increasingly operates according to a set of global norms dictated by neo-liberal ideologies. This process, which they dub 'academic capitalism', normalizes the values of competition according to narrowing criteria, and entrenches market-like behaviours across the teaching/learning, research and service functions of universities globally. Research and scholarship play an especially important part in this system, serving as markers of brand distinction for individual institutions, and driving knowledge production for a commodified knowledge economy. The emerging global academic market has seen a tightening of intellectual agendas as institutions 'gatekeep' legitimate forms of knowledge in the name of 'quality' and 'academic standards' (Slaughter and Rhoades 2004, 120).[6] While Slaughter and Rhoades document examples of resistance to this development – citing cases in South Africa and Central America, for example (2004, 124) – they also note the isolated and unsustained nature of these enterprises.

It is easier, perhaps, for those whose work is already framed cross-culturally, to contemplate effective forms of scholarship that exploit the integrative aspects of globalization for positive academic effects. We might think of the long-distance, dialogic and shuttling modes of scholarship that developed in the 1980s and 1990s in critical anthropology and postcolonial studies. We might point to the increasing mobility that enables research across the academy to be structured in multi-sited ways (see Chan and Fisher 2008). Nonetheless, Slaughter and Rhoades' analysis will resonate with the daily working experiences of many scholars in the West. And, more significantly, it offers a plausible structural explanation for the diminished resources – time, funding, infrastructure – that scholars in many centres outside the West work with. For our purposes, it also clearly sets out the parameters and stakes for a project that seeks to make alternate and novel scholarly voices heard in the global academy today.

Another institutional limitation concerns the place of architectural theory within the academic curriculum. When the EAAE (European Association of Architectural Education) organizes a workshop on architectural theory (which they have done on a regular basis over the last five years), participants tend to identify themselves in rather different ways. Some see themselves as scholars, others as architects who teach. This difference is consistent with the observation that architectural theory typically occupies one of two positions in the educational programme of future architects. It either aligns with architectural history in survey courses and specialist seminars devoted to 'history, theory and criticism' or it is closely linked with studio courses, providing to studio teachers a space where they can discursively reflect upon the tacit knowledge that circulates in the studio learning environment. In the first case, it is often taught by professors holding a PhD in art history, architectural history or (more rarely) architectural theory; in the second it is the by-product of a design-oriented course that is the responsibility of a practising architect, who might or might not hold a PhD but has developed a theoretical stance more informally.

The two situations are common, not just in Europe but also in the USA (where the first version tends to be more dominant in research universities, whereas the second would predominate in more professionally oriented architectural schools) and elsewhere.[7] Nevertheless, architectural theory as an academic discipline is dominated by the first type of scholar – art or architectural historians who do not practice as architects.[8] It is not hard to conjecture the reason for this: these scholars are the ones whose career paths depend upon their publication output, whereas the professors who teach architectural theory as part of their involvement in their studio work receive promotions on the basis of their architectural projects. Hence, there is a clear difference in publication patterns, with the first type of scholars being much more prolific in writing books and articles, and the second type being better known in terms of their built works.

This situation makes up for a disjuncture between, on the one hand, the academic identity of architectural theory in a book like this, and, on the other, architectural theory as taught in many architectural schools. Depending on the willingness of the responsible professor to address the very wide range of issues that can possibly be covered in architectural theory, students will or will not be offered the opportunity to engage with them. Depending upon the openness of the responsible professor to reflect upon design questions, students will or will not be challenged to bridge theory and design. The resulting teaching practices thus make up a very wide variety of contents and methods, making architectural theory, although often seen as essential, not very stable nor anywhere near canonical.

While a growing number of anthologies, edited collections, authored books and journals participate in defining and delimiting architectural theory, many teachers feel free to venture far away from these supposedly core narratives. Instead, they follow specific trajectories that build upon older approaches (about scale, rhythm, proportions; or about materials, crafts and joints; or about space, tectonics and details), or that highlight an idiosyncratic theoretical angle, engaging specific 'masters' and their ways of doing architecture (Le Corbusier, Mies and Louis Kahn come to mind as very popular reference points for this kind of teaching).

POSITIONING THE HANDBOOK

Three influential anthologies of architectural theory, each building on the Parc de la Villette 'theory moment', were published in close succession in the late 1990s. Kate Nesbitt's *Theorizing a New Agenda for Architecture: An Anthology of Architectural Theory 1965–1995* was published in 1996, and this was followed in 1997 by *Rethinking Architecture* edited by Neil Leach. *Architecture Theory since 1968*, edited by K. Michael Hays, appeared a year later, in 1998. At the time, the publication of these collections was greeted with a sense of excitement, but also, perhaps a sense of closure, one that comes with the attempt to place the unruly and often contentious debates of the prior three decades into some form of order (Lavin 1999). Since this Handbook inevitably engages with the culture of ideas that these collections represent and have actively shaped, framing their endeavours is integral to explaining our own. In stating things in this way, we want to underscore the fact that the organization of this collection – and our editorial relationship to prior approaches – seeks to explore the reach, coherence and porosity of architectural theory as a field of inquiry.

The Hays, Nesbitt and Leach volumes all take the time period around 1968 as their starting point. In *Theorizing a New Agenda*, Nesbitt argues that the three decades since 1965 were characterized by social upheaval, a loss of faith in the modernist project, and 'a certain disillusionment with social reform' within the profession (Nesbitt 1996, 22). The global recession that followed the oil shocks of the mid-1970s helped to spur a period of critical reflection and writing by architects (in part through lack of building opportunities) in Europe and North America. This was accompanied by the creation of new institutions and publications, which in turn advanced the prominence and influence of architectural theory in education and professional practice. Nesbitt notes the proliferation of competing positions that emerged in this period – something that both her extended introduction and the organization of the book reflect (1996, 28). She crossmatches five paradigms (ranging from 'the aesthetic of the sublime' to post-structuralism) with five major themes that the paradigms are employed to address (from place and history to the body). The result is a complex, pluralist map of the field, one that is primarily populated by the writings of architects and architectural academics based in the USA and, to a much lesser degree, in Europe. Nesbitt locates the 'institutions of theory' in New York, Venice and London (1996, 22). This institutional focus might be one of the reasons why, for all her awareness of the social conditions of architecture, she did not register discourses that were important elsewhere in the world, such as those concerned with participation and populism (Tzonis and Lefaivre 1976) or on 'human settlements' (d'Auria et al. 2010).

K. Michael Hay's volume, *Architecture Theory since 1968* also argues that the time period (in this case ending with 1993) is defined by the emergence of new institutions of theory. But he goes a step further to argue that since 1968 'architecture theory' has all but subsumed 'architectural culture' (Hays 1998, x). In this formulation, the social upheavals and uncertainties of the 1960s led to the institutionalization of a permanent critique in architectural culture, one that is achieved through theory as a system of mediation or 'transcoding' between social changes in the world at large and their specific articulation within architectural culture. As a result, architectural culture becomes less a stable foundation for theoretical discourse than its object of desire: it must now be 'constantly constructed, deconstructed and reconstructed through more self-conscious theoretical procedures' (Hays 1998, x). The choice of material in the Hays collection, while overlapping at points with Nesbitt's, is more attuned to a specific critical strategy, one which grants architecture a sense of partial autonomy from the forces in which it is embedded:

> In its strongest form mediation is the production of relationships between formal analysis of a work of architecture and its social ground or context [...] but in such way as to show that architecture is having some autonomous force with which it could also be seen as negating, repressing, compensating for, and even producing as well as reproducing, that context. (Hays 1998, x)

Hays thus gives prominence to the autonomy of architecture as the source of its critical capacity. Both in the years leading up to and following the publication of his volume, the approach summarized above by Hays (and also explored in the journal *Assemblage*) has been the subject of considerable discussion. Some have argued (including, at earlier points, the editors of this Handbook) that the emphasis on the critical discourse of form displaced other considerations and practices; others have claimed that, regardless of the success or failure of the approach, it redirected attention to architecture as system of representation intertwined with the texts, institutions and agents that constitute it as such.[9] Though our volume clearly departs from the discourse of critical form, we nevertheless are operating in the opening Hays' volume helped to create for an architectural theory that questions its historical assumptions – as part of an effort to redefine how the social and the architectural are defined and related to each other.

The third major collection to emerge in the 1990s, Neil Leach's *Rethinking Architecture* (1997), shares with both Hays and Nesbitt an emphasis on the capacity for architectural theory to provoke critical reflection. He describes the end of the twentieth century as a 'moment of recuperation', and (following Jameson) one of 'inverted millenarianism' in which 'premonitions of the future [...] have been replaced by analysis of the past, and by reflection, in particular, on the collapse of various concepts on which contemporary society had been grounded' (Leach 1997, xiii). However, the point of departure in Leach's book is not within architecture, but explicitly outside it: architectural discourse, he suggests, has been 'largely a discourse of form' organized around 'questions of style' (1997, xiv). He proposes rethinking architecture through 'depth models' from other disciplines that transcend the limitations of such an approach. His categories, though in some cases overlapping directly with Nesbitt's (such as phenomenology, postmodernism, post-structuralism), are examined from the standpoint of critical theorists and philosophers who write about architecture but have no training in it (1997, xvi). The critical step here, different from, but as powerful as, the space clearing potential of 'posts-' and 'turns', involves creating a negative characterization of the discipline in order to move outside it. For Leach, this exteriority creates the possibility of rethinking the discipline's internal priorities. This approach elaborates the rich potential of connections with other disciplines. The absence of an internal perspective also means that the specificities of architecture (such as its engagement with form, construction or material) are not considered central elements of discussion.

While this Handbook overlaps with these three volumes in terms of its time frame and thematic content, from an editorial standpoint it has been organized and produced in a fundamentally different way. The Handbook is not a collection of existing texts. Rather, it presents original texts on topics that we, as editors, considered significant to the field of architectural theory today. The invited authors engage with a cross-section of existing literature, assessing significant debates and posing challenging questions that indicate future directions for study and investigation.

In developing the framework for the Handbook, we have built upon and reconsidered the assumptions that underpin the previous anthologies. From a temporal standpoint, our initial intention was to pick up where these collections left off, by dealing with the turbulent period from around 1989 to the present. However, once the project was underway – a process that involved extensive meetings amongst ourselves and the 16 section and project editors – it became clear that the complicated intellectual and institutional histories of the participants would make such neat divisions impossible. A sense of (sometimes critical) dialogue with the past, rather than a periodizing break with it, is a consistent feature throughout. This is reflected in the temporality of the contributions, almost all of which reach into (and in some cases extend beyond) the last three decades as the frame for their discussions. As with the Nesbitt, Hays and Leach volumes, the period from the mid-1960s to the present is regarded in this collection as one of intensifying change, with profound transformations coming in the decade immediately after those volumes were published.

However, we do not regard 1968 as singular moment of epochal change, but instead see it, together with more recent changes occurring around 2000, as a contradictory moment of intensification that opens onto a much more divided and polarized world – one in which the unanticipated consequences of prior waves of capitalist modernization increasingly dominate the future imaginings of the global present: the fall of the Berlin Wall in 1989, the collapse of the Soviet Union, and the realignments of alliances in Europe and elsewhere; the revitalization of religious and nationalist movements, with sometimes fundamentalist and aggressive overtones (including the events surrounding 9/11 and its aftermath); systemic changes in the global financial system (the 'Big Bang' in 1987) followed by the rise or fall (and rise) of various economic bubbles, each increasingly more exaggerated and precarious than its predecessor (culminating with the collapse of 2008); the related generalization of digital technology; the shift in economic growth patterns towards China and India; further rapid urbanization in the global South (with half of the world's population now living in cities); increasingly polarized geopolitical conditions; growing popular consciousness of an environmental crisis that is planetary in scale.

The complexity of the current moment requires an impure, inclusive approach enlivened by the possibilities produced by the critical intersection and juxtaposition of competing positions. Some of the approaches and debates featured in the previous volumes have also been brought to the fore in this Handbook, along with others that remained more or less in the background: the overlaps and tensions between memory, history and tradition (Section 4); the role of the profession and the institutions of architecture (Section 5); the discourses on sustainability and how they relate to late-capitalism (Section 7); the important interaction between architecture and the transformation of the urban field (Section 8). Finally, the Handbook is notable for the way it explores the interaction between architectural theory and architectural projects – not just by including mostly 'theoretical' (paper) projects, but also by discussing how the Handbook's themes are relevant to the professional production of architecture, to how architects deal with commissions, and to how diverse groups interact with their built environments.

WORLDING, PROVINCIALIZING, GATHERING

Our ambition is for the Handbook to act as a vehicle that broaches an expanded and more porous definition of architectural theory. This ambition, as we have also suggested, is necessarily anticipatory and retroactive. That is, it engages with the worldly possibilities of theory as much as it values existing discourse. In this respect, an expansive and porous definition of theory is also a matter of retrieving features that were already present, though dormant, within archaic definitions of the term. 'Theory' used to connote openness, participation, generosity and mobility as well as authority and clarity. The term is derived from the Greek *theoros* and *theoria*, which embody ideas of viewing and of sacred duty (Bill 1901, 197). The idea of 'spectator' seems to have been the original meaning, later to be supplemented by that of a 'state delegate to a foreign festival' (Bill 1901, 198). Religious and sacred duties were subsequently added to this delegate function, giving rise to a second meaning: 'commissioner sent on sacred service'. So the plural *theoroi* came to designate delegates sent to sacred foreign festivals to view, to participate and to represent their home state. Herodotus and Thucydides, amongst others, used the term in a simpler way to refer to 'journeys of travel and sightseeing' (Bill 1901, 199). The function of *theoroi*, as Wlad Godzich puts it, was to 'see-and-tell' in a way that offered an 'official and more ascertainable form of knowledge'. As such *theoria* provided 'a bedrock of certainty: what it certified as having seen could become the object of public discourse' (Godzich 1986, xiv).

This etymology gave rise to different understandings of theory. The conventional, scientific use of the term tends to emphasize the authorizing, ground-truthing and systemic aspects of its archaic meaning. This is the kind of theory that travels, and is valid because it travels, because it transcends contingencies, and all that they stand for – materiality, tactility, contamination, circumstance. On the other hand, theory, as a nickname for those eclectic (post-structuralist, postmodern) interdisciplinary styles of scholarship, activates the mobile, estranging, relative and contingent aspects of the archaic meaning.

These two understandings of theory have, in the recent past, been seen as incompatible and mutually exclusive. On the one hand, theory aspires to be an authorizing practice giving rise to a globally applicable system of concepts. On the other hand, 'theory' functions as set of tactics and styles of reading and thinking that work to disrupt that system. This tension and oscillation between the authorizing and disruptive dimensions of theory underpins what Miller (1987) and de Man (1982) called the 'triumph' of and 'resistance' to theory, and the wider ends-of-theory debate. It also resonates with Tafuri's resistance to avant-garde architectural theory as a kind of illusory rhetorical superstructure for the discipline, and with the subsequent post-critical debates in architecture. This Handbook positions itself as part of this oscillation, rather than entrenching one stance or other. In this respect we are motivated by the complex tensions between the general and the contingent, the global and the situated, that are precisely *held* within the classical sense of *theoria*. The ancient Greek *theoroi* who traveled, saw and reported, were under a duty to produce understandable reports that could 'enlarge the community's view' (Rausch 1982, cited in Rabate 2002, 114). This theory-making was a cosmopolitan project that established carefully calibrated relationships between the distant and the near, the foreign and the familiar. Rodolphe Gasché's (2007) recent meditation on the ongoing relevance of theory cites Hans-Georg Gadamer's famous essay 'In Praise of Theory' as a way of articulating this. 'Theoria', Gadamer suggested, 'is not so much the individual, momentary act as it is a comportment, a state and condition in which one holds oneself' (Gadamer 1990, 96; cited in Gasché 2007, 200).[10]

How, then, should we qualify our actions in this expanded terrain of architectural theory? How do we summarize the motivations behind undertaking a new collection of this kind? What kind of architectural theory could grasp the complexity of that midsummer's afternoon in Park de la Villette? What does it mean to theorize architecture in an ends-of-theory or post-critical moment? What might be the scope and remit of this new era of architectural theory? By way of concluding our first introduction to this Handbook, we want to invoke three different, though related, concepts as a means of fleshing out the idea of an architectural theory in an expanded field: provincializing (Chakrabarty), worlding (Spivak), gathering (Latour). Each of these concepts usefully refers to conditions – such as building, making, inhabiting, mapping, describing territories – that make them amenable to architectural reflection. But they each in different ways articulate a mode of practice and style of thinking that is attentive to the complexities and contradictions around matters of difference in a globalizing world.

Chakrabarty's (2000) term 'provincializing Europe' is not merely a matter of articulating histories from non-European points of view (this is a long-standing project and many such histories have been written). Rather, the term refers to a simultaneous acknowledgment of the indispensability and inadequacy of the European intellectual heritage for thinking through conditions that pertain in everyday life outside of Europe. This doubled stance that simultaneously decentres and activates principles such as rationality, secularism or social justice, demands heightened attention to the situated and practising nature of theory. It calls for being constantly attuned to the particularities of difference and the generalities of concepts and categories and how they might be mutually accommodated.

Spivak (1990) adapts ('vulgarizes', as she puts it) Heidegger's term 'worlding' for similar purposes. She uses the term to draw attention to the epistemic violence implicated in imperialism, in particular 'the assumption that when the colonizers come to a world, they encounter it as uninscribed earth upon which they write their inscriptions' (1990, 129). The idea of the 'Third World' is, for Spivak, a striking instance of this homogenizing process. Yet, this process also contains within it possibilities for a 'counter-worlding' or a new 'worlding of the world' in which alternate, situated possibilities for being in the world are articulated. As in Chakrabarty's logic of provincialization, this is a self-contradictory process that involves 'un-learning' the privileges of speaking from the centre as much as it does learning and propagating new forms of knowledge.

Latour's (2004) reappropriation of Heidegger's conception of 'gathering', brings us to the most architectural framing of these three related themes. Latour's consideration of contemporary technology, leads him to consider the way certain things have gathering or relational effects. The work of theory, for Latour, is not merely a matter of 'debunking', but one of assembly. The theorist 'is one who offers the participants arenas in which to gather'. The critic is 'the one for whom, if something is constructed, then it means it is fragile and thus in great need of care and caution'.

We do not propose that 'provincializing', 'worlding' and 'gathering' is a recipe for practising theory in contemporary times. Rather, we aim to draw out the richness of each of these verbs and examine their consequences for thinking about architecture today. We propose that architecture always already involves a form of provincializing, worlding and gathering. We propose that each of these concepts, as they have been respectively adapted, vulgarized and wrenched from their original (European) intellectual context, will help to displace the narrowed framing of post-structuralist architectural theory, and help configure a newly sensitized framework for thinking about architecture in contemporary times.This is, we think, what the contributors to this volume have attempted to do: they have responded to and elaborated the editorial themes and issues in ways that anchored them in worldly concerns that question the hegemony of what is often seen as the centre of the discipline. They have considered architecture as a material practice that gathers not only techniques and materials, but also people and their social interactions.

FOUR GUIDING THEMES

In developing the content of this collection, we have identified a sequence of interpretive and methodological strategies to translate the critical potential of these three verbs into a more tangible editorial framework: a set of orienting devices that also collectively represent, in the broadest sense, the goals of the collection. This framework can be defined by a commitment to interdisciplinarity and cross-cultural analysis, rethinking architecture's characteristic divide between theory and practice, and the pursuit of open-ended and provisional investigations. We briefly outline each of these below.

INTERDISCIPLINARITY

Our approach to interdisciplinarity in this collection has been shaped by its complicated institutional history and the challenges it poses for architectural scholarship. The discourse on space, indebted to the pioneering work of Henri Lefebvre, holds particular significance in relation to the interdisciplinarity of architectural theory. Through the work of Lefebvre and others who followed him, space in the humanities and social sciences has assumed a new prominence in social theory: no longer regarded as a container, frame or context for social processes, but a social process in itself that is intertwined with the development of capitalism. In its diverse meanings and analytic potential, space is at once material and imaginary, and spans scales from the body to the planetary. As such, it offers a bridge between the realm of architectural scholarship and the theorization of space and social processes in other fields.

At the same time, the discourses on space carry with them concerns about dissimulation (architectural theorists operating as social scientists) and displacement (where the specificity of architectural practices dissolves into a more generalized interest in social processes) (Robbins 1994; West 1993). Others have suggested that recent forms of interdisciplinarity in architectural research are in part a manifestation of the institutional authority it now holds within the universities: with the expansion of programmes in architectural history and theory, particularly at the PhD level, architectural academics have come to view other disciplines as sources, competitors and intellectual contexts for their research, shifting the focus from buildings and practice in the world at large to debates between disciplines within the academy (Jarzombek 1999, 197).

As we have suggested in the first part of this introduction, the turn towards the so-called post-critical, and the parallel, but quite different, revival of interest in pragmatism (with its emphasis on theory as something that guides, but does not precede, practice) are in part a reaction to interdisciplinarity and its potential to dissolve the historical specificity of disciplinary knowledge and practice (Saunders 2007). We do not advocate interdisciplinarity as a corrective to what some have characterized as a self-enclosed and self-referential discipline. We argue instead that architecture has always borrowed from other disciplines to illuminate its central questions, to augment its legitimacy, to find a language to redefine its agenda. A more fully historicized understanding of architecture's 'interdisciplinary intellections' (Jarzombek 1999, 197) would enable us to better understand architecture's intellectual positioning today. Until the middle of the twentieth century, the fields of reference tended to be well-established disciplines such as archaeology, philosophy or history. Since then, architectural theory has been influenced by more fluid theoretical discourses such as structuralism, post-structuralism, semiotics, cybernetics, (neo) Marxist political theory, cultural studies, gender studies or postcolonial theory. This situation, which is partially responsible for the archipelago-like character of architectural theory, is nevertheless also a rich source of innovation and provocation. Emerging voices in architectural theory present new and original perspectives that are often based on intimate knowledge of neighbouring fields. We therefore regard interdisciplinarity as a way of representing and questioning the multifold processes and practices intrinsic to architecture and its specific history as a discipline and profession.

CROSS-CULTURAL FRAMEWORKS

This handbook has been shaped by the intellectual legacy of postcolonial struggles, most directly in the way we have conceptualized theory's space of knowledge. It has been conventional for theory collections to reinstate the grand evolutionary narrative of nineteenth century historicism as the unquestioned organizing framework for the sequential presentation of master texts, a convention that continues up to the present with several recent volumes on architectural theory. Perhaps the most notable example of the continuing tradition is the two-volume collection edited by Harry Francis Mallgrave and Christina Contandriopoulos, which begins with a chapter on Vitruvius and concludes with a section entitled 'Millennial Tensions' (Mallgrave 2005, Mallgrave and Contandriopoulos 2008). A subsection on the 'End of Theory' creates a threshold to the future grouping, entitled 'Beyond the Millennium'. If the implied break with the past underscores the persistence of architectural theory's developmentalist tropes, the geography of knowledge mapped by the collection as a whole underscores the resilience of architectural theory's universalizing space of Euro-American origins and teleological development.

This collection is indebted to three decades of postcolonial studies that have, in diverse ways, reimagined the bounded spaces of Western knowledge as part of a world space surcharged with historical forces of colonization, imperialism and their aftermath. We therefore do not propose cross-cultural analysis based on a simple inside/outside relation, whereby the traditional Western canon is supplemented with more and more 'external' sources: this approach, in our view, can only serve to reinforce (and re-legitimate) the operations of the original system. Instead, we argue the first step is to uncover the cross-cultural within objects and ideas previously understood as (racially) pure exemplars of 'Western modernity' or 'colonial culture'.

Rethinking the space of European origins and hegemony in this way also transforms the assumptions of diffusionist models of modernity, in which ideas are presumed to travel from core to periphery, and from purity to debased status as they move between contexts. Following Edward Said, what emerges instead is a 'contrapuntal' narrative social space in which the architectural and urban 'cultures of imperialism' are in movement between core and periphery, as they are re-assembled, reworked and reinscribed in both the colonial city and imperial metropole (Cairns 2007). More recently, scholars of architectural and urban modernities have employed a cluster of terms (such as global, alternative, multiple, indigenous, vernacular, domestic or ordinary, amongst others) to denote the conceptual and geographical decentring of monolithic conceptions of history. The terms signal a methodological shift, in which modernity is defined as an encounter rather than a simple transmission across borders: a site of conflict, and of agency and appropriation. The resulting transformation in the space of theory registers in the Handbook through multiple and sometimes contradictory positions, which do not line up in a neat evolutionary flow, but rather express different responses to common issues (such as the technology, aesthetics or sustainability) across cultures.

THE ECONOMY OF REFLECTION AND ACTION

The Handbook also sets out to positively engage with the widely acknowledged theory–practice divide. As editors, we believe this involves questioning the autonomy that is sometimes asserted by those engaged, on the one hand, in critical, theoretical and interpretive work, and those, on the otherhand, involved in the creative and manual work of making a building. While acknowledging that a certain kind of relative and strategic autonomy is necessary for each realm, we have sought in both the organization and content of the collection to foreground the complex economy that the discipline of architecture has always sought to sustain between these realms. One of the underlying premises of the Handbook is that architectural theory can be characterized as a style of thinking that is constitutionally, if not always avowedly, open to the material and pragmatic dimensions of the built environment. And, because architectural modes of building are self-conscious, considered and inherently theoretical, this can be said to be a reciprocal principle.

Here we might think of Rem Koolhaas' essay 'Junkspace' (2003). It is a meditation on the material conditions, design, construction and consumption practices that constitute the generic spaces of late-capitalism. Less essay than slab of stream-of-consciousness prose, 'Junkspace' is theory at the front lines of globalization. It is informed by the pragmatic, craftless construction techniques behind the airconditioned, escalator- and travelator-fed, insulated spaces of the global city: 'verbs unknown and unthinkable in architectural history – clamp, stick, fold, dump, glue, shoot, double, fuse – have become indispensable' (Koolhaas 2003, 410). Frederic Jameson, in his review of the wider *Project on the City* (Chuihua et al. 2003a, 2003b) to which 'Junkspace' formed a centrepiece, suggests that Koolhaas' writing, and this piece in particular, represents a 'new symbolic form' (Jameson 2003, 77). The essay's 'repetitive insistence' and sheer energy speaks directly to 'concrete' – actually, plastic, aluminium, vinyl, glass, plasterboard – realities of a globalizing world. Koolhaas' prose, Jameson argues, is one means of 'breaking out of the windless present of the postmodern back into real historical time, and a history made by human beings' (Jameson 2003, 76). In a more instrumental guise, yet working on a similar set of themes, we might also consider the work of architecture and planning firm, DEGW, and in particular, co-founder Frank Duffy's research on office space, its history and future fortunes (Duffy 1992, 2008; Duffy et al. 1998). The firm has built its professional reputation on the capacity to bring sophisticated research techniques to bear both on the immediate – programmatic, urban, structural – demands of a given brief, and on longer-term strategic thinking on issues relevant to a particular sector, such as corporate work practices. The complex commissions that DEGW undertake form a rich and reciprocal terrain for Duffy's theoretical writings.

Like all economies and systems of exchange, transactions can be conducted illicitly as much as in the open, materials can be as often smuggled as declared, and the process can be as often short-circuited as it is smooth. In making a critical intervention in the economy of reflection and action, we have therefore sought to foreground the theoretical assumptions that underpin areas that are typically regarded as non-theoretical; at the same time, through ideas associated with gathering, we have sought to examine theory as a social practice, thus expanding the architectural meaning of the term 'practice' beyond its typically professional connotations, to one that refers to the routines, habits of thinking, social and intellectual relationships that shape theory.

PROVISIONAL AND OPEN-ENDED INVESTIGATIONS

As noted above, many of the edited collections published over the last two decades that deal with architectural theory have been concerned with mapping the formation and historical development of specific strands of architectural thought through the published writings of architects, critics and practitioners. *The Handbook* differs from these efforts, because it is structured around a series of issues and debates. This collection is not focused on the influence of single texts or individual authors: in working within the genre of the literature review, we present the interpretive work of scholars who construct cross sections through debates that we believe are central to the current intellectual landscape of architectural theory. The chapters in this collection stretch across a much larger set of positions, institutional geographies, and built conditions than is possible to achieve in an anthology of previously published material. While acknowledging the centrality of certain conventions of architectural theory as part of the core problematic of the collection, the contributions are concerned with mapping new tendencies and operating in domains that border on parallel investigations in other disciplines.

We believe that theory must be open to continuous revision and change if it is to represent and intervene in the relationship between the built environment and the changing conditions of the world at large. This collection does not construct a singular, evolutionary model of the field that culminates in an idealized present. While our contributors address the genealogy of the positions they discuss, collective emphasis is on the immediate past as a space of competing and sometimes contradictory positions. We have tried to represent the contingent and situated quality of theoretical discourse across multiple debates. Contributions question the given definitions and typical modes of architectural theory as a means of provoking open-ended investigations into possible outlines of future directions.

NOTES

1 See Brunette and Willis (1994, 27) for an account of the failure of the collaboration, and Derrida's critique of Eisenman's reading of post-structuralism and architecture.

2 See Andrew Benjamin (2007) for further discussion of architecture's autonomy and the role of deconstruction and critical architecture.

3 See Casey (1998, 312–317) for detailed discussion of the philosophical issues. See also Rendell (2006, 117) for discussion of the 'fit' of new functions in the Parc de la Villette follies.

4 The idea of theory as an expanded field draws from Rosalind Krauss' (1979) famous esssay 'Sculpture in the expanded field', and from Anthony Vidler's (2004) subsequent revisiting of that essay in his discussion of architecture and landscape.

5 *Academic Capitalism* (Slaughter and Rhoades 2004) has a predominant US focus, and builds on an earlier book (Slaughter and Leslie 1997) that was framed with material from higher education institutions in Canada, Australia, the UK and the USA. See also their contributions to the collection, *Exchange University* (Chan and Fisher, 2008).

6 Bill Readings' (1996) book *The University in Ruins* was a powerful early warning of the narrowing of intellectual agendas in the name of unaccountable principles such as 'excellence'. It remains an important text in this debate.

7 In the absence of substantive studies on this topic of where and how architectural theory is taught, we base ourselves on our own observations and on our relative familiarity with a wide range of institutions, like, for example, those where the contributors to this Handbook are teaching. Hilde Heynen was involved in the coordination of the architectural theory workshops of the EAAE (Hasselt 2006, Trondheim 2007, Lisbon 2008, Fribourg 2009, Chania 2010).

8 This dominance of non-practising scholars is a rather recent phenonenon. In Joan Ockman's *Architecture Culture 1943–1968* one can count 46 authors who are mainly known as practising architects versus 27 others (art historians, philosophers or critics). In K. Michael Hays' (1998) *Architecture Theory since 1968* the ratio is reversed: 17 practising architects versus 36 non-practising scholars.

9 Hays' collection contains a number of contributions that are critical of the approach he outlines in his introduction. Mary McLeod's contribution to the volume, for example, connects the rise of deconstruction to the politics of the Reagan era. Her argument was originally published in the journal *Assemblage* (also edited by Hays), where it was part of a cluster of articles that challenged the discourses of critical architecture over that journal's history (McLeod 1989). The final issue of *Assemblage* in 2000 also reflected critical on arguments around the approach. See for example, Robert Somol's discussion, entitled 'In the wake of *Assemblage*' (Somol 2000). A range of other authors have focused on issues extending from the role of journals in supporting debates around critical architecture, to the translation of deconstruction in architectural theory (Crysler 2003; Groat 1992; Heynen 2007; Kahn 1994; Schwarzer 1999).

10 See Rodolphe Gasché's chapter 'Under the Heading of Theory' (2007) for an account of the theory debate in literary criticism and its current fortunes.

BIBLIOGRAPHY

Alexander, Christopher (1964) *Notes on the Synthesis of Form*. Cambridge, MA: Harvard University Press.

Baird, George (2004) '"Criticality" and its discontents'. *Harvard Design Magazine* 21.

Benjamin, Andrew (2007) 'Passing through deconstruction: architecture and the project of autonomy', in Jane Rendell et al. (eds). *Critical Architecture.* London: Routledge.

Bill, Clarence P. (1901) 'Notes on the Greek theoros and theoria'. *Transactions and Proceedings of the American Philological Association* 32: 196–204.

Borden, Iain and Jane Rendell (eds) (2000) *InterSections. Architectural Histories and Critical Theories.* London: Routledge.

Bordwell, David and Noel Carroll (1996) *Post-theory: Reconstructing Film Studies.* Madison, WI: University of Wisconsin Press.

Boudon, Philippe (1971) *Sur l'Espace Architectural. Essai d'épistémologie de l'Architecture.* Paris: Dunod.

Bourdieu, Pierre (1970) 'The Berber house or the world reversed'. *Social Science Information* 9(2): 151–170.

Broadbent, Geoffrey and Anthony Ward (eds) (1969) *Design Methods in Architecture.* London: Lund Humphries.

Brunette, Peter and David Willis (1994) 'The spatial arts: an interview with Jacques Derrida', in Peter Brunette and David Willis (eds), *Deconstruction and the Visual Arts: Art, Media, Architecture.* Cambridge: Cambridge University Press.

Cairns, Stephen (2007) 'The stone books of orientalism', in Peter Scriver and Vikramaditya Prakash (eds). *Colonial Modernities: Building, Dwelling and Architecture in British India and Ceylon.* London: Routledge, 51–66.

Callus, Ivan and Stefan Herbrechter (2004). *Post-theory, Culture and Criticism.*

Casey, Edward (1998). *The Fate of Place: A Philosophical History.* Berkeley: University of California Press.

Chakrabarty, Dipesh (2000) *Provincializing Europe: Postcolonial Thought and Historical Difference.* Princeton, NJ: Princeton University Press.

Chan, Adrienne S. and Donald Fisher (eds) (2008) *The Exchange University: Corporatization of Academic Culture.* Vancouver: UBC Press.

Ching, Francis D.K. (1979) *Architecture: Form, Space and Order.* New York: Van Nostrand Reinhold.

Chuihua, Judy Chung, Jeffrey Inaba, Rem Koolhaas and Sze Tsung Leong (eds) (2003a) *Great Leap Forward: Harvard Design School, Project on the City 1.* Cologne: Taschen.

Chuihua, Judy Chung, Jeffrey Inaba, Rem Koolhaas and Sze Tsung Leong (eds) (2003b) *Harvard Design School Guide to Shopping: Project on the City 2.* Cologne: Taschen.

Crysler, C. Greig (2003) '"Strategies of disturbance" and the generation of theory', in *Writing Spaces. Discourses of Architecture, Urbanism and the Built Environment.* London and New York: Routledge, 56–83.

Culler, Jonathan (1994) 'Introduction: what's the point of theory', in Mieke Bal and Inge E. Boer (eds). *The*

Point of Theory: Practices of Cultural Analysis. Amsterdam: Amsterdam University Press.

—— (2000) 'The literary in theory', in Judith Butler, John Guillory and Kendall Thomas (eds). *What's Left of Theory: New Work on the Politics of Literary Theory.* London: Routledge.

Cunningham, Valentine (2002) *Reading After Theory.* London: Blackwell.

d'Auria, Viviana, Bruno De Meulder and Kelly Shannon (eds) (2010) *Human Settlements. Formulations and (re)Calibrations.* Amsterdam: SUN.

de Man, Paul (1982) 'Resistance to theory'. *Yale French Studies* 63: 3–20.

Duffy, Francis (1992) *The Changing Workplace.* London: Phaidon

—— (2008) *Work and the City.* London: Black Dog.

Duffy, Francis, Denice Jaunzens, Andrew Laing and Stephen Willis (eds) (1998) *New Environments for Working.* London: Taylor & Francis.

Eagleton, Terry (2004) *After Theory.* New York: Basic Books.

Gadamer, Hans-Georg (1990). 'In praise of theory', trans. Dennis J. Schmidt and Jonathan Steinwand. *Ellipsis* 1(1): 85–100.

Gasché, Rodolphe (2007). *The Honor of Thinking: Critique, Theory, Philosophy.* Stanford: Stanford University Press.

Geiser, Reto (ed.) (2008) *Explorations in Architecture: Teaching, Design, Research.* Basel: Birkhauser.

Ghirardo, Diane (ed.) (1991). *Out of Site. A Social Criticism of Architecture.* Seattle: Bay Press.

Godzich, Wlad (1986) 'Foreword: the tiger on the paper mat', in *The Resistance to Theory,* Paul de Man. Minneapolis: Minnesota University Press.

Gregotti, Vitorio (1995) 'The historical project of Manfredo Tafuri'. *Casabella* [Special Issue] 619–620: 144–151.

Groat, Linda (1992) 'Rescuing architecture from the cul-de-sac'. *Journal of Architectural Education* 45(3): 138–14.

Harvey, David (1989) *The Condition of Postmodernity.* Oxford: Blackwell.

Hays, K. Michael (1984) 'Critical architecture: between culture and form'. *Perspecta* 21: 14–29.

—— (ed.) (1998) *Architecture Theory since 1968.* New York and Cambridge, MA: Columbia University and MIT Press.

Heynen, Hilde (2007) 'A critical position for architecture', in Jane Rendell et al. (eds), *Critical Architecture,* London: Routledge, 48–56.

Heynen, Hilde and André Loeckx (1998) 'Scenes of ambivalence. Concluding remarks on architectural patterns of displacement'. *Journal of Architectural Education* 52(2): 100–108.

Husserl, Edmund (1931) *Ideas: General Introduction to Pure Phenomenology,* trans. W.R. Boyce Gibson. London: Allen and Unwin.

Jameson, Fredric (2003) 'Future City'. *New Left Review* 21(May/June): 65–79.

—— (2004) 'Symptoms of theory or symptoms for theory?'. *Critical Inquiry* 30(2): 403–408.

Jarzombek, Mark (1999) 'A prolegomena to critical historiography'. *Journal of Architectural Education* 52(4): 197–206.

Johnson, Philip and Mark Wigley (1988) *Deconstructivist Architecture.* New York: Museum of Modern Art.

Kahn, Andrea (1994) 'Representations and misrepresentations: on architectural theory'. *Journal of Architectural Education* 47(3): 162–168.

Koolhaas, Rem (2003) 'Junkspace', in *Harvard Design School Guide to Shopping: Projects on the City 2,* Judy Chung Chuihua, Jeffery Inaba, Rem Koolhaas and Sze Tsung Leong (eds.) Cologne: Taschen, 408–421.

Krauss, Rosalind (1979) 'Sculpture in the expanded field'. *October,* 8 (Spring): 30–44.

Krier, Rob (1988) *Architectural Composition.* New York: Rizzoli.

Latour, Bruno (2004) 'Why has critique run out of steam? From matters of fact to matters of concern'. *Critical Inquiry* 30 (Winter): 225–248.

Lavin, Sylvia (1999) 'Theory into history: or, the will to anthology'. *Journal of the Society of Architectural Historians, Architectural History 1999/2000* 58(3): 494–499.

Leach, Neil (ed.) (1997) *Rethinking Architecture. A Reader in Cultural Theory.* New York and London: Routledge.

Le Corbusier (2000 [1955]) *The Modulor: A Harmonious Measure to the Human Scale, Universally Applicable.* Basel: Birkhauser.

Loeckx, André, Kelly Shannon, Rafael Tuts and Han Verschure (eds) (2004) *Urban Trialogues: Visions, Projects, Co-productions.* Nairobi: UN Habitat.

Mallgrave, Harry Francis (ed.) (2005) *Architectural Theory: Volume I: An Anthology from Vitruvius to 1870.* Malden, London: Wiley-Blackwell.

Mallgrave, Harry Francis and Christina Contandriopoulos (eds) (2008) *Architectural Theory: Volume II: An Anthology from 1871 to 2005.* London: Wiley-Blackwell.

Martin, Reinhold (2005) 'Critical of what? Toward a utopian realism'. *Harvard Design Review* 22(Spring/Summer): 1–5.

McLeod, Mary (1989) 'Architecture and politics in the Reagan era: from postmodernism to deconstructivism' *Assemblage* 8(February): 22–59

Miller, J. Hillis (1987) 'The triumph of theory, the resistance to reading, and the question of the material base'. *Publications of the Modern Language Association* (May): 281–291.

Muratori, Saverio (1967) *Civiltà e Territorio*. Rome: Centro Studi di Storia Urbanistica.

Nesbitt, Kate (ed.) (1996) *Theorizing a New Agenda for Architecture: An Anthology of Architectural Theory, 1965–1995*. New York: Princeton Architectural Press.

Norberg-Schulz Christian (1965) *Intentions in Architecture*. Cambridge, MA: MIT Press.

Norris, Christopher and Andrew Benjamin (1988) *What is Deconstruction?* New York: Academy Editors.

Ockman, Joan (ed.) (2000) *The Pragmatist Imagination: Thinking about Things in the Making*. Princeton, NJ: Princeton Architectural Press.

Owen, Graham (ed.) (2009) *Architecture, Ethics and Globalization*. London: Routledge.

Panerai, Philippe, Jean Castex, Jean-Charles Depaule and Ivor Samuels (2004 [1977]) *Urban Forms: Death and Life of the Urban Block*. London: Architectural Press.

Papadakis, Andreas (1988) *Deconstruction in Architecture*. London: Academy Editions.

Papadakis, Andreas and Clive Aslet (1988) 'The new classicism in architecture and urbanism'. *Architectural Design* 58(1–2).

Payne, Michael and John Schad (eds) (2004) *Life. After. Theory*. London: Continuum International Publishing.

Perez-Gomez, Alberto (1985) *Architecture and the Crises of Modern Science*. Cambridge, MA: MIT Press.

Popper, Karl (2002 [1963]) *Conjectures and Refutations: The Growth of Scientific Knowledge*. London: Routledge.

Proshansky, Harold M., William H. Ittleson and Leanne G. Rivlin (eds) (1970) *Environmental Psychology: Man and His Physical Settings*. New York: Holt, Rinehart and Winston.

Rabate, Jean-Michel (2002) *The Future of Theory*. Oxford: Blackwell.

Rausch, Hannelore (1982). *Theoria: Von ihrer sakralen zur philosophischen bedeutung*. Munich: Wilhelm Fink.

Ray, Nicholas (ed.) (2005) *Architecture and its Ethical Dilemmas*. New York and London: Routledge.

Readings, Bill (1996) *The University in Ruins*. Cambridge, MA: MIT Press.

Rendell, Jane (2006) *Art and Architecture: A Place Between*. London: I.B. Tauris.

Robbins, Bruce (1994) 'Pathetic substitutes'. *Assemblage* 23(April): 86–91.

Rossi, Aldo (1982 [1966]) *The Architecture of the City*. Cambridge, MA: MIT Press.

Saunders, William S. (ed.) (2007) *The New Architectural Pragmatism*. Minneapolis: University of Minnesota Press.

Schwarzer, Mitchell (1999) 'History and theory in architectural periodicals: assembling oppositions'. *The Journal of the Society of Architectural Historians* 58(3): 342–348.

Slaughter, Sheila and Larry L. Leslie (1997) *Academic Capitalism: Politics, Policies, and the Entrepreneurial University*. Baltimore: Johns Hopkins University Press.

Slaughter, Sheila and Gary Rhoades (2004) *Academic Capitalism and the New Economy: Markets, State, and Higher Education*. Baltimore: Johns Hopkins University Press.

Somol, Robert (2000) 'In the wake of *Assemblage*'. *Assemblage* No. 41(April): 92–93.

Somol, Robert and Sarah Whiting (2002) 'Notes around the Doppler effect and other moods of modernism'. *Perspecta* 33: 72–77.

Speaks, Michael (2001) 'Architectural theory and education at the millennium, Part 3 – Theory practice and pragmatism'. *A+U* 9.

—— (2002a) 'Design intelligence and the new economy'. *Architectural Record* (January): 72–79.

—— (2002b) 'Design intelligence: Part 1, introduction'. *A+U* (December): 10–18.

—— (2002c) 'Theory was interesting ... but now we have work'. *arq: Architectural Research Quarterly* 6(3): 209–212.

Spivak, Gayatri Chakravorty (1990) *The Post-colonial Critic: Interviews, Strategies, Dialogues*. London: Routledge.

Tafuri, Manfredo (1976 [1973]) *Architecture and Utopia: Design and Capitalist Development*. Cambridge, MA: MIT Press.

——(1980 [1968]) *Theories and History of Architecture*. London: Harper and Row.

Till, Jeremy (2009) *Architecture Depends*. Cambridge, MA: MIT Press.

—— (on behalf of the RIBA Research Committee) 'What is architectural research?', www.architecture.com/Files/RIBAProfessionalServices/ResearchAndDevelopment/WhatisArchitecturalResearch.pdf, consulted August 2, 2010.

Tzonis, Alexander (1972) *Towards a Non-Oppressive Environment.* Boston: i Press.

Tzonis, Alexander and Liane Lefaivre (1976) 'In the name of the people'. *Forum* 25(3): 5–33.

van Eyck, Aldo (1961) 'Architecture of Dogon'. *Architectural Forum* (September): 116–121.

—— (1967) 'Dogon: mand-huis-dorp-wereld'. *Forum* (July): 30–50.

Vidler, Anthony (2004) 'Architecture's expanded field'. *Artforum* 42(8): 142–147.

West, Cornel (1993) 'A note on race and architecture', in *Keeping Faith. Philosophy and Race in America.* New York and London: Routledge, 45–54.

Introduction – 2: Reading the Handbook

C. Greig Crysler, Stephen Cairns and Hilde Heynen

THE STRUCTURE OF THE HANDBOOK

We have structured the Handbook to stage some of the tensions inherent in thinking architecturally. It is divided into eight thematic sections, each of which is guided or activated by a set of three keywords. We have chosen themes and keywords that rehearse, scrutinize and, we hope, extend major debates of the last decades. We have loosely arranged the terms so that they define a shift in scale as one moves through the collection, beginning with the body and concluding with the transnational territory. The Handbook also attempts to accommodate and mobilize some of the effects that are generated when thinking in close proximity to the processes of making or inhabiting architecture. To this end, we have interleaved a project section between chapter sections. Each project refers to the themes and keywords of the sections that immediately precede and follow it, serving to either link or separate the sections.

The Handbook structure can be summarized as follows.

Section 1: Power/difference/embodiment (Chapters 1–4)

This section, curated by Hilde Heynen and Gwendolyn Wright, considers how architecture participates in power relations and the construction of self and other. Architectural and urban spaces can sustain, question or modify political and social structures of power. Spatial patterns interact with existing cultural constructions of gender, class, race, geography and status, usually upholding established hierarchies with exciting new imagery, and sometimes defying those norms. The chapters in Section 1 reflect upon these issues by discussing the influence of consecutive strands of theoretical development.

Citizenship (Chapter 5)

Ines Weizman recounts the story of a critical culture of drawing and exhibiting (led by such figures as Iskander Galimov and Mikhail Filippov) that flourished in the last years of the Soviet era as a means of articulating what citizenship and, what they call, an 'architecture of the governed' might mean today.

Section 2: Aesthetics/pleasure/excess (Chapters 6–9)

This section, edited by John Macarthur and Naomi Stead, charts architecture's variable historic investment in aesthetic experience. Aesthetics stands for architecture's pleasure principle, one of the oldest and most persistent in architectural theory. This motivational principle cannot always be grounded in the uses to which architecture is put nor in the benefits – whether social, moral or political – it is said to deliver. As a consequence aesthetics are often figured as being 'in excess'. The chapters in this section trace how architecture and art are positioned in relation to one another and in relation to other disciplines.

Consumption (Chapter 10)

Ana Miljacki explores three distinctive, compelling architectures of consumption: Prada's flagship store in downtown New York (OMA), a new supermarkert in booming Nova Gorica, Slovenia (Sadar Vuga Architects), and a vast new shopping centre complex in the suburban outskirts of Istanbul (Foreign Office Architects).

Section 3: Nation/world/spectacle (Chapters 11–14)

Architecture is deeply implicated in the enactment of modernity – rather than simply a descriptive feature of it, states AbdouMaliq Simone in his introductory chapter. The four contributions in this section (edited by C. Greig Crysler), consider the role of architectural representation – as process and artifact – in shaping the terms of national culture and identity, particularly in reference to spectacle. They consider the multiple manifestations of modernity, the spatial politics of globalized nationalism, as well as the role of architecture in the unfolding of spectacular zones of consumption.

Heritage (Chapter 15)

Fernando Diez presents a suite of art gallery projects in Madrid (Herzog & de Meuron), Maine, USA (Machado and Silvetti) and São Paulo (Paulo Mendes da Rocha) that, as Diez argues, demonstrate the way in which 'preservation' has come to replace 'modernization' as the master discourse for architecture.

Section 4: History/memory/tradition (Chapters 16–19)

This section explores the significance of the past and its relationship to the present. Recent interest in public memory and 'memory practices' has placed the meaning of history and memory in tension. The study of vernacular architecture has led to a redefinition of tradition in relation to social processes such as colonization and imperialism, nationalism or global tourism. These tendencies are reflected upon in chapters focusing on preservation, heritage and the vernacular. The section is curated by C. Greig Crysler.

Culture (Chapter 20)

Paul Walker examines contemporary museum projects – the National Museum of Australia (Ashton Raggatt McDougall), Tjibaou Cultural Centre in Noumea, New Caledonia (Renzo Piano Building Workshop), Musée du Quai Branly in Paris (Jean Nouvel) – in terms of relationships between technology, form and (postcolonial) national identity.

Section 5: Design/production/ practice (Chapters 21–24)

Architecture's traditional conceptualization of design as a form of drawing that orchestrated the process of building production abstractly and from a distance has become increasingly strained in recent years. Design thinking and practice in this traditional sense seems increasingly inadequate in the face of emergent dimensions of contemporary metropolitan life: radical compressions of space and time, interpenetration of urban and rural space, international division of labour, digital revolution, etc. Dana Cuff is the editor of this section, which deals with the different faces of the profession today.

Flows (Chapter 25)

Stephen Cairns elaborates Manuel Castells' claims regarding a late-capitalist 'space of flows' by examining architecture's own engagement with the logics of flow through the concept of circulation. The discussion takes the form of a traveling meditation threaded through five airports from Edinburgh to Mumbai.

Section 6: Science/technology/ virtuality (Chapters 26–29)

The transformations in the understanding and practice of contemporary science and technology imply effects ranging from important issues concerning the notion of ethics and the role of human agency to the influence of discourse formation on human subjectivity, society and the human body. These issues, state section editors Arie Graafland and Heidi Sohn, are fundamental to architecture. Subject to the same epistemological transformations, architectural knowledge and architectural discourse face a maelstrom of inner changes with the onset of digital technologies.

Infrastructure (Chapter 30)

Delia Duong Ba Wendel revisits New Orleans in the aftermath of Hurricane Katrina, and presents a compelling account of the shifting relationship between architecture and infrastructure, and how they were variously deployed or withheld in the history of urban development in those neighbourhoods most profoundly affected by that disaster.

Section 7: Nature/ecology/ sustainability (Chapters 31–34)

This section, edited by C. Greig Crysler in collaboration with Simon Guy, explores the theories linking nature and ecology, and the built environment in response to the global environmental crisis. The chapters explore the changing terms of the 'ecology question in architectural design', the role of institutions in shaping postcolonial variants of sustainability in Southeast Asia, and the critical questions raised for architectural and urban theory by the international debates surrounding the 'renewable city'. Issues of sustainability and development are addressed not only as technical/ professional matters, but also in relation to the situated investigation of how nature is represented, theorized and transformed by human agency in architectural and urban design.

Landscapes (Chapter 35)

Kelly Shannon documents the significant collaboration between architecture and landscape architecture in the recent past, and both critiques and demonstrates the rich possibilities of this expanding horizon for architectural practice by discussing territory-scaled projects in the USA, Italy and China.

Section 8: City/metropolis/territory (Chapters 36–39)

This section, edited by Brian McGrath and Grahame Shane, examines the city as it has been theorized, represented and imagined from the perspective of architecture. It opens up to discussions that cover larger scales of analysis (metropolis, megalopolis, metacity), in response to claims that the city can no longer be theorized as a clearly bounded, sub-national domain, and instead must be understood as part of networks and spatial realities that are potentially global in scale. This concluding section brings together discourses on current urbanities, which negotiate between architecture, urbanism and social and political sciences.

Housing (Chapter 40)

Iain Low showcases three innovative housing projects designed for challenging socio-economic situations: San Miguel de la Vega, Caracas, Venezuela (Mateo and Matias Pinto D'Lacoste), Mansell Road, Durban, South Africa (Harber Masson Associates), and Quinta Monroy, Iquique, Chile (Elemental).

CONNECTIONS BETWEEN SECTIONS

We have structured the relationship between sections to capture the tensions and connections between different areas of debate. The sequence of thematic sections is non-linear, with clusters of ideas calling and responding to each other through immediate proximity and a range of subtler connections that extend across the entire collection. By placing questions of power, difference and embodiment at the beginning of the book, we hope to underscore their centrality to everything that follows. The comprehensive introduction to Section 1, by Hilde Heynen and Gwendolyn Wright, provides critical pathways through the most significant transformations in thinking about the relationship between built environments and diverse conceptions of power. These lines of inquiry extend through the other chapters in Section 1 to subsequent chapters across the collection (see for example Itinerary 2 below, which connects the discussion of postcolonial theory in Section 1 to other chapters dealing with nationalism, heritage and collective memory, globalization, sustainability and the metacity).

While Section 1 acts as a threshold to the collection, its central concerns are also materialized in more local relationships: the project on dissidence and citizenship that immediately follows (Chapter 5) by Ines Weizman makes material the politics of professional identity introduced by Heynen and Wright, while the second major thematic section on aesthetics, pleasure and excess challenges the characteristic exclusion of debates on aesthetics from much of contemporary architecture theory, and the generally negative connotations that have been attached to the term since its complicated transit through architectural postmodernism.

A similar juxtaposition occurs between Section 5 (Design/production/practice), Section 6 (Science/technology/virtuality) and the debates that surround them. In positioning these two sections in the middle of the collection, we hope to extend the disciplinary concerns of practice, design and technology into a range of interdisciplinary debates – ranging from the role of buildings in constructing the past for future purposes, to the changing relationship between technologies, landscape and nature.

The sequence of themes and projects concludes with Section 8 (City/metropolis/territory), followed by Chapter 40 on housing. In the same way we regard Section 1 as a threshold into the collection, so too have we considered these chapters less as a boundary marking the end of the collection, than an effort to bring together many of the preceding debates. The chapters in Section 8 and the examples of low-cost housing examined by Iain Low in the last chapter of the collection explore the domestication of systemic forces such as globalization, nation-building, and the production of urban infrastructure and manufactured landscapes.

The project sections highlight processes of design, construction and fabrication of buildings, or how buildings might be used, adapted or otherwise inhabited. Purposely varied in approach and style, they collectively demonstrate a kind of material thinking. So, for example, Ines Weizman's (Chapter 5, Citizenship) examination of political dissidence through a set of little-known and unbuilt experimental architectures in Soviet-era Russia resonates with chapters in Section 1 on power and difference, and those in Section 2 on aesthetics and pleasure. Paul Walker's (Chapter 20, Culture) examination of three well-known and widely discussed contemporary museums connects the chapters on history, memory and tradition in Section 4, and the issues surrounding contemporary architectural production in Section 5. Other project sections examine the work of the global avant-garde (Rem Koolhaas, Foreign Office Architects, Herzog and deMeuron), while others linger in relatively anonymous, generic architectures of airports, supermarkets and malls. Iain Low (Chapter 40, Housing) examines a set of innovative housing projects in South Africa and South America, thereby linking the final section in the Handbook on urban theory with the first on embodiment. None of the project discussions, however, merely affirms, instantiates or illustrates issues being addressed in neighbouring chapter sections. Rather, the relationship between project and text is intended to fluctuate as the responsibility for rehearsing a discursive field, adopting a theoretical stance, or progressing an argument, shifts from one to the other. Collectively, the project sections help in the wider aspiration of the Handbook to diversify the legitimate mediums and reach of architectural theory.

ITINERARIES

Rather than discussing the individual contributions in a linear manner, starting with the first and ending with the last, we activate the term 'itinerary' as a means of charting some of the alternate ways of reading this Handbook. The term 'itinerary' suggests a modest disruption of the more fixed structures such as chapters and sections, by identifying common themes, sub-texts or tropes that cut across them. In this respect, itineraries are pathways (that only occasionally stray from the straight and narrow) rather than lines of flight. But their modestly disruptive effects also resonate with our wider characterization of architectural theory and what it might be to practice architecture today. Following an itinerary can transform our experience of place, but does not overturn architecture's deep complicity in the logics and imaginaries associated with place, such as domesticity, groundedness and materiality. The transformative work of architectural theory is effective, we suggest, neither by willfully transcending nor blindly affirming this complicity. Rather, it is a matter of inhabiting, inspecting and enjoying – as Slavoj Žižek (2001) might say – this tension symptomatically.

The Handbook, then, can be read in various ways. Below we propose three 'itineraries' as possible reading sequences, and as invitations to readers to construct their own.

Itinerary 1: Sustainability

'Whither earthly architectures?' This question, posed by Simon Guy in the title to his introduction to Section 7 on Nature/ecology/sustainability, points to the now vast array of architectural approaches to the environmental crisis signaled by 'sustainability'. Stretched to the limit by competing definitions and disciplinary outlooks, the term has come to stand for everything and nothing, a category heading for a divided field. At this stage it is clearly more productive to define the term through the various conflicts and tensions it signifies. In this itinerary, Guy's question is turned back on the collection as a whole, to explore the diverse and sometimes contradictory ways, authors theorize sustainability and its relation to architecture.

Debates on sustainability emerge at various points across the collection (including Section 7, where they are an explicit focus): as part of the problem of appropriate technology in postcolonial settings; as a way to reconsider and question the history of architecture and its construction of the nature/culture divide; in relation to the rethinking of landscapes provoked by new technologies; and as a way to redefine the politics of urban growth in cities and regions. But sustainability is also referenced through discussions of recent conditions that have given the term a new urgency. The economic collapse that began in earnest in 2008 has served to highlight once again the relationship between architecture and the failed assumptions of endless consumption and its environmental consequences. In her discussion in Chapter 10, Ana Miljacki suggests that it is precisely architecture's relation with cultures and practices of consumption that requires further reflection, a task that architectural theory has largely avoided. The twentieth century, she argues, has 'left us a legacy of architectural and design criticism that has demonized any entanglement of architecture with consumption, and certainly with overt consumerism and speculation'. She suggests that such a reflection would 'delaminate' architecture from consumption and enable the envisioning of 'qualitatively different' alternatives. As Krupar and Al note in Chapter 14, sustainability has itself become a mechanism of growth – most notably in the way it has been employed to retool the identities of corporations as socially responsible and 'beyond petroleum' even as their role in environmental devastation accelerates. They chart the historical transformation of spectacle over the last four decades, and suggest that the enveloping social relationships described by Guy Debord in his famous diagnosis of consumer capital, *Society of the Spectacle*, have been realized in ways that exceed the terms of his original formulation. Many of the counter-strategies he proposed (such as the *dérive* and *détournement*), have become part of the spectacle of the brand and its processes of symbolic identification, destruction and renewal. Like Miljacki, they call for an analytical shift away from ideology critique, and towards a careful analysis of spectacle as situated practice.

Krupar and Al underscore the spectacular integration of sustainability into the changing processes of capitalist modernization in ways that reproduce, rather than challenge, its growth machinery. And indeed, sustainability now operates as a framework for disciplinary modernization, a narrative that turns with renewed force to the myth of technology as a means of resolving social contradictions and saving the environment. As Guy notes in his introduction to Section 7, writing by prominent architects on sustainability has tended to embrace advances in building materials and systems, while also heralding the capacity of professional creativity and innovation to 'transform the profession's competencies'. In Chapter 33, Peter Droege suggests that the modernizing histories and theories of Western architecture are built on silence about oil dependence and its environmental consequences, which he foregrounds and periodizes as the hegemony of fossil fuel modernism: Our theories are saturated with oil.

The rhetoric of techno-scientific modernization embodies the temporal paradox that Duanfang Lu describes in Chapter 13 as 'haunting': though framed as future-directed responses to the crisis of the present, eco-modernities are inevitably entangled with (and selectively reactivate) past histories. Much of the expertise and infrastructure related to the production of sustainable building remains located in wealthy countries of the postindustrial West. As Brown and Maudlin point out in their contribution to Section 4 (History/memory/tradition), the issues surrounding sustainable design have provoked architects to borrow from an imaginary 'pre-modern', 'pre-industrial' and 'non-Western' past in order to solve the present problems of not only the postindustrial West, but – under the rubric of an increasingly universal discourse of sustainability – those of the entire planet. As they suggest, such Orientalist constructions ignore the historical intertwining of tradition and modernity by fixing traditional environments as timeless repositories of local knowledge outside the conditions of capitalist modernization. In the process, local practices are converted into technoscientific principles that, in their abstraction, may simply reproduce the problems they are employed to resolve in a more 'traditional' language.

In Chapter 34, Jiat-Hwee Chang explores the postcolonial tensions between tradition and modernity in the context of debates about sustainable architecture in Southeast Asia.

He draws upon the history of the Aga Khan Awards for Architecture over the last decade as a way to examine a specific constellation of institutional processes and practices that have shaped debates on sustainability in Southeast Asia. He identifies three major shifts, beginning with green developmentalism, stressing the potential of technological modernization; this was followed by an emphasis on a return to traditional building methods; and finally an emphasis on self-help squatter settlements. While the first of these embraces technology and is clearly intertwined with postcolonial modernization programmes, he shows how the subsequent return to tradition and interest in squatter communities as paradigms of sustainability, is also infused with techno scientific assumptions. Across his discussion, Chang shows how the apparently objective technical basis of sustainable architecture is continuously redefined in relation to postcolonial institutions and political histories in Southeast Asia.

Chang's discussion of the 'postcolonial variants' of sustainability overlaps with Dana Cuff's characterization of the discipline of architecture outlined in her introduction to Section 5. She argues that the production of architecture has characteristically involved an opposition between the innovative variant and the model, or some aspect of the discipline's core knowledge, where an 'enduring ideal is mobilized by distress'. Though her argument is not explicitly framed in relation to recent debates on sustainability, the claims of epochal change associated with the term clearly define it as a radical variant from disciplinary norms. But the variant must be converted to a model or precedent to become influential, and this process of normalization – though seldom studied – is arguably at the heart of architectural production. A reflexive understanding of the relation between model and variant as mutually constitutive rather than opposed is, Cuff argues, essential to understanding the creative potential in the 'double bind' that holds them together.

The notion of a disciplinary core that gradually evolves in response to innovations re-emerges in Richard Ingersoll's contribution (Chapter 32). He argues that architecture has always addressed ecological questions because it is unavoidably involved in altering the landscape. The relationship has intensified at moments of rapid environmental change, when normative assumptions about the relationship between nature and culture, buildings and their environments, were disrupted and rethought. Ingersoll's argument challenges the ahistorical claims of epochal (and apocalyptic) change associated with ecological design by arguing such considerations have historically been a central if overlooked aspect of architecture's disciplinary core.

The underlying claim in Ingersoll's chapter – that both buildings and their natural environment are part of a larger interdependent and historically contingent ecology – is shared by a number of other authors, who restate the issue in terms of the relation between buildings and landscapes. In Chapter 28, Antoine Picon suggests that the way we perceive and use technology has shifted from that of the discrete artifact to a field of 'quasi-objects', dependent on networks for their operation. The network is a landscape punctuated by transitory points of access and interface: as a site of interacting social and spatial processes. In her commentary in Chapter 35, Kelly Shannon discusses a cross section of design propositions that take the idea of landscape as socio-technical process as their premise. The built environment in Shannon's account holds a similar status to the quasi-object in Picon's: a mediating condition between the natural and the artificial, 'embracing urbanism, infrastructure, strategic planning, architecture and speculative ideas'.

By questioning the opposition between building and landscape, where technological objects (including buildings) are a 'mere effloresence of networks and fields life' (Picon) defined by the 'intricate layering of flows through sites' (Shannon), these authors question the possibility of discrete, object-centred 'solutions' to environmental problems. In both cases, the landscape is not something that is other to technology, but rather operates as a generator of specific socio-technical effects. The implications are developed further at an urban level in Section 8, which McGrath and Shane introduce by suggesting that the terminology of 'metropolis' and 'megalopolis' no longer adequately describes urbanity today. They argue that the last three decades of deregulated financial speculation and transnational development have led to urban 'patches' that mix elements typically segregated by prior planning models. Their preferred term, 'metacity', stresses urbanization as a differentiated planetary condition that is navigated and changed through new media: 'Distant people can measure the difference between mixtures in patches or islands of the archipelago and make informed choices about their goals, desires and movement paths' (McGrath and Shane, Chapter 36). Ubiquitous technology allows the simultaneous representation of the close-up and the distant, the local and the global, permitting adaptation to systemic changes as (or before) they unfold. The metacity marks the extension of landscape urbanism to a global scale, where it operates as a 'complex adaptive system in disequilibrium' where 'social actors of the city are seen as an integral part of, rather than separate from nature'. It is therefore not so much a formula for designing sustainable cities as a basis for an alternative consciousness of urbanized nature, perceived as dynamic, rather than static, at once local and global and subject to continuous change from below.

As the academic consensus in architecture moves rapidly to embrace the idea of sustainability as the ultimate technical fix, a specialized knowledge base that will enhance the profession's claims to expertise, or a messianic agenda that will unify architecture around a universal common cause, the importance of reasserting social and historical differences is increasingly important. As Simon Guy suggests, the modernizing impulse of the emerging consensus rests on a series of oppositions that obscure the ever more entangled relationship between things and the social natures we all inhabit: 'We need to open up and explore the language we use to talk about sustainability, the techniques and technologies analyzed, the processing and placing of design innovation and the architectural practices that result.'

Itinerary 2: The postcolonial

As we have noted above, one of the defining goals of the Handbook is to enhance cross-cultural awareness and to make the postcolonial an important part of architectural theory today. Several contributions address themes connected to postcolonial theory. Jyoti Hosagrahar does so most explicitly in Chapter 3, which is devoted to 'Interrogating Difference: Postcolonial Perspectives in Architecture and Urbanism'. After a brief discussion of the intellectual genealogy of this theory, she considers how it has informed thinking about buildings and urban space as symbolic cultural landscapes. These landscapes are shown to be political artifacts that are historically constituted and culturally constructed. Their meaning cannot be determined from a single viewpoint, since it is the result of complex negotiations between various interested parties – colonizers and colonized, architects and users, different social strata, different religious groups, etc. None of these groups is capable of monopolizing the form and significance of urban space, even if there are clear asymmetries in the distribution of power among them. Such insights, propelled by the growing scholarship on the architectural and urban culture of former colonies, have necessitated a revisiting of the architectural history of modernity, positing different conceptions of modernity as alternatives for the one that sees modernity as an essentially Western paradigm that originated in Europe and from there started to conquer the world. These alternatives are variably seen as 'multiple', 'divided', 'hybrid', 'indigenous', or, indeed, 'alternative' modernities – pointing towards the need to recognize that local versions of modernity exist that are not bleak imitations of a powerful original, but rather strong conditions that have their own internal logics and dynamics.

This theme of different modernities links Hosagrahar's chapter with Chapter 13 where Duangfang Lu discusses 'Entangled Modernities'. Lu's analysis focuses on historiographic and epistemological issues. She claims that, in order for architects to adequately respond to the entangled modernities that make up everyday reality, they have to adopt a different epistemological stance, taking their leave from the assumption that the only worthwhile outlook on architecture is the Western one. According to her, architects and architectural schools need to accept that other modernities also offer valuable sites of knowledge production; they need to embrace these alternative knowledges and approaches, in order to resist the globalizing tendency leading to social homogenization and environmental destruction.

Hosagrahar in her systematic treatment of the postcolonial paradigm in Chapter 3 also points towards ideas concerning nation and nationhood as prime topics for postcolonial investigations. This is further elaborated by Abidin Kusno in his contribution on 'Rethinking the Nation' (Section 3, Chapter 12). Kusno discusses how architecture participates in the construction of and contestation over national identities, historical memories and the everyday. Using case studies and examples from Southeast Asia, he problematizes the relationship between state and nation, between nationalism and liberalism, and between developmentalism and the everyday, showing how architecture is implicated in these different constellations. If Kusno's focus is on buildings and urban spaces and their impact on cultural constructions of nationhood, AbdouMaliq Simone approaches the same themes with less emphasis on the structuring impact of built realities. In his introductory chapter to Section 3 (Chapter 11, 'Enacting Modernity'), Simone draws attention to the flows of bodies and things, and claims that the absence of infrastructure does not necessarily mean the collapse of social life. As an anthropologist, he is sensitive to the way people make their own world in terms of the materials available to them – and these materials are all too often only immaterial realities such as memories, trajectories or imaginations. According to Simone, it is these practices and arrangements that harbour the possibility of something other and better, a possibility that is not necessarily guaranteed by actual architectural projects and interventions.

Nevertheless, as Hosagrahar, and with her Rajagopalan (Chapter 17) and Boyer (Chapter 18), argue, for many people cultural identity is invested in buildings and monuments. It is important to recognize that this investment is not automatic, nor uncontested. Hosagrahar points to the role of colonial authorities in determining what of the local past in the colonies was worth preserving and what not. Mrinalini Rajagopalan mentions how in postcolonial conditions the preservation of monuments is fraught with contradictions, bringing about the 'disappearance of history' rather than its memorialization.

M. Christine Boyer discusses what she calls 'heritage terrorism' – the siege of the collective memory of people and nations that are considered the enemy (she refers to cases of urbicide in former Yugoslavia, Israel/ Palestine and Iran). Important to her, however, is the consideration that architecture, as the archetypal collective memory, should not simply accept this designation but should ask what it is that the practice of memorialization obscures, suppresses and transforms. Narratives about buildings and their meaning can never be monopolized, they are the sites of contestation and ambivalence and only the recognition of this situation can bring about the respect that is necessary to avoid terrorism.

C. Greig Crysler, in his introduction to Section 4 (Chapter 16), links these arguments with a reflection on the role of different temporalities. He argues that postcolonial thinking has challenged the temporality of progress and innovation that underlies (Western) modernity's claim for superiority and the colonialist assumption that other cultures were lagging behind and needed to catch up with modern standards and with 'development'. Referring to Brenda Yeoh, he suggests that the everyday reality in many colonial cities was a far cry from what colonial powers intended to realize. The desired totality and temporality of the colonizing grasp most often failed to overcome the temporality of tradition and everyday practices, which proved to be much more resilient than the colonial imagination thought possible. Likewise, feminist studies in architecture have increasingly focused on the importance of spatial practices and on the interaction of theory and praxis, as Jane Rendell argues in Chapter 4. If one can point to the fact that feminist approaches and postcolonial reflections are not yet fully integrated in architectural theory, it is clear at least that they share a set of similar motivations: the desire to present an alternative to logocentrism with its colonial and patriarchal overtones, the drive to recognize, name and valorize differences, the will to address and correct unequal power relations, the ambition to understand the agency and tactical moves deployed by those in underprivileged situations.

The will to recognize differences is also at the heart of the project by Ashton Ragatt McDougal for the National Museum of Australia, discussed by Paul Walker in Chapter 20 (the project section on 'Culture'). Walker compares this building to other well-known 'postcolonial' cultural institutions – Renzo Piano's Tjibaou Cultural Centre in New Caledonia and Jean Nouvel's Musée du Quai Branly in Paris – and suggests that it uniquely problematizes its own architectural authority. In so doing, Walker argues, this project refracts the wider dilemmas of postcolonial cultural identity formation. Nevertheless – or maybe as a consequence of this ambition – the building was not well received by all parties. In his project section on 'Flows' (Chapter 25) Stephen Cairns addresses the stark contrast between the pockets of First World space one finds in airports located in places like Mumbai, with the dire Third World housing conditions that are immediately adjacent to the airports. This contrast arguably manifests the postcolonial condition in a *pars pro toto*, as Cairns elaborates in dialogue with Manuel Castells' conception of the 'space of flows'. For Cairns it is remarkable how architecture refuses to deal with the fluidity and transitoriness of this space of flows, always (re)turning to the values of stability, groundedness and longevity – an attitude that in the end negates rather than negotiates the condition of flows.

Brian McGrath and Grahame Shane (Chapter 36) likewise assert that the present-day urban condition is one in which flows of information, people and materials predominate. They suggest that established models of the metropolis – based on a colonial hierarchy of centre and periphery – and of the megalopolis – based upon sprawl and networking – are still operational but can no longer claim to offer valid solutions for contemporary challenges. These challenges have to do with the global rise of urban populations that need equitable access to renewable resources. Architects and urban planners should no longer argue that their designs are solely responsible for shaping the city. Architects can nevertheless play a constructive role in the bottom-up social organization that generate new urban configurations. Vyjayanthi Rao, in her contribution reviewing 'Slum as Theory' (Chapter 38), builds upon McGrath's and Shane's arguments by advocating a rapprochement between research and design. She argues that conventional visions of the city enshrine the plan as normative, and thus miss out the range of everyday practices of placemaking that substantiate the presence of different groups in the city. Urban ethnographies that focus on these practices allow for a rearticulation of the questions of politics, participation and expertise, and open up new spaces of interest to both social scientists and designers. By aligning themselves with these ethnographies, designers revisit the issue of participation outside of normative planning practices. They can thus tap into the imaginary of participation as a key component in the emergence of the mega-city as a valid, ethical model or even a prototype of urban futures. Examples of how such practices of everyday placemaking are put to productive use by architects and planners are discussed in Iain Low's project section on 'Housing' (Chapter 40).

Itinerary 3: Technology and aesthetics

Architecture's relationship to technology is, historically, an ambivalent one. Even, when technology is openly celebrated – as in the case of Le Corbusier's famous aphorism, 'a house is a machine for living in', or Adolf Loos' less-well-known proclamation that the plumber is the 'quartermaster of culture' – we find a disavowal of the fuller consequences of the technological in the greater attention generally lavished on the surfaces that conceal or disguise a building's technologies (see Lahiji and Friedman 1997). Reyner Banham, in his *Architecture of the Well-Tempered Environment* (1984), complained that architectural drawings were the last place to look at in order to explore a building's technological infrastructures. This was despite the mid-century diagnosis of architectural historian Siegfried Giedeon that 'mechanization takes command' (1948). This is, in a way, consistent with a more general conception of technology as standing in opposition to organically defined categories such as the body, life, society or culture. Embedded in this structure is the assumption that these 'life' categories can be credited with some spontaneous and organic principle that technology does not have. Technology, by contrast, is understood to be programmed, regulated and mechanistic. The technological comes to be located in architectural discourse in a complex way; architecture is fundamentally entangled in the technological, yet rarely confronts it head on.

This set of concerns finds its most focused expression, as we would expect, in Section 6, Science/technology/virtuality. The section as a whole is framed by Arie Graafland and Heidi Sohn's introductory essay (Chapter 26). They deploy Timothy Luke's concepts of 'third nature', as an informational cybersphere/telesphere that radically extends the biosphere of the 'first nature', and the industrial, territorial logics of the 'second nature'. This framework usefully locates contemporary debates on digital media, digital fabrication and dematerialization. Refusing, what Richard Coyne (2001) has called the techno-romanticism so often attached to digital technology, Graafland and Sohn critically assess the 'bodiless holograms and empty simulations' of virtual architectures and the complex materiality and embodiments of contemporary everyday life. Antoine Picon (Chapter 28) situates the contemporary engagement with digital technologies within the wider debate on postindustrial production and consumption, and its uneven manifestation globally. His analysis hinges on the waning autonomy of technological artifacts, and the rise of the 'quasi-object' in the context of networked technological systems. This situation has powerful consequences for the logics of autonomy that have long been coded into architectural practice. The new conceptions of materiality, aesthetics, performativity and sustainability that are provoked, demand, Picon argues, new transdisciplinary practices. Some of Picon's principle themes are amplified and extended in Jonathan Hale's discussion of the place of the body and human consciousness within this technological network (Chapter 29). The flip side of the quasi-object is, in a sense, a prostheticized body and mind. Hale explores the sense of threat that such a hybrid prosthesis poses to humanist threads in architectural theory, and goes on to consider new forms of virtual embodiment and consciousness. N. Katherine Hayles and Todd Gannon (Chapter 27) further thicken this thread in their essay 'Virtual Architecture, Digital Media' with their detailed analysis of representational media and the varying 'forensic' and 'formal' materialities associated with the spread of digital media in architectural production.

From here the reader might step neatly onto Christopher Hight's essay 'Manners of Working: Fabricating Representation in Digital Based Design' in Section 5, Design/Production/Practice (Chapter 23). Hight plots the ways in which emerging digital media are transforming the foundational conceptual bases of design practice. The technological thread finds expression in a number of other essays that engage with architecture as a professional practice in Section 5. Paolo Tombesi's discussion (Chapter 22) of outsourcing of significant aspects of design and building production work to India from architectural offices in Australia, for example, powerfully exemplifies the discussions in Picon, Hale, and Graafland and Sohn. While the circumstantial realities of architectural production are elaborated by David Salomon's concept of 'dirty realism' and the ways in which design practices continuously manage the contingencies of the world (Chapter 24).

As is already perhaps evident, those sub-branches of this itinerary that engage with corporeality and the body might tempt the reader to explore Section 2, Aesthetics/pleasure/excess. Section editors, John Macarthur and Naomi Stead point out that aesthetics is 'perhaps the least developed area of modern architectural theory'. And, given that architecture is usually regarded as involving something more than the mere 'management of natural and social situations', readers might reasonably expect to find a sustained articulation of the discipline's interface with 'philosophical aesthetics or theories of art and artistic affect' in architectural discourse. Instead, discussion of aesthetics – under such varied headings as pleasure and entertainment, taste, ennui, distortion and constraint, abstraction, and corporeality – is dispersed through various sub-disciplinary debates, not least the consideration of technology. So it is, perhaps, not surprising to find, for example, the formalism that Hayles and Gannon discuss in the context of architectural technology resonating with Sandra Kaji-O'Grady's essay on 'Formalism and Forms of Practice' in Section 2 (Chapter 8). Kaji-O'Grady examines the impact of formalist theories developed in philosophy, literature and the visual arts on architectural criticism and practice. She teases out the complex ways in which aesthetics has been the site upon which architecture simultaneously stakes and destabilizes its claims as an autonomous practice. Conventional rule-governed approaches that underpin good taste are shown to be in tension with a persistent sub-current in the discipline that experiments with the irregularities, transgressiveness, and even abjection, of bad form. To loop this thread back upon itself, the reader might return from this discussion of the transgressive aesthetics of the formless to the chapters by Hale and Hayles and Gannon and their consideration of the everyday technologies that come into play when architects – such as Diller, Scofidio and Renfro; François Roche and Stéphanie Lavaux; and Philippe Rahm – seek to materialize 'formless' effects architecturally.

Although this lively strand of contemporary practice does not explicitly frame itself in phenomenological terms, it is clear that this work resonates with this significant intellectual tradition in architecture. Jorge Otero-Pailos (Chapter 7) sets out a clear account of this tradition, documenting the key players, and reminding readers of the profound effects this tradition had on the discipline. Otero-Pailos' essay is significant too, for its contribution to our understanding of the ways in which architectural theory, especially through a disciplinary interest in phenomenology, came to simultaneously distinguish itself from architectural history and claim an explicit place in the process of design itself. Bart Verschaffel's discussion (Chapter 9) of the fracturing of once fixed and immemorial aesthetic categories and the emergence of subjective, relational, sensate categories of aesthetic experience in the Enlightenment offers an important grounding to the wider discussion. It historicizes the phenomenological strand in architectural theory, further thickening the relationship with technology through his account of the structure–ornament debate, aired by Picon in Section 6. Fischer's essay (Chapter 2) on the critical and post-critical in architecture offers a useful interface between the philosophical aspects of the collection, and those that engage with or are motivated by matters of practice. Here the practicalities of getting buildings built evidently press upon more metaphysical tendencies in architectural theory. Paola Viganò, on the other hand (Chapter 37), deals with European cityscapes, arguing that urban and regional infrastructures offer the technological support to accommodate contemporary lifestyles, and are thus highly important elements that play a major (if often unacknowledged) role in the construction of the collective imaginary.

Finally, we might consider two further chapters that signal distinctive trajectories from this juncture. Both complicate the technology/aesthetics nexus by situating their discussions in contexts that are heavily over-determined by political tensions. Delia Duong Ba Wendel (Chapter 30) explores architecture's intricate relationship to infrastructure through the lens of Hurricane Katrina and its effects on New Orleans. Wendel diagnoses a history of under-investment in particular parts of that city, and shows that subsequent urban development was profoundly racialized. Well-to-do areas populated by white residents develop with infrastructural underpinnings, while poorer, black neighbourhoods do not. Wendel argues that the devastation of New Orleans was pre-scripted and, furthermore, that a nuanced understanding of the complex entanglement of architecture and infrastructure is required to properly see it. Working with similar themes, but through a more global set of sites, Deborah Natsios (Chapter 39) examines what we might describe as the aesthetics of anxiety associated with the society of control. Drawing on Deleuze's distinction between discipline and control, she plots a myriad of networked micro-sites of control – pizza parlours, museums, border checkpoints – that increasingly structure the urban experience for many. This attention to specific urban sites allows her to extend and ground arguments regarding the collapse of distinctions between public and private spheres, and even outside and inside, in many cities today.

A fourth itinerary: Absences

By way of concluding this readers' guide, we sketch a fourth itinerary plotted against those themes we have not addressed in this Handbook in any sustained way. Such an itinerary, an inevitable corollary of the principle of open-endedness to which we aspire, gestures towards some of the obvious absences in the collection as it stands, and flags directions for future research. Here we might think of practice-based research, architecture and ethics, community based practice and rethinkings of queer theory.

The most important absence probably has to do with 'tacit' architectural theories, which are operational in many institutions of architecture, but which do not present themselves as such. One could argue, for example, that tacit architectural theories are instrumental in the setting up of architectural curricula – determining the relative importance of design, history and technology (to name just these) as constitutive elements of the education of an architect. When reviewing these curricula, one also comes across instances where 'theories' in the authoritative sense of the term are being used, without the counterbalance provided by the disruptive impulse that we described in the introduction as crucial for *theoria.* In courses on building science, for example, norms and standards regarding 'comfort' are uncritically transmitted as if they are based on solid facts rather than on historically constructed agreements (Shove 2003). Likewise courses on universal design (or 'inclusive design' as it is now called) are often taught without taking into account the critique of 'normality' produced by queer studies (Ingraham 2006; McRuer 2006). Implicit architectural theories are also operational in policies for the upgrading of urban centres or for the stimulation of architectural culture (as is the case in many European countries). Though we have been concerned from the outset to acknowledge how institutions shape, and are shaped by, architectural theory, the Handbook does not examine in any depth such instances of 'applied' architectural theory.

We might also refer to the question of design (as) research, an important and growing field with an expanding institutional space. The Handbook recognizes that the question of how to transfer theoretical understandings to the practice of design is important – hence the eight project sections interleaved through the collection. Yet we know that the absence of an elaborate reflection on this theme, beyond the case study format we have employed, might dissatisfy those architectural theorists for whom bridging theory and design constitutes the core of their teaching. It might also dissatisfy those who are working hard to bring design research up to the level of a recognized academic methodology, enriching architectural research by widening the set of available techniques and approaches (Geiser 2008; Till undated; van Schaik 2005).

Another important issue that is notably absent is that of participation and activism. During the 1970s, in the wane of modernism, advocacy planning and calls for participation of users briefly gained prominence on the architectural scene (Tzonis and Lefaivre 1976), soon to be dismissed – or at least ignored – when postmodernism came along (Jencks 1977; Harvey 1989). Underneath the surface, however, practices of participation have continued to be important in urban planning processes and hence in architectural practice (Blundell Jones et al. 2005; Ghirardo 1991; Jenkins and Forsyth 2009). Debates about governance versus government, concerns about stakeholders and honest attempts to provide underprivileged groups with architectural services, continue to be relevant for the discipline – even when such items lack recognition and visibility in the dominant publications (Loeckx 2005). In this Handbook they are just touched upon in the contribution by David Salomon (Chapter 24), but it is good to see that recent publications are making a case again for design as activism (Bell and Wakeford 2008) and for a renewed, in-depth engagement with ethics (Owen 2009; Ray 2005; Wasserman et al. 2000).

Reflecting on the metaphorics and aesthetics of travel, Georges Van den Abbeele (1992) argues that travel effects a kind of transgression of the home, of the situated and the place-bound by heightening the experience of time. The role of the itinerary, in his analysis, is to domesticate the transgression of home by turning the mobility of travel into a narrative. The itinerary (re)spatializes time, rendering it graspable, recountable and mappable. However, and here we can sense something of the disruptive potential of the term, 'the home that one leaves is not the same as that to which one returns' (Van den Abbeele 1992, xix).

BIBLIOGRAPHY

Banham, Reyner (1984) *Architecture of the Well-Tempered Environment.* Chicago: University of Chicago Press.

Coyne, Richard (2001) *Technoromanticism: Digital Narrative, Holism, and the Romance of the Real.* Cambridge, MA: MIT Press.

Geiser, Reto (ed.) (2008) *Explorations in Architecture: Teaching, Design, Research.* Basel: Birkhauser.

Harvey, David (1989) *The Condition of Postmodernity. An Enquiry into the Origins of Cultural Change.* Oxford: Blackwell

Ingraham, Chrys (2006) 'Thinking straight, acting bent. heteronormativity and homosexuality', in Kathy Davis, Mary Evans and Judith Lorber (eds) *Handbook of Gender and Women's Studies.* London: SAGE, 307–321.

Jencks, Charles (1977) *The Language of Post-Modern Architecture.* New York: Rizzoli.

Lahiji, Nadir and Daniel S. Friedman (eds) (1997) *Plumbing: Sounding Modern Architecture.* New York: Princeton Architectural Press.

Loeckx, André, Kelly Shannon, Rafael Tuts and Han Verschure (eds) (2004) *Urban Trialogues: Visions, Projects, Co-productions.* Nairobi: UN Habitat.

McRuer, Robert (2006) *Cultural Signs of Queerness and Disability.* New York: New York University Press.

Owen, Graham (ed.) (2009) *Architecture, Ethics and Globalization.* London: Routledge.

Ray, Nicholas (ed.) (2005) *Architecture and its Ethical Dilemmas.* New York and London: Routledge.

Shove, Elizabeth (2003) *Comfort, Cleanliness and Convenience. The Social Organization of Normality.* London: Berg.

Till, Jeremy (on behalf of the RIBA Research Committee) (undated) 'What is architectural research?', http://www.architecture.com/Files/RIBAProfessionalServices/ResearchAndDevelopment/WhatisArchitecturalResearch.pdf, consulted August 2, 2010.

Tzonis, Alexander and Liane Lefaivre (1976) 'In the name of the people'. *Forum* 25(3): 5–33.

Van den Abbeele, Georges (1992) *Travel as Metaphor: From Montaigne to Rousseau.* Minneapolis: University of Minnesota Press.

van Schaik, Leon (2005) *Mastering Architecture: Becoming a Creative Innovator in Practice.* London: Wiley.

Wasserman, Barry, Patrick Sullivan and Gregory Palermo (eds) (2000) *Ethics and the Practice of Architecture.* New York: Wiley.

Žižek, Slavoj (2001) *Enjoy Your Symptom!: Jacques Lacan in Hollywood and Out.* London: Routledge.

SECTION 1

Power/Difference/Embodiment

1

Introduction: Shifting Paradigms and Concerns

Hilde Heynen and Gwendolyn Wright

Architecture houses and holds human beings in an intimate way, enframing them in a manner not unlike clothing (although admittedly less intimately). It thereby mediates between people and their wider environment, providing a membrane that protects bodies from intruders and climatic incursions such as rain or cold. It also gives them a symbolic presence, at once internal and in terms of the outside world, in which variations can have radically divergent effects on individual psyches. No single person controls this complex mediation; it involves ongoing negotiations about social, cultural, economic and political matters. This is how architecture is intertwined with articulations of power and difference. Power is relevant when discussing the privileged role of the architect, but also when analysing presumptions about the individual and the public, including the client, or when investigating the social and environmental impact of buildings. Architectural and urban spaces can sustain, question or modify political and social structures of power. Spatial patterns interact with existing cultural constructions of gender, class, race, geography and status, usually upholding established hierarchies with exciting new imagery, sometimes defying those norms. This introductory chapter explores how such issues have given rise to consecutive and overlapping strands of theoretical explorations. By doing so it frames and positions the next three chapters, which analyse some of these issues in greater depth.

Theories about architecture entail self-conscious analyses about underlying systems, influences, intentions, conditions and changes over time. If Western theories have evolved and altered considerably since antiquity, the pace and passions of change during the second half of the twentieth century seem unprecedented. Moreover, whereas the centre of gravity in earlier periods was clearly Europe, American voices have become more prominent (Mallgrave 2005; Mallgrave and Contandrioupolos 2008). The intellectual horizons of architectural theory have also shifted. If in the decades before 1970 practising architects, focusing on aesthetics, set the tone (Ockman 1993), since then the advent of post-structuralist literary theory and the emancipatory goals of political/social radicalism brought in other voices with concerns that were quite distinct from design processes as such. These new influences altered many fundamental conceptions about architecture and its effects. Some people have criticized this intellectual stance as too distant and abstract, too far removed from the actual practices of designing and using buildings. Nonetheless, this more intellectualized mode has reset the tone of architectural debate that emanates from publications, conferences and courses (Nesbitt 1996; Hays 1998). The intensity and the very nature of the issues have opened new directions in the last decades of the twentieth century, resulting in a fluid and diverse field of multiple, sometimes incommensurable theories.

The new theorists looked beyond the themes of individual originality, harmonious composition and phenomenological resonance which had up until the 1960s defined architectural discourse. Concurrently, the figure of the theorist became increasingly detached from the practising architect, and architectural theory evolved into a full-fledged, full-time academic discipline. The shift began in the 1970s when neo-marxism provided a widespread critical perspective. Authors such as Alexander Tzonis (1972) and Manfredo Tafuri (1976) introduced a theoretical framework that confronted the link between architectural developments and their socio-political context. They questioned whether an architect's good intentions indeed translated into socio-political benefits, given that the demands of capitalism played a significant role in architecture's history – and its present (see also Aureli 2008).

Michel Foucault, especially in his writings on the hospital (1973) and the prison (1977), provided the next major influence, taken up by Tafuri in his later years and taken to heart by a whole series of architectural scholars in the late 1970s and early 1980s. Foucault explained how expert knowledge affects the social workings of power, and thus how certain architectural configurations (such as the famous panopticon) can play a role in disciplining people's minds and bodies. He opened the way for a series of studies that investigated how diverse buildings and social patterns interact. Most architectural theorists believed that spatial configurations could embody and reinforce human attitudes and interactions, albeit with diverse interpretations of the specific role. Whereas Foucault himself insisted that no architectural form could be inherently oppressive or liberating, since human actions were the critical factor (Wright 2005), not all his followers have taken this point to heart.

Post-structuralism, which challenged prevailing concepts of inherent qualities or simple binary relationships, flourished in Paris from the late 1960s onwards, with, next to Foucault, writers such as Julia Kristeva, Jean-François Lyotard, Roland Barthes and Jean Baudrillard. Deconstructive philosophy, based on the writings of Jacques Derrida, soon formed one particular strand that emphasized the instability and defensive self-regard in all forms of language. Architectural theory absorbed these influences and applied them to visual languages. This absorption occurred with a bit of a time delay, since literary theory and criticism mediated the impact of continental French theory, especially on the American intellectual scene (see Bloom 1979). At first it seemed as if semiotics, the study of languages as systems of signs, would reinvigorate architectural theory at the wane of modernism. Charles Jencks and George Baird (1969) explored the concept of meaning in architecture, followed by other authors who tried to develop more systematic reflections on how architecture worked as a medium of communication (Eco 1972, Norberg-Schulz 1975).

Miscommunication was a major theme in the critiques of technocracy and top-down planning during these same years. The semiotic focus soon tied in with a criticism of the theoretical foundations of architectural modernism, leading Jencks to announce the 'Death of Modernism' – and hence the arrival of postmodernism (Jencks 1977). Architectural postmodernism was not fully in line with postmodern philosophy as described by Lyotard, since it relied upon a teleological understanding of architecture's course, putting postmodernism chronologically 'after' modernism which was at odds with how Lyotard saw the relationship between both paradigms (Lyotard 1992).

It shared nevertheless with philosophical postmodernism a suspicion of presumptions about rationality and transparency. It became increasingly difficult to simply presume these were stable guiding principles in architecture (as they had seemed to be within the Modern Movement). Architects now had to confront the power relations inherent in all such language systems.

Post-structuralism, postmodernism and deconstruction thus taught architectural theorists to question the logocentrism that is entrenched in Western thinking. The Purism, essentialism and universalism that had dominated modernist architectural discourse for the better part of the twentieth century gave way to hybridity, constructionism and relativism. Feminist and postcolonial theories appropriated these concepts and gave them a more direct and activist meaning, emphasizing how difference is embodied and thereby used to separate people according to gender, class and ethnicity. A growing literature on architecture and gender raised fundamental questions about the literal and symbolic embodiment of architectural values and biases. Postcolonial critiques highlighted themes of difference in architecture's geographical and cultural hierarchies – both cultural differences to respect and inequalities to expose.

These volatile forces have constituted the most visible currents in architectural theory in the past few decades. Although they are by no means the only viable way to 'do' architectural theory – as will become clear in the other sections of this volume – they constitute pertinent challenges for architecture and architects. Hence we begin this volume with an extensive discussion of recent paradigms and concerns related to issues of power, difference and embodiment.

ARCHITECTURE AND POWER

Contemporary architectural theories often emphasize how buildings and physical settings reveal, accentuate or challenge various structures of power that are otherwise difficult to discern. This extends from a global realm of economies, ecologies and cultural dominance to the particularities of specific groups and even those of individual subjectivities. If the theoretical frameworks of neo-Marxism and post-structuralism first addressed the macro-scale of how societal relationships intersect with architectural movements and discourses, later approaches narrowed the scope to scrutinize specific building types or spatial configurations in circumscribed times and settings.

An early example of this highly focused work can be found in Reinhard Bentmann and Michael Müller's study of the villa, published in German in 1970 and translated only in 1992 as *The Villa as Hegemonic Architecture* (conspicuously without the chapter on the Israeli-kibbutz ideology'). This Marxist study embedded the analysis of architectural sources (drawings, manuals, buildings) within a broader context that drew upon political, social and economic history, effectively showing how this building type has embodied particular power relationships that endure and others that change over time.

Thomas A. Markus undertook a similar enterprise two decades later in his *Buildings and Power* (1993), which focused on new building types developed between roughly 1750 and 1850, notably schools, prisons, public libraries, museums and factories. Rather than appropriating an overtly Marxist or Foucauldian theoretical framework, Markus used Bill Hillier and Julienne Hanson's space syntax (1984) as an overarching analytical instrument. Space syntax claims to be a specifically *architectural* theory, based on spatial/architectural parameters rather than importing philosophical or social theories from other disciplines. Its basic idea is that spatial configurations have an ordering impact on how social relationships unfold and that it is possible to unravel this connection by studying underlying spatial patterns, such as 'depth' (the number of thresholds to cross before reaching the innermost space in a building) or 'axiality' (the presence of a long visual axis). The core users of space syntax – Hillier, Hanson and their students – have elaborated this model into computational software that is being applied in a variety of historical and geographical cases, albeit with mixed results. Space syntax tends to be used in an abstract, universalist way that does not take account of cultural or social differences among people. Authors such as Markus or Kim Dovey (1999) couple a basic version of the space syntax toolkit with other interpretational frameworks – social history, art history, social theory, hermeneutics – which allows them to deploy it without overly reductive effects.

These various studies have expanded the purview of architectural history and theory away from a few iconic monumental buildings towards a wide range of modest, indeed ordinary and commonly used structures. Few contemporary architectural scholars would agree with Nikolaus Pevsner's infamous dictum that 'a bicycle shed is a building, but Lincoln cathedral is a piece of architecture' (1957, 23). In traditional scholarship, as Markus correctly observed (1993, 26), researchers treated buildings as art, as material objects or as investments, but rarely as social objects. These earlier architectural historians tended to adopt methods and techniques from art history, relegating the study of technical or financial aspects to engineering and real estate. The emphasis on buildings as socially relevant objects, however, requires an interdisciplinary perspective, one that intertwines architectural analysis with methodologies developed in fields like anthropology, sociology, psychology or geography (Lawrence and Low 1990, 2003). Architectural theorists and historians have gradually integrated such parallels, becoming far more precise and refined in the process.

Social and cultural geographies have had a major impact, often emphasizing the effects of imperialism and colonialism on urban space. Brenda Yeoh's book on colonial Singapore (2000) has been influential in showing how British and Asian conceptions of the city contributed to and clashed with one another, a tension that has affected Singapore's present shape. Jane M. Jacobs' study on postcolonialism and the city revealed how different spatial interpretations lead to volatile social geometries of power, signification and contestation in every part of the world (1996).

Blank: Architecture, Apartheid and After (Judin and Vladislavic 1999) was one of the first books on architecture to fully integrate a broad-based social perspective into discussions about contemporary architecture without neglecting historical legacies. The very layout of the book juxtaposes diverse perspectives among South African architect-activists and theorists, some of whom lambast the spatial legacies of racism in cities and townships, while others explore alternative possibilities for reconciliation. In a similar manner, Eyal Weizman's *Hollow Land: Israel's Architecture of Occupation* (2007) deftly interweaves military and political history, astute three-dimensional mapping, a deconstruction of archeological discourse and a wry disquisition on the Israeli military's appropriation of Situationist theories. Weizman uses the word 'architecture' in a double sense, indicating both the built structures that sustain the occupation (walls, bridges, tunnels, settlements, checkpoints and watchtowers) and a metaphor for the constructed nature of political issues.

To some extent the widened scope of what constitutes 'architecture' connects to a desire to side with or at least stand up for the powerless that first emerged in the 1970s. Initially united under the rubric of advocacy, some radical architects and planners had worked closely with impoverished and disempowered groups in American cities, rural areas and other sites throughout the world, such as 'informal' urban settlements (barrios, bidonvilles, favelas, etc.) in the fast-growing Third World cities. The ongoing interest in David Harvey, Manuel Castells and the legacy of John F.C. Turner reaffirms a vision of radical global changes through specific local interventions. Whereas these issues have had little play among the most visible theorists (e.g. in the so-called 'post-criticality' debate), they are nevertheless taken up by several more politically oriented authors.

Issues of citizens' rights have recently come to the fore, especially in terms of rights for the poor, the powerless and other marginalized groups in specific settings, both urban and rural. [See discussions in this section (Chapter 3) but also in Sections 5 (Chapter 24) and 8 (Chapter 38), as well as in Chapter 40 on housing.] Provocative recent debates have emphasized a spatial dimension to citizenship. In principle, a nation-state defines citizens as those people who are born in and or live within its borders – thus privileging a space-bounded view on citizenship. Yet the fluidity of globalization encompasses transnational movements of people and internal socio-economic disparities, both of which accentuate divergences from 'formal' and 'substantive' citizenship for those who seem to be 'outsiders'. Even long-time residents may not be able to claim the privileges that supposedly go along with that status (housing, social security, etc.). Demands for these rights in cities and rural areas have given rise to what Holston (1999) calls 'insurgent citizenship'. The inverse is also true in that wealthy foreign investors, producers and tourists often exercise considerable influence over the use, access and appearance of specific urban spaces, even when they are neither citizens nor residents.

All these explorations have brought *representation* to the fore. Key questions extend from visual modalities to the subjectivity of user responses and on to political metaphors. Section 5 will discuss the effects of computer drawings and models of future buildings. Here we are principally interested in representation as it relates to subjectivity and to political issues. Recent cognitive and psychological theorists, notably Jacques Lacan, relate representational images to conceptions of subjectivity. Reflecting on such propositions might lead us to emphasize the role of representational spaces in subject formation – arguing for example that girly bedrooms help construct female subjectivities or that master bedrooms support heterosexuality as the norm. Given these interrelations, how might we best think about the subject that creates and the subjects that inhabit a space? Do certain representational techniques tend to reinforce norms, generate alternatives and/or sustain other critiques?

The early dominance of psychoanalytic theory has now extended from inquiries about the architect's individual creativity and a supposedly collective response of the public – both of which have multiple and competing dimensions. Some theorists have questioned the interactions between architectural innovations and various understandings of domesticity (Heynen and Baydar 2005) or the impact of urban renewal on people's sense of home (Porteous and Smith 2001). Others have focused on incentives for daring innovation or the individual's role in the rapid succession of transformations in generic types like housing or infrastructure (Bell 2004; Varnelis 2008). Still others have asked how physical spaces affect concepts of gender and sexuality; race and ethnicity; or class and status (Rendell et al. 1999; Wilkins 2007; Zukin 2009). This leads in turn to questions about the avant-garde concept of *estrangement,* hisorically considered liberatory, and the parallel disdain for familiarity, which seemed an inevitable constraint. Some theorists are now pointing out that certain forms of familiarity might be a necessary base for innovations and comparisons, as is the case with laboratory experiments (Picon and Ponte 2003). Established patterns may reinforce 'traditional' expectations but they also allow a platform for exploring alternatives, even transgressions of established norms, as in the sciences or indeed in legislation. Recent interest in the work of Pierre Bourdieu has brought new subtleties to the debate about cultural capital and discrimination that is fundamental to architectural judgement. Bourdieu's notion of the *habitus* also aligns the structure of architectural settings with that of more practical activities that effect the power of invention (Pinto 2002; Lipstadt 2003).

Many recent theorists continue to explore the political implications of representation in the sense of representative democracies, community participation and the hierarchy of architecture firms. The 1960s to 1970s encompassed active political involvement along with critiques of good intentions by Manfredo Tafuri and Michel Foucault. New strategies for 'participation' and public debate about architectural design – especially the need for choices – emerged in the 1980s. The 1990s then imported ideas about hybridity from Néstor García Canclini and Homi Bhabha, criticizing purity as exclusionary. Several key questions have emerged. Does the public have a right to good architecture in addition to the architect's right to explore new ideas? To what extent and by what criteria do non-architects – clients, users and various members of the public, often competing with one another – judge architecture? How can we distinguish between differences based on culture or group preferences and others that constitute inequalities? If we acknowledge that architects can produce settings geared to rigid discipline and oppression, which may not be immediately visible, how might we conceive of an architecture of resistance (see also Chapter 5)?

All these questions draw upon post-structuralist theory in that they refuse to acknowledge a privileged position for Western man as the subject of a teleological history, as centre and reference point for notions of progress and development. And yet, if the earlier concept of 'modern man' no longer holds, no adequate substitute has emerged. The individual 'self' can be variously understood as a heroic author/architect, a narcissist or as a person who may want to resist or at least question what is imposed, however inarticulate or frustrated those reservations might be. Post-structuralist theory considers all these selves as 'agents' rather than 'subjects' since they are clearly conditioned by and responding to societal and spatial conditions which they can negotiate but cannot overcome. In a similar way, architects (and theorists) are agents whose ideas about creativity, reception and effects are likewise conditioned by their time and circumstances, although they too can choose to emphasize or ignore a particular topic or audience.

Ole Fischer's chapter on criticality (Chapter 2) deals with many of these issues, focusing on a most interesting debate that unfolded during the years since 2000. In the wake of Tafuri's and Foucault's analyses of architecture's interconnection with power, a dominant tendency within architecture and within architectural theory has espoused criticality: the desire to relate *critically* to hegemonic societal powers, either by exposing manipulative societal conditions through formal language – sometimes denouncing the very powers that brought a building into being – or by positioning planning and design interventions in such a way that they benefit or at least take the side of disadvantaged social groups. Both kinds of critical architecture have recently been taken to task for being too convoluted, too intellectualized, too difficult and distanced or simply too boring. In unraveling the intricacies of these debates, Fischer points towards hidden geographies (notably Europe versus North America). Like other cohorts, he draws on Bruno Latour, especially his emphasis on 'connections' rather than static space and mutable 'aggregates' with open borders and relatively fixed agents such as 'the architect' or 'architecture'. Fischer thus pleads for a more honest self-reflection in which architecture is not just a matter of interest, but also a matter of concern (Latour and Wiebel 2005; Latour 2007; Graham and Marvin 2001).

POWER AND DIFFERENCE

Given that power has become a major issue in architectural theory over the last several decades, it stands to reason that *difference* and *embodiment* have come to the fore. These are the warp and woof of power relations; one might even state that some differences are 'produced' by uneven power relations. Patriarchy, imperialism, colonialism and economic dominance emphasize particular characteristics to bolster inequalities between, respectively, men and women, West and East, colonizer and colonized, city and country. These differences do not exist in an abstract way: they are embodied in real persons who can be subjected to real discrimination.

Whereas the heroic generations of modernists believed they could wipe away all differences based upon class, ethnicity or gender – uniting all humanity under the banner of a shared belief in progress and emancipation – it has become clear that differences among people and places are profound and persistent. Likewise, assertions of a necessary break with local and regional geographies no longer hold up. Many contemporary theorists stress the importance of climate and landscape as well as history and culture in people's relations with the built environment (see also Sections 4 and 7). A few postmodernists who criticized the modernist tabula rasa have recently moved towards 'ecological' notions of interconnection, a paradigm that extends from environmental pragmatists to some of the pleas for a 'new urbanism'. Landscapes are no longer presumed to be bucolic; they can be dangerous, vulnerable, urban and even conceptual. Human interventions can take many forms. Debates about 'critical regionalism' that began with Tzonis and Lefaivre's analyses of post-WWII Greek modernism in the 1970s then expanded with Kenneth Frampton's call for abstract expressions of local tectonic and climactic conditions. In contrast, explorations of the distinctive modernist idioms of Latin America, Southeast Asia, the Middle East and other regions now emphasize the incorporation of 'traditional' climactic adaptations together with modern technological innovations (see also Chapter 34). Here, too, those who argue for the essence or genius loci of a place now encounter criticisms that they unintentionally encourage unequal hierarchies, eco-consumerism and tourism. In sum, it is no longer possible to claim that architectural practice or theory can bracket out the complex distinctions and interconnections, both global and local, at the core of environmental issues.

Even without resorting to post-structuralist theories, therefore, the notion of difference has taken on a primary role in many architectural discourses. Engagement with the work of authors such as Derrida, Lyotard or Foucault has given philosophical depth to these issues. For Derrida, *differance* – a play upon the French words for 'differing' and 'deferring' – is an inescapable feature of language: language is built upon differences between words, the meanings of which can never be fixed but are always subject to further clarification. There is no ultimate guarantee that words mean what we want them to mean, since this chain of signification can never be anchored in a transcendent entity (such as 'God') accepted by all users of the language. Lyotard takes this idea one step further by exploring its social consequences. His book *Differend* (1989) investigates situations in which a conflict arises that cannot be resolved because there are no rules of judgement that both parties accept as applicable to the case. If parties do not agree about the rules of the game, the game cannot be played in a fair way. Lyotard argues convincingly that this situation often occurs because language produces different genres of discourses which are not always compatible with one another. Rather than ignore this differend – whether by subsuming everything under the same denominator of money (capitalism) or by playing one's own game as if it is the master game ruling all others (academia) – he insists that philosophy must bear witness to the differend. Lyotard's 'language games' resemble Foucault's 'discursive formations,' indicating a loose constellation of interconnected theories about what can be spoken and comprehended in a given historical context. Foucault suggested that such discursive formations may determine what kind of ideas can gain foothold, and hence which ones are closely related to regimes of power. Not incidentally, he insisted that power did not radiate out from one person or one centre (a king or a government); it is an ongoing process in which finely dispersed structural forces regulate everyone's behaviour, including those who exercise considerable power over others, in a continuous concatenation of actions and reactions.

Postcolonial theories have used these ideas in order to unravel how colonialism used specialized or expert knowledge production and how colonized people negotiated, contested and twisted colonial spaces. Edward Said's *Orientalism* (1978) has been a major reference. Said argued that imperial practices were closely intertwined with modes of knowledge production that looked back to the Enlightenment project of modernity. Indeed, colonial discourse was intrinsic to European self-understanding since knowledge about foreign peoples and territories (two closely linked topics) allowed Europeans to position themselves as modern, civilized, superior, developed and progressive while local colonized populations supposedly possessed none of these qualities (Venn 2000). Said's *Orientalism* refered specifically to a body of scholarly knowledge and practices that characterized the Orient as the 'other' or antithesis of the Occident, roughly equating it with the mysterious, the exotic, the excessive, the irrational, the alien. This 'other' was seen as the negation of everything that Europe imagined or desired itself to be. Since Europe's 'modern' virtues would continue to progress, the differences would always remain intact. Historians such as Gwendolyn Wright (1991) or Zeynep Çelik (1997b) have brought these topics to the fore in architectural history and theory. Yet even today few accounts of modernity and modernism acknowledge this crucial role of colonialism in the self-understanding of Western culture. Although some 'alternative modernities' have been introduced in recent years, the pivotal role of colonialism has been conveniently ignored in the conventional historiography of the Modern Movement.

Jyoti Hosagrahar discusses these themes in Chapter 3. She acknowledges that postcolonial perspectives in architecture and urbanism do not comprise a well-defined body of knowledge, although they do share an intellectual starting point in what she calls 'intellectual decolonization': the active rejection of spaces and discourses based in hegemonic dualities (modern versus traditional, centre versus periphery, universal versus local, Western versus non-Western). Postcolonial thinking explores multiplicities and hybrids, studying precisely those spaces and practices that cannot be qualified as either 'modern' or 'traditional' since they occupy a position in between. Such an approach raises questions about the conventional categories and narratives in all aspects of architectural history. (Why is Europe almost always the focus of general histories of architecture? Why do we presume that innovations always radiate outward from a vital centre to peripheral hinterlands that can only copy and, often as not, 'misinterpret' that modernity?)

Postcolonialism thus provides insights into the multiple ways that archiecture is implicated in the socio-political processes of nation-building and the economic geopolitics of globalization, in the present as in the past. How do we judge improvements that may benefit local populations, even as they endanger environments and entrench dominant powers? This dilemma, so conspicuous in colonial and neo-colonial settings, underlies every architectural intervention. We see that the history of architecture is also inscribed in the trajectories of 'minor' architects who negotiate between the requirements of powerful political authorities on the one hand and the specific local realities of materials, skills and cultural traditions on the other. This in turn calls attention to the challenges and accomplishments of contemporary architects and urbanists who 'design from the margins', those who practise on the edges of the places where avant-garde architectural culture is produced and promoted, especially those who work in and for places where the goals of social responsibility, sustainability and multiplicity require new kinds of reflection and new forms of architectural creativity.

Difference is also a crucial term for feminist theories, as Jane Rendell explains in Chapter 4. Feminist architects began to develop gendered critiques of architecture in the 1970s. This was at first inspired by an activist, political mood that aimed to break down the barriers for women in the architectural profession and, simultaneously, to expose and alleviate gender discrimination in the 'man-made' built environment. Feminist concerns gradually shifted towards a critique of conventional understandings of architecture based on monumental buildings and the master works of canonized male architects. Architectural historians began to study women architects and the role of female patrons in the production of architecture. Feminist architects developed new forms of interdisciplinary praxis that questioned the boundaries of architecture as a discipline. Difference and location became central concerns as these theorists insisted that knowledge is always situated, and so one must always consider the standpoint from which insights are being developed. Knowledge is not free-floating; it is embodied in persons, who are differently situated in terms of class, race, culture and gender. These circumstances are not incidental; they directly affect the kinds of knowledge that are produced and disseminated. Converging with postcolonial perspectives and other analyses of power, feminism and gender studies have radically altered the parameters of architectural theory.

These intellectual explorations have thus brought the stability of 'architecture' as a concept into question. Architecture is shown to be a contested territory, no longer the undisputed legacy of 'the canon' – whether this is the chronicle of 'masterworks' running from the Egyptian pyramids to the Seattle Public Library or the privileged terrain of white males who have defined avant-garde culture. Diverse groups are asserting their right to make architecture productive and meaningful on their own terms. These terrains include feminist collectives working to protect women against male violence, subaltern practices seeking to redefine what constitutes heritage, 'minor' designers exploring the aesthetic terrains of specific regions, and writers mapping the intersections of autobiography, critical writing and poetic spatial practices. These diverse voices have not achieved a profound change in conventional practices and disciplinary boundaries, but they have had a significant impact on architectural theory, in that they show how conventional understandings of architecture are – wittingly or unwittingly – bound up with patriarchy and cultural hegemony.

The language of these critical voices has become more precise and pointed since the 1960s as analysts have drawn upon broader intellectual tendencies. Recent theories have incorporated a revived environmentalist movement and new conceptions about cities as dynamic, heterogeneous ecologies (see also Sections 7 and 8) in questioning established canons, hagiographies and teleologies that had long been taken for granted. Architects' intentions are suddenly less important than other influences, both new and established, conscious and unintended. Even specific words have changed. Whereas early verbs asked how architecture and urban spaces reflect, support or modify political and social structures of difference, other more nuanced terms now ask how they *intimidate*, *divide*, *buttress*, *enhance*, *challenge* and *destabilize* – all of which can be positive or negative in different circumstances.

The appropriation of languages outside of architecture has thus shifted considerably in the past 40 years. To some extent the discussion has touted the significance of architecture and spatial configurations, both urban and natural, not just within the discipline but in the world at large – including other academic disciplines from the sciences to the humanities. Architectural analogies of the 1960s continued to draw from the biological and social sciences. Christopher Alexander initiated the use of computers to apply mathematical set theories, hoping to extrapolate a new language that could assure a building's 'fit' in modern societies. The rise of the New Left then unleashed vehement critiques of the design professions, refuting promises of amelioration as empty metaphors. Architects and theorists alike evoked the *people*, the *public*, the *social* and the *community* in beginning to acknowledge diverse, even competing needs or desires. While an activist trajectory continued, taking new paths, architectural theory in the 1970s often converted politics into more abstract intellectual concerns, as explored by Ole Fischer in Chapter 2. The idea of an oppositional strategy of negation emphasized words like *difference*, *rupture*, *fragmentation* and radical *heterogeneity* as ways to sustain alternative utopian possibilities. Familiar architectural analogies were scrutinized, especially terms like *structure* or *stability*, although clever language games sometimes became facile. Recent interests have shifted to theories about translation/bilingualism and vernacular or local languages for everyday life. Through these debates the term *discourse* often replaced that of language, again encompassing various meanings from a distinctive internal 'jargon' (as Adorno used the term) to Foucault's ideas about culture/power, Lyotard's fascination with discursive genres and Habermas's theories about conversation.

Gradually the modernist idea of utopia as a brave new world underwent significant changes. Whereas architects such as Le Corbusier or Frank Lloyd Wright had no qualms in depicting idealized versions of the future (Fishman 1977), the utopian impulse bore itself out in the 1960s, giving way to dystopian scenarios that saw the future in terms of loss and catastrophe – or at least as a much more ambivalent place to be than the Radiant or Broadacre City. Superstudio, Archizoom or OMA used architectural tools (drawings, models, mappings) to investigate the liberatory but also oppressive forces of spatial configurations (Van Schaik and Macel 2005). A fascination with technology gave rise to multiple experiments that investigated the possibilities of megastructures, inflatables, domes, spaceships, underwater worlds and desert cities. If these experiments barely touched upon mainstream architectural culture and remained politically ineffective (Scott 2007), they help explain the simultaneous neo-colonial export of high-tech infrastructure and manufactured-housing systems that would supposedly transform and 'solve' the problems of the Third World.

By the 1980s and 1990s, the very idea of utopia seemed compromised beyond redemption. Postmodernism presented itself as a down-to-earth architectural strategy that was more interested in salvaging elements of the past than in discovering possibilities for the future (Jencks 1977; Klotz 1984; Jameson 1989; Ghirardo 1996). 'Post-humanist' theorists repositioned the architectural avant-garde, deriding efforts to improve conditions as naive and futile. Yet here and there, utopia re-emerged, often bound up with the notion of *difference* itself: something different had to be possible, something more than just a repetition of what already existed, something that harboured a promise that could not yet be articulated. One group of authors came up with the term *Embodied Utopias* as a way to think the future – or re-configure the past – not in an abstract, spiritual way, but rather as social and corporeal practices, recognizing the importance of bodies that are ethnically, sexually, culturally and socially inscribed (Bingaman et al. 2002).

EMBODIED DIFFERENCES

Architecture's engagement with the body can be traced back to antiquity. Western classicism envisaged the orders as emulating the human body. Recent architectural theories have reconfigured the body as a model for rhythm and proportions, as a reference point for discussions of scale, as a vulnerable body in need of physical and symbolic shelter, as a sensuous body that perceives buildings in visual but also in haptic ways, as a working body that requires functionally apt spaces, as a comfort-seeking body that desires tempered environmental conditions or as a body with special needs that necessitate prosthetic help from technology and from architecture (Rykwert 1972; de Sola-Morales 1997; Hauptmann 2006). All these aspects of the body have given rise to an extensive literature that will be further explored in Sections 2 and 6 of this Handbook. However, this literature often posits an unmarked, quasi-idealized body as the subject of architecture, a body without a sex, a gender, a skin colour, an age, a language, a culture, a physical defect or even a class. Even today, the bodies in architectural theory are all too often – unconsciously and therefore unmarked – presumed to be male, middle-aged, middle-class, white bodies that struggle with anxieties about cars and computers, but know next to nothing about child bearing, racial profiling, social exclusion or cultural subordination.

The contributions in this section insist that we recognize how physical spaces inscribe power constellations and differentiations onto human bodies with consequences that directly affect everyday practices and experiences. The institutional realities of architectural education, the structuring of the profession and the organization of architectural media all share in the disparities and discriminations described in these pages: they privilege middle-class, Anglo-Saxon, able-bodied, white males while making it harder for all those lacking one or more of these features to be successful in their chosen field (assuming for a moment that 'choosing a field' would be a concept applicable beyond the confines of global middle-class economy). If (post)critical positions (Fisher), postcolonial perspectives (Hosagrahar) and feminist critiques (Rendell) have something in common, it might be this insistence that differences matter in everyday situations and that architecture, one way or another, is involved in this mattering.

Architecture is not the only discipline to explore this fascinating if tangled phenomenon. Cultural geographers also argue that 'bodies and places are woven together through intricate webs of social and spatial relations that are made by, and make, embodied subjects' (Nast and Pile 1998, 4). What architectural theory can add to these understandings is a more specific analysis of how spatial articulations contribute to this making of subjects. Going further, it asks how architectural discourse is implicated in the production of differentiated spaces that shape differentiated subjectivities. Examples include Beatriz Colomina's analysis of the gendered architectural spaces of Loos and Le Corbusier (1994), Leslie Kanes Weisman's explanation of 'discrimination by design' (1992) and Zeynep Çelik's writings about colonialism's fundamental role in modernism (1997a; 1997b). This type of scrutiny also interrogates the implicit relations between 'architecture' and 'race'. For example, Darell Fields (2000) mines the aesthetic discourse of G.W.F. Hegel to understand how 'blackness' and 'architecture' are intertwined. (Fields contends that Hegel put architecture beneath other forms of the fine arts because of its association [through 'Egypt'] with 'blackness'.) Lesley Lokko (2000) examines the metaphor of 'light' in Western discourse: light as the source of vision and understanding, as the medium through which architecture is imagined and experienced, which makes it the opposite of 'dark', 'black' and 'night'. The fundamental role of both metaphors in language and experience (ranging from tropes of rationality and Enlightenment to practices of slavery), makes it difficult to construct alternate architectures that might overcome these inherited associations. This is nonetheless the challenge facing architects and theorists who seek to articulate an architecture that is meaningful from the point of view of *other* traditions and *other* collective memories. For Lokko, the question is 'how to draw on these traditions [e.g. those associated with the body and with orality], interpreting them in ways that not only satisfy the "past/present/future" dichotomy "solved" by the tradition of orality, but offers something new, something to enable to process of "becoming"' (Lokko 2000, 33).

Some authors have adopted the term 'heterotopia' to describe such alternate modes of architectural thinking and practice. They take the word from Foucault who described heterotopias, somewhat enigmatically, as 'real places, effective places, places that are written into the institution of society itself, and that are a sort of counter-emplacements, a sort of effectively realized utopias in which the real emplacements, all the other real emplacements that can be found within a culture, are simultaneously represented, contested and inverted' (Foucault 2008, 17). He suggested that such sites can accommodate, albeit briefly, practices that one way or another fall outside the dominant culture. This notion has been taken up in very different ways in a fast-growing literature on heterotopia (see for example Dehaene and De Cauter 2008) that usually emphasizes a subversive and emancipatory potential but sometimes warns of a disciplinary – even oppressive – condition. Craig Wilkins (2007), who writes on space, architecture, race and music, wants to go beyond the latter aspect, which he feels Foucault overemphasized. He proposes instead to think in terms of 'celebratory heterotopias' where people act collectively to resist cultural alienation and, in the process, produce euphoric spaces and empowered subjects who actively and continually renegotiate differences among themselves (Wilkins 2007, 108ff, 111). This, for him, is the architectural/urban equivalent of bell hooks' 'choosing the space of the margin' (hooks 1989b). Both authors call for rethinking the experience of space in ways that are closer to African-American bodies.

The workings of the body are evoked not just by Wilkins, but also by many others discussing how spaces can accommodate practices related to power and difference. Important in this respect is our choice of the term 'embodiment' over 'body' in the title of this section. This choice is theoretically charged, because it implies that we understand bodies not as given objects but as entities inscribed by structural differentiations, by social and cultural imprints such as gender, race, class, etc. Indeed, no one's body is ever 'just' a body, completely determined by historical and cultural circumstances. The fact that bodies act out or 'perform' the differentiations of gender, ethnicity, class, etc., means they can also subvert these labels and explore alternatives (Thrift and Dewsbury 2000). For example, women are never 'just' women since they can choose and 'perform' versions of femininity in which shifts, ironical gestures or parody allow them to undermine the very norms of femininity they are embodying (Irigaray 1985b; Butler 1993). In a similar way, colonized people and racial minorities have some leeway in how they act out the roles society has assigned to them, such that mimicry and exaggeration can parody and, to a certain extent, resist derogatory labels (Taussig 1992).

As Jane Rendell argues in Chapter 4, the 'performative turn' in architecture and architectural theory has lagged behind other disciplines (she names art and literature.) A similar statement can be made about the impact of queer theory – a collective tag used for studies based on lesbian and gay sexualities. Queer theorists, according to Kathy Rudy (2000), share some assertions that open up exciting ways to rethink social reality. They emphasize the role of interpretation in understanding all aspects of human life – hence questioning and challenging what is usually taken to be 'normal'. Sexual identities and gender are understood as historically contingent, socially constructed categories that rely in part on performance, which leads to a political activism that is often aggressive and confrontational. Lastly, queer theorists refuse to discuss sexual behavior from an ethical point of view: for them, all consensual sex is good and every attempt to restrict it should be seen as partial to a hegemonic force that keeps the idea of 'normal' intact. As a mode of thought, queer theory therefore encompasses a wide range of critical practices and priorities which mobilize 'queer' as a verb to unsettle assumptions about sexed/sexual being and doing (Spargo 1999, 40). Given these assertions, queer theory might well challenge architectural theory to confront the spatial paradigms that seem to reinforce the robustness of 'normality,' since architecture solidifies social norms and institutional regulations into stone. Architectural theory has not directly engaged this challenge. Although we have two books (Betsky 1997; Bonnevier 2007) and a couple of illuminating articles (Urbach 1999; Reed 1996) that explicitly deal with architecture from a queer point of view (or with queer theory from an architectural point of view), this literature does not match the extensive geographical analyses of queer space (Brent Ingram et al. 1997; Duncan 1996; Browne et al. 2007; Hemmings 2002; etc.).

Admittedly, one must first ask whether or how a certain 'space' is 'queer'. Architectural theory examines the articulation of physical spaces into rooms, buildings, streets and cityscapes, demonstrating how these seemingly stable spatial entities shore up 'normality'. Hence it is difficult to recognize 'queerness' as a possible attribute of any of these spaces, because 'queering' means subverting normality (see Chauncey in Sanders 1996). Aaron Betsky (1997) provides a case in point. Although Betsky starts out by affirming that queer space is 'a misuse or deformation of a place, an appropriation of the buildings and codes of the city for perverse purposes' (5), half the book is devoted to descriptions of historical building types – from Roman baths to Bavarian fairy tale castles – that he feels exemplify queerness. His interpretation thus oscillates back and forth between characterizing specific *spaces* as queer and recognizing that only certain *uses* make a space queer, usually just for the time of those uses. Christopher Reed tackles the problem head-on by stating that 'queer space may be a contradiction in terms'. He opts out of this contradiction by adding the qualification 'imminent':

> No space is totally queer or completely unqueerable, but some spaces are queerer than others. The term I propose for queer space is *imminent*: rooted in the Latin *imminere*, to loom over or threaten, it means ready to take place. For both advocates and opponents, the notion of queerness is threatening indeed. More fundamentally, queer space is space in the process of, literally, *taking place*, of claiming territory. (Reed 1996, 64)

This imminence brings us back to the topic of performativity. The geographers Thrift and Dewsbury (2000) discern four current manifestations of performance: the work of Judith Butler, non-representational theory, the discipline of performance and the reworking of academic practices as performative. All four, it seems to us, offer useful insights for architectural theory. Judith Butler argues that gender is not inherent to bodies, but acquired through repeated performances of femininity or masculinity (Butler 1993), a recognition taken up by architectural authors such as Dana Arnold (2002, 129–31). Non-representational theory, exemplified by the works of Gilles Deleuze, emphasizes the flow of everyday life as embodied, contextual, technologized and creating affect or emotions. This outlook valorizes an everyday set of skills which are highly performative, in that they allow something that exists or is latent to become other than what is expected. The influence of non-representational theory, mediated through the works of authors such as Elisabeth Grosz, is very much present in architectural theory, as becomes evident in Section 6 of this volume and in a book on *The Body in Architecture* (Hauptmann 2006). The discipline of performance, the third manifestation, has deepened the recognition of theatricality as a metaphor for all kinds of human behaviour. The metaphor provides architectural theory with a means to grasp and perhaps utilize the multiple kinds of resonance in a term like 'authenticity', rather than insisting on one inherent meaning (Verschaffel 2001) or as a way to frame diverse interactions between architectural spaces and social patterns (Harris 2005; Heynen and Loeckx 1998). Lastly, some architectural writers and practitioners are reworking their own teaching, research and presentations towards more performative methods.

But then, architects' presentations have always been highly stylized performances, typically using a multitude of seductive images to construct a narrative of inspiration, conceptualization, reworking and materializing, barely supported by words. This assemblage of revelations then magically coalesces into architectural designs that become buildings. The evident theatricality of this kind of performance is transformed and radicalized in what Jane Rendell calls 'site-writing', which turns lecturing (about) space into – literally – 'spacing' a lecture (lecture understood as a combination of reading, writing and performing/creating), where words as spatial inscriptions gain dominance again over images (Rendell 2005).

If embodied differences thus gave rise to critical interrogations about all kind of architectural and academic practices, there is another strand in recent architectural discourse about the body that seems strangely remote from the heavily theorized endeavours that inform postcolonial and gender studies. The propagators of *universal design* adopt a more upbeat, seemingly self-evident and straightforward tone that raises new criteria for an inclusive approach to architectural design (Preiser and Ostroff 2001). This field arose from a double motivation. On one front, the fact of an increasingly aging population, especially in Western countries, poses a challenge in terms of the suitability of conventional homes and other environments for people with weakening physical capacities, which in turn challenges designers to develop new building typologies and spatial strategies. On another front, political assertions of rights have extended to disabled people's demands for equal accessibility and the ability to enjoy all types of services and spaces. The adagio of universal design states that, since good design practices respect the diversity of all human beings in terms of spaces and objects that are accessible and useful to all, they will enhance the overall quality of design. Accessibility, safety, convenience and satisfaction are the key terms in this discourse, which is increasingly gaining a foothold in architectural and design curricula.

The universal design discourse may seem like a belated offspring of modernist functionalism, one that replaces the able-bodied, white, adult male as the subject of architecture with a more diverse but hence rather enigmatic character that is supposed to encompass all types of human differences. Because this discourse rarely engages theoretical issues, it tends to come across as undertheorized and even simplistic. To some degree, universal design does share modernism's laudable emancipating objectives, together with the belief that architecture can change the world, without acknowledging how these convictions are bound up with the forces of cultural hegemony and benevolent paternalism, such that any improvement will have some unexpected repercussions. Even more important is the basic assumption that it is possible to 'design for all'. As we have seen, architecture and design interventions always embody differences, accentuating, reflecting, framing, installing or transforming them in myriad ways. Thus it seems highly unlikely that we can simply do away with them. As some protagonists themselves admit, the word 'universal' in universal design is an ironic choice (Pedersen and Crouch 2002). Recent theoretical analyses should make us wary about goals that seem self-evidently beneficial for everyone and about strategies that claim to be universally valid. Yet, all the same, as architects and as theorists, we should never let circumspection lead us to abandon aspirations for a more just, inclusive and, yes, a more beautiful world.

CONCLUSION

Recent turns in architectural theory all share a reaction against *totalizing* analyses, whether they be Marxism or the modernist project itself, as Habermas has called it. Given the earlier dominance of the Frankfurt School's critical theory, this trend is sometimes labelled post-criticality (see Chapter 2). Architectural theory now recognizes diversity, discontinuity, contingency and inevitable if unpredictable changes over time. Many people seem to celebrate these qualities as inherently liberatory. Topics like gender, race and culture have shifted from oppositional dichotomies to include and embrace a spectrum of differences. Interest in cities and ecologies has further amplified these ideas (see Sections 7 and 8). The present condition is often described as an archipelago or a patchwork, evoking both multiplicity and fragmentation. Pragmatism has re-emerged as one sign of this effort to take account of diversity, 'things in the making' over time, and experimentation within a system (Saunders 2007). As William James put it in 1907: 'Pragmatism unstiffens all our theories, limbers them up and sets each one at work.' This trend also draws from other more recent sources, including Bruno Latour's Actor-Network-Theory which traces the multiple, mostly unanticipated associations between humans and 'things' as agents in the world (Latour 2007). An historian of science, Latour was thinking of microbes or information, but this type of analysis can clearly be put to work for architecture as well.

Architectural theory continues to evolve. There is growing attention to praxis, materiality and hybrid processes rather than fixed 'positions'. While this section highlights intellectual debates, we are also drawn to the many ways that theory has become more connected to real life experiments, especially small incremental changes, and to the exigencies of practice. If an earlier generation focused on exposing the negative effects of architecture, thoughtful architects and intellectuals around the world are now combining various theoretical concerns to suggest creative new forms and strategies, respectful of histories and cultural diversity, cognizant of the myriad interrelations between power, difference and embodiment.

2

Architecture, Capitalism and Criticality

Ole W. Fischer

ON THE IMPOSSIBILITY OF BEING 'CRITICAL'

In 1994, at the ANY conference in Montréal, Rem Koolhaas raised fundamental doubts about the critical potential of architecture as a discipline: '*The problem with the prevailing discourse of architectural criticism is this inability to recognize that there is in the deepest motivations of architecture something that cannot be critical*' (cited in Kapusta 1994). This statement, a short objection against the concept of autonomous architecture and against theory as a form of intellectual resistance could be seen as a prelude of the realist cynicism of *S, M, L, XL* (Koolhaas and Mau 1995) and the subsequent publications of OMA – if it would not have triggered an ongoing debate on the disciplinarity of architecture, and thus the question as to the interrelationship of theory, practice and society.

Taken literally, Koolhaas is right, of course, because the realizations of architectural projects consume large investments of capital, material and labour, and the architect has a clear-cut commission from his client (private or corporate), cooperates with engineers and contractors and collaborates with government officials (including building inspectors). Architecture is slow in realization, it resists change – in spite of the constant talk about dynamics, flexibility and variation – and it proves to be long-lasting. The complexity of architectural projects demands a high degree of specialization and division of labour, which leads to hierarchical structures and blurring of distinct authorship, which are typical of contemporary service and the administration sector. However, this is also true for other collaborative cultural productions, such as music, theatre or filmmaking, which does not necessarily inflect their 'critical' content or function in society.

A closer look at Koolhaas' remark may yield results at another level of architectural discourse – at the uncertain state of architecture between engineering, service industry and art. The concept of autonomy as a precondition for the critical function of the arts derives from modern aesthetics from Kant to Adorno, but is limited in architecture by criteria such as satisfying needs, utility, function or programme, if not to speak of construction, technology or economy. Therefore the comment of Koolhaas on the 'deepest motivations of architecture' might be a reminder of its specificity to relate and integrate these internal and external factors of the discipline in a productive way, which means architecture is necessarily connected and engaged with society on multiple levels, and therefore inevitably affirmative and contiguous, or in the words of Koolhaas himself: it is the task of architecture '*to reinvent a plausible relationship between the formal and social*' (Koolhaas and Whiting 1999, 50).

The critical analysis of the 1960s and 1970s laid bare architecture's deep involvement with order, control, power and hierarchy (for instance Foucault 1977) and it debunked architecture's official history as religious, feudal and bourgeois representation, as capitalist distribution, and as politics of the body – in short: as an *ideological* instrument in the service of the ruling classes (see also Bentmann and Müller 1992). Seen from this perspective, Koolhaas' doubts and objections seem to be far more dialectical and 'critical' in regard to the material basis and cultural superstructure of architectural interventions than the search for a 'critical project' within the discipline might imply.

Finally, the questioning of the 'critical' potential of architecture and the provocative plea for affirmation, surrender and opportunism by Koolhaas has to be read in relation to the specific historic context and its 'hidden opponent' – that is the author, text or discourse to which the statement tacitly refers: in this case the group of architects and theorists involved with *ANY* magazine and the project of 'criticality' in architecture that they propagated.

CRITICALITY, POST-CRITICALITY, POST-THEORY?

'Critical architecture' has played a major role in the debates of architectural theory in the past three decades, at least at the influential universities on the east and west coasts of North America (see for instance Lillyman et al. 1994; Ockman 1985; Speaks 1996). Under the banner of 'criticality', the theory of architecture was recognized and professionalized as a regular academic discipline, with its own programmes and chairs, with distinct 'critical' magazines such as *Oppositions*, *ANY* or *Assemblage* – reflected by such European platforms as *AA Files*, *Quaderns* or *Archplus* – and with a series of publications, exhibitions and symposia, all of which lead to the effect that 'criticality' became a synonym for the theory of architecture. The current questioning of 'criticality' by a younger generation of architectural theoreticians addresses the 'critical theory' of K. Michael Hays and the 'critical practice' of Peter Eisenman, who, in analogous relation to minimalist and concept art, set out to reposition the discipline of architecture on explicitly theoretical foundations. Here, the term 'theory' refers to a conglomerate of philosophical, sociological and linguistic texts mainly by European authors – such as Althusser, Barthes, Lacan, Adorno, Habermas, Lefebvre, Foucault, Baudrillard, Derrida and Deleuze – that, through the agency of comparative literature, were transformed in a process of selection, fragmentation, translation and re-interpretation into an instrumental and operative meta-criticism that is suitable for a 'critical reading' of a wide range of social, cultural or artistic phenomena, including architecture.

The 'critical' edge of this 'theory' stems from the linguistic, psychoanalytical and neo-Marxist origins of these texts, which, in different ways, follow the traditions of progressive thought since the Enlightenment. These include the *Critiques* of Kant, who – in the literal sense of critique as strict self-examination or separation – defined the limits of the human faculty of cognition to create a new foundation of philosophical thought and help people achieve a freedom of reason. Marx's *critique of ideology* sought to expose the contexts of delusion of society and culture by attributing them to conditions of domination and production to help people achieve an economic-political awareness. In addition, Freud's *analytical criticism* described the limits of individual and collective consciousness so as to emancipate people from the power of the subconscious, the repressed, and compulsion. Always, criticism manifests itself as a clash between the established, dominant status quo of culture and society and divergent possibilities, deviant latencies and the excluded *other* as a search for enlightenment, alternatives and changes.

The question facing 'critical architecture', however, is: 'critical – of what?' (Martin 2005). Strictly speaking, there are at least two divergent approaches within this academic debate that call themselves 'critical'. The first endorses the idea of the autonomy of the discipline with regard to external factors such as society, function or historical significance, and hence a reduction to the formal manipulation of the internal elements of architecture. The argument for autonomy is based on a linguistically post-structuralist model that interprets architectural elements as self-referential signs whose differentiation commences a process between figuration and abstraction (Eisenman 2000). The 'criticism' consists precisely in repudiating previous systems of legitimization toward uncovering a generative process between sign and form that leads to the (architectural) sign 'becoming unmotivated', a resolution of established meanings and thus an opening up of the architectural discourse. The concept of autonomy is disassociated from modern concepts such as technological progress or social interaction as well as from postmodern notions of interdisciplinarity between the humanities, presenting itself instead as 'inner-architectural' criticism, as a methodical-critical analysis of the architectural structure. The second argument opposes reification, mediation and fetishization of architectural objects, and searches for strategies designed to evade the pressure of visual commodification of the 'late capitalist' culture industry (Hays 1984). On the basis of a Freudo-Marxist analysis of post-industrial consumer society – in the footsteps of Walter Benjamin, Theodor W. Adorno and Jacques Lacan – we see dialectical-critical positions that claim that a critical architectural practice is possible within the prevailing social order by opening up an 'in-between-space' in which architectural forms are more than just the result of market forces. The strategies of this cultural and social criticism by architecture comprise a deceleration of perception, a silence of architecture, a refusal of pictoriality, staging and branding, an uncovering of architecture's staging devices as in Brecht's theatre, and the demonstrative exhibition of social constructions, conventions and negative effects such as objectification, alienation or discrimination. Both these academic strands of 'critical architecture' share the constant indexing of their 'critical' state against the discipline, their 'critical' intentions resist dominant social, economic and cultural forces, and the generative processuality of form by means of a complex system of references from the object to theory and vice versa.

After pop and media theory and (neo) pragmatism (Ockman 2000) had already questioned the idea of 'critical architecture' in the 1990s, the current debate about a 'post-critical' stance was kicked off by an essay by Robert Somol and Sarah Whiting in *Perspecta* (2002), in which the two authors distinguish between a 'critical project – here linked to the indexical, the dialectical and hot representation' and an 'alternative genealogy of the projective – linked to the diagrammatic, the atmospheric and cool performance'. Somol and Whiting's critique of critique was taken up, augmented and expanded by other theorists of the same generation, such as Michael Speaks (2002), Sylvia Lavin (2003) and Stan Allen (2004), and yet it is concerned with more than an academic generational conflict or a new style: the revision of the 'critical' tradition of theory concerns the relationship between architecture and society, or, to be precise, between architecture and power, capital and media. Realism, pragmatism, and professionalism appear as the new subjects of 'post-theory' – proactively challenging the utility and efficacy of critical thought, intellectual resistance and elaborative theoretical constructs in a competitive global market of architectural design. To 'solve', not to 'problematize', marks the new 'post-critical' approach: the ideal of autonomy as a precondition of architectural 'criticality', which distances itself from building, is replaced by an immersion into practice. As a result, the relationship between theory and project seems to be reversed: whilst the 'critical' discourse favours theoretical writings, abstract conceptual models, and variously superimposed, textually based graphics (like a palimpsest), the 'post-critical' protagonists prefer to draw attention to shapes, images and the performative qualities of built objects. Diagrams, slogans, logos, and new media are deployed as a kind of 'mental PowerPoint' to reduce the complexity of architectural projects to recognizable icons, core messages, or brands, and thus to promote a fast, approximative perception and an intensive experience or atmospheric 'feeling' – particularly with regard to a broad audience of occupants, consumers and clients – as a deliberate contrast to the strained 'critical reading' of advanced, complex theoretical texts and built fragments of thought that, in terms of their conception, refuse to bow to emotional appropriation, everyday use, visual representation, or easy consumption, and require an 'explanation' by the professional critic.

In addition, as the common reproach of post-critics goes, 'critical architecture', which set out to question authors, power discourses, and social constructions, has itself meanwhile become a dominant institution, rather than producing unexpected interpretations, new perspectives and alternative concepts for action. Since, in this 'regime of criticality', theory plays a determining role in design, it reduces the architectural project to a 'sample', 'illustration' or index of the theoretical concept. The 'critical' author-architect inscribes a theoretical derivation into the project and limits the role of the occupant, viewer or critic to a 'reading' and 'reproduction' of this architectural 'text'. If, for example, we refer to such prominent 'critical' architects as Tschumi, Eisenman or Diller and Scofidio, we see a significant extent of coherence in the articles, reviews and publications on their work, because they regard themselves as 'conceptual architects' they view 'theory' and 'critical content' as essential factors of their design production. Yet this self-referential fallacy between academic discourse and 'critical practice' threatens to become inappropriate for architectural topics that go beyond the realm of established 'critical' themes, which, inversely, implies that 'critical architecture' degenerates into a style. What is more, the 'critical discourse' over the past thirty years has experienced an accelerated race for 'new' theories that, in view of its fast changes, give the impression of arbitrariness and fashion. Even the most severe critics of 'the system' have had to realize that criticism, revolt and subversion are part of the stabilizing repertoire of 'late capitalism': critical gestures have quickly been internalized, commodified and recycled for niche products or marketing strategies. In many respects, established academic criticism has proved to be an ineffective tool of resistance, liberation and change.

On the other hand, the leviathan of monolithic, hegemonic 'critical architecture' drafted by 'post-critics' seems to be a phantasmagoria itself, the projection of a great antagonist onto a small group of academic architects and theorists with limited influence on the discipline at large. This common 'uber-opponent'[1] obscures the considerable differences between the various positions in post-criticism, ranging, as it does, from first: an affirmative post-theory geared to performance, implementation and operationality that analyses future fields of design activity as a kind of neo-liberal think-tank and develops strategies of work organization, architectural intervention, and marketing, to second: a post-critical stance that progressively banks on the digital revolution, new materials and media, to third: an architecture of 'new sensuality' and affect (compare Deleuze 2005), focusing on staging moods, immersions and atmospheres.

In a sense, the 'post-critical' involves a repetition of the phenomenon of transatlantic cultural transfer: whilst under 'critical architecture' European philosophical texts, political hypotheses, and linguistic methods were fed into the American academic discourse, later to be re-exported as 'theory', now the oeuvre of individual architects, such as OMA/Rem Koolhaas, MVRDV, UNStudio, FOA/Alejandro Zaera-Polo, or Herzog & de Meuron, serves 'post-critical' authors as evidence of a contemporary 'projective' practice. Since the fall of the Berlin Wall, Europe has seen the emergence of a generation of architects who have proactively embraced the changed political and economic conditions in the deregulated markets of the EU and the transition countries, seeking to redefine the profession in terms of production, organization and effect. In different ways they have allowed architecture to benefit from IT, processing technology and material sciences, corporate management, marketing and consulting, combining them with strategies from art, media and fashion in order to position the strong architectural object as an event and identity-forming experience, thus lending added cultural value to architecture in the eyes of the public and decision-makers. Compared with these new operative instruments, the 'critical' apparatus proves to be inefficient in setting itself apart in an economy of attention and gaining a competitive edge over 'anonymous' investor architects and epigones by means of a politics of the proper name. In addition, the collapse of actually existing socialism and the crisis of the European left have created a general suspicion of ideology and any kind of 'theory' and 'criticism'. The consequence is a widespread weariness towards theory among staunch European architects, particularly those who had direct dealings with representatives of 'critical architecture' such as Herzog & de Meuron with Aldo Rossi, Rem Koolhaas with Peter Eisenman, or Alejandro Zaera-Polo with Michael Hays. What looks like smart European 'post-critical' pragmatism from the vantage point of American post-theorists is often nothing but indifferent scepticism, entrepreneurial realism, or a rhetorical retreat to seemingly impartial objectivity, professionality and 'architectural expertise' – in other words, a severe disenchantment with criticism that extends into the academic discourse of European universities and trade journals (Van Toorn 1997).

'CRITICAL THEORY' VERSUS 'CRITICAL' THEORY

Ensconced in the 'post-critical' project lies a double strategy: on the one hand, it is an attempt to overcome the schism between academic theory and design practice and to make contemporary architectural objects, phenomena and strategies accessible (once again) for reflection; on the other hand, 'post-critical' theory hinges dialectically on 'criticality' and attempts to set itself apart from it antithetically, as the prefix 'post' already suggests. However, as already stated, in 'critical' architectural theory, two different concepts of criticism overlap. One historical vector comes from the realm of socio-psychological philosophy and neo-Marxist criticism of society and culture, as espoused by the 'Frankfurt School', who coined the concept of 'critical theory' as opposed to the 'traditional theory' of scientific positivism and orthodox Marxism (Horkheimer 1937). This is the vector that informed the 'critical architecture' opposing reification, mediation and fetishization of architectural objects. A second epistemological trail leads to the theory-based textual criticism of comparative literature, which refers back to phenomenological, hermeneutic, semiotic and structuralist models, and later also post-structuralist, psychoanalytical and feminist reading strategies (such as deconstruction). This second trail inspired the 'critical architecture' based on the autonomy of architecture and the enhancement of the status of theory. While this mode of criticism aims to analyse, interpret, explain and possibly subvert human sign systems (hence existing cultural artifacts), socio-philosophical 'critical theory', on the other hand, seeks to accomplish a self-reflective analysis of 'societal totality', hence a criticism of the preconditions of science, culture and politics in capitalist society in order to change it as a whole. The core presumption of 'critical theory' is the failure – in consideration of the totalitarian ideologies of Fascism and Stalinism – of bourgeois enlightenment, whose promises of knowledge, self-determination, and rational analysis of nature and myth are said to have dialectically transformed into 'instrumental reason', into an economic-technological system of rule in which the irrationality of the myth returns as 'positivistic' affirmation of the existing (Adorno and Horkheimer 1972). Nevertheless there is much common ground between socio-political 'critical theory' and 'critical' literature/language theory, ranging from the choice of topics to mutual borrowing of methods, texts and authors who may be counted among both groups.

Manfredo Tafuri, the Marxist architectural historian from the 'School of Venice', played a major role in the construction, in this double sense, of a 'critical' architecture/theory in the 1970s. On the basis of the cultural criticism of the Frankfurt School, particularly Benjamin and Adorno, he defines the history of architecture as part of a broader materialist historiography as much as architectural theory as a critique of ideology, which is not limited to the formal analysis of individual objects or designs but rather discusses architecture as the obfuscation of social conditions. At the same time, however, he avails himself of linguistic and structuralist methods that go back initially to Barthes, Lévi-Strauss, Eco and Foucault, from where he proceeded to Lacan, Derrida and Deleuze. His eclectic meta-criticism that passes from the level of aesthetic form to the level of language of architecture (that is, semantics, structure and typology), and on to the level of language about architecture, coincides with the theoretical approaches of the New York Institute of Architecture and Urban Studies (IAUS) co-founded by Emilio Ambasz and Peter Eisenman. For them, Tafuri's analytical critique of language, his negative dialectics of modernity and his philosophical scepticism towards given societal realities and utopias seemed eminently suitable as a theoretical legitimization of 'critical' architecture, disseminated by the IAUS magazine *Oppositions* (Hays 1999) and pursued in the projects of the New York Five (Drexler et al. 1972). Tafuri's interest in the concept of autonomy met with that of architects like Aldo Rossi, Oswald Mathias Ungers and Peter Eisenman, albeit from a different perspective: these representatives of 'critical' architecture/theory consider autonomy on the level of form and structure, as a challenge to the function, meaning, construction, visuality and mediation of architecture. They framed architecture linguistically as an 'autonomous language' or as a culturally 'given' artifact independent of the author's intentions. Tafuri uses autonomy against the background of the Italian '*autonomia*' movement of anarchic communists and actionistic groups of the 1960s as a demand for socio-political engagement and economic, cultural and political participation, in opposition to the ruling capitalist system outside the established (and thus already compromised) institutions, such as the state, political parties or trade unions – indeed as an extension of class struggle. Ultimately, '*autonomia*' meant literally the self-organization of tenants in building cooperatives and the direct action of do-it-yourself and urban squatting, in short, the strive for 'architecture without architects' (Rudofsky 1964). For Tafuri, with reference to Horkheimer and Adorno, any kind of production within the capitalist order is always already contingent, collaborative and instrumentalized, which is why he insists on the autonomy of architectural history/theory from design practice (and thus constraints of justification) and on the critic's detachment from the object – very unlike the 'operative' theory of the 'critical' architect or the 'post-critical' version of 'engaged' criticism.

The misunderstanding between formal linguistic self-criticism of 'critical' architecture, and Tafuri's critique of ideology founded on economic, political and cultural arguments, could not be greater. The fact that Tafuri, who diagnoses the historical failure of modern architecture to enter into a critical relation with capitalism, has been used to legitimize American 'critical' architecture/theory seems to be one of history's ironies, as Diane Ghirardo (2002) has already observed. And yet the protagonists of 'critical' architecture even hijacked Tafuri's resigned assessment regarding the 'end of architecture', using it to justify the autonomous, abstract, absolute operations with the drained architectural elements, finally proclaiming with Derrida the 'end of the end' (Eisenman 1984). Still, in the early 1970s Tafuri had made a full-scale attempt to clarify the role of criticism (and language) in architecture on the IAUS platform *Oppositions* (1974): there he distinguished, firstly, between language as technical neutrality (functionalism) and, secondly, the emptiness of signs after the dissolution of meanings (Rossi), and, thirdly, an architecture that sees itself 'critically', ironically or as a mass medium reduced purely to 'information' – and this category encompasses the projects of Stirling, Venturi and the New York Five, which he criticizes as subjective experimentalism, cynicism, or hermetic 'language games'. The fourth position espoused by Tafuri claims the interchangeability and futility of positions one to three, as 'criticism' remains inside the 'language of architecture', merely endlessly reproducing what has been said and what already exists[2] instead of analysing and realizing the underlying principles and possibilities of architectural and critical 'production' within the existing societal structures. To him, it is the task of architecture to change the reality of society with the 'plan' (urbanistic as well as political) to reorganize the production and distribution of labour and capital, which at the same time, however, implies that the architect must cooperate with public decision-makers and integrate into economic-political and administrative processes as an 'engineer' or 'producer' (in compliance with Benjamin's 1934 formula of 'the author as producer').

In a way, it is the European developments in architecture of the 1990s, as outlined above, that confirms the path of political, economic, administrative and technical integration predicted by Tafuri, albeit under contrary political circumstances of globalization. And whereas in the early 1970s Tafuri prophesized the imminent end of architectural avant-gardes as a result of the disillusioning effect of 'critical theory' – with the impossibility of a 'critical' project having been proven (Tafuri 1980, 91) – today an end of (critical) theory would appear imminent as a result of an operative practice that, ironically or ignorantly, embraces progress and technology, pursues instrumentalization through marketing and mass media, and flirts with its status as a commodity, spectacle or fashion – giving up in the end any attempt to criticize capitalism. Despite his utter resignation, even Tafuri betrays signs of admiring the discreet charm of omnipresent, adaptable and excessive capitalist production. But the decline of a culturally and politically critical consciousness in architecture is not caused by the 'temptations of the market' alone but also by the historical evolution of 'critical' architecture/theory: besides architectural formalism, post-structuralism challenged neo-Marxist 'critical theory' as one out of numerous political ideologies and demystified the autonomy of the critic vis-à-vis social conditions as a theoretical construction. What remains is a postmodern relativity of 'everything goes' and also the dominance of the linguistic analogy in the academia of the 1980s and 1990s, whose degree of abstraction is responsible for the loss of sensorial, material, atmospheric, temporal, aesthetic, emotional and performative qualities that are today being re-addressed by 'post-critical' authors.

AUTONOMY, CONTIGUITY AND NEGATION

George Baird (1995) has argued for acknowledging a more parallel and continuous development of modern, postmodern, structuralist and post-structuralist tendencies in architectural theory, rather than framing it as a revolutionary process of paradigm shifts. Exemplary for this complexity and ambiguity might be the position of Aldo Rossi. Seen from a European perspective, he is a left intellectual – a member of the Partito Comunista Italiano as well as one of the professors of Politecnico di Milano dismissed for his support of the student revolt of 1968/1970 – and father figure of neo-classical postmodernism. From a North American perspective, he belongs to the neo-avant-garde of the 1970s together with Eisenman, Hejduk and Tschumi. Rossi himself, however, believed in the continuation of the modern project, and with the *Architecture of the City* (1984) he wanted to reconstruct the discipline by proving its foundations in enlightenment rationalism, combining an ideological critique of history with a typological critique of architectural forms of the city that he considered as its fundamental reality. Therefore Rossi insisted on the autonomy of architecture – in the double sense of first a pre-existing historic fact of monumental, permanent primary elements and structural residential areas of the city detached from functional, technological, societal or economic determination, and second, a specificity of architecture as such, as a form of scientific knowledge. This self-reflection of architecture on its own history, formal logic and typological ideas enabled a revision and reassessment of Italian rationalism of the 1930s that implied the purging of its Fascist political content, especially with regard to Giuseppe Terragni, an interest Rossi shared with Eisenman (Eisenman 1998).

Rossi's autonomy project seeks to re-contextualize the architectural object within the (European) city and the 'collective memory' of its citizens, but at the same time de-contextualize it from political, economic and societal reality, even from contemporaneity, as Rafael Moneo noted, who went on, with reference to Tafuri, to sketch out the danger for architecture to be reduced to 'inoperative parameters' and 'pure game' (Moneo 1976, 18). But Rossi's attempt to take architecture away from the heated political discourse of the late 1960s and early 1970s, which risked the discipline dissolving into social work, functionalist technological positivism or technocratic instrumentalization, is driven by the melancholic insight that the critical alternatives of the modern movement are no longer available. Neither the utopian project of the radical avant-garde nor the emancipatory social reformist practice seem an option because both have been proven to be either ineffective or complicit with capitalist instrumental access to world, labour and humans. From this dystopian perspective of the impossibility for architecture to picture or produce an alternative reality within the existing societal relations, the Rossian project of autonomy – as a process of disciplinary separation, typological abstraction and archaic reduction – opens a fallback position of architectural practice evading social reality, a reality that forcefully returns back into these formal manipulations and poetic analogies, as Rossi's work demonstrates,[3] but an evasive position that aligns with the philosophical concept of *negation*, as introduced by the Frankfurt School 'critical theory' and transferred to architecture by Tafuri: '*This [simple] truth is, that just as there cannot exist a class political economy, but only a class criticism of political economy, so too there cannot be founded a class aesthetic, art, or architecture, but only a class criticism of the aesthetic, of art, of architecture, of the city itself*' (Tafuri 1976, 179).

Within the capitalist regime Tafuri (1980) denies any possibility of envisaging the 'architecture for a liberated society' or maintaining a critical stance within design, but he emphasizes the *negative* aspect of ideological critique for the history and theory of architecture. This is a clear reference to the *Negative Dialectics* of Adorno (1973), who conceptualized the task of philosophy as to unmask societal contradictions and to situate these as historic products in notional mediation, though with the important difference that Adorno concedes for art an autonomous space beyond the instrumental rationality of capitalist production (Adorno 1984). Art gains autonomy through its negation of operational 'use' or 'function' as well as its distance from societal reality, yet at the same time art remains for Adorno a social practice or a product of societal labour and therefore determined by history, production process, techniques, influence, context, etc. Because of a historic split between signs and images, they have become operational in modern society, but Adorno proposes a reconstruction of their independence with the dialectical concept of mimesis. The resemblance of art to itself evades the identity thinking of linguistic categories and enables genuine experience of 'otherness' within modern instrumentalized society – what makes art 'critical'. On the other hand, art relates mimetically to society and recognizes societal reality – what makes art similar to the criticized. While the similarity is necessary to enable involvement by the observer, it is the formal autonomy that exposes the concealed social reality (repression, exploitation, estrangement, etc.) and puts art in opposition to and in negation of society (Heynen 1999, 174–192). This dialectic renders modern art abstract, dissonant, discomforting and anti-utopian; to picture a positive image of society (like socialist realism) has grounds in false premises just as much as 'committed' art, since the representation as much as the 'message' demand complicity with the audience. Adorno excludes affirmative, contingent, tangible art from his aesthetics, for without the distance of autonomy they turn into reified, popular, conformist commodities of 'culture industry' that reproduce the manipulative contexts of delusion.

Adorno's *Aesthetic Theory* (1984) implies a selection of specific genres capable of autonomy and negation, such as serious music, dramatic literature and abstract visual art (in short: elitist high culture). Architecture, however, functional, contingent or operative, hardly ever conforms to these conditions, even if it retreats to formal abstraction and 'post-functionalism' (Eisenman 1976). Yet Walter Benjamin – as much as Adorno a point of reference for Tafuri – scrutinizes the concept of autonomy as a relict of prehistoric magic ritual that survived in the bourgeois cult of the singular, crafted, auratic work of art – determined by restricted access, private ownership and authorial authenticity – and he contrasts it with the simultaneous collective reception of reproduced artifacts such as photo, film and architecture. In his famous 1936 essay on 'The Work of Art', Benjamin substitutes the contemplative immersion of the individual observer into the work of art of idealistic aesthetics with the dispersion of reproductions amongst the urban masses, where reception takes place in the state of distraction (Benjamin 2008). It is precisely the contingency by use and function that qualifies architecture for Benjamin as the 'prototype' of 'tactile' – in contrast to 'optical' – reception of the (new) mediated art of the masses. The daily, habitual, casual experience of reproduced art – or architecture – replaces 'cult value' with 'exhibition value', hence transforming art from a commodity fetish to an ubiquitous exercise for human perception that is able to reconstitute the historic unity of critical stance and delight. Whilst Adorno concentrates on the critical role of the work of art, as promising a different societal reality, Benjamin's hope resides in art's cognitive role as an experimental field for new forms of (aesthetic) demand, since he conceptualizes art received in distraction as an unconscious training for new skills of 'apperception' by the masses that precede the change in societal relations. And if Adorno excluded the economy of art from his theoretic reflection in order to emphasize its distance from reification and instrumental adjustment of the world, then Benjamin located a revolutionary aspect in the process of technological (re)production, distribution and mass consumption of art that constitutes a collective audience, reconciles art and science, and restructures human perception, imagination and consciousness. That is: he differentiated the dialectical relations between technology, arts and politics already laid out by historic materialism.

WITHIN THE INTERIOR SPACE OF CAPITAL

Adorno and Benjamin presented two alternatives for a critical artistic practice within capitalist society: on one hand there is the notion of resistance embedded in the autonomous work, and on the other hand there is the search for concepts to stimulate opposition from contiguous factors of production, programme or use. From a Marxist point of view, architecture is as much a part of society's productive forces (hence its economic base) as its cultural superstructure (hence its reproduction of capitalist hegemony). This dialectic was explored by the French sociologist Henri Lefebvre (1991, 26), who considered '(social) space as a (social) product' resulting from productive forces, modes of production and relations of production (that is, from human labour and its organization, from the instruments of labour respective technology and from resources). Following the theory of materialist dialectics, he defined the production of space as a historical process where different societies and therefore modes of production crystallize in different historical spaces; at the same time he aimed at a 'unitary theory' of space that covers physical, mental as well as social aspects. Since he regarded space not only as a product 'secreted' by society but also as a productive force of capitalism that reproduces social relations, he differentiated between three interrelated levels: first, 'spatial practices' of production and reproduction; second, 'representations of space', that is the conceptualized, codified, mental space manifested in signs contiguous to power and order; and third, 'representational space', which contains the life of inhabitants and users (Lefebvre 1991, 33). In this scheme, architecture belongs to the second category, which minimizes its critical potential, but opposition and subversion re-enter with everyday practice – the individual, imaginary and historic dimension of 'representational space'. This reflection on everyday life was augmented by Michel de Certeau (1984), who pursued the 'productive' side of consumer culture existent in the individual practice of bricolage, deviance and ruses. Yet, in contrast to Lefebvre, de Certeau understands 'practice' primarily as linguistic termini in the sense of 'pragmatics' and 'performance', and, following the speech act theory based on de Saussure, he differentiates between the system of written language (*langue*) as hegemonic, institutional and strategic, and the individual use of spoken language (*parole*) as temporal, trickery and tactical.[4] De Certeau denies, with reference to Foucault (1977), the possibility of an autonomous position within the strategic system of power, but he concedes the tactical use of space to create individual freedom operating within the structure set by strategy. Exemplary for the transfer from speech act to spatial practice is the pedestrian walking in the street as 'enunciation of the city' (de Certeau 1984, 97), subverting with the individual choice of path the dominant order imposed by planning, though the same example demonstrates the problematic equation of practising language (or everyday activities) with economic production and political participation – not unlike the mix-up of formal and political autonomy in 'critical' architecture.

This reflection on everyday life, space and practice is part of the sociological critique against post-war functionalism and modernist planning methods of the 1960s, which parallels Lefebvre with Jane Jacobs (1961) or Alexander Mitscherlich (1965). However, Lefebvre was not recognized in the English-speaking architectural debate until the 1990s, when he was called upon by authors, such as Margaret Crawford (1999) or Mary McLeod (1997), who distanced themselves from paternalistic New Urbanism and formalist avant-gardes (of postmodern, neo-modern or deconstructivist fashion). Sceptical of the dominant linguistic theories in academia that reduce architecture to questions of signification and form finding, this sociological critique calls for a return to 'the real' of lived experience without being patronizing, to an examination of popular culture without being populist, and for taking action under existing social conditions without selling out. Sharing the optimistic assessment of everyday life by Lefebvre and de Certeau as rich, complex and transformative, this architectural and urban practice addresses ordinary programmes (housing, retail, conversions, street furniture) and small-scale interventions that question normative understandings of space and place, of private and public, of politics, participation and citizenship. Still, there remains a crucial gap between this informal urbanism, pragmatic realism and micro-political activism and the dialectics of Lefebvre, who introduced the concept of the everyday as a complementary vector of modernity in order to project a fundamental change in hegemonic societal relations.

The persistence of a utopian perspective, even a nondeterministic one full of tensions and contradictions, also separates Lefebvre from de Certeau, as much as their contrary understanding of 'place': de Certeau favours space (*espace*) as operative, actualized, oriented, over the notion of place (*lieu*) as stable, ordered and defined, with the first comparable to spoken narration and the second to written text, while Lefebvre defends the 'differential space' of place, history and individuality against the 'abstract space' of capitalist society, which he describes as universal, instrumental and homogenous – the space of commodities and power, administered by consensus and disintegrating traditional locality, relations and practices. This critique of the spatial homogenization was taken up, though with reference to de Certeau, by Marc Augé (1995), who developed the oppositional model of 'place' versus 'non-place', with which he distinguishes between the construction of identity by individuals interacting with each other in authentic places defined by history, centrality and recognition versus the non-personal, homogenized, generic environments of supermarkets, airports and hotel lobbies – the deterritorialized, transitional spaces of consumption and traffic.[5] Yet whilst Lefebvre associated 'differential space' with instability and social change, it was already de Certeau who returned to a phenomenological notion of identity and authenticity in the discourse on 'place' (Heidegger 1994, Norberg-Schulz 1980), which became the dominant paradigm in the anthropology of Augé, as his call for an 'organic social' demonstrates.

Even if Augé does not blame contemporary architecture alone for the withering away of place, his dirge on the loss of cultural differentiation and locality meets with the concept of 'critical regionalism' in architecture. The term, originally coined by Alexander Tzonis and Liane Lefaivre (1985), was propagated by Kenneth Frampton (1983) – an early member of the IAUS in New York – as an answer to universalization and 'scenography' of consumerist semiotic postmodernism, significantly introduced by a passage from Paul Ricoeur. With a detour to Benjamin's concept of 'aura', the authors suggested slowing down the process of visual commodification by working with local materials, techniques and typologies and by referring to context, history and season – altogether features that have to be experienced on site and that are difficult to reproduce in images. In contrast to earlier regionalism or (postmodern) vernacular tendencies, here the 'critical' denotes first a reflexive understanding of local inspiration and the notion of place, a dialectic of technological 'civilization' versus 'culture' exemplified in the work of Alvar Aalto or Alvaro Siza. Carried by Habermas' belief in modernity as an unfinished project of emancipation (Habermas 1983), Frampton asks how to reconcile regional diversity and specificity with the universal progress of reason (Frampton 1983). A second notion of the 'critical' became more prominent in the last revision of *Modern Architecture* (Frampton 2007, 344–389) where Frampton argues for the reconstruction of 'civic form' and 'public appearance' in the sense of Hannah Arendt (1958) as a sphere of direct encounter and interaction of citizens like the ancient Greek agora (see also Baird 1995) against depoliticized mediation and commodification of the contemporary (built) environment. Yet regionalist as well as organicist tendencies are as much a product of rigorous modernization as they carry an anti-urban, anti-technological and anti-pluralistic undercurrent that sets an ideal oneness of community and culture against the experience of estrangement, fragmentation and loss in society, what makes them an ideological construct in need of a dialectical analysis as much as the enlightenment project they stem from (Dal Co 1979). Already Marx had hoped to overcome capitalist division of labour and estrangement with free, self-fulfilling production, and gave rise to an anti-technological resentment exposed in the Arts and Crafts movement and later through expressionism, organicism, regionalism and contemporary consumer-producer models. Apart from its cynicism, Koolhaas' counter- attack on the identity, authenticity and historicity of the (European) city has its merit in pointing out the liberating effects of thinking architecture beyond memory and place or utopist planning theories (1994). In contrast to Benjamin, however, who conceptualized the emancipatory potential of technical reproduction and the urban culture of the everyday, Koolhaas does not offer a critical project – such as the 'politicization of art' – any longer.

OUTLOOK: WHAT IS *LEFT* IN ARCHITECTURE?

How can architecture be resistant to the omnipresence of global capitalism and consumerist culture? Since crisis is an existential part of the process of capitalism, critical gestures are internalized, recycled and exploited as formal novelty and comment ('recuperation'), such as urban guerilla tactics for product placement and branding (Von Borries 2004), or situationist experiments for staging urbanity and creating events. However, if utopian planning, even in actually existing socialism, has not been able to project an architectural and urban alternative to imperialist representations of power and capitalist consumer culture, but instead has reproduced totalitarian environments, does this mean that a critical practice in architecture is as much 'falsified' as scientific Marxism (Popper 1945)? What about El Lisitzky's experimental Cloud Iron, exploring an architecture that articulates communal ownership of the ground and the new economic base of society? Or the examples listed by Tafuri: the 'Siedlungen' of the German Weimar Republic, the housing blocks of Red Vienna, the park and urban redevelopments of Olmsted, all taking a social stance within the system? If it is rather the social content of architecture than the formal autonomy that constitutes a 'critical' project within the discipline, then even the 'projective' could become part of the continuation and legacy of modernity as an unfinished project, as Hilde Heynen suggests.[6]

If critical thought is still to play a role and be possible in architecture, and critical practice is to be possible at all, criticism – and above all critics – must become aware of the mechanisms, conditions and dependencies of critical thought and critical production, make lucid its objectives and instruments, and understand how these questions are connected with each other and with the socio-economic, cultural and political whole, all of which go far beyond the current hefty academic exchange of 'critical' and 'post-critical' arguments. One example is the self-criticism of Bruno Latour (2004) who examined the crisis of critique against the background of the aggravated rhetoric of war (against terrorism) in 2003. With some concern, he notes the instrumentalization of criticism by political opinion-makers and controlled media, who have appropriated arguments and strategies of critical theory in order to use them for manipulative purposes, having understood that its analytical force promotes suspicion of *any* kind of argumentation, even if it goes against the interests of the enlightened public itself.

Precisely because the critical theory of the past three decades has challenged the legitimization of classical concepts of enlightenment such as 'truth', 'scientific method' or 'reality', unmasking them as social constructions, it contributes to the relativization and construction of 'realities' that have led to the perversion of the emancipatory goals of criticism, to a loss of meaningfulness, perspicuity and reality, and to anti-Empiricism instead of a renewal of empirical thought. But if criticism turns into a critical gesture or, worse, into arbitrariness, relativity and conspiracy theories (that is, into an instrument of disinformation political manipulation of public opinion and a product of media consumption) criticism must review its attitude, instruments and methods in order to adjust them once again to its original topics and objectives: instead of abstraction, deconstruction and subtraction of 'matters of fact', Latour demands realism, construction and addition – a critical theory that '*takes care of things*' (2004, 233).

Architecture has yet to take stock of the 'critical arsenal' in Latour's sense. Even if we look sceptically at this martial metaphor, critical theory and practice as potential, enrichment, participation and discourse – as 'gathering' in a political, spatial and disciplinary sense that interprets the contiguity of architecture with society, culture, media, technology, economy and production as a gift and not as a handicap, in order to progress out of this condition to arrive at specific architectural interventions and theoretical concepts – thus displays starting points that must be further pursued. We will then explore how the theory of architecture must be fundamentally re-formulated to move beyond the loop of the established academic machine of the 'critical', 'post-critical', 'post-theoretical' or, quite simply, cynical, affirmative camps and towards constructive criticism. In the redefinition of a critical agenda, the distinction between an operative criticism that examines the mode of handling the architectural material (that is, the architectural project, object, questions of form, structure, programme, construction, materialization, image, effect, atmosphere, etc.) and a content-based criticism that reflects on architecture as an exemplification of cultural, political and economic societal conditions has to be resolved. Instead of going on to separate meaning (or aesthetics) from performance (or politics) and mistake one for the other, a new critical theory in architecture will involve reflective and projective modes, contemplative critique and active intervention. The difference between theory and practice will not play such a major role as maintained by Tafuri, for a theoretical text is just as much a design and a cultural product, is as involved in interactions and dependencies, and is as much a part of a market as an architectural project.

Such a conception of criticism will gather and focus precisely these different factors, levels, and discourses of architecture so that the naturally ensuing interaction, friction and conflicts, arrive at emergent realities instead of settling for monolithic discourse systems and firmly codified disciplinary roles. By self-critically reflecting on its own status and the conditionality of architecture, dialectically examining replication and autonomy, visualizing the construction of 'reality' as one of various possible 'truths', this criticism will lift the architectural discussion above the formal expression of a contemporary mood, above service, fashion or lifestyle, recontextualizing it in society, culture and everyday experience. Critical thought deals with the public sphere, clients and their (political) views, production, funding and ownership, questions of accessibility, participation, urbanity and public space. It seeks concurrence, density, engagement, exchange, discussion and conflicts, and takes part in negotiating private and public interests, albeit not in isolation from the search for architectural quality and its criteria. In short, it scrutinizes the plausible relationship between form and society, as Koolhaas has already observed.

NOTES

1 George Baird goes so far as to talk about an oedipal complex of the younger generation, hinting at the manifold personal links between the authors of critical and post-critical theory (Baird 2004, 17–18).

2 The title of the essay should be understood in this sense: An architecture that locks itself in the endless loop of language, excluding all other links (*contiguity*), that speaks only of itself, is decoration, representation and social conversation – *L'Architecture dans le Boudoir* – is maximum formal freedom by maximizing rationalistic terror, a strategy that Tafuri compares to the literature of the Marquis de Sade and that alludes directly to the chapter dedicated to de Sade 'Excursus II: Juliette or Enlightenment and Morality' in Horkheimer and Adorno's *Dialectics of Enlightenment*.

3 The well-known 'Monte Amiata' housing block in the Gallaratese quarter of Milan designed by Aldo Rossi in 1969–1973 was originally a condominium investor project that referred typologically and spatially to the access arcade of Italian worker housing of the nineteenth century. Ironically it was seized by urban squatters in 1974 (Fezer 2003)

4 de Certeau (1984, 26): 'The actual order of things is precisely what "popular" tactics turn to their own ends, without an illusion that it will change any time soon. Though elsewhere it is exploited by a dominant power or simply denied by an ideological discourse, here order is *tricked* by an art. Into the institution to be served are thus insinuated styles of social exchange, technical invention, and moral resistance, that is, an economy of the "*gift*" (generosities for which one expects a return), an esthetics of "*tricks*" (artists' operations) and an ethics of *tenacity* (countless ways of refusing to accord the established order the status of a law, a meaning, or a fatality).'

5 Augé (1995, 77–78): 'If a place can be defined as relational, historical and concerned with identity, then a space which cannot be defined as relational, or historical, or concerned with identity will be a non-place. The hypothesis advanced here is that supermodernity produces non-places, meaning spaces which are not themselves anthropological places and which, unlike Baudelarian modernity, do not integrate the earlier places: [...]'

6 Hilde Heynen (in Rendell et al. 2007, 53): 'The driving force behind this position [projective theory] is the indignation concerning the fact that social reality continues to be oppressive and unjust, and the conviction that, as long as this situation remains persistent, the need for critique remains as urgent as ever.'

3

Interrogating Difference: Postcolonial Perspectives in Architecture and Urbanism

Jyoti Hosagrahar

INTRODUCTION

Postcolonial perspectives in architecture and urbanism offer ways of thinking about built form and space as cultural landscapes that are at once globally interconnected and precisely situated in space and time. With intellectual roots in the struggles against Western European colonization of Asia and Africa in the nineteenth and early twentieth centuries, much of the scholarship has focused on the global South that has been disdained or marginalized in received literature. Postcolonial thought questions the dominance of universalizing paradigms and simplistic categorizations in conventional scholarship in architecture and urbanism focused on Western Europe and North America. Dichotomies such as those between West and non-West, traditional and modern, have persisted as rigid oppositions that deny both the interdependence and the inequalities in the relationship. Postcolonial perspectives challenge the notion of a universal modernism that privileges those in positions of power and authority, legitimating their right to define fundamental values, policies, operations, and identities. They acknowledge instead the multiple dimensions of subordinate experiences. In so doing, postcolonial perspectives particularize universal narratives and globalize narrowly parochial ones.

Postcolonial scholarship began in the 1950s as a fiercely political opposition to colonial rule: giving voice to the oppressed, while exposing the violence and brutality of those in power. Scathing indictments against oppression critiqued the complex and insidious ways in which colonialism operated and the corrosive impacts it had on people and their landscapes – producing a condition that the French anthropologist, Georges Balandier spoke of as 'the Colonial Situation' (1966 [1955]). Although a crude and violent assertion of control over passive subjects has been all too prevalent in colonial circumstances, postcolonial scholars have recognized power as a complex and all-encompassing web of relationships that operates in space to control people's behavior, relationships, and identities. As Ashis Nandy (1988 [1983]) has explained so well, the historical inequalities and cultural domination have been such that the indigenous identity must contend with its subjectification as its 'intimate enemy.'

The intellectual discourse of postcolonial critique and affirmation extended from the social sciences to philosophy, film, and other art forms. Using the language, tools, and tropes of the colonizers to highlight experiences and perspectives other than the dominant ones, the subordinate and the marginalized spoke back to power, and in the process, decentred their discourse. Thus postcolonial thought as an intellectual perspective is not so much the result of a chronological sequence of events after colonialism as it is a way of thinking about the relationship between a dominant power and its subjects under colonialism.

Postcolonial perspectives in architecture and urbanism do not form a well-defined body of knowledge or a fixed set of stylistic tropes even today. While historical, geographical, and cultural distinctions are paramount, the influences come from a variety of disciplines as well. It is, as yet, a dynamic approach that does not have a clear or agreed upon beginning, boundary, or path. Some scholars define postcolonial studies as precisely focused on European colonization of the nineteenth and twentieth centuries. Others have a wider view that now includes the experiences of nations that have never been colonized, such as Turkey; the repercussions of earlier colonization in Latin America; recent imperialism such as those by the US, Japan, or the USSR; as well as the multiple effects of colonial experiences on Europe and the US. In its broadest definition, postcolonial perspectives give voice to all types and sites of struggles against hegemonic power. Its challenge is in legitimizing, enabling, and empowering alternative narratives and forms. Many critical readings about domination based on gender, race, caste, ethnic, or religious groups, could thus be subsumed under postcolonial thought.

In this chapter, I adopt a middle ground. I argue for an intellectual decolonization, an active rejection of spaces and discourses based in hegemonic dualities: a realm that is neither so broad as to include every type of critical perspective under its umbrella nor so narrow as to exclude any interpretations that do not pertain specifically to Western European colonialism. Through writing and theorizing, but equally through design and planning interventions, postcolonial theory has relocated discussions of modernity to marginalized locales and emphasized the interplay of culture and power in imagining, producing, and experiencing the built environment. This chapter considers writing within the broad realm of postcolonial perspectives as well as critical practices with similar objectives. I also include the work of scholars from a variety of fields other than architecture who have influenced thinking about built form and space. A wealth of scholarship has emerged in recent years that highlights the distinctive experiences and histories of specific regions. Given my personal experience, research, and practice, this chapter emphasizes scholarship and examples from South Asia more than other regions. It begins with a discussion of the key intellectual issues and concerns of postcolonial theory. I will then focus on four topics of critical importance: historiography and representation, nationalism and nationhood; globalization; and preservation and cultural identity. This leads to a discussion of postcolonial themes in recent design practice, seen across a broad geographical and cultural terrain. At a time when sustainability is an urgent global concern, postcolonial theory becomes especially important in giving salience to the global–local interconnections to address equity, access, and environmental resources.

KEY IDEAS AND INTELLECTUAL INFLUENCE

The first and still most admired writer in this field was the philosopher and revolutionary,

Frantz Fanon best known for his book, *The Wretched of the Earth* (2004 [1961]). Fanon, born in Martinique and educated in Paris, was a vocal critic of France's colonization of Algeria while it was still a colony. He denounced the psychopathology of colonialism and warned of possible violence in the aftermath of national independence struggles. Fanon's powerful work on race and colonialism inspired and influenced anti-colonial liberation movements for decades.

Edward Said's *Orientalism* (1978) was a seminal work that further shaped the landscape of postcolonial thought. His brilliant literary exegesis of learned Orientalist scholars shows how they created the very idea of the mysterious 'Orient'. They disdained all indigenous scholars as inevitably biased and parochial; bestowing interpretive authority of major historical texts to outside experts. Said contended that this axis of knowledge and power still affects every realm of modern life across the world. Along with other scholars, Said's work showed how identities were culturally constructed rather than inherent characteristics. Said thus led the way for later critical theorists to read architecture and urban spaces, both historical and contemporary, as cultural documents that could reveal hidden biases.

In Said's work, as well as in that of many other postcolonial thinkers, Michel Foucault emerged as an important theoretical influence. Foucault challenged established notions about the relationship between culture, power, and knowledge (see also Chapters 1 and 2). His 'networks of power' identified cultural practices that served to dominate in ways that went far beyond direct acts of physical aggression including architectural spaces that worked as 'machines for the control of the self'. His analysis of the all-encompassing panoptic controls of prisons and asylums as well as his notion of heterotopias as 'other' spaces that allowed people to step briefly outside the expected norms of behaviour were concepts especially important to architecture (Foucault 1977; 2008).

The 1980s saw revisionist thinking in the humanities and social sciences that included a growing coterie of non-Western intellectuals, many of whom had been trained in universities in the West. The Subaltern Studies Collective, started in the mid-1980s, marked a dramatic move into the global intellectual terrain. Speaking from and on particular landscapes of South Asia, they challenged conventional histories of colonized or subject populations with 'histories from below' that presented various non-elite populations as active agents of social and economic change.[1] Ranajit Guha, Gyan Pandey, Partha Chatterjee, Gyan Prakash, and Gayatri Spivak have been among the most prominent members of the Collective (Guha and Spivak 1988; Guha 1997). Strongly influenced by Marx and Gramsci, the work of this group has sought out the experiences of marginalized people. The significance of their work to architecture and urbanism has been twofold. First in legitimizing 'other' histories that are non-Eurocentric and making visible people and landscapes that received accounts had been blind to; and second in recognizing the subtle ways in which even the most marginalized populations actively shape and negotiate the spaces they inhabit.

Race was a central aspect of Western Europe's colonization of Asia and Africa, making racial difference an important aspect of postcolonial analysis. Focusing on questions of power and identity, scholars have probed the positive and negative self-conceptions of diverse groups within a larger and/or hostile society (Appiah and Gates 1995; Hall and du Gay 1996). Literary critics like Henry Louis Gates (2006) have pointed out the cultural prejudices inherent in literary theory, arguing that black American literature should be evaluated on the criteria of its origin rather than measured against Eurocentric literary canon. Contrary to such a view of a black cultural aesthetic has been Kwame Anthony Appiah's (2003) critique of Afrocentrism as a mirror image of Eurocentrism and equally preoccupied with ancient histories. These varied commentaries on the constructions of black culture and African-ness have had a profound impact on identity politics. For architecture and urbanism, such debates have raised questions about subjective experience and cultural relativity of aesthetics in architecture and urbanism as opposed to supposedly objective and universal measures for their evaluation.

Colonial anxieties about purity of oppositional categories such as black and white, colonizer and colonized, modern and traditional were countered by ever increasing forms of hybridity as new ideas, people, images, and capital moved around the world with greater frequency. Transnationalism and interconnectedness meant increasingly 'impure' mixtures of diverse, supposedly contradictory, even forbidden elements, or experimentation driven by the desire to find new kinds of strength and beauty. Homi Bhabha (1994) has recognized the unpredictability of hybridization, the impossibility of total control as itself a source of power. Bhabha's intricate view of hybridity and infiltration of cultural symbols, values, and practices and his emphasis on identities as heterogeneous provide an understanding of multiple, contradictory, and fluid modern identities.

The grand history of Europe had for decades been equated with the universal history of humankind and many have continued to accept accounts of a linear and universal modern originating from Western Europe and disseminating to other places. Postcolonial intellectuals have been instrumental in offering complex readings of modernity and modernism from the margins. Arjun Appadurai (1996) has been immensely influential with his work on modernity and globalization (discussed in greater detail later in this chapter). In his recent book, *Provincializing Europe* (2007), Dipesh Chakrabarty has addressed the idea of Europe not as a specific geographical region but as the mythical site of the original modern. His effort to provincialize Europe is not to reject the legacy of Enlightenment thought that he considers indispensable to a social critique of justice and equity but to de-centre the mythical Europe by looking at the many Europes from the margins.

Addressing global interconnections, local experience, and visual difference, postcolonial approaches in architecture and urbanism look far beyond form, function, and style. In depicting particular places as international and cosmopolitan as well as local and provincial, postcolonial critics do not dismiss the commonalities of modernism but have highlighted the uneasy negotiation between sameness and difference in particular locales. Postcolonial theory has informed thinking about buildings and urban space as symbolic cultural landscapes that are historically constituted, culturally constructed, political artifacts whose forms are dynamic and meanings constantly negotiated.

HISTORIOGRAPHY AND REPRESENTATION

From Vitruvius to Venturi, architectural theory has relied on a particular set of historical premises and examples that were considered universal even though they were rooted in the experiences and intellectual traditions of Western Europe and North America. This Eurocentric canon looked down on all other cultures, dismissing their architecture as static, backward, or 'decadent'.

Postcolonial thought questions the received canon of European architectural history as the *only* history of architecture and is also critical of a linear history that traces the 'progress' of architecture from primitive to modern. One genre of writing has critiqued the ways that design and policy reinforced established identities and relationships of power and also looked at interventions in the colonies. In *The Politics of Design in French Colonial Urbanism* (1991), Gwendolyn Wright has analysed design strategies in France and in three French colonies (Morocco, Indochina, and Madagascar) from the 1880s through to the 1930s. Seemingly antagonistic design strategies – historic preservation, contextual design, and a highly rationalized modernism – all served imperial goals.

Highlighting the overarching and particular histories of different colonies, she has also emphasized the significance of this imagery at home to promote tourism and public support for the colonialist project. In *An Imperial Vision* (1989), Thomas Metcalf has looked at architecture as a symbolic representation of British power in India and as an instrument for articulating cultural difference.

Another genre of postcolonial inquiry has focused on the conflicts, negotiations, and experiences of different groups of subordinate populations in response to dominant interventions to control and define identities. Historiography in this mode of inquiry has used eclectic sources to piece together narratives from the other side. For instance, my study of nineteenth century Delhi (Hosagrahar 2005) showed that Indians appropriated neoclassical elements into traditional building fronts, negotiated the limits of Haussman-ic clearances of dense urban neighborhoods, and subverted colonial building regulations to transform the city into one that was both traditional and modern. Accounts of defiance and negotiation by those in the margins destabilize the singular authority of those in power. Through form, use, and meaning, architecture and built form have contributed to imagining and constructing identities. Some scholars have critically examined the ways that those in authority have used space to define oppositional identities to reinforce their position of power. Others have explored the ways these enforced and essentialized identities have been contested and negotiated by subordinate groups.

Timothy Mitchell's *Colonising Egypt* (1988), a seminal work, critically examines Europe's encounter with the Orient, the preconceptions and perceptions on both sides. In his insightful analysis of the representation of Cairo at the World's Fair in Paris in 1889, Mitchell has argued that colonial displays affected Western perceptions of urban life, especially in the colonies, creating an artificial vantage ('the-world-as-exhibition') that combined sensual pleasures with the assurance of safety. Zeynep Çelik (1992) later accentuated the gendered aspect of these displays of the non-West that further reinforced power relations between the colonizers and the colonized.

The colonial construction of difference was premised on the purity of the opposing groups: colonizer and colonized, Orient and Occident, modern and traditional. The reality, however, was always much muddier. Some postcolonial histories have reversed this ideal of purity to look at hybrids. Anthony King (1976) initiated this approach early in his career, analyzing British cantonments in India as a hybrid 'third culture': neither entirely British nor entirely indigenous. A subsequent book, *The Bungalow* (1984) followed the development of a house form from its humble origins as rural hut in Bengal through its many colonial avatars in South and Southeast Asia to its incarnation as a 'cozy' middle-class house in the United States. This book showed architecture as a global project in which the buildings and forms that developed in one place influenced those in another, weaving as it did themes of prejudice and exoticism, visibility and invisibility into a complex narrative. Other recent studies have also regarded the seemingly dichotomous categories such as 'colonizer' and 'colonized', or 'modern' and 'traditional' as fluid and shifting, seeking out areas of hybridity, ambivalence, and crossing over of cultures. In emphasizing interconnections and infiltrations, they have highlighted the active engagement of the subordinate groups in the making of their landscapes and identities. Swati Chattopadhyay's (2005) interpretation of colonial Calcutta, for example, has offered valuable insights into the way the Bengali middle-class appropriated the forms and tropes of the colonizer to increase their own authority and status.

Against the notion of a singular Western modernity imposed on the world, scholars increasingly advocate the concept of multiple, overlapping, and incomplete modernities. This in turn precludes simplistic characterization of forms and meanings (see for instance Morton 2000). Postcolonial thought is not about a rejection of European modernism. Rather, it necessarily engages with modernist universals and the discourses of European intellectual traditions. Acknowledging these as a global heritage, postcolonial perspectives make sense of this heritage from and for the margins. Postcolonial theories have created modulated terms to describe the multiplicities of modern life and, to a lesser extent, its hierarchies. Dilip Parameshwar Gaonkar (1999) speaks of 'alternative modernities,' and Gyan Prakash (1999) of 'divided modernities.' Lu in this volume (Chapter 13) underscores complex, impure interconnections with 'entangled modernities.' Such phrases challenge the received canon that puts Europe at the centre, rejecting adaptations and secondary gestures toward multiculturalism or 'global openness'.

In fact, all modernities are indigenized interpretations of an imagined ideal. This is why I titled my book *Indigenous Modernities* (Hosagrahar 2005). Rejecting the notion of an alternative to the dominant and single notion of modern, I hold that all modernities are indigenized interpretations of an imagined ideal. The concept of 'indigenous modernities' recognizes and legitimizes a multiplicity of 'other' experiences of modern life, its spatial forms and cultural expressions, as being on a par with conventional ones. And Western Europe moderns too, are localized indigenous realizations of a mythical ideal.

Postcolonial perspectives not only globalize local histories and provincialize histories masquerading as global but have also informed global comparisons. For those convinced that particular European architectural histories are *the* only histories of architecture, the canonized built forms are, by definition, complete, autonomous, and universal. In this view, the built forms of other places, especially in the colonies and ex-colonies, are dependent and place specific and hence not worthy subjects of historical inquiry. Nineteenth-century European historians presumed they were presenting a global perspective. Even today, few European or American historians pause to ask how colonial histories might have affected Western aesthetic ideals and hierarchies.

Early histories of modern architecture, notably Sigfried Giedion's *Space, Time and Architecture* (1967 [1941]) glorified a teleology that showed modernism emerging triumphant from western architectural history. Giedion gave considerable attention to the US as well as Europe, but virtually ignored non-Western cultures. Later editions, and a plethora of similar histories of modernism that soon followed, occasionally added non-Western sites designed by European and North American 'masters'. Mark Jarzombek and Vikramaditya Prakash offer a valuable counterpoint to the architectural histories of Bannister Fletcher and Giedeon in *A Global History of Architecture* (Ching et al. 2006). In order to emphasize the connections, contrasts, and influences in architectural movements throughout history, this book organizes 5000 years of architectural history on a global timeline from pre-history to the present.

Postcolonial perspectives, however, have not yet managed to dominate the teaching of architectural history, as became clear from a special series of issues of the *Journal of the Society of Architectural Historians* (2002–2003). The series highlighted how the primacy of European monuments and narrative of stylistic development still remains the central architectural canon almost everywhere. It was also apparent that local architectural histories and building traditions received short shrift in comparison. Sibel Bozdogan (2001), Gülsüm Baydar (1998), and I (Hosagrahar 2002) have each pointed out the Orientalist bias in the canonical histories of architecture. In recent years, 'non-Western' intellectuals teaching in architecture schools in North America and Australia (many of whose writings are discussed in this chapter) have brought postcolonial critique and transformations to bear on the teaching of grand European histories of architecture – so it is well possible that the coming years will see a serious shift in dominant teaching topics and methods.

NATIONALISM AND NATIONS

The emergence of nations in the twentieth century has been a matter of much debate among scholars (see also Chapters 11 and 12). The works of Benedict Anderson (1999 [1985]) and Partha Chatterjee (1993) have led the way. Anderson described how nations were 'imagined' into existence rather than teleologically determined by language or religion. Chatterjee has pointed out how nations were cobbled together from colonies and imagined into existence by colonizers in their efforts at empire building and later by nationalists. Military conquest and European geopolitical competition shaped national boundaries regardless of the diversity of indigenous groups they encompassed, creating among citizens fragmented loyalties between modern nations and other forms of traditional communities.

Architectural styles had historically played an instrumental role in visualizing national identities in Western Europe. For the Western European colonizers building in the colonies, the choice of style was deliberate. In addition to displaying the authority of the empire, they carefully sought to construct narratives of difference between what they saw as the enlightened colonizers and the primitive, decadent, and despotic colonized. The newly independent nations also used architecture in their search for a national identity in their own terms. They rebelled against a colonial characterization of their societies as primitive and backward, and at the same time did not want to cast themselves in the mould of the colonizers whose forms they identified with oppression. The literature suggests that the anxiety to visually express the identity of the new nation as both modern and unique in its heritage resulted in four types of responses.

First, the rise of anti-imperialist movements during the twentieth century often fuelled the idea of reclaiming (or constructing) a pristine and idealized precolonial past rejecting architectural forms associated with Western Europe and Greek and Roman classicism. For instance, in her study of modern nation building in Turkey and its complicated relationship with an Ottoman past, Sibel Bozdogan (2001) has showed how the architects such as Sedad Eldem served as key figures in the new republic responsible for creating a 'Turkish' identity that made references to a vernacular Anatolian heritage. A second response has been for the nation to portray itself as a global modern by inviting acknowledged 'masters' of modern architecture in Western Europe and North America to construct iconic symbols in the International Style such as in Chandigarh and Dacca. Vikramaditya Prakash's (2002) critical study of Le Corbusier's design of Chandigarh has explicated a newly independent India's struggle to define itself as a leader in science and technology. He has shown the ways the conflicting views and imaginations of key figures, political ideologies, and urban processes were negotiated to construct the modernist narrative of the nation and shape the seemingly global form of the city. A third response has been more fragmented. Changing nationalist agendas and narratives can lead to a diversity of architectural and urban preferences, that each mediate in a different way the construction of national identity (see for instance Kusno 2000 about Indonesia). Finally, in recent years, design interventions by high profile designers from Western Europe and North America in places that had hitherto been relegated as traditional have helped to establish their national identity as significant players in a globalized world. Architects recognized as global stars have moved 'the margins' to transform them into museums of architectural wonder or laboratories for architectural experimentation. Iconic buildings such as those by Herzog and de Meuron and Rem Koolhaas in Beijing, Norman Foster's design for the sustainable city of Masdar in Abu Dhabi, and Arup's technological and planning wonder in the eco-city of Dongtan in China are examples of such projects that have been instrumental in building new identities for these nations.

Citizenship is a concept related integrally to nationhood – loyalty and allegiance to an imagined community in return for the rights of legitimate membership. Going far beyond received notions of modern nation-states as the principal domain of citizenship, scholars have examined the complexity of citizenship and multiple allegiances in the context of transnational migration, recent trends in globalization as well as the growing importance of cities. Essays in a collection edited by James Holston, *Cities and Citizenship* (1999), have pointed to the crucial significance of the right to reside in the renegotiating of cities, democracy, and new alignments of local and global identity. The absence of citizenship or the systematic denial of it to some people significantly marginalizes them. From refugee camps and shelters of those fleeing war and ethnic persecution to the vast landscapes of slums, scholars have highlighted the urban spaces of illegitimacy, appropriation, and informality where the hegemony of their marginal identities are reproduced and contested (Roy and Al Sayyad 2004).

PRESERVATION AND CULTURAL IDENTITY

As visualizations of inherited values and histories, preservation of cultural heritage takes centre stage in discussion of identity (see also Chapter 17). Western European notions of preservation, when transported to the colonies, rationalized the assertion of power and a single linear historical account that reinforced colonial hierarchies.

Colonial officials appropriated the right to classify heritage structures and define which monuments were worthy of preservation as artistic representations of a people and their identity. The British in India glorified ancient history as part of a narrative of early glory and medieval decline justifying British imperialism that promised to guide India once again to the glory that was (Hosagrahar 2002). For the French in North Africa, preservation of the *medina* of cities like Rabat, Fez, and Tunis, frozen and timeless, juxtaposed against modernist urban improvements in the new developments outside the walled city, articulated the identity of one as a place of decadence and the other as one of progress (Beguin et al. 1983; Abu-Lughod 1980; Wright 1991; Hamadeh 1992).

For modernists seeking the comforting binary of traditional and modern, an imagined 'authenticity' is of central concern. Any signs of modernity in heritage places they dismiss as signs of 'failure', 'incompleteness', and 'in-authenticity'. Such pictorializing of heritage and tradition to give it visual appeal has often been at the cost of locals compromising their needs and even excluding residents from inhabiting and using certain parts of the city. The process of constructing exotic and picturesque heritage has, at times, falsified a place. Not only does it disallow modernization and change but it also selectively preserves or reconstructs those elements that enhance an image of the place as belonging to another epoch.

Perhaps nowhere has the process of constructing a medieval city been a more insidious and deliberate a project than in Cairo. As the authors of *Making Cairo Medieval* (Al Sayyad et al. 2005) have observed, art historians, architects, urban planners, conservationists, literary writers, and travellers together constructed an identity of the old city of Cairo as 'medieval'. The process involved selective restoration and rehabilitation to shape the city forms to fit the imagined ideal: a dual operation that simultaneously modernized and medievalized Cairo. Remaking Cairo as medieval served both the Western European powers that partially colonized Egypt as well as nationalist goals.

Tourism has been an important driver for commodifying and marketing heritage. Selectively preserving, reconstructing, and controlling activities have served to make historic settings exotic and picturesque in Asia, Africa, and Latin America, raising the question, as the collection *Consuming Tradition* (Al Sayyad 2001) does, of who decides what kind of change is acceptable in historic landscapes. Falsification and exaggeration in pictorializing heritage places are equally prevalent in North America where Michael Sorkin (1996) has pointed out that they are comparable to theme parks for entertainment.

A discussion of heritage sites raises important questions of what gets designated as heritage, by whom, and which identities are privileged. The designation of architecturally unremarkable places as important landmarks in specific histories and communities recognizes subordinate histories. Aapravasi Ghat in Mauritius was inscribed as a World Heritage Site by UNESCO in 2006. It was the landing place during much of the nineteenth and early twentieth century for almost half a million indentured labourers arriving from India to work in the sugar plantations of Mauritius, or other places in the British Empire. As such, it has strong associations in the memories of the indentured labourers and their families. Transnational populations in historic cities, like North Africans in Paris, or South Asians in Leicester, prompted in part by the intertwined histories of the two regions, have necessitated the rethinking of a single authentic identity of a place to become instead an ongoing historical account.

One aspect of preservation that remains a dilemma for many cities in Asia, Africa, and Latin America, is the absence of clear distinctions between traditional built forms and informal ones. While officials intervene to preserve vernacular settlements identified as traditional; informal settlements have often been the target of clearances. Although many have observed continuities of settlement patterns between neighborhoods in historic cities and squatter settlements, the latter have been considered as urban problems and planning failures.

GLOBALIZATION

From a postcolonial perspective, globalization does not appear as a determining force that has flattened out other urban processes, but rather as a phenomenon producing flows of capital, goods, labour, and information that forcefully shape the forms of specific cities and neighbourhoods and leaves others behind, reproducing in new ways the global inequalities and dependencies of colonialism. Anthony King (1990) was one of the earliest to make connections between modernization, the continuing interdependencies between the ex-colonial powers of Western Europe and the colonies in Asia and Africa, and the formation of global cities, cultures, and spaces. King began by tracing the connections between urbanism, colonialism, and the world economy further, developing Wallerstein's theories of the world-economic system. King emphasized cultural and spatial dimensions, showing how contemporary patterns of globalization have historical roots in the nineteenth- and twentieth-century colonialism of Asia and Africa. Thus, cities like London, New York, and Tokyo have become internationalized spatially and demographically as well as economically with ethnic enclaves, transnational communities, and spaces of global culture (King 2004).

Arjun Appadurai's work (1996; 2001) has been immensely influential in the understanding of the cultural experience of modernity and globalization. Two aspects of his work have been key. First is his engagement with image, media, and representation as social practices in the global cultural processes that highlight the role of fantasy in the making of the new global order. He has alerted us to the ways that the imaginaries collapse accepted separations between subject and object, resonating with the postmodernist view of the fragmented visual experience. Second, is Appadurai's contribution, along with Carol Breckenridge and the journal, *Public Culture* they co-founded, to understanding transnationalism and public culture. Together, they have been incredibly important in bringing to the fore cultural transformations in cities through investigations of a wide range of everyday appropriations and interpretations of power and identity in the city, from the terrorist attack in Mumbai to the football clubs of Buenos Aires. Another related initiative of Appadurai, a non-profit, Partners for Urban Knowledge, Action and Research (PUKAR), has been valuable in viewing Mumbai as a conceptual base and laboratory to investigate cultural forms of globalization.[2]

Other postcolonial approaches have emphasized the broader regional and transnational dynamics that have shaped particular places. In a collection edited by Gyan Prakash and Kevin Kruse (2008), the authors, focusing on expanding urban networks, have argued that cities like Johannesburg and Vienna were shaped by the particular histories of their global engagements. Sheila Crane's essay in their collection, for instance, has interpreted the colonial and postcolonial histories of Marseilles and Algiers not as self-contained entities but as interconnected forms shaped by similar forces. Nuanced readings of corporate landscapes emerging from the new globalization have emphasized the heterogeneity within the apparently homogenous monoculture of global cityscapes. Reinhold Martin and Kadambari Baxi for instance, have focused on imaginaries in the construction of corporate towers for multinational corporations in their book, *Multi-National City* (2007).

Nineteenth- and twentieth-century colonialism resulted in global movements of people in addition to goods and ideas. South Asians in Malaysia, Singapore, the Caribbean, and the UK; and North Africans and Vietnamese in France, among others, formed immigrant and diasporic communities. The struggles of these subordinate groups to cope with environments that were sometimes hostile and segregated defined the identities of the communities and their spaces. Equally significant are critical readings of the cosmopolitan transnationalism of cities like Los Angeles (Davis 2000) or Hong Kong (Abbas 1997).

Global flows of architects, design concepts, technologies, and materials from Western Europe and North America to the countries of Asia, Africa, and Latin America have resulted in new conceptualizations of globalized architectural practices where ideas and innovation are considered the purview of architectural schools and practices in Western Europe and North America, while drawings and detailing are subcontracted to specialized agencies in India and China (see Chapter 22). Jeffrey Cody's *Exporting American Architecture* (2003) has provided rich insights into architectural importation in China, looking at the global-local interactions and the technologies of production even in discussions of ordinary buildings and neighborhoods. The Harvard Design School Project on the City directed by Rem Koolhaas has explored urbanism in rapidly urbanizing metropolises as a global phenomenon with particular forms in each place including the Pearl River Delta in China (Chung et al. 2001) and Lagos, Nigeria (Koolhaas 2008).

DESIGNING FROM THE MARGINS

No predefined criteria identify postcolonial approaches in design. I see practice not merely as an enactment of theory but also as advancing postcolonial thinking in the spatial realm. Most contemporary practitioners of architecture and planning do not make any explicit references to postcolonial theory. Rather, they critique accepted premises, categories, and forms arising from specific Western European and North American experiences, and propose alternative visions, processes, or narratives of modernism. Such designers see architecture as globally constituted engaging the interconnections between 'locality' and 'globality'. They seek not simply to take forms imagined elsewhere and locate them in distant places with minor adaptations but rather to renew and enrich understandings of dominant tendencies from the margins. They challenge the principles of universal design by embracing 'otherness', place, time, issues, and cultures rather than ignoring or subordinating them to the dominant paradigms of modernism.

From the perspective of received canons of architectural history, recognizing important innovations and designers in other locales is itself a huge step. Journals such as *Mimar* have played a critical role in privileging concerns such as low-cost housing, and priorities such as materials, technologies, climate, and cultural needs different from those common in Western Europe and North America. For instance, Hasan-Uddin Khan and Sherban Cantacuzino's *Charles Correa* (1987), and Brian Taylor's *Geoffrey Bawa* (1995) have contributed both to design knowledge and to critical discussions by identifying imperatives and narratives that construct modernism other than the dominant universalist ones. The writings have helped to document and globalize the work of architects who otherwise might have been considered totally embedded within their national contexts. Looking at postcolonial efforts to design from the margins in the last two and a half decades, I see four key themes as most significant: an emphasis on the particularities of region, site, and context; in-depth knowledge of a place and people; social responsibility in design; and sustainability.

One important postcolonial approach in design is a response to the characteristics of region, site, and context arguing for an identity that was modern but particular to a place. Deeply concerned about homogenization, many architects around the world have sought design solutions that are more specific and more appropriate to their context and have contributed to richer, more localized interpretations of modernism. Some, such as Glenn Murcutt in responding to Maori architecture, have modified and developed vernacular spaces and building practices. Others, such as Ken Yeang and T.R. Hamzah, or William Lim have paid special heed to climatic conditions and investigated what modernism means in the tropics. Still others, such as Balakrishna Doshi and Charles Correa have offered approaches to housing and street design that are dynamic and progressive, drawing on careful study of historic cities in India. Their work has been especially important in recognizing housing and city building as social and economic processes as much as form-making endeavors. With professional training in Europe and North America, these architects have critically examined their positions as 'outsiders' to the communities they have designed for and attempted to educate themselves to be cultural 'insiders.'

The Aga Khan Award for Architecture has been notable for celebrating the appropriateness of contextual design (see also Chapter 34). Currently on its eleventh cycle, the award has recognized and encouraged design innovation that has addressed prevailing concerns in the Islamic world. Despite numerous criticisms, the AKAAs have influenced new generations of designers to consider contextual and cultural relevance of design rather than mimic those arising out of the culture of the metropole or replicate traditions without inquiry or improvement.

How architects gain knowledge about the place they are designing in and how well they know it is a crucial question. In contrast to colonial architecture and planning interventions, and the increasing globalization of architectural practices in recent years, some designers have largely concentrated their work on a single region and devoted themselves to responding to the central issues arising there. Laurie Baker for instance, spent over thirty-five years of his life in India developing techniques of building with bricks that were low cost, used simple technology requiring minimal training, and were climatically comfortable in a hot humid climate. A French anthropologist, Peter Dujarric drew on his studies of Senegalese traditional motifs and crafts as well as village architecture in the design of a cultural centre, the Alliance Franco-Senegalaise in Kaolack, that aimed to celebrate and represent the essence of Senegalese culture.

At once local and global, rationalizing, improving, and modifying local technologies has resulted in greater opportunities for South–South flows of knowledge. Such lateral exchanges challenge the singular authority of Western Europe and North America as the centres of innovation (see also Chapter 13). For instance, Nader Khalili (1996) an Iranian-born architect, developed a type of shelter that could be built with sandbags and barbed wire and that could be used as emergency shelter in the event of a disaster. This design for disaster housing has been successfully used in Africa.

Another postcolonial approach to design has been to consider seriously social responsibility in design, with some viewing the social process of design as important as the form of the final outcome. Challenging a dependent view of architecture as largely an artistic endeavour whose aesthetics are driven by principles derived from movements originating in Western Europe and North America, some architects have addressed the spatial and cultural needs of underprivileged communities. With an activist agenda, some design efforts have focused on marginal localities with their particular problems, and limitations as legitimate subjects of design. From the provision of shelter for victims of natural disasters to refugee housing in conflict, from improving slum environments to providing improved infrastructure, design interventions, such as those of Architecture for Humanity (2006), have aimed at improving people's lives through community design (see also Chapter 38). Eschewing the conventional role of the autocratic expert, designers of this persuasion call attention to the creative force of collaborative knowledge building and design.[3]

A postcolonial agenda in the community development projects is advanced by the emphasis on enabling, empowering, and partnering with the community so that residents become active agents of transformation rather than passive objects of improvement that only increases their dependency. Clearly such efforts have conceived architecture as socially embedded processes more than completely visualized forms. For instance, the Grameen Bank, a microfinance organization in Bangladesh, has succeeded in creating low-cost housing by entrusting impoverished rural women with group loans for rebuilding their homes.[4] Their housing project won a World Habitat award and, moreover, by recognizing the creditworthiness of a group largely considered invisible and incapable, it had helped to empower them. With the idea of inculcating pride and self-sufficiency, Gawad Kalinga has assisted thousands of slum dwellers in the Phillipines to improve their living conditions with brightly painted homes, beautiful parks and playgrounds, colourful gardens, and clean surroundings.[5]

An increasingly important dimension of social responsibility in design is enhancing sustainability. Although 'sustainability' is a term that is variously interpreted, it has generally been synonymous with green building and energy efficient technologies. Only recently have equity and diversity as complex, interconnected ambitions been at the forefront of design and planning. Postcolonial perspectives on sustainability challenge the universality of technology-dominated innovations rooted in the experiences and practices in Europe and North America. Capital-intensive infrastructural services and building technologies demand huge investments of both finance and technical know-how, further reinforcing historical dependencies and marginalities. Equally, postcolonial thought, cognizant of the turbulent influence of modernity and uneven globalization everywhere, rejects simplistic assumptions about indigenous people following timeless practices and living in harmony with nature.

Minimalist interventions to rationalize, improve, and modify simple, local technologies and processes are to be preferred above importing new systems from abroad. From the perspective of enabling self-sufficiency, a simple and low-cost technology for a scavenging-free two-pit pour-flush toilet for safe and hygienic on-site disposal is a valuable contribution without high investment in expensive underground drainage. Sulabh International has been remarkably successful in constructing such public toilets in cities all over India.[6] Collective design involving marginalized groups has served to organize and empower them, as well as develop solutions that are likely to be sustained by them. Mumbai-based SPARC has successfully supported movements to organize slum dwellers and pavement dwellers, especially the women, to find collective solutions for affordable housing and toilet facilities.[7]

Sustainable Urbanism International's (SUI) exploration of cultural sustainability has included expanding the notion of heritage far beyond monuments to look at the intersections of nature, culture, and built environment.[8] Their integrated view of sustainability has highlighted the ways that local knowledges, building practices, and hydrological systems have been integral to a cultural landscape. Identifying such heritage has been a collaborative effort with local residents that has helped them recognize forms, practices, and skills they have lost or are fast losing, and can help generate livelihoods. Efforts to revive and conserve historic lakes and wells, a heritage-sensitive masterplan for cities to develop on a compact model based on the built forms and standards derived from historic neighborhoods, and reviving and adapting traditional technologies of earth construction for new structures all integrate heritage conservation with design, development planning, and natural resource management.[9] From the perspective that these too are valuable resources, and that each place needs to find its own version of innovative architecture, SUI's minimalist design and planning interventions have aimed to bring necessary improvements for local economic development.

CONCLUSION

Far from being isolated artistic endeavours, postcolonial thought has contributed to interpreting architecture and urban space as cultural artifacts that are symbolic landscapes constituted by layers of meanings and identities. As sites of assertion, contestation, and subversion of difference, built form and space have been instrumental in reinforcing and negotiating hierarchies and relationships. Postcolonial perspectives show the ways in which seemingly unique and narrowly particular forms and histories are situated in global interconnections; and forms and histories presumed to be universal, such as Western European modernisms, are in fact provincial and particular.

Above all, postcolonial theory is a way of thinking about knowledge and power. It has emphasized ways that knowledge about the world is generated in specific relationships between those with power and those without as a way to justify and perpetuate those conditions of domination. This chapter concludes not by summarizing the status of postcolonial theory but rather with the implications of adopting such a perspective in research and design. What future directions does postcolonial thought point to? Looking ahead, I see the repercussions in architectural thinking and design as fourfold.

First, thinking about architecture in an expanded realm acknowledges interconnections across time, space, and scales – as well as inequities. As a symbolic landscape, the significance of a single building extends far beyond its site to the community, city, and nation. Postcolonial thinking encourages the questioning of established cultural categories, disciplinary boundaries, and hierarchies of control. With the new modernities of globalization, new forms of dominance and subordination, and inclusion and exclusion, have emerged. The structures and hierarchies of colonialism have morphed into the new landscapes of globalization.

A postcolonial engagement in design has prompted designers to challenge universal paradigms of modernism. It prompts them to sully accepted binaries like modern and traditional; art and technology; craft and globalization; heritage and development; conservation and development; improvization and design; local and global; nature and built form; and expert and community.

Second, postcolonial thinking challenges with multiplicity and hybridity the tyranny of singular narratives of modernity. Rather, it encourages alternative interpretations of modernism and legitimizes other modernisms originating outside its canonized loci. Rather than expect purity and authenticity, postcolonial thought accepts hybrids. By highlighting histories, experiences, built environments, and people invisible in the canonical histories, postcolonial efforts have engaged with dominant accounts. A postcolonial agenda for design thinking involves as Gwendolyn Wright (2002) has suggested, considering the politics of space: 'Comodernities', as a way of thinking about modernism that allows for respectful dissent and plurality of trajectories rather than a continued acceptance of Western hierarchies alone. The objective of postcolonial critique has not been to reject the central narrative or to replace it with another, equally singular and authoritative history, but rather to expand, enrich, and renew it from the margins.

Third, postcolonial perspectives alert us, implicitly or explicitly, to the sources of architectural knowledge. Particular treatises, histories, and forms of Western Europe (and, more recently, North America) have become canonized as architectural knowledge. Recognizing the relationship between knowledge and power, postcolonial thought legitimizes other architectural knowledges. Giving voice to subordinate struggles against the structures of hierarchy, the legitimization of their experiences, has been an express objective. Beyond considering Western Europe's colonization of Asia and Africa, the ordinary and everyday architecture of prostitution houses and flop houses or critical studies of race, class, and gender, postcolonial perspectives influence investigation of other types of power relations using the idea of negotiating power and identity rather than assuming them to be given categories.

Finally, postcolonial inquiry in design brings to centre stage a transformative agenda for architectural and planning interventions seeing their objective as empowering and enabling the ordinary and the marginalized to reconsider their subjectivities as agents of positive change and to renegotiate their positions of relative powerlessness. Considerations of sustainability of environmental and cultural resources are central to this view.

Postcolonial perspectives espouse a transformative agenda for architecture and urbanism that enables and empowers multiplicity in the processes of material production, practices of their inhabitation, and structures of representation. The attempt to break free of colonial hierarchies includes investigating the colonial dimensions of concepts like modernism, postmodernism, tradition, heritage, and sustainability – all of which are rooted in Western European experiences of modernity. Interrogating difference demands an investigation into the origins of the conceptual frameworks and spatial categories that define the discipline. Therein lies our future – and our hope – of a more just and equitable world that demands globalizing knowledge production in architecture and planning.

NOTES

This chapter has benefitted enormously from the comments and suggestions of Gwendolyn Wright, Hilde Heynen, and Greig Crysler who read and re-read several versions of the chapter. Anthony King also read an earlier version of the chapter. I am very grateful to them for giving so generously. Irene Urmeneta and Damien Carriere ably assisted in compiling the bibliography.

1 The term 'subaltern' was a term used by the British to refer to junior officers in the army and literally means subordinate. The work of Eric Stokes, Eric Hobsbawm, and James Scott was also influential here.

2 See www.pukar.org.in/

3 See for instance the special issue on alternative architecture by *Journal of Architectural Education*, May 2009.

4 See www.grameen-info.org/

5 See www.gk1world.org/

6 See www.sulabhinternational.org/

7 See www.sparcindia.org/

8 See www.sustainurban.org/; www.arch.columbia.edu/labs/sustainable-urbanism directed by Jyoti Hosagrahar

9 See report, Sustainable Urbanism International. 'Site Management Plan for Sustainable Conservation and Development of Hoysala Heritage Region'. 5-volume Monograph to the Government of Karnataka, 2011.

4

Tendencies and Trajectories: Feminist Approaches in Architecture

Jane Rendell

This chapter provides an overview of shifts in the debate around feminism and architecture over the past 40 years, from the 1970s, when (arguably) feminist debate in architecture first emerged, to the 1990s, when discussions concerning the relationship between gender and space gained strength in the academy, to the contemporary moment. We will see how the key concerns raised by gender and feminist theorists are evident in a wide range of architectural texts and practices, from the analytic to the productive, the interpretative to the speculative, and from those which are clearly aligned with the feminist movement, to those which do not necessarily identify themselves as 'political' or motivated by issues concerning discrimination against women. One of the most original and radical aspects of feminist and gendered critiques of architecture has been to draw attention to the body, to reveal how architectural knowledge is embodied and how the practice of architecture is material not only in terms of its engagement with the production of artifacts but also through animate bodies and corporeal processes.

In the first part, *Tendencies*, I outline how architecture's engagement with gender difference has changed in emphasis in the past 30 years, in response to the multifarious demands of 'feminisms' and the changing place of political work in the profession and the academy. In the second part, *Trajectories*, I turn my attention to the present moment, and sketch out the terms and concepts, processes and modes of analytic enquiry and interpretation, critical and creative production, which currently feature across the work of a wide range of architectural writers and practitioners interested in feminism and gender.

TENDENCIES

The early stages of the architectural debate emerged out of the more overtly politicized discourse of feminism(s), where feminists of different persuasions took varying positions: some liberal, arguing for equal representation in architecture, others radical, calling for the overturning of the patriarchal profession of architecture and its replacement by a form of feminist practice with a different set of values. Within architectural practice, several forms of feminist design emerged, from socialist to essentialist. Published research on gender and architecture first started to appear in the late 1970s, largely written by women and from an overtly political feminist angle. Much of this work brought ideas about gender and women's studies generated in other fields – particularly anthropology, art history, cultural studies and geography and philosophy – to bear on architectural studies. This provided an interdisciplinary context for a gendered critique of architecture, one which expanded the terms of the discourse by making links with methodological approaches in other academic disciplines and which positioned gender theories, often drawn from other fields of study, as useful tools and models for critiquing architectural culture – history, theory, criticism and design. In the UK, the economic recession of the early 1990s produced a situation where a number of architects chose to pursue alternative forms of practice, such as projects, which fused architecture and art, and those which encouraged the role of ethnic minorities and women as clients. The GLC (Greater London Council) had, in an earlier period, supported non-mainstream forms of architectural practice, for example cooperatives, but as this tail-end of socialism disappeared, it was replaced by a cultural climate where state subsidies were removed and all forms of architectural practice were forced to compete in the open-market, thus making it extremely hard for such groups to survive.

Meanwhile in academia, over the same time frame, feminism and women's studies developed into gender studies. From a positive angle, this could be viewed as the recognition of the importance of the dialectical relationship between men and women, masculinity and femininity, and the role of gender as a category of analysis, but seen more negatively, the flourishing of gender studies presided over the slow disappearance of a politically orientated feminist discourse that was more 'grassroots'/'direct-action' in its approach. In architectural history, the 'herstory' mode of recovering or bringing into visibility the work of female architects, patrons and users, shifted its focus to critiquing the gendering of the discipline itself, the notion of a canon and its associated tools of historical analysis, choosing instead to analyse the gendering of architecture and its multiple forms of representation. This rethinking of the methodology of architectural history was also inspired by feminist art historians such as Griselda Pollock (1981; 1988; 1992; Parker and Pollock 1987). Feminism, in this time period, deepened understandings, across disciplines, of the role of gender in producing forms of representation (both of architecture as a subject matter and the gendered subject his/herself), producing a situation where the signifying structure was no longer taken for granted, and subjects, selves and spaces were understood to be performed and constructed rather than natural and self-evident. This can be understood as part of the larger change in feminist cultural analysis described by Michèle Barrett (1992), for example, which moved from focusing on the causes of oppression to understanding the representation of those different modes of oppression, and representation itself as a tool of oppression.[1]

The mid- to late 1990s saw the publication of a substantial number of texts investigating architecture and gender, but expanding the field to explore concerns with sex, desire, space and masculinity, and with a more explicit theoretical framing (Agrest et al. 1996; Coleman et al. 1996; Colomina 1992; Hughes 1996; McCorquodale et al. 1996; Sanders 1996). What such books had in common was their multifaceted nature. They were all edited collections, compositions of different voices, which, rather than simply describing the work of female architects or prescribing the architecture that feminists should produce, were characterized by a more speculative attitude toward the relationship of architecture and feminism.

Feminisms

One of the most important aspects of the relation between feminism and architecture is the diversity of the positions adopted. Some could be considered to follow principles of 'equality' (those who have sought to advance their recruitment and status within the ranks of the architecture profession as it exists) while others prefer principles of 'difference' (those who have questioned the nature of architectural practice and instead redefined their architectural design practice in ways that differ radically from existing models). In dealing with issues of difference, there have been several approaches to looking at the ways in which gender impacts on architecture.

One has been to critique architectural value systems as implicitly patriarchal and to focus on the problems inherent for women as users of 'man-made' environments (Little et al. 1988; Roberts 1991). Socialist and Marxist feminists involved in critiquing the 'man-made' environment in the late 1970s and early 1980s promoted a series of approaches to architectural design. The work of the American feminist planner and historian, Dolores Hayden, for instance, identified how certain features of the man-made environment discriminate against women, such as inhospitable streets, sexist symbolism in advertising and pornographic outlets (1986). Hayden proposed removing these sexist features and replacing them instead with childcare facilities, safe houses and better public transport to ensure a more equitable society. Matrix, a London-based feminist architectural cooperative, set up in the early 1980s, was also concerned with the problems experienced by women users of the man-made environment as well as designing spaces for women users which improved upon aspects of safety and accessibility in the public and domestic realms (Matrix 1984). The cooperative advocated a design process where users were involved in the design from the outset, and architects, rather than imposing their designs, acted as enablers helping future occupants realize their own spatial needs and desires.

Implicit within this work is a critique of architectural value systems and a suggestion that women have different priorities in the design of built spaces and the organization of their production (Weisman 1992). Although aligned to a socialist viewpoint, this position closely fits with the agenda of radical feminism where femaleness and femininity are seen to encompass a set of qualities, which are quite different from maleness and masculinity (Kennedy 1981). Such feminists see the values of contemporary societies which are patriarchal, which organize and monopolize private property to the benefit of the male head of the family, as reflected in the often phallic building forms that they produce, the quintessential example being the skyscraper. Conversely they suggest that cultures, which revere the feminine principle and treat women at least as equals produce built forms related to the morphology of the female body (Lobell 1989).

A number of feminist designers have also drawn architectural inspiration from the female body, designing womb-like and curvaceous forms rather than phallic towers, spaces which focus on aspects of enclosure, exploring the relationship between inside and outside through openings, hollows and gaps. American critic Karen Franck, following Nancy Chodorow, has argued that women's socialization fosters a different value system emphasizing certain qualities such as connectedness, inclusiveness, an ethics of care, everyday life, subjectivity, feelings, complexity and flexibility in design. Franck has cited the work of women architects such as Eileen Gray, Lilly Reich and Susana Torre's projects such as 'House of Meaning' and 'Space as Matrix' as exemplary of this approach (Franck 1989). Promoting the idea that women designers and users value different kinds of spaces – ones which foster the flexibility required by women's social roles – also suggests analogies between spatial matrices and the fluid spatiality of the female body (Torre 1977, 186–202).

In this time period, a commitment to developing an understanding of the differences among women was key to the agenda of both black and lesbian feminists. The Combahee River Collective, for example, worked to form a more adequate feminist theory of racial difference, which involved developing thematics common to the work of many black women writers, such as a focus on the strength of black women as opposed to their more commonly perceived status as victims, the relation of everyday experience to theoretical concepts, and the positive aspects of relationships between women (Combahee River Collective 1982; see also Davis 1982; hooks 1989a; Collins 1990). For lesbian feminists, the difference between women was to be understood in terms of sexual preference as well as sex; and lesbianism a form of female culture and community as well as a **sexual practice**. For writers such as Adrienne Rich, lesbianism was experienced in the form of both 'continuum' and 'existence' (1983; Fuss 1991), while others emphasized the importance of female friendship (Bunch and Pollock 1983; Bunch 1987; Raymond 1986). The work of the black lesbian poet, Audre Lorde is exemplary here in that it engages with the emotional as well as the rational in order to draw out the interlocking relations of different forms of oppression due to race and sexuality, as well as class and gender (Lorde 1996).

Herstory

Feminist architectural history has also adopted a number of different approaches aligned with various political positions. Following reformist or liberal tactics aimed at establishing conditions of equality for women, some feminists have been concerned with women's exclusion from architecture and sought to produce an alternative history of architecture by uncovering evidence of women's contributions (Boutelle 1988), either as architects of large institutional buildings in the public realm, or within the building industry and also through their roles as patrons, as the work of Alice T. Friedman has explored (1989; 1997). The work of Lynne Walker (1984) in the United Kingdom and Gwendolyn Wright (1977) in the United States has emphasized an important aspect of the historical recovery of the contribution of women to architecture. Both historians have highlighted the ways in which women have had to fight for inclusion in the predominantly male profession, from their acceptance in institutions of architectural education, to establishing themselves in offices as professional architects.

Other feminists have focused their critique on the gendered nature of architectural history itself, arguing that only the buildings of the great male masters have been categorized as 'architecture' and included in architectural history. By reclaiming the history of low-key buildings, everyday housing, domestic, interior and textile design, spaces or practices typically associated with women and regarded as trivial, such feminists show that it is not only the buildings of the public realm, financed by wealthy patrons, the nobility and merchants of the past and the wealthy capitalists of today, that are worthy of being part of history. In challenging what constitutes architecture, this work is strongly linked to the perspectives of Marxist geographers, namely David Harvey and Edward Soja, and Marxist philosopher, Henri Lefebvre, who have argued that space is socially produced and also that space is a condition of social production (see for example Harvey 1989; Soja 1989; Lefebvre 1991). Feminist geographers, such as Liz Bondi (1990; 1992; 1993), Doreen Massey (1994), Linda McDowell (1993) and Gillian Rose (1993), have developed and extended much of this work, arguing for attention to gender as well as class difference in the production of space.

Interdisciplinarity

Drawing on gender theory, from fields such as psychoanalysis, philosophy, cultural studies, film theory and art history, increasingly developed the work of feminists in architectural studies through the late 1980s and 1990s, particularly in architectural history, theory and criticism. By the mid- to late-1990s, interdisciplinary feminist criticism had extended the field of architectural discourse, blurring the boundaries between theory and history, and between criticism and practice.

The implications of feminist work on representation and gender in other fields; namely psychoanalysis, philosophy, cultural studies, film theory and art history raised two main issues for the practice of architectural history; first, new objects of study – the actual material which historians choose to look at; and second, the intellectual criteria by which historians interpret those objects of study. An important body of work coming out of US scholarship, specifically East Coast universities such as Princeton and publications such as *Assemblage* and *ANY,* highlights the relevance of such methodological issues. Critics such as Beatriz Colomina (1994), Zeynep Çelik (1997a) and Mabel Wilson (1996) have focused on developing sustained feminist critiques of the traditional male canon. Using feminist interpretative techniques, they place issues of gender, race and ethnicity at the heart of the architectural practice of such male masters as Adolf Loos and Le Corbusier.

Theoretical approaches suggest new aspects of architecture to explore, equally new architectural objects provide new sites through which to explore theory and suggest new kinds of interpretative modes. Drawing on the work by queer theorists such as Judith Butler and Eve Kosofsky Sedgwick (1991), notions of 'performativity' have provoked those in spatial disciplines to look at how place and gender are performed. For Butler, sex and gender are both social and historical constructions, gender is not to culture as sex is to nature; sex as natural fact does not precede the cultural inscription of gender. To think of the body only in terms of the biological, anatomical or physiological, is limited. Instead, Butler considers gender to be a performance that produces the illusion of an inner sex. Butler (1990) suggests that 'gender trouble' is culturally produced through 'subversive body acts' or 'the body in drag' that exhibit the artificiality of gender and so subvert the system from within through parody. This notion of the 'performativity' of gender shows how the performance of gender may operate subversively to radically critique the naturalness of the biologically sexed body. Working with queer theory to rethink understandings of architecture in relation to the spatial practice of 'coming out', Henry Urbach has focused on the history of the design of the closet, to develop an argument concerning secrecy and display with relation to homosexuality (Urbach 1999).

Drawing on post-structuralism and psychoanalysis, gender and queer theory has developed a body of work which problematizes such seemingly stable terms as architecture, male and female, and examines architecture and masculinity as mutually reinforcing ideologies. In a profession where masculinity is collapsed into the neutral figure of the 'architect', and sites of current architectural education and discourse: the office, the media, the institution and the profession, are also considered gender neutral, recognizing gender as a social construction in order to critique the heterosexual patriarchal bastion of architectural practice has been of key importance. Joel Sander's critique of a project by architectural practice SOM, Cadet Quarters, US Air Force Academy, Colorado Springs, showed how representations of masculinity are central to the work of these contemporary architects (Sanders 1996, 68–78), while Diana Agrest (1993), using examples from the treatises of Renaissance architects who advocated the use of particular proportion systems for setting out the formal geometries of buildings, demonstrated how the male body was used to represent the ideal set of proportions, while the female body was either rejected from the practice of architecture or suppressed within it.

Over this period, feminist research shifted understandings of the role of theory from inside to outside architecture, from design prescription to design critique, connecting architecture not only to production, but also to reproduction through representation, consumption, appropriation and occupation. Such work has highlighted new directions for feminist architectural practice to concentrate not only on the end product but also the process of design itself, thus pointing to the importance of the dialogue between theory and practice in architecture, which we might call 'feminist architectural practice'.

Feminist architectural practice

The work of feminist architectural practices such as muf in the United Kingdom and Liquid Incorporated in the United States, have strived to relate feminist theory to architectural design, built practice to written text, and dealt with issues of femininity and decoration, relations of looking and the materiality of fluids, and most importantly embodiment (muf 1996; 2001; Landesberg and Quatrale 1996). The drawn and written projects of American architect and critic, Jennifer Bloomer have been highly influential in this respect, dealing with the difference of the 'feminine'. Her texts have a spatially structured materiality, operating as metaphoric sites through which imaginative narratives are explored, as well as employing metonymic devices to bring the non-appropriate into architecture. For Bloomer (1993), different modes of writing express new ways of understanding architecture through the intimate and personal, the subjective rather than objective, through sensual rather than purely visual stimulation. Bloomer's text *is* her architecture; her textual strategies are used to interpret architectural drawings and spaces but also to create new notions of space and creativity, allowing links to be made between architectural design and theory. Her work has greatly influenced other architectural designers, whose projects draw on feminist theoretical concerns, to stimulate new forms of design, from the choosing of site to the articulation of services.

Another important aspect of feminist architectural practice has been the testing of architecture's professional and disciplinary boundaries, as demonstrated through the work of architects who have developed the artistic aspect of their practice, such as Maya Lin, or collaborated with artists and other spatial practitioners in the public spaces of the city (Felshin 1995; Lacy 1995). Dance, film, art and writing have provided architecture with new feminist ways of working (Thomas et al. 2002), and clearly as well as the makers of works (the architectural practitioners, designers, urbanists, artists), the role of audience, user and critic have become vital to constructing the meaning of feminist practice.

Questions of subjectivity have been very important in feminist architectural practice, with the work of French feminists Hélène Cixous, Luce Irigaray and Julia Kristeva, being highly influential. Irigaray's work on mimicry (1985a, 133–146) argued that, if women are not speaking subjects in the existing symbolic order, then the only way for women to represent themselves is through an acknowledgement of this condition – through mimicking or parodying their objectified position. Architect Elizabeth Diller, addressed this issue through a project that demonstrated how feminist critiques of women's role as domestic labourers can be used to inspire creativity (Diller 1996). Diller's architectural project involved a complex choreography where, by performing a series of folding movements similar to origami, a number of shirts were ironed into perfectly useless forms. As a parody of the precision of housework and the reworking of such skills for a new function, this can be read as feminist architectural practice.

Over the last 30 years then, feminist architectural design and feminist architectural history and theory have changed internally and in relation to one another. On the one hand, feminist architectural history has developed from a recovery of evidence of women architects to embrace the role of theory, specifically critical and gender theory in interpreting architectural representations historically. On the other hand, feminists have opened up definitions of architectural design to include process as well as product, drawing and writing as well as building, so that the distinctions between design, history and theory are now, more than ever, less than clear-cut.

However, there is still resistance from within the profession to modes of practice seen to be irrelevant to the task of providing buildings in the most cost-effective way possible. Women's exclusion from the architectural profession and education has been a historical problem connected with explicit sexism; today, although more women are entering the profession, a discrepancy between the number of women entering architectural education and those who become practising architects remains. A study in Australia, for example, which showed that although women made up 43 percent of architecture students, less than 1 percent were firm directors, connected this to the fact that women might choose not to take 'traditional practitioner paths'. The problem remains particularly acute for African American women licensed to practice architecture in the United States, where, although the figure has quadrupled over the past 15 years, they still account for only 0.2 percent of the total population of approximately 91,000 licensed architects.

TRAJECTORIES

The past decade has continued to see a flourishing of activity in feminism and architecture, driven by interdisciplinary concerns. One of the key aspects of change has been the role of theory, which has shifted from a tool of analysis to a mode of practice in its own right. The term 'theory' is here not understood to refer to modes of enquiry in science through either induction or deduction but rather to critical theory (see Chapter 2). Critical theories are forms of knowledge which differ from theories in the natural sciences because they are 'reflective' rather than 'objectifying' and take into account their own procedures and methods; they aim neither to prove a hypothesis nor prescribe a particular methodology or solution to a problem but to offer self-reflective modes of thought that seek to change the world (Geuss 1981, 2). I extend the term 'critical theory' to include the work of feminists and others whose thinking is self-critical and desirous of social change – who seek to transform rather than describe (Rendell 2003). Much feminist practice in architecture has developed ways of working with the 'useful' aspect of theory, not necessarily from a pragmatic point of view, or through modes of applying theory, but rather by practising theory in a speculative manner – which combines critique and invention, and is performative and embodied.

Trajectories is divided into four subsections, each one of which highlights a particular theme important to the current intersection of feminism and architecture. These themes: critical spatial practices, other spaces, difference and location, and the performative turn, feature as the focal points of scholarly energy, professional disagreement and original new research.

Critical spatial practices

As just discussed, the opposition between history/theory/criticism (or activities which write about architecture) and design (or activities which produce architecture) has started to dissipate, especially in the academy, and increasingly outside it in practice, though not yet perhaps at the heart of the profession. Within academia, the rise in what has been termed 'practice-led/-based research' (Rendell 2004) as well as the influence of the writings of Henri Lefebvre and Michel de Certeau on spatial practice, has produced an understanding of practice as a process which occurs not only through the design of buildings but also through the activities of using, occupying and experiencing, as well as modes of writing and imaging which describe, analyse and interrogate (de Certeau 1984; Lefebvre 1991).

It is possible to draw connections between de Certeau's strategies and Lefebvre's representations of space on the one hand, and de Certeau's tactics and Lefebvre's spaces of representation on the other, and suggest a distinction between those practices (strategies) that operate to maintain and reinforce existing social and spatial orders, and those practices (tactics) that seek to critique and question them. I favour such a distinction and have called the latter 'critical spatial practice' – a term which serves to describe both everyday activities and creative practices which seek to resist the dominant social order of global corporate capitalism (Rendell 2006). This has been the aim of much of the increasing collaborative and interdisciplinary practice across art and architecture, where the construction of relationships between disciplines and a focus on the process as well as the product of design has started to play a key role and shape debate in the production of the public realm.

Described as an architectural practice, muf, for example, is frequently criticized for not producing any 'architecture' or buildings, but this is because its way of working is itself a critique of architectural design methodologies that emphasize form and object-making. muf's working method highlights the importance of exchange across art and architecture, the participation of users in the design process and the importance of collaborating with other producers. For muf, the architectural design process is not an activity that leads to the making of a product, but is rather the location of the work itself (muf 2001, 25). muf's methodology is established out of a critique of the brief, and through the ensuing development of a dialogue between clients, artists, architects and various other material fabricators, between those who produce the work and those who use it. In architecture, to position a building as a 'methodology' rather than as the end result of the method or process that makes it, is a radical proposition.

Other spaces

Feminist critique has been particularly effective in mobilizing the possibilities of Derridean deconstruction in architecture (Derrida 1976, 6–26). The radical move deconstruction offers is to think 'both/and' rather than 'either/or', putting deferrals and differences into play and suggesting instead 'undecideability' and slippage. This has allowed a thorough and ongoing critique of a number of binary oppositions, but most specifically the separate spheres or the 'public–private' division of gendered space manifest in different cultures at various historical periods. This work has drawn attention to the spaces both marginalized within gendered binaries in mainstream architectural discourse, such as the domestic and the interior, and/or positioned as terms which exceed this binary distinction, such as the margin, the between, the everyday, the heterotopic and the abject (McLeod 1996; Campkin and Dobraszcyk 2007; Campkin and Cox 2008).

The interior and the domestic have been perhaps the most thoroughly explored of these 'other spaces' as they have both been directly associated with the private home, and as such subordinated to the public city, in both patriarchal and capitalist cultures, and within the discourse of modernity. There is a huge heritage of feminist literature, which critiques the separate spheres, and revalues the private sphere, but what is significant in this newer work, is the lack of defensive positioning. The arguments are not necessarily foregrounded in the separate spheres debate, nor launched from a specifically feminist position, and often forge alliances with texts that are not part of the feminist lineage (Heynen and Baydar 2005; Heynen 2002; Rosner 2005).

The research on the interior has a different resonance, with, I think, another set of reasons surrounding its current emergence. First, the newfound confidence of interior design or interior architecture, a professional and academic discipline which has long been marginalized in relation to architecture. The reader *Intimus*, for example, sketches out an intellectual context for interior design, which celebrates its difference from architecture and, in so doing, draws on a rich and far more densely textured field of reference (Taylor and Preston 2006). Second, the interior is both a space and an image (Penner and Rice 2004; Penner 2005), and as Rice discusses (2007), its emergence in the bourgeois culture of late-nineteenth-century Europe links it closely to the birth of psychoanalysis as a discipline. The significance of current interest in the interior might then be understood in terms of the position it occupies as the site of convergence between space and subjectivity, place and psyche.

Difference and location

The 1990s saw a rise in the relevance and pertinence of identity politics focusing on class, gender, race, ethnicity and sexuality. Emerging through, and at times diverging from, this discourse, has been the work of post-structuralist feminists. This work has been particularly important for architecture in offering metaphorical insights; new ways of knowing and being have been discussed in spatial terms, developing conceptual and critical tools such as 'situated knowledge' (Haraway 1988) and 'standpoint theory' (Flax 1991) to examine the interrelations between location, identity and knowledge (Probyn 1990; Benhabib 1992). The groundbreaking personal/poetic writing of black women such as bell hooks is seminal here, as well as the work of Rosi Braidotti (1994) whose figure of the 'nomadic subject' describes not only a spatial state of movement, but also an epistemological condition, a kind of knowingness (or unknowingness) that refuses fixity.

This subtle understanding of position as physical, emotional and ideological, and difference as multiple rather than binary, as well as a diversified knowledge of the role of colonializing practices/discourses, is present in new understandings of positioned knowledge from a range of theorists including Seyla Benhabib, Sue Best, Rosalyn Diprose, Jane Flax, Moira Gatens, Sandra Harding, Elspeth Probyn, Linda Nicholson, Andrea Nye and Gayatri Spivak. As this work makes clear, identities are contingent and situated, constructed in response to particular times and places. The notion of gender difference as essentialist – as ahistorical and ageographical – is thoroughly critiqued. Many of those with an Anglophone perspective have been wary of the 'feminine' for its association with biological essentialism, but for those with a training in continental philosophy and in the French language, it is clear that the 'feminine' is not only biological but also cultural, and has been associated with the other and with lack (following Jacques Lacan), and as the site of difference itself (Jacques Derrida). Indeed one feminist critic has wondered whether the role of females in producing architectural space can be examined without recourse to the 'feminine' (Bergren 1994). Unleashed afresh, the feminine is a term, which has recently allowed feminists a vibrant engagement with aesthetic experience.

An important and timely volume, *Altering Practices*, edited by Doina Petrescu (2007) brings the debate around feminism and architecture right up to date, with a discussion of the 'poetics and politics of the feminine'. In taking account of the feminine, rather than, or at least as well as, the feminist, essays in this book acknowledge the role of aesthetics as well as ethics, form as well as function, in architecture, turning the focus to the processes through which practices of space are gendered. The focus on the other, and within the book the development of an understanding of practices which aim to change, transform or alter, as forms of practising 'otherwise' or 'otherhow', evidences the diverse range of feminist work current in architecture in a clear, articulate and political way. Petrescu's own practice as an architect with aaa (atelier d'architecture autogérée), and the ECObox project based in the La Chapelle area of Paris, is transdisciplinary, locally focused and works to produce small changes on a micro level in the community (Petrescu 2005).

The question of difference has not only been taken up and explored by feminists, but also by those in postcolonial theory (see also Chapter 3). In architecture, work in this area has transformed from 'critical regionalism' into a more profoundly politicized and radical arena. Lesley Lokko has addressed issues of black identity in her edited book *White Papers, Black Marks: Architecture, Race, Culture* (2000), which holds fast to a strong sense of desire for political change while recognizing the often contingent and situated conditions of race and identity. Felipe Hernandez's work, although not explicitly about gender, also makes an important point in this field. Hernandez has chosen to develop the critical concept of 'transculturation' generated by the Cuban anthropologist, Fernando Ortiz, in the early 1940s, in relation to his own research on Latin American architecture. This a pointedly political alternative to the more usual use of the 'holy trinity' of Homi Bhabha, Edward Said and Spivak, whose theoretical writings are the backbone of postcolonial studies, yet whose own locational positions in the West are less often taken into account. For Hernandez, the location of theory is an important part of his project (Hernandez 2003; Hernandez et al. 2006).

The work of women architects from South Asia presented in the 2000 *An Emancipated Place* conference held in Mumbai, likewise challenged conventional, and usually minority world-dominated, ways of defining architecture and the role of the architect (Somaya et al. 2000). Rather than adopt a purely conceptual perspective, different modes of practice were presented as alternative models with 'holistic and inclusive' values instead of didactic ones. These included projects which addressed issues such as participation, enabling, sustainability and conservation of tradition and heritage. In these works, the architect's working mode turns out either to be acting as a community developer or as organizers of a participatory process (e.g. Yasmeen Lari, Brinda Somaya, Afroza Ahmed, Gita Balakrishnan), or creating 'a balance in life' (between nature and architecture) (e.g. Meena Mani, Namita Singh, Anupama Kundoo, Parul Zaveri), or conserving heritage settlements and buildings (e.g. Yasmeen Lari, Sandhya Sawant, Abha Narain Lambah) and crafts (e.g. Minnette De Silva, Parul Zaveri). The attitude towards architecture expressed in *An Emancipated Place* highlights the material reality of the area – a poverty-stricken framework in rural and urban areas – and the need for architects who can address environmental and humanitarian concerns not as a choice but as a necessity and effective intervention in this context. In this conference, it was the other place in terms of geographical location and architecture construction, which provided difference rather than only gender.

The performative turn

In visual and spatial culture, feminists have drawn extensively on psychoanalytic theory to further understand relationships between the spatial politics of internal psychical figures and external cultural geographies (Friedman 1998; Fuss 1995; Rogoff 2000; Silverman 1996). The field of psychoanalysis explores these various thresholds and boundaries between private and public, inner and outer, subject and object, personal and social, in terms of a complex understanding of the relationship between 'internal' and 'external' space. The writings of philosopher Elizabeth Grosz (1994; 2001) and geographer Steve Pile (1996) have been particularly influential in this respect.

Although psychoanalysis has given architectural research insight into the theoretical interpretation of buildings, images and texts, what is new in the feminist work in this area, is the interest in the production of subjectivity and the performative qualities of criticism. Amelia Jones and Andrew Stephenson (1999), for example, take issue with the tradition that the interpreter must be neutral or disinterested in the objects, which s/he judges, and posit instead, with reference to spatial mobility, that the process of viewing and interpreting involves 'entanglement in intersubjective spaces of desire, projection and identification'. Peggy Phelan's commentaries on performance art (1993) have developed a mode of writing criticism that declares its own performativity and the presence of the body of the critic in the writing as 'marked'. In Della Pollock's highly informative discussion of the key qualities of performance writing (1997), she includes being subjective, as well as evocative, metonymic, nervous, citational and consequential as exceptional aspects of this type of writing. And in Gavin Butt's edited volume (2005) the attempt by critics and practitioners to 'renew criticism's energies' occurs specifically through a 'theatrical turn'.

The level of performativity and self-reflectivity in architectural debate has tended to lag behind other disciplines, namely art and literature. Although, there has been, in architecture, some degree of exploration of the relation between criticism, history and theory (Nesbitt 1996; Hays 2000; Leach 1997; Borden and Rendell 2000), there has been very little explicit discussion of the situated-ness of the critic, and therefore the relation between criticism and practice. My own practice of 'site-writing' (Rendell 2010) aims to address this issue. Site-writing explores the position of the author, not only in relation to theoretical ideas, art objects, and architectural spaces, but also to the site of writing itself. My suggestion is that in operating as a mode of practice in its own right, this kind of criticism or critical spatial writing, questions the terms of reference that relate the critic to the work positioned 'under' critique, transforming over time depending on their specific locations, constructing as well as tracing the sites of relation between critic and work.

Feminists in cultural, literary and post-colonial criticism, such as Cixous (Sellers 1994) and Gloria Anzaldúa (1999), have woven the autobiographical into the critical in their texts, combining poetic writing with theoretical analysis to articulate hybrid voices. 'Voices' can be objective *and* subjective, distant *and* intimate, drawing on spaces as they are remembered, dreamed and imagined, as well as observed, in order to take into account the critic's position in relation to a work and challenge criticism as a form of knowledge with a singular and static point of view located in the here and now. Mieke Bal's exploration of the critic's 'engagement' with art explores this territory in art history, as someone coming from literary criticism, her interest in narrative opens up ways of thinking about subject positions in criticism (Bal 2001, xi; Bryson 2001, 12). In architecture, Guiliana Bruno (2002), another interdisciplinary traveller, moving this time from film criticism to architecture, also points to the situated nature of writing about architecture, outlining both a personal journey in the introduction to her *Atlas of Emotion*, as well as suggesting that the book itself adopts a spatial structure. For my own part, rather than write *about* the work, I am interested in how the critic constructs his or her writing in relation *to* and in dialogue *with* the work. The focus on the preposition here allows a direct connection to be made between the positional *and* the relational.

The work of Katja Grillner and her colleagues at KTH Stockholm, has been developing in similar directions, examining how writing constructs as well as reflects meaning (Grillner et al. 2005). The role of writing as a form of practice in its own right, has been explored by Rolf Hughes in his discussion of the prose poem as a hybrid genre which combines critical and creative writing practices in relation to what is called practice-led or based research (Hughes 2006). Katerina Bonnevier operates a performative writing which stages theoretical analysis and historical research to re-examine queer space (Bonnevier 2007). Taken as a whole, this research considers the modes in which we practice theory and criticism to be more than a description of content, but to define critical positions, the 'architecture' of theory then takes into account the structure, processes and materials of the medium employed – these are considered integral to the construction of the writing, showing that theory and criticism are themselves material practices.

The influence of Marxist methodologies in architectural history has played a key role in critiquing a type of architectural history, which placed the designer and the form of the building at the forefront of the discipline. Historical materialism pointed instead to the 'social production of space' – to the role of the construction industry, cultural/social context, as well as the reproduction of space through its representation and use. Such methodologies have been adopted/adapted by certain feminists in the field to highlight the gendering of processes of production and reproduction, but also through feminism's own version of materialist analysis, to develop an understanding of the role of body as matter (Rawes 2007a; 2007b).

This understanding of 'materiality' has started to produce work where material is not only seen as the social and economic context for architecture but also viewed as an active ingredient in the processes of making architecture. This might appear rather obvious in relation to architectural design, but feminist explorations of the different potential of architectural materials from the conceptual design to the level of the detail remain limited; the theoretical work of Katie Lloyd Thomas (2007) is an exception. Sarah Wigglesworth Architecture is one practice, which has consistently explored new potentials for materials, most famously in the use of an unusual range of material including quilting and straw, at 9 Stock Orchard Street, the Straw House, 2001. It is also the case that the processes of researching and writing architecture have been informed by material concerns, placing emphasis on embodiment, narrative and voice, and articulating texts that are patterned, and that create topographies of intersecting epistemologies and ontologies (Araujo et al. 2007).

CONCLUSION

This apparently highly integrated situation where theory and practice are in dialogue, as I have described it here, could be understood as an expression of the new-found confidence of feminism in architecture, that the gender debate has infused architecture to such an extent that there is no longer any need to directly address issues of oppression. This condition, however, is potentially highly dangerous for two reasons.

First, it could obscure the vital contribution of feminist forbears, producing a new version of 'hidden from history' and diffusing feminism's political imperative. It is interesting to note here that we have seen perhaps fewer sole-authored publications by feminists in architecture than in other disciplines such as visual culture, art history and cultural geography. The recent edited collections which have deepened the exploration of certain gendered dimensions of architectural design and culture have operated in a different mode of authorship, collaborative rather than sole, and in a more nuanced way looking at themes that derive from feminist enquiry but, for the non-informed and often non-feminist reader, are not obviously associated with it, such as domesticity, materiality and pattern. Such collections have been edited by feminists (and I include myself here) who ten years ago would have made their feminist agenda explicit whereas now they seemingly no longer feel the need to do so, perhaps because they wish to explore other questions. However, the danger is that, unless the references to feminist theory are made clear, we are unwittingly 'unwriting' architecture's feminist genealogy. This then poses questions about acknowledgement, and raises the issue of appropriation and the danger of invisibility. This last point leads to a much graver problem, which is the lack of economic support for making visible – for publishing work – produced outside the narrow confine (physically and conceptually) of the so-called developed, more accurately described as minority, world. The range of published material on feminism and architecture is currently biased in favour of the minority, and so creates an inaccurate construction of the global culture of gendered spatial practice.

Second, and perhaps of an even more serious nature from a humanitarian perspective, is the impression suggested by minority world publications, that gender oppression is no longer an issue. To focus myopically on gender, would suggest a certain blindness to today's context where in some places far more urgent forms of oppression, marginalization and difference demand our attention right now. However, some of these remain directly connected with sex and gender, while in others these aspects are less obvious, but yet still a factor, for example operations of resistance against neo-conservative and neo-liberal politics at work in architecture, connections between military domination and oil consumption, the uneven distribution of wealth between the majority and minority world, and the rapid unfolding of environmental catastrophes and events, such as the current food crisis, related to them. We need then to recognize that the operation of this debate is global, and to ensure that as feminists the particular dimensions of gender struggles at a both macro and micro level are kept firmly on the agenda.

NOTE

1 The volume *Gender Space Architecture*, which I co-edited at this time, offered something slightly different: an attempt at an interdisciplinary introduction which consisted of a carefully selected, comprehensive collection of seminal texts from the 1970s to the 1990s, organized both chronologically and thematically, which attempted to chart historical changes within feminism and caused by the impact of feminism within the discipline of architecture, as well as map feminist developments in other disciplines which might be of relevance to architecture. See Rendell et al. (1999).

Section 1 Bibliography

Abbas, Ackbar (1997) *Hong Kong. Culture and the Politics of Disappearance*. Minneapolis: University of Minnesota Press.

Abu-Lughod, Janet (1980) *Rabat: Urban Apartheid in Morocco*. Princeton: Princeton University Press.

Adorno, Theodor W. (1973) *Negative Dialectics*. London: Routledge [translation of *Negative Dialektik* 1966].

—— (1984) *Aesthetic Theory*. London: Routledge [translation of *Ästhetische Theorie* 1970].

Adorno, Theodor W. and Max Horkheimer (1972) *Dialectic of Enlightenment*. New York: Herder and Herder [translation of *Dialektik der Aufklärung: Philosophische Fragmente* 1944].

Agrest, Diana (1993) *Architecture from Without: Theoretical Framings for a Critical Practice*. Cambridge, MA: MIT Press.

Agrest, Diana, Patricia Conway and Leslie Kanes Weisman (eds) (1996) *The Sex of Architecture*. New York: Abrams.

Allen, Stan (2004) Commentary in response to 'Stocktaking 2004: Nine questions about the present and future of design', *Harvard Design Magazine* 20: 5–51.

Al Sayyad, Nezar (ed.) (2001) *Consuming Tradition, Manufacturing Heritage: Global Norms and Urban Forms in the Age of Tourism*. London: Routledge.

Al Sayyad, Nezar, Irene A. Bierman and Nasser O. Rabbat (eds) (2005) *Making Cairo Medieval*. Lexington: Lexington Books.

Anderson, Benedict (1999 [1985]) *Imagined Communities: Reflections on the Origin and Spread of Nationalism*. London: Verso.

Anzaldúa, Gloria (1999 [1987]) *Borderlands/La Frontera: The New Mestiza*. San Francisco: Lute Books.

Appadurai, Arjun (1996) *Modernity at Large: Cultural Dimensions of Globalization*. Minneapolis: University of Minnesota Press.

—— (2001) *Globalization*. Durham, NC: Duke University Press.

Appiah, Kwame Anthony (2003) *In My Father's House: Africa in the Philosophy of Culture*. Oxford: Oxford University Press.

Appiah, Kwame Anthony and Henry Louis Gates, Jr. (eds) (1995) *Identities*. Chicago: University of Chicago Press.

Araujo, Ana, Jane Rendell and Jonathan Hill (eds) (2007) Pattern, Special Issue of *HAECCEITY*.

Architecture for Humanity (2006) *Design Like You Give a Damn: Architectural Responses to Humanitarian Crisis*. New York: Metropolis Books.

Arendt, Hannah (1958) *The Human Condition*. Chicago: Chicago University Press.

Augé, Marc (1995) *Non-Places. Introduction to an Anthropology of Supermodernity*. London: Verso [translation of *Non-Lieux. Introduction à une anthropologie de la surmodernité* 1992].

Arnold, Dana (2002) *Reading Architectural History*. New York and London: Routledge.

Aureli, Pier Vittorio (2008) *The Project of Autonomy. Politics and Architecture within and against Capitalism*. New York: Princeton Architectural Press.

Baird, George (1995) *The Space of Appearance*. Cambridge, MA: MIT Press.

—— (2004) '"Criticality" and its discontents', *Harvard Design Magazine* 21: 16–21.

Bal, Mieke (2001) *Louise Bourgeois' Spider: The Architecture of Art–Writing*. Chicago: University of Chicago Press.

Balandier, Georges (1966) 'La situation colonial' [1955], translated as 'The colonial situation: A theoretical approach', in Immanuel Wallerstein (ed.) *Social Change: The Colonial Situation*. New York: Wiley, 34–61.

Barrett, Michèle (1992) 'Words and things: Materialism and method in contemporary feminist analysis', in Michèle Barrett and Anne Phillips (eds) *Destabilising Theory: Contemporary Feminist Debates*. Cambridge: Polity Press, 201–219.

Baudrillard, Jean (1976) *L'échange symbolique et la mort.* Paris: Gallimard.

Baydar, Gülsüm (1998) 'Toward postcolonial openings: rereading Sir Banister Fletcher's "History of Architecture"', *Assemblage* 35: 6–17.

Beguin, François, Denis Lesage and Lucien Godin (1983) *Arabisances: Décor architectural et trace urbain en Afrique du Nord 1830–1950.* Paris: Dunod.

Bell, Michael (2004) *Space Replaces Us. Essays and Projects on the City.* New York: Monacelli.

Benhabib, Seyla (1992) *Situating the Self: Gender, Community and Postmodernism in Contemporary Ethics.* Cambridge: Polity Press.

Benjamin, Walter (1999) 'The author as producer', in *Selected Writings. Volume 2. Part 2 1931–1934,* Cambridge, MA: Harvard University Press, 768–782 [translation of 'Der Autor als Produzent' 1934].

—— (2008) *The Work of Art in the Age of its Technological Reproducibility, and Other Writings on Media.* Cambridge, MA: Harvard University Press.

Bentmann, Reinhard and Michael Muller (1992) *The Villa as Hegemonic Architecture.* London: Humanities Press [translation of *Die Villa als Herrschaftsarchitektur* 1970].

Bergren, Ann (1994) 'Dear Jennifer', *ANY,* 4: 12–15.

Betsky, Aaron (1997) *Queer Space. Architecture and Same-Sex Desire.* New York: William Morrow.

Bhabha, Homi K. (1994) *The Location of Culture.* London: Routledge.

Bingaman, Ami et al. (eds) (2002) *Embodied Utopias. Gender, Social Change and the Modern Metropolis.* London: Routledge.

Bloom, Harold et al. (1979) *Deconstruction and Criticism.* New York: Continuum.

Bloomer, Jennifer (1993) *Architecture and the Text: the (S)crypts of Joyce and Piranesi.* New Haven: Yale University Press.

Bondi, Liz (1990) 'Feminism, postmodernism, and geography: a space for women?' *Antipode* 22(2): 156–167.

—— (1992) 'Gender symbols and urban landscapes', *Progress in Human Geography* 16(2): 157–170.

—— (1993) 'Gender and geography: crossing boundaries', *Progress in Human Geography* 17(2): 241–246.

Bonnevier, Katerina (2007) *Behind Straight Curtains: Towards a Queer Feminist Theory of Architecture.* Stockholm: Axl Books.

Borden, Iain and Jane Rendell (eds) (2000) *InterSections: Architectural History and Critical Theory.* London: Routledge.

Borden, Iain, Jane Rendell and Barbara Penner (eds) (2000) *Gender Space Architecture. An Introduction.* London: Routledge.

Boutelle, Sara (1988) *Julia Morgan: Architect.* New York: Abbeville Press.

Bozdogan, Sibel (2001) *Modernism and Nation Building: Turkish Architectural Culture in the Early Republic.* Seattle: University of Washington Press.

Braidotti, Rosi (1994) *Nomadic Subjects.* New York: Columbia University Press.

Brent Ingram, Gordon et al. (eds) (1997) *Queers in Space. Communities, Public Places, Sites of Resistance.* Seattle: Bay Press.

Browne, Kath et al. (eds) (2007) *Geographies of Sexualities.* Aldershot: Ashgate.

Bruno, Guiliana (2002) *Atlas of Emotion: Journeys in Art, Architecture and Film.* London: Verso.

Bryson, Norman (2001) 'Introduction: Art and Intersubjectivity', in Mieke Bal, *Looking in: The Art of Viewing.* Amsterdam: G+B International, 1–39.

Bunch, Charlotte (1987) *Passionate Politics: Feminist Theory in Action.* New York: St. Martin's Press.

Bunch, Charlotte and Sandra Pollock (eds) (1983) *Learning our Way: Essays in Feminist Education.* New York: The Crossing Press.

Butler, Judith (1990) *Gender Trouble: Feminism and the Subversion of Identity.* London: Routledge.

—— (1993) *Bodies That Matter: On the Discursive Limits of Sex.* London: Routledge.

Butt, Gavin (ed.) (2005) *After Criticism: New Responses to Art and Performance.* Oxford: Blackwell.

Campkin, Ben and Paul Dobraszcyk (eds) (2007) Architecture and Dirt, Special Issue of *The Journal of Architecture,* 12(4).

Campkin, Ben and Rosie Cox (eds) (2008) *Dirt: New Geographies of Cleanliness and Contamination.* London: Tauris.

Canclini, Nestor Garcia (1995) *Hybrid Cultures.* Minneapolis: University of Minnesota Press [translation of *Culturas hibridas* 1989].

Castells, Manuel (1977) *The Urban Question: A Marxist Approach,* Cambridge, MA: MIT Press [translation of *La question urbaine* 1972].

Castells, Manuel (1996) *The Rise of the Network Society. The Information Age: Economy, Society and Culture.* Oxford: Blackwell.

Çelik, Zeynep (1992) *Displaying the Orient: Architecture of Islam at Nineteenth-Century World's Fairs.* Berkeley: University of California Press.

—— (1997a) 'Gendered spaces in colonial Algiers' [1992], in Diane Agrest, Patricia Conway and Leslie Kanes Weisman (eds) *The Sex of Architecture.* New York: Abrams, 127–40.

—— (1997b) *Urban Forms and Colonial Confrontations: Algiers under French Rule*. Berkeley: University of California Press.

Chakrabarty, Dipesh (2007) *Provincializing Europe: Postcolonial Thought and Historical Difference*. Princeton: Princeton University Press.

Chase, John, Margaret Crawford and John Kaliski, (eds) (1999) *Everyday Urbanism*. New York: Monacelli.

Chatterjee, Partha (1993) *The Nation and its Fragments: Colonial and Postcolonial Histories*. Princeton: Princeton University Press.

Chattopadhyay, Swati (2005) *Representing Calcutta: Modernity, Nationalism, and the Colonial Uncanny*. New York: Routledge.

Ching, Francis D., Mark Jarzombek and Vikramaditya Prakash (2006) *A Global History of Architecture*. Hoboken, NJ: Wiley.

Chung, Chuiha Judy, Jeffrey Inaba, Rem Koolhaas, Sze Tsung Leong (eds) (2001) *Great Leap Forward. Harvard Design School Project on the City*. Cologne: Taschen.

Cody, Jeffrey W. (2003) *Exporting American Architecture, 1870–2000*. London: Routledge.

Coleman, Debra, Elizabeth Danze and Carol Henderson (eds) (1996) *Architecture and Feminism*. New York: Princeton Architectural Press.

Collins, Patricia Hill (1990) *Black Feminist Thought*. London: Unwin Hyman.

Colomina, Beatriz (ed.) (1992) *Sexuality and Space*. New York: Princeton Architectural Press.

—— (1994) *Privacy and Publicity. Modern Architecture as Mass Media*. Cambridge, MA: MIT Press.

Combahee River Collective (1982) 'A Black Feminist Statement', in G.T. Hull et al., *All the Women Are White, All the Blacks Are Men, But Some of Us Are Brave: Black Woman's Studies*. New York: The Feminist Press.

Crawford, Margaret (1999) 'Blurring the boundaries: Public space and private life', in John Chase et al. (eds) *Everyday Urbanism*. New York: Monacelli, 22–35.

Dal Co, Francesco (1978) 'Criticism and Design', *Oppositions* 13: 1–16.

—— (1979) 'From parks to region: Progressive ideology and the reform of the American city', in Giorgio Ciucci et al. (eds) *The American City from Civil War to the New Deal*. Cambridge, MA: MIT Press.

Davis, Angela (1982) *Women, Race and Class*. London: The Women's Press.

Davis, Mike (2000) *Magical Urbanism. The Latinos Reinvent the Big US City*. New York: Verso.

de Certeau, Michel (1984) *The Practice of Everyday Life*. Berkeley, CA: University of California Press. [translation of *Arts de faire* 1980].

de Sola-Morales, Ignasi (1997) 'Absent bodies', in Cynthia C. Davidson (ed.) *Anybody*. Cambridge, MA: MIT Press, 18–24.

Dehaene, Michiel and Lieven De Cauter (eds) (2008) *Heterotopia and the City: Public Space in a Post Civil Society*. London: Routledge.

Deleuze, Gilles (2005) *Cinema 1: The Movement Image*. New York: Continuum [translation of *Cinéma 1, l'image-mouvement* 1983].

Deleuze, Gilles and Felix Guattari (1983) *Anti-Oedipus: Capitalism and Schizophrenia*, Minneapolis: University of Minnesota Press [translation of *L'Anti-Œdipe. Capitalisme et Schizophrénie* 1972].

Deleuze, Gilles and Felix Guattari (1987) *A Thousand Plateaus. Capitalism and Schizophrenia II*. Minneapolis: University of Minnesota Press [translation of *Mille Plateaux. Capitalisme et Schizophrénie II* 1980].

Derrida, Jacques (1976) *Of Grammatology*. Baltimore: Johns Hopkins University Press [translation of *De la grammatologie* 1967].

—— (1981) *Dissemination*. London: Athlone Press [translation of *La dissémination* 1972].

Diller, Elizabeth (1996) 'Bad press', in Francesca Hughes (ed.) *The Architect: Reconstructing Her Practice*. Cambridge, MA: MIT Press, 74–94.

Dovey, Kim (1999) *Framing Places. Mediating Power in Built Form*. London: Routledge.

Drexler, Arthur, Colin Rowe and Kenneth Frampton (1972) *Five Architects: Eisenman, Graves, Gwathmey, Hejduk, Meier*. New York: Wittenborn.

Duncan, Nancy (ed.) (1996) *BodySpace. Destabilizing Geographies of Gender and Sexuality*. London: Routledge.

Eco, Umberto (1972) *La structure absente. Introduction à la recherche sémiotique*. Paris: Mercure de France.

Eisenman, Peter (1976) 'Post-functionalism. Editorial', *Oppositions* 6: i–iii.

—— (1984) 'The end of the classical: The end of the beginning, the end of the end', *Perspecta* 21: 154–173.

—— (1998) *Giuseppe Terragni: Transformations, Decompositions, Critiques*. New York: Monacelli.

—— (2000) 'Autonomy and the will to the critical', *Assemblage* 41: 90–92.

Fanon, Frantz (2004) *The Wretched of the Earth*. New York: Grove Press [translation of *Les damnés de la terre* 1961].

Felshin, Nina (1995) *But Is It Art? The Spirit of Art as Activism*. Seattle: Bay Press.

Fezer, Jesko (2003) 'Gallaratese Occupata!', *An Architektur 10*: 37–8.

Fields, Darell W. (2000) 'Historical errors and black tropes', in Iain Borden and Jane Rendell (eds) *Intersections. Architectural Histories and Critical Theories.* London: Routledge. 39–54.

Fishman, Robert (1977) *Urban Utopias of the Twentieth Century: Ebenezer Howard, Frank Lloyd Wright and Le Corbusier.* New York: Basic Books.

Flax, Jane (1991) *Thinking Fragments: Psychoanalysis, Feminism and Postmodernism in the Contemporary West.* Berkeley: University of California Press.

Foucault, Michel (1973) *The Birth of the Clinic: An Archaeology of Medical Perception.* New York: Pantheon [translation of *Naissance de la clinique: une archéologie du regard médical* 1963].

—— (1977) *Discipline and Punish: The Birth of the Prison.* New York: Pantheon [translation of *Surveiller et punir: Naissance de la prison* (1975)].

—— (2008) 'Of other spaces' [1967], in Michiel Dehaene and Lieven De Cauter (eds) (2008) *Heterotopia and the City: Public Space in a Post Civil Society.* London: Routledge. 13–30.

Frampton, Kenneth (1983) 'Towards a critical regionalism: six points for an architecture of resistance', in Hal Foster (ed.), *The Anti-Aesthetic. Essays on Postmodern Culture*, Port Townsend: Bay Press, 17–34.

—— (2007 [1980]) *Modern Architecture. A Critical History.* London: Thames & Hudson.

Franck, Karen A. (1989) 'A feminist approach', in Ellen Perry Berkeley (ed), *Architecture: A Place for Women.* Washington: Smithsonian Institution Press. 201–16.

Frank D. Ching, Mark M. Jarzombeck, Vikramaditya Prakash (2007) *A Global History of Architecture.* Hoboken, NJ: Wiley.

Friedman, Alice (1989) *House and Household in Elizabethan England.* Chicago: University of Chicago Press.

—— (1997) *Women and the Making of the Modern House.* New York: Abrams.

Friedman, Susan Stanford (1998) *Mappings: Feminism and the Cultural Geographies of Encounter.* Princeton: Princeton University Press.

Fuss, Diane (1991) *Inside/out: Lesbian Theories, Gay Theories.* London: Routledge.

—— (1995) *Identification Papers.* London: Routledge.

—— (2004) *The Sense of an Interior: Four Rooms and the Writers that Shaped Them.* London: Routledge.

Gaonkar, Dilip Parameshwar (1999) *Alternative Modernities.* Durham: Duke University Press.

Gates, Henry Louis (2006) *Thirteen Ways of Looking at a Black Man.* New York: Vintage.

Geuss, Raymond (1981) *The Idea of Critical Theory: Habermas and the Frankfurt School.* Cambridge: Cambridge University Press.

Ghirardo, Diane Y. (1996) *Architecture after Modernism*, London: Thames and Hudson.

—— (2002) 'Manfredo Tafuri and architecture theory in the U.S., 1970–2000', *Perspecta 33: The Yale Architectural Journal*: 38–47.

Giedion, Sigfried (1967 [1941]) *Space, Tme and Architecture; The Growth of a New Tradition.* Cambridge, MA: Harvard University Press.

Graham, Stephen and Simon Marvin (2001) *Splintering Urbanism: Networked Infrastructure, Technological Mobilities and the Urban Condition.* London: Routledge.

Grillner, Katja et al. (eds) (2005) *01.AKAD.* Stockholm: AKAD and Axl Books.

Grosz, Elizabeth (1994) *Volatile Bodies: Toward a Corporeal Feminism.* Indianapolis: Indiana University Press.

—— (2001) *Architecture from the Outside: Essays on Virtual and Real Space.* Cambridge, MA: MIT Press.

Guha, Ranajit (ed) (1997) *A Subaltern Studies Reader, 1986–1995.* Minneapolis: University of Minnesota Press.

Guha, Ranajit and Gayatri Chakravorty Spivak (eds) (1988) *Selected Subaltern Studies.* New York: Oxford University Press.

Habermas, Jürgen (1983) 'Modernity – an incomplete project' [1980], in Hal Foster (ed.) *The Anti-Aesthetic. Essays on Postmodern Culture.* Port Townsend: Bay Press, 3–15.

Hall, Stuart and Paul du Gay (eds) (1996) *Questions of Cultural Identity.* London: Sage.

Hamadeh, Shirine (1992) 'Creating the traditional city: a french project', in Nezar AlSayyad (ed.) *Forms of Dominance: On the Architecture and Urbanism of the Colonial Enterprise.* London: Avebury.

Haraway, Donna (1988) 'Situated knowledges: the science question in feminism and the privilege of partial knowledge', *Feminist Studies*, 14(3): 575–603.

Harris, Dianne (2005) 'Social history: identity, performance, politics, and architectural histories', *Journal of the Society of Architectural Historians*, 64(4): 421–23.

Harvey, David (1989) *The Condition of Postmodernity.* Oxford: Blackwell.

Harvey, David (2001) *Spaces of Capital: Towards a Critical Geography.* Edinburgh: Edinburgh University Press.

Hauptmann, Deborah (ed.) (2006) *The Body in Architecture*. Rotterdam: 010.

Hayden, Dolores (1986) *Redesigning the American Dream*. New York: Norton.

Hays, K. Michael (1984) 'Critical architecture: Between culture and form', *Perspecta 21: The Yale Architectural Journal*: 15–29.

—— (ed.) (1998) *Architecture Theory since 1968*. Cambridge, MA: MIT Press.

—— (ed.) (1999) *Oppositions Reader*. New York: Princeton Architectural Press.

—— (ed.) (2000) *Architecture Theory since 1968*. Cambridge, MA: MIT Press.

Heidegger, Martin (1994 [1952]) 'Bauen Wohnen Denken', in *Mensch und Raum. Das Darmstädter Gespräch 1951* (reprint), Braunschweig: Viehweg, 88–102.

Hemmings, Clare (2002) *Bisexual Spaces: A Geography of Sexuality and Gender*. London: Routledge.

Hernandez, Felipe (ed.) (2003) Transculturation in Latin America and architecture, special issue of *Journal of Romance Studies*, 2(3).

Hernandez, Felipe, Mark Millington and Iain Borden (eds) (2006) *Architecture and Transculturation in Latin America*. Amsterdam: Rodopi.

Heynen, Hilde (1999) *Architecture and Modernity: A Critique*. Cambridge. MA: MIT Press.

—— (ed.) (2002) 'Architecture, gender, domesticity', Special Issue of *The Journal of Architecture*, 7(3).

Heynen, Hilde and Gülsüm Baydar (eds) (2005) *Negotiating Domesticity: Spatial Productions of Gender in Modern Architecture*. London: Routledge.

Heynen, Hilde and André Loeckx (1998) 'Scenes of ambivalence. Concluding remarks on architectural patterns of displacement', *Journal of Architectural Education*, 52(2): 100–108

Hillier, Bill and Julienne Hanson (1984) *The Social Logic of Space*. Cambridge: Cambridge University Press.

Holston, James (ed.) (1999) *Cities and Citizenship*. Durham: Duke University Press.

hooks, bell (1989a) *Talking Back: Thinking Feminism, Thinking Black*. Boston: South End Press.

—— (1989b) *Yearnings: Race, Gender, and Cultural Politics*. London: Turnaround Press.

Horkheimer, Max (1937) 'Traditionelle und kritische theorie', *Zeitschrift für Sozialforschung*, 6(2): 245–297.

Hosagrahar, Jyoti (2002) 'South Asia: Looking back moving ahead, history and modernization', *Journal of the Society of Architectural Historians*, 61(3): 355–369.

—— (2005) *Indigenous Modernities: Negotiating Architecture and Urbanism*. London: Routledge.

Hughes, Francesca (ed.) (1996) *The Architect: Reconstructing Her Practice*. Cambridge, MA: MIT Press.

Hughes, Rolf (2006) 'The poetics of practice-based research', in Hilde Heynen (ed.) Unthinkable Doctorates? Special Issue of *The Journal of Architecture*, 11(3): 283–301.

Ingram, Gordon Brent et al. (1997) *Queers in Space*. Seattle: Bay Press.

Irigaray, Luce (1985a) *Speculum of the Other Woman*. New York: Cornell University Press [translation of *Speculum de l'autre femme* 1974].

—— (1985b) *This Sex Which Is Not One*. New York: Cornell University Press [translation of *Ce sexe qui n'en est pas un* 1977].

Jacobs, Jane (1961) *The Death and Life of Great American Cities*. New York: Random.

Jacobs, Jane M. (1996) *Edge of Empire: Postcolonialism and the City*. London: Routledge.

Jameson, Frederic (1989) *Postmodernism or the Cultural Logic of Late Capitalism*. Durham: Duke University Press.

Jencks, Charles (1977) *The Language of Post-Modern Architecture*. New York: Rizzoli.

Jencks, Charles and George Baird (eds) (1969) *Meaning in Architecture*. London: Barrie & Rockliff the Cresset P.

Jones, Amelia and Andrew Stephenson (eds) (1999) *Performing the Body/Performing the Text*. London: Routledge.

Judin, Hilton and Ivan Vladislavic (eds) (1999) *Blank: Architecture, Apartheid and After*. Rotterdam: NAi Publishers.

Kapusta, Beth (1994) 'The Academy speaks (to the Academy)', *The Canadian Architect* 39(8): 10.

Kennedy, Magrit (1981) 'Seven hypotheses on male and female principles', 'Making room: Women and architecture', *Heresies: A Feminist Publication on Art and Politics* 3(3), issue 11: 12–13.

Khalili, Nader (1996) *Ceramic Houses and Earth Architecture: How to Build Your Own*. Hesperia, CA: Cal-Earth Press.

Khan, Hasan-Uddin and Sherban Cantacuzino (1987) *Charles Correa*. New York: Concept Media.

King, Anthony. D. (1976) *Colonial Urban Development: Culture, Social Power and Environment*. London: Routledge & Kegan Paul.

—— (1984) *The Bungalow: The Production of a Global Culture*. London: Routledge.

—— (1990) *Global Cities. Post-Imperialism and the Internationalization of London*. London: Routledge.

—— (2004) *Spaces of Global Cultures: Architecture, Urbanism, Identity.* London: Routledge.

Klotz, Heinrich (1984) *Revision der Moderne: Post-moderne Architektur, 1960–1980.* Munich: Prestel.

Koolhaas, Rem (1994) 'Generic city', in Rem Koolhaas and Bruce Mau (1995) *S, M, L, XL*, New York: Monacelli, 1246–1264.

—— (2008) *Lagos: How it Works.* Amsterdam: Lars Muller.

Koolhaas, Rem and Bruce Mau (1995) *S, M, L, XL*, New York: Monacelli.

Koolhaas, Rem and Sarah Whiting (1999) 'Spot check. A conversation between Rem Koolhaas and Sarah Whiting', *Assemblage* 40: 36–55.

Kusno, Abidin (2000) *Behind the Postcolonial: Architecture, Urban Structure, and Political Cultures in Indonesia.* London: Routledge.

Lacan, Jacques (1966) 'Le stade du miroir comme formateur de la fonction du Je', in Jacques Lacan. *Écrits 1.* Paris: Seuil, 89–97.

Lacy, Suzanne (ed.) (1995) *Mapping the Terrain: New Genre Public Art.* Seattle: Bay Press.

Landesberg, Amy and Lisa Quatrale (1996) 'See angel touch', in Debra Coleman, Elizabeth Danze and Carol Henderson (eds) *Architecture and Feminism.* New York: Princeton Architectural Press, 60–71.

Latour, Bruno (2004) 'Why has criticality run out of steam? From matters of fact to matters of concern', *Critical Inquiry*, 30(2): 225–248.

—— (2007) *Reassembling the Social: An Introduction to Actor-Network-Theory.* Oxford: Oxford University Press.

Latour, Bruno and Peter Wiebel (eds) (2005) *Making Things Public. Atmospheres of Democracy.* Cambridge, MA: MIT Press.

Lavin, Sylvia (2003) 'In a contemporary mood', *Hunch* 6/7: 294–296.

Lawrence, Denise L. and Setha M. Low. (1990) The built environment and spatial form. *Annual Review of Anthropology* 19: 453–505.

Leach, Neil (ed.) (1997) *Rethinking Architecture.* London: Routledge.

Lefebvre, Henri (1991) *The Production of Space.* Oxford: Blackwell [translation of *La production de l'espace* 1974].

Lillyman, William, Marilyn Moriarty and David Neuman (eds) (1994) *Critical Architecture and Contemporary Culture.* Oxford: Oxford University Press.

Lipstadt, Hélène (2003) 'Can "art professions" be Bourdieuean fields of cultural production? The case of the architecture competition', *Cultural Studies*, 17(3–4): 390–419.

Little, J., L. Peake and P. Richardson (eds) (1988) *Women in Cities: Gender and the Urban Environment.* London: Macmillan.

Lobell, Mimi (1989) 'The buried treasure', in Ellen Perry Berkeley (ed.) *Architecture: A Place for Women.* Washington: Smithsonian Institution Press, 139–57.

Lokko, Lesley Naa Norle (ed.) (2000) *White Papers, Black Marks: Architecture, Race, Culture.* London: Athlone.

Lorde, Audre (1996) 'The master's tools will never dismantle the master's house' [1979], in *The Audre Lorde Compendium.* London: Pandora.

Low, Setha M. and Denise Lawrence-Zúñiga (eds.) (2003) *Anthropology of Space and Place: Locating Culture.* Malden, MA: Blackwell.

Lyotard, Jean-François (1984) *The Postmodern Condition.* Minneapolis: University of Minnesota Press [translation of *La Condition Postmoderne* 1979].

—— (1989) *Differend. Phrases in Dispute.* Minneapolis: University of Minnesota Press [translation of *Le Differend* 1983].

—— (1992) 'Note on the meaning of "post-"', in Jean-François Lyotard, *The Postmodern Explained: Correspondence 1982–1985.* Minneapolis: University of Minnesota Press, 75–80 [translation of 'Note sur les sens de "post-"' 1986].

Mallgrave, Harry Francis (ed.) (2005) *Architectural Theory: Volume I: An Anthology from Vitruvius to 1870.* London: Wiley-Blackwell.

Mallgrave, Harry Francis and Christina Contandrioupolos (eds) (2008) *Architectural Theory: Volume II: An Anthology from 1871 to 2005.* London: Wiley-Blackwell.

Markus, Thomas A. (1993) *Buildings and Power.* London: Routledge.

Martin, Reinhold (2005) 'Critical of what? Toward a utopian realism', *Harvard Design Magazine* 22: 104–109.

Martin, Reinhold and Kadambari Baxi (2007) *Multi-National City: Architectural Itineraries.* New York: Actar.

Marx, Karl (1976) *The Capital.* New York: Vintage [translation of *Das Kapital. Kritik der politischen Ökonomie*].

Massey, Doreen (1994) *Space, Place and Gender.* Cambridge: Polity Press.

Matrix (1984) *Making Space: Women and the Man Made Environment.* London: Pluto Press.

McCorquodale, Duncan, Katerina Rüedi and Sarah Wigglesworth (eds) (1996) *Desiring Practices.* London: Black Dog.

McDowell, Linda (1993) 'Space, place and gender relations, part 1 + part 2', *Progress in Human Geography*, 17(2): 157–179; 17(3): 305–318.

McLeod, Mary (1989) 'Architecture and politics in the Reagan era: From postmodernism to deconstructivism', *Assemblage* 8: 22–59.

—— (1996) 'Everyday and "other" spaces', in Debra Coleman et al. (eds) *Architecture and Feminism*. New York: Princeton Architectural Press, 1–37.

—— (1997) 'Henri Lefebvre's critique of everyday life: An introduction', in Steven Harris and Deborah Berke (eds) *Architecture of the Everyday*. New York: Princeton Architectural Press, 9–29.

Metcalf, Thomas R. (1989) *An Imperial Vision: Indian Architecture and Britain's Raj*. Berkeley: University of California Press.

Mitchell, Timothy (1988) *Colonising Egypt*. Berkeley: University of California Press.

Mitscherlich, Alexander (1965) *Die Unwirtlichkeit unserer Städte. Anstiftung zum Unfrieden*. Frankfurt/Main: Suhrkamp.

Moneo, Rafael (1976) 'Aldo Rossi: The idea of architecture and the Modena Cemetery', *Oppositions* 5: 1–30.

Morton, Patricia A. (2000) *Hybrid Modernities*. Cambridge, MA: MIT Press.

muf (1996) *Architectural Design*, 66(7–8): 80–3.

muf (2001) *This Is What We Do: A muf Manual*. London: Ellipsis.

Nandy, Ashis (1988 [1983]) *The Intimate Enemy: Loss and Recovery of Self Under Colonialism*. New York: Oxford University Press.

Nast, Heidi and Steve Pile (eds) (1998) *Places Through the Body*. London: Routledge.

Nesbitt, Kate (ed.) (1996) *Theorizing a New Agenda for Architecture: An Anthology of Architectural Theory 1965–1995*. New York: Princeton Architectural Press.

Norberg-Schulz, Christian (1975) *Meaning in Western Architecture*. New York: Praeger.

—— (1980) *Genius Loci: Towards a Phenomenology of Architecture*. New York: Rizzoli.

Ockman, Joan (ed.) (1985) *Architecture, Criticism, Ideology*. Princeton. NJ: Princeton Architectural Press.

—— (ed.) (1993) *Architecture Culture 1943–1968*. New York: Rizzoli.

—— (ed.) (2000) *The Pragmatist Imagination: Thinking about 'Things in the Making'*. New York: Princeton Architectural Press.

Parker, Rozsika and Griselda Pollock (eds) (1987) *Framing Feminism: Art and the Women's Movement 1970–85*. London: Pandora.

Pedersen, Annette and Christopher Crouch (2002), 'Introducing universal design to a colonial context', in Jon Christophersen (ed.) *Universal Design. 17 Ways of Thinking and Teaching*. Drammen: Husbanken, 289–314.

Penner, Barbara (2005) 'Researching female public toilets: Gendered spaces, disciplinary limits', *Journal of International Women's Studies* 6(2): 81–98.

Penner, Barbara and Charles Rice (eds) (2004) 'Constructing the interior', Special issue of *The Journal of Architecture* 9(3): 267–273

Petrescu, Doina (2005) 'Losing control, keeping desire', in Peter Blundell Jones, Doina Petrescu and Jeremy Till (eds) *Architecture and Participation*. London: Spon, 43–64.

—— (ed.) (2007) *Altering Practices: Feminist Politics and Poetics of Space*. London: Routledge.

Pevsner, Nikolaus (1957) *An Outline of European Architecture* [1942]. Harmondsworth: Penguin.

Phelan, Peggy (1993) *Unmarked: Politics of Performance*. London: Routledge.

Picon, Antoine and Alessandra Ponte (2003) *Architecture and the Sciences: Exchanging Metaphors*. New York: Princeton Architectural Press.

Pile, Steve (1996) *The Body and the City: Psychoanalysis, Subjectivity and Space*. London: Routledge.

Pinto, Eveline (2002) *Penser l'art et la culture avec les sciences sociales: en l'honneur de Pierre Bourdieu*. Paris: Sorbonne.

Pollock, Della (1997) 'Performing writing', in Peggy Phelan and Jill Lane (eds) *The Ends of Performance*. New York: New York University Press, 73–103.

Pollock, Griselda (1981) *Old Mistresses: Women, Art and Ideology*. New York: Pantheon.

—— (1988) *Vision and Difference: Femininity, Feminism and the Histories of Art*. London: Routledge.

—— (1992) 'Trouble in the archives: Introduction', *Differences: A Journal of Feminist Cultural Studies*, 4(3): iii–iv.

Popper, Karl R. (1945) *The Open Society and Its Enemies*. London: Routledge.

Porteous, J. Douglas and Sandra E. Smith (eds) (2001) *Domicide: The Global Destruction of Home*. Montreal: McGill-Queen's University Press.

Prakash, Gyan (1999) *Another Reason: Science and the Imagination of Modern India*. Princeton: Princeton University Press.

Prakash, Gyan and Kevin M. Kruse (eds) (2008) *The Spaces of The Modern City: Imaginaries, Politics, and Everyday Life*. Princeton: Princeton University Press.

Prakash, Vikramaditya (2002) *Chandigarh's Le Corbusier: The Struggle for Modernity in Postcolonial India*. Seattle: University of Washington Press.

Preiser, Wolfgang F.E. and Elaine Ostroff (eds) (2001) *Universal Design Handbook*. New York: McGraw-Hill.

Probyn, Elspeth (1990) 'Travels in the postmodern: Making sense of the local', in Linda Nicholson (ed.) *Feminism/Postmodernism*. London: Routledge. 176–189.

Rawes, Peg (2007a) *Irigarary for Architects*. London: Routledge.

—— (2007b) 'Plenums: Re-thinking matter, geometry and subjectivity', in Katie Lloyd Thomas (ed.) *Material Matters: Architecture and Material Practice*. London: Routledge, 55–66.

Raymond, Janice (1986) *A Passion for Friends*. Boston: Beacon.

Reed, Christopher (1996) 'Imminent domain: Queer space in the built environment', *Art Journal* 55: 64–70.

Rendell, Jane (2003) 'Between two: Theory and practice', in Jonathan Hill (ed.), Opposites Attract: Research by Design, Special issue of *The Journal of Architecture* 8(2): 221–238.

—— (2004) 'Architectural research and disciplinarity', *ARQ* 8(4): 141–147.

—— (2005) 'Architecture-writing', *The Journal of Architecture*, 10(3): 255–264

—— (2006) *Art and Architecture: A Place Between*. London: Tauris.

—— (2010) *Site-Writing: The Architecture of Art Criticism*. London: Tauris.

Rendell, Jane, Barbara Penner and Iain Borden (eds) (1999) *Gender, Space Architecture: An Interdisciplinary Introduction*. London: Routledge.

Rendell, Jane, Jonathan Hill, Murray Fraser and Mark Dorrian (eds) (2007) *Critical Architecture*. London: Routledge.

Rice, Charles (2007) *The Emergence of the Interior: Architecture, Modernity, Domesticity*. London: Routledge.

Rich, Adrienne (1983) 'Compulsory heterosexuality and lesbian existence', in E. Abel and E.K. Abel (eds) *The Signs Reader: Women, Gender and Scholarship*. Chicago: University of Chicago Press.

Roberts, Marion (1991) *Living in Man-Made World: Gender Assumptions in Modern Housing Design*. London: Routledge.

Rogoff, Irit (2000) *Terra Infirma*. London: Routledge.

Rose, Gillian (1993) *Feminism and Geography: The Limits of Geographical Knowledge*. Cambridge: Polity Press.

Rosner, Victoria (2005) *Modernism and the Architecture of Private Life*. Columbia: Columbia University Press.

Rossi, Aldo (1984) *The Architecture of the City*. Cambridge, MA: MIT Press [translation of *L'architettura della città* 1966].

Roy, Ananya and Nezar Al Sayyad (eds) (2004) *Urban Informality: Transnational Perspectives from the Middle East, Latin America and South Asia*. Oxford: Lexington.

Rudofsky, Bernhard (1964) *Architecture without Architects: An Introduction to Nonpedigreed Architecture*. New York: Museum of Modern Art.

Rudy, Kathy (2000) 'Queer theory and feminism', *Women's Studies* 29: 195–216.

Rykwert, Joseph (1972) *On Adam's Hut in Paradise. The Idea of the Primitive Hut in Architectural History*. New York: MOMA.

Said, Edward W. (1978) *Orientalism*. New York, Pantheon.

Sanders, Joel (ed.) (1996) *Stud: Architectures of Masculinity*. New York: Princeton Architectural Press.

Saunders, William S. (ed.) (2007) *The New Architectural Pragmatism*. Minneapolis: University of Minnesota Press.

Scott, Felicity (2007) *Architecture or Techno-Utopia. Politics After Modernism*. Cambridge, MA: MIT Press.

Sedgwick, Eve Kosofsky (1991) *The Epistemology of the Closet*. New York: Harvester Wheatsheaf.

Sellers, Susan (ed.) (1994) *The Hélène Cixous Reader*. London: Routledge.

Silverman, Kaja (1996) *The Threshold of the Visible World*. London: Routledge.

Soja, Edward (1989) *Postmodern Geographies: the Reassertion of Space in Social Theory*. London: Verso.

Somaya, Brinda et al. (eds) (2000) *An Emancipated Place. Proceedings of the Conference and Exhibition: 'Women in Architecture 2000 Plus'*. Mumbai.

Somol, Robert and Sarah, Whiting (2002) 'Notes around the Doppler effect and other moods of modernism', *Perspecta* 33: 72–77.

Sorkin, Michael (ed.) (1996) *Variations on a Theme Park: The New American City and the End of Public Space*. New York: Hill and Wang.

Spargo, Tamsin (1999) *Foucault and Queer Theory*. Cambridge: Icon.

Speaks, Michael (ed.) (1996) *The Critical Landscape*. Rotterdam: 010.

Speaks, Michael (2002) 'Design intelligence. Part 1: Introduction', *A+U Architecture and Urbanism 387*: 10–18.

Tafuri, Manfredo (1974) 'L'architecture dans le boudoir: The language of criticism and the criticism of language', *Oppositions* 3: 37–62.

—— (1976) *Architecture and Utopia. Design and Capitalist Development.* Cambridge, MA: MIT Press [translated from *Progetto e Utopia* 1973].

—— (1980) *Theories and History of Architecture.* London: Granada [translation of *Teorie e storia dell'architettura* 1968].

—— (1987) *The Sphere and the Labyrinth: Avant-gardes and Architecture from Piranesi to the 1970s.* Cambridge, MA: MIT Press [translation of *Sfera e il labirinto* 1980].

Taussig, Michael (1992) *Mimesis and Alterity. A Particular History of the Senses.* London: Routledge.

Taylor, Brian (1995) *Geoffrey Bawa.* London: Thames & Hudson.

Taylor, Mark and Julieanna Preston (eds) (2006) *Intimus: Interior Design Theory Reader.* Chichester: Wiley–Academy.

Thomas, Katie Lloyd (ed.) (2007) *Material Matters: Architecture and Material Practice.* London: Routledge.

Thomas, Katie Lloyd, Teresa Hoskyns and Helen Stratford (2002) 'Taking place', *Scroope: Cambridge Architecture Journal* 14: 44–48.

Thrift, Nigel and John-David Dewsbury (2000) 'Dead geographies – and how to make them live', *Environment and Planning D: Society and Space*, 18, 411–432.

Torre, Susana (ed.) (1977) *Women in American Architecture: A Historic and Contemporary Perspective.* New York: Whitney Library of Design.

Turner, John F.C. (1977) *Housing by People.* New York: Pantheon.

Tzonis, Alexander (1972) *Towards a Non-Oppressive Environment.* Boston, MA: i Press.

Tzonis, Alexander and Liane, Lefaivre (1985) 'The grid and the pathway; the work of D. and S. Antonakakis' [1981], in *Atelier 66. The Architecture of Dimitris and Suzana Antonakakis.* New York: Rizzoli, 14–25.

—— (2003) *Critical Regionalism. Architecture and Identity in a Globalized World.* Munich: Prestel.

Urbach, Henry (1999) 'Closets, clothes, disClosure' [1996], in Jane Rendell, Barbara Penner and Iain Borden (eds) *Gender, Space, Architecture: An Interdisciplinary Introduction.* London: Routledge, 342–352.

Van Schaik, Martin and Otakar Macel (eds) (2005) *Exit Utopia: Architectural Provocations 1956–1976.* Munich: Prestel.

Van Toorn, Roemer (1997) 'Fresh conservatism and beyond', *Archis* 12(11): 15–22.

Varnelis, Kays (ed.) (2008) *The Infrastructural City. Networked Ecologies in Los Angeles.* Cambridge, MA: MIT Press.

Venn, Couze (2000) *Occidentalism. Modernity and Subjectivity.* London: Sage.

Verschaffel, Bart (2001) *Architecture is (as) a Gesture.* Luzerne: Quart.

Von Borries, Friedrich (2004) *Who's Afraid of Nike-Town? Nike-Urbanism, Branding and the City of Tomorrow.* Rotterdam: Episode.

Walker, Lynne (1984) *British Women in Architecture 1671–1951.* London: Sorello.

—— (1989) 'Women and architecture', in Judy Attfield and Pat Kirkham (eds), *A View from the Interior: Feminism, Women and Design.* London: The Women's Press.

Weisman, Leslie Kanes (1992) *Discrimination by Design.* Chicago: University of Illinois Press.

Weizman, Eyal (2007) *Hollow Land: Israel's Architecture of Occupation.* London: Verso.

Wilkins, Craig L. (2007) *The Aesthetics of Equity. Notes on Race, Space, Architecture and Music.* Minneapolis: University of Minnesota Press.

Wilson, Mabel O. (1996) 'Black bodies/white cities: Le Corbusier in Harlem', *ANY* 16: 35–39.

Wright, Gwendolyn (1977) 'On the fringe of the profession: Women in American architecture', in Spiro Kostof (ed.) *The Architect: Chapters in the History of the Profession.* Oxford: Oxford University Press, 280–309.

—— (1991) *The Politics of Design in French Colonial Urbanism.* Chicago: University of Chicago Press.

—— (2002) 'Building global modernisms', *Grey Room* (7): 124–134.

—— (2005) 'Cultural history: Europeans, Americans, and the meaning of space', *Journal of the Society of Architectural Historians* 64(4): 436–440.

Yeoh, Brenda (2000) *Contesting Space: Power Rrelations and the Urban Environment in Colonial Singapore.* Oxford: Oxford University Press.

Zaera-Polo, Alejandro (2004) 'A scientific auto-biography, 1982–2004: Madrid, Harvard, OMA, the AA, Yokohama, the Globe', *Harvard Design Magazine* 21: 5–21.

Zukin, Sharon (2009) *Naked City: The Death and Life of Authentic Urban Places.* New York: Oxford University Press.

5

Citizenship

Ines Weizman

MOBILIZING DISSENT: THE POSSIBLE ARCHITECTURE OF THE GOVERNED

A gigantic ship loaded with Russian monasteries, church spires, and Kremlin-like fortresses is 'beached' at the edge of a generic block-city. The oarsmen who propel the ship are unaware that their vessel is no longer mobile. The ship of fools was a common trope in the Soviet art of the Glasnost years. It also acquired several architectural articulations. In 1989, Iskander Galimov and his collaborator Michael Fadeyev submitted a red-toned gouache painting on this theme together with a set of detailed architectural plans, sections and structural calculations as their entry to an ideas competition for a Russian Centre in Bologna (Figure 5.1). The proposal won first prize. Yet, while the competition jurors described it as a 'venturous architectural idea' – presumably enjoying the unusual format of the submission, the intricacy of the painting, its surrealist humour, and the familiar icons of Russian architecture – they missed the critical dimensions of

Figure 5.1 (Below) Iskander Galimov in collaboration with Michail Fadeyev, Russian Centre in Bologna, Italy, 1989.

the proposal. Galimov and Fadeyev's proposal was not an urban intervention in an Italian city, but rather a bitter comment on the end of the Soviet Union. This architectural proposal was also a bitter farewell note. Two years later, Galimov successfully found asylum in Austria. Conceived at the end of a decade of growing political crisis in the Soviet Union, the architectural language with which this work is articulated is typically allegorical. It is a form of expression adopted by, what I will refer to in this chapter as, a generation of dissident architects. Since the mid-1980s, when control over artistic expression in the Eastern Bloc somewhat eased, Galimov experimented with the use of architectural allegories, assembling an eclectic archive of the icons of architectural history into imaginary structures. He understood his work as a simultaneous call to expand the limited choice of available references in Soviet architecture and to rebel against its ideological underpinnings. In this architectural proposal, he aims critical barbs both forwards and backwards in time, at the old Soviet system and its all-too-rapid adoption of the safe refuge of myopic nationalism.

As a form of political practice, dissidence is largely associated with the last decades of the Cold War and has seemingly laid dormant since its end. 'Dissidence': to mean a form of political practice that, unlike revolutionary politics, does not seek to overthrow and replace government, to take over power, or to govern, but a practice determined to radically and fundamentally contest the way in which subjects are governed. Dissidence, in this sense, can be conceived as the possible politics of the governed, and dissidence articulated through architecture and spatial practices as a possible mode of contestation. If political relations are reproduced spatially, through the very organization of the city, its infrastructure, its streets and dwellings, as well as through the social formations and behaviours it underwrites, we must ask: how can architecture act against dominant political interests? How can architecture be used as a tool of dissent? It is because of their assumed association with political power that I believe architects engaged in dissent are worthy subjects in engaging the issue of citizenship.

There are potential problems and inevitable paradoxes with dissidence as a political practice. To start with, no one, not least architects, feels easy with this designation. Most architects interviewed for this chapter claimed that their form of protest had nothing to do with the heroism and sacrifice of 'political dissidents' which for many former Soviet citizens meant imprisonment and torture. However, we find in forms of aesthetic practice, an indirect evasive, and devious relation to power that I will explore as architecture's dissidence. Furthermore, some former Cold War political dissidents expressed a sense of estrangement and alienation from the new world they have inadvertently helped bring into being. Others, worse, became active promoters of the relatively unrestrained, conservative, market-led, or religious-national ideology, that characterized it. What are the limits and potentials of this form of practice?

The aim of this chapter goes beyond the historical evaluation of the largely unwritten history of dissident architecture, but is to mobilize a reading of dissident practices from the meltdown years of the Cold War, to reflect upon the possibilities of contemporary architecture.

***

An example of what I would understand as dissident practice can be detected in a film by the then East German (GDR) filmmaker Peter Kahane, titled *The Architects* (Figure 5.2). It is an example of a particular kind of dissidence against, what in the context of Cold War era Eastern Europe has often been called, 'state-sponsored cynicism'. The film concerns a group of young architects who, feeling all their hopes for creative work in the GDR to be lost, are given a miraculous opportunity to realize a design for a new urban centre. Yet this fiction could not surpass reality. Initially enthusiastic about their new design proposals that carefully considered and challenged the GDR's predominant modernist planning doctrines (proposals that from today's perspective would be described as 'postmodern'), the architects were to endure a painful series of compromises in negotiations with the Party representatives. They rejected the 'innovations' of the architects' design, refused to understand its references to humanism, scale and history, and reduced it to the default state language of production, efficiency and statistics. When, at the end of the film, the foundation stone for a highly amended and reduced version of the original proposal was laid, the architects' collective, and the family of the main protagonist, had broken apart. The tragedy of the film, which would probably have been painful for audiences in GDR cinemas if it was ever shown, is intensified by the historical 'untimeliness' of the film. Kahane had struggled since 1985 with the state censorship and various media bureaucracies in East Berlin, only to be granted the permission, budget and filming rights in summer 1989, a mere few months before the collapse of the GDR. As filming began while the Berlin Wall was being demolished, Peter Kahane's project was left in a whirlwind of emotions and contradictions. Regardless of the momentous events, Kahane decided to complete the film as planned, making it a curious document of the time of collapse. When the film was released to cinemas in February 1990, its subtle dissident message seemed obsolete. The film was a box-office flop. *The Architects* encapsulates a complex set of dissent practices, both filmic and architectural, that saw professionals risking their careers, as well as friends and families.

During the Cold War, architectural dissent was articulated by refusal (to participate in state projects), by subversion of the norms and language of dominant/dominating architecture, or by a retreat into the private domain of paper architecture or hidden pedagogy.

The violent suppression of the protest movement, probably first in East Germany in July 1953 and last in Prague 1968 seemingly foreclosed the possibility of internally-generated 'reform communism' in the Eastern Bloc. In those years leading up to the violent clashes with the government's military forces, a vivid, although secret, underground cultural scene had formed in many cities of the Soviet Bloc. In the 'second part' of the Cold War, after 1968, Eastern European dissidents continued to assess the effectiveness and aims of their practices, but rather than seeking to reform it, they increasingly questioned the very foundations of the communist system as such. In response, Eastern European states observed, intimidated, imprisoned, killed or forcefully expatriated dissidents and other non-conformists. With the increasing fortification of the Iron Curtain, every form of opposition or critique was subsumed under the aegis of the ideological war. Individuals, organizations and governments in the West (from both conservative and critical left strands) began to support the struggles of Eastern European dissident groups, harnessing them into a wider Cold War antagonism. If dissidents were not seeking to take over power, they were, nevertheless, often supported and manipulated by those who did. Dissident practices were vulnerable to such traps and contradictions, and were rarely simple expressions of bottom-up resistance to the imposition of top-down power. Dissidence, then, contains a structural paradox that saw the state and the dissident entangled in a mutual embrace.

In the 1980s the Cold War antagonism deepened as a result of the aggressive neoliberal politics lead by Thatcher and Reagan who also accelerated the nuclear arms race in order to drag the Soviets in to the spending spree that would eventually bankrupt them. In 1982, the Reagan administration placed the Soviet Jewry issue near the top of its bilateral agenda with the Soviet Union and pursued it relentlessly. The 'Let My People Go!' campaign cast Jewish refuseniks/dissidents as the last link in a chain of Jewish martyrdom. It encouraged millions of Soviet Jews to demand the right to migrate from the Soviet Union to Israel as a 'human right'.

Figure 5.2 (Below left and right) Screenshots, *The Architects*, dir. Peter Kahane, 1990. Complicating the reading of the film is the fact that the script is based on the real story of Michael Kny, who in the early 1980s together with his superior Wolf-Rüdiger Eisentraut, began to design an urban centre for Berlin Marzahn, the largest housing estate in the GDR built in a prefabrication system. When Kny was commissioned to design a series of public buildings in Marzahn he refused the hard-edged modernist blocks, as was typical, but interleaved them with new glass panels and a variety of other materials to articulate new building typologies containing a variety of programmes such as a post office, a library, a cinema and a department store. To get his design proposals approved, the architect recalled, in an interview with the authors, that he had to camouflage his intentions by either presenting simplified or misleading plans to his political commissariat. The architectural drawings and models that featured in the film were produced by Kny himself: some were documents of the architect's projects at the time, others were especially drawn as requisites for the film, thereby representing a unique occasion and motivation for the architect to develop some of his ambitions for the commission.

Eventually, in Reagan's second term, many Jews, including long-term refuseniks and prisoners of conscience, were allowed to leave. Many did not stay in Israel. Many of those who did make it there became conservative Zionists. Most famously, the symbol of these dissidents, Natan Sharansky, became a right-wing politician in Israel and a supporter of the settler movement.

***

This analysis focuses specifically on dissidence in the former Eastern Bloc in the 1980s. This period, that I would like to

describe as the 'meltdown' of the Cold War, presents particular difficulties for film and architecture. Creative practices such as these appear to be intertwined in a complex field of cultural references, connotations, precedents and 'ideological double speak'. This phenomenon came to typify the creative milieu of the 1980s, when Party leaders could no longer sustain cultural isolation from the West, and had begun to loosen censorship guidelines and permit more criticism of official culture. One side effect was that the meaning of almost every creative gesture came to be read as a form of political allegory, a form of critique that, if correctly interpreted or decoded, crossed the lines of the permitted. As a consequence, every such gesture aroused government suspicion, and party bureaucrats struggled to (over) read the messages embedded within art. It was the way for citizens to exercise, what Slavoj Žižek described as the 'totalitarian laughter' by which 'cynical distance, laughter, irony, are, so to speak, part of the game [...] and the ruling ideology is not meant to be taken seriously or literally' (Žižek 1994, 311). The censors' calculation that increased openness would also effect people's confirmation of established values and the status quo, eventually got snarled in its own cynicism.

The practice of the then East German architects Christian Enzmann and Bernd Ettel in 1983–1984 could be described as a literal 'propaganda in action'. In their work, imagination and fantasy did not remain in the domain of the private, but rather burst the elastic boundary between private dissidence and its public expression with dramatic effect, and grave personal consequences. The two architects, research fellows at the architecture school in Weimar, smuggled competition briefs into the GDR from West Berlin and smuggled out their competition entries with the help of a network of Austrian monks. The format of their drawings, letter-sized sheets, were chosen to deal with the

constraints of their perilous travel from East to West Berlin. The inevitable unlucky moment occurred in 1983 when one of the jury members reviewing Enzmann and Ettel's competition entry in West Berlin was, it is widely assumed, a Stasi informer and alerted the East German authorities. The competition was the first in a series for the outdoor museum and monument to the victims of the Third Reich now known as 'Topography of Terror' in Berlin. Rather than only making the reference to the dictatorship of the Third Reich, the architects drew a wall-strip punctuated by watchtowers to make an obvious connection to the infrastructures of surveillance of the GDR regime (Figures 5.3 and 5.4).

Incredibly, while this smuggling operation was underway, the young architects participated in two more competitions in East Berlin, proposing even more radical sets of architectural proposals that explicitly confronted the regime. Their submission for a competition for Bersarin Platz in Berlin, presented as black line rendered axonometrics, proposed an overstated urban allegory: a cannon-like device placed at the centre of the square. The device was apparently designed for 'shooting' citizens over the Wall to freedom. But a net, positioned within the cannon's ballistic trajectory, made sure that the citizens would never complete their escape over the Wall, and would be captured and imprisoned. The architects chose to confront the regime seemingly oblivious of obvious risks, expressing their dissent in drawing and in full awareness of the consequences. Aiming to push the system to the limit of its intolerance, perhaps in order to expose these political limits that were still very real during the gradual meltdown of the Eastern Bloc, or, eager to find an indirect route to the West, they preferred to go to prison on the way out of the country. These actions mark, in my opinion, the limits of dissidence. Dissident practices are exemplified by a rather delicate interplay between private

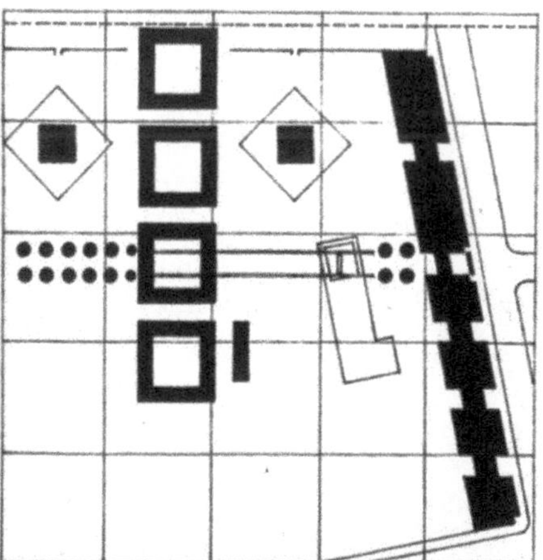

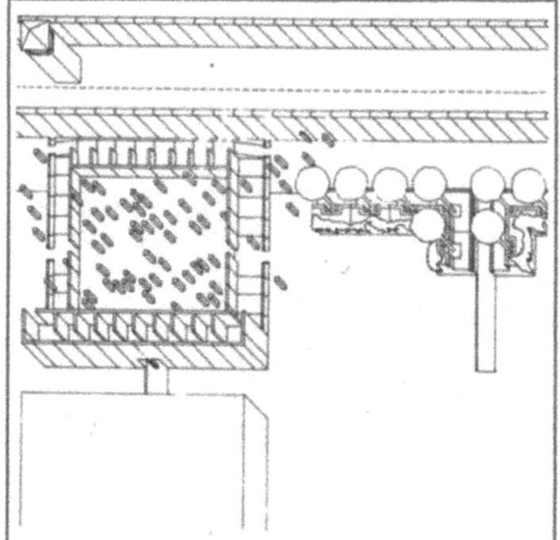

1. Limitation

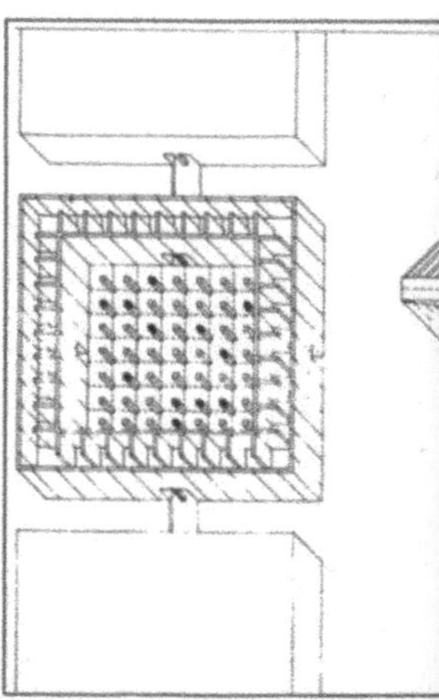

2. Selektion

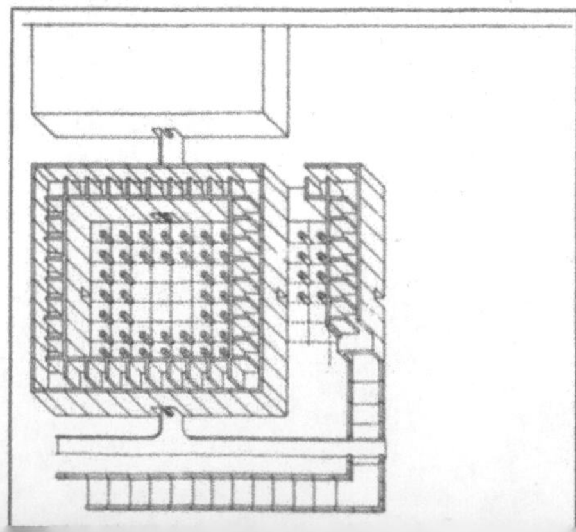

action and the public, and overt or camouflaged, annunciations. The power of Enzmann and Ettel's work has not only pushed, but in fact pierced this boundary. Here there was melodrama, breaking the rules of the game rather than playing it differently. No one in the GDR, and not many in the West, curiously, were aware of the competition drawings. By seeking to generate 'crisis', the two self-testified enemies of communism practised the outmost tactic of revolutionary socialism. The two architects were arrested and charged with offending the GDR and imprisoned for 20 months. After their release in 1986 they were left unemployed until they managed to exit to West Berlin at the end of 1988, merely a year before the fall of the Wall.

From the mid-1970s, groups of architects otherwise employed in state-run architectural collectives, or as academic staff in architecture schools, met in private houses – 'kitchens' as they later liked to say – to produce drawings that were meant to challenge the stifling, standardized language of Soviet architecture. These drawings also sought to introduce 'culture', understood largely as national and religious tradition, into architectural articulations of allegories, legends, and postmodern contextualization. Such kitchens, private and intimate, were seen as subversive micro-sites where some form of autonomy from state power was articulated, where fantasy would be unrestricted by reality, and where smuggled journals from the West could be safely gleaned. The motto of these kitchen architects was 'fantasy against utopia'.

Figure 5.3 (Below left) Christian Enzmann and Bernd Ettel, Competition, Prince-Albrecht Areal, Berlin-West, 1983/1984.

Figure 5.4 (Below) Christian Enzmann and Bernd Ettel, Competition, Bersarin Platz, Berlin-East, 1984.

Figure 5.5 (Below) Alexander Brodsky and Ilya Utkin, Columbarium Architecture (Museum of Disappearing Buildings), 1990, 42 x 31 inches, Courtesy Ronald Feldman Fine Arts, New York.

Figure 5.6 (Below right) Iskander Galimov, Michail Fadeyev, St Petersburg, 1991.

Figure 5.7 (Opposite top) Ilya Kabakov, The Man Who Flew Into Space From His Apartment, 1981–88, mixed media installation, 110 x 95 x 147 inches, Photo: D. James Dee, Collection of Musée National d'Art Moderne, Centre Georges Pompidou, Paris, Courtesy Ronald Feldman Fine Arts, New York. Another very strong visualization of this urge of the individual trying to break out from the tired claims of the state for the communist utopia (again by slingshot) is probably Ilja Kababkov's 1985 installation The Man Who Flew into Space from his Apartment. The installation consisted of a fabricated room decorated with communist paraphernalia, a makeshift slingshot and an artfully ruptured ceiling indicating the trajectory that the absent 'hero' evidently traversed as he catapulted himself into space. Being covertly installed and deinstalled in private apartments around Moscow, the work itself was shown only to an underground audience of artists, architects and intellectuals. Numerous such exhibitions and installations have taken place throughout the former Soviet Bloc with very few surviving records or accounts that testify to their existence.

In the 1980s, in the East and West alike, national histories started to regain new appreciation in architectural culture. In the West, figures such as Aldo Rossi, Michael Graves and Leon Krier critiqued modern architecture's pretensions to technological utopianism, universality and rationality and advocated, in the name of postmodernism, a return to the values of urbanity, history and

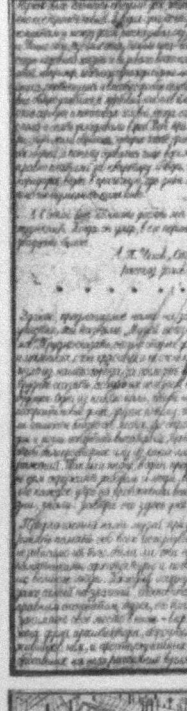

site-specificity. But in the East, this same critique, aimed at a modernist architecture thoroughly embedded in state ideology, was seen as a form of dissent. The very idea of utopia was seen as totalitarian.

Perhaps the best-known dissident practices of this kind came to be seen internationally through the annual international architectural design competitions run by the Japanese magazines *Japan Architect* and *Architecture and Urbanism* (A+U). Established in 1981, the competitions attracted many architects and students from the Soviet Union, many of whom were among the top prize winners. In 1984, a group of architects, most of whom were from the Moscow Architectural Institute (MArkhI), collected work for an exhibition in Moscow and consolidated this work under the title 'paper architects'. Michael Belov, Alexander Brodsky and Ilya Utkin, Mikhail Filippov, Nadia Bronzova and Yuri Avvakumov were leading figures in this group. Brodsky's and Utkin's elaborate

drawings and etchings depicting outlandish, often impossible, structures and cityscapes became well-known representatives of this group. Brodsky and Utkin exploited the tight format of the Japanese design competitions, specifying only one page per submission, by developing the narrative dimensions of their fantasies. In the spirit of those works, in 1984, the architects submitted a proposal to the Union of Architects of USSR Competition. 'Columbarium Habitabile', was a proposal for a museum in which plans, models and other documents associated with Moscow's historical architecture could be stored and hence 'preserve the memory of all disappearing buildings' (Figures 5.5 and 5.6). Their proposal for an impossibly large archive parodied the reality of the dilapidating and neglected historical cities of the Soviet Union. The scale of the proposal was hardly comprehensible through the drawings as the size of people and architectural models (or are they full-scaled buildings?) vary in unaccountable ways. Furthermore, every corner of the page was filled with etched marks that conveyed a sense of extended time. This included the time invested in making the drawings themselves, the time consumed in the very medium of etching itself, and the seemingly endless overworking of the image, which represents an expenditure

Figure 5.8 (Below left and right) Mikhail Filippov, The Third Rome, Design of the new Church of Christ the Saviour, Section, 1989. The drawing series for The Third Rome depicted architectural elevations, sections and plans for a new cathedral on the site of the former Cathedral of Christ the Saviour in Moscow. The original had been demolished on Stalin's orders in 1931 to be replaced by a vast administrative centre and congress hall, the Palace of the Soviets. The Palace of the Soviets project itself was never completed. The sole remains, a deep foundation pit, was converted into a gigantic open-air swimming pool. The critical aspects of this work reside in the oppositional gesture that removed the swimming pool, and so the vestiges of the Palace of the Soviets itself, to reinstate the cathedral.

that would appear entirely inefficient in the functionalist environment of socialism. The etchings also create a temporal illusion suggesting that they have been created in the past. The antiquated and operose work of the needle cutting into the plate (that also allows for the reproduction and further circulation of the work), and the romanticism and melancholia of the architects' motives create a sense of despair that in its sheer 'inefficiency', absurd lethargy and bizarre search for beauty describes a political statement (Figure 5.7).

Similarly, and yet with less absurdism and conceptual references, another member of the group, Mikhail Filippov, takes his bearings from the eighteenth century Baroque. In 1989 Fillipov, equipped with the skills of a painter, sculptor and architect, reminiscent of the tradition of the great Russian painters, prepared a drawing consisting of a series of large-sized plans called 'The Third Rome' (Figure 5.8).

More subtly, Filippov, like Brodsky and Utkin, also deployed an antiquated representational technique to critical effect. Eschewing hard-line modernism, and working with pencil and watercolour, in minute detail, Filippov used the medium to draw attention to the blind spots of the technocratic regime. He also deliberately employed gigantic impractical sheet formats as if conceived as sites of liberation from the sterile collectivity of communism, as unfettered terrains for his private imagination. This is a form of dissent by retreat.

The political stances that these architects adopted, and the particular approaches to dissidence that they practiced was, following the end of the Cold War through the early 1990s, profoundly transformed by circumstance. Mikhail Filippov and his supporters, and soon also Ilya Utkin, promoted historicist architecture. Filippov's idea to discover the traces of fallen Ancient Rome, as was articulated in his Soviet era

'Third Rome' project, now merged with a strange post-Soviet melancholy. Perhaps he was searching for the unfulfilled potentials of communism in the daily reality of post-Cold War life.

In this drawing, Filippov anticipated a coming post-Cold War reality that saw, by the mid-1990s, the reconstruction of a historical replica of the Cathedral of Christ the Saviour and, by the early 2000s, the construction of such bizarre historicist projects as the Triumph Palace apartment building, nick-named Stalin's Eighth Sister (a belated sibling to the famous Stalinist-era 'seven sister' towers).

For many of the 'paper architects', and the artists and intellectuals associated with them, the years of the political transformation of Glasnost around 1987 were not only a period of questioning of the relationship between art, architecture and politics, but about the ideological and ethical function of 'creative practice' per se. It was a period of reflection about the very responsibilities and potentials of architecture. This situation has become particularly acute when, during the later part of the 1990s, the free market economy was redrawing Russia's physical and social landscape.

In the 2000s, when the government was seeking to rebuild the status of Russia as a global power, it opted to employ the best of Western architects. Western architects embraced these opportunities and submerged themselves in the newly found opulence. But the new 'turbo capitalism' also seemed, for many of the artists and architects based in Russia, to be simply too vulgar and 'corrupt' to offer new forms of creative practice. The 'innovations' of capitalism were rejected like the 'utopias' of communism. Many local Russian architects have again reverted to historicist styles and traditions – now pitched against what they saw as the ills of 'Anglo-Saxon capitalism'. Figures such as Alexander Belov are also typical of this

conception of architecture that aimed to withdraw from politics (in order never to return) as all governments and political institutions were viewed with suspicion (Figures 5.9, 5.10 and 5.11).

***

These narratives of architectural dissent seem to be part of a world long gone, but the paradoxes they contain might still be relevant today. They demonstrate the possibility of architects, not only to refuse to participate, but to practise critically, showing the multiple ways by which the 'paradox of subjection' could be avoided. What I aimed to promote here is a reflective kind of architectural practice, political and transformative, one aware of its dangers, pitfalls and limitations.

Figure 5.9 (Below left) Alexander Brodsky, Installation for 'You Prison', Sandretto Re Rebaudengo Foundation, Turino, 2008.

Figure 5.10 (Below) Alexander Brodsky, Apshu Café, Moscow, 2003.

Figure 5.11 (Below right) Alexander Brodsky, 95° Restaurant, Klyaz'minskoe Reservoir, 2000. In the early 1990s, Alexander Brodsky made use of the low budget allocated for the renovation of the Apshu Café by using only building materials and fragments from historic buildings demolished in Moscow to allow for new development. In 2001, Brodsky designed a summer restaurant (95° Restaurant) in the Klyaz'minskoe Reservoir, bringing alive a search for the archetypical, fantasies of boat-houses or temporary waterside buildings. Apparently rejecting the idea of the new, traditional and cheap materials are used to give a sense of decay, an impression that is enforced by the 5 degrees of inclination of the wooden structure that relates to the surrounding trees and gives it the sense of the unstable and temporary.

The possible significance of this rather partisan narration of some 'dissident practices' of the Cold War era might go beyond the historical evaluation of its largely unwritten history. It should lead us into asking what architectural dissent might mean today. Indeed, if the question is to be raised again, it must be raised against a completely different political and social reality and also against a different architectural culture. When today's projects articulate architectural gymnastics resembling product design exhibitions, and material has completely surrendered to the demand of form, it might be interesting to ask what can architecture still do in articulating the question of citizenship, that is the contemporary architecture of the governed. Furthermore, mobilizing the term 'dissent' into the architectural field of the possible, might seek thus the potential of politically engaged architecture to go beyond the current limits of its documentary/critical stand and engage the political problems of the present with its own tools.

BIBLIOGRAPHY

Žižek, Slavoj (1994) 'How did Marx invent the symptom', in Slavoj Žižek (ed.), *Mapping Ideology.* London: Verso.

FURTHER READING

Arch+. Zeitschrift für Architektur und Städtebau, "Architektur ohne Architekten", April 1990, No. 103.

Architectural Association (1988) *Nostalgia of Culture. Contemporary Soviet Visionary Architecture.* London: The Architectural Association.

Boym, Constantin (1992) *New Russian Design.* New York: Rizzoli.

Catalogue of Soviet Exposition `V Biennale di Architettura' Venezia 1991 (1991) *Arte Dell'Architecttura in Unione Sovietica.* Rome: Gangemi Editore.

Falk, Barbara J. (2003) *The Dilemmas of Dissidence in East-Central Europe.* Budapest, New York: CEU-Press.

Feher, Michel (2007) *Nongovernmental Politics.* Zone Books, MIT Press.

Klotz, Heinrich (ed.) (1990) *Paper Architecture. New Projects from the Soviet Union.* New York: Rizzoli.

Nesbitt, Lois (2003) *Brodsky & Utkin. The Complete Works.* New York: Princeton Architectural Press.

Project Russia (2006) Alexander Brodsky, No 41, 3/2006, Moscow.

Revzin, Grigory (2000) *Catalogue of the Russian Pavilion,* La Biennale di Venezia VII International Architecture Exhibition, Mikhail Filippov, Moscow.

SECTION 2

Aesthetics/Pleasure/Excess

6

Introduction: Architecture and Aesthetics

John Macarthur and Naomi Stead

This section of the Handbook covers what is perhaps the least developed area of modern architectural theory, that is, the relation of architecture to aesthetics and the idea of art. This might seem surprising to those outside the discipline, because if architecture is something more than the management of natural and social situations, we might expect to find a justification for this claim in philosophical aesthetics or theories of art and artistic affect. Instead, we find a dispersed discussion of pleasure and entertainment, of taste, of ennui, of distortion and constraint, of abstraction and corporeality. We read discussions of affects that might be considered aesthetic and of practices that might be called artistic, but in the later twentieth century there is little serious attention given in architectural discourse to the older questions of whether architecture is an art, how it relates to the other arts, whether it aims to please the senses, and if so, how.

This situation is not entirely one of negligence on the part of architectural theorists. Its cause is, in the first place, a subterranean fault-line in modern Western culture between two concepts usually thought complementary: art and aesthetics. Do architecture and other artistic practices come first and then aesthetics studies which explains them? Or is there an innate aesthetic feeling, in the first place for nature and human beauty, which then becomes the basis for the etiolated and arcane practices we call art? This is a question of precedence that turns into one of comprehensibility. As Barnett Newman rather testily puts the painters' side of the argument, 'aesthetics is for the artist as ornithology is for the birds' (Newman 1952). Architecture has in recent decades been firmly on the art side of the divide, believing in the autonomy of architecture and that its particular and specific values and historical trajectory are immanent in the problematics thrown up in everyday architectural practice (see Chapter 2). The architectural theory of such matters is more likely to occur in discipline-based journals than, say, the *Journal of Aesthetics and Art Criticism*; Bernard Tschumi's famous discussion of the pleasures of architecture (1994) describes feelings a layperson could not share, for reasons we will expand on below. Similarly, while architectural discourse has a general interest in painting and the other arts, it sees itself as a different species to birds like Newman. Painters, musicians, dancers, architects all draw on the authority of 'art' in different ways at different times, and this raises the further questions of whether there is 'art-as-such', of which architecture is a form, or whether 'art' is just a category into which we place painting, architecture, and so on.

The poor fit between art, 'the arts', and aesthetics is as much historical as conceptual. Western architecture is an idea, a discipline, and a defined corpus of buildings going back to the ancient Mediterranean. The other disciplines have similarly long and concrete histories, but none would have been called 'art' until the Renaissance nor thought of as a set with systematic differentiations until the *paragone*, the ritual debate that began in the seventeenth century on the merit of the different arts. Aesthetics emerged out of British empiricism across the eighteenth century and had no particular place for art. Aesthetics is the study of our reflection on the pleasure or displeasure of sensory experience. Its paradigm is nature, and art is gathered up into aesthetics through the ancient idea of mimesis, or the role of art to imitate the beauties of nature. Aesthetics, however, did offer the basis for a general concept of art-as-such by positing an aesthetic faculty of mind. In the older, open set of 'arts' based on disciplinary knowledge and socio-economic structures like guilds, it was not incongruous that Filippo Brunelleschi was a goldsmith, nor that his architectural practice was not distinguished from his mechanical engineering or his studies of optics. Aesthetics differentiated these practices and, what is more, proposed to rank 'arts' such as goldsmithing, architecture, painting, and poetry relative to how they served the aesthetic faculty. These systems of the arts, such as those formulated by the Abbé Batteux, Jean le Rond d'Alembert, and Immanuel Kant, are quite risible and largely confined to the eighteenth century. They have echoes and effects later in history in the Arts and Crafts' rejection of them, in the curriculum of the Bauhaus, and so on, but their more significant effect is the introduction of externalities into the old rivalry between the arts: for instance, the idea that architecture differs from (is better than) sculpture because the former deals with space in a way that is a fuller exercise of the sensorium, or, conversely, the idea that sculpture differs from (is better than) architecture because it is not instrumental (see Eisenman's interview with Richard Serra in Serra 1994). These historical and conceptual uncertainties are the unstable ground across which the architectural theory of aesthetics, art, and pleasure is dispersed. We will now attempt to map and organize that discourse as a context for the three chapters that follow.

These three chapters divide the field of aesthetics in architecture into three parts. Chapter 7, by Jorge Otero-Pailos, addresses architectural phenomenology, the most prevalent and influential modern discussion of the perceptual basis of architectural experience. Chapter 8, by Sandra Kaji-O'Grady, examines concepts of artistic technique, namely, form, formalism, and formlessness in architecture through the lens of systematic and serial practices in architecture, art, and music. Chapter 9, by Bart Verschaffel, examines disciplinary coherence, looking into the interrelation between architecture and the other arts, and between aesthetics and art history, by examining the figures and practices of the artist, the architect, and the engineer. In the first part of this introductory chapter, we will talk through and around these three chapters, placing their subject in historical context, and discuss some of the factors that have led to the re-emergence of interest in architectural aesthetics. This re-emergence has three underlying conditions: the historicization of earlier systems of normative aesthetics, which have become relativized in this process and thus opened as a new theoretical material; a growing interest in the place of architecture within a hierarchy or system of the other arts, which has overlapped with contemporary artists' fascination with architectural themes and techniques; and a thoroughgoing 'post-critical' moment in culture that has heralded a revaluation of beauty, among other things, as we see with the popularity of Umberto Eco's *On Beauty: A History of a Western Idea* (2004).

The second half of this introduction will be dedicated to an issue not directly addressed in the three chapters to come, which is that of pleasure, and the joint problem or, rather, the paradox it presents in architectural aesthetics. The majority of discussions of aesthetics in architecture are concerned with the anti-aesthetic, of which there are two distinct kinds: first, in the sense of the exploration and manipulation of negative affect (not the traditional sensual pleasure in beauty, but its contrary – disgust, boredom, or ennui, at ugliness, formlessness, or the abject), and, second, the anti-aesthetic as that which attempts to go beyond the aesthetic. Leaving aside aesthetic questions, and the aesthetic norms and canons of architectural tradition, the anti-aesthetic eschews the idea of architecture as something to be known simply through being 'felt', and it champions this outside or excess to the aesthetic as a space of critical potential. So in this schema of anti-aestheticism, the question of pleasure produces a confusion – is this a pleasure at negative feelings? Or is it an anti-aesthetic pleasure? The matrix of responses to these questions, which think the anti-aesthetic through pleasure, offers another way through this complex field. But first to the origins of modern aesthetics, as they bear on architecture.

HISTORICAL PERSPECTIVES – KANT

Immanuel Kant's aesthetics, contained in the *Critique of Judgement*, remains the strongest philosophical expression of modern ideas on aesthetic feelings and practices. Kant argues that beauty exists in judgements of taste and is fundamentally subjective: beauty is what we feel; it is not a quality of objects in themselves. In the 'Analytic of the Beautiful', Kant gives four conditions that are required to be satisfied if we are to be sure that our judgement is aesthetic, as opposed to an act of reason or a realization of morality (1911, 1–22). The first moment of this analytic is that we must have no interest in the actual existence of the object, only noting the pleasure it gives us. Kant distinguishes this pure pleasure from 'agreeableness', where a desire is satisfied, and from the pleasure we have in the good, which we ought to have. The second stricture is that when we make the judgement that a tree is beautiful, we imagine that no person should disagree. The judgement of beauty is thus universal, but it is so without a concept. That is to say there is no concept of the beauty of trees on which we have prior agreement. If that were the case, our judgement would be rational, not aesthetic, as we would be comparing the object to its concept. The third definition says that in beauty we admire the form of the purposiveness of an object, but not its purpose. To admire the beauty of a tulip is to admire the form of its completeness and is distinct from the botanist's admiration of the flower as a mechanism of reproduction. The fourth point is related to the second, supposing not only that none should disagree with our judgement but also that all will necessarily agree with us – a 'common sense' that is a commonality of the relation of sensation to feeling, which means that beauty is necessarily intersubjective.

Fine art for Kant is a kind of human productivity that imitates God's creativity. It has the appearance of being natural, yet at the same time we know that it is not (1911, 45). He still has the older sense of art as making and makers' knowledge, but this is not aesthetic for the reason of the third moment of the analytic of the beautiful; that is, craft has a purpose. Kant similarly rules out of aesthetic judgement what he calls the 'agreeable arts', as in entertaining conversation, in which we have an interest because it is conducted with the aim of enjoyment. Fine art objects are by contrast intrinsically final, whole in themselves without reference to the use or pleasure they might entail. In this, nature is the model of art and superior to it, but Kant also thinks that there are aesthetic ideas, which exist only in the fine arts (1911, 48).

Fine art is the result of genius, where an artist, by their talent, goes beyond imitating the established rules of art and thinks newly created aesthetic ideas such as new conceptual knowledge.

Kant's aesthetics and his definitions of fine art remain the definitive explanation of our uses of beauty and art in the modern world. With his rigorous subjectivism, he does, however, make a 'division of the fine arts' and a 'comparative estimate of the worth of the fine arts' (1911, 51, 53). Within this exists Kant's definition of architecture and its aesthetic potential:

> [Architecture] is the art of presenting concepts of things which are possible only through art, and the determining ground of whose form is not nature but an arbitrary end – and of presenting them both with a view to this purpose and yet, at the same time, with aesthetic finality. In architecture the chief point is a certain use of the artistic object to which, as the condition, the aesthetic ideas are limited (1911, 51).

Architecture's limits, then, are manifold. Aesthetic ideas are the obverse of concepts for Kant: reason dealing in concepts, and the imagination in ideas. Thus, architecture's presenting 'concepts of things only possible through art' (in the broader sense of artifice), rather than semblances of nature, already takes it down a peg. It is common for laypeople and readers of Kant to think that architecture cannot be art because it must be useful. However, Kant is more subtle than this. If architecture necessarily implied utility (or pleasingness), it would not be a fine art at all, whereas in his system of the arts it is included and seen to be superior to music. Its problem, rather, is that although we can consider a building as possessing its own finality, without thought of its use, architecture nevertheless has a concept of this subsequent use. This means we might consider how well or how badly it performs a use in which we have no interest, and this would be a judgement of reason, not an aesthetic judgement.

HISTORICAL PERSPECTIVES – THE TWENTIETH CENTURY

In part, the lacuna of aesthetics in architectural theory was caused by the failure of the very great claims made for it in the early to mid-twentieth century. The modern aesthetics of architecture claimed a basis in psychology, and thus the possibility of an empirical proof of the aesthetic merits and failures of buildings. This led to precepts, prescriptions for practice and normative concepts of form, which, despite claims to scientific status, tended towards the customs of pre-existing European and American architecture. The aesthetics of architecture became a reactionary field, most often practised by non-architects, and one largely pitched against the theoretical developments published in progressive architecture journals and described elsewhere in this Handbook. For most of its history, in most cultures, architecture has been a rhetorical culture, concerned with meaning, authority, and propriety, and in its more saturnine moments with the limits and failures of meaning. Architectural theory, especially in the post-war period, has returned to this rhetorical conception, but in a critical mode: thinking of architecture as a nexus of power and knowledge, of ideologies and spatial disciplines, of industrial production, colonial management, and the normalization of subjects. By contrast, if one thinks of architecture as a matter of sense, as a source of sensuous pleasure, and, what is more, a pleasure that ought to be necessarily and universally shared, then architectural aesthetics could, and has been, a normative discourse. The best-known treatment published in our period, Roger Scruton's *Aesthetics of Architecture* (1979), is opposed to cultural relativism and claims aesthetical justification for a particular strand of Western architecture: classicism. Similarly, texts such as those of Rudolf Arnheim describe some of the basic techniques of architects – of scale, movement, texture, frontality, threshold, and so on – as having a direct and certain description in human psychology, and in view of which various architectural cultures merely cloud our understanding (1977). For most of the late twentieth century in architectural discourse, *aesthetics* meant this kind of foundationalism, or equally troubling simplistic sociological surveys of popular and professional preferences for one building over another.

Given the perceived dangers of essentialism, progressive discourse has tended to avoid the word *aesthetic* when addressing kindred topics such as the pleasure of architecture, desire as a spatial structure, sensuous embodiment, and buildings as devices of seduction. Safely bracketed by the word *negative*, *aesthetics* is sometimes used in variously ecstatic accounts of abjection, ascesis, monstrosity, mundanity, pain, and violence. Along with these concepts are studies of various sites of 'architectural' pleasure, such as shopping arcades, parks, fairgrounds, brothels, and bachelor pads. In general, then, the older, dowdy aesthetics focused on the concept of beauty and hence the claims to innate value that architectural theory has been impatient with. Only a few commentators, such as Anthony Vidler (1992; 2000) have been concerned to show how much a 'negative' and apparently non-normative aesthetics is in fact based on the older concepts of sublimity and picturesqueness and ultimately triangulated with beauty. This is a situation of the arts as a whole where an interest in beauty and pleasure was understood as anti-intellectual, and aesthetics as the attempt by reactionaries to normalize an uncritical account of art. Beauty has since returned as a respectable interest with its own intellectual trajectory to do with the eclipse of 'critical' culture (in the sense of cultural works critical of cultural norms and institutions) and the rise of a new criticism, expository and evaluative (Elkins 2003). We will return to this issue towards the end of this introduction, in a discussion of the current 'post-critical' moment and its repercussions for aesthetics in architecture.

The nails in the coffin of normative architectural aesthetics were driven by historians who relativized its prescriptions but treated these as moments of intellectual history. For example, the aesthetic and psychological theories of Heinrich Wölfflin, August Schmarsow, Geoffrey Scott, and others at the turn of the twentieth century were long considered arcane predecessors to the mid-century founders of canonical modern history, such as Sigfried Giedion (1941; 1948; compare with 1981) and Nikolaus Pevsner, whose ideological comportment had, by 1980, lost them all credibility. However, when looked on with some historical objectivity by intellectual historians such as Harry Mallgrave, Eleftherios Ikonomou, and Mark Jarzombek, figures such as Wölfflin are now understood as crucial to architectural history; their aesthetic ideas are no longer assessed as programmes to be enacted, but as problematics that drove and can now explain the intellectual history of architecture's recent past. Thus contextualized and relativized, the aesthetic theories themselves become a new resource.

Jorge Otero-Pailos's chapter in this volume (Chapter 7) follows in this tradition as he critiques the architectural phenomenology of the mid- to late-twentieth century. In this phenomenology is an example, perhaps the dominant example in our recent history, of an architectural aesthetics properly said, and it constitutes one of the three lines of inquiry that can describe the whole of the field of architectural aesthetics, and that are covered in the three chapters in this section. Although generally preferring the term *poetic* to *aesthetic*, phenomenology is the dominant mode in architecture where the question of sense and affect is posed. It proposes to explain directly how the spaces we inhabit make us feel. Architectural phenomenology proposes that one should recognize and value unmediated experience, and the ongoing currency of this idea is witnessed in the popularity of Juhani Pallasmaa's *The Eyes of the Skin: Architecture and the Senses* (1996). The idea that architecture can be made better through understanding our perception of space and putative spatial archetypes begins in the eighteenth century, takes its modern form in the late-nineteenth century in empathy theory, grows in empirical psychology in the mid-twentieth-century, and is reviving today in an uptake of neuropsychology. However, the dominant idea for understanding architecture as a matter of sense in the mid- to late-twentieth century was phenomenology. This was only loosely related to the philosophical phenomenology of Edmund Husserl, Henri Bergson, and Maurice Merleau-Ponty. Otero-Pailos' short history of architectural phenomenology reveals it as a strange concoction of proper phenomenology, pop psychology, old-fashioned humanism, and, more recently, evolutionary psychology, which makes kin of writers as diverse as Christian Norberg-Schulz, Ernesto N. Rogers, Kenneth Frampton, and Charles Moore. Otero-Pailos shows that the ideas and historical trajectory of architectural phenomenology are best understood as a battle for intellectual hegemony in the academy. Paradoxically, this sensibility for direct experience requires cultivation through a highly theorized account of architectural history. Phenomenology nevertheless remains the strongest case we have of architectural thinking claiming the authority of a fundamental outside, something beyond the particular concepts of art or architecture specific to a culture or time.

ARCHITECTURE AND THE VISUAL ARTS

An important contextual shift that has contributed to the new interest in architectural aesthetics is the interplay of architecture and the visual arts. Architecture is currently more likely to be understood as an art than at any time since art nouveau. This shift is a part of a wider retreat of architecture from ideas of social and functional utility, which is beyond our present discussion, but, as much as this, it has to do with the increasing value within architectural discourse of claiming the name of an art. Whatever one thinks of the practical or social utility of building, of its representational powers or its abilities to create or normalize spatial conditions, architects treat these as so much material that can be manipulated. The social and material matter of building is, to a certain extent, material for the architect in the same way that lived life is material for a novelist or filmmaker. A house may be a place to live and a real-estate investment, but to an architect it is more like what the theme of adultery, say, or the prodigal son, might suggest to a novelist. Architectural techniques (such as scale, directionality, sequential planning, typological recognition) assume that the manifold social and material relations of a building can be momentarily totalized as a 'material' that can be worked with these same architectural techniques. This situation is familiar to us through the concept of media, having a conceptual model in the sculptor's work with chisels on marble, with the cinematographer's use of camera movement to make narrative, and the whole conception of the fine arts that has, since the eighteenth century, been organized around media and their appropriate techniques.

To think of architecture as an art does not require a basis in aesthetics, and indeed, the concept of architecture as an art is in a degree of conflict with an aesthetic view. Strictly put, aesthetics considers our reflection and judgements on our sensuous experience, and thus makes no in-principle distinction between our judgement of the beauty of a tree, a painting, or a symphony. Kant goes to some lengths to show that art presents aesthetic ideas nature does not possess, but these are ideas nonetheless applicable to our aesthetic feeling for nature. Following on from this, the whole aesthetic enterprise assumes the homology of aesthetic judgements of art and nature. Aesthetical thinking is therefore sceptical of axiomatic distinctions between forest clearings and buildings, let alone historically and culturally limited distinctions between architecture and sculpture. Much of the architectural theory that deals with matters that are roughly aesthetic, in fact takes as its premise the existence of art as a discrete kind of human activity, and a set of 'the arts' that can be understood through their differences and complementarities. Aesthetic concepts are often wheeled in to make these differentiations, but at a second order. Most architects will thus distinguish what they do from sculpture around a concept of space. Modern architects generally accept the postulates of early-twentieth-century thinkers that space is an object of sense that can be directly perceived, despite the lack of an orifice for space to enter the body. Rather, the eyes, hands, ears, locomotive potential, skin, and the whole body make *space* the principal percept of the sensorium understood as a whole. But if they know these arguments, most architects will use them to explain a more basic point, which is why an architectural concept of space differs from sculpture and the relative positions of its fabric. In short, space is generally understood as the medium of an (architectural) art, one that distinguishes it from other arts and their media, and aesthetic arguments are marshalled to this end.

This is a situation not of architecture alone, but rather of all the arts. Michael Fried's strongly conventionalist view of painting holds that all its issues and problems are imminent in its historical and conceptual development and the idea of painting as an art, and the existence (or not) of an aesthetic faculty are weak external contexts (1967, 1998). Fried's is a more considered and argued version of what most architects have thought of architecture since the widespread notion of 'architectural autonomy' arose in the 1970s. Here, a history-of-ideas approach to architecture, whether variously Marxian like the work of Manfredo Tafuri (1987; Tafuri and Dal Co 1979) or hermeneutic like that of Joseph Rykwert (1972; 1980), served an interest in self-referential form as varied as the ur-classicism of Aldo Rossi or the ur-avant-gardism of Peter Eisenman. Autonomous architecture looked like art – one might say it took its conceptual model from the idea of art – and assumed there were 'sister arts', but there was little at stake in their interaction. This situation has changed since the 1990s, with an increasingly high value placed on interdisciplinarity in both architecture and the visual arts: the design-like practice of artists such as Andrea Zittel, Jorge Prado, and Thomas Demand, and the artistic comportment of architects such as Rem Koolhaas and Herzog and de Meuron (Ursprung 2002). The value placed on interdisciplinarity in contemporary culture began in a critique of disciplines as arbitrary constraints on creativity, which led to various collaborations of architects and visual artists. Jane Rendell's book *Art and Architecture: A Place Between* documents the issues and some indicative practices (2006). As this process has accelerated, its terms have changed, and issues around the basis for collaboration have led to a reassertion of disciplines, which Rosalind Krauss calls the differential specificity of media in contemporary art. Now that media are no longer given as material constraints, artists make rooms, painters work in photomedia, and much art is ephemeral; media has become a conceptual issue, and many of the deeper questions of aesthetics have re-emerged from the practical intersections of art disciplines.

In Chapter 8, Sandra Kaji-O'Grady explains the architectural concept of form and formalism as it developed in the 1960s alongside formalist poetics and minimalism and serialism in the visual arts and music. Serialism explains some of the recent history of architectural concepts of form and form-making procedures, and it is also an interesting parallel to some of the intermedial exploration of the present day. In this discussion, Kaji-O'Grady opens the issue of the anti-aesthetic that so characterizes twentieth-century culture, for the affect supposed by many kinds of formal procedure is not pleasure in the simple sense of eighteenth-century aesthetics, or even heightened awareness, but rather boredom, ennui, disgust – kinds of affects that are much more than merely negative. This level of conceptual practice in architecture asks whether it needs affect at all, if, rather than pleasing us, architecture can present the limit of the human. It is thus anti-aesthetic in a second sense of thinking that art can take us beyond the aesthetic. By beginning in sensuous forms, architecture might take us to forms of non-conceptual cognition.

Understood in its strongest forms of autonomy from use, art cannot have a purpose in pleasing. Thus, there is ultimately a conflict between understanding architecture as an autonomous art discipline working through a historically unfolding formal problematic and aesthetics, which would show that all this has a purpose in confronting the sensorium in some other useful way. This conceptual conflict needs to be understood historically. It is the rise of aesthetic theory, and particularly Kant's concept of purposiveness without purpose, that gives terms to the claims of architecture's autonomy from sense and hence, paradoxically, from aesthetics. The fourth chapter of this section will thus open the question of the disciplinarity of architecture. Bart Verschaffel shows in Chapter 9 that the concepts of artistic media and sensory affect cannot be resolved without considering the concept of architecture per se, as a discipline or form of knowledge understood as a relation between knowledges.

There are real and complex histories of how architecture has or has not been an institution at different times in different cultures, but this history is not what interests us here. Rather, Verschaffel shows that one cannot understand architecture merely as a set of operations, nor in the affects that architecture might produce, but that the discipline needs also to produce a logical concept of itself and these relations. If we look to history or to comparative cultural analysis, it might seem that architecture exists (or not) almost by accident, in the differing ways that building has been organized in various cultures and times. To speak of these relations with the definite article as 'the discipline of architecture' might be ultimately ideological. Nevertheless, this ideology requires a continuing process of becoming coherent. Architecture seeks a licence for its institutional existence, and thus autonomy, by claiming autochthonous concepts such as *design* and a persona, *the architect*. That we find it useful to speak of the architecture of the Australian Aborigines, or the architects (rather than masons) of the Gothic cathedrals of Europe, is a matter not of historical truth or anachronism, but of a demand for conceptual coherence. The *discipline* is that contingent totality from which we can project a future practice and use the resources of our numerous pasts. To this extent, architecture continually produces its own essence as a discipline, distinguishing itself from engineering and the visual arts, finding in its own history fundamental distinctions that might be visible only in retrospect.

The three chapters that follow each have particular aims and, especially in the cases of Otero-Pailos and Kaji-O'Grady, quite specific intellectual histories to map. Nevertheless, it is our proposition that in this section of the Handbook we have laid out three axes – of sense perception, artistic technique, and disciplinary coherence – that can be used to survey the field of the architectural theory of matters aesthetic. There are further contexts and issues in the field that are not addressed directly in the chapters, and we will attempt to cover them in the remainder of this introduction. Earlier, we raised the issue of architecture as a critical discourse and the recent eclipse of this idea, an issue also treated elsewhere in the Handbook. We can align a number of other important contexts around this concept and its historical shift: the anti-aesthetic tone of much critical discourse, and the history that, despite appearances, connects the post-critical return of beauty and aesthetic thinking with an earlier concept of pleasure.

PLEASURE

Although the high-theory discourse of the 1970s and 1980s was resolutely anti-aesthetic, this was an alliance of two kinds of anti-aesthetic that can be exemplified in two very different kinds of pleasure. The first of these was anti-aesthetic, which was largely popularist in that it opposed the operation of aesthetics as a distinct mode of thought, particularly that there was a contemplative aesthetic pleasure different in kind from everyday enjoyment. The second would be better called a negative-aesthetics of pain, disgust, ordinariness, and boredom, that is, an aesthetic developed from the original anti-aesthetics of the sublime and the picturesque. The pleasures of this negative aesthetic, the pleasure of a proximate distance from abjection and terror, are not so different from eighteenth-century explanations of the enjoyment of tragedy or sublime landscapes, but they are exactly the pleasures that the first true anti-aesthetes opposed.

In the 1960s, Robert Venturi and Denise Scott Brown became the most prominent debunkers of the formalist aesthetic of modernism by explaining what architects could learn from the popular built environment (Venturi et al. 1972). The original empirical formulation of aesthetics by the Earl of Shaftesbury, David Hume, and Edmund Burke assumes not only individual preference but also the communication and display of this in an intersubjective *taste*. In eighteenth-century doctrines of civic humanism, such as those of Joshua Reynolds, the discussion of what was within and without the bounds of taste was considered an important way to construct the social realm. Venturi and Scott Brown exploded the consensus of their day, famously taking the good and bad examples from Peter Blake's *God's Own Junkyard* (1964) and asserting opposed preferences. Blake diagnosed the problem of 1960s America by showing how far civic space had degenerated from Jeffersonian architecture. Venturi and Scott Brown responded that they preferred the lively inauthenticity of the commercial strip to the 'good form' of the University of Virginia. They argued that architecture should give over its elitism and self-reference and establish a broader constituency in the republic of taste. The British Townscape movement, which explicitly revived the picturesque as an analytic of vernacular urban qualities (Cullen 1961), had influenced Venturi and Scott Brown, who started out in the real sociology of suburb culture, studying with Herbert Gans (1968; 1974). A variety of sociologically-based studies began to show that the pleasures of modern architecture escaped most people, and that if such architecture had any cultural meaning it was to identify the powers of commerce and government. Although there have been numerous denunciations of the social disasters of modern architecture, Philippe Boudon's study of the modification of Le Corbusier's worker's suburb Pessac was significant in showing how popular taste had the power to deflate the form-follows-function arguments by which architects avoided discussing their aesthetic judgements (1972).

Pierre Bourdieu's concept of cultural capital, in which educational attainments and aesthetic discretion are shown not merely to distinguish classes but also to be actually exchangeable in the real economy, did much to strengthen a social critique of architecture (Bourdieu 1984; Bourdieu and Darbel 1990; Dovey 1999; Stevens 1998). Bourdieu, however, draws back from describing culture merely as a calculus of class and wealth. As much as his aim is to critique the given-ness of legitimated culture, it is also to defend everyday concepts of enjoyment from an aesthetic concept of pleasure as something demanding, rare, and difficult to obtain. In his scathing attack on Jacques Derrida's reading of Kant's aesthetics, Bourdieu claims that aesthetics makes the ascesis of scholarship the model for all human enjoyment. In architecture, these kinds of sophisticated defences of popular taste led to critiques of architecture such as Diane Ghirardo's collection *Out of Site* (1991). Earlier versions of this anti-aesthetic tended to celebrate the spectacular and the excessive, the 'unrefined' aspects of popular taste, but this shifted in the 1990s to an interest in *everydayness* and an admiration for the matter-of-factness and expediency of the vernacular built environment, an interest that continues into the present (Harris and Berke 1997). While claiming authority from Michel de Certeau (1984) and Henri Lefebvre (1991), this everydayness has much to do with the rediscovery of the sociological aims of Team 10 and the Smithsons' interest in ugliness, much of which can be traced back to the first aestheticization of vernacular architecture in the picturesque (Lichtenstein and Schregenberger 2001; Risselada and van den Heuvel 2005). At the beginning of the twenty-first century, we could map this area of investigation between Rem Koolhaas's celebration of the low quality, excess, and ephemerality of the commercial architecture he calls 'junkspace' (2002), and Atelier Bow-Wow's careful mapping of what they call 'pet architecture', the small-scale eccentric vernacular caused by the spatial parsimony of Tokyo's land-tenure system (2002). Both constitute an outside to critique architectural practice and its aesthetic norms, but to the extent that both have moved some distance from a simple account of pleasure, they merge with the other kind of anti-aesthetic.

One of the general antimonies of aesthetic discourse is that of the facile and the demanding. From Arthur Schopenhauer to Walter Benjamin, writers have claimed that aesthetic feelings should be easy or difficult, common or rare, contemplative and abstract or immediately haptic. If the first anti-aesthetic we have described champions an account of pleasure as something natural and immediate, its opposite, an account of the pleasure of architecture as something ascetic, abstract, and demanding to experience, draws on a line of philosophical thinking from Kant and Schopenhauer to Theodor Adorno. The high point of this strand of thinking in architecture is the deconstruction of the 1980s, which modelled itself on post-structuralism in literature and cultural studies but quickly took up the name of Derrida's philosophical mode – probably because of the awful pun involved. Sandra Kaji-O'Grady's chapter in this section explains how much of the concept of form in deconstruction derives not from a philosophy of language but from serialist accounts of form as procedure, taken from the visual arts and music. Nevertheless, the language and literary side of post-structuralism was also fundamental, especially around the concept of pleasure and excess, derived by Bernard Tschumi from Roland Barthes, Derrida, and Georges Bataille, and we will now turn to this important strand.

TRANSGRESSION AND *JOUISSANCE* IN ARCHITECTURE

Tschumi's influential article-cum-artwork of 1975, 'Advertisements for Architecture', includes an image of Le Corbusier's modernist Villa Savoye in ruins, before its restoration, under the title 'Sensuality has been known to overcome even the most rational of buildings' followed by the subtext 'Architecture is the ultimate erotic act. Carry it to excess and it will reveal both the traces of reason and the sensual experience of space' (1996, 533). Although the statement is intended to shock and confront, Tschumi is not critiquing the Villa Savoye, nor anyone's opinion of it, but rather the existence of the canon, its foundation in beauty, its projection into a future. Tschumi appears to be transgressing the values of the discipline, but this is in fact a second order where transgression becomes a value in itself. Bataille's surrealist anthropology of the 1930s was being rediscovered at this time by Barthes and by Derrida (Bataille 1996; Derrida 1981; Caille 2001). Bataille's interest in the cultural anthropology of debasement and sacrifice was theorized by Derrida as the possibility that the radical disruption of a limited economy, say that of a literary genre or of norms of sexual conduct, could explode into the 'general economy' and make all existence equally unruly. When Tschumi publishes an image of a person being thrown out of a window under the title 'To really appreciate architecture you may even need to commit a murder', he raises this same possibility – where architectural ideas and concepts might develop to a stage where they have no happy relation with the rest of life. 'Advertisements for Architecture' is a polemical theoretical text, but one can see its consequences in Tschumi's Parc de la Villette project in Paris, where the brief of uses is disaggregated and homogenized on a logical process bearing no relation to the actual buildings' programmes. Similar ideas are at stake in Peter Eisenman's House VI: the conjugal bed is split down the middle, and formal schemas from Le Corbusier and Gerrit Rietveld are overlayed and inverted so that an upside-down green stair crosses a more usable red one.

These architectural 'pleasures' cannot be separated from the idea of valuing innovation and progress in art, or, to a degree, the denigration of obsolete culture. One of the principal problems of aesthetics is how to account for change in art, Hegel famously thinking of it as a continual development towards its sublation into pure spirit. Since Hegel, Nietzsche, and Marx, it has been common to compare artworks not only on their pleasingness or their aesthetic ideas but also on whether they progress or retard the development of human spirit. Deconstruction was explicitly avant-gardist, or neo-avant-gardist – another aspect of its punning name lay in references to the constructivism of the early twentieth century, and Tschumi's form vocabulary is borrowed from Russian avant-gardists in particular. Given this, another way to understand the pleasures Tschumi supposes architecture can provide is to think of them within the temporal structure of avant-gardism. The term is borrowed from military parlance and means being ahead of a main force, confronting and testing the enemy the better to prepare the main body of the army coming behind. Avant-gardists therefore see and act differently from the rest of us, but this is because they are literally ahead of us, already dealing with our immediate future. As John Rajchman has explained, the unlikely pleasures of avant-garde architecture, finding a split down the middle of your bed and so on, are synecdoches of future pleasures (1998). The unpopularity and even the incomprehensibility of avant-garde architecture connote a future in which it will be popular and in which our current feelings will be obsolete. The model here again is the historical avant-gardes such as futurism and constructivism, variously rabidly individualist or collectivist, that were anti-humanist in their belief that not only society but also the body and the emotions could be constructed. Despite new names, the affect this kind of anti-aesthetic supposes lies firmly within the history of the sublime.

As Burke said of the sublime, these difficult pleasures are nevertheless supposed to be enjoyed in the present, as Nietzsche might have said, by those who are up to the demanding task. Tschumi's concept of architectural pleasure draws heavily on Roland Barthes. In *The Pleasure of the Text* (1975a), *S/Z* (1975b), and *Sade/Fourier/Loyola* (1997), Barthes develops a concept of the distortion, transposition, and invention of language, which he calls its systemacity, as the basis of the reader's pleasure in writerliness. The idea is the familiar one of formal constraint, as in poetic scansion, but understood structurally through Roman Jakobson's idea of poetry's systematic misalignment of the axes of grammar and syntax in speech. In part, Barthes's project was a defence of the literary avant-garde – for example, the novels of his friend Alain Robbe-Grillet, which are difficult to read as language and also on occasion describe sex crimes. Following the one-time surrealist George Bataille's recuperation of the pornography of the Marquis de Sade as literature, Barthes asks what it is that the reader enjoys in descriptions of sexual torture, coprophilia, and so on. The answer is that the pleasure one expects of narrative and sequence carries one through de Sade's interminable list of degrading acts to a point where being the reader becomes unbearable, and what is *writerly* and *readerly* are revealed as naked constructions of the text. Then there is a moment of excess or refusal, and any self-possessed 'pleasure' in reading collapses into a kind of literary joy that parallels the orgasms pursued so systematically by de Sade's characters. In the literary pornography of de Sade and Bataille, a transgression of language and structure follows out of the transgressive sexual acts their texts represent, and the space of representation itself collapses. Barthes distinguished the *pleasure* of the readerly text (his example is Balzac's *Sarrazine*) from the *jouissance* of the writerly texts he admired.

Perhaps it is the difficulty of translating *jouissance* that left Tschumi's article with the title 'The Pleasures of Architecture', but it is certainly this arc from syntactic procedure to new affects that he and other architects such as Daniel Libeskind, Zaha Hadid, Coop Himmelblau, and Eisenman sought. The Barthesian model of orgasmic architecturalness is an extreme and even pompous claim for the *enjoy-ability* of architecture, but to an extent, it is a hyperbole useful in describing a wider and slightly more plausible claim: the idea that a libidinous attitude to space could act as a critique of the sociopolitical basis of building. Much progressive architecture since the 1970s has been anti-aesthetic in the sense of claiming to escape normative aesthetics into an embodied critical state that is, nonetheless, embodied like an affect. For some decades in the late twentieth century, the strongest term of approbation for an architectural work such as this was *critical*, a term that followed Walter Benjamin's call to 'politicize the aesthetic' (1973 [1935]), and the Frankfurt School's idea of critical theory.

THE CRITICAL

The political side of critical architecture is the concept of ideology critique drawn from Marxism, which suggests that we consistently naturalize and misunderstand the interests that cause the world to be the way that it is. It should then be possible, according to the Marxist position, to undo such misapprehensions by revealing the interests at stake, so as to then reorganize socio-economic structures. But how is this ideology critique possible by architectural means rather than by, say, journalism or forensic accountancy? What is critical architecture at the level of affect? A certain displacement or distance between the programme of uses and the architectural programme might suffice, but this sounds like the older distinction of *architecture* over *building* as a matter of value. What is new in so-called critical architecture is a reversal of the values of affect. If architecture, under the model of a traditional aesthetics, pleases by *placing* the subject, a critical architecture *misplaces* one. The subject of the architecture is separated from the subject of the building and that displacement, like Barthes's critique of the assumed roles of reader and writer, collapses the self-evidence of living in the world as it is. The model of a critical architecture is then well served by a concept of pleasurable excess. Trained architectural consideration is always in excess of need or of the uses imagined for a building and thus implies a critique of the necessity of building per se, and this can be affecting. But to find those extreme examples where we might be able to call this affect pleasure (or anti-pleasure) – those occasions where a building might actually be uncanny and disorienting, aid in seduction, or cause compulsive shopping – then we have something that looks like evidence for the claim that architecture can spring from syntactic procedures to the general condition of the economy or to the structure of thought since the enlightenment or to other much larger extra-architectural matters.

Some of the most interesting and useful contemporary architectural theory arises out of this strand of thought. This includes Anthony Vidler's early translations of Barthes's ideas on de Sade into eighteenth-century architecture (1987) and his later theorization of the psychopathologies of space (1992; 2000), Denis Hollier's writing on Bataille (1989), Mark Wigley's engagement with the philosophy of Derrida (1993), and so on. As much as these works bear on aesthetic issues, they bear on the whole condition of architecture, and we have already moved a long way beyond the remit of this section. The last point we need to make, however, is that this moment of critical architecture is over, at least in part because of the return of aesthetics in the simpler older sense.

THE POST-CRITICAL

The so-called post-critical moment is a watershed across the humanities. In it, the long line of licence between political critique, and the criticism practised in literature or architecture, has finally snapped. In the most interesting overview, Ian Hunter (2006) claims that all critical theory continued the persona of the metaphysician at the same time as it critiqued metaphysics. The literary tropes and inaccessibility of Derrida are in Hunter's view a continuation of seventeenth-century spiritual exercises based on scholarly ascesis. There are few today who think that the exercise of architectural issues in a building commissioned and built under the normal conditions of capitalism has any political potentiality. It is an often heard complaint that architects use theory aesthetically, and in the terms of our present discussion this is the aesthetics of demandingness. In these terms, the good architect will struggle to a personal epiphany, and the difficulties of theory are a train parallel to design on which these personal qualities can be evidenced. These are matters dealt with elsewhere in the Handbook (see Chapter 2), but it is interesting that a crucial article by Robert Somol and Sarah Whiting (2002) gives a role to Dave Hickey, the art critic who (along with others) has made beauty hip again (Hickey 1997; 2009). This looks to us like a dialectic, a return to an easier, lighter, and commonsensical account of aesthetic feeling, with a history going back to David Hume.

The eclipse of the ascesis of high theory and its etiolated concept of difficult and sometimes painful architectural pleasures is perhaps no different to the earlier critique of the dry authoritarianism of modernist formalism. Modernist architecture is on the ascendant in most of the world, having achieved in late capitalism and commercial branding the success that evaded its earlier socialist mode. It would be a pity if the new-found popularity of modernism translated directly into a popularist account of architectural aesthetics. The most interesting theory of architectural aesthetics today is not theory at all; it is criticism. The collapse of the grander claims for critical architecture has allowed a space for the return of practical criticism of architectural works, and this, in time, will encourage reflection on how and why we judge some buildings more pleasing than others.

7

Architectural Phenomenology and the Rise of the Postmodern

Jorge Otero-Pailos

The term *architectural phenomenology* came into wide use in the post-war period to refer to the study of architecture as it presents itself to consciousness in terms of so-called archetypal human experiences, such as the bodily orientation of up and down, the perceptions of light and shadow, or the feelings of dryness and wetness. It has since cohered into architecture's primary discursive mode for examining questions of perception and affect, as opposed to the analytic tradition of analysing buildings in terms of stylistic rules of composition. By relegating style to a secondary plane, it undermined one of the foundational categories according to which most architectural history is written. At the time when most modern architects took history for granted as something to be ignored, architectural phenomenologists made history into a question rather than a given, something exciting to ponder and theorize. As such, architectural phenomenology played a central role in the turn towards history that has come to define the postmodern period. More than simply a discourse, it was also a social assemblage that drew together architects who placed a premium on experience as a form of intellectuality, and who collectively reconsidered theory as more than a mere explanation of practice – indeed, as practice's primary means of advancement.

Certainly, interest in experience was not new to a profession that, after all, is concerned with making structures fit for human habitation. A number of crucial nineteenth-century debates in physiology, psychology, and philosophy shaped how modern architects understood experience (see Crary 2001). By that time, scientists had come to prove that the bodily senses were unreliable, and that they could therefore not claim an essential objectivity or epistemological certainty. The idea of fragmented human perception became emblematic of the wider human experience of modernity, and early-twentieth-century architects made its architectural expression into the hallmark of modernism. At the same time that modernists in many ways defined themselves in relation to the fragmentation of human perception, they never ceased to consider it a problem to be resolved architecturally through buildings that could restore the lost unity of human experience. Peter Behrens's work for AEG in Germany first advanced the notion that dislocating effects of modern technology on the senses could be assuaged through visual technologies, like graphic design or architectural 'styling', an idea that later influenced the ideology of the

Bauhaus (Anderson 2000). In the United States, Albert Kahn's work for Ford, and the wider discourse of 'industrial democracy' developed during World War I, also fed on a similar belief in the restorative power of architectural design (Bentel 1992). In many ways, architectural phenomenology was a continuation of these earlier efforts to restore the lost unity of experience architecturally, but it was also different insofar as it posited authentic experience as something timeless and fundamentally external to modernity. If modernism was the architectural expression of the experience of modernity, then architectural phenomenology attracted architects disillusioned with modernism to the paradoxical promise of finding a premodern type of experience on which to ground the expression of a new postmodern architecture.

By the early 1960s, a young post-war generation of North American and European architects had seized the idea that architecture should participate in the liberation of human experience from the constraints of the social status quo. Raised during the ascendancy of post-war modernism in the West, they viewed its austere institutionalized aesthetics as the emblem of an oppressive and closed social order. They thought individual experience had been impoverished by the process of industrialization, and became disillusioned with the modernist faith in technology as the driver of emancipation. In a radical break from modernist ideology, some members of that generation sought to reground the future of modern architecture in the premodern past, a time when, they believed, individuals had experienced architecture, and their world in general, in richer and more wholesome ways. The protagonists of this turn towards the past called it postmodernism, celebrating what they saw as a major triumph over the aesthetic and intellectual constraints of modern architecture. Aesthetically, the postmodern style incorporated allusions to premodern architecture into technologically modern buildings, consciously undermining, often with a degree of irony and humour, the modernist emphasis on the correspondence between the building's structure and its façades. The postmodern style has received a great deal of scholarly attention, but the same is not true about its intellectual history. To accomplish the turn towards the past intellectually, postmodern architects had to replace the piloting concepts of modernism, from the abstract ideas of space and form, towards new notions of history and theory. Out went the conviction that technology drove history, and in came the sense that architectural history was driven by the search for authentic, original human experiences. They replaced the belief that architecture would become more sophisticated as technology moved towards the future teleologically, with the notion that architecture would become more advanced as it returned to the ontological origins of human experience. They conceived contemporary experience in terms of historical continuity rather than rupture.

The protagonists of this intellectual shift were not a self-identified group armed with an emblematic manifesto, but rather a series of independent architects whose collective achievements are only understandable retroactively as constituting a new intellectual formation, architectural phenomenology, which recast history as the experiential content of modern architecture. This collective discourse achieved the greatest coherence in the United States, in the academic circles that formed around the figures of Jean Labatut, Charles Moore, Christian Norberg-Schulz, and Kenneth Frampton, whose teachings and writings made their impact on architectural culture slowly and deliberately, over decades rather than years. As some of the most influential pedagogues and international best-selling authors, they led the transformation of Western architectural culture during the so-called postmodern period, changing how architects learned and understood the relationship of modern architecture to its history. Their ability to produce such a discourse helped legitimize the recuperation of historical architecture as an inspiration for modern design, and underpinned the emergence of the postmodern style. But more importantly, their ingenious construction of new experiential protocols for researching and writing architectural history had an intellectual impact that lasted long after the postmodern style went out of fashion. They made the study of architectural history into the hallmark of the intellectual architect, or, as we say today, the architect theorist. Yet, however staunchly committed to the intellectualization of architecture, they were also firm believers in the primacy of lived experience over detached mental analyses as a means to understand the history of architecture. They were thus caught in the paradoxical position of having to intellectualize their resistance to the emergence of theory as something separate from practice. Their ambivalence sowed the seeds of anti-intellectualism into contemporary architectural theory.

Postmodernism in architecture was both a stylistic movement and an intellectual sea-change that germinated in the post-war period, took root in the 1970s, and flourished in the 1980s. While postmodernism is easy to identify stylistically, its intellectual contours are not as straightforward to discern. My aim is to clarify the nature of architectural phenomenology as one of the major unexamined intellectual sources of postmodern architectural thought. The name obscures as much as it reveals its derivations, making them seem primarily philosophical, when in fact they were also aesthetic and included practices such as camouflage, graphic design, and photography. It is difficult for us today to look upon a camouflage pattern, a supergraphic paint scheme, or a carefully framed picture of a construction joint as anything more than various aesthetizations of theory, that is, as post-facto representations of intellectual work. Yet before the rise of what we now call architectural theory, these practices were included in what was considered legitimate intellectual work in architecture, not something secondary to mental acts, but as their primary source and governing standard. Architectural phenomenology refers to this ambiguous intellectual realm, and to the process whereby architects grew self-aware of its ambiguity, testing, contesting, celebrating, and exploiting it for the purpose of defending the belief that architectural practice embodied a unique mode of intellectuality that could not be separated from aesthetic experience.

Architectural phenomenologists endeavored to systematically analyse the intellectual content of architecture – the intentions in architecture, to use Christian Norberg-Schulz's terminology – in terms of visual and experiential codes. The form of their analytical work ranged from elaborate photo essays to graphic and building designs, as well as more conventional texts, making it clear that architectural ideas circulated as much through words as images. This revelation about the nature of discourse gave intellectual weight to key themes of postmodernism, such as the new attentiveness to image-like two-dimensional building surfaces and decorations. As a result of their relentless search for an experiential source to intellectuality, architectural phenomenologists tested the accepted limits of what was deemed purely conceptual work. During the post-war era, that limit was synonymous with architectural history, which figured as the model for scholarship, intellectual work, and, most importantly, detachment from aesthetic production. Postmodernism's wider turn towards history was understood to be an intellectualization of the discipline. In that context, architectural phenomenology held the line against architectural historians, offering the prospect that architects might employ their unique experiential and aesthetic means to investigate the intellectual content of history. By raising the prospect of other ways to produce history, architectural phenomenologists effectively called into question the accepted conventions of architectural historiography, such as the reliance on secondary written documents to establish such facts as dates of construction, lines of patronage, and costs. For architectural phenomenologists these were irrelevant secondary details that distracted historians from their main task of ascertaining the historic significance of buildings. Instead, they raised the possibility that a building's historic significance, or its 'meaning' to use their preferred term, might be more accurately ascertained through the direct physical experience of the building itself. Their collective probing of the methods and purposes of architectural history raised its intellectual stakes. Their experientialist historiography was a key factor in the development of a distinctly new theoretical kind of history by architects and for architects. Architectural phenomenology played a central role in setting into motion what we now call theory, not only intellectually, through the expansion and rearticulation of architecture's modes of scholarship, but also socially, by staking out a new position for architect-historians within the academy as the custodians of architecture's peculiarly ambiguous mode of intellectuality.

Architectural phenomenology's insistence on this ambiguity, conceived as the unity of theory and practice, pitted it against the very idea of an autonomous architectural theory that it helped spawn. By the mid-1980s, this put architectural phenomenologists in the paradoxical position of having to theorize their own demotion of theory. For the younger generation of postmodern thinkers eager to take up the position of architect-historians, the ambiguity of experientialist historiography began to appear as an intellectual liability rather than an asset. The eclipse of architectural phenomenology was as spectacular and swift as its rise. It became synonymous with an anti-intellectual affirmation of the primacy of practice over theory. When a student show at the Architectural Association in London was criticized under the title 'All Phenomenology and No Substance', it was not necessary to read to the end of the review to know that the critic considered it all 'superficiality and subjectivism' (Fraser 1995), and without any theoretical grounding. Detractors of architectural phenomenology portrayed its hypostatization of sensory experience as an essentialist, ahistorical, anti-theoretical, irrational, and subjective flight from all scholarly conventions and discourse. Significantly, practising architects felt as compelled to defend architectural phenomenology as architect-historians – a testament to its lasting influence in the profession even after it became intellectually suspect. Oswald Mathias Ungers (1926–2007), chairman of the architecture department at Cornell University during the critical years between 1969 and 1975, came forward with 'I Am Trying to Save the Phenomenology of Architecture' (Bouman and van Toorn 1993), defending the idea that architects could grasp the historical significance of places, and express it architecturally, by experiencing their primordial form. His was a defence of the idea of genius loci as the experiential origin of meaning in architecture, an idea that had been chiselled by Norberg-Schulz (1980) into a foundation stone of architectural phenomenology. At stake in these debates over the intellectual worth of architectural phenomenology were two of the most important themes in postmodernism: history and theory. Indeed, architectural phenomenology emerged as the recognition of the fact that these two ideas were inextricably (even if ambiguously) bound, and that a renewed understanding of history within architecture required a reformulation of the discipline's paradigms of intellectuality.

It is hard for students of architecture today to grasp why the mere mention of architectural phenomenology generates such polarizing responses in their teachers. Some enthusiastically embrace it – usually the design faculty – commonly using it to signify, more or less restrictively, the ideas of paying close attention to the role that sensory experience plays in our understanding of architecture, and of designing in such a way as to reinforce recognizable patterns of experiencing buildings. Others emphatically reject it – typically the history and theory faculty – as a soft type of history and theory at best, and at worst as a dangerous form of detheorized history and dehistoricized theory, which takes the critical bite out of intellectual work in order to operatively legitimate architecture's status quo. Students entering the academy encounter architectural phenomenology as a dividing line between theory and design, and therefore also as the element that enables the distinction between those two divisions of architecture. But that line has a history. It comes to us laden with associations with particular people, practices, places, schools, building projects, publications, and conferences. The trouble is that, despite the divisive role of architectural phenomenology, or perhaps because of it, we lack an unprejudiced account of its history, and of its role in shaping the intellectual developments we have come to know as postmodernism. The fact that architectural phenomenology has carried on without a proper description of itself is somewhat ironic, especially given the fact that, as its name suggests, it appropriated so much from phenomenological philosophy, which was, after all, initiated by Edmund Husserl as a method for the unprejudiced description of phenomena as they appeared in experience.

One of the prejudices standing in the way of a history capable of assessing the role of architectural phenomenology within postmodernism is the notion that intellectual changes happen abruptly. Intellectually speaking, postmodernism did not occur in architecture all at once. Rather, it happened in phases that were marked by the coalescing of disparate ideas and practices into coherent and identifiable patterns of thinking and doing. These phases are sufficiently different from one another to warrant different names and to be studied in detail and in relative independence. Architectural phenomenology was an early phase in the intellectual development of postmodernism. It was important not only for setting the stage for later structuralist and post-structuralist phases of postmodernism but also for radically expanding what was deemed legitimate intellectual work in architecture. It was the testing ground where new intellectual positions, such as that of the architect-historian, staked their claim to be a form of architectural practice by retaining various modes of aesthetic production, from graphic design to photography, and by simultaneously detaching themselves from professional building design and construction. It was also the testing ground for new sets of theoretical questions regarding the authenticity of the human experience of architecture and place, and the stability of history as a grounding source of design. Significantly, these questions were turned into their negative form during the later deconstructivist phase of postmodernism, but remained its defining themes. By the mid- to late 1980s, architect-historians were examining how unfamiliar and uncanny the experience of architecture and place could also be, as proof of the inauthenticity of all claims to experiential authenticity (Vidler 1992). They attacked the idea of history as the foundation for design as well, emphasizing the unsettling discontinuities and distortions inherent in historical master narratives.

Following in the line of such post-structuralist contributions, it is important to emphasize not just the lines of conceptual continuity but also the manner in which discontinuities and ruptures structured the transformation from the early to later phases of postmodernism. One cannot assume that architectural phenomenology always bore an overt similarity to what we know as (late) postmodern theory. The very history that concerns us would escape us if we were to selectively seek to match the dividing lines within contemporary architectural discourse onto the past, or to selectively fish out ideas from the post-war period, on the basis that they bear an outward resemblance to those we are familiar with, and to artificially cast them as the roots of a long arc to the present. Perhaps Robert Venturi, whose *Complexity and Contradiction in Architecture* (1966) is widely held to be the intellectual inauguration of a new postmodern thinking, has been the greatest beneficiary of this trend to edit history in the likeness of the present. Yet that approach can never account for the fact that sometimes ideas can also have their roots in their apparent opposites. Quite apart from Venturi, the thought that a building is a complex and contradictory object was also revealed in the need, felt by so many of his contemporaries, to constantly and obsessively affirm its stable identity – the first response to change is very often denial. Certainly in the case of postmodernism, the double disavowal of the possibility of a unified architectural object and a unified self were preceded by an intellectual probing of its opposite condition: of architecture as the stable setting of authentic human experience, one firm and basic enough to help people orient themselves in their new postmodern surroundings, grounding their sense of self, their identity, in particular places. By being careful not to impose the present condition onto the past, we begin to notice just how different postmodernism was at the outset from what it later became.

The most obvious discontinuity between the early and late phases of postmodernism is generational. The change in approaches and responses to the questions concerning the status of history and theory in architecture corresponds to a replacement of the players according to the inevitable logic of human ageing. Architectural phenomenology was the product of a generation born during the interwar period and reaching maturity in the post-war era, at a time when French existentialism stood as the emblem of intellectual sophistication in the West. Jean-Paul Sartre was particularly relevant to the new generation, both in his insistence on political commitment and in his demand that people should reject bad faith, stop leading lives according to the false conventions of prewar society, and opt instead for the pursuit of an authentic existence. Sartre contributed to youth subculture of the 1950s by encouraging individuals to express themselves through their actions, to take responsibility for those actions, and to have a strong sense of political commitment. His late post-war writings, which emphasized the importance of communal projects as the path to achieve personal authenticity, resonated with architects more than his earlier works, which were more narrowly concerned with individualistic morality. More importantly for our purposes, Sartre demonstrated the vitality of phenomenology when in Germany it 'seemed to have become a matter of past record, to be left to the historians of philosophy' (Spiegelberg 1982, 473).

Although popular with the young generation, Sartre's brand of existentialism suffered in American academia for being too Marxist and too staunchly hostile to religion in a country where most philosophers, although not overtly religious, 'were not far removed from the spiritual traditions of their families and communities, and they were averse to a philosophy that trampled too indelicately on remaining religious sensibilities' (Fulton 1999, 135). In American architectural circles, Sartre's phenomenological sources, which seemed less politically charged, became far more influential than existentialism *tout court*. Paradoxically, religion served as the Trojan horse within which phenomenology entered American architectural discourse. During the dark period of McCarthyism, Catholic schools served as safe havens from communist suspicion where young architects were given the latitude to study Sartre, Merleau-Ponty, and other phenomenologists (McCumber 2001). It was those young Catholics who first brought an interest in phenomenology to American architecture – the influence of Catholics can be traced in the intellectual trajectory of Labatut, Moore, Norberg-Schulz and Frampton. Religion thus played a central role in the architectural reception of phenomenology, although it remained muted under the more secular language of philosophy.

The second generation of postmodern architect-historians, trained in the wake of 1968, matured in an academic environment with different intellectual references. French thought remained important for them, but they were attracted to younger Parisian thinkers, including Jacques Derrida, Gilles Deleuze, Roland Barthes, and others. Many of these thinkers, reacting to the sway of Sartre, sought to undermine him by establishing their own direct interpretations of Marxism and of German phenomenology. In Barthes's first book, *Writing Degree Zero* (1953), there was an open acknowledgement of his indebtedness to Sartre when he stated his goal as to impart a more correctly Marxist dimension to the existentialist notion of commitment. Derrida's introduction to his translation of Husserl's *The Origin of Geometry* (1989 [1962]), made it impossible for late postmodern architect-historians to speak of deconstruction without having to acknowledge phenomenology, and by extension architectural phenomenology (Krell 1997).

Of the second generation of postmodern architect-historians, Mark Wigley carried out the most sustained and self-reflective analysis of deconstruction from the perspective of architecture (1993), and he was also one of the harshest critics of architectural phenomenology (1992). Mark Jarzombek (2000), Hilde Heynen (1999 [1993]) and K. Michael Hays (1991) are also among those who made noteworthy contributions to situating late postmodern thinking in opposition to architectural phenomenology, but inevitably in relation to it. This younger generation reproached architectural phenomenology for mishandling the postmodernist themes of history and theory, and for having essentialized both into a specious notion of universal human experience. Operating from a Foucaultian intellectual frame of reference, they sought to rectify this shortfall by historicizing the concepts of history and theory within the larger evolution of architectural discourse, showing architectural phenomenology's claims to universality to be contingent on unexamined Western Enlightenment ideals, and proving its depiction of experience as a natural human condition to be highly artificial. They also viewed architectural phenomenology as operating in political bad faith, insofar as it purported to stand for place-based architectural practices found in marginal regions of the world, but actually only allowed non-Western architects entry as long as they spoke its Western language of universal experience.

Significantly, charges about politics flew in both directions. The older generation of architectural phenomenologists often presented post-structuralists as having no political commitment, and as having turned the postmodernist notion of pluralism into a toothless relativity where every idea was given equal value. This mutual reception (or rejection) across generations helped in forging the sense of an overblown gulf between the early and the late phases of postmodernist architectural thought. There were noteworthy attempts at reconciliation, such as the work of Michael Benedikt (1987; 1991), but, insofar as they did not account for how social relations distort intellectual history, they could not explain why they fell on deaf ears. The moment of greatest tension between these two generations of postmodern thinkers was the late 1980s, when both were active with equal force and capacities. That is the time when postmodernism, intellectually speaking, is thought to have irrupted in architectural discourse – basically at the time when postmodernism, as an aesthetic style expired. In the absence of a social history, the deconstructive phase of postmodernism appeared to have arrived magically, motivated out of some internal discursive logic beyond the reach of any human agent.

Architectural phenomenology's discursive ramifications are daunting in scope. It exists both inside and outside of the academy, somewhere between publications, academic genealogies, built projects, discursive practices, and personal friendships. On the European side, Ernesto Nathan Rogers (1909–1969) was a key figure for the development of architectural phenomenology. Rogers was considered 'the hero-figure of European architecture in the late Forties and early Fifties' (Banham 1959). He was a partner in the renowned BBPR firm, the editor of *Casabella Continuità*, Italy's premier architectural journal, and an active member of CIAM. Rogers introduced one of the major ideas of architectural phenomenology: the belief that history, the kind of history that matters in architecture, was contained within buildings as a cumulative collective experience, and could therefore only be accessed experientially. It was a transposition of the old idea that art contains the intentions of the artist into a collective and historical plane. His notion of tradition undermined the modernist emphasis on form. If modernism was to be the permanent revolution it promised to be, then it demanded the constant, physical revision of obsolete formal elements. Modernism, for Rogers, was the experience of the revolution of history in the present, as the continuous transformation of tradition. Modern architecture could only achieve its promise of liberation from the past by internalizing it, by resynthesizing its present forms within an existing tradition. In his view, to adjudicate modernism only to the architecture originating after the 1920s, as Reyner Banham and other historians had done, was to negate its liberating potential, by reducing it into forms (Rogers 1959).

Rogers cultivated exchanges among the circle of young architects and phenomenologists that formed around *Casabella*, including architects Giancarlo de Carlo, Vittorio Gregotti, Guido Canella, Aldo Rossi, Ezio Bonfanti, Gae Aulenti, and Joseph Rykwert, who worked as a junior architect in the BBPR studio during the early 1950s, as well as some philosophy students like Salvatore Veca. Under Rogers, a small but influential group of young European architects was forged who explored phenomenology as an intellectual framework for rethinking modernism. Each of them absorbed Roger's notion of tradition and developed it in their own way. Most of them however (notably Vittorio Gregotti and Aldo Rossi) dropped phenomenology in favor of the more clearly Marxist teachings of the Frankfurt School – the notable exception being Rykwert (see Gregotti and Otero-Pailos 2000; Molinari 2000).

Whereas architectural phenomenology in continental Europe petered out after Rogers, it took root and was developed in the United States thanks to the work of Labatut. Trained in the prestigious Parisian atelier of Victor Laloux, Labatut emigrated to the United States in 1927 where he transformed the stale Beaux-Arts pedagogy of the American academy into a vibrant new anti-formalist approach to modern architecture that remained grounded on historical precedents. The key to his success was his ability to formulate a third alternative to the modernist dyad of abstraction and figuration, which he called Eucharistic architecture, referring to buildings where one could experience a timeless spiritual content within building materials. Eucharistic architecture incorporated images drawn from popular culture, such as the figure of George Washington or the image of Christ, into otherwise abstract spatial compositions as a means to attract and focus the attention of visitors on the experience of material textures, lighting conditions, and sound atmospheres. Ultimately, his designs were meant to entice visitors to turn their attention inward, towards their body, where they could empathically experience the spirit of architecture, or in the words of philosopher Jacques Maritain, Labatut's friend and interpreter, 'the movement of immobile things' (1961).[1]

Way before his students Robert Venturi and Charles Moore embraced American kitsch, Labatut had made the case that the historical sources of architecture should be expanded beyond the reduced vocabulary of classicism to include roadside commercial advertising billboards and other emblems of popular culture. The key to that expansion was Labatut's four-step process to *learn* to experience existing things in a modern way, *assimilate* the inner experiential lessons, *forget* the outer form of the object, and *create* the same experience within a different form (Labatut 1979). To carry out this process, Labatut developed a sophisticated design methodology to distort and break up the unity of inherited forms according to camouflage techniques that he learnt while serving in WWI, such as contour and object matching. In this way, non-architectural figurative objects as well as historic architectural styles could be given new abstract and modern architectural forms. At the end of WWII, Giedion proclaimed modern architecture to be in crisis on account of its inability to satisfy cultural demands for symbolism. He presented Labatut's work as an exemplary way out of the predicament and towards a New Monumentality (Giedion 1944).

Charles Moore was one of Labatut's most talented students. A mercurial personality who reveled in the play of irony and deadpan humour, he became the poster child of America's freewheeling postmodernism, and an extraordinarily influential teacher. His buildings are famous for their ironic juxtapositions of high and low cultural references, simultaneously celebrating kitsch, consumer culture, and classicism. Moore has unjustly been relegated to the status of a superficial, touchy-feely architect who operated from the hip, without a well-developed theory of architecture. But Moore's anti-theoretical position was a highly sophisticated theory about the primacy of personal experience and memory in the intellectual understanding and aesthetic interpretation of architectural history, which became central to the development of architectural phenomenology. Unlike Labatut, Moore was a prolific writer. Two key texts mark his theorization of architectural phenomenology. His PhD dissertation, *Water and Architecture* (1957), was the first analysis of Gaston Bachelard's work within American architectural discourse. In it, Moore developed the notion that all architecture originated in archetypal psychological experiences, which he called poetic images. For him, the postmodern recuperation of historical precedents in contemporary architecture entailed a search for those poetic images. But this search could not be conducted in a detached intellectual way. It was a matter of experiencing buildings directly. The second key text was *Body, Memory, and Architecture* (1977), co-authored with Kent Bloomer, in which he made the case for shedding the modernist definition of architecture in terms of the abstract concepts of space and form in favour of, as the title indicates, concrete bodily experiences, and place-bound memories. Here, the more concretely experiential notion of memory replaced the abstraction that is history. There were key intellectual milestones in the path that lead from the first to the last texts, but they were buildings, not books: especially the three houses that Moore designed for himself at Orinda (1962), Sea Ranch (1965), and New Haven (1966). In these houses Moore developed and perfected the aedicule, a small temple or house within a house, as the archetypal poetic image of inhabitation (an interest which he developed after reading Summerson's 'Heavenly Mansions' (1963)). The aedicule figured as the elemental architectural frame for human orientation. Wherever it was built, it served to ground human memories in that particular place. Indeed, Moore built one every time he changed residence. The theorization of architecture as a set of archetypal mnemonic experiences became a leitmotif of postmodernism. The intellectual status of the building itself hangs in the balance of Moore's work. He refused to cede intellectuality over to pure mental acts, considering it essential to situate it in the more ambiguous realm of the experiencing body.

Moore's most influential years as a teacher were spent at Yale, first as Chair of the Department of Architecture (1965–1967), followed by a term as Dean (1969–1970) and as Professor (1970–1975). At the time, Yale was along with Northwestern University, the most important centre for the study of phenomenology in America, a social circle centred around the figure of John Wild, the most prominent American phenomenologist of the postwar years. The Society for Phenomenology and Existential Philosophy (founded in 1962) was highly visible at Yale (Edie 1969). Under Moore, the architecture school welcomed other Yale phenomenologists like Karsten Harries, who devoted much of his later career to teaching philosophy to architects. The 1960s political student activism was felt particularly strongly at Yale. Phenomenology presented the possibility of a social commitment without all the Marxist rhetoric. Wild increased the distance between phenomenology and Marxism by arguing that 'the connection between existentialist thought and any definitive political philosophy, as it is now presented to us, is wholly arbitrary and unstable' (1955, 166). Clearly responding to the pressures of McCarthyism, Wild presented phenomenology as 'ideological armament' against the infiltration of Marxist thought into the United States, and therefore as the philosophical counterpart to the Cold War arms race (1955, 5–6). The search for experience, made architectural phenomenologists at Yale appear above the fray of politics and business, engaged in a disinterested pursuit of the essence of architecture. Socially, this helped them claim the higher ground of impartiality *vis-à-vis* corporate modernist architects, and to gather toward themselves all the power generated by the post-war struggle to humanize modern architecture.

The political ambiguity of phenomenology's career, covering the full spectrum between European Marxism and American McCarthyism, came in part from its central claim to be a search for an unbiased description of human experience, an account free from prejudice, and therefore free from politics. Put differently, phenomenology claimed the ground of a pre-political discourse. In American architecture schools, this ground had already been staked out by the experientialist discourse of art psychology, through the writings of art historians like Rudolph Arnheim (Jarzombek 2000).

Christian Norberg-Schulz was Giedion's brightest and certainly most famous student. Based in Oslo, Norberg-Schulz's books were nonetheless incredibly popular in the 1970s in the United States, and indeed in much of the world. His obsession with rootedness and authenticity contrasts with his cosmopolitan life and upbringing as an architecture student first at the ETH in Zürich, then at Harvard where he was steeped in Arnheim's gestalt theory of perception. His first books *Intentions in Architecture* (1965), and *Existence, Space and Architecture* (1971) were heavily influenced by Arnheim. The derivation can be seen as much in the texts as in the images, which Norberg-Schulz set against each other in precise ways in order to describe and illustrate various archetypal experiences of architecture. Arnheim asserted that all thinking involved visual perception (in the form of a mental image) and, conversely, that visual perception was commensurate with intellectual work (Arnheim 1969; Beardsley 1971). Diagrams, according to Arnheim were the link between the visual and the textual, and he therefore spent much of his time trying to figure out the diagrammatic structure of paintings. His theories served to add legitimacy to the central tenet of architectural phenomenology that practice and theory are inseparable and ambiguously related.

Norberg-Schulz became best known for *Genius Loci: Towards a Phenomenology of Architecture* (1980), in which he defined architecture as the expression of the spirit of the place in which it is built. The book instantly made Norberg-Schulz into the main interpreter of Heidegger for architectural audiences. Like other architectural phenomenologists before him, Norberg-Schulz presented the thesis that architecture was the expression of human experiences. Where he differed was in situating the origin of those experiences in nature. According to his theory, the original structure of human experience was given in the landscape. He equated those original experiences with the *genius loci*, such that in order to express the history of the place in contemporary designs, one should not necessarily look at historic buildings, and should instead go back to the original source in the topography. Following Arnheim, but also influenced by the work of Kevin Lynch, Norberg-Schulz advanced the notion that visual diagramming was the key to the exegesis of the intellectual content of the landscape. Norberg-Schulz used carefully framed photographs as the basis for presenting the visual patterns he saw in landscapes, referring to them first as 'topological figures', then '*genius loci*', and finally '*alétheic* images'. The last term made reference to Heidegger's notion of *Alétheia* or self-disclosed truth. But this was an instrumental misreading of Heidegger, who after all mounted one of the most powerful critiques of representation as the dominant intellectual paradigm of modernity (Heidegger 1977 [1952]).

Quite apart from the clearly essentializing tendencies of his photo[historio]graphy, Norberg-Schulz blazed new trails into architectural historiography bringing with him the visual habits and ambiguous intellectuality of the architect. His books represented a new theoretical way of doing architectural history that shifted the status of photographs from illustrations to narrative interpretations, and demoted the text to mere accompaniment. Although he remained committed to the primacy of practice, and considered himself an architect, the fact is that his intellectual work was entirely contained within the format of the printed book. Quite against his own intentions, Norberg-Schulz made great strides in carving out a position for architectural theory as something detached from practice.

As architectural phenomenologists slowly codified the ambiguous realm of architectural intellectuality into graphic design principles and ideas, they also began to expose some of its contradictions. Kenneth Frampton attempted to resolve some of these tensions. Born into the English working class with a privileged mind, Frampton was educated at the Architectural Association, and soon found himself drawn into the world of architectural criticism, graphic design, and publishing. He was technical editor of *Architectural Design* from 1962 to 1965, and after his arrival at Princeton University in 1964, he became a well-known figure in New York architectural circles. He continued his career in publishing as co-founder and editor of *Oppositions* in 1973, with Peter Eisenman and Mario Gandelsonas. Frampton achieved international recognition in the early 1980s for his theory of Critical Regionalism, which was mostly received as an architectural aesthetic that celebrated the synthesis of industrial building with local craft. But in reality Critical Regionalism was also intended to be a new theory for understanding (or rather producing) the history of architecture that led up to it. Critical Regionalism proclaimed that modern architecture had ended multiple times, in a series of unresolved crises caused by the inability to give proper architectural expression to key advances in industrial building technology. Modern architecture had, in that sense, ceased to exist (or failed to be born), and all that was left was building. Critical Regionalism was meant as a call to redress the asymmetry between building and architecture, by rethinking what architecture could be. Frampton actually had carried out this rethinking before he landed on the term 'Critical Regionalism', in a series of seminal essays written roughly during the 1970s, including 'Labour, Work and Architecture' (1969), 'Industrialization and the Crises in Architecture' (1973), 'On Reading Heidegger' (1974), 'Constructivism: The Pursuit of an Elusive Sensibility' (1976), and 'The Status of Man and the Status of His Objects: A Reading of The Human Condition' (1982). In these essays he borrowed heavily from Hannah Arendt's phenomenological analysis of the public sphere to argue that architecture was the elevation of building to an aesthetic, which people could experience as the *res publica*. The existence of architecture, he thought, was ethically necessary as common experiential foundation for the individual development of fully human lives; that is lives capable of experiencing a shared social reality. The trouble was that in the age of industrialization, it had become impossible to elevate building above the mere labour of construction. Following Arendt's analysis of surplus labour in a capitalist society, Frampton wondered how one could make the labour of building yield an aesthetic surplus. His answer came towards the end of his career with the theory of tectonics, which basically focused attention on construction joints as the sites where the first signs of aesthetic surplus could be detected.

With tectonics, Frampton in a sense came full circle to the beginnings of his career, when, working on graphic designs for *Architectural Design*, he had first explored the question of how *not* to represent a building, but to graphically produce an experience that was in excess of the building itself, yet tantamount to it. Frampton's notion of surplus experience, as variously revised into Critical Regionalism and Tectonics, was perhaps the last serious attempt to work out postmodernism's themes of history and theory aesthetically. Ultimately, Critical Regionalism was a theory of the crisis of aesthetics as model for intellectuality, and as such, it represented the last vital gasp of architectural phenomenology.

To unpack postmodernism's central notions of history and theory requires understanding its intellectual history. Rogers, Labatut, Moore, Norberg-Schulz and Frampton, Rykwert, Vesely and others looked to philosophy in general and phenomenology in particular, for a coherent intellectual framework through which to recast historic architectural forms into an experiential content. Architectural phenomenology coalesced into a coherent discourse through the intertwining of the search for authentic experience and the search to reconcile modernism with its own history. It was not a wholesale rejection of modernism. Rather, it was ambivalent. Its denunciations of modernism often co-existed with enthusiastic pleas for architecture to be built according to true modernist principles.

Architectural phenomenologists defended the uniqueness of the architect's individual experience, yet they also resisted the idea that experience was purely individualistic. Believing that architects should retain commitments outside the self, architectural phenomenologists pined for a community of shared values and beliefs in which to ground self-expression. They were part of a wide 1960s interest in the intersection of 'community' and architecture, ranging from the cries of neighbourhood preservation organizations against urban renewal to psychosexual utopias of communal life like Drop City. Kenneth Frampton's British New Left politics led him to interpret the capitalist opposition to organized labour as an erosion of community. Inspired by the Arts and Crafts ideology (and socialism) of William Lethaby and William Morris, he envisioned a return to medieval guild societies, with modern architects as master masons at the centre. Christian Norberg-Schulz's Catholicism led him to identify modernism's hypostatization of objectivity with the secularization of society, a process he thought led to the collapse of social order and to visual chaos. He called for modernism to return to the 'spiritual roots' that he thought were the source of all meaningful and visually ordered architecture. For Charles Moore, who had to publicly repress his homosexuality in order to survive the conservatism of the Cold War, the severe minimalist aesthetics of modernism meant the denial of corporeal pleasure and interpersonal contact. To rebuild community, he believed, modern architecture had to become erotic, transgressing aesthetic codes to stimulate the senses of visitors with intimate sensual experiences. Each of these three architects felt that the dominant forms of post-war modernism excluded the defining experiences of their social community and, by extension, of their generation.

In their search to differentiate themselves from the modernist tradition they were educated into, they faced a new set of problems: The question was less how to create something new, and more how to avoid repeating something old. To renew modernism they felt they had to turn away from modernism's aesthetic conventions. This trait differentiated architectural phenomenologists from many of their contemporaries, most notably the New York Five, who revived the 'original' modern style and forms of the historical European avant-gardes. Architectural phenomenologists sought to establish their connection to the origins of modernism not by adhering to its historical style but by attempting to experience the world in the same way as the modern masters – that is, originally, authentically, and ahistorically.

Paradoxically, their awareness of modernism's history led them to search for an ahistorical constant underpinning all modern architectural expression. While working independently of one another, they all arrived at the conclusion that sensorial experience was this timeless constant – a supposition that surprisingly ran counter to phenomenology's insistence on the historicality of experience. For them, all architecture ever built was organized according to an elemental language of basic bodily experiences. To reconnect modern architecture to the rest of architectural history meant understanding the deeper pre-linguistic experiential language that, they believed, was the organizational principle of every building ever built. On the surface, their individual quests to understand architecture in term of experiential content seem as varied as the aspects of architecture that they each focused on: Labatut was obsessed with how the visual perception of scale, and the tactile sensing of texture changed in relation to one's movement; Moore was absorbed by how small interior spaces could feel enormous; Norberg-Schulz was fixated on expressing the relationship of the building to its site in terms of visual patterns; and Frampton was preoccupied with how small tectonic details could visually express the structural logic of an entire building culture. Despite the differences in terms of what aspects of architecture they focused on in their writings, the intellectual operations they performed in those texts shared important commonalities.

Architectural phenomenology, the discourse that wove together sensorial experience and architectural history, achieved coherence by interlacing three thematic strands. The first theme, *experience*, entailed the conviction that the senses were not historically determined. The fact that buildings are designed with the human body in mind, allowed architects to posit elemental sensorial experiences as the transhistorical origin of all architecture. Severed from historic specificity and essentialized, bodily experience became the point of entry for spiritualist and religious interpretations of architecture, which began to turn against modernism's secular objectivity. The second theme, *history*, involved the modernist belief that historical buildings were expressions of a deeper structuring reality, which was thought to remain constant across time. Architects rejected historicist claims, such that architectural expression is solely determined by its historical context. Instead they explored new forms of historiography meant to identify and understand precisely those aspects of architecture that might not be historically determined. The third theme, *theory* emerged as an early instance of interdisciplinarity. To support the thesis that experience was the 'essence' of architecture, architects searched for evidence in other disciplines, most notably in phenomenological philosophy. In these early examples of 'scholarly' work, before architecture PhD programmes were established and the rise of theory in the late 1970s, intellectuality appeared as an ambiguous but unique realm, at the intersection of the professional architect's and the historian's practice. The experimental nature of this intellectual realm transformed the tradition of architectural historiography, resulting in important new theories and modes of writing architectural history, which incorporated the visual and experiential sensitivity of architectural design.

Woven together, these three strands defined architectural phenomenology and its legacy. The number of architects who participated in shaping architectural phenomenology is clearly greater than four. My intention is not to assign to Labatut, Moore, Norberg-Schulz, and Frampton the status of 'founders' of architectural phenomenology. Quite the contrary, their works were formed through their relationships to a wide social web. Their names have become synonymous with architectural phenomenology in the same way that the names of certain composers are associated to certain genres of music. Each individual gives us access to a broad assemblage of mentors, collaborators, commentators, enemies, and students, who also participated in the broader restructuring of modernism. These individuals were in contact with each other but resisted seeing themselves as a group. Socially, architectural phenomenology was not a self-identified homogeneous block, but rather a discontinuous social assemblage. Yet this social disjointedness did not prevent it from achieving coherence as a shared intellectual framework, which initiated the intellectual transformation we have come to know as postmodernism.

Although its centrality in architectural theory has been much diminished, architectural phenomenology continues to be the primary discursive mode for dealing with questions of perception and affect. Alberto Pérez-Gómez, a professor of architectural history and head of PhD studies at McGill University in Montreal, is among the most influential figures of a younger generation of architectural phenomenologists, trained by Joseph Rykwert and Dalibor Vesely at the University of Essex, which includes David Leatherbarrow, Helen Powell, and Daniel Libeskind (Thomas 2004). Pérez-Gómez arrived in Essex from Mexico, where he had studied architecture and been exposed to the writings of Spanish phenomenologist José Ortega y Gasset. His 1979 dissertation, later published as *Architecture and the Crisis of Modern Science* (1979; 1983) in an obvious reference to Husserl (1970), portrayed architectural phenomenology as the way to surmount the contradictions of modernity. For Pérez-Gómez, modern architecture had its roots in neoclassicism, which in turn was the culmination of a long Cartesian tradition to make architecture into a science by imposing abstract mathematical theoretical models upon practice. For him, Jacques-Nicolas-Louis Durand's (1760–1834) attempt to reduce architectural design to the 'science' of combining interchangeable modular parts according to functional requirements, signified the negation of the poetic artistic content of architecture, which could only be restored through a phenomenological return to authentic experiences of buildings (Pérez-Gómez 1979; 1983). Pérez-Gómez's search for an undistorted experience of architecture in history was the subject of much criticism, inspired by Manfredo Tafuri, for distorting historiography itself in an 'operative' way (McLeod 1987).

Architectural phenomenology is today well established as a legitimate scholarly enterprise that is well represented in masters and PhD programmes in architecture, especially in second-tier schools, even if it is conspicuously absent in the leading centres of theoretical reflection. The appearance of discrimination fuelled the creation of sectarian societies aimed at promoting architectural phenomenology. Associations such as EDRA (Environmental Design Research Association) appeared as umbrella societies for architects interested in phenomenology to network.[2]

By the early 1990s, new publications begun to appear that maintained the flame of architectural phenomenology. Significantly, as architectural phenomenology appeared to lose its academic footing in architecture, phenomenological geographers and philosophers came to the rescue. For instance, philosopher and geographer David Seamon founded the *Environmental and Architectural Phenomenology Newsletter* (1990), and established the *SUNY Series in Environmental and Architectural Phenomenology* (Seamon and Coates 1993). Philosopher Karsten Harries (1983, 20) encouraged architectural phenomenologists with infinitely quotable pronouncements such as 'Architecture is at least as likely to edify as philosophy'. The 'ethical function' of architecture, he argued replaying an old cliché, was to get society beyond modernity's 'arbitrariness' by making people *feel* the 'wholeness' of the 'original' language of the senses and the imagination (18). Michael Zimmerman (1985), a phenomenologist who became interested in architecture while teaching at Tulane University in the 1970s, encouraged architects to pursue an 'ego-less attunement to Logos'. Don Ihde, philosopher and Dean of the School of Humanities and Fine Arts, and professor of philosophy at SUNY Stonybrook, tried to recover the sense in which architectural phenomenology was intellectually postmodern (Ihde 1988). Philosopher Edward Casey, another professor at SUNY Stonybrook, tried to associate architectural phenomenology with the more popular architects of the moment, arguing that Peter Eisenman and Bernard Tschumi created places that emerged out of human experiences of being 'implaced' in an unfolding, dynamic processes of 'embodiment' (1997). Casey's selective and instrumental account of the intersections between architecture and phenomenology is evidence of how social struggles distort knowledge. His genealogy of architects was an attempt to validate his own position in relation to the changing social structure of architecture, of who was 'in' and who was 'out'.

Perhaps in response to the new encroachments of philosophers and geographers on the intellectual territory staked out by architects, a number of recent conferences have attempted to reclaim the history of architectural phenomenology as a movement led by architects. The 2001 symposium 'Architectural Observations: Phenomenological Aspects of Architecture and its Education', which took place at the department of architecture of TUE University in Eindhoven, the Netherlands, is representative of this trend. Participants included Alberto Pérez-Gómez (McGill, Montreal), Juhani Pallasmaa (Helsinki), Tony Fretton (TU, Delft), Dalibor Vesely (Cambridge University), Dan Hoffman (Arizona State University), Wim van den Bergh (TU, Eindhoven), Kim Shkapich (Cooper Union, New York), and Aliki Economides (McGill, Montreal).

With its promise to recover the fullness of a lost experience of reality, architectural phenomenology became the catch basin for all disillusionment with modernity. The architect-historians of the 1970s exploited that disillusionment to establish their authority over architecture. They cast themselves as the ideal observers of architecture by claiming that immediate experience was not immediate at all, but rather reality was always hidden behind veils of self-deceptions, and distorting technological manipulations. They claimed that the immediate experience of buildings required a level of aesthetic competency only they had achieved, but that everyone could learn. Architectural phenomenology produced new architectural standards of intellectual, aesthetic, and historiographical competency. Through its objective and discursive mechanisms, it organized the attention of architects towards what mattered (intellectuality, aesthetic experience, history), and structured the functional relationships between these matters. It posited a transhistorical pre-verbal experiential language as the synthesis of these matters, and as the source of all architectural expression. This interest in pre-verbal language was instrumental in opening architects to the emergent discipline of structural linguistics and to semiotics. While the idea that this pre-verbal experiential language of architecture could be expressed in many styles opened modern architects to historic architecture and spawned postmodernism, the phenomenological ideal of aesthetic purity dovetailed into the modernist discourse of abstraction and survived the demise of the postmodern style. Today, architectural phenomenology undergirds the sensualist neo-modernist fantasy of an essential experiential origin to architecture. Paradoxically, the theoretical project that began as a search for a historically conscious modern architecture achieved its opposite. These lessons are paramount to theory today, when the post-critical pursuit of architectural expression outside of history and culture is again on the rise. If a critical historiography can be provisionally sketched out, along Pierre Bourdieu's definition, as an attempt to 'explore the limits of the theoretical box in which one is imprisoned [...] to provide the means for knowing what one is doing and for freeing oneself from the naïveté associated with the lack of consciousness of one's bounds' (1993, 184), then to write the history of architectural phenomenology is also to recognize that we are not entirely free from its grasp.

NOTES

1 My translation. Maritain, Letter to Labatut, (March 13, 1961), Box 7, *Jean Labatut Papers*, (Princeton University Department of Rare Books and Special Collections).

2 The Environmental and Architectural Phenomenology group held network meetings at Environmental Design Research Association conferences, beginning with the one held in April 6–9, 1990, at the University of Illinois, Champaign-Urbana.

8

Formalism and Forms of Practice

Sandra Kaji-O'Grady

There is no single and agreed definition of form or of formalism, but rather a series of arguments and examples spanning the nineteenth and twentieth centuries drawn from philosophy and applied to the criticism and practice of literature, music, the visual arts, and architecture. In its first appearance, in nineteenth-century German philosophical aesthetics, formalism was concerned with the mode of perception of forms in the absence of any meaning. It referred to a property of the seeing of objects, as Kant proposes. In the simplest terms, formalism is a methodological attitude – a mode of criticism – that derives its explanations from the formal relationships between parts of a work, be they musical notes, words, colours, marks, or volumes.

K. Michael Hays writes that the formalist position as it pertains to architecture is characterized by:

> The comparative absence of historical concerns in favor of attention to the autonomous architectural objects and its formal operations – how its parts have been put together, how it is a wholly integrated and equilibrated system that can be understood without external references, and as important, how it may be reused, how its constituent parts and processes may be recombined ... architectural operations are imagined to be spontaneous, internalized – that is, outside circumstantial reality – and assimilable as pure idea ... the way in which a building as a cultural object in time is possessed, rejected, or achieved is not addressed. (1984, 16)

Formalism comes into clearest view when seen in opposition to hermeneutic or contextual criticism, wherein the object of study is situated in a broader network of heterogeneous and often contested human relationships within society. Indeed, Russian formalism, which was concerned with poetry, developed in the 1910s in reaction to what was seen as the failure or inadequacies of the practice of interpreting literary texts by relating them to the historical circumstances and politics of the era in which the work was written, its philosophical or theological milieu, or the experiences and frame of mind of its author. Russian formalism was anti-realist, denying that morality or philosophy should be the concern of literature.

German formalist aesthetics, too, emerged antagonistically in response to classical theories of imitation and representation in the arts – proposing formal compositions as an exercise in creating from nothing according to an internal logic. Form was no longer thought of as an expression of content but as co-existing with the idea. In the twentieth century, American formalist art critic Roger Fry contended that art should be directed not at illusion but at being genuinely creative. Fry writes of the post-impressionists that 'they do not seek to imitate form, but to create form ... they aim not at illusion, but at reality' (1961 [1912], 189). Art aims at new realities, and artworks are new entities that enter the real world in their own right. For architectural historian Alan Colquhoun, formalism is 'that type of thought which stresses rule-governed relationships rather than relationships of cause and effect ... it is concerned with the "how" of things, not with the "why"' (1994 [1987], 76). The artist Joseph Kosuth similarly claims that art is 'abstract in relation to cultural meaning, in the way that the noises we utter called words are meaningful only in relation to a linguistic system, not in relation to the world' (Siegel 1985, 224).

Throughout the twentieth century, the fates of formalism and contextual hermeneutics – in architecture, as elsewhere – are intertwined, with proponents of each arguing over the philosophical authority or richness of its critical engagements and, even more vehemently, for the ethical and political consequences of its position. As Pérez-Gómez observes: 'For more than two centuries, architects, critics and theoreticians have been arguing functionalist and formalist positions, opposing art to social interests and ethics to poetic expression' (2006, 4). Current post-critical theories in architecture as promulgated by Somol and Whiting attempt a synthesis between aspects of resistance available in formalist autonomy and the complexities of society and technological change that they believe need to be addressed. In 'Notes Around the Doppler Effect and Other Moods of Modernism', Somol and Whiting contend that: 'If critical dialectics established architecture's autonomy as a means of defining architecture's field or discipline, a Doppler [post-critical] architecture acknowledges the adaptive synthesis of architecture's many contingencies' (2002, 75). The kind of synthesis they propose is elusive, for the two positions are mutually exclusive. Formalism is not simply an alternative framework for understanding works of art. Indeed, for those who support the hermeneutic approach to aesthetics it is logically impossible. Mieke Bal, for example, explains that 'Aesthetics is also a context, which is why formalism necessarily fails' (1992, 566).

Formalism ultimately fails to bracket out context at the same time as it fails to account for it in the aesthetic experience, yet as an operative and influential narrative across the arts its success is unquestionable. Formalist criticism in both art and architecture has, over the course of the last century, established priorities and set limits to discourse; shaped disciplinary history and borders; and had tangible effects on the way architecture and art are produced and realized, in addition to how they are apprehended.

Formalism developed from a mode of criticism into a way of making and experiencing art and architecture, as well as a definition of art and of contemporaneity. It was, however, not homogeneous. Formalist criticism tends not towards descriptive and neutral accounts of the formal attributes of a work, as one might initially expect, but typically advocates one approach over others. Formalism has been used to promote, provoke, or dismiss one art or architectural practice over another, not so much on aesthetic grounds as on ethical or moral differences. This is most readily observed in the influence of the pre-eminent art critic Clement Greenberg, whose advocacy for a particular mode of formalism in painting reached a very wide audience and was such that he incited practices, in and out of painting, intended variously to refute or confirm his view.

Greenberg called on Kant's *Critique of Judgement* to give authority to his argument, yet shifted the exercise of taste towards a moralizing attempt to distinguish between the impure kitsch and the abstract and formal. Greenberg combined the idea of autonomy – in the form of the purity of the medium – with revolution in the form of progressive moves towards an ever more purified discipline. For Greenberg, the essence of painting lay in its flatness, and he supported abstract art that eschewed perspectival illusion, specifically the 'American-type' painting of abstract expressionism carried out in the late 1940s and early 1950s by Jackson Pollock, Barnett Newman, Robert Motherwell, and Willem de Kooning (1966). In this work, Greenberg found support for his belief that the way a painting is made and its purely visual aspects are of much greater import than its narrative content or its relationship to the visible world. Rosalind Krauss (1990), before breaking from his influence, concurred with Greenberg that what is specific to painting is its 'directness, the immediacy, the instantaneousness of showing'.

The support Greenberg gave for various artists is not always congruent with his theoretical arguments, and there is no clear path from one to the other. Rauschenberg's 'White Paintings' of the early 1950s, for example, seem to bring to a conclusion Greenberg's contention that the essential medium of painting is its flatness. Rauschenberg believed the 'White Paintings', purged as they are of any marks, colours, or images that might imply illusionistic depth, 'take you to a place in painting art has not been' (Hopps 1991, 230). Yet the critic dismissed the 'White Paintings' as having crossed the line between a determinate negation and the Dadaist realm of the gratuitous negative gesture. In 'Recentness of Sculpture', Greenberg subsequently implied that Rauschenberg's monochromes were responsible not only for the advent of minimalism but also for the rise of pop, assemblage, and other types of what he dismissed as 'novelty art' (1967, 24–26). Greenberg and his protégé Michael Fried viewed the minimalist sculpture that engaged with gravity and process and construction as a betrayal of formalism, thus missing its import. What had occurred was a shift from the optical formalism of abstract painting to a phenomenological formalism in which, artist Robert Morris proposes, 'the body measured the work as much as the eye' (1989, 343). Minimalism continued both a formalist attachment to autonomy and reduced conventions and an interest in inner reactions and projections in the face of external forms.

It is not surprising, of course, that there remains a great deal of subjective judgement and argumentation around the apprehension of works submitted to the formalist gaze. John Cage, who found Rauschenberg's 'White Paintings' an inspiration for his own silent compositions, viewed them as works concerned with process, since they allowed the incorporation of the temporal and changing in the way shadows and dust registered on their surfaces (1961, 236). The paradox is at the heart of art history generally, but, more specifically, is also embedded in the neo-Kantian tradition in which formalism is a condition of the subject, not of the object. The composition or appearance of the object is not, in fact, the issue. The issue lies with how our mind organizes and makes sense of what it sees and experiences. The object is the cause and the effect of the psychological condition of human empathy with the external world. Thus the same work of art may be interrogated by diverse critical positions, and problematically claimed to represent that position. When we add to individual subjectivity, the variables that come with different disciplines and their conventional media (sound versus text or colour, for example) and the different modes of engagement audiences may have with works (distracted and accidental versus the framing of the gallery or concert), then formalism takes on an even wider range of hues.

In architecture, formalist criticism was very early on conflated with form as the physical appearance of the building. Form was a key preoccupation in the development of modern architecture, and the history of the term is thoroughly accounted for by Adrian Forty in his entry on form in *Words and Buildings* (2000, 149–172). What is evident in this short history is that the discussions around form and formalism in architecture depart from those taking place in art, in that they return again and again to the relationship between form and function. Function is not viewed as an external force to be bracketed out along with other contextual aspects but as an internal force through which form emerges. Beginning with Viollet-le-Duc in the nineteenth century, good form was conceived as the outcome of the rational procedure of a careful consideration of function and structure (Hearn 1995, 12–13). Early formalist theories in architecture emphasized principles of unity and harmony in the composition of formal elements and the use of conventional systems of scale and proportion tied to a material and structural rationale.

Against the eclectic use of different styles and decorative elements, theorists such as Otto Wagner (1992 [1902]) put forward the argument that the shaping of form (*Formgebung*) should be consistent with its purpose and material – a purity of form could be achieved through using the simplest means and ensuring a correspondence with purpose and construction. These nineteenth-century ideas are the basis of twentieth-century modernist architectural practice. As Mies van der Rohe explained in 1923:

> We know no forms, only building problems. Form is not the goal but the result of our work. There is no form in and for itself ... Forms as goal is formalism; and that we reject. Nor do we strive for a style. Even the will to style is formalism. (Neumeyer 1991, 242)

Such theories, which see form as a by-product of construction or 'building problems', have an uncertain relationship with aesthetics and aesthetic judgement. As Viollet-le-Duc understood it, a rational design method may not always result in a beautiful and satisfying formal outcome, but a beautiful building is necessarily rational (Hearn 1995). A rational design method certainly does not account for the emergence of a modernist and international style in architecture in which we see a similarity of form across diverse programmes and construction methods. There is something of a contradiction in the emergence of *functionalism* as an aesthetic style.

One alternative to the view that formal beauty is the product of rational construction is to see it as something excessive, a supplement to necessity. The question is not resolved in contextual criticism either, where works of art or architecture are entirely the product of external forces. As Hays explains, hermeneutic or cultural criticism leaves architecture as 'essentially an epiphenomenon, dependent on socio-economic, political, and technological processes for its various states and transformations' (1984, 16).

The early discussions of form that saw architects breaking away from the repetition of historic styles are the background against which subsequent debates and questions play out. It is also this backdrop that goes part of the way to explaining the particular vehemence of critics of formalism in architecture. Opponents to formalism in architecture tend to focus not on the contradictions inherent in its arguments but on the perceived dereliction of the ethical responsibilities of the architect. It is, evidently for some, tolerable to bracket out questions of social context or function when writing a building review or a scholarly essay, but an outrage to make these excisions when designing a building.

Formalist ambitions in the practice of architecture are, consequently, denied, or dismissed as socially irresponsible, culturally irrelevant, solipsistic, and arbitrary. To some critics, formalist architectures such as that proposed by Peter Eisenman are simply not architecture. Michael Sorkin, for one, criticizes Eisenman's proposal for a House El Even Odd as far 'from any reasonable standard of legibility as habitable architecture' and snipes, 'Who, after all, really wants to live with or in a Sol LeWitt?' (1991, 38). While the three-dimensional grids and cubes that are the shared formal motif of LeWitt's sculptures and Eisenman's houses of the 1970s are acceptable as art, they are not, evidently, acceptable as architecture because these forms do not derive their purpose from the function or meaning of inhabitation and the logical processes of building. Likewise, the pursuit of the liberal individualism of the modern formalist artist, celebrated in figures such as Jackson Pollock, has no parallel in a discipline constrained by social expectations; function; assumptions about professionalism; budgets; and regulatory mechanisms pertaining to planning, safety, and amenity. Some architects may aspire to the uncompromising stance of fictional protagonist architect Howard Roark of Ayn Rand's *The Fountainhead*, but they are likely to find themselves sued or dismissed rather than venerated. The 'starchitects' produced by the contemporary cult of celebrity may have greater latitude and be sought out by clients for their individual style, but this does not mean they operate independently of clients and budgets, or outside of regulatory frameworks and construction processes.

These tensions are not merely questions of professional conduct, for, as philosopher Jacques Derrida points out, the use value of architecture is a foundational assumption of the discipline. Derrida proposes that:

> Architecture must have a meaning, it must present it and, through it, signify. The signifying or symbolical value of this meaning must direct the structure and syntax, the form and function of architecture. It must direct it from outside, according to a principle (arche), a fundamental foundation, a transcendence or finality (telos) whose locations are not themselves architectural ... The experience of meaning must be dwelling. (1986, 68–69)

For this reason and for its materiality, duration, and tradition, Derrida considers architecture to be antithetical to the philosophical practice of textual deconstruction and a last 'fortress of metaphysics'. This, no doubt, is what makes formalist experiments in architecture, such as the infamous hanging column and upside-down staircase of Peter Eisenman's House IV, so controversial. It is in gestures such as these – which shall be returned to in detail in this chapter – that the very limits of formalist theory for practice can be revealed. It is also through such inflammatory elements that the debates between advocates for formalism and those proponents of contextualism move from the realm of arcane skirmishes between academics and come to the attention of the entire profession. In the remainder of the chapter, some of the key attempts to develop and apply formalist positions in architecture will be discussed with reference to built and unbuilt projects. All of the approaches to be discussed affirm the centrality of the formal to architecture and would attest to a degree of disciplinary autonomy that would see formal development as internal to architectural history. Their ambitions are, however, wildly divergent.

A first group is concerned with the question of what constitutes good form and with establishing the principles by which good form can be distinguished from bad. Like Greenberg, this group articulates disciplinary boundaries in terms of the distinction between high art and kitsch, and between the avant-garde and the merely repetitive or nostalgic. We can trace the lines of thinking of this approach from the philosophical treatises of Kant, through Heinrich Wölfflin, Roger Fry, Clive Bell, and Clement Greenberg in art, and in architecture from Rudolf Wittkower to the work in the 1960s of Colin Rowe and Alan Colquhoun. Crucial to Greenberg's argument is the idea that formalist practice entails its own disciplinary critique. Greenberg argues that:

> The essence of Modernism lies ... in the use of the characteristic methods of a discipline to criticize the discipline itself – not in order to subvert it, but to entrench it more firmly in its area of competence. (1966, 101)

Formalism thus establishes a model for the very internal organization of the discipline itself – that is, the location and porosity of its disciplinary boundaries and the sources that drive historical change. Greenberg advocates for incremental rather than revolutionary change. Greenberg argues that: 'Nothing could be further from the authentic art of our time than the idea of a rupture of continuity. Art is ... continuity and unthinkable without it' (Carrier 2002, 33). Colquhoun, similarly, notes in relation to the twentieth-century architectural avant-garde that their formalist tendencies made it possible to argue against 'seeing architecture as continuously developing according to a historical law of technical and social revolution' proposing instead that modern architecture has 'reached a threshold which enables it to give form to the eternal laws of aesthetics' (1994, 76). Colquhoun was keen to see modernist architecture as a new expression of classical laws of harmonious proportion. The Gestalt figural reversal of classical 'good form', for example, that Rowe and Colquhoun discern in Le Corbusier's villa plans of the 1920s, confirms their belief in the continuity of formal principles internal to the discipline, even where these have become more demanding or complex.

Rowe and Colquhoun's interests go beyond 'good form' to questions of meaning and the relationship between architectural ideas and forms. Following Wittkower, Rowe's early writings, as Anthony Vidler observes (2003, 7), are largely concerned with drawing modern architecture back to the classical tradition. After contact with Robert Slutzky, a painter and teacher at the Cooper Union in the 1950s, Rowe concerns himself with Gestalt theory, with painting and with transparency. The layering of cubist collages provides the starting point for an attack on the glass façades of Gropius' Bauhaus building. In his later writings, Rowe takes formalism to be a special way of reading a text or a painting, or a building, which demands that transparency – the direct gaze towards a meaning – be redirected into opacity. In architecture, this would mean 'reading' a building as a kind of abstract text that emerges out of the dialectic between fact and effect, or between what Robert Slutzky phrased 'that which appears and that which signifies, form and meaning' (Rowe and Slutzky 1963). Given that architectural forms are more ambiguous than words in relation to their meanings, buildings could be experienced as a cause for multiple meanings. This is what Rowe and Slutzky mean when they advocate for 'phenomenal transparency' – the simultaneous taking place of phenomena that permeate each other without destruction – over 'literal transparency', when, for example, the structure of a building can be perceived through the application of glass (1963). Taken a step further – as Rowe's successor Peter Eisenman does – buildings can be read as mere pretexts for multiple mental constructs, and the idea given precedence over the object to the extent that the conceptual building is more significant than its realization.

Indebted to Colin Rowe's idea that architecture is a form of text to be read, Eisenman understands Rowe to be advocating the substitution of semantics (or content) with syntax and argues that formalism is such a gesture. By this, Rosalind Krauss proposes (1987, 173), Eisenman intends 'a consideration of form as a signal or notation'. Eisenman's approach, however, reunites formalism with a line of inquiry that begins with Russian formalism and continues through the Prague School to structuralism, post-structuralism, and deconstruction. This lineage and Eisenman's contribution to it is central to the 'critical architecture' or 'critical formalism' of the 1970s and 1980s, in which it is argued that an architecture of autonomous formalism might disrupt social norms and disciplinary assumptions by producing defamiliarizing spatial conditions. Eisenman's approach stands in stark contrast to the late modernist functionalism of the 1960s, which had seen in architecture renewed commitment to positivist research into behavioural sciences, systems theory, and technologies – all used to argue the inevitability of form in regard to its function.

The Russian formalists believed that, in contrast to everyday language, poetic language forces a defamiliarization through the difficult syllable and odd syntax. Literature is that which deviates from average speech because it intensifies, invigorates, and estranges mundane speech patterns. Likewise, Rosalind Krauss, in 1987, proposes that Eisenman's reading of formalism on linguistic terms allows him to produce architecture as a 'cognitive object ... [that] had the power to cause in its reader or viewer reflection upon the modes of consciousness' (168).

Eisenman's essay on 'Post-Functionalism' (1976) condenses his design preoccupations into a manifesto for an architecture that is self-referential, autonomous, and concerned with its own formal operations and disciplinary materials. Architectural practice, echoing Greenberg, is to be at once a critique of architecture and a theoretical project. As Eisenman makes clear, his renewal of the project of architectural autonomy, consists of two parts:

> First, the search for a way to make the elements of architecture the wall, the beam, the columns self-referential; and second, the development of a process of making that could produce self-reference without referring to the formal conventions of modernism. (1987, 172)

The first part of this project sees Eisenman attempt the articulation of a system of signs removed from their materiality and use function. He proposes that to make something conceptual in architecture requires interrupting the pragmatic aspects so that their functional derivation becomes secondary to a primary reading as a notation in a conceptual context. This is realized through 'cardboard architecture' – architecture that does not express its physicality as structure and material, and focuses on forms as signals of information – and by treating every part of the building as a marker or sign. Thus in the Frank house of 1972 there is a stair too low to descend without stooping, an extremely narrow door, and a column that interrupts the placement of the table in the dining-room table. House VI has a split in the floor of the master bedroom, which forces the clients to sleep apart in single beds. The overt challenge to functionalism entailed by these dysfunctional features has made the houses infamous and emphasizes the privilege given to the rules and processes of formal composition.

The second part of the project, the development of a self-referential process, has its origins in serial music. Essential to the process of defamiliarization was what poet Viktor Shklovsky called the laying bare of technique – the making transparent of the author's manipulation of the material, its artifice. The 'total serialism' of the composer Pierre Boulez takes up a similar idea about technique in music. Its highly artificial procedures are subsequently adopted in the visual arts in the late 1960s in the work of artists such as Sol LeWitt, Mel Bochner, Donald Judd, and Hanne Darboven, which is where Eisenman came into contact with them. The establishment of rules or procedures to be followed in the process of composition and performance was, with reference to Boulez, referred to in exhibitions and criticism as serial art, procedural art, and epistemological conceptualism. Exhibitions of serial art included *Art in Series* (1967), *Serial Imagery* (1968), and *Systemic Painting* (1966), and featured work by LeWitt, Morris, Judd, and Bochner among others. John Coplans (1968), Mel Bochner (1967), and Rosalind Krauss (1971) each make critical contributions to serial art in essays in *Artforum*. Eisenman's understanding of serial art and the intended consequences of using constraints and predetermined rules is gleaned from Sol LeWitt, about whose work he wrote in 'Conceptual architecture' (1971, 51–57). LeWitt argued that the rules used to generate unexpected outcomes appear logical, but in fact expose the arbitrariness of systems of meaning and representation. LeWitt proposes that 'all the planning and decisions are made beforehand and the execution is a perfunctory affair. The idea becomes the machine that makes the art' (1978 [1967], 166). Furthermore, 'Irrational thoughts should be followed absolutely and logically' (1969, 80).

Eisenman's Houses I–VI, like LeWitt's sculptures, use cubes and grids that are subjected to processes of permutation or transformation. The houses are also indebted to John Hejduk's seven houses of his so-called

Texas period (1954–1956) – these are similarly concerned with the formal variations that might be achieved using the constraint of a nine-square grid. While LeWitt and Hejduk lay out the variations individually, Eisenman layers the permutations within the one object, thereby achieving a more complex divided volume. This is then nominated as the building, and the process is restarted for each house. Each sequence demonstrates the cumulative effect of iterative and additive procedures. In the subsequent houses, Eisenman is critical of the presumption in his process of the cube as a pure and original state (1984, 63). Instigating a new process, which he calls decomposition, Eisenman deploys strategies of superimposition, addition, and nonsequentiality. Eisenman proposes the final plan of House X as a 'series of traces' that 'refer in a sense forward to a more complex and incomplete structure rather than backward to a unitary, simple, and stable structure' (1983, 48). His goal is 'the revelation of formal consistencies or regularities often through inconsistencies or incongruities ... in which the beginning and end point remain undefined and the chief principle was uncertainty: a working forward in time and backward in space' (1983, 46). Eisenman replaces the cube as the starting point with an 'el-shape' whose impure geometry suggests to him that it figures as a fragment and impure geometry. He believes the results cannot be immediately understood or perceived by the viewer because the previous moves are 'not simply the sum of a recognizable series of geometric or spatial conditions' (1984, 66).

In *The Architectural Uncanny*, Vidler suggests two different ways of understanding Peter Eisenman's houses. One is to the see the series of projects as 'an exercise in the rational exploration of certain pre-established formal constructs: a self-conscious logical sequence with a beginning and an end' (1992, 118). Alternatively, it is plausible to see them as 'posed self-consciously against anthropomorphic analogies, closed formal systems and functionalist derivations', in such a way that these designs 'overturn the classical system of representation' (1992, 118). The second view, in which formalism opposes meaning and humanist values, strikes the greatest challenge to the architectural discipline, and many of Eisenman's critics took seriously the challenge posed by his work. The most articulate opponents can be found in Mario Gandelsonas's proposal for a neo-functionalism and Kenneth Frampton's call for an architecture of place-creation – both essays were published in the journal *Oppositions* while Eisenman was an editor (Hays 1998).

Alongside and in opposition to the pursuit of good form, and taking a different approach than that evidenced in critical formalism, are experiments and theories in formlessness or bad form. Many of these developed out of an engagement with psychoanalysis that extends back to Adolf Loos' writings on order and cleanliness in the 1890s and the Freudian art criticism of Adrian Stokes in his 1930s meditations on the Renaissance and Venice. Psychoanalytic theory has since been taken up in a number of ways. Mark Cousin's series of articles on 'The Ugly' (1994; 1995) explore the theoretical conditions that pitch the ugly as the opposite of beauty and condemn it as error and evil. For Cousins, the principles of classical architecture – rhythm, repetition, and harmony – are all efforts to repress the disorganization that defines the ugly. Teresa Stoppani's 2007 essay on dust makes even further-reaching claims for the formless in architectural history and theory, offering a history of dust in classical architecture to the present. In *The Architectural Uncanny* (1992), Anthony Vidler comprehensively examines the abject and horror in domestic spaces across architectural history. Several scholars, including Ellen Lupton and Abbott Miller (1992), Mark Wigley (2001), and Nadir Lahiji and Daniel Friedman (1997), have diagnosed in modernist architecture an aestheticization of hygiene that reveals anxieties around waste and formlessness.

Thomas Mical argues in his *Surrealism and Architecture* (2005) that modernist architecture was essentially involved in formlessness:

> Architecture must remain void to function and incomplete to produce effects, because architecture can only be completed in the spatial immersion of the subject ... The semiotic impulses of the self, fluid and formless, move easily through the formless continuity of modern domestic spaces and urban contexts. This is the locus of the formless in architecture – modernism's space without qualities, emptied of inner experience, the vaporous undecipherable spaces of the 'in-between' where the paradoxes of interiority and exteriority are to be resolved by the perceptive subject. (2005, 5–6)

There are critical precursors to this reading. Sigfried Giedion and Laszlo Moholy-Nagy worked independently early in the twentieth century to link the unconscious and intuition to unbounded overlapping spatial relationships that blur boundaries between inside and outside that they referred to as formless or aformal. As Giedion wrote in 1927, 'The houses of Le Corbusier define themselves neither by space nor by forms: the air passes right through them. The air becomes a constitutive factor! ... There is only a single, indivisible space. The separations between interior and exterior fall' (1995, 84). Other iconic projects and architectural movements, such as Friedrich Kiesler's Endless House of 1959, have been recently reconsidered in terms of their formlessness. Linking the Smithsons to the surrealist art of Tàpies, Dubuffet, and Tzara, Irénée Scalbert (2008, 24) proposes that: 'Behind Banham's interpretation of Brutalism as the short change of functionalism, a whole world was concealed: that of the formless and of the "informel", of which aformalism and the intrusion of topology represented but one facet'.

The above engagements with formlessness were primarily through criticism and historical revision, though they were evidently a preoccupation of practitioners as diverse as Gaudi and the Brutalists. It is not until after the exhibition *L'informe: mode d'emploi*, curated by Rosalind Krauss and Yve-Alain Bois and held at the Centre Pompidou in Paris during the summer of 1996, and the publication of the catalogue of that exhibition, *Formless: A User's Guide*, that formlessness became a widespread and intentional ambition for architects. The exhibition led to renewed interest in themes of abjection, sublimation, and fragmentation across the arts, and in particular into the work of Georges Bataille, whose strange 'dictionary' was published serially in the journal *Documents* during the late 1920s. It is from Bataille that Bois and Krauss take their concept of the formless as that which speaks to us of what is belittled, denigrated, repressed. Bataille's examples of the formless include abject fluids such as spit and vomit, that which is mutable and in process of decay, and handmade forms that resemble these, such as blobs.

The exhibition was not intended to reify or classify the formless; rather, around two hundred pieces of evidence were laid out without regard to style, period, or oeuvre. The aim of the curators was to reframe modernist works of art in such as way that our understanding of modernism would be radically altered. Their chief target was form, and the mainstream modernism – both artists and critics – that subscribed to a notion of good form. Clement Greenberg was number one on their hit list. They contended that Greenberg promoted a myth based on four foundational postulates: that art ought to be 'purely visual', that pictures reveal themselves instantly, that art is addressed to the subject as an erect being, and that works of art should be bounded and ordered. These postulates give Bois and Krauss a set of characteristics with which to put forward alternative works that are horizontal, unbounded, disordered, and temporal.

The formless exhibition only marginally addressed architecture, including projects by artists that literally attacked architectural structures – Robert Smithson's Partially Buried Woodshed (1970) and projects by Gordon Matta-Clark, for whom Smithson was a mentor. Although Matta-Clark's 'anarchitectural projects' involved cutting negative spaces into buildings, it was not so much the structure of architecture he wished to attack as its social function. These cuts induce vertigo, but Matta-Clark saw his cuts as opening up social information. 'By undoing a building', Matta-Clark said, '[I] open a state of enclosure which had been preconditioned not only by physical necessity but by the industry that [proliferates] suburban and urban boxes as a context for insuring a passive isolated consumer' (Lee 2000, 26). The position architecture held in this exhibition – as a target of operations that yield formlessness at the price of their ongoing role as architectures of use and inhabitation, rather than as a vehicle for formlessness – correlates with Bataille's views on the discipline.

Bataille proposed architecture as a metaphor and model of an order that ought to be destroyed. In his *Documents* entry on 'Architecture' of 1929, Bataille argues that philosophy, mathematics, and architecture have generated a system of petrification that fixes into a unified whole what was initially concrete, sensuous, and liquefied. Bataille proposes 'it is obvious, that mathematical organization imposed on stone is none other than the completion of an evolution of earthly forms ... In morphological progress men apparently represent only an intermediate stage between monkeys and great edifices. Forms have become more and more static, more and more dominant' (1992 [1929], 26). Architecture, Bataille concludes, is concerned with the systematic, with the regulation of the plan, and with inspiring fear and control as a mechanism for social order. It denies its own ruination and opposes itself to all disturbing elements.

If we follow Bataille, then architecture and formlessness are oppositional categories – a formless architecture is an oxymoron, yet critics and architects have pursued a formless architecture through that which disturbs, is mobile, and eludes definition. Following the exhibition, the projects most enthusiastically championed as formless have been less about the destruction of architecture as an authoritative practice, and more clearly targeted at the Greenbergian postulates of boundedness, visuality, and immediacy and the erect viewing subject. Diller and Scofidio's Blur Building of 2002, for example, literally conceals its edges and obfuscates visuality. Described by the architects as 'an inhabitable cloud', it consists of a steel tensegrity structure rising above Lake Neuchâtel in Switzerland on four columns and enveloped in 31,500 water vaporizers that conceal it all in a fog. The architects propose (2002, 180) that the Blur Building takes on the unpredictability, the terror, and the grandeur of weather, both imitating it and responding to it. Hans Ibelings diagnoses the Blur Building as an example of a more widespread tendency in recent architectural culture to pursue an architecture of 'nothing', in which to approach the 'dissolution of architecture' (2002, 87). The tendency is, in fact, an older one with precursors including the 'air architecture' pursued by the artist Yves Klein in the 1950s that consists of microclimates constructed from warmed and cooled air, walls of fire and water, gases, odours, magnetic forces, light, and sound. Coop Himmelblau's dream of an architecture that bleeds and burns, realized in their Burning Wing, is another.

François Roche and Stéphanie Lavaux (R&Sie) have similarly directed their practice towards breaking down the boundaries between object/subject and object/territory through the transformation of materials and states. Their Dusty Relief/B-mu (2002), proposed for the Contemporary Art Museum in Bangkok, is designed to collect the city's pollution cloud of dust on the surface of an aluminium latticework using an electrostatically charged system (Ruby and Durandin 2004, 137). R&Sie's extension to the School of Architecture in Venice, titled Aspiration Aqua Alta (1998) uses capillary action to suck up the liquid of the canal between two transparent plastic foils that make up the building envelope, thus transforming the material of the building from plastic to stagnant water with algae and foam, at the same time making visible the threatened sinking of Venice. These projects pursue 'non-form' or temporary form through making their architecture from material from each situation – the human subject, the object, climate, and territory. The vegetal and biological are brought into their projects as dynamic elements that disturb fixed form. While all architecture is ultimately subject to the ravages of time and decay and the ruin has long been a fixture of romanticism and the picturesque, R&Sie's projects are distinguished by a desire to accelerate and magnify these processes.

Again, it is necessary to emphasize that formlessness, like formalism, is something brought to the object, a way of apprehending it, not a property subsisting in the object.

Rafael Moneo, for one, sees formless architecture in both 'fragmented deconstructivist operations' and 'indifferent neutral containers' with minimalist aspirations, clearly referring to the architecture of Herzog and de Meuron (1997, 74). So while the projects of R&Sie can be approached from the thematic of formlessness, it is equally fruitful to consider their work in relation to a series of experiments in open-endedness that includes both phenomenal incompletion and experiments in the establishment of a rule-bound design process whose outcomes were predetermined but unknown. Take, for example, Robert Morris's Continuous Project Altered Daily, carried out during 22 days in March 1969 in the warehouse of a gallery owner in New York City's Upper West Side. Morris gathered a great range of materials, with which he took up an ongoing dialogue and interaction. Indeterminacy had become a literal aspect of the physical existence of the thing. 'Under attack,' he writes, 'is the rationalistic notion that art is a form of work that results in a finished product … What art now has in its hands is mutable stuff which need not arrive at the point of being finalized with respect to either time or space. The notion that work is an irreversible process ending in a static icon-object no longer has much relevance' (1993, 68).

There are some obvious problems with all these attempts to undo form and formalism, with formlessness – regardless of the success with which a building may be realized as a cloud of vapour or a precarious aggregation of dust. The oppositions that are to be undone – the characteristically modernist opposition of form versus content being the number-one target – are in effect replaced by other equally Hegelian, idealist oppositions: formed versus formless, object versus process, solid versus liquid. The 'shattering of signifying boundaries, the undoing of categories' that Krauss (1993, 157) insists are achieved through the informe, evidently persist. Critics objected to the notion of 'antiform' when the idea was first mooted in the 1960s. Allan Kaprow (1968, 32) writing of the felt sculptures of Robert Morris, found that literal non-form is inconceivable.

A tendency since the late 1990s in architecture has been to merge formalism with other concerns and to find a synthetic solution. Experiments in software-generated architectures, for example, have seen formal complexity argued as the inevitable outcome of the resolution of material and environmental parameters. Indeed, the appearance of the neologism 'performalism' in the title of a 2008 exhibition of architecture in Tel Aviv makes clear the coupling of formalist approaches with 'performance' (Grobman and Neuman 2008). Featuring work by Preston Scott Cohen, Eisenman Gehry Partners, Greg Lynn FORM, OCEAN, Open Source; Reiser & Umemoto, Kolatan and MacDonald – the curators of *Performalism* – propose that: 'The main argument of the exhibition is that digital architecture's formalism, realized through a multidimensional use of performance, offers a field of action by far wider than mere formalism, actually defining new needs and a new inessential concept of subjectivity' (Grobman and Neuman 2008).

While the technologies of the digital era allow more complex and multiple performative parameters to be incorporated in the design process, work of the kind being celebrated in this exhibition has its origins in Frei Otto's concept of 'finding form' through experiments intended to arrive at the optimization of materials and structure (Otto and Rasch 1995). Processes in nature, framed by genetic and biological sciences, are commonly referred to in the contemporary work, where they are used to develop forms that are active and responsive to changing environments – that optimize their performance in the same way that plants and animals do. Again, social, regulatory, and political forces are bracketed out in this recent version of formalism, while quantitative environmental parameters are embraced as formal drivers. The resulting work is notable for the curvilinear and complex forms that depart from Cartesian geometries, some of which require material and fabrication techniques not yet available, and some of which are considered 'ugly' and formless by architects that remained committed to the orthogonal forms of modernism. Sceptics have derided this new architecture as a variant of formalism that uses technology and environmental motivations for its justification. Catherine Ingraham, for example, has noted that the 'computational naturalism' of these digital architectures perpetuates a 'classical formalism' in which programme, inhabitant, and occupant are cast aside for form-making (2006, 209). It is significant that formalism is used both by Ingraham and the promoters of Performalism in the pejorative – their 'mere formalism' echoing earlier dismissal of the term as found in James Ackerman's 'meaningless formalism' (1974, 239), Susannah Hagan's 'autistic formalism' (2001, 196), or Pérez-Gómez's 'epidemic of empty formalism' (2006, 5).

Performalism, and the dismissive and moralizing critical response to it, reminds us that formalism is neither a dead argument nor a fixed moment in history but is constantly reworked in light of new theories and practices. Performalism is of its time. New techniques that promise the visualization and realization of geometrically more complex and plastic forms than previously possible coincide with environmental concerns that demand buildings designed to expend less energy and material. The take-up of the formalist position, or its variants, at any time is closely related to the social and historical contexts that it seeks to exclude from the act of interpretation. It is this that is perhaps the greatest irony of the cycles of formalist criticism and practice. It has long been noted that Greenbergian formalism, and the abstract art he championed, succeeded because it coincided with the Cold War period, when the overwhelming desire was for a form of American art that seemed to demonstrate the individualism and 'freedom' of the intellectual and artist from the demands of the state, and which contrasted most dramatically with the social realism supported by the Soviet and other communist states. Indeed, Serge Guilbaut argues that in the American situation it was 'because of avant-garde art's self-proclaimed neutrality, it was soon enlisted by governmental agencies and private organizations in the fight against Soviet cultural expansion' (1983, 11). Strategically also in relationship to Europe, the formalist criticism of Greenberg, along with abstract expressionism, offered affect and immediacy as an antidote to the intellectual sophistry of the European tradition. It proposes the work as an index of the physical process of its making and symptomatic of an intuitive or emotive gesture. Abstract expressionism was framed as a conscious rejection of the intellectualism it eschewed as a decadent cul-de-sac serving to sever the artist from feeling.

The correlation between Greenberg's synthesis of formalism and Marxist history and his agency in creating a market for abstract expressionism supports the case that criticism – regardless of its stripes – has a crucial role in the consumption of art and architecture, both in its appreciation and its purchase in the market. David Carrier suggests that philosophic art criticism, such as that of Clement Greenberg, emerges whenever untraditional criteria of evaluation are re-quired by the changing art of the time (2002);

that is, art criticism arrives when connoisseurship fails and consumers need guides to identify aesthetically valuable work. We see a similar pattern in architecture in the 1970s and 1980s. The attempts at architectural autonomy through the formalist experiments of the 1970s and 1980s, often derided as 'paper architecture', coincided with a growth in architectural theory in publishing and in architectural education. This phenomenon must be understood in light of not only the student revolution of 1968 but also a period of economic downtown in the building industry globally. The perceived destruction throughout the 1950s and 1960s of older neighbourhoods in centres of architectural discourse such as London and New York saw some architects distancing themselves from the commercial practices that oversaw insensitive redevelopment. Arguments for architectural autonomy, be they put forward by the Italian architectural historian and theorist Manfredo Tafuri or Peter Eisenman, were strongest at a time when architects felt most compromised by the vagaries of capitalist development and when the profession was losing its ground to developers and project managers. The second half of the twentieth century saw repeated calls for formalist practice as a means for achieving, if not the complete autonomy of the discipline, some expression of resistance to the instrumentalism of capitalist society. These remain significant, if incomplete attempts.

9

Art in (and of) Architecture: Autonomy and Medium

Bart Verschaffel

The business manager of St. Peter's:

'Well, young man, our boss, Pope Julius II, recommended you as being quite gifted. You know we are in difficulties in building the cupola; those architects don't know how to proceed. How many cupolas have you built?'

Michelangelo:

'Cupolas? None, I am a painter and sculptor, Sir, but...'

Business Manager:

'What? A painter and a sculptor? Oh my dear fellow I am sorry, we want an expert cupola-builder'.

This conversation would have happened if Michelangelo were alive today; but he was wise enough to have lived in the sixteenth century. And so he built the cupola, without ever having studied architecture; because the confidence of Pope Julius II in an artist's versatility showed real understanding of a creative mind. (Kiesler 1929, 15)

Tafuri already said so: 'The World of architectural culture grows even more distant from architecture itself'. This ideological fog appears in all possible forms, the most dangerous being the legitimization of architecture as a form of direct service to the ideals of a certain society, a kind of political commitment, the fundamental misconception of the modern movement, or at least of its theoretical rigidity. Architecture cannot be legitimized by society, unless by that society's need for the Other within itself, the need to transcend itself by plunging into the unknown, by breaking its habits and certainties. Architecture simply stands outside constituted society. (Bekaert 2003)

INTRODUCTION

Architecture is well institutionalized as a discipline, but the field of architecture has a 'weak identity' and is in constant need of *legitimization*. In architecture and architectural education many different competences and positions are involved, and these cannot easily be synthesized or be mastered by a single person. Architecture is related to but also differs from art, and lives somewhere in between the incompatible 'extremes' of *art* and *engineering*. This manifests itself first on an institutional level: in some countries architecture exists as an independent field, but more often it is either considered as a technical discipline and integrated in a faculty of engineering, or it is considered an art discipline and integrated in a school of art. In many countries both traditions co-exist, but not without conflict. The heterogeneity of the field of architecture also shows in the social 'persona' of the architect: 'I find myself involved in a variety of fields – architecture of course – but also in urban masterplanning, exhibition installation, furniture and product design, as well as writing architectural thought and criticism. Nevertheless, I identify myself as an "architect"' (Ito 2003, 250). The 'artist' and the 'engineer' have strong identities that are opposites and mutually exclusive; the architect seems too much of an artist to be a reliable engineer, but professionally too much dependent on programmes, external forces, and limitations to be considered as a real (that is, a 'free') artist. The identity of the architect is traditionally unclear and hybrid, and today 'our young students acquire a confused picture of the architect's responsibilities' as well. The architect's *persona* nevertheless defines what is possible for architecture today.[1] Is it so that nowadays 'the modern architect no longer requires any knowledge of management, the building site, organization, the construction process, or the materials used', so that the only thing left for architects is 'the creation of images of the construction to be realized, preferably with a general and flexible client brief' (Coenen 2003, 142)? The architect as a socially well-adapted artist? The relevance of architecture as a social and cultural practice is dependent on what is, in the current circumstances, institutionally accepted or expected from an architect – as distinct from what is possible for an artist, for example? Looking into this may help to decide what an architect is in today's society, what the architect's responsibilities are, and whether, or how, architecture can in the present circumstances be considered a cultural and critical practice (see *Hunch* 6/7, 2003).

ARCHITECTURE IS ...

The institutionalization of architecture as a discipline is based on a certain body of (technical) knowledge, a tradition and/or history one ought to relate to (that is, familiarity with the 'canon' of architecture), a social position and responsibility linked to and representative of the discipline (a legally protected professional position restricted by an initiation procedure), and a certified building production (not everything that is built is considered as 'architecture').

A body of knowledge ...

In the history of the West, and from antiquity onwards, architecture has been considered as *a science*. This basically implies that architecture stands above the knowledge of the artisan or the practice of mere craftsmanship, but it also implies that the science of architecture proper is specific to itself, and different from the building sciences. What characterizes architecture both as different from mere craftsmanship, and as different from the techniques of building and construction, is drawing or 'design'.[2] The 'design', or the process of selecting and representing information and spatial constellations, exploring and deciding on possibilities through visualization – be it with pencil and paper or with three-dimensional renderings – of the layout, structure, form, and aspect of things to be made or built, has long been considered to be the heart of architecture and architectural education.

The importance attached to 'drawing' brings architecture nearer to the arts. But as much as architecture has done to be considered as an artistic discipline, it has also claimed an exceptional position among the arts, as being productive and not imitative, and as being the 'mother' of the arts.[3] The artist and the architect make a different use of *disegno*, and this difference lies at the heart of the divergence and conflict between the myth of the artist and the myth of the architect, both of which are still effective today. Architecture has become a specific discipline, by distancing itself not only from artisanship but also from the other arts. The architect's 'manual labour' is strictly *limited* to the art of drawing or *disegno*. The architect is a designer and not an executive.[4] As long as this person draws or makes *modelli*, even beautifully and creatively, the architect stays within the intellectual discipline of architecture. When he makes sketches as a preparation to paint or to carve, the architect will *also* be an artist, as many classical architects have been. It has proven much more difficult for sculptors or painters to emancipate completely from mere artisanship because they must themselves still do at least part of the manual labour of painting or carving. That is why the mythology of the artist and art theory have developed the distinction between two different kinds of making: the skillful production of the artisan-imitator, whose production is individualized but not marked by their specific hand, and the 'real' artist, whose making is creative and exceptional, because it is *virtuoso* (spontaneous, effortless, non-repetitive) and 'inspired'.[5] The handwork of the genius is not craftwork but, rather, creation. The architect's competence and skill, on the contrary, resides in the intellectual activity of making plans and models, and directing and supervising their execution. The architect does not practise building directly. It is remarkable and significant that the myth of the architect and the myth of the artist, in spite of their similarities and historical relation, break apart here. Even today's star architects are never portrayed, and they rarely pose themselves, as romantic inspired genius figures who create something from nothing: such great architects are more like adventurers, or leaders of a team, exploring the new and the possible and pushing them to the limit, stealing the secrets of nature from the gods in order to achieve their own ends. The architect is not a god but more a hero – Daidalos – who risks being punished for his *hubris* by failure or being struck by madness. But the architect as such is not an artist. The architect may also be a painter and paint in the morning, as Le Corbusier did, but architecture is definitely something else.

A tradition and/or history one ought to relate to ...

The idea of 'architecture' is linked to the classical, Aristotelian idea of perfection and/or perfect work: the idea that human making (as an imitation and emulation of 'natural growth') can reach beyond its mere 'function', so that the functioning and use of things is integrated in a complex whole that is not just well-made and useful but also beautiful and perfect. Giorgio Vasari created the classical 'Gallery' of 'great masters' who succeeded in this endeavour and made perfect and therefore exemplary work in art and architecture. The discipline of architecture is founded – parallel to how a scientific paradigm is formed (Kuhn 1974) – not just by an agreement on theoretical principles or a body of knowledge but also by the acceptance of a specific set of *normative examples*: the canon of architecture. To be able to practise architecture one needs to be familiar with this selection of historical examples. To make architecture is to take part in – to imitate and compete, or to emulate – this endeavour of making perfect work.

A social position ...

It is interesting to note, even in light of today's concerns, that for Vasari and his contemporaries architecture is not yet a profession but a task and a responsibility – not unlike the task of being a politician today. There are no schools where one can learn everything one needs to know to become a politician (see *Hunch* 6/7, 2003). It is a task that certainly requires specific competences and knowledge, but which can be assumed by people coming from very different backgrounds and training. The same is true for architecture historically, and is even true today: some highly respected contemporary architects were first carpenters, journalists, artists, actors, or engineers. It is true, though, that architecture has not only been institutionalized as a discipline but also become a profession. In most countries, one has to be trained as an architect and know about architecture in order to be permitted to practise architecture. At the same time, everybody will agree with Leon Battista Alberti that, although design may be the heart of architecture, the architect should not master a specialized and limited field of knowledge but know *everything* – just as a politician should. This is, of course, impossible, and so there are at least fifty different curricula, each one-sided and incomplete, that lead to the title of architect.

A certified building production ...

The institutionalization of architecture implies that not everything that is built is considered 'architecture'. This has, in principle, nothing to do with the quality or meaning of a building. Architecture – good or bad, success or failure – is a building that is, beyond its functionality, somehow aware of the project of making perfect work, and somehow refers to the canon. The architect works, from Alberti onward, with a *musée imaginaire* of the discipline in mind: a collection of all the buildings – including many famous unbuilt or destroyed buildings – referring to the project of architecture, whose adventures are told by the history of architecture. The notion of architecture presupposed by architectural theory and criticism, and the notion of architectural history – the development and the virtual 'museum' of architecture – are *operative concepts*. To become well grounded in architecture means becoming acquainted with this historical frame of reference and the valuation and hierarchy of reputations it commends. The notion of architecture itself is therefore ideological: it is used to exclude and to include a specific mode of building production, isolating a certain corpus of buildings by referring to aesthetic principles, and neglecting their material (economic, social) conditions. The notion of architecture is therefore also *a cultural concept:* the process of legitimatization relates a certain building production to an intellectual and discursive tradition. Manfredo Tafuri's critique of the discipline of architecture starts from the fact that in making or approaching buildings as architecture one inevitably – probably purposefully – abstracts the building from its 'real' historical, social, economical, technical context, transfers it to the timeless, a-historical Gallery of Famous Buildings, and deduces its meaning and value from its place there.[6] The building appears in splendid isolation in the ideological construction called architecture. One certainly has to agree with Tafuri that architectural history is operative, and that today's architectural journalism and criticism isolates just a small part of a huge building production, with the effect of leaving the social and economical impact of this total production, what is really happening, almost unnoticed and undiscussed.

THE SPECIFICITY OF ARCHITECTURE

The specificity of architecture compared to the work of art can clearly be seen in the fact that, with the institutionalization and the becoming-modern of the arts, the artist and the artwork function totally and exclusively within the art institution: to succeed, an artwork cannot be anything other than, or in addition to, a work of art. When it functions at the same time as a decorative object in an interior, or as an ornament on a building, or as an official monument, it loses its autonomy, and fails as a work of art. The status of being pure or autonomous art, guaranteed by a position inside the art institution, automatically lends each art work a kind of radicalism: being autonomous implies the radical negation of the world.[7] The foundation of art as a discipline imposes a system whereby a certain class of images and objects are abstracted from their use value – as objects of devotion, private or public commemoration, political propaganda, economical speculation – and considered and interpreted purely as 'works of art', actually belonging in the history of art and the museum, even if *de facto* they hang in a church or a commercial gallery.

One can argue that as far as a piece of architecture exists internally in the discursive space of the discipline of architecture – founded by the history of architecture, and enacted in the space of architectural criticism, magazines and catalogues, exhibitions and tourism, school books and the canon – the work of architecture is just like a work of art. But unlike the artwork – which can only properly operate within the institutionalized, homogeneous space of the art world and has little use and meaning when it functions merely as an anonymous thing, image, sign or object – the work of architecture is usually *also* a *building*. As such, it has a considerable mute presence and impact, an appearance and a meaning for its inhabitants and users, also when those are completely unaware of its status as architecture. This means that although Tafuri is certainly right in arguing that architecture is an operative concept, this ideological discursive operation *never results in an effective isolation of the work of architecture from the world*. And this fact is even – although never elegantly – acknowledged within the internal discourse of architecture. Paper architecture certainly exists, and some people will claim that architecture is nothing but design. But it remains very difficult to argue principally that it is wrong or improper to approach architecture also as a building-in-the-world, and that one should consider a project or a building exclusively as a 'statement' in the conversation of architecture, or a 'move' in the game of architecture.

EROSION OF THE FOUNDATIONS

If we agree that the institution of architecture is the outcome of the collective undertaking of making perfect or beautiful work (whatever the social conditions for this sharing may be), and of some agreement or consensus of the canon (whatever power mechanisms may have played out in installing that consensus), the question arises of how the discipline of architecture can survive *the erosion of its foundations*. Architecture has been institutionalized, has become 'official', and is now protected by the existence of academies, schools, prizes, magazines, text books. At the same time, though, this whole development has also been criticized externally and internally, up to the point that, now, all the principles and presuppositions that founded the discipline of architecture have been radically put into question or have been 'deconstructed'. I briefly point to three lines of critique.

The fall of the rules and the canon: subjectivism in aesthetics

Classical architectural theory follows an 'objective' aesthetic: beauty is an objective quality belonging to work that is perfectly executed following certain rules and models. The perfection of the work can be ascertained, exactly like health or a physical deformation can be determined. After the subjective turn in philosophy and taste in the eighteenth century, however, beauty and ugliness are no longer considered to be objective qualities of an object or image, and cannot be known with certainty. They are a matter of sensation, perception and feeling experienced by the beholder. When beauty is not an objective quality but exists only as an experience, the idea of a canon of beautiful models cannot make much sense anymore. From then on, architecture is about causing effects in the beholder, and using and controlling the empirical qualities of the building to produce and stimulate sensations. When Edmund Burke discusses in his *Inquiry into the Origin of our Ideas of the Sublime and the Beautiful* the effects of 'magnitude' and 'light in building', he explains that it is not the real or objective magnitude that counts, but the skill to 'deceive' the beholder's eye so that his or her imagination 'rises to infinity', just as darkness, certain types of disorder, and emptiness also cause it to do (Burke 1998 [1757]; see also Hipple 1957). He devotes lengthy pages to arguing that proportion is not the cause of beauty, not in vegetables, nor animals, nor in the human species, and it is clear that the next victim of his argument is architecture. When Burke writes that 'we begin to feel that mathematical ideas are not the true measures of beauty', then the classical idea of architectural beauty is over. Burke introduces into theory ideas and insights that were in the eighteenth century explored in 'paper architecture' by artists such as the Bibiena family and Giovanni Battista Piranesi, as well as Étienne-Louis Boullée and other French revolutionary architects. His insights have later been used in literature and in cinema to transform closed, familiar and protected spaces – such as interiors and cities – into labyrinth-like, deep, infinite spaces, that are *unheimlich* or architecturally 'uncanny' (Vidler 1992).[8]

Despite its prominence in the intellectual debates and cultural theory of the last decade, the meaning and usefulness of the category of the sublime – for the interpretation of architecture or for architectural theory – seems limited. This is because of something Burke himself already indicates: it is quite difficult for an object to represent or to suggest infinity. Architecture becomes uncanny in conditions where it loses its reference to the human body and human presence, or when this presence is threatened. These conditions can be imagined and visualized in drawings, theatre settings and movies.[9] A few recent buildings – 'canonized' museum buildings and/or monuments such as Libeskind's Jewish Museum, the hall of Frank Gehry's Guggenheim Museum in Bilbao, or the Holocaust Memorial of Peter Eisenman in Berlin – making excessive use of void spaces and clashes of scale, may *appeal* to the sublime, but most examples make a poetical-symbolical *reference* to the sublime instead of causing the 'natural' *experience* of the sublime. One can try the monumental and the colossal, but sublime architecture cannot easily be built.

More relevant for architecture, as well as for understanding shifts in taste and in architectural culture, is the notion of the 'picturesque'. The picturesque shares many presuppositions with the notion of the sublime, but happily lacks its metaphysical aura and strong connection to negative theology – which made it much less popular in late-twentieth-century philosophy and cultural theory. The picturesque also refers not to a classical objective beauty but to subjective appreciation: the picturesque is 'a beauty that we like', and therefore like to represent or look for in paintings. The human mind finds pleasure in the new and surprising (not in drama but in anecdote); the irregular (but not in the chaotic); softness (not in darkness but in the sunset); the effects of time (the ruin) but not in history; the homely, peasants and old houses and domestic animals (and not in heroes and palaces and hunting). The picturesque is the world one would like to see from the window of one's house. The picturesque certainly is a 'weak' aesthetic theory. It is only recently that its importance for understanding contemporary Western architecture and dwelling culture is being (re)discovered (Macarthur 2007). The picturesque undoubtedly is an aesthetic category crucial for understanding and appreciating important architectural movements such as nineteenth-century eclectic architecture, the Arts and Crafts movement, the garden-city movement, and both the postmodern recuperation of commercial vernacular architecture as well as postmodern architecture.[10]

In a broader sense, the subjective turn has led to distinct forms of architectural theory that, though unrelated to the history of architectural styles, have a latent aesthetic approach to architecture. This is implicit in any architectural theory based in phenomenology or anthropology (for example Norberg-Schulz 1980). But does the notion of *genius loci* somehow imply *feeling meaning*? The subjective turn unexpectedly also leads to semi-scientific design theories that aim to cause feelings of 'well-being' via architecture. Roger Scruton (1995), for example, suggests that good architecture ought to generate the effect of a feeling of comfort and a peace of mind.

The fall of rules and the canon: cultural relativism

The notion of classical architecture was regularly criticized from within, both in theory and in practice, when it became clear that Roman and Greek architects themselves did not follow the rules they supposedly invented. How then could one impose these rules on modern architecture? Besides, some genial artists had demonstrated that they were capable of freely inventing new rules – at least in the arts, with Michelangelo as the famous case. Piranesi convincingly argued that Roman architecture is creative beyond the rules derived from Greek temple architecture, and even before that, Joseph Emanuel Fischer von Erlach wrote a 'true' history of architecture that clearly could not contain the variety of buildings within the classical canon. One cannot reject everything that is different as barbaric or primitive. Should not all buildings be considered equally true and beautiful – certainly when those newly discovered exotic architectures often are very picturesque and pleasant to look at? Does all architecture not have the same rights? All this leads directly to architectural eclecticism as propagated by César Daly and others in the nineteenth century.[11] Daly himself believed that eclecticism would somehow lead to a 'Synthesis', and that eclectic experiments would lead to a modern style, the universalist architecture of the future. The 'truth' would somehow mediate between 'the useful' and 'the beautiful'. Daly's project of Synthesis, though, was never more than a programme, but his theory effectively legitimized playing with and finding pleasure in plain stylistic plurality and mixture. It took another century to realize and admit that not every culture carries its own bit of architectural truth, as Daly thought: there is no set of truths in different architectural cultures that can be made compatible and consistent. More recent critiques of the traditional canon and the very notion of a canon, by vernacular movements, by gender studies, by postcolonial theory, have each widened the scope of buildings and projects now taken into account by the architectural discourse. Informal and vernacular architecture, industrial constructions and ruins, the follies of Las Vegas, cheap modernism, colonial architecture, web design – the theories and argumentation of each new approach are very different, but the end effect runs along the same lines as Daly's eclectic argument: *Tout est Architecture!* (Le Corbusier). *Alles ist Architektur*! (Hans Hollein) (see Buckley 2007). The final question is, though, what does it mean to accept that architecture can be made without architects, and that anti-architecture and even paper architecture must all be equally considered as architecture? That anything goes?

The fall of the rules and the canon: engineering as 'true architecture'

A third criticism of the idealization of architecture invokes the truth that seems to reside in 'use' and 'function'. Authors writing in the classical tradition – such as Philibert de L'Orme or Marc-Antoine Laugier – already made reference to pragmatism and the common sense of the master builders of the past as a 'reality principle'. The prophets and pioneers of modern architecture, from Eugene Viollet-Le-Duc and John Ruskin to Adolf Loos and Henri Van de Velde, admired the unperverted authenticity and common sense of the craftsman and the farmer-builder. This role of the craftsman and the farmer, honest and unspoiled by culture, truthful because they are *natural* and 'uncultivated', is in the twentieth century taken over by the engineer. The antidote for the artistic Beaux-Arts tradition is the rational architecture of *l'esthétique de l'ingénieur.* The engineer-redeemer replacing the architect-demiurge (Schnapp 2008).

> Engineers are the direct and immediate agents of human progress to a greater extent than any other social category. With their discoveries and painstaking tinkering with inventions, they improve everything that humankind has devised so that life may fulfill its potential for intelligence. ... Beyond the diversity of values and personalities, beyond disparities in social class and intellectual sparkle, one always recognizes in the engineer a quiet, level-headed, thoughtful human subject, a subject used to coolly resolving all situations with good will, perseverance, and a sense of duty infused with the best of popular virtues. (Bardi 1938)

The attractiveness of the engineer as a role model was certainly related to the process of introducing new building materials and adapting to the industrialization of building. The growing private building activity of the nineteenth century surely needed more technically-trained architects, and designing and building machines, including *machines à habiter*, is what engineers do ... But this shift is accompanied by a cultural revolution: a choice was made to reduce meaning to function, to move to a design practice which did not bother with culture, taste, and historical reference, to a non-style with no memory. Engineering is expected to produce a natural beauty, residing in the elegance of construction and the economy of means (Colquhoun 1989). The ideal of engineering embodies the phantasm of tautological architecture: an architecture without ornament, a *naked architecture*: 'realism without fantasy'. In this way, engineering is not just a field of specialized technical knowledge in the service of building and architecture. It also is a style, that whispers, 'that which is beautiful is true', and vice versa. It also whispers that *architecture is a lie.* One shouldn't trust those 'geniuses' who 'disfigure the practical art of building into absurd architecture' (Silber 2007).

The figure of the engineer, however, is as ambiguous as technology itself is.[12] Engineering traditionally stands for a sense of reality and economy, matter-of-factness and sobriety, and opposes no-nonsense thinking against wild artistic fancy. But at the same time, the figure of the engineer comes dangerously close to the magician again, as the one who can make the impossible real. Engineering nowadays does not function only as the 'reality principle' in architectural education, bringing the architect back down to earth, but promises also unlimited innovation and endless possibilities. The rationalism represented by industrial engineering of the nineteenth century could perhaps pretend to be necessary and true. But since postmodernity, with its many new materials, its lessons from Las Vegas and from consumerism, the roles seem reversed. Even engineers do not believe anymore that the form can simply follow the function. The engineer now challenges the architect to design what is technologically possible – the highest skyscraper ever, and so on – because engineering needs to actually build extremes to prove the possibilities of new technology. The architect feels hired just to invent a spectacular form and a story to sell it. After modernism, architecture relies on engineering for almost everything *except* aesthetics: the appealing outlook is what architecture has to add. Architecture is, again, ornament – free style.

SURVIVAL WITHOUT A CANON

Architecture has lost its foundation, but curiously enough the discipline survives. One can do without a canon. One simply agrees to disagree, changes history for 'contemporaneity', and integrates deconstruction as a standard practice into the theory legitimizing the discipline. 'Contemporaneity is not a style, nor a religion or an esthetics. It is the moment we are living in. We can be enthusiastic or not about it, and we still, all of us, remain contemporary!' (Katarxis undated).[13] Institutional critique has now become mainstream theory. All this may not be so different from what has happened in the arts. Modern art also works against the canon and the museum as a matter of principle. A genuine work of art relates critically to the very notion of art and even more to aesthetic values, otherwise it becomes kitsch. But all this does not imply that the art institution is in danger. As Marcel Duchamp and Andy Warhol have demonstrated, and Arthur Danto (1981) has theorized, everything that is said and done within the art institution, no matter how 'critical' or transgressive, is automatically recuperated as art. 'With a zero event, an artistic super-event is staged, in other words art has begun to function like a performance' (Baudrillard 2007). The same logic works, *mutatis mutandis*, in architecture. The loss of the canon, the absence of rules and the many disagreements of principle are not threatening. The institution does not rely on consensus anymore.

THE QUESTION OF AUTONOMY

Historically, the idea of the autonomy of art first appears in the principle of *l'art pour l'art* and the idea of absolute beauty: art should not be used in any way (Davies 2007). This positive strategy, however, is ideologically suspect because autonomous beauty silently accepts the world outside as it is. Aesthetic admiration and aesthetic pleasure are intrinsically affirmative. But then, as Georg Simmel wrote in 1897 in *Jeinseits der Schönheit*, 'then the great slaughter began': 'With the great negation sign as its only weapon' modern art negated everything everybody else used to affirm (Simmel 2008, 329). Not only aesthetic ideals or the idolatry of the canon, or retinal pleasure, but the art institution itself should be negated. Aesthetic qualities, along with objective perfection, become irrelevant and even suspect. For a work of art, being beautiful is a problem. A work of art should be 'a *deceptive object*' (Cauquelin 1996, 106).[14] Expanding Theodor Adorno's critical stance, variations of deconstructionism have radicalized this principle of negation to the point that every statement and every image that succeeds in evoking a 'presence' is wrong as such, because it covers the unbearable with representation. This leads, in political thinking, to the impasse of a Heideggerian 'waiting' or a Giorgio Agamben-like 'empty messianism', and turns in art theory and criticism into aesthetisizing the 'imperfection' of the work: the work of art should almost not exist, it should not be more, bigger, more solid, better made, or be more interesting than necessary to express a 'no'. And this consequently leads to an art production consisting of small gestures, subtle rearrangements, fragile and temporary constructions, and anorectic images, where the critical stance gives way to aesthetisizing the experience of the 'void' in small doses, and to an overall aesthetics of the sublime.

Architecture cannot follow here. What is possible for the artist in art is not possible for the architect in the world. Compared to the radicalism of the arts, architecture will always be half-hearted and ideologically unreliable. Architecture can perhaps be radically *positive* – there are indeed a few very dangerous examples of totalitarian architecture. But it is more relevant that a work of architecture can never be just or fundamentally a 'no'. One might provocatively call the September 11 terrorist attack on New York's World Trade Center an artistic statement, but it can never be considered as an architectural statement. It is of course possible to negate a building radically, but no building can *express* radical negativity. The Belgian architect and theoretician Wim Cuyvers made a 45-minute walk on a huge rubbish dump filming with a hand-held camera his stepping feet in one long shot. The video shows the exposure of a human body to an original chaos – the world without or before architecture. These images of the zero degree of world-making, though, may make good art, but they are nothing more than the 'In the beginning ...' of the founding myth of architecture. The video is not architecture. A work of architecture, because it exists as a fact or an object before it functions as a sign, before it means or says anything, and because it is always somehow useful for humankind, is fundamentally an affirmation. This is what Giorgio Grassi (1976) has called the intrinsic realism of architecture: architecture is always sustaining, necessary, positive, affirmative. The problem with the prevailing discourse of architectural criticism is this inability to recognize that 'there is in the deepest motivations of architecture something that cannot be critical' (Rem Koolhaas cited in Kapusta 1994). This is why the complete and sudden demolition of a building has a strong mythical dimension, and why its destruction can be recuperated as an artistic gesture: the destruction of a building always is a *pars pro toto* of the annihilation of the world itself, and announces the return of the condition visualized by Cuyvers.

The position of architecture is therefore ambivalent. Architecture takes part in the critical-creative production of culture. Architecture is not neutral economic production like baking bread or cutting hair, but is like saying something: every piece of architecture implies a statement, it implies political and social choices, and it implies responsibility. But the architect also never operates in the clean and autonomous discursive space of the institution of architecture. That is why making a building in the world is different from creating an art work or installing a sculpture in public space. The institutional space of architecture is not closed and self-contained. A building or an environment is always also a matter of use, pleasure, beauty, and money, and not just of architectural meaning and significance. Certainly, architecture has its own institutional space and discourse, its own gallery of fame. There even exists a kind of architecture that is clearly made for this gallery, and doesn't want anything more than to exist and be discussed in architectural magazines. But a building is never just architecture and always more than a subject of architectural discourse. It always has a second life in the world and in time, outside the disciplinary space. One can rightfully consider art as a game, with its own playground, time, and rules – a game so creative and imaginative that, finally, the constant re-invention and changing of the rules is what this game is now about: not just being creative by making a work of art never seen before, but constantly radically redefining what art can be. Architecture, on the contrary, is never really a game.

Rem Koolhaas has made a lucid and despairing analysis of the artistic irrelevance that conditions contemporary star architecture. The game of money and power and the development of a global building industry have disconnected the discipline of architecture from the project of making the world. The market economy has taken away most of the basis of architecture and the vast majority of the grounds for its claims. The architect no longer works for the common good nor for a public administration with good intentions. Clients are now individuals and companies, who have all kinds of interests but are rarely connected to morals. Architecture's claim to dignity and moral value, 'which used to revolt us so much', has already evaporated (Van Winkel and Verschaffel 2004). One could expect that, in these circumstances, Koolhaas would quit architecture and start a new life – in philosophy, for example, as did Ludwig Wittgenstein, or as an artist. But rather than quit architecture and opt for 'artistic purity', in parallel to his activities as a building architect (in the firm OMA, the Office for Metropolitan Architecture), activities which are necessarily full of compromises and frustrations, he founded AMO. AMO is a study centre that operates independently of or in cooperation with academic institutions, and practices architecture and design as a purely intellectual discipline, unconnected to building and independent of the building industry. Koolhaas's shadow office – where the same people use the same competences and intelligence to think about the same issues as those on which OMA is working, but now disconnected from the real world of money and power – defines a model exactly because AMO does not look for shelter under the 'autonomy of art'. This pragmatic solution has a general relevance. AMO institutionalizes, next to the 'unreality' of architectural schools and academic discourse, but *within the discipline of architecture itself*, a position for architectural thinking or design.

Being aware of the impurity of architecture, being aware of the effects and seriousness of architectural practice, can perhaps lead to strategies that use the inevitable presence of architecture in the world for a cultural production that is not artistically but politically motivated. The so-called radicalism of the arts goes along with splendid isolation, arbitrariness, and irrelevance. Artists nowadays can say what they want but cannot be critical anymore. Architects on the other hand can perhaps still manage this, a little, but only if they are smart enough to play the double game.

TO CONCLUDE

The most privileged case, the test to check how art and architecture relate, is the modern-art museum.[15] The museum is the test field for what art and architecture can possibly be and do for each other. The recent boom of museum architecture is therefore significant, and indicates the problem. The new contemporary-art museum has to solve the problem of assigning a place to the arts today. The solution is a standard solution: a lot of open, undefined, wide and high white-cube-like closed spaces, flexible, without architecture, where everything is possible; with spectacular entrance and circulation areas and a rooftop restaurant, along with an icon-like outside. In other words, a 'decorated shed'. This gives the impression that there is a neat labour division, and that architecture respectfully holds back and retreats to secondary spaces and the façade, to give art as much freedom as possible. In reality, what is probably happening is that art is locked up in its playpen, and the museum, transformed on the outside into a sculpture-like artistic object in the city, is really the site of fratricide.

NOTES

1 For some classical overview studies on the history of the architect and the making of the 'persona' of the architect, see Kostof (1977), Ricken (1977), Ackerman (1991), Callebat (1998), and Saint (1983; 2007).

2 For a recent overview, see Burioni (2008), especially Chapter2, 'Die Architektur und die Künste des *disegno* (1550–1568)'. See also Williams (1997). For a recent discussion of Vitruvius as 'Ur-text' see Patterson (2006). For an analysis of modern design practice, see Cuff (1991). Also of interest is Niels Prak (1980).

3 The question of 'mimèsis' in classical architectural theory is very complex and runs into twentieth-century theory in a way too complex to be dealt with here. See Rykwert (1972) and an overview of recent theory stemming from Walter Benjamin's thought on mimèsis in Hilde Heynen (1999).

4 Jeffrey T. Schnapp interestingly remarks that architects are portrayed with regular design tools as accessories, to stress the intellectual side of their profession. This is mitigated, however, by the common alternative of smoking an object-type-pipe or a cigar, indicating a position in between artistic frivolity and rationalized pleasure. Cf. Schnapp (2008). Prak (1983) made it clear that, even if the architect identifies primarily with designing, the studio work is only a limited part of the job.

5 Cf. the classical compendium by Sillig (1827) and Kris and Kurz (1979). See also Wittkower and Wittkower (1963) and Soussloff (1997).

6 For a recent discussion of Tafuri's theoretical heritage with an extensive bibliography, see Leach (2007) and Solà-Morales (2000).

7 The most radical versions of this thesis stem from the critical theory of Theodor Adorno (2004).

8 Vidler argues that modernist architecture, detached from its social-political programme and aesthesized into a 'style', is experienced as 'unheimlich' or uncanny: one 'feels' the repression of the political. See also Vidler (2000).

9 Some will argue that it is the basic anthropomorphism of architecture, or the recognition of the 'presence' of the scale and Gestalt of the human body, that lends meaning. See, for example, Rykwert's recovery of classical anthropomorphism in Rykwert (1996).

10 Charles Jencks (1977) explicitly presents postmodernism as a strategy of radical eclecticism, integrating vernacular or populist and historical references.

11 On the recent 'rehabilitation' of César Daly, see Schoonjans (2007) and Geert Palmaers (2005).

12 Cf. Saint (2007), particularly Chapter 6, 'A Question of Upbringing', for a discussion of the architectural school culture in the nineteenth and early twentieth centuries. For historical examples of 'imaginative engineering' and technology, see Scott (2007).

13 'Katarxis is a new webzine dedicated exclusively to a New Traditional Architecture and Urbanism: one that in its vernacular and classical expressions, incorporates a re-evaluation of the many World Cultures; includes the humanist heritage of the West and the East; and acknowledges the evidence of New Sciences, and the positive logistics of the contemporary world'.

14 Anne Cauquelin (1996): 'la provocation ne vise plus le public, mais *l'art lui-même* dans ses aspects établis: c'est à l'art tel qu'il est encore sujet de croyances que les artistes s'attaquent, et c'est en cela que le décept, le fait de décevoir, est pour les artistes un outil approprié'.

15 There has been a boom in publications about (art) museums, almost as much as a museum boom – among the many, Davis (1990). For a critical evaluation of museum architecture from Centre Pompidou to the Tate Modern, see Davidts (2006).

Section 2 Bibliography

Ackerman, James (1974) 'Transactions in Architectural Design', *Critical Inquiry* 1(2): 229–43.

—— (1991) *Distance Points: Essays in Theory and Renaissance Art and Architecture*. Cambridge, MA, and London: MIT Press.

Adorno, Theodor (2004 [1972]) *Aesthetic Theory*. Gretel Adorno et al. (eds) with a translator's introduction by Robert Hullot-Kentor. New York: Continuum.

Anderson, Stanford (2000) *Peter Behrens and a New Architecture for the Twentieth Century*. Cambridge, MA: MIT Press.

Arnheim, Rudolf (1969) *Visual Thinking*. Berkeley: University of California Press.

—— (1977) *The Dynamics of Architectural Form*, based on the 1975 Mary Duke Biddle lectures at the Cooper Union. Berkeley: University of California Press.

Atelier Bow-Wow (2002) *Pet Architecture Guide Book*, vol. 2. Japan: World Photo Press.

Bal, Mieke (1992) 'Telling, Showing, Showing Off', *Critical Inquiry* 18(3): 566.

Banham, Reyner (1959) 'Neo-Liberty: The Italian Retreat from Modern Architecture', *The Architectural Review* 746(March): 231.

Bardi, Pietro Maria (1938) '*Missione del ingegneri*', quoted by Jeffrey T. Schnapp (2008) in 'The Face of the Modern Architect', *Grey Room*, 33(Fall): 8–9.

Barthes, Roland (1967 [1953]) *Writing Degree Zero*. London: Jonathan Cape.

—— (1975a [1973]) *The Pleasure of the Text*. Translated by Richard Miller. New York: Hill and Wang.

—— (1975b [1970]) *S/Z*. Translated by Richard Miller. London: Jonathan Cape.

—— (1997 [1980]) *Sade/Fourier/Loyola*. Baltimore: Johns Hopkins University Press.

Bataille, Georges (1985) *Visions of Excess: Selected Writings 1927–1939*. Edited and translated by Allan Stoekl. Minneapolis: University of Minnesota Press.

—— (1992 [1929]) 'Architecture', *Documents* 1(2): 117. Translated by D. Faccini as 'Architecture', *October* 60: 25–26.

—— (1996) 'The Notion of Expenditure', in Allan Stoekl (ed.) *Visions of Excess: Selected Writings 1927–1939*. Minneapolis: University of Minnesota Press, 116–129.

Baudrillard, Jean (2007) 'Architecture and the Void, Art and Life', *Domus* 897: 81–88.

Beardsley, Monroe C. (1971) 'On Arnheim's "Visual Thinking"', *Journal of Aesthetic Education* 5(3): 186.

Bekaert, Geert (2003) 'Quel nom est architecte?', *Hunch* 6/7: 78.

Benedikt, Michael (1987) *For an Architecture of Reality*. New York: Lumen Books.

—— (1991) *Deconstructing the Kimbell: An Essay on Meaning and Architecture*. New York: SITES/Lumen Books.

Benjamin, Walter (1973) 'The Work of Art in the Age of Mechanical Reproduction' [1935] in Walter Benjamin, *Illuminations*. London: Fontana, 219–253.

Bentel, Paul (1992) 'Modernism and Professionalism in American Architecture, 1919–1933'. PhD dissertation, MIT, Cambridge, MA.

Blake, Peter (1964) *God's Own Junkyard: The Planned Deterioration of America's Landscape*. New York: Holt, Rinehart and Winston.

Bochner, Mel (1967) 'The Serial Attitude', *Artforum* 6(4): 28–33.

Boudon, Philippe (1972) *Lived-in Architecture: Le Corbusier's Pessac Revisited*. Translated by Gerald Onn, with a preface by Henri Lefebvre. London: Lund Humphries.

Boulez, Pierre (1971 [1964]) *Boulez on Music Today*. Translated by S. Bradshaw and R. R. Bennett. London: Faber.

Bouman, Ole and Roemer van Toorn (1993) 'I Am Trying to Save the Phenomenology of Architecture: Interview with Oswald Mathias Ungers', *Archis* 2(February): 58–65.

Bourdieu, Pierre (1984) *Distinction: A Social Critique of the Judgement of Taste*. Translated by Richard Nice. Cambridge, MA: Harvard University Press.

—— (1993) *The Field of Cultural Production*. New York: Columbia University Press.

Bourdieu, Pierre and Alain Darbel (1990) *The Love of Art: European Art Museums and Their Public*. Translated by Caroline Beattie and Nick Merriman. Stanford: Stanford University Press.

Buckley, Craig (2007) 'From Absolute to Everything: Taking Possession in "Alles ist Architektur"', *Grey Room* 28: 108–22.

Burioni, Matteo (2008) *Die Renaissance der Architekten. Profession und Souveränität des Baukünstlers in Giorgio Vasaris Viten*. Berlin: Gebr. Mann Verlag.

Burke, Edmund (1998 [1757]) *A Philosophical Inquiry into the Origin of Our Ideas of the Sublime and the Beautiful. With an Introduction and Notes by Adam Phillips*. Oxford: Oxford University Press.

Cage, John (1961) *Silence*. Middletown, CT: Wesleyan University Press.

Caille, Alain (2001) 'The Double Inconceivability of the Pure Gift', *Angelaki: Journal of the Theoretical Humanities* 6(2): 23–39.

Callebat, Louis (ed.) (1998) *Histoire de l'architecte*. Paris: Flammarion.

Carrier, David (2002) *Rosalind Krauss and American Philosophical Art Criticism: From Formalism to Beyond Postmodernism*. Westport, CT: Greenwood Publishing.

Casey, Edward S. (1997) *The Fate of Place: A Philosophical History*. Berkeley, Los Angeles, London: University of California Press, 205–210.

Cauquelin, Anne (1996) *Petit Traité d'Art Contemporain*. Paris: Du Seuil.

Çelik, Zeynep (2007) 'Kinaesthetic Impulses: Aesthetic Experience, Bodily Knowledge, and Pedagogical Practices in Germany, 1871–1918'. PhD dissertation, MIT, Cambridge, MA.

Coenen, Jo (2003) 'What's Left of the Architect Today', in *Hunch: The Berlage Institute Report* 6/7.

Colquhoun, Alan (1989) 'Architecture and Engineering: Le Corbusier and the Paradox of Reason', in *Modernity and the Classical Tradition. Architectural Essays 1980–1987*. Cambridge, MA, and London: MIT Press, 89–119.

—— (1994 [1987]) 'Rationalism: A Philosophical Concept in Architecture', in *Modernity and the Classical Tradition: Architectural Essays 1980–1987*. Cambridge, MA: MIT Press, 57–87.

Coplans, John (1968) 'Serial Imagery', *Artforum* 7(2): 34–43.

Cousins, Mark (1994) 'The Ugly: Part 1', *AA Files* 28: 61–64.

—— (1995) 'The Ugly: Part 2', *AA Files* 29: 3–6.

Crary, Jonathan (2001) *Suspensions of Perception: Attention, Spectacle, and Modern Culture*. Cambridge, MA: MIT Press.

Cuff, Dana (1991) *Architecture: The Story of Practice*. Cambridge, MA: MIT Press.

Cullen, Gordon (1961) *Townscape*. New York: Reinhold.

Danto, Arthur (1981) *The Transfiguration of the Commonplace: A Philosophy of Art*. Cambridge, MA: Harvard University Press.

Davidts, Wouter (2006) *Bouwen voor de kunst? Museumarchitectuur van Centre Pompidou tot Tate Modern*. Ghent: A&S Books.

Davies, Stephen (2007) 'Aesthetic Theory. Definitions of Art', in Berys Gaut and Dominic McIver Lopes (eds) *Aesthetics. The Routledge Companion to Aesthetics* (2nd edn). London and New York: Routledge. Part II, Ch. 18.

Davis, Douglas (1990) *The Museum Transformed: Design and Culture in the post-Pompidou Age*. New York: Abbeville Press.

de Certeau, Michel (1984) *The Practice of Everyday Life*. Translated by Steven Rendall. Berkeley: University of California Press.

Derrida, Jacques (1981) 'Economimesis', *Diacritics* 11: 3–25.

—— (1986) 'Point de folie – Maintenant l'architecture', *AA Files* 12: 65–75.

Diller, Elizabeth and Ricardo Scofido (2002) *Blur: The Making of Nothing*. New York: Harry N. Abrams.

Dovey, Kim (1999) *Framing Places: Mediating Power in Built Form*. London and New York: Routledge.

Eco, Umberto (2004) *On Beauty: A History of a Western Idea*. London: Secker & Warburg.

Edie, James M. (1969) 'Introduction', in James M. Edie (ed.) *New Essays in Phenomenology*. Chicago: Quadrangle Books.

Eisenman, Peter (1971) 'Conceptual Architecture: Towards a Definition', *Casabella* 359–360: 51–57.

—— (1976) 'Post-Functionalism', *Oppositions* 6: 9–12.

—— (1983) *House X (Bloomfield House)*. New York: Rizzoli.

—— (1984) 'The Futility of Objects: Decomposition and Processes of Differentiation', *Lotus International* 42: 63–75.

—— (1987) 'Misreading', in *Houses of Cards.* New York: Oxford University Press.

Elkins, James (2003) *What Happened to Art Criticism?* Chicago: Prickly Paradigm Press.

Forty, Adrian (2000) *Words and Buildings: A Vocabulary of Modern Architecture.* London: Thames & Hudson.

Frampton, Kenneth (1969) 'Labour, Work and Architecture', in Charles Jencks and George Baird (eds) *Meaning in Architecture.* New York: George Braziller, 151–167.

—— (1973) 'Industrialization and the Crises in Architecture', *Oppositions* 1: 57–82.

—— (1974) 'On Reading Heidegger', *Oppositions* 4: unpaginated.

—— (1976) 'Constructivism: The Pursuit of an Elusive Sensibility', in *Oppositions* 6: 25–44.

—— (1982) 'The Status of Man and the Status of His Objects: A Reading of the Human Condition', *Architectural Design,* 52(7–8): 6–19.

Fraser, Murray (1995) 'All Phenomenology and No Substance', *The Architect's Journal* 382(17): 42–43.

Fried, Michael (1967) 'Art and Objecthood', *Artforum* 5(10): 12–23.

—— (1998) *Art and Objecthood: Essays and Reviews.* Chicago: University of Chicago Press.

Fry, Roger (1961 [1912]) 'The French Post-Impressionists', *Vision and Design,* London: Pelican. pp. 188–93.

Fulton, Ann (1999) *Apostles of Sartre: Existentialism in America, 1945–1963.* Evanston: Northwestern University Press.

Gans, Herbert (1968) *People and Plans: Essays on Urban Problems and Solutions.* New York: Basic Books.

—— (1974) *Popular Culture and High Culture: An Analysis and Evaluation of Taste.* New York: Basic Books.

Ghirardo, Diane (ed.) (1991) *Out of Site: A Social Criticism of Architecture.* Seattle: Bay Press.

Giedion, Sigfried (1941) *Space, Time and Architecture: The Growth of a New Tradition.* Cambridge, MA: Harvard University Press.

—— (1944) 'The New Monumentality', in P. Zucker (ed.) *New Architecture and City Planning.* New York: Philosophical Library, 547–568.

—— (1948) *Mechanization Takes Command: A Contribution to Anonymous History.* New York: Oxford University Press.

—— (1981) *The Beginnings of Architecture.* Princeton, NJ: Princeton University Press.

—— (1995 [1927]) *Bauen in Frankreich/Building in France.* Translated by J. Duncan Berry. Los Angeles, CA: The Getty Center for the History of Art and the Humanities.

Grassi, Giorgio (1976) 'Realismus in der Architektur', *Archithese* 19: 18–24.

Greenberg, Clement (1966) 'On Modernist Painting', in Gregory Battock (ed.) *The New Art: A Critical Anthology.* New York: E. P. Dutton.

—— (1967) 'Recentness of Sculpture', in Maurice Tuchman (ed.) *American Sculpture of the Sixties,* Greenwich, CT: New Graphic Society, 24–26.

Gregotti, Vittorio and Jorge Otero-Pailos (2000) 'Interview with Vittorio Gregotti: The Role of Phenomenology in the Formation of the Italian Neo-Avant-Garde', *Thresholds* 21(Fall): 40–46.

Grobman, Yasha and Eran Neuman (2008) *Performalism: Form and Performance in Digital Architecture,* Tel Aviv Museum of Art, June 27, 2008–September 13, 2008, www.tamuseum.com/museum/exhibitions.asp (accessed July 1, 2008).

Guilbaut, Serge (1983) *How New York Stole the Idea of Modern Art: Abstract Expressionism, Freedom, and the Cold War.* Chicago: The University of Chicago Press.

Hagan, Susannah (2001) *Taking Shape: A New Contract between Architecture and Nature.* Oxford: Architectural Press.

Harries, Karsten (1983) 'Thoughts on a Non-Arbitrary Architecture', *Perspecta: The Yale Architectural Journal* 20: 9–20.

—— (1997) *The Ethical Function of Architecture.* Cambridge, MA: MIT Press.

Harris, Steven and Deborah Berke (eds) (1997) *Architecture of the Everyday.* New York: Princeton Architectural Press.

Hays, K. Michael (1984) 'Critical Architecture: Between Culture and Form', *Perspecta* 21: 16.

—— (1991) 'The Structure of Architectural Phenomenology', in *Newsline: Columbia University Graduate School of Architecture, Planning and Preservation* (December–January).

—— (ed.) (1998) *Oppositions Reader: Selected Readings from a Journal for Ideas and Criticism,* New York: Princeton Architectural Press.

Hearn, M. F. (ed.) (1995) *The Architectural Theory of Viollet-le-Duc: Readings and Commentary.* Cambridge, MA: MIT Press.

Heidegger, Martin (1977 [1952]) 'The Age of the World Picture', in *The Question Concerning Technology and Other Essays*. Translated by William Lovitt. New York: Harper and Row, 115–154.

Heynen, Hilde (1999 [1993]) 'Worthy of Question: Heidegger's Role in Architectural Theory', reworked into her book *Architecture and Modernity*. Cambridge, MA: MIT Press, 8–24.

Hickey, Dave (1997) *Air Guitar: Essays on Art & Democracy*. Los Angeles and New York: Art Issues Press.

—— (2009) *The Invisible Dragon: Essays on Beauty Revised and Expanded*. Chicago and London: University of Chicago Press.

Hipple, Walter (1957) *The Beautiful, the Sublime and the Picturesque in Eighteenth-Century British Aesthetic Theory*. Carbondale, IL: Illinois University Press.

Hollier, Denis (1989) *Against Architecture: The Writings of Georges Bataille*. Translated by Betsy Wing. Cambridge, MA: MIT Press.

Hopps, Walter (1991) *Robert Rauschenberg: The Early 1950s*. Houston: Menil Foundation.

Hunter, Ian (2006) 'The History of Theory', *Critical Inquiry* 33(1): 78–112.

Husserl, Edmund (1970 [1936]) *The Crisis of European Sciences and Transcendental Phenomenology*. Translated by David Carr. Evanston: Northwestern University Press.

—— (1989 [1936]) 'The Origin of Geometry' in Jacques Derrida, *Edmund Husserl's Origin of Geometry: An Introduction*. Lincoln: University of Nebraska Press, 157–180.

Ibelings, Hans (2002) 'Towards the Absolute Zero: The Diller + Scofidio Cloud at Expo.02', *Archis* 4: 86–88.

Ihde, Don (1988) 'Phenomenology and Architecture', in Stephen Perella (ed.) *Form; Being; Absence: Architecture and Philosophy: Pratt Journal of Architecture*. New York: Rizzoli International Press, 63–67.

Ingraham, Catherine (2006) *Architecture, Animal, Human: The Asymmetrical Condition*. New York: Routledge.

Ito, Toyo (2003) 'To Be an Architect', in *Hunch: The Berlage Institute Report* 6/7.

Janicaud, Dominique (1991) *Le tournant théologique de la phénoménologie française*. Combas: Éditions de L'Éclat.

Jarzombek, Mark (2000) *The Psychologizing of Modernity: Art, Architecture, History*. Cambridge: Cambridge University Press.

Jencks, Charles (1977) *The Language of Post-Modern Architecture*. New York: Rizzoli.

Kant, Immanuel (1911 [1790]) *Kant's Critique of Aesthetic Judgement*. Translated by James Creed Meredith. Oxford: Clarendon Press.

Kaprow, Alan (1968) 'The Shape of the Art Environment', *Artforum* 6(10): 32–33.

Kapusta, Beth (1994) 'The Academy Speaks (to the Academy)', *The Canadian Architect* 39(8): 10.

Katarxis (undated) Entry on 'Contemporaneity'. http://luciensteil.tripod.com/katarxis/id17.html.

Kiesler, Frederick (1929) 'Michelangelo 1929', in *Selected Writings*. Stuttgart: Gerd Hatje.

Koolhaas, Rem (2002) 'Junkspace', *October* 100: 175–190.

Kostof, Spiro (ed.) (1977) *The Architect: Chapters in the History of a Profession*. New York and Oxford: Oxford University Press.

Krauss, Rosalind (1971) 'Stella's New Work and the Problems of Series', *Artforum* 10(4): 40–44.

—— (1987) 'Death of a Hermeneutic Phantom: Materialization of the Sign in the Work of Peter Eisenman', in Peter Eisenman (ed.) *Houses of Cards*. New York: Oxford University Press, 166–184.

—— (1990) 'The Blink of an Eye', in David Carroll (ed.) *The States of 'Theory': History, Art and Critical Discourse*. New York: Columbia University Press, 175–199.

—— (1993) *The Optical Unconscious*. Cambridge, MA: MIT Press.

Krauss, Rosalind and Yves-Alain Bois (2000) *Formless: A User's Guide*. Cambridge, MA: Zone Books/MIT Press.

Krell, David Farrell (1997) 'A Malady of Chains: Husserl and Derrida on the Origins of Geometry and a Note to the "Archeticts" of the Future', *Architectural Design* 67(5–6): 12–15.

Kris, Ernst and Otto Kurz (1979) *Legend, Myth, and Magic in the Image of the Artist: A Historical Experiment*. (English translation prepared by Alastair Laing and reviewed by Lottie M. Newman; preface by E. H. Gombrich.) New Haven, CT: Yale University Press.

Kuhn, Thomas (1974) *The Structure of Scientific Revolutions*. Chicago: University of Chicago Press.

Labatut, Jean and André Girard (1951) 'Adventure in Light-Color-Polychromy: A Church Prototype. An Interview', *Liturgical Arts* 20(1): 2–8, 16–18, 20–21, 23–27.

Labatut, Jean (1944) *The Universities Position with Regard to the Visual Arts*. Princeton: Princeton University Press.

—— (1973) 'An Approach to Architectural Composition', *Modulus* 9: 58–63.

—— (1977) 'Conversations with Jean Labatut/ Interview by Michael Wurmfeld', in *Princeton's Beaux Arts and its New Academicism: From Labatut to the Program of Geddes*. Princeton: PDQ Press, 1–17.

—— (1979) 'History of Architectural Education Through People', *JAE: Journal of Architectural Education*, 33(2): 21–24.

Lahiji, Nadir and Daniel Friedman (1997) *Plumbing: Sounding Modern Architecture.* New York: Princeton Architectural Press.

Leach, Andrew (2007) *Manfredo Tafuri, Choosing History.* Ghent: A&S/Books.

Lee, Pamela (2000) *Object to Be Destroyed: The Work of Gordon Matta-Clark.* Cambridge, MA: MIT Press.

Lefebvre, Henri (1991) *Critique of Everyday Life.* Translated by John Moore. London and New York: Verso.

LeWitt, Sol (1969) 'Sentences on Conceptual Art', *Art-Language* 1: 80.

—— (1978 [1967]) 'Paragraphs on Conceptual Art', in Alicia Legg (ed.), *Sol LeWitt.* New York: The Museum of Modern Art. p.166.

Lichtenstein, Claude and Thomas Schregenberger (eds) (2001) *As Found: The Discovery of the Ordinary: British Architecture and Art of the 1950s.* Baden: Lars Müller.

Lupton, Ellen and J. Abbot Miller (1992) *The Bathroom, the Kitchen, and the Aesthetics of Waste.* New York: Princeton Architectural Press.

Macarthur, John (2007) *The Picturesque: Architecture, Disgust and other Irregularities.* London and New York: Routledge.

Maritain, Jacques (1977) *Creative Intuition in Art and Poetry.* Princeton: Princeton University Press.

McCumber, John (2001) *Time in the Ditch: American Philosophy and the McCarthy Era.* Evanston, IL: Northwestern University Press.

McLeod, Mary (1987) 'On Criticism', *Places: A Quarterly Journal of Environmental Design* 4(1): 4–6.

Mical, Thomas (2005) *Surrealism and Architecture.* New York: Routledge.

Molinari, Luca (2000) 'Between Continuity and Crisis: History and Project in Italian Architectural Culture of the Postwar Period', *2G* 3(15): 4–11.

Moneo, Rafael (1997) 'Recent Architectural Paradigms and a Personal Alternative', *Harvard Design Magazine* 2: 71–75.

Moore, Charles W. (1957) *Water and Architecture.* PhD thesis: Princeton University.

Moore, Charles W. and Kent C. Bloomer (1977) *Body, Memory and Architecture.* New Haven: Yale University Press.

Moran, Dermot (2000) *Introduction to Phenomenology.* London and New York: Routledge. p. 204.

Morris, Robert (1989) 'Words and Images in Modernism and Postmodernism', *Critical Inquiry* 15(2): 343.

—— (1993) *Continuous Project Altered Daily: The Writings of Robert Morris.* Cambridge, MA: MIT Press.

Neumeyer, Fritz (1991) *The Artless Word: Mies van der Rohe on the Art of Building.* Translated by Mark Jarzombeck. Cambridge, MA: MIT Press.

Newman, Barnett (1952) quoted by the Barnett Newman Foundation, www.barnettnewman.org/chronology.php, consulted January 19, 2010.

Noever, Peter (ed.) (2004) *Yves Klein: Air Architecture.* Ostfildern: Hatje Cantz.

Norberg-Schulz, Christian (1965) *Intentions in Architecture.* Cambridge, MA: MIT Press.

—— (1971) *Existence, Space and Architecture.* New York: Praeger.

—— (1980) *Genius Loci: Towards a Phenomenology of Architecture.* London: Academy.

Otto, Frei and Bodo Rasch (1995) *Finding Form: Towards an Architecture of the Minimal.* Fellbach: Edition Axel Menges.

Pallasmaa, Juhani (1996) *The Eyes of the Skin: Architecture and the Senses.* London: Academy.

Palmaers, Geert (2005) *Eclecticisme. Over moderne architectuur in de negentiende eeuw.* Rotterdam: 010 Publishers, 98–147.

Patterson, Richard (2006) 'What Vitruvius Said', in J. Madge and A. Peckham (eds) *Narrating Architecture.* London and New York: Routledge, 341–359.

Pérez-Gómez, Alberto (1979) 'The Use of Geometry and Number in Architectural Theory ... (1680–1820)'. PhD dissertation, University of Essex.

—— (1983) *Architecture and the Crisis of Modern Science.* Cambridge, MA: MIT Press.

—— (2006) *Built Upon Love: Architectural Longing after Ethics and Aesthetics.* Cambridge, MA: MIT Press.

Prak, Niels (1980), *Geschiedenis van het ontwerp-onderwijs.* De Bilt: Cantecleer.

—— (1983) *Architects: The Noted and the Ignored.* New York: John Wiley.

Rajchman, John (1998) *Constructions.* Cambridge, MA: MIT Press.

Rand, Ayn (1996 [1943]) *The Fountainhead.* New York: Penguin.

Rendell, Jane (2006) *Art and Architecture: A Place Between.* London and New York: I. B. Tauris (distributed in the US by Palgrave Macmillan).

Ricken, Herbert (1977) *Der Architekt. Geschichte eines Berufs.* Berlin: Henschelverlag.

Risselada, Max and Dirk van den Heuvel (eds) (2005) *Team 10 1953–1981: In Search of a Utopia of the Present.* Rotterdam: NAi Publishers.

Rogers, Ernesto Nathan (1957) 'Tradizione e attualità nel disegno', *Zodiac* 1.

—— (1959) 'L'evoluzione dell'architettura: Risposta al custode di frigidaires', *Casabella Continuità* 228(June): 2–4.

—— (1964) 'The Phenomenology of European Architecture', in Stephen R. Graubard (ed.), *A New Europe*. Boston: Houghton Mifflin. pp. 438–42.

Rowe, Colin and Robert Slutzky (1963) 'Transparency: Literal and Phenomenal', *Perspecta* 8: 45–54.

Ruby, Andreas and Benoît Durandin (eds) (2004) *Spoiled Climate: R&Sie Architects*, Basel: Birkhäuser.

Rykwert, Joseph (1972) *On Adam's House in Paradise: The Idea of the Primitive Hut in Architectural History*. New York: Museum of Modern Art.

—— (1980) *The First Moderns: The Architects of the Eighteenth Century*. Cambridge, MA: MIT Press.

—— (1996) *The Dancing Column: On Order in Architecture*. Cambridge, MA: MIT Press.

Saint, Andrew (1983) *The Image of the Architect*. New Haven: Yale University Press.

—— (2007) *Architect and Engineer: A Study in Sibling Rivalry*. New Haven and London: Yale University Press.

Scalbert, Irénée (2008) 'Architecture as a Way of Life: The New Brutalism 1953–1956', www.team10online.org/research/papers/delft1/scalbert.pdf, accessed July 2008, 1–30.

Schnapp, Jeffrey T. (2008) 'The Face of the Modern Architect', *Grey Room*, 33(Fall): 6–25.

Schoonjans, Yves (2007) *Architectuur en vooruitgang. De cultuur van het eclecticisme in de 19e eeuw*. Ghent: A&S/Books.

Scott, Felicity D. (2007) *Architecture or Techno-utopia: Politics after Modernism*. Cambridge, MA, and London: MIT Press.

Scruton, Roger (1979) *Aesthetics of Architecture*. Princeton: Princeton University Press.

—— (1995) *The Classical Vernacular: Architectural Principles in an Age of Nihilism*. New York: Saint Martin's Press.

Seamon, David and Gary J. Coates (1993) 'Promoting a Foundational Ecology Practically Through Christopher Alexander's Pattern Language: The Example of Meadowcreek', in David Seamon (ed.), *Dwelling, Seeing, and Designing: Toward a Phenomenological Ecology*. Albany: State University of New York Press, 331–351.

Serra, Richard (1994) *Writings/Interviews*. Chicago and London: University of Chicago Press, 140–155.

Siegel, Jeanne (1985) 'Joseph Kosuth: Art as Idea as Idea', in *Artwords: Discourse on the 60s and 70s*. Ann Arbor, MI: UMI Research Press, 221–231.

Silber, John (2007) *Architecture of the Absurd. How 'Genius' Disfigured a Practical Art*. New York: Quantuck Lane Press.

Sillig, Julius (1827) *Dictionary of the Artists of Antiquity, Architects, Carvers ... Painters (etc.)*. London: Black & Armstrong.

Simmel, Georg (2008 [1897]) 'Jenseits der Schönheit,' in *Jenseits der Schönheit*. Frankfurt Am Main: Suhrkamp Schriften zür Ästhetik.

Solà-Morales, Ignasi de (ed.) (2000) 'Being Manfredo Tafuri', *ANY: Architecture New York*, 25–26.

Somol, Robert and Sarah Whiting (2002) 'Notes around the Doppler Effect and Other Moods of Modernism', *Perspecta* 33: 72–77.

Sorkin, Michael (1991) *Exquisite Corpse: Writings on Buildings*. London: Verso.

Soussloff, Catherine (1997) *The Absolute Artist. The Historiography of a Concept*. Minneapolis: University of Minnesota Press.

Spiegelberg, Herbert (1982) *The Phenomenological Movement: A Historical Introduction*. The Hague, Boston and London: Martinus Nijhoff Publishers.

Stevens, Garry (1998) *The Favored Circle: The Social Foundations of Architectural Distinction*. Cambridge, MA: MIT Press.

Stokes, Adrian (2002 [1934]) *The Quattro Cento and Stones of Rimini*. Pennsylvania: Penn State Press.

Stoppani, Teresa (2007) 'Dust Revolutions. Dust, Informe, Architecture (Notes for a Reading of Dust in Bataille)', *The Journal of Architecture* 12(4): 437–447.

Summerson, John (1963) 'Heavenly Mansions: An Interpretation of Gothic', in *Heavenly Mansions, and Other Essays on Architecture*. New York: W. W. Norton, 1–28.

Tafuri, Manfredo (1976) *Architecture and Utopia. Design and Capitalist Development*. Cambridge, MA: MIT Press [translated from *Progetto e Utopia* 1973].

—— (1987) *The Sphere and the Labyrinth: Avant-gardes and Architecture from Piranesi to the 1970s*. Cambridge, MA: MIT Press [translation of *Sfera e il labirinto* 1980].

Tafuri, Manfredo and Francesco Dal Co (1979) *Modern Architecture*. Translated by Robert Erich Wolf. New York: H. N. Abrams.

Thomas, Helen (2004) 'Invention in the Shadow of History: Joseph Rykwert at the University of Essex', *Journal of Architectural Education* 58(2): 39–45.

Tschumi, Bernard (1996 [1977]) 'The Pleasure of Architecture', in Kate Nesbitt (ed.) *Theorizing a New Agenda for Architecture: An Anthology of Architectural Theory 1965–1995.* New York: Princeton Architectural Press, 532–540.

Ursprung, Philip (ed.) (2002) *Natural History*, Published on the occasion of a travelling exhibition held at the Centre Canadien d'architecture, Montréal, October 23, 2002–April 6, 2003. Baden, Switzerland: Lars Müller.

Van Winkel, Camiel and Bart Verschaffel (2004) '"Ik ben verbluft over de rechten die het artistieke zich aanmeet": Vraaggesprek met Rem Koolhaas' ['I am stunned by the prerogatives art dares to claim': A Conversation with Rem Koolhaas], *De Witte Raaf* 109: 6–8.

Venturi, Robert (1966) *Complexity and Contradiction in Architecture.* New York: Museum of Modern Art.

Venturi, Robert, Denise Scott Brown and Steven Izenour (1972) *Learning from Las Vegas.* Cambridge, MA: MIT Press.

Vesely, Dalibor (1988) 'On the Relevance of Phenomenology', *Form, Being, Absence. Architecture and Philosophy: Pratt Journal of Architecture* 2: 59–62.

—— (2004) *Architecture in the Age of Divided Representation: The Question of Creativity in the Shadow of Production.* Cambridge, MA: MIT Press.

Vidler, Anthony (1987) *The Writing of the Walls: Architectural Theory in the Late Enlightenment.* Princeton: Princeton Architectural Press.

—— (1992) *The Architectural Uncanny: Essays in the Modern Unhomely.* Cambridge, MA: MIT Press.

—— (2000) *Warped Space: Art, Architecture, and Anxiety in Modern Culture.* Cambridge, MA: MIT Press.

—— (2003) 'Transparency: Literal and Phenomenal', *Journal of Architectural Education* 56(4): 6–7.

Vischer, Robert et al. (1994) *Empathy, Form, and Space: Problems in German Aesthetics, 1873–1893.* Introduction and translation by Harry Francis Mallgrave and Eleftherios Ikonomou. Santa Monica: Getty Center for the History of Art and the Humanities. Distributed by the University of Chicago Press, Chicago.

Wagner, Otto (1992 [1902]) *Modern Architecture: A Guidebook for His Students in This Field of Art,* Translated by Harry Francis Mallgrave. Chicago: University of Chicago Press.

Werner, Frank (2000) *Covering and Exposing: Coop Himmelb(l)au.* Basel: Birkhauser.

Wigley, Mark (1992) 'Heidegger's House: The Violence of the Domestic', *Columbia Documents of Architecture and Theory (D)* 1: 91–121.

—— (1993) *The Architecture of Deconstruction: Derrida's Haunt.* Cambridge, MA: MIT Press.

—— (2001) *White Walls, Designer Dresses.* Cambridge, MA: MIT Press.

Wild, John Daniel (1955) *The Challenge of Existentialism.* Bloomington: Indiana University Press.

Williams, Robert (1997) *Art, Theory, and Culture in Sixteenth-Century Italy: From Technè to Metatechnè.* Cambridge: Cambridge University Press.

Wittkower, Rudolf and Margot Wittkower (1963) *Born Under Saturn: The Character and Conduct of Artists.* New York: Random House.

Zimmerman, Michael E. (1985) 'The Role of Spiritual Discipline in Learning to Dwell on Earth', in David Seamon and Robert Mugerauer (eds) *Dwelling, Place and Environment: Towards a Phenomenology of Person and World.* Dordrecht, the Netherlands: Martinus Nijhoff Publishers, 247–256.

10

Consumption

Ana Miljački

Though the critics who have doubted consumption's capacity to deliver economic growth and associated improvements in living standards appear to be vindicated by the global financial crisis of 2008, the question of how to critically describe or theorize the relationship between consumption and architecture at the end of postmodernism remains open.

At the beginning of the twenty-first century, 'consumption' encompasses an expansive collection of practices. We consume money, nature, things, ideas, atmospheres, experiences and architecture. Some of the recent considerations of those practices have begun to reposition the term and its intellectual currency away from the simplistic, though widely-held, caricature of consumption as the global medium by which the unknowing masses are manipulated for the benefit of transnational corporations.[1] Within a more strictly architectural discourse, Rem Koolhaas, Jeffrey Inaba and Sze Tsung Leong's (2002) *Guide to Shopping*, and the shiny, Albert Ferré et al's edited (2005), collection *Verb Conditioning: The Design of New Atmospheres, Effects and Experiences* have begun to describe the

Figure 10.1 (Below) Prada Epicenter, New York, OMA and 'Prada Vomit' mural by 2x4. (2x4)

extent to which consumption has been complexly integrated into the shaping of contemporary architecture and its public constituencies.

We live in the age of entanglements, which means at least two things. First, consumption has gotten more complexly intertwined with architecture than it was at the time when, Marxist architectural critic, Manfredo Tafuri asked architects and historians to understand the status of the architectural object and the role of the architect in ideological terms as resting upon wider structures of production.[2] Second, we are becoming proficient at describing these and many other types of entanglements without abstracting and simplifying them to the point of flattening them completely.

Bruno Latour invited the readers of his book *Reassembling the Social* (2005) to take a mental test.[3] If we thought that the time would come when we would be able to distinguish ends from means, facts from values and humans from non-humans – trusting that clarity was merely a question of progress – we could still consider ourselves modern. If we hesitated at all when presented with this idea, we were likely to be postmodern. But if, indeed, we believed that the world was getting ever more entangled, we might have entered another paradigm, one that Latour called 'non-modern'. The possibility that such a non-modern stance offers is the capacity to see and describe complex relationships between architects, money, technological innovation and various types of uses and reception. This does not imply an abandonment of the fact of modernism, as a period with a particular ethos, concept of time and a specific idea of progress. In fact, a type of periodization is important

Figure 10.2 (Below) Prada Epicenter, New York, 'Parallels' mural by 2x4. (2x4)

here, even if we lack a convenient name for the contemporary. Terms such as Marc Augé's (1995) 'supermodernity', Hans Ibelings' (1998) 'supermodernism', Zygmunt Bauman's (2000) 'fluid modernity' or Latour's (2005) 'non-modern', each attempt to describe an important difference between the contemporary and the modern (understood historically).

If modernism was underwritten by the idea that progress and the arrow of time would eventually deliver things to perfection, or to a perfectly rational and organized world, today we can no longer confidently tap into the authority and certainty of that project. Furthermore if, following Latour and others, we come to appreciate the entanglements between things, then a categorical critique of consumption in architecture seems no longer plausible or useful. A perspective that foregrounds relationality certainly offers more scope to consider the agency of design. The binding together of ideas, people, materials and agencies as allies or, their dispersal as rivals, demands a greater attention to the logics and workings of design, however prominent, modest, explicit or tacit their expressions might be. What follows are a set of three reports, or stories, that say something about the place of architecture in the terrain of this contemporary consumption.

WALLPAPER

The New York flagship store for Miuccia Prada's luxury clothing and lifestyle accessories was conceived in close collaboration by Prada and Rem Koolhaas' firm OMA as a space that would transcend

Figure 10.3 (Below) Prada Epicenter, New York, showing the 'Guilt Incorporated' mural by 2x4. (2x4)

the usual storage, counter, and cash register functionality of retail outlets. Named the Prada New York Epicenter, located in downtown Soho and opened in 2001, the store was conceived as a kind of quasi-public space. A portion of the store was dedicated to the display of high fashion and was intended to contribute to the cultural event calendar of the city. The design of the New York Epicenter, and others in the Prada chain in Tokyo, San Francisco and Los Angeles, explicitly downplayed the Prada brand itself – a decision that has been regarded as both an act of brand confidence and a sophisticated move to rejuvenate the brand. The discrete presence of the brand and the careful integration of non-retail space in the design (along with some sophisticated event planning) have seen the New York Epicenter come to serve as *the* space for exhibitions, fashion events and parties. The Prada store is ambiguously positioned as a species of privately wrought public space.

The New York Epicenter has consistently programmed its quasi-public spaces with various low- and high-tech novelties, surreal and sometimes even Brechtian estrangement devices. One significant component of this programming is a wall mural that changes every six months. Always visible from outside, and for many the sole reason to visit the store, the graphics of the murals mingle critical atmosphere with striking aesthetic effects. The New York-based graphic design firm 2x4 is the 'keeper' of the murals, designing and installing the images on a six-monthly cycle. Their 'Prada Vomit' mural (Figure 10.1), as it was nicknamed, launched

Figure 10.4 (Below) The 'Guilt Incorporated' mural scheme, drawing of the large wall graphic presented as a single long graphic, and with a close up of two portions of it. (2x4)

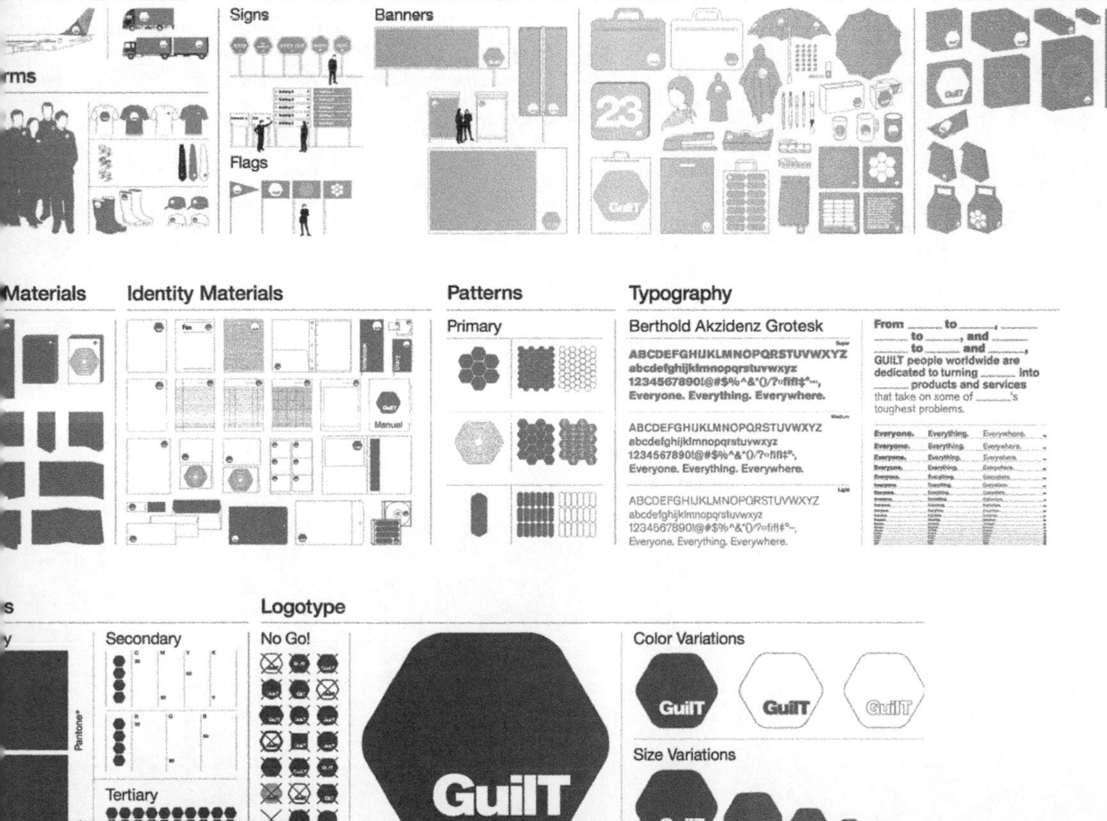

Figure 10.5 (Above) A model of the 'The Matrix Enfolder' portion of the Mercator Center in Nova Gorica, Slovenia, by Sadar Vuga Architects. (Sadar Vuga Architects)

Figure 10.6 (Below) Inside of the Matrix Enfolder, Mercator Center in Nova Gorica. (Sadar Vuga Architects)

Figure 10.7 (Below right) A view of the 'Matrix Enfolder' from the bottom level of the parking structure. Mercator Center in Nova Gorica. (Sadar Vuga Architects)

the series and featured pixilated and self-consciously picturesque floral figures that framed a series of more jarring, mildly pornographic images. In another wallpaper, an army of Chinese women is pictured dressed in standard work attire, individually and collectively assuming now widely recognized victorious workers' postures (Figure 10.2). These women nod at once towards the contemporary coolness of Chinese socialist realist chic, and the literal aspects of globalized divisions of labour that see average Americans intimately familiar with the 'Made in China' labels in their everyday wardrobes.

The 'Guilt Incorporated' mural was another, equally multivalent image to feature in the New York Epicenter (Figures 10.3 and 10.4). The title of the mural referred to the brand identity concocted by 2x4 for an imaginary company, consisting of the usual range of branding paraphernalia such as logos, letterheads, signage, livery and colourings.

The graphics were multiplied to cover the wall, inviting interpretation on an individual level, while also providing a commentary on the ideological role of the contemporary graphic design. Since it is hard to imagine any of Prada's hard-core regulars feeling actual guilt about purchasing Prada products, the term 'guilt' here has the status of a meta-concept, perhaps not unlike the way consumption functions for the collective imaginary of well-to-do urbanites more generally. But it is also possible that, after the (all-too-brief) shock effect of the mural wears off, Guilt Incorporated operates hedonistic cover that smoothes the way to accepting the prices of luxury goods. There should be no illusion: the dissimulation of Prada's explicit brand in the spaces of the Epicenter store is recouped through the quasi-critical aura of these murals, and the atmosphere of the events that they frame. Prada's brand is a kind of post-brand that corresponds to the new form of quasi-public space that has been crafted for a new consuming constituency. In this space the messages delivered by 2x4 follow the logic of consumption highlighting the extent to which contemporary aesthetic and political experiences are fused.

WALL

As a retail typology, the supermarket and its younger cousin the hypermarket are at the exact opposite end of the retail spectrum from the Prada Epicenter. The large quantity of goods, organized in seemingly simple rows, but nonetheless 'scientifically' positioned for the greatest impact on the attention of family cooks, demanding kids and every other shade of shopper, have been packaged for years in big box architectures that some say litter, but certainly help constitute, the ex-urban landscape all over

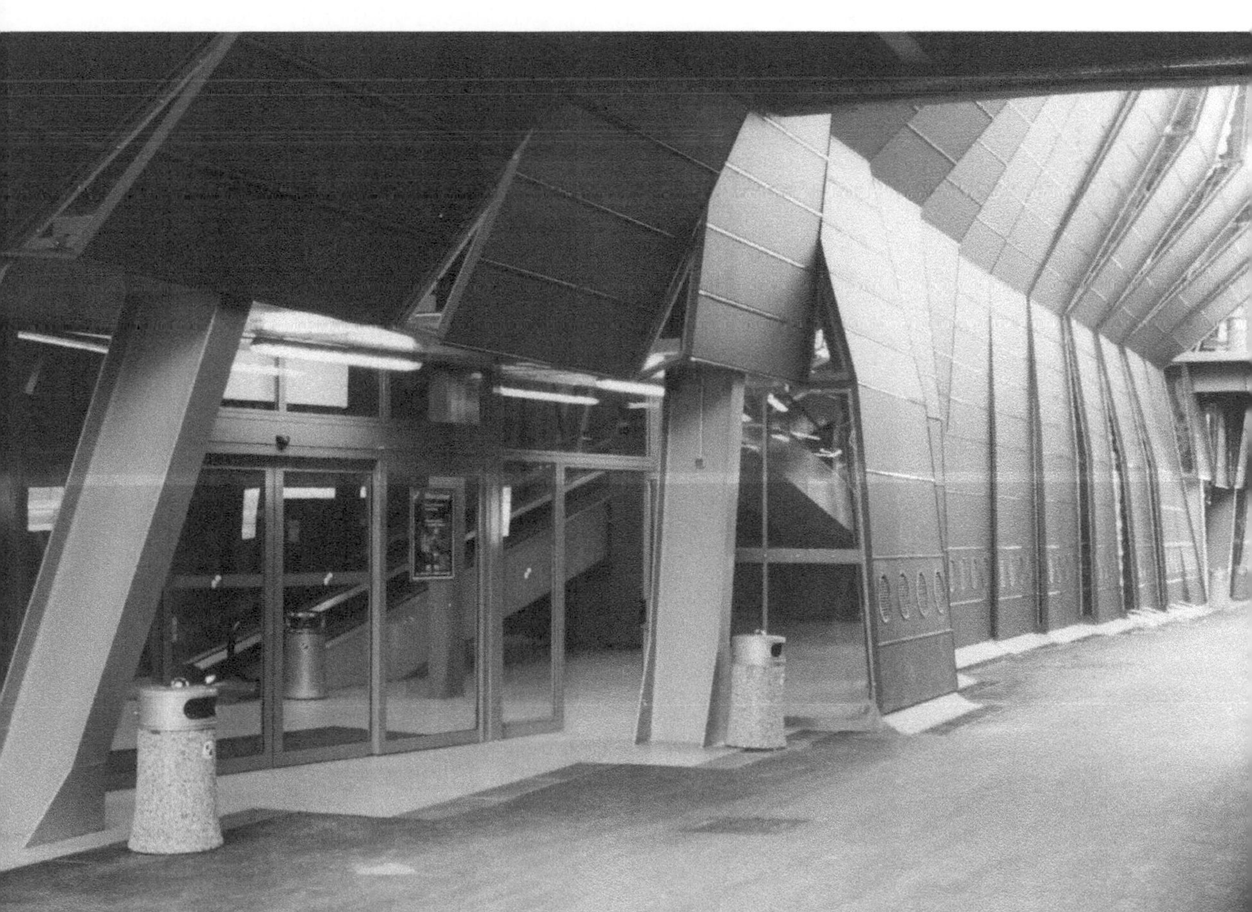

the world. Although socialism had its version of supermarkets – dedicated to large-scale, collective delivery of goods, with an ethos of something like 'reasonable consumption' – nothing signalled New Europe's (the old East Europe) turn of fortune more than the arrival of shopping malls, big box architectures and large billboards on the outskirts of its towns. In an environment where big box architectures were being rapidly constructed, differentiation between them became an urgent imperative. The quality of design and the image of such consumer spaces became as significant as that differentiation was urgent. It is no coincidence, then, that a number of the most interesting architectural interventions across the urban landscape of the New European states, such as Slovenia and Croatia, bear the logo of Mercator, one of the most progressive retail companies to emerge in the post-socialist former Yugoslavian states.

Mercator was a private company established in 1949 as Živila Ljubljana. It was nationalized in the immediate post-war years and grew to be one of the largest wholesalers and, consequently, a 'known' and trusted brand during the socialist era of Yugoslavian 'Brotherhood and Unity'. The privatization of Mercator began in 1993, kicked off by a public share offering that resulted in over 60,000 private shareholders. The company has been spreading its network of businesses and hypermarkets, supermarkets and stores across the former territory of Yugoslavia. Not only is the company setting a standard for responsible corporate behaviour in the region, in terms of its environmental consciousness, its dealings with local producers of food and other goods, and its socially-minded fundraising campaigns, it is also one of the most innovative clients for young Slovenian and Croatian architects.

Figure 10.8 (Below) Three parts of the Mercator Center in Nova Gorica. (Sadar Vuga Architects)

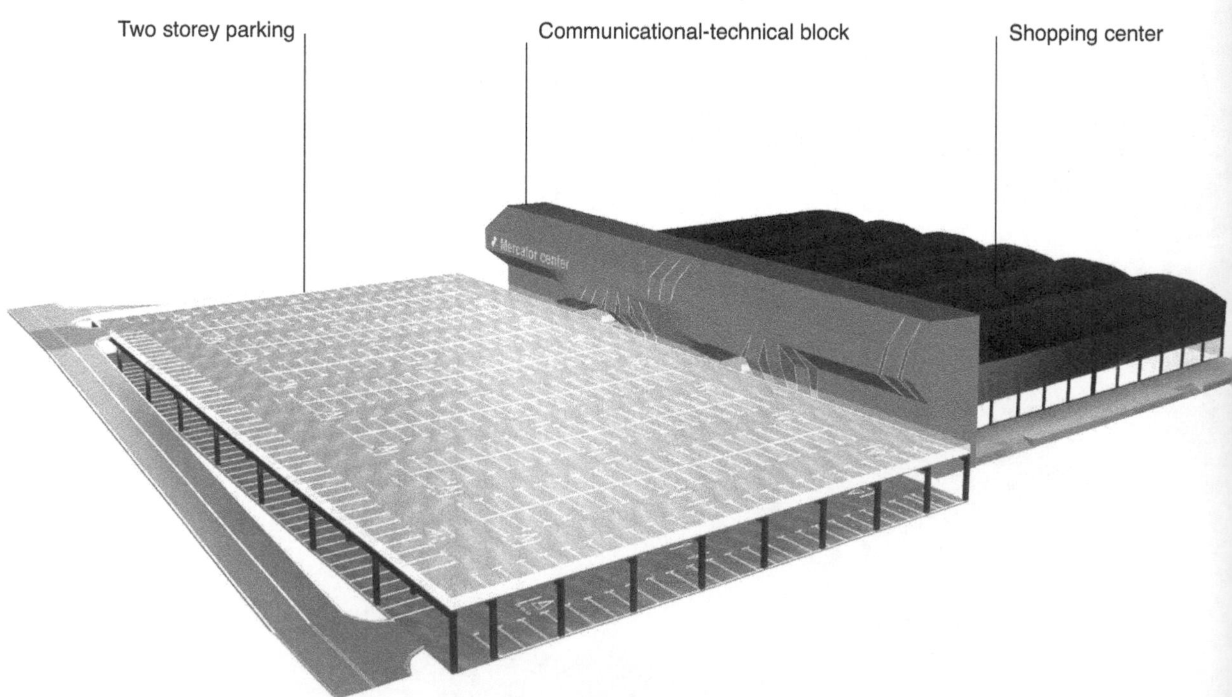

The challenge that Mercator offers its architects is twofold: facilitating consumption while expressing something of the Mercator group's corporate philosophy, and if there were such an entity as corporate citizens of the world, then also its value as a player in the new, or at least re-emergent, civil societies of the Balkans. Recognizing what Victor Gruen, the so-called 'father of the mall', understood implicitly – that the mall was not inevitable, but that it took an architect to imagine it and sell it – Mercator invites and pays for architectural innovation.[4] In this region, where the configuration of hypermarkets, their standards of operating, and their disposition within the ex-urban shopping landscape have not been stabilized through years of practice (as they have been in North America), a company with a real investment in the local context is in a position to inventively steer and shape the future of that landscape.

Mercator Center in Nova Gorica, Slovenia, was designed and built in 2000–2001 by Sadar Vuga Architects, widely regarded as leaders of Slovenia's first post-transition wave of architects.[5] The first sketches for the project involved the production of a new ground and a new façade, masking an old warehouse and recreating the basic box-in-the-parking-lot effect, when seen from the highway. The bulk of the intervention is a plug between the warehouse and the new parking structure, that Sadar Vuga earnestly titled 'Matrix Enfolder' (Figure 10.5). Parking is accommodated on several levels, yet on the exterior Sadar Vuga almost nostalgically present an image of a parking lot. The semiotic game they are playing, including a reference they make to the American landscape of big box stores circa 1950s, invites other readings that further entangle the history of the type with

Figure 10.9 (Below) A side view of the Mercator Center in Nova Gorica. (Sadar Vuga Architects)

its newest context (Figure 10.6). The project appears from the local expressway as an undulating façade, a giant billboard that signals the presence of Mercator (together with the denotative sign for the store). The undulating façade marks the entry into the shopping centre, and helps to monumentalize the building. Its large scale and strangeness in this landscape has a branding function, signifying a modern company dedicated to efficiency and contemporary design.

Sadar Vuga Architects explain the logic of the undulating wall via the old narrative of function (Figures 10.7–10.10). The wall is filled with circulation: stairs and connections between the parking lot and the mall. But the ultimate architectural product has multiple readings made possible through a basic functionalist differentiation of three programmatic elements: parking, shopping, circulation. The Matrix Enfolder also performs as a wind barrier and furthermore its form helps bring natural light into the

Figure 10.10 (Above) Mercator Center in Nova Gorica, Slovenia. (Sadar Vuga Architects)

Figure 10.11 (Below left and right) Meydan Shopping Centre grounds seen from above, Ümraniye, Turkey. (Metro Asset Management)

deep plan of the mall. From certain oblique angles the assemblage of elements, each with its own character, supports a three-dimensional reading of the project (synthetic grounds of the parking, an expressive thin element, and the old shed), while the frontal view from the highway gives the effect of a folded, two-dimensional plane. The Nova Gorica Mercator Center, reads as a 'mall' when approached by car, but when it is examined more carefully in section, it becomes clear that the typology of the mall has been inflected in rather unexpected ways. Many recent accounts of contemporary Slovenian architecture have placed Sadar Vuga's work squarely within current European discourse. Yet their work at the Nova Gorica Mercator Center suggests a conceptual and typological thinking that engages with pre-1989 Eastern Europe. It is possible that as Mercator in Nova Gorica is accepted into mainstream European discourse, at least two things get smuggled in with it. On the one hand, Sadar Vuga's play with signification and typological innovation elevates a project as 'mundane' and generic as a supermarket. On the other hand, the ghost of a collectivist utopia seems to be embodied in Mercator's shareholder-owned and locally invested company structure. There is little doubt that architectural innovation helps Mercator's profits directly and indirectly. However, this project also demonstrates that the adaptation of earlier (seemingly outmoded) forms of retail architecture to fit the newly commercialized landscape of New Europe, and the reconciliation of market and collectivist logics, has seen an architecture deployed in a way that is not simplistically determined by profits.

GROUND

Having exploded onto the architectural scene in the 1990s with their project for the

Yokohama Ferry Terminal, Foreign Office Architects (FOA) has since cultivated itself as a global practice. As the firm's name suggests, the practice sees itself as being unmoored from any particularly place, with a perspective that values the 'foreign'. In 2005, FOA was invited by the METRO Group to participate in an architectural design competition for a new shopping mall in Ümraniye, a fast-growing suburb of Istanbul, Turkey. The METRO Group is a large German-based retail and wholesale corporation, rivalling Tesco in the UK and Carrefour in France in scale and global reach, and had been expanding since the early 2000s in former Eastern European countries, as well as Turkey. The Meydan shopping mall, as the project was to be known, was conceived by the METRO Group as a new mall prototype for application in future projects in the Middle East (Figures 10.11–10.15). In a recent book on the project, *Meydan Shopping Square: A New Prototype by FOA* (2008) – a book produced by the client and somewhat marred by the its generally self-congratulatory tone – the METRO Group refigure the problem of big box architectures, and their proliferation on the edges of urban centres generally, as an opportunity to intelligently shape and steer the rapid growth of Middle Eastern cities (Cesarz and Ferreira-Erlenbach 2008).

Figure 10.12 (Below) Meydan Shopping Centre, exterior view, Ümraniye, Turkey. (FOA, photograph by Friedrich Ludewig)

The major innovations of FOA's proposal stem from the decision to locate the parking decks below the pedestrian plane. This allowed the pedestrian ground plane to be continuous with the surrounding streets, better integrating the complex into its suburban context. The ground plane itself is a relatively continuous surface differentiated by folds and undulations of varying severity.

Figure 10.13 (Above) Meydan Shopping Centre, interior view of the supermarket. (FOA, photograph by Friedrich Ludewig)

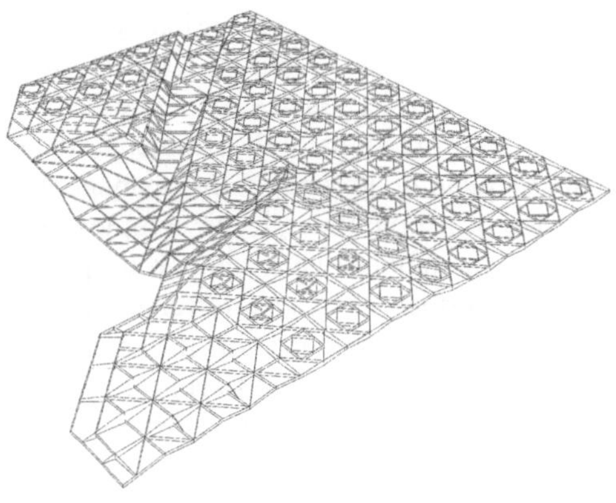

Figure 10.14 (Above) Axonometric drawing of the Meydan Shopping Centre roof, showing the change in angle and the basic logic of the structural grid. (FOA)

Figure 10.15 (Below) Section of the Meydan Shopping Centre. (FOA)

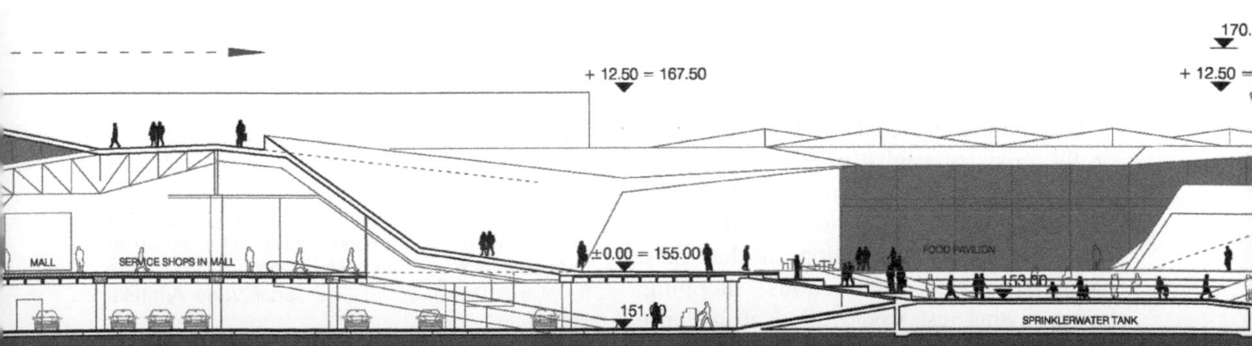

These help to articulate variously scaled public spaces such as parks, skating rinks (in winter), paved squares, sports areas and other, less functionally-determined, zones. The undulating ground helps manage the passage of people through the complex, and is also continuous with some roof planes offering further navigable terrains. A geothermal unit embedded in the complex, claimed to be the largest in Europe, heats and cools the interior spaces. The different possibilities for public space and passage make the Meydan project a convincing new prototype in a context where public culture and shopping are deeply related.

The dream behind the Meydan project in many ways echoes Victor Gruen's hopes for the mall. Gruen imagined the mall to be strategically located on the inter-city highway networks of the US, functioning as engines of urban growth, and thereby promoting new forms of consumerism along with a newly conceived (suburban) civic imaginary. While we know that Gruen's formula has produced a slew of 'dead malls' in the US, and is widely regarded as threatening the compact urban forms of the new and future Europe, the METRO Group's Meydan project does offer an important reformulation of that old model. More carefully embedded in existing urban fabrics, integrating public space in more imaginative ways, enriching the functional diversity, and keyed into a local geothermal energy source, the Meydan mall offers the town of Ümraniye an infrastructure that it just might be equipped to use on its own, one that is less likely to be left high and dry as an obsolete infrastructure by shifting global financial flows. The Meydan mall is, in effect, less brittle an urban form because it is not so exclusively tied to the logics of global capital and consumption.

The limit scenario of the financial crisis, or the crisis of capitalism, is possibly the most useful mental test of the architectural and urban value of projects produced to facilitate daily consumption in that most banal sense of conspicuous shopping; however, this test would allow us to once again delaminate architecture from the conditions of its possibility at the beginning of the twenty-first century. It is only in describing multiple agents involved in the production of architecture (including patrons, cultural forces and existing historical narratives) that a series of qualitatively different relationships between consumption and architecture can begin to be rendered with enough complexity to allow for patterns of contemporary architectural agency to emerge.

NOTES

1 The Introduction to a recent compendium on consumption (Clarke et al. 2003) suggests that 'consumption' as a term and concept is remarkably slippery, at different times being associated with pleasure, economic necessity and outright destruction. It is a theme that has preoccupied many of the key figures in Western thought: Karl Marx and political economists in both Leninist and Frankfurt School veins, anthropologists like Emile Durkheim, Marcel Mauss and Georges Bataille, and the more recent chroniclers and theorists of everyday life under capitalism, Henri Lefebvre, Roland Barthes, Jean Baudrillard and Michel de Certeau (see Clarke et al. 2003).

2 If Manfredo Tafuri considered anything transferable from the lessons of historical modernism to his contemporary context, then the misconception of architecture's ideological role in modernism has to be seen as its most important lesson. Hence, part of the conclusion of *Architecture and Utopia* calls for a real demystification of architecture's position within the system of relations of production, and a real understanding of architecture's capacity to affect the political and economic realms. See Tafuri's (1979) *Architecture and Utopia.*

3 The spirit of this challenge can be found in a number of Latour's writings in the 1990s and 2000s, and is expressed most famously in his *We Have Never Been Modern* (1993).

4 Perhaps the most compelling aspect of Alex Wall's (2006) recent study of Victor Gruen's work is his view of Gruen as an extremely savvy promoter and salesman of his own ideas.

5 See a series of texts by Europe's young critics on the work produced in Slovenia since the Slovenian independence in *Six Pack* Exhibit Catalogue (Ljubljana: Dessa, 2005). See Sadar Vuga Arhitekti 2006.

BIBLIOGRAPHY

Augé, Marc (1995) *Non-Places: Introduction to an Anthropology of Supermodernity*. London: Verso.

Bauman, Zygmunt (2000) *Liquid Modernity*. London: Polity.

Cesarz, Michael and Manina Ferreira-Erlenbach (eds) (2008) *Meydan Shopping Square: A New Prototype by FOA: A Metro Group Project in Istanbul*. Berlin: Jovis.

Clarke, David B., Marcus A. Doel and Kate M.L. Housiaux (eds) (2003) *The Consumption Reader*. London: Routledge.

Ferré, Albert et al. (eds) (2005) *Verb Conditioning: The Design of New Atmospheres, Effects and Experiences*. Barcelona: Actar.

Ibelings, Hans (1998) *Supermodernism: Architecture in the Age of Globalization*. Rotterdam: NAi Press.

Koolhaas, Rem, Jeffrey Inaba and Sze Tsung Leong (2002) *The Harvard Design School Guide to Shopping/Harvard Design School Project on the City*. Cologne: Taschen.

Latour, Bruno (1993) *We Have Never Been Modern*. Cambridge, MA: Harvard University Press.

—— (2005) *Reassembling the Social: An Introduction to Actor-Network-Theory*. Oxford: Oxford University Press.

Sadar Vuga Arhitekti (2006) *Tendencies* (Design Document Series 17). Seoul: Damdi.

Tafuri, Manfredo (1979) *Architecture and Utopia*. Cambridge, MA: MIT Press.

Wall, Alex (2006) *Victor Gruen: From Urban Shop to New City*. Barcelona: Actar.

SECTION 3

Nation/World/Spectacle

11

Introduction: Enacting Modernity

AbdouMaliq Simone

Is it possible to gather up the discrepant materials, sentiments, forms and efforts of various peoples and 'send them off' into a horizon that everyone values as either necessary or better? Or is any assemblage always provisional and haphazard – full of tensions and make-shift 'deals' where the contributions of components are always subject to negotiations among their 'messy' inclinations and histories? These questions, at the heart of architecture and urbanism's long preoccupation with modernity, continue to haunt a world increasingly convinced that it was never 'modern' and re-emphasize the contestations always at work in how things – materials, language, bodies – are brought together. In other words, the concerns of the present seem to deal with the troublesome practices and designs that attempt to assemble coordinated understandings and actions about what can be done, where and how.

These questions have stretched the notions of architecture to encompass mathematics and finance which attempt to generate models about how vastly divergent locations, economies, and ways of doing and valuing things can circulate through each other, and generate surplus value through the unpredictable products of such circulation. Architecture has also engaged various political ecologies and discourses of sustainability which attempt to visualize complex interdependencies among bodies, infrastructure, climates and environments. All deal with fundamental questions about what it is possible for people and things to do with each other, what they can make, for whom, and what the implications of this making will be.

In this section, Abidin Kusno, Duanfang Lu, Shiloh Krupar and Stefan Al take up these questions by exploring various facets of the relationship of architecture to modernity, the nation and power in three chapters. Each has marked resonance and cross-cutting reiterations. Kusno emphasizes the volatile and always to be worked out relationship between the nation and the state. Lu focuses on how to think about and engage the tricky multiplicities of modernity. Krupar and Al focus on how architecture shifts from the performative display of ideological solidities to the enwrapping of affect and experience into more viral forms of power through stretching the operations of spectacle. In all of these explorations, architecture cannot be held as some stable instrument of discourse or techné, but itself becomes a shifting array of effects.

For if a critical locus of modernity has been the concrescence of the individual as a stabilized object of discipline and reflection, as well as the predominant mode of consciousness, then architecture is deeply implicated in the very enactment of modernity – rather than simply a descriptive feature of it.

As Lefebvre (1991a) indicates, actions initiated or compelled from an environment act in the elaboration of space. Space is not something that actors are 'set' in or 'emerge' from. Rather, actors and environments mutually participate in the constitution of overlapping, switching and modulated registers of operation in which perception is steered and behaviour habituated to apprehend specific boundaries, distinctions and trajectories – in terms of the experience of inside and out, here and there, now and then. The individual is an architectural instrument and an object of architecture. At times this relationship between instrument and object is self-reinforcing and transformative, and so the details of how this relationship is conducted become critical in thinking about potentialities and constraints, openings and confinement.

For Lu, in her concise and sweeping review of how modernity appears in the world and its impact on it, this terrain of the relational reveals just how modernity has been capable of acting like a trickster – changing skins and masks, replicating itself in seemingly contradictory ways. At the same time, it is forced to consort with ghosts – ways of thinking and doing things it supposedly got rid of, but really cannot afford to if it is to be, as Lu says, an epochal force from which no society can escape. For the trick of modernity is to have acted as a system of comprehensiveness and completion, positing a linear trajectory of development in which novelty, abstraction and the arbitrariness of representation can all be handled without upending the rational calculations of what was to come.

In architecture, it entailed the appropriation of vernacular forms and experiences, and incorporating them into a frame of abstraction that sought to erase the traces of origin and use. The erasure is not so much of the reference itself. Rather, it is as if the abstraction acted as some deep structure which could give rise to heterogeneity of expression. Therefore, differences in people's ways of doing things and seeing the world weren't really different, but were rather various forms of certain generic cognitive and moral principles that varied in terms of their level of development. Everyone was heading for the same place, but at different times, and this lag constituted a platform that justified different regimes of regard and rule.

During the past several decades there has been an attempt to get out of this scheme of developmental lags by positing the existence of multiple or alternative modernities that embody the purported efforts of all people to exceed the terms of a given recognition and to take advantage of unanticipated and dense relations with the world. Such aspirations are particularly exemplified in and by cities.

In cities, different settlement histories are at work and intersect in different ways. Within these histories are different capacities for making things happen. New ground is charted and sometimes different ways of life contract. They hold their place in more narrow versions of themselves. Particular kinds of neighbourhoods, with particular kinds of residents and ways of doing things, may extend themselves across the city. They may disappear in some places and reappear in others. They may fracture and regroup as smaller enclaves in different parts of the city, or simply integrate themselves into other more predominant forms of social identity. A highly mixed neighbourhood of different kinds of residents and activities may simply become available to mixtures of a new kind. What starts out as a highly homogenous, for example suburban area, may over a matter of decades become highly mixed or vice versa. In other words, the various processes of so-called 'urban modernity', such as gentrification, sustainability, diversification and growth – to name a few of the keywords attached to critical urban processes – do not necessarily take place in necessarily stable and clearly recognizable ways.

Lu chooses to use the notion of 'entangled modernities' to deal with this multiplicity. This proves to be an important strategic move. Otherwise, to talk about many modernities is to implicitly emphasize a notion of equivalence. Not that all modernities are the same. But differences then become subsumed to various versions of modernity, of a general equivalence, or as Jean-Luc Nancy (2000) says, a new form of the One, as a monstrosity that precludes renewal. Rather, Nancy emphasizes that we are in a world that is in itself broken, and that the multiplicity of bodies and experiences that might recognize a commonality can only do so in the sense of being exposed to and sharing-out this brokenness. The notion of multiple modernities makes divergent, parasitical exchanges somehow equal. It doubles the practice whereby modernity itself was an accumulation of gifts – taken through imperial manoeuvers and then effaced as gifts, as something compelling the continuity of some ongoing exchange. History is made to seem self-transparent, without debt.

After all, it was through bestowing a general equivalence to the colonies – through the granting of independence and nationhood – that the West was able to deal with a wide range of struggles and aspirations whose terms and feelings were not always recognizable in any conventional language. This granting of sovereignty, of recognition, then made the terms of interaction understandable. Even though nations of the 'developing world' did not have the capacities and power of their 'equivalents', they were not fully part of the 'world of nations'.

Lu avoids these problems of equivalence by exploring the coupling of the postcolonial and the postmodern, and the ways in which the supposed dissipation of grand narratives opens up the way for mimetic play. Here, diverse national and regional settings take things from each other and haunt each other with unexpected versions of themselves – something aided by the proliferation of mimetic machines and technologies which continuously reconfigure the space of the relationships between self and other, North and South. Here, the West cannot get rid of ghosts.

As we know, mimesis is a tricky game of doubling. As Taussig (1993) points out, the mimetic always releases features, capacities and dimensions that the original was incapable of – but which must have been there all along, as well as the sense that the 'reality' of the original did not have to be what it was. After all, this is the possibility of transformation and renewal. Modernity then is always anxious about itself. In the same place and time, another set of conditions, another way of doing things, and another reality has always already been possible – and in an important way, was always already *in place.*

For example, it is precisely this virtual presence of *cityness* in each and every major and mundane action undertaken to structure urban life that is made peripheral – even if the viability of urban economies, governance and innovation requires that *cityness* as an essential resource. Thus, in cities there is always a certain *doubleness* of time – a sense that behind the present moment, there is another time operating, other things taking place, unfolding, waiting, getting ready or slipping away, and that we know only a fragment of what is proceeding. The seemingly coherent landscape of the city is the result of a process where unruly eruptions, interference and murkiness are negated or erased. With this erasure, whatever appears coherent about the city is fundamentally tenuous and uneasy. It is always uncertain as to the extent to which 'urban development' adequately conceals both the operations of erasure, as well as what was erased, denied or pushed aside.

This haunting is not dissimilar to that long embodied in some of the critical works of African American scholars from DuBois' *The Soul of Black Folks* to Tony Morrison's *Beloved.* In this work, the lost souls of slaves never have a home to return to or even a final destination in mind. There can never be a putting to an end of what has transpired, for there is always more to what happened which can never be fully experienced nor put to rest. Modernity assumes that eventually all that had been left out can be brought in and integrated, and that, perhaps more importantly, the 'debt' owed through exclusion and appropriation could be paid off simply by inclusion. But as Hortense Spillers (2003) points out, there are desires that have no home in language.

For the sacrifices made, for recouping losses that cannot be recouped, for making spaces in circumstances that did not provide any, there are desires that cannot be accommodated by modernity. Not that these desires point to a space outside modernity, but a facet that it cannot acknowledge – an absolute limit in its ability to take everything in, which after all is something on which it has been predicated. In order to act as all-encompassing, modernity has had to preclude, for example, the transmigration of souls or the fact that different times and ways of being could inhabit each other. These become the ghosts of an endless haunting which Lu then sees these as the presence of many different kinds of knowledge.

So, if, as Maurizio Lazzarato (2004) indicates, the subject is the concern of the soul under modernity, the soul is again a concern for architecture. For as Anselm Franke and Hila Peleg (2008) point out, there is an ecstatic dimension to the mimetic play in postcolonial relationships where the individual becomes the space that is imitated, displays and exhibits it in a way that no analytical distance is possible and the experience of distinctions – of background/foreground; self/world – is suspended. The vast spread of evangelical Christianity across the world, where not only is the distance between performer and audience, preacher and congregation, God and human beings, eroded, but the spaces of daily operations become products of a 'speaking in tongues', of a direct possession by the holy spirit and the concretization of that spirit. Here, there are no historical distinctions or continuities, and instead the interchangeability of life and death.

As Filip de Boeck (2005) says about the everyday culture of Kinshasa, in a city with little of anything institutional to provide it coherence, any sense of anchorage in viable infrastructure, governance or economy, there is nothing to hold its attention in a particular direction. As a result, everything is taken in bits and pieces from the world – memories, recitations, disconnected signs, dreams of Europe, fetishes, images from anywhere – and put to work as materials for organizing plural worlds that individuals have to step in and out of. In some respects, this is similar to what Nigel Thrift (2005) calls 'fugitive materials' – traditions, codes, linguistic bits, jettisoned and patchwork economies, pirated technologies, bits and pieces of symbols – that increasingly find their way into all cities. But in Kinshasa, the second world of mystique and of the imaginary is so prolific that it overtakes any discernible sense of reality.

If there is to be justice in the entangled relations that have characterized modernity, then as Badiou (2005) indicates it occurs in the midst of a flux of places – there is no right place or time. Soul, here, is a notion of space, a space no one figure occupies or determines, something that exceeds the normal disposition of bodies, and in which everyone must travel, without sign posts, without the language of diplomacy, and in which everyone must bear gifts.

Abidin Kusno (Chapter 12) takes up the relationship of architecture to the unstable coupling of nation and state. The elaboration of the political as the navigation among the bifurcations of nation and state has long dominated postcolonial thought. Increasingly, politics is the space where subjects operate in between notions of community and the heterogeneous realities of a populace and, as such, it is the space where a 'people', a collective subject becomes visible. Here visibility becomes a resource for people, as they recognize particular ways of being together, of what it is possible to do together. As such, it is a resource particularly important for the state to harness and control. In consequence, as AbdelMalik Sayad (2006) indicates, strategies of visibility can be seen as a menace.

Kusno talks about the use of architecture as a technology of power, particularly in terms of the visualization of the national 'geo-body', and perhaps the very notion of the national subject. But the very need to make such a body visible again raises the notions of ghosts. For under slavery and colonial rule, on plantations, in work camps and in cities, colonized subjects made a sense of collective life in the shadows. As long as they offered up representations of themselves to the gazes of their 'masters' that emphasized dysfunction, confusion and fragmentation, they were largely free to experiment with various ways of being together, of making economies, and domestic and social life.

These were largely invisible because the slave quarters, the popular neighbourhoods, the hostels and dormitories – although the objects of colonial rule – were not considered legitimate places where the rulers would go. It is from these contexts that revolts emerged, and where particular ways of framing aspirations, moral sentiments and political practices were largely developed. Even if trade unions, universities, religious institutions and bureaucracies were the contexts in which key leaders of anti-colonial, anti-slavery and liberation movements were trained and began to organize, they, nevertheless, had to deal with these invisibilities.

In the aftermath of independence, nations required a series of interlocking apparatuses in order to concretize the formation of a 'people' – i.e. systems to regulate borders, define responsibilities and rights of its citizens, and to extract from them capabilities, loyalty and resources. It is not a world where people with their differences were assembled and reassembled in various configurations of possibility. Rather, they were individualized under the pretence of legislative equality. Thus, the nation had to continuously perform a certain excess – with ceremony, celebration, commemoration, and above all the spectacular in the built environment.

The built environment is a particularly significant modality through which the nation performs its ubiquity, its immediacy (its presence in people's lives) and instantaneity (its ability to know what its citizens really want and need) – all of the dimensions of a simulated divinity. The construction of cities with their freeways, complexes and monuments is the materialization of the nation's pervasive ability to enter into the very heart of its citizen's lives.

As an instrument of modernity – in building 'modern nations' – the built environment is used as language of summation, of bringing to a close what can be remembered and what can be said about what the nation is – its eventuality and composition. While it is important to always recognize what a nation has endured, it is important that such attention not crowd out certain implications of the endurance.

Taking the example of nations emerging from colonization, there is an incessant question as to how the resourcefulness and implications of another past were not actualized – i.e. the invisibilities of the efforts made under difficult circumstances to 'become a people'. It is not that these possibilities were precisely defined, as in a revolutionary programme or set of policies, but rather a sense that something could have happened which did not, and which perhaps is not completely laid to rest. In its efforts to concretize the parameters of nationhood, the state uses the built environment to structure particular worlds in which citizens will interact and thus curtail 'that which is yet to come', as well as discipline citizens seen to be getting out of hand. The built environment will be used to justify claims and privileges of all kinds; it will be re-interpreted and re-framed in light of new information and events; it will be qualified and even demeaned as repetitions of old ways become visible in the present.

It is not an easy question to consider just what states are to do with these more invisible aspirations and practices, or even the possibility embodied by the nation as a 'deep horizontal comradeship'. Such aspirations easily can turn into claims of a particular authenticity, and Kusno warns of how the coupling of regionalism with nationalism can spawn a darker form of patchworked nationalism, where the need to realize the authentic legacies and aspirations of a people can only be worked out through authoritarian management. At the same time, as has been evidenced through much of modernist architectural discourse, supposedly universalistic rational and legal systems of thought and governance mask highly parochial cultural sentiments.

The state appropriates the built environment as an instrument of self-aggrandizement, it converts horizontal comradeship into an authoritarian right to rule, and deploys universalistic, rational frameworks of development, design and governance for highly particularistic interests. But also somewhere in-between these manoeuvers, there is a space where modernity might offer, as Kusno puts it, a radically new time which can translated into popular mobilization.

Using the example of the Indonesian poet, Mas Marco Kartodikromo, Kusno talks about how different notions of citizenship could emerge from the engagement with colonial urban modernity. This engagement could be an 'insurgent' one, in that it constituted an arena that provided new challenges for a wide range of vernacular practices. It was an incitement to exceed the terms of what was familiar while, at the same time, went beyond the implications and meanings that this modernity embodied.

Such insurgency has become a particularly vital practice on the part of architects throughout the postcolonial world as the struggles for a right to the city, for the provision of urban services and housing, for participation in the governance of cities, and the fight for the legitimacy of a wide array of local economies and entrepreneurial practices become arenas in which new forms of collective life are enacted.

As Kusno concludes, making an analytical difference between state and nation 'allows architecture to be seen as a site of tension, struggle, and compromise between them'. It also enables it to be a vital instrument in the exploration of what Ann Stoler (2008) calls 'relational histories' – where imperial formations are rethought as 'polities of dislocation and deferral that cut through the nation-state by delimiting interior frontiers as well as exterior ones' (205). Here, it is important to understand the highly particular trajectories of ruin and wastage to which specific sites and people have been subjected. The ways particular landscapes have been rendered toxic or inoperable, the particular kinds of wounds and incapacities that have been experienced and carried over, the continuities of colonial relations that are relocated into the midst of the metropole through urban planning and particular forms of spatial politics – all must be considered through detailed examinations of particular entangled relationships within various domains of power; all of which employ architectural concepts and designs to configure and enforce their particularities.

Deep horizontal comradeship is also to be located outside of the binaries of state and nation. Often, localities will be articulated to macro-cultural solidarities that extend themselves across international domains but do not consolidate themselves as specific political sovereign territories. Rather, these solidarities attempt to convey an already embodied realization and, as such, make the international order one replete with contradictory repertoires of engagement and transaction. Yet, in such a field, the 'nation' can become a locus and site of innovation – i.e. an innovation of mediation between accelerated individuation and the internationalized processes from which such individuation is operationalized and played out.

For many Muslims, the *ummah* – a deep horizontal comradeship that crosses the temporary convenience of nations – remains a real aspiration. Sometimes the *ummah* is thought of as a nation with an actual unified government, ruled by *shari'ah* or the return of a caliphate. But mostly it is considered to be a nation that exceeds the trappings of governmental and juridical particularity, a fundamental locus of identification and means of consolidating an unyielding sense of togetherness.

Ironically, in the hardscrabble world of geopolitics, much attention has been placed on the Gulf as a strange attractor of star architects and mega-urban projects. But much more importantly, in terms of this discussion, the Emirates, in particular, represent the concrete diffusion of a form of the *ummah* through massive investments in the built and financial environments of the Muslim world; where Dubai, instead of being a territorialized urban entity, becomes a concept to be diffused across the North and West Africa, as well as the Horn. In other words, through its massive current account surpluses, and its increasing status as a critical financial centre offering alternatives to the US dollar denominated bonds and security, the Emirates can not only intervene into built environments around the world, but establish 'parallel' worlds within them. These become in some important ways the concrete machinery through which an *ummah* is further recognized.

On the other hand, there are more ephemeral lines of articulation which link a range of diffuse struggles, people, memories and erasures into a form of what Gavin Williams (2002) calls 'like-being'. In his meditation on the relations between Salvadoran gang members in Los Angeles who have never even seen El Salvador and the remnants of their ancestors who may or may not have been directly involved in the Farabundo Marti National Liberation Front (FMLN), as well as the perpetuities of violence that seem to efface any difference between war and peace, Williams talks about the spectral promise of the continuation of the struggle for transformation. In other words, different situations across the world, barely linked by common nationality, ethnicity or events, may in their own ways participate in an opaque resemblance or an 'actively unprogrammed contagion' and yet, still operate in concert, still remain phantom subjectivities at work in remaking the world. Again, the issue of modernity consorting with ghosts.

Krupar and Al (Chapter 14) take up the processes through which the operations of spectacle have been progressively translated into the notion of brands. Whereas spectacle, affected through manipulations of the built environment that brought people together in large scale acts of exhibition, witnessing and consumption, once cemented particular ideological foundations for people acting in concert, the objective of branding is to increasingly act directly on experience and affect. It attempts to circumvent the need for an audience being together, either actually or virtually, to witness a particular performance. Rather, a much more viral operation is in mind, a way in which power can address itself not only to a social body, but to microphages and synapses, as well as to cognitive phase spaces and forms of attentiveness. Starting with critiques of Guy Debord, they explore notions of interactive spectacle which suture the use of the spectacle as an instrument for creating a sense of unification and wholeness to the more diffuse consumption of prolific commodities in a maneuver that weakens social bonds and 'corrals mutually indifferent consumers'.

Key here for architecture is the increasing disjunction of the surface from function and semantic depth, so that the surface becomes a scene with its own autonomous operations, and thus the promoter of relations among a wider range of actors. The object of consumption is to be attuned to ever more particular and proliferating sensibilities, inclinations and situations. Maximizing profit is seen as best accomplished through crossing the distinctions between labour in commerce, education and the arts – where all of these fields are drawn upon so that branding conveys the sense of a comprehensive experience. In order to wrap up so many different facets of living within the brand, decisions, productive systems, forms of engagement with social fields and modalities of representation must be diverse, flexible and dynamic. These are all processes that the Situationists valorized as antithetical to the spectacle, but are now part and parcel of the efficacy of the brand.

The brand attempts to be a particular architecture of mediation in the uncertain relationships between the need to maximize the rate of profit, threatened by overproduction and rising costs of production, the need to flexibly develop and engage new fields of consumption, and the enhanced potentialities to create unforeseen worlds of consumption that ensue from what Lazzarato (2004) calls the 'cooperation between minds'. Finance requires architecture of circulation in order to move widely. Capital must be put to use to cultivate opportunities that enable it to spread out, to be applied to a wide range of situations. This is why it is also placed and positioned in, for example, real estate development, both for the accumulation of rents and as objects of speculation. Place embodies a particular interaction of knowledge, labour, technology, infrastructure and resources. It takes time to cultivate the capacities of place, but once done, place exerts capacity quickly when knowledge is a scarce commodity.

In a world where production systems are increasingly deterritorialized, displaced and parcelled out – where they take place among a wide range of places – they are socialized through networks. In other words, how communication takes place, how different experiences in different places are translated in terms of each other, how people in different places come to see each other as mutual participants in the same place – is the accomplishment of networks that exceed particularistic forms of identification and that create the experience of being in 'one world'.

The problem for capitalist production systems is how this knowledge of networks, of mutually constitutive experiences of simultaneity, is to be priced. Extra-economic conditions of competitiveness become colonized through the value-form, yet they must maintain the creativity of the extra-economic engagements of arts, education and psychology. It is these challenges which 'brandscapes' try to mediate, as they seek to create specific experiences of being together, transformed and enlivened without the necessary adherence to the dictates of particular places, codes, allegiances or even ideological baggage. Participants can feel like they are part of a cutting edge and a new frontier.

Spectacle has also become, according to Kruper and Al, the elaboration of an 'atmos-fear' – i.e. 'a pedagogical device that produces fear, legitimates state power and mobilizes a political economy of disaster'. As Massumi (2005) points out, fear makes it as if that which is feared has already occurred. The identity of any possible object, what something might be – i.e. how anything, however mundane could become an object of danger or terror – increasingly determines the affective quality of the actual situation. Here, people are to live under a constant state of emergency, to be prepared to experience threats everywhere and thus subsume critical analysis and political mobilization to exigencies of quick decisions.

Institutional analysis becomes increasingly based on stochastic models of randomness and catastrophe, where it becomes increasingly difficult to know in advance what is likely to happen based on a thorough and careful analysis of present conditions. Thus the emphasis is on probabilities and pre-emption – i.e. seeing in the present an entire future trajectory of particular behaviours, characters and inclinations which are read into as portending future threats. Thus even the most banal circumstances can be imbued with a sense of danger.

In this reorientation of temporality, the immediacy of present experiences becomes even more valorized, and thus the object of architectural work. Experiences are to be made more dynamic, direct, singular, affecting and intense – efforts which are often translated into the creation of large energy-intensive atmospheres which attempt to operate at all senses, registers and scales of apprehension. Here, 'brandage', as Kruper and Al indicate, envisions experience to be authentic presence, and location as an essentialized truth. Somehow the 'real' can be really captured if only the right images of it can be conjured and conveyed. Yet as Kruper and Al point out, this aspiration assumes an undifferentiated subject that can be transformed through particular operations of the image and is prompted by deterministic economic readings that tend to fix viewers to the image as a delimiting false consciousness.

Instead, they emphasize the need to re-conceptualize the spectacle through governance, as the objective of governance is to steer social systems in ways that modify their structural operations, their interests, and their understandings about what they do in specific circumstances and settings. The structural constraints inscribed in institutions and production systems – i.e. what they think it is possible to do – are not inherent. Rather, these constraints are contingent upon the characteristics of specific spatio-temporal horizons of actions through which institutions and spectacles operate.

As such, political processes are essentially precarious and unstable. In politics, social relationships tend to be isolated from the complex and continuous web of causal connections from which they emerge. These social relationships are, then, set up as both explicit objects and instruments of politics. Such manoeuvers undoubtedly generated unanticipated consequences – and this is why in part there has been such emphasis on intervening at the level of affect and pre-cognition. For these consequences can make other subjects, projects and interests visible that have not been visible before. While attempting to steer complex institutional arrangements and relationships through a complex environment, new dilemmas and consequences are continuously being generated.

Again, this is why brandscapes attempt to play to a state of immediacy and emergency, of imaging the culmination of the 'real' in which everyone can directly participate. As the authors indicate, these projects pile up unintended and un-monumental leftovers, as well as what Virilio (2007) calls an 'accretion of accidents', where wreckage piles up everywhere. And thus continues the long process of modernity making refuse, where spaces of positivity, 'well-rounded lives' and 'actors with capacities' are attained with the inextricable by-product of wasting others.

As Kuper and Al point out, giving consumers the sense of immediacy, of proximity to 'real intensities' and 'real things', as well as directing design interventions to the level of feeling and affect tries to circumvent the particular complexities of politics now played out over a potentially unwieldy multiplicity of places and institutions. At the same time this sense of 'directness' constitutes a form of mediation between the need to put capitalist knowledge to work to increase accumulation and profit and, at the same time sustain the openness, sympathy, collaboration and publicity inherent to the 'general intelligence' relied upon by capital to open up new worlds of consumption. But in doing so, this operation may also contribute to the dissipation of particular modalities of representation where populations were stabilized within the ambit of the state and municipality, through a deal where they were accorded certain rights in return for their assuming specific responsibilities to the state. In other words, they had the right to be represented by an apparatus which formally committed itself to represent their interests and needs.

But as Papadopoulos and Tsianos (2007) point out, the continuous shifts and radical re-articulations of the trajectories of individual lives affected in post-liberal sovereignty, as well as the substantial relocation of governance to individuals as self-responsible agents, has significantly worn away the capacities of representational bodies to mediate. This is not only a matter of politics being constituted in a more networked system, as Arditi (2003) argues – where there is a constellation of sites for the enactment of the political and the constitution of politics, as well as a sense of regularity in the dispersion of sites of political enunciation. For increasing numbers of urban residents, there exists no real mediating body that sorts out, regulates, or explains how individual bodies and lives are to be coordinated with each other, how they are to share space, or what their obligations are to each other (Sánchez 2008).

Cities everywhere become the collection of micro-territories that have little to do with each other even if in many respects they share the same fate. Brandscapes engineer a world where bodies could be reached and affected without the cumbersome baggage of representational systems. The autonomy of signs can be operationalized to generate singular impacts on bodies as deterritorialized fields of intervention. Thus, brandscapes contribute to a situation where how bodies interface with other bodies is something that has to be invented on the spot. As result, many of those interactions are increasingly violent, banal, arbitrary, parasitic or simply just do not take place. How people then are 'sorted out'; how they discover viable practices of determining how they are to be with each other remains largely undecidable.

THE PATHS AHEAD

So what can be done about such fabricated undecidables? For the majority of the world's urban dwellers, this is a matter of strategy. It is a matter of knowing when and how the relational interdependencies of their lives can be made visible and when things should be kept out of view, or at least known in ways that cannot be easily pinned down. These oscillations require an environment, and as such, the urban built environment comes to support or impede certain strategic potentials.

The reflections of these authors on the volatile relationships among modernities, nations and peoples, images and experiences, reaffirm the importance of a process of urbanization long made peripheral to analysis and productive engagement. Too often the focus on contemporary everyday life and cities limits itself to big developments, vast suburbs or overcrowded slums. But what of those districts that continue to absorb and even support very different ways of life, aspirations and capacities?

While the dense and messy landscapes of these districts may be fast disappearing, cities remain full of intricate conjunctions of times, space and bodies that demonstrate, even if only metaphorically, the contested yet generative relationships among things not really able to fit together or to do much without each other. People are able to see and experience just how tentative the 'taken for granted' actually is – but at the same time are better able to 'write' their own experiences and experiments into it.

The seemingly haphazard, incomplete and strewn out arrangements of buildings, infrastructure and activity that continue to persist in many cities provides an important visualization of what people have to deal with in order to make a viable life in the city. They can show how water and power appear and disappear, what bodies and objects manage to get through in order to encapsulate themselves in a sense of individual agendas and aspirations. They show the terrain, conditions and conjunctions along which the changing projects of people and things try to get along – not always very successfully. It is an environment that cannot be summed up, nor subsumed under a singularly formatted representation or necessity. The navigations of residents trying to engage and disengage, trying to both stabilize and rearrange the conditions in which they situate themselves, are not the smooth uninterrupted sailings of fast cars on superhighways.

Rather, they criss-cross and side-step the markings and sediments of many different movements, constituting a place always signaling its availability to deals, small initiatives and grand designs. The intersections of work and home, market and play, open spaces and shadow worlds, are intertwined folds along which traverse people, things, waste, resources, services, talk, civilities and tensions, and shifting pockets of affective intensities and quiet. All entail things 'stepping' through and around each other; something evident day in and day out. As many residents in Matete (Kinshasa) or Penjaringan (Jakarta) say, it is a world that can be worked with. And even though the work is hard and sometimes people get nowhere in particular, it is a world where residents feel that they manage to count for something – that there is something indeed to manage.

We know from many places in the world that the absence of infrastructures and mediations do not necessary mean the collapse of social life. Sometimes, people themselves are the important infrastructure. In other words, their selves, situations and bodies bear the responsibility for articulating different locations, resources and stories into viable opportunities for everyday survival. In cities with few ready-made formats capable of specifying just how individuals are to obtain shelter, food, money and status, the particularities of an individual's family and ethnic background, their personal character and style, their location in particular arrangements of residence and circulation with others, all become the stuff of shifting circuitries of connection along which pass information, cash, obligations, possibilities and support. In such an existence, it is difficult for individuals to think of a life for them, to plan a specific trajectory, or to know in advance just what implications a particular course of action might produce.

It is possible to draw lines across these apparently haphazard and improvized urbanities. There can be organizational principles – but what they are and for whom, again, are strategic concerns. There are few overarching necessities capable of compelling strict attention or mass adherence. But this doesn't mean that the form of the necessary or the form of apparently unmediated need or experience cannot function as a kind of shadow in which many different options and ways of doing things can percolate or hide.

The breaking up of surfaces once counted upon to represent some specific use or meaning takes on an important role in postcolonial struggles. In other words, depth doesn't necessarily mean substance, and surface isn't necessarily condemned to being the facile, ever-shifting vehicle of commodification. For example, Pheng Cheah (1999) has written about the 'spectral nationality' that hangs over and haunts peoples of the postcolony. No matter how the course of nationhood in much of the global South has found itself dissipated and fractured by war, indebtedness, exploitation, or nearly comprehensive incorporation in the circuitries of global capital, a dream-image of a way of life whereby a people exceeds the particularities of their local circumstances and relations is concretized in and through nationality as a disembodied techné. Here, the surface of the nation still has use in keeping alive certain aspirations for people being 'more than they are'. It does not embody, it does not represent – it keeps things open, keeps things from being foreclosed or prematurely wrapped up. If then the spectral is thought to exert real effects, what are the nature of their 'architectures' and conditions of existence?

What, then, does a daily living architecture point to? The three contributions here lead us to this question. Especially if the nation is a means of experiencing new kinds of connections among people with whom one shares a city; something more just; something with more space for the majority to not only realize the levels of consumption attainable for a minority but to also make all of the years of living by their wits count for something else.

The existent spatial arrangements and social relations of the city could not themselves constitute the incipient form of such a nation. If one looks at the realities of urban life for the majority of the urban residents in the global South, the conditions that currently exist would hardly nurture hopes and ideas about the nation or the stuff of its materialization. Instead, the present urban realities would make those aspirations 'dead in the water' before they had any chance of suggesting a viable way to be realized.

Neither would urban residents go out of their way and risk everything to insist on an all or nothing realization of dreams and ways of doing things that starkly announced themselves to be either antagonistic to the world's dominant models or an alternative to them. If they did so, they would likely experience a kind of 'second defeat'. The first defeat being that the original hopes that lay behind the initial struggles for independence and nationhood in most instances never really materialized.

Likewise, manifestations of the spectral, this dream of the nation, in the daily practices and arrangements of the 'not-yet-citizens' of the 'real nation' could not simply be placeholders for what is to come. In other words, all of the creative efforts urban residents make to survive in cities and to keep open the possibilities for a better life are not just compensations for the lack of jobs, services and livelihoods, and neither are they necessarily the kernels of new way of being in the city that simply needs more time, political support and money in order to be realized. Rather, as Cheah (1999) implies, something must be set in motion that addresses the turbulent and uncertain experiences of the present; something that constitutes a reminder of a way of life and being together that could have taken place but did not. Something set in motion that brings about a continuously renovated, flexible and improvized series of tactics that 'look everywhere' for opportunities to take 'things forward'. In other words, there has to be a way to lead people's thoughts, actions and commitments into versions of themselves for which there are not any clear terms of recognition or clear links to the hopes and dreams to which people aspire.

Therefore, the objective for those who continue to aspire to be something more than they are in the present is not to become anything in particular in terms of the prevailing notions about what can be taken account, what makes sense, or what is logically possible. The idea is to keep things open, keep things from becoming too settled or fixed. The messed up city then is not simply a mess. In the very lack of things seeming settled, people keep open the possibility that something more palatable to their sense of themselves might actually be possible.

12

Rethinking the Nation[1]

Abidin Kusno

What is so important about the nation? First, the nation is not about to disappear. Instead it remains an important component in the cultural organization of our social and political life regardless of whether it is necessarily a good or bad thing. We know well enough that nationalism has the capacity to create a condition for violence and exclusion, but we also have to acknowledge that nationality and the nation-state have the power to enforce sovereignty, supra-local solidarity as well as individual and collective rights of citizenship. The nation is also important because it is a cultural artifact that represents humanity's tendency to come together as well as to divide into conflicting groups. This tension between the nation's interest to incorporate and its power to exclude is just one among many tensions that make nationalism a rich and productive concept for architecture. Indeed, like other powerful ideas that make our modern world move, nationalism does not stand outside architecture. Instead it is instrumental in the shaping of architectural ideologies and practices.

Architecture is linked to nationalism when its semiotic functioning organizes solidarities for a limited sovereign community as well as distinguishing the community from 'outsiders'. The capacity of architecture to perform such a role of subjection for the nation, however, relies not only on the ways in which architecture is produced and represented, but also on how it is imagined, received and ignored collectively. Since architecture lies within the framework set by the nation, we can also suggest the possibility of architecture transforming the framework within which its meanings are constructed. In this sense, architecture's involvement in nationalism would neither always be on the side of dominant power nor is it essentially conservative in nature. On the contrary, architects have also acquired considerable skill in using architecture to confront oppressive nationalist power and propose alternative 'insurgent' social and political positions to restore what they believe to be the 'goodness' of nationalism. Similarly, no matter how progressive an architectural form and space may look, it is still adaptable to the functioning of fascistic political regimes.[2] Interwoven into this nation and architecture relation is the tension between the imagined fullness of nationalism and the contradictory and often insurgent realities of everyday life. The narratives of everyday life often produce different affiliations and practices that work against or outside the unifying national narrative of architecture. The relations between architecture and nationalism thus consist of a series of unresolved tensions, and they are cut across by the everyday with its own relatively autonomous, contextually determined and socially produced sense of what is necessary to lead a meaningful life. Yet it is these tensions, possibilities and limits in engaging with social life that make the nation an important and productive subject for architecture.

In this chapter, I discuss the implications of nationalism for architecture by reflecting historically, on how architecture participates in the construction of and contestation over national identities, historical memories and the everyday. I explore the theoretical frameworks and analytical concepts of studies of architecture and nationalism, and consider their interaction with such powerful forces as colonialism, capitalism and modernity.

While exploring the importance of nationalism to architecture, this essay has four main objectives. The first is to show that nationalism is increasingly viewed by architectural theorists and historians as an attribute of the state. Under this condition, architecture is seen as the state's ideological artifact for the exercise of power. While this premise has produced important works on architecture and nationalism, it has also limited the intellectual horizon of architectural studies. The analytical focus on the state stems from the conflation of the 'nation' and the 'state' even though these two different entities have distinct histories and interests. Unlocking the relation between the nation and the state will open up a way to conceive different national practices and narratives that work critically beneath or above the state.

The second objective, related to the first, is to problematize the tendency to regard postcolonial nationalism as the enemy of modern liberalism. Under this condition, nationalism is often associated with either traditionalism or totalitarianism, and with such a premise we tend to forget the profound modernity of postcolonial nationalism, especially in relation to its history of anti-colonial movements.

The third purpose is to dispose of the idea that globalization has eroded nationalism especially in regard to the remarkable recent spread of mega architectural projects in the major cities of postcolonial countries. The concentrated spectacles of these projects are clearly generated by global capitalism, but it is also a product of historical memories and nationalism. But unlike the nation-building of the early Independence era, the mega architectural projects of today tend to become incorporated within the existing order of capitalism rather than interrogating that order.

The last purpose is to consider the extent to which the nation is an external entity to everyday life. I believe that the spread of governmental technologies in the last three decades in response to the disintegrative forces of 'neo-liberalism' has resulted in the deepening reach of the developmental state into the interior of everyday life of both urban and rural communities. The core of the issue, however, is neither the autonomy of the everyday life nor the total control of the state. Instead, the everyday of the communities, represented in this chapter by the marginalized groups, have also acquired tactics of insurgency, albeit to a different degree in different areas, in pressuring the state to deliver the promise of nationalism to guarantee individual and collective citizenship.

To address these issues, I will draw a good deal of my illustrative materials from non-Western countries, mainly because the speed of change in the ways nationalism is conceived there has been so rapid as to throw light on the dynamic relations between architecture and nationalism. In this contribution, I confine my attention to postcolonial countries in Asia generally and to Indonesia specifically. The reasons are both practical and theoretical. While my main specialization is on that region, I trust that some of the issues I touch on will invite responses from those knowledgeable about other parts of the world. The choice of cases and the thematic focus is aimed at engaging with the political present and to contribute to thinking about future research on this significant topic.

THE NATION AND THE STATE

Nation and representation

Studies of the relations between architecture and nationalism have been enduring concerns since the early twentieth century. The main framework of the research (almost exclusively on the Western hemisphere) has been divided between interest in the national discourse of architectural modernism on the one hand and romantic regionalism on the other. A few studies have focused on the mutually constitutive relations of these two architectural movements in the formation of national identity. However, since World War II, scholarship on architecture and national identity has shifted orientation and emphasized different processes. Architectural historians such as Anthony King (1976, 2004), Diane Ghirardo (1980), Gwendolyn Wright (1991) and Barbara Miller Lane (1968) among others, have defined the parameters of investigations of the relation between architecture and nationalism as they evolved in the shadow of Western imperialism and the subsequent need to deal with nationalism's fascist ideology during the Nazi era. In the last decade of the twentieth century, a new generation, including Nezar AlSayyad (1992), Sibel Bozdogan (2001), James Holston (1989) and Lawrence Vale (1992) among others, have approached architecture and national identity from a broadly conceived (post)colonial perspective, bringing different insights into an understanding of the formation of national identities. The contributions of these works lie primarily in their interdisciplinary approach to architecture. Following their path, younger scholars have begun to write architecture and nationalism in part stimulated by the work of Benedict Anderson (1991 [1983]) who wrote his *Imagined Communities* with principal concerns, examples and reflections drawn from the national worlds of the 'peripheral' South.

Anderson's insights into the nature of nationalism are particularly suggestive. For him, the crucial issue is not the fact that the imagining of the community (of a nation) depends on the employment of an idealized national culture, but on how it is represented and experienced as 'national' representation. Anderson shows how representations such as those of the newspaper, novel, map, census and museum configured the imagination of people with political effects acting upon who they are and how they might relate to each other. We could say that the idea of representation is not just visual and textual, but also spatial and architectural. Architecture is spatially and formally configured, and that configuration by ways of semiotic arrangement may shape identity and identification. Architecture is one of the 'technologies of power' such as the map, census and museum, which contribute to the visualization of the national 'geo-body' (Thongchai 1994). We thus can see how architecture, like the map and museum, narrates the theme of the nation under a particular political regime. And conversely, we can see architecture, like the commercial market generated print (and today virtual) materials, such as newspapers, novels and advertisement, sell lifestyle and consciousness which both sustains and challenges the regulatory regime of the nation state.

However, as much as optimism may radiate from buildings invested with a national theme, uncertainty known as 'architectural indeterminacy' and 'the arbitrariness of the sign' continue to hover over the meaning of the building (Saussure 1983; Barthes 1997 [1979]; Eco 1980). Irrespective of the issue of semiotics as style of sign, where the state has the monopoly of resources, the spatial scale of the building and urban form as well as the nature and number of 'national' buildings – such as theatres, museums, opera houses, schools and stadia can also be used as a sign of nationalism. On the other hand, architecture may also function merely as a physical setting for various representations to exert their power. The contents of the nationally constituted map and museum as well as newspapers and novels are read and understood, collectively and individually, in the materiality of an 'architectural' setting. In other words, everyday architecture of non-representational practices which carries no national semiotics could also provide a setting for the kind of consciousness that we identified as 'the national'. (For a discussion on non-representational practices, see: Lu's contribution to this section). Whether architecture operates as a 'representation' or a 'setting' for the formation of 'imagined communities', we need empirical, ethnographic and historical works and analyses of discourses and receptions (with a mix of interdisciplinary approaches beyond visual analysis) which are far from easy to do. How does the architectural mode of addressing its audience allow one to imagine a limited sovereign community as well as envision other equivalent sovereignties? How does architecture challenge the dominant power of the state and envision a different national imagining? Before exploring these questions, let me first tease out the often unspoken assumption of scholarship on architecture and nationalism.

Architecture and state power

Dominant studies on architecture and nationalism tend to focus on how the nation-state uses architecture to represent itself in official nationalist propaganda. Several works on architecture and nationalism have demonstrated the strength of state power through cases ranging from Nazi Germany to colonial 'forms of dominance' and experiments of architecture under postcolonial conditions (AlSayyad 1992; Bozdogan 2001; Lane 1968; Vale 1992). For instance, the designation of particular sites as the embodiment of collective national imaginings has given rise to works on capitol or governmental buildings (Vale 1992; Ksiazek 1993; Kalia 1987). As Lawrence Vale indicates 'a variety of national regimes have used architecture and urban design to express political power and control' and designers too 'have manipulated the urban built environment to promote a version of identity that would support and help legitimize this rule' (Vale 1992, viii).

In this framework, the state expects architecture to supply the image of the nation and thus the imagination of belonging to the sovereign world of nations. The state, often via media, invests meaning and narrative to create both the architectural content (the function and the programme) and form (the organization of space and the stylistic choices of architecture) with 'formative' power to interpellate human subjects as national. The importance of focusing on the state's politics of architecture and urban design is the sense that architecture is never autonomous and 'whether or not the architects claim to care about politics, many politicians use architecture and urban design as political instruments' (Vale 1992, 275). This line of thought represents a basic premise of most scholarship on architecture and nationalism, especially when it comes to an analysis of fascist ideology, empire and nation-building. This approach has contributed to our understanding of architecture as an ideological superstructure emanating from the state working together with architects within the contexts of colonial and postcolonial national conditions and of capitalist or socialist revolutions.

However, it is useful to recognize that the focus on how architecture is politicized and put to use by a political regime to raise legitimacy and national sentiment tends to read the nation as a shorthand expression for nation-state. It rarely draws an analytical line between fascism and nationalism, and in related and indirect fashion, between the people-nation and the state-apparatus. The blurring of the analytical line also runs the risk of portraying nationalism as an expression of an authoritarian culture. In this fashion nationalism has been given a taint of pathology and irrationality.[3] Interest in charisma, irrationality and megalomaniac creativity of characters such as Saddam Hussein, Mao Zedong or Sukarno has turned nationalism into the enemy of modern liberalism.

Moreover, it is also useful to acknowledge that underlying most of the studies on architecture and nationalism is the tendency to think of the state as the ultimate agent. Focusing on the power of the state to control representations, questions of reception have largely been left out and, with some exceptions, there are very few with attention to how different subjectivities come to be formed. But how could we talk about the semiotic functioning of architecture to interpellate readers as national subjects and to allow viewers to picture in their mind the limited form of their 'imagined community'? Furthermore, the gap and the tension between the national subject and the state apparatus (which raises the question of the difference between what Mamdani (1996) called citizen and subject) have often been overlooked. But how can we tease out the gap between the national population and the state apparatus through architecture? One way to move beyond the existing state-based approach to architecture and nationalism is to first recognize the 'goodness' of the nation.

The goodness of the nation

In *Imagined Communities* (1991 [1983]), Anderson discusses historically how the nation came to consist of two interrelated but contradictory identifications. The first one is the people-nationalism forming from below a 'deep, horizontal comradeship' that could inspire and transform the state. The second one is the official nationalism sanctioned by the state often in the interests of the ruling elites (who claimed to rule in the name of people). Given the antagonistic relations between the nation and the state, Anderson (in *Language and Power*) suggests that one should not read '"nation" as merely a convenient shorthand expression for "nation-state"' (Anderson 1990: 94). The popular 'participatory interest' of the nation often comes as an opposition to the interest of the state which, according to Anderson, 'has to be understood as an "institution", of the same species as the church, the university, and the modern corporation' (Anderson 1990: 95). And the state also has its own memory and 'harbors self-preserving and self-aggrandizing impulses' often against the nation (Anderson 1990, 95). Anderson further argues that the conflation of a popular, participatory nation and an older adversarial state is rather recent.

> On the one hand, the imagined community of the nation, whose legitimacy and right to self-determination have become accepted norms in modern life, finds the gauge of that autonomy in a state 'of its own.' On the other hand, the state, which can never justify its demand on a community's labor, time, and wealth simply by its existence, finds in the nation its modern legitimation. (Anderson 1990, 95)

In Anderson's formulation, the nation is a community because 'regardless of the actual inequality and exploitation that may prevail in each, the nation is always conceived as a deep, horizontal comradeship' (Anderson 1991, 16). The nation-state, on the other hand, is 'a curious amalgam of legitimate fictions and concrete illegitimacies' (Anderson 1990, 95). On this basis, one could read *Imagined Communities* as an epic of a love and hate relationship between the nation and the state, and ultimately a reflection on the radical possibilities of nationalism. Regardless of the problem with the binary opposition between the state and the nation which often invites an overlooking of their mutually constitutive relation, the tension-filled dialectics between them offers a way of analyzing nationalism in a more complex way.

For instance, following Anderson, Pheng Cheah (2003) refers to the postcolonial state as a ghost that not only haunts but also possesses the nation. Thus, 'the living nation will always be haunted by ghosts that cannot be exorcised ... especially after independence' (Cheah 2003, 303). In this duel between the (colonial) state and the (anti-colonial) nation, Cheah shows how postcolonial intellectuals' narration of their nation is continuously haunted by the fact that popular participatory interest of the nation has been domesticated if not killed by its own state. Cheah calls this mutual haunting between the nation and the state 'spectral nationality'. To us, the dialectical relation between the state and the nation formulated by Anderson could be seen as an invitation to think about architecture as playing a role not merely of supporting state power, but also the possibility of helping the formation of a 'national imagination' in the larger task of inspiring and transforming the state.

To explore architecture and nationalism beyond a 'state-centered approach' (Mitchell 1999),[4] we would need to not only consider issues around subject formation (how identities are formed in and through the architectures of the state), but also how architecture while working for the nation-state (within different settings of economic arrangement) challenges authority and thus provides an alternative vision for the nation. In the following section, I will provide a concrete example of how architecture might relate to the national (instead of the state) imagination. But let me first provide the context of its emergence, which is the colonial condition where nationalism and the colonial state were most visibly at war.

The colonial gift of nationalism

As much as architecture has been the place to look for the construction of and contestation over national identity, it has also been marked by histories of colonialism (AlSayyad 1992).[5] We have heard stories of how architecture was used by the imperial power in the service of colonial continuation. Various architectural strategies were indeed devised to communicate to the colonized their relations to the imperial power to which they belonged as subjects. Scholars working on colonial politics of urban design and planning have identified at least two different but interrelated strategies of dominance (Rabinow 1989; see also Wright 1991). One is the 'middling modernism', a technique of development based on universalistic criteria that is free from association with the local and the particular. On the other hand, a competing approach called 'techno-cosmopolitanism' used the local and the particular as the starting point for the assumption of development.

What is crucial for us is that with these different approaches to the colony, the representation of imperial power is subjected to competing strategies of development. While the programmes were often creative and new, they were never quite coherent and never immune to unintended consequences. Recent works on colonial architectural discourses have pointed to the ambiguities and the difficulties of developing the colony as the subject of imperial rule (Kusno 2000; Wright 1991). However, despite the difficulty, there is at least one coherent approach in the ways the colonial state constructed identities for its subjects. The colonial Leviathan introduced the concept of fixed territorial boundaries and the whole way of classifying, or simplifying its subjects under a territory of a 'nation' (Thongchai 1994; Scott 1998). This colonial mode of territorial governance set up the idea of the nation as a proper unit of imagination along with the idea of a national culture and tradition. In other words, the territorial power of the West produced a symbolic mapping of the national space for the colony.

Let me now offer an architectural example of how a building might be implicated in the mapping of the nation and how a colonial architectural movement might shape nationalist imagination. At the beginning of the twentieth century Dutch architects, under the influence of 'techno-cosmopolitanism', carried out experiments of various styles (such as syncretic Indies architecture and art deco) in the various urban centres of colonial Indonesia (Kusno 2000). This architectural experiment was built on the idea of an ethically based 'modernizing mission' and it effectively undermined the neo-classical style that had once dominated the architectural language of Dutch colonialism. The core of this new practice was the extensive use of indigenous building styles – recreated into a kind of inter-island vernacular-modern architecture. The architects quoted unrelated fragments of regional building elements from different parts of the archipelago and composed them into a coherent trans-archipelagic 'Indies architecture'. This Rabelaisian type of architecture brought together various elements from different parts of Indonesian islands and created thus a pan-Indonesian building style. This syncretic architecture (most clearly illustrated in the first university in the colony, the Bandung Institute of Technology, Figure 12.1) was supported by the colonial state even though the Dutch architect, a man born in Indonesia, was arguably quite sympathetic with the emerging anti-colonial nationalist movement.

Figure 12.1 (Below) The Institute of Technology at Bandung, 1920; Architect Henri MacLaine Pont. (Iwan Sudrajat)

The 'Indies' mode of architectural representation (which expanded to churches, central markets, museums and theatres for the use of Indonesians) was meant to symbolically show the 'natives' that they too could develop with their own 'national' architectural language and resources but of course under the guidance of the 'ethical rule' of the colonial state. On the other hand, this style of architecture was also intended to supply a paradigmatic representation of Dutch imperial rule in the early twentieth century as different from its British and French counterparts (see also Gouda 1995). The Indies architectural style was used as a means to show how different Dutch 'Indonesia' was from French 'Indochina' or British 'India'. In a way, we could say that the Indies architecture (perhaps unintentionally) had opened up a condition of possibility for Indonesians to imagine a national 'form'. Indies architecture operates like a semiotic 'map' that integrates territories and defines them as the cultural body of the 'nation'.

How did this experiment in architecture under colonial conditions relate to nationalist movements for Independence? How did this colonial architectural representation contribute to the formation of Pan-Indonesian anti-colonial nationalism, which would lead us to acknowledge the divergence between the intention and the outcome? It is hard to find the evidence of the relation between Indies architecture and the nationalist movement (clearly visual analysis alone is not sufficient to account for this relation), but after independence, this type of architecture was almost immediately forgotten. The international style modernist architecture of the 1950s was instead mobilized by the first president Sukarno, himself an architect, to register the importance of the newly emerging nation-state (see Insurgent Nationalism, below). There were surely many political reasons why the syncretic Indies architecture vanished from national memory. The reasons need not detain us here, but the crucial thing was what happened to it after the end of Sukarno's rule. As the country entered the 1980s under the rule of Suharto's New Order (1966–1998), architects had begun to make reference to the Indies as an earlier experiment towards Indonesian architecture. The somewhat unconscious rationale behind the retrieval of the mixed and hybrid architecture of the colonial era was the urgency felt among Indonesian architects to respond to the tendency of the state to identify ethnic Javanese architecture as the ultimate symbol of Indonesian architecture (Kusno 2007).

This story raises the issues of a colonial legacy. It acknowledges the 'gift' of colonial Indies architecture to overcome the ethno-centric political culture of the Suharto era. The question however is no longer whether postcolonial nationalist imagination of architecture is imaginary or derivative. Instead it shows the effort on the parts of the post-colonial architects, in a subtle architectural form of insurgency, to challenge the state's parochial idea of nationalism. The story indicates not only the extent to which post-colonial national formation is filled with a contradiction of both identification with and rejection of colonialism, but also the extent to which architecture can contribute to addressing the problem of ethno-nationalism and to propose instead a more inclusive supra-local Indonesian architecture in order to give an idea of 'good nationalism'. In short, the story shows not only the effect of colonial representation on postcolonial architecture, but also the extent to which the contextually determined architecture's involvement in nationalism does not always represent the side of dominant power.

The case of 'Indies architecture', above, indicates a remarkable invention of a regionally based vernacular tradition as the source for a national culture in both colonial and postcolonial contexts (see also Chapter 19). Since the connection between regionalism and nationalism carries both present and past political delicacies, regionalism is never quite a straightforward retrieval of pre-colonial sources as is sometimes assumed in the study of architecture and nationalism. Instead, it is inseparable from colonial 'orientalist' constructions of local cultures [which Rabinow (1989) has called 'techno-cosmopolitanism']. Regionalism and nationalism thus are categories of identity and politics. Their colonial formation raises a broader question about the production of an architectural knowledge in the post World War II era that conflates 'regionalism' with postcolonial 'nationalism'. In what follows I show how nationalism and regionalism have become the categories of identities for architecture of the postcolonial world, a process which in turn has created modernism as the cultural domain of the developed world.

Architecture regionalism and the peripheralization of nationalism

In the 1980s, when the State of Indonesia promoted local identity in Indonesian architecture, the region of Asia (as well as several other parts of the postcolonial world) saw the proliferation of discourses on 'cultural heritage' and 'regionalism'. In Southeast Asia, a series of workshops on architecture and national identity were staged (sponsored by universities, state agencies, professional associations and transnational foundations such as the Aga Khan Award for Architecture). Two premises appear to have emerged through events. The first is the conflation of 'nationalism' and 'regionalism' (itself a development out of earlier colonial 'techno-cosmopolitanism' as well as concurrent discourses on 'architecture regionalism' in the West) and the second is the association of 'nationalism' and 'regionalism' with countries outside the developed West (see also Crysler 2003).

Since the end of World War II, the interest in the relation between architecture and nationalism has shifted from what used to be a principal concern for architecture in the (Western) Euro-American continent to the decolonized world of Asia and Africa.[6] In the US for instance, up to the 1950s, American-based architectural critics (prompted in part by economic depression and fears of communism, fascism and immigration), still searched for architecture that would adequately represent America as an exceptional country. One could tease out the romantic imagination of Frank Lloyd Wright who at various points in his career wished to see his organic 'agrarian' architecture become the national identity of the US. However, by then powerful urban corporate elites had followed influential European architects in exile in the US in promoting the 'international style' in architecture. Seeing this international architecture as 'buildings free from the local and particular', they associated 'national' landscapes with the development of fascist politics (Noble 2002: 181).

By the end of 1950, the question of nationalism in American architecture had largely disappeared, following what Keith Eggener (2006) has called the 'naturalization' of European-based modern architecture as American architecture. In 1952, with the institutionalization of the International Style in the US, H.R. Hitchcock declared that: 'American architecture has come to occupy a special prominence in the world ... [It] is not an isolated phenomenon: in architecture, as in many other things, we are the heirs of Western civilization' (as quoted in Eggener 2006, 255). This universalizing and explicitly evolutionary assumption of American triumphalism produced two interrelated discourses. The first is the placing of the US at the centre of a 'universalizing' modern architecture; the second is the relegation of 'regionalism' (once the focus of American architecture) to the new nations in the periphery, assumed to be still struggling with and bounded by issues of nationalism.

Thus, when we discuss nationalism and architecture, we run the risk of making it appear as essentially a problem of postcolonial countries. As Billig (1995, 6) points out:

> Gaps in political language are rarely innocent. The case of 'nationalism' is no exception. By being semantically restricted to small sizes and exotic colours, 'nationalism' becomes identified as a problem: it occurs 'there' on the periphery, not 'here' at the centre. The separatists, the fascists, the guerillas are the problem of nationalism.

The fact that most of the work on architecture and nationalism since the 1950s is largely restricted to cases other than those of liberal democratic countries indicates the positionality of nationalism in the geopolitics of the world.[7] By the 1980s, nationalism is accepted as a counterpoint to globalism and in a similar vein, regionalism is often taken as a framework for architecture in the periphery and set in contrast to modernism.[8] As I have indicated above, this association of regionalism with nationalism tends to spawn a darker form of postcolonial nationalism in which the desire for freedom (from imperialism) is displaced into the realm of the authoritarian state.

Writing in a climate of Euro-American liberalism, Kenneth Frampton (1996 [1980]) in his discussion of 'critical regionalism' starts with a long quotation from Paul Ricoeur's 'Universal Civilization and

National Cultures' written in 1961 which highlights the fact that: 'Every culture cannot sustain and absorb the shock of modern civilization. There is the paradox: how to become modern and to return to sources; how to revive an old dormant civilization and take part in universal civilization' (as cited in Frampton 1996 [1980], 314). We have here the universality of Euro-American civilization waiting to be identified by and reconciled with local and national cultures of different places. The Eurocentrism in this conception of civilization need not concern us here. The point is that nationalism is identified as a central dilemma for the nations in the periphery as they seek 'to take part in universal civilization'.

Similarly, in a contribution to *Postcolonial Space(s)*, perhaps the first book on architecture and postcolonialism, Alan Colquhoun (1997) (after an elaboration on eighteen century European thoughts) indicates that in the late nineteenth and early twentieth century, regionalism was seized on in particular by cultural nationalists to create 'authentic' architecture even though this means an 'invention of tradition' (Hobsbawm and Rangers 1983).[9] For Colquhoun, regionalism constitutes an ideological backbone for the widespread nationalist movements, especially from politically and culturally dominated countries. Like Frampton, he draws an antagonistic connection between regionalism and rationalization and, in related fashion, the affinity between regionalism and nationalism and the importance of overcoming both (thus the proposal for 'critical regionalism' from Frampton).

However, by positing nationalism as quite different from the rational legal form of domination (such as capitalism and bureaucracy) Colquhoun overlooks two possibilities. First is the appearance of cultural nationalism in what is supposedly a universalistic rational-legal system of domination. As I have shown earlier, the construction of regional-nationalist "Indies architecture" is inseparable from the orientalist history of the colonial state and the sustained interest of the colonizer in other cultures. The, second is the profound aspiration of postcolonial nationalists to actualize freedom beyond the iron cage of traditional 'regionalist' forms of community. The putative antithesis between the Enlightenment's universalism and nationalist particularism obscures the aspiration of postcolonial nationalists to actualize freedom (as well as the failure to retain and actualize such aspirations) by engaging with modernity. In the following section, I show the character of postcolonial aspirations for modernity by a consideration of how the shock of the new has shaped the imagination of popular nationalism.

INSURGENT NATIONALISM AND THE EVERYDAY

Tracing figures of insurgent nationalism

In a remarkable series of writings in the early 1920s by Mas Marco Kartodikromo, an Indonesian anti-colonial 'dandy' who was finally detained by the state and died in a penal colony, there are mixed poetic and political references to the modern urban visual environment of colonial cities in Java (for a fuller account, see Kusno 2010). The city where Mas Marco lived was by then undergoing a series of 'modernizations' such as the broadening of asphalt roads, the lighting of streets, the construction of European suburbs, the (middling modernist) zoning of the city, the proliferation of shops, restaurants, hotels and cinemas, and not least, the experiment of new architecture. The lively main streets which offered asphalt roads, motorcars, billboards, offices, hotels, the movie house, restaurants, fashionable shops, dancing halls and other wholesale ensembles of imported commodities had come to colonial Indonesia in the early twentieth century as a central agent of modernization (Shiraishi 1990; Mrazek 2002).

Mas Marco did not criticize these developments in the city. Instead he addressed this landscape of colonial modernity with a mix of shock and an exhilarating sense of engagement. What is crucial for us is how he juxtaposed the novelties of the modern built environment (as many of the buildings appear 'modern' with remarkable traces of proto-art-deco architectural styles) with the traditional royal palace, as if to make a point that his urban generation is on the move, leaving behind the feudalistic cultural tradition of Java sanctioned by Dutch colonial power.[10] Mas Marco himself rejected traditional iconography and preferred to dress himself up in Western suit with skullcap, coloured shoes and many pens in his pocket. With enormous excitement he embraced the modern urban environment and used it to develop his anti-colonial subjectivity.

As the colonizers developed the city to become modern centres of the colony they also opened up a space for the colonized to develop a critical consciousness based on the sense of being discriminated against and left behind. Mas Marco demanded a share of modernity often in the form of 'collective consumption', which was re-materialized in the national struggle for independence. He publicized colonial injustices, organized protests and demanded equality and 'rights to the city'. He demanded the promises and the products of modernity which had transformed him.

Once we consider how the colonial built environment (including its architecture) was received by the colonized, it would be difficult to argue that in the colony non-local 'modern' architecture is essentially a 'form of dominance'. The lived experience of colonial subjects seems to indicate that responses to the rhythms of colonial architecture and urban form are more ambiguous and unpredictable. The arrival of new visual environments and the provision of new infrastructures and urban cultures provide important settings for the colonized intelligentsia to develop a vision for their imagined future. We know well that in most cases colonial cities were divided cities, but this division also quite often brought elements together and established an exchange between them. This exchange may have not been planned, but it is capable of constituting a political imagination. For Marco, the colonial city represented less the form of dominance, but more an aspiration for an egalitarian modernity which led him to a duel with the colonial state.

We can say that Marco articulated a different form of citizenship as he engaged with colonial urban modernity. The development of the colonial city (one could add, signified by the proliferation of new architecture) stimulated not only his desire to consume urban modernity, but also his anti-colonial national consciousness. In the context of colonial relations, the promise of modernity to deliver a radically new time can be translated into incendiary actions. It is not just a utopian wish but also an insurgent one.

In his comprehensive study of Brasilia as a modernist city, James Holston (1989; 1999) explores the idea of insurgency as a form of citizen response to the state-project of modernist architecture and urbanism. The master plan of the city which imagined a coherent future of the Brazilian nation finally gave in to paradoxes and contradictions in social life. Brazilians who lived in Brasilia brought with them their cultural practices of everyday life and eventually transformed Brasilia into something different from the modernist urban paradigm. Insurgency, in Holston's formulation, represents urban practices 'that often derive from and transform the (state directed) project but are in important ways heterogeneous and outside the state' (Holston 1999: 167; see also Simone 2004). In some ways, Mas Marco was like the occupants of Brasilia. He introduced a form of insurgency into the colonial city that demanded an accommodation unintended by the colonizer. Perhaps Mas Marco is more radical for he believed that anti-colonial struggles for independence ought to be based on practising what he called the 'science of communism' which would lead effectively to the overthrowing of the colonial state.

From Mas Marco, we learn that the tension between the (colonial) state agenda from above and insurgency from below are not always only related to nationalism. The international communism of his time seems to play a major role in his self-conception of modernity. Acknowledging the breadth of motivation of those who transform the meaning of the colonial city, prompted us to consider the possibility of seeing the nationalist in the early decolonization of the postcolonial world as constituting a *transnational* insurgency against the imperial centre of the West which, after decolonization, had continued to assert its power over the newly independent states (see also Smith, 2000).

In the following section I look at the architectural discourses of the early decolonization of the 'Third World' and instead of understanding them as an expression of state authoritarianism, I consider them as a form of insurgency against the geopolitical order of the time (even though their practices had marginalized members of their own communities). By doing so, I show how utopian modernist architecture and urban design played an insurgent role for the formation of transnational anti-colonial nationalism. One could argue that focusing on the agency of state leaders might replicate again the approach of 'seeing-like-a-state'. Yet, we can also ask what would the state-directed modernist discourses of nation building in the decolonized world be like if we see the leaders of the decolonized world as insurgents demanding their own path of development against the tutelage of the West? The question of whether the decolonization constitutes a form of 'people nationalism' can only be determined contextually according to specific times and social locations. Nationalist leaders of Asia and Africa in the 1950s consciously sought to create a transnational solidarity, underscoring the breadth of nationalist imaginings (see also Chakrabarty 2000a). Can the decolonized state be seen as practising transnational 'insurgent nationalism' against the imperial West?

Few things show more clearly the state practices of insurgency than the decolonized world of Indonesia under Sukarno. I approach Sukarno as representing 'insurgent nationalism' for he operated in the context of coming to terms with the colonial state he inherited on the one hand and fighting against the forces of Western neo-colonialism on the other. In his aspiration for a new beginning for a new nation, Sukarno in some ways was not merely inheriting an old colonial state, but he also sought to transform it, by ways of constituting a transnational 'Third World' solidarity.

Can the Third World nation-states be seen as performing nationalist insurgency?

As an architect, Sukarno appropriated some aspects of modernist architecture and urbanism for the capital city of Jakarta in order to reverse the developmentalist narrative of the not-yet modern nation. Sukarno interpreted modernist architecture as national architecture and one that would enable Indonesians to see and represent their identities as supra-local and part of the larger transnational community to which they belong as members (see also Smith 2000). He had very little patience for the resources of regionalist 'vernacular' architecture, and had little interest in using any of their potential for the building of 'national' character. His nation was to be released from the gravity of tradition and the weight of the past. Many of the buildings he put up in Jakarta have the quality of flying, of soaring high, and of screaming up to the sky with very little attachment to the ground (compare to Brasilia, see Holston 1989; and to Chandigarh, see Kalia 1987).

Appropriating the vocabulary of modernist architecture of his time, Sukarno believed in the semiotic capacity of modernist architecture to shock and to awaken Indonesians so as to create in them new subjectivities. The violence of colonial apartheid and the experience of regional conflict prompted him to envision a new city, even though this could only be built within the existing fabric of the now 'old' colonial centres. Upholding the popular national imagination which was looking for a sign of change, Sukarno commanded the construction of a modernist city, for it represented (at least in his mind) a new time even though realities of violence, poverty and frivolity continued to mark the urban life of Jakarta. Yet, central to the investment in new architecture for the heart of the colonial city was also the attempt to counter memories of war, conflict and colonialism, and most importantly perhaps, the post-war imperial webs of the United States and the Soviet Union.

Looking across different countries, we could say that Mao Zedong, Jawaharlal Nehru, and Sukarno, as well as other leaders of the decolonized world, invested modernist architecture in their (capital) cities as a way to eradicate memories of the past as well as to find a position against the pressures from the geopolitics of the post World War II era. They turned their 'insurgency' to modernism even as they conceived this strategy as a catalyst of the strength of their 'national' historical traditions. The context for this construction of a coherent self was the pressure to assert a transnational collective anti-imperialism as the Cold War arrangements started to encroach on the decolonized world. The Bandung Conference of Asia-Africa in 1955 (which mobilized figures such as Gamel Abdel Nasser, Jawaharlal Nehru, Kwame Nkrumah, Chou En Lai, Ho Chih Minh and Sukarno) represented such an aspiration for a new world.[11] Several of these postcolonial subjects conceived the city as the site for the mobilization of 'independence', 'revolution' and 'anti-imperialism'. In all these attempts, modernist architecture (especially for Sukarno) served as a semiotic device to signal the self determination of the newly liberated countries.

These leaders of the early decolonization period tried to show to the world that their new nations were not weak or a due-to-fail state which needed to be controlled by the primitive or advanced accumulation of capital via Western aid under the notion of 'democracy', 'freedom' and 'development' (see Harvey 1989a, b). In some ways, the Asia-Africa Conference in Bandung was an attempt to configure a version of 'global assemblage' for the Newly Emerging Forces to counter the neo-colonial modernity prescribed by the West. (For a different formulation of global assemblage see Ong and Collier 2004.) However, this nationalist insurgency to sustain the liberation of Asia and Africa against 'Western imperialism' was in stark contrast to the wish of Washington, which by then had made every effort in the region to create a base for 'development' under the supervision of loyal and capitalistically prosperous authoritarian regimes. The early moment of decolonization that I have outlined above is historically important for an understanding of the contemporary version of mega modernist architectures that have been erected in postcolonial countries to represent their national identity. We can perhaps say that contemporary modernist architecture (but now inflected by the market) is the inversion of the early state modernist city building. In Indonesia, where the Asia-Africa conference was held, at least all that was revolutionary and Sukarnoist – all that had brought early Indonesia to economic deprivation as the story goes – was declared the negative model for the neo-liberal oligarchic urban reform of Suharto's New Order (1966–1998). The Sukarno regime's slogan of 'go to hell with American aid' was replaced by the New Order's efforts to welcome foreign investments and to promote General Suharto as 'the father of development'.

With prosperous (authoritarian and capitalist) regimes in place, cities in the decolonized world have since become the sites for economic, political and cultural investment by foreign capital. Thus, as much as architecture and the city has been the place for the utopian visions of the nation, they also have become a playground of the market economy.

The paradox is that this type of postcolonial city works in the context of amnesia, of forgetting less the colonial past than its own recent memories of insurgency against the web of neo-colonialism.

TRANSNATIONAL ASSEMBLAGE

Neo-colonial global market nationalism

The proliferation of a market-generated built environment, while displacing earlier forms of state-nationalist modernism, has not prevented today's nationalists from imagining liberation from neocolonial relations. For instance, the ex-prime minister of Malaysia, Mahatir Mohamad, when he launched his Multimedia Super Corridor in the 1990s stated:

> Without being a duplicate of any of them [meaning other developed nations], we can still be developed. We would be a developed country in our own mould. Malaysia should not be developed only in the economic sense. It must be a nation that it is fully developed not only in the economic sense. It must be a nation that is fully developed along all dimensions: economically, politically, socially, spiritually, psychologically and culturally. (As cited in Marshall 2003, 171)

Behind the image of the high-tech city, Mahatir was concerned with overcoming the 'West' and taking charge of Malaysia's own modernity (see also Bunnell 2004). His emphasis on 'development' was aimed at taming the 'West' by ways of consolidating national autonomy. Mahatir was thinking about his project as a platform for Malaysia to become a nation free from dictates of developed countries. But the geopolitical context in which Mahatir operated is very different from that of Sukarno. Sukarno's insurgent nationalism and his appropriation of modernist architecture to resist neo-colonialism have all been incorporated into anxious strategies for marketing the city and the nation. Today, we have an instance of how nationalism harnessed the market economy to achieve a sense of national autonomy. No matter how patriotic is Mahatir's call, it represents a need for the state to (in the words of Eisenger, 1988) 'identify, evaluate, anticipate and even help and create markets for private producers to exploit, aided if necessary by government as subsidizer or co-investor' (as cited in Bunnell et al. 2002, 6).

The city competition for national revival is not specific to postcolonial countries. It is a global phenomenon which takes place in both the centre and the periphery (see also Driver and Gilbert 1999). Various scholars, despite their different concerns, see the 'global urban projects' as a sign of a profound disorientation as well as integration with our capitalist times. I agree with their assessments, and indeed we need to talk about the spectacle of these mega-urban architectural projects in Asia today as a recent product of neo-liberal economic or financial globalization, of the transnationalization of property markets, of ethno-cosmopolitanisms, and new technologies of governance through 'ecologies of flexible capital and expertise' (Ong 2006; Olds 2002; Bunnell et al. 2002).

However, the imagistic architectural and urban design that we have seen in Mahatir's Kuala Lumpur while bound up with the neo-liberal circulation of capital could also be said to be motivated by a desire to give a visual coherence and individuality to the city and the nation as an 'exemplary centre' (Geertz 1980). We could, in the manner of a research agenda, also alternatively relate ourselves to the happenings of mega architectural projects in Asia. Instead of understanding them as a product of hegemonic 'global' forces and new strategies of regulation, perhaps we could also see them as a 'cultural' enterprise for postcolonial Asia to come to terms with its turbulent past and as a nationalistic mnemonic response to Western hegemony?

Long distance nationalism

What will come out of the reconstruction of new time and space of the Asian region and of the shift from the state to the market modernism – what 'national' identities are being and will be produced – are still unanswerable questions. The neo-liberal global assemblage is bound up with inter-city competition and such reconfiguration has produced a distinctive type of nationalism, namely, 'long distance nationalism' (Anderson 1998). The exchange between resources of 'home country' and those of the transnational citizens of the metropole have increasingly been seen as providing a supposedly more independent trajectory for architecture and urban development in the region. By way of concluding this chapter, let me consider the long distance nationalist network of India and its residents on the other side of the Asia Pacific Rim, Vancouver. The imagistic urban design which involves 'long distance nationalism' has also pointed to the mutually constitutive relations among regions in Asia.

The *Asian Pacific Post* reported in 2004 that: 'a low-profile Indo-Canadian tycoon from Vancouver is set to embark on Asia's largest real estate development – a new C$3 billion Indian smart city located [in Bangalore] in an area three times the size of Stanley Park'.[12] This large parcel of land will be developed into an 'internet-friendly city' which will consists of residential areas filled with 'bungalows, townhouses and apartments in enclaves modeled after luxurious western subdivisions with names like "Venice", "Hampton", and "Soho"'.[13] Three other similar projects are expected to come in Mumbai, Delhi and Kolkata. They are all made for 'the overseas Indians returning home and the burgeoning middle-class in the subcontinent'.[14] The developer of the smart city also understands that for the Non-Resident Indians: 'Buying real estate here is not just an investment option but also *a matter of emotion*. But once they are back in India, they certainly don't want to compromise on their living standards. They want to live in the same environment they were used to in the West'.[15] Manoj Benjamin, the chairman of the project, describes his project in India as a 'labor of love' and that 'our goal is to develop the New India, modernizing housing and businesses and realizing a self-sustaining city of the future for this country and its inhabitants'.[16]

What we have here is a story of how transnational 'postcolonial' forces today intertwine with the national or the local in the construction of urban utopias.[17] It is also a story of how the emotion of 'long distance nationalism' encourages a non-resident Indian to take up the role of leading India to what he envisions to be its future.[18] He intends to show to the outside world the capacity of India (or better, the Indian) to 'export Western technology (in order) to modernize the city'. The West is positioned as some kind of a portable model, the parts of which can be easily cut and pasted for the construction of the future smart city of Asia.[19] Through certain images of the Western oriented architectural styles, the Indo-Canadian tycoon in Vancouver intends to bring India a new time by refashioning a new space even as this means creating a techno-paradise for the Indian elite to stay away from the crisis-ridden city occupied by the underclass.

Finally, if the Vancouver tycoon gives us the spectacles of the future in his discourse of the Smart City, there is one more dimension that reveals the urgency of the present. The Indo-Canadian tycoon proclaims that in regard to his Smart City, 'there is nothing like this happening in Asia today ...' for he believes that his Indian smart city will be more adventurous than the East Asian equivalent.[20] This proclamation is made possible by today's peculiar geopolitical situation. The rise of China today (with its frenetic construction of global urban projects) compels the tycoon to make comparisons. He shows a sense of difference from but also a clear identification with contemporary Asia. He reveals to us that his 'spectre of comparison' is less with the West than with the gigantic neo-modernist East Asian urban projects. After displacing the West, the Indo-Canadian tycoon is seeking to re-orient Asia from its East Asian mediation to the Indian sub-continent.

CONCLUSION: HARD TO IMAGINE

The architectural consequences of 'long distance nationalism' that I illustrated above are produced out of references to and with consequences for more than two national territories. In a crucial way, it captures the thrust of this entire section that there are many nations within one state and such a condition allows different configurations of social relations that both challenge and strengthen the nation-state in both colonial and postcolonial times. This chapter has tried to show how an attention to the analytical difference between the state and the nation (cut across by imaginations and realties of the everyday) would allow architecture to be seen as a site of tension, struggle and compromise between them.

I do not suggest that we need to separate the state from the nation (just as we often do to 'civil society' and the 'state'), but the conflation of the state and the nation has overlooked the profound contradictions between them. Almost all nation-states today and in the past contain, almost always uneasily, numerous sub- and transnational attachments, as well as the practices of the everyday with its own sense of what is necessary to lead a meaningful life (see also Yeoh 1996; Jacobs 1996). There is thus a need to shuttle in and out of the nation-state to capture the practice of popular nationalism and the everyday. And in some cases, we need to reframe some seemingly statist discourses as an expression of anti-statist nationalism. For instance, I disposed of the usual framework of seeing President Sukarno as representing the state in order to capture his underlying nationalist insurgent war against the legacy of colonial state and the neo-colonial forces of his era. Sukarno was historically formed under the influence of populist nationalism against the colonial state, but in the postcolonial era he had to come to terms with the colonial state which he inherited and once criticized. In preserving the tension between the state and the nation, questions of agency in the form of collaborations, resistances and insurgencies in architecture and urbanism could be addressed.

But Sukarno is just one among many other national subjects who contributed to the meaning of architecture. How about the common people who built, lived and invested meaning in the everyday urban structures coded with national symbolism? Here we may find a generation of urban poor whose principle motivations – especially after the state's ignorance of poverty-removal housing programmes – may be those other than supporting the state-led nationalism. The question of reception however remains a most difficult terrain to explore in architecture for, as Umberto Eco (1980) once indicated, architecture is more than a sign to concentrate on. Instead it is also functional space filled with the distractions of everyday life. We could also ask about the position and reception of the market-generated mega architectural projects of our time. If they could be seen as another relation between the state and the nation operating in the context of neo-liberalism, we still do not know how they are experienced, used and contested by people who actually live and work in and through them. Even though architecture could be seen as an apparatus that interpellates individuals to become national subjects, we still need to consider how the inhabitants have adhered to a regime of senses promoted by various scales of architecture and urban production. While architecture may be used by particular agents of the state in an attempt to visualize the concept and content of the 'nation', there is no certainty that it will be understood and received as such by the intended audience. How do architecture and nationalism interact with the global homogenizing forces of capitalism and the discursive heterogeneity of the 'relatively autonomous' everyday life?

Finally, what about the 'other spaces' that lie outside the official nationalist urban kaleidoscope such as those of the decaying area beyond the imagistic mega projects and the sections of the city where most of the poor live? How about the dispersed representations of nationalism that operate in the other spaces outside the purview of the concentrated spectacle promoted by the state? Yet, as we have seen earlier in the divided colonial city of Mas Marco, it is often because of these other spaces of the everyday where the majority lives that nationalism encounters both its potential and its limit.

NOTES

1 I would like to thank the editors (especially Greig Crysler) and Anthony King for their helpful comments on the earlier version of this essay. Thanks also to AbdouMaliq Simone for the useful conversation over the past year(s) on architecture, cities and the nation.

2 As Susan Buck-Morss has pointed out: 'Despite all the political rhetoric that has been invested in arguing that one can differentiate decisively between variants of modern culture – that certain architectural styles are inherently "fascist", that constructivist principles are intrinsically "progressive", or that heroic iconography is uniquely "socialist" – these cultural forms have shown themselves remarkably resilient, adaptable to the most diverse social and political purposes' (Buck-Morss 1995, 4).

3 Recent works have looked at the ways in which the 'rationally' based modernist architecture is localized, adapted and transformed to satisfy specific conditions of nationalism in different locales. They also considered why and how the presumably 'irrational' authoritarian regime used quite 'rationalistic' modernist architecture to represent charismatic domination. Mussolini, with indirect input from 'rationalist' architects appropriated systematically Roman architecture to represent his fascist regime (Fuller 2007, Lasanky 2004; Ghirardo 1980). Ataturk in the 1930s Ankara brought together 'modernism with nation building and state power' (Bozdogan 2001), and maestros such as Louis Khan and Le Corbusier were invited to 'modernize' and 'nationalize' South Asian and Latin American society via their monumental government complexes (Holston 1989; Kalia 1987; Prakash 2002). Similarly, Sukarno brought home modernist architecture to represent his authoritarian Guided Democracy (Kusno 2000; see also Hess 2006 for the case of Kwame Nkrumah in Ghana).

4 State-centred approach, according to Mitchell (1999: 81), 'presented the state as an autonomous entity whose actions were not reducible to or determined by forces in society'.

5 Nezar AlSayyad formulates the process of national identity via colonialism in this way:

> When the people of the dominated, colonized societies started to rebel against this colonial world order, they had little to cling to in their drive to establish their own sovereignty, and they were forced to use the ideology and terms of the existing colonial world, with its baggage of concepts like independence, national identity, and freedom. (AlSayyad 1992, 19)

There is a question of history and agency in this formulation. The postcolonial identity is discussed in terms of the colonial discourses that construct it. The postcolonial society is regarded as the effects of colonial power relations and thus the national formation is problematic, contradictory and unstable.

6 In the Western hemisphere, interests in issues of national identity in art and architecture have moved to the 'peripheral' regions of Europe. An art historian reports: 'Recent years have seen the publication of a wealth of new international studies devoted to Art Nouveau, Arts and Crafts, national romanticism and the construction of national identity through art in the late nineteenth and early twentieth centuries. In particular, these have sought to redress the traditional western orientation of post-World War II accounts of the period, demonstrating that central, northern, southern and eastern Europe produced artistic centres that were as creatively original as those of the West, and highlighting the dynamic, pan-European interaction of cultures, artists and ideas that took place' (Kallestrup 2006: ix; see also Bowe 1993; Facos and Hirsh 2003).

7 This tendency continues until recently when, due to the discourse of European Union, migration, and globalization, several Western European countries began to search for and promote the distinctiveness of their respective national architectures. Hilde Heynen indicates that several countries in Europe are fiercely trying to promote a national architecture – or at least their national architects as can be observed in the publicity campaign by the Netherlands, in heavily subsidizing publications on Dutch architecture which are indeed globally distributed and the yearbooks published in the Netherlands, in Flanders, in Germany, and similar publications in France (Hilde Heynen correspondence 6/12/08).

8 Keith Eggener (2006: note 14) reports that during the late 1940s and 1950s when America was

constructing its image of triumphalism especially through modern architecture, regionalist architecture was discussed in relation to Mexico, Brazil, Finland and Switzerland.

9 Alan Colquhoun (1997, 13) refers to regionalism as an architectural approach which believes that 'architecture should be firmly based on specific regional practices based on climate, geography, local materials, and local cultural traditions'. Colquhoun indicates the influence of this approach as a continuation of the earlier eighteenth century ideological conflict between Enlightenment and romanticism. He also points out that regionalism gained its urgency as the world (following Weber) was felt to be undergoing 'disenchantment' due to capitalism's rationalization and secularization of social life (Ibid. 15). In this sense, regionalism ought to be understood in relation to the tyranny of rationality, capitalism and bureaucratization. Colquhoun however did not mention that this awareness of the linear progression (or digression) of time and the need to produce 'Kultur', came in tandem with imperialism and European colonialism of different parts of the world. The access to and regulation of a variety of cultures around the world raises the tension between the idea of sovereignty and development which included the need to adapt modern technology to preindustrial places.

10 For a discussion on the co-construction of Javanese conservative culture by both the Dutch colonial state and the Javanese King, see Pemberton (1994).

11 See the report soon afterward by African-American writer Richard Wright in *The Color Curtain* 2007 [1956] and *White Man, Listen!* 1955 [1957].

12 'Vancouver Tycoon to Build Asian City', *Asian Pacific Post*, October 7–20: 1.

13 Ibid. 1.

14 Ibid. 5.

15 Ibid. 5. Emphasis added.

16 Ibid. 1 and 5.

17 For a recent account of the global-local nexus of architecture and urbanism as representing post-colonial conditions, see King (2004).

18 Benedict Anderson (1998, 58–76) has written about the emergence of various forms of 'long distance nationalism' among diasporic community generated largely by a curious combination of the community's economic success and social/political displacement in the metropole.

19 For a discussion on the process of 'cut and paste' in other major cities in Asia, see King and Kusno (2000).

20 'Vancouver Tycoon to Build Asian City', op.cit. 1.

13

Entangled Modernities in Architecture

Duanfang Lu

American children hear no stories about ghosts. They spend a dime at the drugstore to buy a Superman comic book. This 'Superman' is an all-knowing, resourceful, omnipotent hero who can overcome any difficulty. ... In a world without ghosts, life is free and easy. Americans can gaze straight ahead. But still I think they lack something, and I do not envy their life. (Fei Xiaotong, 1943, quoted in Arkush and Lee, 1984)

During a visit to the United States in 1943, Chinese anthropologist Fei Xiaotong noted the differences between China, where contemporary life was engulfed in the thick layers of the accumulated past, and America, where people were future-oriented but nonetheless dominated by an alienating order (Arkush and Lee 1989, 174–181). Ghosts, in Fei's vision, represented the presence of the specter of the past that continuously haunted the present and made up the very core of being Chinese: 'Life in its creativity … melds past, present, and future into one inextinguishable, multilayered scene, a three-dimensional body. This is what ghosts are' (1989, 178). In contrast, living in brightly lit American rooms, Fei wrote, 'gives you a false sense of confidence that this is all of the world, that there is no more reality than what appears clearly and brightly before your eyes' (1989, 181). Fei's comments encapsulate a grasp of the modern that wrestles with the differences of histories, cultures, nationalities, and ethnicities. Indeed, despite the 'false sense of confidence' in the universality, rationality, and homogeneity of the modern given by dominant discourses, recent accounts have revealed in modernity the constant wrestling with 'ghosts' of all sorts that have been there from the very beginning and will not go away.

To think the modern is to think the present, which is necessarily caught in the ever-shifting social, political, and cultural cross-currents. For many decades, modernization was depicted in social sciences as a broad series of processes of industrialization, rationalization, urbanization, and social changes through which modern societies arose. This approach has been heavily criticized for its Eurocentric assumptions in recent years. It assumes, for example, that only Western society is truly modern and that all societies are heading to the same destination. With the epistemological break triangulated by postmodern, post-structuralist, and postcolonial theories, the dominance of progressive historicism and its associated binaries (modern/traditional, self/other, centre/periphery, etc.) is being challenged.

Questions about modernity, understood as modes of experiencing and questioning the present, are being re-thought.

This chapter will trace a number of recent theoretical and methodological shifts in understanding architecture's relation to modernity. Rather than attempting an exhaustive survey, it is a provisional and partial review of our current state of understanding regarding modernity's multiplicity and globality in architecture. Specifically, it recognizes that there has been a significant turn away from singular, linear, teleological, Eurocentric models to those of 'multiple', 'alternative', 'global' or 'other' modernities. This shift has encouraged new ways of understanding the modern in relation to the 'North-South' divide and forms of social difference such as class, ethnicity, and gender. It has also opened up a new research agenda on the complicated relationship between architecture and modernity. In this chapter, I will sketch the key tendencies that have arisen in architectural researchers' responses to this broad shift and expand the concept of 'entangled modernities' as the main interpretive framework. The term has been chosen over other competing vocabularies in order to go beyond the assumption of exclusive European authorship in the making of modernity and to emphasize sites of encounter, crossing, and negotiation. While ideas such as 'multiple modernities' imply that there was *one* modernity originating in Europe which was subsequently inflected with different national/cultural variations, 'entangled modernities' stresses the multiple meanings of the modern from their inception at different locales and their tangled relations.[1] Echoing and expanding Fei's vision of ghosts, I hope to use the term to grasp the intrinsically paradoxical differences at the very heart of the modern, on one hand, and the geo-historical entanglements of modernities from a global perspective, on the other.

The chapter is divided into four parts. The first provides an overview of the understandings of the modern in twentieth-century Western architectural discourse. The second reviews recent architectural scholarship on non-canonical histories of modernities. The third highlights developments in the study of the quotidian fabric of the modern. The final part sketches out an analytical framework which posits the recognition of different modernities at the level of epistemology.

INTERROGATING MODERNITY

The term 'modern' originated from the fifth-century Latin term *modemus* which was then employed to distinguish the Christian present from the pagan past. From the fifteenth to eighteenth century, three vital transitions – the discovery of the Americas, the Renaissance, and the Reformation – formed 'the epochal threshold' to modern times in Europe (Habermas 1981, 5). With a new sense of the ascendancy of the present over the past, discourses on modernity proliferated: from Marx's 'melting' version in which the explosive drives of capitalism liberated humanity from its own illusions, to Weber's 'iron cage' vision in which a purposive rationality ushered in a disenchanted world; from the Baudelairian appreciation of the aesthetic pleasure brought by the effervescence of modernity, to the Nietzschean claim of narcissistic self-absorption against an absurd modern world. The hallmarks of Europe's self-acclaimed modernity include: the grounding of human experiences in reason, the ordering of meaning based on science and technology, the idea of history as linear and teleological, and the obsession with newness and constant change. For many commentators, modernity is a condition that at once empowers people and constrains them. On the one hand, as 'all that is solid melts into air', new conditions and sources are created for bold, free human developments in all directions. On the other hand, new constraints are generated by the processes of the spread of capitalism, rationalization, and commodification, and by a desire to escape from freedom which has generated anxiety and uncertainty – thus 'the miracle, the mystery, and authority' are perpetually created, which will be addressed by the other two chapters in this section.

While the processes of modernization began around the fifteenth century, the kinds of art, literature, architecture, and music we term 'modernism' did not appear until the late nineteenth century. Marshall Berman (1982) characterizes modernity as a historical experience that seeks to ceaselessly transform the very conditions that produce it. In the same vein, modernism has been a reaction to societal modernization, which is modern in its celebration of newness and the break from tradition, and anti-modern in its critique of modernization's betrayal of its own human promise. In architectural discourse, the very idea of modernism is culturally and historically constructed into a heroic interwar modernism and a revisionist post-World War II modernism, which are characterized by different manifestations of the modern in architecture. The modern movement in architecture originated from the avant-garde spirit shared by modernist painting, music, and literature. Compared with their literary and artistic counterparts, whose counter-modern gestures called the authority of Western rationality into question, early modernist architects were more allied with societal and industrial modernization. Their manifestos and practices often affirmed the beliefs and values of modernization being attacked by other streams of modernism: progress, technology, and rationality (Conrads 1970). Walter Gropius (1965, 19) in his description of the Bauhaus programme, for example, proclaimed that: 'A breach has been made with the past, which allows us to envisage a new aspect of architecture corresponding to the technical civilization of the age we live in; the morphology of dead style has been destroyed; and we are returning to honesty of thought and feeling'.

Similar expressions can be found in the writings of the modern movement's other polemicists such as Le Corbusier, Nikolaus Pevsner, and Sigfried Giedion, the manifestos of the Congrès Internationaux d'Architecture Moderne (CIAM), and subsequent canonical architectural histories (e.g., Le Corbusier 1927; Hitchcock and Johnson 1932; Giedion 1941; Pevsner 1968; Benevolo 1971). The modern in interwar modernism as described in these accounts had a number of basic characteristics. First, it was Euro-American in that its revolutionary impulse hinged on the material, technical, and economic advancements taking place within the Western spatial system. Second, it was simultaneously universal – the new forms, spatial principles, and technologies of modernism were viewed as a matter of knowledge and expression of zeitgeist which held an epochal force that no society could escape. Third, by repudiating of traditional restrictions and decoration, reconceptualizing space-time, following the logic of function, and modulizing its components, modernist architecture embodied modern modes of living, thinking, and production based on rationality, efficiency, calculation, and the obsession with novelty and abstraction. Fourth, most modernist architects shared the moral pretension of advancing social and political goals through practices ranging from the design of furniture, the house and the street to the planning of the whole city. In the polemical picture of the modern movement, the founders of modernist architecture often resembled the omnipotent 'Superman' who, like God, 'made all things new' in their heroic creation of architectural language in 'a world without ghosts'.

The development of the modern movement can be seen as a progressively narrowing process through which a cohesive position on modernism gradually became dominant and a shared set of terms to which avant-gardes addressed themselves were stabilized. Hence its self-interpretations were necessarily reductive. Recent studies, however, reveal modernist discourse as a site where the intrinsically paradoxical aesthetic, political, cultural, and moral differences both competed and tangled with each other.

The Weissenhofsiedlung is an appropriate example. First exhibited in the city of Stuttgart in the summer of 1927, the Weissenhofsiedlung was part of a series of exhibitions with the overall title of 'Die Wohnung' (The Dwelling) directed by Mies van der Rohe.[2] While the Weissenhof is often considered the moment when modernist architecture first became institutionalized, its origins were conflicted, pitting advocates of housing reform against some architects such as Mies van der Rohe while placing them in league with others such as J.J.P. Oud (Kirsch 1989). The Weissenhof architecture featured flat roofs, white walls, cantilevered balconies, roof gardens, sun terraces, and large verandas. These characteristics were later labeled 'International', a style frequently critiqued for deprival of any reference to specific locality in the decades that followed, but they were initially inspired by Mediterranean, Middle-Eastern, and North African vernacular buildings (Overy 2005). Exhibited in an era when colonialism was at its peak, the Weissenhof architecture was assaulted in racist terms by both traditionalists and proto-Nazi critics. The *Siedlung* was nicknamed 'Little Jerusalem' soon after its opening in 1927 and its style was frequently sneered at as 'orientalist', 'colonial', or 'north African' (2005, 56). A satirical postcard with figures of Arabs and camels montaged on to the view of the Weissenhof estate was circulated throughout the 1930s. Conflicts among Western countries preceding World War II and anti-Semitic sentiment produced additional entanglements. Although the determined polemicists of the modern movement characterized modernism as 'international', French critics considered the promotion of architectural internationalism an attempt by Germany to impose the style upon western and central European nations. The cosmopolitanism associated with the international qualities of architectural modernism was frequently used by Nazi propagandists to demean 'anti-national' and 'rootless' Jewish intellectuals (2005, 56).

Standard history books see the built Weissenhof as 'modern' and the 'blut and boden' reaction as 'anti-modern'.[3] Yet as Jeffrey Herf (1984) points out, the latter should instead be considered as part of a modernism that does not conform to the standard narrative. Herf terms it a 'reactionary modernism'. Similarly, researchers have tended to separate the modern movement's idea of embracing mass production from the attempt to resist industrial modernity through the design of hand-crafted objects. Historically, however, the boundaries between the two were porous and subject to crossings from both sides. The Weimar Bauhaus, for example, developed both mass-reproducible industrial products and one-off, expressionist ones, which reflected the initial idea of establishing the Werkbund: to improve the global competitiveness of German industry by integrating mass-production techniques and traditional crafts. There were also diverse positions regarding issues such as political goals, technology, and tradition among avant-gardes themselves (Tafuri and Dal Co 1986; Hays 1992; Heynen 1999). The multiple constitutive differences involved in the project of modernism signalled competing ideas of whose modernity would become dominant at a dynamic formative moment of industrial capitalism.

While there are differences that occur synchronically in the modern of any given historical era, the rupture between different eras tends to bring new sets of tensions, which demand different sets of questions to be asked and different types of histories to be written. Despite its claims to universality in time and space, interwar modernism was developed when society was plagued by both class and nation-state conflict, and 'ascetic objects' were necessitated by economic depression and post-war rebuilding (Betts 2004). With the establishment of two co-existing superpowers in the Cold War context, the development of the welfare state, and the rise of consumption-orientated society amid post-World War II prosperity in the West, modernist architecture went through a series of changes. The socialist ideals of its

European pioneers were replaced by a commitment to democracy, which was employed strategically to expose the defects of the liberal West's enemies. Under the new political aura, modernist architecture was Americanized and exported to different parts of the world (Loeffler 1998; Cody 2003). Earlier modernist doctrines such as 'form follows function' and 'building = function x economics' were questioned and dismantled. New aesthetics and historiographies were advanced to interrogate capitalist modernity in its new state. Thus Robert Venturi called for 'complexity and contradiction' to address the inadequacy of modernist architecture in a consumer society, and transmuted the Miesian motto from 'less is more' into 'less is a bore' (Venturi 1977 [1966]; Venturi et al 1986, 139). The grand obituary notice regarding the death of modernism was made by Charles Jencks (1977, 9), who declared that the demolition of the Pruitt-Igoe public housing project in the US city of St. Louis on 16 March 1972 signalled 'the day Modern Architecture died'. The polemic of postmodernist design rejects architectural modernism's technological purism and prohibition against historical reference, embracing instead an ironic historicism which takes past allusions and forms as material for double coding or pure play (Jencks 1977). Others have addressed previously neglected problems such as contexualism, authenticity, and identity.

The field of architecture in the West appeared to be coming apart during the two decades after World War II. Practitioners pursued their idiosyncratic interests in face of uncertainty over modernity, generating a diverse body of work which Sarah Goldhagen and Réjean Legault (2000) have aptly described as 'anxious modernisms'. Nevertheless, a new key orientation has emerged out of this anxiety since the 1970s, which may be labelled 'pluralism'. While practitioners of interwar modernism were obsessed with the utopian goals of transforming society through revolutionary architecture, a new breed of postmodernist, deconstructivist, and post-theoretical architects dream of an architecture of multiplicity, heterogeneity, and discontinuity to cope with commercial society (Wigley 1998a; Piotrowski 2008). Manfredo Tafuri (1976; 1980) has judiciously pointed out that twentieth-century utopian designers were doomed to failure, as all utopian architecture since the Enlightenment ended up as a rationalization of the social crises of industrial capitalism. I suggest that some parallels can be drawn regarding the state of pluralism in contemporary architecture. For all their complexities, contemporary Western architectural discourses and practices have been marked by the domination and hegemony of a consumption-driven capitalist system. While fragmentation is found in architectural responses to the latter, many architects nonetheless share a tacit equation of modernity with Euro-American capitalist modernity, the hegemonic assumption about the universality of modernist architecture, and the epistemological distancing of regional building traditions from legitimate design knowledge. Arguments about contextualism, diversity, and contradiction are inevitably used as an apology for the singularity and totality of corporate and financial capitalism. As long as it is bound up with the latter's singular economic and knowledge system, to paraphrase Tafuri, a plural architecture is always an illusion.

THE MODERN IN THE PLURAL

The discussion on postmodernist architecture during the 1970s and 1980s was an important component of wider postmodern debates, but it was heavily shaped by the discipline's own history and agenda. While postmodernism in architecture shares with postmodern cultural theories a rejection of modernist claims to universality and purity, the former does not possess the breath and radicalness of the latter in questioning the very roots of rationality, epistemology, dualisms, logocentrism, and so on. The late twentieth century witnessed many risks which arose from the products of the modernist ethos (Adorno and Horkheimer 1979 [1947]) – from the enormous hazards of ecological calamity to the destructive potential of nuclear war. From a radical viewpoint, postmodern theorists seek to counterbalance the gross limitations of modernity. Jean-François Lyotard (1984 [1979]) defines postmodernity as an 'incredulity toward metanarratives [of Enlightenment]' – the grand narratives that structured Western science and philosophy by grounding truth and meaning in the presumption of a universal subject and a predetermined goal of emancipation. With the eclipse of modernist values, a new postmodern culture celebrates the foundations of identity as fluid, contingent, and ambivalent. Jean Baudrillard's (1981; 1993 [1976]) widely read account of the play of signs and simulacra dissolves the modern notion of political economy by cutting its connection to the 'real'.[4] In contrast, the neo-Marxist critique of postmodernism as the cultural logic of late capitalism seeks to traverse this celebratory tone of postmodern culture with a modernist impulse to reformulate the postmodern as an ontological condition within the changing structures of post-Fordist political economy (Jameson 1991; Harvey 1989a; Lash 1990).

Postmodernism, in many ways, remains an antagonism within the confines of the First World. Postcolonialism extends this interrogation to other political and geopolitical locales, dealing broadly with the complexities of the modern in response and resistance to colonialism and the continuing dominance of Western hegemony. Edward Said's (1978) study of the 'Orient' as an object of colonial knowledge signaled a decisive turning point in understanding the Western discursive construction of the modern by negating non-Western cultures as the Other.[5] While previous models presupposed modernity as a result of economic and technical advancements in Europe, recent studies reveal European expansion through colonization as an indivisible feature of modernity, and non-Western modernities as an integral part of global modernity (e.g., Rabinow 1989; King 1990; Wright 1991; Al Sayyad 1992; Çelik 1992; 1997; Jacobs 1996; Scriver and Prakash 2007). By assuming vantage points outside the West, postcolonial critics have shattered the singular and linear scheme of modernity and revealed various types of epistemic violence associated with it.

New discursive formations on 'multiple', 'alternative', 'global', or 'other' modernities have been proliferating in recent years. In previous canonical discourses, modernization was conflated with Westernization; unmodernized societies were viewed as inferior ones that were considered to be bound sooner or later to evolve to more Westernized ones according to universally applicable rules. More recently, commenting on the passing of socialism, Francis Fukuyama (1992) claims that all nations with distinctive pasts will necessarily reach for a common 'liberal democracy'; with no legitimate alternative to the latter as the universal form of political-economic structure for all societies, we are now facing 'the end of history'. The actual developments of the 1990s, however, contradicted such hegemonic assumptions. As 'pasts' which had long been relegated as 'backward' and 'behind' are resurrected in different parts of the world, it seems that conflicts over modernity previously articulated as Cold War antagonisms between socialist and capitalist models have been replaced with a surge of diverse cultural claims in the era of globalization (Dirlik 2002). In response to this shift, new academic paradigms have emerged to come to grips with the multiplicity and globality of the modern. Earlier interrogations often invoked time and temporality (When is 'the modern'? Are we moving closer to or away from 'being modern'? Is it an 'incomplete project'? Could it be that 'we have never been modern'? Or have we once been modern and are no longer so, as postmodernism has declared it to be?).[6] Current debates on the modern highlight instead the problematic of space and spatiality. Global modernity has been variously conceptualized as an evolving, plural modernity already everywhere and 'at large' (Appadurai 1996), one characterized by 'creative adaptations' in different cultural or national sites that have given rise to 'alternative modernities' (Gaonkar 1999; 2001), and one complicit with late capitalism to produce new inequalities (Dirlik 2007).[7]

Against the context of changing conceptual grounding, two broad methodological shifts have become salient in the analysis and critique of modernity in architecture. The first is the question of representation raised by structuralist theories, postmodern debates, and the Foucaultian notion of discourse, which stress that language is central to the understanding of human society and that knowledge is not universal but historically specific and socially constituted. The second is the question of the authority of history raised by postmodern, post-structuralist, feminist, and postcolonial theories. With the unified and essentialized viewpoints of traditional history repudiated, new forms of history-writing incorporate more voices and representative viewpoints, stressing the diversity of social distinctions such as race, class, gender, and ethnicity. Architectural historiography has been a topic of fundamental significance in this discussion. Conventional historiography in architecture is marked by its codification of aesthetically exemplary buildings into stylistic categories, and the ordering of heterogeneous design practices into progressive movements. The discursive move from the assumption of an objective 'history' to the study of histories as forms of representation has raised a series of self-reflexive questions (Bozdogen 1999). Dell Upton (1991), for example, dissects the analytical assumptions of architectural history that were invented to legitimize architects as professionals in the modern commercial economy. He proposes instead a 'landscape' approach which takes the entire material world as its object of inquiry and stresses the multiplicity and fragmentation of meaning. The productive interactions between architectural history and cultural theory have recently been addressed by Iain Borden and Jane Rendell (2000), Dana Arnold (2002), and Dana Arnold, Elvan Altan Ergut and Belgin Turan Özkaya (2006).[8]

As notions and effects of rationality, power, and domination undergo a radical reassessment, an expanded and more sophisticated understanding of the dark sides of modernity has developed. The formal rationality of modernity and its human consequences are highlighted by recent studies on high modernism (Holston 1989; Scott 1998; Buck-Morss 2000).[9] Researchers have revisited early texts on the modern by authors such as Walter Benjamin, Charles Baudelaire, Georg Simmel, and Siegfried Kracauer as sources to fuel the contemporary critique of modernity (e.g., Frisby 1988; 2001; Benjamin 1991; Heynen 1999; Hvattum and Hermansen 2004; AlSayyad 2006). The intersection between a deinstitutionalized understanding of governing techniques and a reformulation of space as a fundamental category of politics has produced new conceptual frameworks for examining the spatial experiences of modern rationality. A growing body of literature has addressed architecture's relation to fascist modernities (Herf 1984; Hewitt 1993; Ben-Ghiat 2001), socialist modernities (Hudson 1994; Reid and Crowley 2000; Castillo 2003; 2008), and colonial modernities (see Chapter 3). Together this scholarship has revealed multiple limitations and paradoxes associated with the processes of modernization ranging from bureaucracy, imperialism, and racism, to the mass organization of genocide.

With canonical narratives which privilege Western modes of thinking and aesthetics being challenged, research on the heterogeneous trajectories of modern architecture in non-Euro-American societies has begun to grow. Up until three decades ago, standard history books focused on the development of modern architecture in the West. Academic inquiry into the built environment in non-Western societies concentrated on traditional forms. Little attention was devoted to their modern architecture, which was considered as a lesser form of Western modernism. This orientation has changed with the critique of orientalist perspectives and the recognition of multiple paths to modernity. Studies on modern architecture's complex relations to modernization, development, power, and identity construction have increasingly built up our knowledge on how modernism was developed, interpreted, transformed, and contested in different parts of the world (e.g., Lang et al. 1997; Burian 1997; Kusno 2000; Fraser 2000; Bozdogan 2001; AlSayyad 2001; Prakash 2002; Zou 2001; Rowe and Kuan 2002; Carranza 2002; Ruan 2002; Crinson 2003a; Noobanjong 2003; Guillén 2004; Andreoli and Forty 2004; Lu 2006; 2007a; 2007b; 2010; Isenstadt and Rizvi 2008; Zhu 2009). Sibel Bozdogan (2001), for example, illustrates the alliance of modernism with nation building and state power through a nuanced reading of the development of modern architecture in early republican Turkey. Mauro Guillén (2004) highlights modernist architecture's powerful role in introducing societies into modernity by addressing the phenomenon of 'modernism without modernity': modernist architecture in Latin America arising at a time when societies lacked the typical prerequisites for modernism, such as industrialization and modern construction technologies.

Research on modern architecture in non-Western societies has been conceptually significant in overcoming the earlier hegemonic assumption which identified the West as the sole yardstick to measure the beginning and end, success and failure of modernism. It shows how canonical architectural historiography has universalized experiences with modernity that were actually peculiar to the Euro-American context. It demonstrates, instead, that there are multiple ways of being modern, which are not imperfect, incomplete versions of an idealized full-blown modernity, but social forms and processes with their own trajectories, discourses, social institutions, and categories of reference. Furthermore, the previous model of modernization pictures local histories as disconnected variations, each confined to an *a priori* state-defined space following an internal logic. To quote Eric Wolf (1997 [1982], 6), this is a 'model of the world as a global pool hall in which entities spin off each other like so many hard and rounded billiard balls'. In contrast, by mapping the concrete routes to and through modernity (e.g., the travel of modern architectural knowledge and technology, globalized architectural practice, and foreign aid building programmes), recent accounts point to the importance of multiple patterns of entanglements between different locales (Lu 2000; 2007b; 2010; AlSayyad 2001; Cairns 2004; Isenstadt and Rizvi 2008). In fact, certain geopolitical forms of modernity (e.g., Soviet, Chinese, Indian, and Japanese) have proven to be more influential than the Euro-American ones in shaping the modern in some regions.[10]

EVERYDAY MODERNITIES

While modernity is often treated as an abstract and overwhelming phenomenon, growing attention has been paid to the everyday as an approach to the modern in recent years. Everydayness, as Henri Lefebvre proclaims, is a philosophical category that most intimately corresponds to experiences of modernity. Often defined as what it is not – neither the extraordinary nor the heroic; neither the formal nor the spectacular; neither the transcendent nor the philosophical – the everyday is an unarticulated habitat of the modern subject. It is through this amorphous and seemingly insignificant arena where average people do ordinary things that most social processes occur. Recent calls to adopt the everyday as an approach to modernity have taken diverse forms in response to different epistemological, methodological, and political concerns. The move has been related to a now-familiar turning in historiography and social analysis from privileging the actions of the state and public organizations to attending to the microcontexts of society, with the French Annales School of historiography and the German *Alltagsgeschichte* ('everyday life') school of social history as its two prominent variants. From the feminist contention that 'the personal is political' to the postcolonial recovery of the voices of the subaltern, the shift in focus has underscored the deinstitutionalization of 'the political' in modern society. As discussed in Chapter 1 of this volume, in the wake of Foucault, we see power inscribed on the body of the person and saturating in all the relations of everyday life: the home, the church, the school, the prison, and the discourse of sexuality. The Gramscian theory of hegemony has also contributed to this move in important ways.[11]

Notably, French sociologist Pierre Bourdieu (1977; 1990) has developed a systematic framework to analyse everyday practice in direct reaction to structuralism. According to Bourdieu, the richness of everyday life does not stem from objective social laws, nor arise from the subjective decision-making of free subjects. Instead, it is a result of the operation of *habitus*, a set of bodily dispositions acquired through a gradual process of inculcation which incline individuals to act and react in certain ways. As Bourdieu (1990, 68) puts it: 'It is because agents never know completely what they are doing that what they do has more sense than what they know'. Bourdieu's theory of practice has had a major impact upon anthropology, education research, and cultural studies. For spatial disciplines, his theory provides a solid ontology for an improved understanding of the spatial and temporal embeddedness of everyday life. Geographer Nigel Thrift (1996, 6), for instance, argues that practice, practical sense, and practical consciousness are all related to 'being in the world'. As such, any adequate analysis of spatial practices must include into it the non-representational dimension of knowing, of which Bourdieu's theory of practice provides a constitutive account. Also influential among spatial disciplines is Lefebvre's critique of everyday life (1984; 1991a; 1991b), which points to an alternative approach to the everyday as an open-ended and provisional arena created by the political economy of modernity. At the core of his arguments, Lefebvre holds that a sizable transition, from an industrial to urban base of capitalist production, has taken place in our time. Such a transition, which Lefebvre terms 'the urban revolution', has enabled capitalism to expand into every aspect of daily life. The everyday as such is a product of controlled consumption but nonetheless holds desires necessary to generate transformation. Lefebvre's emphasis on the materiality of the quotidian environment helps to rebuke the dominion of language over lived experience: 'Everyday life is sustenance, clothing, furnishing, homes, neighbourhoods. ... Call it material culture if you like' (Lefebvre 1984, 21). Others have addressed the issue of agency in everyday practice (de Certeau 1984; Scott 1985; 1990; Ortner 1994).

The architectural interpretations of the quotidian fabric of modernity have been shaped by the circumstances of different times. The question of housing was central to interwar modernism (Heynen 1999; Lane 2007, Chapter 8). Architects claimed that new architecture was the best tool to alleviate housing scarcity and rehumanize the modern city. They espoused new technologies to create the ideal 'minimal dwelling' and promoted modernist villas among the middle class as newly desired objects. By the late 1960s, however, most architects had abandoned social agendas that characterized modern architecture of the previous era; housing gradually developed into a separate discipline. Terms connected to the growing influence of phenomenology, such as dwelling and *genius loci*, began to permeate architectural discourse. The expanding hegemony of structuralism and its derivatives, sometimes reduced architecture to the realm of text which could be manipulated freely on a formal level. The tendency worked well for design practice increasingly dominated by commercial culture but exacerbated the alienation of architecture from lived space. The attempt to move beyond the bondage of architecture to French linguistic theory has been an important incentive behind the growing architectural interest in the everyday approach during the 1990s. Steven Harris and Deborah Berke's edited volume *Architecture of the Everyday* (1997) represents such an attempt by describing an anti-heroic architecture that engages with lived experience and draws strength from its relation to recent theories of the everyday, notably the Lefebvrian and feminist critique of everyday life.[12] Theories and practices of the Situationists were revisited to reflect on the logic of continuously mystified commercial culture through innovative imaginations of the everyday (Sussman 1989; Sadler 1991; Plant 1992; Andreotti and Costa 1996; Wigley 1998b; Kavanaugh 2008).[13] Architects and planners have also examined 'everyday urbanism' as the basis of an informal, bottom-up approach to urban space (Crawford 1994; Chase et al. 1999; Kelbaugh 2000).[14]

Meanwhile, recent attempts to grasp the modern entailed in mundane life by investigating domestic space have proved to be productive. An acute sense of 'homelessness' has long been taken as an important attribute of modernity in Western thought (Berger et al. 1974). In his discussion of the 'places' of modernity in Germany, for example, Francesco Dal Co (1990, 27) depicts the modern subject as a 'wholly homeless' nomad who is hostile to the idea of 'home'. Yet such a metaphor of homelessness, according to Hilde Heynen (2005, 2), only 'reinforces the identification of modernity with masculinity'. While 'ordinary' dwellings were previously studied under the category of 'vernacular architecture', feminist writers, along with scholars of other fields, have worked to bring the research into domestic architecture back to the core of the studies of modernity studies in the last three decades. They show that the rise of modern society has been associated with the re-definitions of private and public spheres (e.g., Wright 1981; Hayden 1981), the articulation of new gender relations in domestic settings (e.g., Cieraad, 1999; Heynen and Baydar 2005), the development of new urban dwelling types in response to the experiences of uprooting (e.g., Blackmar 1989; Groth 1994), and the impact of consumption patterns upon housing and interior design (e.g., Spigel 2001; Isenstadt 2006). Compared with approaches of the previous era, current researchers put more emphasis on how people make meaning in their life worlds and assert their subjective agency in often heavily gendered domestic spaces. They also highlight the domestic sphere as the site where modernity is materialized and particularized. Jordan Sand's book *House and Home in Modern Japan* (2003), for example, uses domestic space to analyze everyday experiences with the modern and the new bourgeois culture during the formation period of Japanese modernity.

Significantly, a flourishing literature of everyday and domestic spaces in socialist societies has offered more nuanced renderings of various dimensions of 'real existing socialism'. Focusing on the mechanisms of state power and planned economies, Western Cold War scholarship often depicts state socialism as a culture of dictatorship and surveillance, and a type of 'unmodernity' when measured with normative standards of capitalist modernity (Pence and Betts 2008, 7–8). Recent research into everyday experiences in socialist societies has debunked this totalitarian model and provided new insights into what modernity meant for socialist society. By looking into people's everyday practices of will and resistance and seemingly trivial artefacts of the domestic environment, Victor Buchli (2000), Susan Reid and David Crowley (2000), Mart Kalm and Ingrid Ruudi (2005) and others have revealed the dynamic interplay of individual subjectivity and the project of building modern socialism in the Soviet Union and other socialist bloc states. Linking socialism to global reconceptualizations of the modern, Katherine Pence and Paul Betts (2008) take issue with the long-standing Cold War modern/unmodern dichotomy between West and East Germany and prompt reconsideration of East German socialism as modern. They show that despite being 'a severely circumscribed field of interaction', the GDR society was characterized by diverse lived spaces, occupied and transformed by ordinary people. My own book *Remaking Chinese Urban Form* (Lu 2006) brings into light a broad range of everyday textures and tensions under Maoist socialism by examining how the work unit (*danwei*) developed as a primary urban form which integrated work, housing, and social services, and how its characteristic spatiality in turn staged a modernity alternative to that of both the West and the Soviet Union.

Recent studies of everyday modernities have enriched current rethinking of the modern on three fronts. First, an important premise of the everyday approach concerns the liminal realm of human experience in which people are aware of certain occurrences but have not quite articulated them at the level of explicit consciousness. While other accounts of modernity focus on well-articulated social/structural mechanisms of one sort or another, the everyday approach seeks to discern how nuanced recognitions, social relations, and symbolic struggles are forged in the liminal space between the unseen and the seen, the submerged and the apprehended, and the unspoken and spoken (Comaroff and Comaroff 1997; Upton 2008). Second, while previous studies of modernity explore the development and effects of elite culture, recent accounts of everyday modernities demonstrate that avant-gardes were not the sole originators of modernity; instead, modern identities are the creations of ordinary people through myriad heterogeneous daily practices. Third, while previous models of modernization prioritizes nation and civilization as their units of analysis, studies of everyday and domestic modernities, by looking into the actual doings of people rather than stereotypes, show that experiences of the modern are differentiated by class, gender, ethnicity, and local settings, even within the same national space.

ENTANGLED KNOWLEDGES

The historiographical turn from singular, Eurocentric, linear, teleological models of the modern to those of 'multiple', 'alternative', 'global', or 'other' modernities has provided new understandings of the complex relationship between architecture and modernity. I nevertheless suggest that there are a few epistemological problems left by this new framework: On what grounds should we read one modernity in terms of another? Is there not a real danger of misconstruing other modernities when viewing them solely from positions provided by metropolitan theory? And more importantly, is it possible to develop more sensible architecture based on mutual persuasions between different modernities?

I argue that the recognition of other modernities has to be posited at the level of epistemology in order to imagine an open globality based not on asymmetry and dominance but on connectivity and dialogue on an equal basis. It is important to recognize not only the histories of different modernities, but also the *legitimacies of different knowledges*. My call is made not out of purely epistemological concerns but rather out of a concrete historical situation. As recent postcolonial scholarship has made clear, no chapter in Western modernity is complete unless it includes the history of the epistemological violence that European colonial power inflicted upon other peoples. During the course of constructing the contemporaneity of other cultures as the primordial prehistory of the dominant self, the West dwarfed other knowledges as irrational narratives that should be exorcised for lack of epistemological validity (Said 1978). With this calculated refusal, the way was paved for the spread of the sovereignty of Western knowledge throughout the world, with enduring consequences until today. On the one hand, other regional intellectual traditions, 'once unbroken and alive', are treated as purely matters of historical research devoid of any theoretical lineage (Chakrabarty 2000a, 6). On the other hand, the regionality of Western thought masquerades as uncontestable universalism, its cognitive formula assuming a central role even in places where realities are completely disjoint from happenings in the metropolis (Radhakrishnan 2000). One of the violent effects of the denial of other knowledges has been the establishment of a false historical dichotomy. 'Western knowledge' vis-à-vis 'native experience' in social sciences (most notably in anthropology and area studies) assumes that any epistemic category making sense of the native belongs to the West. This cognitive inclination is still robust despite the sophistication of recent theoretical constructs (Robinson 2005).

The global sovereignty of Western modern architecture and the suppression of other architectural knowledges have had destructive consequences for built environments around the world. The past five decades have witnessed waves of theoretical debates that sought to address the ubiquitous problem of placelessness, with the idea of critical regionalism developed by Kenneth Frampton and others being one of the most influential academic propositions since the 1980s (Tzonis and Lefaivre 1980; Curtis 1982, 331–343; Frampton 1983; 1992 [1980], 314–327; and 1998 [1983]). Systematic assessments of critical regionalism have been made elsewhere (e.g., Colquhoun 1997; Eggener 2002; Hartoonian 2006). My polemic here is to use critical regionalism as an example to highlight a fundamental failure of contemporary architectural discourse in responding to the reality of other knowledges. According to Frampton (1998 [1983], 23), '[t]he fundamental strategy of Critical Regionalism is to mediate the impact of universal civilization with elements derived *indirectly* from the peculiarities of a particular places [emphasis as in the original]'. To achieve this, Frampton suggests taking inspirations from local specifities such as the light conditions, topography, climate, place-form, and so on, with the tectonic and tactile dimensions stressed. John Utzon's Bagsvaerd Church is cited as an example 'whose complex meaning stems directly from a revealed conjunction between, on the one hand, the *rationality* of normative technique and, on the other, the *arationality* of idiosyncratic forms [emphasis as in the original] (1998 [1983], 25).

Frampton's prescriptions are certainly helpful in moving beyond postmodernism's nihilistic play of signs for consumption and to pursue a more sincere and sensitive architecture. My concern has been that the operation of critical regionalism preempts the possibilities of local architectural knowledges, as if the latter do not exist at all. While Frampton is highly critical of the *tabula rasa* tendency of modernist design, the local is treated here as an epistemological '*tabula rasa*', which can at best provide some 'arational' idiosyncrasies for metropolitan architectural virtuosity. The drama of critical regionalism can only be played out with reference to 'universal modernism', which is presumed to be the only genuine knowledge emanating from rationality. This scenario, however, is utterly ironic when we consider that the majority of people on Earth still live in varied types of sophisticated 'regional architecture' designed and constructed by local builders who do not have access to 'normative' modernist building knowledge and technique. For them, so-called 'universal modernism' is merely another regional reality.

Yet in critical regionalism as articulated by Frampton, the inherited regional culture is posited as a necessary object for destruction, rather than living knowledge with the same epistemological significance as 'universal civilization' – read here as Western 'scientific, technical, and political rationality'. As such, critical regionalism falls within the bounds of Eurocentric epistemology: other cultures are construed as unregenerate irrationality waiting to be expelled, although part of them may be dissected and then reassembled only to revitalize the fading spirit of Western rationality. By eschewing the possibilities of other knowledges altogether and projecting modernism's anxiety with its inner crisis onto other locales, critical regionalism's cultivation of regional cultures turns out to be another operation to sustain modernism's schizophrenic obsession with itself.

Could the rich regional building traditions not merely be raw material for metropolitan manoeuvers but living knowledges with their own epistemological claims? Is it possible to launch a critique of modernism that acknowledges the contemporaneity of multiple epistemic spaces? And could different knowledges be contested and updated not just with reference to Western thoughts and forms but with historical reference to one another? My study on the aftermath of the people's commune movement in China (1958–1960) points to such possibilities (Lu 2007a). During the commune movement, concurrent with sweeping institutional changes, architects boldly experimented with modernist design in rural China, but their proposals rarely progressed from paper. The failure of the commune plan problematized the issue of modernist architecture. As the country was short of steel and concrete, and little state funding was available for rural construction, designers recognized the importance of combining both modern and traditional methods. There arose a new need for collective self-understanding and other knowledges besides those of the West. Hence, 1963 saw a sudden expansion of knowledge of traditional built forms in different parts of the country. Surveys of vernacular architecture were conducted and published, and efforts were made to integrate local building conventions with modern design. Meanwhile, the influential *Architectural Journal* (*Jianzhu xuebao*) started extensive coverage of architecture in Third World countries. The 1963 issues covered architecture in Indonesia, Cambodia, Burma, Cuba, North Korea, Vietnam, and Albania, while the 1964 issues added Egypt, Mexico, Ghana, Guinea, and Syria to the list. Unlike typical Western representations, Chinese authors focused on modern developments in architecture rather than on the traditional forms of these nations. They paid particular attention to how designers adapted buildings to local social, geographical, climatic, and cultural conditions. In a 1963 report on Cuban architecture, for instance, innovative roof systems for industrial structures and well planned residential districts in Havana were extolled (Liu 1963). Occasionally, a 'sameness' was drawn between building traditions in China and those in other developing countries (Cheng 1963).

Through such discursive parameters, the architectural practices of other developing countries were linked with those of China, creating a world of synchronic temporality and shared spatiality. As these coeval knowledges fuelled new imaginings of modern Chinese architecture, the early 1960s saw a flourishing of design projects with a strong local flavour. The new orientation destabilized the previous discursive framing of 'Western modernist architecture', which became a subject of intellectual contention. This conceptual twist was reflected by Huanjia Wu (1964), who commented on the 'ten greatest buildings in the 1960s' selected by the American journal *The Architectural Forum*. Wu found the work of 'master architects' (including Le Corbusier, Louis Kahn, and Eero Saarinen, among others) 'chaotic', 'ugly', and 'sick'. Saarinen's expressionist TWA Flight Centre, for example, was denounced for the lavish abuse of technology for purely visual concerns.

These comments were certainly made under specific historical and political circumstances, but they help to illustrate the matter of fact that there is an 'exterior' to an allegedly 'universal modernism', where it may be challenged or even deemed irrelevant. It is from this discursive space that we can start to confront the regionality and finitude of modernism on the basis of other experiences. From the above example, we see that the crisis of modernist architecture in China in the early 1960s differed greatly from the crisis in the West during the same period. Chinese architects were forced to face the historically constituted condition of scarcity after the failure of commune design; it was from this vantage point that they posited modernism among other knowledges and developed a new vision of Chinese architecture. The rich regional building traditions revealed through this example are not 'ghosts' of the past to be disenchanted but knowledges that continue to build upon the present.

My position here is both similar and dissimilar to that of Dipesh Chakrabarty in his book *Provincializing Europe* (2000b). Colonial historicism was the colonizers' way of saying 'not yet' to non-European peoples, who were forced to wait until they became 'civilized enough to rule themselves' (2000b, 8). Chakrabarty argues that the contemporary historicist framework commits the same error by considering the persisting world of peasants, which involves 'gods, spirits, and supernatural agents as actors alongside humans', an anachronism in Indian political modernity. He sets out to dismantle the linear notion of time by reconceptualizing the present as 'constantly fragmentary' with diverse ways of being in the world. Like Chakrabarty, I stress the contemporaneity and synchronicity of multiple life worlds. Yet unlike Chakrabarty, who focuses on reinstituting a coevalness between irrational supernaturalism and political modernity in India, I seek to build on the coevalness of different rationalities and knowledges. Chakrabarty is correct in his claim that it is better to see reason as 'one among many ways of being in the world', but his designation of the native life world as a phenomenological immediacy fraught with blind faith and superstition tends to repeat the false historical dichotomy between an inherited domain comprised of native religions and customs, and a colonized domain comprised of Western political economy and science. Yet in reality, even Western modernity has never been completely disenchanted – a powerful Christian religion, for example, is always coeval with capitalist modernity in the United States.

My contention is that much in native life worlds, like in the Western ones, are constituted by rationalities and knowledges developed and accumulated over time, despite their being construed in terms of the divine or super-human. The rich and sophisticated regional building traditions across the world are the testimony to this. Yet our architectural discourse and educational system have effectively delegitimized these other knowledges. With the specificity of modern Western forms disguised as authentic universalism, modernist design is defined as the only 'valid' knowledge taught in design studios everywhere. Other regional building traditions are either ignored or reduced to material for stylistic borrowings or historical research, devoid of any potential as resources for thinking about the present. As long as Western-centric epistemological assumptions remain dominant and other knowledges are considered residual, I argue, we are still very much in the shadow of Sir Banister Fletcher's 'Tree of Architecture'.[15]

What is more problematic is architecture's actual means of production in late modernity. Designers are mass produced based on more or less similar curriculums. Jet travel and new information technology allow architects to design projects at distance with ease (McNeil 2009). 'Starchitects' are driven to produce the same theatrical effect everywhere instead of attending to the unique differences of each site. A new level of abstraction is achieved as people, places, and local knowledges are effectively bypassed by globalized processes of architectural production. This shift mirrors the dominant tendency of our time, in which the abstract 'space of flows' is imposing its logic over scattered lived places (Castells 1996, 428). The faceless flows of capital bear little relationship to the real economy, responding largely to unpredictable turbulences triggered by speculation, illogical swings of crowd behaviour, and the random processing of constantly updated information by financial wizards (1996, 474). It is in face of this ultimate irrationality intrinsic to financial capitalism that self-consciously bold forms are relentlessly created for no reason other than to throw up higher, more spectacular, or more technologically sophisticated projects into the global image economy (Lu 2008). Like never before, modern architecture – as a way of building, a knowledge product, a style-of-life consumer item, and a symbol of modernity – has reached every corner of the planet. Even in remote rural areas, peasants choose to build modern-style buildings in concrete instead of adopting local forms and materials. As a result, indigenous building knowledges and technologies have been disappearing rapidly in many places. It is reported that buildings now account for forty percent of total energy consumption in developed countries. The spread of modern architecture (and the lifestyles associated with it), not unlike the spread of chemical pesticides, has reduced cultural diversity and produced destructive ecological effects.

Much research has addressed the problems of ubiquitous placelessness and environmental sustainability in recent years. What I hope to add here is a transformative imagining of these issues at the level of epistemology. Unless other modernities are recognized as legitimate spaces of knowledge production, the march toward social homogeneity and environmental destruction will remain unchecked. It is time to enfranchise other spatial rationalities and architectural knowledges to create a more sustainable, just, and culturally and ecologically rich world. It is time to open our architectural education to a multi-logical programme that encourages dialogue and reciprocity amongst different understandings of dwelling and building.

ACKNOWLEDGEMENTS

The research for this chapter has been supported by Australian Research Council. Parts of the chapter appeared in the Introduction chapter of my book *Third World Modernism* (2010) and *Fabrications*, vol. 19, no. 2.

NOTES

1 The idea of 'multiple modernities' formulated by Shmuel Eisenstadt and others recognizes the multiplicity of cultural programmes, and argues that culturally specific forms of modernity will continue to exert their influence upon value systems, institutions, and other aspects of modern societies (Eisenstadt 2002; Sachsenmaier et al. 2002). Although it is a positive move from the pervious unilinear model of modernization, the 'multiple modernities' model assumes that the instances of the modern outside the West are the localizations of an original Western modernity. The idea of 'entangled modernities' was proposed by a small number of scholars as a modified model out of the dissatisfaction with the multilinear approach of 'multiple modernities' (Randeria 2002; Therborn 2003; Arnason 2003). So far, the concept has been most clearly spelled out by Göran Therborn (2003), who argues that different modernities do not just co-exist but entangle with each other. Therborn's approach, however, is very much an 'old school' Marxist one; his emphasis on time and institutional processes may be seen as an effort to restore their primacy over space and non-institutional processes. A systematic explication of the notion has yet to be developed. The final part of this chapter, 'Entangled Knowledges', considers the notion at the level of epistemology.

2 Intended to be a permanent demonstration of the possibilities of modernist housing design, the estate consisted of housing types ranging from detached single-family houses designed by Le Corbusier and Hans Poelzig to row houses designed by J.J.P. Oud and Mart Stam.

3 I want to thank Greg Castillo for bringing up this point.

4 While Marxian political economy stresses production and a system of needs, Baudrillard claims that we are now in a new era of simulation in which the play of signs replaces the logic of production as the key constituent of postmodern society. One's wage, for example, is merely a sign of one's position in the system, which bears no relation to what one produces (Baudrillard 1993 [1976]).

5 Demonstrating the possibilities of challenging the very roots of Western rationality and epistemology through the study of texts, representations, and their institutional bases, Said's approach has generated a great degree of theoretical transferability (see Chapter 2).

6 I am indebted to Sibel Bozdogan for bringing my attention to these questions.

7 These new formulations of global modernity represent a broad political spectrum: from those who intend to promote global management of cultural differences (e.g., Shmuel Eisenstadt), postcolonial scholars who proclaim native cultures and knowledges (e.g., Arjun Appadurai and Dilip Parameshwar Gaonkar), to New Leftists who call for systematic understandings of global capitalist modernity (e.g., Arif Dirlik).

8 The *Journal of the Society of Architectural Historians* (JSAH) and the *Journal of Architectural*

Education (JAE) published in 1999 special issues on 'Architectural History' (edited by Eve Blau) and 'Critical Historiography' (edited by Kazys Varnelis) respectively; both argue for theoretical openings for the transformation of architectural history.

9 Anthropologist James Scott defines 'high modernism' as 'a particularly sweeping vision of how the benefits of technical and scientific progress might be applied – usually through the state – in every field of human activity' (Scott 1998, 90). Notably, his study reveals the 'quasi-religious faith in a visual sign or representation of order' (1998, 114) held by social planners in different parts of the world.

10 The seemingly long-established Chinese norms of neighbourhood design, for instance, were indeed results of transnational interactions, informed by events, sources, and inspirations from various parts of the globe, and the impact of the Soviet model was more significant than others during the early period of Chinese socialism (Lu 2006, Chapter 2).

11 While 'ideology' in traditional Marxist thoughts indicates the specific forms of consciousness imposed by the ruling class upon subordinate groups, Antonio Gramsci (1971) argues that a class's hegemony cannot be reduced to a process of ideological domination but has to consist in the creation of a 'collective will' resulting from the active adoption of the interests of the popular classes by the hegemonic class. Gramscian notions of hegemony have heavily influenced the development of the field of cultural studies.

12 For a concise review of Lefebvre's critique of everyday life, see McLeod (1997). For an attempt to explore the limits of contemporary theories in approaching the everyday in concrete ways, see Upton (2002).

13 Existing in 1958–1972, the Situationist International was a constellation of French artists, urbanists, and writers who sought to constitute an *anti-art* as a critique against the consumer society and quotidian oppression in post-war Europe by creating 'situations' – events 'staged to catalyze liberatory transformation' (McLeod 1997, 23). The strategies they proposed, such as *dérive* (drift – a mode of navigating space aimed to making new urban connections) and psychogeography (the study of the laws and effects of the geographical environment to generate new possibilities), are full of spatial implications (Andreotti and Costa 1996).

14 One of the early calls was made by Margaret Crawford (1994) in a catalogue essay published in *Assemblage*, which celebrates the quotidian practices and residential landscapes resistant to the forces of late capitalist economy in East Los Angeles.

15 The 'evolutionary tree' in Fletcher's famous frontispiece to *A History of Architecture on the Comparative Method* (1897) depicts the evolution of Western architecture as dynamic and historical while considering the architecture of other cultures non-historical and having no impact upon the 'History of Architecture'.

14

Notes on the Society of the Brand

Shiloh Krupar and Stefan Al

In the forty years since Guy Debord published *Society of the Spectacle,* many of his key assertions have been fully realized. However, the underlying conditions that led to the triumph of the spectacle have undergone dramatic changes (Harvey 1989a; Pinder 2000; Giroux 2006). In addition to innovations in digital technology which have vastly transformed the production and reception of spectacle, the Keynesian model of technocratic state power attacked by Debord has been significantly modified, if not replaced by the global diffusion of corporate spectacle and branding in the neo-liberal context, along with the rise of the security state, redefinitions of national sovereignty, and the all-pervasive environmental threat of 'risk society' (Beck 1992). These shifts demand modification of the way the political instrumentality, environmental politics, and corporate image culture of spectacle are theorized.

The contemporary reconfiguration of spectacle as the brand, and its architectural, urban manifestations, also inspire an internal critique of spectacle. Architectural branding seeks to mobilize emotional expression, seduction, customization, perception, enjoyment, and pleasure; brandscapes strive to create opportunities for 'experiences', playful interactivity, sensuous embodiment, and individualizing procedures that claim the status of public life. In this respect, Marxist ideology critique, with its emphasis on false consciousness of the image and on symptomatic, base-superstructure analysis, is not able to adequately address the processes of subject formation and the specific social and historical conditions in which spectacle emerges. Furthermore, Marxist criticism of spectacle has been appropriated to legitimate the capitalist context of brand promotion, and brandscapes typically employ Debordian methods to create architectural 'atmosphere'.

This chapter explores architectural culture and branding to suggest external and internal reasons for reformulating spectacle. In a Situationist-inspired fashion, the chapter's section headings comment on Debord's *Society of the Spectacle* and the literature on brandscapes in the form of annotations, notes in the margin, and 'culture jamming diagrams'[1] that distill some of the contradictions of our branded world.

The narrative arc builds on a discussion of the genealogy of the spectacle, the rise of the starchitect, branded cities and services. While we are sympathetic with Debord and committed to Marxist criticism, particularly regarding the architect as producer of spectacle, the last two sections on 'atmosphere' and 'atmosfear' delineate some of the flaws of the Marxist approach and the different historical conditions that now exist in relation to spectacle. We conclude with suggested adjustments in methodology that avoid a simple dismissal of spectacle and realms of cultural production. We attempt to reconcile a critical position regarding the brand with recognition of the value of branded architecture.

SPECTACULAR ORIGINS OF THE BRAND: FROM PHANTASMAGORIA TO NEO-LIBERAL EXPERIENCE ECONOMY

The idea of 'spectacle' was most famously put forward by Debord, who sought to reinvigorate the Marxist project in the post-World War II period, which saw the rise of mass media, consumerism, and information technology. Debord's theory of spectacle has remained central to critical readings of the 'image stage' of contemporary architectural culture in relation to national development, modernization, changing structures of state power, and the globalizaton of corporate culture. The afterlife of the ideas and practices of Debord and the Situationist International (SI) is quite striking, particularly in the profusion of cultural activism and social critique over the last decade. The conceptual scaffolding of Debord's *Society of the Spectacle* and its understandings of 'spectacle', historical or theoretical, provide an important entry point into the contemporary world of the brand and the neo-liberal 'experience economy'.

In the aftermath of the radical movements of 1968, critics on the Left began to explore how culture served to encode and reproduce dominant capitalist interests. Institutions such as the *New Left Review* or the Birmingham Centre for Cultural Studies pursued the study of forms of popular culture as ideological mechanisms that maintained the operations of capital. Deeply influenced by the post-war Paris milieu of French modernist avant-garde movements, among them Dada and surrealism, Debord and the SI reacted against environmental design and criticized large state-led urban projects for operating within the logic of 'spectacle'. Drawing on earlier Marxist work on the dreamworld of capitalism and the Frankfurt School's critique of the culture industry, Debord and the SI explored the city, everyday life, and new modes of consumer society around them. Debord argued that 'spectacle' defined a new stage in capitalism in which images have replaced commodities as the objects and engine of consumption (Debord 1994 [1967]; McDonough 2002). To make this argument, critics including Debord relied heavily on the concepts of reification and commodity fetishism, picking up on a thread of Marx's *Capital* long ignored, except in the work of Georg Lukács. The spectacle was a means to reconfigure arguments about alienation and address the pervasiveness of consumer culture. The triumph of the spectacle Debord describes refers to the dispersed and integrated field of image-relations dominating social life (Debord 1994 [1967], 42). It also addresses the means and methods employed by capitalist institutions to relegate subjects passive and depoliticized. Spectacle 'perfected' the separation between the 'real' contradictions of capitalist production and the mediated dreamscape of consumer culture. Debord's theory is ultimately a theory of false consciousness; images mediate social relations so that ultimately, and falsely, images become the social relation.

Debord's *Society of the Spectacle* served as a manifesto for the SI during the post-World War II era and was linked to the development of several SI social-aesthetic practices, devised to interrupt the cultural systems of advanced capitalism. The 1950s witnessed a growth in the construction and installation of assemblages, environments, happenings, situations, funk, and even junk art, all strategies that attempted to collapse high/low art distinctions and merge art and the urban environment in the spirit of radical avant-garde movements. Anticipating techniques associated with the postmodern, such as pastiche and quotation, Debord and the Situationists practiced the 'dérive' – trips with no destination or random tours from unknown subway stations – in order to inhabit geography in ways unimagined by city planners and designers (McClure 2004). The Situationists also ventured to 'interrupt' the totalizing power of spectacle via the 'détournement', literally 'detouring' or re-purposing parts of the spectacle to expose its internal logic. Culture jamming is a modern-day equivalent. 'Jammers' graffiti on billboards or utilize graphic design conventions to denaturalize or 'jam' taken-for-granted signs and advertising, often with surreal effects that provoke and challenge onlookers.

The diversity and historical situatedness of spectacle is vast. The term 'spectacle' covers a multitude of phenomena: festivals and theatre, the mass media, religious and courtly spectacles in the Middle Ages, imperialism's spectacular 'others', spectacular bodies/genders/sexualities, sport entertainment, the staging of politics and protest (Roberts 2003). Debord's society of the spectacle has more immediate origins in the nineteenth century, particularly the urban architectural spaces of universal expositions, World's Fairs, and the Parisian Arcades, where Walter Benjamin argued the phantasmagoria of the commodity began in the radiant displays and shop windows (Roberts 2003; Giberti 2002; Morton 2000). Visual entertainments, such as dioramas and stereoramas, intensified desire, captured attention, and obscured the realm of the factory. Tony Bennett (1995) describes an exhibitionary complex – a network of exhibitionary spaces and disciplinary knowledge – that anticipated Debord's society of spectacle, connecting nineteenth- and early twentieth-century department stores, art galleries, natural history museums, the cinema, traveling anthropological exhibits, and other temples of luxury consumption.

The centrality of the state – historically emerging forms of state power and technologies – is also notable in Debord's account of spectacle. Studies of the Fascist period leading to World War II or the imperial state of the nineteenth century have often used the concept of spectacle to foreground the state, documenting the ways the state appears as the apex of civilization or the enlightened guarantor of progress, monopolizing violence to legitimate claims of superiority. Debord too explored the organization of state power and made a distinction between the 'concentrated' and 'diffuse' forms of spectacle, modeled after state totalitarianism and capitalist-democratic society respectively. Debord's concentrated spectacle by and large refers to the spectacle of political religion, exemplified by fascism's regeneration of society through the idea of the party as the embodiment of the general will (the 'People-as-One') and the built environment as a total work of art. The concentrated spectacle attempts to transform history back into nature and re-unify the separation imposed by actors and spectators. The diffuse spectacle, on the other hand, is linked to the spirit of capitalism and the dis/enchantment of the world historically orchestrated by the marketplace and the technological realization of magic tricks and profane illusion (Roberts 2003). The spectacle of the commodity simultaneously atomizes social bonds and corrals mutually-indifferent consumers, accumulating dead objects in place of the living festive body of people (Roberts 2003). More recently, in response to changing state power and neo-liberal culture, Debord wrote about 'integrated spectacle' in *Comments on the Society of the Spectacle* (1990), linking mass media and surveillance technologies. Debord's account of spectacle's evolution into an integrated state – the integration of the concentrated and diffuse spectacle – rehearses prevailing contemporary models of integrating business solutions in the name of innovation and efficiency. Similarly, the concept of the 'interactive spectacle' captures the interconnections between new virtual technologies, new forms of seduction and domination, and new possibilities for identification and even democratization (Best and Kellner undated).

The brand's semiological processing of the Fordist world of standardized commodities emerges under these new social-economic conditions, providing new principles of social organization by customizing and differentiating products and places for the purposes of increasing consumption (Harvey 1989b; Jameson 1991; Klein 2002). Naomi Klein (2002) details the important role of branding in the corporate world since the 1990s. Marketing adds 'brand value' to companies; brand value is the symbolic 'trust' of a company, the result of its symbolic associations with lifestyles, feelings, events, and environments, produced by marketing. In the case of an exceptional brand such as Coca-Cola, brand value can easily exceed the market capitalization of the company (Neumeier 2006). Klein refers to this contemporary form of spectacle as the 'new branded world' of globalization (Klein 2002). Branding has become so integrated in the very fabric of companies that their own operations often serve as an ad for the brand: superstar CEOs, design consistency, holistic mission statements, a propensity for monument-building. Brands monopolize ever-expanding stretches of cultural space, eclipsing actual physical products as mere filler for the lifestyle essentials provided by brand consumption.

Many corporations consider architecture a terrain capable of shaping consumer experience and, therefore, of building a brand. Architecture is a crucial element in the definition of brand experience; it can effectively convey the message of the brand and bridge the gap between the corporation and consumer. Branded architecture not only showcases products but associates them with lifestyles, emotions, and atmospheres (Neumeier 2006). Moreover, a general move from commodity production to the offering of services has further accelerated consumption and led to what is often coined the 'experience economy' (Pine and Gilmore 1999). Branding signals a shift from wrapping promotional activities around concrete services to creating themed enhancements, mega-projects, multi-use complexes, and lifestyle enclaves. The idea of the 'festival marketplace', first implemented in cities such as Boston and Baltimore during the 1960s and 1970s, demonstrates an early 'brandscape' that would try to install the corporation as the centre of a new branded civic space, blurring public and private. Invented by the socially conscious developer James Rouse, the concept was considered a leading strategy destined to revitalize dilapidated downtowns in American cities.

The transformation of the brand from a two-dimensional, static, abstract, and deterritorialized graphic marketing device to brandscape has extended the reach of the brand umbrella and blurred the professions of architecture and marketing. The brandscape aims to cultivate identities for people/places and produce authentic transformations by 'tapping into' the environmental unconscious or desires of communities. Under pressure to negotiate commercial interests and regional particularities, architects often adopt marketing research methods – the hyper-rational means of codes and statistics – as a way to engage the public realm in the account planning and designing of architecture (Klingmann 2007, 109). In some cases, the anthropological practice of ethnographic observation substantiates the architect's role as a master of product placement, facilitating the selling of products, buildings, and brands through user input and data on locality. The contemporary corporatization of architectural practice works to subordinate the structural layout of buildings and programming of space to an image, based on well-researched themes or commercial concepts (O'Brien 2002). However, many architectures of high-end consumption, like Prada or Armani stores, seem less concerned with being economical and more interested in recruiting 'starchitects' to engineer complex, experimental, expensive, and high-profile buildings. The starchitect provides architectural 'autographs' and signature buildings that inspire a spectacle of excess.

POP! GOES THE STARCHITECT: FASHION, FAME AND SIGNATURE BUILDINGS

The
indi-
vidual
who in the
service of the
spectacle is
placed in stardom's spotlight is in fact the opposite of
an individual, and as clearly the enemy of the
individual himself as of the individual
in others. In entering the spec-
tacle as model to be identi-
fied with, he renounces all
autonomy in order himself to
identify with the general law
of obedi- ence to the
course of
thi ngs.

(Debord 1967: Thesis 61)

Architecture is reproduced and disseminated in various forms, in photography, on stamps, in guidebooks, and so forth. The media of the field – the critics, journals, magazines, galleries, museums, firms, and schools – spectacularize building designs through networks of publicity. In the field of professional architecture, the competition is one longstanding ritual of publicity and public demonstration of allegiance between architecture and the state or corporate elites. Competitions are usually held for buildings of local and national importance and provide the means for increasing the cultural capital of the individual architect, the profession as a whole, and the high-profile sponsor (be it a state, corporation, or elite organization) without the expense of actually producing the building. The drawings and models drafted for the competition are central to the event, virtually substantiating the avant-garde claims to fame of the participants and accruing their own value through circulation (Colomina 1996). Whether the project is executed or not, the designs have symbolic endurance, especially when reproduced and sold in architectural boutique books, the installation spaces of future urbanisms. The competition facilitates the making of architect-celebrities through media exposure; the building designs function as designer objects for huge state projects or monumental endorsements of multi-billion-dollar corporations (Stevens 1998). Such alliances raise the profile of the architect and, in many cases, help push projects through public review processes, depending on location. The figure of the starchitect shows that fame is essential to the architect's role in modern society. The starchitect's fame represents the ambition for an authentic correspondence between talent and creativity in the face of the reproducible image's banality (Jarzombeck 2008).

Architects are, in a sense, imaging machines that scan, process, and project images and words (Wigley 2008). Those who script slogans and design logos and brandscapes are some of the most successful in the field today. An early example of the professional blending of architecture and branding is Le Corbusier, who effectively publicized his ideas through essays and forms of self-promotion that essentially branded the persona of the architect. Le Corbusier developed a distinctive aesthetic by distilling his work into easily digestible concepts and catch phrases, choosing a memorable professional name, personal colour (white) and material (concrete), and marketing a modern lifestyle through his own stylistic synchronization of work and leisure (Klingmann 2007, 155; Colomina 1996). He declared himself to be a revolutionary architect throughout his career, demonstrating how avant-garde practices – manifestos, revolutionary gestures, and proclamations of the new – can be complicit with capital's accumulation in/through image.

Today a growing number of architects with high-cultural academic backgrounds use their expertise to work with mainstream developers on shopping architectures that blur consumerism and elite culture, eschewing any lofty ideas about taste within the profession. Concomitantly, high-end brands are utilizing high-brow architecture and design as marketing devices and showcase 'habitats'. Fashion labels in particular employ signature architects to recreate their identities and convert their sales rooms from the stuffy elitist boutiques of the past to hip congregational spaces that inspire consumers via an integrated cultural system of style (Sorkin 2005; also Klingmann 2007, 125). The collaborative couplings of Ando-Armani, Gehry-Miyaki, and Koolhaas-Prada are exemplary of this trend. The professional overlap between the fields of architecture and fashion stretches the brand beyond any fixed essence and operationalizes architecture as a curatorial process.

Koolhaas elevates the brand in his architectural practice and pedagogy, whether strategizing with European intellectuals on a design for the EU flag, publishing a dizzying array of statistics and photos of shopping or global cities, or ironically amplifying the copyright of his own concepts and research materials. As Michael Sorkin (2005) notes, the brand syndrome also operates at a more surreptitious level than the starchitect; architectural offices are asserting their corporate status by adopting logo-like acronyms, following SOM, such as KPF, NBBJ, and HOK. The corporate branding of architectural offices is intended to promote the international operation of the firms, enlarging the neo-avant-garde's practice through assuming corporate power over the image of the city (Smith 2006; Frampton 2005). Signature buildings serve as media logos and instant Pop signs for the firms and their clients (Foster 2008). The architectural form, usually a decorated shed inflated to sculptural blob via elaborate surfaces of high-tech materials and electronic manipulations, decoratively dominates the surrounding landscape. For example, the Denver Art Museum, designed by Daniel Libeskind, markets the museum as its logo, plastering the triangular outline of its building-as-shipwreck form on T-shirts, umbrellas, notebooks, and ties. The Erasmus Bridge, popularly known as 'the Swan', serves as the sign for the city of Rotterdam, Netherlands. In 2004, Ben van Berkel, designer of the bridge and co-founder of the UNStudio firm, disputed the abuse of his design, by which he meant the sale of miniature replicas or the use of the bridge's image in photographs or commercial logos. The official city logo, now the only legal reproduction of the Erasmus Bridge, serves as a shelter for the architectural design's celebrity, similar to the privatized spaces of Las Vegas casinos which ban paparazzi photographers in order to protect the privacy of movie stars.

BRANDED CITIES AND SERVICES

"Target Market: The groups of customers a company has decided to serve."

(Neumeier 2006: 178)

> "... architectural practice ought to capitalize on these diverse qualities [lifestyles, attitudes, social ractices] by creating open-source scenarios* that rovoke rather than prevent the active engagment of people in the scripting of their own narratives."
>
> (Klingmann 2007: 80)

*See End User Agreement for use of this concept

Architecture and architects are not the only branded entities. Cities are increasingly developing brands in an attempt to participate and differentiate themselves in the new experience economy (Florida 2002). In a classic essay, David Harvey describes a shift from urban managerialism to urban entrepreneurialism as a new mode of governance of cities. Harvey (1989c) forecasted that cities would act as entrepreneurs and actively participate in economic development and employment growth, rather than focus on the local provision of services, facilities, and benefits to urban populations. Global inter-urban competition for resources, spurred on by new communication technologies and flexible organizational forms, has encouraged cities to develop cultural opportunities, recreation, education, and entertainment as a way to attract capital (Vale and Warner 2001). As Debord poignantly asserted, the city is being reconstructed according to the diktat of the image. Architecture helps to supply and intensify that image economy or 'iconomy' by fixing brand identity in place, as a stakeholder in the built environment (Smith 2006).

Cities actively participate in marketing and branding their image, dovetailing with the efforts of corporations to exteriorize their corporate value systems and generate their own physical contexts. For example, the Las Vegas Convention and Tourism Authority is dedicated to branding Las Vegas and distributing it nationally and internationally. Exceeding 300 million dollars in total resources alone, the organization has turned Las Vegas into one of the most recognized brands in the world, known to many people via the slogan: 'What happens here, stays here'. This strong brand status is one of the reasons the city surpassed Mecca in 1999 as the most-visited tourist destination in the world. Cities sometimes promote their unique experiential qualities; examples of this include the making of tourist maps and the organization of heritage trails or themed tours. The construction of public-private developments, such as sports stadiums, convention centres, and the organization of mega-events, also facilitate city branding. Cities aggressively compete to host the Olympics and other high-profile sporting events, which are perceived as large-scale advertisements catalysing future urban development. Other common marketing strategies involve attracting feature films and television series to shoot episodes in the city. Cities go out of their way to accommodate film crews and companies, with the hope that such depictions of the city will attract the attention of mass media audiences. Cities also pursue high-profile cultural institutions. The paradigmatic example is the Guggenheim museum in Bilbao, designed by starchitect Frank Gehry. It is often lauded for its great transformational ability as a tourist magnet and, consequently, has been coined the 'Bilbao Effect'. Critics refer to the building as a commercial 'franchise' project designed by an architect obsessed with exuberant shapes to the extent that the building is 'an image accumulated to the point where it becomes capital' (Foster 2002, 41).

The branding of cities reflects a larger reformulation of the architectural profession's model of practice: the maximization of profit and stretching of brands through the departure from traditional divisions of labour in commerce, education, the arts, or elsewhere. The cross-programming of spaces, expressed in terms like infotainment or the corporate university, fosters wealth-generating bundles, requiring interdisciplinary (re)arrangements of the architectural field. The entertainment architecture of Las Vegas, for example, requires partnerships between graphic designers, product designers, product researchers, and a growing number of architects who use their high-cultural expertise to blur any distinction between mass consumerism and elite culture. The Jon Jerde Partnership's 'CoCreativity', an iteration of Disney's 'Imagineering', is another instance of interdisciplinary teamwork, integrating planning, urban design, landscape design, object making, and other activities in the export of themed attractions and shopping enclaves (Klingmann 2007, 99).

Branded cityspaces package services, often ones formerly assumed by the state, in terms of lifestyle 'choice'. The authoritarianism and hypercentralization of such choices promote forms of identity and individualism under the sign of an invented public realm. The brand moves away from being a static thing to a living edifice built by participants in the market, contributing the values and meanings necessary for people's lives, rituals, and relations (Frank 2000). The Venturis promoted the identification of 'the civic' with 'the commercial' in their endorsements of automobile-oriented commercial architectures of urban sprawl. In their early advocacy of Pop art and critique of elitism in architecture, the suburban strip served as an exemplary model of populism, capable of capturing attention with a sensorium of corporate trademarks conflated with public symbols (Foster 2008, 167). The populism supported by Pop artists and postmodern architects, with their combination of reverence and cynicism or irony, has currently given way to the neo-conservative equation of political freedom with free markets. The brandscape intensifies this association by suggesting consumption engenders self-realization. Contemporary corporate development practices attempt to participate fully in the visitor's active psychoaesthetic process of lifestyle creation by serving customized environments and services that seem to anticipate the visitor's needs; atmosphere intensifies the disciplinary effects of such sealed-off spaces (O'Brien 2002).

BRANDSCAPE ATMOSPHERE: THE DOUBLE DÉTOURNEMENT

"Architecture must advance by taking emotionally moving situations rather than emotionally moving forms, as the material it works with"

Report on the Construction of Situations, 39

The advent of the brandscape signals a renewed emphasis in architecture on surface and the experience of the subject. Rather than idealizing object-oriented design, detachment, functionalism, and the purity of form, brand architecture picks up on a different post/modern legacy: the production of affect and consumer experience through the deployment of scenographic elements, symbolism, and feeling. In the brandscape, the logic of the plan is abandoned in favour of choreography and 'atmosphere', a field of effects produced through the curation of the surface (Lavin and Furjan 2005). Atmospheric architecture, through 'filling the air with special effects (opacities, luminocities, mists, colors)', attempts to amplify spectators' bodily awareness of the 'kinetic, tactile field in which they are fully immersed' (Lavin and Furjan 2005).

Modernist architecture placed less emphasis on symbolic values and somatic experiences than form shaped by programme and function. The role of symbolism in architecture was re-examined most famously by Venturi, Scott-Brown and Izenour in 'Learning from Las Vegas' first published in 1972. Inspired by the Las Vegas Strip, they claimed that architecture was not only 'duck' (object-like) but 'decorated shed' (surface-oriented). By their account, the scenographic urbanism of the Las Vegas Strip, and the surrounding parking lots, demonstrates that the image had detached itself from the architectural object and become an autonomous object in its own right (Venturi et al. 1986). Historically the idea of the decorated shed overlaps with vernacular architecture, and

Baroque, Renaissance, and Gothic architecture, where decoration was integrated into the form of the building. By contrast, the decorated shed today employs new technologies of communication and decoration, such as the poster and the video screen. This has widened the 'gap' between building and ornamentation, to the extent that surface images have turned into quasi-architectural objects (Wigley 1990).

An even earlier architectural precedent of brandscape atmosphere, Gottfried Semper's concept of 'Bekleidung' articulated the idea of the detachable surface (Fausch 1994). In the second half of the nineteenth century, Semper defined architecture as decorative covering as opposed to structure. Semper's history of modernism shifted architecture from the tradition of the wooden shelter to that of woven fabrics, subordinating structure to the creation of atmosphere and dressing. In *Principle of Dressing*, Semper states: 'I think that the *dressing* and the *mask* are as old as human civilization ... The denial of reality, of the material, is necessary if form is to emerge as a meaningful symbol, as an autonomous creation of man'. According to Semper, textiles and surfaces deployed in architecture were to mask the structure and its material reality in favour of ornament and symbolism; the structural wall served to scaffold symbols, signs, and sensations (Wigley 1995). This approach, anticipating semiotics and postmodern architectural strategies, would become central to the production of brandscapes. Fernandez-Galiano (2005) notices: 'Gottfried Semper's *Bekleidung* – the building as clothing – has been turned into a wrapping for lifestyle, and those architectures most radically entrenched in materiality, tactility, and gravitas are most quickly pressed into the service of spectacle'.

Brandscape atmosphere endeavours to establish a psychological connection with the user through 'emotional design', a particular process of design that is user-centred, engages with the body, and is loaded with cultural associations through marketing (Neumeier 2006; Norman 2004). For instance, the design consultancy firm IDEO prides itself in creating experiences not products, employing sociologists, ethnographers, and architects. This type of human-centred design extends back to the 'semantic turn', the origins of which are linked to a dispute between functionalists and 'product semantic' practitioners at the Ulm School of Design during the 1960s. The 'semantic turn' acknowledged that humans respond more to meaning than form. As a result, designers sought to differentiate, customize, or 'wrap' products in meaningful signs (Krippendorff 2006). The legacy of this shift contributes to the contemporary prominence of the designer as a figure that enlists architects, entertainment engineers, and stage designers in the ongoing quest to bridge the psychological gap between product and user.

Ironically, the brandscape's emphasis on the embodied and experiential echoes the anti-spectacular practices of the Situationists. The call for an atmospheric architecture that affects the user psychologically is quite similar to the Situationist idea of unitary urbanism. Intended to counter spectacle, unitary urbanism is the 'theory of combined use of arts and techniques as means contributing to the construction of a unified milieu in dynamic relation with experiments in behavior' (Situationist International 2006, 52). It is concerned with the atmospheric effects of rooms, hallways, streets, and the activities enfolded in those places: 'The most elementary unit of unitary urbanism is not the house, but the architectural complex, which combines all the factors conditioning an ambiance'. The construction of atmosphere seeks to transform the user and thus 'must take into account the emotional effects that the experimental city is intended to produce' (Debord 2006, 38). SI-affiliate Constant Nieuwenhuys conceived the city as 'uncontrolled atmosphere' in his 'New Babylon'. The project offers a glimpse into a world of continuously changing atmospheres constructed by users rather than designed by architects. This was an alternative to the 'décor' fashioned by post-war capitalism, such as the large state-led urban planning projects of Paris and their international counterparts in Brasilia and Chandigarh. The Situationists lamented authoritarian construction and the havoc it wreaked on the urban environment of Paris, such as the *Périphérique*, *banlieues*, tourist developments, holiday camps, cultural centres, and factories. These areas, according to the Situationists, alienated people, isolating individuals together. Thus they attacked modernist architecture's main proponent: 'We will leave Monsieur Le Corbusier's style to him, a style suitable for factories and hospitals, and no doubt eventually for prisons' (Chtcheglov 2006, 2). Besides criticizing Le Corbusier for promoting social segregation and allegedly desiring 'to squash people under ignoble masses of reinforced concrete', the Situationists rejected functional efficiency as a whole for 'attempting to entirely eliminate play' (Chtcheglov 2006: 2). Unitary urbanism, on the contrary, would integrate art into the realm of urbanism, and in this way blur the boundaries between function and fun.

Brandscapes attempt to accomplish the same, utilizing SI-associated ideas to blur architecture and brand, logo and building, corporate identity and civic space. City marketing in Toronto, for example, organizes 'city walks' that indoctrinate the visitor into the brandscape of Toronto as the 'performance city'. Carefully-curated trails lead tourists around town so that they might discover the city and hear the untold stories of diversity. 'Urban annotation tours' are strikingly similar to the Situationist dérive: 'the practice of a passional journey out of the ordinary through a rapid changing of ambiance' (Debord 2006, 40). The purpose of the dérive, however, was to counter official stories and city maps provided by the government and offer an experimental way to explore the psychogeography and 'other' side of the city. The intended effect was to induce a certain consciousness in citizens rather than to promote the marketing of city image. 'Walks' with non-commercial intent run the risk of being co-opted for marketing purposes, or of inspiring further touristic consumption of the city. In some cases, marketing campaigns make-over brands using guerrilla marketing tactics, enacting anti-spectacle practices identified by the Situationists, albeit in commercialized form (Klein 2002).

It is therefore important to adjust Marxist theories of spectacle in order to account for the cooptation of Situationist techniques, which were historically developed to criticize spectacle but now frequently serve as vehicles of the brand. In terms of methodology, Marxist criticism of spectacle – the binding and blinding of the viewer by the image – does not adequately address the processes of subject formation suggested by the brandscape; ideology critique and the concept of 'false consciousness' do not effectively capture how architecture can inspire people to participate in the making of image infrastructures and the expansion of capital (Stallabras 2006). The interactive narratives and physically-immersive designed environments of brandscapes are more mobile and potentially democratic than the regulative ideal Debord once posited of the image – its concrete separation from and mediation of material presence. Affirmative accounts of spectacular architecture insist that the image can actually intensify, cultivate, or perform 'the local', 'lived experience', 'community', and 'aura'. These positive assessments of the brandscape applaud the architect's interest in the transformation of the subject, as opposed to the perfection of the object or performance of the building, and encourage a re-assessment of spectacle as material, embodied, and social-relational (Klingmann 2007). By attempting to create experiences of authentic presence, brandscapes even suggest that the 'real' is produced as an effect rather than obfuscated by the image or separated by the spectacle.

Furthermore, brand literature utilizes Marxist analyses of the capitalist production of space, like those of Henri Lefebvre and David Harvey, as endorsements for architecture's participation in the experience economy, projecting a singular historical trajectory of capitalist development that culminates in the brandscape (Wigley 2008). In stark contrast to a modernist architectural discourse that emphasized standardization, rationality, objective standards, and ideas about justice (even if this amounted to a style rather than political action), contemporary architectural branding combines the ethics and values of multinational corporations – diversity, innovation, flexibility, 'jamming', dynamism, and performance – with the rhetoric and practices of the avant-garde (Sorkin 2005). Anna Klingmann's *Brandscapes* and the *Harvard Design School Guide to Shopping* are attempts to understand, utilize, and potentially subvert the programme of the brand. For example, the Prada flagship store in New York, designed by OMA, attempts to combine shopping and retail programme with social functions, much like Bernard Tschumi's (1994) cross-programming techniques of 'event architecture'. The conditions surrounding Debord's arguments about the emergence and workings of spectacle have changed significantly; architectural branding and atmosphere lead an avant-garde revival of the theory of spectacle in the service of commercial legitimacy rather than criticism of capitalism.

ATMOSPHERE

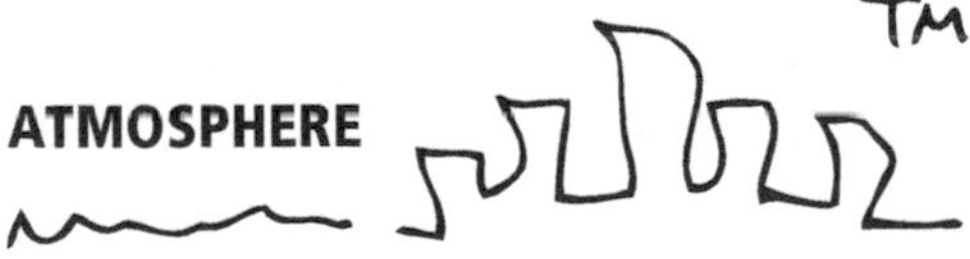

Debord wrote of expanding, highly technocratic state power and its penetration of everyday life. His model of spectacle emerged out of Keynesian models of state power, the rise of consumer society in the West, and the emergence of spectacular forms of state-led modernization in the developing world (Holston 1989; Scott 1998; Mitchell 2002). Debord was reacting against large state-led urban projects and eschewed direct references to state power in favour of critical displays of commodity culture. By contrast, spectacle today is more aptly 'corporate spectacle' in the neo-liberal context. The consumerist version of spectacle operates in tandem with the spectacle of violence and state-led/legitimating retribution, interlocking images of war, terrorism, and collective destruction with narratives of state power. Brandscapes increasingly orchestrate 'atmosfear': embodied psychogeographies of fear, insecurity, paranoia, and despair that help maintain the neo-liberal environment by insulating policy-making from democratic process. Whereas spectacle previously involved the production and reception of architecture in relation to nation-building projects, 'atmosfear' serves as a pedagogical device that produces fear, legitimates authoritarian state power, and mobilizes a political economy of disaster.

Harvey warned about the contradictions and unequal social geographies that are evident within the entrepreneurial city, such as large spectacular developments that cater to tourists, surrounded by increasingly impoverished residential neighbourhoods. This 'splintered urbanism' is evident in the stark contrast between gated communities and ghettos or satellite labour camps (Graham and Marvin 2001). Those who do not fit within the city brand and those who labour to maintain the lifestyle image paraded by sparkling development projects are deliberately kept out of sight and heavily policed. The brandscape is in this sense a carceral landscape, part of a geography of exclusion, surveillance, and control. Segregation contributes to social homogeneity and lack of diversity in branded spaces, to the extent that they are qualified as 'urbanoid', a combination of urban and paranoid (Goldberger 1996). Luminous portions of the city and branded spaces celebrate their 'human park as refuge' qualities, sculpting their secessions from society and fears of social disintegration in intimate bio-forms. For example, Greg Lynn has experimented with the structures of complex organisms, from butterflies to jellyfish, insects to turtles, artichokes to orchids (Lütticken 2001). Widespread interest in amalgams of high-tech and nature, of the cutting edge and the primeval, encourages the splitting off of a section of land for private property enclosures that can be franchised, such as the highly-sanitized eco-city 'new urbanism' developments so popular in developing countries. The phantasmagoric ideal of 'California', globally pursued by the rich, provides another example of an extensive themed archipelago of utopian luxury that relies on a 'planet of slums', exploiting the labour of maids and parasitically built on/by the desolate encampments of migrant construction workers (Davis and Monk 2007).

In the current context, reduced and redefined state regulation extends vast powers to corporations, resulting in fortressed lifestyles and consumer spectacles that sell the nation-state or global cities and fuel the political economy of 'starchitecture' and security, from Shanghai to Los Angeles, Berlin to Johannesburg (Crysler and Krupar 2011; Low 2003). Dreams of plenitude have turned into nightmares of perpetual war, signalling what some critics call the shift from the 'terrorism of spectacle' to the 'spectacle of terrorism' (Giroux 2006; Davis 1998; Massumi 1993). The spectacle Debord imagined as colonizing everyday life more aptly refers to the independent spaces of exception and exclusion conjoined in a composite image of deregulated transnational state power (Agamben 2003; 2005; Diken and Laustsen 2005; Graham 2004; Gregory and Pred 2007; Retort 2005). Detailed descriptions of horrific threats and repetitious visual displays of terrorist attacks work to consolidate the national body and sanction the rise of the security state, where collective provision is shifted from welfare to aggression and protection. The ascendancy of neo-liberal models of deregulated governance, with their attendant weak citizenship, social-economic polarization, and exhausted regimes of mass consumption, produce vast assemblages of surveillance over the general population, which suffers from debt, poverty, different forms of incarceration, and insecurity about economic survival (Gilmore 2007; Caldeira 2000). This, combined with the spectacle of environmental threat – its diffuse, all-pervasive, invisible, undetectable, immeasurable, but nevertheless apparent side effects in everyday life, generates a form of 'survival citizenship' whereby basic biological existence as a prerequisite for political participation is no longer guaranteed by the state (Petryna 2006).

Ulrich Beck (1992; 2002; 2006) diagnoses the wide array of contemporary ecological crises, including Chernobyl, global warming, mad cow disease, the Asian financial crisis, and 9/11, as symptoms of global 'risk society', wherein the state has subcontracted the power to define and respond to issues of safety and socially-produced risks to limited circles of technological experts and private charity groups. Neo-liberal state structures, evolving under conditions of world risk society, ironically exhibit an aura of self-regulation and self-legitimacy while in fact organizing irresponsibility, manufacturing uncertainties, and unevenly distributing insecurities. Other critics attribute the current transformations of the state to the resurgence of primitive accumulation and the rise of disaster capitalism (Harvey 1989b; Klein 2007). Accumulation through dispossession – the privatization of publicly-owned assets or assets not previously subject to the market – enjoys a long history dating back to the enclosure movements and colonial seizures. However, as Klein (2007) elaborates, a predatory form of capitalism now trolls the globe, using the desperation and displacement created by catastrophes and ever-looming virtual risks to generate new business opportunities in damage control, prisons, encampments, policing, and security services. Disasters provide opportunities to privatize state capacities and use organs of the state to subsidize particular corporations rather than regulate them, funnelling wealth into private hands, rigging markets, and/or deflecting attention from large-scale risks brought on by relentless growth.

A parallel but seemingly more benign phenomenon than the spectacle of primitive accumulation is the emergence of states and corporations that are branding themselves as green and environmentally-friendly. Corporations have become main advocates for workplace rights, diversity, environmental consciousness, and other expressions of corporate social responsibility in the neo-liberal context; hot buzzwords include such concepts as reduce, recycle, re-use, and re-think (Munshi and Kurian 2005). Authoritarian capitalist countries also promote themselves as sustainable and eco-friendly, following the lead of eco-cities such as Curitiba, Brazil, where urban planners have continually displaced democratic decision-making and political debate with fast-tracked remediations of the built environment (Lubow 2007). Beijing's 'Green Olympics' aimed to create an eco-city of control and surveillance, entrenching what some critics refer to as 'ecological authoritarianism' (Reiss 2007). Fear and greenwashing are complementary. Green developments not only utilize surveillance cameras, biometric technologies, and other security devices but also function as promotional, cost-efficient 'overlay environments' for military bases, detention facilities, and other carceral landscapes. In fact, some of the most innovative 'eco-friendly atmosfear' is produced in the field of incarceration, i.e., the much-touted 'sustainable prison' and OmniView's zero-blind-spot panopticon prison design.

Yet as Rem Koolhaas reminds us, there is always a discrepancy between the progressive image of any brandscape or atmosphere and the retrogessive environment created by the architecture (Koolhaas 2002). Koolhaas describes the formal aspects of branding's effects as 'junkspace': the in-between space, the space that is not designed. In addition to this formal assessment, junkspace also refers to the actual waste and pollution caused by energy-intensive atmospheres; it is the piling up of unintended and unmonumental material leftovers, from the scale of the brandscape to the latest Pottery Barn spatula. The inter-urban race for spectacle has obvious grave ecological consequences, even if eco-city enclaves attempt to stave off such deleterious ecological impacts and hazards.

Consuming disaster through films and literature based on disease or disaster produces and perpetuates atmosfear. Images of catastrophe dominate broadcast media news, popularizing globalization as the quest to survive. The once-arcane field of forensics has taken hold of the popular imagination; a panoply of TV shows with a forensic approach emphasizes the viewer's role as investigator, presenting exhibits of evidentiary traces that prompt the viewer to reconstruct criminal behaviour or disastrous chains of events (Rugoff 1997). From another perspective, the anticipation and integration of catastrophe into the designs of iconic buildings, such as a stadium engineered to collapse in a particular way, also contribute to an atmosphere of fear (Ellin 1997; Massumi 1993). Above all, the phenomena of 'dark tourism', with its interrelated network of evocative spaces, such as 'black spots', 'dissonant heritage sites', and 'sites of conscience', contributes to an expanding experiential complex of atmosfear (Lennon and Foley 2000; Stone and Sharpley 2008). Museums that commemorate death and disaster sites, in particular, mobilize embodied psycho-geographies of fear, torture, nostalgia, novelty, anxiety, insecurity, and attraction to death, authenticity, and renewal. A high-profile example: visitors to the US Holocaust Museum in Washington, DC receive a Jewish ID card at the entrance which inspires the visitor's identification with a museological prosthesis that is maimed, murdered, and reborn throughout the exhibition (Crysler and Kusno 1997; Crysler 2003). In some cases, the need to witness poverty, riots, and disaster draws tourists to areas of ongoing political turbulence, such as the tours of urban poverty in the favelas of Brazil. Pilgrimages to strife-torn destinations, politically risky regions, and urban danger zones can include humanitarians and activists, adrenalin-rush pursuers, and journalists seeking firsthand accounts (Adams 2003).

Prison tours and the commercial use of former sites of incarceration, where state-sanctioned infliction of punishment, pain, and privation took place, are also popular 'dark tourist' activities, along with visits to celebrity murder sites, concentration camps, execution chambers and death rows, the killing fields of war, bombing ranges, military arsenals converted to nature refuges, and places where people were swept away in lava or floods, crushed by earthquakes, starved to death or tortured (Strange and Kempa 2003; Lippard 1999, 118–134). While people visit these sites for a variety of reasons, 'disaster consumption' overflows with a culture of fear and panic. Disaster capitalists and corporate-politicians inflate threats to justify comprehensive and intrusive public monitoring for profits. The Bush administration's War on Terror produced fear of a generalized 'other' that is about to attack. Such enemy images are deterritorialized, flexible state constructions that legitimize the global intervention of military powers as self-defence. According to Retort's evocative polemic against the comingling of spectacle and primitive accumulation, the military neo-liberalism of the imperial US – its constant pursuit of primitive accumulation through bombardment, temporary occupation, and the establishment of military bases – works with the perpetual emotion machines of the media to create a state of aftershock from the massive incomprehensible virtual violence (Retort 2005; 2006). This world of images – this spectacle of permanent militarization – relies on weak citizenship, wherein citizens are sutured into a deadly simulacrum of community.

New historical conditions of spectacle do not merely seek to make people passive consumers, as Debord related. Pedagogical power naturalizes a state of exception which threatens the potential for meaningful non-violent, democratic political intervention (Giroux 2006). Whether through processes of invasion (of crime, migrants, terrorists, etc.) or the spread of an invisible spatial network of camps, the spectacle of terrorism constitutes subjects as the effect of a potential violence perpetuated indefinitely by the virtual (Stoneman 2007; Weber 2002; Smith 2006). Spectacle becomes a mode of 'fast-track' communication charged with subjectifying power and organizing a general state of emergency. The governmentality of spectacle increasingly regulates subjects by teaching them to spurn the patience required to form critique, in the process providing an education in the limits of conscience. In addition, as demonstrated by the profits Hollywood collects from relentlessly rehearsing and exorcizing apocalypses, terrorism and spectacle converge in an hallucinatory fashion as technological magic, as a total work of art, as atmosfear. The spatial consequences are dystopic and vast, ranging from private armies like Blackwater (re-branded "Xe" in 2009) to face-recognition technologies and the permutations of the 'camp'. How atmosfear takes hold and pedagogically influences people, however, depends on existing social conditions, institutional arrangements, and modes of government.

PARTING WORDS ON METHODOLOGY AND THE FUTURE OF SPECTACLE

Debord's *Society of the Spectacle* prefigured Marxism-based cultural studies, which continue in various forms today. However, the Debordian approach has numerous shortcomings. The problem of methodological abstraction can lead to totalizing assertions about the capitalist mode of production. The ongoing denigration of the visual as seductive, illusory, and detached from reality perpetuates spectacle's linkage to the 'tricks' of the phantasmagoria (magic lantern). From the camera obscura at the center of Marx's critique of ideology to Baudrillard's simulacra, the critic attempts to reveal 'the authentic real' lurking behind the image. The critic, in a position of privileged distance, performs the critical operation of 'decoding' the mythic processes of signification in order to unmask reality. There is little to no discussion in these accounts of the institutional contexts or subject-forming processes of spectacle, particularly how points of spectacular mediation were conceived and put into practice. The audience is treated as largely passive, duped by the narcotic allure of the spectacle, or in the thrall of the production of fear and shock. An example of this approach can be found in the Marxist critiques of post-modern architecture and themed environments. While this literature should not be dismissed, the case studies invariably rely on a critique of the ideology of such spaces, regardless of historical-geographical particularities, they are deemed to be variations on the theme park: inauthentic, simulated, fake, and devoid of social life (Baudrillard 1991; Bégout 2003; Gottdiener 2001; Sorkin 1992). However, we make sense of the world through images; the symbolic is part of everyday life. Images are social relationships, and spectacle is an embodied interactive process.

Theories of governmentality, which investigate how populations are defined and regulated through moralizing discourses grounded in the actions of specific agents and institutions, offer important ways to reconceptualize spectacle (Dean 1999; Butler 1997). Post-Marxist critics like Bennett (1995) and Jonathan Crary (2001) consider how new regimes of perception and attention are organized by architectures of sensation and affect; spectacle does not repress reality, it produces the real in present-day articulations (Foster 1996; Brown 2006; P. Harvey 1996). Spectacle becomes particularly strategic as a technology of power – as pedagogy – during times of crisis and change, when structural conditions necessitate the reorganization of national bodies of subjecthoods. Theorists who adopt this approach suspend grand meta-assumptions about mediation and the reproduction of capitalism in favor of *in situ* analyses, informed by ethnographic and/or archival research that questions how spectacle is produced and received in specific settings. Two contemporary studies exemplify this methodological shift. Daniel Goldstein's ethnographic research on spectacle in Bolivia (2004) shows how forms of insurgent citizenship and vigilante justice are performed in street festivals, challenging the neo-liberal state for failing to provide security. Annette Fierro's more architecturally-focused study (2003) of the 'glass state' of the modern French republic begins by analyzing construction details as assemblages of power and knowledge that anticipate and help produce different orders of spectacle.

The governmentality approach is particularly useful when applied to the brandscape and its dystopian twin 'atmosfear'. Governmentality detours questions of representation that assert the separation of images from reality; instead, spectacle is productive of subjectivity rather than merely repressive. Spectacle constitutes forms of collective self-identification and population management through sense experiences, ranging from visual to aural to touch, smell, and the sensations of embodied emotions, including those associated with real and virtual spaces. The brandscape's turn to atmosphere, weather, and other mediums signals a line of flight from the individuated ocularity long associated with the spectacle, re-organizing architectural practice in the process (Dorrian 2008). The dialectic of spectacle and primitive accumulation, as evidenced in glittering state-led modernization projects or the aftermath of devastating environmental disasters, shows architecture's ongoing investment in spectacular rupture, especially avant-garde practices that aim to produce shock and hijack the spectacle. Embodied psychogeographies of delight and terror regulate the body and discipline identity in different, but often overlapping, ways. Brandscape and atmosfear demand a mobile, yet grounded critique attuned to shock, affect, embodiment, emotion, subjectivity, intensity, light, locomotion, and atmosphere.

Debord's theory also needs to be revised to account for new historical conditions, especially branding's co-opting of techniques formerly used to criticize spectacle. For unitary urbanism, subjective experience was not the means to an end, but the endless possibility of serendipity and utopian community; Constant's New Babylon project of the 1950s/1960s, with its immense structures, would have abolished the need to stay in a fixed place. The brandscape ultimately works in the reverse, modelling social reform (or revolution) as secession from society and instrumentalizing subjective experiences to promote brand identification and particular lifestyles. The model of state power backing Debord's arguments has changed dramatically since 1968; the role of the state in the contemporary neo-liberal moment directs attention to the intense regulatory functions and political utility of spectacle. As more and more public goods and services are subsumed under corporate private ownership, dismantling the social commons and stripping people of what they collectively owned, the brandscape offers a replacement, performing one of neo-liberalism's primary goals: to assess and isolate individuals while collectively diluting the idea of society. What is the alternative to brand citizenship or atmosfear in the context of omnipresent branding of politics and the nation-state? Any attempt to answer this question faces the challenge of retaining a commitment to Marxist analysis while moving away from the reductionism of Debord's position. In writing this chapter, we experienced firsthand the difficulty in resisting the totalizing language of '*the* spectacle' employed by Debord, especially in our account of the shifting historical conditions of spectacle.

The recuperation of the theory of spectacle by branding, and the appropriation of anti-spectacle techniques as vehicles of the brand, demand that we continually review the purposes, productions, and techniques of spectacle. It is an oversimplification and an error to see spectacle as something totally illusionist and mechanically performed by 'the system', as if there were no skills, desires, or fascinations involved in branded architecture. Starchitects, after all, are not just coincidentally picked from a pool; many of them are indeed fascinating and intellectually stimulating architects. In addition, the effects of spectacle are by no means predictable and static. Some critics insist digital media and 'overexposure' to images actually erode consumer attention and desire. New screen technologies offer users the potential means to subvert user-centred designs and the highly-scripted spaces of the brandscape. In addition, techniques of street theatre, such as mimicry, overidentification, and amplification, offer ways to deconstruct spectacle through proximity to the spectacle. The histrionic anti-branding sermons of performance artist Reverend Billy, for example, not only produce critique on the street but facilitate impromptu festival, ecstatic ritual, and even church – a mobile 'Church of Stop Shopping' – in place of the branded world. Architects, too, present counternarratives that challenge capital, even branding 'sustainability' or blurring professional practice with a mission of social redistribution, such as the NGO Architecture for Humanity.

The contemporary field of architecture, as an arena of social practice, is productively haunted by the collapsing future. In the face of immeasurable fallout from 'the financial meltdown of October 2008' and other crises of the capitalist world as we know it, forms of thrifty architecture and coupon consumerism may surpass the spectacle of excess and atmosfear. But whether government interventions and salvage operations merely cater to more corporate bailouts and perpetual war or conspire toward a 'post'-post-Keynesian new world (a new New Deal?) remains to be seen. What seems certain is that Debord's critique of spectacle will continue to trip the conceptual smoke alarm, inspiring critical annotations on the society *after* the brand, and experimental fusions of 'stop shopping' and 'stop shocking'.

NOTE

1 'Culture jamming', 'adbusting', and other tactical media strategies are often employed by anti-brand, anti-corporate globalization artists and activists. Practitioners alter billboards and/or utilize graphic design conventions to de-naturalize and/or mutate taken-for-granted advertisements and brand logos canvassing the built environment.

Section 3 Bibliography

Adams, Kathleen M. (2003) 'Global cities, terror, and tourism: The ambivalent allure of the urban jungle', in Ryan Bishop, John Phillips and Wei Wei Yeo (eds) *Postcolonial Urbanism: Southeast Asian Cities and Global Processes*. New York: Routledge.

Adorno, Theodor W. and Max Horkheimer (1979 [1947]) *Dialectic of Enlightenment*. Translated by John Cumming. London: Verso.

Agamben, Giorgio (2002) 'Marginal notes on commentaries on the Society of the Spectacle', *Means Without End*. Minneapolis: University of Minnesota Press, 73–90.

—— (2003) *Cities Without Citizens*. Philadelphia: Slought Books.

—— (2005) *State of Exception*. Chicago: University of Chicago Press.

AlSayyad, Nezar (ed.) (1992) *Forms of Dominance: On the Architecture and Urbanism* of the *Colonial Enterprise*. Aldershot: Avebury.

—— (ed.) (2001) *Hybrid Urbanism: On the Identity Discourse and the Built Environment*. Westport, CT: Praeger.

—— (2006) *Cinematic Urbanism: A History of the Modern from Reel to Real*. New York: Routledge.

Anderson, Benedict (1990) *Language and Power: Exploring Political Cultures in Indonesia*. Ithaca: Cornell University Press.

—— (1991 [1983]) *Imagined Communities: Reflections on the Origin and Spread of Nationalism*. London: Verso.

—— (1998) *Spectre of Comparisons: Nationalism, Southeast Asia and the World*. London: Verso.

—— (2002) 'Bung Karno and the fossilization of Sukarno's thought', *Indonesia* 74: 1–19.

Andreoli, Elisabetta and Adrian Forty (eds) (2004) *Brazil's Modern Architecture*. London: Phaidon.

Andreotti, Libero and Xavier Costa (1996) *Theory of the Dérive and Other Situationist Writings on the City*. Barcelona: MACBA and ACTAR.

Appadurai, Arjun (1996) *Modernity at Large: Cultural Dimensions of Globalisation*. Minneapolis: University of Minnesota Press.

Arditi, Benjamin (2003) 'The becoming other of politics: A post liberal archipelago', *Contemporary Political Theory* 2(3): 307–325.

Arkush, R. David and Leo O. Lee (eds) (1989) *Land Without Ghosts: Chinese Impressions of America from the Mid-Nineteenth Century to the Present*. Berkeley, CA: University of California Press.

Arnason, Johann P. (2003) 'Entangled communisms: Imperial revolutions in Russia and China', *European Journal of Social Theory* 6(3): 307–325.

Arnold, Dana (2002) *Reading Architectural History*. London: Routledge.

Arnold, Dana, Elvan Altan Ergut and Belgin Turan Özkaya (eds) (2006) *Rethinking Architectural Historiography*. New York: Routledge.

Badiou, Alain (2005) *Being and Event*. Translated by Oliver Feltham. New York: Continuum.

Barthes, Roland, (1997 [1979]) 'The Eiffel Tower', in Neil Leach (ed.) *Rethinking Architecture: A Reader in Cultural Theory*. New York: Routledge.

Baudrillard, Jean (1981) *For a Critique of the Political Economy of the Sign*. St Louis, MO: Telos Press.

—— (1991) *America*. London and New York: Verso.

—— (1993 [1976]) *Symbolic Exchange and Death*. London: Sage.

Beck, Ulrich (1992) *Risk Society: Towards a New Modernity*. New Delhi: Sage.

—— (2002) 'The terrorist threat: World risk society revisited', *Theory Culture Society*, 19(2): 39–55.

—— (2006) 'Living in the world risk society', *Economy and Society* 35(1): 329–345.

Bégout, Bruce (2003) *Zeropolis: The Experience of Las Vegas.* London: Reaktion.

Benevolo, Leonardo (1971) *History of Modern Architecture.* Cambridge, MA: MIT Press.

Ben-Ghiat, Ruth (2001) *Fascist Modernities: Italy, 1922–1945.* Berkeley, CA: University of California Press.

Benjamin, Andrew (1991) *The Problems of Modernity: Adorno and Benjamin.* London: Routledge.

Bennett, Tony (1995) *The Birth of the Museum: History, Theory, Politics.* London: Routledge.

Berger, Peter L., Brigitte Berger and Hansfried Kellner (1974) *The Homeless Mind: Modernization and Consciousness.* New York: Vintage Books.

Berman, Marshall (1982) *All that Is Solid Melts into Air: The Experience of Modernity.* New York: Simon and Schuster.

Bertrand Monk (eds), *Evil Paradises: Dreamworlds of Neoliberalism.* New York: The New Press.

Best, Steven and Douglas Kellner (undated) *Debord and the Postmodern Turn: New Stages of the Spectacle.* www.uta.edu/huma/illuminations/kell17.htm (accessed August 13, 2008).

Betts, Paul (2004) *The Authority of Everyday Objects: A Cultural History of West German Industrial Design.* Berkeley, CA: University of California Press.

Billig, Michael (1995) *Banal Nationalism.* London: Sage.

Blackmar, Elizabeth (1989) *Manhattan for Rent, 1785–1850.* Ithaca: Cornell University Press.

Bloom, Nicholas (2004) *Merchant of Illusion: James Rouse, America's Salesman of the Businessman's Utopia.* Columbus: The Ohio State University Press.

Borden, Iain and Jane Rendell (eds) (2000) *Intersections: Architectural Histories and Critical Theories.* London: Routledge.

Bourdieu, Pierre (1977) *Outline of a Theory of Practice.* Cambridge: Cambridge University Press.

—— (1990) *The Logic of Practice.* Cambridge: Polity Press.

Bowe, Nicola Gordon (ed.) (1993) *Art and the National Dream: The Search for Vernacular Expression in Turn-Of-The-Century Design.* Dublin: Irish Academic Press.

Bozdogan, Sibel (1999) 'Architectural history in professional education: reflections on postcolonial challenges to the modern survey', *Journal of Architectural Education* 52(4): 207–216.

—— (2001) *Modernism and Nation Building: Turkish Architectural Culture in the Early Republic.* Seattle: University of Washington Press.

Brown, Wendy (2006) *Regulating Aversion: Tolerance in an Age of Identity and Empire.* Princeton, NJ: Princeton University Press.

Buchli, Victor (2000) *An Archaeology of Socialism.* Oxford: Berg.

Buck-Morss, Susan (1995) 'The city as dreamworld and catastrophe', *October* 73 (Summer): 3–26.

—— (2000) *Dreamworld and Catastrophe: The Passing of Mass Utopia in East and West.* Cambridge, MA: MIT Press.

Bunnell, Tim (2004) *Malaysia, Modernity and the Multimedia Super Corridor: A Critical Geography of Intelligent Landscapes.* New York: Routledge-Curzon.

Bunnell, Tim, Lisa Drummond and K.C. Ho (eds) (2002) *Critical Reflections on Cities in Southeast Asia.* Singapore: Time Academic Press.

Burian, Edward R. (ed.) (1997) *Modernity and the Architecture of Mexico.* Austin: University of Texas Press.

Butler, Judith (1997) *The Psychic Life of Power.* Stanford, CA: Stanford University Press.

Cairns, Stephen (ed.) (2004) *Drifting: Architecture and Migrancy.* London: Routledge.

Caldeira, Theresa (2000) *City of Walls: Crime, Segregation, and Citizenship in São Paulo.* Cambridge: Cambridge University Press.

Carranza, Luis (2002) 'Editor's introduction: expressions of modernity in Latin American architecture', *Journal of Architectural Education* 55(4): 199–200.

Castells, Manuel (1996) *The Rise of the Network Society.* Oxford: Blackwell.

Castillo, Greg (2003) 'Stalinist modern: Constructivism and the Soviet company town', in James Cracraft and Dan Rowland (eds) *Architectures of Russian Identity, 1500 to the Present.* Ithaca: Cornell University Press, 131–149.

—— (2008) 'East as true West: redeeming bourgeois culture, from Socialist Realism to Ostalgie', *Kritika: Explorations in Russian and Eurasian History* 9(4): 747–768.

Çelik, Zeynep (1992) *Displaying the Orient: Architecture of Islam at Nineteenth-Century World's Fairs.* Berkeley, CA: University of California Press.

—— (1997) *Urban Forms and Colonial Confrontations: Algiers under French Rule.* Berkeley, CA: University of California Press.

Chakrabarty, Dipesh (2000a) 'Asia and the twentieth century: What is "Asian modernity"?', in Kwok Kian-Woon, Indira Arumugam, Karen Chia and Lee Chee Keng (eds) *'We Asians': Between Past and Future.* Singapore: Singapore Heritage Society, 15–32.

—— (2000b) *Provincializing Europe: Postcolonial Thought and Historical Difference.* Princeton: Princeton University Press.

Chase, John, Margaret Crawford and John Kaliski (eds) (1999) *Everyday Urbanism.* New York: Monacelli Press.

Cheah, Pheng (1999) 'Spectral nationality: The living on [*sur-vie*] of the postcolonial nation in neocolonial globalization', *Boundary 2* 26(3): 225–252.

Cheah, Pheng (2003) *Spectral Nationality: Passages of Freedom from Kant to Postcolonial Literatures of Liberation.* New York: Columbia University Press.

Cheng, Xiaofang (1963) '*Jianpuzhai jianzhu*' [Cambodian architecture], *Jianzhu xuebao* [Architectural Journal] 7: 22–26.

Chtcheglov, Ivan (2006) 'Formulary for a new urbanism', in Ken Knabb (ed.) *Situationist International Anthology.* Berkeley, CA: Bureau of Public Secrets.

Cieraad, Irene (1999) *At Home: An Anthropology of Domestic Space.* Syracuse, NY: Syracuse University Press.

Cody, Jeffery W. (2003) *Exporting American Architecture, 1870–2000.* London: Routledge.

Colomina, Beatriz (1996) *Privacy and Publicity: Modern Architecture as Mass Media.* Cambridge, MA: MIT Press.

Colquhoun, Alan (1997) 'The concept of regionalism', in Gülsüm Baydar Nal-bantoglu and Wong Chong Thai (eds) *Postcolonial Space(s).* New York: Princeton Architectural Press,13–23.

Comaroff, Jean and John L. Comaroff (1997) *Of Revelation and Revolution: The Dialectics of Modernity on a South African Frontier Vol. 2.* Chicago: University of Chicago Press.

Conrads, Ulrich (1970) *Programs and Manifestoes on 20th-Century Architecture.* Translated by Michael Bullock. Cambridge, MA: MIT Press.

Crary, Jonathan (2001) *The Suspension of Perception: Attention, Spectacle, and Modern Culture.* Cambridge, MA: The Press.

Crawford, Margaret (1994) 'Mi Casa es su Casa: The politics of everyday life in East Los Angeles', *Assemblage* 24 (August): 12–19.

Crinson, Mark (2003a) *Modern Architecture and the End of Empire.* London: Ashgate.

Crysler, C. Greig and Abidin Kusno (1997) 'Angels in the temple: The aesthetic construction of citizenship at the United States Holocaust Memorial Museum', *Art Journal* 56(1): 52–64.

Crysler, C. Greig (2003) *Writing Spaces: Discourses of Architecture, Urbanism, and the Built Environment, 1960–2000.* London and New York: Routledge

Crysler, C. Greig and Shiloh Krupar (2011) *Waste = History* (unpublished manuscript).

Curtis, William J. (1982) *Modern Architecture Since 1900.* Englewood Cliffs, NJ: Prentice-Hall.

Dal Co, Francesco (1990) *Figures of Architecture and Thought: German Architecture Culture, 1880–1920.* New York: Rizzoli.

Davis, Mike (1990) *City of Quartz: Excavating the Future in Los Angeles.* London and New York: Verso.

—— (1998) *Ecology of Fear: Los Angeles and the Imagination of Disaster.* New York: Metropolitan Books.

Davis, Mike and Daniel Bertrand Monk (2007) 'Introduction', in Mike Davis and Daniel Bertrand Monk (eds) *Evil Paradises: Dreamworlds of Neoliberalism.* New Press.

De Boeck, Filip (2005) The apocalyptic interlude: revealing death in Kinshasa. *African Studies Review,* 48, 11–32.

de Boeck, Filip and Marie-Françoise Plissart (2004) *Kinshasa: Tales of the Invisible City.* Ghent: Ludion.

de Certeau, Michel (1984) *The Practice of Everyday Life.* Berkeley, CA: University of California Press.

Dean, Mitchell (1999) *Governmentality: Power and Rule in Modern Society.* Thousand Oaks, CA: Sage.

Debord, Guy (1990) *Comments on the Society of the Spectacle.* London and New York: Verso.

—— (1994 [1967]) *The Society of the Spectacle.* Translated by David Nicholson Smith. Cambridge, MA: MIT Press.

—— (2006 [1957]) Toward a Situationist International, in Ken Knabb (ed and trans). *Situationist International Anthology.* Berkeley, CA: Bureau of Public Secrets.

Diken, Bülent and Carsten Bagge Laustsen (2005) *The Culture of Exception: Sociology Facing the Camp.* London and New York: Routledge.

Dirlik, Arif (2002) 'Modernity as history: post-revolution China: globalization and the question of modernity', *Social History* 27(1): 16–39.

—— (2007 [2006]) *Global Modernity: Modernity in the Age of Global Capitalism.* Boulder, CO: Paradigm Publishers.

Dorrian, Mark (2008) 'The way the world sees London: Thoughts on a millennial urban spectacle', in Anthony Vidler (ed.) *Architecture Between Spectacle and Use.* New Haven, CT: Yale University Press.

Driver, Felix and David Gilbert (eds) (1999) *Imperial Cities: Landscape, Display, Identity.* Manchester: Manchester University Press.

Dube, Saurabh (2002) 'Introduction: enchantments of modernity', *The South Atlantic Quarterly* 101(4): 729–755.

Eco, Umberto (1980) 'Function and sign: The semiotics of architecture', in Geoffrey Broadbent, Richard Bunt and Charles Jencks (eds) *Signs, Symbols, and Architecture*. London: John Wiley and Sons Inc., 11–70.

Eggener, Keith L. (2002) 'Placing resistance: a critique of critical regionalism', *Journal of Architectural Education* 55(4): 228–237.

—— (2006) 'Nationalism, internationalism and the "naturalisation" of modern architecture in the United States, 1925–1940', *National Identities* 8, 3 September: 243–258.

Eisenger, Peter K. (1988) *The Rise of the Entrepreneurial State*. Wisconsin: University of Wisconsin Press.

Eisenstadt, Shmuel N. (ed.) (2002) *Multiple Modernities*. New Brunswick: Transaction Publishers.

Ellin, Nan (1997) *Architecture of Fear*. New York: Princeton Architectural Press.

Facos, Michelle and Sharon L. Hirsh (eds) (2003) *Art, Culture, and National Identity in Fin-de-Siècle Europe*. Cambridge: Cambridge University Press.

Fausch, Deborah (1994) 'Towards "an architecture of our times": Scaffold and drapery in the architecture of Venturi, Scott Brown and Associates', in Deborah Fausch et al. (eds) *Architecture: In Fashion*. New York: Princeton Architectural Press.

Fernandez-Galiano, Luis (2005) 'Spectacle and its discontents', in William Saunders (ed.) *Spectacle and the Commodification of Architecture: A Harvard Design Magazine Reader*. Minneapolis, MN: University of Minnesota Press.

Fierro, Annette (2003) *The Glass State: The Technology of Spectacle in Paris, 1981–1998*. Cambridge, MA: MIT Press.

Fletcher, Sir Banister (1897) *A History of Architecture on the Comparative Method*. London: B.T. Batsford.

Florida, Richard (2002) *The Rise of the Creative Class: And How It's Transforming Work, Leisure, Community and Everyday Life*. New York: Basic Books.

Foster, Hal (1996) *The Return of the Real*. Cambridge, MA: MIT Press.

—— (2002) 'Master Builder', *Design and Crime and Other Diatribes*. London and New York: Verso.

—— (2008) 'Image building', in Anthony Vidler (ed.) *Architecture between Spectacle and Use*. New Haven, CT: Yale University Press.

Frampton, Kenneth (1983) 'Prospects for a critical regionalism', *Perspecta* 20: 147–162.

—— (1992 [1980]) *Modern Architecture: A Critical History*. 3rd edn. London: Thames & Hudson.

—— (1996 [1980]) 'Critical regionalism: modern architecture and cultural identity', in *Modern Architecture: A Critical History*. New York: Thames & Hudson.

—— (1998 [1983]) 'Towards a critical regionalism: Six points for an architecture of resistance', in Hal Foster (ed.) *The Anti-Aesthetic: Essays on Postmodern Culture*. New York: The New Press, 17–34.

—— (2005) 'Introduction: The work of architecture in the age of commodification', in William Saunders (ed.) *Spectacle and the Commodification of Architecture: A Harvard Design Magazine Reader*. Minneapolis, MN: University of Minnesota Press.

Frank, Thomas (2000) *One Market Under God*. New York: Doubleday.

Franke, Anselm and Hila Peleg (2008) *The Soul (Or, Much Trouble in the Transportation of Souls)*. Introduction to Manifesta 7. Trento.

Fraser, Andrea (2006) 'Isn't this a wonderful place? (a tour of the tour of the Guggenheim Bilbao)', in Ivan Karp and Corrine Kratz (eds) *Museum Frictions: Public Cultures/Global Transformations*. Durham, NC and London: Duke University Press.

Fraser, Valerie (2000) *Building the New World: Studies in the Modern Architecture of Latin America, 1930–1960*. New York: Verso.

Frisby, David (1988) *Fragments of Modernity: Theories of Modernity in the Works of Simmel, Kracauer and Benjamin*. Cambridge, MA: MIT Press.

—— (2001) *Cityscapes of Modernity*. Cambridge: Polity Press.

Fukuyama, Francis F. (1992) *The End of History and the Last Man*. New York: Free Press.

Fuller, Mia (2007) *Moderns Abroad: Architecture, Cities and Italian Imperialism*.

Gaonkar, Dilip Parameshwar (1999) 'On alternative modernities', *Public Culture* 11(1): 1–18.

—— (ed.) (2001) *Alternative Modernities*. Durham, NC: Duke University Press.

Geertz, Clifford (1980) *Negara: The Theatre State in Nineteenth Century Bali*. Princeton: Princeton University Press.

Ghirardo, Diane (1980) 'Italian architects and Fascist politics: An evaluation of the rationalist's role in regime building', *Journal of the Society of Architectural Historians* 39: 109–127.

Giberti, Bruno (2002) *Designing the Centennial: A History of the 1876 International Exhibition in Philadelphia*. Lexington, KY: University of Kentucky Press.

Giedion, Sigfried (1941) *Space, Time and Architecture: The Growth of a New Tradition*. Cambridge, MA: Harvard University Press.

Gilmore, Ruth Wilson (2007) *Golden Gulag: Prisons, Surplus, Crisis, and Opposition in Globalizing California*. Berkeley, CA: University of California Press.

Giroux, Henry A. (2006) *Beyond the Spectacle of Terrorism, Global Uncertainty and the Challenge of the New Media*. Boulder, CO: Paradigm Publishers.

Goldberger, Paul (1996) 'The rise of the private city', in Vittullo Martin (ed.) *Breaking Away: The Future of Cities*. New York: The Twentieth Century Fund.

Goldhagen, Sarah Williams and Réjean Legault (eds) (2000) *Anxious Modernisms: Experimentation in Postwar Architectural Culture*. Montréal: Canadian Centre for Architecture.

Goldstein, Daniel M. (2004) *The Spectacular City: Violence and Performance in Urban Bolivia*. Durham, NC: Duke University Press.

Gottdiener, Mark (2001) *The Theming of America: Dreams, Media Fantasies and Themed Environments*. Boulder, CO: Westview Press.

Gouda, Frances (1995) *Dutch Culture Overseas: Colonial Practice in the Netherland Indies 1900–1942*. Amsterdam: Amsterdam University Press.

Graham, Stephen (ed.) (2004) *Cities, War and Terrorism: Towards an Urban Geopolitics*. Oxford: Blackwell.

Graham, Stephen and Simon Marvin (eds) (2001) *Splintering Urbanism: Networked Infrastructures, Technological Mobilities, and the Urban Condition*. London and New York: Routledge.

Gramsci, Antonio (1971) *Selections from the Prison Notebooks,* Edited and translated by Quintin Hoare and Geoffrey Nowell-Smith. London: Lawrence & Wishart.

Gregory, Derek and Allan, Pred (2007) *Violent Geographies: Fear, Terror and Political Violence*. New York and London: Routledge.

Gropius, Walter (1965) *The New Architecture and the Bauhaus*. Cambridge, MA: MIT Press.

Groth, Paul (1994) *Living Downtown: The History of Residential Hotels in the United States*. Berkeley, CA: University of California Press.

Guillén, Mauro F. (2004) 'Modernism without modernity: the rise of modernist architecture in Mexico, Brazil, and Argentina, 1890–1940', *Latin American Research Review* 39(2): 6–34.

Habermas, Jurgen (1981) 'Modernity versus postmodernity', *New German Critique* 22: 3–14.

Harris, Steven and Deborah Berke (eds) (1997) *Architecture of the Everyday*. New York: Princeton Architectural Press.

Hartoonian, Gevork (1997) *Modernity and Its Other: A Post-Script to Contemporary Architecture*. College Station, Texas: Texas A&M University Press.

—— (2006) Critical Regionalism Reloaded, *Fabrications* 16(2): 123–29.

Harvey, David (1989a) *The Condition of Postmodernity: An Enquiry into the Origins of Cultural Change*. Oxford: Basil Blackwell.

—— (1989b) 'From managerialism to entrepreneurialism: The transformation in urban governance in late capitalism', *Geografiska Annaler* 71(B): 3–17.

—— (2005) *The New Imperialism*. New York: Oxford University Press.

Harvey, Penelope (1996) *Hybrids of Modernity: Anthropology, the Nation-State, and the Universal Exhibition*. London and New York: Routledge.

Hayden, Dolores (1981) *The Grand Domestic Revolution: A History of Feminist Designs for American Homes, Neighborhoods, and Cities*. Cambridge, MA: MIT Press.

Hays, Michael K. (1992) *Modernism and the Posthumanist Subject: The Architecture of Hannes Meyer and Ludwig Hilberseimer*. Cambridge, MA: MIT Press.

Herf, Jeffrey (1984) *Reactionary Modernism: Technology, Culture, and Politics in Weimar and the Third Reich*. Cambridge: Cambridge University Press.

Hess, Janet Berry (2006) *Art and Architecture in Postcolonial Africa*. Jefferson: McFarland & Company.

Hewitt, Andrew (1993) *Fascist Modernism: Aesthetics, Politics, and the Avant-Garde*. Stanford: Stanford University Press.

Heynen, Hilde (1999) *Architecture and Modernity: A Critique*. Cambridge, MA: MIT Press.

—— (2005) 'Modernity and domesticity: tensions and contradictions', in Hilde Heynen and Gülsüm Baydar (eds) *Negotiating Domesticity: Spatial Productions of Gender in Modern Architecture*. London: Routledge.

Heynen, Hilde and Gülsüm Baydar (eds) (2005) *Negotiating Domesticity: Spatial Productions of Gender in Modern Architecture*. London: Routledge.

Hitchcock, Henry-Russell and Philip Johnson (1932) *The International Style*. New York: Norton.

Hobsbawm, Eric and Terence Rangers (eds) (1983) *The Invention of Tradition*.

Hodge, Brooke (2006) *Skin and Bones: Parallel Practices in Fashion and Architecture*. New York: Thames & Hudson.

Holston, James (1989) *The Modernist City: An Anthropological Critique of Brasilia*. Chicago: Chicago University Press.

—— (1999) 'Spaces of insurgent citizenship', in James Holston (ed.) Cities and Citizenship. Durham, NC: Duke University Press, 155–76.

Hudson, Hugh D., Jr. (1994) *Blueprints and Blood: the Stalinization of Soviet Architecture, 1917–1937*. Princeton, NJ: Princeton University Press.

Hvattum, Mari and Christian Hermansen (eds) (2004) *Tracing Modernity: Manifestations of the Modern in Architecture and the City*. New York: Routledge.

Isenstadt, Sandy (2006) *The Modern American House: Spaciousness and Middle-Class Identity, 1850–1950*. Cambridge: Cambridge University Press.

Isenstadt, Sandy and Kishwar Rizvi (2008) *Modernism and the Middle East: Architecture and Politics in the Twentieth Century*. Seattle: University of Washington Press.

Jacobs, Jane M. (1996) *Edge of Empire: Postcolonialism and the City*. New York: Routledge.

Jameson, Fredric (1991) *Postmodernism, or, the Cultural Logic of Late Capitalism*. Durham, NC: Duke University Press.

—— (2003) 'Future city', *New Left Review* 21 May–June: 79–66.

Jarzombeck, Mark (2008) 'The (trans)formations of fame', in Anthony Vidler (ed.) *Architecture Between Spectacle and Use*. New Haven: Yale University Press.

Jencks, Charles (1977) *The Language of Postmodern Architecture*. 4th edn. New York: Rizzoli.

Kalia, Ravi (1987) *Chandigarh: In Search of an Identity*. Carbondale: Southern Illinois.

Kallestrup, Shona (2006) *Art and Design in Romania, 1866–1927: Local and International Aspects of the Search for National Expression*. New York: Columbia University Press.

Kalm, Mart and Ingrid Ruudi (eds) (2005) *Constructed Happiness: Domestic Environment in the Cold War Era*. Tallinn: Estonian Academy of Arts.

Katz, Cindi (2008) 'The death wish of modernity and the politics of mimesis', *Public Culture* 20(3): 551–560.

Kavanaugh, Leslie (2008) 'Situating situationism: Wandering around New Babylon with Mille Plateaux', *Architectural Theory Review* 13(2): 254–270.

Kelbaugh, Douglas (2000) 'Three paradigms: New urbanism, everyday urbanism, post-urbanism', *Bulletin of Science, Technology & Society* 20(4): 285–289.

King, Anthony D. (1976) *Colonial Urban Development: Culture, Social Power and Environment*. London: Routledge and Kegan Paul.

—— (1990) *Urbanism, Colonialism, and the World-Economy: Cultural and Spatial Foundations of the World Urban System*. London: Routledge.

—— (2004) *Spaces of Global Cultures: Architecture, Urbanism, Identity*. London: Routledge.

King, Anthony D. and Abidin Kusno (2000) 'On Be(ij)ing in the world: Postmodernism and the making of transnational space in China', in Arif Dirlik and Xudong Zhang (eds) *Postmodernism and China*. Durham, NC: Duke University Press.

Kirsch, Karin (1989) *The Weissenhofsiedlung: Experimental Housing Built for the Deutscher Werkbund, Stuttgart, 1927*. New York: Rizzoli.

Klein, Naomi (2002) *No Logo*. New York: Picador.

—— (2007) *The Shock Doctrine: The Rise of Disaster Capitalism*. New York: Metropolitan Books.

Klingmann, Anna (2007) *Brandscapes: Architecture in the Experience Economy*. Cambridge, MA: MIT Press.

Klotz, Heinrich (1988) *The History of Postmodern Architecture*. Translated by Radka Donnell. Cambridge, MA: MIT Press.

Knabb, Ken (2006) (ed.) *Situationist International Anthology*. Berkeley, CA: Bureau of Public Secrets.

Koolhaas, Rem (2002) 'Junkspace', *October* 100 (Spring): 175–190.

Krippendorff, Klaus (2006) *The Semantic Turn: A New Foundation for Design*. Boca Raton, FL: The CRC Press.

Ksiazek, Sarah (1993) 'Architectural culture in the fifties: Louis Kahn and the National Assembly Complex in Dhaka', *Journal of the Society of Architectural Historians*, 52 (December): 416–435.

Kusno, Abidin (2000) *Behind the Postcolonial: Architecture, Urban Space and Political Cultures in Indonesia*. London: Routledge.

—— (2007) 'The afterlife of the empire style. the Indies architecture and art deco', in Peter J. Nas (ed.) *The Past in the Present: Contemporary Architecture in Indonesia*. Rotterdam: NAI Press in association with KITLV Leiden, 131–145.

—— (2010) *The Appearances of Memory: Mnemonic Practices of Architecture*. Durham, NC: Duke University Press.

Lane, Barbara Miller (1968) *Architecture and Politics in Germany, 1918–1945*. Cambridge, MA: Harvard University Press.

—— (ed.) (2007) *Housing and Dwelling: Perspectives on Modern Domestic Architecture*. London: Routledge.

Lang, Jon, Madhavi Desai and Miki Desai (1997) *Architecture and Independence: The Search for Identity – India 1880 to 1980*. Delhi: Oxford University Press.

Lasanky, Medina D. (2004) *The Renaissance Perfected: Architecture, Spectacle and Tourism in Fascist Italy*. University Park, PA: Pennsylvania State University Press.

Lash, Scott (1990) *Sociology of Postmodernism*. London: Routledge.

Lavin, Sylvia and Helene Furjan (eds) (2005) *Crib Sheets: Notes on the Contemporary Architectural Conversation*. New York: The Monacelli Press.

Lazzarato, Maurizio (2004) 'From capital labor to capital life', *Ephemera* 4(3): 187–208.

Le Corbusier (1927) *Towards a New Architecture.* Translated by Frederick Etchells. London: John Rodker.

Leach, Neil (ed.) (2002) *The Hieroglyphics of Space: Reading and Experiencing the Modern Metropolis.* London: Routledge.

—— (ed.) (1997) *Rethinking Architecture: A Reader in Cultural Theory.* New York: Routledge.

Lefebvre, Henri (1984) *Everyday Life in the Modern World.* Translated by Sacha Rabinovitch. New Brunswick: Transaction Books.

—— (1991a [1974]). *The Production of Space.* Tr. Donald Nicholson-Smith. Oxford: Basil Blackwell.

—— (1991b) *Critique of Everyday Life.* Vol. 1. 2nd edn translated by John Moore. New York: Verso.

Lennon, John and Malcolm Foley (2007) *Dark Tourism: The Attraction of Death and Disaster.* London: Thomson.

Lippard, Lucy R. (1999) *On the Beaten Track: Tourism, Art, and Place.* New York: The New Press.

Liu, Yunhe (1963) 'Guba jianzhu' [Cuban architecture], *Jianzhu xuebao* [Architectural Journal] 9: 20–27.

Loeffler, Jane C. (1998) *The Architecture of Diplomacy: Building America's Embassies.* New York: Princeton Architectural Press.

Low, Setha (2003) *Behind the Gates: Life, Security, and the Pursuit of Happiness in Fortress America.* London and New York: Routledge.

Lu, Duanfang (2000) 'The changing landscape of hybridity: A reading of ethnic identity and urban form in late-twentieth-century Vancouver', *Traditional Dwellings and Settlements Review* 11(2): 19–28.

—— (2006, 2011) *Remaking Chinese Urban Form: Modernity, Scarcity and Space, 1949–2005.* London: Routledge.

—— (2007a) 'Third World modernism: Modernity, utopia and the people's commune in China', *Journal of Architectural Education* 60(3): 40–48.

—— (2007b) 'Architecture and global imaginations in China', *Journal of Architecture* 12(2): 123–145.

—— (ed.) (2008) *Rethinking architectural spectacle* (special issue), *Architectural Theory Review* 13(2).

—— (ed.) (2010) *Third World Modernism: Architecture, Development, and Identity.* London: Routledge.

Lubow, Arthur (2007) 'Recycle city: The road to Curitiba', *New York Times Magazine.* www.nytimes.com/2007/05/20/magazine/20Curitiba-t.html (accessed August 13, 2008).

Lütticken, Sven (2001) 'Parklife', *New Left Review* 10: 111–118.

Lyotard, Jean-François (1984 [1979]) *The Postmodern Condition: A Report on Knowledge.* Minneapolis: University of Minnesota Press.

Mamdani, Mahmood (1996) *Citizen and Subject: Contemporary Africa and the Legacy of Late Colonialism.* Princeton: Princeton University Press.

Marshall, Richard (2003) *Emerging Urbanity: Global Urban Projects in the Asia Pacific Rim.* London: Routledge.

Massumi, Brian (1993) *The Politics of Everyday Fear.* Minneapolis: University of Minnesota Press.

—— (2005) 'Fear (the spectrum said)', *Positions* 13(1): 31–48.

McClure, William (2004) 'Triumph of the spectacle', *Borderlands* 3(1).

McDonough, Tom (2002) 'Introduction: ideology and the Situationist utopia,' in Tom McDonough (ed). *Guy Debord and the Situationist International: Texts and Documents.* Cambridge, MA: MIT Press.

McLeod, Mary (1997) 'Henri Lefèbvre's critique of the everyday: An introduction', in Steven Harris and Deborah Berke (eds) *Architecture of the Everyday.* New York: Princeton Architectural Press, 9–29.

McNeil, Donald (2009) *The Global Architect: Firms, Fame and Urban Form.* New York: Routledge.

Mitchell, Timothy (1999) 'Society, economy, and the state effect', in George Steinmetz (ed.) *State/Culture: State-Formation after the Cultural Turn.* Ithaca: Cornell University Press, 76–97.

—— (2002) *Rule of Experts: Egypt, Techno-Politics, Modernity.* Berkeley and Los Angeles, CA: University of California Press.

—— (2007) 'Dreamland', in Mike Davis and Daniel Bertrand Monk (eds) *Evil Paradises: Dreamworlds of Neoliberalism.* New York: The New Press.

—— (2008) 'The spectacle today: A response to RETORT', *Public Culture* 20(3): 573–581.

Morton, Patricia (2000) *Hybrid Modernities: Architecture and Representation at the 1931 Colonial Exposition, Paris.* Cambridge, MA: MIT Press.

Mrazek, Rudolf (2002) *Engineers of Happy Land: Technology and Nationalism in a Colony.* Princeton: Princeton University Press.

Munshi, Debashish and Prya Kurian (2005) 'Imperializing spin cycles: A postcolonial look at public relations, greenwashing and the separation of publics', *Public Relations Review* 31: 513–520.

Nalbantoglu, Gulsum B. and Wong Chong Thai (eds), *Postcolonial Space(s).* New York: Princeton Architectural Press.

Nancy, Jean-Luc (2000) *Being Singular Plural.* Trans. by Robert Richardson and Anne O'Byrne. Stanford: Stanford University Press.

Nas, Peter J. (ed.) (2007) *The Past in the Present: Contemporary Architecture in Indonesia*. Rotterdam: NAI Press in association with KITLV Leiden, 131–145.

Neumeier, Marty (2006) *The Brand Gap: How to Bridge the Distance Between Business Strategy and Design*. Berkeley, CA: New Riders Press.

Noble, David (2002) *Death of a Nation: American Culture and the End of Exceptionalism*. Minneapolis: University of Minnesota Press.

Noobanjong, Koompong (2003) *Power, Identity, and the Rise of Modern Architecture: From Siam to Thailand*. Florida: Universal Publishers.

Norman, Donald (2004) *Emotional Design*. New York: Basic Books.

O'Brien, James (2002) 'Las Vegas today – Rome in a day: Corporate development practices and the role of professional designers', *Journal of Architectural Education* 54: 68–79.

Olds, Kris (2002) *Globalization and Urban Change: Capital, Culture and Pacific Rim*. Oxford: Oxford University Press.

Ong, Aihwa (2006) *Neoliberalism as Exception: Mutations in Citizenship and Sovereignty*. Durham, NC: Duke University Press.

Ong, Aihwa and Stephen Collier (eds) (2004) *Global Assemblages: Technology, Politics, and Ethics as Anthropological Problems*. Oxford: Wiley-Blackwell.

Ortner, Sherry B. (1994) 'Theory in anthropology since the sixties', in Nicholas B. Dirks, Geoff Eley and Sherry B. Ortner (eds) *Culture/Power/History*. Princeton, NJ: Princeton University Press, 372–411.

Overy, Paul (2005) 'White walls, white skins: Cosmopolitanism and colonialism in inter-war modernist architecture', in Kobena Mercer (ed.) *Cosmopolitan Modernisms*. London: Institute of International Visual Arts, 50–67.

Papadopoulos, Dimitris and Vassilis Tsianos (2007) 'How to do sovereignty without people? The subjectless condition of postliberal power', *Boundary 2* 34(1): 135–172.

Pemberton, John (1994) *On the Subject of 'Java'*. Ithaca: Cornell University Press.

Pence, Katherine and Paul Betts (eds) (2008) *Socialist Modern: East German Everyday Culture and Politics*. Ann Arbor: University of Michigan Press.

Petryna, Adriana (2006) *Life Exposed: Biological Citizens After Chernobyl*. Princeton, NJ: Princeton University Press.

Pevsner, Nikolaus (1968) *The Sources of Modern Architecture and Design*. New York: Praeger.

Pinder, David (2000) 'Old Paris is no more: Geographies of spectacle and anti-spectacle', *Antipode* 32(4): 357–386.

Pine, Joseph and James Gilmore (1999) *The Experience Economy: Work is Theatre and Everyday Business a Stage*. Boston: Harvard Business School Press.

Piotrowski, Andrzej (2008) 'The spectacle of architectural discourses', *Architectural Theory Review* 13(2): 130–42.

Plant, Sadie (1992) *The Most Radical Gesture: The Situationist International in a Post-modern Age*. London: Routledge.

Prakash, Vikramaditya (2002) *Chandigarh's Le Corbusier: The Struggle for Modernity in Postcolonial India*. Seattle: University of Washington Press.

Quinn, Bradley (2003) *The Fashion of Architecture*. Oxford: Berg Publishers.

Rabinow, Paul (1989) *French Modern: Norms and Forms of the Social Environment*. Cambridge, MA: MIT Press.

Radhakrishnan, Rajagopalan (2000) 'Postmodernism and the rest of the world', in Fawzia Afzal-Khan and Kalpana Seshadri-Crooks (eds) *The Pre-Occupation of Postcolonial Studies*. Durham, NC: Duke University Press, 37–70.

Randeria, Shalini (2002) 'Entangled histories of uneven modernities: Civil society, caste solidarities and legal pluralism in post-colonial India', in Yehuda Elkana, Ivan Krastev, Elisio Macamo and Shalini Randeria (eds) *Unraveling Ties: From Social Cohesion to New Practices of Connectedness*. Frankfurt: Campus Verlag, 284–311.

Reid, Susan E. and David Crowley (eds) (2000) *Style and Socialism: Modernity and Material Culture in Post-War Eastern Europe*. Oxford: Berg.

Reiss, Spencer (2007) 'Smog and mirrors: China's plan for a green Olympics'. *Wired Magazine* 15. www.wired.com/science/planetearth/magazine/15-08/ff_pollution (accessed August 7, 2008).

Report on the Construction of Situations (2006) in Ken Knabb (ed.), *Situationist International Anthology*. Berkeley, CA: Bureau of Public Secrets.

Retort (Iain Boal, T.J. Clark, Joseph Matthews and Michael Watts) (2005) *Afflicted Powers. Capital and Spectacle in a New Age of War*. London and New York: Verso.

—— (2006) 'An exchange on afflicted powers: Capital and spectacle in a new age of war', *October* 115: 3–12.

—— (2008) 'The totality for grownups', *Public Culture* 20(3): 583–593.

Roberts, David (2003) 'Towards a genealogy and typology of spectacle: Some comments on Debord', *Thesis Eleven* 75: 54–68.

Robinson, Jennifer (2005) *Ordinary Cities: Between Modernity and Development*. New York: Routledge.

Rowe, Peter G. and Seng Kuan (2002) *Architectural Encounters with Essence and Form in Modern China*. Cambridge, MA: MIT Press.

Ruan, X. (2002) 'Accidental affinities: American beaux-arts in twentieth-century Chinese architectural education and practice', *Journal of the Society of Architectural Historians* 61(1): 30–47.

Rugoff, Ralph (ed.) (1997) *Scene of the Crime*. Cambridge, MA: MIT Press.

Sachsenmaier, Dominic, Jens Riedel and Shmuel N. Eisenstadt (2002) *Reflections on Multiple Modernities: European, Chinese and Other Interpretations*. Leiden: Brill.

Sadler, Simon (1991) *The Situationist City*. Cambridge, MA: MIT Press.

Said, Edward W. (1978) *Orientalism*. London: Routledge.

Sánchez, Rafael (2008) 'Seized by the spirit: The mystical foundation of squatting among Pentecostals in Caracas (Venezuela) today', *Public Culture* 20(2): 267–305.

Sand, Jordan (2003) *House and Home in Modern Japan: Architecture, Domestic Space, and Bourgeois Culture, 1880–1930*. Cambridge, MA: Harvard University Press.

Saussure, Ferdinand de (1983) *Course in General Linguistics*. La Salle, IL: Open.

Sayad, AbdelMalik (2006) *L'immigration ou les paradoxes de l'altérité. 2. Les enfants illégitimes*. Paris: Éditions Raisons d'Agir.

Scott, James C. (1985) *The Weapons of the Weak: The Everyday Forms of Peasant Resistance*. New Haven: Yale University Press.

—— (1990) *Domination and the Arts of Resistance: Hidden Transcripts*. New Haven: Yale University Press.

—— (1998) *Seeing Like a State: How Certain Schemes to Improve the Human Condition Have Failed*. New Haven: Yale University Press.

Scriver, Peter and Vikramaditya Prakash (2007) *Colonial Modernities: Building, Dwelling and Architecture in British India and Ceylon*. London: Routledge.

Shiraishi, Takashi (1990) *An Age in Motion; Popular Radicalism in Java, 1912–1916*. Ithaca: Cornell University Press.

Simone, Abdou-Maliq (2004) *For the City Yet to Come:* Urban Change in Four African Cities. Durham, NC: Duke University Press.

Situationist International 2006 [1958] 'Definitions', in Ken Knabb (ed and trans). *Situationist International Anthology*. Berkeley, CA: Bureau of Public Secrets.

Smith, Michael Peter (2000) *Transnational Urbanism: Locating Globalization*. Oxford: Wiley-Blackwell.

Smith, Terry (2006) *The Architecture of Aftermath*. Chicago: The University of Chicago Press.

Sorkin, Michael (1992) *Variations on a Theme Park: The New American City and the End of Public Space*. New York: The Noonday Press.

—— (2005) 'Brand aid, or, the Lexus and the Guggenheim', in William Saunders (ed.) *Spectacle and the Commodification of Architecture: A Harvard Design Magazine Reader*. Minneapolis: University of Minnesota Press.

Spigel, Lynn (2001) *Welcome to the Dreamhouse: Popular Media and Postwar Suburb*. Durham, NC: Duke University Press.

Spillers, Hortense (2003) *Black, White, and in Color: Essays on American Literature and Culture*. Chicago: University of Chicago Press.

Stallabrass, Julian (2006) 'Spectacle and terror', *New Left Review* 37 (Jan-Feb): 87–106.

Stevens, Garry (1998) *The Favored Circle: The Social Foundations of Architectural Distinction*. Cambridge, MA: MIT Press.

Stoler, Ann Laura (2008) 'Imperial debris: Reflections on ruins and ruination', *Cultural Anthropology* 23(2): 191–219.

Stone, Philip and Richard Sharpley (2008) 'Consuming dark tourism: A thanatological perspective', *Annals of Tourism Research* 35(2): 574–595.

Stoneman, Scott (2007) 'Pedagogy in a time of terror: Henry Giroux's *Beyond the Spectacle of Terrorism', The Review of Education, Pedagogy, and Cultural Studies* 29: 111–135.

Strange, Carolyn and Michael Kempa (2003) 'Shades of dark tourism: Alcatraz and Robben Island', *Annals of Tourism Research* 30(2): 386–405.

Sussman, Elizabeth (ed.) (1989) *On the Passage of a Few People through a Rather Brief Moment in Time: The Situationist International 1957–1972*. Cambridge, MA: MIT Press.

Tafuri, Manfredo and Francesco Dal Co (1976) *Architecture and Utopia: Design and Capitalist Development*. Cambridge, MA: MIT Press.

—— (1980) *Theories and History of Architecture*. New York: Harper and Row.

—— (1986) *Modern Architecture*. 2 vols. New York: Rizzoli International.

Taussig, Michael (1993) *Mimesis and Alterity: A Particular History of the Senses*. London and New York: Routledge.

Therborn, Göran (2003) 'Entangled modernities', *European Journal of Social Theory* 6(3): 293–305.

Thongchai, Winichakul (1994) *Siam Mapped: A History of the Geo-Body of a Nation*. Honolulu: University of Hawaii Press.

Thrift, Nigel (1996) *Spatial Formations.* London: Sage.

—— (2005) 'Movement space: The changing domain of thinking arising from the development of new forms of spatial awareness', *Economy and Society* 33(4): 582–604.

Tschumi, Bernhard (1994) *Event-Cities.* Cambridge, MA: MIT Press.

Tzonis, Alexander and Liane Lefaivre (1981) 'The grid and the pathway', *Architecture in Greece* 15: 164–178.

Umbach, Maiken and Bernd Hüppauf (eds) (2005) *Vernacular Modernism: Heimat, Globalization, and the Built Environment.* Stanford, CA: Stanford University University Press.

Upton, Dell (1991) 'Architectural history or landscape history?' *Journal of Architectural Education* 44(4): 195–199.

—— (2002) 'Architecture in everyday life', *New Literary History* 33(4): 691–707.

—— (2008) *Another City: Urban Life and Urban Spaces in the New American Republic.* New Haven: Yale University Press.

Vale, Lawrence (1992) *Architecture, Power and National Identity.* New Haven: Yale University Press.

—— (2001) *Imaging the City: Continuing Struggles and New Directions.* New Brunswick, NJ: Center for Urban Policy Research.

Venturi, Robert (1977 [1966]) *Complexity and Contradiction in Architecture.* New York: Museum of Modern Art.

Venturi, Robert, Denise Scott-Brown and Steven Izenour (1986) *Learning from Las Vegas: The Forgotten Symbolism of Architectural Form.* Cambridge, MA: MIT Press.

Virilio, Paul (2007) *The Original Accident.* Cambridge: Polity Press.

Weber, Samuel (2002) 'War, terrorism, and spectacle: On towers and caves', *South Atlantic Quarterly* 101(3): 449–458.

Wigley, Mark (1990) 'The decorated gap', *Ottagono* 94: 36–55.

—— (1994) 'White out: Fashioning the modern', in Deborah Fausch et al. (eds), *Architecture: In Fashion.* New York: Princeton Architectural Press.

—— (1995) *White Walls, Designer Dresses: The Fashioning of Modern Architecture.* Cambridge, MA: MIT Press.

—— (1998a) *Constant's New Babylon: The Hyper-Architecture of Desire.* Rotterdam: 010 Publishers.

—— (1998b) 'Whatever happened to total design?', *Harvard Design Magazine* 5: 1–8.

—— (1998c) 'The architecture of atmosphere', *Daidalos* 68: 18–27.

—— (2008) 'Toward a history of quantity', in Anthony Vidler (ed.) *Architecture between Spectacle and Use.* New Haven: Yale University Press.

Williams, Gareth (2002) *The Other Side of the Popular: Neoliberalism and Subalternity in Latin America.* Durham, NC and London: Duke University Press.

Wolf, Eric R. (1997 [1982]) *Europe and the People without History.* 2nd edn. Berkeley, CA: University of California Press.

Wright, Gwendolyn (1981) *Building the Dream: A Social History of Housing in America.* New York: Panmeon.

—— (1991) *The Politics of Design in French Colonial Urbanism.* Chicago: University of Chicago Press.

Wright, Richard (1995 [1957]) *White Man, Listen!* NewYork: HarperCollins.

—— (2007 [1956]) *The Color Curtain: A Report on the Bandung Conference.*

Wu, Huanjia (1964) 'Ping xifang shizuo jianzhu' [A review of ten buildings in the West], *Jianzhu xuebao* [Architectural Journal] 6: 29–33.

Yeoh, Brenda (1996) *Contesting Space: Power Relations and the Urban Built Environment in Colonial Singapore.* New York: Oxford University Press.

Zhu, Jianfei (2009) *Architecture of Modern China: A Historical Critique.* London: Routledge.

Zou, Denong (2001) *Zhongguo xiandai jianzhu shi* [Modern Chinese Architectural History]. Tianjin: Tianjin kexue jishu chubanshe.

15
Heritage

Fernando Diez

In the 1980s, after the steep disciplinary decline of architecture's and urbanism's authority, architects found themselves with a reduced field of influence in social decisions concerning the environment, the cities and architecture itself. As this erosion progressed and the 'classical' fundaments of modern architecture weakened (Eisenman 1984), the notion of 'preservation' proved itself to be a convincing source of legitimation. Silently, unnoticed, 'preservation' replaced 'modernization' as the driving force behind social decisions concerning the most important commissions and prestigious sites. As architects found that this enabled them to

Figure 15.1 (Below left and right) Evita Fine Arts Museum, Córdoba, Argentina, 2007. Gramática-Morini-Pisani-Urtubey and Lucio Morini. Old central hall. (Gustavo Sosa Pinilla)

Figure 15.2 (Opposite top) Evita Fine Arts Museum. Connection between new and old halls. (Gustavo Sosa Pinilla)

most effectively claim and defend a disciplinary field of influence they began to accept, some with enthusiasm, others with resignation, the new predominance of conservation over renovation. For the first time since the early twentieth century, the past became a source of meaning stronger than the future. A new field of professional practice flourished, and so did its priests, claiming exclusive rights and knowledge. Project architects compromised with change looked worried. Conservation versus renovation had already become a difficult issue.

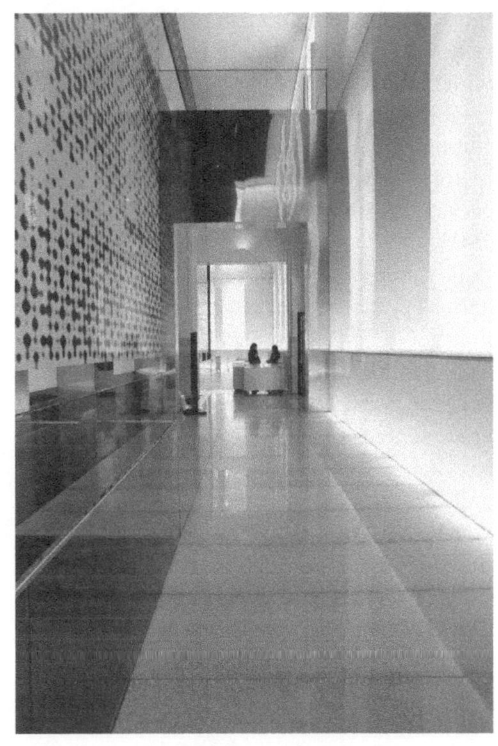

When renovation and re-use expanded as questioned but potent alternatives to compulsive museumification, the time arrived to acknowledge the almost unavoidable picturesque effect of heritage re-use. An issue that has been little noticed and less commented upon, perhaps, because of the bad press of picturesque sensibility, so intensely criminalized as ornament before. We know the ruin is a classical picturesque motif. In the fabrication of the monument, the picturesque is not just a way of looking, but an action, which reminds us of the difference that Riegl established between 'historic monument' and 'monument'. The first coming out of the way history affects a building, the second conceived as such from the beginning (Riegl 1903).

Recent projects for late-nineteenth-century and early-twentieth-century buildings show that new design approaches are developing, establishing a new symbolic relation with the very near past. Some meaningful projects are opening paths to understand this new relation – infusing the idea of monument, and even ruin, into buildings that just a few years ago would only have been considered, maybe refined, but otherwise ordinary buildings. In recent books, Iñaki Abalos has already revealed this unnoticed comeback, the emerging of a contemporary picturesque sensibility that is willing to intensely merge landscape and architecture. Abalos looks at the picturesque in a positive way, referring to romantic precedents such as Alexander von Humboldt and Frederick Olmsted, but also to the expressionism of Bruno Taut and some of the later works of Le Corbusier. And finds in the work of such different contemporary architects as Miralles y Pinos, Peter Eisenman and Toyo Ito, traits of this new picturesque sensibility (Abalos 2008). The ruin is back, and so are its essential invocations, the past, the landscape, the footprint of time and rust, stained and torn surfaces in complex and random patterns. It shows a new interest in a referential abstraction that obtains figurative patterns from the context. Place is given new importance as a source of meaning, and thus heritage is not only considered because of its memorial aspects but because it can

Figure 15.3 (Below left and right) Bowdoin College Art Museum. Machado and Silvetti Associates, Maine, USA, 2008. (Facundo de Zuviría)

give character to a project, otherwise lost in the overflowing storm of contemporary images.

If in previous centuries the useful life of a building averaged 500 years, the twentieth century reduced it to almost 50 years. Mid-twentieth-century powerhouses (such as Tate Modern) and other industrial or even residential buildings are now obsolete, abandoned old buildings increasingly seen as objects of nostalgia. Inverting the notion that the modern movement had painfully made dominant, that the old and obsolete had to be replaced by the new. Unexpectedly, the desire that the past should be erased by the present surrendered to the necessity for the present to be saved by the past.

Since the 1990s, heritage is growing at an ever faster pace. It has acquired menacing proportions, threatening to devour the present. Françoise Choay says that what she calls the 'inflation of heritage' (Choay 1992) cannot be explained only as a consequence of the interest in the past and collective memory, suggesting it is the consequence of our contemporary loss of faith in the ability to build our own heritage. Beyond the already acknowledged commercial exploitation of heritage by tourism and its reproduction in many ways, from the relatively rigorous museum reproductions to the more deceiving thematic simulations that oscillate from mimesis to parody (Silvetti 2003/2004), heritage has experienced an expansion in terms of time, place and theme. One reason for such a geometrical overgrowth could be found in its simulation. As Jean Baudrillard has noticed, the more we simulate reality, the less effective it is in convincing us it has any meaning (Baudrillard 1981; 1997). In other words, increased reproducibility exerts an effect on the credibility of heritage, and thus on its value. The more it breeds, the less meaning it has, the more dubious it feels. The distance between the fake and the replica is only circumstantial, and authenticity, as is reality

itself, is harder to perceive as society cannot avoid cloning successful things and events. The anxiety for success is what feeds this process, the symptomatic response to the weakening faith in the authenticity of contemporary life – a kind of mirror-effect, in which everything is the anticipated expectation of already existing desires. Hannah Arendt had warned us of the destructive power of a future planned on the statistical survey of our present.[1]

As a state of suspicion surrounds any new product or work of art, and that includes architecture, the past emerges as a possible antidote, as a safe-conduct to authenticity. The intrinsically contradictory needs for conservation and renovation collide in the contemporary authenticity machine *par excellence*: the museum. As the modern temple for legitimacy, the museum expanded its dominance over every field of human interest. Its obvious purpose is to legitimate its contents; to declare authenticity where it is rapidly disappearing. Its less visible purpose is to legitimate its promoters; to give them visibility above the saturated noise of mass media. Private and public institutions as well as cities and commercial corporations increasingly find in heritage, and thus the museum, the means to get both attention and credibility. But since heritage inflation generates its own doubts, subtle design resources are necessary in the most visible and prominent settings, and thus massive architectural talent is needed to dig deeper in the resurrection of the past. In such circumstances, architects find themselves caught between two contradictory demands. They are asked to rescue the authenticity of a building of the

Figure 15.4 (Below left and right) Bowdoin College Art Museum. Long section. (Machado and Silvetti Associates)

Figure 15.5 (Opposite top) Bowdoin College Art Museum. New entry and old pavilion. (Facundo de Zuviría)

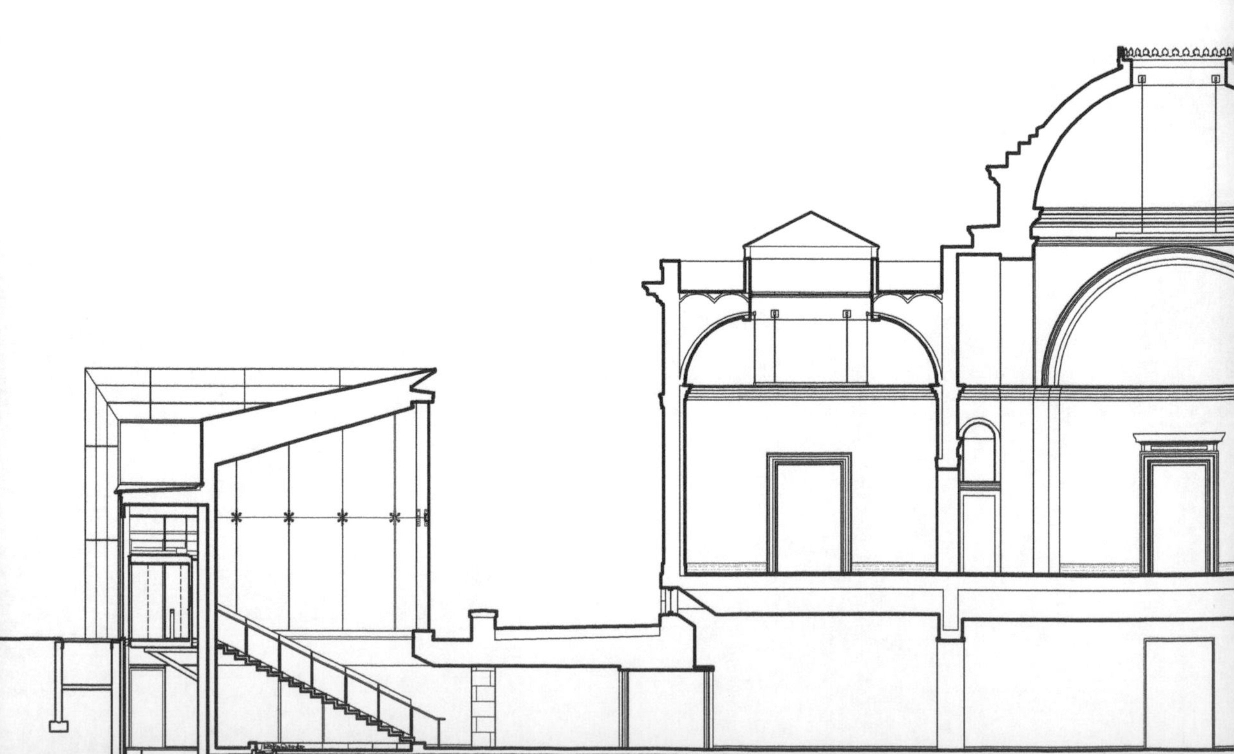

recent past, transforming it into true heritage, and at the same time, they are asked to transform it into a modern installation capable of containing complex contemporary programmes, finding out how to make a museum from an old building that quite often must be presented as rescued from abandonment and ignorance, performing for their clients, once again, the heroic act of archeological discovery and rescue.

Even more demandingly, architects are implicitly asked to meet a secret but unavoidable need: to transform otherwise boring old museums or simple ordinary buildings into new, shining, sexy images that will be able to attract the attention of the media. This part of the programme cannot always be written down, but is the prerequisite for the success of the promoter as well as the architect. Such transfiguration requires a subtle equilibrium between restoration and renovation, between symbolic effectiveness and functional programmatic needs – an almost magical act that can only be accomplished with carefully controlled design decisions, in which the chosen materials and surfaces are as important as bold additions and surgical destruction. A merging of past and present that demands the kind of picturesque contemporary sensibility that Abalos describes, displaying the ability to master emerging aesthetic figures, some of which can be identified in these paradigmatic recent projects.

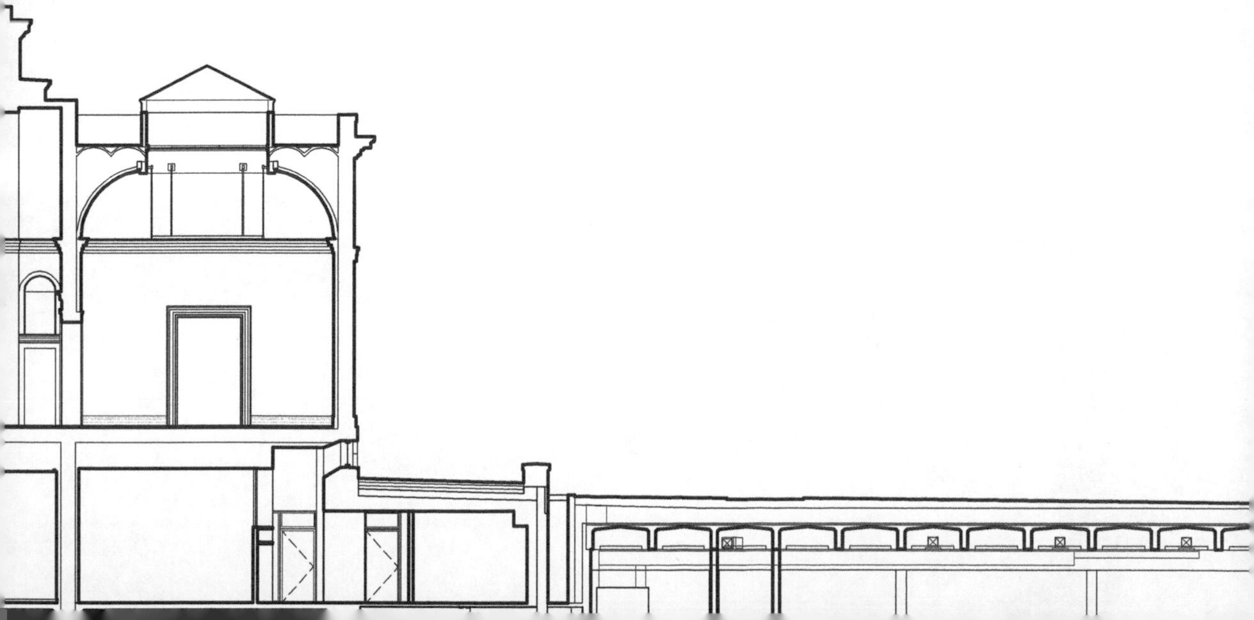

THE CONTRASTING FRAME

The most controversial intervention on Córdoba's built heritage, the transformation of the 'Ferreyra Palace' into the Evita Fine Arts Museum (Córdoba, Argentina, 2007) has produced a preservation scandal as well as spectacular architecture with undeniable power of attraction (Rodriguez 2008). The Ferreyra Palace was a private residence commissioned from the French beaux-arts architect Ernest-Paul Sanson and finished in 1914. The biggest residential mansion of the city, surrounded by gardens occupying a whole block, it remained a testimony of old Argentine glories and wealthy times, as well as a treasure of classic beaux-arts architecture. Critics say the building in itself would have been an extraordinary museum just filled with the original furniture and works of art, an untouched surviving testimony of private life at the beginning of the century. But means and ends merged in this operation to recycle the building into an arts museum. In fact, it is difficult to say whether the new programme was the excuse to expropriate the house to convert it into a public asset, or if it was the means for the government to leave a legacy of its long administration. In any case, the building was already unanimously recognized as valuable heritage, praised by Nicklaus Pevsner after a visit in the 1960s.[2]

Gramática-Morini-Pisani-Urtubey and Lucio Morini's project consisted of a radical intervention in the interior, demolishing the upper floors of the first span of the building

Figure 15.6 (Below) Pinacoteca de São Paulo. Paulo Mendes da Rocha, Eduardo Argenton Colonelli and Weliton Ricoy Torres, São Paulo, Brazil, 1998. Exterior view. (Nelson Kon)

Figure 15.7–8 (Below right) Pinacoteca de São Paulo. Steel bridges connect halls crossing old patios. (Nelson Kon)

to produce an intense vertical hall space with new stairs and elevators. This hall greets the public with tight smooth vinyl surfaces that cover the walls and windows, producing a contrasting effect between the very smooth backlighted surfaces and the brilliant glass panels and floors, and the elaborate surfaces of classical architecture and ornate Venetian floors of the old main hall. To declare the contemporariness of the new museum, destruction is ruthlessly applied, concentrated on restricted areas while the rest of the building is carefully restored, especially the outside. For the innocent visitor, the destruction is not that visible (as it is in Caixa Forum) because all scars of destruction have been erased. Instead, the spectacular contemporary atmosphere strikes the eye with the sophistication of the surfaces of bright new materials and rigorously controlled digital light management. The old windows appear as phantoms behind the pristine smoothness of the tight vinyl, and the brilliant op-art serigraphed glass panels oppose the black cow hide that covers the stairs arising towards the deep black of the old attic at the top of the highly verticalized space. The strong impact of these contrasting surfaces works as the prelude and the frame of the preserved surfaces, explicitly pointing to the saved heritage, making forcibly visible their textures, spatial qualities and nature. If masterly achieved, the smooth neutrality of the new exhibition rooms of the upper floor left no traces of the scale and textures of the former domestic spaces. Although the building was already seen as sacred heritage by specialists and the cultural elite, it could have been a boring one for the wider public, and this may have been the reason why such a *contrasting frame* of the old was considered necessary, bringing back into discussion the inherent conflict between culture democratization and refinement presented by Umberto Eco (1964) in the 1960s. Feeding the building with the desired appeal was the claim that

the sacrifice of such substantial parts of the interior, if regrettable, was somehow considered necessary to produce enough attention – and investment – to give it the desired visibility. A spectacular requirement not that different from so many of Guggenheimean Krens' inspired operations (Sorkin 2002/2003).

THE CONSCIOUSNESS OF LANDSCAPE

The Walker Art Gallery was originally designed by Charles Follen McKim (from McKim, Mead and White) as a free-standing pavilion finished in 1894, surrounded by the university lawn. The new enlargement and improvements for the Bowdoin College Art Museum (Maine, USA, 2008) by Machado and Silvetti are especially interesting because of the remarkable unity of the elegant pavilion, standing against the open, free space of the park (Corona Martínez 2007). Maybe this particular relation is already naturalized in our experience of American campuses, but it is the legacy of an old and deep alliance between architecture and landscape in which dominant perspectivs from and towards architecture establish the symbolic status of a specific site, producing what those in the 1970s were fond of calling *place*. This almost geographical consciousness, which reminds us of Palladio's Villa Capra, was an essential quality of the old building that the architects explored in different alternatives. Asked to substantially enlarge the exhibition and service areas and to provide access for the disabled (which meant either ramps or outside elevators) a drastic intervention was unavoidable. They found that the first project devised would have harmed some of the subtle but powerful qualities of the building: a sunken

Figure 15.9 (Below) Caixa Forum. Ground level plan. (Herzog & de Meuron)

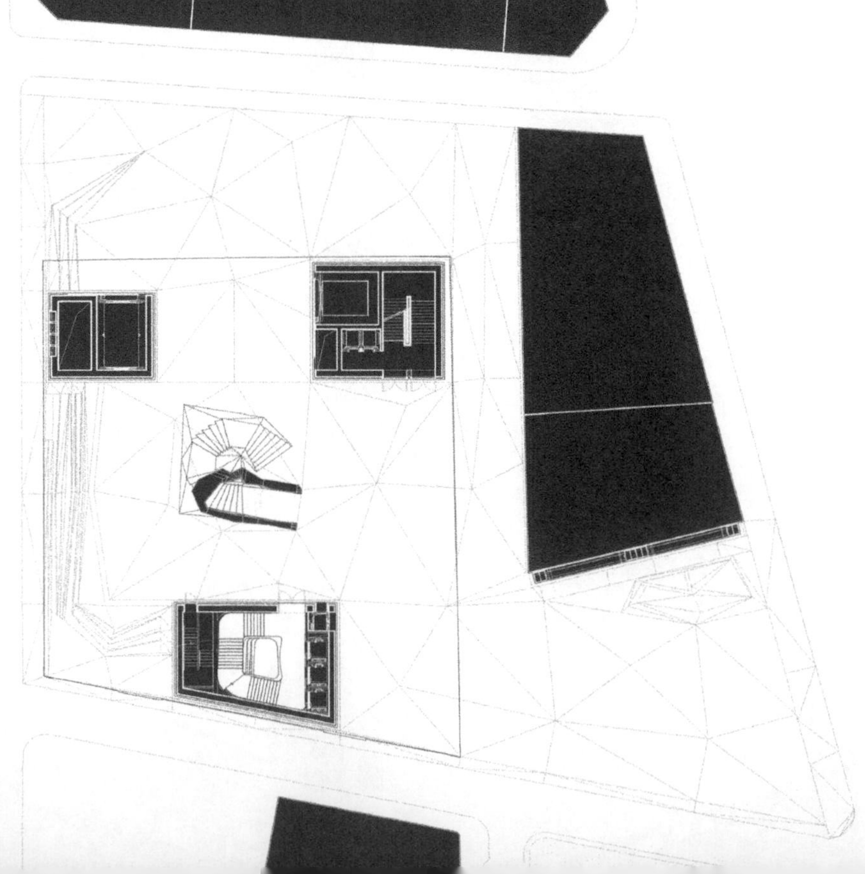

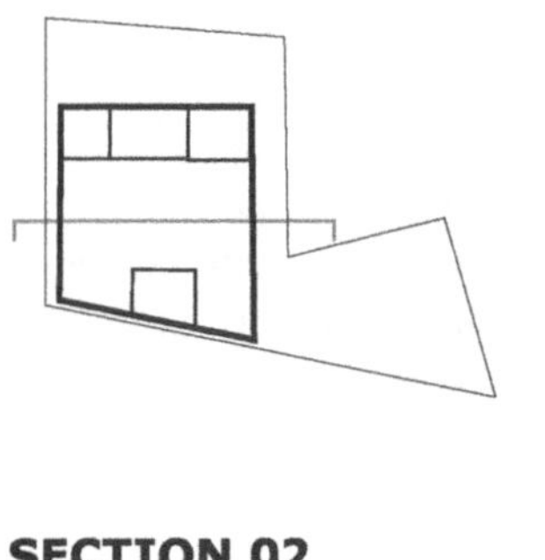

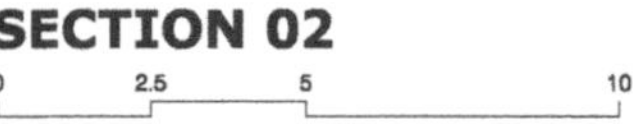

Figure 15.10 (Above right) Caixa Forum, Madrid, Spain, 2008. Jacques Herzog, Pierre De Meuron and Harry Gugger. Section location. (Herzog & de Meuron)

Figure 15.11 (Below) Caixa Forum. Section. (Herzog & de Meuron)

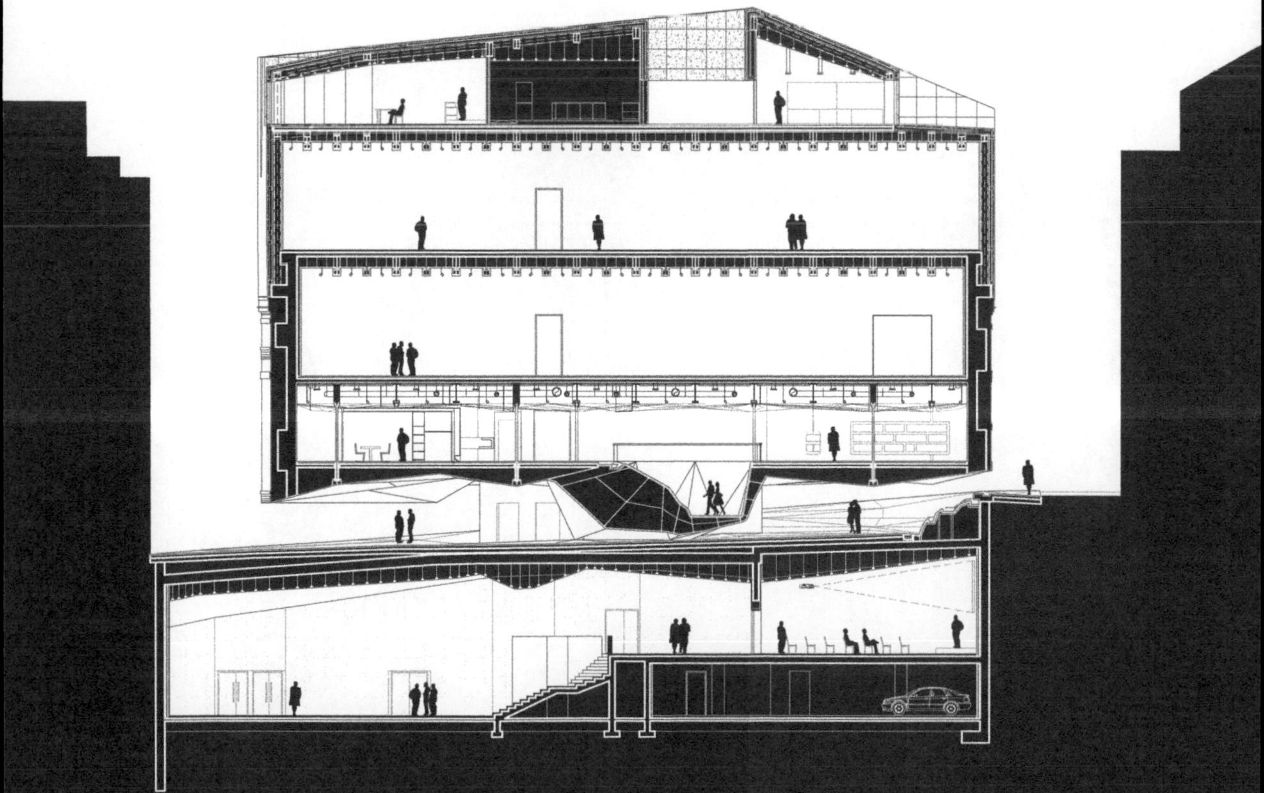

entrance beneath the front porch would have deprived it of the podium and stairs that establish such a strong relation with the landscape. This first project proved that there were no possible direct new entrances to the building without damaging the unity of the pavilion. Instead, the definitive design erects an independent, light aedicule at a side of the building to produce an entry that descends towards new rooms beneath ground level, preserving the main building's isolation. Having to add seven new exhibition rooms and several administrative and curatorial spaces, the challenge for the architects seemed to be how to preserve the conceptual relation of the free-standing pavilion with its surroundings. Descending to the basement through elegant double stairs, the visitor is guided to the new exhibition rooms – a complex operation that required levelling down the original basement floor. The old stone foundations had to be surgically cut to achieve the desired height for the room's ceilings. Putting most of the programme under ground level and concentrating the additions on only one side of the existing building proved to be an effective strategy to preserve the pavilion's graceful appearance and unity.

The controlled size and the intense transparency of the new entrance pavilion neutralizes any interference with the way the lawn frames the main building. At the same time, the glass and bronze in which it is built, attracts visual attention and the visitor's movement, inviting him to recognize the classical tension between the free-standing pavilion and the void that surrounds it, inducing a consciousness of the landscape that surrounds it. The glass and bronze pavilion stands as a means of entrance, but more significantly, it gives a gravitational stability to the villa, in the same way as a satellite makes more evident the central position of the planet it orbits. The intentional contrast between the solid and heavy materiality of the pre-existing building and the light and reflecting surfaces of bronze and glass, virtually pointing at the old building, forces us to acknowledge the status of the museum, not just as a fine arts museum, but as a monument, a noble building now old enough to be regarded as heritage itself.

Figure 15.12 (Below) Caixa Forum, Madrid, Spain, 2008. Jacques Herzog, Pierre De Meuron and Harry Gugger. The old masonry with its sealed windows and the Corten steel upper levels. (Caixa)

THE READY-MADE RUIN

Paulo Mendes da Rocha had to transform the 1896 building originally designed by Francisco de Paula Ramos Azevedo as a school for arts and crafts into the Pinacoteca de São Paulo (São Paulo, Brazil, 1998). The building had been in use for many years, but its exterior walls had never been plastered, so its bricks, still visible, deteriorated, and

lacked the classical subtle finishing details (Wisnik 2008). The architect decided to preserve this unfinished provisional aspect by reconstructing the rotten bricks. Contrasting their heaviness with the light steel and the active structural appearance of bridges that cross the patios of the old building, to create a completely new pattern of movement breaking the neo-classical room order of the beaux-arts plan (Zein 1998).

There is very limited destruction. Instead Mendes da Rocha performs a ready-made act framing the already deteriorated aspect of the unfinished fabric, carefully restoring the bricks into their randomly rotten pattern. This is not a simple task, since it must be more carefully performed than a conventional restoration, as it must be decided where the limit is between reconstruction and structural stabilization. In the reconstruction of the spoiled it is difficult to avert restoring reflex that can change the randomly varied provisional patterns, and sometimes it may seem impossible not to fall into recreation. In the Pinacoteca this delicate work is completed by framing the *ready-made ruin* with the smoothness of glass and steel. As the former patios are transformed into interior public spaces, their rough terracotta bricks become a differentiating texture from the exhibition rooms that preserved the plastered white walls with classical patterns.

Contrasting surfaces and textures are to contemporary heritage what the frame is to a work of art, or what the modern gallery is to the statements of conceptual art. The ready-made can only acquire its status from its displacement from its natural context, and Mendes da Rocha trusted more in the powerful authenticity of the frozen unfinished walls than in any new texture that could have been made.

THE FABRICATED RUIN

The project of Caixa Forum Art Center (Madrid, Spain, 2008) by Jacques Herzog, Pierre De Meuron and Harry Gugger produces an urban piazza to work both as an atrium and allow for the necessary perspective of the building, allowing it to emerge in the city with an objectual quality. The building itself, an old powerhouse built on massive brickwork, is treated with surgical coldness. The costly and complex elimination of its first metres allowing for an open-plan transparency at the ground level is the means for a better connection with the narrow city streets, but also the excuse for the carefully planned destruction of its tectonic qualities. This operation is necessary to *fabricate the ruin*, declaring that the otherwise ordinary industrial building is now part of the city's built heritage. And to produce at the same time the intense aesthetic contrast that declares the contemporariness of the new building. The mummified skin of red bricks is the effective source of such meanings, its openings dramatically sealed to remind us of the uselessness of the old structure. The rough texture of the red brick walls is contrasted with the transparency of the glass, the white smooth interior finishings, and the rough coronation of rusted steel. Being corrupted and stable at the same time, the Corten steel is the contemporary metaphor of the old, a rusting process in which time has been frozen, showing the power and control of modern technology and, contradictorily, representing decay. All these resources and powerful textures – including the green vegetal wall by Patrick Blanc – are the means for a spectacular architecture that proved able to storm the media with unforgettable images. A goal, if not explicitly declared, that was completely accomplished.

Accommodating new uses and more floor space and updating the old with modern technological equipment may be a part of the challenge. But rescuing the authenticity of the recent past, producing at the same time the excitement of the new, is the real demand behind practical and functional explanations. If that is achieved through the destruction or the framing of the old is only a matter of circumstance. From the more subtle and controlled elegance of Machado & Silvetti's contrasting pavilion (built at the side) to the spectacular halls of Evita Museum (built inside) to the delicate glass and steel framing of the unfinished building by Paulo Mendes da Rocha (sewing together interiors and exteriors), to the outspoken aggressiveness of Caixa Forum aesthetics, some destruction seems to be necessary. The question is, how much?

Through these projects it becomes evident that a new field of work re-using recent heritage has opened up. Society seems no longer comfortable to consider heritage just in a contemplative way, to regard it as already dead architecture. It asks for consecration of recent heritage, but also for its authenticity to become a source of character for the newest contemporariness. These projects invite us to start listing the emerging design tactics and the new aesthetic figures that effectively frame and point to the newer ruins of the near present.

NOTES

1. 'The justification of statistics is that deeds and events are rare occurrences in everyday life and in history [...]. The application of the law of large numbers and long periods to politics or history signifies nothing less than the wilful obliteration of their very subject matter [...]. Deeds will have less and less chance to stem the tide of behavior, and events will more and more lose their significance [...]. Statistical uniformity is by no means a harmless scientific ideal; it is the no longer secret political ideal of a society which, entirely submerged in the routine of everyday living, is at peace with the scientific outlook inherent in its very existence' (Arendt 1958, 42–43).

2. Declared Pevsner after his visit: 'One has no idea of its size. It is surrounded by a medium size garden on one of the main avenues of the city. Its central hall is 100 per 100 feet wide. The hall of Reform Club, to give an example, is 52 per 52 feet wide, Buckingham Palace's Ball Room is 120 per 60 feet wide and 45 feet high. Ferreyra Palace's hall height is 75 feet, larger than all. That gives an idea of its size'.

BIBLIOGRAPHY

Abalos, Iñaki (2008) *Atlas Pintoresco Vol. 2: Los Viajes.* Barcelona: Gustavo Gili.

Arendt, Hannah (1958) *The Human Condition.* Chicago: The University of Chicago Press.

Baudrillard, Jean (1981) *Simulacra and Simulation*, Translated by Sheila Glaser. The University of Michigan Press.

—— (1997) *La Ilusión y la Desilusión Estéticas.* Caracas: Monte Avila Editores Latinoamericana.

Choay, Françoise (1992) *L'Allégorie du Patrimoine.* Paris: Editions de Suil.

Corona Martínez, Alfonso (2007) 'Sobre algunos edificios recientemente reformados'. *Summa+100*, Buenos Aires, June 38–63.

Eco, Umberto (1964) *Apocalittici e integrati Casa Ed.* Valentino Bompiani.

Eisenman, Peter (1984) 'The end of the classical: The end of the beginning and the end of the end', *Perspecta* 21.

Riegl, Alois (1903) *El Culto Moderno a los Monumentos.* Boadilla del Monte: A. Machado.

Rodriguez, Florencia (2008) 'El patrimonio se construye hoy', *Summa*+96, Buenos Aires, Sept. 2008, 66–89.

Silvetti, Jorge (2003/2004) 'The muses are not amused, pandemonium in the house of architecture', *Harvard Design Magazine* 19(Fall 2004): 22–33.

Sorkin, Michael (2002/2003) 'Brand aid', *Harvard Design Magazine*, Fall/Winter.

Wisnik, Guilherme (2008) *Paulo Mendes da Rocha*, Recent Work, 2G N0.45, Gustavo Gili, Barcelona.

Zein, Ruth V. (1998) *'Other Brazilian Architectures'*, 2G N.8 *Latin American Architecture*, Barcelona, 14–23.

SECTION 4

History/Memory/Tradition

16

Introduction: Time's Arrows: Spaces of the Past

C. Greig Crysler

The three terms that animate the chapters in this section constitute different, if overlapping routes to the past. Though history, memory and tradition continue to hold distinctive meanings in relation to each other, in practice they are increasingly difficult to separate. For much of the 20th century, normative definitions represented history as the dominant of the three terms, referring to authoritative narratives produced by experts according to agreed scientific standards. Both memory and tradition were cast as subjective and hence biased, or primitive, unchanging and outside historical time (Bennett 2004, 1; Olick and Robbins 1998, 109; Yoneyama 1999, 27).

The so-called 'crisis of history' and the end to 'grand meta-narratives' marked by globalization and the rise of postmodernism have brought all three terms together in new critical formations (de Certeau 1986; Lyotard 1984 [1979]). The progressive, evolutionary time associated with narratives of national culture has been called into question by the troubled history of the nation-state, its failed modernization projects and wars, descents into authoritarianism, and the aftermath of colonialism: historical time has been undone by its own tangled history (Olick 2005; 2007). Memory has emerged as a corrective to the silences, lapses and exclusions of official history. In its transit from unreliable messenger to critical counter-narrative, memory has acquired a surplus of history, just as history has adopted memory as a reflexive index of its own shortcomings (Huyssen 1995; 2003, 2). And tradition, characteristically positioned as something to be progressed away from (the ugly and ill places of the premodern world) or as points of origins for grand sagas of progress, has in recent scholarship also become intertwined with both memory and history. Thus it is possible to speak both of 'traditional history' as an established version of historical inquiry, and 'histories of tradition' (both material and epistemological) and even 'traditional memories' as the nostalgic afterglow of premodern recollections (AlSayyad 2004).

But it is not only the boundaries between regions of the past that have become less distinct: recent investigations into 'present pasts', 'histories of the future', 'histories of the immediate present', and the 'future of nostalgia' suggest that the past is constructed in the present. Events, spaces, even entire societies that once seemed securely fixed in time may, under certain conditions, slip from one temporal domain into another (Huyssen 2003, Rosenburg and Harding 2005;

Vidler 2008; Boym 2001). Critics have suggested that time is speeding up, in some cases to such an extent that both the past and future are disappearing into an endless present (see for example, Virilio 1986 [1977]; 1991). Paradoxically, claims that the past and future are disappearing have occurred alongside the accumulation and storage of memories. Museums linked to the selective construction of national memories have proliferated internationally. Digital technology has enabled a vast expansion in collective memory, while simultaneously acting as the potential source of a 'general accident' that is global in scale (Ulmer 2005, xvii; Virilio 1999). Memories are not only preserved, but codified and produced in 'memory machines' ranging from digital archives to the heritage and preservation of landscapes and built environments (Shanken 2009). Traditions are invented and produced within spaces of accelerating time, where they act as bulwarks against the momentum of contemporary change, or are selectively appropriated, deterritorialized and resynchronized within the encompassing reach of global capitalism.

Over the last three decades, arguments that denaturalize time by examining it as a cultural construction have emerged together with the so-called 'spatial turn' in the social sciences and humanities. Scholars in a wide range of disciplines have challenged the tendency to define time as the foundation of social change, with space as its mere container or reflection. The theoretical developments associated with the 'spatial turn' in the social sciences and humanities signal a commitment to understand time and space together, and to foreground the question of how, and on what terms, the former is related to the latter (Deutsche 1996; Gregory and Urry 1985; Massey 1994; 1995). Time, as it registers in social processes extending from the speed of production to the routines of everyday life, is understood as being shaped by the production, organization and use of space. (Giddens 1979; Harvey 1989; King 2004; Lefebvre 1991 [1974]; Thrift 1996). The underlying argument is thus not so much about a call to turn away from time in favour of space, but rather, to reconceptualize how the two are defined and related to each other in specific disciplinary and social settings.

Conceptions of time have played an important role in organizing the relationship between specializations in architecture. Otero-Pailos has argued, for example, that preservation studies have focused on time separate from space, while design cultures since modernism have tended to prioritize space apart from time (Otero-Pailos 2005; see also Till 2009). Others have claimed that design activity synchronizes time and space, regardless of whether the terms of that process are recognized as such or not (Wigley 2000). Rethinking time as a cultural production has challenged these assumptions and unsettled the foundations of architectural history. As Jyoti Hosagrahar notes in the first section of this collection, architecture's version of historicism, with its presumption of the forward movement of time in the West, has become the focus of critical operations that seek, following Dipesh Chakrabarty, to place the idealized times and spaces of colonial culture back into the worlds they seek to transcend (Chakrabarty 2000). Postcolonial perspectives, Hosagrahar writes, 'particularize universal narratives and globalize narrowly parochial ones'.

If we accept that time and space are inseparable, any consideration of past times is simultaneously a consideration of material and imagined spaces. In the discussion that follows, I contextualize the three chapters in this section by situating them in relation to time's arrows, or the vectors of temporality that cut across a wide range of disciplines and intersect with architecture. The past emerges as a non-unified field of multiple and contradictory temporalities, or 'time zones.' I focus on three different lines of motion: accelerating time (spaces of flux, disappearance, the end of history), everyday times (spaces of everyday life, tradition and the vernacular), remembered times (spaces of memory, commemoration, preservation and collective amnesia). Each of these time zones are sites of debate and counterargument, which continue to transform not only the way architectures and urbanisms of the past are defined and represented, but how the past is used to shape the material conditions of the present and future. I draw these concerns together in a fourth and concluding zone, where I connect changing conceptions of the past to institutional times, as synchronized by the canon and the curricular mechanisms of architectural education.

ZONE ONE: ACCELERATING TIME

The fantasy of an 'incredible shrinking world' of frictionless space is one of the narrative planks upon which the story of capitalist globalization has been built (MacGillivray 2006). In its first and most familiar variant, the discourse of globalization is tied to a crisis in the capitalist mode of production, exacerbated by the oil shocks of the 1970s, and the recession that followed. These provoke systemic changes that ripple outwards from the post-industrial countries of the First World, transforming the cities and economies of newly industrializing countries (Harvey 1989; 2006). World City theorists such as John Friedmann (1986) and Saskia Sassen (2000) postulate an emerging system of 'command and control' through which the energy of a planetary circuit board is relayed (see also Castells 1996a). Though transcending the more obvious restatement of the First World modernization determining (and setting the pace) for all the rest, these accounts nevertheless propose a version of centre and periphery relationships, comprised of a stellar constellation of world-girding cities. The discursive criteria for admission to the ranked order of nodes in a global network has become the object of intense competition for cities both within and outside the new 'world order', leading scholars to argue that the analytic model is complicit with the processes it describes (Hart 2002; Oncu and Weyland 1997; Smith 2001).

These arguments mark an attempt to reconceptualize the relationship between time and space, by showing how the expansion and reorganization of capital involves a 'spatial fix' (or displacement) that is intertwined with the acceleration of various constructions of time (travel, production, investment, data transmission, etc.). This interpretation was further advanced in the 1991 English language publication of *The Production of Space* (also a reference point for many authors in this collection) some twenty years after its initial appearance in France. As Shields has noted, *The Production of Space*, though opening up new theoretical horizons related to the role of representation in social change through the anti-foundational 'trialectics' of the perceived, conceived and lived, also contained its own historical ellipsis: Lefebvre arrived at his formulation after a long march through epochal history that began with Ancient Greece and culminated with the 'differential space' of the globalizing present (Shields 1999).

Lefebvre's work gave new coherence to the so-called spatial turn, or the 'spatialization of social theory' and related attempts to move beyond the economic functionalism of Marxist urban political economy. As Edward Soja argued in his influential 1989 book, *Postmodern Geographies*, the Lefebvrian discourse on space offered a way to challenge the 'unbudgeable hegemony' of nineteenth-century historicism, which Soja claimed represented space as a simple reflection of evolutionary time, or ignored it altogether. In his reformulation, space and time are joined together in reciprocal determination – where, for example, urban space is shaped by the processes of capitalism and in turn, 'acts back' on those processes through redefined patterns of occupation and use. Similar arguments were made by David Harvey who argued, like Soja, that space was a social process, an ideological representation and an organization of knowledge, all of which had the capacity to influence social change and hence the experience of time (Harvey 1989; 2000; 2001).

Despite the complexity of their arguments, both Harvey and Soja retained the mode of production as a motive force, and in the end reproduced the base/superstructure models they sought to transform. In the process they tended to reduce cultural production – whether of cities, architects or artists – to dizzying ideological manifestations of accelerating time, including feminist interventions, which were either ignored or treated as playful mystifications of space-time compression (Deutsche 1996; Massey 1994).

As Nancy Stieber has noted, the development of Marxist arguments about time and space in the social sciences invited connections with architectural history, where a longstanding discourse of time and space, equally Hegelian but with a different spiritual essence, was already in place (Stieber 2006). Modernist historians such as Sigfried Giedion made the relationship between time and space central to modern architecture. However the forces that determined the specific nature of the relationship remained elusively located in the zeitgeist of the age, less specific but equally foundational as the mode of production in Marxist discourses. And while the parallel formulations may have created the linguistic grounds for potential exchange across disciplines, Stieber has suggested the result has been less a broadening of architectural research than a displacement of its object of study: as historians have moved to reframe their research in Marxist terms, they may have replaced one model of foundationalism with another.

Copies without origin

The 'acceleration of acceleration' as a means to conquer the 'friction of space' leads in some accounts to a world dissolving into a condition of pure flux, one in which the past is uprooted, deterritorialized and commodified on a global scale (Auge 1995; Castells 1996a). Marxist critics connected to the lineage of the New Left and its commitment to examine the ideological role of culture, argued that the entire basis of capitalist production had shifted from the production of things with use value to the production of signs with exchange value (Baudrillard 1975; Gottdiener 1986, 2001; Poster 1988). The focus on capital's realization problem – most effectively pursued by Jean Baudrillard – turned the political economy of writers like Harvey and Soja into pure simulation: for Baudrillard, any analysis based on a mode of production tied to industry, a proletarian workforce, and struggles between capital and labour could only be regarded as a simulacrum (or a sign that refers to other signs, in this case Marxist narratives of production and class revolution) (Baudrillard 1975, 117). Instead, we have arrived at what Baudrillard famously termed 'the mirror of production' based on economies of desire managed by 'symbolic analysts' in concert with marketing experts, advertising agencies and other forms of expertise related to the production of a pervasive, if constantly shifting, spectacle of consumption (Reich 1991; Krupar and Al, Chapter 14 in this volume).

In a dilation of the semiosis explored by hyperrealists such as Baudrillard (1975; 1981; 1983), Eco (1986), Žižek (1989; 2004), and Jameson (1991; 1994; 1998), much of what fell under the rubric of high postmodernism in architectural culture was almost immediately absorbed into the mainstream of commercial production to provide a nostalgic backdrop that was surprisingly in tune with the 'morning in America' of the Reagan presidency, with eclectic historical references generalized far beyond the elite circuits of architectural culture that first generated them (McLeod 1989). Thus another mirror of production emerged – one which seemed to confirm the end point of Manfredo Tafuri's *Architecture and Utopia*: architecture as a 'self-advertising sign', with its use value in communication, first promoted as a challenge to the symbolic alienation of high modernism, but quickly becoming the visual currency of an emerging brandscape of flexible production and a newly intensified consumer capital (Tafuri 1976; see also Foster 1985).

If the past of hyperreality is, in these analyses, absorbed into a 'desert of the real' where signs refer only to other signs that are more real than the real itself, so too is the future dissolved into the present in degenerate form. The archetypal figure of this dissolution is perhaps the theme park, which became a paradigmatic example of the 'degenerate utopia' of the themed environment: the future colonized by the mirror of production in the global present. Disneyland – perhaps most notably in the work of Lois Marin – was cited as evidence of the impossibility of imagining utopian futures in any form outside those of capital. The 'no place' of eighteenth-century social thought had, in Marin's view, been converted into an ideological reproduction of the capitalist present (Marin 1984). The point is amplified in Sorkin's influential 1992 collection which understands spaces of consumption converging in an endless variation of the theme park typology (see also Sorkin 2001). Others, most notably M. Christine Boyer in her account of the city of collective memory, locate the loss of critical consciousness in the spectacular appropriation and reordering of the past through processes of gentrification (Boyer 1994).

Frederic Jameson argued that the intensification of consumption in segregated spaces was producing an entirely new ontology of capital. His widely-read analysis of the Bonaventure Hotel in Los Angeles interpreted the building's interior as an allegorical urban hyperspace, one so wide-ranging in its reorganization of space and time that it transcended historically ingrained perceptual capacities. The resulting space made it impossible for the body 'to locate itself, to organize its immediate surroundings perceptually, and to cognitively map itself and its position in a mappable external world.' (Jameson 1991, 44) Here the body is trapped in its own history, leading to an 'alarming disjunction' between it and the decentred built environments of multinational capital. The disjunction is ideological, making the material conditions and processes of late capitalism unknowable in the delirium of accelerated modernity. Other critics similarly argued that increases in the speed and ubiquity of digital communications and international travel enabled individuals to imagine themselves as members of trans- or post-national communities no longer constrained by the territorial boundaries of the nation-state, whether through the mechanisms of what Anderson called 'long distance nationalism', or via Arjun Appadurai's Weberian scheme of ideal typical 'scapes' of finance, ethnicity, culture, media and politics (Anderson 1992; Appadurai 1996).

For Jameson, the proposed counter-strategy (derived from Kevin Lynch's image of the city (1960)) involves an aesthetic of cognitive mapping, part of a 'pedagogical political culture that would endow individual subjects with a heightened sense of their place in the global system' (Jameson 1991, 54). Unlike modernist interventions, the Bonaventure does not rise above the fallen city in a utopian statement of difference, but rather, refracts the surrounding chaos through its secure logic (42). Jameson would later find similar qualities, defamiliarized through their intensification, in the large urban projects of Rem Koolhaas. These, he argued, employ strategies of 'replication' in relation to what already exists. Projects such as the Eurolille development are treated as creative reworkings of 'post-civil society' where an anonymous envelope marks off a space of apparently random juxtapositions, and in doing so replicates the falling away of clear divisions between public and private, city and building, that in turn define the enabling conditions of metropolitan delirium (Jameson and Speaks 1992). The dual strategy of replication and intensification reorients the temporal basis of architectural design: here the future resides in a 'dirty realism' of the present, rather than in utopian visions of a better world.

A similar redirection occurs in Koolhaas's studies of locations outside the US, particularly his writing based on the case of Singapore (a 'metastasizing modernism'), and the studies he and his students have undertaken of rapidly urbanizing cities such as Lagos, Nigeria, as part of the *Project on the City* (Felix and Wolting 2005; Koolhaas 1997, 2007). The conditions of rapid and weakly regulated urban growth are embraced, in Matthew Gandy's words, as a means to 'highlight the homeostatic complexity of newly evolving socio-economic structures, with the city conceived as a series of self-regulatory systems' (Gandy 2005, 39). Thus collapsed or unequal infrastructure and unplanned urbanization, together with various forms of congestion and crowding all become positive conditions that liberate the intrinsic ingenuity of the city's inhabitants from totalizing systems and allow 'self-organizing' mutations of local invention and spatial change to emerge (Koolhaas 1997).

The characteristic viewpoint is from above. Kaleidoscopic patterns formed by stalled traffic and informal housing signal an orientalist cybernetics of feedback loops and laissez-faire self-regulation (Godlewski 2010). Koolhaas converts Lagos into a positive model through the same aesthetics of geometric abstraction deployed by Bernard Rudofsky in *Architecture without Architects* some thirty years earlier (Rudofsky 1964). The principle of modernist immanence expands to a metropolitan scale, as the 'Third World city' becomes visible not as something to progress away from, but rather, as an imagined future towards which all other cities are inexorably moving.

Elsewhere, the strategy is reversed: rather than transmuting one city into an origin for the future of the city *per se*, a diverse group of cities are represented as components of a single metropolitan type. Thus in the catalogue for the *Cities on the Move* exhibition that Koolhaas co-curated (under the subheading 'Southeast Asian Cities of Chaos and Urban Change') (Koolhaas 1999), Tokyo, Seoul, Malaysia, Hong Kong, Singapore and Bangkok amongst others, are gathered together under the heading of the 'East Asian City' and presented within generic categories such as work, leisure, shopping, entertainment, infrastructure and sex. The simulated meta-city that results is intended to evoke the urban decay and uncontrollability of the contexts it borrows from. As Koolhaas said in an interview published in the exhibition catalogue: 'We'll do newness and airport construction, but we'll also do decay, sex and drugs, just like in a real city ...' (Koolhaas 1999, 17).

The future orientalism of the Lagos study and the *Cities on the Move* exhibition is also represented in a cluster of articles appearing in *ANY* magazine and other journals in the late 1990s, where China appears as a force so powerful and overwhelming that it can only be channeled or latched onto. History is again eradicated by speed (Kwinter 1992). As the theorist Jeffrey Kipnis writes: 'The New Asian City warps past any Marxian notion of "formation" or "construction"; it is an artifaction of speed and dominance, unholy and beyond history' (Kipnis 1996, 170). Others, such as the literary theorist Ackbar Abbas, argued that history was disappearing through its spectacular visibility in heritage projects and simulated reconstructions of the past in Hong Kong immediately prior to reunification with China. The replacement history, or the 'culture of disappearance' ironically obscured Hong Kong's actual history as a future-directed economic power rising to regional dominance as a financial centre (Abbas 1997).

ZONE TWO: EVERYDAY TIMES

The conditions associated with the 'culture of disappearance', the financescapes of 'modernity at large' and the 'unholy artifaction' of rapid urbanization cited above are aptly summarized by the spiralling mounds of capitalist residue in Koolhaas's soliloquy on junkspace (Koolhaas 2002). As a frenzied audit of the effects of global consumption diagnosed through its waste, this exaggerated repetition of disposable banality defines a strategy of resistance to accelerated modernity: further acceleration is employed as means to defamiliarize and shock. The result, according to Jameson, is an 'orgasmic breaking through into time and history again, into a concrete future' (Jameson 2003, 77).

As Ole Fischer notes in Chapter 2 of this collection, arguments about the acceleration of time and the related loss of history have also led to a range of responses that, in different ways, attempt to slow down, freeze or even reverse the perceived effects of modernization. The process by which an entire category of buildings is first defined as 'other' to architecture and then assimilated back into its disciplinary structure is at the centre of the arguments presented by Brown and Maudlin on tradition and the vernacular for this section. The term 'vernacular architecture' embodies the contradiction of buildings that are classified as being at once outside and within architecture. Their chapter explores the construction of vernacular architecture in relation to multiple oppositions: 'the antiquated against the contemporary; the archaic against the modern; the traditional against the innovative'. The term also signals an opposition between low culture and high, 'layman and professional, the anonymous and the authored as well as the spontaneous and the planned, the circumstantial and the conceptual and the passed-down and the designed' (Brown and Maudlin 2011, Chapter 19 in this volume). The result, they argue, is the creation of two distinct, self-contained fields, with architecture and architectural history in one, and vernacular studies in the other. The divide, as they note, is also characterized by differing temporalities, with vernacular buildings understood in terms of the slow adaptation of existing forms and the use of inherited knowledge, while architecture is identified with innovation and the production of forms that are considered finished (and frozen in time) once construction ends. The relationship between the vernacular and architectural history also operates in relation to an instrumental divide, with the former acting as a timeless essence for the latter, an origin from which progressive developments in the field of architecture can be measured.

Vernacular modernisms

The vernacular has thus developed historically in opposition to the modern and a chain of related terms: the industrialized, professional, the official and the elite, as well as disciplinary formations of architectural design and history, amongst many others. As Wright notes, the coherence of the opposition between the vernacular and modern depends on artifice: 'For both, the abstraction of an eternal present depends on two imaginary temporalities, distinct but closely intertwined. One is a vision of traditional stability and unity in a past that is about to be lost forever … this illusion in turn allows, even encourages, fantasies about the present, whether they derive from self-righteous efforts to preserve or re-create that imagined world, or from boldly innovative images that proclaim a radical new departure…' (Wright 2003, 166). The various ways in which the vernacular/modern duality has been constructed and mobilized has become a significant area of research in its own right. Considerable attention has been devoted, for example, to the ways in which colonizing powers made the selective appropriation and reuse of 'local' or 'indigenous' building practices an integral part of pacification strategies (AlSayyad 1992). These were intertwined with articulations of colonial modernity, where characteristic building practices, first defined as 'traditional' or evidence of the vernacular, were appropriated and infused with industrial technology, whether as exhibition pavilions at World Fairs in the imperial metropole, or in the key public spaces built alongside preserved fragments of the 'traditional city' in the colonies. (Morton 2000; Rabinow 1989; Wright 1991)

The juxtaposition sought to provide visible evidence of the progress that colonial knowledge and power could bring – a practice that, as various scholars have shown, has also been a consistent feature of the spatial operations of postcolonial nationalism (Kusno 2000; Vale 1992). Though initially developed through research on colonial settings of the French and British empires, arguments about vernacular modernisms in colonial settings have expanded to include a rich array of settings and power dynamics beyond these initial studies. Mia Fuller's analysis of the fascist new towns constructed in the Italian colonies and the mainland under Mussolini provides a complex reading of the intersections between authoritarian state power and the vernacular, while Michelangelo Sabatino, also examining the Italian context, has revealed how the vernacular creatively mediated and transformed the tensions of modernization across political regimes (Fuller 2007; Sabatino 2011).

As Umbach and Hüppauf note, the growth of research on the vernacular within historical forces such as colonization has occurred alongside a growing body of literature that continues to examine it as a form of particularity against the universalist claims of modernity, as defined through abstraction, forward temporality and rationalization (2005). Indeed, the processes associated with globalization have in some respects deepened the status of the vernacular as a reaction formation, grounded in a longing for local authenticity (Massey 1994, 147). The normative opposition thus remains an active part of vernacular debates, one of many positions in a field Wilson and Groth describe as polyvocal (2003). For Umbach and Hűppauf, the main tension remains between those who want to resolve the heterogeneity of modernity through multiple stages (and in the process, position the vernacular in the distant past as a point of origin), and those who regard heterogeneity as the operating principle of modernity itself. In the latter formulation, architectural strategies attempt to cope with, create or master the 'modern condition' (6). Rather than representing the vernacular as a vanishing form threatened by encroaching modernization, it is redefined as a 'generative principle', operating variously as an attempt to transform modernity's effects, an image of the future, and the medium through which the modern is imagined (7–8). In this view, the individual, the emotional and the regional – all characteristics attributed to the vernacular – are constitutive of modernity rather than destroyed or debased by it (11).

The rhetoric of practice

In the debates outlined above, the vernacular is repositioned as a process of creative translation, mediation and appropriation, one that can be examined both from above (by studying the incorporation of the vernacular into dominant norms and forms), and from below (in ways that reveal the slippage between dominant intentions and diverse conditions of use). The official and 'unofficial', the intended and appropriated are understood dialectically (even 'contrapuntally') across (post)imperial space rather than as separate conditions (Said 1993, 66). A similar transformation has occurred in relation to the everyday. As with the vernacular, the key insight has been to rethink the everyday as a practice of representation that links together embodied experience, subject formation and space. The influence of Michel de Certeau has been significant here, particularly his 1984 book, *The Practice of Everyday Life*, and for those in the built environment disciplines, the widely cited article, 'Walking in the City'. The everyday is regarded as an 'enunciative function', and hence part of relational system of meaning in the 'rhetoric of practice' (de Certeau 1984, 97). Perhaps most significantly, the everyday, as a 'way of operating' and process of 'topographic appropriation' is now within, rather than outside the space of modernizing discipline. The two are bound together, with the practices of everyday life redefined as '... tricky and stubborn procedures that elude discipline without being outside the field in which it is exercised ...' (96) The everyday thus becomes integral to social life, rather than its static and subordinate margins.

The concept of the everyday as a space of re-appropriation and counter-practice has yielded a rich array of studies extending from spectacular spaces of consumption (Elsheshtawy 2010; Hou 2010; Shields 1991; 1989) through the realm of the urban homeless (Ruddick 1996; Rosler 1991) to that of the maximum security prison (Rhodes 2004). It has also transformed the understanding of power relations in colonial contexts. Brenda Yeoh's innovative book on colonial Singapore examines how colonial regulations were applied to the verandahs of shop houses, laneways, markets and others spaces in an attempt to impose order on public and semi-public areas in tandem with the science of sanitary improvement (Yeoh 1996). While her study is not framed explicitly in terms of the vernacular and the everyday (she writes of 'daily life' and 'Asian perceptions'), she arguably helped to open up the reformulation of both terms in relation to the colonial city because her research is founded on their interdependence with colonial modes of control. The target population ignored and resisted regulations until they were eventually withdrawn or applied in different ways elsewhere in the city, where they were again in continuous tension with established perceptions and habits of colonized populations. The constant slippage between the desired outcome and actual conditions reveals the unstable, fungible nature of colonial power, and the resilience of everyday spaces and practices, which remain outside the imagined totality and temporality of the colonizing grasp. Like the vernacular, the everyday in such accounts is therefore not a space of tacit, enduring routines that have somehow evaded the control of dominant interests; rather it defines the point at which networks of knowledge and power are recognized, manoeuvred around, appropriated and transformed in unpredictable ways.

Contingency and change

Henri Lefebvre's research on the everyday, emerging in response to the technocratic management of society in post-war France, has also been widely influential in relation to analyses of urban space and the public sphere. He shares with de Certeau a focus on practice, and an optimism about the future, furthered by his commitment to dialectical analysis stressing contestation and the unsettling of given categories of action. Defined by both the bland routinization of everyday life and open-ended moments of festival and play, in its multiple contradictions Lefebvre's everyday 'reveals the human that still resides within us' and with it, the potential of human agency to effect change (McLeod 1997, 16). In the movement between the repressive and liberatory, his formulation embraces the temporality of both the critical present and the socially just future.

The implication of Lefebvre's synthesis has been explored along numerous lines by other scholars, but perhaps most forcefully in relation to his parallel arguments about the 'right to the city', or (as in David Harvey's words) 'the right to change ourselves by changing the city' (Harvey 2008, 23; see also Mitchell 2002).

Though Harvey and others have remained largely committed to the primacy of class in social change, the everyday created openings to reconsider agency in ways that moved beyond the assumptions of economic foundationalism. The influential 1999 book on 'everyday urbanism' co-edited by John Chase, Margaret Crawford and John Kaliski, for example, turned attention towards situated analysis of everyday spaces and practices tied to political contingencies on the ground. The authors show how multiple or 'counterpublics' shape and reshape the spaces of everyday life through practices 'founded on contestation rather than unity, and created through competing interests and violent demands as much as reasoned debates' (Crawford 1999, 25). A rich array of case studies and critical reflection has emerged around these arguments, further redefining the relationship between the everyday, design and the public sphere (see for example Harris and Berke 1997; Hou 2010; Schmidt et al. 2008). Far from conceptualizing the everyday as a nostalgic reservoir of simpler times, or an outpost of authentic social relations in the midst of capital's increasing grip, it emerges here through the rhythm of agency and change. It is perpetually in tension with, and hence just beyond, the limits of existing conditions.

This approach to the everyday has also proven influential in rethinking the terms of architectural production, by acknowledging its basis in the contradictions and contingencies of everyday life. As Jeremy Till argues in *Architecture Depends* (2009), this requires architects to leave behind 'delusions of autonomy' and engage with occupants, users and builders in their 'messy, complex lives … mess is law' (61). A praxis of contingency, Till argues, takes responsibility for architecture's enabling conditions, and is frankly acknowledged as situated and partial (as well as partisan). As with the positions outlined above, Till finds optimism in working more humbly, 'gathering the past in order to shape better (but not perfect) futures' (61). It is a standpoint that is grounded in a revised conception of time. The production of architecture derived from partial, rather than absolute truth is also one that gives up the struggle for timelessness in the rhetoric of spatial representation. The most pungent manifestation of the immersion in the time of contingency centres on what Till calls 'rubbish theory' or a recognition of architecture's intrinsic status as waste (70). Threading a praxis of contingency through waste requires the architect to assume responsibility for the ruinous status of objects typically abstracted from the dynamic movement of time: in this view, architecture conceived outside time is waste(d) before it is built (75).

Global traditions

A similar rethinking of the 'semantics of time' has been underway in relation to the discourse on traditional environments, also discussed in detail in Brown and Maudlin's chapter for this section. Tradition has historically been located in idealized spaces outside imperial 'civilization' or capitalist modernization. Over the last three decades it has been defined as an active process of change within, rather than outside, these conditions. When viewed through the lens of organizations such as IASTE (International Association for the Study of Traditional Environments) and its journal (*Traditional Dwellings and Settlements Review*), debates on tradition are as polyvocal as those associated with the vernacular: salvage narratives appear alongside those that explore the global production of tradition under the terms of expanding global tourism and large scale gentrification (Crysler 2003).

Against these antinomies, a series of other approaches move beyond understanding tradition as something about to be lost, or as already fully converted to multiples without origin. Here, as in some of the most challenging research presented at recent IASTE conferences, tradition is examined along the lines of what Ong and Collier have called a 'global assemblage': a constellation of practices that is 'heterogeneous, partial, unstable, situated, and whose temporality is emergent because its composite form is shifting, in formation or at stake' (Ong and Collier 2005, 5). Tradition emerges as an interdisciplinary 'problem space' (5). Situating the interconnected fields defined by tradition, the vernacular, the ordinary and everyday within the temporalities of capitalist modernization has also provided a way to rethink the spaces of global cultures. In *Ordinary Cities* (2006), Jennifer Robinson argues that the category of the global city should be replaced with that of ordinary cities, as a way to redirect attention towards the situated conditions, practices and routines of everyday life (10). The ordinary – as an inclusive replacement for the global – is intended to 'reterritorialize the imagination' around the complexity and diversity of city life that results from a 'discrepant cosmopolitanism' and modernities uncoupled from their connection to the West (Robinson 2006; see also Duanfang Lu's arguments in Chapter 13; Cheah and Robbins 1998).

ZONE THREE: REMEMBERED TIMES

Studies concerned with the disappearence of history have emerged alongside those claiming that another domain of the past is expanding at an unprecedented rate. By some accounts, the world is now in the grips of a ballooning and global 'memory industry', characterized by exponential growth in museums, archives and institutional sites, and an equally expansive body of scholarly research in 'memory studies', an umbrella term for the specialized subfields concerned in different ways with memory, its spaces, practices and institutions (Baxter 1999; Berliner 2005; Klein 2000; Olick and Robbins 1998; Shanken 2009; Winter 2006).

The simultaneous claim that history is disappearing and memory is expanding is paradoxical only if the two phenomena are understood separately. When viewed together, the growth of memory studies may be understood as a response to the faltering legitimacy, and even the destructive potential of progressive history. Thus the times and spaces of memories are inseparable from the institutions of history (Boyarin 1994). Pierre Nora, whose exhaustive study of collective memory in France helped to inaugurate the current expansion of the field, argued that in the absence of bounded communities of collective memory, 'sites of memory' were needed to preserve the past from its ineluctable rationalization and destruction by history (Nora 1989). As Andreas Huyssen notes: 'Whatever the specific content of the many contemporary debates about history and memory may be, underlying them is a fundamental disturbance not just of the relationship between history as objective and scientific and memory as subjective and personal, but of history itself and its promises' (Huyssen 2003, 2).

While the burgeoning scale and breadth of research on memory is a contemporary phenomenon, one of the central assumptions that underpins much of the current literature can be traced to at least the beginning of the twentieth century, when memory – and more broadly what is regarded as worthy of preserving to sustain memories – was redefined as something that is socially constructed in the present. The core insight as it relates to the co-dependence of past and present was forcefully outlined in Alois Riegl's 1903 book, entitled *The Modern Cult of Monuments* (1982 [1903]). Here Riegl argues that the past becomes visible as 'historic value', through determinations in the present. Other seminal figures in debates about collective memory, such as the French sociologist Maurice Halbwachs (whose landmark text on collective memory was first published in 1925), argues that memory is not intrinsic or given, but rather produced in shared social spaces of everyday life. For Halbwachs, memory was both socially grounded and collective: a 'matter of how minds work together in society, how their operations are not simply mediated, but are structured by social arrangements'. (Halbwachs 1925, cited in Marot 2003 [1999], 30) Marot notes that Halbwach's redefinition of memory resonates with the foundational assumptions of Freud's approach to the unconscious. In both cases, memory is decompartmentalized as a private, individual chamber and retheorized as one of reconstruction, an 'activity of localization and configuration within socially elaborated frames or reference systems' (Marot 2003, 31).

Recent research on the role that cities and built environments play in activating, sustaining and modifying memory share key assumptions with wider developments outlined above: first, the production of memory intensifies in times of rapid social change and hence is dependent upon – even driven by – the temporality of modernization, often in the context of nationalism and nation-building (Boyarin 1994). Second, memories are constructed from specific, socially situated positions in the present, and are by extension embedded in, and productive of power relations. A third and overarching assertion challenges the relationship between memory and immanence by arguing that memories are attached to artifacts through shared, if contested processes of signification, rather than discovered and released by the skillful analyst (Crinson 2005, xviii).

M. Christine Boyer deals with the latter question in her discussion of 'Collective Memory under Siege' for this section. She takes issue with scholars who represent collective memory as an objective but hidden condition that is summoned forth through the experience of place, excavated from the ground, or meditatively released from the fabric of buildings. These approaches are problematic because they give memory an independent life as a thing in itself, something that is defined as an objective condition outside representation, rather than a social practice used to secure or challenge specific interests. She suggests that while memory cannot be embedded in the fabric of the building, it is entirely possible that a building can be constituted in discourse as a 'storehouse of memories' for political reasons. Once this conceptual shift is made, the role of the analyst is to examine the work that 'memory talk' does in specific contexts, to reveal the interests it upholds and the authority it warrants (see also Yoneyama 1999, 28; Coombes 2003, 3). Physical spaces (and their absent counterparts, voids) become the points at which memory discourse is gathered: they are the signifying anchors, and the intersection points for competing recollections. As Boyer reveals, sometimes deadly struggles occur when memories 'take place' and are institutionalized as visible evidence of collective identity (see also Bevan 2006; Boyer 1994; Goldstein 2004; Retort 2007; Kusno 2010).

Boyer's discussion of Rwanda, South Africa and Beirut emphasizes the impurity of memory, the diverse ways in which it is recalled and represented, and the constant transformation of the past in the present as accounts are 'both marked and manipulated by the experience of violence'. From this standpoint, all memory is ultimately collective, to the extent that it must enter into a system of representation that is shared, and culturally determined. 'Memory practices' attempt to bridge the gap between the experience of the event to be remembered and its expression as a memory: our recollections do not pre-exist the discourses and practices that constitute them as such. The destruction of memory is therefore not only a question of attack on its referents through war and civil strife, or something that occurs when the populations who embody memories pass away: both remembering and forgetting are basic conditions of representation. Every discourse creates a centre and margins. To narrate is to make choices which result in exclusions, fissures, and silences (Spivak 1990, 18–19). 'Total recall' is impossible. Memory and forgetting are inseparable, paradoxically bound together through their intrinsic lack of closure: thus we 'forget to remember or remember to forget' (Davis and Starn 1989, 2).

Suspension and stasis

If we accept that memories are attached to places through institutional practices, discourses, informal recollections and everyday routines, then any space may become a locus for the competing recollections that are brought to it. However, memories are always recollected and articulated in the context of asymmetries of power, made tangible by struggles against, within and between various agencies and governmental bodies that seek to regulate meaning. Such struggles invariably seek to 'freeze' artifacts at a particular moment of truth, and in doing so, preserve them from the entropy of time. In this sense, the archive – whether constituted through documents held in an antiseptic storehouse, or through buildings located within designated portions of a city – is against time. Not only are the materials within the archive rescued from destruction, significant effort is made to prevent them from ageing, and hence showing time's passage (Blouin and Rosenberg 2008; Foster 2004; Wigley 2005).

Preservation may be about stopping time, but as Robert Garland Thomson has suggested, it also about claiming time. As the field of preservation has grown in scope and complexity, it has become increasingly detached from the temporal brackets associated with its emergence. The 'historic' in historic preservation has now been compressed to the point where

> 'preservation has begun to transcend its connection to history ... and indeed reveal(s) itself as an argument about the meaning of the term 'historic'. The change can be measured in the (disappearing) minimum age for admission to the category of heritage: the modern, the vernacular, the everyday ... everything is now susceptible to preservation's seizure of time' (Thomson 2004, ix).

The potentially infinite expansion of the field embodies a shift away from nineteenth century models of periodization as the basis for historical classification to more mutable, situated determinations (Koolhaas 2004). The historic past ceases to be the metaphorical foreign country cited by Lowenthal in the title of his influential book (1985) on the same subject. Rather, it is now understood as a relational tense that is linked to the present through future speculation. The future anterior of preservation (to paraphrase the title of an innovative journal of the same name and subject) does not survey a past that 'has been', it examines constructions of the past 'that will have been' (Otero-Pailos 2005, iv).

The redefinition of preservation as a practice tied to the politics of the present has telescoped into a re-examination of its relation to historical forces such as colonization, imperialism and postcolonial nationalism. In her contribution to this section, Mrinalini Rajagopalan moves across the history of preservation in order to disclose its changing affiliations with power. Though extending to the nineteenth century, her discussion is at the same time a synchronic account of the re-theorization of preservation as a social rather than technical process. Preservation guidelines in colonial cities were, Rajagopalan argues, a facet of the orientalist representation of indigenous history, encoding relations of difference and similarity on terms that would support the reorganization of colonized societies, while also producing the grounds against which imperial identity could be legitimated historically. She suggests that successive waves of modernization, produced through postcolonial nationalism and globalization have led to radically different constructions of what should be preserved. Rajagopalan's expanded definition of preservation includes the interchange between bureaucracies, educational settings, legal structures and the changing epistemologies of architectural history. It is both a corpus of institutional practices and a set of procedures that suspend objects in time, so they may act as points of origin for myths of conquest, and aspirational symbols in the discourse of market and nation.

Memory as voidspace

Some of the most powerful 'memory work' of the last three decades has been concerned with making the invisible visible, by describing urban space in ways that summon up the history of forgotten struggles, moments of collective violence and subjugation (Barton 2001; Bell 2009; Koshar 2000; Rosenfeld 2000). This has led to an emphasis on the trace, the palimpsest, and material signifiers that point to former moments whose meaning is obscured or mythologized in the present.

The insights of Walter Benjamin have been particularly influential in this regard. For Benjamin, modernity is a refinement of barbarism, a 'catastrophe of failed emancipation' (Lindner 1986, cited in Gilloch 1996, 13). He argues that the truth of an object reveals itself at the moment of its oblivion – only then, as mythical objects start to dissolve into the dust of modernity, do their hidden contradictions become apparent. The the history of the present is read backwards through the decaying fragments of the past, which in their rotting surfaces reveal an unadorned history of violence (Benjamin 1979; Buck Morss 1997).

But material fragments can also act as sites of forgetting, as voids into which unwanted or painful memories are discharged. Thus, for example, Karen Till argues that present-day Berlin's spaces of memory 'give shape to felt absences, fears and desires that haunt contemporary society' (Till 2005, 9; see also Ladd 1997; Till 2008). Memorials, heritage buildings and artifacts dissolve rather than preserve the past. They are the proverbial garbage cans of history, places where unwanted or troublesome memories are relegated, and hence removed from everyday life and forgotten even as they are memorialized. This argument has also been made by Kristin Ann Hass in relation to the Vietnam Veteran's Memorial. She argues that the polished black granite surface of the memorial acts simultaneously as mirror and void, offering the potential for symbolic recognition of individuals within a larger group of mourners, while also permitting a ritualized discharging of memories.

These are left behind through their mnemonic surrogates, a vast accumulation of objects (over 50,000 at last count) that have been carried to (and deposited at) the wall in acts of individual commemoration (Haas 1998).

The potential for minimalist architecture to engender multiple meanings has been interpreted as a sign of progress in the memorial-building industry, and lauded as a more inclusive and egalitarian strategy. The art critic Michael Kimmelman declared that 'minimalist abstraction, with its allegorical pliancy, turns out to function in a memorial context as the best available mirror for a modern world aware of its own constantly changing sense of history' (Kimmelman 2002). The unadorned physical voids inside the Jewish Museum in Berlin have also been described as powerful allegories of the unfilled gaps in the city's urban fabric and history (Huyssen 2003, 68). The voids operate together with other spatial experiences that are designed to provoke feelings of unease, even dread, as well as hope and release. The museum's 'Axis of the Holocaust' for example, grows narrower and darker as it reaches its conclusion at the chimney-like Holocaust Tower. The building's spaces encourage multiple associations with traumatic events. Their mimetic potential resides in the production of negativity without a positive goal: in doing so the distance between the present and some future moment of reconciliation is exposed, but not resolved (Heynen 1999b, 208) For Adrian Parr, the voids may even act as the starting point for Deleuzian 'lines of flight' away from the repressive grasp of rationalized history (Parr 2008). Such interpretations necessarily stress the experiential properties of the building separate from the exhibitions that now inhabit it, and in doing so point to another gap that remains unresolved.

The sensuous character of the Jewish Museum and the memorial spaces in the landscape outside, connect it to a growing number of museums around the world that seek to impart memories of sometimes violent historical events through embodied experience. Institutions such as the United States Holocaust Memorial Museum (USHMM) in Washington, DC, the Museum of Tolerance in Los Angeles, California and the Apartheid Museum in Johannesburg, South Africa, engage in the institutional production of both memory and history, not only in their curatorial agendas, but also in the architecture that contains (and now) merges with them (Coombes 2003; Crysler 2006;

Crysler and Kusno 1997; Findley 2005; Young 1991, 1993).

The national museum as apocalyptic phantasmagoria clearly marks a departure from its nineteenth century counterpart. Though arriving at an affirmation of the nation-state, the climactic story does not foreground the genius and achievements of an idealized (white male) national body (Bennett 1995, 2004; Maleuvre 1999). Museums of national trauma tell their stories through the nation-state's failures, redemption and rebirth. As such, they mark an important shift that transcends their focus on violence: history is organized around the experiences of populations who were once marginalized or excluded altogether from the official spaces of national representation (Brown 2006; Sen 2006; Taylor and Gutman 1992).

The central representational strategy involves structuring history to solicit empathetic identification between diverse visitors and the groups represented. The practice has been described by Alison Landsberg as one of prosthetic memory. The term is useful analytically because it signals the attempt to fit the museum onto the body of the visitor like a glove. The museum's enveloping somatic experiences, whether critical or celebratory – nevertheless seek a sensuous engagement that extends well past the ocular-central, sequential intake of museum rationality that was characteristic of the great exhibitionary complexes of the nineteenth century (Bennett 1995; 2004). For Landsberg and others, the intended process of self-abstraction and introjection provides the basis for cross-cultural understanding (Landsberg 2004; Findley 2005). The 'museum as differencing machine' provides experiences in which visitors are encouraged to feel their way into the museum body that surrounds them (Bennett 2006, 46).

Such institutional conversions and reprocessings do not operate autonomously, but in relation to other discourses of national history in the world outside the museum, well beyond the orbit of its carefully staged temporality (Myers 2006). Thus it is possible to therapeutically consume and discharge memories of state-led violence within the self-enclosed space of the museum as part of a pedagogy of tolerant, multicultural national citizenship, even as cross-border, extra-legal violence is enacted in the name of those same values on distant territories. Indeed, curatorial spaces of mourning and redemption in one place may actively displace memory of lives lost to the same violence elsewhere, thereby reterritorializing the effects of global warfare as an occasion for nation-building (Butler 2004; Brown 2006).

ZONE FOUR: INSTITUTIONAL TIMES

The organization of time and space constructed by architectural education is rarely a subject for critical reflection. Yet assumptions about temporality play a powerful role in the defining spaces of architectural knowledge within larger curricular structures. Time provides the context for architectural design, the taxonomic structure for architectural history and theory, and the framework for creative production in the studio. A general shortage of time in architectural education is socially produced through continuous deadlines and ambiguously defined expectations of quality. Time's scarcity makes it valuable, and something that must be managed and even produced by students through self-discipline and innovations in efficiency (Crysler, 1995; Stevens 1998). On the one hand 'taking too much time' may result in failure; on the other hand, in a culture of scarcity, those who efficiently manage and create stockpiles of time are at a definite advantage. They are able to forestall the future (deadline) by stretching out the present.

Mark Wigley suggests that design education is 'all about time'. The verbal narratives students provide for their design projects act as synchronizers of space and time. The construction of time occurs simultaneously with the production of space, and acts as its legitimating framework:

> Architecture is normally presented as an environment for events rather than an event in itself. Things happen in and around buildings, but the structure supposedly just stands there. A sense of time is carefully constructed by every architect. Each is an expert in the nuances of such a construction. They tell stories about time that have the effect of naturalizing their projects. The building must appear to naturally fit into a certain time. The project is located 'in' time. Time becomes an interior, a space, a site for the project. (Wigley 2000, 37)

The struggle for time is not limited to the realm of studio education. Faculty are also governed by differing temporalities of production. The careers of academic practitioners are synchronized through patrons and commissions that are in turn tied to the expansion and retraction cycles of the economy; research has its own temporal clock, which oscillates between continuous increases in the pace of production demanded by the institution, and the diverse temporalities of the publishing industry (with 'slow' presses, and extended peer review processes operating in tension with the professional pressure to accumulate citations and the instantaneous speed of internet mash-ups). (See also Dana Cuff's arguments in Section 5 about the modes and temporality of disciplinary change.) The experience of time in architectural education therefore shifts in pace and intensity depending on the sub-area and one's relative position in the institutional hierarchy (which permits different levels of control over time). More broadly, the general scarcity of time creates the conditions of (im)possibility for critical reflection on the practices and institutions of architecture.

Periodization and pedagogy

Euro-American architectural education has been continuously redefined through its changing relation to past, present and future times. For example, in the late nineteenth and early twentieth century, architectural training in the West was anchored in tradition and precedent related to historical models, by the mid-century historicism had largely been supplanted by the future-directed approaches of modernism, a transformation in institutional organization that was matched by the marginalization, if not complete disappearance of architectural history from the curriculum. Some two decades later, the past returned again, through the debates associated with postmodern historicism, reestablishing the link between studio instruction and 'history for architects' (Wright and Parks 1990). More recently, the rise of digital technology and renewed interest in ecology and sustainability suggest that the temporal axis of architectural education may once again be shifting towards the future times of techno-utopia, marked by a renewed faith in the problem-solving potential of science and the machine (Jarzombek 1999; Pyla 2008). Others have argued that the environmental crisis demands a return to 'pre-modern' times (see the arguments around this position outlined in Section 7).

The foregoing suggests that architectural education operates within envelopes of time whose parameters are unstated but widely held. Research on canon formation has extended these arguments historically, revealing how imperial time and space is constituted in narratives of architectural history. For example, at the height of British imperialism, when Banister Fletcher produced his famous tree of architectural history, entire regions of the world were defined as 'non-historical' and therefore outside temporal progression. As Gülsüm Baydar Nalbantoglu notes, when Fletcher's survey was updated posthumously for the seventeenth edition, all the 'non-historical' styles were converted into history, but on terms determined in advance by the encompassing logic of Fletcher's system. In this sense, non-compliant styles disappeared even as they became visible historically (Nalbantoglu 1998).

This system's adaptability, and its capacity to represent new incorporations as natural extensions of the existing order, have enabled it to persist as the foundational framework in the construction of historical time in architecture. The temporal system of synchronization has itself been preserved through modifications that leave its core premise frozen in time. Recent attempts to overturn the exclusionary, ethnocentric basis of texts such as Fletcher's through the production of a 'global architectural history' involve systematic reconceptualizations of how time is defined and represented. The recently published *Global History of Architecture*, for example, replaces Fletcher's evolutionary tree with an historical chronology of crisis and change that extends at regular intervals back to 3000 BC (Ching et al. 2006). A sequence of 'temporal cuts', imposed at regular intervals across the millennia, are intended to create openings onto successive movements of crisis and modernization, thereby positing intervals of dissolution and redefinition occurring synchronically across global space as a principle of historical time. The virtual collection of objects that becomes visible within the structures of architectural knowledge depends on processes of synchronization. Exemplary objects are positioned through discourse in relation to conceptions of time. Thus a politics of architectural knowledge involves not only questions of space, but also those of time, and the often overlooked assumptions that inform its representation.

The canon of architectural history, when organized according to formal and stylistic attributes, is defined by the criteria buildings represent as taxonomic projections. The shift in architectural history over the last two decades away from formal systems of classification and towards forms of understanding that stress buildings as social space has resulted in a parallel rethinking of temporality. Buildings are increasingly understood as the medium of social change, rather than reflections of given formal categories: they are shaped by the social processes in which they are embedded. This shift does not eliminate the processes of synchronization in historical representation, but rather, changes the terms upon which they are based.

CONCLUSION

The zones of the past traced above underscore the materiality of time: temporality is intertwined with the production, occupation and use of space. Time enables the past to 'take place'. If the arguments outlined above are indebted to the insights surrounding the 'spatial turn' and the reciprocal relationship between time and space, recent scholarship points toward the ascendency of another turn, one which moves away from the interdependence of time and space, and towards the realm of affect. The aim of what Nigel Thrift has called 'non-representational theory' seeks to displace the historic determinations of language and subjectivity as sources of meaning, through an emphasis on prelinguistic experiences of affect (Thrift 2007). This area of investigation, sometimes referred to as speculative realism, is expanding with the same intensity and breadth of influence attributed to memory studies. In many ways it is diametrically opposed to the latter's assumptions: the 'affective turn' seeks to redistribute subjective qualities outside the self.

Affect is, in the Deleuzian formulation that has proven most influential in outlining its anti-subjective character, 'hazy and atmospheric', a non-discursive sensation (Deleuze 1996, cited in Navaro-Yashin 2007). It is perhaps not surprising that affect has also become synonymous with the rhizome, and is now associated with the same liberatory potential that rhizomatic form metaphorically signaled in architectural discourse a decade ago (Crysler 2003; Buchanan and Lambert 2005). Affect, like its fibrous correlate, cannot be sited, cornered or controlled; above all, it is against history and is 'antigenealogy' (Navaro-Yashin, 2007). It opens up the possibility of an ontology of the material world, in which physical spaces radiate emotion, and objects have agency (Stewart 1996; 2007; see also McClough and Halley 2007; Ripley et al. 2009). Indeed, the affective turn, in its embrace of the body and emotion as a way of knowing the world, seems almost irresistible, occupying the same critical high ground as museums of national trauma. Yet, as Clare Hemmings notes, 'while affect may constitute a valuable critical focus in context, it frequently emerges through a circular logic designed to persuade "paranoid theorists" into a more productive state of mind, for who would not prefer affective freedom to social determinism?' (Hemmings 2005, 548).

The interdependence, even equivalence between the material and immaterial in the affective turn, notes Navaro-Yashin, resonates with (and in some cases is represented through) Actor Network Theory (ANT). In the mode of analysis advanced by Bruno Latour, ANT involves the flattening of time in an effort to generate symmetry between different modes of agency. But Navaro-Yashin goes further and suggests that Latour's claims of non-human agency are invoked transcendentally:

> Latour argues, without ethnographic specification or historicization, that subjects and objects are always already entangled with one another, imagining a 'flat' or horizontal network of assemblages between humans and non-human entities for all times … (Navaro-Yashin 2007, 9)

In the process, the network becomes an all-inclusive, pervasive phenomenon, capable of reaching across time and disciplines. Navaro-Yashin suggests that the potentially limitless assemblages of ANT need to be complemented with a theory of sovereignty and history that 'cuts' the dimensions of interpretation in relation to specific circumstances.

IN THE RUINS OF INNOVATION

At once a challenge to the deterministic 'sociologism' of some accounts of space and time, and a framework for the negation of one 'turn' by another, the growing emphasis on affect (and the related interest in human/non-human networks) also underscores what might be called the ruinous potential of academic knowledge. In his book, *The University in Ruins*, Bruce Readings describes the shift underway from the liberal humanist university of national culture to the transnational university of corporate excellence (Readings 1996). The shift has only intensified since Readings' book was published, with the metaphor of ruin now operating less as future vision than description of a disintegrating institutional present (see for example, Newfield 2008). Readings' metaphorical ruins recall the writings of Walter Benjamin, who employed the same figure to signify the violence of progress and the ever-accumulating storm of debris left in its wake. Though I have cited this argument in relation to the physical artifacts of the built environment (as well as the voids that mark their destruction) in earlier sections of this chapter, Benjamin returns to the metaphor of ruins to describe the production of knowledge. He argues that the drive for innovation leaves an accumulating pile of discarded paradigms in its wake (Benjamin 1970).

The process of ruination cuts across the theory workshops of architectural culture, where 'new' theories routinely replace old ones in quick succession, backed up by the continuous recourse to space-clearing periodizations and, as pointed out in the introduction to this volume, an accelerating production of 'posts' (the postmodern, post-critical, post-human, amongst others). In this, architecture participates in the 'cascading temporalities of forgetting' (Connerton 2009, 78) in which not only paradigms, but careers and entire institutions are lionized and then forgotten, even as a part of architectural education demands committing names and biographies to memory. The paradox is also repeated at a societal level, where, as the articles in this section show, the expanding production of history, memory and tradition occurs alongside temporalities of forgetting. The authors traverse the gap between memory and forgetting: a space where, as Connerton notes, 'hypermnesia' is continuously provoked by 'a political economic system which systematically generates a post-mnemonic culture', or a modernity that forgets (147).

ACKNOWLEDGEMENTS

I would like to thank Shiloh Krupar, Wanda Liebermann and Katerina Ruedi Ray for their comments on previous drafts of this chapter. I am also grateful to Kahwee Lee and Shiloh Krupar for their bibliographic suggestions for the final part of the chapter on the 'affective turn'. Responsibility for the text is, however, entirely my own.

17

Preservation and Modernity: Competing Perspectives, Contested Histories and the Question of Authenticity

Mrinalini Rajagopalan

The coupling of the concepts of preservation and modernity, as complementary rather than contradictory phenomena has been a fundamental aspect of theories of architectural preservation. Whilst the preservation of monuments has a long history spanning back many centuries, it was the particular pressures sparked by the Industrial Revolution and modernization that generated philosophical inquiries into the meaning of the historic monument as well as inspiring policies for its preservation. Since its inauguration in the modern era though, preservation theory has responded to and indeed been shaped by various forces. These include the colonial encounter; the identity politics of nationalism; the commodification of heritage through tourist practices; and the use of heritage as a catalyst for urban redevelopment and gentrification. The dialectic that shapes preservation discourse as essentially focused on the objects of the past, but ineluctably shaped by the concerns of the present is a central theme of this chapter.

Two core concepts will frame the discussion of preservation as an institutional process as well as epistemological debate in this chapter. The first is the concept of authenticity, which has operated as a foundational conception in theories of preservation both historically and in the present. It received considerable attention from philosophers and historians in the late nineteenth century, as industrialization was fundamentally changing the physical environments of the Western and non-Western world, and architectural monuments began to occupy a prominent place in narratives of civilizational progress and national identity. The etymology of the word authenticity can be traced to the Greek root 'authentes', meaning author, and the earliest uses of the concept of authenticity were linked to evaluating objects and artifacts as original and genuine as opposed to counterfeits or reproductions (Benjamin 1969; Matero 2007). In addition, by the late eighteenth century, the rise of capitalist economies and nationalisms around the world had led to the idea that modern societies were those that were marked by the individual rather than the collective. The radical rise of individualism in the era of modernity was not only marked by the ownership of property and the freedom of choice, but also the laying of claims to a particular set of 'authentic' histories and traditions that would differentiate modern individuals from premodern societies defined by kinship networks and collective living. In the modern era, authenticity thus functioned as a marker of not just objects but also of 'modern individuals' who were able to position themselves within the trajectory of civilizational progress rather than as simply a member of a collective mass (Berman 1970; Hobsbawm and Ranger 1983; Handler 1988). From France's efforts to establish national policies to protect historic monuments or the nostalgic lamentation for traditional architecture in Britain to the popular movement to save structures like Mt. Vernon by deeming them 'national monuments' in North America, the mid- to late nineteenth century was marked by a renewed interest in the preservation of architectural monuments as authentic documents of irretrievable pasts. As the historian Francois Choay has argued, the ruptures caused by the Industrial Revolution propelled scholars to recalibrate the history of human creation as two distinct phases: 'a "before", to which the historic monument was relegated, and an "after", where modernity began' (Choay 2001). Such teleological conceptualizations of modernity were also, however, deeply embedded within the structural violence of colonialism, whereby the physical and cultural resources of the non-Western world were appropriated and or redefined to serve the ideology of colonization (Said 1979; Fanon 1963). The trope of authenticity was a recurrent theme in the narrative of colonial domination as well, with the representation of certain indigenous architectural styles and urban forms, as 'vernacular' or 'premodern' (Wright 1991; Çelik 1997); or the classification of vastly different architectural objects from diverse contexts into ethnic or linguistic rubrics such as Islamic, Hindu, or Buddhist by colonial historiographers (Guha-Thakurta 2004; Abu-Lughod 1987). Indeed architectural preservation worked alongside other technologies of the nineteenth century such as photography and the spectacle of World's Fairs to represent the cultural resources of the colonized world as the primitive other to the modernizing Western world (Morton 2000; Pelizzari 2003).

While authenticity formed the epistemological foundation for the theories of preservation, it was also the basis for several conservation charters, policy documents, and legislative tracts that marked the formalization of preservation initiatives in many parts of the world. Therefore, the second concept that guides this discussion of preservation and modernity is the role that institutional regulation has played in the selection, classification, and management of monuments from the nineteenth century onwards. Rather than force a false (and inaccurate) separation between the theoretical debates surrounding the historic monument and the policies of architectural preservation, this chapter is meant to highlight the connections between them and emphasize that the theory and practice of architectural preservation have been and continue to be deeply imbricated within one another. In other words, it is impossible to understand the calls for architectural preservation as championed by Viollet-le-Duc in France or John Ruskin in Britain, without understanding the parallel emergence of museums and archives dedicated to conserving the partrimony of these nations or the professionalization of archaeology as a discipline. The urgency to preserve historic monuments as 'authentic' documents of the past, was a product of modernization rather than a reaction to it. Moreover, in order to implement the values of authenticity and historical accuracy so that they could be commonly understood by amateurs and experts alike, these abstractions had to be instrumentalized and managed via the bureaucracy of modernity such as institutions, charters, policy regulations, etc.

This chapter is arranged according to four loose chronological sections that mark significant shifts in preservation theory and policy. Following from the origins of preservation theory as an elite Western European discourse, the first section titled 'Preservation as a Discourse of Nation and Empire' explores the global transmission and local appropriations of preservation in various contexts through the processes of colonialism and nationalism. The ideologies of preservation that underwrote the narratives for nascent nationalisms as well as the dominance of empire in various parts of the world is the focus of this first section. The second section, 'Preservation in the Post-War World', looks at the internationalization of preservation discourse following World War II. Authenticity was the dominant theme of policy initiatives espoused by institutions such as UNESCO, ICOMOS, ICCROM, etc. for the cataloging, salvaging, and stewardship of monuments around the world. The significant shifts in historic preservation brought on by the emergence of postmodernism as a philosophical discourse and architectural movement is the substance of the third section titled, 'Preservation and Postmodernism'. Here I address the greater inclusion of various types of agents as well as objects into the previously narrow canon of preservation, due to the fragmentation of linear notions of history; the co-option of preservation to strengthen national and ethnic identities; as well as the further commodification of heritage through the processes of tourism and themeing. The final section of the chapter, 'The Globalization of Preservation' focuses on the production and management of architectural heritage as a commodity in the cycles of global capitalism. Whilst this chapter argues that the beginnings of modern preservation theory have been inflected by global processes, such as colonialism, since the nineteenth century, this last section focuses on the increasing collusion between preservation practices, urban renewal, tourism, and gentrification in late-twentieth-century constructions of place.

PRESERVATION AS A DISCOURSE OF NATION AND EMPIRE

The simultaneous emergence of nationalist consciousness and historic preservation in the nineteenth century was neither coincidental nor unrelated. Eric Hobsbawm and Terence Ranger have identified this historic period with the 'invention of traditions' with new nations laying claim to unique origin narratives that were dependent upon long-enduring histories and attendant cultural symbols such as architecture, literature, food, rituals, and costumes (Hobsbawm and Ranger 1983). As Timothy Mitchell has argued: 'One of the odd things about the arrival of the era of the modern nation-state was that for a state to prove that it was modern, it helped if it could also prove that it was ancient' (Mitchell 2002, 179).

The use of architectural preservation as a scaffolding for representing the collective past of a nation is perhaps nowhere more evident than in nineteenth-century France, particularly with Viollet-le-Duc's techniques of preservation, which were articulated less as a means to conserve the physical form of a historic monument but rather, to reveal the universal principles of cultural progress that had led to its creation. In France, industrialization was understood as the inevitable outcome of civilizational progress and the historic monument was seen as a signifier of the nation's teleological development into modernity (Jokilehto 1999). In other words, the key role of preservation was to provide a sturdy narrative of the history of national development (Rabinow 1989). This view led French preservationists such as Viollet-le-Duc to follow a radical interventionism when it came to restoring monuments to their original form and style – an ideology that would shape the preservation movement in France as well as its many colonies (Dupont 1966;

Huxtable 1983). Pierre Nora has argued that the consolidation of tangible sites of heritage at this time went hand in hand with the creation of other historical institutions such as archives and museums, whereby an older model of experiential and spontaneous memory was substituted with official sites and documents of history (Nora 1989). Nora's concept of the modern institutionalization of memory as history was apparent in the destruction of large parts of Parisian fabric by prefect of the city Baron Haussman on one hand, and on the other hand, the protection of selected monuments by the Historical Monuments Office, of which Viollet-le-Duc was an active member (Rabinow 1989).

Narratives of preservation as a nationalist cause also emerged in various nineteenth-century descriptions of heroic individuals struggling to save their nation's patrimony. For example the history of preservation in the United States has placed much emphasis on the agency of individuals such as Ann Pamela Cunningham in the rescue of Mt. Vernon and John D. Rockefeller's contribution to the restoration of colonial Williamsburg, thereby crediting them as visionaries who saved the nation's historic structures (Hosmer 1965).[1] As Max Page and Randall Mason have argued, the saving of Mt. Vernon has been seized as the ur-moment of historic preservation in the United States, thus mythologizing the characters as well as their motivations in a larger narrative of national consciousness (Page and Mason 2004). However, as Daniel Bluestone reminds us, the prominent role of women in nineteenth-century preservation in the United States was motivated by their 'stewardship of domestic and national morality and as part of their role in educating children for citizenship' (Bluestone 1999, 301).[2] Indeed, it is important to understand the work of the Mt. Vernon Ladies Association as not simply an act of historic preservation but within the nineteenth-century social context where upper-class American women actively took on the role of social and moral reformers. The urgency to preserve Mt. Vernon cannot be separated from the nineteenth-century anxieties over increased immigration and the concomitant desire to canonize the nation's origins as marked by elite-male privilege.

Similarly in the early twentieth century, Germany historic preservation was given impetus by the concept of *Heimat* (or homeland), which was embedded in the belief that historic monuments, landscapes and cities had the ability to arouse national sentiment and belonging in the nation's citizens (Umbach and Hüppauf 2005; Koshar 1998). This concept of belonging was aggressively co-opted by the Third Reich who used urban planning and architectural monumentality to represent myths of racial purity and to justify the authority of the Nazi regime, which often meant a radical reinscription of historical meaning.[3] The architectural vocabulary of monumental classicism, was favoured over historical eclecticism on the grounds that the former represented racial purity, socialism and anti-capitalist sentiment, a representation of power that would also be replicated by other fascist regimes, such as that of Benito Mussolini in Italy (Koshar 1998; Fuller 2007).

For the emergent nation-states around the world in the nineteenth century, architectural preservation served as a tectonic record of their unique and glorious pasts. In doing so, historic monuments underpinned hegemonic national narratives that could not rely on the fragmented and contested memories of the various peoples that they claimed to represent. Indeed as Pierre Nora has remarked, '[modern memory] is, above all, archival. It relies entirely on the materiality of the trace, the immediacy of the recording, the visibility of the image' (Nora 1989, 13). It was precisely in their canonization as historic monuments that many buildings gained currency as authentic markers of the nation's past, thereby also linking authenticity to modern institutions of authority, such as the nation-state.

In addition to nationalism, theories of preservation that acknowledge its role within (rather than in opposition to) modernity have benefitted from the study of colonial processes. Over the last two decades, a wide range of scholars have argued that industrialization and imperialism were concomitant projects that shaped preservation discourse in the centres of Euro-American domination as well as the colonies. Studies of preservation in North Africa, Indochina, India, etc. followed Edward Said's conceptualization of orientalism and the European imperialist construction of the non-West as 'other' (Said 1979). Post-Saidian theories regarding preservation have marked a distinct shift from the assumption of cultural geography and historical value as naturalized categories of valuation to a broader understanding of the invention of cultures and geographies through Eurocentric notions of difference. Architectural preservation was only one of many ways through which the systems of difference, between colonizer and colonized, were established and maintained. Others included the display of history via the spectacles of World's Fairs and exhibitions; the display of physiognomic difference between the races in museums; and the use of literature and painting as systems of imperial domination (Said 1993; Mitchell 1988; Morton 2000; Bennett 2004).

One example of such strategies of othering, as outlined in seminal studies by Timothy Mitchell, was the representation of Cairo in the World's Fair of 1881 in Paris, as a dusty and exotic panorama complete with Oriental dancing girls and donkeys for transportation (Mitchell 1991). Such 'authentic' representations of Cairo bore little resemblance to the actual city which was rapidly modernizing at the time as per the vision of its ruler, Khedive Ismail (Adham 2004). Despite these indigenous attempts at modernization, the colonial apparatus of historic preservation in nineteenth-century Cairo (the Comité de Conservation des Monuments de l'Art Arabe), was committed to freezing the city's heritage so that it could comply with Victorian perceptions of a 'medieval, Islamic' city in contrast to Europe's own historical past and present – a process that Irene Bierman has referred to as the 'medievalization of Cairo' (Bierman 2005). Colonialism thus had a profound influence on the manner in which non-Western 'heritage' was constructed along orientalist lines in the West. Thus, whilst authenticity was seized in Europe and North America to denote national uniqueness or as a claim to modernity; in the colonial context, authenticity appeared as a spectacle that marked the colonized as outside the modern.

As it was with the 'medievalization' of Cairo, the histories and geographies of many other colonial cities were also subject to aggressive edition and redaction. For example the formalization of historic preservation in India began with the establishment of the Archaeological Survey of India (ASI), by the British colonial government in the late nineteenth century to catalogue architecture and antiquity in the subcontinent.[4] Colonial notions of India's past were based on a crude, evolutionary logic of history and the separation of ethnographic groups into distinct and immutable categories. Thus ancient India was defined as Hindu and Buddhist, followed by a medieval period dominated by Islamic rule, which in turn was superseded by the colonial period of modernity. This notion of history was translated into a scientific taxonomy through which India's monuments were classified into strict categories, that left little room for interpretations of cultural or aesthetic syncreticism (Metcalf 1989; Asher and Metcalf 1994). The inequality of power in the colonial context allowed the colonizers to represent conjectural theories of ethnic and racial difference as scientific knowledge.

Modern technologies (photography and museums) along with the rise in tourism played a large role in the commodification of colonial heritage as well as the construction of national identities. For example, in addition to the picturesque depictions of 'ancient' India on postcards, photographs, and paintings that circulated widely in the British empire; reproductions of architectural details were exhibited in British museums as a means to illustrate Indian history (and Britian's place within it) to audiences in the colonial metropole (Pelizzari 2003; Breckenridge 1989). Heritage management also played a large part in staging national spectacles such as those organized by Benito Mussolini in fascist Italy, where in an effort to position himself as the modern successor of past Italian emperors, he recreated tableaux of what he perceived as 'traditional Renaissance towns' and 'revived' Renaissance festivals all over the country (Lasansky 2004).

The development of preservation theory in the late nineteenth and early twentieth century must be understood as an important thread within other epistemological constructions of modernity, architecture, and urbanism. For example, the Euro-American notions of history as civilizational progress that undergirded preservation ideology were also echoed in texts such as *Space, Time and Architecture* (Giedeon 1941); in the construction of 'modernism' as an ahistorical period as well as architectural style in the debates advanced by the members of CIAM; and in Le Corbusier's proposals for functionalism in architectural and urban design; and calcified by the International Style exhibition at the Museum of Modern Art in New York in 1932 (Mumford 2000). The development of heritage practices around the world worked in tandem with (rather than in opposition to) these other memes that championed the teleological notions of historical progress, and represented the rupture between 'historic' and 'modern' periods as absolute truths.

PRESERVATION IN THE POST-WAR WORLD

The interwar and immediate post-World War II periods were marked by several divergent trends in preservation theory and practice. On the one hand, there was a significant destruction of heritage due to aerial bombardment in parts of Europe, extensive suburbanization and related urban blight in the United States, and violence and chaos left in the wake of decolonization in several parts of the world. On the other hand, this was also a moment marked by the increasing professionalization of architectural preservation across the world. The celebratory narrative of individual agency and philanthropic heroism that had dominated preservation since the nineteenth century in the United States, gave way to increasingly urgent calls for the establishment of schools of preservation. In 1940, the founders of the Society of Architectural Historians claimed historic preservation as central to the workings of the Society and the following year it dedicated a roundtable to the issue of preservation (Bluestone 1999).[5] By the mid-1970s and early 1980s dozens of new public history certificate and degree programmes had emerged across the United States to train historians for careers in museums, archives, historic preservation agencies and public policy settings.

The professionalization of preservation in the post-war United States was also supported by federal sponsorship and urged on by the destruction of vast areas of historic fabric in many US cities due to the impact of large-scale urban renewal projects. The programs of the New Deal offered much government support and funding for the National Park Service and other bodies dedicated to historic preservation. As Charles Hosmer has suggested, the rampant destruction of historic areas through New Deal road-building and urban renewal projects led to calls for a more systematic approach to preservation (Hosmer 1981). However, the federal designation of 'national' heritage sites during this time was often accompanied by the exclusion or marginalization of subaltern groups such as women, African-Americans, and Native Americans from the landscape as well as the history of the American nation-state (Shackel 2001).

Heritage narratives also became the basis for revisionist architectural histories that favoured typologies of style and aesthetics. For instance Daniel Bluestone has argued that the 'Chicago School' of architecture was a historical construction that followed in the wake of a 1933 exhibition curated by the MOMA and titled 'Early Modern Architecture, Chicago 1870–1910' (Bluestone 1994). The exhibition helped to canonize as a style a diverse group of architects who may not necessarily have identified themselves with a particular 'school'. Once institutionalized as such, this narrative served as to legitimate the city's history, especially during the 1950s and 1960s, when the expansion of inner city public housing was perceived as a threat to the 'historic fabric' made up of Chicago School architecture (Bluestone 1994). In the post-war building boom, architects worked with property developers, and politicians in the hope that the revival of the downtown might reverse inner city decline and improve Chicago's post-war reputation, illustrating Max Page and Randall Mason's claim that, preservation in the United States has been driven by a 'local, "civic patriotism" that has been closely allied with boosterism' (Page and Mason 2004, 10).[6]

Growing concerns in the post-World War II period about the destruction of heritage through rapid urbanization were also echoed in the many schemes to 'rebuild' Britain after the war. The large scale destruction of entire swathes of urban fabric during the Blitz, overcrowding in cities, and the spread of Corbusier-inspired modernist new towns were some of the many challenges faced by planners and preservationists in Britain. In 1947, a committee on Reconstruction in the City of London proposed to rebuild the urban fabric with historic buildings retained alongside new construction in a relatively harmonious manner, signalling a new trend in urban reconstruction that invoked picturesque visions of medieval townscapes (Holden and Holford 1951). Gordon Cullen, the noted English architect, urban designer and founder of the Townscape movement, supplied many of the designs for the committee's report, which included the creation of public squares and parks, shady avenues and quaint riverfront development in order to provide a cohesive image of London after the war (Cullen 2006 [1961]).[7] Cullen's ideas were framed as a counter to the dehumanizing and anonymous nature of modernist architecture (particularly the new towns and housing towers), which was beginning to be roundly criticized in publications like the *Architectural Review* during the 1950s (Hall 1988; Ellin 1996).[8]

A key development of the interwar and post-World War II years was the 'internationalization' of preservation theory as well as practice, through the drafting of Charters such as the Athens Charter (1931) and the Venice Charter (1964) as well as the establishment of global organizations such as UNESCO (1945), ICCROM (1956), and ICOMOS (1965). Whilst there is no doubt that even the late-eighteenth-century preservation debates were forged within a climate of global processes, such as colonialism and nation building, the international preservation movements of the 1930s and later sought to standardize the meaning of heritage and the practices of its conservation. For example, the Athens Charter of 1931 produced by the First International Congress of Architects and Technicians of Historic Monuments, had the primary goal of devising a set of preservation mandates that would standardize the divergent and sometimes haphazard methods of reconstruction around the world. To this end it called for the recognition of monuments as authentic historic documents, worthy of preservation but not objects that could be copied and rebuilt in the modern day.[9]

The damage to historic urban fabric left in the wake of World War II prompted the Hague Convention to draft the Convention for the Protection of Cultural Property in the Event of Armed Conflict in 1954. This was followed by the Venice Charter in 1964 which was drafted by a team of international delegates as a guiding framework for historic preservation around the world. The document employs authenticity as a fundamental criterion in the classification of monuments as heritage (Jokilehto 1985) and begins with a definition of heritage as tradition:

> Imbued with a message from the past, the historic monuments of generations of people remain to the present day as living witnesses of their age-old traditions. People are becoming more and more conscious of the unity of human values and regard ancient monuments as a common heritage. The common responsibility to safeguard them for future generations is recognized. It is our duty to hand them on in the full richness of their authenticity. (Venice Charter, cited in Williams et al. 1983, 198)

By carefully avoiding any reference to the nation, region, or local interpretations of historic monuments, the Charter advances its case for a universal definition of heritage that can be applied to various global contexts. The use of the Athens and Venice Charters as the basis for preservation work carried out by international organizations such as UNESCO, ICOMOS and ICCROM has furthered a monolithic and largely Eurocentric definition of tradition, heritage and authenticity, concepts which are culturally complex and deeply contested.[10]

The Venice Charter was written in the same year that Bernard Rudofsky's exhibition 'Architecture without Architects' was presented at the Museum of Modern Art in New York. The exhibition featured an eclectic collection of photographs of vernacular and indigenous architectural forms around the world that were built by 'non-pedigreed' builders and whose forms were determined by factors such as climate, community needs, and local building materials rather than aesthetic style or the professional genius of the architect. Besides opening a conversation about vernacular built forms, the exhibition challenged the conventional dichotomies between high and low architecture; building and design; modern and traditional; etc. These binaries had previously been calcified by architectural historians such as Nicholas Pevsner who in his book, *An Outline of European Architecture* (Pevsner 1943), had made the famous distinction between a building (using the example of a bicycle shed) and architecture (as in the Lincoln Cathedral). Whilst Rudofsky's exhibit and its celebration of vernacular forms signalled a clear departure from these modernist paradigms, it should be understood within a growing discourse about the everyday, which had been set in motion by philosophers such as Henri Lefebvre and Michel de Certeau (Upton 2002).

The post-war appropriation of vernacular architecture as heritage was also given much impetus by the emergence of new nation-states all over the world. For example in Egypt, the preservation of the Pharaonic past went alongside the building of new villages that mimicked vernacular forms and the technology in an effort to aggrandize the Egyptian peasant as an important subject of the nation-state (Al Sayyad 1995; Mitchell 2002). In other contexts such as Cambodia, concepts of heritage and authenticity were appropriated for macabre postcolonial representations of a new nation for an ethnically pure Khmer race (Edwards 2007). Meanwhile, the designation of monuments as World Heritage sites, brought in much needed tourist dollars for newly decolonized countries such as India, Morocco and Indonesia.

Post-war schemes represent a turning point in the discourse of preservation, not least because they mark the beginnings of urban movements that would depart from the academic debates regarding authenticity and historical value and move towards a strategy of 'development'. The scenographic ambience of tradition was deployed as an important part of a new vocabulary of urbanism in the Western and non-Western world, and paved the way for the further conflation of urban development, tourism and preservation.[11] For example, the preservation of the entire city of Bath in England, was spearheaded by the planner Patrick Abercrombie, who was most interested in highlighting the Georgian historic fabric of the city. Abercrombie's plans for Bath, however, clearly departed from the conservative approach that early British preservationists such as John Ruskin and William Morris had advocated by coupling aggressive development projects, such as the building of a civic centre and the development of new road networks, with historic conservation. Similar schemes of urban redevelopment were carried out for other historic cities in England and Scotland, most notably Warwick and Edinburgh (Pendlebury 2003). Preservation in the interwar and immediate post-war period thus set the stage for the themeing of urban environments as national, regional and local sites of heritage consumption.

PRESERVATION AND POSTMODERNISM

The 1970s defined a period of dramatic change in the conceptualization of the historic monument particularly calling into question accepted modalities of authenticity and linear notions of history. Postmodern philosophers such as Jean-François Lyotard theorized the end of historical master narratives and totalizing political and social theories, while others like Francis Fukuyama claimed the collapse of the Berlin Wall marked the 'end of history' driven by grand ideological conflicts between East and West (Lyotard 1984 [1979]; Fukuyama 1992). Meanwhile, architectural theorists such as Charles Jencks, proclaimed the end of architectural modernism and its espousal of universal absolutes, and called for its substitution with a spatial and formal pluralism that would also create more humane public space (Jencks 1977). Robert Venturi et al.'s polemic architectural text, *Learning from Las Vegas*, made similar claims, arguing for the abandonment of elitist definitions of architecture as high art and the embrace of the 'ugly and ordinary' (Venturi et al. 1977 [1972]). By the mid-1970s architects had abandoned modernist diktats such as 'Form Follows Function' or 'Less is More' for the playful use of symbols and historic icons to create a formal vocabulary that had wide and even popular appeal (Scott-Brown 1971). The exact end-point of architectural high modernism and its abrogation by postmodernism has been a continuing, albeit controversial, motif in architectural historiography. While some scholars, such as Jencks, have seen the dramatic demolition of the Pruitt-Igoe housing complex in St. Louis, Missouri as the 'death of modernism' yet others have pointed to Arthur Drexler's 1975 exhibition 'The Architecture of the Ecole des Beaux-Arts' at the Museum of Modern Art in New York as a trenchant critique of modernism at the very institution that had served to inaugurate architectural modernism in the 1930s. Whilst both these narratives of rupture have recently received critical treatment from historians who dismantle the dichotomy between modernity and post-modernity, it suffices to say that by the 1970s, modernism was eschewed as both philosophical discourse as well as architectural aesthetic.[12]

The theory and practice of architectural preservation did not remain unaffected by the emerging debates regarding postmodernism. Scholars such as Mario Carpo have argued that because postmodernism as a philosophy was based upon the fragmentation of master narratives including that of history and the collapse of centralized systems; it also provided a renewed impetus to preservation movements around the world. Relieved of the burden of standing as signifiers of a particular historical moment or as markers of cultural and social progress, monuments could now be construed as repositories of various and often contested meanings (Carpo 2007). Indeed Carpo suggests that, 'new monuments can have no power of historical orientation because the postmodern vision of history no longer provides any preset line of progress along which historical signs may be clearly situated ...' (Carpo 2007, 53). The recognition, and subsequent rejection, of the cultural and professional elitism that had so defined high modernism, was echoed by preservationists who began to turn a critical eye towards the narrow histories that preservation discourse had produced thus far.

Preservation policies were also not left unaffected by the social movements of the time; such as the civil rights movement in the United States, the increasing visibility of subaltern and aboriginal groups and the various campaigns that sought to expand national histories to include previously marginalized populations. These changes in the perception of history were well reflected in the Burra Charter, first drafted in 1979 (and later revised in 1981, 1988, and 1999) at the meeting of the Australian National Committee of ICOMOS in Burra, Southern Australia, where the definition of heritage was expanded to include 'natural, indigenous and historic places' of cultural significance.[13] Scholars have rightly remarked that the Burra Charter marked the shift to an 'archaeological model of heritage' (Miele 2005) where the cultural value of heritage would be determined by its context rather than *a priori* aesthetic hierarchies or hegemonic constructions of taste. In a similar vein, at the twentieth session of UNESCO held in Paris in 1978, the committee recognized the importance of emerging forms of media and communication and new economies of heritage consumption (such as tourism) in shaping 'culture industries' of the time (UNESCO 1982).

Preservationists in 1970s, also began to turn their attention to the buildings of the modern movement – a contentious development, considering that high modernism was, at least in theory if not always in practice, based on the rejection of historicity and historicism. Dominant tendencies in Euro-American modernism had emerged out of the belief in a universal aesthetic (i.e. the International Style) and attempted a scientific and rational response to the social world (as exemplified in Corbusier's dictum that the modern house is a 'machine for living'). However, by the 1970s many modernist buildings had accrued value as artifacts of historic importance and many were even adopted as cultural vestiges of modern nation-states. For example, Kevin Murphy claims that the preservation of the Villa Savoye in the mid-1960s can be seen as a campaign via which the 'building came to stand for French political autonomy and cultural attainment in the twentieth century' (Murphy 2002, 71). By absorbing Villa Savoye (as a pure example of early modernism) into a national schema of cultural symbols, France was able to make the claim that it had been an important site for the origins and growth of the modernist movement in the early twentieth century. In other words the Villa Savoye was preserved as a 'national' monument but one whose value was assessed in terms of its international import (Murphy 2002).

Similar to the nationalist desires that underwrote the appropriation of Villa Savoye, was the staging of Tel Aviv as a 'Bauhaus' city in the late 1980s and 1990s. As with the canonization of the Chicago School, here too a diverse set of modernist architectural practices from the 1930s was absorbed into a singular rubric of Bauhaus style modernism in the 1984 exhibition, 'White City: International Style Architecture in Israel, A Portrait of an Era'. Later, in 1994, the city underwent renovations, was painted white and turned into a museum of sorts for the 'Bauhaus in Tel Aviv' celebrations. Alona Nitzan-Shiftan suggests that the process situated the cultural legacy of Israel in an easily recognizable trajectory of European history while divorcing it completely from 'Arab' or Palestinian contexts and histories (Nitzan-Shiftan 1996). Even so, the concept of an international modernism was always framed here as elsewhere as a national phenomenon.[14] Furthermore, such representations deliberately locate the beginnings of modernism in Palestine with the growth of Zionism in the early twentieth century, thus erasing the indigenous Palestinians from this historical narrative of modernity. In 2003 when a part of the city built in the 1930s was declared a World Heritage Site by UNESCO, these intertwined mythologies of Zionism and architectural modernism were further calcified (Fuchs and Epstein-Pliouchtch 2008).

On the one hand, the preservation of modernist architecture often served to reinforce chauvinist narratives of the nation-state and emphasize its awakening into modernity. On the other hand, the emergence of revisionist and postcolonial histories in the 1970s also challenged the framing of national identity as monolithic and uncontested, by arguing that the imagination of the nation-state as an 'imagined community' (Anderson 1983) necessarily involved the marginalization of certain subjects. As Partha Chatterjee has remarked, the nation-state is in fact a fragile product of modernity, one that is constantly challenged by those 'fragments' that are excluded from its imaginary as well as its self-fashioning (Chatterjee 1993). Recent theories of preservation have tried to navigate a hegemonic ideal of nationhood whilst accommodating the histories of marginalized subjects and events.

The American historian, Dolores Hayden has called for a practice of preservation that would take into account the untold or invisible histories of ethnic minorities, immigrants and women – groups that have been traditionally ignored as contributors to the historic landscape (Hayden 1988). She urged the writing of new urban histories that took into account the revisionist social histories of the 1980s, which focused on the Latino or Japanese-American legacies of cities such as Los Angeles. She also records a change in the general understanding of preservation (in the United States) during the 1980s, as it became less targeted towards an exclusive and limited audience of architectural conservationists, historians, or developers interested in preservation, and more to larger communities that included 'humanities councils, historical societies, public history programs and individual scholars across the country' (Hayden 1988, 45). These new agendas of preservation as public history can be seen within the larger debates around multiculturalism and the need (particularly in the United States) to acknowledge the contribution of ethnic minorities and immigrants to the building of the nation and its cities.

The fragmentation of meta-narratives provoked by postmodern thinkers, opened up the discourse of preservation to include a wide variety of historical sites as well as agents into the otherwise narrow canon of heritage in many parts of the world. Indeed, postmodernism as a philosophy would redirect the concept of authenticity from purely aesthetic or historical values to include context-based definitions of value (as in the vernacular) as well as previously marginalized voices as new authorities of heritage. However, these postmodern histories were also mediated through and often strengthened through the nation-state, further reifying the institutional bureacuracies of modernity.

THE GLOBALIZATION OF PRESERVATION

In recent decades the theories and practices of preservation have had to position themselves within the epistemologies and processes of globalization. While some scholars have argued that globalization has recreated cities as the primary spaces of capital flows and transnational networks of financial management (Sassen 1991; Castells 1989); still others contend that the global processes of economic exchange and technological innovation are not without cultural and social ramifications (Appadurai 1996). Preservation discourse in the context of globalization has been marked by a variety of responses and theoretical models. For example, some scholars have paid attention to the increasing commodification of heritage and the blurring of lines between theme parks and heritage enclaves (Sorkin 1992; Zukin 1991). Indeed, many urban theorists argue that following the neo-liberal economic policies espoused by many nations in the 1980s, cities have capitalized on their cultural and historic resources to lure more capital investment into their urban centres (Harvey 2006; Smith, N. 1996). For example, by the late 1980s in the United States, partnerships between public and private interest groups had invested several millions of dollars to revitalize 650 'Main Streets' or historic downtowns in various small cities across the country (Stipe 2003). Meanwhile, the erasure of architectural and cultural artifacts due to recent ethnic conflicts such as in the case of Bosnia-Herzogovina, or the destruction of the Buddha statues in the Bamiyan valley of Afghanistan have evoked global rebuilding efforts that stress the universal value of local heritage (Herscher and Riedlmayer 2000; Adams 1993; see also Boyer in this section). Similarly, the commemoration of traumatic histories and spaces of the nation-state, such as the Japanese-American concentration camp at Manzanar in California, signals the importance of preservation in expanding nationalist histories, but also calls into question the role that 'dark tourism' plays in further commodifying such spaces for public consumption (Dubel 2001). Contrary to expectations that global processes would signal the end of the nation-state, even a cursory look at preservation apparatuses shows that the global management of heritage is continually mediated through national institutions and preservation continues to strengthen agendas of national, ethnic and even religious identity.

The challenges of assuming a universal definition of contested concepts such as authenticity emerged again with the drafting of the Nara Document of Authenticity (1994), which acknowledges the diversity of global cultural practices to be accommodated in the prescriptive maxims of preservation.[15] Whilst the Nara Document is written in response to the processes associated with globalization, it echoes the anxieties of early preservationists who saw industrialization as a homogenizing force and a threat to authenticity. For example, at the 1994 Nara conference, David Lowenthal argued that heritage was at risk from practices such as tourism, which often results in eroding the historical context in which it operates, but can also generate a deep ambivalence regarding authenticity in the tourists themselves (Lowenthal 1995). Referring to an example where a visitor was disappointed with the experience of a protected heritage town in France, but reacted favorably to the fascimile of Cro-Magnon paintings at Lascaux II, Lowenthal laments that, 'the erosion of ambience and context so demeans the authentic that contrived verisimilitude becomes preferable' (Lowenthal 1995, 124).

Indeed, the challenges to an absolute definition of authenticity have come from diverse institutional quarters, including the International Network for Traditional Building, Architecture and Urbanism (INTBAU), which lists the Prince of Wales as one of its founding patrons.[16] At a 2006 conference INTBAU sought to revise the Venice Charter, and especially its limitations regarding rebuilding, replicating or reproducing heritage sites, by arguing that much of these limitations came from the Charter's roots in modernism and the desire to isolate historical sites as separate and distinct from the new modern era via preservation.[17] In effect, INTBAU seeks to redefine heritage as continuing and lived tradition – an ideological position that has led it to support the recreation of neo-traditional villages in England, as well as the adaptive reuse of historic buildings. INTBAU takes an explicitly anti-modernization stance in urban and architectural development, going so far as to advocate the creation of model Victorian villages such as Poundbury in England – an authentic facsimile that is based upon a non-existent 'original' Victorian village. The neo-traditional movement in Britain has been paralleled by New Urbanism in the United States with the creation of towns such as Seaside in Florida and Disney's meticulously planned 'small town' of Celebration also in Florida. These urban enclaves which capitalize on the nostalgia for the Main Streets and long-lost communities in the United States and have been roundly criticized as little more than residential theme parks for wealthy bourgeois communities. (Davis and Monk 2007; Ross 1999).[18]

Since the 1980s, the debates regarding preservation have been expanded by anthropologists, sociologists and geographers who have examined the management of history via socio-political processes rather than the collection and display of antiquarian 'objects' (Lowenthal 1998; Al Sayyad 2001; 2004). Embedded within these discussions is the recognition that 'authenticity' and 'tradition' are concepts that are constantly redefined through complex processes of valuation, negotiation, and mediation. A key actor in the discussion of tradition as a new mobilization of history has been the International Association of the Study of Traditional Environments (IASTE), an interdisciplinary group that focuses on the continuing use and shifting meanings of 'tradition' particularly in the vernacular architecture of non-Western contexts (Al Sayyad and Bourdier 1986). In recent years, IASTE has focused its energies on the critical discussion of 'tradition' – a concept that had been gaining currency both in the postmodern creation of new cities and urban development in the United States and Britain as well as its emergence in the creation of new global practices of consumption such as tourism, the creation of gated communities and theme parks, etc. In a recent book on the subject of tradition, Nezar Al Sayyad (founder of IASTE) has argued that the acceleration of the heritage economy as a globalized process cannot be separated from the colonial histories of many nation-states, the rejection of modernism as a failed architectural discourse and the post-war instability of many nation-states around the world (Al Sayyad 2001). Following Anthony King's assertion that the colonial city was the forerunner of the contemporary global city (King 1990), IASTE has sought to insert the critical discussion of urban processes such as gentrification, urban themeing, the use of heritage as civic boosterism, etc., within the larger debates regarding historic preservation as a project of modernity (Crysler 2003).

The global politics of preserving colonial heritage, however, is fraught with several contradictory phenomena involving memorialization and the creation of tourist narratives. One of many examples, is the case of Hong Kong, where rampant property speculation and new development threatens and even renders moot the preservation of colonial heritage. Ackbar Abbas has termed the persistent liminality of Hong Kong's heritage as a 'space of disappearance', where the physical preservation of buildings and other historic objects has instead been replaced by the memorialization of colonial Hong Kong through photography exhibits and even cinema which capitalize on the nostalgia for a seemingly cosmopolitan yet colonial Hong Kong. Echoing Baudrillard's thesis that in the postmodern world, the replica often renders the original moot, Abbas posits that preservation 'is not memory. Preservation is selective and tends to exclude the dirt and the pain,' and the end goal of preservation often serves to 'bring about the disappearance of history' (Abbas 1997, 66). Hilde Heynen has argued similarly that the increasing attention to memorializing the past is coupled with an amnesia for the past or the lack of interest in history. She claims that the heritage industry may in fact pose a threat to 'historical objects' particularly in the urban realm, where authenticity is often bypassed for the creation of an 'image' that is palatable to tourists and will help the overall aesthetics of urban space (Heynen 1999a).[19]

The blurring of lines between monument and memorial, heritage and tourism, history and memory, is perhaps most apparent in the new directions that preservation has assumed in postcolonial contexts such as South Africa and its efforts to reconcile its apartheid past with postcolonial development. Constitution Hill, a mixed-use urban redevelopment project and heritage centre, is only one example of the collusion between sites of memorialization and monumental rebuilding projects. Built within the remants of the most notorious prison complex from the apartheid era, Constitution Hill attempts to insert South Africa's democratic postcolonial future into its history which includes a long struggle for basic human rights (Gevisser 2008). The critical reframing of concepts such as 'authenticity' and 'tradition' have also been echoed in new ventures in South Africa heritage display which prefer to illustrate the impossibility of reconstructing a singular historical narrative. For example, District Six in Johannesburg, an area where 'blacks', 'coloureds', 'whites', and 'Indians' once lived together, was later demolished because it did not conform to the strict racial segregation mandated by the apartheid regime (Coombes 2003). A museum in a former church remaining on the site is dedicated to reconstructing the history of apartheid in District Six through the fragmentary voices of its residents. The displays reveal the contested nature of historical reconstruction, particularly in the context of traumatic pasts. Here, authenticity is produced through the immediacy of the experience offered to the visitor by the voices of the original residents of District Six.

Whilst it can be tempting to read the increasing collusion between commodification and peservation as a recent phenomenon of globalization, it should be remembered that, as a product of modernity, preservation has always been embedded within and fashioned by distinctly global processes such as colonialism, capital networks of trade and cultural exchange and nationalist narratives. Similarly, like the nineteenth-century yearnings of Victorians for a pre-industrialized past; the present-day discourses and practices of preservation continue to be motivated by the same nostalgic impulses to recover lost histories, spaces or icons that may never have existed in the past. Most importantly preservation theory as well as policy continues to be defined by the quagmire of 'authenticity', a concept that has renewed purchase in the socio-cultural flux wrought by the forces of globalization.

CONCLUSION

Any discussion of architectural preservation as a theoretical discourse must acknowledge its roots in late-ninteenth-century conceptualizations of modernity. On the one hand, theories of preservation were forged at the intersection of phenomena such as the role of tradition in defining modernity; the colonial management of cultural resources in large parts of the developing world; the use of history to legitimate the emergence of nation-states; etc. On the other hand, the practices that defined heritage were reliant upon and indeed shaped by the bureacratic apparatuses and institutions of modernity, such as museums and archives. In addition, modern theories of preservation have had to contend with the ambivalences between the definitions of monument as a historic object and the monument as a commodity – a challenge that has only been accelerated through the phenomena of global tourism, urban boosterism, and the increasing commercialization of heritage across the world. It may be argued then that the central questions that dominate the field of preservation theory today are not much different from those that John Ruskin, William Morris, Viollet-le-Duc and Alois Riegl pondered more than a century ago: How is authenticity to be determined in a historic monument and what institutional practices would best ensure the posterity of monuments for the future?

David Scott has argued that any imagination of the past is ineluctably linked to the present, and that *how* we tell histories is as important as *what* we tell (Scott 2004). In terms of preservation theory, this would mean looking closely at the epistemological as well as institutional frameworks that produce heritage. For example, we might ask how the narrow and ultimately subjective framing of authenticity has replicated Euro-centric notions of heritage as well as history in various parts of the world. Or how the institutional narratives of heritage have played a role in fossilizing some representations of the past while silencing others. In this brief (and by no means exhaustive) chapter I have focused on scholarship that theorizes the monument as both an object of historic preservation as well as a product of modernity. It was the disconnectedness and anxiety brought on by modernity that necessitated a deliberate project of archiving the past and the search for locating history in 'authentic' documents of the past. If in recent decades the processes of globalization and the postmodern crisis of history have on one hand led to the rampant commodification of heritage it has also been coupled with a renewed interest in establishing universal norms for defining authenticity via heritage. The theories and practices of preservation over the last century have attempted to grapple with these paradoxes.

The theoretical discourse of preservation has also been enriched by analyses of institutionalized power. Foucault's path-breaking work on the disciplinary regulation of knowledge as a means of consolidating power (Foucault 1972) and Said's conceptualization of the use of culture as a means of maintaining imperial hegemony (Said 1979) have prompted the critical investigation of preservation practices as deeply embedded within and produced by complex power structures. It is no longer possible to study the heritage practices in postcolonial contexts such as Malaysia or Morocco, without also acknowledging their colonial roots. Similarly, official histories of the nation must be studied alongside related subaltern histories. And the scientific display and management of heritage is often intertwined with commercial interests and phenomena such as gentrification. Indeed, the discourse of preservation has benefitted much from the recent spate of literature that relies on case studies (from diverse global contexts) to illuminate the local and contextual particularities of preservation. However, the literature on preservation continues to remain divided over historical studies and preservation policies, the latter of which are often treated in an ahistorical or non-theoretical manner. Indeed, preservation discourse could be made much richer by new insights into the theories that have shaped the policies followed by UNESCO and other institutions in various contexts around the world. And while the histories of preservation have been greatly influenced by the 'interdisciplinarization' of discourse – i.e. its critical reconceptualization as a social, cultural and political phenomenon – the theoretical frameworks of preservation have received less attention in terms of such interdisciplinary analyses.

The future development of preservation discourse will require architectural historians and theorists to understand preservation as ineluctably imbricated within the forces of globalization, neo-liberalism and cosmopolitanism rather than a process that stands in opposition to them. To return to David Scott's notion that all constructions and perceptions of history are filtered through the anxieties as well as the expectations of the present, new theories must recognize that the meanings and manifestations of heritage are not static, but constantly produced by contemporary social, political and economic forces. A critical appraisal of preservation must also take into account the institutional regulation of preservation policies as well as the epistemological production of concepts such as 'authenticity' as mutually constitutive rather than as operating in separate realms of discourse and action. From the 'authentic' depiction of Cairo's streetscapes at the World's Fair of 1881 to the preservation of apartheid landscapes in late-twentieth-century South Africa, the complexities of heritage preservation have been persistent and enduring. The challenges of this century promise to be just as recondite and will demand understandings of preservation that go beyond the aperçus of universal objectification and absolute definitions.

NOTES

1 Charles Hosmer's, *Presence of the Past: A History of the Preservation Movement in the United States before Williamsburg*, an encyclopaedic overview of historic preservation in the United States, specifically does not include native American sites in the history of preservation on the basis that movements to preserve them follow a different pattern from the more iconic sites such as Mt. Vernon and Williamsburg. However, this type of historical representation squarely places Native American heritage outside of the 'national' narrative that is

imagined around early preservation movements, thereby marginalizing it as non-historical or ahistorical.

2 Preservation was often used as a didactic means to construct national identity as in the case of Litchfield – a New England town built in the vocabulary of Colonial Revivalism. Alan Axelrod argues that although the town was seen as a realistic representation of eighteenth century life in a Puritan society, it is more accurately a version of what elite society during the late nineteenth and twentieth century perceived as colonial (Axelrod 1985). He suggests that the social origins of the town can be traced back to nineteenth-century anxieties about modernization, rapid urbanization (and related concerns over increased immigration) which left Americans longing for a mythic past and for stable and ethnically homogenous communities. The belief in the ability of historic environments to educate and provide a morally restorative environment to the lay-public is evident in Harriet Beecher Stowe's memorialization of Litchfield as an idealized North American Utopian community in her 1878 novel *Poganuc People* – an idealized representation of a homogenous American community that was later appropriated as an emblem of American patriotism in the McCarthy era (Axelrod 1985).

3 As Rudy Koshar points out, 'whole urban fabrics were torn from their previous historical associations and transformed into total symbols of a myth-inspired racial community: Munich was the capital of the Nazi movement; Nuremberg, the city of party rallies; Goslar, the center of peasantist "Blood and Soil" ideology ... and Berlin ("Germania"), the capital of Hitler's new racial empire' (Koshar 1998, 156).

4 It should be noted here that while the colonial authorities may be credited with the formal establishment of an archaeological apparatus, this formalization would have certainly been preceded by many indigenous, albeit less formal methods of preservation. For example, in India, the posterity of many historic buildings that were also religious structures was ensured by the continuation of local rituals of worship and memorialization. It was also not uncommon in precolonial India for local regents and monarchs to provide stipends for the upkeep of monuments. An often cited example of such 'indigenous' preservation is the decision of Daulat Rao Sindhia, the ruler of Gwalior, to forbid the quarrying of stone from the Arhai din ka Jhonpra mosque (originally built in 1192 by the earliest Islamic rulers of the Indian subcontinent) as early as 1809 (Flood 2007).

5 A proposal put to the Society lamented that very little was being done in schools of art and architecture to properly educate graduates about the techniques of restoration and preservation, and argued that 'the business of caring for, restoring, and sometimes unearthing the nation's historical structures is a field into which, up till now, men and women have simply drifted by chance and temperament. The time has come when this casual source of personnel is inadequate to the demand' (Mason 1955).

6 Daniel Bluestone has argued that historic preservation in the United States was often accompanied by large-scale destruction of urban fabric that was deemed less worthy of preservation. For example, the designation of the Robie House in 1957 as a historic monument was accompanied by the demolition of more than 880 buildings in the Hyde Park neighbourhood to make way for the renewal of the University of Chicago campus (Bluestone 1994).

7 Cullen's book, *The Concise Townscape,* was an urban 'pattern book' of sorts where whilst bemoaning the dearth of interesting 'townscapes' that could sustain vibrant communities, he appealed for increased density and pedestrian-centred urban design, the 'town' as the centre for social diversity and activity.

8 Recently scholars have suggested that the desire to recover a 'lost' sense of urban and national community, was also deeply linked to the transition of England from an imperial power to a post-imperial nation-state. Jane M. Jacobs has argued that post-war efforts to redefine the urbanism of London in a local, traditional or vernacular idiom was propelled by a nostalgia for pre-war stability that was associated with a lost British imperial might. These anxieties coupled with growing demands for local empowerment translated into a post-war planning aesthetic that highlighted London's history as an imperial and commercial centre of power (Jacobs 1996).

9 International Network for Traditional Building, Architecture & Urbanism www.intbau.org/venicecharter.html (accessed August 1, 2008).

10 Whilst UNESCO was amongst the first organizations to propose 'global' policies for preservation, the early conferences, such as the first held in 1931 in Athens, were largely European in emphasis. The Venice conference of 1964 included only three non-European countries: Tunisia, Mexico, and Peru. Fifteen years later the World Heritage convention had been signed by twenty-four countries representing five continents, however the origins of these now 'global' policies regarding preservation remain mired in their Eurocentric origins (Choay 2001).

11 One of the first urbanists who proposed creatively using history in order to create 'ambient' urban environments was the nineteenth-century Viennese town planner Camillo Sitte. Like Gordon Cullen and Leon Krier who followed in the twentieth century, Sitte proposed using history to evoke a sentimentality

and a sense of community within urban subjects (Sitte 1979).

12 In critiquing the myth that Pruitt-Igoe marked the decisive end of the modernist movement, Kate Bristol has convincingly argued that the demolition of the complex had more to do with the deep structural problems of racial inequality and poor planning that had plagued the housing project from its very origins. Bristol also charts how the demolition of Pruitt-Igoe was appropriated as a dramatic signifier of the end of modernism and how this narrative gained increasing purchase with every re-telling (Bristol 1991). Similarly, Felicity Scott has argued that Arthur Drexler's curation of the Beaux-Arts exhibition, did not intend to replace architectural modernism with a historicist vocabulary of aesthetic forms. Instead, Scott posits that Drexler, partly sensing the imminent demise of modernism had hoped to open a debate that would historicize modernism as a phase of architectural production (Scott 2007).

13 www.nsw.nationaltrust.org.au/burracharter.html (accessed August 1, 2008).

14 For example Michael Levin, the curator of the 1984 exhibition had asked the following question in the exhibition catalogue: 'What is national in the International Style?' The answer provided was that the modernist architecture of Tel Aviv was an aesthetic expression of the Yishuv (early Zionist settlers in Israel pre-1948) to build a nation that was 'old-new' (Fuchs and Epstein-Pliouchtch 2008). In Levin's submission then, Tel Aviv may have been thoroughly International in its modernist legacy but it was also a vernacular modernism, in that it could have only been produced through the Zionist experience of the early twentieth century.

15 The difficulty of proposing an absolute and universal definition of 'authenticity' for preservation policy around the world, was witnessed in many of the discussions at the Nara Conference. For example, Nobuo Ito spoke directly to the difficulties of translating the concept into Asian languages such as Japanese, where there does not exist a corollary for the term. It is also interesting to note that the connotation of authority that is embedded within authenticity can be interpreted less favourably as authoritarianism in Japanese (Ito 1995).

16 INTBAU was in fact a product of a project titled 'The Prince's Foundation for the Built Environment' and initiated by the Prince of Wales in 2000.

17 Although it advocated protecting the objects of the past, the Venice Charter was seen by INTBAU as little more than another instrument through which modernism was glorified as the triumphant new epoch – one that would sever all ties with history and begin anew. The 2006 conference even went so far as to suggest that the Venice Charter may have been nothing more than a post-war product of the Cold War, when the 'West covertly funded cultural institutions with the aim of promoting modernism and creating a clear contrast with the Soviet bloc's preference for social realism and traditional architecture' (www.intbau.org/venicecharter.htm).

18 In 1988, the year that DOCOMOMO International was founded as the key body for the preservation of modernist architecture, Leon Krier was appointed to draft the masterplan of the neo-traditional village of Poundbury in England. Five years later in 1993, Andres Duany and Elizabeth Plater-Zyberk drafted the official charter of the Congress of New Urbanism, although their first New Urbanist town – Seaside in Florida – had been completed in the 1980s. The canonization of the modern movement as a historical category developed alongside the rejection of modernism as a viable cultural resource. And even as modernist architecture was co-opted to satisfy the narratives of nationalist as well as ethnic identity on the one hand it was also the catalyst for movements that actively replaced the cold universality of modernist aesthetic with the use of historic symbols and forms.

19 Heynen cites the example of St. Peterschurch in Leuven (Belgium) which was 'restored' in the 1990s – a process which actually led to the destruction of the only 'original' or 'authentic' pieces of the church from the fifteenth century, the 'sculptured stone walls of the south porch' which were never completed and at the moment of restoration were very dilapidated and decaying. Thus 'memory and amnesia seem to operate in conjuncture rather than opposition' (Heynen 1999a, 369).

18

Collective Memory Under Siege: The Case of 'Heritage Terrorism'

M. Christine Boyer

> Since memory is actually a very important factor in struggle … if one controls people's memory, one controls their dynamism. And one also controls their experience, their knowledge of previous struggles (Foucault 1989, 89–106)[1]

Since architectural collective memory is literally carved or erected in stone, and thus tangible, monolithic, recognizable and permanent, it has been called the archetypal collective memory (Olick 2007, 89). If collective memory is under siege in the twenty-first century, as will be argued here, what then does architectural collective memory actually signify? What fundamental assumptions about history, memory, identity and the nation underlie architectural practice when it ventures into the process of memorialization or stages theatrical performances of material evidence and artifacts of recall? If trauma of war is a special form of memory, registering affects but not meaning, how then do architects negotiate the distinction between intangible memories and more formal acts of collective memorialization (Kaplan 2005)? Collective memory under siege requires sensitive interpretation of past events and imputed representations, as well as careful negotiations over the future of a nation or people. Never set in stone, it belongs to a field of argumentation located at the heart of modern ethics.

THE RISE OF THE 'MEMORY MACHINE'

'Memory' as an intellectual debate was absent from the 1968 *International Encyclopedia of Social Sciences* published under the direction of David L. Sills; it did not appear in the collective work *Faire de l'histoire* edited in 1974 by Jacques Le Goff and Pierre Nora; nor in 1976 was it among the *Keywords* assembled by the cultural historian Raymond Williams (Traverso 2005, 10). Since then, however, the word 'memory' has become an obsession, diffused across cultural, social and political studies, the humanities and history, architecture and archaeology. But what does the word actually refer to? What kind of memory is at stake? If only individuals remember, then what is collective memory? Perhaps collective memory is a sensitivity but not an operational concept, then what does it sensitize us to and what does this imply for the building of memorials and the design of commemorative spaces?

In 1984, Nora (1989; 1984–1992) described *lieux de memoire* [realms of memory], to be 'an unconscious organization of collective memory' reflecting national, ethnic or group commonalities. His seven-volume attempt to catalogue every memory site in France reflects a certain nostalgia for a mythical 'Frenchness' lost in the process of modernization or eradicated in the uniformity of globalization. His affirmative albeit backward-looking approach to memory has spawned a veritable 'memory machine' retrieving and inventing traditions in many different places around the world, remarking on how the past has been remembered or forgotten, how narratives have been constructed and landscapes of memory confabulated (Müller 2002, 18). 'Memory tourism' has transformed historic sites into museums, turned the 'past' into a consumer object to be recuperated and utilized by commercial interests, and exploited as spectacles in theme parks and the cinema.

Where did this obsession with memory come from? Nora claims we speak so often of memory because there is so little of it. As I argue in *The City of Collective Memory* (Boyer 1994), when a gap in time appears between the memory of an event and its actual experience, attempts are made to write these absent moments down, to preserve all the little-known facts as much as possible, to erect monuments and establish commemorative celebrations. A gap in time enables memory to act as resistance to the acceleration of time or to be used as a tool in search of moral redemption for past grievances and regrets, or to provide a source of identity in an increasingly alienating and modernizing world. Such a gap in time appeared in the late twentieth century, after a century of wars, totalitarian regimes, genocides and crimes against humanity, when the last 'witnesses' of these atrocities and their memories were disappearing (Young 1993).

The Holocaust of World War II has been positioned as the generator of the 'memory machine'. Much has been written about Germany's efforts both to reconcile controversial memories of its National Socialist past and its attempts to transform the centre of Berlin into a new memory district with Daniel Libeskind's design for the Jewish Museum, Peter Eisenman's Memorial to Murdered Jews of Europe, and Peter Zumthor's cancelled Topography of Terror Documentation Centre. Karen Till (2005, 8–9) makes the following argument: 'If the Holocaust and its memory still stand as a test case for humanist and universalist claims of Western civilization, then one might argue that these place-making processes in Berlin are central symbolic and material sites of the crisis of modernity, uniquely embodying the contradictions and tensions of social memory and national identity in the late twentieth century and early twenty-first'. Such a statement is beset with conceptual and interpretive contradictions and double standards which this chapter tries to explore. How have humanist and universalist claims been deployed to keep amnesia not memory alive? What role does Western civilization play in the crisis of modernity, and does memory of the Holocaust act as a symbolic centre for proclaimed clashes of civilizations in the Middle East today? If Berlin represents an 'unstable optic identity' of the nation, as Till believes (2005, 5), what is the relationship between the eye of the spectator and the logic of governmentality, between individual memory and collective memory, not just in Berlin but in any other memorial site?

INDIVIDUAL/COLLECTIVE MEMORY

Since it is difficult to define collective memory, some suggest abandoning its universalizing meaning replacing it with myth, tradition or commemoration. Others want to restrict its application to public discourse about the past or to narratives that speak in the name of collectivities. A third possibility is to limit its reference to mnemonic processes and practices such as memorial sites and public monuments (Olick 2007, 33–34).

Everyone seems to agree that individual memory, the kind that people carry around in their heads, differs from collective memory. The French sociologist Maurice Halbwachs, the founding father of contemporary memory studies, called the first 'autobiographical memory'. He believed, however, that the actual act of remembering always takes place as group memory. This latter process of remembering together he called 'collective memory'; it operates as a framework limiting and binding intimate acts of individual recall (Halbwachs 1992, 53). So he mused 'the mind reconstructs its memories under the pressure of society' (1992, 51).

There are in the end as many collective memories as social groups, social differentiations and societal pressures. This is the trouble with collective memory, as Jeffrey Olick explains, it refers to too many things: collected individual recollections, official commemorative events, and features of shared identities. And it is located in too many places: subjective reminiscences, myths, language, traditions, popular culture and the built environment (Olick 2007, 21). Olick believes however in the validity of a collective perspective, for without such the constitutive narratives of mythology, tradition, heritage cannot be explained. Moreover, techniques for recording memory such as language, the archive, the museum and monuments are social constructions; they constitute the mnemonics of collective memory and characterize ways of knowing about time, history, memory and identity (Olick 2007, 28–30; Preziosi 1993).

Jan-Werner Müller points to another problem: the very language with which we discuss collective memory treats it as a 'thing' to be 'shared', 'confiscated', 'repressed' or 'recovered'. Thinking memory can be excavated or empirically known as a fact leads to instrumental control over its contents. Since individuals remember, not collectivities, unearthing personal memories generates too many therapeutic narrations or souvenirs. On the other hand, overgeneralizing attempts to define collective memory as a social fact fail to grasp how 'memory' actually is deployed in politics, and how control over individuals' perception is achieved (Müller 2002, 19).

Extending this troubled belief in excavation, a popular metaphor likens memory to a palimpsest: not a velum scraped clean for new use but horizontal strata of ancient texts brought to the surface in the present, revealing their simultaneous co-existence. Freud conceptualized an individual's memory as such a storage system in which all that had gone before was retrievable. His was an archaeological gaze, a structure of vision engendering a new vocabulary of surface and depth, hidden and revealed, dark and light (Bennett 2004, 88). Transferred to the urban fabric, the users of 'palimpsest' assume that lost memories haunt a city's collective memory albeit in unsettled arrangements, they are ghosts of a restless past possessing some places. Constructing places of memory is one way to work through such traumatic remains, Karen Till argues, to give shape to metaphysically absent but intensively felt fears and desires. It situates memories in place, stops their prowling around. People return to these haunted places, she believes, to make contact with their loss, places that contain unwanted presences and past injustices. In these situated places they work through contradictory emotions of shame, guilt, fear, sadness, longing, anxiety and they hope for a better future (Till 2005, 5–15). Just how an absent, immaterial haunting signifies individual or collective meaning remains a conundrum.

Andreas Huyssen (2003, 7–8) also deploys this palimpsest metaphor to explore how urban space shapes collective imaginaries.

His approach is somewhat ambivalent for he notes that memory work too often focuses on individual remembering bringing a 'hypertrophy of memories' to the surface while an excessive marketing of memory creates 'memory fatigue'. A melancholic fixation on traumatic memory, moreover, radiating out from master-signifiers in the 1990s – the ubiquitous Holocaust discourse, South African post-apartheid debates, child abuse revelations and more – restricts the study of memory to the prison house of the past where pain, suffering and loss reside. It represents an inability to think the future in the present, to understand the political layers of memory discourse. Memory studies cannot deny traumatic pasts, but a better way to deal with them, Huyssen (2003, 1–10) argues, is the discourse of human rights based on truth commissions and judicial proceedings or in the healing practices of designing objects and commemorative public spaces.

HISTORY/MEMORY

Halbwachs maintained that memory is different from history, although both are intent on elaborating the past they may be antonyms. 'Historical memory' as representation comes down to us through written records, photographic evidence, cinematic narrations, the cityscape and material artifacts. It is 'petrified memory', no longer steeped in experience or relevant to the present (Heynen 1999a, 369–390). Memory, on the other hand, is alive and actual; there is no need to write it down, preserve it for posterity, for it is of the present moment, shared in a group, passed on by word of mouth.

Commemorative celebrations enacted in public space, and memory traces stored in archives and memorials, act as prompts to individual memory. Even though the historical past may not have been experienced, these celebrative events and traces help to keep the past alive and meaningful in the present. Shared in public and socially exchanged, collective memory gives rise to an ongoing process of reinterpretation, preservation and transformation.

While Halbwachs and Nora linked places of memory to spatial artifacts, landscapes, sites, monuments and museums, there are as well narrative forms of memory. In times of war or political conflict, narrations of the nation, of an ethnic or religious group, and memory of past grievances and misrepresentations may play more important roles than spatial or architectural representations, since intangible memories are easily manipulated and controlled by elite groups or government officials bent on securing political power. In such cases Charles Maier (1993, 136–152) claims 'the surfeit of memory is a sign not of historical confidence but a retreat from transformative politics'. The past is expected to redeem what the future may not be able to appease.[2] Memory may have corrosive effects on political policies.

The opposing divide between history and memory has not remained as Halbwachs and Nora theorized.[3] Many researchers now recognize that history and memory are both embedded in narrative frames, constructed for specific purposes and reworked for present needs. Thus researchers have tried to find substitutes for the term 'collective memory' offering lists of alternatives. For example, 'mimetic memory' refers to the transmission of practical knowledge from the past, 'material memory' looks at traces of the past stored in objects, 'communicative memory' studies language and communication, and 'cultural memory' transmits cultural meaning from the past. And memory work is differentiated as 'official memory', 'vernacular memory', 'public memory', 'popular memory', 'family memory', 'historical memory', until the list becomes meaningless (Olick and Robbins 1998, 111–112). Sites of memory have fared no better, just about anything is included from archives to museums, parades to moments of silence, gardens to ruins, fast days to family icons (Young 1993, xviii). The struggle remains constant: to avoid defining collective memory too broadly so it encompasses everything a group of individuals remembers or making too fine-grained distinctions that obliterate the ability to understand how memory of a group influences individual perceptions, how memory can be politically manipulated by those in power.

Sidestepping attempts to draw up a definitive list of memory concepts, another approach studies the historical development of the material means of memory transmission. These researchers focus on the shift from processes of mnemonic memorization to external storage devices in the development of archives, libraries and museums in the nineteenth century and to the creation of electronic files and databases in our computer age. Mnemonic devices are also affected by time and subjected to constant renegotiation and change: archives are enlarged, museums of local history expanded, and material traces of memory are more inclusive (Preziosi 1993; Lury 1998).

While memory and history may be mutually dependent on each other, Müller claims historians should be correctors of memory. Knowing their histories will be contested, they nevertheless should wake their readers from the nightmare of too much memory, too partial, too shifting, too traumatic and too subjective. Historians are not witnesses; they hold no memory of atrocity and oppression. To conflate the two holds serious political and ethical consequences (Müller 2002, 22–25). History, Enzo Traverso clarifies, may be born of selective and subjective memory, but it puts the past at a distance and writes it down in the present according to the rules of objectivity, contemporary concerns, global rationalizations. History and memory are not opposites, as Halbwachs and Nora imagined, but held in dialectical tension. The sources of history are constantly enlarged by memory: contesting its blind spots, bringing silenced and subjugated voices into play, replacing amnesia with remembrance and reconciliation. The process is far from easy (Traverso 2005, 18–41)!

NATIONAL IDENTITY AND 'URBICIDE'

One of the problems haunting the term 'collective memory' is the issue of national identity. Ernest Renan (1920 [1882]) pointed out more than a hundred years ago, that in the formation of national identity remembrance and forgetting depend on each other, shared memory and shared forgetting.[4] With the rise of the nation state, certain memories are mobilized while alternatives are repressed and regional differences assimilated. Official narrations are idealized or invented and guarded with care: access to papers and national archives may be limited and allegiance to the hegemonic form of memory tightly controlled. There is no unitary collective mental set for the nation to possess, no 'pristine memory' to recall, only selected memory and numbing amnesia to manipulate as an instrument for better or worse by those in power, or those seeking power (Müller 2002, 22, 29–30, 32).

Although counter-memory resists such restrictions and overgeneralizations of national identity, offering competing pasts and narrating different events, it takes place within the framework of political power. And counter-memory, the recovery of suppressed memory, is not always liberating. When collective memory is conjoined with inflamed national passions, the memory-power nexus, residing in national and political memory and in civil and individual memory, becomes a highly contested terrain (2002, 1–35).

Bogdan Bogdanovic, the architect, designer of monuments to the peaceful co-existence of different cultures and memories in post-war Yugoslavia, a former mayor of Belgrade, used the term 'urbicide' to describe war against cities in the Balkans during the 1990s. The sieges and bombardments of Vukovar, the World Heritage city of Dubrovnik and the historic centres of Sarajevo and Mostar involved intentional attacks on their urban fabric because these cities were symbols of multiplicity – shared spaces of ethnic, cultural, religious and civic values – the antithesis of the Serbian ideal.[5] Bogdanovic might have used 'memoricide': murder of the past through the mutilation and eradication of geographical and architectural markers on the land. Memory was literally blown up during the Balkan wars as homes, neighbourhoods, monuments, mosques, churches and cultural artifacts were erased, mnemonic devices such as maps redrawn to display an ethnically reconfigured future, and schoolbooks rewritten to tell official tales (Müller 2002, 9, 17). Ilana Bet-El (2002) claims the words 'I remember' and the dark recollections that swirled around different speakers of remembrance in Yugoslavia, when collected together and carefully manipulated, turned into weapons of hatred, fear and then war.

Whatever one's ethnic position, the death knell for Yugoslavia was sounded by Slobodan Milosevic's speech to angry Serbs in Kosovo Polje on April 24, 1987. He admonished Serbs to stay there, on their land, where their memories lay, but not to stay suffering as in the past but to change the situation (Bet-El 2002, 208; Bevan 2006). Milsovic's carefully chosen words evoked the memory of the battle of Kosovo in 1389, when the Serbs were defeated by the Ottomans. But alongside the upsurge of Serbian nationalism, stood the proud memories of Croats resting on Teutonic conquests, Habsburgian culture, and more recent Serbian oppression; and next to them rose up the Bosnian Muslims with their memories steeped in Ottoman supremacy and religious oppression; and next were the Albanian Kosovars with memories of battles with Serbs stretching back to the seventeenth century. Memories pitted against memories became tools of ethnic identity and inflamed passion, of unalleviated pain and suffering. There was failure on all sides to recognize the power of memory to spiral into war and murderous destruction.

'Urbicide' is a term that also applies to deliberate strategies of the Israeli army deploying bulldozers to systematically destroy water tanks, roads, electricity generating plants, hospitals, schools, homes and cultural symbols in Ramallah, Hebron, Bethlehem, Jenin and other Palestinian cities, plus the construction of a network of bypass roads to Israeli settlements on the West Bank. To eliminate such targets deemed necessary for military self-defence, also brings death and disease to innocent civilians. The war of the bulldozer is meant to drive Palestinian people away, to deny their collective, individual, cultural and historical rights to the land, to place them in permanent poverty, to seclude them behind a wall and thus eradicate them from sight – an 'unstable optic' of national identity at play (Salmon 2002; Graham 2002; Segal et al. 2003; Hanafi 2001; Sorkin 2005).

'Urbicide' can also be applied to the war in Iraq where insurgents quickly understood that the asymmetrical power of US technological superiority might be thwarted even neutralized, by taking refuge in complex and uncertain urban terrains. They quickly moved the battlefield into Iraq's sixteen largest cities. The conclusion is simple, as one US military commander has said: 'We have seen the future war, and it is urban'. Technological superiority, fighting war at a distance, reflects the US military strategy of zero soldier deaths, while it increases the death of civilians and destruction of their cities as so much collateral damage (Wielhouwer 2004).[6]

THE RHETORIC OF MEMORY AND THE SPECTACLE OF WAR

The expression 'heritage terrorism' is exemplary of the rhetoric of memory. It was coined by Neal Ascherson of *The Observer* (March 2001) during the international outrage over Mullah Mohammad Omar's wanton destruction of the giant Buddha statues carved into the rock cliffs of Bamiyan in the second century AD, and includes his threat to eliminate all 'offending' pre-Islamic artefacts left in museums throughout Afghanistan (Ascherson 2001; Jan 2001; Flood 2002; Nemeth 2007;

Gerstenblith 2006).[7] Mullah Omah proclaimed, in defence of his decree, that the statues were not part of the beliefs of Afghanistan for there were no Buddhists left in the country; since they were only part of its history 'all we are breaking are stones'.[8]

Iconoclastic acts of cultural catharsis are as old as human hatred, and Ascherson (2001) claims the Taliban's acts of vandalism against idols were motivated by religious and nationalistic aims. These blind zealots unleashed horrendous acts of 'heritage terrorism', he criticized, in order to prove that no other religion but Islam ever held sway in Afghanistan and deliver proof to future generations by eradicating all traces to the contrary. Lynn Meskell (2002, 557–574) labels this 'negative heritage', 'a conflictual site that becomes the repository of negative memory in the collective imaginary'.[9] The Taliban sought to clear the slate of memory. Afghanistan had never been Buddhist, never part of a semi-Greek Bactrian empire, never a territory of Britain or Russia, never a twentieth century nation embarking on a path of modernization. While outrage over the Buddha monuments added a new phrase to military skirmishes, the meaning of 'heritage terrorism' may be far from clear. 'Terrorism' is after all an empty signifier, one that can be filled with a variety of actions by non-state insurgents who 'we' dislike because 'they' violently oppose our way of life, our democracy, our civilization, our modernity, our freedom (Badiou 2006, 19). Applying the adjective 'heritage' only reinforces this antagonism – our culture against theirs, two nihilisms at war, the East and the West. Ignored in this struggle are complicated connections and unresolved ethical arguments in the definition of permissible wars and impermissible terrorism.

Was it necessity to drop the atomic bomb on Hiroshima and Nagasaki in order to shorten the conflict and spare even more innocents from perishing in war (Asad 2007, 26)? Since this question remains unanswered, how can architects build a memorial to that horrendous event and if they do, what do they think it signifies? Lisa Yoneyama (1999) raises such questions by looking at the architect Kenzo Tange's 1949 plans for a Peace Memorial Park on the site of the first atomic blast in Hiroshima. This plan was celebrated by CIAM as the 'humanization of life' at the core of the city and republished in their catalogue *The Heart of the City* in 1952 (Tyrwhitt et al. 1952, 106, 137–8). Tange told his fellow architects the source of his design came from the realization among those who survived the 'most extraordinary man-made disaster ever witnessed' that the entire world faced a new problem transcending all others. The release of atomic energy might advance humankind but it might obliterate all life on earth. Eternal world peace had to prevail to deter another disaster. Tange's Peace Park was planned consequently to memorialize the inaugural moment of the nuclear age.

To this effect, and for the eyes of spectators who gather to celebrate peace, Tange placed a coffin-shaped stone monument under an arch in the Peace Park, on which were carved 200,000 names of those who died and an epigraph: 'Please rest in peace, because we shall not repeat the mistake.' But Japanese, Yoneyama explains (1999, 15–16), does not have a symbol for 'we'; so in 1952 public controversy erupted over what 'we' referenced, and whose and what mistake was made. The Japanese believed they were innocent victims of the atomic blasts. No one, Yoneyama notes, associated Tange's 1949 designs with his similar fascist scheme for the same site in 1942. This ambitious Commemoration Building Project for Construction of Greater East Asia Co-Prosperity was intended to celebrate the Japanese Empire and Pan-Asian prosperity. No one remembers this scheme, or Japan's pre-war imperialism, colonialism and militarism. Instead they make 'anemic elisions' of wartime atrocities substituting the sceptre of 'A-Bomb Nationalism' (Yoneyama 1999, 4). The Japanese hold tight to this national myth believing in a 'phantasm of innocence' as Tange's statement implies, severing any linkage with guilt, any responsibility for the

Japanese military record of rape and plunder. By remembering the atomic attacks as crimes against an anonymous and universal 'humanity', Yoneyama argues, they keep 'amnesia' alive. By conflating the bomb and peace, 'Hiroshima's postwar design thus spatially represented the master narrative of the post-World War II order in the Asia Pacific region'.

Critical remembering is seldom produced by war; instead a spectacular politics is put into play. 'The spectacle [Retort tells us] is deeply (constantly) a form of violence – a repeated action against real human possibilities, real (meaning flexible, useable, transformable) representation, real attempts at collectivity' (Retort 2005, 131). Accumulated into an image, whether it is the mushroom cloud of an atomic bomb or the imploding of the World Trade Center towers (WTC) on 9/11, war and the deployment of spectacular imagery have been linked together for a long period of time. The spectacle as image is key to the management of symbolic power, and this image-power nexus is highly concentrated in symbolic sites of memory: places, monuments, icons, logos, signs that rule over the cultural imaginary. Hence these icons are prone to destruction in war and reconstruction in peacetime.[10]

The visual immediacy of the Twin Towers with smoke billowing from their tops, imploding in real time and then remediated and multiplied through split screens, scrolling headlines, radio feeds and cellphones turned the event into an immediate spectacle. The perpetrators designed their acts as theatrical performances, intentionally selecting the date and images to spellbind their audiences.[11] 'Shock and awe' tactics of the retaliatory and retributive Iraq war of 2003 were likewise televised as image-spectacles seared into memory as performances and repetitively looped in an endless war of images (Grusin 2004). The deployment of spectacular imagery, however, leaves vast realms of experience unnarrated and inaccessible to memory, allowing illusions and false options to prevail.

No one thought the WTC towers were a site of remembrance until their destruction on September 11, 2001. These cultural icons became the targets of terrorist attacks because they defined the market culture and capitalist ideals of those who created them; they fit the definition of 'the spectacle' like a glove.[12] But in the wake of their collapse, the WTC site was mobilized for spectacular purposes and absorbed into the collective imaginary. It quickly emerged as a tourist destination with the requisite paraphernalia of souvenirs, memory maps and architecturally designed viewing stands.

Unanswered questions shadow the 'war against terrorism' waged in retaliation, making the mission of creating an enduring monument at the WTC site – or reconstructing 16 acres at Ground Zero – hard to accomplish. Likening the sites to 'ground zero' of a nuclear explosion with radiating rings of effects has not helped (Boyer 2002). When this article was written in 2007, no one was in control of the site, reconstruction was far behind schedule, and the design was plagued with disappointments. The warring parties remained unappeased: families of the dead, business interests, government agencies, the larger community.

The once proud masterplan of Daniel Libeskind has been eviscerated. His dream in 2002 entailed a sacred ground with quiet meditative spaces dug deep into the indelible footprints of Tower One and Tower Two. Crystalline structures jumbled over the site, two large public places, A Park of Heroes and a Wedge of Light commemorated lost lives, while an elevated pedestrian walkway around the entire perimeter offered a vision of its tragic expanse. Now the emotional value of his ideas has been reduced to Michael Arad's and Peter Walker's memorial plaza 'Reflecting Absence' of 2004. A simple 'forest grove' of trees at street level contains two large voids marking the famous footprints. At the centre of each void is a recessed pool of water filled by a cascade flowing down its perimeter walls. Surrounding the pool is a continuous ribbon of names of the dead arranged in no particular order. 'Standing there at the water's edge, looking at a pool of water that is flowing away into an abyss, [Arad and Walker claim] a visitor to the site can sense that what is beyond this curtain of water and ribbon of names is inaccessible.'

More accessible, three tall towers designed by the world's most renowned architects, Lord Norman Foster, Lord Richard Rogers and Fumihiko Maki, accompany David Childs' Freedom Tower and 7 World Trade, and will stand along two sides of the site. The ensemble promises nothing more than a bland office park. Nor has the 'Reflecting Absence' design been without criticism: some family members want the memorial to be above ground not sunken thirty feet below, while government leaders have placed a cap on cost overruns causing further design alterations. Any attempt to preserve a site necessarily ignores other uses, other engagements with meaning and memory. Arad poignantly remarked as his plans were unveiled: 'Every way you find to resolve this satisfies some but causes pain and anguish to others.'[13]

THE STRUGGLE OVER AMNESIA

In the aftermath of 9/11, the national attention of the US shifted to Afghanistan, then to Iraq, but left unattended wars, famines and catastrophes in Africa as well as other parts of the world. Estimates hold that 5.4 million people have been killed in the war in the Congo, development indices throughout the continent are on a precipitous decline, while HIV/AIDS, starvation, landmines and the continued exploitation of natural resources continue unabated (Caplan 2003). It is not generally understood that the downward spiral of poverty may be connected to the upward rise of terrorism, both lethal to the memory of the past. In order to understand how memorialization is a complicated task we look closely at three areas recovering from amnesia: Rwanda, South Africa and Beirut.

Rwanda

How do countries such as Rwanda remember the brutal and painful history of genocide between 1990 and 1994 that killed nearly a million people, mostly Tutsi, without rekindling divisions that led to the killings? How do Rwandans keep alive an understanding of how and why these killings occurred? Pat Caplan, an anthropologist from the UK, traveled to Rwanda in search of answers, visiting four major genocide memorials and many smaller sites of memory (Caplan 2007). She found the Kigali Genocide Memorial typical of many Holocaust museums, done very professionally and movingly.

The museum building is surrounded by terraced gardens with streams and pools; a list of names, far from complete, is inscribed on a standing wall; a series of huge mass graves appear in the garden, one still receiving bones for dignified burials in coffins as they are excavated and recovered, then brought to the site. Inside the museum, the first room explores the historical background to the Rwanda genocide. It begins with the period of Belgium rule, when boundaries between Tutsi and Hutu were established and identity cards required, and when the minority Tutsis were used as a vehicle of indirect rule by the Belgiums. The second room covers the 100 days of massacre, the third narrates stories of resistance, the fourth (a circular room) contains photographs of those who were killed, and the last room offers life stories of children killed, their favorite foods, sports, best friends and what became their fate. The upper floors of the museum are devoted to other genocides: the Herero in Namibia by the Germans, the Armenians by the Turks, the Bosnian Muslims by the Serbs (Caplan 2007, 20).

The second memorial, in Butare, was far from self-explanatory. In a university setting, a huge mass grave is enclosed in a low-roofed structure with open walls on which are displayed photographs. Caplan had to ask a guard to explain what happened, why suddenly one day in 1994, soldiers arrived and started killing, and why so many professors and students joined in killing 400 of their students and colleagues. She visited two church memorials: one at Ntarama was left largely untouched. Bones and clothing were strewn about, a wall still stained in blood where babies' heads had been smashed, an outhouse where a few clothes had been hung and bones heaped about. Far from being a dignified burial, the untouched evidence juxtaposed with meagre intervention remains poignant. The second church, at Nyamata, had the same type of jarring juxtapositions. It appeared at first to be cleared of evidence of massacre except that slowly she realized the light streaming down from the tin roof came from bullet holes and that the altar cloth was stained in blood, and a small room off the sanctuary was piled high with bones. A mass grave behind the church held catacombs where bones and skulls had been sorted neatly by type then arranged on shelves (Caplan 2007, 21).[14] There are different ways to memorialize genocide. Some advocate excavation of bones and their reburial in order to bring closure for themselves and to publicly blame those responsible; others prefer to allow bones to lie where they have fallen, in order to remember the vast absences that genocide created never to be filled (Holtorf 2006, 101–109).[15]

What if the collapse of collective memory, was itself the reason why ethnicity became such a powerful instrument of genocide? What if 35 years of amnesia, of memories collectively repressed gave rise to these atrocities? And what if failure of the international community to intervene to stop the killings makes memory an insufficient tool to guarantee that killing will not re-occur? The writer Benjamin Sehene (1999) believes most Rwandans suffer from a lost collective memory. He blames Christianity for destroying the memory of a civilization rooted in myths and built on hierarchy, a tyranny but one imbued with a sense of restraint. In such an atmosphere, things were left unsaid, hatreds were self-censored, and three ethnic groups, the Hutus, Tutsis and Twas, lived in peace. In 1931, however, the Catholic Church deposed Musinga, the Tutsis' last divine-monarch, because he refused to be converted. They tore into shreds all the religious traditions, rituals and myths of the ruling Tutsis – their collective memory and esoteric rights – that were the pillar of Rwandan society. Just before and after independence in 1962, the Hutus attempted to redress the social balance after centuries of feudal domination. They began a bloody revolt in 1959, massacring 20,000 Tutsis and forcing thousands to flee into Burundi and Uganda. Effecting a transfer of power to a Hutu regime, everything with a Tutsi connotation was banned, including thousands of words cut from the language; a quota system was installed allowing only nine percent of all positions in higher education or civil services to be held by Tutsis. Government and military service were restricted as well. 'But a past that is forgotten is bound to repeat itself because forgetting involves a refusal to admit wrongdoing. In Rwanda, amnesia led to successive pogroms against the Tutsis which began in the 1960s and ended in their genocide' (Sehene 1999, 3). Subtle points lie awake in the deep structure of memory, they rise to the surface time and again, making political power struggles inevitable and memorialization an impossible task.

South Africa

The memory problem for South Africa in the 1990s rested on how to remember the apartheid period since the regime displayed exemplary techniques of concealment and silencing. In post-conflict societies, it often takes decades to bring individual untold memories back from the past, to reconnect these voices with the present. Nombulelo Elizabeth Makhubu's son Mbuyisa Nikita Makhubu was captured in a photograph carrying in his arms the body of Hector Pieterson after the South African police shot and killed the 13-year-old boy on 16 June 1976 during the Soweto uprising. This photograph has become an icon of resistance against apartheid. But Nombulelo told the South African Truth and Reconciliation Commission (TRC) another story in 1997: her son disappeared in 1977, fleeing from police persecution and has never returned. She wanted to know can anyone bring him back from the silence, from no-place: does anyone know what happened to him, how did he die, when did he die, where did he die? With these simple questions revealing her 20 years of pain, she – and many other mothers in truth seeking processes – tore the memory of the Soweto uprising and apartheid from the process of symbolization, commemoration and memorialization and from the collusion of acts of violence with silence, secrecy and lies. She brought memories of the event back into the present by reminding the Commission there were still questions to be answered, memories to be listened to, and stories to be told. This is how Helena Pohlandt-McCormick (2006) writes about the memory of apartheid in South Africa, how she links remembering and accountability together with habits of secrecy, dissimulation and manipulation which belong equally to official narrations of apartheid as well as to resistance politics. Before any process of memorialization can take effect, silencing has to be undone.

The official apartheid record (primarily the Cillié Commission Report) is full of statistics, a cold analytical account of events.[16] It seeks to discredit the student uprising in Soweto and to legitimize the actions of the police, explaining why it was necessary to shoot and kill so many school children. The stories individuals tell, on the other hand, are a mixture of pride and anger, suffering and retribution. They are full of memory drifts and protections against 'wounds in the tissue of memory' incurred by the violence of apartheid. The destruction of archives, the disappearance of bodies, the concealment of evidence of political dissidents, the one-sided teaching about apartheid, make it difficult for individuals to place their memories of the Soweto uprising or any other apartheid happening in the context of the historical event. Pohlandt-McCormick's accounting of the difference between public and private memory, thirty years after the Soweto uprising, reveals two types of information that go into the creation of memory: the original perception of the event and the official manipulations after the event. She finds many silences in South Africa: some caused by the experience of trauma that make words fail, others by complicity and guilt that needs to hide from the truth. When stories are told from memory and in official accounts, they blend together, both marked and manipulated by the experience of violence. How then to start the process of memorialization?

The iconic site of Robben Island off the coast of Cape Town, reveals the tensions and difficulties. Used as a place of exile for prisoners, lepers and the insane for over 400 years, it is symbolically associated with Nelson Mandela who, beginning in 1964, spent eighteen of his twenty-seven years of imprisonment there. The island was also the place of exile for most black male opponents to the apartheid regime. And it was on this island that Frederik de Klerk and Mandela began their negotiations culminating in a 'government of national unity' (Coombes 2003). As the birthplace of South African democracy, it became a key site of public discourse about memory, trauma and recovery. Should it be transformed into a casino, an amusement park, a rehabilitation centre for street children, a university to teach about liberation and peace? Most ex-prisoners rejected any commercial use, and suggested the prison become a museum and the island a conservation area. But museological practices needed to be restrategized if they were to document and display intangible heritage sources, not artifacts in any normal sense of the word.

In May 1993 an exhibition 'Esiqithini' (meaning 'on the island') was co-organized by the natural history museum of Cape Town and an archive committed to recovering the legacy of the liberation struggle. Tensions erupted into controversy: should the exhibit be scientifically objective and primarily about the island's natural and social history or should it be about emotively sensitive displays from the life of prisoners involving them as vital interpreters? The main feature of the exhibition became the 'apple-box archive' so-called for the way prisoners carried off their belongings once released. Still controversy continued: an exhibition drawing more international than local interest hardly addressed the hardships ex-prisoners still faced (Davison 2007, 144–160, 281–282).

Museological practice and therapeutic story-telling came into conflict over how to appropriately memorialize the site. Christopher Colvin, an anthropologist, visited the Robben Island Museum in 1998 and found the actions of his tour guide peculiar (Colvin 2005, 153–166). This ex-prisoner kept repeating the following phrase in various renditions: 'brothers and sisters, do not be afraid of me … I love you'; at other times saying 'he had died for them' as he reiterated a list of barbaric experiences such as suffocating heat in the summer, rat infestations in winter, tormenting work in the lime quarry, smarting cold salt water showers. Called 'therapeutic narration', this verbal accounting is meant to be emotional, not a rational sifting of documentary and anecdotal evidence, simultaneously reassuring and discomforting. In this extreme manner, Robben Island, its prison museum and tour guides become a memorial to the triumph of the human spirit over forces of evil, the triumph of love and redemption. To touch memory is a delicate gesture making the process of memorialization an impossible task.

Beirut

During sixteen years of civil war in Lebanon, 1975–1991, oblivion of memory set in, many even questioned whether atrocities happened at all or referred to the period of war as 'a series of nightmares' (Haugbølle 2002).[17] After the war, a law of general amnesty made an attempt to wipe the slate clean without attributing the war to any one cause or group; citizens were inhibited from discussing the war less their conversations became incitements to sectarian behaviour. They were told to get on with their lives, and forget the war. Eventually an effort was made to 'look the beast in the eye' and to deal with the memory of war lest it return to hold them hostage.[18] For some, collective amnesia gave way to recall in films, memoirs, novels, poetry, the press, through architectural reconstructions and commemorative ceremonies. Others tired of the war, only wanted to forget. And some, believing there was no shared national history to heal egregious wounds, sought to repress memory absolutely, fearing it would give rise to a renewal of war. So many prohibitions against recall and remembering require one to ask how collective memory is being constructed, how the war is actually talked about, and what might be the political and ethical implications of these constructions and words?

There are painful statistics to recall in Lebanon: 150,000 dead, 200,000 injured, 17,000 missing, one million émigrés and thousands uprooted and displaced. Within the city limits of Beirut, apartment houses were flattened, residential districts bombed, the downtown district turned into a major battlefield, while a 'green line', a no-man's-land, divided the city in two: east and west, Muslim and Christian. In the post-war period, sites of remembrance were quickly lost in the downtown area, once referred to as the 'centre of the country'[19] as properties were condemned, acquired and levelled then reconstructed by a governmental/private company Sociètè Libanaise pour le development et la reconstruction de Centre Ville de Beyrouth (Solidere), spearheaded by the late prime minister Rafiq Hariri (Sawalha 2002, 36). Beginning in 1994, Solidere commissioned well-known international architects to give a new face to the city, obliterating more connections to its past. The company's declared aim is to rebuild Beirut as it was before the war: 'Paris of the Mediterranean' and to re-plan and rebuild the public space where Beirut's 'intercommunal mixing ... Christians and Muslims continued to meet together at official functions and served on the same committees, courts, and mixed tribunals'.[20] Solidere's slogan 'Beirut, an ancient city of the future'[21] means the restoration of only selected buildings, the preservation of some façades while changing the functions, use and street plan of the whole (Sawalha 2002, 73–74).

Living in an urban memory of pastiche architecture is not to everyone's liking. Beginning in November 1994, the Lebanese press reported, on a nearly weekly basis, 'the wrecking of mosaics, walls, columns, and other archaeological monuments in Beirut. Working around the clock for more than a year, bulldozers dug into the city, filling dump trucks that promptly emptied their loads into the Mediterranean Sea. More than 7 million cubic feet of ancient Beirut have been lost forever' (Naccache 1996). In the end Solidere's bulldozers levelled more structures than did the entire civil war. The archaeological strata and the visible surviving townscape of the late-Ottoman and early-modern French Mandate periods were gone. Some maintain this colonial townscape did not belong to Lebanese national patrimony. Only with the rise of memory studies in the last twenty years, and especially as writers and the media began to lament the hole in memory that Solidere's erasures produced, has any mention of this history and the concept of heritage and patrimony been discussed at all.[22]

Whatever the point of view, many Lebanese have difficulty acknowledging truth about the war, calling the civil war 'the events' or 'the war of others' (Fisk 2000). Yet one voice, Alexandra Asseily, pushed Solidere to construct a garden of forgiveness amidst the ruins of the old Roman city. Although halted by the resumption of hostilities in 2006, it is planned to be a series of rectangular gardens of jasmine, orange and lemon trees, zigzagging through central Beirut along the green line that divided Beirut from north to south during the war. Asseily claims: 'I had an idea that there was something to be done to release all this pain. People died without acknowledgement, not only in this period of time but before and beyond. And there were all these moments in time that were passed over.'[23]

CONCLUSION

Clearly 'heritage terrorism', 'urbicide' and 'wars on memory' or 'selected amnesia' are unbalanced reactions – they not only threaten the memory and material artifacts of individuals and specific groups, they are fraught with problematic over-responses when retribution and restitution are provoked (Holtorf 2006). Destruction of material memory tokens engenders outrage not thoughtful consideration. After the Bamiyan Buddhas were blown up, some Muslim clerics condemned the destruction as 'an act of cultural genocide against humanity.'[24]

The anonymous destruction and construction, eradication and preservation, cannot be neatly separated, one gives rise to the other and both transform the sense of the past and places of memory in specific ways. Change, development and modernization inevitably entail loss – the same loss that engenders the 'memory machine' and the writing of history. Are the West's reactions overwrought, when amnesia covers over its own destructive crimes against memory and heritage in the wake of modernization, when it refuses to intervene in wars against civilian populations and the genocide of ethnic groups? Which is more important: the preservation of stones or the lives of people?

'Modern memory is, above all, archival. It relies entirely on the materiality of the trace, the immediacy of the recording, the visibility of the image' (Nora 1989, 13) But who has the right to make the final selection of what material artifacts are preserved and what destroyed, whose memories are narrated and whose obliterated? There is an on-going struggle over popular memory as Foucault (1989, 93) warned: how to obstruct the flow of oral testimony when too many memories seek inclusion, how to control the frameworks within which memory is formed, how to reprogramme 'what they must remember having been'. Linked to this is an endless struggle over how to write and memorialize history; how to archive, access and interpret the accumulation of discourses engendered by the 'memory machine', bubbling up from below or imposed from on high, written in words by scholars or in stones by architects. Conflicts over how to re-present collective memory, and what that re-presentation signifies, never abate.

If memory is considered to be the central medium through which identity is formed – individual, group or national – then has sufficient attention been given to why certain memories are taken up and used at specific times? Perhaps the exploding interest in collective memory has placed too much attention on symbols of cultural, religious or ethnic identity of a nation, group or people, because deliberate iconoclastic attacks on cultural heritage and cultural differences have not only increased but become primary war aims in their own right (Boylan 2001). Because post-conflict reconstruction and remembering never take place in a vacuum, a builder of places of memory must be aware of lingering resentments, unrecognized privileges, double standards in treatment of former enemies. In recovering from identity violence, memory can be productive or destructive, lead to renewal of war or peace and must be handled with utmost care.

There is no such thing as a therapy of place-making, as some maintain, nor do memory and temporality invade urban space through monuments, sculpture or architecture as others argue. Memory and temporality are not disembodied abstractions that haunt or invade anything; they are too various and pluri-vocal to be locked up in stone or settled in place. Memories collected in the public sphere represent a multiplicity of arguments: debatable, contestable, suppressible, includable and transformable. In this contentious complexity, architecture as the archetypal collective memory must ask what its practice obscures, suppresses, transforms, what its icons and symbols are imputed to signify, and how its processes of memorialization are linked to other discourses stored in the archive of memory and time.

NOTES

1 See quotation: 92.

2 Quoted by Müller 2002, 16.

3 For an overview of memory studies see Olick and Robbins 1998, 105–140.

4 Quoted by Müller 2002, 12, 21, 33.

5 'Urbanity is one of the highest abstractions of the human spirit [Bogdanovic claims]. To me, to be an urban man means to be neither a Serb nor a Croat, and instead to behave as though these distinctions no longer matter, as if they stopped at the gates of the city.' 'Interview with Bogdan Bogdanovic, Serbian architect', *Rencontre européennei* 7 (February, 2008); quotation: 1; 'Urbicide' was used by Marshall Berman to describe the willful use of the bulldozer by Robert Moses in the destruction of the South Bronx in the 1950s and 1960s, see Berman 1983; 'Urbicide' en.wikipedia.org/wiki/urbicide.

6 Quoted by Boyer 2008, 51–78.

7 See also 'Buddha Statues Destroyed Completely' *The News* (March 13, 2001): unpaginated.

8 'All We Are Breaking Are Stones' *AFP* (February 27, 2001): unpaginated.

9 See quote: 558.

10 The horrors of 9/11 were intentionally visible, marking them as distinct from other aerial attacks. There were no cameras at Dresden, Hamburg or Hiroshima (Retort 2004, 5–21; Weber 2002, 449–458).

11 For more about the spectacle and the WTC towers see Retort 2005.

12 The spectacle is capital accumulated to such a degree that it becomes an image. See Debord 1983.

13 Michael Arad, January 14, 2004. Quoted by Pedersen 2004.

14 Death squads of Tutsis lured Hutus to the place of sanctuary in churches and then systematically slaughtered them. So churches became the centre of

struggle over the creation and preservation of memory as memorials to genocide (Longman and Rutagengwa 2006).

15 See also quotation: 103.

16 Pohlandt-McCormick 2006, Chapter 6 'Violence and the Construction of History' in 'I Saw a Nightmare'.

17 Quotation from novelist Ghad Al-Samman (1997) in Sawalha 2002, 52.

18 Desmond Tutu, seeking truth and reconciliation in post-apartheid South Africa, explained 'None of us have the power to say, "Let bygones be bygones" and, hey presto, they then become bygones. Our common experience in fact is the opposite – that the past, far from disappearing or lying down and being quiet, is embarrassingly persistent, and will return and haunt us unless it has been dealt with adequately. Unless we look the beast in the eye we still find that it returns to hold us hostage' (quoted by Haugbølle 2002, 8).

19 'wast al-balad'.

20 Quoted by Bloch-Jørgensen et al. 2006, 67.

21 'Beirut madina ariqa lil mustaqbal'.

22 An essay based on a public lecture presented by Saliba (2000).

23 Alexandra Asseily quoted by Fisk (2000).

24 '"Medival" Taliban Lashed over Buddhist Demolition' *AFP* (March 2, 2001): unpaginated www.rawa.org/statues.htm

19

Concepts of Vernacular Architecture

Robert Brown and Daniel Maudlin

For most people the term 'vernacular architecture' means buildings such as English thatched cottages and clapboarded New England salt-boxes, mud huts in Africa, or the tin and concrete-block ziggurats of the Brazilian favela: things from the rural past and things from foreign places that are associated with the identity of the people who built and live, or lived, in them. In addition, for some, the vernacular may also call to mind the work of contemporary architects whose buildings are in the style of a certain region. These popular perceptions broadly mirror those distinctions between architecture and buildings held by architects and architectural historians for whom, typically, vernacular architecture has been categorized as the study of 'traditional buildings': buildings that are, or were, the authentic product of a specific place and people, have evolved in form over time, and are produced by non-expert 'ordinary people' through shared knowledge passed down over time. The vernacular has, therefore, been widely understood as '"the architectural language of the people" with its ethnic, regional and local dialects: the product of "non-experts"' (Oliver 2006). Since the rise of modernism in the twentieth century, architectural writers have tended to admire what they regarded as traditional buildings for the immediate relationship between form and function that they believed controlled their 'design': practical responses to practical considerations. Indeed, the term 'vernacular architecture', as opposed to traditional, vernacular or folk buildings, first appeared in the post-war period of the 1950s and 1960s when architects sought to appropriate simple traditional buildings to legitimize prevalent functionalist theories of design. Vernacular architecture was characterized as a functional shelter for people, animals and stores, 'built to meet needs', constructed according to the availability and performance of materials and formed in response to environmental and climatic conditions (Oliver 2006; Al Sayyad 2004).

However, since the folklorists of the early twentieth century, traditional buildings have also been studied within the fields of ethnography, cultural geography and material culture where they have been interpreted as artefacts of human culture. Influenced by these wider fields of cultural study, in the latter part of the twentieth century architectural writers such as Amos Rapoport and Paul Oliver extended our understanding of the elements that contribute towards the production and evolution of traditional buildings to include cultural practices and social rituals, or the study of 'cultural impact' (Rapoport 1969; Oliver 2006). Thus, according to Oliver, the cultural impact upon a building is the totality of human values, activities and artefacts which affect the formation of the building and which give meaning and direction to the lives that occupy it (Oliver 2006). By this interpretation, vernacular architectures, whether built of stone, timber, mud or tin, are not simply exemplars of the modernist tenet that 'form follows function' but complex social and cultural relations spatially constituted (Jackson 1989). The terms 'social' and 'cultural' typically refer to the activities of a localized, sub-national, people and place in the study of traditional buildings. Indeed, prior to modernism, the identification of vernacular architecture with a distinct people and place had been a prevalent theme of post-Romantic Western architecture. In recent years, the study of vernacular architecture has become, or become again, the study of the cultural impact of a specific people upon building practices in a specific place (a geographic area defined by historic socio-cultural boundaries). The designation of traditional buildings as cultural assets has had political implications. Vernacular architectures are often used interchangeably by governments to establish and enforce national and sub-national identities. However, our understanding of the local has also changed to recognize that spatial constructs of culture are shifting as the phenomenon of globalization and the formation of new global networks, both physical and virtual, impact upon our perception of both place and identity (Castells 1996b; Mathews 2000).

The equation of vernacular architecture with traditional buildings is only part of the picture. Indeed, the definition of the term 'vernacular architecture' is not universally agreed and may be extended to include the 'everyday': city neighbourhoods, provincial market towns, roadside diners, suburban housing developments, generic edge-of-town retail barns and anonymous industrial complexes. In the late 1980s and 1990s, architectural writers found new theoretical foundations for the study of everyday buildings in the writings of cultural theorists such as Michel de Certeau and Henri Lefebvre (de Certeau 1984; Lefebvre 1991). The everyday can refer to the anonymous 'provincial' versions of fashionable architectural styles by unknown, or forgotten, architects and builders such as the classically proportioned eighteenth-century farmhouses of the American east coast (Glassie 2000). However, the everyday also describes a wide range of anonymous contemporary buildings and places. It is what Robert Venturi described as the 'ugly and the ordinary', from the mass-produced domesticity of trailers and the suburban 'condo' development to the 'decorated sheds' of the edge-of-town strip mall (Venturi et al. 1977 [1972]). The contemporary everyday may also include buildings that are personal gestures of individuality: the attention-grabbing kitsch of Venturi's duck-shaped roadside diner, the idiosyncratic American motels enjoyed by Umberto Eco or the hand-made 'outsider art' eco-homes of the hippies' earth-ships in New Mexico. The vernacular can also be extended to ordinary, anonymous places, 'non-places', such as vacant lots, the backs of buildings, the undersides of bridges and the verges of highways that are appropriated by urban subcultures (street gangs, skateboarders, graffiti artists) (Auge 1995; Borden 2001; Chase et al. 1999). Moving further still from the thatched cottage, the everyday vernacular may also include functionally-determined industrial structures such as oil refineries, power stations and the prairie-spires of giant grain-silos across the American Midwest.

VERNACULAR ARCHITECTURE AS OTHER

From the traditional to the everyday, the term 'vernacular' incorporates a broad mixture of unrelated buildings. However, common to all vernacular buildings is that they are positioned by architects and architectural historians outside of what is considered 'architecture'. They are 'other'. The vernacular is removed from the self-authorized discourse and practice of the architectural mainstream whether positively, as a source of learning and inspiration or critique of professional practice, or negatively, when seen as a threat or dismissed as unworthy of attention (Orum-Nielsen 1995; Vesely 2006). This relationship between the sanctified and unsanctified is not new, and has been with us at least since an ideological battle between tradition and innovation arose when the Romans copied the Greeks (Lowenthal 1985). Such oppositions evoke the linguistic roots of the term 'vernacular' as a local language in juxtaposition to the official Latin of the Roman Empire.

This sense of the 'other' in architectural discourse positions the vernacular as antiquated, archaic, traditional (and fixed), as low culture and non-professional versus a contemporary, modern, innovative, high culture and professional pantheon of architectural praxis. 'Architecture' is not only different from the vernacular, it is superior: socio-economic and aesthetic hierarchical distinctions are both implied and explicit. From a culturally relativist point of view, these judgements are to be understood as deeply rooted in the history of Western culture, from aesthetic theory to the history of art and architecture (the canon of what is art and what is not), architectural education, practice and building production. However, as Marcel Velligna notes, the marginalization of the vernacular is not confined to 'architecture'; within the fields of ethnography, cultural anthropology and material culture there is a disposition to 'us' and 'them' dichotomies that serve to 'define the vernacular in opposition to categories like the formal and especially, the modern, and that essentially relegate vernacular traditions to a time and space that is distinctly different from the latter' (Upton 1993; Vellinga 2006).

Discussions of the vernacular as 'other' therefore place it in a series of oppositions to 'architecture': the antiquated against the contemporary; the archaic against the modern; the traditional against the innovative. It is a conflict presented as distinctions between low culture and high culture, layman and professional, the anonymous and the authored as well as the spontaneous and the planned, the circumstantial and the conceptual and the passed-down and the designed. The creation of such dualities restricts our understanding, narrows discussion and reinforces existing bias and preconceptions. It is misleading to view the relationship between 'vernacular architecture' and 'architecture' as opposites which reluctantly meet at a typological barrier. Positioned behind this boundary are fixed constructs of time, place, production, origin, intent and ownership, authenticity, heroism, morality and truth, which fail to recognize the interdependence of products and processes across the built environment. Such a barrier distorts our understanding of architecture, or as critiqued here, what has been separately defined as both vernacular architecture and 'architecture'.

This predisposition towards categorization, the drawing up of boundaries and territories, can itself be interpreted as a peculiarly Western intellectual activity. As Torgovnick (1999; cited in Forty 2006, 11) argues, we make sense of our world '... in the act of defining the other'. Arguably, such tendencies arise out of Western philosophical, scientific and religious traditions, which objectify and structure the world into a hierarchal order; such actions are characteristic of what Bellah (2003) defines as axial (i.e. Western) cultures. This tendency is further reflected through essentialism, a belief in '... the true essence of things, the invariable and fixed properties which define the "whatness" of a given entity' (Fuss 1989; cited in Morton 2003, 73). Such practice is equally endemic to academic discourse, through which boundaries define both disciplines and their operations (Crysler 2003). This tendency towards categorization is a reductive act which ignores the individuality, complexity and shift of knowledge. Moreover, this cataloguing runs the danger of putting all concepts, paradigms and approaches into one inflexible restrictive structure (Spivak 1990), and ultimately homogenizing them while reducing their distinctiveness (Crysler 2003). While useful to navigate conditions and negotiate meaning, categorization puts in place narrow, fixed definitions and rigid, inflexible boundaries which are limiting and cannot deal with ambiguities that defy easy explanation or organization. The depth, complexity and range of vernacular architectures, and their cultural meanings, have therefore been rendered inaccessible to 'architecture' through the creation of the hold-all category of the 'other'.

ARCHITECTURE, ART AND THE VERNACULAR

The categorization of vernacular architecture as 'other', those buildings that are not 'architecture', has created a hierarchy of two distinct, self-contained, professional and academic fields – architecture, and with it architectural history, and vernacular architecture studies – each with its own parameters, methodologies, typologies, professional bodies and academic societies. Famously, the architectural historian Nikolaus Pevsner opened *An Outline of European Architecture* (1943) with: 'A bicycle shed is a building: Lincoln Cathedral is a piece of architecture … Nearly everything that en-closes space on a scale sufficient for a human being to move in is a building; the term architecture applies only to buildings designed with a view to aesthetic appeal'. One is revered as conceptual art and design while the other is dismissed as merely inhabited space. The study of architecture and architectural history since the post-war period of Pevsner has predominantly focused upon cathedrals – and the building of canons of known works by known architect-artists – whilst the study of bicycle sheds, especially traditional ones, has become the remit of vernacular architecture studies. Pevsner, writing in the 1940s, was clear that what we now characterize as 'vernacular architecture' is not architecture at all; just buildings. However, in the 1950s, the term 'vernacular architecture', a contradiction in terms for Pevsner, emerged in order to re-examine architecture through the prism of traditional buildings: 'vernacular architecture' signified the appropriation of traditional buildings by post-war architectural writers concerned with functional determinism. Through the structural analysis of traditional buildings, texts such as Sybil Maholy-Nagy's *Native Genius of Anonymous Architecture* (1957) sought to demonstrate that the principle of functional determinist that underpinned modernism was a universal, *a priori* architectural condition (Heynen 2008). The subtitle of Bernard Rudofsky's highly influential 1964 MOMA exhibition, and best-selling catalogue, *Architecture Without Architects: A Short Introduction to Non-pedigreed Architecture*, makes clear Rudofsky's intention to position traditional buildings within 'architecture' through the interrogation of authorship. Rudofsky was very selective in his choice of examples in order for his functionalist agenda to have the required impact on modernist architecture 'at home' (Scott 2001). Functional determinism, and a preoccupation with the relationship between site, structure and materials, has been highly influential upon the formulation of vernacular architecture studies as an academic field. Subsequently, traditional buildings have been assimilated into professional architecture as forms have been interpreted and understood in the Euro-American language of architecture (Crysler 2003). Writing in the late 1960s, architects Paul Oliver and Amos Rapoport expanded

Rudofky's interest in the form and function of traditional buildings to consider the cultural impact, or human dimension, of traditional buildings. Since *Shelter and Society* (1969), Paul Oliver has repeatedly demonstrated that traditional buildings are a rich cultural resource: highly complex objects that can express multiple meanings through form and decoration, enclose inhabitable space and frame human ritual and the performances of daily life (Oliver 1969; 2003; 2006). Oliver has further argued that '"vernacular building" and "monumental architecture" should be considered together as part of an interdependent totality' (Crysler 2003). However, this goal is still only partially achieved across architectural practice and education. Published in the same year, Amos Rapoport's *House Form and Culture* (1969) was also highly influential. Rudofsky, Oliver and Rapoport were formative in the development of the field of vernacular architecture studies. Within the academic field that has emerged, the value of traditional buildings has been based upon the comparably narrow criteria of age, authenticity and 'ethical' criteria of 'purity of form', 'truth to materials', and 'economy of means', all of which are employed to establish the worth of a building (Vellinga 2006). Underlying such judgements is 'an inclination to disregard those vernacular traditions that do not satisfy the[se] criteria' (Oliver 2006).

As such, for many, the field of vernacular architecture has often considered the influence of, or contact with, design and the architect-artist as an indication of decline and the corruption of regional evolved traditions (Arciszewska and McKellar 2004). Within the history of buildings this has created an academic no-man's-land between recognized works of architecture and 'authentic' traditional buildings occupied by the anonymous everyday buildings that make up the vast bulk of the historic built environment. In Britain for example, the national building boom of the eighteenth century, which visually defined a new national culture connected by revolutions in industry, transport and communications (print), has been considered by vernacular architecture specialists as the beginning of the end.

The pioneering work of Oliver and Rapoport established links between architecture and other areas of cultural studies. The study of traditional buildings has always been common to a number of academic disciplines outside of architecture. Across subjects such as ethnography, cultural anthropology, cultural geography, social history and material culture, vernacular architectures are considered as aspects of human settlement (as opposed to the aesthetic formal concerns that have preoccupied architectural discussions on the vernacular). These fields share a common academic heritage in the establishment of folklore studies in the early twentieth century (often with a national bias such as Scottish or Irish studies). Informed by the European nationalist movements of the later nineteenth century, folklorists had a post-Romantic fascination with pre-industrialized European societies and their traditions. Folklorists collected or recorded the material culture and intangible heritage (music, poetry, dance, ritual) of what they identified as authentic pre-industrial folk cultures. Like a pot or shoe, traditional buildings were recorded and collected as artefacts of material culture; an object that can be read in order to learn about human life. Significantly, though both Oliver and Rapoport came from architectural backgrounds, their pioneering early works were first published as cultural geography texts. In 2007, a shift away from architecture, and its internal debates, towards a broader interdisciplinary approach within the field of vernacular architecture studies was signalled when the Vernacular Architecture Forum, based in the United States, changed the title of its journal from *Perspectives in Vernacular Architecture* to *Buildings and Landscapes*.

Through *Buildings and Landscapes,* the Vernacular Architecture Forum has also extended its typological boundaries beyond traditional buildings to embrace contemporary everyday buildings and places whether the suburbs, the mall, trailer parks, casinos or factories. Where architectural thinking has extended to contemporary everyday buildings it has taken two distinct approaches. Venturi's *Learning from Levittown* analysis of 1970s' mass-production and suburban housing did not aim to claim the status of art for those houses but to value them as cultural artefacts that provided 'signs' by which we can understand the post-industrial consumer. The practices and places of the everyday discussed by cultural theorists such as Michel de Certeau and commentators like Umberto Eco, an enthusiastic explorer of the world of kitsch, logically include ordinary and anonymous buildings as indicators of mass-consumer practices, a way to understand the activities and values of 'ordinary' people (Eco 1986). Ideas such as de Certeau's notion of 'bricolage' have filtered into architectural thinking and provided a cultural framework within which we can consider the evolved, non-designed conflation of structures and spaces that create places such as the city neighborhood (de Certeau 1984). Subsequent cultural theorists have re-emphasized the role of political-economic power in Western culture and argue that 'the field of cultural studies has vastly overestimated the power of consumers by failing to keep in view the determining role of production on cultural consumption, the capitalist cultural industries produce only an apparent variety of products whose variety is finally illusory' (Garnham 1997). In turn, this theoretical repositioning of the consumer in relation to cultural production has influenced recent interpretations of the meaning and processes of everyday architectural production (Maudlin 2009).

In contrast, the everyday has also been absorbed by architects as a specific visual aesthetic – a source of inspiration. Modernism, in particular the architects of the Bauhaus, embraced the processes and products of industrial mass-production for their aesthetic as well as their functional qualities (famously at both the Farnsworth House and Seagram Building, Mies van der Rohe had occasion to chose aesthetics over function). This twentieth-century industrial vernacular aesthetic was further developed by post-war British architects such as Alison and Peter Smithson (Hunstanton School, Norfolk, 1954), James Stirling (Leicester University Engineering Building, 1959) and Norman Foster and Richard Roger's early work as Team 4 (Reliance Controls Factory, Swindon, 1967). The aesthetics of the everyday and consumption took on a different guise in the 1980s when architects influenced by Venturi's *Learning Las Vegas,* such as Michael Graves, embraced kitsch and pop culture. Lefaivre and Tzonis (2001) referred to the act of 'defamiliarization' in critical regionalism, in which specific elements of the vernacular are re-employed in a contemporary, though intentionally unfamiliar – i.e. abstract – manner, is also reflective of this engagement; it allows mainstream architecture to 'touch' the vernacular whilst 'keeping its hands clean' (Cairns 2006). Contemporary vernacular architecture is equally active in such appropriation, with fragments and forms of 'polite' architecture finding their way into popular culture for aesthetic and symbolic affect, often without any reference to the intentions underlying their original production.

The distinction between the vernacular and 'architecture' has to a large extent been formed out of historic professional, academic and social constructs. Distinct from the operative Masonic lodges and apprenticeship systems of builders and the building industry, 'architecture' as an artistic, scholarly and socially exclusive activity can be identified in Abbot Suger's conception of the medieval royal chapel of St. Denis, in the Renaissance humanist writings of Alberti, and in the eighteenth-century works of gentleman-architects such as Lord Burlington and Thomas Jefferson. However, 'architecture' fully emerged as a profession with the foundation of governing bodies across Europe and North America in the early to mid-nineteenth century. In doing so, the profession established itself as the gatekeeper of not only who enters into the profession, but also of what constitutes 'architecture'. This delineation has been sustained by a self-referential architectural press and the architectural awards system, each of which has helped to define and reinforce what is 'architecture' (Prak 1984; Spector 2001).

These practice-centred distinctions have been further perpetuated by architectural education. The emphasis upon canons of works, visual form and its implied meaning (as intended by the architect-artist) over the role and meaning of the building for the lives of its inhabitants has also dominated the teaching of design and architectural history in schools of architecture. Concerns such as business management, building economics, build-ability and the collaborative nature of building production, have also been marginalized in favour of prioritizing a conceptual and perceptual (i.e. artistic) focus (Crinson and Lubbock 1994; Cuff 1998 [1991]). Consideration of the cultural contexts of architecture that lend themselves to the interrogation of anonymous everyday buildings (old and new) and an engagement with issues relating to environment, psychology, gender, ethnicity and global cultures has been excluded from what Kingsley (1988) has called the 'great men, great monuments' approach, i.e. white, Western, male, architect-generated architecture. Equally, while we may criticize twentieth-century architectural education for a tendency to ignore the vernacular, it has also been the case that the scientific research methodologies of non-architectural disciplines that incorporate traditional buildings, such as archaeology and ethnography, compound this exclusion through the production of work that is 'often expressed in a technical language and published in inaccessible places' (Dyer 1997). However, architectural education has shifted considerably over the last two decades. The increased emphasis placed upon the human contexts of architecture in degree programmes, as opposed to exclusively abstract formal considerations, has seen a move away from the canonical, artist-and-object approach to history and theory towards a broader understanding of the built environment which encompasses many of the cultural aspects of vernacular architecture studies. Accordingly, the use of traditional canonical histories as key texts has declined in favour of more holistic approaches such as Spiro Kostof's *A History of Architecture* (1995 [1985]) and *The City Shaped: Urban Patterns and Meanings Through History* (1991), Simon Unwin's *Analyzing Architecture* (1998), and more recent attempts at reformulating the canon in global terms such as *A Global History of Architecture* (Ching et al. 2006).

THE PRIMITIVE HUT AND THE SEARCH FOR AUTHENTICITY

The search for architecture's origins in the vernacular is a recurring theme in architectural theory where it appears as a notional primitive hut, a place of origin, rather than actual traditional buildings. The primitive is called upon to represent both the local (as place of origin) and the universal (as archetypal). First articulated in Laugier's *An Essay on Architecture* in 1753, the origin myth of the 'primitive hut' has been explored by successive architects and theorists, from William Chambers in mid-eighteenth-century Britain, to Gottfried Semper and Otto Wagner in the nineteenth century, through to Le Corbusier's primal forms, the writings of Bernard Rudofksy or Sybil Moholoy-Nagy and Joseph Rykwert's *On Adam's House in Paradise* in the twentieth century. The appeal of the primitive hut is not so much what it is, but rather what it represents: the pure, the archetypal; it is a structure responsive to its inhabitant's needs and aspirations without stylized preconception, something shared by all in the collective unconsciousness. Further, it is seen as a source of renewal (Cairns 2006; Rykwert 1972) and salvation in the face of the impure, the decadent, and the eclectic that can arise from and infiltrate aesthetic and formal practice. As such, the primitive has served as a known and immutable point of reference, providing a critique of contemporary practice when it becomes too self-indulgent (Forty 2006). The primitive hut has also made repeated appearances as a place of salvation and the object of longing in the writings of popular literary authors from Henry David Thoreau's Walden (1854) to Michael Pollan's *A Place of My Own* (1997) (both are narratives of its realization).

Central to the construct of the primitive has been the notion of authenticity, which has surfaced as a consistent theme in contemporary debates relating to both the vernacular and contemporary architecture. The romanticizing of the primitive grants it an inherent dignity, unencumbered by the contingencies and impurities that too often compromise the noble aspirations of primitive man's/woman's counterpart, the architect. However, the authentic is elusive. Defined as of 'undisputed origin, genuine, done in the traditional or original way', it can also be that which is done 'in a way that faithfully resembles the original' (Pearsall 1998). Peter Blundell Jones' inquiry into this search for the authentic, notably in terms of tectonic and social authenticity, concluded that an absolute sense of the authentic may be unobtainable, owing to selective (and various and repeated) manipulations of form, tectonics and meaning (Jones 1991a, 1991b, 1991c and 1992; Handler 1986). Identifying the authentic is especially problematic when operating across boundaries, principally cultural but also geographic, economic, political, professional and social boundaries, arising from a tendency to presume that the cultural determinants that inform buildings are fixed and belong to specific social-cultural groups; this is compounded by a propensity to look at other cultures as having 'internally consistent essences' (Bozdogan 1999). As Lefaivre and Tzonis (2001) point out, we make constructs by imposing criteria informed by our prior beliefs and desires. In essence, we see what we want to see through selective 'codes by which we delineate, symbolize, and classify the world around us' (Lowenthal 1985). These preconceptions are a particular challenge when crossing boundaries (whether cultural, economic, political or social), where we tend to rely on our own experience when evaluating a new condition. Though such ethnocentrism is common, this frame of reference may lead to misleading or reductive interpretations and conclusions (Tuan 1974; Rapoport 1989; Spivak 1990). Such preconception perpetuates the myth of a single point of origin for the primitive (Coyne 2006), and overlooks the diversity and flux which exist within cultures: they are all 'continually in a process of hybridity' (Bhabba 1990; cited in Menon 2001). The privileged status accorded to the primitive again illustrates the artificial barriers and underlying bias that divide the vernacular and 'architecture' and further delimits our understanding of the built environment. As Rykwert notes, 'the primitive hut has appeared as a paradigm of building: as a standard by which other buildings must in some way be judged', invoked by architects as 'right because it was first' (1972, 13). Such deification conflicts with the more recent advocacy of the vernacular as a dynamic, evolving tradition (Asquith and Vellinga 2006) and with modernism's positivist, progressive central tenet.

TRADITION AND MODERNITY

Arguably, the most long-standing and vociferous debate within architecture is the dichotomy between tradition and modernity. As previously discussed, this conflict goes back at least to the Romans, and again re-emerged during the Renaissance as a battle between the ancient and the modern (the classicists and scientists). The historicist debate was exemplified in the nineteenth century by Gottfried Semper's indecisiveness on whether 'architecture's traditional types, its language of forms, must be discarded in a new architectural order, or whether their life can be extended by a process of abstraction on the existing condition' (Mallgrave 1988). To the architects and designer-makers of the Art and Crafts movement at the turn of the twentieth century, tradition was understood as something valuable but imperilled, a fragile vessel of cultural identity and memory that needed to be protected and perpetuated against the forces of industrialization and urbanization.

Architectural discourse in the twentieth century continued to present tradition and modernity in terms of opposites: with tradition presented first as the negative and later as the positive. To some extent a reaction against nineteenth-century historicism, the early advocates of modernism professed to believe in modernity and the future, rationalism, technological progress and social advancement. These positive modern values were positioned as a direct and deliberate departure from tradition and the past, irrationality, technological inferiority and reactionary politics (Crysler 2003). However, in the post-war period, tradition began to be presented positively as the cure to the perceived failures of international modernism. For a new generation of architectural writers such as Paul Oliver, Amos Rapoport and Bernard Rudofsky, global traditional cultures and their buildings embodied a sense of place and cultural authenticity that had been destroyed, forgotten or corrupted in modern capitalist society; 'tradition was an Eden-like paradise about to be lost to modernity' (Crysler 2003).

Subsequently, there has been a tendency within the field of vernacular architecture studies to define tradition through reference to posterity, accumulation and continuity. Central to this definition is the assumption that tradition means 'unquestioning conformity' (Lewcock 2006) and orthodoxy (Oliver 2006). This static interpretation of traditional or vernacular architecture has been compared to a paralysed body (Upton 1993). Such reductive interpretations ignore one of the meanings of the word, '"to bring across", and to provide guidance – guidance, indeed, for contemporary actions' (Rowe 1996). In *The Past is a Foreign Country*, Lowenthal (1985) set out a range of often conflicting views; for example, he suggests that for the British, the past is revered for its continuity and accumulation and is central to the identity of place and themselves, while for Americans, the past has typically been a 'reminder of decadence and dependency' and is dismissed by many as irrelevant. This interpretation of tradition is reflected within the contemporary heritage sector. Heritage organizations are concerned with history and employ a definition of the vernacular which pertains only to traditional buildings and ignores current vernacular activity, such as self-build housing. In Britain, Paul Oliver has argued that both governmental and independent heritage organizations have interpreted 'vernacular architecture' as 'traditional buildings' due to the underlying assumption that the primary value of traditional buildings is as vessels of half-forgotten cultural memories that, therefore, must be protected from change and loss (Oliver 2006). The British system for preserving old buildings through the statutory Listed Building process supports this idea, fixing a notional point in a building's history as its completion, typically the date of listing sometime in the later twentieth century (Lowenthal 1985).

The twentieth-century critical presentation of modernity and tradition as two forces in opposition encapsulated a familiar set of dichotomies: old/new, east/west, progress/conservation or stagnation. But, in practice, since the early twentieth century modernity and tradition have been fused in a set of complex interrelationships characterized by ambiguity and fluidity (Upton 1993). Modernist architects embraced aspects of tradition while simultaneously rejecting it in favour of modernity and progress. Adolf Loos argued that 'tradition represented the process of critical thought that eventually brought everything to an equivalent plane of rationalized perfection' (Crysler 2003). Alvar Aalto's use of traditional, local (Finnish) materials is well known and he is often presented as a point of origin for the regionalist strand within contemporary architecture (Pallasmaa 2007 [1988]; St John Wilson 2007 [1995]). Modernist notions of spatial organization and formal abstraction also informed the post-war reinterpretation of traditional buildings as 'vernacular architecture', as evidenced in the abstracted black and white photography of Rudofsky's *Architecture without Architects* (Scott 2001). Modernist housing schemes in both interwar Vienna and post-war Britain combined modernist forms and mass-produced materials with traditional settlement patterns (Heynen 1999b). Indeed, in Britain, with its strong Arts and Crafts legacy and sense of national character embedded in a mythologized rural past, the dialogue between tradition and modernity, especially the 'spirit of place', persisted throughout the modernist experiment and informed British architects' fascination with Aalto and Scandinavian modernism. Tradition informed the work and thinking of many modern British architects and planners: from the 'village greens' of Taylor and Green's 1950s public housing projects; to Alison and Peter Smithson's urban model of the 'grille', based on the Yorkshire village of West Burton, presented at the tenth CIAM congress at Dubrovnik in 1955; and the picturesque 'snaking lines' of the traditional English village eulogized in Gordon Cullen's 1961 *Townscape* (Powers 2007; Maudlin 2009).

Janet Abu-Lughod has further argued that the conception of tradition and modernity as geographic, as well as temporal, opposites was formed from an anachronistic 'Western' colonial and immediate postcolonial, world view (1992). Intrinsic to the structuring of these oppositions were the perceived attitudes and values that different cultures have towards the past and future. In the 1960s, Amos Rapoport argued that Western culture tends to be more oriented towards the future, while in 'non-Western', 'traditional' cultures modern ideas and practices are seen as a threat to valued traditions (Rapoport 1969). Since the 1960s, the experience of economic development in India and throughout Africa has demonstrated a desire for 'Western' buildings which are valued as symbols of modernity. While ecological issues of climate change and sustainability have questioned the assumption that modernization equates with progress, increasingly the imperative for sustainable design has also led architects globally to question the twentieth century's commitment to technological progress and to reconsider modernity by looking to their own past to solve the problems of the immediate future. However, the differentiation between tradition and modernity cannot be grafted on to a perceived conflict between a monolithic 'West' and 'non-Western' cultures: a problematic and changing relationship between tradition and modernity is a global issue. Abu-Lughod presents a world of multiple modernities characterized by hybridity and global interdependence within which tradition is an active process (1992); what Ananya Roy has described as the 'corrupting impact of history upon modernity' (2001, 7). Tradition can be better understood not in terms of opposition but as a creative, adaptive and reflective process within modernity (Asquith and Vellinga 2006; Bronner 2006).

PLACE, CULTURE AND IDENTITY

Nezar Al Sayyad has observed that 'for anything to be considered vernacular, it has always been assumed that it must be native or unique to a specific place, produced without the need for imported components and processes' (2004). This long-standing role of traditional buildings (defined as and, at times, defining the term 'vernacular architecture') in 'Western' architecture as a signifier of people and place was established in the late eighteenth century when the study of folk cultures and their products first gained validity as a field of intellectual enquiry and aesthetic pleasure. Emerging out of the picturesque tradition of the cottage ornée, most famously Marie Antoinette's pastoral-fantasy *hameaux* at Versaille, the Romantic movement celebrated regional traditional buildings as representative of place and valued artefacts of folk culture. Prior to romanticism, traditional buildings, especially cottages, were viewed as pieces of pastoral scenography or with disgust (Macarthur 2007). The architect-designed 'picturesque cottage', constructed from elements of vernacular architecture, first appeared in the mid-eighteenth century as part of the range of exotic *fabriques* positioned around the circulation routes of designed landscape gardens with the intention of evoking particular literary or historical associations. The picturesque celebrated the irregularity and variety of vernacular buildings and took an amoral aesthetic pleasure in scenes of rural poverty and material decay. Writing in the mid-nineteenth century, John Ruskin condemned this amoral position as the 'heartlessness of the picturesque ... a facile preoccupation with visual qualities which blind the weak minded to human suffering' (Macarthur 1997). Romanticism, however, set the specific national or regional significance of folk cultures against the universalizing principles of European Enlightenment thought and the cultural authority of classicism and classical architecture. The architectural perspective in romanticism was identified by Goethe in his analysis of Strasbourg cathedral which he argued was culturally significant because of its relevance to the history and people of Strasbourg, even though by the artistic standards of eighteenth-century critical analysis the building did not meet the criteria for 'good' architecture. Like Goethe in Germany, proto-Romantic English theories of the picturesque such as Uvedale Price's *Essay on the Picturesque* also sought to emphasise the specific aesthetics of place, including local building traditions, over universal, European, standards of taste (1794).

The picturesque and romanticism were the first European intellectual movements to embrace the 'other' and to set indigenous traditional buildings, and the value of place and people, in direct opposition to the universal forms and values of Classicism. Traditional buildings became revered as artefacts of a nation's culture. The desire for a nationally and regionally expressive architecture persisted in the national Historical Revival styles of the nineteenth century and the Arts and Crafts vernacular revival of the early twentieth century. While championing the hand-produced against mass production and an emerging machined aesthetic, the Arts and Crafts movement was equally a celebration of the local in opposition to the universal. The primitivist trend within modernism in the 1940s prompted another conflict, this time against the universality of the International Style. The modernist appropriation of the vernacular introduced traditional buildings to a generation of architects but it also redirected the study of vernacular architecture by architects away from a culturally sensitive, folkloric approach, towards a preoccupation with structures and materials.

However, outside of the artist-and-object concerns of authorized architectural discourse, romanticism has remained at the heart of vernacular or everyday architectures and has informed the persistent revival of traditional forms through the nineteenth and twentieth centuries, especially in suburban domestic architecture. A recent manifestation of this recurring theme is the neo-traditional developments associated with New Urbanism. New Urbanism emerged in North America in the 1980s and purported to advance the fundamental qualities of 'real towns' through a new form of urban development that restored a sense of community through diversity. This meant mixed-income housing, with public spaces, public buildings, small-scale businesses and retail outlets. Neo-traditional design was common but not fundamental to New Urbanism. Nonetheless, New Urbanism remains associated with neo-traditional architects such as Robert A.M. Stern. New Urbanists introduced 'traditional neighbourhood development' design codes

(TNDs) at developments such as Seaside, Florida, from 1978, and Kentlands, Gaithersburg, Maryland, 1988 (Haas 2008). In Britain, New Urbanism is famously represented by the village of Poundbury, Dorset, developed by Prince Charles with the neo-traditional architect and polemicist Leon Krier. Through the 1990s, neo-traditionalism has come to dominate commercial suburban developments in Britain and North America (Maudlin 2009). Regionalist architectural writers such as Liane Lefaivre, Juhani Pallasmaa and Kenneth Frampton have criticized this everyday neo-traditional architecture for its lack of authenticity in the reproduction of traditional buildings. Frampton, for example, argues that 'superficial historicism can only result in consumerist iconography masquerading as culture' (Frampton 2007 [1982], 377). While Tzonis has observed that 'like other kitsch works these [houses] feed settings of emotion and starve rationality – the message can be received without a translator' (Tzonis 2003, 19). Tzonis uses kitsch pejoratively, implying these buildings are cynically produced to please the aesthetically uneducated and artistically uninformed.

Intended as an aesthetic and critical counterpoint to commercial neo-traditionalism, the regionalism debate in contemporary architecture, a strand often traced back to Aalto, re-emerged with Lefaivre and Tzonis' articulation of Critical Regionalism (2003). Since Aalto, the process of site-specific aging, especially in materials, has been valued within regionalism both for its inherent beauty and for fostering a sense of time and place (Lynch 1993 [1972]; Mostafavi and Leatherbarrow 1993; Pallasmaa 2005). Central to the concept of critical regionalism was that it was critical of itself. As such, Tzonis and Lefaivre sought to identify a departure from conventional historicist regionalism in the works of architects such as Renzo Piano and Santiago Calatrava, which interrogate and reinterpret traditional materials and forms (Tzonis et al. 2001; Lefaivre and Tzonis 2003). The term critical regionalism was also employed by Kenneth Frampton, who proposed a building ethos that would embrace the liberating possibilities of modernization (in relation to technology and information) while resisting the homogenizing tendencies of production and consumption of a globalized world (Frampton 1986).

The conflict between the local and universal is also witnessed at the scale of the city, pitting the evolved, multi-layered historic European city – flawed, often-idealized but still working – against universalist city-planning models, such as the rational planning principles of the Athens Charter developed by the International Modern movement in the twentieth century. Influenced by texts such as Gordon Cullen's *The Concise Townscape* (2006 [1961]), Christopher Alexander's *The Pattern Language* (1977) and *The Timeless Way of Building* (1979), the high density, multi-functional districts and picturesque formal irregularity of the historic European city reinvigorated city planning in North America and Britain in the 1980s and led to planning models such as New Urbanism. In *The Death and Life of Great American Cities* (1965 [1961]), the vernacular of the American city neighbuorhood was celebrated by Jane Jacobs for its intimate human qualities, which Jacobs similarly ascribed to a traditional mixture of building types, building usage and social diversity. Described as 'weak urbanism', this model of a 'collage city' suggests an urban landscape of haptic experience that is intimate and participatory, and which accommodates a physical language of diversity, fragmentation and self-expression (Pallasmaa 2000, 82; Rowe and Koetter 1978). In the 'collage city' public acts of re-appropriation of 'public' space reflect de Certeau's notion that everyday activity is a form of resistance against the dominant socio-economic-political forces that control the city and its inhabitants; highly influential in the United States, *Everyday Urbanism* puts de Certeau's argument into practice (Chase et al. 1999). The traditional urban forms advocated by Cullen and Alexander and the *bricolage* of the city neighbourhood described by de Certeau establish a distinct 'here', in opposition to the perceived commodification and homogenization of place in the 'modern', especially modernist, city. These historicist urban models refer to a mythologized past, which, through their emphasis upon the specifics of place, evade the challenges of contemporary urban life such as spaces of 'super-modernity' and 'non-places' defined by transience, simultaneity, ever-increasing speed and an emerging de-territorialized global culture (McQuire 2000; Auge 1995; Parent 1996).

The 'other' is perhaps most evident in the delineation of cultural and ethnic boundaries; we are what they are not, and we are where they are not. The association of traditional and neo-traditional buildings with peoples and places can quickly lead to questions of identity, with vernacular architectures appropriated as convenient symbols of national and sub-national identities (Leach 2002 [1998]). The relationship between vernacular architecture, place and identity is therefore open to exploitation and the cultural value invested in regional architecture, historic or contemporary, must be questioned. National governments tend to adopt vernacular building traditions to support their national identity building political agendas. According to Nezar Al Sayyad, arguments against the contemporary forces of globalization, that character needs to be preserved through the use of traditional materials and forms, are generally weak, 'invoked to preserve particularly national or regional agendas' (2004, 6). In today's increasingly globalized world, dwelling is a widely differentiated experience, while some people are trapped in space others live an increasingly transient existence where cultural identity is reduced to networks of subcultures. In this complex contemporary context, the creation of contemporary places that use local vernacular architectures to evoke place-specific identity brings new social problems of exclusivity and exclusion.

At the global level, debates concerning culture, identity and place have, again, been conceived historically in terms of the 'other'; as the opposites of 'us and them', between the 'West' and 'non-Western' countries. In this duality, the 'West' is a geographic and cultural point of self-reference coined to distinguish Europe, Europeans and its 'white' former colonies in North America and the Antipodes, from the Occidental: those non-European, and alien, countries and peoples to the East (and elsewhere). This cultural condition is compounded and enforced by 'Westerners'' sense of cultural, and racial, superiority that has supported the colonial activities of European nation states. What 'Western culture' has classified as 'non-Western' indigenous architectures have historically been perceived by 'Westerners' as exotic, decadent, at times erotic – such as nineteenth-century depictions of gypsy or Arab cultures – and perhaps to be feared. From the Middle East, to Africa, India, Australia and North America, colonized cultures have also been derided as primitive (in the pejorative sense) and inarticulate (Hvattaum 2006). But, equally these 'non-Western' cultures and their traditional buildings have been admired by the 'West', often the colonial masters, for their perceived moral innocence and cultural authenticity. What is defined as authentic local culture (in opposition to external forces) is often imposed from outside. The outsider sees what they want to see, with little consideration given to local circumstances, operations or perceptions (Eggener 2002). Extended to its extreme, indigenous voices are silenced through this projection and the celebration of local identity becomes an act of intellectual imperialism (Spivak 1990).

Postcolonial governments in the 'Third World' have also appropriated this duality as a socio-political strategy, positioning themselves and their actions in terms of resistance to the hegemony of the 'West'. Global cultures outside of the 'West' have been apprehensive about the threat the 'West' presents to valued traditions. 'Western-influenced' modernization is distrusted where capitalism is perceived not simply as an economic system but as an ideology informing both politics and culture (Rowe 1996). Thus, the counterpoint of architectural identity-building can also be identified whereby 'non-Western' countries adopt 'Western' architectural styles as a statement of modernity. Within this oppositional construct attempts by 'non-Western' societies to resist such 'Western' ideological incursions through the maintenance of indigenous icons of cultural identities, including traditional buildings, have been described as 'defensive structuring' (Rapoport 1986).

Simplistic 'us and them' posturing has frequently been employed by national governments where traditional architectures are evoked and enforced by legislation to mask internal political divisions and domestic socio-economic difficulties. Referring to the 'West' and 'non-West' as unified categories and bounded territorial domains, set in opposition to each other, does not acknowledge the cultural differences and complexities within each or their interdependence (Abu-Lughod 1992; Crysler 2003). Concurrent with these ambiguities and complexities is what it means to be acting locally in an age of instantaneous communication; enabling architects in one culture in one part of the world to interact with another culture without ever leaving home, from Western conceptual architects brought into the developing world to deliver a branded vision, to computer technicians working at night in the developing world to generate construction drawings for practices in the West (Cuff 1999). These same means enable even the poorest of communities and organizations to interact globally, for instance, the National Slum Dwellers Federation in India and their equivalent in African nations, utilizing twenty-first-century technology to share experiences, knowledge and skills in their fight for improved living conditions.

INCOMPLETENESS, TRANSIENCE AND FLUX

Recent scholarship has repositioned 'tradition' as a process of change within a world of multiple modernities. Through such interrogations of prevalent concepts of vernacular architecture, ambiguity emerges as central to our understanding of buildings. Re-examining vernacular architecture also brings to light the concepts of incompleteness and transience in building and suggests their centrality to all architectures. Traditional buildings are often perceived as unchanging, fixed in a specific place and time since their initial completion, frozen and untouched over the course of their lives (Vellinga 2006). While incompleteness and transience is readily recognized in culturally dispossessed contemporary everyday buildings, whether the dwellings of the favela or the expanding suburbs, the fixing of 'tradition' by the heritage and tourism industries artificially disassociates traditional buildings from the changing cultural processes by which they were formed and are continuously reformed. Equally, professional architects typically aspire to achieve a timeless-ness in their buildings, illustrating architects', and historians', preoccupation with defining and fixing form (Duffy 1998). Architects tend to consider a building as complete upon the completion of building works. The occupation of the building and its subsequent adaptation, alteration, decoration and personalization by people is then often perceived in terms of decline; the unpopulated images of shiny new buildings in the architectural press are presented as a record of the building as a 'pure' art-object at its temporal zenith.

However, these notions of fixed architecture begin to unravel when interrogated in the context of the life-cycle of individual buildings and the built environment. A lesson that can be learned from a re-examination of the vernacular is that all buildings are incomplete and subject to change, as the occupants constantly alter and adapt their surroundings in response to changing cultural, economic, social and technological conditions and, increasingly, ecological concerns (Brand 1994). Indeed, thinking about buildings as completed objects is evidence of a tendency to focus on the conception and implementation of a building as its defining act and ignores a life-cycle-based view of architecture, which acknowledges that changes occur in form, use, operation and maintenance over time (Brown et al. 2005). All architecture can be understood as incomplete, shifting and transient (as can the socio-historical interpretive structures and categories through which we represent it). Both 'vernacular architecture' and 'architecture' are responsive to people, place and tectonics over time. Buildings are not merely physical form but cultural and social constructs which relate to wider, changing ecological, economic, political and technical sensibilities and concerns (Heath 2007). These concerns are constantly shifting. Equally, built forms and their meanings are subject to change over time and space, in response to these ongoing and evolving cultural conditions. The complex cultural relations that exist between buildings and people within the urban framework of the city have been repeatedly interrogated by Iain Borden and Jane Rendell (Borden and Rendell 2000; Borden 2001; Borden et al. 2003).

In addition to the temporal transience of building and buildings, the relationship between 'architecture' and the vernacular, between design and non-design, is also in a constant state of flux. Conceptual architecture, and architects, are constantly informed and refreshed by the vernacular, and the vernacular is constantly influenced and changed by the work of architects and designers. The conception of architecture and the vernacular as neatly opposed categories must again be questioned and reconceptualized in terms of hybridity, change and ambiguity (Upton 1993). There is no architecture, other than the unrealized and notional, that is untouched by conditions of the vernacular, such as materials and labour, and there is no vernacular building that is entirely uninformed by design, even if simply the inscribing of an outline of a plan in the ground. If the framing of the vernacular as 'other' is reconceptualized then vernacular architecture can be understood as a living condition within architecture, not tangential to it.

CONCLUSION

Whether thatched cottages or trailer parks, vernacular architecture is typically defined as those buildings that are outside the mainstream of professional, 'authorized' architecture. Throughout the twentieth century, the study of vernacular architecture tended to focus on its formal qualities, particularly of traditional buildings, reflecting an emphasis on functional determinism. Too often marginalized were the changing underlying cultural or social forces which generate the built environment, frame its interpretive structures and give deeper meaning to it over its life. While it has been granted legitimacy as a distinct field, the vernacular has tended to be registered only as a source for the appropriation of form, or as cultural activity unrelated to the theory and practice of architecture. Architecture can now be reconceptualized as a more inclusive and continuous field that includes the traditional and the everyday: the vernacular is a living condition within architecture. Rejecting the imposed positioning of vernacular architecture as 'other' can articulate a more permeable, and malleable definition of architecture. The artificially constructed dualities that have defined vernacular architecture as 'other' – art/anonymity, tradition/modernity, specific/universal, complete/incomplete – can be framed as questions with which to interrogate the processes and conditions within architecture. Concepts that are used to articulate the vernacular are fundamental to our understanding of all architectures; concepts that relate to the production and life of buildings such as incompleteness, shift and transience; and concepts that explore the relationships between buildings and people such as time, memory, place and identity.

Section 4 Bibliography

Abbas, Ackbar (1997) *Hong Kong. Culture and the Politics of Disappearance.* Minneapolis: University of Minnesota Press.

Abu-Lughod, Janet (1987) 'The Islamic City: Historic Myth, Islamic Essence, and Contemporary Relevance', *International Journal of Middle Eastern Studies* 19(May): 155–176.

—— (1992) 'Disappearing Dichotomies: First World–Third World; Traditional–Modern', *Traditional Dwellings Settlements Review*, 3(2): 7–12.

Adams, Nicholas (1993) 'Architecture as the Target', *The Journal of the Society of Architectural Historians* 52(4): 389–390.

Adham, Khaled (2004) 'Cairo's Urban *déjà vu*: Globalization and Urban Fantasies', in Yasser Elsheshtawy (ed.) *Planning Middle Eastern Cities: An Urban Kaleidoscope in a Globalizing World.* London: Routledge.

Al, Stefan (2010) 'The Strip: Las Vegas and the Evolution of Spectacle', PhD dissertation manuscript, UC Berkeley.

Alexander, Christopher (1977) *The Pattern Language – Towns, Buildings, Construction.* New York: Oxford University Press.

—— (1979) *The Timeless Way of Building.* New York: Oxford University Press.

AlSayyad, Nezar (ed.) (1992) *Forms of Dominance: On the Architecture and Urbanism of the Colonial Enterprise.* Aldershot: Avebury.

—— (1995) 'From Vernacularism to Globalism: The Temporal Reality of Traditional Settlements', *Traditional Dwellings and Settlements Review,* 7(1): 13–24.

—— (ed.) (2001) *Consuming Tradition, Manufacturing Heritage: Global Norms and Urban Forms in the Age of Tourism.* London: Routledge.

—— (2004) 'The End of Tradition, or the Tradition of Endings?', in Nezar Al Sayyad (ed.) *The End of Tradition?* London: Routledge, 1–29.

Al Sayyad, Nezar and Jean-Paul Bourdier (eds) (1989) *Dwellings, Settlements and Tradition: Cross-Cultural Perspectives.* Lanham, MD: University Press of America.

Anderson, Benedict R.O'G. (1983) *Imagined Communities: Reflections on the Origin and Spread of Nationalism.* London: Verso.

—— (1992) *The Werthem Lecture 1992. Long Distance Nationalism. World Capitalism and the Rise of Identity Politics.* Amsterdam: CASA (Center for Asian Studies).

Appadurai, Arjun (1996) 'Disjuncture and Difference in the Global Economy' in *Modernity at Large. Cultural Dimensions of Globalization.* Minneapolis: University of Minnesota Press, 27–47.

Appiah, Kwame (2007) *Cosmopolitanism: Ethics in a World of Strangers.* New York: Norton.

Arciszewska, Barbara and McKellar, Elizabeth (2004) 'Preface', in Barbara Arciszewska, and Elizabeth McKellar (eds) *Articulating British Classicism: New Approaches to Eighteenth-Century Classicism.* Aldershot: Ashgate, ix–xxv.

Asad, Talal (2007) *On Suicide Bombing.* New York: Columbia University Press.

Ascherson, Neal (2001) 'Heritage Terrorism' Is a Way of Sticking Two Fingers to the West', *The Observer,* Sunday, March 4.

Asher, Catherine and Thomas Metcalf (1994) *Perceptions of South Asia's Visual Past.* New Delhi: American Institute of Indian Studies.

Asquith, Lindsay and Marcel, Vellinga (2006) 'Introduction', in Lindsay Asquith and Marcel Vellinga (eds) *Vernacular Architecture in the Twenty-First Century – Theory, Education and Practice.* Abingdon: Taylor & Francis, 1–20.

Auge, Mark (1995) *Non-Places: Introduction to an Anthropology of Supermodernity.* Translated by John Howe. London: Verso.

—— (2004) *Oblivion.* Translated by Marjolijn de Jager. Minneapolis: University of Minnesota Press.

Axelrod, Alan (ed.) (1985) *The Colonial Revival in America*. New York: Norton.

Badiou, Alain (2006) *Polemics*. London: Verso.

Barton, Craig E. (ed.) (2001) *Sites of Memory Perspectives on Architecture and Race*. New York: Princeton Architectural Press.

Bastea, Elena (2004) *Memory and Architecture*. Albuquerque: University of New Mexico Press.

Baudrillard, Jean (1975) *The Mirror of Production*. St. Louis: Telos Press.

—— (1981) *For a Critique of the Political Economy of the Sign*. New York: Semiotexte.

—— (1983) *Simulations*. Translated by Paul Foss, Paul Patton and Philip Beitchman. New York: Semiotexte.

Baxter, Charles (1999) *The Business of Memory: The Art of Remembering in an Age of Forgetting*. St. Paul, MN: Graywolf Press.

Bell, Duncan (2009) 'Introduction: Violence and Memory', *Millenium: Journal of International Studies* 38(2): 345–360.

Bellah, Robert (2003) *Imaging Japan – The Japanese Tradition and its Modern Interpretation*. Berkeley. University of California Press.

Benjamin, Walter (1969) 'The Work of Art in the Age of Mechanical Reproduction' in *Illuminations*. Translated by Harry Zohn. New York: Schocken Books.

—— (1970) 'Thesis on the Philosophy of History', in *Illuminations*. London: Cape, 245–255.

—— (1979) 'The Critique of Violence,' in *One-Way Street and Other Writings*. Translated by Edmund Jephcott and Kingsley Shorter. London: Verso, pp. 132–154.

Bennett, Tony (1995) *The Birth of the Museum. History, Theory, Politics*. New York and London: Routledge.

—— (2004) *Pasts Beyond Memory: Evolution, Museums, Colonialism*. London: Routledge.

—— (2006) 'Exhibition, Difference and the Logic of Culture', in Ivan Karp et al. (eds), *Museum Frictions. Public Cultures/Global Transformations*. Durham, NC: Duke University Press, pp. 46–69.

Berliner, David (2005) 'The Abuses of Memory: Reflections on the Memory Boom in Anthropology', *Anthropological Quarterly* 78: 18–23.

Berman, Marshall (1970) *The Politics of Authenticity: Radical Individualism and the Emergence of Modern Society*. New York: Atheneum.

—— (1983) *All That Is Solid Melts into Air: The Experience of Modernity*. New York: Verso.

Bet-El, Ilana R. (2002) 'Unimagined Communities: The Power of Memory and the Conflict in the Former Yugoslavia', in Jan-Werner Müller (ed.) *Memory & Power in Post-War Europe*. Cambridge University Press, 206–222.

Bevan, Robert (2006) *The Destruction of Memory. Architecture at War*. London: Reaktion Books.

Bhabha, Homi (1990) 'The Third Space', in Jonathan Rutherford (ed.) *Identity: Community, Culture, Difference*. London: Lawrence and Wishart.

Bierman, Irene (2005) 'Disciplining the Eye: Perceiving Medieval Cairo', in Nezar Al Sayyad, Irene Bierman and Nasser Rabat (eds) *Making Cairo Medieval*. Lanham, MD: Lexington Books.

Bloch-Jørgensen, Kasper, Stine Vijlby Jensen and Metter Vinggaard (2006) 'Achieving Reconciliation in Lebanon?', *International Development Studies*, BAS (May).

Blouin, Francis X. Jr. and William G. Rosenberg (2007) *Archives, Documentation and Institutions of Social Memory: Essays from the Sawyer Seminar*. Ann Arbor, MI: University of Michigan Press.

Bluestone, Daniel (1994) 'Preservation and Renewal in Post-World War II Chicago', *Journal of Architectural Education*, 47(4): 210–223.

—— (1999) 'Academics in Tennis Shoes: Historic Preservation and the Academy', *Journal of the Society of Architectural Historians*, 58(3): 300–307.

Borden, Iain (2001) *Skateboarding, Space and the City: Architecture and the Body*. London: Berg Publishers.

Borden, Iain and Jane, Rendell (2000) *InterSections: Architectural Histories and Critical Theories*. London: Routledge.

Borden, Iain, Tim Hall and Malcolm Miles (eds) (2003) *The City Cultures Reader*. London: Routledge.

Boyarin, Jonathan (1994) *Remapping Memory: The Politics of TimeSpace*. Minneapolis: University of Minnesota Press.

Boyer, M. Christine (1994) *The City of Collective Memory. Its Imagery and Architectural Entertainments*. Cambridge, MA: MIT Press, 407–420.

—— (2002) 'Meditations on a Wounded Skyline and Its Stratigraphies of Pain', in Michael Sorkin and Sharon Zukin (eds) *After the World Trade Center*. New York: Routledge, 109–120.

—— (2008) 'Urban Operations and Network Centric Warfare', in Michael Sorkin (ed.) *Indefensible Space: The Architecture of the National Insecurity State*. London and New York: Taylor & Francis, 51–78

Boylan, Patrick J. (2001) 'The Concept of Cultural Protection in Times of Armed Conflict: From the Crusades to the New Millennium', in K.B. Tubb and N. Brodie (eds) *Illicit Antiquities*. London: Routledge, 43–76.

Boym, Svetlana (2001) *The Future of Nostalgia.* New York: Basic Books.

Bozdogan, Sibel (1999) 'Architectural History in Professional Education: Reflections on Postcolonial Challenges to the Modern Survey', *Journal of Architectural Education* 52(4): 207–215.

Brand, Stewart (2004) *How Buildings Learn: What Happens After They're Built.* New York: Viking Penguin.

Breckenridge, Carol, A. (1989) 'The Aesthetics and Politics of Colonial Collecting: India at World's Fairs', *Comparative Studies in Society and History* 31: 195–216.

Bristol, Kate (1991) 'The Pruitt-Igoe Myth', *The Journal of Architectural Education* 44(3): 163–171.

Bronner, Simon (2006) 'Building Tradition: Control and authority in vernacular architecture', in Lindsay Asquith and Marcel Vellinga (eds) *Vernacular Architecture in the Twenty-First Century – Theory, Education and Practice.* Abingdon: Taylor & Francis, 23–45.

Brown, Robert, Kalra, Ripkin and Theis, Michael (2005) *The Rough Guide to Community Asset Management.* London: MLC Press.

Brown, Wendy (2006) *Regulating Aversion. Tolerance in the Age of Identity and Empire.* Princeton, NJ and Oxford: Princeton University Press.

Buck Morss, Susan (1997) 'Historical Ruins', in *Dialectics of Seeing. Walter Benjamin and the Arcades Project.* Cambridge, MA: MIT Press, 159–204.

Buchanan, Iain and Greg Lambert (2005) *Deleuze and Space.* Edinburgh: University of Edinburgh Press.

Butler, Judith (2004) *Precarious Life. the Powers of Mourning and Violence.* London and New York: Routledge.

Cairns, Stephen (2006) 'Notes For an Alternative History of the Primitive Hut', in Jo Odgers, Flora Samuel and Adam Sharr (eds) *Primitive – Original Matters in Architecture.* London: Routledge, 86–95.

Caplan, Pat (2003) 'Anthropology in the New World (Dis)order', keynote lecture given at the Conference of Anthropologists of Southern Africa, University of Cape Town, August 24.

—— (2007) '"Never Again": Genocide Memorials in Rwanda', *Anthropology Today* 23(1) (February): 20–22.

Carpo, Mario (2007) 'The Postmodern Cult of Monuments', *Future Anterior* 4(2): 51–60.

Castells, Manuel (1989) *The Informational City: Information Technology, Economic Restructuring, and the Urban-Regional Process.* Oxford: Cambridge University Press.

—— (1996a) *The Rise of the Network Society.* Oxford: Blackwell Publishers.

—— (1996b) 'Globalization, Flows, and Identity: The New Challenges of Design', in William S. Saunders, (ed.) *Reflections on Architectural Practices in the Nineties.* New York: Princeton Architectural Press, 198–205.

Çelik, Zeynep (1997) *Urban Forms and Colonial Confrontations: Algiers Under French Rule.* Berkeley, CA: University of California Press.

Chakrabarty, Dipesh (2000) *Provincializing Europe. Postcolonial Thought and Historical Difference.* New York and London: Routledge.

Chase, John, Margaret Crawford and John Kaliski (1999) *Everyday Urbanism.* New York: The Monacelli Press.

Chatterjee, Partha (1993) *The Nation and Its Fragments: Colonial and Postcolonial Histories.* Princeton, NJ: Princeton University Press.

Cheah, Pheng and Bruce, Robbins (1998) *Cosmopolitics. Thinking and Feeling Beyond the Nation.* Minneapolis: University of Minnesota Press.

Ching, Francis, Mark, Jarzombek and Vikramaditya, Prakash (2006) *A Global History of Architecture.* Chichester: John Wiley.

Choay, Francois (2001) *The Invention of the Historic Monument.* Cambridge: Cambridge University Press.

Clough, Patricia Ticineto and Jean Halley (2007) *The Affective Turn. Theorizing the Social.* Durham, NC: Duke University Press.

Colvin, Christopher J. (2005) '"Brothers and Sisters, Do Not Be Afraid of Me" Trauma, History and the Therapeutic Imagination', in Katharine Hodgkin, Susannah Radstone (eds) *Memory History Nation: Contested Pasts.* Edison, NJ: Transaction Press.

Connerton, Paul (2009) *How Modernity Forgets.* Cambridge: Cambridge University Press.

Coombes, Annie E. (2003) *History after Apartheid, Visual Culture and Public Memory in Democratic South Africa.* Durham, NC: Duke University Press.

Coyne, Richard (2006) 'Digital Commerce and the Primitive Roots of Architectural Consumption', in Jo Odgers, Flora Samuel and Adam Sharr (eds) *Primitive – Original Matters in Architecture.* London: Routledge, 229–239.

Crawford, Margaret (1999) 'Blurring the Boundaries: Public Space and Private Life,' in John Chase, Margaret Crawford and John Kaliski, *Everyday Urbanism.* New York: Monacelli Press, 22–35.

Crinson, Mark (ed.) (2005) *Urban Memory. Historical Amnesia and the Modern City.* New York and London: Routledge.

Crinson, Mark and Jules Lubbock (1994) *Architecture – Art or Profession? Three Hundred Years of Architectural Education.* Manchester: Manchester University Press.

Crysler, Greig C. (1995) 'Critical Pedagogy and Architectural Education', *Journal of Architectural Education* (May): 208–217.

—— (2003) *Writing Spaces: Discourses of Architecture, Urbanism and the Built Environment, 1960–2000.* New York: Routledge.

—— (2006) 'Violence and Empathy: National Museums and the Spectacle of Society', *Traditional Dwellings and Settlements Review* (Spring): 19–38.

Crysler, C. Greig and Abidin Kusno (1997) 'Angels in the Temple. The Aesthetic Construction of Citizenship at the United States Holocaust Memorial Museum', *Art Journal* (Spring): 52–64.

Cuff, Dana (1998 [1991]) *Architecture: The Story of Practice.* Cambridge, MA: MIT Press.

—— (1999) 'The Political Paradoxes of Practice: Political Economy of Local and Global Architecture', *arq* 3(1): 77–88.

Cullen, Gordon (2006 [1961]) *The Concise Townscape.* Oxford: Elsevier.

Davis, Mike (1992) *City of Quartz. Excavating the Future in Los Angeles.* New York: Vintage Books.

Davis, Mike and Daniel Monk (eds) (2007) *Evil Paradises: Dreamworlds of Neoliberalism.* New York: New Press.

Davis, Natalie Zemon and Randolph Starn (1989) 'Introduction' *Representations* 26 (Spring): 1–6.

Davison, Patricia (2007) 'Museums and the reshaping of Memory', in Sarah Nuttall and Carli Coetzee (eds), *Negotiating the Past: The Making of Memory in South Africa.* Oxford: Oxford University Press.

de Certeau, Michel (1984) *The Practice of Everyday Life.* Berkeley: University of California Press.

—— (1986) *Heterologies. Discourses on the Other,* Translated by Brian Massumi. Minneapolis: University of Minnesota Press.

Debord, Guy (1983) *Society of the Spectacle.* Detroit: Black & Red.

Deutsche, Rosalyne (1996) *Evictions: Art and Spatial Politics.* Cambridge, MA: MIT Press.

Dubel, Janice (2001) 'Remembering a Japanese-American Concentration Camp at Manzanar National Historic Site', in Paul A. Shackel (ed.) *Myth, Memory and the Making of the American Landscape.* Gainsville, FL: University of Florida Press.

Duffy, Francis (1998) *Architectural Knowledge: The Idea of a Profession.* London: E & FN Spon.

Dupont, Jacques (1983) 'Viollet-le-Duc and Restoration in France', in Norman Williams, Edmund Kellogg and Frank Gilbert (eds) *Readings in Historic Preservation: Why? What? How?* New Brunswick, NJ: Center for Urban Policy Research.

Dyer, Christopher (1997) 'History and Vernacular Architecture', *Vernacular Architecture* 28: 1–8.

Eco, Umberto (1986 [1967]) *Travels in Hyperreality.* London: Picador.

Edwards, Penny (2007) *Cambodge: The Cultivation of a Nation 1860–1945.* Honolulu: University of Hawaii Press.

Eggener, Keith (2002) 'Placing Resistance: A Critique of Critical Regionalism', *Journal of Architectural Education* 55(4): 228–237.

Ellin, Nan (1996) *Postmodern Urbanism.* Cambridge, MA: Blackwell Publishing.

Elsheshtawy, Yasser (2010). *Dubai: Behind an Urban Spectacle.* New York and London: Routledge.

Fanon, Frantz (1963) *The Wretched of the Earth.* New York: Grove Press.

Felix, Bruno and Femke Wolting (2005) *Lagos Wide and Close: An Interactive Journey into an Exploding City.* Amsterdam: Submarine Channel.

Findley, Lisa (2005) *Building Change. Architecture, Politics and Cultural Change.* New York and London: Routledge.

Fisk, Robert (2000) 'City Life: Beirut – Garden of Reconciliation but not Truth for a Civil War', *The Independent* (April 14): 19.

Flood, Finbarr Barry (2002) 'Between Culture and Culture: Bamiyan, Islamic Iconoclasm, and the Museum', *The Art Bulletin* 84(4) (December): 651.

—— (2007) 'Lost in Translation: Architecture, Taxonomy, and the Eastern "Turks"', *Muqarnas* 24.

Forster, Kurt W. (1982) 'Monument/Memory and the Mortality of Architecture', *Oppositions* 25.

Forty, Adrian (2006) 'Primitive: the Word and Concept', in Jo Odgers, Flora Samuel and Adam Sharr (eds), *Primitive – Original Matters in Architecture.* London: Routledge, 3–14.

Foster, Hal (ed.) (1983) *The Anti-aesthetic. Essays on Postmodern Culture.* Seattle: Bay Press

—— (1985) '(Post)modern Polemics', in *Recodings. Art. Spectacle, Cultural Politics.* Seattle: Bay Press,121–138.

—— (2004) An Archival Impulse. *October* 110(Fall): 3–22.

Foucault, Michel (1972) *The Archaeology of Knowledge.* Translated by Sheridan Smith. New York: Pantheon Books.

—— (1989) 'Film and Popular Memory', in *Foucault Live.* New York: Semiotext(e).

Frampton, Kenneth (1986) 'Place, Form, Cultural Identity', *Domus* 673: 17–24.

—— (2007 [1982]) 'Ten Points on an Architecture of Regionalism: A Provisional Polemic', in Vincent B. Canizaro (ed.) *Architectural Regionalism: Collected Writings on Place, Identity, Modernity, and Tradition.* New York: Princeton Architectural Press, 374–386.

Friedmann, John (1986) 'The World City Hypothesis' *Development and Change* 17(January): 69–84.

Fuchs, Ron and Epstein-Pliouchtch, Marina (2008) 'Myth, History and Conservation in Tel Aviv.' Paper presented at the Tenth International DOCOMOMO Conference, Rotterdam.

Fukuyama, Francis (1992) *The End of History and the Last Man.* New York: The Free Press.

Fuller, Mia (2007) *Moderns Abroad: Architecture, Cities and Italian Imperialism.* London and New York: Routledge.

Fuss, D. (1989) *Essentially Speaking: Feminism, Nature and Difference.* New York and London: Routledge.

Gandy, Matthew (2005) 'Learning from Lagos', *New Left Review* (May–June): 36–52.

Garnham, Nicholas (1997) 'Political Economy and the Practice of Cultural Studies', in Marjorie Ferguson and Peter Golding (eds) *Cultural Studies in Question.* London: Sage Publications, 45–68.

Gerstenblith, Patty (2006) 'From Bamiyan to Baghdad: Warfare and the Preservation of Cultural Heritage at the Beginning of the 21st Century', *Georgetown Journal of International Law* (Winter): 1–58.

Gevisser, Mark (2008) 'From the Ruins: The Constitution Hill Project', in Achille Mbembe and Sarah Nuttall, (eds) *Johannesburg: The Elusive Metropolis.* Durham, NC: University of North Carolina Press.

Giddens, Anthony (1979) *Central Problems in Social Theory.* Berkeley: University of California Press.

Giedion, Sigfried (1941) *Space Time and Architecture.* Cambridge, MA: Harvard University Press.

Gilloch, Graeme (1996) *Myth and the Metropolis: Walter Benjamin and the City.* Cambridge: Polity Press.

Glassie, Henry (2000) *Vernacular Architecture.* Bloomington: Indiana University Press.

Godlewski, Joseph (2010) 'Alien and Distant. Rem Koolhaas on Film in Lagos, Nigeria', *Traditional Dwellings and Settlements Review,* 7–19.

Goldstein, Daniel M. (2004) *The Spectacular City. Violence and Performance in Urban Bolivia.* Durham, NC: Duke University Press.

Gottdiener, Mark (1986) *The City and the Sign: An Introduction to Urban Semiotic.* New York: Columbia University Press.

—— (2001) *The Theming of America: Dreams. Media Fantasies and Themed Environments.* Boulder, CO: Westview.

Graham, Stephen (2002) 'Clean Territory: Urbicide in the West Bank', www.openDemocracy.net (August 7).

Gregory, Derek and John Urry (1995) *Social Relations and Spatial Structures.* London: Macmillan.

Grusin, Richard (2004) 'Premediation', *Criticism* 46(1) (Winter): 17–40

Guha-Thakurta, Tapati (2004) *Monuments, Objects and Histories: Institutions of Art in Colonial and Postcolonial India.* New York: Columbia University Press.

Haas, Tigram (2008) *New Urbanism and Beyond: Designing Cities for the Future.* New York: Rizzoli.

Halbwachs, Maurice (1992) *On Collective Memory.* Translated by Lewis A. Coser. Chicago: University of Chicago Press.

Hall, Peter (1988) *Cities of Tomorrow: An Intellectual History of Urban Planning and Design in the Twentieth Century.* Malden, MA: Blackwell Publishing.

Hanafi, Sari (2001) 'Targeting Space through Bio-politics: The Israeli Colonial Project', *Palestinian Report* 10(32) www.palestinereport.ps/article.php?architect=267 (February 18).

Handler, Richard (1986) 'Authenticity', *Anthropology Today* 2(1): 2–4.

—— (1988) *Nationalism and the Politics of Culture in Quebec.* Madison, WI: University of Wisconsin Press.

Harris, Steven and Deborah Berke (1997) *Architecture of the Everyday.* New York: Princeton Architectural Press.

Hart, Gillian (2002) *Disabling Globalization. Places of Power in Post-Apartheid South Africa.* Berkeley and Los Angeles: University of California Press.

Hartman, Saidya V. (1997) *Scenes of Subjection. Terror, Slavery and Self-Making in Nineteenth Century America.* New York and Oxford: Oxford University Press.

Harvey, David (1989) *The Condition of Postmodernity.* Oxford: Blackwell Press.

—— (2000) *Spaces of Hope.* Berkeley and Los Angeles: University of California Press.

—— (2001) *Spaces of Capital: Towards a Critical Geography.* New York and London: Routledge.

—— (2006) *A Brief History of Neoliberalism.* Oxford: Oxford University Press.

—— (2008) 'The Right to the City.' *The New Left Review* (Sept–Oct): 23–40.

Hass, Kristin Ann (1998) *Carried to the Wall. American Memory and the Vietnam Veteran's Memorial.* Berkeley, Los Angeles and London: University of California Press.

Haugbølle, Sune (2002) 'Looking the Beast in the Eye: Collective Memory of the Civil War in Lebanon', unpublished Master Studies, St. Antony's Collective, University of Oxford, www.111101.net/Writigns/listingwritings.php?typerawcmd=a+Haugbolle.+T-6k>

Hayden, Dolores (1988) 'Placemaking, Preservation and Urban History', *Journal of Architectural Education* 41(3).

Heath, Kingston (2007) *Exploring the Vernacular in Contemporary Regional Design: Cultural Process and Environmental Response*. Oxford: Architectural Press.

Hemmings, Clare (2005) 'Invoking Affect. Cultural Theory and the Ontological Turn', *Cultural Studies* 19(5): 548–567.

Herscher, Andrew and Andras Riedlmayer (2000) 'Monument and Crime: The Destruction of Historic Architecture in Kosovo', *Grey Room*, 1(Autumn).

Heynen, Hilde (1999a) 'Petrifying Memories: Architecture and the Construction of Identity', *The Journal of Architecture* 4(4): 369–390.

—— (1999b) *Architecture and Modernity*. Cambridge, MA: MIT Press.

—— (2008) 'Anonymous Architecture as Counter-Image: Sibyl Moholy-Nagy's Perspective on American Vernacular', *The Journal of Architecture* 13(4): 469–491.

Hickey, David (1997) *Air Guitar. Essays on Art and Democracy*. Los Angeles: Art Issues Press.

Hobsbawn, Eric and Terence Ranger (1983) *The Invention of Tradition*. Cambridge: Cambridge University Press.

Holden, C.W. and W.G. Holford (1951) *The City of London: A Record of Destruction and Survival*. London: Architectural Press.

Holtorf, Cornelius (2006) 'Can Less Be More? Heritage in the Age of Terrorism', *Public Archaeology* 5: 101–109.

Hosmer, Charles (1965) *Presence of the Past: A History of the Preservation Movement in the United States Before Williamsburg*. New York: Putnam.

—— (1981) *Preservation Comes of Age: From Williamsburg to the National Trust, 1926–1949*. Charlottesville, VA: National Trust for Historic Preservation in the United States by the University Press of Virginia.

Hou, Jeffrey (ed.) (2010) *Insurgent Public Spaces: Guerilla Urbanism and the Remaking of Contemporary Cities*. New York and London: Routledge.

Huxtable, Ada Louise (1983) 'Resurrecting a Prophetic Nineteenth Century Practitioner,' in Norman Williams, Edmund Kellogg and Frank Gilbert (eds) *Readings in Historic Preservation: Why? What? How?* New Brunswick, NJ: Center for Urban Policy Research.

Huyssen, Andreas (1995) *Twilight of the Memories. Marking Time in a Culture of Amnesia*. London and New York: Routledge.

—— (2003) *Present Pasts Urban Palimpsests and the Politics of Memory*. Stanford: Stanford University Press.

Hvattum, Mari (2006) 'Origins Redefined – A Tale of Pigs and Primitive Huts', in Jo Odgers, Flora Samuel and Adam Sharr (eds) *Primitive – Original Matters in Architecture*. London: Routledge, 33–42.

Ito, Nobuo (1995) '"Authenticity" Inherent in Cultural Heritage in Asia and Japan', in K.E. Larsen (ed.) *Nara Conference on Authenticity (Japan 1994. Proceedings)*. Rome: UNESCO, ICCROM, ICOMOS.

Jackson, Peter (1989) *Maps of Meaning*. London: Routledge.

Jacobs, Jane (1965 [1961]) *The Death and Life of Great American Cities*. London: Penguin.

Jacobs, Jane M. (1996) 'Negotiating the Heart: Place and Identity in the Postimperial City', in *Edge of Empire: Postcolonialism and the City*. London: Routledge.

Jameson, Frederic (1991) *Postmodernism or the Cultural Logic of Late Capitalism*. Durham, NC: Duke University Press.

—— (1994) *The Seeds of Time*. New York: Columbia University Press.

—— (1998) *The Cultural Turn. Selected Writings on the Postmoderm 1983–1998*. London: Verso.

—— (2003) 'Future City', *New Left Review* 21(May–June 2003): 65–79.

Jameson, Frederic and Michael Speaks (1992) 'Envelopes and Enclaves: The Spaces of Post-Civil Society (An Architectural Conversation)', *Assemblage* 17(April): 30–37.

Jan, Abid Ullah (2001) 'Blowing Statues vs. Satanic Savagery', The Independent Center for Strategic Studies and Analysis (June 26).

Jarzombek, Mark (1999) 'Molecules, Money and Design. The Question of Sustainability's Role in Architectural Academe', *Thresholds* 18: 32–38.

—— (2000) *The Psychologizing of Modernity. Art, Architecture and History*. Cambridge: Cambridge University Press.

Jencks, Charles (1977) *The Language of Postmodern Architecture*. New York: Rizzoli.

Jokilehto, Jukka (1985) 'Authenticity in Restoration Principles and Practices', *Bulletin of the Association for Preservation Technology* 17(3/4).

—— (1999) *A History of Architectural Conservation.* Oxford: Butterworth Heinemann.
Jones, Peter Blundell (1991a) 'In Search of Authenticity', *The Architect's Journal*, October 30: 26–30.
—— (1991b) In Search of Authenticity – Part 2', *The Architect's Journal*, November 6 : 32–6.
—— (1991c) 'In Search of Authenticity – Part 3', *The Architect's Journal*, December 4: 21–5.
—— (1992) 'In Search of Authenticity – Part 4', *The Architect's Journal*, January 8 and 15: 29–32.
Judn, Hilton and Ivan, Vladislavic (eds) (1998) *Blank. Architecture, Apartheid and After.* Rotterdam: NAI Editions.
Kaplan, E. Ann (2005) *Trauma Culture: The Politics of Terror and Loss in Media and Literature.* New Brunswick: Rutgers University Press.
Karo, Ivan, Corine a Kratz, Lynn Szwaja and Tomas Ybarra-Frausto (eds) (2006) *Museum Frictions. Public Cultures/Global Transformations.* New York and London: Routledge.
Kern, Stephen (1983) *The Culture of Time and Space, 1880–1918.* Cambridge, MA: Harvard University Press.
Kimmelman, Michael (2002) 'Out of Minimalism, Monuments to Memory,' *New York Times* (January 13): A1.
King, Anthony D. (1990) *Global Cities.* London: Routledge.
—— (2004) *Spaces of Global Cultures.* London and New York: Routledge.
Kingsley, Karen (1988) 'Gender Issues in Teaching Architectural History', *Journal of Architectural Education* 41(2): 21–25.
Kipnis, Jeffrey (1996) 'Beijing and Seoul', in *Anywise.* New York: Anyone Corp, 168–175.
Kirkbride, Robert (2009) *Architecture and Memory. The Renaissance Studioli of Federic de Montefeltro.* New York: Columbia University Press.
Klein, Kerwin (2000) 'On the Emergence of Memory in Historical Discourse', *Representations* 69: 127–150.
Koolhaas, Rem (1997) 'Singapore Songlines', in *SMLXL.* New York: Monacelli Press, 1008–1089.
—— (1999), 'Cities on the Move,' in *Cities on the Move. Urban Chaos and Global Change. East Asian Art, Architecture and Film Now.* London: Hayward Gallery.
—— (2002) 'Junkspace,' *October* 100(Spring): 175–190.
—— (2007) *Lagos: How it Works.* Basel: Birkhauser.
Koolhaas, Rem and Hans-Ulrich Obrist (1991), 'An Accelerated Merzbau', in *Cities on the Move.* London: The Hayward Gallery, 16–19.
Koshar, Rudy (1998) *Germany's Transient Pasts: Preservation and National Memory in the Twentieth Century.* Chapel Hill, NC: University of North Carolina Press.
—— (2000) *From Monuments to Traces. Artifacts of German Memory 1870–1990.* Berkeley, Los Angeles and London: University of California Press.
Kostof, Spiro (1991) *The City Shaped: Urban Patterns and Meanings Through History.* London: Thames & Hudson.
—— (1995 [1985]) *A History of Architecture: Settings and Rituals.* Oxford: Oxford University Press.
Kusno, Abidin (2000) *Behind the Postcolonial: Architecture, Urban Space, and Political Cultures in Indonesia.* New York: Routledge.
—— (2010) *The Appearances of Memory. Mnemonic Practices of Architecture and Urban Form in Indonesia.* Durham, NC: Duke University Press.
Kwinter, Sandford (1992) 'Rem Koolhaas, OMA. Urbanism after Innocence', *Assemblage* 18 (August): 83–85.
Ladd, Brian (1997) *The Ghosts of Berlin. Confronting German History in the Urban Landscape.* Chicago: University of Chicago Press.
Landsberg, Alison (2004) *Prosthetic Memory. The Transformation of American Remembrance in the Age of Mass Culture.* New York: Columbia University Press.
Lasansky, Medina (2004) *The Renaissance Perfected: Architecture, Spectacle, and Tourism in Fascist Italy.* University Park, PA: Pennsylvania University Press.
Laugier, Marc-Antoine (1977 [1753]) *An Essay on Architecture.* Translated by Wolfgang Herrmann and Anni Herrmann. Los Angeles: Hennessey & Ingalls.
Leach, Neil (2002 [1998]) 'The Darkside of the Domus', in Andrew Ballantyne (ed.) *What is Architecture?* London: Routledge, 88–102.
Lefaivre, Liane and Alexander Tzonis (2003) 'Tropical Critical Regionalism', in Alexander Tzonis, Liane, Lefaivre and Bruce Stagno (eds) *Tropical Architecture – Critical Regionalism in the Age of Globalization.* Chichester: John Wiley, 1–13.
Lefebvre, Henri (1984 [1968]) *Everyday Life in the Modern World.* Translated by Sacha Rabinowitz. New Brunswick, NJ: Transaction Books.
—— (1991 [1958]) *Critique of Everyday Life.* Translated by John Moore. London: Verso
—— (1991 [1974]) *The Production of Space.* Translated by Donald Nicholson-Smith. Malden: Blackwell Publishing.
—— (2004 [1992]) *Rhythmanalysis: Space, Time and Everyday Life.* London: Continuum.

Lewcock, Ronald (2006) 'Generative Concepts in Vernacular Architecture', in Lindsay Asquith and Marcel Vellinga (eds) *Vernacular Architecture in the Twenty-First Century – Theory, Education and Practice*. Abingdon: Taylor & Francis, 199–214.

Libeskind, Daniel (1999) *Daniel Libeskind. Jewish Museum. Between the Lines*. New York: Prestel.

Longman, Timonthy and Rheoneste Rutagengwa (2006) 'Religion, Memory, and Violence in Rwanda', in Oren Baruch Stier and J. Shawn Landres (eds) *Religion, Violence, Memory and Place*. Gary: Indiana University Press, 132–149.

Loukaitou-Sideris, Anastasia (2009) *Sidewalks: Conflict and Negotiation over Public Space*. Cambridge, MA: MIT Press.

Lowenthal, David (1985) *The Past is a Foreign Country*. Cambridge: Cambridge University Press.

—— (1995) 'Changing Criteria of Authenticity', in K.E. Larsen (ed.) *Nara Conference on Authenticity (Japan 1994. Proceedings)*. Rome: UNESCO, ICCROM, ICOMOS.

—— (1998) *Possessed by the Past: The Heritage Crusade and the Spoils of History*. Cambridge: Cambridge University Press.

Lury, Celia (1998) *Prosthetic Culture Photography Memory and Identity*. London: Routledge.

Lynch, Kevin (1993 [1972]) *What Time Is This Place?* Cambridge, MA: MIT Press.

Lyndon, Donlyn and Charles, Moore (1994) *Chambers for a Memory Palace*. Cambridge, MA: MIT Press.

Lyotard, Jean-François (1984 [1979]) *The Postmodern Condition: A Report on Knowledge*. Minneapolis: University of Minnesota Press.

Macarthur (1997) 'The Heartlessness of the Picturesque: Sympathy and Disgust in Ruskin's Aesthetics', *Assemblage* 32(April): 126–141.

—— (2007) *The Picturesque: Architecture, Disgust and other Irregularities*. London: Routledge.

MacGillivray, Alex (2006) *A Brief History of Globalization: The Untold Story of our Incredible Shrinking Planet*. Philadelphia: Running Press.

Maholy-Nagy, Sybil (1957) *Native Genius of Anonymous Architecture*. New York: Horizon Press.

Maier, Charles (1993) 'A Surfeit of Memory? Reflections on History, Melancholy and Denial', *History & Memory* 5(2): 136–152.

Maleuvre, Didier (1999) *Museum Memories: History, Technology, Art*. Stanford: Stanford University Press.

Mallgrave, Harry (1988) 'Introduction', in Otto Wagner, *Modern Architecture*. Translated by Harry Mallgrave. Santa Monica: Getty Center for the History of Art and the Humanities, 1–54.

Marin, Louis (1984) *Utopics: Spatial Play*. Translated by Robert A. Volirath. New Jersey: Atlantic Highlands.

Marot, Sebastien (2003 [1999]) *Urbanism and the Art of Memory*. London: Architectural Association.

Massey, Doreen (1994) 'Flexible Sexism', in *Space, Place and Gender*. Minneapolis: University of Minnesota Press, 212–248.

Massey, Doreen (1995) *Spatial Divisions of Labor: Social Structures and the Geography of Production*. New York: Routledge.

Matero, Frank, G. (2007) 'Loss, Compensation, and Authenticity: The Contribution of Cesare Brandi to Architectural Conservation in America', *Future Anterior*, 4(1).

Mathews, Gordon (2000) *Global Culture/Individual Identity*. London: Routledge.

Maleuvre, Didier (1999) *Museum Memories: History, Technology, Art*. Stanford: Stanford University Press.

Maudlin, Daniel (2009) 'Constructing Identity and Tradition: Englishness, Politics and the Neo-Traditional House', *Journal of Architectural Education* 63(1): 51–64.

McLeod, Mary (1989) 'Architecture and Politics in the Reagan Era: From Postmodernism to Deconstructivism', *Assemblage* 8(February): 22–59.

—— (1997) 'Henri Lefebvre's Critique of Everyday Life: An Introdction,' in Steven Harris and Deborah Berke (eds) *Architecture of the Everyday*. New York: Princeton Architectural Press, 9–29.

McQuire, Scott (2000) 'Blinded by the (Speed of) Light', in John Armitage (ed.) *Paul Virilio – From Modernism to Hypermodernism and Beyond*. London: Sage Publications, 142–160.

Menon, A. G. Krishna (2001) 'Thinking "Indian" Architecture', in Andrzej Piotrowski, and Julia Williams Robinson (eds) *The Discipline of Architecture*. Minneapolis: University of Minnesota Press, 83–102.

Merrifield, Andy (2006) *Henri Lefebvre: A Critical Introduction*. New York: Routledge.

Meskell, Lynn (2002) 'Negative Heritage and Past Mastering in Archaeology', *Anthropological Quarterly* 75: 557–574.

Metcalf, Thomas (1989) *An Imperial Vision: Indian Architecture and Britain's Raj*. Berkeley, CA: University of California Press.

Miele, Chris (ed.) (2005) *From William Morris: Building Conservation and the Arts and Crafts Cult of Authenticity 1877–1939*. New Haven, CT: Yale University Press.

Mitchell, Timothy (2002) *Rule of Experts: Egypt, Techno-Politics, Modernity*. Berkeley: University of California Press.

Morton, Patricia (2000) *Hybrid Modernities. Architecture and Representation at the 1931 Colonial Exposition.* Cambridge, MA: MIT Press.

Morton, Stephen (2003) *Gayatri Chakravorty Spivak.* London: Routledge.

Mostafavi, Mohsen and David Leatherbarrow (1993) *On Weathering – The Life of Buildings in Time.* Cambridge, MA: MIT Press.

Müller, Jan-Werner (ed.) (2002) *Memory & Power in Post-War Europe: Studies in the Presence of the Past.* Cambridge: Cambridge University Press.

Mumford, Eric (2000) *The CIAM Discourse on Urbanism, 1928–1960.* Cambridge MA: MIT Press.

Murphy, Kevin (2002) 'The Villa Savoye and the Modernist Historic Monument', *Journal of the Society of Architectural Historians* 6(1).

Myers, Fred (2006) 'The Complicity of Cultural Production: The Contingencies of Performance in Globalizing Museum Practices', in Karp, Ivan et al (eds), *Museum Frictions. Public Cultures/Global Transformations.* Durham, NC: Duke University Press, pp. 46–69.

Naccache, Akbert F.H. (1996) 'The Price of Progress', www.archaeology.or/9607/abstracts/beirut.html

Nalbantoglu, Gulsum Baydar (1998) 'Towards Post-colonial Openings: Rereading Sir Banister Fletcher's *History of Architecture', Assemblage* 35: 5–17.

Navaro-Yashin, Yael (2007) 'Affective Spaces, Melancholic Objects. Ruination and the Production of Anthropological Knowledge,' *Journal of Royal Anthropological Institute* 15: 1–18.

Nemeth, Erik (2007) 'Cultural Security: The Evolving Role of Art in International Security', *Terrorism and Political Violence* 19: 33–34.

Newfield, Christopher (2008) *Unmaking the Public University: The Forty Year Assault on the Middle Class.* Cambridge, MA: Harvard University Press.

Nitzan-Shiftan, Alona (1996) 'Contested Modernism: Erich Mendelsohn and the Tel Aviv Chug in Mandate Palestine', *Architectural History.* 39.

Nora, Pierre (1984–1992) *Les Lieux de Mèmoire,* 7 vols. Paris: Gallimard.

—— (1989) 'Between Memory and History: Les Lieux de Mémoire', *Representations* 26(Spring): 23.

Olick, Jeffrey K. (ed.) (2005) *States of Memory/ Continuities, Conflicts and Transformations in National Retrospection.* Durham, NC: Duke University Press.

—— (2007) *The Politics of Regret On Collective Memory and Historical Responsibility.* New York and London: Routledge.

Olick, Jeffrey K. and Joyce Robbins (1998) 'Social Memory Studies: From "Collective Memory" to the Historical Sociology of Mnemonic Practices', *Annual Review of Sociology* 24: 105–140.

Oliver, Kelly (2004) *The Colonization of Psychic Space. A Psychoanalytic Social Theory of Oppression.* Minneapolis: University of Minnesota Press.

Oliver, Paul (ed.) (1969) *Shelter and Society.* New York: Praeger.

—— (2003) *Dwellings: The Vernacular House World Wide.* London: Phaidon.

—— (2006) *Built to Meet Needs – Cultural Issues in Vernacular Architecture.* Oxford: Elsevier.

Oncu, Ayse and Petra Weyland (1997) *Space, Culture and Power. New Identities in Globalizing Cities.* New York: Zed Books.

Ong, Aihwa and Stephen Collier (1999) *Flexible Citizenship. The Cultural Logics of Transnationality.* Durham, NC: Duke University Press.

—— (eds) (2005) *Global Assemblages: Technology, Politics, and Ethics as Anthropological Problems.* Malden, MA: Blackwell.

Orum-Nielsen, Jorn (1995) 'Denmark's Living Housing Tradition', in David Benjamin (ed.) *The Home: Words, Interpretations, Meanings, and Environments.* Aldershot: Avebury, 243–265.

Otero-Pailos, Jorge (2005) 'Historic Provocation: Thinking Past Architecture and Preservation' *Future Anterior* 2(3): ii–vi.

Page, Max and Randall Mason (2004) *Giving Preservation a History: Histories of Historic Preservation in the United States.* London: Routledge.

Pallasmaa, Juhani (2000) 'Hapticity and Time – notes on Fragile Architecture', *Architectural Review* 78–84.

—— (2005) *Eyes of the Skin: Architecture and the Senses.* Chichester: John Wiley.

—— (2007 [1988]) 'Tradition and Modernity: The Feasibility of Regional Architecture in Post-Modern Society', in Vincent B. Canizaro (ed.) *Architectural Regionalism: Collected Writings on Place, Identity, Modernity, and Tradition.* New York: Princeton Architectural Press, 128–140.

Parent, Claude (1996) 'Architecture: Singularity and Discontinuity', in Paul Virilio and Claude Parent, *Architecture Principle – 1966 and 1996.* Translated by George Collins. Paris: Editions de l'Imprimeur, 153.

Parr, Adrian (2008) *Deleuze and Memorial Culture. Desire, Singular Memory and the Politics of Trauma.* Minneapolis: University of Minnesota Press.

Pearsall, Judy (ed.) (1998) *The New Oxford Dictionary of English.* Oxford: Oxford University Press.

Pedersen, Martin C. (2004) 'Goodbye Memory Foundations, Hello Reflecting Absence', Urban Journal posted January 21. http://sixthcolumn.blogspot.com/2005/06/reflecting-absence-indecency-of-911.html.

Pelizzari, Maria A. (2003) 'From Stone to Paper: Photographs of Architecture and the Traces of History', in *Traces of India: Photography, Architecture, and the Politics of Representation, 1850–1900.* New Haven, CT: Yale University Press.

Pendlebury, John (2003) 'Planning the Historic City: Reconstruction Plans in the United Kingdom in the 1940s', *The Town Planning Review* 74(4).

Pevsner, Nicholas (1943) *An Outline of European Architecture.* London: Pelican Books.

Pohlandt-McCormick, Helena (2006) '"I Saw a Nightmare ..." Doing Violence to Memory: The Soweto Uprising, June 16, 1976', Gutenberg-e.org and Columbia University Press. www.gutenberg-e.org/pohlandt-mccormick/archive/

Pollan, Michael (1997) *A Place of My Own.* London: Bloomsbury.

Poster, Mark (1988) *Jean Baudrillard. Selected Writings.* Stanford: Stanford University Press.

Powers, Alan (1996) 'Teaching History in Schools of Architecture in the Age of Electicism', in Adam Hardy and Necdet Teymur (eds) *Architectural History and the Studio.* London:?uestion Press: 17–25.

—— (2007) *Britain: Modern Architectures in History Series.* London: Reaktion Books.

Prak, Niels (1984) *Architects: The Noted and the Ignored.* Chichester: John Wiley.

Preziosi, Donald (1993) *Brain of Earth's Body.* Minneapolis: University of Minnesota Press.

Price, Sir Uvedale (1794) *An Essay on the Picturesque, as Compared with the Sublime and the Beautiful; and on the Use of Studying Pictures, for the Purpose of Improving Real Landscape.* London.

Pyla, Panayiota (2008) 'Counter-histories of Sustainability', *Volume* 18(4): 14–18.

Rabinow, Paul (1989) *French Modern: Norms and Forms of the Social Environment.* Cambridge, MA: MIT Press.

Rapoport, Amos (1969) *House Form and Culture.* Englewood Cliffs, NJ: Prentice Hall.

—— (1986) 'Culture and Built Form – A Reconsideration', in D. G. Saile (ed.) *Architecture in Cultural Change – Essays in Built Form and Cultural Research.* Lawrence: University of Kansas.

—— (1989) 'A Different View of Design', *The University of Tennesse Journal of Architecture,* 11. Reprinted in Nick Wilkinson (ed.) (1995) *33 Papers in Environment Behaviour Research.* Pune: Sangram Press, 457–469.

Readings, Bruce (1996) *The University in Ruins.* Cambridge, MA: Harvard University Press.

Reich, Robert B. (1991) The *Work of Nations. Preparing Ourselves for 21st Century Capitalism.* New York: A.A. Knopf.

Renan, Ernest (1920 [1882]) 'What is a Nation?'.

Retort (2004) 'Afflicted Powers: The State, the Spectacle and September 11', *NLR* 27(May–June): 5.

—— (2005) *Afflicted Powers: Capital and Spectacle in a New Age of War.* New York: Verso.

Rhodes, Lorna (2004) *Total Confinement. Madness and Reason in the Maximum Security Prison.* Berkeley and Los Angeles: University of California Press.

Riegl, Alois (1982[1903]) 'The Modern Cult of Monuments. Its Character and its Origin', *Oppositions* 25: 21–51.

Ripley, Colin, Geoffrey Thun and Kathy Velikov (2009) 'Matters of Concern', *Journal of Architectural Education* 62(4): 6–14

Robbins, Bruce (1999) *Feeling Global. Internationalism in Distress.* New York and London: New York University Press.

Robinson, Jennifer (2006) *Ordinary Cities: Between Modernity and Development.* London and New York: Routledge.

Rosenberg, Daniel and Susan Harding (eds) (2005) *Histories of the Future.* Durham, NC and London: Duke Univeristy Press.

Rosenfeld, Gavriel D. (2000) *Munich and Memory. Architecture, Monuments and the Legacy of the Third Reich.* Berkeley, Los Angeles and London: University of California Press.

Rosler, Martha (ed) (1991) *If You Lived Here: The City in Art, Theory and Social Activism.* Seattle: Bay Press.

Ross, Andrew (1999) *The Celebration Chronicles: Life, Liberty and the Pursuit of Property Values in Disney's New Town.* New York: Ballantine Books.

Rowe, Colin and Kim Koetter (1978) *Collage City.* Cambridge, MA: MIT Press.

Rowe, Peter (1996) 'Design in an Increasingly Small World', in William Saunders (ed.) *Reflections on Architectural Practice in the Nineties.* New York: Princeton Architectural Press, 220–230.

Roy, Ananya (2001) 'Traditions of the Modern', *Traditional Dwellings and Settlements Review* 12(2): 7–20.

Ruddick, Susan M. (1996) *Young and Homeless in Hollywood: Mapping Social Identities.* New York and London: Routledge.

Rudofsky, Bernard (1964) *Architecture without Architects. A Short Introduction to Non-Pedigreed Architecture.* Garden City, NY: Doubleday and Co.

Rykwert, Joseph (1972) *On Adam's House in Paradise.* New York: Museum of Modern Art.

Sabatino, Michelangelo (2011) *Pride in Modesty: Modernist Architecture and the Vernacular Tradition in Italy*. Toronto: University of Toronto Press.

Said, Edward (1979) *Orientalism*. New York: Vintage Books.

—— (1993) *Culture and Imperialism*. New York: Alfred A. Knopf.

Saliba, Robert (2000) 'Deconstructing Beirut's Reconstruction: 1990–2000 Coming to Terms with the Colonial Heritage', www.Csbe.org/Saliba-Diwan/essay1.htm (April 19).

Salmon, Christain (2002) 'The Bulldozer War', www.counterpunch.org/salmon0520.html (May 20).

Sassen, Saskia (1996) *The Global City: New York, London, Tokyo*. Princeton, NJ: Princeton University Press.

—— (2000) *Cities in a World Economy*. Thousand Oaks, CA: Pine Forge Press.

Sawalha, Aseel (2002) 'Remembering the Old Good Days: The Reconstruction of Urban Space in Postwar Beirut', Unpublished PhD dissertation, The City University of New York.

Schmidt, Christian, Stefan Kipfer and Richard Milgrom (eds) (2008) *Space, Difference, Everyday Life: Reading Henri Lefebvre*. New York: Routledge.

Scolari, Massimo (1998) 'The New Architecture and the Avant Garde', in K. Michael Hays (ed.) *Architectural Theory Since 1968*. Cambridge, MA: MIT Press, 126–141.

Scott, David C. (2004) *Conscripts of Modernity: The Tragedy of Colonial Enlightenment*. Durham, NC: Duke University Press.

Scott, Felicity (2001) 'Bernard Rudofsky: Allegories of Nomadism and Dwelling', in Sarah Williams Goldhagen and Réjean Legault (eds) *Anxious Modernisms: Experimentation in Postwar Architectural Culture*. Cambridge, MA: MIT Press.

Scott-Brown, Denise (1971) 'Learning from Pop', *Casabella*, 359–360(December):14–23.

—— (2007) *Architecture or Techno-Utopia: Politics after Modernism*. Cambridge, MA: MIT Press.

Segal, Rafi, Eyal Weizman et al. (2003) *Territories Islands, Camps and Other States of Utopia*. Berlin: KW – Institute of Contemporary Art.

Sehene, Benjamin (1999) 'Rwanda's Collective Amnesia', 1–4. www.unesco.org/courier/1999_12/uk/dossier/txt08.htm

Sen, Amartya (2006) *Identity and Violence. The Illusion of Destiny*. New York and London: W. Norton and Company.

Shackel, Paul A. (2001) *Myth, Memory, and the Making of the American Landscape*. Gainsville, FL: University Press Florida.

Shanken, Andrew (2009) 'The Memory Industry and its Discontents: The Death of a Keyword,' in Marc, Treib (ed.) *Spatial Recall: Memory in Architecture and Landscape*. London and New York: Routledge, 219–239.

Shields, Rob (1989) 'Social Spatialization and the Built Environment: The West Edmonton Mall' *Environment and Planning D: Society and Space* 7(2): 147–164.

—— (1991) *Places on the Margin: Alternative Geographies of Modernity*. London: Routledge Chapman Hall.

—— (1999) *Lefebvre, Love and Struggle: Spatial Dialectics*. New York and London: Routledge.

Sitte, Camillo (1979) *The Art of Building Cities: City Building According to its Artistic Fundamentals*. Westport, CT: Hyperion Press.

Smith, Mark M. (2007) *Sensing the Past, Seeing, Smelling, Tasting and Touching in History*. Berkeley: University of California Press

Smith, Michael Peter (2001) *Transnational Urbanism. Locating Globalization*. Oxford: Blackwell.

Smith, Neil (1996) *The New Urban Frontier: Gentrification and the Revanchist City*. London: Routledge.

Soja, Edward W. (1989) *Postmodern Geographies. The Reassertion of Space in Critical Social Theory*. New York and London: Routledge

Sorkin, Michael (ed.) (1992) *Variations on a Theme Park: The New American City and the End of Public Space*. New York: Hill and Wang.

—— (2001) *Some Assembly Required*. Minneapolis: University of Minnesota Press

—— (ed.) (2005) *Against the Wall*. New York and London: The New Press.

Spector, Tom (2001) *The Ethical Architect – The Dilemma of Contemporary Practice*. New York: Princeton Architectural Press.

Spivak, Gayatri Chakravorty (1990) 'The Postmodern Condition: The End of Politics. With Geoffrey Hawthorn, Ron Aronson and John Dunn', in Sarah Harasym (ed.) *The Post-Colonial Critic: Interviews Strategies Dialogues*, 17–35.

Spruce, Duane Blue and Tanya Thrasher (eds) (2008) *The Land Has Memory. Indigenous Knowledge, Native Landscapes and the National Museum of the American Indian*. Chapel Hill, NC: University of North Carolina Press.

St John Wilson, Colin (2007 [1995]) *The Other Tradition of Modern Architecture: The Uncompleted Project*. London: Black Dog Publishing.

Stevens, Garry (1998) *The Favored Circle. The Social Foundations of Architectural Distinction*. Cambridge, MA: MIT Press.

Stewart, Kathleen (1996) *A Space on the Side of the Road. Cultural Poetics on an 'Other' America*. Princeton, NJ: Princeton University Press.

—— (2007) *Ordinary Affects*. Durham, NC: Duke University Press.

Stieber, Nancy (2006) 'Space, Time, and Architectural History', in Dana Arnold, Elvan Altan and Belgin Turan Ozakaya (eds) *Rethinking Architectural Historiography*. London and New York: Routledge, 171–182.

Stipe, Robert E. (2003) *A Richer Heritage: Historic Preservation in the Twenty-First Century*. Chapel Hill, NC: University of North Carolina Press.

Sturken, Marita (2007) *Tourists of History. Memory, Kitsch and Consumerism, from Oklahoma City to Ground Zero*. Durham, NC: Duke University Press.

Tafuri, Manfredo (1976) *Architecture and Utopia*. Cambridge, MA: MIT Press.

Taylor, Charles and Amy Gutman (eds) (1992) *Multiculturalism and the Politics of Recognition: An Essay*. Princeton, NJ: Princeton University Press.

Thoreau, Henry David (1854) *Walden; Or Life in the Woods*. Boston: Ticknor and Fields.

Thrift, Nigel (1996) *Spatial Formations*. Thousand Oaks, CA: Sage.

—— (2007) *Non-Repesentational Theory. Space, Politics, Affect*. New York and London: Routledge.

Thomson, Robert Garland (2004) 'Preservation in Search of the Historic: New Methods, Expanding Boundaries', *Future Anterior* 2(1): ix–xii.

Till, Jeremy (2009) *Architecture Depends*. Cambridge MA: MIT Press.

Till, Karen E. (2005) *The New Berlin. Memory, Politics, Place*. Minneapolis: University of Minnesota Press.

—— (2008) 'Artistic and Activist Memory Work: Approaching Place-based Practice', *Memory Studies* 1(1): 99–113.

Torgovnick, Marianna (1990) *Gone Primitive: Savage Intellects, Modern Lives*. Chicago: University of Chicago.

Traverso, Enzo (2005) *Le passé, modes d'emploi histoire, mémoire, politique*. Paris: La Fabrique éditions.

Tuan, Yi-Fu, (1974) *Topophilia – A Study of Environmental Perception, Attitudes, and Values*. Englewood Cliffs, NJ: Prentice-Hall.

Tumarkin, Maria (2005) *Traumascapes. The Power and Fate of Places Transformed by Tragedy*. Melbourne: Melbourne University Press.

Tyrwhitt, J., J.L. Sert and E.N. Rogers (1952) (eds) *The Heart of the City: Towards the Humanization of Urban Life*. London: Lund Humphries.

Tzonis, Alexander (2003) 'Introducing an Architecture of the Present', in Liane Lefaivre and Alexander Tzonis (eds) *Critical Regionalism: Architecture and Identity in a Globalized World*. New York: Prestel, 1–19.

Ulmer, Gregory (2005) *Electronic Monuments*. Minneapolis: University of Minnesota Press.

Umbach, Maiken and Bernd-Rüdiger Hüppauf (2005) *Vernacular Modernism: Heimat, Globalisation and the Built Environment*. Stanford: Stanford University Press.

Unwin, Simon (1998) *Analyzing Architecture*. London: Routledge.

Upton, Dell (1993) 'The Tradition of Change', *Traditional Dwellings and Settlements Review* 5(1): 149–165.

—— (2002) 'Architecture in Everyday Life', *New Literary History* 33.

Vale, Lawrence (1992) *Architecture, Power, and National Identity*. New Haven: Yale University Press.

Vellinga, Marcel (2006) 'Engaging the Future: Vernacular Studies in the 21st Century', in Lindsay Asquith and Marcel Vellinga (eds) *Vernacular Architecture in the Twenty-First Century – Theory, Education and Practice*. Abingdon: Taylor & Francis, 81–94.

Venturi, Robert, Denise Scott-Brown and Steven Izenour (1977 [1972]) *Learning from Las Vegas: The Forgotten Symbolism of Architectural Form*. Cambridge, MA: MIT Press.

Verdery, Katherine (1999) *The Political Lives of Dead Body. Reburial and Postsocialist Change*. New York: Columbia University Press.

Vesely, Dalibor (2006) 'The Primitive as Modern Problem: Invention and Crisis', in Jo Odgers, Flora Samuel and Adam Sharr (eds) *Primitive – Original Matters in Architecture*. London: Routledge, 17–32.

Vidler, Anthony (2008) *Histories of the Immediate Future: Inventing Architectural Modernism*. Cambridge, MA: MIT Press.

Virilio, Paul (1986 [1977]) *Speed and Politics. An Essay on Dromodology*. New York: Semiotexte.

—— (1991) *The Lost Dimension*. New York: Semiotexte.

—— (1999) *The Politics of the Very Worst: An Interview by Philippe Petit*. Translated by Michael Cavaliere. New York: Semiotexte.

Waters, Malcolm (1995) *Globalization*. New York and London: Routledge.

Weber, Samuel (2002) 'War, Terrorism, and Spectacle: On Towers and Caves', *The South Atlantic Quarterly*, 101(3) (Summer): 449–458.

Westwood Sallie and John Williams (1997) *Imagining Cities: Scripts, Signs, Memory*. New York and London: Routledge.

Wielhouwer, Peter W. (2004) 'Preparing for Future Joint Urban Operations: The Role of Simulation and the Urban Resolve Experiment', Command and Operations Group, USJFCOM/19.

Wigley, Mark (1991) 'Prosthetic Theory: The Disciplining of Architecture', *Assemblage* 15: 6–29.

—— (2000) 'The Architectural Cult of Synchronization', *October*, 94(Autumn): 31–61.

—— (2005) 'Unleashing the Archive', *Future Anterior* 2(1): 11–15.

Williams, Norman, Edmund Kellogg and Frank Gilbert (eds) (1983) *Readings in Historic Preservation: Why? What? How?* New Brunswick, NJ: Center for Urban Policy Research.

Wilson, Chris, and Paul Groth (2003) *Everyday America. Cultural Landscape Studies after J.B. Jackson.* Berkeley, Los Angeles and London: University of California Press.

Winter, J. (2006) 'Notes on the Memory Boom: War Remembrance and the Uses of the Past' in Duncan Bell (ed.) *Memory, Trauma and World Politics: Reflections on the Relationship between the Past and the Present.* Basingstoke: Palgrave, 54–74.

Wright, Gwedolyn (1991) *The Politics of Design in French Colonial Urbanism.* Chicago: University of Chicago Press.

Wright, Gwendolyn (2003) 'On Modern Vernaculars and J.B. Jackson,' in Wilson, Chris and Paul Groth (eds), *Everyday America. Cultural Landscape Studies after J.B. Jackson.* Berkeley: University of California Press.

Wright, Gwendolyn and Janet Parks (eds) (1990) *The History of History in American Schools of Architecture.* New York: Temple Hoyne Buell Center for the Study of American Architecture and Princeton Architectural Press.

Yeoh, Brenda S. (1996) *Contesting Space. Power Relations and the Urban Built Environment in Colonial Singapore.* Oxford and New York: Oxford University Press.

Yoneyama Lisa (1999) *Hiroshima Traces: Time, Space and the Dialectics of Memory.* Berkeley: University of California Press.

Young, James E. (1991) *The Art of Memory: Holocaust Memorials in History.* New York: Prestel.

—— (1993) *The Texture of Memory: Holocaust Memorials and Meaning.* New Haven: Yale University Press.

Žižek, Slavoj (1989) *The Sublime Object of Ideology.* London: Verso.

—— (2004) *Organs without Bodies: Deleuze and Consequences.* London and New York: Routledge.

—— (2010) *Living in End Times.* London: Verso.

Zukin, Sharon (1991) *Landscapes of Power: From Detroit to Disney World.* Berkeley, CA: University of California Press.

20

Culture

Paul Walker

In a key text, 'The End of Modernity, The End of the Project?', philosopher Gianni Vattimo suggests that there are no longer any robust ways of legitimating the architectural project:

> The task posed is to find legitimations for the project that no longer appeal to 'strong', natural, or even historical structures. For example, one can no longer say that there is a golden number, an ideal measure that can be used in the construction or the planning of cities, nor even that there are natural needs, since it is increasingly absurd to try to distinguish them from new needs induced by the market and therefore superfluous, not natural (Vattimo 1997, 151).

This wearing away of what had appeared to be the realities of function, planning,

Figure 20.1 (Below) The National Museum of Australia, designed by Ashton Raggatt McDougall, seen from Lake Burley Griffin. (National Museum of Australia 2001, photograph by George Serras)

and history leads in Vattimo's view to 'the need for a new monumentality'. Sigfried Giedion once also used the term 'new monumentality', but Vattimo's formulation is distinct from Giedion's. Both acknowledge the displacement of utility as the principal means by which design is to be validated. But for Giedion this is replaced by another fundamental, 'the eternal need of the people for symbols', while for Vattimo it is not. For now there is no singular 'people' but rather a multiplicity drawn 'from all the communities that have found a voice in [...] the conflict of interpretations in which we live'.

Vattimo argues for a 'weak' strategy, what he calls a strategy of the ornamental, for the ornament is that which is tangential to a traditional view of art or architecture's propriety, this latter being related to the authority of truth.

The focus of this Project Section is on the relationship of architectural design to what could be called institutional design, or intent. In particular, it is concerned with three museums, a building type which has a particular tradition of monumentality tempered in recent years by an expectation that museums should also be accessible to broader audiences and multiple communities. The three museums are new. Each is concerned with the legitimacy of the nation state's authority in relation to questions of culture. One is a new national museum in a postcolonial

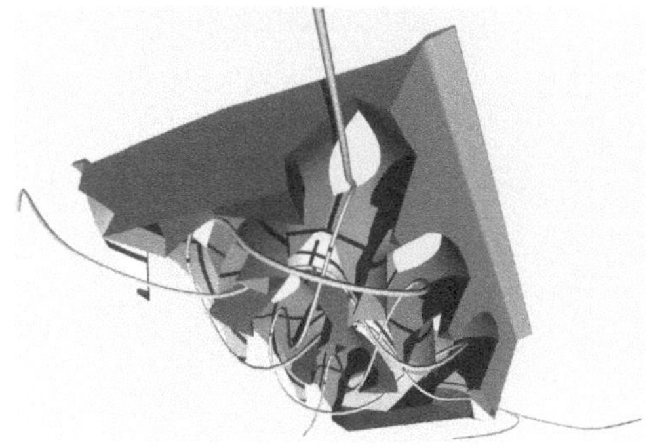

settler society, Australia, where cultural issues have been problematized in recent politics, both in relation to the indigenous people (aboriginality) and the cultural diversity arising from post-war migration patterns (multiculturalism). The second is an institution built as part of a complex political rapprochement between a metropolitan power and the indigenous people in a territory, New Caledonia, which remains in possession of that power. The third is a museum in Paris devised for collections of objects from former French colonies, and intended to establish new relationships between the state and the countries from which the objects came, and between the state and its citizens who came from those countries.

For each building, the design will be investigated in terms of how it claims architectural legitimacy in both cultural reference and in technical invention. In one, the National Museum of Australia, the first seems to dominate; while in the others, the Tjibaou Cultural Centre and the Musée du Quai Branly, the second seems to balance the first. The ways in which these strategies correspond to institutional agendas will also be considered: the three buildings are for institutions motivated by emergent but different postcolonial circumstances. But these circumstances are themselves uncertain and changing.

Figure 20.2 (Below left and right) The Garden of Australian Dreams, designed by Richard Weller of Room 4.1.3, in the NMA's courtyard. (National Museum of Australia 2001, photograph by George Serras)

Figure 20.3 (Opposite top) Worm's eye view of the knot in the extrusion that generated the interior volume of the NMA's orientation gallery. (Ashton Raggatt McDougall)

THE NATIONAL MUSEUM OF AUSTRALIA

The National Museum of Australia (NMA) opened in Canberra in 2001. It was designed by the Melbourne practice Ashton Raggatt McDougall. Set on a peninsula in Lake Burley Griffin, the NMA's context is the parkland of Canberra's core in which are scattered a capital city's conventionally monumental buildings. The NMA's design departs from that of its institutional siblings: it is one of multiplicity, complex forms and many references (see Reed 2002; Hamann 2002; Jencks 2001). Although it is a relatively small building for its site, it has been stretched and pushed toward the lake edge so that in distant views it works at the city's expanded visual scale (Figure 20.1). The building's external forms, however, are brightly coloured and covered with graphic devices – including what appear to be giant scaled Braille bumps – producing what critic Naomi Stead (2004) has described as 'the semblance of populism'. There are also multiple architectural references: the plan of the Gallery of the First Australians makes a controversial reference to the plan of the Jewish Museum in Berlin; glazing details of vast windows in the orientation gallery are derived from those of the Sydney Opera House; elements of the Australian Institute of Aboriginal & Torres Strait Islander Studies (a research facility integrated into the museum complex) are from Australia's Parliament House (1988, Mitchell Giurgola Thorpe), and the Villa Savoye, rendered black (see Hutson 2006). The space at the middle of the site contains the Garden of Australian

Figure 20.4 (Below) The tall, iconic forms of the Tjibaou Cultural Centre, with a traditional Kanak building in the foreground. (Lindy Joubert)

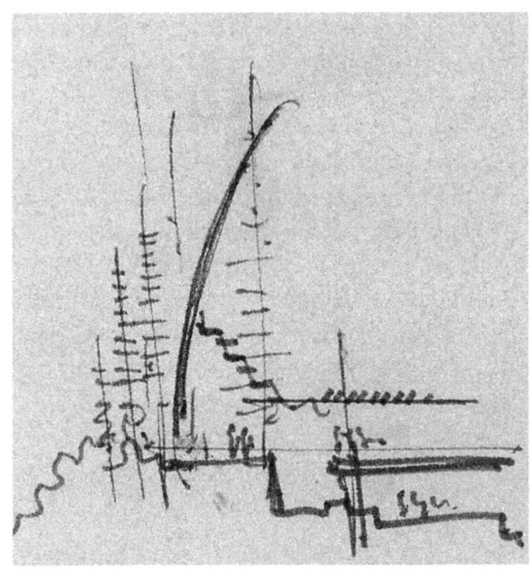

Dreams, designed by landscape architect Richard Weller of the practice Room 4.1.3, also characterized by its delirious piling up of graphically embedded quotations (Figure 20.2) (Weller 2001).

But gestures to architecture's own history and status are not the only drivers of the NMA's design. A key conceptual element is an extrusion of pentagonal section that loops through the project. Depending for its configuration and construction on advanced digital design applications, this is only ever actually realized in its absence, for instance as a giant conceptual knot, that as a spatial 'negative' shapes the white, plastered interior surfaces of the orientation gallery (Figure 20.3). The extrusion also cuts through building

Figure 20.5 (Above left) Tjibaou sectional sketch. (RPBW Renzo Piano Building Workshop)

Figure 20.6 (Below left) Detail view of the Tjibaou building in its densely planted site. (Lindy Joubert)

Figure 20.7 (Below right) Piano's work is noted for its attention to building technique. (Lindy Joubert)

volumes, with reveals clad in red enameled steel. It produces a semblance of the new, but here, unlike much recent architectural deployment of new technologies in form-making, there is no pretence that the problem of legitimation has been put aside. At the entry to the museum, one side of the extrusion loops up in a great arc of red, white and orange steel that then gestures toward the centre of Australia. This is the 'Uluru line', an addition by Ashton Raggatt McDougall to Walter Burley Griffin's Canberra axes. This new line connects the city to the broader country and history of Australia, but is as complicated and entangled as Canberra's original axes are lucid and direct. It is also a Rainbow Serpent from an Aboriginal dreaming, a landscape tributary from the Red Centre, and so on.

The overwhelming visual multiplicity of the museum building corresponds directly to the institutional intent set out by the museum during its development phase. In 1999 – reflecting an institutional embrace both of multiculturalism and aboriginal cultural and political self-awareness – the NMA's foundation director, Dawn Casey, wrote of the museum as 'a mosaic; a compelling picture made of different parts; a number of diverse stories that collectively make up a great anthology' (Casey 2001). But the Australian federal government has been unsettled by the museum's proposition of radical cultural dissonance in Australia, and two years after it opened, the government initiated a review. Echoing Casey's words, the review praised the museum for its inclusiveness of

Figure 20.8 (Below) Interior of Tjibaou exhibition space. The Centre's programme is to preserve and encourage Kanak culture and promote cultural exchange in the South Pacific. (ADCK-Centre Culturel Tjibaou/Renzo Piano Building Workshop, architects. photograph by Michel Denancé)

'the mosaic' of Australian experience. But it also harshly criticised it for inadequately representing Australia's achievements (National Museum of Australia 2003, 66–67). Casey was removed. The museum review also recommended demolition as a strategy: not of the building but of the apparently less problematic target of the Garden of Australian Dreams. This did not proceed.

The putative failure that the NMA review uncovered was a failure to adequately manifest accepted and singular historical narratives of nationhood, to reflect beliefs that Australia's dominant national politics for the previous decade had made a matter of doctrine. Surviving the museum review intact, the building design did not guarantee the survival of the museum's institutional strategy.

THE TJIBAOU CULTURAL CENTRE

Like the NMA, the Tjibaou Cultural Centre in Noumea is tendentiously related to its political context. But New Caledonia's post-colonial experience is unlike Australia's insofar as the colonialism which is its context is overt: New Caledonia is still 'French'.

The Tjibaou Cultural Centre was an outcome of arrangements negotiated between Kanak political movements and the French government in the late 1980s. Jean-Marie Tjibaou was a Kanak political leader in these negotiations. Deeply interested in Kanak cultural identity and development, he was assassinated in 1989. The ostensible programme of the centre bearing Tjibaou's name is to preserve Kanak culture, encourage contemporary

Figure 20.9 (Below) Musée du Quai Branly from Quai Branly, with the Eiffel Tower looming to the west. (Stephen Cairns)

works of Kanak expression, and to promote cultural exchange in the South Pacific. But cultural centres are not traditional to Kanak culture, and as one of Mitterand's Grands Projets – the only one outside metropolitan France – the Tjibaou Cultural Centre has a role representing French largesse (see Findley 2005).

The building design was procured through an international competition won by Renzo Piano Building Workshop. Piano included a noted anthropologist with expertise on the Kanak in his team, and after the competition the design was developed through consultation with Kanak (Findley 2005, 51–2, 56). The Centre's architecture can be construed to reflect its programme of promoting local indigenous culture through reference to the traditional forms of the tall, conical roofs of Kanak chiefs' houses, and to the linear plan arrangement of village houses along a central 'street', transformed into a contemporary tectonic language (Figure 20.4). This presence together of the traditional and the new in the Centre's architecture has been embraced by Kanak as relevant to their own condition. In the words of Tjibaou himself: 'We want to proclaim our cultural identity. We want to tell the world that we are not survivors of prehistory; even less, archaeological remains, but

Figure 20.10 (Below) The Patrick Blanc-planted wall on the research block on Quai Branly, with a typical nineteenth century Parisian building adjacent. (Paul Walker)

Figure 20.11 (Opposite top) On rue de l'Université, the museum building is imprinted with *Jimbala and Gemerre*, a work by Lena Nyadbi from the Kimberley region of Australia. (Paul Walker)

Figure 20.12 (Below right) The approach to the Musée du Quai Branly's public entry through the landscaping by Gilles Clément. (Paul Walker)

men of flesh and blood' (Tjibaou cited in Kasarherou 1995, 91).

But generally Piano's work is positioned in architectural culture in terms of exquisite building technique and disavowal of theory rather than in relation to its occasional attention to local cultural identity (Figures 20.6 and 20.7). While the particularly Kanak aspect to the Tjibaou's architecture is clear, Piano's own comments on its local references are curiously general. In an interview published in *Architecture and Urbanism* in 1996, Piano mentions being attracted to the prospect in the project of a language of lightness akin to his own architectural interests:

> I think the Pacific area is a place typical for culture of lightness and repetition of gesture. It is very true in Japan, but also true in many other countries surrounding the Pacific area, or the Pacific Rim. It is also true in Western America if you think about Charles Eames, Richard Neutra, the case study houses, and their sense of immateriality of lightness (Piano 1996, 92).

Elsewhere, Piano has erroneously described the Kanak as dispersed through the Pacific and specific to New Caledonia merely through their 'concentration' there (Piano 1997, 174).

This dissolving of Kanak culture into a generic Pacificness – taking in a third of the globe in Piano's words quoted above – disavows the significance of the specific local references in the design of the Tjibaou Cultural Centre. It renders the tall roof forms clustered in a linear sequence curiously unproblematic, as if when quoting it Piano had simultaneously elided Kanak cultural particularity.

While acknowledging the bravura of Piano's work and the welcome his building has received from Kanak, Mike Austin (theorist and historian of Pacific architecture) has pointed to the problematic treatment by Piano of the Kanak hut: not only is the roof covering lost and the frame structure beneath fragmented, most importantly the centre-post is missing at Tjibaou (Figure 20.5). Symbolically, this emasculates the architecture. Austin – whose own analyses of Pacific island traditions in architecture have emphasized the importance of openness in their constructed spaces – finds the Tjibaou Centre's enclosure of the linear space at the centre of the village to be equally problematic. Austin is also troubled by Piano's unreflective equation of the Kanak forms deployed at Tjibaou with contemporary conceptions of sustainability and passive environmental performance (Austin 2000, 26–27).

These criticisms do not hold that some authentic Kanak culture could have been recuperated at the Tjibaou (Findley 2005, 64–65). But nor does the Tjibaou Cultural Centre exhaust the conditions under which Kanak (people, culture) could be contemporary. One of the most interesting readings of the Centre is by Diane Losche (2003), who considers it in an 'expanded field' encompassing other, less celebrated Kanak

Figure 20.13 (Below) The main volume of the Musée du Quai Branly is suspended above Clément's forest/garden. (Paul Walker)

cultural centres. These are characterized not by beautifully presented artefacts and iconic architectural gestures meant for global consumption but rather by exchanges that occur through performance and ritual (Figure 20.8). Taking as a given that to engage with the modern world is in such contexts to engage with international tourism, Losche concludes that the conventional monumentality of Tjibaou and the liveliness she found at a counter-example on the New Caledonian island of Lifou are mutually dependent. Without thc support of Tjibaou, Lifou would disappear, but without Lifou and its living cultural flux, Tjibaou's monumentality would descend into deathliness.

MUSÉE DU QUAI BRANLY

Opened in 2006, the Musée du Quai Branly was envisaged by the French government and President Chirac as symbolic of 'France's new relationship with the non-European indigenous world' (Naumann 2006, 90). But its location at a site in central Paris, not far from the Eiffel Tower in the midst of an urban district closely associated with the great French world expositions of the nineteenth century raises the question of what is disavowed or forgotten in its project of new cultural and political connections, and what is remembered or newly asserted (Figure 20.9).

Architect Jean Nouvel claims to have conceived the building as 'a selective dematerialization' so as to leave the museum's exhibited objects conceptually sitting in the forest (Nouvel 2002, 202). The landscaping

Figure 20.14 (Below) Plan of the permanent exhibition level of the museum. Projecting exhibition boxes on the north side, and the 'soft' walls of the central circulation spine are apparent. (Ateliers Jean Nouvel)

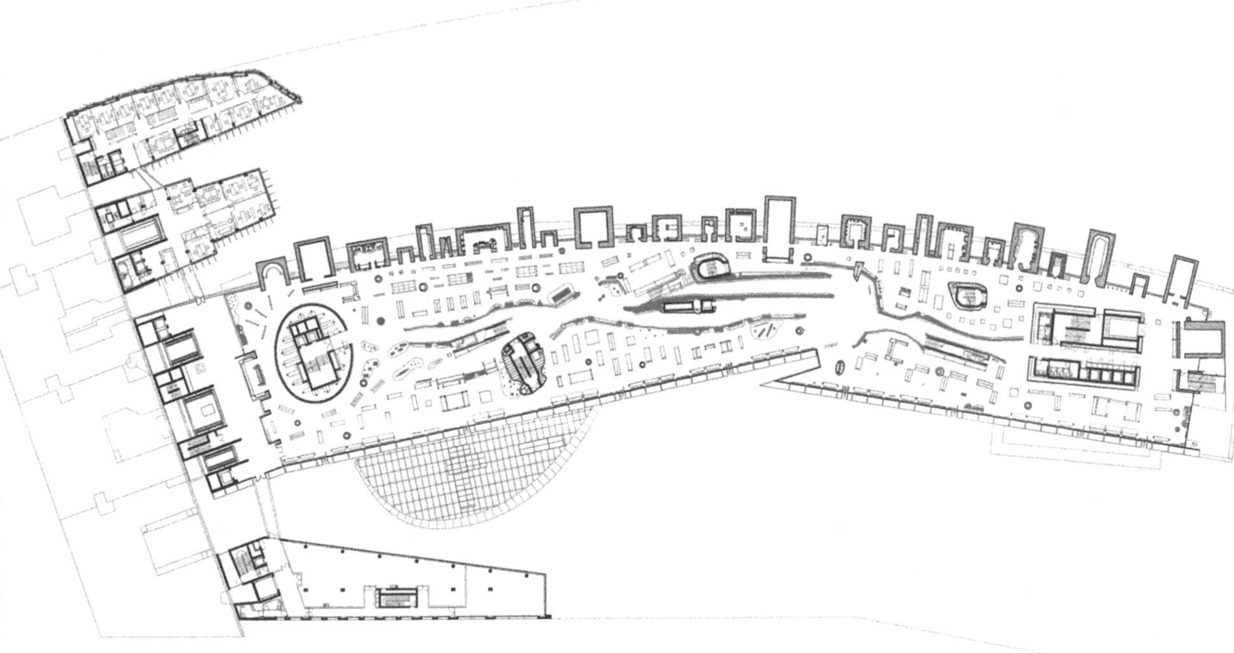

at Quai Branly, by Giles Clément with 'vegetative walls' by Patrick Blanc (Figure 20.10), establishes a kind of artificial jungle in which the museum floats: planting has yet to reach its maturity, but – based in broad drifts of trees and shrubby and herbaceous plants – it is organized in a horticultural citation of wildness. The main bulk of the museum building is suspended above this garden, anchored to the ground at the east by a café and service spaces, and at the west by temporary exhibition areas and the museum entry (Figures 20.12 and 20.13). Two other wings at this end of complex house administration and research.

To access the museum, visitors traverse Clément's 'forest', and discover the museum entry deep in the site. To reach the main part of the museum – the elevated volume for the permanent collections – they then take a long, irregular ramp that delivers them to the middle of the exhibition space. Collections are organized in this space on a geographic logic, in areas connected by a circulation spine (Figure 20.14). This is defined by walls softly formed to make seats and niches for video screens: the vaguely organic qualities of the design of these walls are emphasized by their being entirely clad in leather. Surfaces and details are otherwise conventionally tech-ish. Though illumination levels are low, light enters from the outside through both the north and the south walls of the vast museum volume, filtered on one side by a moiré screen, and on the other by translucent images of tropical vegetation.

Nouvel himself has described the ambience created by these devices as 'spiritual' (Nouvel 2006, 14). While this implies a disposition of respect in the design towards the objects that it houses, it is nevertheless troubling, returning the non-West to its role of irrational otherness (see Clifford 2007 and Price 2007 for analysis of museological issues raised by the Musée du Quai Branly).

A comparison with Nouvel's earlier Fondation Cartier is telling: the Cartier's transparency proclaims inquiry, intellect, accessibility as core to its contemporary arts programme; its landscape, also by Clément, has a rhetoric not of the a-cultural but of the elegiac or the archaeological. The Blanc plant wall at the Fondation Cartier is but an isolated fragment, an unexpected delight. At the Musée du Quai Branly, the engulfing of a wall on one side of the complex with plants becomes problematic, as it implies a comparison with the wall on the other side of the site covered with a work titled *Jimbala and Germerre* by Lena Nyadbi, a contemporary Gija artist from Australia's Kimberley region (Figure 20.11). The introduction of a presence for Aboriginal Australia at the heart of a key European capital through this work and the others by indigenous Australians incorporated into the museum's architecture is a startling fact, realizable only through the deployment of advanced logistics and assembly techniques (Naumann 2006, 91; see also Armstrong 2006).

Nevertheless, it risks reinvigorating the old trope of the noble savage, being given new credence in a contemporary equation of indigeneity with environmental sustainability: the reassertion of the equivalence of the non-Western indigenous and the natural through current discourse on 'environment' will have profound implications for the post-colonial world.

CONCLUSION

The three buildings considered here manifest contrasting attitudes in recent architecture to the discipline's own history, from the apparent ahistoricism of the Musée du Quai Branly to the multiple architectural references of the NMA. While its design incorporated sophisticated IT applications to envision and document the 'boolean string' of the 'absent' pentagonal extrusion, the NMA could be placed at the end of a line of post-modern architecture marked by direct and allusive references to earlier canonical works. But the deployment in the NMA design of these citations in the same direct, graphic way as references from popular culture (the club colours of sports teams, for example) mocks any attempt to establish a sound foundation for architecture in its own genealogy. While Ashton Raggatt McDougall's work constantly and affectionately cites architectural precedent it never seeks legitimacy in design conventions; rather, it problematizes authority. The strategy of multiplicity and uncertain authority corresponded with the NMA's institutional agenda at the time the building was commissioned, so that the staging of national histories and national memories can only be provisional. But the NMA's subsequent trajectory suggests that it is politically difficult for such an institutional position to prevail. History, memory and tradition are political matters, and doubt has little political currency.

In contrast to Ashton Raggatt McDougall, Nouvel and Piano generally eschew any reference to disciplinary history in their work. Rather, both could be construed as continuing to approach architectural design as the technically innovative solution of programmatic and building 'problems', a kind of unself-conscious neo-modernism. Tjibaou, however, departs from this a-representational stance. There, the citation in the building design of a local and culturally specific building tradition entails a conflation of primitivism and contemporaneity. This also occurs at the Musée du Quai Branly in the overlaying of parts of the complex with images derived from works by Australian indigenous artists. These projects throw into particular relief the Design/Production/Practice thematic of Section 5 of the Handbook. In both the Tjibaou Centre and the Musée du Quai Branly, the conjunction of contemporary technique and culturally specific image attends a political programme intending to transcend a problematic history. At Tjibaou, this is the history of settler relations with the Kanak; more grandly at Quai Branly, it is the history of interactions between a metropolitan state and the non-Western indigenous world. Even more than at Tjibaou, the unprecedented conjunction of image and building at the Musée du Quai Branly entailed technical sophistication. Only on these terms could works drawn from distant and very specific cultural traditions in Aboriginal Australia be realized in the metropolitan context of central Paris. While this represents the unprecedented cosmopolitanism the present affords, it risks rehearsing old colonial relations that the Musée du Quai Branly purports to disavow.

BIBLIOGRAPHY

Armstrong, Claire (ed.) (2006) *Australian Indigenous Art Commission*. Sydney: Art & Australia.

Austin, Mike (2000) 'The Tjibaou Culture Centre in New Caledonia' in Michael J. Ostwald and R John Moore (eds) *Re-framing Architecture: Theory, Science, and Myth*. Sydney: Archadia Press, 25–29.

Casey, Dawn (2001) 'The National Museum of Australia', in Darryl McIntyre and Kirsten Wehner (eds) *National Museums: Negotiating Histories*. Canberra: National Museum of Australia.

Clifford, James (2007) 'Quai Branly in Process', *October* 120: 3–23.

Findley, Lisa (2005) *Building Change: Architecture, Politics and Cultural Agency*. London: Routledge.

Hamann, Conrad (2002) 'Enigma Variations', *Australia Art Monthly*,138: 5–9.

Hutson, Andrew (2006) 'The Vivid Cast', *Fabrications*, 16(2): 84–98.

Jencks, Charles (2001) 'How to Speak Australian', *Architecture*, 90(8): 82–91.

Kasarherou, Emmanuel (1995) 'Men of Flesh and Blood: the Jean-Marie Tjibaou Cultural Centre in Noumea', *Art and Asia Pacific*, 2(4): 90–95.

Losche, Diane (2003) 'Cultural Forests and their Objects in New Caledonia, the Forest on Lifou', *Australian and New Zealand Journal of Art*, 4(1): 77–91.

National Museum of Australia (2003) *Review of the National Museum of Australia, Its Exhibitions and Public Programs. A Report to the Council of the National Museum of Australia*. Canberra: Commonwealth of Australia.

Naumann, Peter (2006) 'Naturally in Paris', *Architecture Australia* 95(5): 88–95.

Nouvel, Jean (2002) *Jean Nouvel 1994-2002: the symbolic order of matter/El Croquis*, 112/113. Madrid: El Croquis Editorial.

—— (2006) 'Recent and Three Buildings: Interview with Jean Nouvel', *GA Document* 93: 8–19.

Piano, Renzo (1997) *Logbook.* New York: Monacelli Press.

—— (1996) 'Renzo Piano Building Workshop: Cultural Center Jean Marie Tjibaou', *Architecture and Urbanism* 315: 92–102.

Price, Sally (2007) *Paris Primitive: Jacques Chirac's Museum on the Quai Branly.* Chicago: University of Chicago Press.

Reed, Dimity (ed.) (2002) *Tangled Destinies: National Museum of Australia.* Mulgrave: Images Publishing.

Stead, Naomi (2004) 'The Semblance of Populism: National Museum of Australia', *The Journal of Architecture*, 9(4): 485–496.

Vattimo, Gianni (1997) 'The End of Modernity, the End of the Project?' in Neil Leach (ed.) *Rethinking Architecture: A Reader in Cultural Theory.* London: Routledge: 148–154.

Weller, Richard (2001) 'The National Museum, Canberra, and Its Garden of Australian Dreams', *Studies in the History of Gardens & Designed Landscapes,* 21(1): 66–84.

SECTION 5

Design/Production/Practice

21

Introduction: Architecture's Double-Bind

Dana Cuff

According to cultural observers, contemporary life changes at heretofore unheard of speed and is rife with uncertainty. From Marshall Berman to David Harvey, Reyner Banham to Paul Virilio, risk and radical transformation characterize everyday life in our postmodern era. How is it then that architects, and the professional institutions that represent them, continue to paint a portrait of a timeless profession? More than law or medicine, architecture ardently upholds its unchanging core as demonstration of the field's essential nature. Even within the arts, in contrast to painting or sculpture, architecture grounds itself on tradition, precedent, and an established body of knowledge.

Indeed, the architectural office in the nineteenth century is recognizably similar to that of the twenty-first century. The most recent comprehensive study of architectural practice and education opens thus:

> The education of architects – the men and women who design our skyscrapers and plazas, churches and museums, our schools and our homes – rests on traditions as old as history. … This sense of kinship with centuries of traditions, thoughts, and personalities is, in fact, the true tie that binds those who practice architecture with those who teach it and study it. (Boyer and Mitgang 1996, 3)

This depiction is particular to architecture; it is not possible to substitute other professions or arts and make similar statements. Thus, the way in which architecture's core is uniquely conceptualized is in some sense productive of the discipline. The practices that persist within architecture are more than emblematic, they are constitutive, and chief among those timeless practices is design.

It was to this end – conceptualizing the core – at least in part, that Vasari wrote *The Lives* and that the Academia del Disegno was founded in sixteenth century Florence. Both projects meant to establish the arts, including architecture, within Tuscan cultural politics by defining the essential nature of great artists. Through the academy, disegno signified the intersection of intellect and creation, its artists exhibiting more than craft by virtue of schooling in the collected works and ideas of the visual arts. Disegno itself implies both concept and realization, a conjunction of idea, if not theory, with practice, and more literally with drawing. The identical construction appears nearly 500 years later in a book titled *Why Architects Draw*: 'Drawing is at once an idea and an act, an autonomous concept and a mode of social production' (Robbins 1994, 7). Drawing has been an essential component of the definition of an architect. In eighteenth-century America, the building trades evolved as proto-architectural practices through the craft apprenticeship system, largely through training in drawing schools (Woods 1999, 53–58). The enduring role of the drawing-as-design reflects this fundamental formulation of architecture. In contemporary education and practice, where young practitioners may no longer learn to draw except in digital media, a reverential space is attributed to the sketch as the embodiment of concept and artistic gesture. The central role of the drawing, the special status of design as theory and practice, architecture as an art – these constructs mark the discipline and resist change. One of the most provocative challenges to the core regarding representation is the ability to work, perhaps for the first time since medieval crafts, in a one-to-one fashion, without representational intermediaries. Three-dimension printers, rapid prototyping, and digital fabrication linked to modelling software are making it possible to move directly from digital data to the manufacture of building components (Kolarevic 2003).

The academy, along with the professional organizations (e.g. RIBA, AIA, HKIA), is a primary channel for the core's persistence. The education of an architect is monitored by professional organizations that seek consistency among institutions, monitoring the production of architects, and hence the market for services. Schools across the globe operate on relatively similar grounds, with the studio at the heart of a student's experience. The studio, or atelier from the Beaux Arts tradition, is a mainstay of the profession. Through studio education, unique to architecture in the contemporary academy, design is upheld as the most important component of professional training. Intrinsically, the studio emphasizes practice over theory, creativity over knowledge of precedent, coming up with solutions over analysing problems, individual work over collective action, drawing and modeling over other media.

Fundamentally, the studio is design and design is at the core of the core. The 2009 convention of North American architecture schools was in fact titled: 'The Value of Design: Design is at the Core of What We Teach and Practice'. The theme describes design as equivalent to innovation, asserting it as the means for architecture to become more 'significant within society.' In the studio, design is taught by a 'master', typically a practitioner who brings his experience to each novice's individual critique. The one-on-one form of practical training, master to pupil, is based on modelling (like music and clinical medicine) as Donald Schon points out in *The Reflective Practitioner* (1983). Such a traditional approach is complicated to sustain in light of internet-based remote learning, virtual classrooms, and digital game-based learning.

While a persistent professional core retains the primacy of design and drawing, architecture cannot be represented as a homogeneous field. The characterization above is an outmoded anathema to young designers with critical practices. Indeed, experimentation marks most published works of contemporary design. Technological innovations in particular launch new directions in architecture, providing a vitality characteristic of architecture's cutting edge. In my own research, I have spent two decades exploring architecture's breaks with tradition and those practices that represent upheavals within the profession (Cuff 2000a; 2001; 2003). Here, I want to adopt the counter-perspective: What purpose, in the Foucauldian sense, does a stable core serve in architecture?

Architecture's essentialism has been formulated over centuries into a model or ideal type. In his seminal text on the changing nature of practice, sociologist Robert Gutman (1988) reasons that architects 'promulgate the idealized version of an architectural life' to avoid shattering important myths about their social status. Another sociologist, Magali Larson (1977), argued more specifically that architects managed their profession's identity for the express purpose of maintaining a market for services. The idealized portrait is tacitly embedded throughout the profession; it entails a string of individual heroes, the Vitruvian core values (commodity, firmness, delight), the origins of architecture in Rome and Greece, the profession capable of integrating all trades, the intertwining of art and technology, the gentlemanly nature of the profession, the downplaying of business concerns, the benefits of the small office, the patron, financial gain as a side effect of practice – and the list continues. Gutman argues that those beliefs are self-defeating because they interfere with the architect's ability to cope with the complications of architecture's contemporary conditions. Still, architectural offices, the professional organizations, and schools cling to them all the same, suggesting structural resistance on the part of these institutions. It is my contention that this tenacious core is necessary in a rather paradoxical sense: to sustain a profession that is defined by its creativity. The conservative, universalist model of architecture serves as a datum against which contemporary architects can demonstrate their unique and forward-moving practices.

In addition to political economy explanations of the stubborn core, there exists, within architecture, a contradiction that has not received adequate critical attention. This contradiction pits architecture's enduring ideal against a profession in crisis, based on writings about architecture (not from the professional institutions) that describe a perpetual state of agitation. In these depictions, architecture is on the brink of disaster or a fomenting revolution. Observers from the nineteenth century as well as the twenty-first century announce architecture's radical shifts, ranging from new stylistic eclecticism, to a digital revolution, to societal rejection. Such histrionic formulations of architecture reinforce the spectacular status of the creative enterprise. Architecture's literature offers a storyline for a profession – an occupation sanctioned by society and requiring specialized study that is inherently experimental. The intrinsic novelty is balanced by historical continuities that lie at the core which thus serves as a datum for both the individual and the discipline.

The unremitting crisis of architecture can be variously explained. As a writerly production, architectural transformation is far more noteworthy than the status quo, thus biasing journalism toward a more calamitous view of circumstances. But there are also disciplinary grounds for such claims. Given the above-stated premise that architecture, relative to other disciplines, is conservative, then discourse about innovation becomes exceptional. Experimentation can be explained in either of two ways. First, supposedly stable practices are in fact undergoing constant change creating anxiety (nothing is supposed to be changing, but everything seems to be changing). This is the Marx-cum-Berman notion that 'all that is solid melts into air'. Alternatively, because the ideal blinds us to seeing the change occurring all around us, making that change apparent requires exaggeration. This could be characterized as the Freud-cum-Debord version of architecture represented as spectacularly new.

Let us call this the problem of model and variant within architecture. Leaving variant aside for a moment, what is generally conceived as a durable core is in fact a model architectural profession that has been cumulatively created. The model practice, like the model practitioner, stand in relation to any particular reality. The model is a compass that points out discrepancies between contemporary circumstances and architecture's exemplary status.

In architecture, that discrepancy is not the gap to be narrowed as it might be in other professions. Compared to other professions, architecture exhibits a particular, ambiguous relationship between model and circumstance. In medicine, the scientific knowledge base and technologically-dependent practices presume modern, positivist notions of progress (Bledstein 1976). In law, there is a fundamental dependence upon precedent yet its evolution is the very substance of legal practice at the highest levels. In business, schools of thought proliferate to offer instruction on managing innovation within organizations (Kelley 2001). Architecture is more akin to the arts with regard to the balance struck between static and dynamic models. At least since the mid-nineteenth century, non-conformity has held its own idealized status within the arts. Much has been written on the avant-garde and on the emergence of movements that represent significant new directions such as abstract expressionism and conceptual art. At least in the past century, artists broke free not from their own rigid characterizations but from institutional conservatism (Greenberg 1939; Lippard 1973). The model architect is not the one who makes measured progress, nor one who must depend on precedent (though neo-traditionalists might dispute this claim), but the inventor of variants that can inflect the model itself. As such, an architect like Bruce Goff is surely a variant but not a particularly influential one, whereas Frank Gehry, originally cast as an iconoclast, is now positioned as a pioneer of digitally-enabled formalism.

We could also frame model and variant within the context of stability and crisis. If the persistent core draws disciplinary boundaries, assures a market for services, renders subjective identity, and lays the foundation for advancement, then crisis sets the stage for transformation. In material terms, the crisis that produces a tabula rasa offers an open field for innovation, and a reduction of complexities inherent to working in context. In socio-political terms, crisis uniquely holds the potential for radical change, akin to a collective version of shock treatment. The clean slate, physical and/or mental, is the abstract precursor for change, whereas in fact, the practical precursor is a well-defined set of norms.

When the two stereotypes of crisis and normative practices are placed in relation to one another, the clichéd depictions of architecture shatter, creating new insight into the profession. Architecture strikes a fragile balance between an enduring ideal intermittently mobilized by distress. This is architecture's double-bind, which as Gregory Bateson defined it (1972), is a recurrent paradox created by conflicting demands that cannot be ignored. And it is a significant one, a special pathology defined by practice. The double-bind reflects the stasis and change that are part of architecture's material circumstances. To unravel this braided logic, the first step is to grasp the way in which the double-bind is practised; the second is to interrogate the idealized static qualities of the profession.

PRACTICE IN A DOUBLE-BIND

When Frank Gehry's Bilbao Guggenheim opened in 1997, the *New York Times* architectural critic, Herbert Muschamp, declared an architectural miracle had occurred (Muschamp 1997). The building represented a new optimism, a new direction for architecture, a variant on the model of the orthogonal and the museum as an institutional building type in which architectural restraint was displaced by pure exuberance. Walt Disney Concert Hall opened in 2003 in Los Angeles to similar fanfare muted only slightly by pragmatic questions about the building's reflective glare and budget overruns. More to the point, critics felt the need to address whether Disney Concert Hall was actually novel, or whether it was derivative of Bilbao. 'For a building instantaneously acclaimed as a vanguard masterpiece, the Walt Disney Concert Hall is surprisingly traditional'. wrote Raymund Ryan in *The Architectural Review* (2004). In *Slate Magazine* the *LA Times* architecture critic Christopher Hawthorne asked: 'Is the long-delayed Disney Hall, then, just a consolation prize for Los Angeles? Does one of the biggest cities in the world find itself in the odd position of playing second fiddle to a Basque regional capital with a population under 400,000?' (Hawthorne 2003). His answer was an equivocal, 'Not exactly', arguing that the concert hall was not the newest new (the ideal variant), but a better rendition of a its predecessors (the variant inflects model).

The double-bind, a kind of architectural schizophrenia, is that great works of contemporary architecture must be new and yet show their origins simultaneously. The architect develops a body of work, which by definition exhibits some family resemblance within itself as well as within the discipline, yet each project must be unique. To become more than an iconoclast, an architect like Frank Gehry, or for that matter, Zaha Hadid or Glenn Murcutt, needs followers. Then, as followers grow into creative variants of the master, the master is folded into the professional core.

Architects generally acknowledge the importance of their forebears, insofar as they also depart from them. Take Robert Venturi's comment in the preface to *Complexity and Contradiction in Architecture*, for example: 'As an architect I try to be guided not by habit but by a conscious sense of the past – by precedent, thoughtfully considered' (Venturi 1966, 13). Venturi here parrots French sociologist Pierre Bourdieu's notion of the habitus, when he suggests that habits are unselfconscious practices that comprise the routines of everyday life. Only when we step back from them, as if from an academic perspective, can we understand and potentially transform the directives of the habitus. The architect's practices-as-habit and her production-as-precedent reflect two strands of the normative core of the discipline.

MODEL AND VARIANT

At least since modernism it has been commonplace to assert the radical nature of architecture's production, yet by definition radical departures occur in relation to a static backdrop – an abstract model of constancy that stands in contrast to variants in practice. Without that stable element, variation would not be identifiable. For example, when Zaha Hadid won the Pritzker Prize in 2004, she was a variant in many ways: a woman, relatively young, Middle Eastern, with few built projects to her name. Her exceptional body of work was described by a Pritzker juror thus: 'Over the past 25 years, Zaha Hadid has built a career on defying convention – conventional ideas of architectural space, of practice, of representation, and of construction'. The assumption is that the jury and the architectural readers share an understanding of those conventions from which Hadid's work departs.

The conventions – dimensions of practice that defy transformation, are as informative as those that create a more fluid portrait of contemporary practice. In fact, the interpretation of radical departures must be tied to an analysis of norms. While variously interpreted as the essential nature of practice or as the inertia of tradition, static qualities can be more productively assessed. It is commonly argued, for example, that the conservative tendency to draw boundaries limiting architecture to buildings (not including interiors, furniture, cities, etc.) serves to repress threats to professional identity (Larson 1977). But this is not a sufficient explanation, for it omits other considerations such as the need for a clear model or variants to the boundaries themselves. The double-bind of practice is related to notions of an expanded field, where 'field' or discipline is the correlate of a professional model, its expansion determined by what I have called variants in practice. Anthony Vidler similarly observes, 'And yet, underlying the new architectural experimentation is a serious attempt to reconstrue the foundations of the discipline ...' (2004, 143). When architects lobby to maintain drawing in the professional curriculum, it is less a matter of professional turf defence than an attempt to define the shifting locus of a professional core. If, as mentioned before, drawing represents something timeless within the architects' practices, it assists collective understanding of legitimate innovation. Hadid's paintings of architectural space are striking precisely because they are cousins to the architectural sketch and not to computer rendering. Tadao Ando's architectural drawings are remarkable because they embody the construction document in their communication of technical details, as well as the sketch or Ando's way of thinking about buildings.

These examples liken themselves to Kuhn's normal science (1962), those small, steady steps by which the core of a discipline evolves. Even when architecture is presumed to be in crisis, few think the field will undergo the type of paradigm shift that can occur with new scientific discoveries. Instead, design variants can instigate a new school of thought that can become dominant without refuting its competitors. Within architecture's crisis mentality, a dire state of affairs is variously attributed to the economy, stylistic confusion, a lack of creativity, poor construction, the state of education, and so on. This professional anxiety can serve as a call to action that intellectuals and practitioners produce and listeners grasp. A convincingly significant message of catastrophe demands collective response. The digital revolution, the surveillance city, the World Trade Center site, the Katrina-ravaged Gulf Coast, global warming – each has been variously construed as a crisis that requires architectural remediation (see also Chapters 33 and 39). Disaster scenarios hold the potential for innovation: the old ways have not worked, so new solutions are necessary. It can start with a challenge to the model – we need to incorporate environmental sciences into our design thinking – but it will inherently lead to changing our production – green buildings have yet to offer the formal and disciplinary innovation that we can reasonably expect. The double-bind rears its head, as the professional organization attempts to maintain control over architecture's boundaries while architects experiment with new ideas. The variants to the model can take different forms. LEED ratings that seemed so forward-looking when they were established are now part of the model for sustainable building and are criticized for restricting real green innovation. Landscape urbanism is a type of expanded field, while the use of recycled building materials conforms readily to our professional habits, easily becoming part of an architect's repertoire. Somewhere in between the discipline and its techniques are core considerations about the nature of the architect's work. Architects rethink 'the project' or 'the site' as having boundaries that extend to the forests where lumber is harvested or to a programme that changes every generation.

THE PROJECT AS VARIANT

The architectural project is defined as the work of the architect, so the way that boundaries are placed around that work is at issue. The long history of the profession can be told as the evolution of the project, whether we consider the division of design from execution generally associated with the Renaissance, or the attempts to thwart interior design's professionalization in the twentieth century.

To modify the model, innovative variants challenge the project's boundaries rather than its material quality. *Wired Magazine* discusses this distinction, in relation to Gehry's work once again. 'As part of the first generation of architects to go digital, Gehry used new technologies to make possible buildings so complex they previously existed only in the imagination', writes Jessie Scanlon. By contrast, the firm SHoP 'views digital tools as a way to streamline the design and engineering process, minimizing labor hours and materials waste in order to make high-end, customized architecture more affordable'. Basically, SHoP expands the idea of 'the project' to include more of the building process, fewer of the standard architectural consultants (because they do the work in-house instead), and more of 'the nitty-gritty of construction'. The ubiquitous trope, pitting tradition against innovation, concludes the essay with a description of SHoP's new office space. 'From the roof of the new office, the young partners look out on a century of architecture. They see the Brooklyn Bridge and City Hall. The Woolworth Building, once the tallest in the world, stands across the street'. And SHoP's own vision of cheaper, smarter, better architecture will shape the waterfront to the south. 'Before that can happen, we have to break down the conventions of the profession', admits [partner] Pasquarelli, 'and rebuild it, piece by laser-cut piece'. The difference here is that *Wired* is noting innovative practices, rather than forms. It is through projects then that variants take shape, and experimental practices can be tested. Those that take hold reshape themselves into norms, until eventually whole skylines reflect architecture's slowly evolving model.

CONCLUSION

As architecture's discipline, work, and technique evolve, it meets resistance in those domains where professional vulnerability might be exposed. It is at the level of architectural work where innovative practices and projects destabilize the boundaries of the profession. If the discipline's autonomy solidified over the past decade, it is apparent today that the boundaries are permeable once again. But what of its core? It seems impossible to characterize architectural practice as timeless in light of formal, technological, and global conditions all around us. Yet most firms are organized similarly to their forebears a hundred years ago; design remains the charge of talented individuals; clients continue to dominate the building process. That relatively homogeneous core of the profession, however, provides the datum from which to gauge a heterogeneous, uneven experimentation among practitioners. The practice of design among architects has witnessed significant variation over the past fifty years. Some of these variations have destabilized the otherwise steady identity of architecture. Starting with environmental design in the 1960s, the space of practice has moved in response to changing ideas about theory, form, politics, and economics of architecture. The more provocative contemporary architectural practices have leapt the boundaries of the discipline constructing a 'cultural island' wholecloth in Abu Dhabi, while at the same time designing jewellery for Tiffany or teapots for Alessi marketed through Target discount stores.

The most widely acknowledged external forces impinging upon architecture and cities today are digital technology, globalization, environmentalism, and local politics. There are some significant mutations occurring within architecture as well: the shift from two-dimensional digital modelling to three-dimensional fabrication, or the increasingly rich discourse about practices that question our disciplinary bounds (e.g. landscape urbanism, branding, interactive design). Certainly, the speed with which change occurs in architecture and in other fields has accelerated in postmodernity. We might expect, given this understanding of the double-bind, that accelerated change would be paired with a more deeply entrenched core. Some might argue that neo-historical movements within architecture, such as new urbanism, reflect this entrenchment. Instead, if we focus not on architecture-as-discipline, but take architecture to be what it does, that is its production – be that drawing, design, theory, or buildings, then as a discipline we can examine its current status in relation to its past condition, or more appropriately, its innovative variants in relation to its stable but evolving base. This base, in the realm of practices, does not need to be more entrenched now, merely to balance its more effervescent variations. Instead, worthy variants can more quickly be communicated, evaluated, copied, and incorporated into the core.

Early in the essay, the question was posed: What purpose does a stable core serve in architecture? In contrast to Robert Gutman's sociological assessment of its self-defeating effects, I have argued that a clear, shared model for architecture is as essential to the production of difference and innovation as the invention itself. This model, an ideal type in the Weberian sense, is an abstraction that is understood through concrete practices. Where Anthony Vidler sees an expanded field for architecture is in a rethinking of the core. He identifies three realms of concentrated, productive experimentation: ideas of landscape, biological analogies, and new concepts of programme. But he does not argue that these are radical departures, but instead, 'these new conceptual models are themselves deeply embedded in the history of architectural modernism, and each has already been proposed as a unifying concept at one time or another over the last two centuries' (2004, 143).

As the title of this section suggests, the chapters that follow examine design, production, and practice in architecture. Paolo Tombesi examines the impacts of globalization upon architecture's inherently proximate production. Its multidimensional localism resists the erosion of geography, setting up a double-bind which generates new experiments in pre-fabrication and modularity. Christopher Hight elucidates the transformation of drawing in relation to production, from drawing as representation to the embodiment of material intelligence. Such a radical shift in possibilities will alter not only the architects' practices but the disciplinary core, as Hight points out in the conclusion. Lastly, David Salomon's chapter looks to the end of modernism's cleanly defined production to find new forms of complex, ambiguous, and improvisational practices. All the chapters in this section are infused with a reading of the contemporary circumstances, recognizing their own historical location within the changing world of architectural work.

22

Prometheus Unchained: The Multiple Itineraries of Contemporary Professional Freedom

Paolo Tombesi

ARCHITECTURE OF GLOBALIZATION VS. GLOBALIZATION OF ARCHITECTURE

The contemporary debate in architecture is replete with associative references to globalization, a condition specifically interpreted as the underlying narrative behind the merging of otherwise culturally and economically distinct regions, and the descriptor of transnational flows of people, products and ideas. Over the last quarter of a century, its appraisal has divided architectural theorists and critics. Some have denounced the commercial imperatives driving its stride and the cultural homogenization following its wake; others have asserted its inevitability while celebrating alleged emancipatory functions over traditional categories of architectural behaviour and urban thinking.[1] Against this dialectical background, architectural globalization has assumed distinct although perhaps involuntary connotations, foregrounding relative historical 'newness' and privileging selected phenomenological patterns defined by individual projects, identifiable protagonists and linguistic choices, possibly over industry-broad examinations of the weight carried by the 'foreign' in building design, or professional analyses of the actual mechanisms behind the work under scrutiny. As a result, there is a wealth of exegetic efforts on the material expression of architecture in a globalized world (mostly derived from ostensibly emblematic figures, projects and sites), but a paucity of information on how related work is actually structured and carried out, and what makes it significant vis-à-vis the rest (or the previous history) of the built environment. It thus seems appropriate to verify some of the tenets implicit in the formulation of the discourse just outlined, and eventually suggest ways to address possible dislocations between perceptions and reality. To facilitate this plan, the 'globalization' underlying this text is going to be initially interpreted – by design – in a very specific way: not as a cultural condition informing architectural consciousness, but principally as a collective process of technical organization grounded in space, reliant on technology and human capital, and responding to identifiable needs or wants.

PLUS ÇA CHANGE ...

Many of the traditional elements of the architectural discipline suggest that the ability to move widely across territories, borrowing from and influencing cultures while leaving physical marks, has long been one of the defining characteristics of architecture. Indeed, the very catalogue of built examples throughout history bears persistent testimony to the global reach of numerous compositional models, rules and methods – from Greek-Roman architecture to Neo-Palladianism, Romanesque to Catalan vaulting, bungalows to Streamline Moderne.[2]

Both the dissemination and the appropriation of specific features have always depended on a multitude of factors: not only spheres of political influence but also geographies of patronage, location of centres of training, application of knowledge gained from travel, appropriateness of environmental conditions, opportunities generated by trade and expansion and, last but not least, ideological belonging (Cody 2003; Wright 1991; Rabinow 1989; Isenstadt and Rizvi 2008; Willis 2005. See also Chapter 3). Architects have traditionally travelled beyond their familiar territories in search of ideas or work, or to follow their commissions; and to such an extent as to render that of the 'foreigner' a most comprehensive category in the history of the profession.

The turbulent history of the twentieth century has contributed to intensify this almost natural movement, causing many architects to set off towards, or remain in, distant lands, either to fight, to escape conflict or to aid reconstruction, in fact spreading, often by involuntary example, the dissemination of the modern ideals with a supranational thrust already evident in the international meetings and exhibitions organized since the nineteenth century (Goad and Willis 2003; Loomis 1999; Wharton 2001). Irrespective of the motives behind the journey, the transient condition of many contributors and intellectual disciples de facto transformed leading design offices and organizations into international laboratories for the critical development and future dissemination of ideas.

Physical presence, however, was not always needed. In the absence of human capital, architecture and construction handbooks have effectively fulfilled a surrogate didactic function: English manuals and patents were used to build the new world in North America and Australia. In turn, mail order designs developed in the United States served the needs of buyers from as far as South Africa and the Philippines (Woods 1999, 86), while the Sweets' Product Catalogue was used by Modern European designers as a source of inspiration for detail engineering.[3] Indeed, normative technological frameworks have been employed as instruments of cultural influence through architecture: if Russian printed instructions have dictated the urban lines of the communist world, from Cuba to Vietnam, the US Marshall Plan for post-war reconstruction in Europe funded the production and publication of such texts as the *Manuale dell'Architetto* (1946), Italy's most popular professional drafting guidebook for 50 years, which contains several plates featuring US building systems.

Reviewing these points suggests that the contemporary condition of architecture could be nothing else but a reiteration of established patterns of cultural agency and professional exchange.

SOCIAL PARTICIPATION AS PHYSICAL LIMIT

Things, however, take on a different connotation the moment we consider architecture not as a series of culturally connected artifacts or as an occupational label but rather as an embedded métier consisting of specific routines that contribute to a process of building production. From this perspective, architectural practice has always been an eminently local, place-based operation; an 'industry', that is, which generates its products – in this case interpretative ideas, advice and physical information – in close enough proximity to the place where such products are needed and put to use by clients, consultants and construction executors.

The reason is twofold. On the one hand, it has to do with the nature of the design challenge: since construction is a cumbersome physical and organizational endeavour, taking advantage of the socio-technical conventions already in use locally simplifies the task; but this requires familiarity with the context. On the other hand, localism relates also to the socially complex and thus operatively uncertain nature of the building development process, a process that architects, by definition, are supposed to instruct and monitor. Before and throughout it, proper information must therefore be generated or managed at an almost constant pace, often by being physically present on site.

It is such a distinctive lack of operative (rather than intellectual) autonomy that made it traditionally difficult for architectural firms to operate 'in practice' beyond the territorial limits of physical transactions: information producers and information users had to inhabit, by-and-large, the same social domain.

If one had the space, it could be shown that such a constraining relationship did not apply equally to all building markets. Government-based, design-related bureaucracies, for instance, could historically afford the disadvantages of distance better than independent architects, because construction projects were part of explicit and long-planned programmes, not a result of occasional client initiatives. By contrast, stretching territorial boundaries in private practice was hard. If the architect, or the studio, could not reach or move to a new centre of activity, the limits of the practice were expanded by producing an additional structure of work, either by establishing a branch office or by associating with a 'local' firm in charge of documentation and site administration. The history of architectural firms in the United States contains many of these examples, from George Post's New-York-based firm opening an office as far away as Cleveland in the 1880s (Balmori 1987; Bradford Landau 1998), to Caudill Rowlett Scott devising specific collaboration strategies in the 1950s to cover the US school market from Texas (Tombesi 2006; King and Langdon 2002), to Albert Kahn sending employees from his Detroit office to Moscow in 1930 to supervise Soviet technicians drafting the plans of Russia's five-year industrialization programme factories (Bucci 1993).

It is perhaps against this background that the importance of two distinctive features in the cultural evolution of world architecture can be appreciated. One is the development of prefabricated buildings that could be organized and manufactured into components from the centres of the world, then to be shipped all over its peripheries.[4] The other is the modern reinvention of proportional systems, such as Le Corbusier's Modulor, which had the potential to bypass distance by establishing rules that made the control of their application secondary, thus privileging cultural kinship over technical supervision (Le Corbusier 1980; Pottage 1996).

TECHNOLOGY AS A FORM OF SPATIAL LIBERATION

All the arguments brought forth thus far serve to introduce a hypothesis: the traditional 'grounded-ness' of practice can be the crucial element against which to introduce and frame the substantive changes that have characterized the evolution of architectural activities over the last twenty-five years. It could be said, in fact, that while architectural work has not become intrinsically 'worldlier' during this period, it has certainly become easier to identify and request, provide and monitor, transport and disseminate. This is largely due to the advent of a new technological paradigm revolving around microprocessors, digital systems and, more generally, the convergence of a whole raft of data organization, storage, retrieval and transmittal, optical scanning and printing technologies.[5]

Since 1983 – when *Time Magazine* declared the PC 'person of the year' and Autodesk released the first versions of Autocad[6] – computer aided drafting (for lack of a better term) has established the conditions for an increasingly efficient standardization of notational practices and design routines as well as an augmented capacity to retain knowledge. Moreover, with the parallel development of telecommunications infrastructure, it has also enabled completely new modes of information-transfer across space. Fibre-optic networks, digital links and file transfer protocol sites have now fundamentally reduced the need for physical contiguity for project-based transactions, forever changing the territorial spatialization of design practice. With paper no longer an essential support to the transfer of design decisions (or the dissemination of their outcomes), the Prometheus of architectural practice has been unchained from the tyranny of place.

The importance of attaining such freedom of movement must be placed in context. And the world context of the last forty years has been characterized by the concurrent growth of several factors bearing an impact over the demand for distant services.[7] One factor is the progressive expansion of long-distance travel and the parallel rise of people movement, particularly in the form of mass tourism, a phenomenon that has triggered new development and renovation activity in virtually every locale that can be reached by vacationers or event-goers.[8] Another factor is the deregulation of world financial markets since the 1971 demise of the Bretton Woods agreement, tying countries' currency exchange rates to gold reserves. Deregulation has provided impetus to the search for global investments (including real estate), the growth of transnational capital flows, and the appearance of a new breed of development sponsors, often located away from the old centres of money. A third factor is the emergence of an international division of labour spurred by transnational corporations, with the consequent creation of strategic basins of employment, needs for production infrastructure, service centres, and distribution nodes. The geographic restructuring of production has led to the industrial take-off of low-income regions (such as China and India), which has produced hyper-urbanization trends in areas initially unequipped, in terms of physical structure as well as numbers of building professionals, to cope with the type and the statistics of new construction demand (Tombesi 2004).

Although largely enabled by information technology, then, the foundations of a contemporary architectural practice defined by global activities and presence must be related not only to advances in communications and wiring but also to the evolution of travel, the need for building infrastructure, the advent of new political and cultural realities, and the location of economic actors as well as the availability of technical cadres.

POTENTIAL MOVEMENT AND REAL FLOWS

The ability to be intensely and unprecedentedly mobile does not mean that every architectural firm is or aspires to that goal. Although it is true that the architectural sector as a whole has embraced the use of digital technology in its everyday practices, the adoption of technology does not in itself imply (let alone prescribe) a global outlook or global clients.[9] Indeed, from a statistical perspective, architecture is still a very locally-based occupation. A comparatively much larger number of firms may be active in foreign markets than a few years ago, but in absolute terms only a small portion of professional establishments work beyond their home region.[10] This should not come as a surprise when considered against the demographics of architectural practice. In 2007, for example, almost a quarter of the architectural firms registered with the American Institute of Architects consisted of sole practitioners, and at least 61 percent had fewer than five employees. Of this section, earning just 8 percent of the industry's billings, only a small proportion of offices trespass international boundaries as a matter of professional course.[11] The professional scene in Europe is even more fragmented, with 74 percent of all building design-related firms made out of individual practitioners, and only 1 percent employing more than twenty people.[12] Those who naturally travel for work are the very large firms, which, interestingly, are only in part a product of recent globalization trends. They belong to a fairly established group, have by-and-large been involved with large-scale transnational work for a long time, and are the ones we seldom hear from or read about in the architectural press.[13]

The top architecture-only providers tend to be comparatively small, but equally embedded in the international arena, and perhaps equally concerned with design volume. Out of the Top 100 global practices surveyed in the British *Building Design*'s World Architecture report every year, less than one-fifth would be recognizable to the public as clear contributors to the architectural discourse.[14] The same goes for the rankings produced by *World Architecture* magazine until a few years ago, or by *Architectural Record* today. Partly this is a reflection of the fact that involvement in these surveys is voluntary, and not everyone wants to disclose office data, especially when there is no need for publicity. But, whatever the reasons and the justifications, there is clearly an industrial as well as cultural divide between the bulk of architectural services traded worldwide and the international work that occupies front pages in the architectural press, or catalyses the attention of the public. Generated after all by a limited number of firms, the second has a presence that surpasses by far its actual mass.

This contrast between the myriad of small locale-bound practitioners all over the world, the rarefied industrial heights reached by substantial but anonymous world-encompassing design organizations, and the clamour generated by the marketed avant-gardes of the architectural discipline, clarifies important aspects of architectural globalization by highlighting its statistical contradictions. In spite of the somewhat dominant rhetoric, it is plausible to say that global architecture concerns a relatively small group of players, particularly when taking into account the entire population of practitioners. Even if one could determine that the architectural offices working abroad or making international news were in the thousands, this figure would pale against the 900,000 firms currently active only in Europe.[15] Besides, the firms that are most successful economically worldwide are not, as a whole, the ones that produce architectural opinions. But since there is no doubt that architecture has found a way to travel physically and above all culturally around the world, making unimaginable audiences aware of its presence and conferring some of its champions starchitect status and following,[16] the rationalization of this condition cannot derive simply from demographic or financial figures. One must look for a more complex way to bring the evolution of architectural discussion to bear on the reality of practice.

Indeed, the perception of a globalizing practice could result from the collaboration of three quite different realities:

1) the reality of technological reach, which allows people to work and 'profess' distantly;
2) the concurrent reality of telecommunications and media, which makes possible the amplified dissemination of one's design actions to extended audiences (when indeed not expected or normatively required); and
3) the reality of the building industry in a world of production and commerce, which determines the actual (growing) extent of global professional

markets, and the role assigned to a certain type of architecture in the land improvement process.

Regardless of how many firms actually manage to work away from their home territory, the socio-technical possibility/opportunity is there for them to do so, and so is the faculty to advertise and reflect, as it were, upon the event.

Treating architectural globalization as a collective psychological state grounded in selective reality rather than as integral transformation of the *modus operandi* of the entire architectural industry helps normalize conflicting evidence. In fact, while it is indisputable that the composition of building needs and wants around the world is changing, and that this change affects construction output and transnational contributions, the phenomenon under the lens could be more properly described as a nominal condition, open to every design agency, and engendered by the theoretical ability of architects to access spaces of global disciplinary interaction and design communication. From this perspective, the contemporary situation of practice is historically peculiar in its capacity to define and sustain a market of transnational services, defined by relatively low entry barriers, which functions as an arena where design and design-related activities can be exchanged entrepreneurially between economies, either as goods aimed at facilitating market expansion or generating symbolic capital, services provided to assist industrial and economic take-offs, or commodities shipped from abroad to achieve relative production advantages.

THE INTERNATIONAL TRADING OF ARCHITECTURE: CRITICAL CATEGORIES FROM A COMMERCIAL PARADIGM

The framework just introduced describes contemporary global practice on the basis of what defines it most specifically from an operational standpoint: the negotiation of border crossing rather than the technical ability to cross. In fact, while traditional architectural markets have always been defined within accepted spatial and cultural boundaries (determined also by political and economic spheres), which could be occasionally stretched, the same may not be said for the new global arena. Irrespective of the sense of freedom transmitted by the image of the wandering architect appearing everywhere, proper reading of current international work cannot be achieved simply by focusing on architectural intent (type of design approach), product (type of buildings commissioned) and service (scope of the work required). It also demands critical consideration of how administrative frontiers are crossed and the mode of design supply such crossing entails.

For this to be understood properly, it is necessary to make a temporary foray into the world of economic trading. The basic travel book for this journey is provided by the General Agreement for Trade in Services (GATS), the framework devised in the early 1990s by the World Trade Organization (WTO) to discuss and regulate the international trading of services, including design-related ones.[17] For the exchange of work between nations, the GATS considers a series of transactional possibilities that encompass both physical and virtual elements. According to the WTO, services can be traded internationally in four different ways:

1) Through the temporary movement of 'natural persons', that is by allowing a foreign individual to enter a country in person to supply a service.
2) Through commercial presence, by allowing foreign suppliers to enter a country and establish companies in their market sector (e.g., foreign banks setting up operations).
3) Through 'consumption abroad', by allowing the citizens of a country (or national entities) to travel in order to buy a service from a foreign supplier.
4) Through 'cross-border' supply, by allowing the same subjects to deal with a foreign company from across national borders (that is, through telephone calls or digital connections).[18]

Improbable as it may seem, these four alternatives summarize effectively the channels available for architectural exchange, thus providing a conceptual ordering tool for globalization.[19]

The first category, allowing for the trading of individuals' services, is the one most easily (and somewhat mistakenly) adaptable to the picture of practice we are culturally accustomed to, which associates buildings with single architectural authors, or clearly identifiable design consultants. In its explanatory material, even the WTO uses architectural designers (together with fashion models) as examples of the persons that may travel abroad for service-supplying purposes. In this case, the ability to deliver the service is supposed to be intrinsic to the individual, much as if it were a performance. There are plenty of examples of architects who lend their names, ideas, culture or experience to building projects or organizations away from home. In the past, this kind of travel was normally accompanied by relatively long stays – think of Bramante, Benjamin Latrobe, Frank Lloyd Wright or Bruno Taut. Today, the trading of individual services does not necessarily reflect long-term strategies; rather, it relies on contingent markets that can be entered temporarily and departed quickly, without the same level of personal investment. Contracted services, in this case, can range widely, from styling suggestions to highly technical specialist contributions, from initial consulting by recognized design leaders to design workshops. Quantitatively, though, the flow of 'natural persons' today is mainly concerned with the movement of the architectural workforce – salaried personnel, that is, which follows employment opportunities within a firm rather than autonomously.

The second category underlies fully-fledged attempts on the part of architectural firms to expand their market by increasing geographic coverage, perhaps initially as a result, but in the end irrespective of specific projects. Compared to the first category, this type of border-crossing requires longer-term planning, and reliable expectations about markets for services. For this reason, the map of globalization implied by this trading mode has been associated, at least since the end of World War II, with corporate firms, connected to and moving alongside the economic interests of their mother country and its allies, thus reflecting patterns of foreign policy, economic allegiances, and colonial or pseudo-colonial relationships. Today, the establishment of foreign subsidiaries of large architectural firms still defines corporate architecture, but perhaps of a less overtly political and more market economy-based nature. The locational geography of global firms, in fact, is more likely to reflect opportunities generated by localized urban growth, definition of international service hubs, imbalances in the demand/supply equation of specific building products in particular regions, or simply the strength of the architectural firm in a given design specialty (for example airports, stadia, hospitals or retail).[20]

In spite of all this, much of the work undertaken by architects and firms around the world falls under the other two categories suggested in the GATS model: 'consumption abroad' and 'cross-border' services. Consumption abroad provisions indicate clients' capacity to travel overseas to purchase architectural services. In turn this implies architectural firms' ability to work on and bill projects remotely, from their home base, without being required to move their entire administrative structures on-site, as it were. While the multinational locational nature of many companies is an undeniable factor in the growth of transnational design work, the increase in public profile attained by architecture in recent years cannot be overlooked as a generator of international commissions, strategically focused on the drawing power of the object (Ockman and Frausto 2005). Securing the services of renowned architectural subjects has become an effective way to generate visibility, which can then be employed to either commercial or political ends. This has been happening with the

Olympics at least since 1992, with numerous municipalities and local institutions around the world hiring international names in the attempt to get signature projects, and with all the major companies (such as the Central Chinese Television, or the Swiss furniture manufacturer Vitra) bringing public architectural personae in to build not only headquarters but also symbolic capital.[21]

Casting international flows as the sole product of celebrity-focused drivers, though, would be a mistake. The global exchange of services also reflects the specialization of design expertise, with place-specific offices holding a quasi-monopoly of distinctive forms of knowledge organized according to unique protocols, which can work across the world from their original locations without having to establish new permanent offices. Gehry Partners is the utmost example of an architectural structure with the power to work mostly from home; but the same is true for technical firms such as the façade specialists Front (from New York) or Atelier One (from London).

As a further development of this possibility, the WTO recognizes that domestic entities may choose to deal across national borders with foreign companies simply through the use of communication technology (or, more unlikely, transportation services). All the design competitions open to international entries on the basis of a brief available on the internet or submissions wired through it would be part of this category, as well as the highly specialized services complementary to design, such as façade testing, simulation or modelling, which are becoming increasingly necessary in certain sectors of the architectural market.

Over the last few years, however, cross-border services have acquired a specific, and quite different, strategic connotation, in fact employed by the WTO in its didactic illustrations of the global market, as a tool enabling new forms of the international division of labour to emerge.[22] In this case, the remote exchange of services serves to allow drafting workshops based in lower labour cost areas of the world to supply construction documentation assistance to architectural firms based in higher-cost locales rather than professional advice to a client. This version of design globalization is clearly the result of economic logics internal to architectural practice: the IT-enabled strategic decentralization of salaried workforces allows components of the profession to reduce their project costs either by subcontracting part of their responsibilities at a diminished rate (thereby increasing the competitiveness of their services), or by facing labour shortages without increasing overheads.[23]

Yet the international division of labour is not necessarily about wage differentials or lean employment. There are many instances, in fact, where services can be, and indeed are also being transacted between units of the same organization, or the same temporary project coalition, located in different parts of the world.

FROM ONE TO MANY: EMERGENCE AND SIGNIFICANCE OF NETWORK STRUCTURES

The point just made provides an opportunity to highlight value and limitations of the GATS framework. The formation of design coalitions consisting of different individuals and companies is a distinctive aspect of architecture production. Multiple firms with different structures based in varied locations come together on any project in different ways; they are even more likely to do so in an international context defined and made possible by technological ‘agility’ but nonetheless constrained by distance, relevant knowledge, building supervisory needs and, above all, professional jurisdictions. The opening of a global market, in fact, has sharpened rather than relaxed local licensing and qualification transfer requirements, since this is the only way to control access and govern participation in the local industry. While the European Community allows 'freedom of establishment and service' within its territory for all its citizen architects, the rest of the world makes for a complex legal mosaic.[24] For all these reasons, the more international the work becomes, the more likely it is to involve collaborations between foreign and local firms as well as the foreign and local workforce, distributing weights and responsibilities according to the occasion. Often, this means lead foreign designers acting as individual consultants, foreign-based offices producing the initial proposal and coordinating the design intent, local executive architects looking after document production and site activities, and design or trade specialists engineering solutions from their own scattered locales. The picture of global practice that comes out of project reality is not as neat as any of the categories articulated under the GATS system. It has a hybrid nature, and it is the product of all possible arrangements combined through ad-hoc assembled contributions, often concurrently.

Acknowledging such a variety of work provisions and opportunities in practice serves a double purpose. On the one hand, it helps explain why studying globalization is difficult, and in most cases relative, because what appears on the surface does not necessarily correspond to the industrial organization that supports it, or the resources (intellectual as well as human and financial) actually invested on the project.[25] On the other hand, the multiplicity of design actors on any project suggests the reasons why structure and premises of the GATS system could be contractually correct in theory but operationally and culturally obsolete in the firm-centred image of practice they indirectly underpin. It could be easily argued, in fact, that today's practice in architecture is characterized by the ability to network and establish alliances as much as the act of moving. And this is not only in light of the countless instances in which projects require to be developed by dense transnational groups rather than individual firms, but also in light of the cultural relevance increasingly assigned to the weaving of accessible webs of architectural expertise, particularly when from around the world. By keeping everyone local and yet practically engaged with their foreign counterparts, networks can realize the communal ambitions of canonical twentieth century architectural fellowships, such as CIAM and Team X, while overcoming the organization of commercial world trading through cooperation rather than competition (Risselada and Van der Heuvel 2006; Zardini 1997).

MAPPING THE FLOW: GEOGRAPHIES OF SOCIO-TECHNICAL VARIANCE

Although the taxonomy of the GATS framework is too rigid to reveal the organizational patterns of contemporary project structures (and therefore contemporary practice), it is still useful to outline and reflect on the relationship between the typology of contributions to global design activity and their prevalent geographies. Underlying patterns can be best highlighted by considering such contributions in terms of branding, ideas, knowledge and labour (Figure 22.1).

In the case of individual architects working abroad (GATS category 1), the representation from advanced capitalist economies is overwhelmingly prevalent but internally varied. Within this cluster, significant differences in terms of geographic origin and subgroup composition can be gauged by considering specific value-adding functions.

The location of international brand names indicates a relatively rarefied geography, coinciding for the most part with a few 'world cities'. Their services, by contrast, tend to be exchanged all over high-income societies and poles of intense urban agglomeration.

The passage from top branding to the actual development of new ideas and design propositions defines a larger, more 'democratized' territory, partly organized around the regional expansion of the same leading locales (North America, Northern and Central Europe, Japan) but also encompassing Australia's Western seaboard, Southeast Asian centres and the main urbanized areas of South America. Low-income realities across Africa, Latin America and Asia become fertile, albeit largely unsung, laboratories for those who perceive architecture as an opportunity for social activism and a tool of participatory development.

Instead, the individual supply of technical knowledge and experience tends to follow a locational geography defined almost vicariously, either by the clustering of services in the same urban locales inhabited by top practices, the clustering of technological capital in a given territory, populated for example by research institutions or specialized industry, or the clustering of applicative opportunities (that is areas of intense urban growth where shorthand expertise is needed). However, as mentioned earlier, the most relevant and pervasive of all global individual flows is the movement of architectural workforce, with people criss-crossing the world in (almost) all directions to trail salaried opportunities. Given what was explained at the beginning of this text about the firms active in foreign lands, such opportunities mostly coincide with the employment needs of large offices. If project managerial positions characterize the job market in areas of urban growth, architectural graduates integrate the entry positions available in the geographic 'outposts' of practice with curriculum-enhancing pilgrimages towards the established centres of architectural elaboration.[26]

In terms of architecture-only offices acquiring a stable presence in areas beyond their domestic home base (category 2), the global landscape is difficult to capture at once.

Figure 22.1 (Below) GATS categories, forms of engagement and professional territories. (Paolo Tombesi)

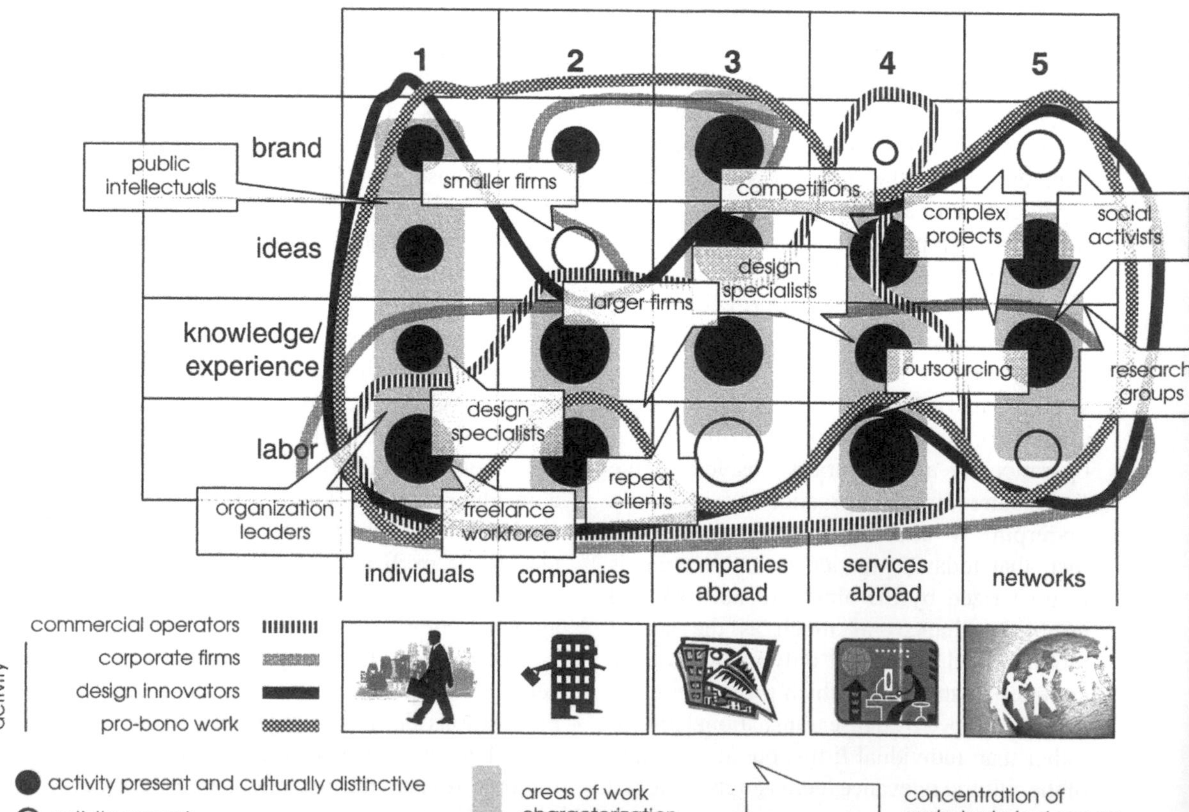

London and New York clearly function as global gateways for the accumulation of architectural intelligence, where leading firms almost have to be present in order to access large clients and global regional markets. Eastern China and the Arab Peninsula (and now increasingly Eastern Europe/ Central Asia) make obvious ports of call based on sustained construction activity and proximity with areas of future growth.

The relationship between firms and expansion locales, though, is not entirely market-led. Studies on architectural firms' participation in world markets have found correlations between cities from where major firms practice and macro-areas of relative professional influence, suggesting that globalization is not as placeless as some purport it to be (Knox and Taylor 2005). In addition, there are a number of smaller firms active in at most two locations as a strategic decision to become 'local' in both. While in many cases this decision reflects architectural niching ambitions, sometimes it betrays a search for new labour pools – a phenomenon that, over the years, has highlighted links between the Americas, the UK and South Africa, the US or the Netherlands and India, Central and Eastern Europe, Singapore and its neighbours.

Foreign shopping – or the third GATS category – defines the most composite, intricate dimension to map. This particular way of crossing boundaries encapsulates every strand of design globalization, it is not size-specific, and is anarchic in nature by responding not only to structural conditions but also discrete project-related opportunities. Branding and symbolic capital services are exchanged equally between affluent societies, whereas more technical architectural services indicate a persistent move from mature, urbanized economies to developing, less urbanized ones. However, as the contribution required from the selected firm moves towards the production aspects of the design service, the probability of encountering establishments from cost-effective economies, such as South Asia, Latin America (and, until recently, Eastern Europe), increases drastically. A similar pattern applies to services exchanged electronically (category 4), and seems to depend on the level of expertise and technology required. The location of most highly technical consulting remains in the 'old world,' whereas graphic processing, data conversion and document production are increasingly located in lower-wage areas, even if controlled by Western interests. It looks as international open design competitions may be the only true ambassadors of a borderless world inhabited, at least in principle, by architectural equals.

Such a perception is bound to change if one looks at the collaborative practices operating outside the established boundaries of economic trading (category 5). If transnational coalitions have become the norm in complex projects, where either knowledge or public perception of expertise is required, collective design research networks or professional solidarity structures (such as Architecture for Humanity, Architectes sans Frontières or Emergency Architects) reveal the global organizing potential of the entire social architectural body.

COMBINING THE MORPHOLOGICAL DIFFERENCES OF PRACTICE

This morphology of global practice is both complex and intriguing. As the 'realms of activity' sketched in Figure 22.1 show, architectural actors inhabit multiple locations in a composite world, which can be read properly only by keeping the technical aspects of the work connected to its cultural results and motivations. This suggests the interpretative risks involved in letting particular dimensions slip out of sight. The architectural products to which we are increasingly exposed are not the natural yield of cohesive trajectories of civilization. They are spurred by determinate and often uneven urban circumstances, they are made possible through the presence of restrained and yet distinctive socio-technical infrastructure, and are certainly facilitated by political engineering.[27] That this global architectural land reflects its own lie is both clear and important to remember, because it contradicts – at least at macro-level – the idea that globalization fuels, or is fueled by, de-territorializing effects. Locales may not always be reflected in the architectural output they have to accommodate, but they play a critical function in the opportunities or pressures they provide, and the international alliances they underpin.

The primacy originally assigned to information technology in the globalization of practice must also be qualified, since the number of architectural employees brought into contact with international projects by digital systems is at least compensated by the armies of itinerant architectural journeymen physically mobilized around the world. The relative weights of these 'natural person' flows balance earlier contentions concerning the limited uptake of international commissions by traditional architectural establishments. The firms (and the brand names) involved in global markets are finite, but the employment they generate is noteworthy (and possibly relevant from a cultural standpoint), particularly when considering turnover rates. As David Harvey noted a few years ago in *Spaces of Hope* – a critical text in relation to the hypotheses put forth in this chapter – the reduction in the cost of overcoming physical space could be at least as significant as the 'so-called information revolution per se' (Harvey 2000, 63).

Perhaps a way to blend digital and physical movement is to reiterate information technology's contribution to the standardization of architectural design and documentation methods. The commercial dissemination of graphic software has de facto created the conditions for a world market of architectural technicians able to move from workstation to workstation. The point is worth stressing in light of ever more efficient but cumbersome technologies such as BIM, which could eventually make digital networks economically and technically preferable to the movement of the architectural workforce. New geographic alliances between pure design firms and documenting offices are already being forged on this basis. The ultimate beneficiaries and critical linchpins of such a system, however, could be the design and engineering specialists who have become the consultants of everyone (and hence the partial authors of almost everything) in a global market, thus acquiring unmatched brokering power across the board.[28] Still, the bulk trading of architecture-related services supports predictable views of globalization and socio-economic exchange patterns: design glamour and technological innovation travel across areas of comparable wealth; advanced economies are net exporters of technical knowledge and conceptual decisions, whereas lower-income regions invert the trend when it comes to the export of data processing and document production activities.

If there is a value in weaving the tapestry presented in these pages, it is not to be found in the simple confirmation of historical conditions and subsequent trends. Instead, the degree of structural change that architectural practice may experience as a result of globalization of work warrants attention. To this end, at least four elements are worth stressing.

The first element is the sustained growth of construction markets in previously peripheral parts of the architectural world, such as China, where the scope of urban change has created a wealth of opportunities for truly reflective local practice. This has led to the emergence of new offices that epitomize original ways of working and are making proselytes overseas.

The second element represents a change in the idea of what a foreign office is. In the space of twenty-five years, the dominant paradigm has matured, from the existence of professional structures 'existing' abroad to implying structures consistently 'working' abroad, but mainly on individual projects scattered around rather than embedded within stable markets.[29] The structural agility implied in this way of practising has generated two relevant consequences. The first is direct support to local executive architect establishments, which must act in a subsidiary capacity to mobile non-local designers. Pairing-up can provide an opportunity to learn from the exchange, but also to grow in terms of public recognition by leaping into a new arena of practice. For the same reason, the mechanics of fame, cultural influence and professional advancement allegedly valid for hundreds of years are inverting their terms. As Rosanne Williamson has written (1991), many architectural lineages were created around fixed locations and office structures that witnessed the passage of time and people, thus building experience and legacies. Today, the ever mobile foreign office has become a preferred training ground (when not almost an academy) for ambitious architectural graduates, as the place where curricula can be built more quickly, and exposure to transnational horizons most easily pursued.

On the other hand, practice alliances have generated new entry paths into large-scale (or corporate) architecture for firms that started as drafting workshops. Through the experience acquired by collaborating with multiple architectural clients, successful service providers (such as Satellier in India and Atlas in Vietnam), have evolved into highly professional entities that offer more complex services in the design process. And given that their market basin and rate of growth are wider and higher than most successful corporate architectural firms, they could become the harbingers of a new, indirect way of getting to the centre of the profession – no longer through building type innovation, as was the case in the twentieth century, but rather through geographic industrial restructuring and the socio-technical division of labour (see Tombesi et al. 2007). Even though the global flows of decisions and projects suggest the existence of power blocs and what some writers have called 'epistemic elites', these may not be as clearly definable by territory and label as one would tend to assume. Understanding globalization thus means understanding the nuances of the work and the mechanics of operative knowledge.

DO GOOD OR DO WELL? GRADING ARCHITECTURAL TRADING

Producing discerning analyses of globalization does not exonerate one from evaluating the activities, products and by-products of the foreign body in architecture. Is contemporary 'beyond-local' practice a good thing or a bad thing? How can this be determined? Does the process raise specific issues for a theory of architecture that purports to be in line with the times? Answering any of these questions requires first agreement on the materials necessary to form a judgement – problematic in itself. In fact, how important are the simulative and discursive tactics enabled by technology to be at the very base of cultural globalization, particularly one so naturally reliant upon images? Can architecture-related experiences be properly 'mediated' through such communication channels, and recreated effectively for intellectual use? In a sense, it is the very iconography of contemporary architecture that warns against the dangers of assenting too quickly. The mediatic industry that manufactures transnational icons seems to assign a significant function to the act of editing for visual consumption. By contrast, accomplishments that are not as self-explanatory and require deeper analysis, do not appear to be the object of equally assertive cultural marketing. (It is comparatively more difficult, for example, to be exposed to acts of architectural counter-heroism, such as unassuming structures in poverty stricken regions requiring Herculean organizational efforts, incremental progresses in waterless sanitation facilities, didactic pilots for construction with harvestable materials, practice-based training in remote locales, or even examples of dangerous imported mediocrity – all of which, one could argue, are as much part of a globalized architectural world as the first set.)

Perhaps a combined theory of architecture as intellectual medium, physical end and emancipatory tool – technically inquisitive rather than politely accepting – could be the way to structure a militant relationship with the architectural simulacra of globalization. Such a relationship could also allow the deconstruction of related design practices on the basis of the WTO-derived strands discussed earlier. In this case, the benefits and costs of transnational work could be weighed up against rhetorical questions of utility: What purpose(s) does the architecture developed – or the energies spent in developing it – serve? The moment this question is asked, the double dimension of the analysis, at once internal and external to the discipline, becomes evident: contributing to the discussion of architecture as cultural practice is other than contributing to the context in which the work is located. And yet a building cannot abstain from being part of either dimension, regardless of the type of emphasis placed on the work. For this reason, every artifact should contribute to forming a view of globalization naturally organized by layers, not necessarily positioned to coincide precisely with one another, but still part of the same discourse.[30]

The thickness thus acquired by the topic evens things out. If the globalization of architecture can at times reflect the reduction of buildings to commercial billboards and material for easily consumed social spectacles, it can also be seen as an essential platform for valuable intellectual exchange and the addressing of real professional, territorial and infrastructural imbalances. In a world where the ratio architects/urban residents sways between 1/400 and 1/100,000 depending on the region, the ability to organize and move swiftly has assisted in urban development and sheltering efforts, brought proper expertise where expertise was needed, disseminated experiences, raised awareness on specific issues, organized action on an unprecedented scale, and contributed to building capacity in areas that had little.[31]

This is different from saying that the proliferation of international flows is not to have any detrimental effects on grounded practice that are worth keeping in check. It should be asked, for instance, at which point the international division of labour that is sweeping through architecture is likely to weaken local professional traditions, and eventually replace the need for regionally specific training and architectural cultivation. (At which point, in other words, do richer countries start determining the profile of the architectural workforce in poorer ones?) It could also be debated whether the possible reduction of the professional design workforce in mature economies, occasionally emerging now but foreseeable in the future as a result of technological advances, will continue to be neutralized by the need for skilled architectural workers in distant territories and specific market sectors. In fact, these trends could end up altering permanently the traditional, self-regulating mechanisms of the profession – particularly the natural distribution of work that characterizes closed economic systems – by making access available to large non-local reservoirs of human resources, being trained on-the-job as we write.[32]

In addition to such issues, what are the guarantees that the adoption of the foreign (or the hiring of the foreigner) is not used as a strategy to bypass informed critical positions on urban development (as happened in London in the 1980s and is happening in China today), wrestle real control away from the architect, or override planning regulations in light of the extra-ordinary aura conferred to the project by the exoticism of its proponents?[33] Responding to the questions posed is clearly beyond the scope of this text and the space available to this contribution. Throwing them as open issues on the table, however, is useful for two reasons. Firstly, to show how easily the discussion of architectural globalization could trespass into other territories, defined by ecologies of value and policies of action different from those officially debated in architecture; secondly, to stress how important such very transcending of architecture could be for its actual worth to be assessed.

The reference to broader reflective dimensions involving capacity-building, technical ownership, governance and control, cultural agency, and authority and authorship, provide architectural theory with the ability to see through the depth of the work under examination, by contaminating scale and presence, for example, with scope and process. The challenge, in this case, would be to find the right balance between the hermeneutics of the immediately *visible* and the mechanics of the elusive *real*. To this end, the time may have come to consider reframing the breadth of certain positions.

In 1983, Kenneth Frampton's essay on critical regionalism articulated the idea that local architectural practice could resist the homogenizing pressures of globalization by concentrating on a set of dialectical oppositions between the experiential and the visual. Despite its broad territorial focus, the agenda evoked an almost underground connotation, as it was explicitly directed at those 'architectures of cultural resistance' that could only exist within the 'interstices of practice'. Today it is useful to ask whether or not this position is still worth prioritizing, or whether a critically regional perspective should be adopted not so much as to support and celebrate the production of work informed by a particular ethos but rather to place local architectural sectors as a whole in a position to engage with and yet withstand an increasingly competitive transnational professional market. A critically regional practice in line with the times, that is, could now be identified as the banner under which industrial policies should be designed to let architecture prosper in all its components.

Such an attempt to problematize architectural globalization, by highlighting the political economy of its unfolding rather than contemplating its cultural drivers, outcomes and champions, may call for the review of certain disciplinary dispositions towards the analysis of design artifacts as well as the centrality given to individual authors thus far in the debate. In return, it could elicit altogether new perspectives on the production of architectural canons and the lines of enquiry generated by it.

NOTES

1 These positions are clarified in a few titles that are also significant chronologically: Kenneth Frampton's essay 'Towards a Critical Regionalism. Six Points for an Architecture of Resistance' (1983) constitutes a point of departure for the critical discussion on globalization, the perspective of which can be usefully compared to Hans Ibelings' *Supermodernism: Architecture in the Age of Globalization* (2002), written nearly twenty years later. William Saunders' edited *Reflections on Architectural Practices in the Nineties* (1996) contains a broad cross-section of relevant opinions on the transformations of architectural work, particularly 'Architecture and Globalization', Rem Koolhaas's contribution to the volume, which is instructive to read in relation to Fredric Jameson's recent commentary on the inverted terms 'Globalization and Architecture' (2007). The *Harvard Design Magazine* Reader *Commodification and Spectacle in Architecture* (Saunders 2005) presents a powerful range of contrasting positions on the function and value of architecture as both a public and private good.

2 A contemporary reflection on the global pervasiveness of architectural thinking can be found in *Casabella*'s special issue on 'Critical Internationalism' (630–631, January–February 1996). The *Atlas of Vernacular Architecture of the World*, edited by Marcel Vellinga, Paul Oliver and Alexander Bridge (2007), provides a spectacular account of the macro-geographic diffusion of given construction types, technologies and materials, often intimating precise relationships between the adoption of determinate techniques and existing environmental conditions. One of the most exhaustive examinations of the techno-cultural use of a single architectural element (or notion) is developed by Anthony King in *The Bungalow: The Production of a Global Culture* (1984).

3 In the monograph on his work, for example, Albert Frey recounts the detail of the sliding door of the Ville Savoye in Le Corbusier's office, which borrows from technical illustrations contained in the Sweet's Catalogue (Rosa 1990).

4 Scholarly literature on the global flows of prefabricated buildings is patchy. Miles Lewis's 'The Asian Trade in Portable Buildings' (1993) provides a glimpse of the richness of the topic. For a British perspective, see: Herbert (1978) *Pioneers of Prefabrication: The British Contribution in the Nineteenth Century*. A more divulgative account is in

Barry Bergdoll and Peter Christensen (2008) *Home Delivery: Fabricating the Modern Dwelling*.

5 John Paterson's relatively unheralded book *Architecture and the Microprocessor* (1980) could be considered a significant anticipation of things to come.

6 See: *Time Magazine*, 121, 1, January 3, 1983, special section on Machine of the Year (Roger Rosenblatt, 'A New World Dawns,' Otto Friedrich, 'The Computer Moves In'); www.time.com/time/magazine/0,9263,7601830103,00.html (accessed 09/18/08); Tony Long (2007) 'Dec. 26, 1982: Time's Top Man? The Personal Computer,' *Wired*, December 26, 2007 (www.wired.com/science/discoveries/news/2007/12/dayintech_1226). For a technical history of CAD, see: http://mbinfo.mbdesign.net/CAD-History.htm (accessed September 19, 2008).

7 For a most comprehensive review of the topic see: Peter Dicken (2007) *Global Shift: Mapping the Changing Contours of the World Economy*.

8 In *Reaching Beyond Gold: The Impact of Global Events on Urban Development* (2007), Tim Van Vrijaldenhoven has outlined a figure-packed record of the organization of large public events since the nineteenth century, which gives a sense of the evolving relationship between tourism, population and urban settings.

9 By the same token, achieving global fame does not necessitate digital inclinations or foreign commissions, as the work of the Egyptian Hassan Fathy, the Norwegian Sverre Fehn or the Australian Glenn Murcutt easily proves.

10 In the 2007 *Architectural Record's* report on the Top Architecture Firms in the US, only 38 percent of the top 100 firms generated over 10 percent of their revenues internationally; with the next 150 offices, the same percentage dropped below 20 percent.

11 See the 2006 *AIA Firm Survey*. Washington DC: AIA Press, 2007.

12 See: CRESME Ricerche (2008) *Worldwide Architecture 2008* report, produced on behalf of the Italian Consiglio Nazionale degli Architetti, Pianificatori, Paesaggisti e Conservatori for the International Union of Architects (UIA) XXIII World Congress, Turin, 2008.

13 The 150 top 'global' design firms listed in 2008 by *Engineering News Record* contain four architecture companies; the list of the top 200 'international' firms, instead, features nineteen of them.

14 http://emag.digitalpc.co.uk/cmpi/worldarch08.asp (accessed September 27, 2008)

15 Eurostat data reported by CRESME Ricerche in *Worldwide Architecture 2008*.

16 See: Gabriella Lo Ricco and Micheli Silvia (2003) *Lo spettacolo dell'architettura. Profilo dell'archistar ©*, unfortunately not yet translated.

17 The General Agreement for Trade in Services (GATS) was signed by WTO members in 1993 and made operative in 1995. Specific sectoral negotiations started in 2000, at the end of the Uruguay Round. See: World Trade Organization, *The General Agreement on Trade in Services: objectives, coverage, and disciplines*, www.wto.org/english/tratop_e/serv_e/gatsqa_e.htm (accessed September 27, 2008); World Trade Organization, Council for Trade in Services, *Architectural and Engineering Services*, Background Note by the Secretariat, July 1998, 16, www.wto.org/english/tratop_e/serv_e/w44.doc (accessed September 27, 2008).

18 It is helpful to bear in mind that none of the categories is defined by technology; yet the availability of specific technologies defines the viability of the work arrangement (and the actions involved in it). If one replaced jets and file transfer protocol sites with horse carriages and postal services, for example, the conceptual framework of the trading system envisioned by the GATS would still stand. But the time required to exchange the information necessary to conceive, develop and implement remote collaborations would increase proportionally to the distance between work structure and project location, until it became unviable.

19 Contrary to general perception, the GATS recommendations are not prescriptive; they form a common platform for transnational negotiations, but countries' adherence to them is voluntary. For an early review of the geography of national commitments in architecture, see: International Investment and Services Directorate Industry Canada, *Canadian Architectural Services: A Consultation Paper in Preparation for the World Trade Organization GATS Negotiations*, www.international.gc.ca/assets/trade-agreements-accords-commerciaux/pdfs/architecture_e.pdf (accessed September 27, 2008).

20 In some cases, though, the demand for visually idiosyncratic products in commercially competitive local markets has produced windows of foreign opportunity for young, smaller firms, typified by the ability to work on ideas and with vocabularies that are novel to the context.

21 On the relationship between architects, cities and capitalist economy, see Zulaika (2001), Sklair (2005) and McNeill (2005). The production of architectural icons is addressed in a special issue of the journal *City*, 10(1) April 2006, and in *Harvard Design Magazine* 17 (Fall 2002/Winter 2003).

22 Froebel Folker, Heinrichs and Kreye (1980) use the expression 'new international division of labour' to describe the relocation of manufacturing operations to Third World countries, which gathered momentum in the 1970s and was facilitated by new technologies and better transport. According to these authors, multinationals used the shift to

respond to intensified competition in world markets, reduced rates of economic growth and lower profitability. Relocation, however, only affected basic manufacturing processes involving low levels of skill.

23 The literature on architectural outsourcing has been growing in the last ten years. For an early introduction, see Tombesi (2001). A scholarly analysis of historical legacies is presented in Tombesi, Bharat and Scriver (2003). David Del Villar's DDes thesis at the Harvard GSD, *Understanding Outsourcing Architectural Services* (2007), gives a broad empirical overview of the global industry, eventually mapped also by *Domus* magazine in the February 2007 issue ('Outsourcing', 900: 26–53).

24 In order to be able to sign as the architect of record for the church he was designing in Rome, for example, Richard Meier had to sit the registration exam in 2000, in Naples, where he had previously received a professional degree *honoris causa*. (For an overview of the differences in international practice requirements, see Chapters 4 and 5, 'Professional Practice' and 'Transnational Practice', Collegi d'Arquitectes de Catalunya (2005), *Architectural Practice around the World*, COAC, Barcelona, www.coac.net/internacional/ang/docs/APAW.pdf (accessed September 27, 2008))

25 On the Dallas Center for the Performing Arts (now the AT&T Performing Arts Center) completed in 2009, for example, the client required that the name of Rem Koolhaas and OMA be retained as architects of the building, even though the project has been developed by Joshua Prince-Ramus, the former director of OMA's New York office, after he left to found his own practice REX, and the executive architect Kendall Heaton. Numerous other examples could be made for iconic buildings around the world.

26 Geographic labour is a topic highly debated in professional circles, also because of the technical or cultural background professional workers carry with them. If Australian architects appear to be sought by British firms working in the Middle East, architectural IT technicians from the sub-Indian continent have been hired in mass from US offices in the 1990s, and now form the backbone of distant subcontracting from home. See Mascheroni (2007), Tombesi et al. (2003).

27 Aside from the institutional documents previously cited in the text, and the by-now several analyses of professional demand in specific areas of the world under development, the work examining the traits of the architectural industry from the point of view of globalization is not abundant. For this reason, studies on the structural differences between architectural regions are critical. See, in particular, Winch (2002).

28 The multi-engineering firm Arup and the curtain wall manufacturer Permasteelisa are the two most natural champions of this category, with the first growing almost a hundred new office locations and 10,000 employees in forty years, and the second going from being in receivership in the early 1980s to acting as the world leader in building envelope design today, with a group of sixty companies located in twenty-seven countries.

29 Incidentally, the firm carrying exactly this name, Foreign Office Architects, is a perfect reflection of the description.

30 At the moment, the publication that best reflects this ambition is the one edited by Mitra Khoubrou, Ole Bouman and Rem Koolhaas, *Volume 12: Al Manakh – Dubai Guide, Gulf Survey, Global Agenda* (2007), which brings together local building events, regional development and world poverty indicators.

31 For a review of professional numbers in relation to building output and architectural schools, see Tombesi (2004) and Col-legi d'Arquitectes de Catalunya (2005) *Architectural Practice around the World*, COAC, Barcelona, www.coac.net/internacional/ang/docs/APAW.pdf (accessed September 27, 2008).

32 If so, architectural globalization could not only generate regions of underemployment, but also have a long-lasting impact over domestic issues of minority groups' representation in the profession, of the type Kathryn Anthony has written about, even simply by increasing employment options (2001).

33 On the topic see Nield (2008).

23

Manners of Working: Fabricating Representation in Digital Based Design

Christopher Hight

> It would be possible, I think, to write a history of western architecture that would have little to do with either style or signification, concentrating instead on the manner of working. A large part of this history would be concerned with the gap between drawing and building. In it drawing would be considered not so much a truck for pushing ideas around from place to place, but as the locale of subterfuges and evasions that one way or another get round the enormous weight of convention that has always been architecture's greatest security and at the same time, its greatest liability. (Robin Evans 1997, 186)

One often hears two complimentary claims concerning digital representation[1] in architecture. The first declares a 'revolution'. The second sees digital technology as just another tool. The first echoes a modernist leitmotif of crisis and rupture. The second presumes that whatever changes occur in the way the architect works, the discipline is essentially continuous if evolving. In the former, technology determines the history of architecture. In the latter, computers are simply enfolded within techniques for designing buildings. For both, architecture has a continuous identity as both practice and object, the former declaring a break with this tradition (although its history is one of sequential crises) and the latter reinforcing its essential identity (although often seen as under continuous threat). Thus both statements depend on a vague convention between representations and construction. Indeed, a double mimetic is at once reinforced and obscured. First that architectural representations are determined by a notion of the 'real' building and second that all drawings and building are copies of an ideal identity of 'architecture' and its 'architect'. All architectural representations therefore gain their meaning from their resemblance to this identity, either by mirroring it or shattering it. The digital radicals present their tools as offering alternatives only by naturalizing normative references to conventional buildings, while the other side treats the building as determining design. Not only does this uncritically foreclose theoretical problems of representation, it curtails examination of the nature of transformation within the discipline as a manner of practice rather than official knowledge (what in the French is distinguished as *savoir* and *conaissance*).

Given these limitations, it might be better to approach the implications of digital design from an oblique angle to this dualism. One approach to the problem might be to extend Robin Evans's line of thought in 'Translations from Drawing to Building', offering a theoretical account of the recent history of digital design that concentrates on transformations in 'manners of working' and to explore the 'gap' between architectural representation and its presumed objects as a site for the production of architectural knowledge (Evans 1997). In other words, rather than focus purely on tools and aesthetic aspects of representation, one would look to practices they engender in relationship to the historical conventions of the discipline. Drawing techniques can do more than simply coordinate defined territories. The space between drawing and building is a material manifold around which the diverse forms of intelligence are recursively precipitated, enfolded and interlinked into constellations of design knowledge.

Although written amidst the displacement of the drawing board by graphical user interfaces, the implications of Evans' text have never been adequately examined in relationship to digital design in spite of its apparent influence upon its practices.[2] Therefore, extending the vector of 'Translations' might serve several purposes. Firstly, one might develop the problematic of translation he offered to provide a richer account of digital media within recent design. Secondly, one can compare Evans's historical examples with recent digital processes, examining what manners of working they transform and what they conserve. Thirdly, focusing on the 'manner of working' displaces histories of architecture based on style and signification upon which many polemics of digital design tacitly rely. Finally, one might delineate another space of translation, one between Evans's text and its influence upon architects. This space offers a productive but non-operative relationship between 'manners' of historical/theoretical work and the practices of design.[3]

THE SPACE OF TRANSLATION AS THE SPACE OF ARCHITECTURAL KNOWLEDGE

Robin Evans has had notable effect upon advanced architectural design, especially given his all too early death. His career orbited around leading British schools, in addition to North America. Significantly, his work combines a keen critical and theoretical insight that paralleled many of the problems of representation found in French post-structuralism that had fascinated architects since the 1970s, but from within the discipline and with a distinctive attention to empirical detail in addition to virtuoso rhetoric. 'Translations' is one representative of his long research agenda into design as a practice and mode of inquiry based around representation and technique; this research culminated in his posthumous 1995 book *The Projective Cast: Architecture and its Three Geometries*. Indeed, Evans' arguments must be adapted to account for the recent practices which it informed, veering away from the linguistic metaphor of translation. Stan Allen, architect and Dean at Princeton, has argued for understanding the relationship between drawing and building as a process of 'transposition' into heterogeneous domains instead of 'translation' into set linguistic codes (Allen 2000, 32).[4] In Allen's work, Evans' 'Translations' appears as an early entry into what has become a broader theoretical attempt to shift away from the armatures of critical theory, semiology and deconstruction/literary criticism in which meaning and signification play a central role. Allen argues architectural drawings are not only notational but 'impure' hybrids between conventions and the singularity of its design. The truth of an architectural drawing is determined neither by its instrumentally nor by its qualities as an autonomous aesthetic object. Therefore, Allen argues, it is not a question of what is lost in translation since neither the drawing nor the building can be considered as a model. Instead, the singularity of architectural drawing lay in its 'transitive' invention of something other than itself (Allen 2000, 36).

In 'Translations' Evans argued that instruments of representation are not transparent to the problems of the building. Drawings, he notes, are normally the first and last objects the architect produces.[5] Not only do buildings routinely vary from their drawings, one learns to be an architect principally by learning to make drawings. Moreover, like a music score, the architectural drawing is not pictorial but notational in regards to construction (Allen 2000, 32), following strict conventions. Symbols denote a 'built' material condition (i.e., two thin parallel lines indicate a glass window) that it rather tenuously depicts (that is, they do not look very much like glass). As if that were not enough, architectural drawings reverse the mimesis of classical representation since they are typically projective in two senses: they project something that does not exist and to do so they employ techniques of projective geometry to describe on a sheet of paper this virtual three-dimensional construction.

Moreover, Evans argues the architectural drawing is a bizarre sort of diagram that does not point out a clear course or measure the territory of a state (in this case a static kingdom of architecture) but rather a map of guerrilla tactics, the 'locale of subterfuges and evasions' (Evans 1997, 186). Normative practice hides its own tracks, relying upon the 'enormous weight of convention' to evade falling into the gap between drawing and buildings. But Evans suggests this is merely an obfuscation of the gap that requires an astonishingly complex set of moves as well as suspension of reflective thought. The ability of the drawing to be at once incommensurable with construction but appear as if it were seamless to it is the pivotal 'subterfuge', or gap, upon which architectural knowledge and practice depend. If so, the potential of 'digital tools' in regards to transforming the subject of architecture is given neither by their strangeness nor adherence to convention, but by the innovations in translation they produce between the 'manners of working' inherent to these tools, the habits of architecture, and the field of conventionalized diagrams we call 'buildings'.

For Evans, this complex relationship distinguishes architecture from most visual arts (which enjoy a direct relationship to its object) as well as from building trades (Evans 1997, 155–156).[6] In fact, modern institutions of instruction and regulation of practice are based on a strict separation of powers; the architect draws and the contractor builds. Examining the standard AIA contract and its historical revisions reveals an increasing distance between the architect's responsibilities and competencies from issues of construction.[7] Prior to the establishment of formal programmes of instruction and the parallel rise of professional governing bodies in the latter half of the nineteenth century, one would apprentice in an established practice and thus be far closer to the problems of building. Schools of architecture arose at least in part out of a need to clearly distinguish mass-produced building from the discipline of architecture, resulting in a much greater investment into various means of representation as the locus for the development of architectural knowledge (Pai 2002, 13–39; see also Cuff 1991, Chapter 4). This separation of architectural representation from the slowly evolving conventions of construction has allowed dramatic transformation in design and expansion in modes of architectural practice and knowledge, which can be considered to include writing, multimedia, exhibitions, programming, and so on. One can experiment and proliferate drawings far faster and wider and, when coupled with printing and distribution technologies, allow ideas to spread and evolve at increasing rates. While some claim the need to overcome the distinction, the gap between practices of drawing and thought and those involved with building are constitutive of the modern organization of architectural knowledge and practice.

Of particular concern to Evans was the Baroque problem of drawing complex curved volumes (of course, these sorts of geometries characterize much recent digital design). Specifically, he focuses on Philibert de l'Orme's dome of the Royal Chapel at Anet (1547–1552) as a concrete manifestation of this space of translation. Between de l'Orme's floor and dome lay the ineffable territory of architecture practice, with the occupant momentarily aligned with and experiencing the written and geometric evasions of the architect.[8] In the building, the ribbed geometry of the dome's vaults seems mirrored in the paving pattern on the floor (Figure 23.1). Indeed, de l'Orme described the floor as a didactic device that reproduced the drawing that generated the dome's geometry. However, Evans reverse-engineers de l'Orme's design process from the constructed dome to its drawings. Rather than explain the dome, he discovers that the floor's design is manipulated to echo the dome's aesthetic effect of 'rotary acceleration' and 'coherent diffusion' but not its actual geometry (Evans 1997, 173). To stand on de l'Orme's floor and under his dome is to experience the space of translation as an architectural effect. This effect operates on a subject triangulated by these fugitive vectors and inscriptions.

Moreover, Evans argues, all subsequent historical written and drawn descriptions trusted de l'Orme and assumed the dome was a simple projection of the floor, the discipline and its history are enfolded into the building's obfuscations. In this way, the chapel serves as a synecdoche for the more general 'subterfuge' that allows architectural practice to imagine such gaps do not exist or can be overcome. The power of de l'Orme's architecture lay in the manifestation of the gap upon which all architecture is constructed.

Evans' empirical approach is commensurable with constructivist theory that understood subjectivity and its ordering of things through such a gap of representation.[9] Indeed, de l'Orme's architecture functions as what philosopher Gilles Deleuze called a diagram,

Figure 23.1 (Below) Plan and perspective section of Philibert de l'Orme's Royal Chapel at Chateau d'Anet (1547–1552) by J.A. de Cerceau. (British Library Department of Prints and Drawings)

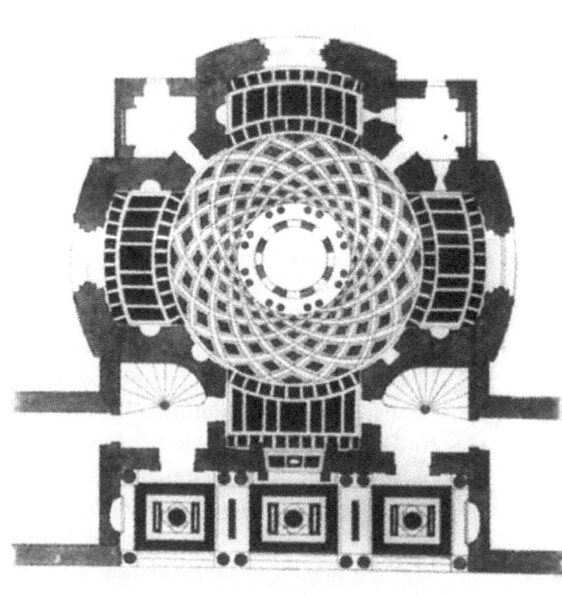

a 'map of relations between forces … within the very tissue of the assemblages they produce,' one that can be generalized to describe the functioning of the discipline of architecture (Deleuze 1988, 36–37). With Felix Guattari, Deleuze offered the diagram as a way of displacing semiotic emphasis on signification, drawing upon a careful analysis of artisan practices as a diagram between the artisan's tacit knowledge, or 'know-how' (*savoir*) and the material properties of that which is being formed out of series of operations and applied forces. The knowledge of the artisan is of the 'manner of working' with material properties and singularities, such as boiling points, melting points, catalytic reactions. These traits are assembled into 'worlds' of material relations (Deleuze and Guattari 1987, 404–412). As media theorist Fredrich Kittler and philosopher of science Bruno Latour have both argued, instruments and media are more than 'tools' for an author; instead they are actants within material and cultural practices which themselves operate within larger networks of institutional and discursive relationships (Kittler 1999; Latour 2005, 63–86). These networks configure the possible modes of authorship and its objects of practice. Evans suggests we pay greater attention to the architectural equivalent of such assemblages. Tools are not transparently instrumental to an end but instead are themselves diagrams that do not produce a more or less accurate depiction of a possible reality, but rather construct systems of relationships to be actualized in time. That is, they do not just signify or mean anything so much as a construct of the site for the fabrication of architectural practice and its objects. The conventions of architectural drawing, allow the multitude of 'know-hows' (*savoir*) employed in the representation and construction of architecture to be related and transformed and in turn, informs the discipline as formal system of knowledge (*connaissance*).

The space of the drawing is a space of translation, but one that cannot be reduced to two discrete sets of pre-existing regimes of signs (or languages). Instead these relationships are made intelligible through the notations themselves. The manner and material conditions through which these knowledges are interlinked matter in delimiting the sorts of things that can be thought through their use. In modernity, the orthographic projection of the plan has been the dominant device coordinating the expertise of design and those of construction. If all the information required to construct a building must be available in such a drawing this tends to normalize the generation of the design as an orthogonal array of surfaces and components. As designs and buildings become more complex, the creative role of these clients, engineering 'consultants', artists, and fabricators increases and the drawing becomes the site of integration of these know-hows and knowledges.

In that regard, the advent and economic availability of drawing software coupled to the emergence of the World Wide Web in the early 1990s may indeed mark a threshold condition in the history of architecture. It is not insignificant that Maya Hambly (1988) could offer an exhibition and historical compendium of drawing instruments spanning 1580–1980 in which all the artefacts can be classified in similar categories. Whether from the sixteenth or twentieth century, they remain recognizable as versions of each other. An architect from 1580 could use the equipment from 1980 with little adaptation to his manner of working (putting aside for the moment the important development of technologies of reproduction and dissemination). Such could not be said for the cinquecento architect confronted with the interface for parametric software. A paper drawing is seen all at once, while the digital drawing is only seen partially, indeed can be 'made' by combining other files that can be drawn and reworked by others, often simultaneously, sent from thousands of miles away, whose only shared language may be that of the program command line. Other basics have radically altered: how one draws a line (placing points instead of moving a ruler), what one draws the line with (a button festooned chunk of plastic), what one 'draws on' (not ink but pixels, not a reflective white surface but a radiating black screen) and even the angle of approach (a vertical 'window' instead of a horizontal table). An architect with a compass and quill or one with a circle template and Rapidiograph both still draw on white paper (or its Mylar surrogate – a transitional material to the darkly luminous screen of the computer monitor), a substrate that theorist and Dean at Columbia University, Mark Wigley has noted is both a very specific material and one that erases its presences as a material. Paper, Wigley argues, 'occupies a liminal space between material and immaterial … [allowing] it to act as a bridge across the classical divide between material and idea' (Wigley 2001a, 29). In that way, paper is the perfect accomplice for the subterfuge of the drawing inscribed upon it. Today, paper emerges from the plotter to document the act of drawing, not as the substrate for its practices. Early versions of AutoCAD made this difference a structural feature of its workflow: one drew in a 1:1 scaled infinitely large 'model space' and used another window in the program to import and scale this model onto a representation of a standard page in something called 'paper space'. No work could be done in 'paper space'; it was simply a frame scaling the digital model. This technical fact raises complex theoretical questions. One used to start an entirely new drawing in order to shift from a large-scale organizational diagram to a detail; now one simply copy-pastes, 'zooms in' and adds more information. Indeed, while choice of scale in a paper world was calibrated to disciplinary conventions about the kind of information each scale represents (1:100 is an organizational site plan, 1/2′:1′ is a material detail); what one constructs in a digital program is always 1:1. This tends to detach the conventional correspondence of scale in drawing with a modernist manner of working that typically moved from macro-scaled ordering in plan to material effects of the detail. As Antoine Picon details in his recent book, *Digital Culture in Architecture*, (2010) this is reflected in the degree to which ornamentation has returned to architectural discourse in a way that blurs classical distinctions of detail and organization, decoration and structure (Herzog and De Meuron's Beijing Olympic Stadium, for example). It is only through a tremendous evasion of critical reflection and concrete evidence that we can believe that the subject who uses and who is constructed through her use of these instruments has not been as significantly transformed as those things which can be drawn with them.

Therefore, following Evans' suggestion to focus on these 'manners of working' rather than meaning, we should examine the itinerant transformations in 'know-hows', and do so through empirical description of these processes in order to understand their differentiations and consistencies without recourse to comparisons to an ideal model of architecture. Such a history would require the historian to transform his 'manner of working' to engage material design practice. This suggests that historians or theorists benifit from a working knowledge of the software and approaches in order to engage contemporary practice. Commenting on recent architecture without knowing the basics of software is like a historian writing about 'Renaissance' architecture without any understanding of linear perspective. Moreover theorizing 'manners of working' cannot depend solely on now normative post-structuralist emphasis representation, ideology, signification or meaning derived from literary criticism or political ideology. Instead, it requires anthropological, empirical and detailed analyses of the practices and use of these instruments, and their relationship to the larger networks within which they weave.

As a necessarily sketchy diagram of what such a history might constitute, I will approach the recent history of digital design as a threefold process.[10] First, the parsing of the field of relations as found in the conventions of the discipline as a known territory; second the de-territorialization of this field; and thirdly, the 're-territorialization' of these relationships in new configurations. To do so,

I will present case studies for each of these stages. The first is found in the linguistic combinations and proportioning found in the proto-computational work of Peter Eisenman; the second is tracked through the relationships of forces manifested in NURBS and animation software and architects like Greg Lynn and Foreign Office Architects; the last is provided by recent interest in parametric, scripting and genetic algorithms.[11] Each engages the gap between representation as tools of thought and the building through which those instruments are normatively calibrated.

CHARTING THE ORTHOGRAPHIC HORIZON

Robin Evans' argument implicitly targeted another text crucial to post-war understandings of the relationship between diagrams and buildings: Colin Rowe's 'Mathematics of the Ideal Villa' (1999 [1947]). Rowe was a key second-generation critic of modernism, whose work often re-evaluated the relationship of modernist architecture to the classical ordering of the Italian Renaissance. In 'Mathematics' (written under the tutelage of Rudolf Wittkower), Rowe famously argued that a common proportioning schema underlay both Le Corbusier's Villa Stein at Garches and Palladio's Villa Malcontenta.[12] In the second half, Rowe complicates this reading. However alike Palladio and Le Corbusier's ordering grids may seem, their translation of into two divergent construction technologies produced two different fields of effects for its subjects. Palladio's load bearing masonry always re-centred the subject in space, while Le Corbusier's steel/concrete frame dispersed the subject across an 'inferential' field of relations. Rowe thus pushed the intelligibility of architectural order and its relationship to the subject to two poles: to the material embodiments of these diagrams through construction and to abstract diagrams of ordering (Hight 2008, 12).

The architect and theorist, Peter Eisenman drew upon Rowe's 'Mathematics' article to argue that the architecture of Le Corbusier and Palladio belonged to a single semiotic of architecture he called 'the Classical' (Eisenman 1984, 155). In a series of House projects numbered I to X, Eisenman sought to develop an autonomous architectural system through drawing and then find the limits of this system. Beginning with grids like those Rowe found in Palladio and Corbusier, Eisenman performed a series of basic formal operations (rotation, doubling, Boolean additions, intersections etc.). These operations did three things. Firstly, they mobilized axonometric and orthographic projection to generate complex geometries. An abstract grid drawn in axonometric was iteratively redrawn and its lines differentiated through a series of game-like rules internal to the process of drawing. Secondly, these operations abstracted the components of architectural drawing from the conventions of their construction to make apparent or even undermine the motivated condition of architectural signs. For Eisenman, the typical architectural drawing was paradoxically determined by its 'use' for construction (a circle is a column) and 'extrinsic significance', of cultural and metaphysical value (i.e., that column is like a human body) (Eisenman 1979, 15–16; 118–128). Thirdly, these processes relocated the object of architectural intelligibility away from the drawing's realization as construction into the construction of the drawing. Appropriating criticism of Le Corbusier's early works as 'cardboard architecture' as a positive, Eisenman problematized the relationship between conventions of construction and the abstract ordering of architectural drawing (for example, the difference between the discontinuous line that signifies a 'door' and material assembly of wood, metal and glass of the constructed entryway).

In House VI, these operations produced a 'column' that did not touch the ground (undermining motivations of meaning), slots in the floor that rendered it impossible to place a large bed in the master bedroom (undermining use), and an Escher-esque upside-down staircase (undermining orientation). In the constructed House IV, such elements undermine the ability to read the constructed condition as a realization of the drawing, as they are traces of the autonomous design processes through which they were produced rather than signifiers of values anterior or construction conventions posterior to the act of drawing. Eisenman's parsing of the autonomous deep structure of architecture had given way to the use of drawing techniques to open 'the possibility of a true dislocation of architectural conventions while remaining within the metaphysical discourse of architecture' (Eisenman 1987, 82).

In House X (Figure 23.2), these techniques are pushed to a critical threshold. Though a commissioned project, House X was never built, instead an axonometric cardboard model serves as the final constructed form not just for the house, but the entire series and implicitly, of the classical tradition. Eisenman's axonometric model is a critical joke whose humour derives from the following of convention to absurdity, a literal cardboard architecture that seeks to push the dialectics between drawing and building to a super-critical threshold through the conventions of orthographic projection.

An axonometric drawing produces the illusion of volume by rotating a plan and then projecting the lines at ninety degrees to their proper height. Unlike perspective, all the elements in an axonometric drawing maintain the same scaled measure. Eisenman's axonometric model is constructed by using the same procedure in reverse; the horizontal surfaces all parallel the ground plane while the vertical elements are projected at forty-five degrees to their normal (ninety-degree) angle. The effect is uncanny. From one privileged point, the viewer is aligned with the model according to the convention of axonometric drawing and therefore the model reproduces the effect of an axonometric drawing; walls and floors appear to meet at right angles, cubic volumes appear correctly proportioned. And yet, if the axonometric drawing produces an illusion of volume, the axonometric strangely flattens its actually volumetric forms, resembling a drawing. Moreover, from any other point-of-view, the angled vertical elements become apparent; skewed to forty-five degrees as if collapsing from a mighty wind (Figure 23.3). The measurable and seemingly objective quality of axonometry is revealed as merely representing another *a priori* value (that architecture represent the truth and rationality).[13] And while a model is conventionally presumed to simulate a 'full-scale' building, here it collapses into the representations of drawing while simultaneously imbued with a presence because of its revelation of the otherwise obfuscated conditions of such representations (Hubert 1981).

Figure 23.2 (Above) Peter Eisenman, House X, axonometric model, 1982. (Peter Eisenman Architects)

Indeed, the axonometric model is analogous to painted examples of anamorphosis, such as the skull at the bottom of Holbein's Ambassadors. Lacan (1981 [1973], 79–92) argued that such anamorphic conceits are a manifestation of the *objet petit à*, that which must remain a blind-spot or be seen only askew because it is a trace of the real which when seen reveals the constructed nature of the subject's sovereignty.[14] If the blotch resolves into a skull at only one angle, the axonometric model resolves into a proper representation of the building from only one position. To rotate around the axonometric model of House X is to be precipitated into the space of translation. It reveals the 'real' building as no less a representation than its drawings are a construction. In turn, the viewer stands neither in an anthropocentric Palladian space nor is diffused across the inferential space of Le Corbusier's plan libre but is suspended in the space of architectural translation, one that has opened into a yawning abyss that the obfuscations of drawing can no longer cover and which the conventional relationships between architectural signs and the construction they signify can no longer bridge.

VECTORS OF DE-TERRITORIALIZATION

In the early 1990s, animation and NURB-based modelling software entered into architectural discourse, in part through an intellectual genealogy traceable through

Figure 23.3 (Below) Peter Eisenman, House X, axonometric model, 1982. (Peter Eisenman Architects)

Eisenman back to Rowe's 1947 article. Indeed, many presented the software as a diagrammatic ordering device, one analogous to the role played by Rowe's proportioning grids. However, most of this software was not designed for architectural problems but to produce film and video animations. Transposing this technology to the discipline of architecture was often done in order to 'destabilize' the conventions of architecture. Ali Rahim (2006, 14) describes such 'technological design practices' as those that employ the computer in an interdisciplinary manner, employing software not intended to solve architectural problems to innovate the sort of problems that architects engage.[15]

Spline/NURB based software[16] allows for more complex production of such geometries by abstracting physical properties into an infinitely elastic line shaped by multiple forces in any direction. Splines emerged from material know-how (*savoir*) rather than ideal geometric know-of (*connaissance*). Although formally defined as late as 1946, their geometries have been used for centuries in crafts such as shipbuilding (Schoenberg 1946, 45–99, 112–141). Spline curves can be created by bending a thin sheet of wood or wire, or by hanging weights on a string, as Gaudi did in his famous structural models of the Sagrada Familia. The curve results from force and material computations (the negotiation of weight, the bending moment of the material, etc.). A digital spline is constructed by locating control points (which can be thought of as virtual weights), the location and strength of which determine the shape. Moving these points alters the virtual force applied and therefore the overall curvature.[17] Moreover, in such software, there is no substantive difference between a curve and straight line. Because a spline's shape emerges by calculating information across its control vertices, as Lars Spuybroek (2004) argues, a straight spline is simply a 'dumb' – that is, uninformed – curve. Here, architecture's normative precept that the straight line and right-angle operate as an ideal, or as a representation of rationality comes into question. The 'page' or drawing space is never blank, rather a new file simply presents a uniformed, neutral, field.

The digital spline can be aligned with a morphogenetic, or what Greg Lynn called 'animate', ethic that understands form as resulting from material processes and forces. Indeed, Jesse Reiser and Nanako Umemoto (2006, 88–89) have presented Gaudi's catenary models of the Sagrada Familia as analogue computational drawing, in which a vaulted geometry arises out of the computation of gravity and thus more structurally rational than, for example, Le Corbusier's use of the right-angle to represent rationality. Following the Catalan architect's lead, Reiser+Umemoto constructed more complex catenary models and adapted this research into digital modelling techniques.[18] When one adds animation features, such as particle dynamics and inverse kinematics, the process of drawing becomes a matter of establishing relational fields between forces and components. This leads to an understanding of software not as a representation so much as a 'machine'.[19] For example, dECOi, NOX and Contemporary Architecture Practice often deploy 'systems' of virtual attractors that swerve trajectories of particles or fields of splines. The architect tunes the geometry by adjusting the various forces and fields involved and their relationships (Rahim 2006, 25–29, 52–53).[20] Like Rowe's proportioning grids, animation and other force-based drawing techniques still produce diagrammatic orders that underlay subsequent transformation into symbols for tectonic elements. However, these relationships emerge through the 'drawing' rather than extrinsic proportions. Like Eisenman's grids, these diagrams delay representation of construction in favour of abstract relations and operations. Unlike Eisenman's early work, these marks are not linguistic signifiers within an isotonic Cartesian grid, but occupy a topological space of (virtual) material forces. Rather than mastery or erasure of the subject, the drawing becomes a map of the relationship between the architect and the field she manages and coaxes the design out of. The 'tool' no longer has a defined objective in a 'building' but rather becomes a search space for the projection of abstractions that might be architecturally ordered.[21]

Such software also raises the same difficulties Evans found in de l'Orme's translation of a two-dimensional geometry into a curved surface. Most spline-based surface modellers do not allow punched openings on a surface.[22] Instead, complexity arises through discontinuities of surface, such as splitting, deforming and folding. Because such surface manipulations do not always already assume that it notates the constructional typology of 'wall', the problem of opening is not that of selecting another component (i.e., window), but instead concerns the more abstract question of how one informs the surface to produce differentiation (and therefore inform) within a continuity. That is to say, while material logics are embedded into the process of drawing, they resist translation into the conventions of construction.

This widened gap between drawing and building can be used strategically as a what Patik Schmacher has described as a mechanism for innovation.[23] A key example is the Yokohama Port Terminal by Foreign Office Architects (FOA), one of the first and largest of such projects to be constructed as a 'conventional building'. Moreover, it was one of a series of projects which mobilized the knowledges of the shipbuilding industry in order to translate spline surface geometries into construction.[24] The translation from drawing to building is also the central concept presented in FOA's monograph of the project, *The Yokohama Project* (Foreign Office Architects 2003). While they present the book as a description of the construction process and workflow (2003, 3–4), this obscures that, rather than translating from drawing to building in a linear way, a recursive process developed in the movement of a luminescent line into steel.

Take for example the opening and ramping system that connects the levels, each representing a bifurcation in the circulation diagram that generated the building's organization.

Figure 23.4 Foreign Office Architects. Yokohama Port Terminal, Yokohama Japan, 1996–2002. Interior view of ramp connecting levels: (A) (Opposite top) Competition entry rendering of ramp condition; (B) (Opposite middle) Ramp condition during design development phase; (C) (Opposite bottom) Photo of similar constructed condition. (A and B, Foreign Office Architects; C, Ramon Prat and ACTAR)

Such openings result by simply 'detaching' one part of a horizontal NURB surface into two abutting surfaces and then moving the control points in the vertical plan to produce an opening in section. This is one of the most basic operations one can perform in spline/NURB modelling. Layering such surfaces on top of each other produces a laminated organization, connected by these openings. In the competition drawings, these connections were rendered as roughly rectilinear ramps (FOA 2003, 87–89). Through the design development process that translated these entirely abstract surfaces of the competition drawings into material thicknesses and constructional geometries, the ramps became increasingly broad, smooth and ambiguously related to the surfaces around them. That is to say, in the move towards building, these elements became more differentiated from existing types. Renderings of the design development and the photos of the constructed vaults of the interior demonstrate how FOA strategically deployed in time the translation space Evans unearthed in de l'Orme's dome (Figure 23.4).

As a result, similar views of the competition scheme, the design development proposal and the corresponding condition in the built object present rather different buildings (Figure 23.5). The continuous geometry of the spline curves in the competition-winning entry were translated into the discrete segments of steel elements. Notably this required closing the genealogical loop of spline-based geometry: just as splines were once used by shipbuilders as physical tools, Yokahama's spline surfaces would be built like a cruise

ship, prefabricated out of large building-size components of welded steel sheets, added from one end of the building to the other (FOA 2003, 96–97). At the same time, the spline geometries of the plan were converted and constructed as composite curves (FOA 2003, 91–93). Moreover, in the design development phase the 'floor' surfaces were given structural depth though triangular pleating of welded steel sheets. These triangulations were created by dropping an orthogonal XYZ grid over the convoluted surfaces; however, this made the construction process inordinately complicated. The triangulations were then redrawn according to the UV coordinate system of the surfaces themselves, drastically simplifying the steel cutting and fabrication (FOA 2003, 93). In this case, drawing operations are integrated into construction, radicalizing the apparent gap between the drawings produced with those instruments, innovating the relationship of knowledges and industries employed to construct a building.

This case study is indicative of more general issues. Because of the distance of NURB-based modelling from conventional orthographic projection, and their translation into construction, it is often necessary to move the drawing into other softwares 'closer' to these conventions (e.g., from Maya to AutoCAD). Even if no information is lost in the process of conversion, the drawing becomes something different within the context of another software package. For example, in moving a spline from Maya into AutoCAD, the geometries are no longer workable in the same way because the geometry changes although it appears similar. On the other hand, simply slicing through a 3-D model rarely produces the precision or material sensibility of a section or plan. The intelligence of the design emerges out of these translation processes between these types of 'drawings', from one file format to another.

Lastly, the mobility and mutability of these 'drawings' and the techniques of drawing also have implications for the way one works with them. Because they are digital, they become mobile across hands, desks and even cultures. One no longer learns to draw after the style of a master, but a way of working through a mediated set of commands and techniques. As Ali Rahim (2006, 14) argues, its effects proliferate across culture and society, 'generating positive feedback, intelligence and adaptations across multiple disciplines and fields of design knowledge'. This opens potentials of network practice, distribution of

Figure 23.5 (Below) Foreign Office Architects. Yokohama Port Terminal, Yokohama Japan, 1996–2002. Evolution of geometry, girders and folds of roof: (A) Competition scheme with isotropic shell and smooth surface; (B) Constructed bi-directional structure and hierarchical organization of girders and folds. Copyright of Foreign Office Architects and courtesy of ACTAR and Foreign Office Architects.

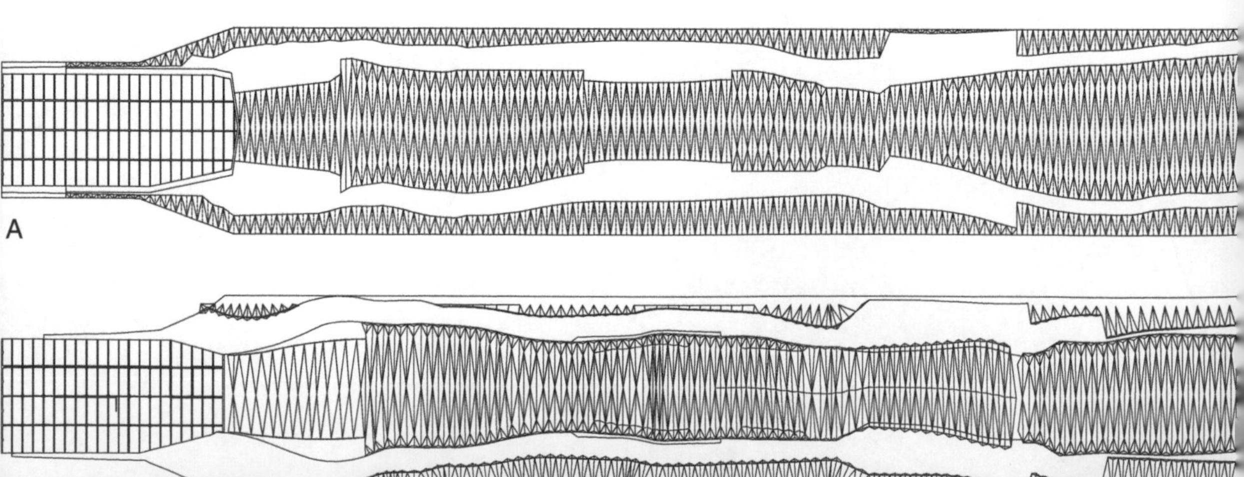

authorship and potential new collaborations not only among architects but between expertise (Hight and Perry 2006a, 5–9).

PARAMETRIC CONSTRUCTIONS

If NURB-based surface modelling was deployed for strategic estrangement from architectural convention to de-territorialize maps of disciplinary knowledge and know-hows, recent use of parametric-based software seems focused on re-territorializing this knowledge into problems of construction. Two general attitudes towards parametric software are worth examining, first as an attempt to bridge the gap between the practices of architecture and construction, but secondly, as a way of opening both to new potentials.

The first species of parametric software is commonly classified as Building Information Management (BIM), which is rapidly being standardized and mandated in the United States and other locales. Moreover, it is often championed as the medium through which to create an 'integrated practice' that bridges the conventional divide between the architect and construction by foreclosing the space of translation between drawing and building.[25] While championed as a tool for greater control and efficiency, BIM presents a major transformation in the nature of architectural practice.

In BIM drawings, every line or symbol in the 'drawing' is really a 'node' within a networked database of information. These symbols are linked to such matters as cost, fabrication and scheduling to be used by other professions in estimating, planning and constructing. Because the drawings begin to refer to a manufactured system at a very early stage, design becomes a problem of assembly. The drawing provides what amounts to a graphical user interface controlling the relationship between these elements. Indeed, one can think of the difference between BIM and standard drawing in computing terms: conventional drawing (by hand or digitally) is roughly like writing code, working abstractly at a 'low' level of basic instructions; drawing in BIM is more like working in a Windows or Mac environment, assembling icons that have a high degree of predetermination by another hand. Aesthetically, much BIM-based work appears as a collage of discrete elements, often without overall coherence. More importantly, it normalizes that collage aesthetic by predicating the possibilities of design on already existing workflows of translation from drawing to building. Thus one can see that the problem of translation has not been resolved, but merely inverted by collapsing the space of translation into a representation of construction conventions.

A different approach manifests in parametric-based softwares like Bentley System's Generative Component or those of Gehry Technologies. Gehry Technologies, a spin-off from Gehry Partners, offers a series of software packages to supplement the engineering software CATIA. The software developed out of the practice's experiences in constructing their characteristic designs of complex curvatures and forms that are not easily translatable into orthographic projections. Here, the 'know-how' accrued over time across many projects within one practice was translated into the design of new representational platforms to be used by many. Every drawn element notates a specific component and its relationship to other components, as a spatial database of relations. In addition to geometric information, material performance, fabrication criteria and other information can be embedded into the 'drawing' as an accurate simulation of the building down to bolt holes. The dataset can be handed to engineers for finite element analysis and development of the structure, to the steel fabricator, to the accountants who keep track of costs. This integrates the various knowledges involved and expands the design phase into the construction period across a more diverse set of participants (Sheldon 2006, 83–86).[26] The conventional manner through which knowleges are related to each other or operate in themselves can be challenged and adjusted based on the requirements of the specific design (Kolarevic 2003, 60). This should not be understood as a return to practices of the 'master builder' because the latter's 'know-hows' are given by strict conventions and routines that only incrementally and slowly evolve across generations of static object types.[27]

According to Robert Aish, one of the program's authors, Bentley System's Generative Components integrates the 'exploratory processes' of drawing with material logics (Kolarevic 2003, 245). In this and other parametric software, 'components' are drawn (simple lines, already complex forms or other components), but are related to other components and populated across large surfaces, forms or patterns through programming 'scripts' (short coded instruction sets). Every component is not only represented as an object, its internal and external relationships and variables are represented by a network graph that allows visualization of the rule set governing its geometric deployment. These geometries can then be 'translated' into another set of software instructions used for numerically controlled fabrication equipment, for example as a cutting pattern in steel plates. Heterogeneous types of information can be integrated within the geometric resolution of a single model, from acoustical to structural to visual and calibrated with each other through the geometric parameters of the model (Menges 2006, 48). Because these systems are defined

Figure 23.6 Achim Menges, Morphogenetic Design Experiment 03, Paper Strip Morphologies, 2004–05: (A) (Below) digital rending of shell; (B) (Overleaf left) screen shot of software showing parametric nodes and relationships; (C) (Overleaf right) laser cutting pattern and constructed prototype. (Achim Menges, www.achimenges.net)

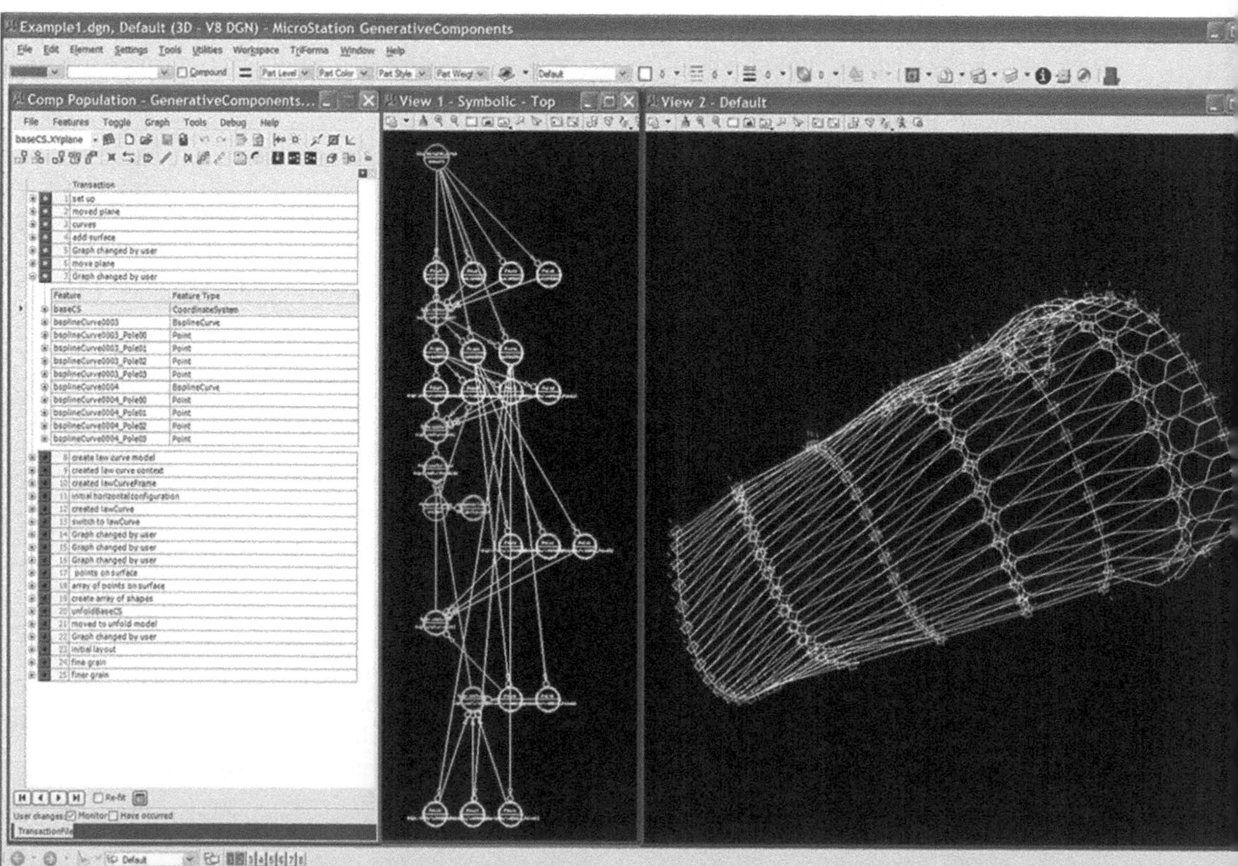

as a series of geometric relationships, they can adapt to changing requirements. In such parametric software, the design results not from a fixed set of *a priori* elements that produce a limited set of possible architectures, but immanent material implications literally inscribed (through scripting) as a set of complex relations (parameters). These relationships are constructed through drawing rather than the drawing serving merely as a graphical user interface for a database (as it becomes in BIM). The process is less like translating from one language (the architect's domain of drawing) into another (construction), but of enfolding and refolding the relationship between these manners of working into a tactical convention immanent to the design rather than extrinsic to its mechanisms of generation.

Moreover, the divisions of knowledge and labour required to assemble the building are organized not upon a conventional interface such as the plan, but arrayed according to the specificity of the design. Importantly, Generative Components is being developed with a collaborative network of SmartGeometry Group.[28] Academic research was integral to development of the software, as were large firms, such as Kohn Peterson Fox and Foster Associates, who collaborated with Bentley to develop the software, using its beta form to design several projects, such as the Smithsonian Institute Courtyard Enclosure (Washington, DC, 2004–2006) or Beijing Airport (Beijing, China, 2003–2008). The drawing becomes a collaborative framework, a common space for potentially new configurations of practices and its objects, a vehicle for the translation of architecture into undetermined projective architectures. The space of interaction between academia and practice suggests that their distinctive modes of practice can be complementary to the development of research and innovation rather than antagonistic. As architects begin to design new media for 'drawing', new potentials for the integration and control over the diverse knowlegdes (know-how and know-of) can be brought to bear upon the architecture (Kolarevic 2003, 248). Notably, these projects are often based on large undulating shells that can be understood as contemporary version of the problem of the Baroque dome with which Evans was concerned in his analysis. Thus, they suggest a similar enclosure of the architectural subject within such a space.

Indeed, the parametric drawing is not a drawing in the sense of a picture to be translated into building; rather it corresponds to Stan Allen's shift to "transposition" from one domain (drawing) to another (fabrication). As documented by Achim Menges in a journal issue focused on the translation from computational processes to construction (Menges 2006, 43), Lars Hesselgren, a founding member of SmartGeometry Group stated:

> We recognized that ... a complete geometric tradition of understanding of descriptive and construct[ive] geometry was being lost through lack of use in a bland ... orthogonal minimalism or indeed, through misuse by being excessively indulged. [Our] objective was [to explore how] geometry could provide a formal resolution of competing forces and requirements.

This suggests an attempt to reclaim and innovate upon the genealogy of work that Robin Evans argued was embodied in de l'Orme's architecture. The diagrammatic aspects of the architectural drawing no longer specify a series of operations upon formal ratios between linguistic elements nor a pre-tectonic virtual field. Instead it is embedded into the material logics of the drawing as a 'manner of working'. Rather than translating drawing into more or less conventional constructional types, the drawing can be translated into unconventional tectonic elements.

This, in turn, closes the recursive loop as the drawing enfolds factors of structural and environmental performance into its processes of generation (Menges 2004, Figure 23.6). As Picon (2010) details, scalar, spatial and visual effects of the architecture are no longer added to construction in the traditional manner of decoration but integrated into the form generation process rendering moot modernist and postmodernist distinctions of structure and ornamentation or between formal effects and material performance. No wonder then that such software is often coupled with attempts to translate biological concepts of complexity and emergence into objects of architectural knowledge, approaching the space of the drawing as an ecological set of relations between elements (Hensel et al. 2006, 19–21). Patrik Schumacher's recent book *The Autopoiesis of Architecture* (2011) argues for "parametricism" as a system of architectural thought. Schumacher, in fact, attempts to "translate" Niklas Luhmann's social systems theory as a means to formalize the design process of architecture as a system of communication between relatively autonomous realms of drawing and construction among others).

CONCLUSION

Parametric and BIM based design is no longer an esoteric pursuit of few outliers but a common approach within schools and increasingly integrated into construction. However, it is critical that we do not naturalize what have already emerged as tropes within parametric design and proliferate them and new conventions. Moving from Boolean linguistics through surface-animation based software to parametric construction tracks architectural representation as a site for manifesting the intelligibility of a design to a material intelligence developed through design.[29] The drawing was first seen as a place where architectural ordering and its significations were made intelligible for the architectural subject via geometry. With the enfolding of animation software and then parametric modelling, geometry becomes the site for the integration of diverse forms of

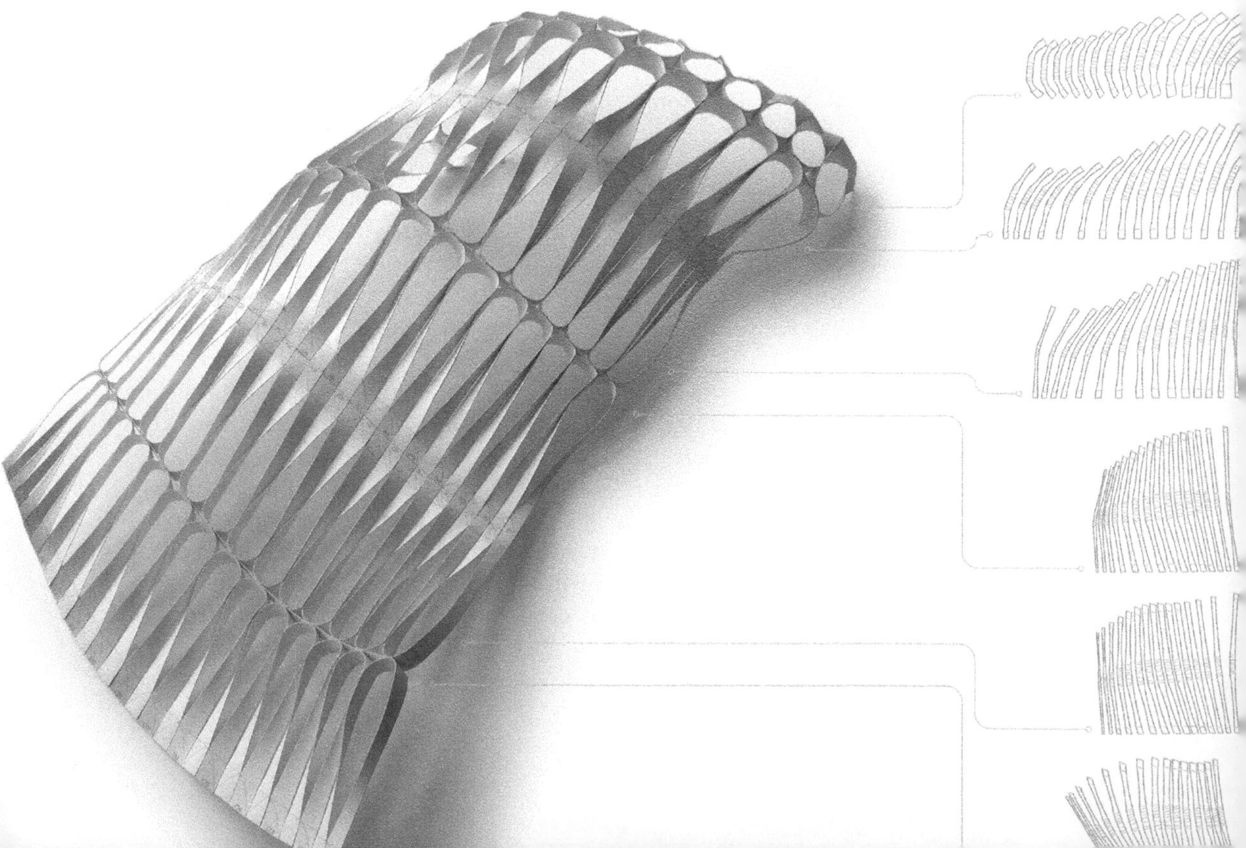

collective knowledge and agencies. In turn, the hand of the architect is redistributed into multiple actors, factors, trades and disciplines. It is not that the software determines the design – or at least no more or less than any drawing medium ever has – but rather that this opens the possibility of translating the space of architectural representation into material constructions that are no longer determined by a normative and finite world of construction types. Disciplinarity should be understood not through the classical metaphor of 'a body of knowledge' but as an ecology of heterogeneous agencies and modes, related to each other in complex and multiple manners through concrete processes in continual translation and transformation.

Taken a step further, this suggests the possibility of strategizing architectural representation as a vehicle to engage and intervene in conditions of the contemporary environment, from landscape to information technology, that are not typically the subject-matter of architecture or its objects (i.e., building). So far all the modes of working examined here presume that the 'building', however transformed, remains the destination of the architect's labour. They do what architects have done for a hundred and fifty years at least: addressing the building in its location within the urban field. Yet these same 'manners of working' could also be the means to enfold new sites and objects of practice, innovating the categories through which we reconstruct the agency of architectural knowledge for the spatial, cultural and economic territories of the twenty-first century.

NOTES

1 In this article, digital design will refer to design processes that employ software modelling and computational processes as key modes for ordering

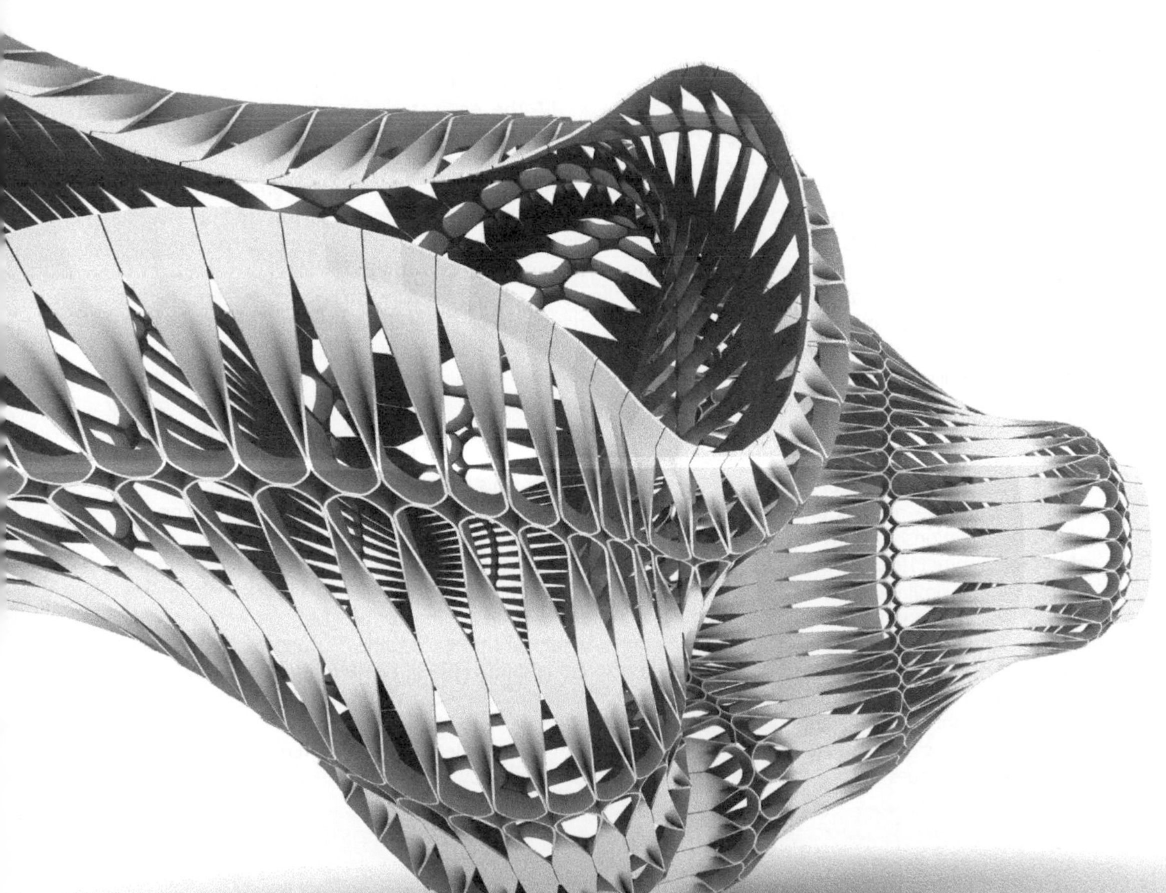

and organization, while digital representation refers to the 'drawn' results of these processes. While some writers such as Terzidis (2006) want to strictly separate between computational processes which rely on scripting to generate designs from 'digital visualization' or modelling based on the user's manipulation of an interface to model a design (seeing the latter as merely an augmented version of hand drawing), this does not help clarify the problem of representation and of its relationship to building.

2 Digital studio curriculums and practices frequently cite the article as a touchstone locating digital techniques within longer genealogies of the discipline. For example, Evans is key to Schumacher (2002) and is on the bibliography of several leading digitally based programmes including at the Architectural Association's Design Research Laboratory.

3 This potential is especially relevant in relationship to the problem of representation for an architectural subject. For example, in the early 1990s, Greg Lynn attempted to argue for the importance of digital techniques in relationship to their representation of alternative, non-humanist, architectural subjects (Lynn 1998, 33–62).

4 While agreeing with and indebted to Allen's thesis, for clarity's sake, I will use the term 'translation'.

5 On the architectural model see Morris (2006).

6 Evans has a notably dated, or naïve, view of artistic production. Stan Allen's argument, adapted from Nelson Goodman, that architecture combines the 'autographic' with the 'allographic' forms of practice offers a similar but better formulation (Allen 2000, 34–35).

7 A trend not entirely reversed in the 2007 AIA Integrated Practice Documents.

8 Evans treats de l'Orme's church as Foucault did Bentham's prison. A direct comparison can be made between Foucault's description of the Panoptican prison as a diagram of disciplinary inscription and Evans' reading of de l'Orme's dome. This field of relationships is called 'panopticonism' in the latter, and perhaps 'orthography' in the former (Foucault 1995, 206–207; Deleuze 1988, 36).

9 The phrase 'ordering of things' is of course a play on the English title for Foucault's seminal account of how the representations structure and establish the relationship between the subject and world in modernity (1977 [1975]). Lacan's psychoanalysis employs a similar void in his arguments of the gaze and subjectivity, while Derrida's deconstruction sought to explore the unbridgeable abyss between the text and its representations. However, all these, Bruno Latour has argued, operate upon the gap first established by Kant's tripartite critique of knowledge and in fact tend to widen it and reify one or the other pole. Instead, he argues for the reality of mediators that construct hybrid assemblages. I borrow this approach to understand the role of instruments of representation (Latour 1992, 55–79).

10 This sequence is taken from that outlined by Corner (1999, 231).

11 These stages follow DeLanda (2001). The extent to which subsequent discourse has followed the progression he outlined is remarkable.

12 Rowe's reading, when coupled with Rudolf Wittkower's polemic on the relationship between Renaissance proportion and Neo-Platonic metaphysics, set the stage for many critiques of modernism. See Hight (2008, Chapters 5 and 6).

13 Here a double-meaning of orthography manifests as the experience of the viewer. In the original Greek, *ortho* means the right-angle and shares a root with *norma;* the interchangeability of 'right-angle' with 'normal angle' reflect this origin (Canguilhem 1994).

14 Strictly, Lacan argues, anamorphosis is the visual embodiment of castration that focuses desire.

15 For more on this historical relationship between architects and non-building construction industries see Kolarevic (2003, 8–10).

16 For clarity's sake, in the text I will only use the term 'spline'; however 'B-Spline' is often used interchangeably, though in fact it is a species of spline geometry based on parametric determinations; 'NURB' curves, or non-uniform rational B-splines, are likewise a species of splines most commonly used in the digital modelling tools I discuss here.

17 The geometry of a drawn spline is calculus based, integrating discrete sets of information (in the form of the virtual forces) along its length. Digital splines have a trait called a 'degree', which determines through how many adjacent points information is related. A one-degree curve integrates information from only immediately adjacent control points, thus producing straight connections, a two-degree curve integrates information from two points to the left and right of each control vertex, thus producing a curve. The greater the degree, the 'smoother' the curve generally becomes because a greater amount of information is being integrated. A change in the middle of line will be distributed across its length. This logic extends to the topological surfaces constructed by lofting two or more spline lines together.

18 Reiser+Umemoto, Catenary Experiments, 1998. The research presented in these experiments is manifested in many of their projects, including their submission to the Yokohama Port Terminal competition (1995), IIT student centre (1997), Kansai National Diet Library (1996); Alishan Tourist Routes (Taiwan, Republic of China 2003).

19 As argued, to rather different formal ends, by Rahim and by Spruybroek.

20 For projects generated using these techniques see for example, Contemporary Architecture Practice, Reebok Flagship Store, Shanghai, China, 2004; NOX, Vision Machine, Nantes, 2000; Greg Lynn FORM, Port Authority Gateway Competition (which used bouncing balls rather than particles); DECOI, Paramorph London, 1999.

21 For a survey of related techniques used in the digital field, refer to Rahim 2000 and 2002.

22 In Maya for example, one can project a square onto a curved surface, but while the shape will render as a hole, there is no real surface discontinuity (as that would necessarily deform the surface geometry).

23 Indeed, Jesse Reiser (Reiser and Umemoto 2006, 233) noted that the danger of digital representation lay not in the ability to produce apparently unbuildable images, or for that matter a transformation of architecture into virtual images, but in the capacity to 'build' the image without any mediation or translation. For him, the collapse of translation is a hyper-real horror.

24 Other examples of recent architectures that employed shipbuilding industry knowledge are Future System's NatWest Media Center (1999), Lords Cricket Ground, London, UK and Gehry's Guggenheim Museum, Bilbao, Spain, and the DG Bank (2000), Berlin, Germany.

25 George Elvin defines 'integrated practice' as combining 'collaboration between disciplines, enhanced concurrency of design and construction phases, and ... greater continuity of involvement' of the design team through out the 'life cycle of the building' (Elvin 2007, 20). All three of these 'foundations' are made possible, he argues, through the use of BIM software throughout the design and construction process.

26 Tools such as Gehry Technologies and similar techniques taken from the aeronautic and automobile industries promoted by Stephen Kieran and James Timberlake (2004) often promise to regain some mastery for the architect; while possibly true this aspect if far less interesting than the redistribution and reformation of boundaries between fields of mastery. cf. Mitchell (1999, 839–841).

27 This return to the 'master builder,' for example, is very much at stake in a symposium conversation, 'Digital Master Builders' in Kolarevic 2003, 64–72.

28 SmartGeometry Group includes Foster Associates and KPF London schools and Bentley Systems itself. The collaboration has survived several re-affiliations of its members to different firms and even to software companies (Menges 2004, 43).

29 The shift I am arguing for here may be related to Michael Speaks' notion of 'Design Intelligence' (2002) as a corollary shift from critical theory's emphasis on representation for the human subject to entanglements between technological, material social and human assemblages. My arguments in this article, however, differ however in Speak's strong proposition of a "post-critical" age that is perhaps symptomatic of a tendency to prematurely conventionalize techniques of digital production into routine production (pun intended).

24

Plural Profession, Discrepant Practices

David Salomon

> Architects need to play a direct role in the policy-making in a community; once a decision has been made and handed to the architect, it's too late. After all, the role of any artist is to help people see things as they truly are.
>
> Samuel Mockbee (quoted in Seymour 2000, 27)

THE HOW AND THE FOR WHOM

In the past, the 'how' and the 'for whom' of architecture have been intimately related. Empirical studies of architectural firms show that the way architects are trained and work – the methodologies and tools they use, how they organize labour and pay structure, the size and location of an office, etc. – directly affects what they work on and who they work for (Blau 1984; Cuff 1991; Tombesi 2003). Three of the most important developments affecting this relationship today are: 1) the emphasis on inter- and intra-disciplinary collaborations – collaborations that emphasize architecture as a social process between different members within the design profession and/or the relationship between design professionals and non-professionals;[1] 2) the use of digital tools for designing, fabricating and communicating design ideas; ones in which the creation and use of information networks are central;[2] and 3) the proliferation of community-based design-build practices where design and aesthetics are seen as a means to address social and political issues, rather than ends in themselves.[3]

Why might architects be interested in doing more collaborative, digital, and design-build work? One answer is that, in contrast to typical professional practice, where a firm responds to requests for their services, each of these models provides architects with the opportunity to get involved at the beginning of the architectural process by making it easier to initiate work themselves – either by designing and building for others, or by generating more speculative work themselves. Such methods are equally relevant for not-for-profit and for-profit projects. The former category is increasingly made possible through the support of larger institutional frameworks – such as schools of architecture – which supply both the human and financial resources necessary to sustain them (ACSA 2000; Gaber and Bennett 2006).[4] Alternatively, advances in design software have made it possible for smaller firms to handle larger and more complex jobs without any sacrifice in quality or time.

New technologies have also enabled firms to be co-owners or developers of projects.

The New York firm SHoP has combined the use of modelling software with for-profit development, acting as both owner and designer on a number of speculative real estate projects.[5] Their progressive solutions were made possible, and profitable, by using computer-aided design and computer-aided manufacturing software that simultaneously produces complex forms, predicts construction costs, and facilitates execution. As developer and architect of The Porter House SHoP added a zinc-clad cube to an existing Renaissance Revival warehouse, transforming the structure into a residential complex (Reeser 2004). By utilizing the representational and managerial capacities of the software 'Solidworks' the firm was able to customize the façade while simultaneously minimizing fabrication and erection time (Figures 24.1 and 24.2). Here, new forms, new practices, and new collaborations between architects, developers, and contractors are rolled into one.

Historically, architects were (and in many places still are) prohibited from taking on this developer role; primarily because their financial connection to a project was understood as being in conflict with their responsibility to protect the public's health, safety, and welfare. Yet, this paradox exists whenever architects offer their service for hire to a client. In both cases, the commitment to the client or project, and the commitment to the public, must be balanced. While this arrangement – and the related technologies – may allow the architect more control (to sacrifice profit for quality, or to accept a lower rate of return in exchange for lower rents), it does not inevitably produce more public or more beautiful objects. In both cases, the flexibility and economy allowed by these means have to be actively tied to a progressive social and aesthetic agenda.

Other firms do not-for-profit projects, updating the community design paradigm begun in the 1960s, working directly for and with communities that are typically underserved by architecture. However, they rarely use the kind of advanced design and fabrication methods used by firms like SHoP.[6] Here the split between design, technology, and service is evident since many of these practices encourage the use of conventional or local materials and building methods – a choice that is understood as a result of pragmatic (i.e., there is no money for such things) and ethical (it would be another case of technological imperialism to use them) considerations. When embedded in schools of architecture, the projects not only embody a different form of practice, but a different pedagogical model from the standard focus on professional and artistic competence. Programmes such as the Rural Studio (Dean 2005) and the BASIC Initiative run out of the University of Washington (Palleroni 2004) emphasize the production of architectural artefacts, but they also focus on building lasting social and cultural awareness in their students. In other words, they emphasize the building up of citizens as much as

Figure 24.1 (Above) SHoP, The Porter House, New York, 2003. The 20,000 sq ft addition hovers over the adjacent building.

the design of buildings (Boyer and Mitgang, 1996).[7]

In each of these three models—collaborative, digital, and design-build—architects are attempting to exert more and earlier influence over the building/space-making process. While the technological, aesthetic, and social emphasis of these trends do overlap one another, the necessary skills and the underlying agendas are rarely combined in a single practice. What they share, however, is the desire to transform architecture's conventional role from an expert for hire (Gutman 1988) to a more proactive approach. This transformation requires the development of new modes of practice that incorporate new techniques and new constituencies to expand the definitions of the professional architect.

IMPURE PROFESSION

For over a century the dominant model for linking architecture's internal processes with its external commitments has been professionalism (Woods 1999; Cuff 1991). Although contested, definitions of a profession include: the ability and autonomy of a group to claim and defend the exclusive possession of a body of expert knowledge; the acquisition of that knowledge via lengthy and highly prescribed training, testing, and licensure; the development of technical skills necessary to put this knowledge to use for the benefit of both clients and the public at large (Larson 1977; Cullen 1983; Cuff 1991; AIA Code of Ethics 2007). This last requirement – responsibility to the public – is not only self-imposed but mandated by the state, which requires that all professions act to protect and advance the 'health, safety and

Figure 24.2 (Below) SHoP, The Porter House, New York, 2003. Construction drawing showing the final location of the numbered panels. The pre-fabricated panels are individually cut, bent and numbered off site and are erected in order as they arrive on site.

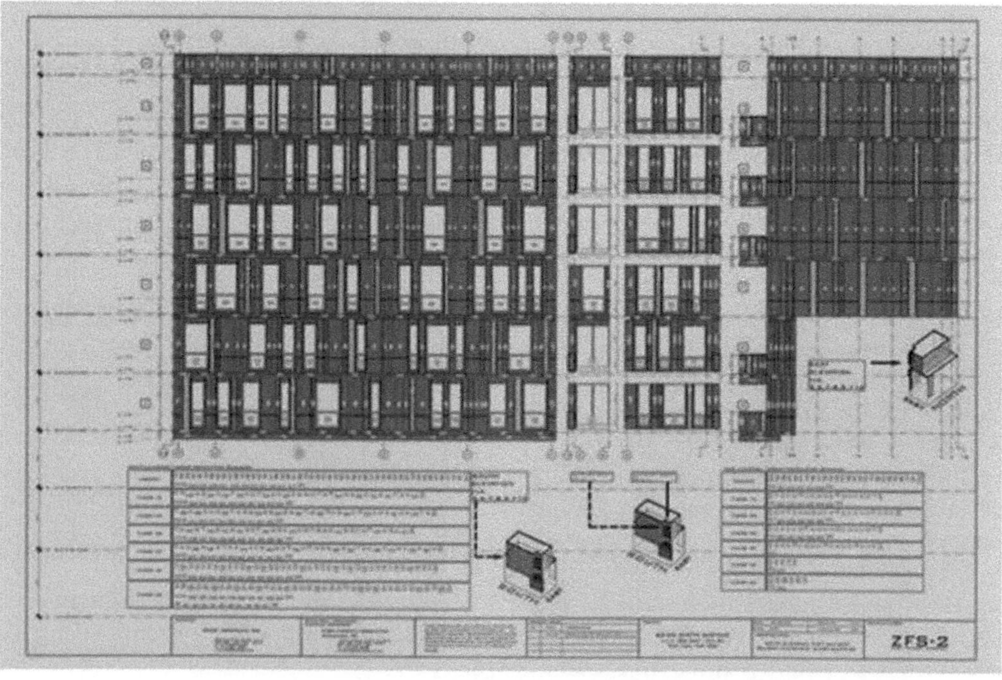

welfare' of the community it serves. In other words, professionals are required to put the public interest over their own personal gain and the individual gains of those who hire them.[8]

Architectural educator Thomas Fisher recognizes that while these requirements are applicable to all professionals, architecture's commitment to the 'public good' extends beyond purely technical issues (more successfully achieved by engineers and planners), and reaches into the aesthetic and symbolic realms (Fisher 1993). The sociologist Magali Larson reinforces this conclusion, arguing that architectural expertise and jurisdiction extend to matters of artistic skill and judgement (i.e. taste). Larson argues that this, and the relationship architecture has with patrons (who are more likely to be interested in the aesthetic and symbolic aspects of architecture, as opposed to clients who are more interested in purchasing a service), not only complicates their ability to act in the public's interest, but divides the field into two. The vast majority of firms are client-oriented, and produce 'buildings', while a much smaller – but more prestigious and influential group – creates 'architecture' (Larson 1993; Gutman 1988).

The limits of professionalism – both in general and specifically for architecture – are well documented by sociologists (Larson 1977; Gans 1983), cultural theorists (Robbins 1993), and architectural critics (Stevens 1998; Crawford 1991). Common complaints directed at professionalism include the unnecessarily esoteric jargon and practices that alienate the public they are chartered to serve, and the self-policing and self-rewarding that lead to an overemphasis on internal innovations rather than ones relevant outside its own borders. In short, an emphasis on technical expertise, political neutrality, and self-discipline have produced out-of-touch practitioners, primarily interested in developments within their own fields. In architecture, this is associated with an interest in formal or aesthetic questions at the expense of social conditions (Ward 1996). Professionalism is thus framed by oppositions such as experts vs. layman, insular vs. activist, and engaged intellectual vs. disinterested technician. These bound dualities are well established and have appeared and reappeared often in architectural discourse, namely: the worldly generalist vs. the narrow specialist, the artistic synthesizer vs. the technical expert, the ethical professional vs. the opportunistic practitioner (Saint 1983; Kostof 2000 [1977]).

Bruce Robbins argues that these binaries are at best stereotypes, and at worst, false choices. Contrary to complaints that professions distance members from 'real world' problems, he argues that professions have always been established and legitimated by broader cultural institutions. Moreover, their continued relevance is dependent upon the effectiveness of the technical skills and competencies they develop in order to achieve larger social goals. In other words, professions have always been open in their constitution, if not in their execution. The importance of this for Robbins is that professionalism and the expertise it generates should not be abandoned for some allegedly purer system. Rather, both sides of the binaries that define professionalism must be aggregated rather than set against one another. One does not have to choose between engagement *or* expertise; between social *or* technical progress; rather, one must be able to use one to achieve the other. Replacing an either/or logic with the logic of both/and results in 'discrepant cosmopolitanism', a multitude of different but interrelated practices that are flexible enough to accommodate the contradictory goals embedded in professionalism, but stable enough to incorporate feedback from sources both inside and outside its borders (Robbins 1993).

DISCREPANT PRACTICES

Related to Robbins' notion of discrepant cosmopolitanism, cultural theorist Kwame Appiah proposes a 'contaminated cosmopolitan' who simultaneously inhabits two or more identities – one of which is typically parochial and personal, the other of which is foreign and/or universal (Appiah 2007); a position which mirrors architecture's traditional understanding of itself as existing at the crossroads of multiple disciplines. Appiah's ideas translate into a set of architectural operations and protocols that can be deployed using architecture's own expertise.

Toward this end, architect and theorist Stan Allen argues that it is more productive for architecture to understand itself as a material practice, rather than a representational or ideological one (Allen 1999). This is not to say that the latter two are unimportant, only that the aesthetic, political, or social projects architecture wishes to take on must grow out of *how* it manipulates both physical and economic materials. Rather than importing theories from other discourses, architecture is more supple, elastic and open when it generates theory from an examination of its own modes of production. In other words, one's theory should follow from how one works, what one works with, and with whom.

Such theory – and the practices from which it grows – also recognizes that one must adapt to the real constraints imposed by material conditions. Allen cites how Le Corbusier and Frank Lloyd Wright adjusted their designs to conform to the physical properties and labour realities of building with reinforced concrete, noting that making such compromises is not a sign of failure, but instead illustrates a kind of design intelligence that recognizes the messiness of architecture's simultaneous negotiation with physical and economic constraints.

While Allen's examples are geared toward the generation of form, his theory recognizes that the practices or operations of architectural design must negotiate competing demands, including issues of use, cost, context, typology, environmental impact, and history. Today, architecture integrates more discrepant elements (both physical and social) into its processes, finds the right techniques for doing so, and develops the forms to express this expanded reservoir of requirements.

In particular, Allen's emphasis on negotiation – but not resolution – is central to the emphasis of the social, networked, and design-oriented practices outlined below. What differentiates these from previous attempts to expand architecture's disciplinary borders is the desire to simultaneously incorporate a variety of different discourses, methods, and cultures into its operating procedures. Instead of searching for one source to tie or ground its production to (e.g., engineering, scientific management, structuralism, semiotics, philosophy, etc.), today architects are learning from numerous areas to expand the discipline and make it more relevant socially (via collaboration), technologically (via digital techniques), and aesthetically (via community-based design-build projects). The dialogue and feedback between these categories produce an impure but robust profession, one which is discrepant yet connected.

PARTICIPATORY PRACTICES

Almost by definition, any architectural act requires the cooperation of a diverse set of people and institutions. What differs from one to the next is the kinds of people and organizations that are involved, and who among them has agency. Conventional professional practice in the United States understands the primary players as the client, the architect, and contractor. It often includes the collaboration between the architect and other design professionals such as engineers and landscape architects.[9] Projects are regulated by governments, which gives the public a degree of control and makes it a part of the process. As environmental issues garner more attention from politicians and citizens, implicit approval is giving way to explicit demands. In other words, public participation is on the rise (Cuff 1996; 1998). Still, many voices are excluded, and decisions are made by the credentialed and the powerful.

To combat this estrangement, the past forty years have seen multiple attempts by architects to work not only with other professionals, but with and for the architecturally disenfranchized (Aeschbacher and Rios 2008). Some of these practices are called 'social', others 'collaborative', and others 'community-based', emphasizing different goals, methods, and degrees of participation.

Social practices

Social architecture is the practice of architecture as an instrument for progressive social change. It foregrounds the moral imperative to increase human dignity and reduce human suffering (Ward 1996). In his provocatively titled essay 'The Suppression of the Social in Design: Architecture as War', Anthony Ward lays out the trajectory of alternative models for architectural practice from the nineteenth century through to the early 1990s, noting the various degrees to which they adhere to his definition of social architecture. For Ward, to achieve a 'truly' social architecture, practitioners must become members of the communities they work for. When architects actively promote the participation of multiple voices in the design process, they simultaneously act as fellow citizens and as engaged professionals. Ward follows C. Richard Hatch, who also emphasizes the social obligations and potential of the architectural process, writing that architecture is 'primarily a social event, as a medium for the creation of a community' (Hatch 1984).

In the 1960s, John Habraken, Kevin Lynch, Christopher Alexander, Lucien Kroll, and Henry Sanoff were among those who realized that architecture was unresponsive to the needs and desires of building occupants (Montgomery 1989; Richardson and Connelly 2005). From the burgeoning field of person-environment studies, there arose an interest in generating data (both statistically and ethnographically) regarding how buildings were used and how they performed, and then feeding back that information into the design process (Montgomery 1989; Schuman 2006). The production of this knowledge allowed architects, in Montgomery's terms, to proactively generate 'new people' that needed their services, and new means for addressing their needs.

In contrast to, and in many cases in reaction to these highly rational and quickly institutionalized social scientific methods (Till 2005; Richardson and Connelly 2005), by the end of the decade advocacy or community-based design positioned itself as 'an alternative style of practice based on the idea that professional technical knowledge without moral and political content is often inadequate' (Toker 2007, 309; see also Ward 1996; Comerio 1984; Till 2005). Community design centres emerged in disadvantaged neighbourhoods to provide legal, design, planning, and even construction assistance (Curry 2000). While these organizations survived through the 1970s, their sharp decline in the 1980s has been attributed to the neo-liberal politics ushered in during the Reagan–Thatcher era which ultimately challenged their legitimacy and slashed their funding (Comerio 1984; Schuman 2006; Toker and Toker 2006).

Without substantial state or institutional support for these efforts, social design has had to find alternative means, and different theories, to stay true to its mandate of serving the general public.[10] One theory that attempts to transcend specific conflicts without negating differences is John Forrester's call to reframe design from a 'problem solving' to a 'sense-making' activity (Forrester 1985). Forrester's logic is picked up by architect Jeremy Till, who argues for the professional discourse of 'logic and completeness' to be replaced with the techniques of 'conversation' and 'story telling'. He argues, that these everyday techniques, structured by participation and feedback among all agents affected by new construction, can provide 'space in which hope is negotiated ... hope [for] a better future for architectural practice' (Till 2005, 41).

While Forrester's and Till's positions re-emphasize the need for collaboration between design professionals and laymen, they do not advocate specific design techniques or forms. In contrast, the planner Randolph Hester outlines more specific design strategies, ones which attempt to integrate the discipline of ecology with the practice of participatory democracy (Hester 2006). Here, democratic participation and ecological stewardship is the greater cause for architects to aspire to. Architects' design skills feed back information from a variety of participants in order to produce truly communal spaces. Hester's formal-spatial techniques recall the vernacular ones found in Christopher Alexander's 'Pattern Language' (Alexander et al. 1977). For Alexander, 'centredness', 'connectedness', and 'density and smallness' are directed toward producing environments that increase the chances of interacting with one's neighbours. Since these environments are spatially and iconographically traditional, if not conservative, they raise questions about their ability to include non-traditional functions and social groups within them. While clearly open to new inputs into the design process, this approach is not tolerant of new forms and sensibilities.

Information practices

The difficulty of simultaneously maintaining a commitment to progressive design, methodologies and clients is evident even in practices that actively use digital devices to do so. For example, many computational tools – such as Building Information Management (BIM) software – are ways for architects to control more of the building process with even less input from other professionals or laymen (Kieran and Timberlake 2004; Willis and Woodward 2006; see also Chapter 23). Even when arguing for more social interaction between architecture and other areas, their processes do not typically include the end users, or any other actors with non-expert information.

Further, digitally-directed practices do not typically foreground a commitment to advancing the public interest. The lack of a clear social agenda is a direct recognition of the failure of modernism's efficient mechanical technologies – and their underlying logic of efficiency through isolation – to make the world a better place.[11] As the sociologist Ulrich Beck has noted, if one of the hallmarks of the so-called first modernity was the rationalization of industrial and everyday activities, the second, or reflexive modernity, is characterized by the proliferation of unexpected and unwanted by-products generated by these optimizing techniques such as economic colonization and global warming. Such side effects, he argues, cannot be solved using the same method that produced them; the problems created by 'functional differentiation can no longer be corrected by further functional differentiation' (Beck 1999, 2). Rather, the simultaneous generation of 'goods' and 'bads' must be examined as complex, dynamic systems in which the relationship between parts is more important than establishing the 'essence' of the parts themselves.

The ability to understand and use such systems – e.g., global markets, ecosystems, buildings, etc. – requires complex mathematical models, increased computational capacities, and sophisticated software. In other words, it needs to break down all information about these systems to the most basic of differentiations: that between on and off, yes or no, 0s and 1s. There is a belief that, 'whereas previous technologies tended to separate trades … software protocols have provided a general language that fosters increased intertwining' (Hight and Perry 2006b, 49).

Networked practices

Architecture has been theorized as a field which harbours both the arts and the sciences. More recently, however, Tierney and Burke have argued that, far from being a locus of the arts, architectural intelligence increasingly exists within a distributed network; a network that is enabled by a 'rich ecology of technology that threatens to overwhelm at the same time it exhilarates and empowers'. Citing Castells' insight that the 'network society is a social structure', they ask, 'What is the position and responsibility of the designer-as-agent within this socially based information system?' (Tierney and Burke 2007, 26; see also Chapter 22).

One possible answer is provided by Hight and Perry in their essay 'The Manifold Potential of Bionetworks' (2006b), in which they argue against the 'standardized organism' of professional practice – 'controlled' by various institutions such as the AIA, RIBA, and National Council of Architectural Registration Boards (NCARB), and for a more diffuse network of practitioners that exchange and feed back information to one another in a less propriety way. Building on the insights of Pierre Levy, Michel Foucault, and Gilles Deleuze, they recognize that this kind of 'molecular' or 'bio' network reflects the current state of the world, in which power is so diffuse that it operates undetected at the micro-scale of the body. This world is characterized, not by 'the centrality [in importance] of knowledge and information, but [by] the application of such knowledge and information to knowledge generation and information processing/communication devices, in a cumulative feedback loop between innovation and the uses of innovation' (Manuel Castells, cited in Hight and Perry 2006b, 50).

Unlike a previous generation of architects interested in cybernetics and feedback loops (Wigley 2001b), the geographically dispersed practices such as Ocean, Open Source Architects (OSA), and kokkugia are less concerned with the broad ecological implications of these systems than in the structural, spatial, and formal possibilities suggested by the natural, epigenetic processes they emulate (Hensel et al. 2004; 2006) The resultant forms – which could not be generated without incredible amounts of computational power – are ones in which a tremendous amount of variation is produced from minimal differences; a model which is analogous to how some social, as well as biological, systems develop (DeLanda 1997).

The work of the firm Servo exemplifies how recursive processes that loop between architectural objects, information systems, and human beings have the potential to generate social effect (Erdman et al. 2006). In a series of seductive installations and proposals, the firm has produced objects and environments in which neither the designer, nor the computer are 'in control' of what one encounters at any moment. The ever-changing aesthetic condition of light, colour, sound, images, and forms, is generated by the conversation that occurs between corporeal and electronic stimuli, sensors and receptors. While the effects within the installation are primarily psychological and physiological, by plugging these environments into larger information networks, they automatically become a part of, and responsive to input from larger corporeal, digital, and social networks.[12] While their contemporary forms and their deployment in museums, galleries, and hotels suggest a limited audience, to dismiss this work would be premature. Such experimental sites are crucial for learning about the implications of feedback-dependent objects in other types of politically charged contexts. While the broader social implications of work like Servo's is not quite clear, the combination of sophisticated forms with sophisticated technologies and passive and active input from users, marks this work as distinct from other networked practices.

Open practices

Both Hight and Perry (2006a; 2006b), and Tierney and Burke (2007) are optimistic about the potential for digitally powered bionetworks to distribute architectural power and control a multitude of agents. The theoretical frameworks which network-inspired practices are based upon – which in addition to Castells' Information Society, include

Hardt and Negri's multitude, Bruno Latour's Actor Network Theory, and Deleuze and Guattari's bodies without organs – are defined by opening up social and political processes to contributions from all sources (see also Gropius 1955). These positions, along with the technologies used to manifest them, have the potential to incorporate local knowledge sets and non-digital information into their feedback loop of innovation.

Just such a loop is described by Cameron Sinclair in his introduction to the book *Design Like You Give a Damn*, a catalogue of proposals and projects done for humanitarian causes (Architecture for Humanity 2006). In tracing the history of his organization he describes the cycle of horror, euphoria, and disappointment in which natural and man-made catastrophes were followed by inspired responses from designers, only to have nothing come of their efforts. Sinclair's disappointment was tempered by the growing realization that his own organization was becoming a database for ideas and solutions that could be studied, improved, and disseminated (if not put in place) before the next crises occurred. Thus, despite being responsible for only a handful of projects, Architecture for Humanity ended up designing a distribution hub for the ever-expanding network of people, institutions, and design ideas relevant for solving future crises. Within this network are experts in the design of objects, logistics, languages, and cultures. While, on the one hand, this archival information could move towards the development of the more abstract or 'universal' solutions associated with modernism (and capitalism), it is precisely Architecture for Humanity's wide and varied distribution of sources – made possible by communication technologies – that offer the potential to augment common knowledge with localized and embodied knowledge. This in turn will produce objects that are both functionally and aesthetically relevant to those who use them. The way things work (well or poorly) and the way they look (foreign or familiar) are crucial to the physical and psychological well-being of the victims of disasters. In other words, technically and economically efficient solutions are not all that is required, but spatial and formal ones – informed by local conditions – are equally important.

DESIGN PRACTICES

Like informational practices, design-oriented practices stress the need to develop new methods for creating architectural projects. And, like social practices, they encourage working closely with specific groups or locales. The key difference between the social practices discussed above (many of which were engaged in design-build programmes) and design practices is the latter's emphasis on the role of aesthetics. In such practices there is an emphasis on design itself – as both a noun and a verb. The focus on aesthetic issues aligns with networked-based practices which also seek to develop relationships between new processes, new organizational structures, and new forms. Design practices' emphasis on using local and/or vernacular methods and materials – as opposed to digital and biological ones – guarantees that different results will be achieved. Finally, in comparison to the ideologically elusive position of informational practitioners, design practices are relatively straightforward in their ambition to have a direct effect on people's lives – both architects and those they work for (Bell 2004).

The simultaneous commitment of design practices to process *and* product, altruism *and* aesthetics, exposes the false dichotomy that typically separates the one from the other. Architectural practices that engage both concepts simultaneously recognize that the ground they occupy includes a responsibility to others that can be fulfilled via the manipulation of form, space, images, sensibilities, moods, and tastes. While often dismissed as superficial if not dangerous, aesthetics are understood as a historically necessary and highly effective means to help solve more important issues via the politicization of art, not the aestheticization of politics (Benjamin 1969 [1936]).[13]

Building aesthetics

The political and social importance of design is recognized by Cuff in her analysis of contentious developments. In these contexts, she argues that it is not the architect but 'the design which moves to the center of debate. Its object-ness externalizes the subjective experience of contending parties, as it absorbs disagreement or embodies commonality'. In order for a design, however, to expand the conversation beyond parochial issues, it must have in it qualities that allow one to recognize it as such. As she notes, 'the architect, as the mid-wife to the design-object, is the key to' producing these representational qualities (Cuff 1996, 21).[14] Architects are central, not because of their professional neutrality, but because of their commitment to the autonomous culture of architecture, that is, to internal formal and disciplinary issues. This expertise allows them to relate forms, images and spaces to social and political issues. Rather than simply solving the problem of a client, the architect here performs like Samuel Mockbee's policy-making artist, a figure who simultaneously shows how things are and how they could be better.

In *Good Deeds, Good Design*, architect Bryan Bell (2004) documents a series of projects by design-build groups, most of them embedded in schools of architecture. Bell makes a slightly different argument regarding the role of design. He notes that the 'technical nature of the built world requires the expertise of architects and planners, it is they who must help people to be involved in [the] decisions' (13). While this is a defence of professional expertise, Bell makes it clear that such help cannot be 'a patronizing gift from the architect,' but the result of a 'mutual exchange between the designer and the client' (13). What makes this exchange mutual is the commitment of designers to enter into a dialogue with local groups, preferably over a period of time and a number of projects.[15]

One example of such a long-term commitment to serving local communities is the BASIC Initiative at the University of Washington. It is comprised of three programmes, the Global Community Studio, the Housing Solutions Studio, and the Local Neighborhoods Studio.[16] The Global Community Studio is organized around an annual design/build project located outside of the United States (most have been in rural Mexico). Students prepare by studying the specific culture they are to visit and the building type they will be making. Design starts the following semester with a two-week on-site charrette with the active participation ofthe people who will use the building. The next two months are spent constructing the building using local materials, local labour, traditional building types, and passive energy techniques. While the overlap between students and local residents is relatively brief, long-term institutional knowledge accumulates as to how to harmoniously merge the embodied knowledge of a locale, the professional skills of architects, and the pedagogical demands (and archival capacity) of an architecture school (Palleroni 2004).

The Washington programme adheres to the historical definition of community design, emphasizing participation and process (Toker 2007). However, unlike the practices of the 1960s and 1970s, and unlike Hester and Allen's work cited above, there is a clear emphasis on architectural expression. Stylistically, both the Global Community Studio and the Local Neighborhoods Studio generate what might be called a 'do-it-yourself' kind of modernism. The detailing, out of necessity and choice, is a rough version of the industrial aesthetic, using inexpensive materials and hand methods to join them. In each case, the designs stand out from their surroundings, even when incorporating the most vernacular types and processes. They are separated from their surroundings just enough so that both their aspirations and limitations are recognizable symbols of the intra- and inter-architectural values that produced them.

Architectural aesthetics are also critical to Rural Studio, a programme founded at Auburn University in 1991 by the late Samuel Mockbee. Architectural students move into the poor rural communities in Hale County, Alabama, get to know the people, their architectural needs, and then design, raise funds for, and build structures for them (Moos and Trechsel 2003; Dean and Hursley 2002). The continued success of the programme can in no small measure be attributed to Mockbee's insistence on the marriage of personal artistic vision, direct community involvement, and a long-term commitment to 'the replacement of abstract opinions with knowledge based on real human contact' (Bates 1995, 99). For Mockbee, the segregated South lent itself to historical and 'mythical' understanding – examined in his own vibrant paintings, as well as in the unique materials and forms found in the designs of the Rural Studio (Moos 2003). Like Bell's work, Rural Studio cannot simply be understood as charity, or as the imposition of architectural values on an unsuspecting client. Neither is it architecture that dispassionately lends specialist knowledge to the will of the people. It partakes of seeming contradictions: using design – representation and organization – to simultaneously announce and improve the public good.

The work of Estudio Teddy Cruz also emphasizes direct community engagement, working with local conditions and materials, and foregrounding the efficacy of artistic

Figure 24.3 (Below left and right) Teddy Cruz, Tijuana River, 1999, photo-construction. This re-mapping of a bird's-eye view of the river is comprised of images of Tijuana, San Diego, and Los Angeles, suggesting the shared histories and destinies of the three.

practices and objects to advance social and political goals. Having investigated the area straddling the border between San Diego and Tijuana since 1994, Cruz's photographic collages represent the improvizational nature of the social and physical conditions found there, while also acting as a model for how to intervene in this paradoxical zone. At once fluid and fragmented, the collages simultaneously embrace and challenge both the hyper-organized and hyper-informal building practices respectively present on the American and Mexican sides of the border. The firm uses the same collage technique to present its architectural solutions, and to describe how proposals evolve (Sokol 2008b; Figure 24.3). In a number of projects, such as Manufactured Sites: A Housing Urbanism Made of Waste/*Maquiladora* (Figure 24.4), the role of the professional architect is to provide a design infrastructure into which citizens literally add their own programmes, labour, materials, and aesthetic. Here, high and low taste-cultures, static and dynamic processes, professionals and laymen all mix to produce a complex yet highly organized landscape, qualities that also describe Cruz's own collages. For both Cruz and Mockbee, artistic output is not only a source for personal reflection but an integral and active agent in (re)forming their respective regions.

CONCLUSION

The diverse firms described above reveal the fragmented state of architectural practice. They also illustrate its desire and ability to expand beyond the false choice between elite designers and socially engaged activists. Yet, while it contains many discrepant entities, the discipline is still far from being discrepantly cosmopolitan, as Robbins defined it. Despite architecture's pluralism, it rarely strives to

transcend this partiality. At the macro level, the discipline does take on progressive aesthetic, technical, and social agendas, but, these attempts are too often isolated and independent from one another. As a result, firms can fall into the trap of conventional professionalism, namely, of limiting themselves to a specialized product or service, relevant only for a specific clientele, building type, or location. Such a position risks becoming unresponsive to forms of intelligence and responsibilities other than the ones it focuses on.

Inventive representational techniques and forms need not be limited to highly capitalized projects, nor should the presence of a community agenda negate technical or formal innovations. Aesthetic shortcomings should be no less troublesome than social or technological ones. The danger of ignoring any of architecture's responsibilities is to retreat into the limited domain of expertise, rather than expanding into a culture of discrepant cosmopolitanism.

Figure 24.4 (Below) Teddy Cruz, Manufactured Sites: A Housing Urbanism Made of Waste/*Maquiladora*, Tijuana, 2005–2008, collage. The proposal takes advantage of the flow of prefabricated parts from the US to Mexican factories (Maquiladoras) where they are assembled and then returned to the US as finished goods. Here leftovers from these factories – along with other industrial refuse – are re-purposed as building materials.

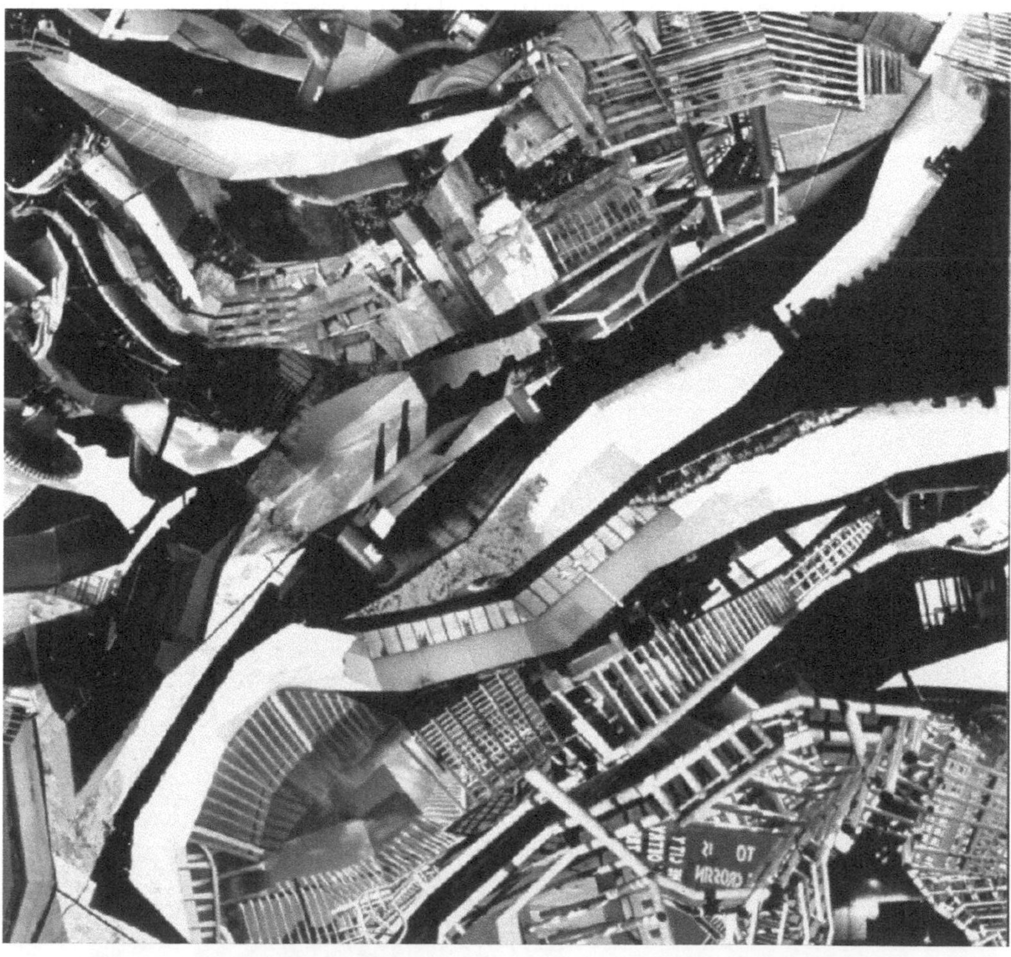

NOTES

1 In addition to describing the person-to-person relationships that exist between those who commission, conceive, and design the building, architecture as a social process can also refer to the effect an architectural artifact has on inter-personal relationships. See Montgomery (1989) for the interest in both these definitions within modern architecture.

2 The contemporary interest in the idea of a network practice is examined in both the special edition of *Architectural Design*, edited by Chris Hight and Chris Perry (Hight and Perry 2006a) as well as in the collection of essays edited by Tierney and Burke (2007). For a pre-history of this movement, see Wigley 2001b.

3 For an overview of contemporary examples of design build practices see Bell 2004; see also Curry 2000. For historical and contemporary examples in Europe, see Blundell Jones 2005. For the changes in the nature of these practices see Toker 2007.

4 There are currently over 40 community design programmes embedded in schools of architecture, over half of which were begun in the 1990s (ACSA 2000). See also Architecture for Humanity (2006) for projects supported by governmental and non-governmental organizations, specifically in response to natural and man-made disasters.

5 This form of practice was only approved by the American Institute of Architects, the voluntary professional association for architects in the United States, in the late 1970s.

6 For the historical shift in community and participatory design programmes from an advocacy to entrepreneurial model, caused by the conservative political policies of the 1980s, see Comerio (1984). For an update on the effects of this, see Toker (2007) and Toker and Toker (2006).

7 Similar programmes that mix a social commitment with technical and aesthetic innovations exist at the University of Washington, University of Texas at Austin, The University of Utah and Kansas State, and the University of Louisiana-Lafayette. There are many other programmes which share the social commitment but not the aesthetic one. See Bell (2004), Curry (2000), Hardin (2006), and Sokol (2008a).

8 The requirements for practitioners in the United States are clearly laid out for architects in the code of ethics supplied both by the AIA (2004) and NCARB (National Council of Architectural Registration Boards, the institution that administers the licensing procedure for architects) (2008). See also Cuff (1991, 39).

9 Linda Pollak makes an important distinction between collaborative and interdisciplinary practices, it being that the former does not demand an overlap or exchange of information, while the latter implies a contested domain of expertise and knowledge that needs to be more actively integrated with one another. She argues that this is this area where expertise is shared, limitations exposed and innovation occurs (Pollak 2002). For examples of required collaboration see the competitions for Downsview Park in Toronto and for Ground Zero in New York.

10 See Toker and Toker (2006) for how the participatory practices of community design have been repackaged by New Urbanism for a clientele on the opposite end of the economic spectrum than the one it was originally created for.

11 See McLeod (1983) for the relationship between modernist architectural theory and scientific management.

12 See Rheingold (2003), who Servo cites as a source for the connection between digital and social networks to produce new social institutions.

13 See Toker (2007) for how New Urbanism has 'hijacked' both participatory methods and imagery to 'aestheticize' the politics of community design.

14 On the importance of representation to achieve other ends, see Martin (2006).

15 See also Bell and Wakeford (2008) for an updated and expanded collection of these kinds of 'public-interest' practices as well as Sokol (2008a) for current academia passed practices.

16 The Global Community Studio is dedicated to working with communities outside the United States; the Housing Solutions Studio works on housing projects for Native American Tribes; the Local Neighborhoods Studio focuses on small-scale constructions in and around Seattle.

Section 5 Bibliography

ACSA (2000) *Sourcebook of Community Design Programs.* Washington, DC: ACSA Press.

Aeschbacher, Peter and Michael Rios (2008) 'Claiming Public Space: The Case for Proactive, Democratic Design', in Brian Bell and Katie Wakeford (eds) *Expanding Architecture: Design as Activism.* New York: Metropolis Books, 84–91.

AIA Code of Ethics (2007) American Institute of Architects, www.aia.org/aiaucmp/groups/aia/documents/pdf/aiap074121.pdf, accessed on January 21, 2010.

Alexander, Christopher et al. (1977) *A Pattern Language.* New York: Oxford University Press.

Allen, Stan (1997) 'From Object to Field', *Architectural Design* 67 (May-June): 24–31.

—— (1999) 'Practice vs. Project', *Praxis* 0: 112–123.

—— (2000) 'Mapping the Unmappable', in *Practice: Architecture, Technique and Representation.* London: Routledge.

American Institute of Architects (2004) 'AIA Code of Ethics', in *Handbook of Professional Practice.* Washington, DC: AIA.

American Institute of Architects, Commission for the Survey of Education and Registration (1954) *The Architect at Mid-Century.* New York: Reinhold.

Anthony, Kathryn (2001) *Designing for Diversity. Gender, Race and Ethnicity in the Architectural Profession.* Urbana: University of Illinosis Press.

Appiah, Kwame (2007) *Cosmopolitanism: Ethics in a World of Strangers.* New York: Norton.

Architecture for Humanity (2006) *Design Like You Give a Damn: Architectural Responses to Humanitarian Crises.* New York: Metropolis Books.

Balmori, Diana (1987) 'George B. Post: The Process of Design and the New American Architectural Office (1868–1913)', *Journal of the Society of Architectural Historians* 46(4): 342–355.

Bates, Randolph (1995) 'Interview with Samuel Mockbee', in Lori Ryker (ed.) *Mockbee Coker: Thought and Process.* New York: Princeton Architectural Press.

Bateson, Gregory (1972) *Steps to an Ecology of Mind.* Chicago: University of Chicago Press.

Beck, Ulrich (1999) *World Risk Society.* Cambridge: Polity Press.

Bell, Bryan (ed.) (2004) *Good Deeds, Good Design: Community Service Through Architecture.* New York: Princeton Architectural Press.

Bell, Bryan and Katie Wakeford (2008) *Expanding Architecture: Design as Activism.* New York: Metropolis Books.

Benjamin, Walter (1969 [1936]) 'The Work of Art in the Age of Mechanical Reproduction', in Walter Benjamin *Illuminations.* New York: Schocken.

—— (1979) 'The Author as Producer', in Walter Benjamin *Reflections.* New York: Harcourt, 220–238.

Bergdoll, Barry and Peter Christensen (2008) *Home Delivery: Fabricating the Modern Dwelling.* New York: Museum of Modern Art.

Blake, C.N. (2000) 'Afterword: What's Pragmatism Got to Do with It?', in J. Ockman (ed.) *The Pragmatist Imagination.* New York: Princeton Architectural Press, 266–273.

Blau, Judith (1984) *Architects and Firm: A Sociological Perspective on Architectural Practice.* Cambridge, MA: MIT Press.

Bledstein, Burton J. (1976) *The Culture of Professionalism: The Middle Class and the Development of Higher Education in America.* New York: Norton.

Blundell Jones, Peter (2005) 'Sixty-eight and After', in P. Blundel Jones, D. Petrescu and J. Till (eds) *Architecture & Participation.* London: Spon, 127–140.

Bourdieu, Pierre (1977) *Outline of a Theory of Practice.* Cambridge and New York: Cambridge University Press.

—— (1990) *The Logic of Practice.* Translated by R. Nice. Stanford, CA: Stanford University Press.

Boyer, Ernest L. and L.D. Mitgang (1996) *Building Community: A New Future for Architecture Education and Practice: A Special Report.* Princeton, NJ: Carnegie Foundation for the Advancement of Teaching.

Boyle, Bernard Michael (2000 [1977]) *Architectural Practice in America 1865–1965 – Ideal and Reality.* Berkeley: University of California Press.

Bradford Landau, Sarah (1998) *George B. Post, Architect: Picturesque Designer and Determined Realist.* New York: Monacelli Press.

Bucci, Federico (1993) *Albert Kahn: Architect of Ford.* New York: Princeton Architectural Press.

Bürger, Peter (1984) *Theory of the Avant-Garde.* Minneapolis: University of Minnesota Press.

Canguilhem, Georges (1994) 'The Normal and the Pathological', in *A Vital Rationalist.* New York: Zone Books.

Choay, Francoise (1997 [1980]) *The Rule and the Model.* Cambridge, MA: MIT Press.

Cody, Jeffrey W. (2003) *Exporting American Architecture, 1870–2000.* London: Routledge.

Cohen, Jean-Louis (2000) 'Urban Projects and Adjustment to the Future', in J. Ockman (ed.) *The Pragmatist Imagination.* New York: Princeton Architectural Press, 42–51.

Colomina, B., A. Brennan and J. Kim Brennan (eds) (2004) *Cold War Hothouses: Inventing Postwar Culture from Cockpit to Playboy.* New York: Princeton Architectural Press.

Comerio, Mary (1984) 'Community Design: Idealism and Entrepreneurship', *Journal of Planning Research* I: 227–243.

Corburn, Jason (2005) *Street Science: Community Knowledge and Environmental Health Justice.* Cambridge, MA: MIT Press.

Corner, James (1999) 'Agency of Mapping: Speculation, Critique and Invention', in *Mappings* D. Cosgrove, (ed.). New York: Reaktion Books.

Crawford, Margret (1991) 'Can Architects Be Socially Responsible?' in Diane Ghirardo (ed.) *Out of Site: A Social Criticism of Architecture.* Seattle: Bay Press.

Cuff, Dana (1991) *Architecture: The Story of Practice.* Cambridge, MA: MIT Press.

—— (1996) 'Contentious Urban Development: Architects and the Public Realm', *Surface Re:Forming Space* 1.

—— (1998) 'Community Property: Enter the Architect or, the Politics of Form', in Michael Bell and Sze Tsung Leong (eds) *Slow Space.* New York: Monacelli.

—— (2000a) Foreword' in Spiro Kostof (ed.) *The Architect.* Berkeley: University of California Press, vii–xv.

—— (2000b) *The Provisional City: Los Angeles Stories of Architecture and Urbanism.* Cambridge, MA: MIT Press.

—— (2001) 'Digital Pedagogies: An Essay', *Architectural Record* 189(9): 200–206.

—— (2003) 'Immanent Domain: Pervasive Computing and the Public Realm', *Journal of Architectural Education* 57(1): 43–50.

Cullen, John (1983) 'Structural Aspects of Architectural Profession', in J. Blau, M. La Gory and J. Pipkin (eds) *Professionals and Urban Form.* Albany, NY: State University of New York Press, 280–297.

Curry, R. (2000) 'History of Community Design', in *The ACSA Sourcebook of Community Design Programs at Schools of Architecture in North America.* Washington, DC: ACSA, 38–43.

Dean, Andrea Oppenheimer and Timothy Hursley (2002) *Rural Studio: Samuel Mockbee and the Architechure of Decency.* New York: Princeton Architectural Press.

Dean, Andrea Oppenheimer (2005) *Proceed and Be Bold: Rural Studio after Samuel Mockbee.* New York: Princeton Architectural Press.

DeLanda, Manuel (1997) *A Thousand Years of Non-Linear History.* New York: Zone.

—— (2001) 'The Case of Modeling Software', in *Verb Processing.* Barcelona: Actar, 131–137.

Deleuze, Gilles (1988) *Foucault.* Minneapolis: University of Minnesota Press.

Deleuze, Gilles and Felix Guattari (1987) *A Thousand Plateaus.* Minneapolis: University of Minnesota Press.

Dicken, Peter (2007) *Global Shift: Mapping the Changing Contours of the World Economy,* 5th edn. London: Sage.

Dutton, T. and L. Mann (1996) 'Modernism, Postmodernism, and Architecture's Social Project', in Thomas A. Dutton and Lian Hurst Mann (eds) *Reconstructing Architecture.* Minneapolis: University of Minnesota Press, 1–26.

Easterling, Keller (2005) *Enduring Innocence.* Cambridge, MA: MIT Press.

Eisenman, Peter (1979) 'Aspects of Modernism: The Maison Domino and the Self-Referential Sign'. *Oppositions* (Winter–Spring).

—— (1983) *House X.* New York: Rizzolli Press.

—— (1984) 'The End of the Classical, the End of the Beginning, the End of the End,' *Perspecta* 21: 154–173.

—— (1987) *House of Cards.* New York: Oxford University Press.

Elvin, George (2007) *Integrated Practice in Architecture.* Hoboken, NJ: John Wiley.

Erdman, David, Marcelyn Gow, Ulrika Karlsson and Chris Perry (2006) 'Parallel Processing: Design/ Practice', *Architectural Design* 76(5): 80–87.

Evans, Robin (1995) *The Projective Cast. Architecture and its Three Geometries*. Cambridge, MA: MIT Press.

—— (1997) 'Translations from Drawing to Building', *Translations from Drawing to Building and Other Essays*. London: AA Publications, 153–194.

Felsen, Martin (2007) 'Complex Populations', *306090: Models* 11: 155–173.

Fisher, Thomas (1993) 'Systems of (Professional) Survival', *Progressive Architecture* (Dec): 7.

Foreign Office Architects (2003) *The Yokohama Project*. Barcelona: ACTAR.

Forrester, John (1985) 'Designing: Making Sense Together in Practical Conversations', *Journal of Architectural Education* 38(3).

Foucault, Michel (1977 [1975]) *The Order of Things: An Archaeology of the Human Science*. New York: Pantheon.

—— (1995) *Discipline and Punish*. New York: Vintage.

Frampton, Kenneth (1983) 'Towards a Critical Regionalism. Six Points for an Architecture of Resistance', in Hal Foster (ed.) *The Anti-Aesthetic: Essays on Post-Modern Culture*. Port Townsend: Bay Press, 17–34.

—— (2007 [1980]) *Modern Architecture: A Critical History*. London: Thames and Hudson.

Fraser, Valerie (2000) *Building the New World: Studies in the Modern Architecture of Latin America, 1930–1960*. London: Verso.

Froebel Folker, Hein, Jurgen Heinrichs and Otto Kreye (1980) *The New International Division of Labour*. Cambridge: Cambridge University Press.

Gaber, Sharon and Daniel Bennett (2006) 'Institutional Support for Community-Based Architecture and Planning Outreach Scholarship at Auburn University', in Mary C. Hardin (ed.) *From the Studio to the Streets: Service Leaning in Planning and Architecture*. Washington, DC: American Association for Higher Education.

Gans, Herbert (1983) 'Toward a Human Architecture: A Sociologist's View of the Profession', in J. Blau, M. La Gory and J. Pipkin (eds) *Professionals and Urban Form*. Albany, NY: State University of New York Press, 303–319.

Geertz, C. (1974) *The Interpretation of Cultures*. New York: Basic Books.

Ghirardo, Diane (ed.) (1991) *Out of Site: A Social Criticism of Architecture*. Seattle: Bay Press.

Goad, Philip J. and Julie Willis (2003) 'Invention from War: A Circumstantial Modernism for Australian Architecture', *Journal of Architecture* 8(1): 41–62.

Greenberg, Clement (1939) 'Avant-Garde and Kitsch', *Partisan Review* 6(5): 34–49.

Gropius, Walter (1955) 'The Architect Within Our Industrial Society', in Walter Gropius, *Scope of Total Architecture*. New York: Harper, 76–90.

Grosz, Elizabeth (2001) 'Cyberspace, Virtuality, and the Real: Some Architectural Reflections', in *Architecture from the Outside*. Cambridge, MA: MIT Press, 75–90.

Gutman, Robert (1988) *Architectural Practice: A Critical View*. New York: Princeton Architectural Press.

Hambly, Maya (1988) *Drawing Instruments 1580–1980*. London: Sotheby's.

Hardin, Mary C. (ed.) (2006) *From the Studio to the Streets: Service Leaning in Planning and Architecture*. Washington, DC: American Association for Higher Education.

Harvey, David (2000) *Spaces of Hope*. Berkeley: University of California Press.

Hatch, C. Richard (ed.) (1984) The *Scope of Social Architecture*. New York: Van Nostrand Reinhold.

Hawthorne, Christopher (2003) *Slate Magazine*.

Hensel, M., A. Menges and M. Weinstock (eds) (2004) 'Emergence: Morphogenetic Design Strategies', *Architectural Design* 74(3).

—— (eds) (2006) 'Techniques and Technologies in Morphogenetic Design', *Architectural Design* 76(2).

Herbert, Gilbert (1978) *Pioneers of Prefabrication: The British Contribution in the Nineteenth Century*. Baltimore: Johns Hopkins University Press.

Hester, Randolph (2006) *Design for Ecological Democracy*. Cambridge, MA: MIT Press.

Hight, Christopher (2003) 'Portraying the Urban Landscape: Landscape in Architectural Criticism and Theory, 1960–Present', in M. Mostafavi and C. Najle (eds) *Landscape Urbanism: A Manual for Machinic Landscapes*. London: Architectural Association, 22–32.

—— (2008) *Architectural Principles in the Age of Cybernetics*. New York and London: Routledge.

Hight, C. and Perry, C. (eds) (2006a) 'Collective Intelligence', *Architectural Design* 76(5).

—— (eds) (2006b) 'The Manifold Potential of Bionetworks', *Perspecta* 38: 40–55.

Hubert, Christian (1981) *The Ruins of Representation*. www.christianhubert.com.

Ibelings, Hans (2002) *Supermodernism: Architecture in the Age of Globalization*. Rotterdam: NAi Publishers.

Isenstadt, Sandy and Kishwar Rizvi (eds) (2008) *Modernism and the Middle East: Architecture and Politics in the Twentieth Century.* Seattle: University of Washington Press.

Jacobs, Fredrika (2002) '(Dis)assembling: Marsyas, Michelangelo, and the Accademia del Disegno', in *The Art Bulletin* September 1.

Jameson, Fredric (2007) 'Globalization and Architecture', in Lee Sang and Ruth Baumeister Ruth (eds) *The Domestic and the Foreign in Architecture.* Rotterdam: 010 Publishers, 94–122.

Jenkins, Frank (1961) *Architect and Patron.* London: Oxford University Press.

Kelley, Tom (with J. Littman) (2001) *The Art of Innovation.* New York: Currency/Doubleday.

Kieran, Stephen and James Timberlake (2004) *Refabricating Architecture.* New York: McGraw Hill.

King, Anthony (1984) *The Bungalow: The Production of a Global Culture.* London: Routledge.

King, Jonathan and Philip Langdon (2002) *The CRS Team and the Business of Architecture.* College Station, Texas: A&M University Press.

Kittler, Fredrich (1999) *Discourse Networks: Film, Gramaphone, Typewriter.* Stanford: Stanford University Press.

Klein, Naomi (2007) *The Shock Doctrine.* New York: Metropolitan Books.

Knox, Paul L. and Peter J. Taylor (2005) 'Toward a Geography of the Globalization of Architecture Office Networks', *Journal of Architectural Education* 58(3): 23–32.

Kolarevic, Branko (ed.) (2003) *Architecture in the Digital Age: Design and Manufacturing.* New York: Taylor & Francis.

Koolhaas, Rem (1995) 'Generic City', in *SMLXL.* New York: Monacelli, 1238–1264.

Kostof, Spiro (ed.) (2000 [1977]) *The Architect.* Berkeley: University of California Press.

Kuhn, Thomas S. (1962) *The Structure of Scientific Revolutions.* Chicago: University of Chicago Press.

Kwinter, Sanford (1998) 'Leap in the Void: A New Organon?', in C. Davidson (ed.) *Anyhow.* Cambridge, MA: MIT Press, 22–27.

Lacan, Jacques (1981 [1973]) *The Four Fundamental Concepts of Psychoanalysis.* New York: Norton.

Larson, Magali Sarfatti (1977) *The Rise of Professionalism.* Berkeley: University of California Press.

—— (1993) *Behind the Postmodern Facade: Architectural Change in Late Twentieth-Century.* Berkeley: University of California Press.

Latour, Bruno (1992) *We Have Never Been Modern.* Cambridge, MA: Harvard University Press.

—— (2005) *Reassembling the Social.* Oxford: Oxford University Press.

Le Corbusier (1980) *Modulor I and II.* Translated by Peter de Francia and Anna Bostock. Cambridge, MA: Harvard University Press.

Leach, N. (2002) *Designing for a Digital World.* London: Academy.

—— (ed.) (2004) *Digital Tectonics.* London: Academy.

Lewis, Miles (1993) 'The Asian Trade in Portable Buildings', *Fabrications* 4(June): 31–55.

Lippard, Lucy (1973) *Six Years: The Dematerialization of the Art Object from 1966 to 1972.* New York: Praeger.

Lo Ricco, Gabriella and Micheli Silvia (2003) *Lo spettacolo dell'architettura. Profilo dell'archistar ©.* Turin: Bruno Mondadori.

Loomis, John A. (1999) *Revolution of Forms: Cuba's Forgotten Art Schools.* New York: Princeton Architectural Press.

Lynn, Greg (1998) *Folds, Bodies & Blobs: Collected Essays.* Bruxelles: La Lettre Volée.

—— (1999) *Animate Form.* New York: Princeton Architectural Press.

Martin, Reinhold (2006) 'Moment of Truth', *Log* 7 (Winter/Spring): 15–20.

Mascheroni, Loredana (2007) 'Outsourcing', *Domus* 900: 28–35.

Mays, Vernon (2007) 'The New Rural Studio', *Architect,* November 1.

McLeod, Mary (1980) 'Le Corbusier and Algiers', *Oppositions* 19/20(Winter/Spring): 56–71.

—— (1983) 'Architecture or Revolution: Taylorism, Technocracy and Social Change', *Art Journal* 43(2): 132–147.

—— (1989) 'Architecture and Politics within the Reagan Era: From Postmodernism to Deconstructivism', *Assemblage* 8: 23–61.

McNeill, Donald (2005) 'In search of the global architect: The case of Norman Foster (and Partners)', *International Journal of Urban and Regional Research* 29(3): 501–515.

Menges, Achim (2004) 'Morphoecologies', *AD: Emergence* 74(3).

—— (2006) 'Instrumental Geometry', in M. Hensel and A. Menges (eds) *AD: Techniques and Technologies in Morphogenetic Design* 76(2).

Miessen, Markus and Basar, Shumon (eds) (2006) *Did Someone Say Participate?* Cambridge, MA: MIT Press.

Mitchell, William J. (1999) 'A Tale of Two Cities: Architecture and the Digital Revolutions', *Science* 285(6): 839–841.

—— (2001) 'Roll Over Euclid: How Frank Gehry Designs and Builds', in J. Fiona Ragheb (ed.) *Frank Gehry, Architect.* New York: Guggenheim Museum, 352–362.

—— (2003) *Me++: The Cyborg Self and the Networked City.* Cambridge, MA: MIT Press.

Montgomery, Roger (1989) 'Architecture Invents New People', in *Architect's People.* New York: Oxford University Press, 260–281.

Moore, Steven (2001) 'Technology, Place, and the Nonmodern Thesis', *Journal of Architectural Education* 54(4): 130–139.

Moos, David (2003) 'Samuel Mockbee: The Architect as Painter', in David Moos and Gail Trechsel (eds) *Samuel Mockbee and the Rural Studio.* Birmingham, AL: Birmingham Museum of Art,13–19.

Moos, David and Gail Trechsel (eds) (2003) *Samuel Mockbee and the Rural Studio.* Birmingham, AL: Birmingham Museum of Art.

Morris, Mark (2006) *Models: Architecture and the Miniature.* London: Academy Press.

Muschamp, Herbert (1997) 'The Miracle in Bilbao', *The New York Times Magazine* Sept 6, 54–59, 72, 82.

National Council of Architectural Registration Boards (2008) *2008–2009 Rules of Conduct.* Washington, DC: NCARB.

Nield, Lawrence (2008) 'Predators and Faise Heroes and Heroines', contribution to the RAIA Convention, Sydney, Australia. Printed in an abridged format as 'False Idols', *Architectural Review Australia* 105.

Ockman, Joan and Salomon Frausto (eds) (2005) *Architourism: Authentic, Escapist, Exotic, Spectacular.* New York and London: Prestel Publishing.

Olds, Kris (1997) 'Globalizing Shanghai: The "Global Intelligence Corps" and the Building of Pudong', *Cities* 14(2): 109–123.

Pai, Hyungmin (2002) *The Portfolio and the Diagram.* Cambridge, MA: MIT Press.

Palleroni, Sergio (2004) *Studio at Large: Architecture in Service of Global Communities.* Seattle: University of Washington Press.

Paterson, John (1980) *Architecture and the Microprocessor.* Chichester: John Wiley.

Petrescu, Doina (2005) 'Losing Control, Keeping Design', in P. Blundel Jones, D. Petrescu and J. Till (eds) *Architecture & Participation.* London: Spon, 43–64.

Picon, Antoine (2010) *Digital Culture in Architecture.* Basel: Birkhauser.

Pogrebin, Robin (2007) 'Built to Last and Lasting', *New York Times* May 12.

Pollak, Linda (2002) 'Building City Landscape: Interdisciplinary Design Work in the Downsview Park Competition', in Julia Czerniak (ed.) *CASE: Downsview Park Toronto.* Munich: Prestel, 40–48.

Pottage, Alain (1996) 'Architectural Authorship: The Normative Ambitions of Le Corbusier's Modulor', *AA Files*, 31(Summer): 64–70.

Rabinow, Paul (1989) *French Modern – Norms and Forms of the Social Environment.* Cambridge, MA: MIT Press.

Rahim, Ali (ed.) (2000) *AD: Contemporary Processes in Architecture* 70(3).

—— (ed.) (2002) *AD: Contemporary Techniques in Architecture* 72(1).

—— (2006) *Catalytic Formations: Architecture and Digital Design.* London: Taylor & Francis.

Reeser, Amanda (2004) 'Complexity and Customization – the Porter House condominium: Sharples Holden Pasquarelli (SHoP)', *Praxis: Journal of Writing + Building* 6: 46–53.

Reiser, Jesse and Nanako Umemoto (2006) *Atlas of Novel Tectonics.* New York: Princeton Architectural Press.

Rheingold, Howard, interview with Jennifer Lee (2003) 'How the Protesters Mobilized', *New York Times,* February 23.

Richardson, T. and Connelly, S. (2005) 'Reinventing Public Participation: Planning in the Age of Consensus', in P. Blundel Jones, D. Petrescu and J. Till (eds) *Architecture & Participation.* London: Spon, 77–104.

Risselada, Max and Dirk Van der Heuvel (2006) *Team 10 – In Search of a Utopia of the Present 1953–1981.* Rotterdam: NAi Publishers.

Robbins, Bruce (1993) *Secular Vocations: Intellectuals, Professionalism, Culture.* New York: Verso.

—— (1996) 'Pathetic Substitutions', in William Saunders (ed.) *Reflections on Architectural Practices in the Nineties.* New York: Princeton Architectural Press, 176–185.

Robbins, Edward (1994) *Why Architects Draw.* Cambridge, MA: MIT Press.

Rosa, Joseph (1990) *Albert Frey, Architect.* New York: Rizzoli.

Rowe, Colin (1999 [1947]) 'The Mathematics of the Ideal Villa', in *The Mathematics of the Ideal Villa and Other Essays.* Cambridge, MA: MIT Press, 1–28.

Ruby, A. and Durandin, B. (eds) (2000) *Spoiled Climate.* Berlin: Birkhauser.

Ryan, Raymund (2004) 'Gehry's Great Concerto', *The Architectural Review* 215(March).

Saint, Andrew (1983) *The Image of the Architect.* New Haven: Yale University Press.

Saunders, William (ed.) (1996) *Reflections on Architectural Practices in the Nineties.* New York: Princeton Architectural Press.

—— (ed.) (2005) *Commodification and Spectacle in Architecture.* Minneapolis: University of Minnesota Press.

Schoenberg, Isaac Jacob (1946) 'Contributions to the Problem of Approximation of Equidistant Data by Analytic Functions', *Quarterly Applied Mathematics* 4.

Schon, Donald (1983) *The Reflective Practitioner.* New York: Basic Books.

Schumacher, Patrik (2002) 'Graphic Spaces: Aspects of the Work of Zaha Hadid', *IDEA – International Graphic Art* 293.

—— (2011) *The Autopoiesis of Architecture: A New Framework for Architecture.* London: Wiley.

Schuman, Anthony W. (2006) 'The Pedagogy of Engagement', in Mary C. Hardin (ed.) *From the Studio to the Streets: Service Leaning in Planning and Architecture.* Washington, DC: American Association for Higher Education.

Scott, James (1998) *Seeing Like a State.* New Haven: Yale University Press.

Seymour, Liz (2000) 'Samuel Mockbee: Reluctant Genius', *Architecture* 89(8): 27.

Sheldon, Dennis (2006) 'Tectonics, Economic and the Reconfiguration of Practice', *AD: Programming Cultures,* 76(4): 83–86.

Sklair, Leslie (2005) 'The Transnational Capitalist Class and Contemporary Architecture in Globalizing Cities', *International Journal of Urban and Regional Research* 29(3): 485–500.

Sokol, David (2008a) 'Learning By Example', *Architectural Record* (October): 120–126.

—— (2008b) 'Repositioning Practice: Teddy Cruz', *Architectural Record,* http://archrecord.construction.com/features/humanitarianDesign/0910cruz-2.asp, accessed on March 17, 2009.

Somol, R.E. and Sarah Whiting (2002) 'Notes Around the Doppler Effect and Other Moods of Modernism', *Perspecta* 33.

Sontag, Susan (1966) 'Notes on Camp', in *Against Interpretation.* New York: Farrar.

Sorkin, Michael (1992) 'See You in Disneyland', in *Variations on a Theme Park.* New York: Hill and Wang, 205–232.

Speaks, Michael (2002) 'Design Intelligence: Thinking in Architecture after Metaphysics', *AD: Versioning* 72(5).

Spuybroek, Lars (2004) *Nox: Machining Architecture.* London: Thames & Hudson.

Stevens, Garry (1998) *Favored Circle: The Social Foundations of Architectural Distinction.* Cambridge, MA: MIT Press.

Tafuri, Manfredo (1979) *Architecture and Utopia.* Cambridge, MA: MIT Press.

Terzidis, Kostas (2006) *Algorithmic Architecture.* London: Elsevier.

Tierney, Therese and Anthony Burke (2007) *Network Practices.* New York: Princeton Architectural Press.

Till, Jeremy (2005) 'The Negotiation of Hope', in P. Blundel Jones, D. Petrescu and J. Till (eds) *Architecture & Participation.* London: Spon, 23–42.

Toker, Zeynep (2007) 'Recent Trends in Community Design: The Eminence of Participation', *Design Studies* 28: 309–323.

Toker, Z. and Toker, U. (2006) 'Community Design in its Pragmatist Age: Increasing Popularity and Changing Outcomes,' *METU Journal of the Faculty of Architecture* 23(2): 155–166.

Tombesi, Paolo (2001) 'A True South for Design? The New International Division of Labour in architecture', *Architectural Research Quarterly* 5(2): 171–180.

—— (2003) 'Super Market: The Globalization of Architectural Production', *Harvard Design Magazine* 17: 26–31.

—— (2004) 'Architectural Feasts or Professional Fausts? A Double Perspective on the Bargains of Globalization', *Architecture Australia* 93(4): 48–50, 93(5): 60–61.

—— (2006) 'Capital Gains and Architectural Losses: The Transformative Journey of Caudill Rowlett Scott (1948–1994)', *Journal of Architecture* 11(2): 145–168.

Tombesi, Paolo, Dave Bharat and Peter Scriver (2003) 'Routine Production or Symbolic Analysis? India and the Globalisation of Architectural Services,' *Journal of Architecture* 8(1): 63–94.

Tombesi, Paolo, Blair Gardiner and Tony Mussen (2007) 'Pariahs or Enablers? The architecture of Design Outsourcing', in *Looking Ahead: Defining the Terms of a Sustainable Architectural Profession.* Manuka, ACT: The Royal Australian Institute of Architects, 36–48.

Van Vrijaldenhoven, Tim (2007) *Reaching Beyond Gold: The Impact of Global Events on Urban Development.* Rotterdam: 010 Publishers.

Vellinga, Marcel, Paul Oliver and Alexander Bridge (eds) (2007) *Atlas of Vernacular Architecture of the World.* London: Routledge.

Venturi, Robert (1966) *Complexity and Contradiction in Architecture.* New York: Museum of Modern Art.

Vidler, Anthony (2004) 'Architecture's Expanded Field', *Artforum* 42(8): 142–147.

Vitruvius (1960) *The Ten Books of Architecture.* Translated by M.H. Morgan. New York: Dover.

Ward, Anthony (1996) 'The Suppression of the Social in Design: Architecture as War', in Thomas A. Dutton and Lian Hurst Mann (eds) *Reconstructing Architecture* Minneapolis: University of Minnesota Press, 27–70.

Wharton, Annabel J. (2001) *Building the Cold War: Hilton International Hotels and Modern Architecture.* Chicago: University of Chicago Press.

Wigley, Mark (2001a) 'Paper, Scissors, Blur', in C. de Zegher and M. Wigley (eds) *The Activist Drawing.* Cambridge, MA: MIT Press.

—— (2001b) 'Network Fever', *Grey Room* 4: 82–122.

Williamson, Rosanne Kuter (1991) *American Architects and the Mechanics of Fame.* Austin: University of Texas Press.

Willis, D. and T. Woodward (2006) 'Diminishing Difficulty: Mass Customization and the Digital Production of Architecture', *Harvard Design Magazine* 23: 70–83.

Willis, Julie (2005) 'In Australia, Between America and Europe, Beaux Arts and Modernism, Scholarship and Qualification: the Melbourne University Architectural Atelier, 1919–1947', *Journal of Architectural Education* 58(3): 13–22.

Winch, Graham M., Denis Grèzes and Brid Carr (2002) 'Exporting Architectural Services: The English and French Experiences', *Journal of Architectural and Planning Research* 19(2): 165–175.

Woods, Mary (1999) *From Craft to Profession: The Practice of Architecture in Nineteenth-Century America.* Berkeley: University of California Press.

Wright, Gwendolyn (1991) *The Politics of Design in French Colonial Urbanism.* Chicago: The University of Chicago Press.

Zardini, Mirko (1997) 'From Team X to Team x – International Laboratory of Architecture and Urban Design', *Lotus International* 95: 76–97.

Zulaika, Joseba (2001) 'Tough Beauty: Bilbao as Ruin, Architecture, and Allegory', *Hispanic Issues,* 24: 1–17.

25
Flows

Stephen Cairns

MANAGING FLOW

The images on this page stand as twin provocations for this chapter. The first image (Figure 25.1 Above) is the work of graphic designer Paul Mijksenaar at Schiphol Airport, Amsterdam. The second (Figure 25.2 Below), by photographer Adam Ferguson, portrays a slum dwelling on the edges of Mumbai's International Airport.

Architecture's investment in the values of stability, groundedness and longevity, while conventional and by no means uniform, is a resilient disciplinary trait. It is an investment that has tended to marginalize those other mutable, ephemeral and fluid conditions that, by necessity, also constitute the medium of architecture. Dealing with fluctuations of air, sound and light, the fluidities of water, the entropic tendencies of matter and the movements of people are all part of architecture. Yet such knowledge has typically been consigned to either technical appendices or assorted marginal spaces of architectural scholarship. Sporadically, it finds metaphorical expression in the 'streamlined', 'folded'

The Mjiksenaar image is one part of a famous wayfinding system that stitches the sprawling buildings of Schiphol into a coherent experience for the millions of travellers who transit through the airport every year. We know from Manuel Castells and others, that the interior spaces of Schiphol are infact continuous – seamlessly so, some scholars would claim – with those of the Mumbai Airport. Yet the slum dweller, however geographically proximate to this space of flows, might as well be on the other side of the earth. These two images provoked me to undertake a journey that might experience something of that space of flows, and the spaces of the slum beyond.

I book my flights through the 'One World' airline network, and am promised seamless inter-continental air travel. I redeem some frequent flier points to cover the booking, and discover that this method of payment is constraining for anything more than the simplest flights. A trip from Edinburgh to Mumbai via Schiphol, for instance, will require intermediate legs to Heathrow and Helsinki.

Edinburgh Airport, Friday 18:00 (Figures 25.3 Below and 25.4 Below right)

Depart Edinburgh. It is cold and wet as the taxi collects me from Princes Street. The beginning of a northerly wind has brought a cold snap, and snowy weather is predicted in the city. The airport is dense with travellers, most of whom seem to be business travellers returning to London for the weekend. I am with a group of experience travellers. Most unpack their laptops, empty their pockets, remove their shoes and belts routinely without being asked. I am offered a curious premonition of my destination by the Indian Head Massage booth that occupies an area opposite the duty free stores.

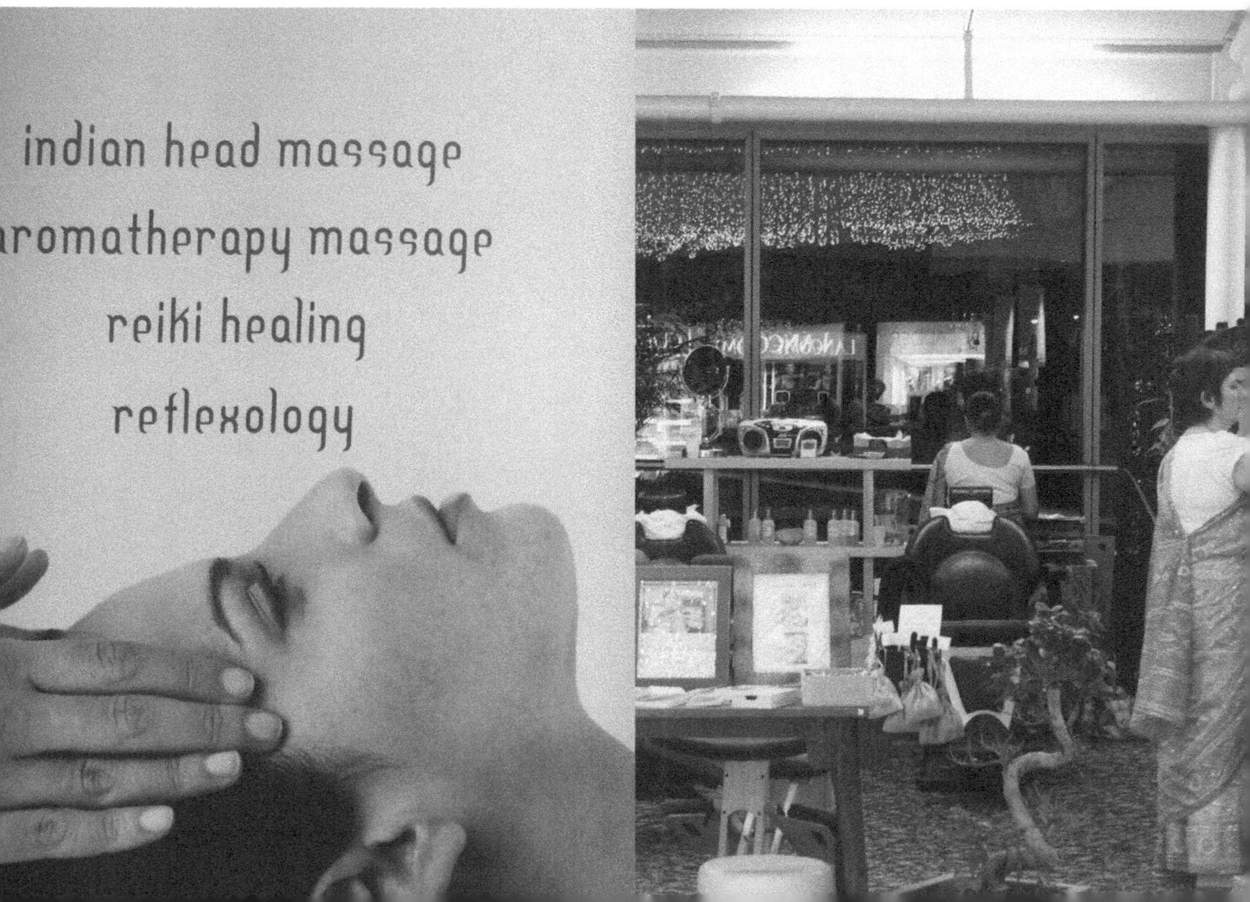

and otherwise 'flowing' architectures of the avant-garde. So, while architecture has always necessarily engaged with flows, historically the focus of its theory and disciplinary self-image has been the stationary.

Privileging statics over flux makes for difficulties in the context of what Manuel Castells famously dubbed the 'space of flows'. His concept of the space of flows describes the increasingly dominant, deterritorializing effects of globalization: transnational flows of people (migrants, tourists, business elites), things, ideas, capital and information. Furthermore, this is a world in which substantial (materialized) flows are supplemented, intensified and often overtaken by virtual flows. How might architecture actively and authentically engage with this shifting condition? Should architecture present itself reactively, say as a material bulwark against the flows of globalization, doggedly asserting the situatedness of place? Should it invest in experiments that seek to articulate flows in a formal language? Or could architecture somehow dissolve these remnants of an architecture-of-stability, in order to reconstitute itself as an architecture *of* flows?

Castells' own analysis is symptomatic of the difficulties that the spatial logic of globalization presents for architecture. He locates architecture prominently but ambiguously in relation to flows. In a rather familiar move, he calls upon architectural styles as evidence of the homogenizing and dislocating effects of the space of flows. But he also sees architecture as a necessary point of *resistance* to the effects of 'social hyperspace', offering 'bridges' between disembedded flows and embedded places (Castells 2009 [1996], 458–459). This resistance work can happen in two key ways. One is borne of an architecture that reactively 'root[s] itself into places, thus into culture'. The other derives from how architecture articulates

'the palaces of the new masters [of flow]'. Castells argues that when architects give form to the abstract notion of spaces of flow (be they transnational flows of people, information or things) their buildings necessarily expose the 'deformity' hidden behind the 'abstraction'. In other words, a materialized architecture works to demystify an otherwise largely virtual (perhaps even invisible) flow. Castells concludes that through this bridging work, architecture may be 'digging trenches of resistance for the preservation of meaning in the generation of knowledge' (Castells 2009 [1996], 453).

I would like to linger on this ambiguous status of architecture in Castells' analysis in order to tease out the wider consequence of considering the role of architecture in the context of a space of flows. I want to locate this discussion in the experience of a significant architectural site of the networked space of flows, namely the airport.

ARCHITECTURE OF NUDITY

For Castells, it is 'airports, train stations, intermodal transfer areas, telecommunication infrastructures, harbors, and computerized trading centers', and other such 'communication exchangers' (Castells 2009 [1996], 453) that are the significant building types of the space of flows. Stylistically for Castells, the most meaningful architecture in the space of flows is what he calls 'the architecture of nudity'.

Castells saw Ricardo Bofill's extension of Barcelona Airport for the 1992 Olympic Games as encapsulating this point. The building, he says, 'simply combines beautiful marble floor, dark glass façade, and transparent glass separating panels in an immense, open space [...]. No cover up of the fear and anxiety that people experience in an airport. No carpeting, no cozy rooms, no indirect lighting. In the middle of the cold beauty of this airport passengers have to face their

London Heathrow Airport, Saturday 08:30 (Figures 25.5 Below left, 25.6 Right, and 25.7 Below)

Depart Heathrow. The transfer from the hotel is smooth and I am deposited at a bus stop some five floors below the departures area. The lift to that level rises through a spectacular slot space between the vast car park and the Terminal 5 building. The density of these buildings and the closeness of their relationship is one consequence of the long planning process that saw Richard Rogers' relatively expansive, low-rise design gradually compress itself into a more compact three-dimensional box. The many lifts, stairs and escalators in the building service a building that has been pressed back by the fabric of the city around it. The departure hall is the upper-most floor, and here the giant engineered capitals to the columns that support the arches spanning the full width of the building are dramatically revealed. The architecture and engineering is elaborate and impressive. I check in at one of the blue electronic booths that float free of their traditional location attached to the baggage handling infrastructure

terrible truth: they are alone in the middle of the space of flows, they may lose their connection, they are suspended in the emptiness of transition. They are, literally, in the hands of Iberia Airlines. There is no escape' (Castells 2009 [1996], 450–451).

The architects' drawing that Castells chooses to illustrate his discussion shows the airport concourse space to be appropriately stark, empty and silent, and supports his idea that architecture must, in some way, critically reveal the disorienting realities of the space of flows. But we know that airport spaces are never like this. They are thick with sub-architectural paraphernalia such as check-in desks and booths, baggage trolleys, seating, security cordons, barriers, vending machines. They are dense with signage (visual and aural) that set out instructions, protocols, regulations, and injunctions about where to be, with whom, with what baggage and when. They are rich with visual and atmospheric effects that, while withheld by the official signage, are delivered emphatically by advertising material. Finally, airport spaces are populated by people – waiting,

Amsterdam Schiphol Airport, Saturday 11:45 (Figures 25.8 Below and 25.9 Below right)

Arrive Schiphol late due to weather conditions in London, and just miss my connecting flight to Helsinki as a consequence. I reschedule the flight for later in the day and rearrange a planned interview with Kees Christiaanse, the Supervising Architect at the airport. Christiaanse develops and works to a masterplan framed by the 'one-terminal concept' inherited from Duintjer, De Weger and NACO (1961–1967), original architects of the terminal. He negotiated this new role with the airport management company, broadening the original remit from that of aesthetic arbiter and appointer of architects, to overall urban design and masterplanning. This remit now incorporates issues such as the relationship of the airport to its immediate hinterlands and to Amsterdam, and its role as a major European transportation

and (increasingly) shopping, entertainment and business hub. Christiaanse also selects architects for internal spaces of the airport buildings, and is charged with maintaining the overall quality of the airport spaces. To this end, he works with a range of design consultants such as Benthem Crouwel Architects, Paul Mijksenaar, who is responsible for the wayfinding and signage, and landscape architects West 8, who are responsible for the public spaces in and around the airport. Each of these consultants have 'life-time commissions' to work more-or-less continuously on maintaining the quality of the airport and keeping it integrated into the space of flows.

For Christiaanse this is a matter of developing Schiphol as an 'airport city' and regional shopping and entertainment centre. The Schiphol Plaza building is a clear demonstration of this, linking as it does to the local, regional and international train system below ground, and to car parks, business centres, shopping malls and hotels above. With aviation functions barely sustainable economically, airports the world over must diversify to remain profitable.

This generates a 'booming market in ideas' that Christiaanse must assess, adjudicate and integrate into the wider urban logic of the complex. Ideas for new integrated business, valet and check-in car parking facilities compete with those for a dog hotel for airport employees and travellers and new themed restaurant and bar facilities within the terminal buildings. Each initiative is assessed for its capacity to smooth the transitions from one form of transportation to another, to generate income, and to keep Schiphol competitive amongst other European hubs.

As Schiphol aims to be the lowest carbon-emission airport in the world, the management of air traffic and terrestrial flows is a complex business.

lounging, rushing, shopping, queuing, stressing – who are almost always wheeling, lugging, dragging or otherwise manoeuvering coats, bags, suitcases and other travel

Helsinki Vantaa Airport, Saturday 23:05 (Figures 25.10 Left, 25.11 Below and 25.12 Below right)

Arrive Helsinki now a full eight hours late and have missed my long-departed flight to Mumbai. The forecast storm, which I experienced the beginnings of in Edinburgh has now caught up with me and Helsinki is enveloped. I arrange for alternate flights and an unplanned overnight stay in Helsinki. My luggage, however, has proceeded without me and is assumed to be in Mumbai by now.

I am issued with an emergency overnight bag and vouchers for a meal and a bus to a hotel. Imagining that I would be spending most of my time in Mumbai, and in the air-conditioned comfort of terminal buildings and aircraft cabins, I find myself underdressed for the Helsinki blizzard. Feeling very exposed, I make my way to the bus and then to the hotel.

The hotel internet connection is expensive and slow. Accompanied only by global news channels and local soap operas, there is little to do other than wait. The following morning the storm has not abated. The advice from the airport is that all flights remain on schedule. Disbelieving, I board the shuttle bus back to the airport. When I arrive, it is clear that the airport terminal is strained. Large crowds of people have checked in and now wait for news of their flights. Queues grow longer and the list of delayed or cancelled flights light up red on the computer screens. I finally depart some six hours late in the knowledge that my planned interviews in Mumbai have been missed.

equipment. The silence of the airport is cacophonous, its nudity is clothed, its emptiness saturated and its disorientations actively compensated for.

While it may be that Bofill's responsibility as architect stopped at the (glass, marble, concrete) inner surfaces of the building envelope, it cannot be imagined that the work of architecture and design ended there too. In fact, building complexes such as airports have become lucrative sites for a myriad of design specialists called on to manage how they are occupied and used. Airports are typically retrofitted by interior designers, industrial designers, furniture designers, graphic designers, advertising creatives, as well as marketing, space branding and wayfinding consultants. Castells' account of Bofill's airport, and its focus on the building envelope, accepts architecture's privileging of the stable aspects of buildings too readily. He can only do this because he ignores the mechanics and choreographics of people and things as they move within the envelope and through the carefully monitored openings that puncture it, as much as he does the thick plenum of the envelope itself within which is

usually suspended the plumbing, ducting, wiring and other conduits that facilitate the material flows of the building.

In short, Castells' interpretation of architecture in the space of flows offers yet another version of a familiar architecture of stability. How might we think differently about architecture in the space of flows?

CIRCULATION

In architectural discourse, the movement of people and more-or-less material substances such as air and water have been largely thought about through the concept of 'circulation'. That conceptualization says much about the tensions I have been discussing thus far. In teasing out the relatively recent history of this concept, architectural historian Adrian Forty shows that circulation, as an architectural concept is a mid-nineteenth century metaphorical borrowing from physiology. Forty identifies an early use of the term 'circulation' by French critic Cesar Daly

Mumbai Chhatrapati Shivaji International Airport, Tuesday 12:45 (Figures 25.13 Below and 25.14 Below right)

Arrive in Mumbai with barely time to clear customs and reboard my return flight to Heathrow. My unusually short stay in Mumbai draws attention to me from officials, and I am asked to wait in a curious interval space still under construction between air- and land-side. I am accompanied only by two labourers who are tiling the walls of what will be a departure lounge. They are as curious of me as I am of them. They work and text on their mobile phones intermittently. I ask them to pose for a photograph, which they are happy to do in exchange for what euros I have remaining in my pocket. (Figures 25.1–25.14 Stephen Cairns, except 25.2 Adam Ferguson, and 25.13 Armeet Panesar).

in his 1857 review of the Reform Club building in London: 'This building [...] is no inert mass of stone, brick and iron; it is almost a living body with its own nervous and cardiovascular circulation systems' (Daly cited in Forty 2004, 89). Then, in 1871, Charles Garnier, architect of the Paris Opéra, develops the aesthetic possibilities of the concept when he writes that the stair 'is one of the most important arrangements in theatres because it is indispensable to the ease of arranging the exits and the circulation, but more because it produces an artistic motif' (Garnier cited in Forty 2004, 90). A little later still, architectural historian Paul Frankl further enriches the concept. He conceives of circulation in terms of a 'great flood of movement that urges us round and through the building' (Frankl cited in Forty 2004, 91), suggesting that architectural spaces are thick with a motile dynamic of their own.

Forty notes that the early formulations of the concept of (human or other) circulation assumes self-contained systems of movement distinct from the building fabric itself (Forty 2004, 90). Furthermore, these early notions of circulation suggest that such systems, while conceptually distinct, are expected to be incorporated, usually invisibly, within the building fabric. Wiring, ducts and pipes are embedded in walls, suspended above ceilings or buried below floors. While stairs, foyers, vestibules, corridors, and hallways – however formal or loosely configured in plan – disguise their overt capacities to direct bodies through a building by inclining, predisposing, prompting, inducing, and tempting bodies kinesthetically. Circulation might have been conceptualized in architecture as a system, but it was intended to be experienced tacitly.

Such early formulations suggest that mobility, fluidity and flows are carefully managed to fit within, and not seriously challenge, those higher order architectural obligations to produce stability, fixedness and containment. This sense is affirmed

when we look more carefully at the metaphorical borrowing itself. Circulation refers to the movement of a 'single fixed volume of fluid travelling around the body' that 'always returned to the same point, the heart' (Forty 2004, 93). By applying the term to architecture, the building was portrayed as a 'bounded and self-contained' entity, a 'self-sufficient', 'sealed system, without orifices' (Forty 2004, 93). The concept of circulation was, arguably, attractive to architectural discourse precisely because it delivered the dynamics of flux and fluidity in a particular, domesticated, form that affirmed the values of stability.

This nascent concept of circulation, once established in architectural vocabulary, was quickly elaborated in the subsequent history of architectural theory. The idea featured in the training manuals of the Beaux-Arts education system, where, by 1902, a chapter was dedicated to 'circulation' as an independent element in architectural composition (Forty 2004, 93). Circulation was integrated with looser concepts such as *enfilade* and *marche*, both of which refer to the sequencing of spaces so as to encourage an experience of movement through them (Van Zanten 1977, 162). Circulation also came to be viewed scientifically by way of the powerful photographic techniques for mapping and calibrating the working body associated with time-and-motion. Such studies supported the development of Taylorist and Fordist industrial production techniques as well as offering new techniques for developing 'scientific management', and 'frictionless living' in the home. The broader interest in scientific management was taken up in modernist architecture by a diverse group of architects, writers and theorists – Gropius, Le Corbusier, Ruskin, Giedion and Sant'Elia – who engaged with the theme from different ideological perspectives (Guillén 2006; see also Pai 2002).

Circulation, as management technique and aesthetic effect, is a central operative concept in contemporary architecture, and often the site of design innovation. For example, a number of avant-garde architectural experimentations have elaborated the original nineteenth-century formulation in interesting, often spectacular, ways. Well-known projects of this kind include Frank Lloyd Wright's Guggenheim Museum in Manhattan (1959), Renzo Piano and Richard Rogers (1976) Beaubourg Centre in Paris, and Rem Koolhaas' Netherlands Embassy in Berlin (2003), all of which 'wrap' a key component of the circulation system around the exterior face of the building for different figurative effects. Other projects, such as UN Studio's Mercedes-Benz Museum (2006), or their earlier Mobius House (1998), intensify the experience of internal spaces through experiments with looping and corkscrew circulatory arrangements (see Kim 2006 for a survey of related contemporary examples). Yet, for all this innovation, the old formulation of circulation remains doggedly in place. We can see this persistence even in projects that actively claim to produce architectures of flow. For example, Zaha Hadid's BMW Plant building (2005) incorporates an open terraced plan that encourages occupants to 'spill through the building and flow into the adjacent buildings' (Hadid cited in Hadid and Gannon 2006, 20). But, as critic Todd Gannon suggests, the 'real achievement of the building' lay in the way it 'marshaled into alignment' all of the services needed to facilitate such bodily flows. So effective was this marshalling, the aesthetic and experience of flow was not 'clamored for by sprinkler pipes, HVAC, signage, and all those workaday elements that undermine so many buildings' (Hadid and Gannon 2006, 22). The effect of a smooth architecture of (people) flow is produced by burying other necessary but stylistically misaligned technologies of flow.

Other projects have had the scope to experiment more aggressively with the conceptual legacy of circulation. James Stirling's Staatsgalerie in Stuttgart (1983) interwove the internal circulation system of the gallery with a public route through the building, enabling a more complex knitting of the building into the surrounding urban fabric. And the design for Foreign Office Architects' Yokohama Port Terminal (2002) was famously 'generated from a circulation diagram' that drew different publics into and through the building (Frerre et al. 2003, 11). This involved marshalling the various temporalities of the different publics, from the general public lingering in the public parks on the building's roofscape, to the traveling public clearing immigration and customs and waiting to depart, to short-term visitors collecting or dropping travellers off, to those that work in the building itself. Both the Yokohama Port Terminal and Staatsgalerie projects are useful departure points for an alternative, architectural *politics* of flows.

POLITICS OF FLOWS

Architecture's insistence on conceiving movement in terms of circulation, and all that this concept connotes, has not escaped the attention of other design-related disciplines. Graphic designer and wayfinding consultant, Edo Smitshuijzen warns the readers of his *Signage Design Manual* (2007) that architects 'are renowned for their ambivalent attitude towards signage'. They 'perceive signage as an assault on the aesthetics of their creation and as an insult to the self-evidence of their spatial design. A lot of them carry an almost sacred but entirely unfounded belief in the functionality of their "wordless" buildings' (Smitshuijzen 2007, 20). This critique from outside the discipline is telling and provocative (see also Smitshuijzen 2007, 29; 62).

In the context of airport spaces, the interdisciplinary relationship that Smitshuijzen broaches is not only unavoidable but also necessary. Airport terminals are well-known instances of flat-horizontal envelope buildings. Indeed most of the buildings that Castells identifies as significant architectural nodes in the space of flows, are of this type. As Alejandro Zaera Polo (one of the Yokohama Port Terminal's architects) notes, the horizontal extent of such building types is substantially greater than their vertical reach. Too expansive to be comprehensible in the horizontal plane by any individual viewer, these buildings are only comprehensible in their entirety from the air. The vast bulk of their interior spaces, being distributed horizontally in the main, are located at some distance from the building envelope and so are not legible in the form or external appearance of the building. They could be considered to be, as Rem Koolhaas memorably put it, 'lobotomized' spaces (Koolhaas 1994 [1978], 296). As a consequence, flat-horizontal buildings are 'less concerned with representation and figural performance than with the organization of material flows: traffic, ventilation, daylight, security'. They are inevitably 'experienced in a fragmented manner' (Zaera Polo 2008, 82). Zaera Polo suggests that with the emergence of such building types we need a new 'politics of the envelope' in which the 'faciality' or, the public expression of the building, is thought anew. But is this concern with how the envelope of an architecture of flows addresses a public, formally or semiotically, enough to constitute an architectural politics of flows? The pressing architectural question that such buildings pose is, surely, less to do with the expressive logic of their external envelopes, than with the communicativity of their vast, distended internal worlds, and how these worlds connect with the often residualized spaces of the exterior. A politics of flows would inspect the foundational assumptions of the circulation concept in architecture and challenge the ongoing consequences of the interiority that are written into that concept. It would examine ways in which such internalized interpretations of flow allow architecture to be complicit not only with the positive features of a space of flows, but also its negative consequences (including new regimes of securitization, conservative reactionism, social polarization, environmental irresponsibility). In other words, I am suggesting that an architecture of flows should move well beyond the roles Castells gives it (reactive expressions of local cultures or demystifying materializations of flows), but also beyond interiorized architectural experimentations constrained by the concept of circulation.

For architecture to engage effectively with the spaces of flows a politics of flows is required. This politics would recognize the relational nature of architecture: how an architectural articulation is constituted out of flows, not simply giving expression to flow. This might mean readjusting architecture's relationship to other design disciplines such as wayfinding and logistics that have already embraced the seemingly vast, hollow spaces of flow. It might mean engaging with other disciplines who deal with mapping and navigating the relational ebbs and flows of the world. It will mean moving beyond the interiority of circulation and engaging with a more open set of metaphors (we might think, say, of respiration or ecology). It should mean a more active engagement with, and ethics of responsibility towards, the great outside of what currently stands for an architecture of flow.

BIBLIOGRAPHY

Castells, Manuel (2009 [1996]) *The Rise of the Network Society, With a New Preface: Volume I: The Information Age: Economy, Society, and Culture.* London: John Wiley and Sons.

Forty, Adrian (2004) *Words and Buildings: A Vocabulary of Modern Architecture.* London: Thames & Hudson.

Frerre, Albert, Tomoko Sakamoto et al. (eds) (2003) *The Yokohama Project: Foreign Office Architects.* Barcelona: Actar.

Guillén, Mauro F. (2006) *The Taylorized Beauty of the Mechanical: Scientific Management and the Rise of Modernist Architecture.* Princeton: Princeton University Press.

Hadid, Zaha and Todd Gannon (2006) *Zaha Hadid: BMW Central Building, Leipzig, Germany.* New York: Princeton Architectural Press.

Kim, Jong-Jin (ed.) (2006) *Activity Diagrams.* Seoul: DAMDI.

Koolhaas, Rem (1994 [1978]) *Delirious New York.* New York: Monacelli Press.

Pai, Hyungmin (2002) *The Portfolio and the Diagram: Architecture, Discourse, and Modernity in America.* Cambridge, MA: MIT Press.

Smitshuijzen, Edo (2007) *Signage Design Manual.* Baden: Lars Müller.

Van Zanten, David (1977) 'Architectural Composition at the Ecole des Beaux-Arts: From Charles Percier to Charles Garnier', in Arthur Drexler (ed.) *The Architecture of the Ecole des Beaux-Arts.* New York: Museum of Modern Art.

Zaera Polo, Alejandro (2008). 'The Politics of the Envelope: A Political Critique of Materialism', *Volume* 17: 76–105.

SECTION 6

Science/Technology/Virtuality

26

Introduction: Technology, Science and Virtuality

Arie Graafland (section editor) and Heidi Sohn (assistant editor)

> The enormous subtlety and the wealth of ineffable nuances involved in human self-presentation originate in the subtlety and richness of the physical world, in low-level processes of biochemical self-organization. These utterly subject-free, but self-stabilizing processes constantly modulate the internal information flow underlying the conscious self-model. It is interesting to note how all current technological attempts at creating truly embodied artificial agents, for example, in robotics, are many orders of granularity away from the *truly* bottom-up solution Mother Nature long ago found on its way to physically realized subjectivity (Metzinger 2003, 291–292).

INTRODUCTION

In 1993 the US government installed its National Science and Technology Council (NSTC), an organ whose main aim is the regulation and coordination of policy on science and technology in the United States. The NSTC claims that a 'revolution' is taking place in the scientific and technological domains: based at the nanoscale, it announces, physics, chemistry, biology, materials science and engineering converge towards the same principles and tools. This view is echoed on the other side of the Atlantic where the Netherlands Bioinformatics Centre (NBIC), characterized by its transnational approaches to science, transfers abstract knowledge developed by mathematicians into applied data, devolved into many different domains. Jean Pierre Dupuy sharply observes that the 'champions' of the NBIC oppose fate itself. By promising immortality, they challenge the very fact that we are born (Dupuy 2000). This is, according to him, a metaphysical programme to place mankind in the position of divine maker of the world. There are apparent threats in these views, as it is evident that what they propose is more than a theoretical matter alone. There seems to be an entire programme to act upon nature and humankind implicit in these perspectives. Very much on these lines, the European Commission issued a report titled *Foresighting the New Technology Wave* (Nordmann 2004) in which it clearly distances itself from the US agenda of improving human performance, as this signals threats to culture and tradition, to human integrity and autonomy.

The different views and perspectives on the impact of an epistemological revolution in science and technology have initiated a heated debate that will reach its watershed in the near future. Are we, as some would like to believe, merely at the moment when our conventional understandings of technology – namely situated as being opposed to organically defined categories such as life, the body and nature – are theoretically shifting, or have the interpenetration and symbiosis of technology and society, of machine and body, produced more than theorizations alone, and have they already reached the practical and material levels? If we consider the possible influence that organizations such as the NSTC or the NBIC may exert on material reality and human life it becomes clear why it is imperative to acknowledge the new theoretical challenges and questions that are brought to the fore in these debates. The implications that accompany transformations in the understanding and practice of contemporary science and technology range from important issues concerning the notion of ethics, to the role of human agency and, ultimately, the influence of discourse formation on human subjectivity, society and the human body. The discursive turn that is taking place heralds a problematic development in our understanding of the human species proper. It heralds the coming-of-age of a convoluted construct: the posthuman. These issues, although pertaining to a higher realm of inquiry, nevertheless are fundamental to architecture. Subject to the same epistemological transformations, architectural knowledge and architectural discourse face a maelstrom of inner changes with the onset of digital technologies. These have revolutionized more than the working methods of architecture, including its projective powers and its design practices, and other aspects of the practical-constructive discipline of building. The technological innovations have deeply influenced contemporary architectural discourse, impregnating it with its new 'problematique'. In recent architectural discourse, there are several strands of theorizations that have addressed this development from a diversity of perspectives, which nevertheless remain limited in scope.

In this section we are primarily concerned with the conceptual and theoretical implications of the technological and scientific 'revolution' on society, culture, subjectivity, and ultimately the human body, since it is in their mutations and hybridizations that we see the imminent danger for architectural discourse. We argue, on the one hand, that an architectural narrative that merges with science, technology and virtuality unleashes a process that may result in its 'disembodiment'. Hence, it is crucial to propose architectural discourses that focus on a narrative exclusively as 'a narrative of technology, science and virtuality', and not on its artificial components. Narrative, as we will elaborate as a prelude to other important notions put forward in the chapters of this section, has the potential to resist abstraction and disembodiment. This introduction prepares and sets the groundwork of contemporary theoretical and epistemological elaborations on science, technology and virtuality, and their impact on society and the body, which the following chapters will address more concretely for architectural discourses. We believe that the formulations brought to the fore in this section ultimately should lead to the very necessary discussions and considerations of the implications that these changes will have on humans proper. Notions of 'converging technologies' – the improvement of human performance through human-computer convergence in nanoscale sciences – are still to be explored in architectural theory and practice.

NEW CONCEPTUAL FIELDS

A common understanding of modernity centres on the belief that human progress should be measured and evaluated solely in terms of the domination of nature, instead of focusing on the transformation of the relationships between 'humans' and 'nature'.

The relationship between humans and nature, however, has without a doubt undergone dramatic changes, boundary dissolutions and definitional mutations – at least in contemporary discourse – rendering the general notions of 'nature' and 'society' obsolete. Donna Haraway, Bruno Latour and Katherine Hayles, among others, have shown in a rather convincing way how, in their obsolescence, 'society' and 'nature' are concepts that are no longer equipped to address their referents. Society and nature have undergone important transformations. Hence, it is becoming paramount to find new definitions and understandings of 'society' and 'nature'.

Latour's research into the practices of the sciences has led him to a redefinition of the concepts of nature, society and technology. His 'sociology of science' aims at dismantling and discharging both the concepts of nature and society. John Urry echoes Latour in his claim that a new, broader concept of 'society' is required, one that approximates what he refers to as 'massively powerful empires' roaming the globe, mass mobility of peoples and objects, and the production and circulation of dangerous human waste (Urry 2000, 13; see also Hardt and Negri 2000). Not unlike Latour, he claims that our experience is given by enduring and increasingly intimate relationships between objects and subjects, rendering the human and physical worlds as elaborately intertwined and inseparable from each other. Hence, the conventional distinctions, or separations, between society and nature or between humans and objects are no longer operative or meaningful.

What is relevant about these theories is that they manage to convey the formation of new conceptual fields. Conceptual fields evolve similarly to material culture, in part because concept and artefact engage each other in continuous feedback loops. Culture circulates through science no less than science circulates through culture. An illustrative example of this is Katherine Hayles' reformulation of chaos theory as both the subject of scientific inquiry and the crossroads where various paths within culture converge. In her understanding, chaos theory, like meteorology, epidemiology, irreversible thermodynamics and nonlinear dynamics, in addition to pertaining to scientific discourse, also serves the function of describing and understanding complex behaviours, defeating the conventional methods of formalizing a system through mathematics. Furthermore, chaos theory may be articulated within developments in the human sciences and postmodern culture, particularly in literature (Hayles 2005). This interpretation extends to the sciences and its domains, encompassing all its subjects and objects, methods and definitions, rebutting the common belief that scientists, for instance, are individuals in white robes, hermetically sealed and isolated within the laboratory, immune to the thousands of experiences that constitute the fabric of everyday life (Hayles 1991; see also Law and Mol 2002).

It is vital to see how language intersects in this. Haraway shows how the multiple languages within the territory of biomedicine concerning the immune system form elaborate icons for principal systems of symbolic and material 'difference' prototypical of the advanced capitalist logic of the 1980s. In this reading the immune system turns into a map drawn with the purpose of guiding recognition and misrecognition of self and other in the dialectics of Western biopolitics (Haraway 1991, 204). Thus, the immune system becomes a historically specific terrain, upon which many diverting forces and elements interact. From global and local politics, military strategic theory, to cutting-edge scientific research subject to awards and prizes; from 'heteroglossic' cultural productions (such as popular dietary practices, feminist science fiction, religious imagery and children's games), to representational techniques and clinical medical practice; from venture capital investment strategies, world-changing developments in business and technology, to the deepest personal and collective experiences of embodiment, vulnerability, power and mortality; the immune system is both an iconic mythic object in high-technology culture and a subject of research and clinical practice. Myth, laboratory and clinic are intimately interwoven (1991, 205). If, as Hayles claims, postmodernism entails a process of denaturalization occurring at multiple sites within culture, then Haraway's description of the immune system as a pastiche of multiple centres and peripheries can be nothing else than a postmodern object: symbolically, technically and politically.

In the light of what appears to be a new conceptual field characterized by its instability and mobility, by its flexibility and propensity to change, the position of architecture within it opens up interesting avenues of inquiry and interpretation. Antoine Picon, in his essay published in *Architecture and the Sciences* (2003), addressed the question of the growing number of images and metaphors from mathematics, physics and molecular biology that have spread among architectural discourse. A large number of these images are related to the growing importance of the virtual dimension in contemporary architecture, as will be elaborated further on. Picon's central question is whether this propensity in architectural discourse is a mere rhetorical figure, or 'habit', or if it is dictated by more profound motives. The use of scientific images and metaphors in architecture is not a recent phenomenon. Picon lists a series of central concepts that originated in different historical settings: the notion of 'structure', for instance, developed from biology and the study of living beings during the nineteenth century. On the other hand, science has also made use of architectural notions throughout its history. Referring to Nelson Goodman, Picon argues that architecture, like science, is about how we make and conceive worlds populated with subjects and objects, where definitions are always historically determined. Architecture and the sciences develop along parallel lines, often meeting in their common attempt to shape categories of visual perception. And in doing so, they construct the notion of subjects and society.

Not surprisingly, contemporary architectural discourse is presently developing a pattern that borrows from a typically postmodern discourse derived from biosciences. In their recent essay 'Upright or Flexible?', William Braham and Paul Emmons advance a comparable discourse within architecture: the image of health as the fortress of hygiene capable of repelling invasions of disease germs that was established in the early twentieth century has been replaced by the picture of an immune system that learns and adapts, and which is weakened or strengthened by other environmental factors. The immune system here is an analogy to a new architecture, which stands in as a microcosm of the larger ecology that it resembles. Relating to seminal texts by Mumford and Giedion, they argue that aspects of changing subjectivity may be demonstrated through building: 'If our bodies are increasingly conceived as dynamic interconnected systems, so too will our buildings be imagined and admired as flexible systems' (Braham and Emmons 2002, 292). They expound the narrative shift from 'upright', quintessentially modern designs to 'flexible', postmodern interpretations by contrasting a type of architecture that is intimately related to the human body: the gymnasium and the fitness centre.

John Russell Pope's 1932 Payne Whitney's Gymnasium built for Yale University was originally designed as an all-male school. Women were only allowed onto the first floor; the rest of the building remained exclusive for male users. Paradigmatic of an 'upright' design, the Payne Whitney Gymnasium resembles its contemporary, the Downtown Athletic Club (DAC) in New York, as interpreted by Rem Koolhaas in his *Delirious New York* (1994 [1978]). Despite the fact that the former example reveals a closer interpretation of a Foucauldian cut, namely through bodily mechanics and discipline, and the latter more of notions of male pleasure, Koolhaas's interpretation of the DAC nevertheless evokes many telling parallels between these two buildings, especially as they influence the role and the shifting understandings of the human body.[1] The logic of corporeal functions within these gymnasiums and clubs – much in line with modernist ideas of hygiene – enhanced the significance of the male body, and underscored the interplay between the structure in spatial and organizational terms of the building and the transformations this produced upon the bodies of its users. Not too far-fetched then, to interpret both these structures as machines, as 'bachelor-machines', in which their specific constructions and designs were intimately related to the idea that these were capable of sequentially, systematically enhancing and perfecting the male body. The body is the focus for a mechanism, which processes sex-specific elements into intensities that attract, exclude or distort each other (Graafland 1996). The social division of the sexes is the breeding ground for the production of circulation, connection and exclusion, producing a quasi-autonomous architectural regime only visible in the inside of the building. According to Koolhaas, notably, the architecture of the DAC – its structure, composition and materialization – plays no role whatsoever. The only interesting or relevant aspects are its processual character, its modes of connection, its pragmatic aspects as social condenser. Literally lifting the bachelor from the 'inferior human breed', easing his development and ascendancy, the Payne Whitney and the DAC also facilitate this ascendance and thrust the bachelor into taking his first steps to becoming posthuman.

The character or attitude embodied in these examples necessarily returns us to Braham and Emmons's formulation of the 'upright' versus the 'flexible'. To explain this they use the example of the Bally Total Fitness chain of gyms that proliferated in the late 1990s. Designed as a set of recognizable components and themes, such as display windows and full-sized mirrors on the exercise floors, or as the loosely horizontal circulation of workout sequences – or circuits – the Bally Total Fitness chain embodies a contemporary 'business practice' characterized by its total flexibility. But it also expresses something quite peculiar about the conceptions of the human body. If we trace the analogy between the total flexibility that lies at the heart of the concept for the Bally fitness centres, the business climate and contemporary digitalized architectures, we can observe a piecemeal disappearance of the evocations of explicit bodily concepts of the 1930s, to be replaced by the notion of a body that, immersed in a discourse of flexibility, has turned into 'disembodied computational information'.

The leap from an 'upright architecture', whose aim was the generation of superior bachelors – early 'upright posthumans' – to a 'flexible' architecture that produces disembodied information, is not a straightforward one. To comprehend the development into the current notion of the posthuman in architecture it is necessary to rethink and to redefine commonly accepted concepts of virtuality, technology, materiality and the human, as there seem to be interesting relationships between science and architecture implicit in this. Similarly to architecture, science is permeated by the virtual in that it is reducible neither to a set of theoretical results, nor to a collection of experimental data. Science appears as the productive tension between theory and experiment and between abstract knowledge and practice. Hence, and as will be explained in what follows, the virtual dimension operates in both architecture and the sciences.

In Chapter 28, 'Technology, Virtuality, Materiality', Antoine Picon will argue that the emerging contemporary subject may be suggested by the partly imaginary figure of the cyborg that presupposes a link between the human and technology so intimate that it leads to their 'hybridization'. Crucial in this is the notion of virtuality. This is not a simple notion, which has, however, been adopted into architectural discourse since the onset of digital technologies in the working environment of the discipline.[2] It is wise to remain within the confines of a quite specific approach to virtuality and its terminology to avoid overlapping connotations. Virtuality is intimately related to a capacity to 'act'; it is a 'potential' awaiting its full actualization, not unlike the bachelor ascending the DAC whose peak condition eventually will develop into the posthuman. Virtual reality is by no means unreal, quite the opposite; yet its full effects are latent, that is, they are not yet fully visible or evident. The virtual in this light is not far removed in discourse from architecture. Elsewhere, Picon has shown how the virtual has been key in those concepts where the notions of project and design have played a formative role. Accordingly, design, order, proportion, ornament, structure and space are all 'potencies' of architecture (Picon 2003).

In Chapter 27, 'Virtual Architecture, Digital Media', Hayles and Gannon will explain that virtuality currently has two central clusters of meaning: one deriving from virtual reality (VR) technologies, the other from the Deleuzian philosophical concept of the virtual as that which is in dynamic tension with the actual in expectancy of its actualization. Following this cluster, Hayles and Gannon also posit architecture as an emergent property of buildings; as the element that lends meaning to a building within an ongoing tradition. In the same way that buildings hold the promise of architecture, documents that surround buildings are equally bound to produce architecture. They have the potential of 'becoming-architecture'. Both the virtual in architecture, and the physicality of these documents, are 'real' in the Deleuzian sense.

It is not difficult to understand why architecture is not a stable construct: it appears through a series of productive tensions or potentials. Picon argues that we live in a seamless technological universe where categories borrowed from landscape theory and history might give us a better understanding of our current condition due to the gradual transitions that are characteristic, and no longer structure or system analogies. Conceptual shifts that took place during the development of cybernetics, for instance, display patterns reminiscent of material changes in artefacts. An artefact materially expresses the concept it embodies but the process of its construction is far from passive, as Hayles and Gannon show.

Contemporary virtual reality may be traced to the Cold War period, when a new phenomenological space was emerging that could be visualized exclusively through the use of screens, maps, diagrams and probabilistic theories of prediction. This period constitutes 'the nucleus of the cybernetic movement' (Dupuy 2000, 44), when it became obvious that the central problems were related to fixing or visualizing a moving target.[3] New visualizations were required and their emergence heralded the destabilization of form, an important issue in contemporary design. Until that period, architectural form was considered the ultimate result of a process of research. Its beauty was the beauty that only an end product could entail, built or unbuilt. Aided or even generated by contemporary computer technologies, digital architectural form can no longer aspire, pretend or achieve this status (Picon 2003, 303). Digital architecture remains the result of an arbitrary stop in a potentially endless process of transformation. And with this process, the human body has changed dramatically from a modernist bodily image to an informational bodiless videogram.

In architecture, many key buildings today are marked by a striking discrepancy between architectural form and tectonics. There is a distance between the initial digital presentation and the constructive reality of many buildings. According to Picon, the development of digital culture and the widespread interest in materiality pose new questions on the relationship between tectonics and the emergence and development of architecture. The tectonic dimensions of buildings as a meta-linguistic phenomenon are related to time, history and memory. But as Picon points out, it is a matter that goes beyond the question of whether we are at the end of tectonics or its rebirth. The question of its relation to memory still needs to be raised.

'THIRD NATURE', TECHNOLOGY AND SOCIETY

In the light of such intense changes in the meaning of architecture, and in line with what Timothy Luke claims, namely that we need another reasoning to capture our present world, it seems almost unavoidable to rethink not only the conceptual underpinnings of terms such as architecture and society, but also, and especially, the very relationships between them. This will revert to questions of what constitutes the categories of the real and the virtual, for instance, and underline the necessity of establishing another, new epistemic notion better suited to approximate contemporary reality. As concepts, architecture, the real and the virtual play a crucial role in the understanding of a 'third Nature', as this pertains to digitalized work processes and digital architectures and, more specifically, their relation to nature and society (Luke 1999). To better grasp the significance and urgency of Luke's formulations of a 'third Nature', it is wise to briefly summarize its preceding but always present two stages, namely 'first Nature', or 'terrestriality', and 'second Nature', or 'territoriality'. 'First Nature' gains its identity from the different terrains forming the bioscape/ecoscape/geoscape of 'terrestriality'. Earth, water and sky provide the basic elements mapped in physical geographies of the biosphere that in turn influence human life with natural forces. These geographies play a direct influence on notions of body and mind. The human brain and the rest of the body constitute an indissociable organism by mutual biochemical and neural regulatory circuits (Damasio 2005, xxi). The organism interacts with the environment as an ensemble. This is to say that the body is far more than a support system: it provides a basic topic for brain representation.

'Second Nature' finds its expression in the technoscape/socioscape of 'territoriality'. The actions of people, cities, economies and states constitute these spaces of territoriality. The epistemological foundations of conventional reasoning in terms of political realism are grounded in the modernist laws of 'second Nature' (Luke 1999).

In taking up the Western philosophical notions of 'first' and 'second Nature', Luke defines 'third Nature' as the informational cybersphere/telesphere, in a way similar to Picon's seamless technological universe, which he qualifies as a topography punctuated by quasi-object terminals. Here, digitalization becomes a primary concern, since it shifts human agency and structure from manufactured matter to a register of informational bits. Human presence is located in the interplay of the first two modes of nature's influence: terrestriality and territoriality. On the other hand, 'third Nature' posits itself well beyond the feasible realm of human consciousness, located more in spheres involving temporality, over and against the 'scapes' implicit in the spatiality of terrestrial and territorial models.

Both architecture and urbanism are directly involved in this new information environment as a 'third Nature' in digitalized work processes and digital architectures and in their relation to first and second Nature. An important effect of it is what Urry calls the 'collage effect': a phenomenon in which the 'event' has become more important than the 'location'.[4] Urry's formulation departs from a critique against media, and centres on the argument that the juxtaposition of stories reveals that most of them share nothing in common except for their newsworthy character (Urry 2000, 127). Urry's 'collage effect' can be made operative in architecture, where the effect of digital media quite literally effaces the notions of space and place, dissolving them into neutral data of locations while simultaneously reducing all forms of embodiment to digital data and event. Arguably, 'telemetricality' has replaced the older aesthetic parameters and the notions of beauty and the sublime in architecture. The growing volatility and ephemerality implicit in telemetricality have supplanted the unique building (as concept) transforming it into a 'series'. This series of possible solutions in rapid prototyping is necessarily the product of an arbitrary stop in the process. But it is the 'final' design that is the end of the prototyping process. This brings to the fore the notion of meaning. As an event, architectural form is supposed to find its ultimate justification in what it can achieve. In referring to Lars Spuybroek's D-Tower, Picon argues that the tower in itself is meaningless. What it does is merely perform: it has neither meaning nor function.

An interesting association might also be established between Luke's 'third Nature' as informational 'spheres' (as opposed to 'scapes') and John Urry's conception of 'instantaneous time' (2000, 126). Instantaneous time is related to the new information and communication technologies based on inconceivably brief instants beyond human consciousness. Codes can be sent over fibre optics instantaneously. There is no longer a shared, stable context that helps to anchor meaning and guide information (Hayles 1999, 47). In contrast to the fixity of print, decoding implies that there are no original texts, no first editions or fair copies. Something similar seems to be occurring in contemporary architectural design, where physicality and body are currently also data or codes to be translated into computer programs. The very notion of 'embodiment' and 'urbanity' in first and second Nature as social construct, as a set of complex social and biochemical relations, is fading away in recent digital design due to the seemingly endless possibilities of digital design techniques.

What seems to be needed then is a new form of 'seeing'. Hayles advances the adoption of a double vision that focuses simultaneously at the power of simulation and at the materialities that produce it, a perspective that corresponds in a certain way to Pesic's notion of 'seeing double' (Pesic 2003). In this, one way of thinking about materialities is through functionality, which according to Hayles may be exemplified with rather inconspicuous applications, such as data gloves or voice activated commands, as the well-known Blur Building of Diller + Scofidio shows. Despite being a clear spatial example, it is nevertheless dependent on computer sensors to locate a given body position. In that sense, it is purely instrumental, and not comparable to social, sensory or political notions of space and urbanity as advocated by Henri Lefebvre or David Harvey.

Arguably the contemporary 'right to the city' might be partially fought out over the web, but political force will need embodiment deployed on the ground, on the streets, rather than on digital highways. Information, like humanity, cannot exist apart from the embodiment that brings it into being as a material entity in the world (Hayles 1999, 49). Embodiment is always instantiated, local, and specific (1999, 196–197). And as such, it encompasses a broad spectrum of problematic relationships and forces that have to converge at some point in order to form coherent directionalities for action. As Harvey points out, there is a witches' brew of political and environmental arguments, concepts and difficulties surrounding these questions that can conveniently become the basis for an endless academic, intellectual, theoretical or philosophical debate (Harvey 2000, 215). No satisfactory solutions will be reached from this debate unless adequate ways of translation between different languages or, even more ideally, some sort of common language is found. This would also entail the establishment of a 'common ground' as Scott Lash advocates. David Harvey refers to 'the web of life' metaphor, something that might indeed be useful in filtering our actions through the web of interconnections that form the living world. This idea, at least in its intentions, comes close to Latour's notions of 'actant-network-theory', or ANT. Harvey, however, operates on a Marxist level, not comparable in any way to Latour's sociology.

The loss of urbanity and body, as well as the fading of social, biochemical and neural regulatory circuits as parameters for architecture and urbanism, is of course of no small significance. It brings questions of action and agency to the fore: how are we to understand our own actions in relation to our organism, nature and society? And how could this translate into possible architectural and urban solutions?

Architecture and urbanism directly deal with the consequences of the shift to our present information age, or post-industrial society. The great advantages promised by these models have necessarily been accompanied by dire problems in most of the larger Western cities, both in Europe and the United States. Contradiction and conflict are the by-products of increased freedom in both choice and mobility; and the connection between the increase in crime and social disorder to the information age is too obvious to disregard. With the arrival and consolidation of the so-called 'new technologies' in the spatial disciplines – architecture and urbanism in particular – we too will have to consider what Fukuyama refers to as the 'great disruption', or the negative trends in society intimately associated with the transition into the information society (Fukuyama, 1999).

The great disruption produced in the transit to a new form of society given entirely to the coding and decoding of information evidences the urgent need to analyse more than the informational techniques alone, but also the effects that these produce on contemporary society. Beyond the concerns of how this disruption may speed up the decline of Western societies, or even of how it has determined the tendency to restore norms, as Fukuyama claims, the transition to an information society renders the very concept of 'society' as problematic for architectural theory. Questions about whether it is feasible – or even necessary – to devise a whole new theory for contemporary architecture are unavoidable today. To be able to rethink architectural theory, however, we need to be willing to rethink the very concepts of technology, science, economy and society itself. On the other hand, notions of action and agency require a revaluation in order to arrive at a different conception of how society, technology and science are interrelated.

In this, the concept of 'action' in relation to Luke's three Natures is key, in spite of its inherent complications. 'Action' should not be understood as an 'act' under the full control of consciousness, but rather as a node, a knot or a conglomerate of many unexpected sets of agencies that have to slowly be disentangled (Latour 2005, 44). Some of the complications of this model are evidenced in the difficulty, if not impossibility, of determining where these systems begin or end, where in these complex systems solutions to environmental and ecological problems may be found, and what kind of agreements will be possible to ameliorate architectural and urban problems. But perhaps most importantly, this demands a complete rethinking of the meaning of agency. The ideas that agency, desire and will belong to the self, and that 'self-will' is clearly and unambiguously distinguished from the will of others, have to be relinquished. In the dissolution of agency as determined by 'self-will', in fact in the redefinition of freedom, we see the posthuman emerge in discourse.

The posthuman is in this regard not necessarily or completely unfree: 'there is no a priori way to identify a self-will that can be clearly distinguished from an other-will' (Hayles 1999, 4). Extending this to society as a whole may also be possible. Collaboration and cooperation in everyday life may be misleading on the level of society since, as Harvey claims, the socio-biological argument that cooperation is, in a sense, an adaptive form of competition also applies to society at large. The apparently dichotomous characteristics of individualism versus collectivism are in fact intimately linked to one another in clearly evolutionary terms. The difficulty in this is that individualism and collectivism render the competitive moment also as the shaping instance of everything else, and use adaptation to absorb collaboration within a competitive framework (in biology) (Harvey 1996, 190). A similar idea is advocated in Fukuyama's work as well. Quoting Richard Alexander, he claims that 'human beings cooperate to compete' (Fukuyama 1999, 175). The origins of cooperation start with kinship; altruism exists in proportion to the degree of relatedness (1999, 169). Culture itself, as the ability to transmit behavioural rules across generations in a non-genetic way, is hardwired into the human brain, and constitutes a major source of evolutionary advantage for the human species (1999, 158).

All the same, it is impossible to conceive of a convincing individualization without first establishing some sort of community as a ground. No ontology is even remotely possible without a ground, without the ground of praxis as 'situated intersubjectivity' (Lash 1999). In that sense, culture and social praxis exert an important influence on the 'groundedness' of community, as is the case with very small groups, and to a greater extent also in specific regions where religion plays a crucial role (Fukuyama 1995).

But larger groups require norms and social rules to function. Harvey considers competition, adaptation, collaboration and cooperation, as well as environmental transformations, as relational social categories rather than mutually exclusive ones. As relational figures, these categories are able to retain their relative autonomy. In the social world, the human capacity of 'self-realization' is socially and economically related to values and to intersubjectivity. The distinction occurs on the level where norms and social capital interact, and especially in the ways that these survive under contemporary capitalist rules. Harvey regards the effects as negative, of course, while Fukuyama, on the other hand, depicts capitalism as capable of creating new norms, breaking apart traditional loyalties, generating new ones and, more generally, creating order. That this 'net creator' of norms is also a moralizing force in society comes as no surprise.

So far, the importance of subjectivity has been traced in its collective aspects to 'intersubjectivity'. There is, however, another issue in this that should not be left unaddressed. The cybernetic aspect of the posthuman that we began to sketch earlier is not necessarily related to interventions in or alterations to the human body. As Hayles argues, even biologically unaltered homo sapiens will count as posthuman. Arguably, the posthuman is all about the construction of subjectivity, or 'human self-presentation' (Metzinger 2003, 292). And in that sense, the posthuman becomes paramount to the disentanglement of one of the main concerns of this text, namely in the posing – or rather proposing – of architectural discourse as a narrative about technology, science and virtuality, and not about its artificial components.

The recourse to memory taps heavily into the very potencies of narrative itself, particularly in its resistance to various forms of abstraction and disembodiment. Narrative as a second order reflection or meta-linguistic phenomenon permits a more embodied form of discourse than any form of analytically driven systems theory as it is conventionally used in contemporary digital architecture. This issue is crucial. What seems to be occurring to contemporary architectural discourse as a narrative about science, technology and virtuality is in fact a process that may result in its disembodiment. Secondly, the discourse on and around the meaning of the 'social' – in the sense of memory and history in the contemporary world – poses new questions for architecture as a built, non-human object.

THE [SOCIAL] BODY AND THE NARRATIVE OF THE SENSES

In order to concretize the role of the body, Urry develops a more detailed examination of the sensuous constitution and a renewed exploration of human sensuous practices, more in line with Marx's critique of the *First Thesis on Feuerbach* (Urry 2000, 78ff.). He also relates how some of the most extraordinary insights of the natural sciences during the twentieth century were incorporated into the social sciences and the humanities, often to their detriment. In *Justice, Nature and the Geography of Difference* (1996), David Harvey addresses similar questions.

Hayles' work on cybernetics is especially informative. According to her, the first wave of cybernetics unleashed by Norbert Wiener held a complex and uncomfortable relation to the liberal subject. Wiener was committed to creating a cybernetics that would preserve autonomy and individuality (Hayles 1999, 140). The second wave of cybernetics, as endorsed by Humberto Maturana, follows the liberal tradition of cybernetics, like Wiener, in that it values the autonomous individual rather highly. But it regards the perception of the observer as determinant in the construction of reality rather than in its passive perception. This construction depends largely on positionality and not on personality. If the world is tied to the observer, it becomes urgent to ask how to maintain boundaries interacting and to what purpose, while maintaining connection to a world which robustly continues to exist regardless of our thoughts about it (1999, 147). Einstein already showed that there is no absolute time independent of the system it refers to. Time and space are not separate from each other. Relatively little social science, however, has incorporated these materials into theory or research (Urry 2000, 121). Urry shows how the social sciences have employed incorrect models of how time is conceived within the natural sciences as a way of arguing for a 'reconfigured sociology' capable of overcoming the division between the physical and social worlds. In this respect, Urry's discourse on the senses is of special significance for architectural discourse. In it he deals with the primacy, or 'hegemony', of the visual over other senses, a hegemony that is also predominant in current architectural discourse and digital practices. According to him, reconfigured sociology should be able to mobilize powerful theory and trigger relevant, solid research in a 'post-societal', 'post-gardening epoch'. It should be a sociology more appropriate to 'game keeping' than to 'gardening', mainly because game keeping is inherently tied to flux, to rapidly changing patterns of habitation and transport, and so on; in short, a sociology appropriate to flexible accumulation. And this is precisely the underlying concept of the Bally Total Fitness chains, where real flexibility lies in the interchangeability of its stores or branches. Failing stores can be closed for the greater good of the chain; new ones can be opened on new sites.

But beyond these examples of flexibility, there is a more serious problem accompanying the arrival and rapid development of so-called new digital technologies in a architectural practice. The conceptualization of and the relation to Luke's 'first Nature' and 'second Nature' has either been lost completely or dealt with in a rather superficial method of data collection. The main discussion here is about the conceptual reduction of first, second and third Nature into one abstract, autonomous data based concept. This reduction is often embodied in the pseudo-architectural concepts or insubstantial datascapes used by Dutch architectural practices such as MVRDV, UN Studio, NOX and ONL. This is indeed related to 'the idealization of architecture as autonomous form' (Braham and Emmons 2002, 302), namely the efforts of the profession to define and protect some independent class of work. Digital architectures, as the Eleventh International Architecture Exhibition in Venice (2008) showed, are indeed 'Out There'. They have moved beyond any notion of first and second Nature. Architecture has become an object of desire, no different from Damien Hirst's art forms. 'Context', that contested concept in sociology, is not a field of influence as many contemporary architectural studios might see it, but instead should be a key element in our efforts to formulate an urban and architectural theory in a post-societal condition.

The question of how to construct a slower, more stable, less volatile and more grounded theory capable of dealing with our senses forcefully leads to our addressing eligible terms in a revisited description and analysis of the very relationship between 'man and nature'. If contemporary biology is about recognition and misrecognition, of coding errors, of the body's reading practices, and of multimillion dollar projects to sequence the human genome, as Haraway suggests, it is then imperative to find and devise what Hayles and Gannon see as 'narratives and concepts' that might work for contemporary ideas in architecture and urban society.

In biomedicine, these narrative transformations translate into a body that ceases to be a stable spatial map of normalized functions. Instead, it emerges as a highly mobile and unstable field of strategic differences. The body in architectural digital design techniques and image reproduction resembles this concept. It seems futile to oppose the slow 'ecological' body equipped with senses to a volatile diagrammatic figure rendered in computational techniques in architecture, by simply 'replacing' its sensory functions. Both figures might rely on impermeable boundaries, which still leave the simple form of rationalist models of cognition intact, as Haraway shows. Here, Winograd and Flores' critique of the rationalist paradigm of embodied – or 'structure determined' – perceptual and linguistic systems and, significantly, of computer design is useful (Winograd and Flores 1986). They argue that the existence of an objective reality composed of things bearing properties and engaging in constant relationships is simply taken for granted in many of these models. A cognitive being gathers information about things, building a mental model with little regard to its phenomenal reality, which can easily become the main concern of the scientist, or the architect for that matter. Knowledge in that sense becomes a storehouse of (architectural) representations that may be called upon to reason and that may be translated into language or design. Thinking in that way is a process of manipulating those same representations into language or form: Italian rationalism created architecture from abstracted visual phenomenal reality, while advanced digital design creates possibilities from software, simultaneously abstracting from the complexities of what we tend to call 'social reality'. If we are to take the relation between physics, the body and the social seriously, then the status of the model will change.[5]

A significant amount of architectural thinking is still advancing along these storehouse lines, with the result that (aesthetic) experience transmits on a permeable level of subjective experience. This does not only imply that one theoretical term is 'better' than another, as for instance Haraway illustrates in her listing of two historical moments in biomedical representation of bodies from the late nineteenth century and the 1980s, but also that many terms or concepts in science and technology are less innocent than they seem initially. Language is never a true follower of intention. Hayles argues that there is an impressive body of work exploring how metaphors, narrative patterns, rhetorical structures, syntax and semantic fields affect scientific discourses and thought.[6] Human history can be read from language, since it gives individuals the opportunity to push back frontiers. It is never a passive instrument; it is an active engagement with a vital medium that has its own currents, resistances, subversions, enablings, pathways and blockages. But in this there are dangers. The body, for instance, might get entangled in a disembodied web of codes and abstractions that cause injury to its sensory and emotional capacities (Graafland 2000, 95). This makes the study of how rational choices are pervaded by emotions more important than ever before. In this regard, a reference to the work of neurophysiologist Antonio Damasio is revealing. His study focuses on patients with brain damage (specifically to the ventromedial part of the prefrontal cortex) and demonstrates how these patients can talk rationally about their effects on other people while remaining totally disconnected from them (Damasio 2005, 209). The brain creates numerous somatic markers: feelings of emotional attraction or repulsion that help the brain to calculate by short-circuiting many of the possible choices that lie before it (2005, 173; see also Fukuyama 1999, 183). But when a thought process reaches a somatic marker it stops calculating and makes the decision. Our brain uses somatic markers for rational decision-making.[7] Norms and intersubjectivity have an extremely powerful emotional hold on humans. Individuals who calculate their self-interest with absolutely cool rationality are considered abnormal and even psychopaths (Damasio 2005, 178). In other words, in our daily life the process of rational choice is pervaded by the emotions, and not only as a source of preferences.

The theorization of human subjectivity and bodily experience in the computer age has yet to begin in architectural discourse. The desire to imitate and extend the calculating and intellectual faculties of the mind has always been present. Despite the fact that the wilder fantasies of the past have been dispersed, today it is still much more feasible to construct machines that are capable of high intellectual performance than to find an automaton capable of expressing ordinary, tangible corporeal sensations like hunger, sorrow or fear in any real way. Hence, our scepticism towards the successors of cybernetics such as Artificial Life (AL) and Artificial Intelligence (AI) in which consciousness is considered the 'late comer' in evolution. Without wishing to discuss this last item at length at this point, what seems dubious is the possibility for us to generate a world in which 'humans and intelligent machines can both feel at home' (Hayles 1999, 239). The computational universe that spreads out before us today might quite literally be nothing more than a 'cybernetic dream' (1999, 239). Enmeshed in lethargy or slumber, our attention might be distracted from the real problems and concerns of our contemporary world. Hayles stresses something similar: the computational universe turns dangerous when it stops being a useful heuristic device and transforms into an ideology that privileges information over everything else as in many digital architectures (1999, 244). Furthermore, information is a socially constructed concept; it is nonsensical to think that just because information has lost its body, humans and the world have lost theirs too. Elaine Scarry's research on language and torture, as will be explained further on, is an illuminating example of the opposite. The penetration of literary criticism into the theories of architecture in the 1980s in deconstructivism, as in Eisenman and Derrida, even notions of 'criticality' and 'autonomy' of a Marxist signature as in Michael Hays and 'post-criticality' with a 'project oriented' signature as in Speaks, Somol and Whiting, all have notoriously neglected the role of bodily argument.

Hayles argues that feelings constitute a window through which the mind looks into the body. If, as she writes, 'feelings and emotions are the body murmuring to the mind', then feelings are 'just as cognitive as other precepts' (1999, 245; see also Damasio 2005, 159).[8] Along these same lines, we find Beaune's reference to Cohen's book on human robots illuminating: '... we cannot now foresee how a future computer could be programmed to blush in suitable embarrassing circumstances, since blushing seems a singularly human phenomenon when we feel exposed' (Beaune 1989, 469). It is, for instance, inconceivable to think or imagine a future robot committing suicide, since suicide implies a foreknowledge of death and some idea of its significance. This is a privilege of human beings (1989, 470).

It may be worthwhile to return to Urry's discourse on the senses. But in order to formulate this it is necessary to conceive of a more developed theory and history of sensuousness. On the one hand, this form of theory is bound to a notion of parataxis and its accompanying structure in theory and criticism. On the other hand, it calls out for a critique of what Hayles refers to as the 'postmodern orthodoxy', which considers the body as a primarily, if not entirely, linguistic and discursive construction, resting on the belief that its materiality is secondary to the logical or semiotic structure it encodes (Hayles 1999, 192). Following on from this, Dupuy constructs a relation between French structuralism and cybernetics; both search for subjectless cognition – cognition without mental content. The unconscious henceforth could be identified with a cybernetic automaton. 'The alliance of psychoanalysis and cybernetics was neither anecdotal nor fortuitous: it corresponded to a radicalization of the critique of metaphysical humanism' (Dupuy 2000, 19). Despite the fact that Louis Althusser indeed developed a 'cybernetic' attitude to a subjectless social structure, namely ideology functioning like a 'cybernetic automaton' (Dupuy 2000, 19), his philosophy places materiality as secondary to the logical structure it encodes. Althusser's epistemological *coupure*, which he constructs out of Marx's early and later writings, is in line with Dupuy's encounter between cybernetics and structuralism. Eileen Scarry refers to this phenomenon by highlighting the discrepancy in the tone of Marx's writing when he acknowledges the body's presence in the elementary sites of artifice, such as raw materials, tools and material objects. The tone becomes more political in more sophisticated sites such as money, capital, the circulation of capital, etc. When Marx moves beyond what she calls 'cellular self renewal' to more compelling forms of self artifice like language, material objects, moral and political consciousness, it continues to be the actual living body itself that is altered (Scarry 1985, 252). It is this notion of body alteration that disappears into Althusser's transformation of ideology as the 'science of man'.[9] What is lost is Damasio's discovery that the body provides a ground reference for the mind (Damasio 2005, 223).

If we were to re-establish an analogy with the sublime in architecture theory, away from the autonomous data-based concepts of digital architectures – to bring back Picon's 'potencies' of architecture – then Scarry's investigations might be of enormous assistance. In them we find a notion of the sublime that can no longer be considered as a Kantian aesthetic experience in which fear and terror are vanquished by the ethical. Scarry's sublime is informed by her studies on the documents compiled by Amnesty International in relation to torture. Her sublime literally encompasses the speechless and irrational terror that emanates from bodily torture. The 'murmuring' of the body is here literally obliterated. Instead, physical pain gains a special status over the mental, the somatic, as well as other forms of perceptual phenomena. Pain is the only sensation that can never be answered or experienced outside of our selves. No external object can ever relate to physical pain in the same way as the body – our body – does. And despite the fact that the experience of physical pain pertains to other human sensorial registers such as desire, hunger, touch, sight and hearing, it differs from all other physical and mental sensations because it has no object beyond or outside our bodies. The lack of an object, and hence the absence of a referential context, makes it almost impossible to express pain in language. This, we believe, overruns the contents of Metzinger's 'self-model of the body'. Humans are subject to an integrated 'mélange of bodily sensations', which encompass '... a host of different types of self-presentational content, like visceral sensations; feelings of hunger, pain, or thirst; proprioceptive and kinaesthetic formats; tactile and temperature sensations; and vestibular information, which are continuously integrated into a supramodal, conscious body image' (Metzinger 2003, 301). We are never in contact with our own body. As an embodied, conscious entity, we are the contents of an image. But this image is a dynamic image in constant flux. Phenomenal experience of immediacy is a graded feature. Thoughts are something that may not even be determined in their full content before being spoken out loud, or actually written down, whereas bodily sensations like pain or thirst are directly given as explicit and 'ready made' elements of the phenomenal self in a much stronger sense.

But beyond 'normal' life, it becomes evident that the conditions of torture that Scarry describes leave little room for Metzinger's integration or 'mélange' of bodily sensations. The supramodal body image shrinks and dissolves into a dominating, speechless experience. Physical pain is not only resistant to language, but it also actively destroys language, deconstructing it into a 'pre-language' of cries and groans (Scarry 1985, 172). To hear those cries is also to witness the shattering of language; it heralds the total disintegration of Metzinger's conscious experience of 'mineness'. Pain and imagination are each other's missing intentional antithesis. They are more than mere opposites. Pain and imagination are above all mutually exclusive: the existence of one requires the elimination of the other. Together, however, they generate the framework of our identities as creative beings, and within them all other intimate perceptual, mental, emotional and somatic sensations. In this way Scarry opens a direction that might lead to Damasio's two-way bridge between neurology and humanities, and to finding out what the brain does during aesthetic experiences (Damasio 2005, xiv). Revealingly, in many languages the term that comes closest to 'pain' is 'work'. As such, 'work' and 'pain' refer to a 'created' object, something that associates it not only with physical pain but also with pleasure, art, architecture, imagination and civilization; in short, to all that which expresses the creative power of man.

CONCLUSIONS

If, after surveying the implications of our new technologies and the computational and informational universes they unlock on our bodies, on our material realities and on our cognitive spheres, we were to reach any form of concluding remarks, we would be forced to phrase these as a sort of warning. Digital technologies and computerization are changing the very notion of 'tool' or 'technology', as Elizabeth Grosz and Katherine Hayles tirelessly remind us, and therefore require a certain degree of precaution. Architectural design will only become more reliant and dependent on these new digital technologies, and this will have the result that our understandings of technology, nature and body will necessarily have to shift to adapt to them.

Contemporary discourses on dematerialization will inevitably change our conceptions of both the body as a material substrate and the 'message'. Information technologies create 'flickering signifiers' – a term that Hayles relates to Lacan's 'floating signifiers',[10] which are characterized by their tendency toward unexpected metamorphoses, attenuations and dispersions (Hayles 1999, 29–30). This, however, does not imply that computational or digital virtual reality is fundamentally different from the virtual reality of writing, drawing or even thinking. The virtual is simultaneously the space of the new, the unthought and the unrealized. And it is precisely here that the real challenge for architecture begins: the 'new' in architecture is certainly not limited to digital techniques as the term in 'digital architecture' suggests, just as the cybernetic aspect of the posthuman is not necessarily related to interventions or alterations to the human body. In architecture, the virtual is present in all its forms, from its processes to its practices, from its concepts and projects to its expressions and representations. The virtual is an integral part of architecture. Nevertheless, and in spite of the fact that these are rarely acknowledged in contemporary architectural theory, there are real and important limitations to this: the capacity of simulations to approach the sensory and the corporeal is still impossible today. If we consider that these corporeal limits and sensory capacities have always been, and continue to be, a vital engine for architecture, it seems far too easy and unjustified to simply ignore them in order to advocate a 'new', digitalized architecture more in tune with other logics than that of our own 'slow' but socially constructed and physically subject-free realized materiality.

To confine architecture to its technologies is to reduce its practice and theorization to a simplified discourse that can only address self-reflexive subjects, bodiless holograms and empty simulations. To the best of our knowledge, this is – if not entirely wrong – nonsense. Discourses that attempt to de-materialize their subject matters are bound to fail in their inability to address the complexities of materialities and bodies: two essential elements of architecture at large. For contemporary architecture, and especially for architectural theory, dematerialization is, if anything, partial, reductive or limited. If architectural theory is at a crossroads, where revisions and redirections are required for its sustained development, it forcefully needs to take the limited scope and application of contemporary discourse into account and be prepared to fully engage the complexities of our present reality.

NOTES

1 A description of the DAC is revealing: its thirty-eight floors were linked to a node of thirteen lifts located on the northern side of the building. The verticality produced by thirty-eight floors allowed people to think of the DAC as a hierarchically arranged set of levels or logics. So the lowest floors were also where the most conventional exercises took place: squash courts, a handball alley, billiard tables, etc. These facilities enabled a rather simple task, namely that of keeping the body fit. The subsequent levels equal the stages in the transformational process of the body: the more intense the workout, the better trained the body and the better trained the body, the higher the athlete ascended within the building. Following this logic it is on the higher levels or floors that a more special territory is revealed, not dedicated to physical exercise alone. On the ninth floor, which significantly housed the Oyster Bar, the athlete undressed and put on his boxing gloves. The plot for this floor then becomes '... eating oysters naked with boxing gloves on' (Koolhaas 1994, 152). A level higher, additional elements are added to this 'social condenser', namely the preventive-medical facilities, a massage section, Turkish baths, sunlamps and six barbers, who 'are initiated into the mysteries of male beauty' (1994, 155). The medical centre, the 'image of health as a fortress of hygiene', is where the process of 'colonic irrigation' unfolds, from where the healthy and purified body is ready to ascend to the top-level sports, to finally link up with the female (element) and the recuperation of the bachelor's body.

2 Deleuze's ideas on the virtual have had a substantial influence on contemporary architectural and art discourse. From Bernard Cache's *Earth Moves* (1995) on through John Rajchman's *Constructions* (1998), Greg Lynn's *Animate Form* (1999), Sanford Kwinter's *Architectures of Time* (2002), Brian Massumi's *Parables for the Virtual* (2002) and Elizabeth Grosz's *Chaos, Territory, Art* (2008) the influence of Deleuze's conceptions of the virtual have played a central role in recent designs of so-called 'folded architectures': a trend that has become prevalent in many architecture schools today (Kittlausz 2005).

3 Norbert Wiener and Julian Bigelow had been working on the theoretical problems posed by anti-aircraft defence. The central problem was that the target was mobile. It was necessary to predict its future position on the basis of partial information about its prior trajectory (Dupuy 2000, 44). The phenomena ranged over a vast number of possibilities: the attack of bombers and enemy armies, the state of military supplies, or economic trends, regardless of whether real or hypothetical (Picon 2003, 293).

4 The notion of event can easily lead to misinterpretation. Eisenman states that mediated environments challenge the givens of classical time, the time of experience. Referring to the Rebstock Park project in Frankfurt, he argues that architecture can no longer be bound by the static conditions of space and place; it must deal with new conditions such as the 'event'. Rebstock is seen as an 'un-unfolding event', comparable to a rock concert where one becomes part of the environment (Eisenman and Rajchman 1991, 9). This is a peculiar reading of Deleuze's *The Logic of Sense* (1990), where he formulates the notion of event as a field of virtual structures. Events are not bodies, but 'incorporeal entities'. They are not physical qualities and properties, but rather logical or dialectical attributes. Events belong to the virtual field, they are 'ideal by nature', and should not be confused with their 'spatio-temporal realizations in states of affairs' (Deleuze 1990, 53). Statements about events

are fundamentally different from statements about physical qualities and properties. Events are not what occurs, but are rather inside what occurs.

5 In the early 1950s the neuropsychiatrist Warren McCulloch defended an ontological position of the model, distancing himself at the time from John von Neumann. A model, for McCulloch, was not a simple instrument of calculation having a purely pragmatic value, determined by the answer to the question 'Does it work?' It had an ontological reality. Cybernetics was concerned with mechanizing the human. It regarded physics not as the rival needing to be challenged – it regarded physics as supplying the model needing to be imitated (Dupuy 2000, 51).

6 Katherine Hayles lists prominent examples: Gillian Beer's *Darwin's Plots*, Donald McCloskey's *The Rhetoric of Economics*, Michael Arbib and Mary Hesse's *The Construction of Reality*, Charles Bazerman's *Shaping Written Knowledge*, and Bruno Latour's *Science in Action* (Hayles 1991, 5).

7 The prefrontal cortices receive signals from several bioregulatory sectors of the human brain and are part and parcel of the reasoning and decision-making apparatus. In that way they are in a privileged position among other brain systems. Somatic markers are created in our brain during the process of education and socialization by connecting specific classes of stimuli with specific classes of somatic markers.

8 See also Metzinger (2003, 82) and Damasio (2005).

9 In Althusser, knowledge is related to sensory knowledge originating from our body in contact with other bodies and our world and related to the way we live our lives. He stresses the deforming ideological side of it, but he hardly addresses the affective issue. Contemporary neuroscience (as in Damasio) shows that feelings are as cognitive as any other perceptual images. They are first and foremost about the body (Damasio 2005, 159).

10 Hayles relates the notion of 'flickering signifiers' to Lacan's 'floating signifiers', in which he stated that 'signifiers are defined by networks of relational differences between themselves rather than by their relation to signifieds' and further that 'signifieds do not exist in themselves, except insofar as they are produced by signifiers'. In other words, they constitute an ungraspable flow 'floating beneath a network of signifiers that itself is constituted through continual slippages and displacements'. A 'flickering signifier' is characterized by a foregrounding pattern and randomness typical of information technologies. Hayles suggests that the signifier cannot be understood as a single marker on a page in a traditional sense but rather as a flexible chain of markers bound together by the arbitrary relations specified by the relevant codes. This explains the interchangeability and arbitrariness between signifier and signified in coding chains, which also account for the difference that 'the intermixture of randomness' produces on patterns (Hayles, *Virtual Bodies and Flickering Signifiers*, available online: www.english.ucla.edu/faculty/hayles/Flick.html – accessed February 23, 2009).

27

Virtual Architecture, Actual Media

N. Katherine Hayles and Todd Gannon

Architectural studies boasts a wealth of material that examines the role of print, paper and other analogue media in forming and transforming architectural practice.[1] While numerous titles on the significance of digital media exist (for example, Beckman, Benedikt, Perry and Hight, Poster, Castronova) that explore their impact on architectural production, no definitive analysis has yet emerged. Indeed, given the rapid pace of change and the development of new digital devices and applications, a definitive work on this topic may never be possible. We offer this chapter as a gathering of resources and a framework within which analyses may proceed. The work done on print media's effects clearly shows that medial effects go beyond architectural practice into such issues as the spread of architectural ideas, the dissemination of architectural writing, and the formation of an architectural canon of forms, styles, and components (for example, Colomina 1996, Carpo 2001). Even this, however, is not a complete inventory. Media effects can be explored in four distinct but interrelated areas: effects on how buildings are conceptualized, effects on how buildings are constructed, effects on the subjectivities of those who envision buildings, and effects on those presumed to inhabit the structures. Given limitations of space, we will focus our analysis on the last two areas – subjectivities of practitioners and assumptions about what constitutes the human, with glances at environmental, spatial, technological, and cultural forces that most deeply affect the transformations.

First, some ground-clearing on our central terms. Virtuality currently has two central clusters of meanings, one deriving from virtual reality technologies (see Hillis 1999 for a summary), the other from the influential Deleuzian concept of the virtual as that which is in dynamic tension with the actual (Deleuze 2005). Both these senses are relevant to our discussion. We begin by offering the hypothesis that all architecture, built or unbuilt, is virtual in the Deleuzian sense. Architecture, we propose, is not building, nor is it some privileged subset of building. Rather, we posit architecture as an emergent property of a range of media, buildings among them. It is that which makes building meaningful to an ongoing tradition. Not building itself, but, as the dictionary tells us, a particular 'art', 'science', or 'manner' of building; as Reyner Banham put it, 'what distinguishes architecture is not what is done … but how it is done' (Banham 1996). Further, we posit that architecture is a function of embodied discourse, that is, discourse instantiated in speech or, more typically, written or graphical documents. 'Document', as the term is used in textual studies, is distinct from 'text' or 'work' because it implies the existence of a physical (or digital) object.

Just as all buildings hold within them the potential of becoming architecture, so the documents that precede, surround, and follow buildings are constitutive players in imagining, planning, and implementing architectural practices and thus also participate in creating architecture. Embodied buildings and embodied documents are physical objects witnessing to architectural acts, but architecture can never be reduced to these objects. Rather, architecture partakes fundamentally of the virtual in the Deleuzian sense, a nimbus of potentialities in dynamic interaction with the actuality of buildings and documents. Both the virtuality of architecture and the physicality of documents and buildings are real, but whereas documents and buildings are location specific, comprising myriad individual instances, architecture is malleable, dispersed, always in flux. As a totality, architecture is ineffable, for as soon as it is written or built, it moves from the virtual to the actual. The collective labour of the discipline acts as midwife to architecture, moving from the raw materials of architectural actual media (whether buildings, construction documents, or philosophical writings) and guiding the emergence of architecture's virtuality into the actuality of things we can read, touch, and traverse.

An important implication that follows from this view is the impact of media on architecture. Like love, the term 'media' evokes universal recognition, yet there is a surprising lack of consensual definitions. For a field such as communication studies, media mean communication technologies such as television, radio, and the internet; for Marshall McLuhan, media were famously configured as 'extensions of man', a definition that cast telegraphy into the same bin as roads. For our purposes, we regard media as materio-semiotic systems that enact the circulation of signs. A neologism coined by Donna Haraway (among others), 'materio-semiotic' connotes objects that partake both of signifying practices and physical instantiation. An earthy example is provided by the rural Midwest landscape one of us (NKH) knew as a child, a time when indoor plumbing was ubiquitous but not quite universal. In that landscape, one occasionally encountered outdoor privies, and not infrequently, visits to them revealed, in the form of a Sears catalogue, the spirit of thriftiness that indelibly marked those who lived through the Great Depression. A materio-semiotic object, the catalogue served a dual purpose: as one lingered while waiting for certain biological processes to occur, it provided casual reading material; later, its material properties (the tearability of the relatively cheap paper, etc.) came to the foreground.

Media, as material systems conveying signs, have two principal strategies at their disposal: circulating signs through people, and circulating people through signs. Typically documents are identified with the first strategy and buildings with the second. Library books circulate among people, for example, while Gothic cathedrals functioned as sign systems through which people circulated as they performed liturgical rituals. The history of books and buildings shows many other possible combinations of strategies. Medieval codices were often chained to podiums, so that it was the people who moved while the books were stationary. Conversely, as Robert Venturi has taught us (Venturi et al. 1977), buildings may be designed to be seen from moving cars, so from a relativistic perspective that takes the viewer's position as constant, the buildings circulate while the person remains sitting in her seat.

Considering both documents and buildings as media – that is, as materio-semiotic systems – has multiple advantages. Defamiliarizing the usual categories that parse buildings as durable architectural entities and documents as ephemera, the medial perspective articulated above encourages interpretations that link semiotic functions to material actualities, so that buildings and books are neither reduced only to discursive entities nor to material objects. Another advantage inheres in the new configurations that emerge when the usual dichotomy between built and paper architecture is broken down and replaced by more flexible and dynamic interactions between virtuality and actuality. As media change – for example, from print-based documents to digital files – the dynamic between architecture's virtuality and the medium's actuality changes accordingly, often with dramatic effects. Virtual architecture, those unbuilt or unbuildable digital constructions of the contemporary generation, becomes not a pseudo-architecture suffering from a lack of physicality but rather an essential architecture unencumbered by physicality. Virtual architecture does not operate outside the pale of the discipline in a lesser realm of the unbuilt (the design equivalent of the undead), as many detractors have insisted. Rather architecture, by virtue of its dynamic interaction with actual media, infuses the physicality of the written and the built with the infinite potential of the virtual. Inhering at the very heart of the discipline, architecture's ineffability, unspeakable as such, is the reservoir that renews the discipline and makes innovation possible.

VIRTUALITY AND MEDIUM SPECIFICITY

> One cannot develop a critical theory of new media if one begins from the assumption that they are somehow immaterial. (Poster 2006, 56)

The rise of the virtual, stimulating a renewed consideration of material specificity, has catalysed new interpretations of materiality. Matthew Kirschenbaum (2005; 2008), for example, has distinguished between forensic and formal materiality. Materiality, referring to the artefactual nature of an object, should not be confused with physicality. As we have argued elsewhere (Hayles 2005), an object has a potentially infinite array of physical attributes. One could, for example, refer to the chemical composition of ink when discussing print technology, and beyond that to the molecular components, their energy states, etc. Physicality alone, then, is insufficient to specify an object. Rather, certain physical attributes are typically of interest in a given circumstance – say, the colours associated with the chemicals in ink. Materiality expresses this conjunction of attention and attributes, focus, and physicality. Attention shifts, focus changes, and materiality transforms. Always embedded in an overt or implied context, materiality, far from being given by an object's physicality, is an emergent event.

Kirschenbaum's formulation of formal and forensic materiality builds on this idea and carries it further by distinguishing between the material substrate of computer technologies (forensic materiality) and the formal sign systems that constitute computer codes (formal materiality). Reconfiguring the usual dichotomy of hardware and software by incorporating their material properties into the definitions, Kirschenbaum draws attention to issues of scale and contingency. Just as any artefact can be parsed in an infinite number of ways, so any two apparently identical artefacts can be seen to differ if the scale of observation is small enough. Two boards, for example, may be judged the same size, but drop to a smaller scale – millimetres rather than inches, nanometres rather than millimetres – and differences previously undetectable become observable.

Kirschenbaum illustrates the point by taking a CD-ROM to a nanotechnology laboratory, where a scanning tunnelling microscope reveals very slight irregularities in the bit patterns. Although we are accustomed to say that information is infinitely and exactly reproducible, this is true only within given tolerances. Along with a context of attention, materiality implicitly references a context of measurement from which observations are generated. Consequently, materiality has borderlands in which it can be transformed, either by a shift of attention or a shift of scale. Like the coastline of Britain in Benoît Mandelbrot's well-known example (1983), materiality cannot be specified in advance and without reference to context, for social, cultural, and psychological aspects interact with technical specifications.

Complementing and complicating this idea of forensic materiality is formal materiality, which in Kirschenbaum's formulation consists of the processes or behaviours in which a computational object engages. Just as one bit is not identical to another bit when the scale of observation is small enough, so the codes that the computer executes may have idiosyncrasies that testify to their origin's historical circumstances, as Kirschenbaum (2008) demonstrates by finding the kernel of an older computer game embedded within the code of a newer one. As with forensic materiality, formal materiality has social, cultural, and psychological dimensions as well as technical ones. Thus both formal and forensic materialities are inherently emergent; in Bruno Latour's terms (2007), they are nature/culture hybrids. As emergent entities, they are path dependent; they have histories, and these histories mark their materiality in ways that break open simple categories such as one and zero bits or executable and not executable code. The material entities become individuals capable of revealing their stories when interrogated with the proper (i.e., forensic) techniques.

What changes when we move from hardware and software to formal and forensic materiality? From the outset, the emergent nature of forensic and formal materiality makes clear that multiple recursive feedback loops cycle between physicality and sociality, media as technical objects and social processes. Adrian Mackenzie (2006) has convincingly argued that software construction is an intensely social process. The framework sketched above broadens this insight to include the technical functioning, social practices and media representations of architectural work. Researchers may understandably choose to focus on a particular aspect of a multiple recursive cycle (as for example Friedrich Kittler does in his emphasis on hardware in such essays as 'There is No Software' [1997a] and 'Protected Mode' [1997b]), but in our view it is a mistake to fetishize any one component as if it alone could explain the dynamics of a complex system. As Donald M. Lowe shows (1995), social, economic, and technological factors work together to form 'the body' in late-capitalist USA. Take, as another example, our claim above that attention is a co-specifying factor in the emergent dynamics, shaping which aspects of physicality become materiality. This might seem to privilege attention as the determining component. Attention itself, however, has historical and culturally specific dimensions that spring from the effects of media and other technologies, as numerous studies have shown. Jonathan Crary's *Suspensions of Perception* (1999) traces the emergence of attention as a medical and industrial concern and explores the complex dynamic between its creation and dissolution; Wolfgang Schivelbush's *The Railway Journey* (1986) demonstrates the effects of rail travel on modes of attention in the late nineteenth and early twentieth century; and Steven Johnson (2006) and we (Hayles 2007) have argued for the effects on attention of contemporary media. To engage a richer sense of the complex dynamics that co-determine media specificity, interactions throughout the system should be understood as entwined with and mutually affecting one another.

Media specificity has been a minority interest in the humanities for most of the twentieth century, with the long dominance of print inducing a kind of somnolence in this regard. (An important exception is textual studies, which has typically engaged with what Jerome McGann [2001] has called 'bibliographic codes', that is, the material aspects of texts.) All this changed, however, with the rapid development of networked and programmable media in the later twentieth century. Signs of crisis are now everywhere apparent as the humanities struggle to come to terms with the importance of media specificity in composition, publishing, credentialing, and a host of other areas. Architecture has been significantly in advance of other areas of the human sciences in investigating interactions between architecture and the objects, subjects, contexts, and media that conspire to produce it. A convenient example can be found in Robin Evans' widely read 1986 essay, 'Translations from Drawing to Building' (1997 [1986]).[2]

Evans' text relates a simple tale: the constructed dome of the Royal Chapel at Anet (1547–1552) by Philibert de l'Orme does not match the drawing of it inscribed in the pavement below nor does their relationship match de l'Orme's description of it in his *Premier tome de l'architecture* (1567). For Evans, these differences do not signal a deficiency in the work, a failure on the part of the architect to translate precisely an architectural concept from one medium to another; rather, the case reveals the differences between the various media (drawings, books, and buildings) that were deployed to produce the architecture in question, as well as the way in which those differences condition and inflect it.

De l'Orme's work hinges on a consonance between the two-dimensional, three-dimensional, and textual instantiations of a complex geometrical pattern, a consonance that Evans's analysis demonstrates to be incorrect geometrically. The work may look like a virtuoso feat of projective geometry (and in fact it is), but this feat was not executed as advertised. Constructing an alibi for de l'Orme, Evans surmises that the architect fudged the floor paving, cropping the aesthetically inferior portions at the projection's edges and scaling up the entire pattern to produce an effect that more closely resembled that of the dome above. De l'Orme's adjustments can be seen as an extension of the ancient Greek practices of visual correction (entasis, the modulation of column spacing, etc.), which likewise torqued, stretched, and adjusted elements to produce a more convincing appearance of their being parallel, perpendicular, evenly spaced, or plumb.[3] Evans demonstrates that de l'Orme's corrective adjustments extend into the *Premier tome* as well, which similarly values the effect of rigorous method over its actual application. We might append de l'Orme's triumphant finish, '... forming by this means compartments that are plumb and perpendicular above the plan of the said chapel',[4] with 'but this didn't look quite right, so we cropped off the outer, ugly bits and made the whole thing bigger'. The addition, while ruining the text's rhetorical effect, would nevertheless have the salutary effect, important for our argument, of revealing the transformational effects of translating between and among media.

In each mediated instantiation of the chapel – the constructed dome, the patterned floor, du Cerceau's engraved drawings, de l'Orme's printed text, Evans' diagrams and photographs – the architectural effect of dizzying geometrical precision was crafted and modulated according to the specific media through which that effect was produced. In the end, we understand that these effects at Anet issue not from a single source but rather from the dynamic interaction of the building's materiality with its myriad mediated representations, as well as with the architect(s) that produce(s) it and the perceiving subjects that engage it.[5] Like writing, each of the media involved made possible and also precluded specific inflections of the thoughts they embody. In many cases, media deployed by architects give rise to ideas that are thinkable only through those media; recall, for instance Peter Eisenman's cunning redrawing of Le Corbusier's Maison Domino. Originally published by the French architect as a two-point perspective, the image was re-drawn by Eisenman as a series of axonometric diagrams (Eisenman 2004). This translation of an iconic drawing from one style of projection to another opened the simple form to a host of new interpretations.

Another avenue along which this line of thinking might develop is architectural photography. Migrating built form to the printed page through the lens of the camera, with its cultural affiliations with truthful representation, made possible modes of architectural thinking unavailable to drawing or writing. Truth travels in step with fiction, producing productive slippages between assumed facts and media representations. As pointed out by Beatriz Colomina, photography and its attendant body of techniques can manipulate reality as much as reflect it. 'Rather than represent reality, it produces a new reality' (Colomina 1996, 80). Colomina goes on to demonstrate in her interpretation of Le Corbusier's serial redrawing of postcards that these new realities signify not as a function of single images but rather through their accumulation and relation to other media: 'a photograph does not have specific meaning in itself but rather in its relationship to other photographs, the caption, the writing, and the layout of the page' (1996, 93–100).

As photography is multiplied in film and made infinitely malleable with digital technologies, these potential 'new realities' are likewise multiplied, and with them their available interactions with other media and their potential to produce new forms of architectural thinking. Let us return for a moment to Eisenman's representations of the Maison Domino (Eisenman 2004); see Figures 27.1 and 27.2. Here, Eisenman uses an abstract drawing technique to produce a series of spare interpretations of Corbusier's already stripped-down original. Taken together, Eisenman's drawings produce an effect of teleological development, an implied history of a primitive form's articulation over time. This effect is particularly effective rendered as an axonometric, which imposes a three-dimensional framework revealing spatial relations while retaining dimensional congruence. Instantiating the argument in Corbusier's more realistic perspective would occlude much of the essential information.[6] Over a series of projects through the 1970s and into the present, Eisenman developed

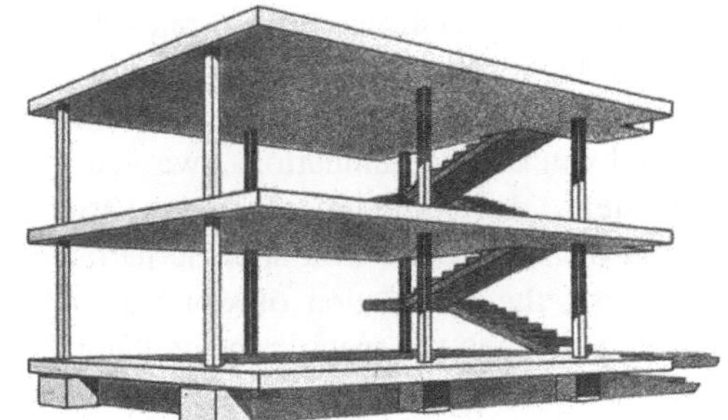

Figure 27.1 (Above) Le Corbusier, Maison Domino, 1914. (© 2010 Artists Rights Society (ARS), New York / ADAGP, Paris / F.L.C.)

this technique further in analyses of the work of Giuseppe Terragni as well as in his own work, producing a series of projects that adopted a narrative syntax to produce the effect of the serial elaboration of primitive forms over time (Eisenman 1999; 2003). With the advent of 3D computer modelling and animation software in the 1990s, such serial elaborations were possible not only in far greater degrees of complexity but also

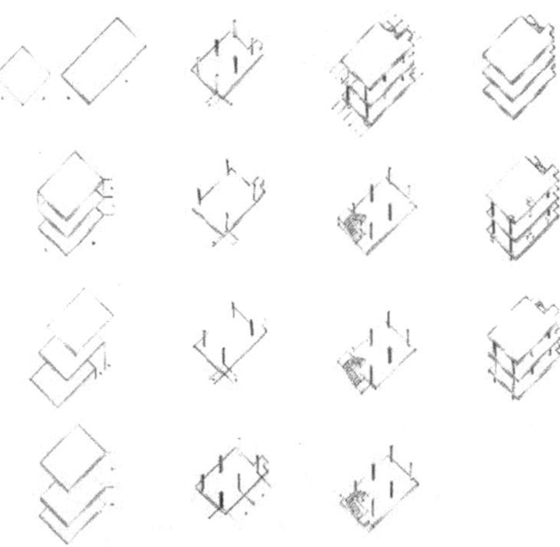

Figure 27.2 (Above) Axonometric diagrams of the Maison Domino, Peter Eisenman. (Eisenman Architects, drawn by Jay Johnson)

with much higher frame refresh rates. From Le Corbusier's single iconic image to Eisenman's step-by-step transformations to Greg Lynn's fluid animations, we see the persistent development through various media of architecture as a specific narrative discourse, the articulation of which is only possible through the specific media that produce it. Coupling these digital animations with soundtracks, live actors, and cinematic techniques, firms operating outside the discipline of architecture such as Imaginary Forces push this discourse still further in their development of architectural pre-visualizations and what has been called 'experience design' (see Krakowsky 2007). The perceivable effects of this discourse do not inhere solely within the objects produced, regardless of whether those objects take the form of buildings, drawings, computer animations, or texts. Rather, these effects obtain from the dynamic interactions that arise in the virtual space between the various media that embody them and the perceiving subjects that engage them.

NEW MEDIA AS ARCHITECTURE

Over the past twenty years, digital technologies have perpetrated a fundamental transformation not only of architectural working methods, but also of the kind of work architects produce and the manner in which that work is interpreted and discussed. Shifts in attention from form to surface, from objects to atmosphere, from meaning to mood, and from critical to post-critical (or projective) practice have been advanced by critics and historians from all camps as symptoms of a more general move away from a discursive paradigm centred upon stable objects and legible meaning to one concerned primarily with fluid environments, ephemeral effects, and ambiguous moods.[7] While others, such as Robert Venturi, have attempted to situate new technologies within old regimes of signification and iconography, we eschew his tendency to cast architecture and media as opposing forces.[8] While architecture might emerge from the interaction of iconography and electronics with generic buildings in the work of Venturi and others, in our view, more interesting work is being done by firms committed not to a conceptual separation of digital media and built form but rather to their seamless integration.

The New York office of Diller Scofidio + Renfro (DS+R) has long been at the forefront of integrating technology and virtuality in architecture as well as in extending architectural practice into neighbouring disciplines such as gallery art, theatre, and film. The firm's precocious facility with virtual effects as well as the trademark elements of their work may be attributed to their long history of collaboration with the theatre and stage production. In contrast to the earnest monumentality of architectural form, the theatre deals unapologetically in artifice, regularly deploying actual construction and virtual projection to construct its illusions. DS+R operates in a similar fashion, and recurrent elements in their projects recall standard theatrical elements and tropes. Their famous mechanical apparatuses, for example, evoke the ad-hoc mechanical tackle of the theatre fly-space. Their aggressive use of architectural drawing conventions (plan and section projections, linear perspective, etc.) to manipulate spatial perception corresponds to the intermingling of architectural technique and theatrical illusion described in early treatises ranging from Vitruvius to Alberti and illustrated in Mannerist examples such as Palladio's Teatro Olimpico in Vicenza or Scamozzi's Teatro di Sabbioneta. In theatre as in the work of DS+R, mechanical and projective devices, from illusionistically painted sets to the split and distorted perspectival recessions of the *scena per angolo* to Diller and Scofidio's early deployment of angled mirrors,[9] come together to produce a range of virtual effects that confound the distinctions between the actual and the virtual and in recent works have become the primary locus of their architectural experimentation.

This tendency is apparent in such hallmark projects as their production design for *The Rotary Notary and His Hot Plate* of 1987, as shown in Figure 27.3. Drawing inspiration from Marcel Duchamp, Diller and Scofidio devised an apparatus composed of an opaque screen that divided the stage parallel to the proscenium and a mirror fixed at forty-five degrees that revealed a plan view of the concealed space to the audience.[10] Viewed head-on (and in the most commonly published photographs), the apparatus effectively flattens into a single plane akin to an elevation drawing, reproducing the gendered separation of bride's and bachelor's domains of Duchamp's 'Grand Verre' while producing a multiplication of the performance space that unleashes a panoply of illusory potential. Moving into the concealed area of the stage displaces the actor's bodies into the virtual space of the mirror apparatus where they are rendered weightless, fragmented, and dismembered. Diller and Scofidio honed their techniques and expanded their repertoire to include video projections in a series of theatrical productions through the 1990s,[11] as well as in installations such as Para-Site at the Museum of Modern Art in New York (1989), Loophole at the Second Artillery Armory of Chicago (1992), and in projects such as the Slow House on Long Island (unfinished, 1992) and the Brasserie at the Seagram Building in New York (2000). In each case, carefully positioned cameras and video monitors displaying both real-time and time-delayed imagery produced on-site as well as remotely, displace and multiply architectural spaces, producing jarring spatial and temporal juxtapositions heightened by their architectural constructions but impossible to achieve through strictly mechanical means. The firm also devised complex presentations of each work, from armatures that blurred distinctions between drawings, models, and the structures designed to support them in earlier works to clever combinations of analogue and digital representational techniques in later presentations. The firm's work developed in scope and ambition through the 1990s and into this century alongside rapid advances in digital technologies, and the office remains at the forefront of experimentation with them that re-imagines the affective potential of architectural projects as well as the technical scope of architectural practice.

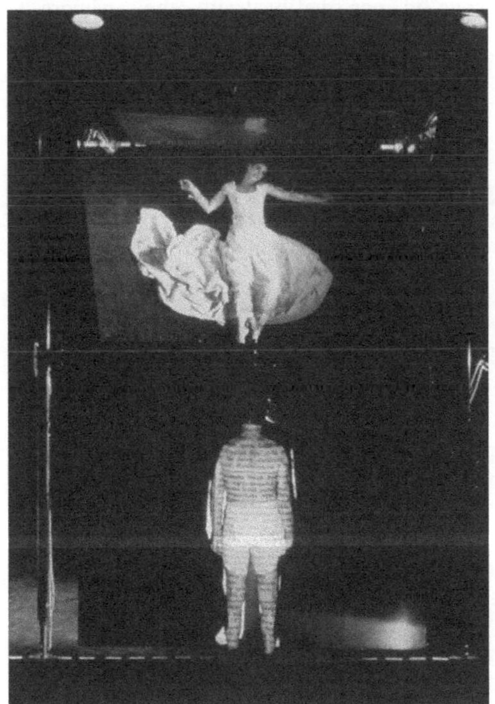

Figure 27.3 (Above) Diller Scofidio + Renfro, *The Rotary Notary And His Hot Plate*, Multi-Media Theatre Work, Philadelphia Museum of Art, PA, 1987. (Diller Scofidio + Renfro)

Perhaps the firm's most ambitious attempt at integrating digital technologies and physical construction is their Blur Building at Yverdon-les-Bains, Switzerland (2002) as shown in Figure 27.4. To construct an artificial cloud in the grounds of Swiss Expo 2002, the firm employed digital technologies in concert with analogue techniques through all stages of conceptualization, design, construction, and operation. Their use of these techniques, from the fusions of analogue and digital drawing methods in presentation materials to the integration

Figure 27.4 (Above) Diller Scofidio + Renfro, *The Blur Building*, Exposition Pavilion for Swiss Expo, Yverdon-les-Bains, Switzerland, 2002. Commissioned by Swiss Expo 2002. (Diller Scofidio + Renfro)

of computer-controlled weather sensors to modulate the complex fog generation system on the project, is well-known and widely published. The project's dissemination in other media, from extensive publication in the popular and scholarly press to the use of its imagery in contemporary products ranging from telephone cards to chocolate bars, has also been noted (see Diller and Scofidio 2002). For the present discussion, the project's unrealized digital components, which aim to eradicate the boundary between virtual and actual spatial environments, are most pertinent.

In the indeterminate space of the Blur Building, familiar architectural depth cues were to be all but erased by the mist. To compensate for diminished visual stimuli, alternative modes of spatial orientation were to have been made available through digitally controlled sound and light effects. As the Blur Building developed, the firm and its many collaborators experimented with a number of integrated media components, from scrolling LED text displays to automated 'braincoats' to interactive online controls, most of which were eliminated due to budget constraints from the final built work. We have noted previously the unfortunate lacunae their absence left in the experience of the built work (Gannon 2002), but, as has been noted by Mark B.N. Hansen, 'in addition to being a temporary built project in the world, the Blur Building exists as a work of embodied conceptual art preserved in the archive of traces that document its making and that include – as a central core of its drama – the media components' (Hansen 2006b, 280). While these unrealized media components did not inflect the constructed spectacle at Yverdon-les-Bains, they are essential to an understanding of the full architectural significance of the Blur Building and point to the burgeoning potential of architecture born out of the interpenetration of new and old media.

Offering much needed protection from the cool mist of the pavilion, Diller and Scofidio's digitally-enhanced braincoats open up new avenues of social interaction and spatial organization, as shown in Figure 27.5. Upon arriving at the pavilion, visitors were to complete a simple questionnaire meant to divine specific personality traits, the answers to which were then uploaded to a central database and to the individual's braincoat. Sensors and transmitters embedded in the coats would communicate with each other as visitors moved through the space, causing visual, aural, and mechanical transformations to the

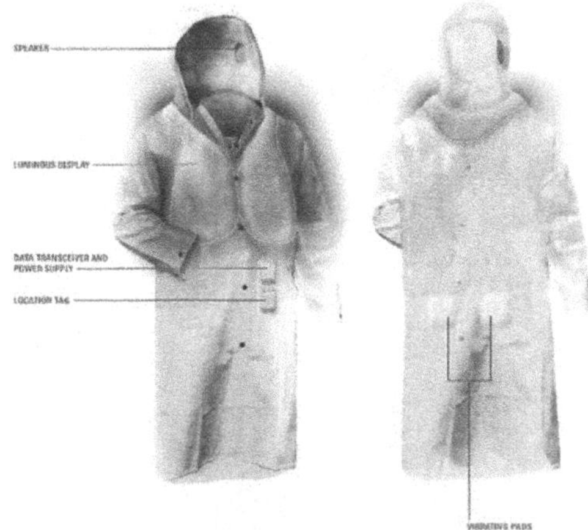

Figure 27.5 (Above) Diller Scofidio + Renfro, *Braincoats*, for the Blur Building at Swiss Expo, Yverdon-les-Bains, Switzerland, 2002. (Diller Scofidio + Renfro)

coat based on proximity to other coats and the programmed information they carried. As a visitor wandering in the mist approached another visitor who had given similar answers to the questionnaire, the system would signal a potential affinity by shifting the colour intensity of each coat toward red and increasing the frequency of audio pulses emitted by the coat.

Contrasting answers would elicit an antipathetic response signaled by a green hue, and exact matches would trigger a vibrating sensation in the coat, 'mimicking the tingle of excitement that comes with physical attraction' (Diller and Scofidio 2002, 217).

The results of this new spatial experiment remain unknown. Like minded visitors might have attracted one another, causing a segregation of inhabitants based on personality that would have resulted in uniform clusters of glowing red coats and rapid aural pulses. Alternatively, visitors might have been turned off by their supposed matches, causing those with similar profiles to repel one another. This might have led to an ironic arrangement of mismatched personalities seeking the comfort of strangers in the closest proximity to one another. More likely, of course, would have been an oscillating swarm of rising and falling pulse tones and a full spectrum of glowing coats as individual visitors pursued individual agendas and entered and exited the system at varying rates – a field of peripatetic denizens blushing, beeping, and vibrating their way through an otherworldly milieu.

In another aborted embellishment, the pavilion was to be equipped with PTZ cameras capable of being controlled by virtual visitors experiencing the space through the internet. While these visitors would not have been able directly to enjoy the full range of physical sensations and alternative social opportunities offered by the braincoats, they would have been afforded a remote view of the spectacle as well as an opportunity to affect the content of the LED displays (and perhaps, by extension, the behaviour of the visitors at Yverdon) through interaction with web-based interfaces. As such, the Blur Building would have inhabited the virtual space of the internet as it simultaneously occupied the physical space over Lake Neuchâtel, with its virtual and actual visitors likewise occupying multiple positions in the manifold virtual instantiations of the space projected around the globe by the internet.

While budgetary constraints precluded the inclusion of these elements in Yverdon, other projects demonstrate the potential of active digital media in architectural design. Linking integrated sensors to computer-controlled lighting elements, Toyo Ito's 1986 Tower of Winds in Yokohama transformed contextual data into 'environmental music' expressed in constantly changing light patterns.[12] Greg Lynn's Embryological House project (2000) invites clients to participate in the design process through an interactive website.[13] More recently, the D-Tower by Lars Spuybroek and artist Q.S. Serafin combines physical construction with web-based components to produce a hybrid, interactive work that colourfully maps the collective emotional state of a small Dutch town.[14] Younger practices such as Höweler + Yoon, Servo, Xefirotarch and others routinely combine digital technologies with physical construction to produce architectural works impossible to consider in strictly analog terms. Far exceeding Venturi's call for a generic architecture adorned with electronic signage, these works (in all their varied instantiations) guide the emergence of an aggressively intermediated architecture that choreographs a complex, integrated ensemble of physical construction, virtual simulation, and pervasive interaction of human subjects and intelligent machines.

VIRTUALITY AND NOTIONS OF HUMAN SUBJECTIVITY

I am teaching a design studio at UCLA. A student has been working on a 3D model of a building and is walking me through the latest changes. It is an early summer afternoon in Southern California and

> the studios, designed with analogue drafting in mind, are bathed in natural light. The sun's glare makes it difficult for me to see the image on the screen, so I ask the student to turn it toward me so that I might get a better view. A second later, without lifting a hand, she asked, 'Is that better?' Flummoxed, I reply, 'You didn't move anything'. Her right wrist flicks the mouse almost imperceptibly, and the 3D image on the screen rotates about its vertical axis. 'How about now?' I reach forward and turn the monitor myself.

Two generations peer at the screen, the older seeing the screen in space, the younger the screen as space. Such anecdotes pepper the literature surrounding the advent of digital technologies in design studios through the 1990s to the present. As more robust platforms and projects such as Second Life come online, these occurrences have become increasingly commonplace. While virtual spaces in built work are only beginning to alter the architectural environment, the virtual spaces in which work is produced have been fully assimilated into workplace practices and, increasingly, into leisure time as well. These professional and leisure practices have had dramatic effects not only on architects but also on artists, writers, and cultural critics. In the cultural imaginary, the virtual in architecture, in vibrant conversation with the actual media of networked and programmable machines, leaps ahead of present construction to envision a built world in which simulated overlays merge seamlessly with actual buildings to create mixed reality environments inhabited by augmented humans.

Such a world is given pride of place in Vernor Vinge's speculative fiction *Rainbows End* (2006) where it is imagined so vividly and pervasively that it almost qualifies as the novel's protagonist. In Vinge's near-future world, buildings are quite plain and even ugly, for they are not designed to be seen in themselves but rather to function as underpinnings onto which virtual overlays are projected.[15] They are in this sense malleable, mutating as the projections change; Juan, a student at Fairmont High School, notices that the 'buildings were mostly three stories today. Their gray walls were like playing cards stacked in a rickety array' (Vinge 2006, 50). There would indeed be little sense in creating elaborate exteriors when what the eye perceives comes not from the building but the computer. Programmable gear provides the projections, texturing, and detailing that transform surfaces into whatever the user has fashioned in his or her 'wearable'. Visions are shared either through VR projections or directly as digital files. Users thus become instant collaborators with architects, creating custom visual effects that advertise their virtuosity in manipulating digital information.

The cumulative effects on human culture and subjectivity are profound. The novel's putative protagonist, Robert Gu, is an older man who had been a world-class poet before he descended into the deep twilight of Alzheimer's. Rescued from darkness by medical advances, he re-awakens to a contemporary world in which most people around him are living in a mixed reality that he can enter only through arduous re-education. The plot foregrounds how class has been reconfigured; the emphasis is no longer on the haves and have-nots but on the digitally facile and digitally obtuse. Just as in former times one was required performatively to display a certain class, gender, and race to have access to a gentleman's club, so now the elite are defined by their skills in manipulating the 'wearables' that create the environments to which other people respond.

The ornate surfaces created by VR projections cover over architectural infrastructures permeated by computational devices. In contrast to their unremarkable exteriors, buildings have remarkable functionalities that, invisible to casual inspection, bestow smart capabilities that make them something like intelligent entities in their own right. 'Cryptic machines are everywhere nowadays', Gu thinks. 'They lurked in walls, nestled in trees, even littered the lawns. They worked silently, almost invisibly, twenty-four hours a day. He began to wonder where it all ended' (2006, 75). Such is the retrofitted

Geisel Library at the University of California's San Diego campus, whose infrastructure includes stabilizers enabling the building to absorb earthquake tremors by counter-movements that ensure continuing stability. A climax arrives when the digital stabilizers are hijacked by a mysterious hacker (who may be, the narrative hints, an emergent virtual entity produced spontaneously by the network's complexity). In answer to a challenge from a rival faction, the hacker literally makes the building walk by converting the stabilizers' countermeasures into coherent directionality. The scene underscores the complexity of agency when it is distributed among embodied individuals, non-human agents, and actual buildings and media.

The novel dramatizes effects documented in a host of non-fictional studies, including rapid technological change and the concomitant obsolescence (Sterling 2005; Harvey 1992); global microsociality emerging from a combination of instantaneous transnational communication and the exigencies of local times and places (Knorr Cetina and Bruegger 2002); crowd sourcing (Howe 2006), here envisioned as 'affiliances', short-term contracts establishing relationships between citizens and corporations for temporary cooperation on a project; government power at once centralized and exercised through distributed networks (Galloway and Thacker 2007); and conspiracies that thrive on asymmetric warfare (Der Derian 2001). Subjectivity is not about interiority expressed through verbal constructions (metaphorized in the poet protagonist, who finds he has lost his gift to make words sing) but about manipulating information so that it forms a pervasive real-time interface with everyday life. Human intelligence has been so thoroughly integrated with intelligence augmentation technologies that 'media', properly conceived, are no longer external affordances but integrated systems rippling across multiple artifactual and biological interfaces (Thacker 2004).

This near-future scenario lies on a trajectory that stretches back at least as far as the early years of the twentieth century. Writing on the influence of media, particularly film and photography, on Le Corbusier's architecture, Beatriz Colomina notes that 'to inhabit' means 'to inhabit the camera. But the camera is not a traditional place, it is a system of classification, a kind of filing cabinet. "To inhabit" means to employ that system' (Colomina 1996, 323). Similarly, 'to inhabit' the structures in *Rainbows End* means to occupy the systems of classification and protocols that enable information to flow smoothly along the networks. Working from the extensive materials in Le Corbusier's archives, Colomina shows that 'the traditional humanist figure, the inhabitant of the house, is made incidental to the camera eye; it comes and goes, it is merely a visitor' (1996, 329). Architectural elements, particularly windows, are consistently superimposed with contemporary media: 'Telephone, cable, radios … machines for abolishing time and space. Control is now in these media' (1996, 332). Colomina argues that 'the window in the age of mass communication provides us with one more flat image. The window is a screen' (1996, 334). Further along the trajectory, the screen in *Rainbows End* leaps out of the frame and projects directly onto ambient surfaces, dynamically engaging with and indeed co-creating environments. The novel performs a world consonant with Anthony Vidler's observation that 'contemporary subject identity, if it is optical at all, finds its subject in screens, in clouded surfaces, in the indeterminacy of non-perspectival structure' (Vidler 2006, 135).

What, then, of contemporary subjectivity? Writing about the earlier twentieth century, Colomina concludes that 'a dematerialization' follows from 'the emerging media. The organizing geometry of architecture skips from the perspectival cone of vision, from the humanist eye, to the camera angle. It is precisely in this slippage that modern architecture becomes modern by engaging with the media' (Colomina 1996, 334). Architecture in the present and near-future, however, does more than displace the 'traditional humanist figure'. Rather, it incorporates the individual (or as Deleuze says, the 'dividual') as a node in a global network of interconnectivity that promiscuously mingles human with non-human agency, local embodiments with global communication flows, virtual overlays with actual buildings and media.

HOW TO FASHION A PRO-HUMAN POSTHUMANISM

> If there is to be a new urbanism it will not be based on the twin fantasies of order and omnipotence, it will be the staging of uncertainty, it will no longer be concerned with the arrangement of more or less permanent objects but with the irrigation of territories with potential; it will no longer aim for stable configurations but for the creation of enabling fields that accommodate processes that refuse to be crystallized into definitive form … it will no longer be obsessed with the city but with the manipulation of infrastructure for endless intensifications and diversifications, shortcuts and redistributions – the reinvention of psychological space. (Koolhaas 1995, 969)

As we confront the issue of contemporary subjectivity, it is worth remembering that humans have been co-evolving with technology almost from the beginning of the species. This complex co-evolutionary spiral has aptly been called technogenesis (Hansen 2006a; Stiegler 1998), producing and produced by the complex feedback loops whereby the production of new tools creates new visions of human beings, which leads to new environments, which puts selective pressure on some features and enhances others, which leads to different practices and related ontogenic changes, which in turn stimulates the creation of yet more tools. As Deleuze has remarked (1995, 178) the pertinent question ought not to be whether the present era is better or worse than what came before (a question impossible to answer comprehensively). Rather, we might better ask what opportunities for constructive interventions are presented to us by our information-intensive environments. One way into the question is to take seriously objections raised to our posthuman condition and consider carefully how undesirable effects can be mitigated and salutary effects enhanced.

The traditional humanist subject was seen as having a body, but (at least in the philosophical tradition) that body was reductively viewed as a support system for the all-important rational mind, as has been shown, among others, by Elizabeth Grosz in *Volatile Bodies* (1994) and George Lakoff and Mark Johnson in *Philosophy in the Flesh* (1999). With the advent of cyberspace, enthusiasts made extravagant claims for leaving the body behind, and transhumanists such as Ray Kurzweil (2006) confidently looked forward to the near future when the body could either be extensively re-engineered for radical life extension or, in Hans Moravec's visions (1990; 2000), dispensed with altogether by uploading consciousness into a computer. In light of such fantasies, we can sympathize with Francis Fukuyama's warning (2006) that there is a human nature and we mess with it at our peril, or Arie Graafland's important comment that we have 'finally lost all ground' (2006, 156). 'What gets lost here', Graafland continues, 'is corporeality in a threefold way: three bodies are lost at the same time, the territorial body of the planet and ecology, and social body or socius, and our human body' (2006, 156). Graafland is correct but only in theory – that is, in reference to theories that erase the enduring biological inheritance we call the body and all the richly sedimented behaviours, inclinations, and proclivities it encodes, chief among them the desire to socialize with other humans, the origin of socius.

Graafland and others who want to resist contemporary erasures of the body may ironically participate in the very movements they would contest, for they accept as given problematic claims from which they extrapolate a dire state of affairs. For example, in arriving at the above conclusion, Graafland cites Chirstine Boyer to the effect that 'in the Cartesian world of computers there is no longer any reference to the body' (Boyer 1996, 117). This statement is both true and false – true if one focuses only on logic gates, idealized bit patterns, and so forth, but false if one considers the full range of affordances in networked and programmable machines, which include multiple body interfaces from the GUI to the mouse and extensive software packages designed specifically with human perceptual systems in mind, for example PET scans and functional magnetic resonance images. Moreover, computers themselves have bodies in the sense of being instantiated entities. As we saw earlier with forensic materiality, these bodies bear the marks of specific histories that place them within social, economic, and political contestations. As Kirschenbaum remarks, '[computers] are material machines dedicated to propagating a behavioral illusion, or call it a working model, of immateriality' (2005, 5). We should not, however, be seduced into taking this illusion for reality. Materiality introduces difference, and difference opens the way for the contingent, the unexpected, the aleatory.

This is the crucial missing point in Boyer's later argument in 'The Body in the City: A Discourse on Cyberscience' (2006), which gives a solid account of first- and second-order cybernetics but in its conclusion accepts ideal abstractions as reality. Discussing artificial life and emergence, she argues that 'this model ushers in by the back door via its bio-social episteme a totalizing desire for omnipotence as a post-humanist fabricator of artificial life or generic cites. Followed to the extreme, signs in this second cybernetics engender the capacity of complex systems to alter, modify, and develop their own programs controlling life and death decisions. This is what "second-order" emergence is all about' (2006, 47). Such a conclusion erases an important aspect of emergence: once evolutionary processes are given a chance to work, they may well produce something no one expected, including those who engineered the evolutionary programs. As materio-semiotic actors, artificial life programs can and do exploit small differences in materialities to enact path-dependent trajectories entirely different from those their creators imagined.

What one makes of these unexpected events is an open-ended question that cannot be answered by referring solely to the technology; the emergent result is radically under-determined with respect to the technology and therefore susceptible to a wide range of interpretations and interventions. John Cage, for example, sought in 'chance operations' (his version of emergence) a release from the limits of the ego and an opening out of human consciousness to the inconceivable diversity that lies all around us, if only we have the mindsets and orientations to perceive it. Gregory Bateson (whom Boyer does not mention) saw in second order cybernetics possibilities for new alignments between human consciousness and the recursive processes that connect us with our environment (Bateson 1980). Our point is not that claims by second-order cyberneticians or researchers in artificial life should be taken at face value, or that we should credit the much more problematic fantasies of the transhumanists. Rather, we want to underscore the importance of interventions that emphasize the positive ways in which current technological trends can open opportunities for progressive actions and empowering practices.

Although limitations of space prevent us from discussing such opportunities in detail, we will point to four areas that seem to us especially promising. The first group is characterized by *theoretical emphases on embodiment and its potentialities*. Richly diverse, these approaches seek to use our present lack of ground as an opportunity to re-envision the relationship between embodied perception, digital media, and artistic and architectural practices. If the body is one important component of our ground, as Graafland argues, perhaps 'losing our ground' is not such a bad thing if it means sloughing off outmoded conceptions of the body that are the residue from a liberal tradition saturated with universalist assumptions about the superiority of the white race, the male gender, and the rational mind. Once we have moved on from this ground, new conceptions of embodiment can coalesce around a number of important sites. Research in brain functioning and imaging technologies, for example, is interpreted in light of art traditions in Barbara Stafford's *Echo Objects* (2007). Gerald Edelman's work (1989), which draws in part on imaging technologies, has stimulated a number of responses from the humanities and arts communities, including those in Joseph Tabbi's *Cognitive Fictions* (2002) and Warren Neidich's 'Resistance is Futile: The Neurobiopolitics of Consciousness' (2006). Mark B.N. Hansen in *New Philosophy for New Media* (2006a) sees in the lack of ground instantiated in digital media positive opportunities for digital artists to foreground embodied responses as the stabilizing component necessary to make sense of artistic digital productions. Bernadette Wegenstein in *Getting Under the Skin* (2006) goes further by conceptualizing the body itself as a form of media, a move also made by Eugene Thacker in *Biomedia* (2004). After recapitulating much of the recent research on the body, Wegenstein remarks, 'We still do not know what the body really is' (2006, 16). Working from a similar idea of enlightened ignorance, Shusaku Arakawa and Madeleine Gins (1979; 2002) treat it as an empowering premise, for it enables them to start with the primacy of embodiment (not from the body, which is always already a social, cultural, and technological construction) and devise architectural structures designed to short-circuit customary perceptions and open onto new sensory experiences and embodied orientations.

A second kind of positive intervention takes the form of *recognizing the irreducible social and cultural complexities of contexts* in which perceptions of embodiment (and the body) are embedded. The celebratory rhetoric surrounding the advent of cyberspace and globalization is contextualized by David Harvey's *A Brief History of Neolibralism* (2007) as part of a transnational movement by the upper classes to recuperate the economic ground lost in the inflationary periods of the 1970s. Harvey convincingly shows that neo-liberalism, although taking different forms in the United States, Chile, Britain, and China, nevertheless represents class warfare by other means. His richly textured analyses provide salutary examples of how underlying patterns can be discerned without treating reductively the social and cultural complexities in which they are embedded. On the negative side, we might think of transhumanist rhetoric as it appears in such prominent spokespeople for the movement as Max Moore. Focused on the transcendent possibilities for individuals, transhumanist rhetoric almost entirely ignores the complex issues that would arise from even modest life extension, including generational conflict, scarcity of resources, and the just allocation of resources when the world population explodes uncontrollably.

A third kind of positive intervention comes in *recognizing new modes of organization that digital media require* and developing theoretical approaches that take their specificities into account. In *Protocol*, Galloway (2005) makes an important contribution in developing what he calls a protocological approach, focusing on the regimens that allow information to flow through the networks or, conversely, that prevent the release of high-value informational assets to unauthorized users. In *The Exploit*, Galloway and co-author Thacker (2007) work from the theoretical models of Deleuze and the sweeping historical panorama of Hardt and Negri's *Empire* to theorize the network as a ground for political action, showing for example that the networks can be integrated into centralized bureaucracy as well as into asymmetric warfare. Other important contributions have been made by Friedrich A. Kittler. Wittily observing that 'the entertainment industry is, in any conceivable sense of the word, an abuse of army equipment' (1999, 96–97), Kittler traces the technological lineages that resulted in the contemporary configuration of the military-industrial-entertainment complex.

Although his methodology is anti-humanistic, in that it refuses the primacy of the human as an adequate explanation for technological development, his approach nevertheless recognizes the importance of social and cultural presuppositions as they are entwined with technological issues of data storage, transmission, and manipulation.

Last but hardly least are theoretical approaches, artistic creations, and architectural practices that *emphasize the importance of recursive feedback loops between embodied practices, social constructions, and the specificities of digital media.* The videographer Paul Ryan, for example, has focused on the tendency of complex systems, particularly turbulent flow, to produce chaotic patterns that endure over time without ever repeating themselves exactly (Ryan 2006). Collaborating with Ryan, Stephanie Strickland and Cynthia Lawson Jaramillo created 'slippingglimpse', a digital art work of considerable beauty and theoretical sophistication (Strickland et al. 2007). Our own contribution in this area develops the concept of intermediation as a framework within which digital literature, art, and architecture may be understood (Hayles 2005; 2008; Gannon and Hayles 2007).

Returning again to Graafland's comment on the loss of ground, we note that complex systems in general lack a ground in the sense that they defy formalization through explicit equations, precisely because every factor interacts with, influences, and is influenced by every other factor. Complex systems do not, however, lack order; rather they instantiate a particularly complex kind of order capable of demonstrating emergent properties. Seeking a ground has historically been represented through such monumental enterprises as Russell and Whitehead's *Principia Mathematica* (1911), which sought to axiomatize mathematics. This grand enterprise was driven by the hope that mathematics could be made logically consistent and formally complete; it would then, so the reasoning went, provide a solid ground upon which all the other sciences (and perhaps the social sciences and even the arts) would build. When the enterprise was proven impossible by Gödel's Theorem and related developments such as the Church-Turing proof, the lack of ground became the catalyst for important artistic explorations typified by M.C. Escher and, later in the twentieth century, the reading and writing protocols associated with deconstruction.

The lack of ground need not mean the end of agency, the loss of order, or the utter transformation of the human into some post-biological version that would be more machine than biological entity. Rather, viewed as an opportunity for constructive interventions, the recognition that complex systems are how the natural world mostly operates opens onto a number of important realizations: that agency is always distributed; that cognition is a much broader function than consciousness and includes many embodied capacities outside the central nervous system; that action always takes place within embedded and recursive systems that can unpredictably amplify the consequences of our actions; and that ethical considerations should therefore always be a component of our considerations. Architecture, deeply entwined with digital media and necessarily attentive to social and cultural constructions, constitutes an ideal site from which to explore and intervene in the recursive feedback loops co-constitutive of materiality, contemporary subjectivity, and digital media.

NOTES

1 Pertinent studies include Colomina (1996), Carpo (2001), compilations by Colomina (1988), Hart (1998), and Rattenbury (2002), among others.

2 As Evans' text is discussed at length elsewhere in this volume, we will limit our discussion to a few salient points. For a fuller treatment, See Chapter 23.

3 For a discussion of visual correction in ancient Greek architecture, see Coulton (1977).

4 de l'Orme (1567, 112), quoted by Evans (1997 [1986], 191).

5 It is interesting to note that Evans produced his analysis of the Royal Chapel without having visited the building, and relied only on mediated representations to develop his argument. Further, his subsequent visit to the chapel compelled him to add a postscript in which he slightly altered his findings, based as much on his visit as on additional photographs he took while there. See Evans (1997 [1986], 188).

6 This observation was often pointed out in graduate seminars led by R. E. Somol at both Ohio State and UCLA, but we know of no published essay in which these thoughts are recorded.

7 The literature on this pervasive phenomenon is vast. For a sampling of the more influential works on the subject, see Riley (1995), Kipnis (2002), Somol and Whiting (2002), Speaks (2001), Lavin (2004), and Baird (2004). Our own contribution focuses on the role digital design technologies play in these shifts in focus (Gannon and Hayles 2007). Elsewhere in this volume, Stefan Al and Shiloh Krupar outline what they see as a shift from object to atmosphere in the development of corporate 'brandscapes'. See Chapter 14.

8 Venturi's position regarding the role of symbolic form was famously advanced in *Learning from Las Vegas* (Venturi et al. 1977) and has been developed to incorporate electronic display technologies in Venturi (1996).

9 For a discussion of the importation of these illusionistic techniques into historical architecture, see Oechslin (1984). We are indebted to Sylvia Lavin for fruitful discussions on the theatre, architecture, and Diller and Scofidio, as well as for directing our attention to Oechslin's essay.

10 The project, and Liz Diller's 1987 discussion of it at the Architectural Association in London, is reproduced in Diller and Scofidio (1994, 103–134).

11 For a documentation of these projects and an illuminating essay, see Goldberg (2003).

12 See Riley (1995, 132–133).

13 The project was exhibited at the seventh Venice Biennale of Architecture in 2000 and can be accessed at www.embryologicalhouse.com

14 See www.d-toren.nl

15 In many ways, Vinge's fiction follows Venturi's lead toward generic buildings adorned with electronic iconography. But his projection of Venturi's ideas into a dystopian near-future gives rise to consequences well beyond the intentions of Venturi's graphic urbanism.

28

Technology, Virtuality, Materiality

Antoine Picon

A NEW TECHNOLOGICAL LANDSCAPE

A reflection on the present state of the relations between architecture and technology cannot dispense with an examination of the changes that have affected technology in the past decades. These changes are not only a matter of innovations like the massive diffusion of digital tools, the development of genetic engineering or the new perspectives opened by the exploration of nanoscale structures. Pathbreaking and spectacular though these innovations may be, they are only part of a more global evolution. This evolution presents a strong epistemological dimension. In other words, it is not only the content of technology but its very definition that has changed during the past decades. What we now call technology differs radically from the technological world that defined classical forms of industrialization, from early-nineteenth-century England to mid-twentieth-century United States, Japan and Germany. Although we are not yet living in truly post-industrial societies, contrary to the assumption made in 1973 by sociologist Daniel Bell,[1] since industrial production has not so much disappeared as relocalized in countries like China, the rise of a service economy in many developed countries has been accompanied by a series of transformations of the perception and understanding of technology.

The first major difference lies in the loss of relevance of traditional technological objects like cars or aeroplanes. In the everyday experience of technology, objects are no longer as determining as they used to be. They have been superseded by more comprehensive and at the same time abstract entities such as networks and fields. Most of the artefacts that surround us today seem to possess only a fraction of the autonomy that machines of the industrial age were imparted with. We tend to live among quasi objects, connectors or terminals that express properties belonging to networks or fields, like the strength of the signal displayed by mobile phones. The case of mobile phones is, by the way, telling. Some of them, such as the Apple iPhone, crystallize strong desires; but they are nevertheless deprived of real autonomy since they would be of no use without a phone plan and a provider's coverage. Interestingly, decades before the development of wireless communication, Buckminster Fuller had already used the phone to illustrate the partial loss of relevance of objects in a society dominated by service. As he noted with great clarity, to own a phone had no real significance. What mattered was to subscribe to a phone plan (Pawley 1990, 23). Contrary to what the French philosopher Georges Simondon stated in his classical book on technological artefacts, contemporary objects or rather quasi objects cannot be considered as 'individuals' (Simondon 1969). In complete contrast to many of their forerunners, such as the locomotive that appears as a fully-fledged character in Emile Zola's novel, *La Bête Humaine* (2001 [1890]), their existence appears as a mere efflorescence of networks and fields life.

The loss of relevance of technological artefacts is probably at the core of our perception of the ever-increasing importance of virtuality. For the networks and fields that are superseding them are less immediately perceptible as traditional objects. They seem to generate possibilities awaiting an actualization through quasi objects like terminals. A wireless network needs for instance computers or mobile phones to become fully present to its users.

Another fundamental characteristic of the new technological sphere that surrounds us is its more and more seamless nature. Wireless networks are there again emblematic of a world in which networks and fields seem to merge in a more and more fluid way. This explains the success of the metaphoric use of verbs like to surf, to browse or to drift when dealing with realities like the internet. They convey something about the attitude to adopt in a continuous technological world.

In this world, components are less and less assembled according to schemes based on geometry and mechanics. The map with its triangulated landmarks, the structure or the engine with their carefully designed parts used to encapsulate some fundamental principles of technological ingenuity. Nothing was more admirable than the systemic arrangement of elements that characterized a Gothic cathedral or a bicycle. Computers and more generally electronic equipment are no longer designed according to these principles. They present themselves as layered assemblages of hardware and software somewhat comparable to sandwiches. Even more than the inner organization of the layers, it is often their interfacing that matters today, and this interfacing is more akin to problems of code writing and translation than to structural design.

From another point of view, the structural dimension is jeopardized by the world of information. Indeed, structure used to be defined at an intermediary scale between the microscopic and the macroscopic. From animal skeletons to buildings, structure was supposed to embody a specific type of order in between these two infinites. Such specificity is now challenged in a world in which information seems to follow similar patterns at every level. This explains the emblematic role played by fractals. No longer perceived as geometric monsters, fractals seem to embody a fundamental characteristic of a world ruled by information, namely its indifference to traditional hierarchies and scales.[2]

Another disturbing aspect of our present situation is the blurring that often occurs between what used to be infrastructural and what was considered as superstructural. In a transportation company, the software application in use to manage the fleet is often more important than the vehicles themselves. In a similar way, to change one's operating system is a more fundamental decision than to switch from one computer to another. The history of the internet is perhaps the best illustration of this blurring between infrastructure and superstructure, for the network changed its backbone a few times during the first decades of its existence, thus suggesting that its real infrastructural level was that of the users connected to it, as if the small branches and the leaves of a tree were at a higher hierarchical level than its trunk (Abbate 2000).

It is in such a context that the crisis of architectural tectonics that I will evoke in a moment must be appreciated. If one adds to it the profound redefinition of the limits between the natural and the artificial that is taking place simultaneously, one finds oneself confronted by a technological universe that is no longer easy to grasp using univocal categories. We live indeed in a techno-natural universe more akin to what philosophers like Bruno Latour or Peter Sloterdijk describe than to the traditional vision of a human sphere circled by a foreign nature.[3]

This universe can no longer be approached using system analogies. A system is always a collection of discrete parts, the relations of which can be characterized in terms of information processing and feedback loops. Cybernetics or neo-cybernetic models are probably no longer relevant to understanding contemporary technology. More traditional systemic approaches, like historians Lewis Mumford's or Bertrand Gille's attempts to describe technological evolution as a series of systems, are even less convincing (Mumford 1938; Gille 1978).

When dealing with a seamless technological universe, it is tempting to use analytical categories borrowed from landscape theory and history. For this universe, with its pervasive presence and gradual transitions, is more akin to a landscape than to a system. Its networks and fields are analogous to a topography punctuated by quasi objects like terminals, just like the countryside is animated by coppices and cottages. But mentioning the countryside here may be misleading, for the contemporary technological landscape is fundamentally urban, almost identical to the city envisaged globally as a landscape.

Contrary to the disinterestedness that was presupposed by former landscape aesthetics, by Kantian theory in particular (Roger 1997), the contemporary technological landscape does not require a lack of involvement from the subject that perceives it. To the contrary, this landscape is indeed inseparable from the redefinition that affects the subject. A possible characterization of the new subject that is emerging under our eyes may be suggested by the partly imaginary figure of the cyborg that presupposes a link between man and his technology so intimate that it leads to their hybridization.[4] Another figure suggested by the advent of digital culture is the detective or rather the decipherer who can make sense of an environment that often presents itself as a riddle (Rosenheim 1997). There again, the capacity to decipher the technological landscape presupposes a familiarity adverse to the Kantian notion of disinterestedness.

THE CRISIS OF TECTONICS AND ITS TEMPORAL DIMENSION

If one turns now to architecture, one of the most striking features of the contemporary scene is the gradual loss of relevance of structure as a guideline for design. Another way to put it is to invoke, after Kenneth Frampton, the notion of tectonics that corresponds in broad terms, beyond Gottfried Semper's somewhat idiosyncratic definition, to structure translated in architectural terms, that is as space defining. If we are to follow Frampton, modern architecture had valued tectonics above all else (Frampton 1995). This did not prevent many modern buildings attempting to free themselves from the strict rules of structures, beginning with some of Le Corbusier's major realizations.[5] But even when they were reduced to a mere spatial ordinance, structural principles and tectonics played an organizational role. They were also instrumental in conveying the plastic and expressive dimensions of architecture. During the first half of the twentieth century, structural details had progressively replaced traditional ornament as a key element in the aesthetic and symbolic appreciation of architecture. This key role was to attain its climax with Mies van der Rohe and his ornamental use of tectonic articulation in projects like the Illinois Institute of Technology Campus for instance.

When the use of the computer began to spread throughout the architectural world in the mid-1980s, one thought initially that it would reinforce the predominance of structure and tectonics through the new possibilities it offered to pass almost seamlessly from the first sketches to the resolution of detailed technical problems. The smooth process it promised to establish seemed at the time synonymous with a deeper degree of coherence between design and structural decisions. This coherence was also to benefit from the perspective of unlimited parametric exploration. A new field was unfolding under the eyes of the designer, a field where multiple tracks could now be followed in order to reach a perfect fit between form and the technology used to realize it.

In many cases, what has happened is the opposite of these over-optimistic scenarios. Indeed, many key buildings are today marked by a striking discrepancy between architectural form and tectonics. Toyo Ito's Mediatheque was supposed to evoke an aquarium in which weeds floated. Although the realized building has retained part of the initial ambition, it is actually made of heavy duty steel plates that are more akin to ship construction, as if design choices were to a large degree independent from the technology enabling their realization (Witte 2002). A similar distance between the soft fabric suggested by the initial digital presentation and the constructive reality of the building can be observed in the case of the Yokohama Terminal. From Toyo Ito's Sendai Mediatheque to Foreign Office Architects' Yokohama Terminal, there seems to be no alternative than to radically distinguish the spheres of architectural form and tectonics. The distinction is at work in many other contemporary signature buildings. Zaha Hadid's Phaeno Center's all-concrete external appearance is, for instance, contradictory with the structural importance of its floor and roof steel girder grids. In that case also, one can observe a discrepancy between form and tectonics.

There is something paradoxical to observe in how today, on the one hand, the computer allows, as initially expected, intimately articulated conception and realization, while it recreates, on the other hand, a striking distance between architectural imagery and the reality of building techniques. More generally, we seem to be in a state of suspension or even a crisis of traditional tectonic assumptions, a situation closely related to the incertitude that affects scale, for it was scale that granted to structure its foundational role. Frank Gehry's practice constitutes probably one of the best illustrations of this crisis, with its spectacular buildings in which architectural form comes first and foremost with little regard for structural constraints. What the computer does is to make possible the realization of form, even if it is far from optimal in structural terms. The use of Catia enables the designer not only to give a rigorous definition to the most complex geometries; it provides the structural engineer and the contractor with the necessary information to build it, whatever the cost.

Beside Frank Gehry's architecture, there are many other instances of indifference, if not conscious rejection of structural constraints. What is at stake is also a critique of the type of legibility that these constraints implied, a critique at work in Michele Sae's new façade for Drugstore Publicis in Paris, with its undulating glazing in complete contrast with the rigid frame of the original building. Although the deconstructivist agenda has stalled as a whole, its rejection of traditional structural organizing rules is still very much present today. Revealingly, such an attitude is shared by engineers such as Cecil Balmond who present it as a quest for an alternative tectonics based on 'non Cartesian' or 'informal' principles (Balmond 2002). Engineered by Balmond, with its complex maze of posts and beams that defies conventional structural understanding, Herzog and de Meuron's Beijing National Stadium appears as an illustration of this quest. It often uses randomness, or at least the appearance of randomness, as a countermeasure to tectonic habitus. The latter is especially conspicuous in another structure designed by Cecil Balmond in close cooperation with an architect: Toyo Ito's 2002 Serpentine Pavilion. Randomness also explains the success of schemes like Voronoi tessellations, which offer important latitude of variation in the size and shape of their cells.

The tendency to free oneself from traditional structural guidelines must be replaced within the broader frame of a technological world in which, as I said before, the distinction between structural and non-structural levels is becoming increasingly porous. As a cultural production, architecture reflects trends that extend far beyond the scope of the building industry. Closer to the reality of this industry, recent technological developments mean that practically anything goes. With the new possibilities offered by advanced welding or glues, many a traditional rule of assemblage can be disregarded. With their increased performances, materials also play a crucial role in this evolution. Epitomized by Gehry's architecture, the capacity of the computer to transform almost every formal choice into a viable constructive assemblage reinforces the possibilities offered to the architect to play with forms without worrying too much about their structural implications. Given the financial limitations that weigh on much of everyday building production, such a possibility is of course limited to relatively expensive commissions like those entrusted to Ito, Foreign Office Architects or Gehry. For reasons of cost control, traditional structural principles still rule the building industry at large. But projects like Ito's Sendai Mediatheque, Foreign Office Architects' Yokohama Terminal, Gehry's Guggenheim Museum or Herzog and de Meuron's Beijing Stadium are the indicators of an ongoing shift.

The new requirements linked to the quest for sustainability concur to this shift. Sustainability is indeed relatively indifferent to the soundness of load-bearing trajectories and the translation of structural choices into legible tectonics. It involves factors like ecological footprints or dynamic energetic behaviour that obey another type of logic, a logic that involves the entire environment instead of remaining within the limits of the built object like traditional structural requirements.[6] There again, the computer is instrumental in enabling designers to identify and master these factors.

Thus the weakening of structural considerations is linked to a more general shift in the understanding of what matters in the physical world, of what represents challenges not yet addressed by human ingenuity. It does not mean, however, that mechanics has lost its relevance, but rather that its status is changing. Mechanics and structural requirements used to be at the cutting edge of man's science and technology. In comparison with biological and ecological stakes, they are now slowly receding into the background. But this background is more constraining than it may seem at first; one can even consider it as a new limit, of a different nature than the scientific front proper. Two examples may facilitate the understanding of what this status means in practice. The first is hard disk mechanical failure. In the domain of hardware, pretty much everything can be fixed except a hard disk mechanical failure because of the difficulty of restoring the exact speed at which the disk used to rotate before the accident. The second example is provided by the potentially dramatic consequences of the poor shape of civil engineering works in the United States. The scope of the problem was suddenly revealed by the New Orleans catastrophe (Ouroussoff 2005). In both cases, the mechanical and structural dimension represents a new kind of limit. By extrapolation, one may very well imagine a world in which structural achievements are no longer synonymous with advanced technology, while structural factors remain determining, more determining in some ways than cutting edge scientific and technological achievements, the applications of which are less pervasive. After all, before displaying 'green' characteristics, a building must still resist static and dynamic loads.

Among the consequences of the suspension of the traditional tectonic assumptions, one finds a spectacular return of ornament as something distinct from tectonic articulation. For all that, today's architectural ornament has not much to do with the definition that prevailed before the dawn of modernity with its sculptural and above all symbolic dimensions. The symbolic dimension is in particular rejected by many contemporary designers. If we are to follow them, new ornament is more akin to a surface or a field condition; it is often similar to a pattern or a tessellation that aims at producing affects that transcend meaning in the ordinary sense (Moussavi and Kubo 2006).[7] Sauerbruch Hutton's Pharmacological Research Laboratories in Biberach, Germany or Office dA's Obzee Heaquarters project in Seoul, South Korea, are typical of this reinterpretation. Even when the elementary ornamental element is actually an image or a series of images, like on the façade of Herzog and de Meuron's Eberswald Technical School Library in Germany, the overall effect is that of patterning or tessellation.

One finds also a new interest taken in materiality, to which I will return in a moment. Materials are pretty much everywhere today. One can even argue, and this will be my point, that there is a strong link between the development of digital culture and the widespread interest in materiality. The recent work of Herzog and de Meuron is quite emblematic of that connection. From the Basel Schaulager to the San Francisco De Young Museum, it has made an intensive use of pixelization, a technique directly linked to the use of the computer.[8]

Ornamentation, materiality: the question arises of the link between these new dimensions and memory. More generally, what seems to become more and more problematic is the relation between the new technological landscape, which is unfolding before our eyes, and memory, a situation somewhat disconcerting because traditional technology, despite the cult of progress that had become associated to it on the dawn of industrialization, was actually inseparable from memory (Stiegler 1998).

In the architectural field, this strong connection was indicated by tectonics. Indeed, tectonics had to do with questions regarding the origin and the development of the arts. This had been made clear by various theorists, such as the French Abbé Laugier whose mid-eighteenth century Essai sur l'Art was centred on the link between tectonics and the emergence and development of architecture (Hermann 1962). The question would remain fundamental, dealing for instance with the interpretation of Greek Doric and its alleged filiation with wood construction, an issue upon which nineteenth-century theorists sharply disagreed.

Tectonics had another connection with memory through the theme of the ruin. Indeed, the ruin raised, in a direct and unambiguous manner, the question of the relation between architecture and time. What the ruination process ultimately revealed was the tectonic dimension of buildings. Often deprived of their former ornaments, the bare walls and columns, the partly collapsed vaults bore testimony to the dissolving effects of centuries. Like the human skeleton, imbued with an almost equal expressive power, the ruin epitomized the flow of historical conditions. Like the skeleton, it conveyed ideas of death and mourning. But it could also carry notions of rebirth and regeneration, hence the frequent use of ruins as the setting of nativity scenes in order to symbolize the redemption of pagan humanity with the advent of Christianity.

Above all, it was through its articulations, through the play between vertical, oblique and horizontal parts, between supporting and supported members, that tectonics related to time, history and memory. Firstly, these articulations had something to do with the way the human body was understood at the time of their design, a link well conveyed by the Spanish structural engineer Eduardo Torroja when he declared that 'vain would be the undertaking of he who hopes to succeed at laying out the structure without having assimilated, all the way to the marrow of his bones, the principles that govern all the phenomena of internal equilibrium' (Torroja 1971 [1960], 28). Through the analogy with the body and the skeleton, an analogy that has become increasingly difficult to sustain today, tectonics held firmly to a temporality marked by notions of birth, growth, decline and renewal, a temporality in profound accordance with the dimensions of memory and history.

Secondly, although tectonic articulations did not constitute, strictly speaking, a language, they followed a kind of syntax. For their designers, as well as for the public accustomed to decipher the interrelations of structural parts, they held a discourse on the very possibility of constructing an argument about how things were sustained, that is again about time, memory, and history. From nineteenth-century architectural theorist Eugène-Emmanuel Viollet-le-Duc to twentieth-century German historian of art Erwin Panofsky, the temptation was great to relate this discourse to the general structures of reasoning prevailing in a given cultural context. Both Viollet-le-Duc (1863–1872) and Panofsky (1951) tried to interpret Gothic structure in the light provided by medieval ways of thinking.

Among the factors that challenge today the possible analogies between structure, discourse and memory, one finds the tendency to replace constructive parts by parametric relations. As George Liaropoulos-Legendre observes: 'Parametric relationships are not parts [...]. Thus a form shaped by parametric modulation has no discrete limb to speak of – you cannot chop it into pieces, nor indulge in the separate application of permutation, substitution and scaling of parts' (Liaropoulos-Legendre 2003, 2, 7). The qualities of smoothness and elegance that digital designers are generally looking for are adverse to syntax-like tectonic expression.

From the nineteenth century on, the link between architecture and memory was often doubled by a connection to the privileged media of memory and history, namely writing. Despite Victor Hugo's famous statement in *Notre-Dame de Paris* that 'ceci tuera cela', (Hugo 1998 [1831], 289) that writing and printing had replaced architecture as the privileged instrument of collective memory, nineteenth-century architecture was actually trying to rise to the challenge represented by writing, often in a very literal way by making an abundant use of inscriptions on its façades. Labrouste's Bibliothèque Sainte-Geneviève is typical of that endeavour with its lists of famous people carved on its external walls.[9]

Can digital media contribute to a permanent inscription? The question must be raised today. One may of course wonder whether we are really being confronted with the end of tectonics. After all, we might very well be only in a period of transition. Realizations like Herzog and de Meuron's Beijing Stadium can be interpreted both as symptoms of the crisis of tectonics and as the first steps taken towards its reinvention, a reinvention marked by the blurring of the structural and the ornamental dimensions. Instead of evoking the definitive abandonment of tectonics, many theorists and practitioners subscribe to this perspective of rebirth (Leach et al. 2004; Reiser and Umemoto 2006). This is for instance the belief that sustains the researches of an engineer like Cecil Balmond (2002). It is, however, striking to observe how a certain indifference towards structure has developed in the past decades. Also, even if a new tectonics approach was to emerge, the question of its relation to memory would still need to be addressed in order to avoid being trapped in an everlasting present. For that purpose, one would have to invent or rather reinvent the equivalent of weight and inertia in the digitally oriented world that surrounds us. For the time being, one has to recognize that this reinvention is not a priority for architecture.

VIRTUALITY AND PERFORMALISM

The ambiguities that surround the relation of contemporary architecture to time and memory find their counterpart in the increasing importance given to the multiple possibilities that arise at every stage of the design process. These possibilities increase the role played by virtuality as a key dimension of architecture.

Of course, design was always about the capacity of architectural drawing to anticipate not a single built reality but a whole range of possibilities. Drawings and even models were never univocal and their power lay to a certain extent in the ambiguity of their relation to reality, an ambiguity that was synonymous with the power to generate various solutions in practice. As such, architectural conception was inseparable from a virtual space constituted by the endless possibilities that arose through the design process and remained to a certain extent present in the final documents describing the project.

The computer marks, however, a new stage, insofar as it places these possibilities at the very core of the design process instead of letting them appear as a side product of the complex interaction between the rules of the art and the invention of the architect. Through objects and techniques like spline curves and parametric design, the dialectics between rules and invention is gradually integrated in the broader frame of the exploration of a theoretically unlimited field of possibilities. Another way to put it is to state that traditional licences that the designer made use of to interpret the rules of architecture are replaced by a systematic quest for variation.[10] Such an evolution, is of course, linked to the crisis of received principles and rules, the principles and rules of tectonics evoked above, but also the aesthetic guidelines that played an essential role in the diffusion of modern architecture, and made its transformation into an 'international style' possible. One often hears complaints about the difficulty we have today in judging the aesthetic value of the forms produced with a computer. This difficulty is an integral part of the spectacular reinforcement of virtuality as a key dimension of architectural design.

In such a context, form becomes comparable to an occurrence, an event that organizes the flow of possibilities around it like an island reshaping the flood of the river that surrounds it. Form used to appear to the spectator; it now happens on the computer screen as a punctuation of the geometric and technical flows generated by software, those very flows that theorists like Greg Lynn have tried to understand better in reference to the pioneering experiments of Muybridge and Marrey with the recording of movement (Lynn 1998).

For someone working in the financial markets, the temporal, event-like structure of what one sees on a computer is even more evident. What a trader deals with using the latest digital equipment are situations on disputed markets that are comparable to battlefields.

From the start, digital culture was about seeing events. It is worth remembering that one of the first major applications of computer networking techniques, the North American anti-missile system SAGE, designed under the direction of MIT computer scientist Jay Forrester, was meant to allow operators to see situations such as a nuclear strike. The profound connivance between nascent digital culture and the Cold War had to do with the role they both gave to events and their possible integrations into scenarios. In the Cold War perspective, analysed by an historian like Paul Edwards (1996), the computer screen was an integral part of the war room.[11]

The relation between digital culture and events runs even deeper. As the French philosopher Pierre Lévy remarked in a pathbreaking essay entitled 'La Machine Univers', a bit of information is not a thing but an occurrence, an atomistic event (Lévy 1987, 124). It corresponds to something that happens rather than something that is following traditional ontological categories.

As something that happens, architectural form can be also apprehended as break from the theoretically unlimited virtual condition that bathes contemporary design process. One could even compare it to a moment of suspension providing a point of view on that virtual condition. Whereas the conditions leading to its occurrence are about endless possibilities and variations, form is all about effectiveness. This duality between the virtual and the effective may account for the somewhat disconcerting co-existence of two discourses on digital architecture, the first one about potential, simulation and scenario, the second about what architecture can actually achieve, or rather perform, in domains ranging from sensory and emotional affects to the technological criteria attached to environmental sustainability.[12] The performative approach is further reinforced by the suspension of the question of meaning that we have already seen at work around ornament. Today's architecture is no longer supposed to convey a message distinct from the effects generated by its presence. As an event, architectural form is supposed to find its ultimate justification in what it can achieve. One of the most emblematic projects in that respect may very well be Lars Spuybroek's D-Tower (2004). The tower in itself has no meaning. What it does is merely perform, changing colour according to the emotions of a Dutch town's inhabitants. One should note that to perform is not the same as the modernist fulfilment of a function. The tower has neither meaning nor function in the traditional sense. It simply does what it does.

Equally representative, in a more distantiated and ironic mode, is François Roche's proposal for the MI(pi) Bar, a pavilion meant to convert urine into tea at the Massachusetts Institute of Technology. There is perhaps no better illustration of the link between architectural form and event than this project that literally erupts from the wall of I.M. Pei's Wiesner building. Even more than the D-Tower, the MI(pi) Bar is meant to achieve its goal with no regards for traditional meaning or function.

TOWARDS A NEW MATERIALITY

Both dimensions, the virtual and the performative, converge on a new accent put on materiality. Indeed, matter is simultaneously, as the precondition of form, the matrix of all possibilities, and, as something imbued with properties that give birth to the various materials we know, the fundamental level on which the effectiveness of architecture is built upon.

Contemporary materiality implies a more proactive conception of materials (Mori 2002). The computer is an integral part of an approach that has led to an increasingly intimate understanding of the mechanics and physics of materials, from the macro to the nanolevels.[13]

There are various ways to approach this evolution. The first one is to focus on the development of composite and smart materials.[14] They have enabled material scientists to combine properties that used to be mutually exclusive. Glass used, for instance, to be transparent, but its transparency went with poor insulating capacities. Now, as a composite product, glass can be both transparent and insulating, and its use for façades is among the fundamental means at the disposal of architects aiming at environmental sustainability. Even more spectacular, transparency was adverse to load-bearing (Bell and Kim 2008).

Composite and smart materials challenge received notions about products such as fabrics (McQuaid 2005). They also blur the distinction between structures and materials. Indeed, they possess a strong degree of organization in contrast with the vision of materials that had prevailed at the dawn of industrialization. They are instrumental in the progressive shift from structural to material design that has taken place in a series of domains. The radical change in the conception of automobile bumpers offers one of the most striking illustrations of this shift. Automobile bumpers used to be designed as structural protections; they are now made of a composite material that limits car-body damage by absorbing a large part of the energy generated by a collision.

Another way to make sense of material evolution is to relate it to the complex scientific and technological environment that prevails today. Based on multiple collaborations between specialists in mechanics, physics, chemistry and computer science, material design is typical of the trend towards interdisciplinarity and heterogeneity that characterize this environment, or better, landscape. As a paradigmatic field of activity, material design presents a definite epistemological turn.[15]

The perspectives offered by material design accentuate the crisis of structural principles. Indeed, a lot of problems that used to be solved using structural design are now treated by the use of appropriate materials. As we just mentioned our car bumpers are for instance no longer akin to fortifications. They are made of composite materials, the deformation of which absorbs part of the energy released in a collision.

In architecture, materials have taken a new importance in the past decades. Their superficial treatment is often inseparable from the quest for ornamentation. Herzog and de Meuron's pixelation techniques are emblematic of the blurring between material and ornament. But the interest taken in the surface and its ornamental treatment goes beyond the question of materials to touch upon the renewed importance given to sensory experience. From the urban to the architectural scale, digital culture is inseparable from a series of interrogations regarding how and what we perceive (Zardini 2005; Jones 2006). This interest is again related to the question of materiality. Indeed, materiality is not only about materials and their use. It encompasses the way we relate to the world; how we construct the perpetually shifting boundary between the subjective and the objective realms. Just like nanotechnologies, sensory experience is an integral part of it.

Speaking of the subjective, as complementary to the objective, the renewed interest in the sensory and the experiential is of course related to the new definitions of the subject that are on trial today. How do cyborgs or cryptographers perceive their environment? This question is repeatedly raised at the articulation of science and art.

When it was invented, the computer, as suggested by its name, was mainly seen as a machine to compute. Later, the proponents of its Cold War uses discovered that it was also a machine that made a certain type of vision possible, the vision one had on the screens of the SAGE system or in an electronically equipped war room. In the past decades, we have become more and more aware of the computer's more general impact on the relation we have to the physical world (Picon 2004).

For instance, visual codes are changing at a surprising speed. We no longer marvel at the capacity of digital media to allow for effects like zooming in and out with a simple mouse click, and we tend to perceive our ordinary three-dimensional world in the same terms, as if ordinary reality was the result of a provisory compromise, or rather a middle-range lens accommodation between the very small and the extremely large, between atoms, or rather pixels, and galaxies. Immediately recognizable forms and objects seem suspended between closely looked at surfaces and textures that evoke some kind of abstract art, and equally abstract satellite-like views that give, again, precedence to surface and texture effects. In both cases, volume perception seems comprised between two kinds of surfaces or skins. The curious status of form in the digital age, both eagerly sought after and somewhat distrusted insofar as it appears as incapable of stable perfection, is to be put in this perspective. Form is not only relative, dependent upon geometric flows; it is also provisory because of the possibility offered at every moment to zoom in and out.

Is this state of things sustainable in the long term? Will we be able to live in a totally clickable or zoomable world in which every configuration is provisory, suspended between larger and smaller instances? A need for stability might very well arise and call for the reinvention, at least for certain purposes, of non-clickable or non-zoomable entities.

A new form of authenticity could come with this non-clickable or zoomable status; after all, paintings in a museum are not clickable. Neither Leonardo's *Mona Lisa* at the Louvre nor Velázquez's *Las Meninas* at the Prado can be viewed at every possible scale. Based on the impulse to click or zoom, but also on the possibility to see this impulse frustrated, the new materiality that is emerging under our eyes will not be simpler and more homogeneous than the one that it is gradually superseding.

The instability of form can be related to the cultural context created by globalization. Globalization can indeed be characterized as a strange short-circuit between the local and the general, a short-circuit that destabilizes middle-range institutions and practices (Veltz 1996). In our global world we see things either from very close or from an extremely distant point of view. Google Earth is typical of this polarization. Despite the variety of scales it proposes to its users, their attention is usually drawn towards local details or general geographic features. It is certainly no hazard, if the computer has been instrumental in the process of globalization. Zooming might be a mere consequence of the crisis of the traditional notion of scale that is related both to computer use and to globalization, a crisis that generates a specific form of perceptive instability. On that level also, digital architecture is in profound accordance with the world that is unfolding around it.

Such instability seems to blur the distinction between abstraction and concreteness, for nothing is at the same time more abstract and concrete than a texture that challenges interpretations based on the ordinary categories of form and object. More generally, in an age marked by particle physics, the age of the computer, the physics of solids and DNA manipulations, materiality is more and more defined as the intersection of two seemingly opposed categories: the totally abstract, based on signals and codes, on the one hand, and the ultra concrete, involving an acute and almost pathological perception of material phenomena and properties, on the other hand. This hybridization between the abstract and the ultra-material is typical of the new or different materiality that is emerging today.

Through questions like that of ornamentation, digitally produced architecture tries to address these spectacular changes and their impact on our approach to materiality. Architecture is, of course, not alone in this quest. Challenged by the crisis of tectonics and the new possibilities opened by material design, engineering is also getting increasingly concerned.

In such a context, professional identities will have to evolve. From Santiago Calatrava to Marc Mimram, the multiplication of hybrid figures between the architect and the engineer is among the symptoms of the evolution to come (Picon 1994; 2007). These figures are of course not the only ones that are emerging today. Engineer-artists or artist-architects are also becoming more common.

In such a context, one may wonder whether architecture will remain what it is now, a discipline that tries to remain distinct from other forms of design. The exploration of new domains like the nanoscale represents an opportunity to go beyond the traditional disciplinary boundaries. This was one of the suggestions made implicitly by the recent Museum of Modern Art exhibition 'Design and the Elastic Mind' (Antonelli 2008). The seamless contemporary technological landscape is perhaps calling for new transdisciplinary practices.

NOTES

1 For a critique of the shortcomings of this type of analysis, see Pierre Veltz's *Le Nouveau Monde Industriel* (2008 [2000]).

2 On fractal geometry, the best introduction remains Benoît Mandelbrot's *Les Objets Fractals. Forme, Hasard et Dimension* (1989 [1975]).

3 See for instance Bruno Latour's *Politiques de la Nature* (2000).

4 On the cyborg and its relevance to architectural and urban questions, see Antoine Picon's *La Ville*

Territoire des Cyborgs (1998); William J. Mitchell's *Me++: The Cyborg Self and the Networked City* (2003); Matthew Gandy's 'Cyborg Urbanization: Complexity and Monstrosity in the Contemporary City' (2005); Erik Swyngedouw's 'Circulations and Metabolisms (Hybrid) Natures and (Cyborg) Cities' (2006).

5 This is for instance the case with the Convent of La Tourette (Ferro et al. 1988).

6 See for instance on that theme, Jacques Ferrier's *Useful: The Poetry of Useful Things* (2004).

7 A stimulating critique of this anti-meaning stance can be found in Robert Levit's 'Contemporary "Ornament": The Return of the Symbolic Repressed' (2008).

8 For a penetrating study of that question, see Rémi Rouyer's 'Architecture et Procès Technique: Les Figures de l'Imaginaire' (2006).

9 On the relation between nineteenth-century architecture and writing, see for instance Barry Bergdoll's *Léon Vaudoyer. Historicism in the Age of Industry* (1994).

10 On the notion of licence, see for instance Alina Payne's *The Architectural Treatise in the Italian Renaissance* (1999).

11 The relation between the computer and the war room was treated in a spectacular way by director John Badham in his 1983 film *WarGames*.

12 On the performative approach, see for instance Branko Kolarevic and Ali M. Malkawi's *Performative Architecture: Beyond Instrumentality* (2005).

13 On the nanolevel perspective in the case of concrete, see Franz Joseph Ulm's 'Béton: Une Entrée en Matière' (2006).

14 See for instance, Ezio Manzini's *The Material of Invention* (1989 [1986]); and Michelle Addington and Daniel Schodek's *Smart Materials and New Technologies for the Architecture and Design Professions* (2005).

15 On the epistemological dimension of contemporary material science and material design, see Bernadette Bensaude-Vincent's *Eloge du Mixte* (1998).

29

Architecture, Technology and the Body: From the Prehuman to the Posthuman

Jonathan Hale

> Visible and mobile, my body is a thing among things; it is caught in the fabric of the world, and its cohesion is that of a thing. But because it moves itself and sees, it holds things in a circle around itself. Things are an annex or prolongation of itself; they are encrusted into its flesh, they are part of its full definition; the world is made of the same stuff as the body.
>
> (Merleau-Ponty 1964, 163)

A discussion of technology in architecture might usefully begin with a redefinition of 'architecture as technology'. Rather than apparently diminishing design to a mechanical process governed by utility, efficiency and economy, this redefinition should also involve a much broader and possibly unfamiliar understanding of technology itself – one that includes its social, cultural and psychological implications. That it has such wide-ranging and yet often neglected dimensions is perhaps more obvious if we include within the category of technology the sum total of all the things that we produce in the pursuit of a better life. For example: our clothes, furniture, equipment, buildings, cities and even landscapes (to the extent that they are actively organized and productive) – in fact anything made, managed, configured, or transformed in the process of modifying the environment for human habitation. This broad definition should also include less tangible tools such as social structures, conventions, habits, forms of entertainment, styles of behaviour – and even language itself. All of these activities and artefacts should be seen first and foremost as tools for reaching out and engaging with the world. As the anthropologist Tim Ingold has defined the term: 'A tool, in the most general sense, is an object that extends the capacity of an agent to operate within a given environment' (1993, 433).

As Heidegger suggests (1977, 12–14) we live in the space opened up and revealed by technology. As human self-consciousness brings with it the realization of what he describes as *Dasein's* 'thrown-ness' into the world (1962, 223), the fact of our being fundamentally not at home in our so-called natural environment forces upon us the need to fashion a 'third space' in which we are firstly to survive, and secondly to thrive. Focusing on the philosophical and cognitive implications of this technology-created zone of habitation between the body and a hostile world, we might conclude that it is actually constitutive of our fundamental sense of self. To be human – and hence to be embodied – is to be already extended into the world, into what Maurice Merleau-Ponty memorably labelled the 'flesh of the world' (1968): a liminal realm where it becomes more and more difficult to say categorically what belongs to the self and what belongs to the environment. Merleau-Ponty's notion of an intertwining of the body and its perceptual field is based on the fact that we perceive the world through the medium of the experiencing body. Hence it might also be said that we experience the world through the 'technologies' of the body's sensory systems. In perceptual terms this means that it is impossible to make a meaningful distinction between our experience of the objects around us and our experience of the body itself in the act of experiencing. As Taylor Carmen has recently explained (2008, 133): 'Flesh is the *identity* of perception and perceptibility, even below the threshold of conscious awareness. As bodily perceivers we are necessarily part of the perceptible world we perceive; we are not just *in* the world, but *of* it.' Apart from recalling the biblical suggestion of the body's organic continuity with the world ('for dust thou art and unto dust shalt thou return'), this statement also throws into question the idea of a fixed and stable boundary between the self and the environment. A more concrete illustration of this idea of a shifting zone of interchange spanning the body–world boundary is provided by Merleau-Ponty in one of his earlier essays on the painter Paul Cezanne: 'The painter "takes his body with him" says Valéry. Indeed we cannot imagine how a *mind* could paint. It is by lending his body to the world that the artist changes the world into paintings' (1964, 162).

By extending this idea of a continuum linking mind, body and world, it becomes possible to question the simplistic received distinction between nature and society, which – as both Bruno Latour (2007 [1993]) and Félix Guattari (1995 [1992]) have suggested – is an artificial, post-rationalized and highly misleading convention. As an alternative to this restrictive binary logic, in the book *Chaosmosis* Guattari posits a new ontological category to describe the merging of the organic and the mechanical that he labels the 'machinic phylum'. Based in part on a statement by the anthropologist André Leroi-Gourhan that the 'technical object was nothing outside the technical ensemble to which it belonged', Guattari (1995 [1992], 36) extended the notion of the ensemble to include the social, cultural and material networks within which technologies are embedded. The principle of the human 'becoming machine' and the machine 'becoming human' was also suggested by Delueze and Guattari in their now famous example of the symbiotic relationship between wasps and orchids. As the orchid is able to mimic the colouring, scent and texture of the female wasp, the male wasp's frustrated acts of mating inadvertently result in the successful pollination of the flower – creating a moment of temporary hybridization across the boundary of plant and animal kingdoms (1988, 10–11).

What Latour describes as technology's tendency to 'mix humans and non-humans' together involves a process of delegating particular acts of human agency onto technical devices – for example where the corporate concierge is replaced by the humble overhead hydraulic door-closer. While the history of industrialization contains numerous examples of machines replicating ever more complex human functions, this process is really only a continuation of the much longer trajectory hinted at already – the desire to extend the capacity of the body to act in the world through the construction of ever more sophisticated tools. We can therefore conclude that all technologies should be seen in terms of their prosthetic relationship with the body, and – more fundamentally – we might agree with Bernard Stiegler that: 'The prosthesis is not a mere extension of the human body; it is the constitution of this body *qua* "human"' (1998, 152–153).

Despite the seeming inevitability of this hybrid human–machine condition, much of the twentieth-century discourse on the prosthetic has been haunted by its apparent threat to our 'true' nature as human beings. As one notable recent collection (Smith and Morra 2006) has recalled, Sigmund Freud saw it as one of the sources of a curiously modern malaise:

> With every tool man is perfecting his own organs, whether motor or sensory, or is removing the limits to their functioning ... Man has, as it were, become a kind of prosthetic God. When he puts on all his auxiliary organs, he is truly magnificent; but these organs have not grown on to him, and they still give him trouble at times ... [P]resent day man does not feel happy in his Godlike character. (1961, 43–44)

Writing on this theme in the 1960s, Marshall McLuhan adopted an apparently more celebratory tone, describing technological devices as the external organs of the body and media as 'the extensions of man' (1964). Later, in *The Medium is the Massage* – that surprisingly postmodern assemblage of iconic images, aphorisms and typographical games – he enthusiastically proclaimed that: 'All media are extensions of some human faculty – psychic or physical' (1967, 26). His examples included the wheel as an extension of the foot; clothing, of the skin; radio, of the ear; print of the eye. Even 'electric circuitry – an extension of the central nervous system' (1967, 40). This last reference hints at the darker side of McLuhan's prognosis as already set out in *Understanding Media*. One response to the technological enhancement of any one of the body's sensory systems is the recalibration of the other senses in a compensatory act of suppression. McLuhan coined the term 'auto-amputation' to describe the negative consequences of this process, as the nervous system moves to protect itself against the dangers of overstimulation. The ultimate consequence of the gradual technological invasion of the body according to McLuhan is summed up in a memorable chapter entitled 'The Gadget Lover', where he effectively reversed the traditional hierarchy between the body and technology as suggested by Freud's statement quoted above – also anticipating Deleuze and Guattari's reference to the uncanny relationship between the wasp and the orchid:

> By continuously embracing technologies, we relate ourselves to them as servomechanisms. That is why we must, to use them at all, serve these objects, these extensions of ourselves, as gods or minor religions ... Physiologically, man in the normal use of technology (or his variously extended body) is perpetually modified by it and in turn finds ever new ways of modifying his technology. Man becomes as it were, the sex organs of the machine world, as the bee of the plant world, enabling it to fecundate and to evolve ever new forms. (1964, 46)

FROM THE EXTENDED BODY TO THE EXTENDED MIND

Before attempting to assess the architectural implications of this apparently apocalyptic scenario, it is worth considering in more measured terms the underlying principles at work over a broader historical trajectory. To better understand the phenomenon of technological embodiment we might first consider examples of the simplest hand-operated tools. Heidegger refers to the use of a hammer, describing how – when skillfully handled – it effectively 'disappears' or retreats from the user's view (1962, 98–107). Perception shifts from the immediate tactile contact between the hand and the wooden shaft of the hammer, out towards the metal surface which is striking the head of the nail. Awareness is soon dominated by the task rather than the tool, which with practice quickly becomes incorporated into an extended body-image.[1] This is perhaps more clearly evident in the use of tools that directly augment sensory awareness, such as wearing glasses to improve vision or, in Merleau-Ponty's famous example, a blind person navigating with the aid of a white cane

(1964, 143–144). In each case it becomes easier to imagine the technology less as a barrier between the body and the world and more as a means to bring the world even closer. As Merleau-Ponty's concept of 'flesh' implies in its intertwining of body and world, its 'thickness' is 'not an obstacle between them, it is their means of communication' (1968, 135).

This notion of the body being physically extended through the use of prosthetic technologies is also echoed in the writings of the American philosopher John Dewey. While highlighting an organic continuity between the body and the 'outside' world, he also hints at an ethical dimension to the relationship between the organism and its environment:

> The epidermis is only in the most superficial way an indication of where an organism ends and its environment begins. There are things inside the body that are foreign to it, and there are things outside of it that belong to it *de jure* if not *de facto*; that must, that is, be taken possession of if life is to continue. On the lower scale, air and food materials are such things; on the higher, tools, whether the pen of the writer or the anvil of the blacksmith, utensils and furnishings, property, friends and institutions – all the supports and sustenances without which a civilised life cannot be. The need that is manifest in the urgent impulsions that demand completion through what the environment – and it alone – can supply, is a dynamic acknowledgment of this dependence of the self for wholeness upon its surroundings. (1980 [1934], 59)

Dewey's reference to the 'higher scale' of property, friends and institutions reminds us just how dependent we are for our sense of self-identity on a whole network of tools and techniques involving both physical and intellectual functions. Of the latter category, an important analysis has recently emerged within the discipline of cognitive science, exemplified in the work of Andy Clark and David Chalmers and their concept of the 'extended mind' (1998). The authors extrapolate from examples of the most mundane experiences, such as wearing a wristwatch or carrying a diary, which like countless similar everyday objects provide a vital support and prompt to our behaviour. Like our clothing and our cars, these objects quickly become integral to our personality and social standing – part of the definition and representation of who we are and what we are capable of. From notepads to photograph albums these external memory-aids act like computer hard-drives onto which we upload important data to be retrieved when the moment demands. The increasingly familiar and distressing experience of losing one's laptop, wallet, address book or mobile phone provides a vivid example of the acute sense of personal loss involved in even a temporary denial of access to what Clark elsewhere has labelled our 'intellectual scaffolding' (2003, 6–11). Clark's ideas also serve as a reminder that the apparently recent appearance of the hybrid human–machine 'cyborg' entity is hardly a new phenomenon. Ever since the first random rock was used as a hammer to smash a nut, bodies have been merging with technologies in even the most basic technical tasks.

The notion of an externalized and distributed intelligence exemplified in the simple act of recording a thought in a notebook also provokes consideration of the evolutionary implications of historically 'primitive' technical activities. Much as a contemporary archeologist might look on the discovery of ancient tool fragments as a store of information about the material culture of a lost society, it is becoming clearer that early human cultures derived considerable cognitive benefits from the developing capacity to exploit external objects as both embodied tools and carriers of technical knowledge. As archaeologists, ethologists and paleoanthropologists argue over the chronology of early innovations in the realms of language and technology, one likely scenario is that tool-use came first. The ability to imagine, plan and execute an ordered sequence of actions in the making of simple tools could form the basis of the core skills needed to communicate through ordered patterns of sound. This conclusion is also supported by recent advances in brain imaging research which show clear evidence of overlapping areas of specialization within the brain for both language and manual skill – a correspondence also previously suggested by Leroi-Gourhan in the 1960s (1993, 86–89). Clusters of neurons in the left cerebral hemisphere, such as Broca's area, dealing with language comprehension may also be involved in the control of the vocal muscles. These areas are also heavily implicated in the so-called mirror-neuron system which is used for both perceiving and executing our generally right-hand dominated manual activities (Rizzolatti and Sinigaglia 2008, 118–123). These new findings are going some way towards alleviating the problems of speculating upon scant archaeological evidence, of which Leroi-Gourhan was all too aware:

> From this starting point, a paleontology of language could perhaps be attempted, but it would only be a skeleton of a science, for there is little hope of ever recovering the living flesh of fossil languages. One essential point that we can establish, however, is that as soon as there are prehistoric tools, there is the possibility of a prehistoric language, for tools and language are neurologically linked and cannot be dissociated within the social structure of humankind. (1993, 114)

This scenario has been recently extended by the cognitive psychologist Michael Corballis in his book *From Hand to Mouth* to help provide a foundation for his controversial account of the origin of spoken language (2002). Looking back approximately two million years to the appearance of the genus *homo* following the genetic divergence of ape and human species, Corballis imagines the gradual emergence of an embodied gestural language of visual signs and symbols.[2] Based on the archaeological evidence of tool-use among early hominid species it is suggested that the increase in levels of manual skill could have facilitated a more articulate form of visual language. This is in the period prior to the anatomical changes necessary for the production of articulate speech. The development of a gestural language could therefore have produced a kind of generalized 'linguistic competence', creating the ideal conditions – as well as a selective evolutionary pressure – driving the development of other, more sophisticated, forms of communication. An embodied language of manual gestures perhaps assisted by secondary emotional vocalizations would later come to be dominated by the more precise articulations of spoken language as we know it today. This process would also have gradually freed the hands for the subsequently more intense process of technical and artistic innovation. In Corballis' view this is only likely to have occurred among anatomically modern humans, beginning sometime around a hundred thousand years ago with the appearance in the fossil record of the species *Homo sapiens*. Evidence for what has been called a 'big bang' of cognitive and cultural evolution begins to appear in the cave art of the upper-paleolithic period (around 40,000–30,000 years ago) which clearly suggests sophisticated social and ritual behaviour (Klein and Edgar 2002; Lewis Williams 2002; Mithen 1996).

The much debated question of whether technical, social or linguistic intelligence is primary in human development (Mithen 1996) overlooks the fact that language itself involves an inherently technical dimension (Ingold 1993). As a means to reach out beyond the body and manipulate elements of the physical – and social – environment, language reminds us of the embodied origins of technology in the effort to extend our human capacities. As the anthropologist Marcel Mauss has also suggested, technology may be seen to originate with the development of 'techniques of the body': 'The body is man's first and most natural instrument. Or more accurately, not to speak of instruments, man's first and most natural technical object, and at the same time technical means, is his body' (2006 [1935], 83). What Aristotle had previously called the 'tool of tools', the hand was to the nineteenth-century anatomist Sir Charles Bell 'the consummation of all perfection as an instrument' (1834, 231). More recently Raymond Tallis in his book

The Hand: A Philosophical Enquiry into Human Being (2003) has described the process by which the emergence of the earliest technologies might actually have been the catalyst for the slow dawning of human self-consciousness. The growing realization of the instrumentality of the hand as the first proto-technology may well have been the stimulus for the development of a cognitive feedback-loop from which what we now call intelligence emerges. As bodily techniques become gradually extended, solidified and communicated in the form of durable material artefacts, these external deposits of human agency become what Levi-Strauss has called 'tools to think'. This dialectical process by which the human is both 'inventor of' and 'invented by' technology was earlier referred to in Friedrich Engels' discussion of the evolutionary function of labour: 'Thus the hand is not only the organ of labour, it is also the product of labour' (1940, 281). The notion of a mutual reinforcement created by the co-development of technology and consciousness, has also been employed by Jacques Derrida (again with reference to Leroi-Gourhan[3]) in his analysis of the archaic impulse of mark-making as a form of externalized memory:

> If the expression ventured by Leroi-Gourhan is accepted, one could speak of a 'liberation of memory,' of an exteriorization always already begun but always larger than the trace which, beginning from the elementary programs of so-called 'instinctive' behavior up to the constitution of electronic card-indexes and reading machines, enlarges difference and the possibility of putting it in reserve: it at once and in the same movement constitutes and effaces so-called conscious subjectivity, its logos and its theological attributes. (1976, 84)

So, to turn a now familiar idea of technology-as-prosthesis around: instead of thinking of technology as an extension of the body, it might be more enlightening to claim that thinking of the body is an extension of technology. That is, the process of becoming self-aware – or becoming aware of 'having' a body and having a choice as to what to do with it – may ultimately be seen as a consequence of the extension of the body through technology.

(DIS-) EMBODIMENT IN ARCHITECTURE

Having established the human and the technological as mutually co-constitutive, it would be reasonable to consider what kind of consciousness – indeed what kind of human – is currently being constructed by the new tools at our disposal? Or at the very least to ask ourselves as architects – as Peter McCleary has suggested: 'What are the characteristics of knowledge derived during the production of the built environment?' (2007, 326). McCleary takes up Heidegger's analysis of the ready-to-hand relationship with tools and equipment and describes a gradual historical transformation from 'transparent' to 'opaque' technologies. As with Heidegger's description of using a hammer, transparency refers to the withdrawal of the tool from the user's conscious awareness – in favour of what Don Ihde has also called an 'embodiment relation' (1990, 72–80). As perception shifts to the task, the user experiences the characteristic resistance of the material being worked, and hence the accumulation of an embodied knowledge about its possibilities and limitations. As technology becomes more sophisticated, more of the human input is delegated to the tool, first, typically, the power source and then gradually the controls, until we arrive at the fully automated black-box machine from which – at the touch of a button – 'finished products' magically appear. At this point awareness is dominated by the experience of the opaque device, with the human input reduced to consulting numerical gauges and digital read-outs in what Ihde has described as a merely intellectual or 'hermeneutic relation'. Embodied knowledge of material reality is thus reduced to an interpretation of data – a linguistic abstraction of reality that we might today describe as digitisation. Another way of framing this trajectory is provided in McCleary's dialectical model of 'amplification and reduction' which also highlights the experiential consequences of an apparent increase in technological efficiency. One of the clearest examples of this comes from the world of communication technologies, where the telephone (and now, of course, the internet) has created a state of instantaneous real-time contact or telepresence – the realisation of what McLuhan famously predicted as the coming of the 'global village' (1967, 63). If we stop to consider the nature of the exchanges made possible by these advances it is easy to see the sacrifices made in terms of the quality of the communication. Where face-to-face contact provides multiple 'channels' of vocal, gestural and contextual information, by contrast the typically crackling, staccato and often interrupted mobile phone call offers only an impoverished form of contact restricted to the audio channel.

The historical shift from transparent towards opaque technologies happens in large part because of the tendency to offload to other agents more and more of what might be called preparatory activities. Contemporary cooking habits provide a useful illustration of this, with the attraction and convenience of the pre-packaged meal. In this case the preparation of the food has already been delegated to another (unseen) human 'actor' (Latour 1987, 1–17; Cockburn 1992, 32–47). The meal itself – like the microwave oven that is used to re-heat it – has thereby become a 'black-box' technology: its design, ingredients, preparation and packaging are no longer an issue for the impatient consumer. No questions are asked of it other than the recommended length of radiation exposure and the appropriate setting of the oven's power-level. The loss here could be seen in terms of Albert Borgmann's notion of 'focal practices' where both the bodily and social dimensions of cooking and eating are apparently being gradually eroded (1984, 196–210). Even a cursory survey of the various processes involved in growing, harvesting and cooking food provides a useful indication of the kind of knowledge that is becoming less and less familiar. According to Borgmann: 'We are disenfranchised from world citizenship when the foods we eat are mere commodities. Being essentially opaque surfaces, they repel all efforts at extending our sensibility and competence ...' (204–205).

As the day to day experience of designing buildings is gradually reduced to the selection of prefabricated components from product catalogues – and as architects become, somewhat like Adolf Loos' plumbers, simply the 'quartermasters of culture' (1982, 45–49) – a void begins to open in the traditional conception of the designer as creator and author. The position of the designer in relation to the builder of buildings is already one of alienation, in the sense that a division of labour has long since taken place in the professionalization of the architect's role. The history of the architectural profession from the Rennaissance to the nineteenth century involved the creation of a protected and rarefied realm of intellectual activity that separated the art from the craft of building. What Antoine Picon has recently described as a contemporary 'crisis of tectonics' is perhaps just the latest consequence of the progressive distancing of the designer from the process of construction. As less and less embodied knowledge is produced during both the educational and professional experience of the practising architect, it is no surprise that the designer now looks elsewhere than the process of building for the sources of formal invention. Given that all architecture must deal – as Kenneth Frampton has suggested – with the tension between its 'representational' and its 'ontological' dimensions it could be argued that the balance has shifted in recent years decisively in favour of the former (Frampton 1990). It is certainly the case that the modernist link between function and expression has been decisively broken in favour of a Saussurean arbitrariness in the relationship between signifier and signified. As both the building's programme and the tectonic systems are no longer expressively embodied in spatial and material form, Venturi's 'decorated shed' has become one of the dominant architectural paradigms – a supposedly functional but anonymous box wrapped in a slick and seamless signifying skin.

The process of bringing an architectural idea to expression in material reality could usefully be seen in terms of the philosopher Andrew Pickering's concept of the 'mangle' (1995). Pickering has described the process of devising and testing a scientific hypothesis through the construction of increasingly sophisticated technological devices as a kind of collision and interaction between human goals and material resistance. He calls this process the 'dance of agency' – an ongoing, open-ended and temporally structured operation involving a dialectic of resistance and accommodation out of which scientific knowledge ultimately emerges. In the act of constructing a building, a similar process can be observed, whereby the tectonic character of a raw material emerges from its resistance to being shaped and transformed into a building component. This notion could also be applied to the architectural design process itself and the way in which concepts are gradually 'worked out' in the material forms of models and drawings. The visual media of architectural representation also possess their own refractory qualities, and thus new formal and spatial opportunities appear unexpectedly through the exploratory process of graphical presentation, simulation and testing.

Pickering describes how the dialectical nature of the dance of agency allows these new possibilities to emerge through an iterative sequence of actions, as each attempted realization is followed by the designer/ scientist accommodating their ideas to the limitations of material reality. He also questions the traditional dichotomy between human and non-human agency, referring directly to Bruno Latour's notion of 'mixing humans and non-humans together'. He is, however, critical of the semiotic emphasis of Latour's model because it seems to imply an equivalence and interchangeability between the human and non-human actors – another echo of Saussure's principle of the arbitrariness of the sign. Pickering instead suggests that the materialities in each case are fundamentally different, in the sense that so-called raw materials possess resistance and inertia but not intentionality. The argument turns on the question of the conscious human intention implied by the use of the word 'agency', such that Pickering's use of the term 'non-human agency' seems to be little more than a metaphor.

The concept of 'material agency' might be more accurately applied to those materials that have already been transformed into products, and thereby already taken on a form of embedded or delegated human intention based on their original designer's agency. In this case, materials are no longer natural but already cultural phenomena, and hence arrive already loaded with a set of preconceptions about how they might be employed. Whether in science or in architecture most so-called 'raw' materials are actually already technological objects and hence the designer/ experimental scientist has to grapple with multiple levels of agency. This is generally the situation that most architects confront when selecting materials for construction projects, as even apparently natural materials like brick and stone carry both physical and cultural properties. Given the ghostly presence of human intention in even the most mundane constructional component, even Louis Kahn's famous invitation to 'ask the brick what it wants to be' may not now seem so uncanny. The only difficulty with applying Kahn's principle in a world of ever more miniaturized digital technologies is whether the answer will have any significant architectural consequences when addressed to embedded sensors, microprocessors and optical fibres.

In the last great period of rapid technological development towards the end of the nineteenth century, the major architectural innovations were still mainly concerned with structural components that possessed obvious tectonic and formal characteristics. As the masonry wall gave way to frame-and-infill systems, architects looked to engineers for guidance on how best to employ them and it could be argued that it has taken almost a hundred years to achieve their successful assimilation. Today the engineer is still seen as the ultimate source of guidance in coming to terms with the latest technologies, although the rapid pace of change has made it much harder for architects to keep up. Another difference now is that the focus of innovation has shifted, away from visible structure and towards 'invisible' servicing systems. With environmental performance now taking precedence over the visual articulation of structure and materiality, designers are still struggling to find a coherent formal language for what Reyner Banham called the 'well-tempered environment' (1969).

DEMATERIALIZATION

The widespread use of CAD in architectural practice could be blamed for further deepening the divisions between the designer as a maker of drawings and the messy realities of the material world. Paradoxically perhaps, one area in which this technology might also bring them closer together is in the area of environmental performance simulation and its ability to visualize normally invisible processes. This has led some designers towards a greater awareness of the relation between internal and external environmental forces, theorized by the Malaysian architect Ken Yeang (1999) as a reciprocal exchange of energies, in a clear echo of John Dewey's description of the organism being 'completed' by its relationship with its surroundings. The effects of climate on architecture – during both design and occupation – have also been described as a form of material agency in both a literal and a metaphorical sense. In Jonathan Hill's discussion of 'weather architecture' climatic forces are given a similar status to the actions of the creative user (2001). Following the philosopher Henri Lefebvre's example, these unpredictable actors are considered alongside the designer as equally important participants in the ongoing 'production of space' (Lefebvre 1991). Likewise the broader status of architectural practice as contingent upon a multitude of uncontrollable real-world phenomena has been powerfully and precisely reformulated in Jeremy Till's book *Architecture Depends* (2009).

These attempts to expose architectural design to factors beyond the designer's control have also led to a greater use of computational modelling in order to process the potentially vast amounts of additional information at the designer's disposal. One consequence of this is that unpredictable patterns of user behaviour resulting from the decisions of conscious human agents are treated as equivalent to the physical characteristics of 'material agency', with predictably problematic results. One of the best known examples of the recent use of the computer to generate three-dimensional architectural design proposals is in the work of Greg Lynn as described in the book *Animate Form* (1999). Through a series of case studies of apparently live projects, Lynn describes his approach to design from the starting point of a seemingly conventional site analysis. Beginning by mapping the site according to degrees of attraction and repulsion, factors such as traffic noise, pedestrian movement and views out to the landscape are captured as forces or vectors which are then allowed to play out against a generic form:

> The forces were allowed to act in free space and interact with one another in a gradient fashion, as they emanate a field of influence without any distinct contour or boundary. The shapes of these forces included linear, vortex and radial directions along with various parameters for decay, acceleration and turbulence. As there was no way to read these invisible forces except in their ability to affect

objects, we introduced a 3-dimensional grid of particles onto the site. (1999, 144)

A further stage in the materialization of this 'dance of agency' involved a more or less literal solidification of the movements of these particles into a folded surface laid over the site:

> After capturing the particle trails as spline elements, we attempted to generate a massing strategy for the site. This involved constructing an accordion-like surface and placing it within the field of forces. We gave the pleated surface varying elasticity at its vertices and intersections of polygons. These elastic vertex connections were assigned based on the density of particles at any given area. (1999, 146)

The range of forms resulting from these carefully orchestrated processes shares many formal similarities with much contemporary 'organic' architecture. This is curious given the apparent care involved in mapping the unique characteristics of each individual context, which suggests that behind the rhetoric of individuality and site-specificity there is actually another stronger force influencing the outcome. In this case it appears that the chosen tools are having a decisive effect on the design, which leads to a similar question about the role of the architect's agency in relation to the agency of the tool designer. On the one hand there is the possibility that the designer may be attempting to step back from the position of author – delegating the decision-making power to the 'black-box' of the computer software. On the other hand, given that Lynn is working with programmes and algorithms of his own devising, this may also allow the architect to tighten his grip on the design process. While presenting the outcome as the result of an apparently impersonal and objective set of pseudo-scientific operations, the designer has actually reinstated his own agency, albeit distributed amongst his tools. Michael Speaks highlights another of the paradoxes inherent in Lynn's approach to design in its reliance on a thematic of movement expressed in ultimately static forms. Formally this seems to situate the work almost too comfortably within the canon of recent architectural history, without questioning whether this technology might also make possible fundamentally new approaches to architectural practice (Speaks 2001).

The origin of Lynn's and other similar generative methods of design (De Landa 2002) can be traced back to the early development of computer technology and the emergence of cybernetics as a discipline from around 1950 onwards. What Norbert Wiener famously labelled the 'science of control and communication in the animal and the machine' began during World War II in the search for a more accurate means of guiding anti-aircraft guns. Katherine Hayles in her book on the 'posthuman' (1999) has given a thorough account of these developments, structured around a narrative of digitisation – the gradual reduction of the living organism to disembodied information and the reciprocal elevation of the machine to an apparently sentient form of nature. The model of the human as information processor is succinctly if somewhat chillingly expressed by Wiener in the introduction to his attempted popularisation of cybernetics called *The Human Use of Human Beings*: 'Man is immersed in a world which he perceives through his sense organs. Information that he receives is coordinated through his brain and nervous system until, after the proper process of storage, collation, and selection it emerges through effector organs, generally his muscles' (1954, 17). One can also see in this formulation a paradoxically nostalgic yearning to return to an age of unself conscious human awareness – a kind of utopian primal bliss when all organisms apparently lived in an instinctive harmony with nature. In this scenario the human being is reduced to the level of W. Ross Ashby's famous *homeostat* – an adaptive electrical device able to respond to changes in its environment in order to maintain its own internal 'ultrastability' (Ashby 1960, 100–121; Cannon 1963).

Attempts to model architectural design as a disembodied process of information handling soon began to proliferate during the growth of the 'design methods' movement in the 1960s. Christopher Alexander's explicit attempts to mathematize the design process in *Notes on the Synthesis of Form* (1964) were actually soon abandoned by the author in favour of an approach based on typological design 'patterns' – returning to the more familiar language of three-dimensional spatial organization. The success of Alexander's later work in inspiring greater user-participation in design highlights another paradoxical aspect of the computerization process. Both user-engagement (or 'community architecture' as it came to be known in the 1970s) and the current use of generative design algorithms betray a nostalgic yearning to return to a time of so-called unselfconscious design (Alexander 1964, 46–70). When vernacular buildings were produced without architects through the gradual development of craft traditions, architecture resulted from an instinctive process that could be compared with the making of birds' nests and termite mounds (Rudofsky 1964; Turner 2000; Hansell 2007).

Continuing Alexander's project of vernacularization with the aid of today's computing power, contemporary designers are currently pursuing similar ends at both extremes of the construction process – by digitizing the processes of architectural design and production at the same time as automating the finished building's environmental control systems. The fact that neither of these endeavours has so far been totally successful is probably due to the fact that the only realistic way to achieve these goals – given the messy complexity of real-world situations – is to massively restrict the number of variables to be taken into account by any one system. By creating highly artificial design scenarios such as in Lynn's work described above – or by building hermetically sealed enclaves that shut out external disturbance (Banham 1969) – it may be possible to create the illusion of perfectly homeostatic and seamlessly responsive architectural environments. These situations are reminiscent of John Searle's infamous 'Chinese Room' experiment, (Dennett 1991) which was intended as a critique of the current claims of artificial intelligence. The coded messages that are being received and processed through the mailboxes of Searle's sealed-off chamber are meant to create an illusion of equivalence between the 'intelligence' of man and machine. It is clear that this effect is actually created by restricting the information input-output capacity to a ludicrously low level.

REMATERIALIZATION

The process of digitization in architecture follows the principles of coding and decoding: by reducing the world to disembodied data it becomes easier to manipulate it within the virtual realm without the inconvenience of material constraints. As an attempt to avoid the consequences of the 'dance of agency' as described by Pickering, this allows various design operations to be executed and tested without dealing with all the complexities of real-world conditions. Once the designer is satisfied with the solution this is then followed by a reversal of the process: the building is constructed by following the instructions contained in the graphical and textual specification – converting the digital model back into material reality. Accepting that this allows the exploration of a realm of abstract geometric, formal or diagrammatic characteristics (Eisenman 1999) it also seems reasonable to ask how much of the world is trapped or lost in these passages through the digital bottleneck? To put this question into context it also worth recalling that architectural practice as a discipline is predicated on the notion that architects create drawings rather than buildings as such, and have therefore always operated via a form of graphic coding. Historically the arcane operations of geometrical projection have allowed architects to cultivate a quasi-mystical persona, and the curious tools of set-square, rule and compass have been seen to possess an almost magical status (Frascari 1993). Architectural drawings likewise come to be seen as mystical artefacts existing on the boundary between the possible and the actual, even to the extent that buildings can be described as 'representations of the drawings that preceded them' (Frascari 1991, 93). The carving out of a special niche for design within the construction process therefore involves a necessary degree of alienation between thinking and building, which is at the same time both liberating and troubling. Marco Frascari traces this tension through the etymology of the word *technology* and its intertwining of the two Greek terms *techne* and *logos*. By reversing the two parts we go from 'knowledge of construction' to the more intriguing 'construction of knowledge', which Frascari also claims explains the links between thinking and making implied by the common root of the words *constructing* and *construing*:

> Drawings must become technographies, which are graphic representations analogously related to the built world through a corporeal dimension and embodying in themselves the Janus-like presence of technology in architecture, where the *techne* of *logos* (*construing*) cannot be separated from the *logos* of *techne* (*constructing*). (1991, 107)

It is this same corporeal dimension of drawing that is celebrated by Juhani Pallasmaa in his book *The Thinking Hand* (2009). He argues that the 'false precision and apparent finiteness of the computer drawing' suggest a misleading correspondence between representation and reality, whereas the vagueness of the hand-drawn sketch actually allows a deeper cognitive connection to be developed through the medium of the designer's body:

> The hand with a charcoal, pencil or pen creates a direct haptic connection between the object, its representation and the designer's mind; the manual sketch, drawing or physical model is moulded in the same flesh of physical materiality that the material object being designed and the architect himself embody, whereas computer operations and imagery take place in a mathematised and abstracted immaterial world. (2009, 95–96)

Both Frascari's and Pallasmaa's interest in the instruments of drawing is echoed in the writing of Malcolm McCullough who has also tried to re-situate and re-materialize the new digital technologies within the broader history of design tools (1996). Focusing on the nature of the human-computer interface and the concept of what has been labelled 'embodied interaction' (Dourish 2004), McCullogh concludes that the success of the computer as a design tool will depend on its achieving a greater continuity with the material world: 'Virtual craft still seems like an oxymoron; any fool can tell you that a craftsperson needs to touch his or her work. This touch can be indirect – indeed no glassblower lays a hand on molten material – but it must be physical and continual, and it must provide control of whole processes' (McCullough 1996, x). Citing Michael Polanyi's *Personal Knowledge* and Henri Focillon's *Life of Forms in Art*, McCullough makes much of the notion of embodied learning and – like McLuhan – the idea of the tool as a *medium* of experience. The key point for McCullough is the way in which the tool feeds back knowledge of the world through the interface of the designer's body and it is this shortcoming in the current computer modelling process that he is keen to rectify. As the rapid simulation of building performance is beginning to allow the architect a more intuitive grasp of environmental design, it becomes conceivable that more of the tectonic qualities of materials will also become possible to simulate – what could be seen as a gradual widening of the digital bottleneck. This point has also been made persuasively by Bob Sheil in the introduction to an issue of the journal *Architectural Design* in which he described the combined use of analogue and digital modeling in the work of a number of young practitioners (2008, 6–11).

The resistance of materials under conditions of transformation is what gives rise to their tectonic qualities, and, as both Bergson (1988 [1890]) and Dewey have suggested, the body's encounter with material resistance is also the ultimate source of our experience of the world: 'Nor without resistance from surroundings would the self become aware of itself.' (Dewey 1980 [1934], 59). Within the residual physicality of the digital realm it may well be possible to identify useful analogues to the material world – perhaps through a more detailed analysis of the technical composition of digital media at the micro- or even nano scale. Similar studies in related disciplines that could perhaps be mirrored in architecture include Vivian Sobchack's studies of the materiality of film (1992; 2004) and Laura Marks' work on digital video (2002).

The other development which suggests a stronger continuity between the screen and the physical world is the realm of digital fabrication which is gradually restoring some of the lost links between thinking and making. By linking the computer of the designer to that of the manufacturer it allows a kind of mass-customisation of components, offering the prospect of a reunification of design and construction in what could be seen as a 'new middle-ages' (Abel 2004, 61–89; Kieran and Timberlake 2004). Rather than simply selecting ready-made construction products in the role of a specifier or 'quartermaster', the use of CAD-CAM technologies potentially extends the designer's control from the structure to the smallest detail. As Mark Goulthorpe has stated in an interview from 2004:

> We should look to expand material imagination through digital media in more abstract ways. Increasingly I think of a project as a distribution of material in space, not as the assemblage of preformed elements. We're moving from collage to morphing, looking to deploy material as material for its spatial and surface effects. As yet, digital technologies do not facilitate the deployment of material-in-space, but they do instigate a reinvention of material process, in that we're not just inventing 'an architecture' but *the possibility of an architecture*'. (Goulthorpe 2008, 131)

We are not yet at the stage of 'printing' buildings, as we are equally not quite ready to print transplant organs, although biomedical scientists are developing bio-polymer 'scaffoldings' that can be used to help seed and support the growth of new tissue structures – Stelarc's 'Third Ear' project being just one high-profile demonstration (Massumi 1998, 341). These developments are beginning to bring about a change in the status of the architectural drawing which is losing some of its rhetorical functions in favour of a return to the medieval idea of the drawing as template (Anstey 2007, 29). Along with this may come a further move away from the traditional idea of architectural authorship brought about by new collaborative models of practice, such as that suggested by the work of SHoP Architects and others working in flexible networks of international partners and consultants (Coren et al. 2003). This shift provides an interesting echo of the notion of distributed bodily agency explored in several of Stelarc's performance projects, where the artist relinquishes control over his own movements through an array of remotely triggered body attachments.

CONCLUSION

In the apparent distance that all new tools create between our bodies and our surroundings lies the beginning of that process of alienation so memorably theorized by Marx and Engels in the nineteenth century. The resulting tension between thinking and making in the theory and practice of design can be traced back through the evolutionary emergence of technology, which, as suggested above, is also closely intertwined with the dawning of human consciousness itself. The fact that some form of alienation is an inevitable component of this development should not foreclose an examination of the current impact of new technologies on the construction – and continual reconstruction – of our basic sense of self.

Theorists and philosophers of technology as diverse as Michel Foucault (1994) and Jonathan Crary (1999) have charted in considerable and convincing detail the contribution of technical equipment, processes and theories to what might be called the restructuring of the modern subject. As each new technology is designed around an idealized pattern of use, so the users must adjust themselves to fit in with these preconceived forms of behaviour. It is here where questions of technology take us from the aesthetic to the ethical realm, as the embedding of human agency within an increasing number of technical objects can unwittingly offer opportunities for the insidious exercise of political power. This scenario was memorably described by Gilles Deleuze as the coming of the 'society of control', in which modes of resistance to political domination disappear behind the 'opacity' of ever more invisible technologies (Leach 1997, 309–313).

For all the potential dangers of what Heidegger described as modern technology's tendency towards 'enframing', it is not yet clear whether we should go as far as Leroi-Gourhan in describing our current condition as a progressive and inevitable 'loss of the hand' (1993, 255). Given that so much of our productive life is spent in front of a computer screen, it may be that a newly re-embodied digital interface may yet allow us to rediscover it. However they may be enhanced, augmented, redefined and reconfigured, our bodies are – as Merleau-Ponty has suggested – the only means we have to go to the 'heart of things' (1968, 135).

NOTES

1 See also recent experimental observations of neural activity during tool use in primates, e.g., Maravita and Iriki (2004).

2 Corballis is continuing a tradition initiated in the eighteenth century by the French philosopher Etienne Bonnot de Condillac (2001 [1746], 113–137).

3 I am grateful to Chris Johnson for pointing out this connection (Johnson 1997).

Section 6 Bibliography

Abbate, Janet (2000) *Inventing the Internet.* Cambridge, MA: MIT Press.

Abel, Chris (2004) *Architecture, Technology and Process.* Oxford: Architectural Press.

Addington, Michelle and Daniel Schodek (2005) *Smart Materials and New Technologies for the Architecture and Design Professions.* Oxford: Architecture Press.

Alexander, Christopher (1964) *Notes on the Synthesis of Form.* Cambridge, MA: Harvard University Press.

Anstey, Tim (2007) 'Architecture and Rhetoric: Persuasion, Context, Action', in Tim Anstey, Katja Grillner and Rolf Hughes (eds) *Architecture and Authorship.* London: Black Dog Publishing, 18–29.

Antonelli, P. (ed.) (2008) *Design and the Elastic Mind.* New York: Museum of Modern Art.

Arakawa, Shusaku and Madeleine Gins (1979) *The Mechanism of Meaning: Work in Progress 1963–1971, 1978. Based on the Method of Arakawa.* New York: Harry N. Abrams.

—— (2002) *The Architectural Body.* Tuscaloosa: University of Alabama Press.

Ashby, W. Ross (1960 [1952]) *Design for a Brain: The Origin of Adaptive Behaviour.* London: Chapman & Hall.

Baird, George (2004) 'Criticality and its Discontents' *Harvard Design Magazine* 21(Fall/Winter): 16–21.

Balmond, Cecil (2002) *Informal.* Munich: Prestel.

Banham, Reyner (1969) *The Architecture of the Well-Tempered Environment.* London: The Architectural Press.

—— (1970) 'A Home is Not a House', in Charles Jencks and George Baird (eds) *Meaning in Architecture.* New York: George Braziller.

—— (1996) 'A Black Box: The Secret Profession of Architecture', in Mary Banham (ed.) *A Critic Writes: Essays by Reyner Banham.* Berkeley: University of California Press.

Bateson, Gregory (1980) *Mind and Nature: A Necessary Unity.* New York: Bantam Books.

Beaune, Jean-Claude (1989) 'The Classical Age of Automata: An Impressionistic Survey from the Sixteenth to the Nineteenth Century', in Michel Feher, Ramona Naddaff and Nadia Tazi (eds) *Fragments for a History of the Human Body, Part One.* New York: Zone Books, 431–480.

Beckman, John (ed.) (1998) *The Virtual Dimension.* New York: Princeton Architectural Press.

Bell, Daniel (1973) *The Coming of Post-Industrial Society: A Venture in Social Forecasting.* New York: Basic Books.

Bell, Michael and Jeannie Kim (eds) (2008) *Engineered Transparency: The Technical, Visual and Spatial Effects of Glass.* New York: Princeton Architectural Press.

Bell, Sir Charles (1834) *The Hand: Its Mechanism and Vital Endowments as Evincing Design.* London: William Pickering.

Benedikt, Michael (1992) *Cyberspace: First Steps.* Cambridge, MA: MIT Press.

Bensaude-Vincent, Bernadette (1998) *Eloge du Mixte. Matériaux Nouveaux, Philosophie Ancienne.* Paris: Hachette.

Bergdoll, Barry (1994) *Léon Vaudoyer: Historicism in the Age of Industry.* New York: Architectural History Foundation; Cambridge, MA: MIT Press.

Bergson, Henri (1988 [1890]) *Matter and Memory.* Translated by N.M. Paul and W.S. Palmer. New York: Zone Books.

Borgmann, Albert (1984) *Technology and the Character of Contemporary Life.* Chicago: The University of Chicago Press.

Boyer, M. Christine (1996) *CyberCities.* New York: Princeton Architectural Press.

—— (2006) 'The Body in the City: A Discourse on Cyberscience', in Deborah Hauptmann (ed.) *The Body in Architecture*. Rotterdam: 010 Publishers, 26–47.

Braham, William and Paul Emmons (2002) 'Upright or Flexible?', in George Dodds and Robert Tavernor (eds) *Body and Building. Essays on the Changing Relation of Body and Architecture*. Cambridge, MA: MIT Press, 290–303.

Cannon, Walter B. (1963 [1939]) *The Wisdom of the Body*. New York: Norton.

Carmen, Taylor (2008) *Merleau-Ponty*. Abingdon: Routledge.

Carpo, Mario (2001) *Architecture in the Age of Printing: Orality, Writing, Typography, and Printed Images in the History of Architectural Theory*. Translated by Sarah Benson. Cambridge, MA: MIT Press.

Castronova, Edward (2007) *Exodus to the Virtual World: How Online Fun is Changing Reality*. New York: Palgrave Macmillan.

Clark, Andy (2003) *Natural Born Cyborgs: Minds, Technologies and the Future of Human Intelligence*. New York: Oxford University Press.

Clark, Andy and David Chalmers (1998) 'The Extended Mind' *Analysis* 58: 7–19.

Cockburn, Cynthia (1992) 'The Circuit of Technology: Gender, Identity and Power', in Roger Silverstone and Eric Hirsch (eds) *Consuming Technologies: Media and Information in Domestic Spaces*. London: Routledge, 32–47.

Colomina, Beatriz (ed.) (1988) *Architectureproduction*. New York: Princeton Architectural Press.

Colomina, Beatriz (1996) *Privacy and Publicity: Modern Architecture as Mass Media*. Cambridge, MA: MIT Press.

Corballis, Michael C. (2002) *From Hand to Mouth: The Origins of Language*. Princeton, NJ: Princeton University Press.

Coren, Christopher et al. (eds) (2003) *Versioning: Evolutionary Techniques in Architecture*. Chichester: Wiley Academy.

Coulton, J.J. (1977) *Ancient Greek Architects at Work*. Ithaca: Cornell University Press.

Crary, Jonathan (1999) *Suspensions of Perception: Attention, Spectacle, and Modern Culture*. Cambridge, MA: MIT Press.

Damasio, Antonio (2005 [1994]). *Descartes' Error: Emotion, Reason, and the Human Brain*. London: Penguin Books.

de Condillac, Etienne Bonnot (2001 [1746]) *Essay on the Origin of Human Knowledge*. Cambridge: Cambridge University Press.

De Landa, Manuel (2002) 'Deleuze and the Use of the Genetic Algorithm in Architecture', in Neil Leach (ed.) *Designing for a Digital World*. London: John Wiley and Sons.

de l'Orme, Philibert (1567) *Le premier tome de l'architecture*. Paris.

Deleuze, Gilles (1990 [1969]) *The Logic of Sense*. New York: Columbia University Press.

—— (1995) 'Postscript on Control Societies', in *Negotiations: 1972–1990*. Translated by Martin Joughin. New York: Columbia University Press, 177–182.

—— (2005) *Difference and Repetition*. Translated by Paul Patton. New York: Continuum International Publishing Group.

Deleuze, Gilles and Félix Guattari (1988) *A Thousand Plateaus: Capitalism and Schizophrenia*. Translated by Brian Massumi. London: Athlone Press.

Dennett, Daniel C. (1991) *Consciousness Explained*. London: Penguin Books.

Der Derian, James (2001) *Virtuous War: Mapping the Military-Industrial-Media-Entertainment Network*. Boulder: Westview Press.

Derrida, Jacques (1976) *Of Grammatology*. Translated by Gayatri C. Spivak. Baltimore, MD: Johns Hopkins University Press.

Dewey, John (1980 [1934]) *Art as Experience*. New York: Penguin Putnam.

Diller, Elizabeth and Ricardo Scofidio (1994) *Flesh: Architectural Probes*. New York: Princeton Architectural Press.

—— (2002) *Blur: The Making of Nothing*. New York: Abrams.

—— (2003) *Scanning: The Aberrant Architectures of Diller + Scofidio*. Foreword by Maxwell Anderson. New York: Whitney Museum of American Art.

Dourish, Paul (2004) *Where the Action Is: The Foundations of Embodied Interaction*. Cambridge, MA: MIT Press.

Dupuy, Jean Pierre (2000) *The Mechanization of the Mind: On the Origins of Cognitive Science*. New Jersey: Princeton University Press.

Edelman, Gerald M. (1989) *The Remembered Present: A Biological Theory of Consciousness*. New York: Basic Books.

Edwards, Paul (1996) *The Closed World: Computers and the Politics of Discourse in Cold War America*. Cambridge, MA: MIT Press.

Eisenman, Peter (1999) *Diagram Diaries*. New York: Universe.

—— (2003) *Giuseppe Terragni: Transformations, Decompositions, Critiques*. New York: Monacelli Press.

—— (2004) 'Aspects of Modernism: Maison Domino and the Self-Referential Sign', in *Eisenman Inside Out: Selected Writings, 1963–1988*. New Haven: Yale University Press, 111–20.

Engels, Frederick (1940) *Dialectics of Nature*. Translated by Clemens Dutt. London: Lawrence and Wishart.

Eisenman, Peter and John Rajchman (1991) *Unfolding Frankfurt*. Berlin: Ernst & Sohn.

Evans, Robin (1997 [1986]) *Translations from Drawing to Building*. Cambridge, MA: MIT Press.

Ferrier, Jacques (2004) *Useful: The Poetry of Useful Things*. Basel: Birkhäuser.

Ferro, Sergio, Chérif Kebbal, Philippe Potié and Cyrille Simonnet (1988) *Le Corbusier Le Couvent de La Tourette*. Marseilles: Parenthèses.

Focillon, Henri (1989 [1942]) *Life of Forms in Art*. New York: Zone Books.

Foucault, Michel (1994) *The Order of Things*. New York: Vintage Books.

Frampton, Kenneth (1990) 'Rappel a l'Ordre: The Case for the Tectonic' *Architectural Design* 3–4: 19–25.

—— (1995) *Studies in Tectonic Architecture. The Poetics of Construction in Nineteenth and Twentieth Century Architecture*. Cambridge, MA: MIT Press.

Frascari, Marco (1991) *Monsters of Architecture: Anthropomorphism in Architectural Theory*. New York: Rowman and Littlefield.

—— (1993) 'The Compass and the Crafty Art of Architecture' *Modulus* 22.

Freud, Sigmund (1961) *Civilisation and its Discontents*. Translated by James Strachey. New York: W.W. Norton & Company.

Fukuyama, Francis (1995) *Trust: The Social Virtues and the Creation of Prosperity*. New York: Free Press.

—— (1999) *The Great Disruption: Human Nature and the Reconstitution of Social Order*. New York: The Free Press.

—— (2006) *The End of History and the Last Man*. New York: Free Press.

Galloway, Alexander R. (2005) *Protocol: How Control Exists after Decentralization*. Cambridge, MA: MIT Press.

Galloway, Alexander R. and Eugene Thacker (2007) *The Exploit: A Theory of Networks*. Minneapolis: University of Minnesota Press.

Gandy, Matthew (2005) 'Cyborg Urbanization: Complexity and Monstrosity in the Contemporary City', *International Journal of Urban and Regional Research*, 29(1).

Gannon, Todd (2002) 'The Light Construction Reader', lecture delivered at Ohio State University, October 2, 2002.

Gannon, Todd and N. Katherine Hayles (2007) 'Mood Swings: The Aesthetics of Ambient Emergence', in Neil Brooks and Josh Toth (eds) *The Mourning After: Attending the Wake of Postmodernism*. Amsterdam and New York: Rodopi, 99–142.

Gille, Bertrand (1978) 'Prolégomènes à une Histoire des Techniques', in *Histoire des Techniques*. Paris: Gallimard, 1–118.

Goldberg, Roselee (2003) 'Dancing About Architecture', in *Scanning: The Aberrant Architectures of Diller + Scofidio*. New York: Whitney Museum of American Art, 44–60.

Goulthorpe, Mark (2008) *The Possibility of (an) Architecture: Collected Essays by Mark Goulthorpe, dECOi Architects*. Abingdon: Routledge.

Graafland, Arie (1996) *Architectural Bodies*. Rotterdam: 010 Publishers.

—— (2000) *The Socius of Architecture: Tokyo, Manhattan, Amsterdam*. Rotterdam: 010 Publishers.

—— (2006) 'Looking into the Folds', in Deborah Hauptmann (ed.) *The Body in Architecture*. Rotterdam: 010 Publishers, 138–157.

Grosz, Elizabeth (1994) *Volatile Bodies: Toward a Corporeal Feminism*. Bloomington: Indiana University Press.

—— (2001) *Architecture from the Outside: Essays on Virtual and Real Space*. Cambridge, MA: MIT Press.

Guattari, Félix (1995 [1992]) 'Machinic Heterogenesis', in *Chaosmosis: An Ethico-Aesthetic Paradigm*. Bloomington: Indiana University Press, 33–57.

Hansell, Mike (2007) *Built by Animals: The Natural History of Animal Architecture*. Oxford: Oxford University Press.

Hansen, Mark B.N. (2006a) *New Philosophy for New Media*. Cambridge, MA: MIT Press.

—— (2006b) *Bodies in Code: Interfaces with Digital Media*. London: Routledge.

Haraway, Donna (1991) *Simians, Cyborgs, and Woman: The Reinvention of Nature*. New York: Routledge.

Hardt, Michael and Antonio Negri (2000) *Empire*. Cambridge, MA: Harvard University Press.

Hart, Vaughan (1998) *Paper Palaces: The Rise of the Renaissance Architectural Treatise*. New Haven: Yale University Press.

Harvey, David (1992) *The Condition of Postmodernity: An Enquiry into the Origins of Cultural Change*. New York and London: Wiley-Blackwell.

—— (1996) *Justice, Nature and the Geography of Difference*. Malden, MA: Blackwell.

—— (2000) *Spaces of Hope*. Edinburgh: Edinburgh University Press.

—— (2007) *A Brief History of Neoliberalism*. London and New York: Oxford University Press.

Hayles, N. Katherine (1991) *Chaos and Order. Complex Dynamics in Literature and Science*. London: University of Chicago Press.

—— (1999) *How We Became Posthuman: Virtual Bodies in Cybernetics, Literature, and Informatics*. London: The University of Chicago Press.

—— (2005) *My Mother Was a Computer: Digital Subjects and Literary Texts*. Chicago: University of Chicago Press.

—— (2007) 'Hyper and Deep Attention: A Generational Shift in Cognitive Modes' *Profession* 187–199.

—— (2008) *Electronic Literature: New Horizons for the Literary*. Notre Dame: University of Notre Dame Press.

Heidegger, Martin (1962) *Being and Time*. Translated by John Macquarrie and Edward Robinson. New York: Harper and Row.

—— (1977) 'The Question Concerning Technology', in *The Question Concerning Technology and Other Essays*. Translated by William Lovitt. New York: Harper and Row, 3–35.

Herrmann, Wolfgang (1962) *Laugier and Eighteenth Century French Theory*. London: Zwemmer.

Hill, Jonathan (2001) 'Weather Architecture', in Jonathan Hill (ed.) *Architecture – The Subject is Matter*. London: Routledge.

Hillis, Ken (1999) *Digital Sensations: Space, Identity, and Embodiment in Virtual Reality*. Minneapolis: University of Minneapolis Press.

Howe, Jeff (2006) 'The Rise of Crowdsourcing', *Wired* 14.06 (see www.wired.com/wired/archive/14.06/crowds.html?pg=2&topic=crowds&topic_set=.)

Hugo, Victor (1998 [1831]) *Notre-Dame de Paris*. Paris: Le Livre de Poche.

Ihde, Don (1990) *Technology and the Lifeworld: From Garden to Earth*. Bloomington: Indiana University Press.

Ingold, Tim (1993) 'Tool-Use, Sociality and Intelligence', in Kathleen Gibson and Tim Ingold (eds) *Tools, Language and Cognition in Human Evolution*. Cambridge: Cambridge University Press, 429–445.

Johnson, Christopher (1997) *Derrida: The Scene of Writing*. London: Phoenix.

Johnson, Steven (2006) *Everything Bad is Good for You*. New York: Riverhead Trade.

Jones, Caroline (ed.) (2006) *Sensorium: Embodied Experience, Technology, and Contemporary Art*. Cambridge, MA: MIT Press.

Kieran, Stephen and James Timberlake (2004) *Refabricating Architecture: How Manufacturing Methodologies Are Poised to Transform Building Construction*. New York: McGraw-Hill.

Kipnis, Jeffrey (2002) 'On Those Who Step in the Same River ...' in *Mood River*. Columbus: Wexner Center for the Arts.

Kirschenbaum, Matthew (2005) 'Every Contact Leaves a Trace; Computers Forensics and Electronic Textuality'. Presentation at the History of Material Texts, University of Pennsylvania, April 4, 2005.

—— (2008) *Mechanisms: New Media and the Forensic Imagination*. Cambridge, MA: MIT Press.

Kittlausz, Victor G. (2005) *Hybride Architekturen: Transfer von Konzepten und Verortungen des Subjektiven in der zeitgenössichen Architektur*. Berlin: Logos Verlag.

Kittler, Friedrich A. (1997a) 'There is No Software', in *Literature, Media, Information Systems*. Translated by John Johnston. New York: Routledge, 147–155.

—— (1997b) 'Protected Mode', in *Literature, Media, Information Systems*. Translated by John Johnston. New York: Routledge, 156–168.

—— (1999) *Gramophone, Film, Typewriter*. Translated by Geoffrey Winthrop-Young and Michael Wurtz. Stanford: Stanford University Press.

Klein, Richard G. and Blake Edgar (2002) *The Dawn of Human Culture*. New York: John Wiley.

Knorr Cetina, Karin and Urs Bruegger (2002) 'Global Microstructures: The Virtual Societies of Financial Markets' *American Journal of Sociology* 107(4): 905–950.

Kolarevic, Branko and Ali M. Malkawi (eds) (2005) *Performative Architecture: Beyond Instrumentality*. New York and London: Spon Press.

Koolhaas, Rem (1994 [1978]) *Delirious New York: A Retroactive Manifesto for Manhattan*. Rotterdam: 010 Publishers.

—— (1995) 'What Ever Happened to Urbanism?', in Rem Koolhaas and Bruce Mau *S, M, L, XL*. New York: Monacelli Press, 959–971.

Krakowsky, Tali (2007) 'Algorithmic Anthologies' *34 Magazine* 8: 207–215.

Kurzweil, Ray (2006) *The Singularity is Near: When Humans Transcend Biology*. New York: Penguin.

Lakoff, George and Mark Johnson (1999) *Philosophy in the Flesh: The Embodied Mind and its Challenge to Western Philosophy*. New York: HarperCollins.

Lash, Scott (1999) *Another Modernity, A Different Rationality*. Oxford: Blackwell.

Latour, Bruno (1987) *Science in Action: How to Follow Scientists and Engineers Through Society*. Cambridge, MA: Harvard University Press.

—— (1988) 'Mixing Human and Nonhumans Together: The Sociology of a Door-Closer' *Social Problems* 35(June): 298–310.

—— (2000) *Politiques de la Nature*. Paris: La Découverte.

—— (2005) *Reassembling the Social: An Introduction to Actor-Network-Theory*. Oxford: Oxford University Press.

—— (2007 [1993]) *We Have Never Been Modern*. Translated by Catherine Porter. Cambridge, MA: Harvard University Press.

Lavin, Sylvia (2004) 'Three Faces of Tel Aviv' *A+U* 06.

Law, John and Annemarie Mol (eds) (2002) *Complexities: Social Studies of Knowledge Practices*. Durham and London: Duke University Press.

Leach, Neil (ed.) (1997) *Rethinking Architecture: A Reader in Cultural Theory*. London: Routledge.

Leach, Neil, David Turnbull, Chris Williams (eds) (2004) *Digital Tectonics*. London: John Wiley and Sons.

Lefebvre, Henri (1991) *The Production of Space*. Translated by D. Nicholson-Smith. Oxford: Blackwell.

Leroi-Gourhan, André (1993) *Gesture and Speech*. Translated by Anna Bostock Berger. Cambridge, MA: MIT Press.

Levit, Robert (2008) 'Contemporary "Ornament": The Return of the Symbolic Repressed', in *Harvard Design Magazine*, 28(Spring/Summer): 70–85.

Lévy, Pierre (1987) *La Machine Univers: Création, Cognition et Culture Informatique*. Paris: La Découverte.

Lewis Williams, David (2002) *The Mind in the Cave: Consciousness and the Origins of Art*. London: Thames & Hudson.

Liaropoulos-Legendre, George (2003) *The Book of Surfaces*. London: Architectural Association.

Loos, Adolf (1982 [1898]) 'Plumbers', in *Spoken into the Void: Collected Essays 1897–1900*. Translated by Jane O. Newman and John H. Smith. Cambridge, MA: MIT Press.

Lowe, Donald M. (1995) *The Body in Late-Capitalist USA*. Durham: Duke University Press.

Luke, Timothy (1999) 'Spaces of Culture', in Mike Featherstone and Scott Lash (eds) *City-Nation-World*. London: Sage.

Lynn, Greg (1998) *Folds, Bodies and Blobs: Collected Essays*. Brussells: La Lettre Volee.

—— (1999) *Animate Form*. New York: Princeton Architectural Press.

Mackenzie, Adrian (2006) *Cutting Code: Software and Sociality*. New York: Peter Lang Publishing.

Mandelbrot, Benoît (1983) *The Fractal Geometry of Nature*. New York: W.H. Freeman.

—— (1989 [1975]) *Les Objets Fractals. Forme, Hasard et Dimension*. Paris: Flammarion.

Manzini, Ezio (1989 [1986]) *The Material of Invention*. Cambridge, MA: MIT Press.

Maravita, Angelo and Atsushi Iriki (2004) 'Tools for the Body (Schema)', *Trends in Cognitive Sciences* 8(2): 79–86.

Marks, Laura U. (2002) *Touch: Sensuous Theory and Multisensory Media*. Minneapolis: University of Minnesota Press.

Massumi, Brian (1998) 'Stelarc: The Evolutionary Alchemy of Reason', in John Beckmann (ed.) *The Virtual Dimension: Architecture, Representation and Crash Culture*. New York: Princeton Architectural Press, 335–341.

Mauss, Marcel (2006 [1935]) 'Techniques of the Body'. Translated by Ben Brewster, in Nathan Schlanger (ed.) *Techniques, Technology and Civilisation*, New York: Berghahn Books/Durkheim Press, 77–95.

McCleary, Peter (2007 [1988]) 'Some Characteristics of a New Concept of Technology', in William W. Braham and Jonathan A. Hale (eds) *Rethinking Technology: A Reader in Architectural Theory*. Abingdon: Routledge, 325–336.

McCullough, Malcolm (1996) *Abstracting Craft: The Practiced Digital Hand*. Cambridge, MA: MIT Press.

McGann, Jerome (2001) *Radiant Textuality: Literature After the World Wide Web*. New York: Palgrave Macmillan.

McHale, John (1976) *The Changing Information Environment*. London: Elek Books.

McLuhan, Marshall (1964) *Understanding Media: The Extensions of Man*, 2nd. edition. New York: New American Library.

McLuhan, Marshall and Fiore, Quentin (1967) Coordinated by Jerome Agel. *The Medium is the Massage: an inventory of effects*. London: Penguin Books.

McQuaid, Mathilda (ed.) (2005) *Extreme Textiles: Designing for High Performance*. New York: Princeton Architectural Press.

Merleau-Ponty, Maurice (1964) 'Eye and Mind', in *The Primacy of Perception*. Translated by Carleton Dallery. Evanston, IL: Northwestern University Press, 159–190.

—— (1968) 'The Intertwining – The Chiasm', in *The Visible and the Invisible*. Translated by Alphonso Lingis. Evanston, IL: Northwestern University Press, 130–155.

Metzinger, Thomas (2003) *Being No One: The Self-Model Theory of Subjectivity*. Cambridge, MA: MIT Press.

Mitchell, William J. (2003) *Me++: The Cyborg Self and the Networked City*. Cambridge, MA: MIT Press.

Mithen, Steven (1996) *The Prehistory of Mind: A Search for the Origins of Art, Religion and Science*. London: Thames & Hudson.

Moravec, Hans (1990) *Mind Children: The Future of Robot and Human Intelligence*. Cambridge, MA: Harvard University Press.

—— (2000) *Robot: Mere Machine to Transcendent Mind*. New York: Oxford University Press.

Mori, Toshiko (ed.) (2002) *Immaterial/Ultramaterial: Architecture, Design and Materials*. Cambridge, MA and New York: Harvard Design School, George Braziller.

Moussavi, Farshid and Michael Kubo (2006) *The Function of Ornament*. Barcelona: Actar.

Mumford, Lewis (1938) *Technics and Civilization*. New York: Harcourt, Brace and Company.

Neidich, Warren (2006) 'Resistance is Futile: The Neurobiopolitics of Consciousness', in Deborah Hauptmann (ed.) *The Body in Architecture*. Rotterdam: 010 Publishers, 188–211.

Nordmann, Alfred (2004) *Foresighting the New Technology Wave: Converging Technologies – Shaping the Future of European Societies*. European Commission Report. http://ec.europa.eu/research/conferences/2004/ntw/pdf/final_report_en.pdf

Oechslin, Werner (1984) 'Between Painting and Architecture: The Artificiality and Autonomy of Scenography' *Diadolos* 14: 21–35.

Ouroussoff, Nicolai (2005) 'How the City Sank' *The New York Times*, October 9, 2005, Section 2, 1–35.

Pallasmaa, Juhani (2009) *The Thinking Hand: Existential and Embodied Wisdom in Architecture*. Chichester: John Wiley and Sons.

Panofsky, Erwin (1951) *Gothic Architecture and Scholasticism*. Latrobe: The Archabbey Press.

Pawley, Martin (1990) *Buckminster Fuller*. London: Trefoil.

—— (1998) *Terminal Architecture*. London: Reaktion Books.

Payne, Alina (1999) *The Architectural Treatise in the Italian Renaissance. Architectural Invention, Ornament, and Literary Culture*. Cambridge: Cambridge University Press.

Perry, Chris and Christopher Hight (2006) *Collective Intelligence in Design*. London: Academy Editions.

Pesic, Peter (2003) *Seeing Double: Shared Identities in Physics, Philosophy, and Literature*. Cambridge, MA: MIT Press.

Pickering, Andrew (1995) *The Mangle of Practice: Time, Agency and Science*. Chicago: University of Chicago Press.

Picon, Antoine (1994) 'Santiago Calatrava: Tettonicao Architettura ?' *Casabella* 615(September): 24–29

—— (1998) *La Ville Territoire des Cyborgs*. Besançon: Les Editions de l'Imprimeur.

—— (2003) 'Architecture, Science, Technology and the Virtual Realm', in Antoine Picon and Alesandra Ponte (eds) *Architecture and the Sciences: Exchanging Metaphors*. New Jersey: Princeton Papers on Architecture.

—— (2004) 'Towards a New Materiality', *Praxis. Journal of Writing+Building* 6: 114–121.

—— (2007) *Marc Mimram architecte ingénieur Hybrid[e]*. Gollion: Infolio.

Polanyi, Michael (1962) *Personal Knowledge: Towards a Post-Critical Philosophy*. London: Routledge.

Poster, Mark (2006) *Information Please: Culture and Politics in the Age of Digital Machines*. Durham: Duke University Press.

Rattenbury, Kester (ed.) (2002) *This Is Not Architecture*. London: Routledge.

Reiser, Jesse and Nakano Umemoto (2006) *Atlas of Novel Tectonics*. New York: Princeton Architectural Press.

Riley, Terence (1995) *Light Construction*. New York: Museum of Modern Art.

Rizzolatti, Giacomo and Corrado Sinigaglia (2008) *Mirrors in the Brain: How Our Minds Share Actions and Emotions*. Oxford: Oxford University Press.

Roger, Jacques (1997) *Court Traité du Paysage*. Paris: Gallimard.

Rosenheim, Shawn James (1997) *The Cryptographic Imagination: Secret Writing from Edgar Poe to the Internet*. Baltimore: Johns Hopkins University Press.

Rouyer, Rémi (2006) 'Architecture et Procès Technique: Les Figures de l'Imaginaire', PhD dissertation, Université de Paris.

Rudofsky, Bernard (1964) *Architecture Without Architects: A Short Introduction to Non-pedigreed Architecture*. London: Academy Editions.

Russell, Bertrand and Alfred North Whitehead (1911) *Principia Mathematica*, Vol. 1. Cambridge: Cambridge University Press.

Ryan, Paul (2006) 'From Video Replay to the Relational Circuit of Threeing' *Leonardo* 39(3): 199–203.

Scarry, Elaine (1985) *The Body in Pain: The Making and Unmaking of the World*. New York: Oxford University Press.

Schivelbush, Wolfgang (1986) *The Railway Journey: The Industrialization and Perception of Time and Space in the Nineteenth Century*. Berkeley: University of California Press.

Sheil, Bob (ed.) (2008) 'Protoarchitecture: Analogue and Digital Hybrids' *Architectural Design* 78(4).

Simondon, Georges (1969) *Du Mode d'Existence des Objets Techniques.* Paris: Aubier.

Sobchack, Vivian (1992) *The Address of the Eye: A Phenomenology of Film Experience.* Princeton, NJ: Princeton University Press.

—— (2004) *Carnal Thoughts: Embodiment and Moving Image Culture.* Berkeley, CA: University of California Press.

Smith, Marquard and Joanne Morra (eds) (2006) *The Prosthetic Impulse: From a Posthuman Present to a Biocultural Future.* Cambridge, MA: MIT Press.

Somol, R.E. and Sarah Whiting (2002) 'Notes Around the Doppler Effect and Other Moods of Modernism' *Perspecta* 33.

Speaks, Michael (2001) 'It's out There ... the Formal Limits of the American Avant-Garde', in Giuseppa Di Cristina (ed.) *AD: Architecture and Science.* London: John Wiley & Sons, 184–189.

—— (2001) 'Design Intelligence and the New Economy' *Architectural Record*, January 2002. pp. 72–9.

Spuybroek, Lars (2004) *Nox. Machining Architecture.* New York: Thames & Hudson.

Stafford, Barbara (2007) *Echo Objects: The Cognitive Work of Images.* Chicago: University of Chicago Press.

Sterling, Bruce (2005) *Shaping Things.* Cambridge, MA: MIT Press.

Stiegler, Bernard (1998) *Technics and Time, 1: The Fault of Epimethus.* Translated by Richard Beardsworth and George Collins. Stanford: Stanford University Press.

Strickland, Stephanie, Cynthia Lawson Jaramillo and Paul Ryan (2007) *slippingglimpse.* http://slippingglimpse.org

Swyngedouw, Erik (2006) 'Circulations and Metabolisms (Hybrid) Natures and (Cyborg) Cities' *Science as Culture* 15(2): 105–121.

Tabbi, Joseph (2002) *Cognitive Fictions.* Minneapolis: University of Minnesota Press.

Tallis, Raymond (2003) *The Hand: A Philosophical Enquiry into Human Being.* Edinburgh: Edinburgh University Press.

Thacker, Eugene (2004) *Biomedia.* Minneapolis: University of Minnesota Press.

Till, Jeremy (2009) *Architecture Depends.* Cambridge, MA: MIT Press.

Torroja, Edoardo (1971 [1960]) *Les Structures Architecturales. Leur Conception, leur Réalisation.* Paris: Eyrolles.

Turner, J. Scott (2000) *The Extended Organism: The Physiology of Animal-Built Structures.* Cambridge, MA: Harvard University Press.

Ulm, Franz Joseph (2006) 'Béton: Une Entrée en Matière', in Jean-Louis Cohen and G. Martin Moeller (eds) *Architectures du Béton. Nouvelles Vagues, Nouvelles Recherches.* Paris: Le Moniteur, 217–221.

Urry, John (2000) *Sociology Beyond Societies: Mobilities for the Twenty-first Century.* New York: Routledge.

Veltz, Pierre (1996) *Mondialisation, Villes et Territoires: L'Économie d'Archipel.* Paris: PUF.

—— (2008 [2000]) *Le Nouveau Monde Industriel.* Paris: Gallimard.

Venturi, Robert (1996) *Iconography and Electronics upon a Generic Architecture: A View from the Drafting Room.* Cambridge, MA: MIT Press.

Venturi, Robert, Denise Scott Brown and Steven Izenour (1977) *Learning from Las Vegas.* Cambridge, MA: MIT Press.

Vidler, Anthony (2006) 'The b-b-b-Body: Block, Blob, Blur', in Deborah Hauptmann (ed.) *The Body in Architecture.* Rotterdam: 010 Publishers, 130–137.

Vinge, Vernor (2006) *Rainbows End.* New York: Tom Doherty Associates.

Viollet-le-Duc, Eugène-Emmanuel (1863–1872) *Entretiens sur l'Architecture.* Paris: A. Morel & Cie.

Wegenstein, Bernadette (2006) *Getting Under the Skin: Body and Media Theory.* Cambridge, MA: MIT Press.

Wiener, Norbert (1954 [1950]) *The Human Use of Human Beings: Cybernetics and Society.* Boston: Houghton Mifflin.

Winograd, Terry and Fernando Flores (1986) *Understanding Computers and Cognition: A New Foundation for Design.* New Jersey: Ablex Publishing Corporation.

Witte, Ron (ed.) (2002) *Toyo Ito. Mediatheque of Sendai.* Munich: Prestel.

Yeang, Ken (1999) 'A Theory of Ecological Design', in *The Green Skyscraper: The Basis for Designing Sustainable Intensive Buildings.* Munich: Prestel.

Zardini, Miko (ed.) (2005) *Sense of the City: An Alternative Approach to Urbanism.* Montreal and Baden: Canadian Centre for Architecture, Lars Müller.

Zola, Emile (2001 [1890]) *La Bête Humaine.* Paris: Gallimard.

30

Infrastructure

Delia Duong Ba Wendel

In the recovery efforts that followed the 2005 hurricanes in New Orleans, architecture and infrastructure were mobilized as strategies of political activism. For the Lower Ninth Ward neighbourhood in particular, long neglected by municipal government and severely damaged by the hurricanes, involving architecture and infrastructure in political negotiations was critical. In an especially vivid example, the neighbourhood's first responses to the disaster employed architecture as a defensive strategy. Confronted with municipal threats to condemn the neighbourhood as unfit for human habitation, neighbourhood activists

Figure 30.1 (Below) Autonomous architecture, uprooted from infrastructural networks. Partial post-hurricane site plan of the Lower Ninth Ward, overlaid onto a 1951 Sanborn Fire Insurance Map. Dwellings (D), churches and commercial facilities (by name), building materials, and water infrastructure noted. Hatched footprints indicate buildings destroyed by the 2005 flooding; solid white footprints indicate buildings dislodged from their foundations. Asterisks locate buildings structurally assessed by the author, as part of Common Ground's counter property-seizure initiative. (Delia Wendel)

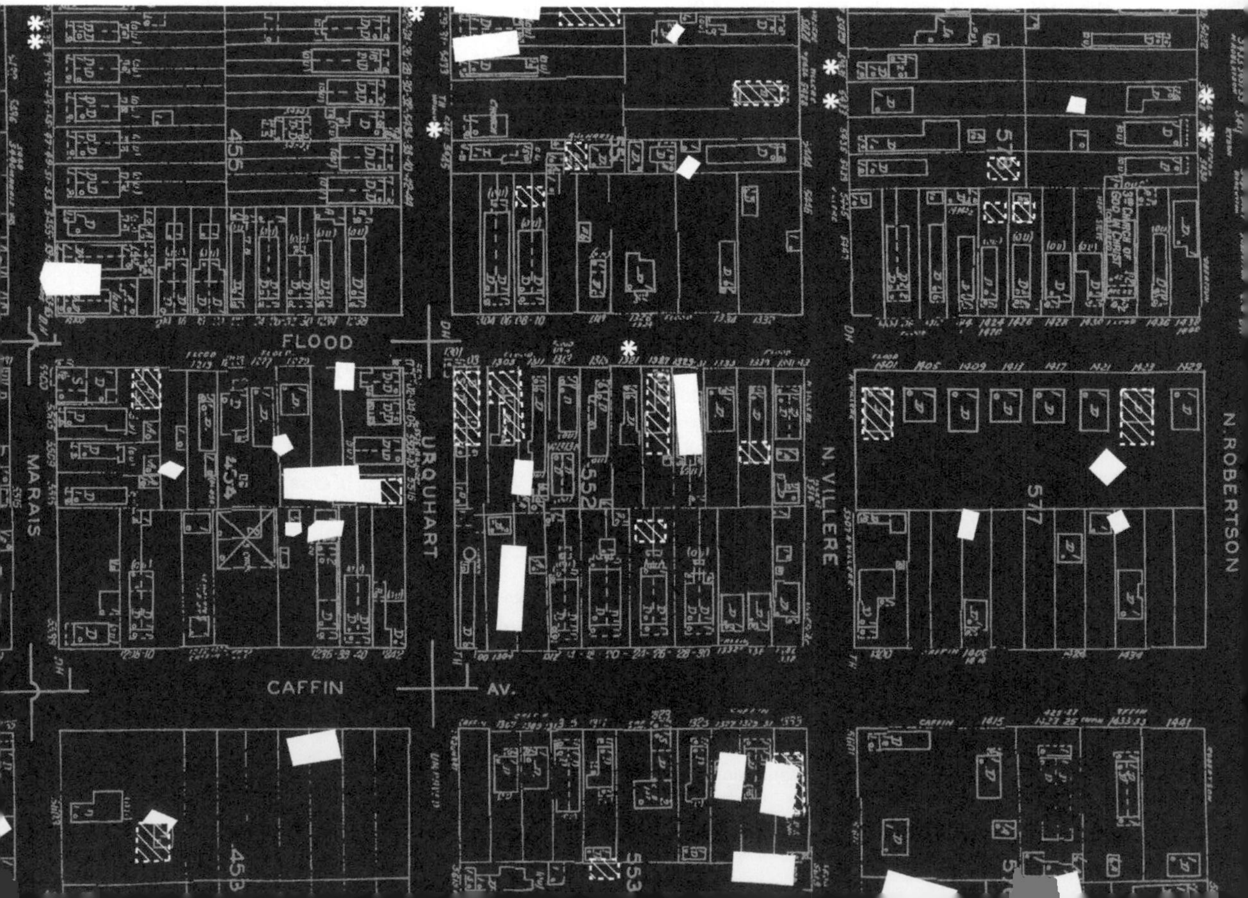

initiated architectural projects to assert the neighbourhood's right to remain. This strategy was marked in its contrast to neighbourhood activism before the 2005 hurricanes, when infrastructure was the focus of negotiations with the city for improved living conditions. This shift from the transactional mode of infrastructure to the secessionist symbolism of architecture can be further distinguished from a second phase of post-hurricane interventions. In late 2006, the community merged these polarized approaches to incentivize financial and public support for the neighbourhood's reconstruction. Infrastructural mechanisms were integrated into architecture, such that architecture operated systemically (and infrastructurally) to address the neighbourhood's crisis. This incorporation of infrastructure in architecture has precedent in architectural history, and toward the end of this chapter, the themes of megastructure and micro-urbanism will be briefly explored to contextualize this third neighbourhood strategy. The following sections illustrate these Lower Ninth Ward strategies to consider the ways in which architecture and infrastructure affect the political empowerment of marginalized neighbourhoods.

ARCHITECTURE AS A DEFENSIVE STRATEGY

The Lower Ninth Ward is located in eastern New Orleans, within four miles of the French Quarter. Before the hurricanes, the area was home to approximately 14,000 residents, the majority of whom were African-American and low- to middle-income homeowners.[1] Established in 1832 as a military outpost, the neighbourhood grew with an influx of freed slaves, rural migrants, jazz and blues musicians and shipping industry workers (Berry et al. 1986; Lewis 2003). One of the notable characteristics of the area is its rich history of community organization in churches (over seventy churches are located within the neighbourhood's two square miles), civil rights groups, and social aid and pleasure clubs that are known for organizing the jazz funerals and second line processions for which New Orleans is famous (DeVore, Dec 2007; Landphair 1999; Regis 1999). Despite this cultural capital, and the fact that African Americans comprised two-thirds of the population in the pre-hurricane city, the Lower Ninth Ward has been marginalized from city politics for decades. This long-term neglect and disinvestment limited the neighbourhood's economic opportunities and affected the quality of social services, housing and infrastructure (Landphair 1999; Sutton, Winter 2005; Wyman 1993).

During the 2005 hurricanes, the Lower Ninth Ward's perimeter levée walls were breached at several locations, causing floodwater levels of between four and twelve feet. This resulted in severe structural and flood damage in over three-quarters of buildings, and weakened both utilities and hazard protection infrastructure (Bates and Green, n.d.: 30; FEMA 2006; Smith and Rowland 2006). Early in the recovery period, the neighbourhood was declared an unviable space by the municipal government, and this impeded rebuilding efforts and infrastructural repairs.[2] However, a comparison of neighbourhoods in New Orleans with similar topographic profiles indicates that the Lower Ninth Ward was not inherently vulnerable to disaster. Rather, its damage was a consequence of a highly localized history of inadequate infrastructure and the construction of shipping channels at its western and northern edges.[3]

The community's first recovery strategies emerged in late 2005.[4] Pressed to act before evacuees could return, activists employed architecture to mark the ground with evidence of residence.[5] Grassroots groups such as Common Ground Collective initiated independent structural assessments to counter the 'eminent domain' seizure of properties by municipal government. The Association for Community Organizations for Reform Now (ACORN) started to rebuild

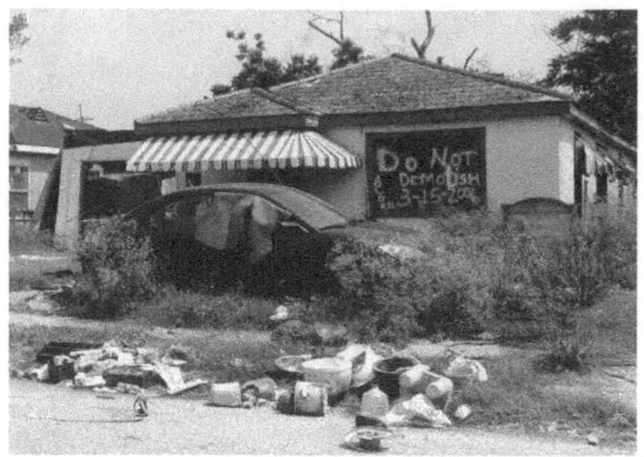

Figure 30.2 (Left) Spray-painted notice by ACORN in defence of eminent domain seizures and premature demolition by the city authorities. In June 2006 when this photo was taken, many residents had not returned because the city authorities prohibited entry to the neighbourhood until May. (Delia Wendel)

Figure 30.3 (Below left) One of two 'Steamboat Houses' built in the Lower Ninth Ward (1905, 1913). Design influenced in part by Mississippi River steamboats. Historically registered in 1977, the houses are often referred to in order to substantiate the neighbourhood's historic credentials. (Delia Wendel)

Figure 30.4 (Below right) One house remaining in a ten- block area that had been densely populated by residences and churches before the 2005 hurricanes. Spray-painted sign on the house reads: 'GUTTING IN PROCESS WILL REBUILD; DO NOT DAMAGE'. (Delia Wendel)

residences, and church groups began denomination-affiliated reconstruction – while the neighbourhood's municipal incorporation was still in question. The New Orleans Preservation Resource Center and the Holy Cross Neighbourhood Association proclaimed the neighbourhood's cultural value with examples of historically registered architecture. Consequently, this diverse range of activists 'untethered' architecture from the land. Characterizations of the neighbourhood's unviability were redirected to the ground, while architectural reconstruction rose above, defiantly under local control.

These reconstruction efforts were informed by the vernacular design logics of neighbourhood residents.[6] Foundations were raised to levels above the 2005 floodlines, water filtration systems were installed, electrical generators were used *in lieu* of functioning utilities, and ventilation continued to be regulated by architectural rather than mechanical means (by deploying a linear, or 'shot-gun', form that naturally drew air through the house). Activists demonstrated extraordinary resourcefulness by rebuilding the neighbourhood largely without functioning water, gas and electrical utilities. Certainly, these tactics were common in other neighbourhoods after the hurricanes. However, unlike the more 'desirable' areas of New Orleans, architecture's autonomy – that is, its disconnection from the infrastructural networks it relied upon – was pronounced in the Lower Ninth Ward. This condition was apparent in the severely damaged landscape, but infrastructural inadequacies had also come to be seen as directly related to the municipality's unwillingness to rebuild the area, and this reinforced the turn to architecture as a means to affirm neighbourhood autonomy.

As the recovery process evolved, it became evident that detaching architectural reconstruction from municipal infrastructure (and planning processes) would only offer short-term relief to threats of eviction and a diminished quality of life. Architecture, even as an embodiment of residents' will, self-sufficiency and history, was not sufficient to guarantee the necessary extension of infrastructural networks to the Lower Ninth Ward. Such was the fortitude of convictions that the neighbourhood was not worth rebuilding. In a context in which land management is critical to civil rights, architectural autonomy was ultimately a limited strategy for comprehensive social justice activism.

INFRASTRUCTURAL NETWORKS

Historically, reparations for the Lower Ninth Ward's marginalization were sought through infrastructure. Infrastructural networks form the complex hardware of our cities, facilitating the movement of people, goods, information, money and natural resources, and protecting against disaster.[7] When Baptiste and Le Moyne mapped New Orleans from the wilderness in 1718, they assessed the land as unfavourable for settlement (Kendall 1922). Today the city remains vulnerable to the flooding of the Mississippi River, storm surges from hurricanes and shrinking coastal wetlands, and sinking due to urbanization and oil infrastructure (IPET, August 2006; 109th Congress Hearing 15 Sept 2005). A natural topography that places the city below sea level, and in a basin surrounded by water bodies, requires complex water pumping and drainage infrastructures to establish the proper grounds for building. That infrastructure should be a point of contention in New Orleans is a consequence of the role it has had in rendering the ground habitable. The possibility of infrastructure's

Figure 30.5 (Below) Delery Street in the Lower Ninth Ward: an unpaved street lacking adequate drainage and sewage infrastructure. Photograph taken in 1959. The Lower Ninth was one of the last neighbourhoods to benefit from the city's streets improvement project. (Louisiana Division, City Archives, New Orleans Public Library)

Figure 30.6 (Below right) View from Deslonde Street toward the Industrial Canal levée wall in the Lower Ninth Ward, nine months after Hurricane Katrina. This area was dense with housing before the hurricanes, and afterward even basic infrastructure was completely destroyed. (Delia Wendel)

catastrophic failure was, in a sense, built into the very fabric of the city. It was in areas such as the Lower Ninth Ward, socially marginal but physically proximate to downtown, that the possibility of failure was entertained (Lewis 2003, 5).

The Lower Ninth Ward's long history of publicly managed infrastructural failures motivated the turn to a defensive architectural strategy after the 2005 hurricanes. At a November 1955 meeting of the New Orleans City Council, Wilfred S. Aubert, then president of the Ninth Ward Civic and Improvement League, listed the following conditions as evidence that the neighbourhood was 'unfit for human habitation':

> Specifically, we refer to poor housing and overcrowded conditions of our schools; the disease-breeding septic tanks, cesspools, outdoor toilets, stagnant water in the gutters; the flooded and muddy streets; the uncollected trash and garbage and the foul odors in the air (Aubert, cited in the *Times-Picayune*, 9 November 1995, 5).

The League petitioned for better street pavements, electricity services, sewerage management, water quality and conveyance, flood controls and public transportation in the neighbourhood. Although the Council met to discuss the desegregation of public space and schools, the League was adamant that the poor quality of its urban infrastructure was equally an issue of social justice. Ten years later, in 1965, Hurricane Betsy's disproportionate destruction of the Lower Ninth Ward consolidated suspicion of municipal indifference toward the neighbourhood (Landphair, December 2007). The following decades of disinvestment only served to reaffirm the Lower Ninth Ward as a low-value space. In the 1980s, a planning firm under contract to the city concluded despondently that the neighbourhood's 'poor physical condition' was the source of its 'negative image and reputation' (EDAW 1980, 1; 114). Despite its control of infrastructure and social services, municipal government did not claim

responsibility for these conditions. And certainly, the years that preceded the 2005 hurricanes did not indicate a change in position. In 2003, Lower Ninth Ward residents rallied against a backdrop of burned-out cars, malfunctioning streetlights and mounds of garbage (McFarley, 15 June 2003). Once again, the neighbourhood organized to protest its substandard infrastructure – this time linking it to high rates of crime in the area. After the 2005 hurricanes funding was hardly forthcoming for an unwanted area of the city that exhibited steady decline during decades of governmental neglect.[8]

Before the 2005 hurricanes, neighbourhood activists were more outwardly concerned with the condition of their infrastructure than with architectural issues such as housing. This was due in part to the implicit understanding that architecture was a matter of private concern.[9] By contrast, infrastructure was synonymous with the public domain. Clearly, infrastructural networks are not merely utilitarian foundations for the efficient operation of our built environments. Infrastructure is intimately intertwined with issues of social justice, in that it connects the conditions of dwelling to wider issues of equitable governance and public

Figure 30.7 (Below) Axonometric drawing of Archigram's 'Plug-In City' project (1963–1964). The rendering presents a megastructure 'kit of parts' comprised of structural frames, 'capsule' housing units to be 'plugged in' to larger structures, and cranes for moving capsules and altering spaces. (Archigram Archives)

Figure 30.8 (Below right) Tokyo micro-urbanism: real estate agency built in the narrow interstitial space between two buildings. The space 'bends' around the shape of the adjacent stair, and occupies only one metre of street frontage. (Atelier Bow-Wow)

responsibility. And as the historical disputes over infrastructure in the Lower Ninth Ward show, in New Orleans high quality infrastructure represents firm socio-political connections to government.

MEGASTRUCTURES AND MICRO-URBANISM

Before I return to the 2005 recovery efforts in the Lower Ninth Ward, allow me to briefly discuss two types of architectural projects that integrate infrastructural mechanisms, as a way of framing the neighbourhood's third reconstruction strategy.

In mid-twentieth-century architectural discourse, megastructures were imagined as architectural frameworks that could override the urban problems of congestion, crime, and municipal and economic dysfunction. Such manic optimism, as illustrated by Archigram's 'Plug-In City' (1963–1964) and 'Walking City' (1963), developed hyper-forms in which architecture performed as infrastructure. The conceit and the dream was that architecture could abdicate from the city, and erect substitutes. Similarly, we could include Cedric Price's 'Fun Palace' (1962), Constant's 'New Babylon' (1962) and Yona Friedman's 'Infrastructures for New York and Los Angeles' (1965) as examples (Banham 1972; Friedman 1965). Megastructures created extensive environments of multiple levels and high complexity for the heightened interaction of people and traffic. Each of these projects imagined vast machinic architectures that were to be provisional and expandable in terms of structure, space and use. They implied a social vision for architecture, in which uninhibited individuals gained flexibility and fun. Despite these intentions, the total design of a seemingly inescapable environment was limiting. The disavowal of existing conditions only

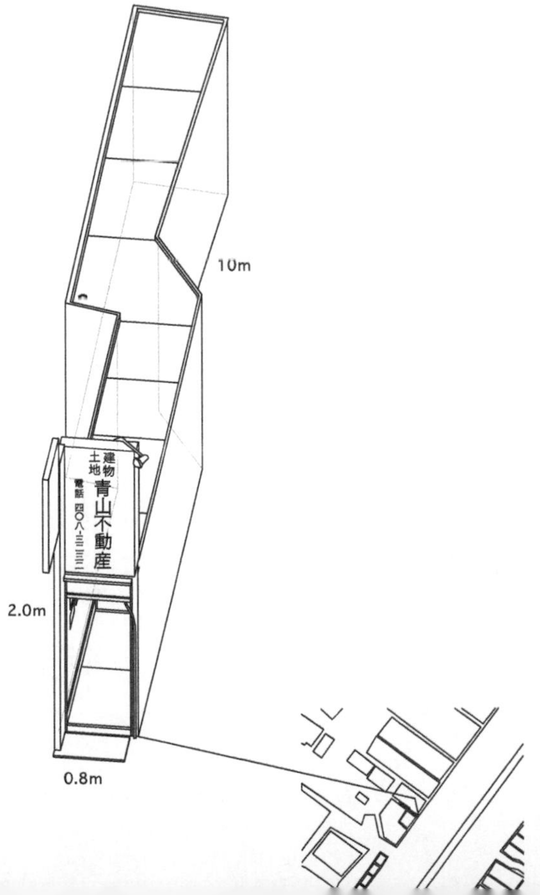

Figure 30.9 (Right) Piet Blom's 'Noah's Ark' thesis was presented by Aldo Van Eyck in 1962, to Team X at the Royaumont meeting on the 'Issue of Urban Infrastructure'. It was rejected by the group as an 'unlivable' and unbounded proposition (Smithson 1968, 679, 687). Nevertheless, the project would continue to be debated in architectural circles for its extreme integration of form (architecture), and 'counterform' (infrastructure). See D. Apon, February 1961. (Jaap Hengeveld Publicaties)

demonstrated irreverence to direct solutions for urban problems.

With similar aspirations, Team X, Christopher Alexander and Japanese Metabolists theorized architecture as networks (Alexander et al. 1977; Maki 1964; Smithson 1968). Urban networks of commodities and transactions revealed the significance of connectedness to the urban

Figure 30.10 (Below left and right) Maps of the Lower Ninth Ward, with buildings before and after the 2005 hurricanes. Data retrieved from the Lower Ninth Ward Neighbourhood Association. (Delia Wendel)

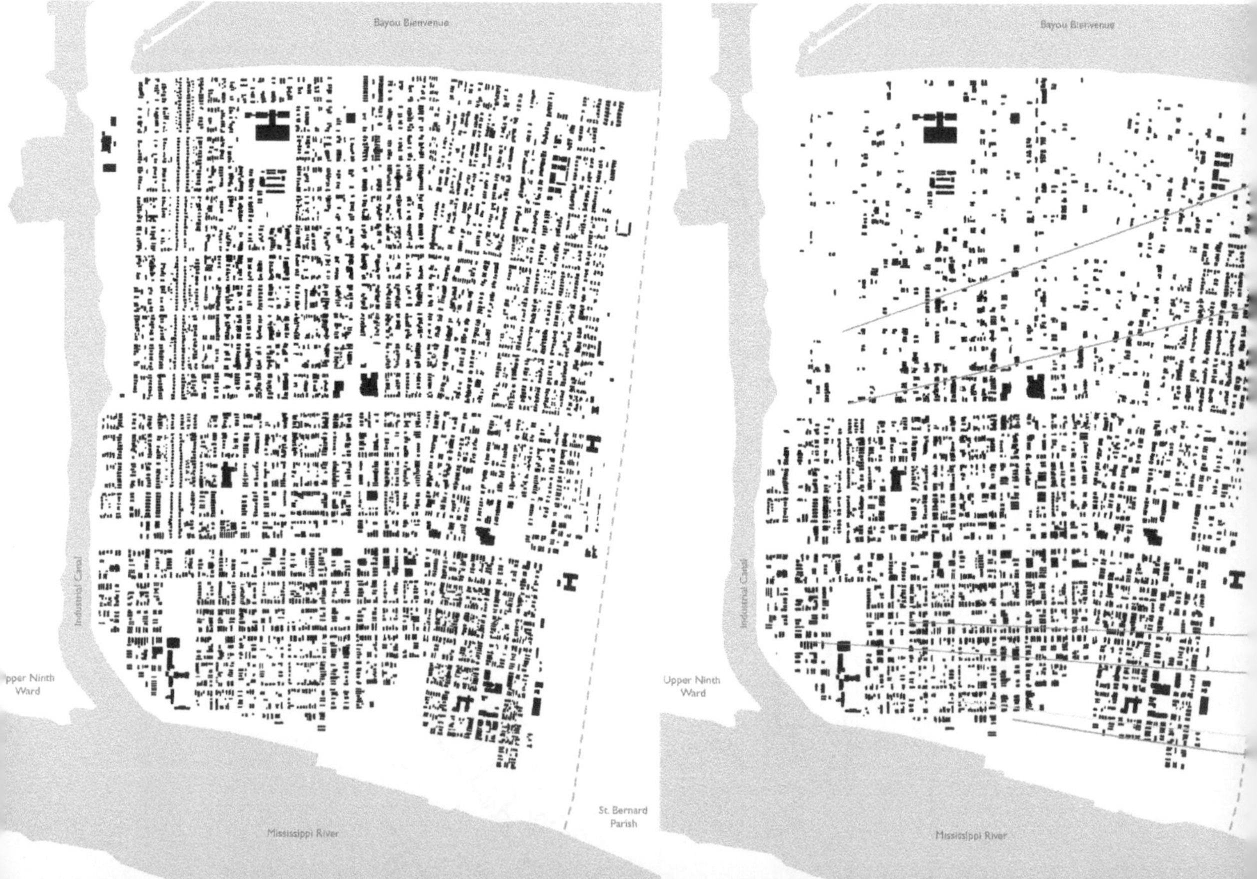

condition, the complexity of modern human relations, and the freedoms in mobile economies (Smithson, 1975). Networked architecture had surpassed the megastructure concept of infrastructure as framework. 'Mat buildings' simulated interconnected flows of money, goods, people and information by pushing the limits of architectural scale to rhizomatic tectonics. These projects organized territories in an anti-monumental manner, unlike the megastructure compression of infrastructure into highly visible mechanistic forms. Kenzo Tange's 'Tokyo Bay Project' (1960), Piet Blom's 'Noah's Ark' (1960), Candilis, Josic and Wood's Toulouse-le-Mirail development (1962), and even Le Corbusier's Venice Hospital (1964) produced architecture as connective tissue, linking programmatic use (transportation, dwelling, shopping, working, etc.) in the city through material and formal continuity (Banham 1976; Sarkis et al. 2001; Smithson 1975). While sensitive to the artifice of the city and the pertinence of technology to urban life, these architectonic networks remained unresolved at the scale of their units. Instead, they presented a vision for the 'maximum possibility' of architecture's transformation of urban infrastructure (and urban life).

Mega- and mat-buildings claimed to administer urban crises through complex formal strategies that assumed infrastructure was everywhere available. The Lower Ninth Ward had already been excluded from this ideal concept of the city. For decades activists unsuccessfully pursued mega-infrastructural development. Conversely, when architecture was employed as a defensive strategy immediately after the hurricanes, activists sought autonomy from municipal oversight and infrastructure. Although this was a statement of refusal rather than a proposed reinvention of the area, mega-projects provide comparable precedents for this desire to override existing conditions. By contrast, micro-urbanism provides a better comparison for an architecture

that has a contingent relation to its political environment.

In the 1990s, micro-urbanism rejected the earlier large-scale approaches to urban renewal. Micro-urbanism operated through ad-hoc and opportunist tactics in the city. In 2001, Japanese firm Atelier Bow-Wow catalogued eighty-one buildings in Tokyo – restaurants, shops, kiosks, dwellings – in their *Pet Architecture Guide Book* (Kaijima and Tsukamoto 2001). The book drew attention to micro-buildings that had 'wriggled' into spaces between larger structures, latching onto existing infrastructures, effectively taking advantage of building and lot mismatches that arose from inconsistent application of planning regulations. This form of city-making values a precise and tactical relationship with immediate contextual fabrics, and the possibilities of non-governed design. Elsewhere this approach has been politicized through agit-prop and anarchist re-uses of space.[10] At its most basic, however, micro-urbanist sites operate within infrastructural networks as 'switches' to initiate more liberating uses of a city's resources, and as 'resistors' to carve out spaces for undervalued urban residents.

Within architectural discourse, the interest in infrastructure stems from the desire to design malleable frameworks that have wide urban effects while also facilitating autonomous activity. This potential has historically been obstructed in the Lower Ninth Ward

Figure 30.11 (Below) Two advertisements depict houses and residents in the Lower Ninth Ward to promote the neighbourhood's sustainable building practices and assert its cultural vibrancy and history. One of several examples of community organization employed to reinvent the neighbourhood as a 'beacon for sustainable development for New Orleans and the world'. (Historic Green New Orleans)

by the lack of municipal support for neighbourhood development. Unlike the micro-urbanism and megastructure approaches, the area is too large to operate within urban interstices and too undervalued to incentivize mega-development. Compared to these precedents, the neighbourhood's own architecture-as-infrastructure strategy developed from similar aspirations. But as the following section demonstrates, significant differences exist in scale and stakes.

ARCHITECTURAL NODES AND INFRASTRUCTURAL NETWORKS

In late 2006, Lower Ninth Ward activists merged earlier strategies to employ architecture to manage infrastructure and public support more broadly. The neighbourhood turned to ecological design. Like megastructures and micro-urbanism, architecture reconfigured infrastructure. Rain-water collection, biologically treated waste systems, brise soleils, weather seals, elevated ground floors, permeable ground treatments for increased water drainage and solar panels for energy collection exemplify the integration of infrastructural mechanisms in architectural form. Two non-governmental foundations initiated this shift by organizing sustainable design competitions and building residential prototypes in the area (Eggler, 16 Apr 2007; Hales, 15 Jul 2006; Krupa, 29 Sep 2007). By integrating what had been exclusively

Figure 30.12 (Below) Brad Pitt's 'PinkProject' installation occupied several razed residential blocks in the Lower Ninth Ward, and inaugurated the 'Make It Right' Foundation's sustainable development initiative. The solar panels lit the area at night, symbolizing a reinvented 'green' iconicity for the neighbourhood. (Delia Wendel)

publicly maintained infrastructure within the private dwelling, at the scale of 150 new residential units, this approach left the previously polarized infrastructure and architecture strategies behind.

The community's interest in this architectural strategy followed seemingly divergent motivations. From an oppositional standpoint, ecological architecture facilitated the local management of infrastructure. The mechanisms architecture employed to capture natural resources and protect against future flooding provided the means to secede from municipal infrastructural networks. This sensibility parallels the 1970s development of 'local' and 'appropriate' practices to counter harmful industrial by-products in marginalized spaces (Carson 1962; Schumacher 1973; and United Church of Christ 1987). Similarly, the vulnerability and governmental neglect experienced after the 2005 hurricanes prompted consideration of ecological models. Although sustainability generally refers to homeostatic systems engineered to protect nature, in this neighbourhood, sustainability refers primarily to the community's survival.[11] Residents were amenable to an unfamiliar architecture that could provide them with self-sufficient systems. With this sensibility under the surface, local oppositional politics connected subtly to a globally popular ecological aesthetic.

From a conciliatory standpoint, ecological architecture primed the neighbourhood's political spokesmanship. The merger of architecture and infrastructure promised to

Figure 30.13 (Below) House on Jourdan Street, Lower Ninth Ward, retrofitted with solar panels. One of ten installations by Sharp Corporation's 'Sola' in 'NOLA' initiative, supported by the Preservation Resource Center and the Louisiana Department of Natural Resources. (enerG Magazine)

reinvent the neighbourhood as a place of value; as 'a beacon for sustainable development for New Orleans and the world' (Global Green 2007). This aphorism aligned the neighbourhood with both regional action against climate change and national environmental concerns. Presciently, in the 1960s, Buckminster Fuller and John McHale introduced this transactional capability, suggesting that systematizing architecture with 'models of flow, distribution and reuse' could efface oppositional politics (Wigley 1996, 3, 5). While the total erasure of decades of discriminatory policies is arguable, in the Lower Ninth Ward ecological architecture was conceived as a positive deception. As a representational strategy, it did not engage directly with the neighbourhood's contentious history of injustice and disinvestment. Instead, it looked beyond these intractable issues to stimulate municipal support via association with celebrity and a popular attitude toward the built environment.

Through both of these rationales, infrastructural networks were drawn into residential architecture and re-politicized, allowing the politics of brinkmanship and negotiation to co-exist. By bridging the architectural divide between micro-urbanist isolationism and totalizing megastructures, this second phase of activism successfully merged the politics of micro-intervention with a vision of maximum possibility. Accordingly, Lower Ninth Ward architecture brandishes the socio-political promise of a recalibrated infrastructural network.

CONCLUSION

As reflected in its struggle over architecture and infrastructure, the Lower Ninth Ward has been teetering somewhere between connectedness and secession for several decades. Historically, publicly provided infrastructural networks were considered a civic right, and the primary means for connecting (physically and politically) with the municipality. To protest the municipality's exclusive control over urban infrastructure, architectural activism fueled the standoff between the neighbourhood and the municipality immediately after the 2005 hurricanes. In the second phase of the neighbourhood's post-hurricane activism, infrastructure was re-tooled at the architectural scale. The integration of infrastructural mechanisms in architectural form provided the Lower Ninth Ward with an increased degree of self-sufficiency. Through the transactional capability of ecological architecture, negotiations with the city were kept open. In this way, architecture acted as a political catalyst to solicit support and funding for the neighbourhood. Megastructures and micro-urbanism provide comparative points for architectural projects that attempt to act systemically, like infrastructure, to address urban problems. But these precedents are limited in that they tend to reinforce a politics of brinkmanship, and are not designed to negotiate with oppositional forces in the city. Through recognition of and engagement with the thickened ground on which it stands, Lower Ninth Ward architectural nodes work in concert with infrastructural networks of reconciliation and empowerment.

NOTES

1 Of the 14,000 residents surveyed in the 2000 U.S. Census, 98.3% were African American, 59% were homeowners (compared to the 46.5% city-wide average), and a third lived at or below the poverty line (GNODC, n.d.; Logan, January 2006).

2 Municipal directives and media representations cited chronic poverty, crime and flooding as reasons not to rebuild the neighborhood. The first municipal rebuilding plan, coordinated with the Urban Land Institute, proposed to shrink the city to provide a safer and cheaper city "for returning residents in the higher neighborhoods" (John McIlwain of ULI, quoted in *The Economist*, 22 Apr 2006). Together with four other neighborhoods, the Lower-Ninth-Ward was to be converted to wetlands and green

spaces using forced buyouts if necessary (Cobb, 23 Jan 2006; Calmes, 15 Sep 2005). The notion of increased safety was interpreted in two ways: first, the lower neighborhoods would physically protect the 'new' New Orleans; and second, by 'neutralizing' these neighborhoods as green space, problems of poverty and crime would be removed. Although no longer under consideration in its entirety, the lack of municipal rebuilding programs and funding for the Lower Ninth Ward suggest that remnants of the proposal remain.

3 Several experts have argued that the Lower Ninth Ward's vulnerability to flooding is not a natural proclivity. Historian John M. Barry has written: "to say you can't re-inhabit the Ninth Ward because of safety is a bit of a phony argument ... If you build a good flood-control system, the entire city is safe. If we don't the entire city is dangerous" (1998, 222). Furthermore, as Lauria and Soll demonstrate, locating the Industrial Canal on the western edge of the Lower Ninth Ward purposefully separated this low-income African American neighborhood from the central city and increased its vulnerability to disaster (1996). Similarly, the manmade Mississippi River Gulf Outlet at the neighborhood's northern edge has been called a 'hurricane superhighway'; a conduit for storm surges that have plagued the area (Breunlin and Regis, Dec 2006). After the 2005 hurricanes, Geologist Roy Dokka compared the neighborhood's topography with less devastated neighborhoods Metairie and Kenner to argue that low land elevation was not the primary cause of damage (Filosa, 1 May 2006). Dr. Mashiriqui supported this, blaming flawed engineering in the Lower Ninth Ward's levee protections (Schwartz, 25 Apr 2006).

4 For additional detail on these defensive architectural strategies, see Wendel 2009. These observations were made during field research in the Lower Ninth Ward, during June-July 2006 and December 2007.

5 There are approximately 3500 residential lots in the Lower Ninth Ward. The neighborhood was the last to be re-opened to residents after the hurricanes under the city's 'Look and Leave' (allowing inspection of properties but with an imposed curfew) and 'Look and Stay' (allowing reoccupation of the neighborhood) decrees.

6 Although vernacular architecture is the focus of this analysis, it is not upheld as universally valuable. The benefits of architectural invention should be weighed alongside those of architectural memory, especially in highly political situations. These debates have a history, of course. For notable examples, see Bernard Rudofsky (1964) who romanticized the vernacular as a counterpoint to modern urban 'mess', and Kenneth Frampton's (1998) reaction to the homogeneity of Modern architecture by privileging architectural responses to local contexts (defined by sun exposure, climate, topography, etc).

7 The infrastructural protections that mediate the tensions between humans and nature in New Orleans constitute an extreme example of a familiar urban condition. When effective, infrastructure facilitates progress. From the First World War, a veritable 'technological society' developed from an unprecedented scale of transformation in the landscape (dams, electrification, land drainage), transportation infrastructure (automobiles, railroads, highways, bridges), communications (radio, television and the Internet), and military and Space innovations. But when infrastructure is substandard, spaces are disconnected from sociopolitical and economic possibility, and more vulnerable to natural hazard. Even in highly developed urban environments the exclusionary effects of infrastructural networks are apparent (Castells 2004; Graham and Marvin 2001). Infrastructural networks are material indicators of a naturalized paradox in our contemporary urban conditions, locating contiguous ascendancy and disadvantage in the landscape.

8 In December 2006, Mayor Nagin vowed that the city would be rebuilt in its entirety, but stated that recovery would be phased to prioritize recovery efforts in the unflooded areas before moving east of the Industrial Canal, to the Lower Ninth and New Orleans East neighborhoods (Filosa, 18 Dec 2006). Nagin declared "market forces" would drive the prioritization of recovery efforts, thereby shifting financial responsibility for recovery to private bodies and residents with means. Nagin acknowledged: "The Lower 9th Ward will probably be the last area. That's just the way citizen investment has gone" (*ibid*). The Mayor's Office of Recovery Management has since identified the Lower Ninth as one of 17 'target recovery zones' in the city, but both the extent of municipal involvement in the rebuilding process and the timeline for reconstruction remain unclear (Mayor's Office, 29 Mar 2007). $136 million has been allocated to this 'target zone', but actions to follow these allocations have been stalled by City Council disputes, federal delays, and fund mismanagement (Eggler, 8 Jan 2009; Guillet, 25 Jun 2007). The situation suggests a high reliance on laissez faire redevelopment strategies, particularly for areas in need of substantial recovery.

9 Although the majority of Lower Ninth Ward residents owned their homes, relegating housing to the private domain, the city was responsible for limiting economic opportunities and social services in this area. Certainly these factors have had impact on the resources of residents to rebuild and maintain their homes. Furthermore, homeownership in this area is not a recent acquisition; the majority of homes were deeded from previous generations.

10 For the founder of the Urban Flash movements in China, microurbanism creates spaces for 'urban nomads', such as: merchants in informal economies, the homeless, migrant workers and politically minded youth (Chi, Nov 2003). Urban Flash tactics draw inspiration from Parent and Virilio's (1996) 'Oblique Architecture' and the Situationists 'detournement' for a guerrilla architecture that operates in the interstices of government-sanctioned capitalist enterprises.

11 Pam Dashiell, president of the Holy Cross Neighborhood Association, reacted to the neighborhood's vulnerability: "[after the hurricanes] it was apparent we needed to be as resourceful and resilient and *sustain* ourselves as best as possible." (Italics mine. Quoted in Russell, 11 Mar 2007).

BIBLIOGRAPHY

109th U.S. Congress, Hearing Before the Committee on Government Reform House of Representatives (15 September 2005) *Back to the Drawing Board: A First Look at Lessons Learned from Katrina.* Washington, DC: US Government Printing Office. Serial No. 109–85.

Alexander, Christopher, Sara Ishikawa, Murray and Silverstein (1977) *A Pattern Language: Towns, Buildings, Construction.* New York: Oxford University Press.

Apon, D (1961) 'Ding-contrading [Thing-Counterthing]', *Forum* 61(5), 179–188.

Aubert, Wilfred S (1955) Help Promised by Councilmen: Ninth Ward Group Asked to Back Bond Issue. *Times-Picayune,* 9 November, p. 5.

Banham, Reyner (1976) *Megastructure: Urban Futures of the Recent Past.* London: Thames & Hudson.

Barry, John M (1998) *Rising Tide: The Great Mississippi Flood of 1927 and How It Changed America.* New York: Simon & Schuster.

Bates, Lisa K. and Rebekah A. Green (n.d.). *(Mis)uses of data: what counts as damage in post-Katrina New Orleans recovery planning.* New Orleans Collaborative Planning: Faculty Research, University of Illinois at Urbana-Champaign.

Berry, Jason, Jonathan Foose and Tad Jones (1986) *Up From the Cradle of Jazz: New Orleans Music Since World War II.* Athens, GA: University of Georgia Press.

Breunlin, Rachel and Helen A. Regis (2006) Putting the Ninth Ward on the Map: Race, Place and Transformation in Desire, New Orleans. *American Anthropologist* 108(4), 744–764.

Calmes, Jackie (2005) The Katrina Cleanup – As Gulf Prepares to Rebuild Tensions Mount Over Control. *Wall Street Journal,* 15 September p. A-1.

Carson, Rachel (1962 [2002]) *Silent Spring.* New York: Mariner Books.

Castells, Manuel (2004) Spaces of Flows, Spaces of Places: Materials for a Theory of Urbanism in the Information Age', in Braham and Hale (Eds.), *Rethinking Technology: A Reader in Architectural Theory* (pp. 440–56). New York: Routledge.

Chi, Ti-Nan (2003) 'Introduction to Micro-Urbanism', *Architectural Design: Urban Flashes Asia* 73(6), 16–21.

Cobb, Kim (2006) Razing versus Rebuilding: Restoring New Orleans, house by house; Volunteers labor to prove that the hardest-hit areas are still habitable. *Houston Chronicle,* 23 January, p. A-1.

DeVore, Donald E (December 2007) 'Water in Sacred Places: Rebuilding New Orleans Black Churches as Sites of Community Empowerment', *Journal of American History,* 94(3), 762–769.

EDAW, Inc (1980) *Ninth Ward Study: Socio-economic Existing Conditions Volume 4*: Prepared for the Board of Commissioners of the Port of New Orleans.

Eggler, Bruce (2009) City Council approves batch of 2007 grants; But clash still simmers on economic fund. *Times-Picayune,* pp. M-1.

_______ (2007) Planning panel approves 'green' project; Low-income housing backed by Brad Pitt. *Times-Picayune,* 16 April, pp. M-1.

FEMA (2006) *Current Housing Unit Damage Estimates: Hurricanes Katrina, Rita and Wilma.* Washington, DC: The Office of the Federal Coordinator for Gulf Coast Rebuilding at the Department of Homeland Security.

Filosa, Gwen (2006) The Lonely Lower 9: 16 months after Hurricane Katrina, hope is rare as people on the streets of the Lower 9th Ward. *Times-Picayune,* 18 December, pp. N-1.

Frampton, Kenneth (1998) 'Towards a Critical Regionalism: Six Points for an Architecture of Resistance', in Hal Foster (Ed.), *The Anti-Aesthetic: Essays on Postmodern Culture* (pp. 17–34). New York: New Press.

Friedman, Yona (1965) 'Infrastructures for New York and Los Angeles', *Arts and Architecture* 82(6): 23–4.

Global Green (2007) USA mission statement for Lower Ninth Ward 'green' development, October 30, holycrossproject.globalgreen.org.

GNODC, Greater New Orleans Data Center (n.d.). *Lower Ninth Ward Neighborhood Snapshot, Post-Katrina Population & Housing Estimates, and Pre-Katrina Information Based on the US 2000 Census.* Online 1 September 2006: www.gnocdc.org/index.html

Graham, Stephen and Simon Marvin (2001) *Splintering urbanism : networked infrastructures, technological mobilities and the urban condition.* New York: Routledge.

Guillet, Jaime (2007) Funding pitfalls surround New Orleans citywide plan. *New Orleans City Business.*

Hales, Linda (2006) Putting New Orleans On the Green Line. *Washington Post,* 15 July, pp. Style-C2.

IPET, Interagency Performance Evaluation Taskforce (2006) *New Orleans Hurricane Protection Projects Data: Post-Katrina Final Report.* Online 27 August 2006: ipet.wes.army.mil/.

Kaijima, Moyoyo and Yoshiharu Tsukamoto (2001) *Pet Architecture Guide Book.* Tokyo: World Press Photo.

Kendall, John Smith (1922) *History of New Orleans, Volumes 1–3.* New York: Lewis Publishing Company.

Krupa, Michelle (2007) Brad Pitt is helping rebuild Lower 9th Ward, but residents have leading role. *Times-Picayune,* 29 September.

Landphair, Juliette (1999) Sewerage, Sidewalks, and Schools: The New Orleans Ninth Ward and Public School Desegregation', *Louisiana History: The Journal of the Louisiana Historical Association* 40(1), 35–62.

______ (2007) '"The Forgotten People of New Orleans": Community, Vulnerability, and the Lower Ninth Ward', *Journal of American History* 94(3), 837–845.

Lauria, Mickey and Michael J. Soll (1996) 'Communicative Action, Power, and Misinformation in a Site Selection Process', *Journal of Planning Education and Research* 15(3), 199–211.

Lewis, Peirce F (2003) *New Orleans : The Making of an Urban Landscape* (2 ed.). Charlottesville: University of Virginia Press.

Logan, John R (2006) *The Impact of Katrina: Race and Class in Storm-Damaged Neighborhoods.* Brown University, Online 20 August 2006: www.s4.brown.edu/Katrina/report.pdf.

Maki, Fumihiko (1964) *Investigations in Collective Form.* St. Louis: Washington University School of Architecture.

McFarley, Jason (2003) Neighbors call for change at 9th Ward rally; City Officials pledge crackdown on litter and crime problems. *Times-Picayune,* 15 June, p. N1.

Mcllwain, John (2006) Flooding back? A misguided new plan to help New Orleans. *The Economist,* 22 April.

New Orleans, Mayor's Office of Communications (29 March 2007) *City Announces First 17 Target Recovery Zones; Areas Will Attract Investment, Residents to Key Resources.* New Orleans: Mayor's Office Press Release.

Parent, Claude and Paul Virilio (1996) *The function of the oblique : the architecture of Claude Parent and Paul Virilio 1963–1969.* London: AA Publications.

Regis, Helen A. (1999) 'Second Lines, Minstrelsy, and the Contested Landscapes of New Orleans Afro-Creole Festivals', *Cultural Anthropology* 14(4), 472–504.

Rudofsky, Bernard (1964) *Architecture without Architects: A Short Introduction to Non-Pedigreed Archtecture.* New York: Museum of Modern Art.

Russell, Pam Radtke (2007) Here Comes The Sun; Solar power starts to shine in Lower 9th. *Times-Picayune,* 11 March, pp. Money-1.

Sarkis, Hashim (ed.) (2001) *CASE Le Corbusier's Venice Hospital and the Mat Building Revival.* Cambridge, Massachusetts Harvard Graduate School of Design.

Schumacher, E.F (1973) *Small is Beautiful.* New York: Harper & Row.

Schwartz, John (2006) How Low is the Lower 9th? Ward's Fate May Lie in the Answer. *New York Times,* 25 April, pp. National: A-24.

Smith, Jodie and James Rowland (2006) Temporal Analysis of Floodwater Volumes in New Orleans After Hurricane Katrina, *Science and the Storms: the USGS Response to the Hurricanes of 2005*: United States Geological Survey.

Smithson, Alison (1968) *Team 10 Primer.* Cambridge, MA: MIT Press.

Smithson, Alison and Peter (1975) 'Team 10 at Royaumont, 1962', *Architectural Design* 45(11), 664–689.

Sutton, Will (Winter 2005) New Orleans' Lower Nine Fades, Fades, Fades Away. *Nieman Reports, 59.*

United Church of Christ, Commission for Racial Justice (1987) *Toxic Wastes and Race: A National Report on the Racial and Socio-Economic Characteristics of Communities with Hazardous Waste Sites.* New York: United Church of Christ.

Wendel, Delia D. B. (August 2009) 'Imageability and Justice in Contemporary New Orleans', *Journal of Urban Design* 14(3), 345–376.

Wigley, Mark (1996) 'Recycling Recycling', *Interstices* 4(November).

Wyman, Russell E (1993) *The Stumpin' Grounds: A Memoir of New Orleans' Lower Ninth Ward*. New Orleans: SUNO Center for African and African American Studies.

SECTION 7

Nature/Ecology/Sustainability

31

Introduction: Whither 'Earthly' Architectures: Constructing Sustainability

Simon Guy

QUESTIONING SUSTAINABLE ARCHITECTURE

> To reflect on the prehistory of sustainability is not to find 'precedents' of practices that give us tips for the present. Rather these reflections aim to mobilize critical perspectives on the shifting definitions of the term and on the practices that are advanced in its name so as to guard against absolutes. Can architects have partnerships with techno-scientific fields without subsuming design to managerialism and anti-intellectual postures? Can ecological problems be debated in architectural circles without resorting to eco-determinism? Can architects embrace an ethical imperative without resorting to moralistic prescriptions or grand metanarratives? Maybe, but to walk between these fine lines it is important for both the profession and academia to constantly interrogate and contest emerging strategies. (Pyla 2008, 16)

It's May 2009 and I'm wandering the aisles of the library at the National University of Singapore to collect more material for this chapter on sustainable architecture for *The SAGE Handbook of Architectural Theory*. Heading initially towards the architecture section, I detour through geography and pick up a classic book by the American geographer David Harvey on *Justice, Nature and the Geography of Difference* (1996). Sociology is nearby, so I pause and discover that the British sociologist Anthony Giddens is now writing about *The Politics of Climate Change* (2009). Browsing the sociology of science section, I am reminded that the French ethnographer of technology Bruno Latour has written on the *Politics of Nature* (2004a). Checking through the indexes of each book I note further references, which send me to other corners of the library, to anthropology, politics and then on to history, until finally I sit down in front of a structurally suspect tower of books to start reading.

And then, I realize that I haven't yet made it to the architecture section. Almost presciently, the first book I discover there is a collection of essays on *Nature, Landscape and Building for Sustainability* (Saunders 2008) taken from back issues of the *Harvard Design Review*. The introduction is by Robert L. Thayer, Jr., who opens by suggesting: 'The interacting notions of nature, landscape, and sustaining design at times might seem simple, but they often slip sideways, like a blob of mercury, when pinned down' (Saunders 2008, vii). Anyone venturing into debates about sustainable architecture is unlikely to disagree with this observation for everyone, it seems, is a green architect now, and each has her own interpretation of the environmental challenge and her own blueprint for a sustainable future. As Susannah Hagan has pointed out, 'a profound and wide-ranging reappraisal of material culture, initially hijacked by geeks and hippies, is being developed within the disciplines of political science, geography, cultural theory, philosophy, economics, the fine arts, the life sciences, and – at last – architecture' (2008b, 100).

Almost fifty years on from Rachel Carson's *Silent Spring*, much ink has been spilled in describing our troubled relationship to nature and how we might forge a new partnership. As Djalali and Vollaard have illustrated (Fig 31.1), ideas about sustainability have been travelling fast, across disciplines, ideologies and geographies, shifting from a residual notion of ecological balance, through an emergent critique of modernization and the identification of alternative modes of design (Hagan's 'geeks and hippies') to a point were we might now arguably identify sustainability as the dominant mode of architectural culture. Following the collapse of public and professional faith in modernism and a long period of uncertainty, drift and discord, characterized by the competing aesthetic styles that have marked the era of postmodernism, the ideal of 'sustainability' appears to have

Figure 31.1 (Below left and right) 'Complex History of Sustainability. A timeline of Trends, Authors, Projects and Fiction', was first published in *Volume 18 After Zero* (Winter 2008). (Amir Djalali and Piet Vollaard and the Archis Foundation)

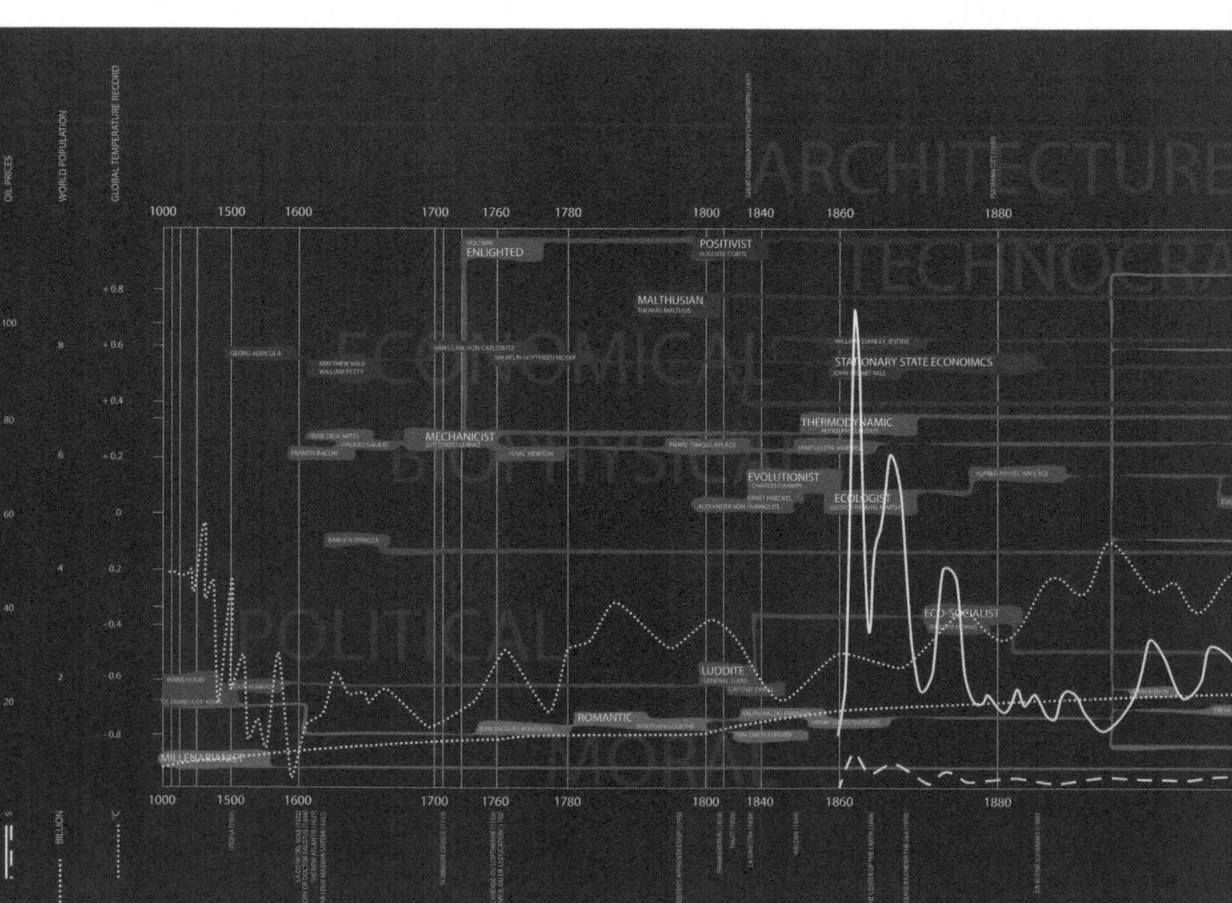

given architecture a new mission and identity. As Arjen Oosterman observes:

> The future is back! Architecture, which has been a bit out of focus lately, is once again alert. Sustainability came to the rescue, setting goals, objectives, tasks and challenges. And the new 'paradigm' is readily absorbed. Architects can save the world again! They advertise their 'sustainable practice' and 'ecological design'. Schools offer master courses in sustainable design, while the building industry provides sustainable solutions and governments compete in a contest of sustainability politics. Sustainability has become a politically correct term, a label that makes whatever you want to do acceptable and good. No questions asked and no doubt involved. (Oosterman 2008, 2)

The purpose of this chapter is to look beyond the 'label' of sustainability, in order to introduce some critical 'doubt' and to ask what for some would be 'politically incorrect' questions about the apparent 'good' of sustainability. This is not a popular option in a sustainability debate in which dialogue about the contested nature of sustainability is viewed as a distraction from the immediacy and immensity of the climate change challenge. From this perspective, consensus is a personal and political imperative to practical problem solving and critical debate is debilitating. As Bruno Latour has put it, "'You have to choose," roar the guardians of the temple. "Either you believe in reality or you cling to constructivism"' (2003, 27). Horrified by any deviation from a design script, often written by an industry of paid consultants with a vested interest in the dominance of one set of solutions over another, such critics claim that we must close down debate about sustainable design and leap into action. Exploring the interpretive flexibility and plasticity of sustainable design, such critics argue, encourages a view that 'everything is equally valid, nothing is wrong,

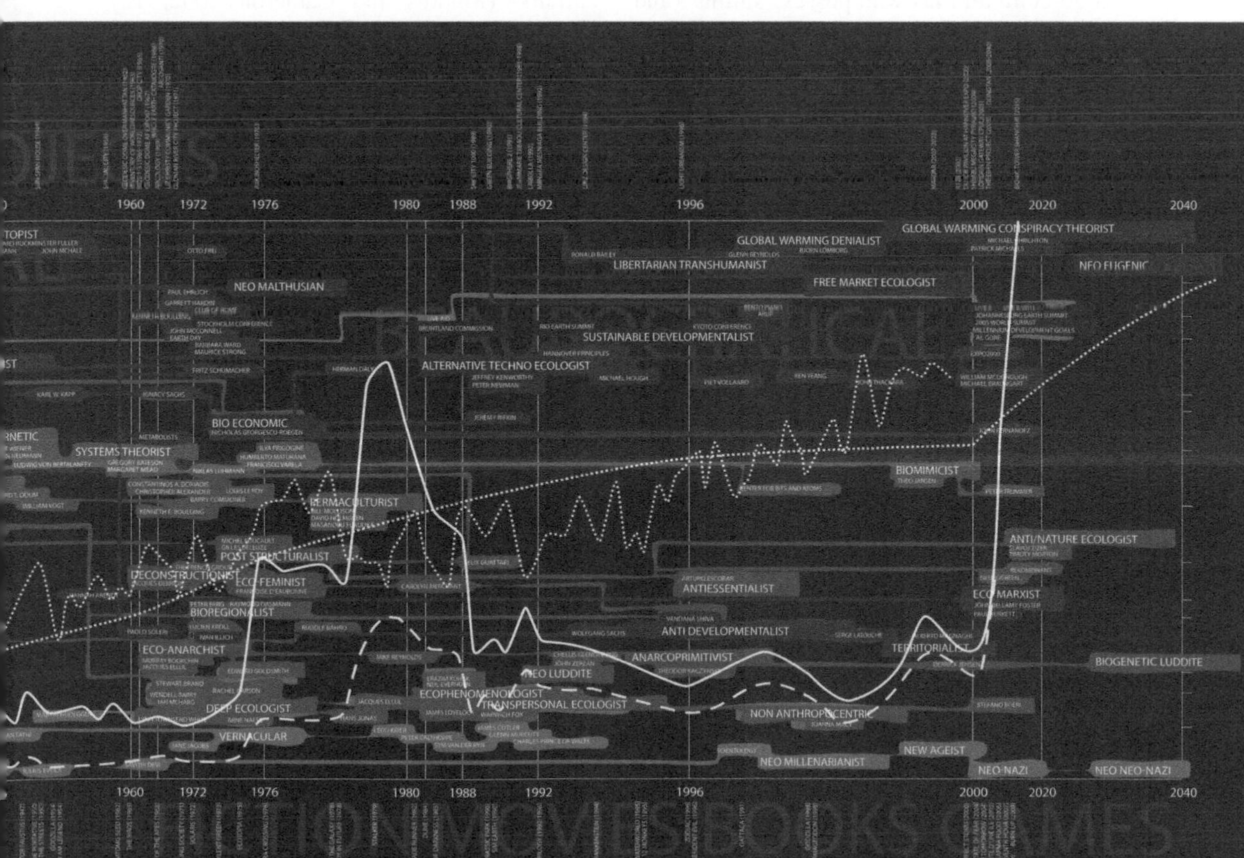

all seems worthy of taking on board, no judgment ensues, and we learn absolutely nothing' (Future Cities 2010). This orthodoxy can mean, as Latour has joked, that 'in order to show that one is not a dangerous outcast, it seems compulsory to swear a pledge of allegiance to "realism" – now meaning the *opposite* of constructivism' (2003, 27).

The position of this chapter is, as Latour goes on to argue, that 'constructivism might be our only defense against *fundamentalism*' (2003, 28). While the term 'constructivism' represents a very broad and highly argumentative church, it does offer an alternative perspective on the co-evolution of 'nature' and 'society' that has emerged across disciplines, from literary studies, history, anthropology, geography, sociology and beyond. This perspective argues that our ideas about nature do not 'somehow touch down uniformly across time and space. Rather they are produced by myriad knowledge-communities who possess similar (and sometimes different) outlooks on nature' (Castree 2005, xiv). Seen this way, sustainable design strategies do not simply express a universal environmental sublime, but are rather the contested outcome of contrasting philosophies and practices rooted in differing accounts of the nature/culture relationship. In order to more fully understand the heterogeneity of sustainable architecture, we therefore have to account for the multiple ways in which environmental problems are identified, defined, translated, valued and then embodied in built forms through diverse design and development pathways. The current 'society–nature dualism', which we have shown structuring debate about sustainable architecture is, as Castree again suggests, blinding us to 'the need for a new vocabulary to describe the world we inhabit' (2005, 224). For Castree, this would not be a vocabulary of 'pure forms' – in architectural terms, the 'performative' or the 'iconic' – but one that 'captures the hybrid, chimeric, mixed-up world in which we are embedded' (2005, 224).

Moreover, following the ecological turn that architecture is following, we also need to critically engage with what George Myerson has termed the 'ecopathology of everyday life' in which 'there is no such thing as simply a blocked drain'. Instead, 'the blocked drain is a symptom of global environmental change, a mundane confirmation of a deeper meaning that has been discovered behind everyday life' (2001, 52). The 'ecopathology' is now powerfully framing architectural theory and practice, and so it is timely to recall the work of Markus and Cameron on architecture and language. They write: 'All natural languages provide their users with multiple ways to represent the same object, state, event or process; the expression of differing perspectives on reality, just as much as the communication of facts about the world, appears to be among the purposes that language evolved to serve' (2002, 3).

The key point here is that 'there are always choices about how to represent a state of affairs' (Markus and Cameron 2002, 12), which leads us to look for 'traces of diverse and perhaps contradictory discourses, in which certain social relations are taken to be "natural", or presupposed as a matter of common sense' (2002, 70). From this standpoint, it is clear that we need to open up and explore the language we use to talk about sustainability, the techniques and technologies employed, the processing and placing of design innovation and the architectural practices that result.

This chapter will attempt to encourage such reflection by introducing some of the key discourses and practices that have shaped the debate, looking backwards and forwards over time in order to highlight the degree of contestation over the concept of sustainability as it is translated architecturally into alternative design practices. This chapter will also engage with these debates geographically, an underdeveloped focus of sustainability studies, to explore what happens when knowledge and practices travel over space as well as time. In this way, the chapter will provide signposts to a variety of literatures on sustainability, deriving from a range of disciplines, and will also serve to introduce and contextualize the other three contributions to this section. In doing so, the chapter will foreground different modes of organizing theories and practices of sustainable architecture, in particular the historical, ideological and geographical, to highlight how a social constructivist perspective might help to make sense of the confusion and contestation that surrounds sustainability debates.

But the chapter will avoid arguing that 'nature' and 'sustainability' are no more than social constructions. As Kate Soper has famously argued: 'It is not language that has a hole in its ozone layer; and the "real" thing continues to be polluted and degraded even as we refine our deconstructive insights at the level of the signifier' (1995, 151). The chapter will therefore also argue that we need to look beyond simple constructivist approaches that focus narrowly on 'competing discourses' of sustainability, by exploring how sustainable architectures are materially assembled, in different ways, as situationally specific responses to localized environmental challenges. In the next section I explore how sustainable architectures are being imagined differently by key contemporary architects, before going on to identify how these discourses are being put into practice.

IMAGINING SUSTAINABLE ARCHITECTURES

There may well be as many types of relationship between nature and architecture as there are architects and buildings (Jodidio 2006, 7).

If there is a consensus emerging in many of the social sciences in relation to sustainability, it is that 'nature' has a politics and that the diverse 'social natures' we all inhabit are 'ever more technologically mediated, produced, enacted, and contested' and 'ever more *entangled* with things' (White and Wilbert 2006, 99–100). Geographers Bruce Braun and Noel Castree argue that this raises fundamental questions for environmental issues ranging from 'national parks to global warming' about 'who constructs what kinds of nature(s) to what ends and with what social and ecological effects' (2001, xi). The sociologist John Hannigan (1995) similarly suggests that society's willingness to recognize and solve environmental problems depends more upon the way these claims are presented by a limited number of people than upon the severity of the threats they pose. This re-framing of nature as a product of social construction, rather than simply an external reality 'out there', redirects our attention away from trying to narrowly define sustainability and towards a process of identifying who is defining environmental problems, in what ways, for what ends.

Turning back to architecture, any cursory review of the literature on sustainable design will find an astonishing collection of claims and concerns expressed across the spectrum of architectural research and practice. Exploring debates about sustainable building, and in particular the ways in which nature is translated and re-scripted into design practices, graphically highlights the ways in which architecture has become a key 'technonatural time-space' which reveals this process of contestation over the meanings of nature (White and Wilbert 2006). But this does not mean that sustainability has been too slippery an idea for designers and planners to interpret and translate into new prescriptions for architecture and cities. Quite the reverse, for as Maarten Hajer has noted, somehow publics, pressure groups, politicians and practitioners still seem able to distill seemingly coherent problems out of this 'jamboree of claims and concerns' (1995, 1–2). To illustrate in relation to architecture, James Wines has shown how:

> Increasing numbers of exceptionally talented architects are exploring a range of approaches and definitions for a new ecological architecture.

> For certain designers, the latest advances in engineering and environmental technology are central to their objectives; while, for others, it is important to return to the lessons of history and the use of indigenous methods and materials. For another group, the resource of topography, vegetation, solar energy and the earth itself are the means to achieve an expanded vision of organic buildings. (Wines 2000, 67)

Such confusion and contestation is well-illustrated in the July 2001 edition of *Architectural Design* which presented a set of 'green questionnaires' completed by eminent architects – Norman Foster, Richard Rogers, Jan Kaplicky, Ken Yeang and Thomas Herzog – each demonstrating these contradictory ways of seeing (Edwards 2001). Each architect was asked about his definition of sustainable design, his key concerns with regards to sustainability, how he would judge success in terms of sustainability and how he used nature as a guide in his design work. For Kaplicky of Future Systems, the 'major aspects of sustainable design are choice of materials and the performance of a building once it is built' (Edwards 2001, 34), whereas for Rogers it must also include a concern for the 'principles of social and economic sustainability as well as the specific concerns of energy use and environmental impact of buildings and cities' (Edwards 2001, 36). For Herzog, it is about 'using renewable forms of energy – especially solar energy – as extensively as possible' (Edwards 2001, 74), while for Yeang it is 'design that integrates seamlessly with the ecological systems in the biosphere over the entire life cycle of the built system' (Edwards 2001, 60).

The relationship of architecture to nature is also contested. Rogers rather vaguely argues that 'nature provides inspiration, information and analogy' (Edwards 2001, 36). Others are quite precise in linking natural and human processes. Yeang, for instance, believes 'nature should be imitated and our built systems should be mimetic ecosystems' (Edwards 2001, 60), while Kaplicky similarly feels 'there is much to learn from [nature's] more efficient use of materials' (Edwards 2001, 34). By contrast, Herzog does not believe that 'architecture can be deduced immediately from nature, since the design process and function of our buildings are quite different from what is found in most plants and animals' (Edwards 2001, 74), while Foster prefers to look to human natures, 'vernacular traditions that are specific to the area in which we are working' (Edwards 2001, 32).

There are similar levels of disagreement about how we might recognize and assess the success of architecture in becoming sustainable. Rogers argues that his practice meets the challenge of sustainability through 'the development of intelligent buildings that can contribute to a substantial reduction in running and maintenance costs during the life cycle of a building' (Edwards 2001, 36). Foster agrees, arguing that 'a "green" building will use as little energy as possible and will make the most of the embodied energy required to build it' (Edwards 2001, 32). He argues it should also create its own energy and have structural flexibility to prolong its life. Foster confidently suggests his own Reichstag building has 'already proved these concepts' (Edwards 2001, 32). Herzog concurs with this emphasis on 'overall performance' but also argues that only 'beautifully made buildings' can really be sustainable and that architects must develop 'new forms of architectural expression which are closely linked to the local condition, such as the microclimate and topography, the natural resources and the cultural heritage of a certain region' (Edwards 2001, 74). Yeang goes further, insisting that a 'successful green building is only one that integrates seamlessly with the natural systems in the biosphere' and warns that 'designers should also beware of making excessive claims about the sustainability of their designs because ecological design is still in its infancy' (Edwards 2001, 60). Kaplicky concurs with Yeang, arguing that as yet 'there have been no truly green buildings built'. He goes on, stating, 'The buildings that are currently being constructed aren't even prototypes for a "green" age. They are only minor attempts at sustainability' (Edwards 2001, 34).

As even this small sample suggests, the mainstream of architecture is in some disagreement about design priorities, the role of technology, the importance of aesthetics, the relationship of natural and built environments and the degree of optimism or pessimism that the current state of sustainable architectural practice should invoke. It is perhaps not surprising that, given this complexity and potential for contradiction, Foster is tempted to define sustainable design as simply just 'good architecture' (Edwards 2001, 32). However, it is again not surprising that Foster's rather optimistic view contrasts sharply with architects such as Wines who want to emphasis that

> ... virtually no form of shelter constructed today (with the exception of habitat built by a few remaining aboriginal cultures) can be credited as authentically green. Everything that technologically dependent societies assume is essential for survival – including the remedial solutions offered by the greenest of green architects – is plugged into the same diminishing sources of power. Every absorber plate and foil insulator required to build a solar collector, every chemical detergent used in a waste-composting plant, every ream of paper needed to spread the ecological message and every drop of jet fuel consumed in transporting environmentalists to international conferences places an additional drain on these resources. (Wines 2000, 226)

It appears, as Kenneth Frampton has put it, that there are 'as many ways of practicing (sustainable) architecture as there are architects' (2001, 128). This raises a range of questions of anyone concerned with how 'future worlds' may be imagined, questioned, debated and delivered. In particular, we need to question how we might distinguish between these distinct philosophical approaches to identify what policy-makers often term 'best practices'; explore their socio-economic, ecological and political viabilities in a range of cultural, political and geographical settings; better understand the politics of these ideologies, how they suggest co-existence with or opposition to the neo-liberal world we currently inhabit; ask whether particular design visions encourage a hopeful or pessimistic perspective on our collective futures; assess the extent to which particular practices open up spaces for wider public engagement in architectural interventions; explore what historical narratives they support or challenge, and what emblematic issues they privilege or marginalize; and question how ideas of sustainability emerging out of debates in the 'West' resonate across geographies and in particular across North and South, and developed and emerging economies.

In sum, we need to more critically explore how these differing ideas of natures connect to alternative design practices and, in turn, how these visions or blueprints of sustainable architecture travel across time and space, and with what effects when they touch down in specific places. In order to get a flavour of these competing pathways of sustainable architecture, we turn now to briefly review some examples of contemporary practice as collected together in a recent international exhibition of future cities.

PRACTICING SUSTAINABLE ARCHITECTURES

> Energy-neutral houses must be something more than symbolic measures for futuristic architects who want to prove *that it can be done*. They must be something more than the sophisticated kind of luxury where exclusive prototypes conceal the fact that most construction goes on as before. (Thyssen 2009, 62)

An exhibition in summer 2009 titled 'Frontiers of Architecture II: Green Architecture for the Future' at the Louisiana Museum of Modern Art in Denmark powerfully illustrated the diversity of contemporary sustainability practice, drawing together projects as varied as slum redevelopments, whole new cities in the desert, computer simulated design, art installations and so on (Holm and Kjeldsen, 2009). Taken together, the Louisiana exhibition celebrated the diversity and ingenuity of contemporary architects and architecture to create 'innovative solutions to the concept of sustainable architecture' (Kjeldsen and Tøjner 2009, 6–7). The exhibition curators framed architectural responses to global environmental challenges by utilizing a concept of four 'laboratories', each working across different locations, prioritizing different sustainability principles and employing distinct design strategies and planning tactics. The experience of visiting these laboratories and observing such a diverse array of urban experiments was akin to the culture shock of long-distance travel as one passes through different countries and continents, grappling with old and new technologies, computed scale shifts from rooms to regions, moving between slums and premium business zones, all the while simultaneously attempting to calculate the varied costs of carbon, culture and human suffering. Turning the pages of the catalogue takes the reader on a similarly disjointed journey through contemporary sustainability practices.

Laboratory One, the 'urban acupuncture' of Ecosistema Urbano, focuses on small scale and renewable interventions to optimize, diversify and regenerate urban public spaces into arenas of social exchange. Their practice looks beyond formal architectural design to solutions that consider 'social networks, environmental and physical components of flourishing, inhabitable urban communities' (Holm and Kjeldsen 2009, 10). The approach is inspired by the work of Jaime Lerner, former mayor of Curitiba, Brazil, a city that he transformed into an icon of master planning through a commitment to controlled growth and integrated traffic management, while encouraging local community self-sufficiency by providing all city districts with adequate education, health care, recreation and park areas.[1] The key to the success of Curitiba is thus not smart technologies, but rather innovative and inclusive urban practices. As Ecosistema Urbano architect José Luis Vallejo argues, 'we miss out on lots of opportunities if we only take an interest in dead materials, wood and stone. Looking at the city, it's people who are the raw material' (quoted in Sattrup 2009a, 13).

Ecosistema Urbano's Eco-Boulevard in Vallecas, a suburb of Madrid, focuses on the insertion of three 'pavilions' made up of trees, open to multiple activities chosen by the public and installed as 'temporary prostheses', to be used only until a more systemic climatic adaptivity has been created (Saieh 2008). The pavilions are designed to be self-sufficient in terms of energy through photovoltaic solar energy collection, and can be dismantled and exported once an area has developed more permanent solutions. According to Vallejo, 'architects have a tendency to forget people and only concentrate on their own ideas' as if they are working in an 'isolated laboratory' (quoted in Sattrup 2009a, 13), which often results in too narrow a focus, thereby missing the opportunities presented by the vitality of the city. They write:

> These days there are quite a few certifications, where you can get a label to stick on your building: this building is energy-efficient, with 702 points. But it's more complex than that: you can put up a zero-energy building that has destroyed a neighbourhood, or does nothing for public space. If you destroy the cultural heritage and value of a place, it isn't sustainable in my view. Creating a living, healthy place to spend time in involves much more than energy reductions. (Quoted in Sattrup 2009a, 14–15)

A greater contrast is hard to imagine with Laboratory Two, the Masdar City project by Foster and Partners, who have become synonymous with what Catherine Slessor has christened the 'Eco-Tech' movement in sustainable design (2001). Here, the focus is on technological ingenuity, utilizing the latest materials, computer aided design and controls, intelligent climatic control and energy-generating technologies to create smart buildings that act autonomously to generate power, modify climates, deal with waste and actively mediate technonatural relations. The Masdar City project involves the planning of a brand new, carbon neutral, low-rise city for just under 50,000 residents and is inspired, it is claimed, by medieval Arab culture and customs combined with the latest smart green technologies. Car-free and with a high density – 200 m between transport links – Masdar will integrate vernacular wind towers with solar cells to supply energy and naturally ventilate the desert city. Developed as a Silicon Valley for renewable energy, the aim is to gather together researchers currently scattered globally to accelerate scientific advances. As such, the emphasis is on reinventing the future through the 'white heat' of smart technologies.

Visiting the project website you can find its architect, Norman Foster, claiming that Masdar 'promises to set new benchmarks for the sustainable city of the future' (Masdar City 2009). Rather than people and urban practices, it is design that is the inspiration here. Interviewed in the exhibition catalogue, Foster's representative Stefan Behling argues that 'consumption is a question of demand and demand is dependent on design' (quoted in Sattrup 2009b, 49). He adds that:

> Your demand for petrol depends on the design of your car, and your demand for a car depends on how the city you live in is designed. So if you can change that, you can change your consumption in the end. The same goes for buildings: it applies to all sorts of things. Architecture and planning can reduce the demand for energy through the way buildings, infrastructure and urban development work. (Quoted in Sattrup 2009b, 49)

Laboratory Three, the 'Atmospheric Home' by Philippe Rahm, takes a different turn again by emphasizing the view that 'architecture is becoming meteorology' (Rahm, quoted in Sattrup 2009c, 91). Rahm is drawing here on a long architectural tradition that connects climate, comfort and function stretching back to Vitruvius and finding contemporary expression in bioclimatic design, that strives to achieve environmental control by working with, rather than in opposition to, the climate. By contrast with high-tech design approaches to mechanically controlling the climate to achieve a predetermined standard of comfort, the bioclimatic design method seeks to utilize ambient energy sources to achieve a more variable and passive indoor environment that relates more closely to local climates. Drawing upon the 'passivehaus' concept, which seeks to control air flow in and out of the building, Rahm builds up his design proposal for the 'Atmospheric Home' around flows of light, heat and humidity to address the 'form, programme and function of architecture' (quoted in Sattrup 2009c, 93). Pointing back to the diurnal rhythms of traditional architectures in the Middle East and Japan, when rooms fluidly followed the social rhythm of the family, Rahm sees the sustainable turn as involving a re-invention of architectural typologies from functions to atmospheres. He writes:

> Working with humidity, for example, creates an atmospheric landscape that also has a lot of sensory potential … Maybe we don't need categories like bedroom, bathroom, kitchen etc. Instead we can talk about dry rooms, medium-dry rooms or moist rooms … In one project we have a kitchen-bathroom-living room. The function becomes fluid (quoted in Sattrup 2009c, 91).

Rahm is not interested in returning to any original nature, but rather wants to trace this fluidity of interior thermodynamic landscapes through thermal simulations in computer models. The aim is to develop a new 'spatial geometry' in order to modulate the sensory landscapes of the home in ways that do not over-consume energy by artificially heating or cooling spaces to an artificially agreed standard of around 20°C. Instead, we learn to follow atmospheric flows and to adapt ourselves, and our architectures, to their climatic variability.

Laboratory Four, a prototype, time-limited, biodegradable pavilion made of bio-plastic by the architect François Roche, is also inspired to follow the lessons of 'nature', but rather than looking back to an architecture of the seasons, prefers to utilize scientific advances in materials technology to mimic the rhythms of natural growth and decay. Here, a new generation of intelligent or 'responsive' materials are being developed that have the ability to store and exchange energy, colour (in response to light, heat, pressure, acidity and energy), and be self-cleaning, water repellent, completely transparent and biodegradable. These potential properties open up a new world of architectural possibilities according to Kasper Guldager Jørgensen, Head of Research and Development at the Danish architectural practice 3XN:

> Instead of building passive constructions and climate screens as hitherto, we can use intelligent materials for dynamic buildings, where functions and information can in principle be installed anywhere; intelligent systems with the scope to adapt to the users. Houses that react to changes in temperature and light, or constructions that can reinforce themselves at peak loads, for example during storms and earthquakes. (Jørgensen 2009, 123)

Roche's experiment involves developing an architectural structure made up of hydrosoluble polymer from agricultural material, strategically designed to slowly 'necrose' by controlling the atmospheric humidity. In this way, the life span of the temporary building can be controlled from its construction to its decomposition. While not directly employing the term 'sustainable' for his work, the practice is similar in spirit to the 'cradle to cradle' design philosophy of William McDonough.[2] In particular, Roche sees direct parallels between his 'chameleon architecture' and the aim of creating more livable environments that are adaptive to fast-changing ecological conditions that are emerging, for instance, rising sea levels. Roche points to the ideas of Rudolph Steiner and concepts of 'natural circulation', in which a building can 'completely disappear without leaving pollution in the process, and even gives nitrogen back to nature' (quoted in Holm 2009, 134). This he argues, represents a radical shift in the balance between architecture and nature, writing: 'Our building doesn't have to be taken down, it will disappear by itself and end up in the sea without leaving traces. That's complete dissolution, and the house will be eaten by the fishes' (quoted in Holm 2009, 134).

PUZZLING SUSTAINABLE ARCHITECTURES

> When you think about the perception of ecological building, it was precisely something to do with wood, contact with nature etc. But the most sustainable construction now is super-insulated and creates its own artificial climate. If you open the window you lose energy. That is really a paradox. (Philippe Rahm, quoted in Sattrup 2009c, 91)

If anything unites these laboratories of sustainability in the eyes of the exhibition curators and catalogue editors, it is an almost modernist belief in the power of technology and design ingenuity to translate current architectural practice into a sustainable paradigm that will overcome the paradoxes highlighted above. As they put it: 'The architects of industrialism knew that form follows function – today maybe we should say that form must follow evolution' (Kjeldsen and Tøjner 2009, 6). The key to this eco-modernity, they argue, is twofold. Firstly, technological innovation: 'Maybe in fifteen years' time there will [be] new sustainable materials that can optimize the various subcomponents of the building over time – and the building will slowly be adapted – formally as well as functionally – to technological advances' (2009, 6). And secondly, the creativity and motivation to 'transform our competencies' (2009, 6). The architects who are daring to think differently, they argue, are 'certainly suffering from no paralysis of the will' (2009, 6). They add: 'Maybe the skyscraper of tomorrow will have moss-clad facades that help us to purify the city air, integrated solar-powered heating, trees and bushes that produce energy and create microclimates and biodiversity for the benefit of animals and birds, and colours that change with the seasons' (2009, 6). Nothing is too great or too small, they argue, to escape from the attention of the green architect – 'nature, the city, the materials, social organization, and even our clothes and shoes' (2009, 6). This is certainly not an argument for small is beautiful, anti-modern environmentalism, but rather for big, bold design moves that demonstrate how architecture has 'rediscovered its status as an applied art' (2009, 6).

A similar view is mobilized by Audacity, who describe themselves as a company who can help you advocate development of the man-made environment, free from the burden of 'sustainababble' and 'communitwaddle' (Audacity 2009). For Audacity founder Ian Abley, the real 'sustainability' issue is one of 'failing to raise the level of machine age industrial development around the world' and instead pandering to 'advocates [of] ever more self-restraint and regulation' (2001, 19). Abley argues for a renewal of industrial modernism to 'produce our way out of fossil-fuelled site based construction' in order to avoid what he terms an 'increasingly thin architectural façade over a stifling parochialism morally justified as sustainable development' (2001, 6). Abley's co-edited collection of essays is notably entitled *Sustaining Architecture in the Anti-Machine Age* (Abley and Heartfield 2001), the tone of which is exemplified by architecture journalist Austin Williams, who argues the need to 'challenge the current positive perceptions about the religion of "sustainability" in architecture' (Williams 2001, 49). Charlick and Nicholson, writing in the same volume, warn that 'much sustainable architecture deals in symbolism' and that the 'green roof or the solar array represents a "green" sensibility, which may extend no further' (2001, 68). Andrew Ross has similarly argued that technologies 'based upon natural elements, or that imitate natural processes … are no guarantee of health, sustainability, or even biodiversity' (1992, 271), and that 'Biomorphic houses designed according to the principles of botanical architecture … are just as likely to be instruments of social apartheid as housing modelled on industrial factories' (1992, 271).

But others equally worry about an eco-industrial model driving sustainable architecture. Ole Thyssen points out that many companies would 'like to build energy-neutral houses. But the goal is growth, and consideration of the environment is a means to an end' (2009, 62). Looking further to the future, Richard Bevan (2009) imagines Heathrow Airport in 2030, an age when personal carbon allowances have become the dominant currency for which the facilities of Heathrow have been utilized as a 'carbon casino' that provides an opportunity for customers to engage in 'eco-gambling' in carbon credits. In this puzzling way, we appear to travel quickly from hopeful 'sensory' architectures to the dystopic image of the 'Carbon Casino Club', creating a market for carbon credits, which further subsidizes the low-cost air travel that arguably refuels a world of eco-capitalism.

And so we end up again with a set of paradoxes: environmentalism is everything and nothing, the central focus and a distraction, a spur to innovation and a hindrance to new ways of thinking, a new opportunity and a barrier. Given that the debate appears characterized both by widespread acknowledgement of the central importance of sustainability to architecture and an interpretive flexibility and plasticity of design practice, we might need to ask a different question. That is, in what ways is knowledge about and commitment to sustainability organized in architectural theory and practice? Taking a constructivist perspective of course means that we could offer different organizing principles with different effects on the narrative of sustainability.

This chapter will now turn to the three other chapters in this section of the Handbook in order to briefly explore alternative modes of organizing the debate about environmental architectures: historical, ideological and geographical.

HISTORICIZING SUSTAINABLE ARCHITECTURE

> To reflect on the prehistory of sustainability is not to find 'precedents' of practices that give us tips for the present. Rather these reflections aim to mobilize critical perspectives on the shifting

> definitions of the term and on the practices that are advanced in its name so as to guard against absolutes. (Pyla 2008, 16)

How then to make sense of the apparent contradictions and coincidences that make up debates around sustainable architecture? Perhaps the classic response of architectural theory is to attempt to develop an historical narrative of sustainability, to chart the shifting priorities that have led to the current moment of competing concerns. Notable among these histories are John Farmer's *Green Shift: Towards a Green Sensibility in Architecture* (1996), James Wines' *Green Architecture* (2000) and James Steele's *Ecological Architecture: A Critical History* (2005), each of which sets out to put into context how architectural ideas and practices have been influenced by environmentalism, by reviewing key ideas, movements and architects and plotting them on a timeline that attempts to make sense of the twists and turns of the debate.

However, an interesting aspect of these histories is that few major architects or styles are left out of the story. Not only are we all green architects now, but it appears that one way or another, we have always been so. As Djalali and Vollaard put it: 'Looking back we see that Western society has always been obsessed by its relationship with the environment, with what is meant to be outside ourselves, or, as some call it, nature' (2008, 33). In their article on the 'complex history of sustainability' in *Volume*, they chart the ideas that preceded but resonate with notions of sustainability and how 'even today there are various trends and original ideas following old ideological traditions' (2008, 33). They illustrate this increasingly complex history through a millennial timeline that moves from Thomas More's *Utopia* and Francis Bacon's *New Atlantis* through a bewildering array of overlapping movements: romantic, industrial, cybernetic, deconstructionist, counter-cultural, developmental, biomimicist, new ageist and so on (see Figure 31.1 on pp. 556–557). While each movement has its own coherent history, taken together they make up a picture that has simply grown more complex over time.

Such historical complexity is illustrated well in Richard Ingersoll's chapter in this volume (Chapter 32), where he attempts to make sense of this patchwork of ideas. Ingersoll argues that while ecological issues have grown in importance in the latter half of the twentieth century, the very act of architecture, involving as it does an intervention into nature, has always held at its heart an environmental paradox. He writes, 'one cannot deny that architecture exists fundamentally as a struggle with natural phenomena' (this volume, 574). In the management of resources like water and materials like timber, architectural achievements have always been at some cost to 'nature'. Human response has always varied; Walden retreated to his primitive hut, Steiner advocated a biodynamic balance, Frank Lloyd Wright pursued organic biomimicry. These are among myriads of attempts to reorient architecture's relationship to the natural world.

But for Ingersoll, two key moments in the late twentieth century bring the ecology question to the fore. First, he argues, the energy crisis of the early 1970s finally mobilized architects in the attempt to stabilize the ecological impact of their buildings. With the realization that half of all energy use was related to buildings, a technological revolution ensued, with an acceleration of experimental designs aimed at reducing the energy demand of the built environment, a trend that continues to this day. And this was not simply a revolution in design, nor was it the preserve of architects. Instead it also led to the creation of new building regulations, materials, technologies, planning approaches, lifestyles and so on. And despite attempts to codify these innovations, no one style or approach succeeded in developing a hegemony and almost all urban development proceeded as hitherto.

However, for Ingersoll, ecology concerns strengthened in the mid-1980s with the discovery of the ozone hole over Antarctica and the growing awareness of the phenomenon of global warming. As consensus grew around climate change, ecological design became a central concern for almost all architects. With the 'Brundland Report' published in 1987, 'sustainable development' became a key focus of design and planning policy, leading to a quantitative revolution in architecture that strived to tame some of the previous design diversity. New, and what Ingersoll describes as 'authoritarian' prescriptions for design emerged, framed by technical audits, energy models and performance codes, each agreed at national and sometimes international levels, with the aim of disciplining 'unsustainable' architecture and promoting 'best practice' environmental design. Over the last twenty years or more, new generations of low-energy building designs have been developed, tested, promoted and occasionally constructed, to the point where the latest technical standards emerging in developed countries are calling for 'zero carbon' constructions. But, with the environmental crisis becoming global, demanding solutions across radically different climates and cultures, and with new digital innovations rapidly expanding the vocabulary of design, Ingersoll can see no end to the proliferation of architectural responses to 'the ecology question'.

Having surveyed the history of architectural attempts to create a new relationship to nature, Ingersoll questions the final value of all the 'good intentions' of designers. Other histories have concluded similarly, with John Farmer questioning whether 'absolute or universal solutions are possible', instead suggesting, 'it may be a question of steering in the right direction' (1996, 185). James Steele is even more pessimistic, in the final sentence of his book reviewing contemporary architectural practices, he reflects on whether 'the final distancing from nature is now underway' (2005, 262). On this evidence, the search for a grand narrative of architectural sustainability seems to be unresolved, with attempts to historicize sustainability appearing to manage little more than to catalogue a confusing proliferation of movements and styles, resulting in a cul-de-sac of confusion and a rather pessimistic outlook. It is precisely for these reasons that other architects and critics have taken a rather different route, one that eschews interpretation and resolves instead to take a particular ideological stand.

ADVOCATING SUSTAINABLE ARCHITECTURE

> To survive on a planet with five billion people requires that a shared system of values is arrived at, so that the ramifications of any action are anticipated, both now and for the future. An architecture that would look at buildings with a similar judgement, and determine beauty through performance might not be so bad … Maybe a green approach to the built environment will succeed not least because it can provide again an architecture for all. (Vale and Vale 1991, 186)

Untainted by the quiet pessimism of the historical perspective, the debate about sustainable architecture has been powerfully shaped by an ever-growing number of optimistic and purposeful environmental manifestos that seek to act as design guides for green architecture. A quick search of Google or Amazon will bring forth many examples, but to name just a few: Brenda and Robert Vale's *Green Architecture: Design for a Sustainable Future* (1991), Victor Papenak's *The Green Imperative: Ecology and Ethics in Design and Architecture* (1995) and Dean Hawkes' *The Environmental Tradition: Studies in the Architecture of Environment* (2001) all present cogent and technically convincing ecological strategies. Quieter in their proselytizing, but nonetheless equally committed to outlining a clear, technically focused way forward, are a wide range of technical best practice books including Smith et al. *Greening the Built Environment* (1998), Peter Smith's *Architecture in a Climate of Change: A Guide to Sustainable Design* (2001) and Edwards and Hyett's *Rough Guide to*

Sustainability (2001). Finally, in this genre, there are a growing number of sustainable architecture monographs containing extensive 'best practice' building reviews, such as Catherine Slessor's *Eco-Tech: Sustainable Architecture and High Technology* (2001), and David Gissen's *Big and Green: Toward Sustainable Architecture in the 21st Century* (2003).

While differing in presentation, practice and priorities, each of these books is committed to identifying a clear pathway through the confusion of the environmental debate by presenting tangible technical evidence, moral persuasion and architectural exemplars. The rhetoric is often one of urgency, a call to action, rather than the more cautious reflective tone of the historical frame explored above. As Vale and Vale write:

> The built environment, then, relates to earth and water, fire and air, and its interactions with each of these elements is such as to involve the transfer of energy. In a world under threat, each transfer of energy needs to be carefully considered to determine its implications, and whether it is really necessary. (Vale and Vale 1991, 42)

The chapter in this volume by Peter Droege (Chapter 33) illustrates this approach, arguing at the outset that the semantic battles over sustainability mean that action is lagging behind the pace of climate change. '*Sustainability* is a bruised and feeble term, twisted in "triple-bottom-line" and other open-ended interpretations' (this volume, 589). Droege could not be clearer in his language when he states, 'naked survival is at stake'. And what is the problem? 'A lack of focus is missing', he argues (this volume, 588). For Droege, the industrial revolution in the West has been fuelled by overconsumption of carbon that has, until recently, invisibly fuelled our extravagant lifestyles. This fundamental dependency has been ignored both in practice and in most of the analysis of urban environmental change. He traces this dependency in the work of modernist architects and their creations as 'caricatures of the fossil-fuel era and its dreams'. Only recently, he argues, has work on the ecological footprint of urbanization and our consumerist lifestyles begun to find expression both in print and in design and planning practice. His conclusion is equally clear: 'The Fossil City approaches its apex', and while 'the dreamlike abuse of fossil fuels continues to mount at a rapid rate', he posits a fourth industrial revolution, a 'transcendence of the fossil fuel age' in which 'high carbon architecture' is displaced by 'diurnally responsive structures' and carbon free cities fueled by renewables (this volume, 594–595).

While Droege's thesis is perhaps at the extreme end of the advocacy spectrum, we can see a shared framing of the environmental challenge and a commitment to radically revise the ecological footprint of architecture and even cities. This emphasis on focused action has, not surprisingly, appealed to many designers, planners and policy-makers. As Hagan has pointed out,

> It is the rationalist majority who now dominate the field. One has only to look at the proceedings of any conference on environmental architecture in the last twenty years to see the overwhelming emphasis on the scientific and quantitative dimensions of the discipline: thermal conductivity of materials, photovoltaic technology, computer simulations, life cycle analysis, and so on'. (Hagan 2001: x)

But this clarity and focus comes at the expense of marginalizing those issues that are not easily calculated and do not easily translate into an energy model. In particular, the focus on best technical practices tends to result in an interpretive squeeze in which problems amenable to technical fixes are foregrounded at the expense of a range of other environmental concerns (Guy and Farmer 2001). As Mark Wigley has suggested, the 'overt politics of ecology – the equitable management of resources – almost always preserves certain regressive ideological formations' (1999, 48). In this case, the 'technocist supremacy', which increasingly dominates environmental policy debates often results in 'non-technical' issues – of health, poverty, and equity for example – being subtly downplayed or sometimes simply ignored. Further implicit in this model of consensus and action is a process of standardization, which means that local conditions and issues, and competing forms of local knowledge and practice, tend to be ignored. It is to this wider issue of place and sustainability that we now turn.

GEOGRAPHIES OF SUSTAINABLE ARCHITECTURE

> Thus, the cities of the future, rather than being made out of glass and steel as envisioned by earlier generations of urbanists, are instead largely constructed out of crude brick, straw, recycled plastic, cement blocks, and scrap wood. Instead of cities of light soaring toward heaven, much of the twenty-first-century urban world squats in squalor, surrounded by pollution, excrement, and decay. (Davis 2006, 19)

It is now a well-known fact that we have passed the point where more people live in cities than the countryside. The majority of this growth is occurring in cities of the South and East, the emerging economies of the developing world. In particular, China and India are developing at a tremendous pace with huge implications for local environments and global climate change. This urban phenomenon has stimulated huge international debate and led to significant activity by Western architects, importing ideas of sustainability tried and tested in developed economies and experimenting with them in very different cultural contexts. This, in turn, has attracted much criticism about the relevance and viability of the transfer of architectural best practice across geographies. Can a universal definition of sustainability be generated, given the diversity of challenges experienced globally? What is the role of local knowledge and practice? Are there alternative, 'indigenous' conceptions of local sustainability that may be more relevant and effective?

This has led to a new twist in the debate about sustainable architecture. Brian Edwards, writing in a special issue of *Architectural Design*, celebrates the fact the sustainability agenda is not 'leading to a single universal style but to a rich and complex architectural order around the world', arguing that this diversity of interpretation can be too easily 'overwhelmed by the internationalization of sustainability as evidenced by scientific literature' and that 'a more appropriate greening of practice occurs when both local and global issues are balanced' (2001, 7). Here we find clear recognition that 'there is no class or style of design which is unequivocally sustainable architecture, and no fixed set of rules which will guarantee success if followed' (Williamson et al. 2003, 127). But Edwards also appears to look to a form of cultural essentialism to explain the alternative formation of sustainability between 'West' and 'East', suggesting that; 'The West tends to "measure" sustainability whilst the South and East simply "feel" it. Asia and Africa act out good green practices by instinct, and their point of reference is not Newton or Einstein but the local shaman or wisdom keeper' (2001, 10). He goes on to argue that, 'As a general statement, the spiritual approach to green design is found in the underdeveloped world and the low-energy, high-material approach in the developed' (2001, 13). This rather 'orientalist' perspective highlights the conceptual challenges of moving the sustainability debate geographically.

The chapter in this volume by Jiat-Hwee Chang (Chapter 34) rehearses many of these issues in his discussion of tropical architecture in Southeast Asia. Chang challenges the 'monolithic' nature of sustainability as represented in current debate and practice. Pointing to the constructivist position outlined above, Chang wants to develop a more pluralistic understanding of sustainable architecture as it is practised, in this case, in Southeast Asia. By reviewing the winners of the celebrated Aga Khan Awards for Architecture, he is able to distinguish between a range of approaches to tropical architecture, each drawing upon their own ideas, traditions and practices. What is so illuminating about Chang's analysis is the way each particular construction of tropical architecture draws on sources from both local and international discourses and practices in different hybridized forms. Hence, he shows how forms of 'green developmentalism' have led to a process of 'rendering technical' essentially social issues, such as equity, as a way of depoliticizing them. In particular, Chang illustrates how a shared belief in 'techno-scientific' principles expressed through shared technical standards, specifications, materials, components and construction methods, developed in metropolitan research and development institutions, allows the West to manage the developing world both economically and culturally. As he argues, 'This reliance on imported expertise, building materials, and building components appears to continue into tropical sustainable architecture given the continued technological gap and inequalities in distribution of resources between the countries in the tropical south and those in the industrial north' (this volume, 605).

Chang notes other traditions that have emerged in response to this 'architectural imperialism', in a return to a neo-traditional tropical architecture that echoes earlier construction forms and utilizes local materials and 'low tech' designs. Architects such as Hassan Fathy and Geoffrey Bawa were lionized for their respect for vernacular architecture, although other critics noted the elite background of these architects and detected a selective interpretation of tradition very distant from the lived realities of peasants that verged on the romantic. Panayiota Pyla concurs, accusing Fathy of imposing on Egyptian architecture a 'homogenizing conception of culture/tradition that did not in fact exist' and noting how Fathy's earth architecture for seven thousand displaced Egyptian peasants known as the Gourni was often rejected due to misinterpretation of local traditions (Pyla 2008, 15).

Chang goes on to identify a third form of tropical architecture, that of grassroots development of the Kampung squatter settlements. Here, respect is accorded to the knowledge and adaptive creativity of the urban poor who build and live in the settlements. Rather than erase these communities, the philosophy is to support what is seen as indigenous, environmentally responsive tropical architecture and a clear alternative to the standardized solutions of technoscientific, international architecture. This interest in slum settlement as 'laboratories' of sustainability is now evident worldwide, through the writing of ethnographers such as Robert Neuwirth and Caroline Moser, the campaigning work of Slum Dwellers International and architectural practices such as Architecture for Humanity.[3] In different ways, each argues for a bottom-up understanding of the creative practices of the urban poor in their struggle for a sustainable way of life, and a reframing of slum dwelling away from that of clearance and modernization and towards a global urban phenomena that continues to grow, and that might have lessons for wider sustainable practice. Others, however, warn again about the dangers of romanticization and a selective filtering of the positives of slum dwelling, that allows the wider political context that frames slum economies to be ignored. As Austin Williams puts it, 'because of the difficulty in creating a believably positive reminiscence of the wartime experience for us in the West, most of the discussion revolves around the closest thing – the "prudent" poverty of the developing world, where the sustainable noble savage lives' (2001, 44).

REASSEMBLING SUSTAINABLE ARCHITECTURES

When we ponder how the global world could be made habitable – a question especially important for architects and designers – we now mean habitable for billions of humans and trillions of other

> creatures that no longer form a nature or, of course, a society, but rather, to use my term, a possible *collective* (contrary to the dual notions of nature-and-society, the collective is *not* collected *yet*, and no one has the slightest idea of what it is to be composed of, how it is to be assembled, or even if it should be assembled into one piece). (Latour 2009, 141)

Looking back and forward over time and across geographies, it is clearly not enough to simply identify a range of new ultra-efficient technologies, design innovations and masterplans. Instead, the challenge of architectural sustainability involves confronting a range of theoretical questions about how we conceive of 'nature', what forms of knowledge we reify, how we prioritize competing ecological issues, and how we relate to particular contexts. That is, how we might juggle the complex balance of resource efficiencies, aesthetics, health, community involvement, equity and so on. As Bruno Latour would put it, it is not simply a 'matter of facts' but of acknowledging 'matters of concern' (2004b, 231). Seen Latour's way, the question shifts to asking how things can be assembled in ways that are more sustainable?

The answer, for geographer Steve Hinchliffe, is to 'pay attention to the ecologies of action, to the interrelations that exist within and between the multiple practices, modes of ordering and materialities' (2007, 186). He argues that, 'there is no magic formula or balance to be struck, producing good ecologies of action can only be experimental, any attempt to assemble a garden, landscape, city, policy, or other grouping will require more than one mode of ordering'. Instead, Hinchliffe highlights the importance of 'a sensibility that is open to those matters and practices that have been temporarily obscured by the requirement to make things happen and to generate coordinated actions' (2007, 186). Thus, we must avoid the tendency of policy and practice to 'render technical', as Chang puts it in his chapter (Chapter 34), a wide range of competing and sometime incompatible, environmental concerns. As Pyla suggests,

> Maybe it is good that sustainability does not have a fixed or coherent definition … because if the technical questions of energy efficiency or the technocratic questions of efficient resource use or even the questions of socioeconomic management end up constituting the definition of sustainability in architecture, this will threaten to reduce design to a series of small decisions (on materials, energy or feasibility) that will ultimately have less to do with design and more with management or with political correctness. (Pyla 2008, 16)

And so we return to the urgent need to rethink the debate about sustainable architectures. As political scientist Andrew Jamison writes: 'More fluid terms are needed: dialectical, open-ended terms to characterize the ebbs and flows, nuances and subtleties and the ambiguities of environmental politics' (2001, 178). David Schlosberg has similarly called for 'statements that are open rather than doctrinaire', that 'conscript' rather than alienate, and that encourage a debate in which 'discourse is never-ending, and solidarity is forever creating new networks and mosaics' (1999, 103). In this way, debate about, and practices of sustainable architecture would enter into what Hinchliffe and Whatmore describe as a 'reconfiguration of ecology, away from statements of fact to engagements with possibilities' (2006, 131). They add: 'Rather than unveiling the truth of the ecology at hand there is a turn to those involved in the co-fabrication of living cities. There is a re-distribution of expertise, or a re-definition of expertise so that it includes lay engagements with place' (2006, 131).

Following this focus on the fluidity of design, we might begin to ask how and why designers are pursuing environmentalism in very particular ways, with very different notions of nature and culture, and with highly variable technological strategies. In doing so, we might chart an agenda for future research and practice that would challenge current orthodoxies, and so better engage in the making and remaking of sustainable architectures (Guy and Moore 2005; 2008).

NOTES

1 See Lerner's website at www.jaimelerner.com.

2 On McDonough's design philosophy, see the McDonough Braungart Design Chemistry website at www.mbdc.com.

3 See the websites for Architecture for Humanity and Slum Dwellers International at www.architectureforhumanity.org and www.sdinet.co.za, respectively.

32

The Ecology Question and Architecture

Richard Ingersoll

The Ecology Question in theories of architectural design gained increased importance during the latter half of the twentieth century in response to the negative environmental impact of architecture and urbanism. Although initially formulated as an ethical issue exclusively in industrialized Western countries, sustainability, or the minimization of the use of non-renewable resources, has become a major technical, political, and legal focus of international debates. Any current discussion of architectural theory invariably returns to the Ecology Question. In some regards, ecology consciousness fits into the general postmodern drift away from determinism, anthropocentrism, and teleology (Wines 2000). In other ways, however, the resulting positions of green functionalism reactivate a role once played by modernist functionalism, implying a philosophical return to positivism. In this chapter I will examine the various trends in the greening of architectural theory, from utopianism, to reformism, to quasi-religious approaches, to technocratic imperatives. The latent apocalyptic presentiments inspired by the current awareness of global warming have unwittingly led many contemporary theorists toward the restoration of the much maligned idea of a master narrative.

To call the theories of sustainability in design 'the Ecology Question,' refers by analogy to Friedrich Engels' polemic in 'The Housing Qucstion'. Similar to the demand for housing as a solution to the social and political problem of the potentially dangerous nineteenth-century working class, the urgency and functionalist premises of twentieth-century environmentalism have been laden with ideological frames worth analysing. What Engels said about Victorian concepts of housing reform seems an appropriate reminder regarding the mission to achieve sustainability: 'It is not that the solution of the housing question simultaneously solves the social question, but that only by the solution of the social question, that is, by the abolition of the capitalist mode of production, is the solution of the housing question made possible' (Engels 1872). His critique could extend to the current tendency to address symptoms without dealing with the superstructure that allowed them to happen, resulting mostly in stopgap placebo solutions.

I will first consider the historical development of the theory of ecology as it relates to architecture; while it is a relatively new topic, and is usually considered ahistorically, it is not without a historical dimension

(Bramwell 1989). From there I will investigate the situations that thrust sustainability from the edge to the centre of the discussion in the fields of design. The subsequent efforts to promote green architecture have bred various agendas for 'ecological correctness'. Solutions range from symbolic gestures toward a oneness with nature to rigorously monitored models of energy performance. If Engels presumed the ultimate flaw of housing solutions came from their inability to change the structure of monopoly capitalism, today one must measure the solutions to the Ecology Question in terms of globalization. The simultaneous emergence of globalism and global warming during the 1990s sets the scene for my conclusion. The confrontation between local and global culture has helped to shift the discourse from a Western-dominated theory to a more multicultural mindset.

BUILDING AGAINST NATURE. A HISTORICAL PERSPECTIVE ON THE INFLUENCE OF ECOLOGY ON ARCHITECTURE

The appearance of ecology within the discourse of architecture hinges on a historic paradox: every act of building betrays the environment, as it requires the displacement of 'natural' relationships. The clearing of the site, the destructive gathering and assembly of materials, and the continued consumption of natural resources to service a finished building set the built environment against the natural. Louis I. Kahn summarized it well with the epigram: 'Everything that man makes, nature cannot make. And everything that nature makes, man cannot' (Latour 1991). This paradox has led some designers with ecological intentions to attempt to imitate nature or enhance natural features. Others have sought natural analogues in their design methods. When faced, however, with leaky roofs, cracking foundations, spalling surfaces, infestations of insects, mould formation, fires, floods, and earthquakes, one cannot deny that architecture exists fundamentally as a struggle with natural phenomena.

Most pre-industrial cultures in the act of settlement laboured to establish an equilibrium between the built environment and the natural. This entailed first of all the management of water: its gathering, distribution, and elimination. Likewise the built environment depended on the resources of the woods and fields. The preparation of building materials usually required skilled transformation by tools. Adobe had to be mixed with straw and other materials into a soft bond; bricks had to be moulded and baked; timber, planed and slotted; stone, quarried and dressed. Even the most natural of materials such as hides and thatch were processed before being assembled. Thus while the ingredients of architecture came as gifts of nature, rarely were they assembled without being reworked through human agency, often damaging the environment. The consequences of deforestation from ambitious building projects proved to be one of the greatest problems of the ancient world (Merchant 1980).

The apparent success of many urban cultures as a producers of monuments and large populations often led to a violent rift in the balance with the environment. The intense agricultural exploitation of Mesopotamia during the second millennium BCE, with two to three harvests per year, contributed to the salinization of the region's soil and the downfall of its settlements (Hillel 1990). The grand pyramid cities of the Maya in Central America collapsed during the ninth to eleventh centuries due to the struggle over limited agricultural resources. In their competitive commissioning of huge monuments they deforested the surroundings, leading to poor agricultural performance in a region with extreme wet and dry seasons (Diamond 2005).

Among the ancient texts concerning building one can discern ecological criteria, especially in the recommendations for siting a building. The Chinese manual, the *Chou-li*, from the first century BCE prescribed a southern orientation, offering solar advantages to the typically broad, colonnaded pavilions. A treatise by Vitruvius, written around 25 BCE, the only surviving ancient Roman source, offered sound advice about avoiding swampy sites and protecting a building from prevailing winds, but otherwise remained silent on environmental issues. The rules that Vitruvius outlined for Greco-Roman architecture followed rational dictates that set buildings apart from nature. The Renaissance treatises of Alberti, Serlio, and Palladio followed suit, pursuing the autonomous issues of style and composition. As Western architecture developed theoretically in alienation from nature, the humanist philosophy of fifteenth- and sixteenth-century intellectuals fixed direction by European knowledge as the anthropocentric worldview (Choay 1997).

Although pre-industrial builders may not have put it down in writing, they usually worked from a legacy of built knowledge based on an inherent understanding of passive solar energy and thermal mass. During the thirteenth century, the Anasazi builders of Pueblo Bonito in Chaco Canyon, New Mexico, followed a perfect southern orientation, stepping up their solar hemicycle structures to allow passive thermal diffusion (Butti and Perlin 1980). While pre-industrial builders occasionally exhausted their local resources, compared with industrial societies they proved relatively harmless in terms of increased entropy on a global scale.

During the mid-eighteenth century, through the polemical texts of Jean-Jacques Rousseau (1712–1778), nature assumed a metaphysical role as the ultimate measure of virtue. This concept reached its apex in the creation of picturesque gardens at the great European houses, such as Stowe, Stourhead, or Erménonville (where the philosopher died and was buried). Rousseau's exaltation of 'natural man' led more to the investigation of the natural rights of humans than to the correct attitude of humans to nature. A century later, the American writer Henry David Thoreau, an amateur naturalist, expressed both a strong defence of human rights in his practice of 'civil disobedience' and a new sensibility to nature in his retreat to Walden Pond. His cabin, built with borrowed tools and recycled boards for $28.12, served as a lesson in economy that paralleled his observations of the wilderness surrounding his shelter.

The dangerous impact of urbanization became increasingly evident after the introduction of the steam engine into industry in the late eighteenth century. Steam power dramatically raised the pro capita use of carbon-based fuels with immediate environmental ills. The Irwell River that passed through Manchester, England, became famous as a stinking sluice for industrial effluvia, while the air of London acquired a permanent black cloud of smog due to the consumption of coal (Marcus 1974). The environmental wisdom of vernacular builders virtually disappeared as industrial processes redefined all dimensions of human existence, from the work place to the home. For the modern urban dweller, the 'ecological footprint', that is, the resources needed to supply an individual's needs, soared from a little over a hectare during pre-industrial times to more than five times that now (Wackernagel and Rees 1996).

During the 1860s, two key terms, 'entropy' and 'ecology', enter the scientific and political vocabulary. The German physicist Rudolph Clausius (1822–1888) coined the term 'entropy' in 1862 to signify the dissipation of matter and energy according to the Second Law of Thermodynamics. Entropy has spread exponentially during the past two centuries with the rise of modern industries and the metropolis. Jeremy Rifkin and Ted Howard have predicted that the unchecked advance of entropy in industrial civilization will lead to the probable heat death of the planet (Rifkin and Howard 1989). According to some theories of sustainable architecture, one should evaluate buildings, their materials and production process, and their performance in terms of whether they raise or lower entropy.

The second key word, ecology, has come to have a greater symbolic function in the culture of architecture. The German zoologist Ernst Haeckel (1834–1919) coined the term in 1866 to specify the theory that everything in nature is interrelated. He built on Charles Darwin's theory of evolution, first published in 1859 in *On the Origin of Species*. From Darwin's expression 'the economy of nature' Haeckel arrived at the Greek word for house, *oikos*, to signify the order of the natural world. This architectural metaphor inferred that the relationships among organisms in nature corresponded to the cooperative organization of a well-run household. While Haeckel's interpretation of the theory of evolution led some to notions of social Darwinism, whereby the survival of the fittest justified social inequality, his worldview generally undermined anthropocentrism, demoting humans to just another species in the chain of life (Foster 2000).

Haeckel had wide influence in the sciences and in politics. Some of his political thoughts, such as 'politics is applied biology', led to the unfortunate racist ideologies adopted by Nazism (Bramwell 1996). He also had a strong effect on art and architecture through his masterful watercolour illustrations of microorganisms, sea creatures, and wildlife, published throughout his life. He gathered them into a hundred plates as *Kunstformen der Natur* (*Art Forms of Nature*) (Haeckel 1899–1904). The organic forms of Art Nouveau in the works of Victor Horta, Hector Guimard, and Antoni Gaudi corresponded to Haeckel's scientific illustrations.

Haeckel's most influential follower and biographer, Rudolf Steiner (1861–1925), sought ties between the natural sciences and spiritual life. Like Haeckel, Steiner revered the holistic positions of Johann Wolfgang von Goethe, to whom he dedicated the principal building in his utopian community at Dornach, Switzerland. He built the Goetheanum from 1913 to 1922 with the followers of his Anthroposophy movement. Steiner avoided using right angles, claiming that they were absent in nature. He explained that his double-domed meeting hall was '... conceived out of the whole. Every single form in this organically conceived building ..., in that it represents a part of the whole, must make evident in its own form that it is indispensable, as manifestly indispensable as the lobe of the ear, or an arm or a head is to the human organism'.

Although Adolph Hitler had despised Steiner for his defence of Judaism, some Nazi ideologues benefited from the philosopher's rich collection of ideas. Walther Darré, Hitler's Minister of Agriculture, authorized hundreds of experimental farms based on Steiner's theory of biodynamic cultivation, making Nazi Germany the first government to adopt ecological policies – in some cases placing the farms next to concentration camps. After arsonists torched Steiner's Goetheanum in 1923, he did not hesitate to use the insurance money to build the Second Goetheanum. Finished in 1928, it rose as one of the Europe's first important non-industrial buildings in reinforced concrete, a material choice that rendered it fireproof. Its angular style, like the facetted cliffs of a mountain, echoed the Expressionist trend in the arts. Steiner explained his strange-looking structure as the product of 'spiritual functionalism', inspired by analogy to natural forms (Adams 1992).

Steiner's buildings at Dornach did not perform in a truly ecological way, but rather presented symbols of ecological sympathy. His theory of education, however, still widely observed in Waldorf Schools throughout the world, and his 'biodynamic' agricultural method, which advocated mulching over the soil rather than digging into it, have remained significant models of holism for later environmental activists. Steiner established a spiritual, quasi-religious approach to the Ecology Question as a reverence for nature.

This ethical position that descended from the Romantic movement in nineteenth-century literature, reappeared in the writings of a number of influential twentieth-century architects. Key among them were Frank Lloyd Wright (1867–1959) and Le Corbusier

(1887–1965). Both men in their youths were steeped in the romantic mission of John Ruskin and the Arts and Crafts movement, but each developed theories on the immanent role of industrialization in the production of modern architecture. Wright wrote his essay 'The Art and Craft of the Machine' in 1901 as a provocation to the purists in the Arts and Crafts movement who rejected industry outright. He praised the arrival of new techniques and materials, while condemning the banality of mass production. Le Corbusier published *Toward an Architecture* in 1923, with a picture of the deck of an ocean liner on the cover. The book, still in print, became the gospel of the machine aesthetic for several generations of modernists.

Despite their dependence on industrial culture both Wright and Le Corbusier became proto-ecologists, the first advocating 'organic architecture', the latter championing the 'green city'. Wright proposed to build into nature; Le Corbusier to build over it. With the Second Jacob's House built in Wisconsin in 1948, Wright created one of the most successful passive solar buildings ever designed: a two-storey hemicycle facing south, its rear lodged in an artificial berm that served as thermal storage (Aitken 1992). Le Corbusier's Purist villas of the 1920s and 1930s proved particularly inefficient in terms of energy. In his later works, however, such as the Maisons Jaoul in Neuilly and the Sarabhai House in Ahmedabad (both completed in 1956), he turned away from the machine aesthetic, using sod roofs and *aerateurs*, movable slots for the convection of cool air. Le Corbusier specifically attempted to create passive, energy efficient dwellings. His Unité d'Habitation in Marseilles, built as a prototype for mass housing in 1947–1952, conserved the ground plane, provided a roof-top garden, and offered light and ventilation from both sides of the building to each unit. The goal of minimizing the amount of space needed for each family by offering dense, loft-like environments proved the opposite of Wright's Broadacre City, with individual houses spreading across the land (Fishman 1982).

Richard Neutra (1892–1970), an Austrian trained by Adolph Loos in Vienna, worked first for Erich Mendelsohn in Berlin and then for Wright at Taleisin before moving to Los Angeles in 1926. He appears to be the first architect to specifically use the word 'ecology' in a theoretical discussion of design. Writing mostly during the 1940s before the political movement for ecology began, he published *Survival through Design* in 1954. Neutra presented the subject of ecology and design as an ethical position but did not specify how to achieve it. His works in the Los Angeles region include some of the finest examples of high modernism in the US. Neutra's houses frequently used an L-shaped configuration of interlocking planes with large plate glass windows facing south, and a pond as a natural cooling feature. Vents at the base and eaves level took in cool air and let out hot. Neutra drew inspiration from the sciences, advocating 'biological realism', by which he meant the creation of environments that served physiological and psychological needs while keeping the dweller in close contact with nature (Neutra 1954).

Neutra's influence in promoting ecology-conscious design proved negligible during the fast-paced years of the American economic boom of the 1950s. In the 1960s, however, ecology entered the political arena. Rachel Carson's 'Silent Spring', first published in the *New Yorker* in 1962, alerted Americans to how they were poisoning the biosphere with DDT pesticides. Groups such as the Sierra Club in California began lobbying for environmental protection, while a widespread movement to ban nuclear testing took to the streets in Europe and America during the same period (Nash 1989).

The Italian architect, Paolo Soleri (b. 1919), who came to work with Wright at Taleisin in 1947, and settled in Scottsdale, Arizona, in 1957, attempted to provide an architectural response to this new ecology movement in the late 1960s. He coined the term 'arcology', meaning to combine architecture and ecology. Through the design of colossal megastructures that hovered over the land like beehives for human communities, Soleri proposed to improve on Le Corbusier's notion of vertical density. He envisioned a city as a single beehive-like organism that would concentrate the distribution of resources and conserve the land. To substantiate his theories he founded Arcosanti in the Sonoran desert in 1970 as a prototype of arcology for five hundred residents. The complex, built into the southern bank of a small canyon, recalls the typology of the Anasazi great houses of Chaco Canyon. Construction of Arcosanti is still underway, mostly by volunteer labour, and has served as an important communal experience for many cohorts of idealistic students seeking an alternative world.

Soleri's models of urbanism have been consigned to the utopian fringes of architecture culture because of their geographic isolation and 'drop-out' character. Like many urban utopias, his arcology implied a strong authoritarian order. The participants at Arcosanti come of their own free will, and while they usually shared the master's desire for a low-entropy lifestyle and environmental responsibility, they were often alienated by Soleri's guru status and autocratic manner. As in most utopias, Arcosanti thrives on good intentions but recreates many of the anthropocentric patterns it presumes to resist, as revealed in the subtitle of Soleri's book: *The City in the Image of Man* (Soleri 1969).

THE ENERGY CRISIS AND THE COUNTERCULTURAL ECOLOGISTS

The first international crisis to quicken interest in the Ecology Question came not from an environmental catastrophe but from the Yom Kippur War of October 1973. Arab oil-producing nations agreed upon a fuel embargo against the US and other supporters of Israel that lasted for six months, devastating the world economy for several years. The ensuing energy crisis throughout the 1970s stimulated research into energy efficiency.

The most surprising discovery came from Richard Stein's 1978 study funded by the American Insitute of Architects, *Architecture and Energy*, which demonstrated that the greatest energy extravagance resulted from the way buildings were produced. Construction and the production of materials as 'embodied energy' accounted for more than ten percent of all annual energy use. Materials such as aluminium contain an extremely high level of embodied energy due to the long process required to make them. While architects have always considered cost issues, few took into consideration the fact that a reinforced concrete structure contained half the embodied energy of an equivalent steel structure. Imported materials and long-distance transport also greatly increased the energy expenditure, as did demolitions and the dumping of inert materials (Stein 1978).

In design, the mandate for energy efficiency did not lead to approaches based on holism, but rather promoted measures such as increased insulation, better solar orientation, and improved building envelopes. The building codes in regions such as Calfornia were changed to encourage higher degrees of insulation, which significantly reduced energy use. This did not necessarily result in better design, and certainly did not encourage more integration with natural systems. The new standards of construction lowered energy consumption by twenty percent, but the huge increase in development during the next two decades far outweighed the gain in energy conservation.

The energy crisis inspired government-funded research into alternative energy. Tax incentives led to such extraordinary landscape transformations as the Altamont Pass Windfarm in Northern California. It was installed in the mid-1970s, and the wind-swept chaparral slopes carry nearly five thousand eolic turbines. At the consumer level, solar water heaters, which at the beginning of the twentieth century had been a common sight in Southern California, were revived as awkward additions to the rooftops of single-family houses. In Israel at the end of the 1970s, ninety percent of all homes installed solar water heaters through a programme of tax incentives, dramatically cutting energy use. Photovoltaic cells, which of all alternative energy sources have the greatest potential as architectural features, were introduced at this time, but were not yet affordable. Many experiments in solar energy were applied to new buildings, such as the water-filled black tubes of the Trombe wall that created thermal mass. Thus a large part of the new ecological approach to design remained within the realm of scientific research.

The San Francisco Bay Area remained one of the most active places for research and activism concerning the Ecology Question. The region had a strong history of environmentalism, as the home of the national parks movement and the Sierra Club. During the 1960s, Friends of the Earth branched off from the Sierra Club to become the most outspoken lobby for environmental causes. The Bay Area also generated *The Whole Earth Catalogue*, developed by Stewart Brand in 1968, which became the Bible of countercultural lifestyles and ecology consciousness (Kirk 2007). Other activist groups such as Greenpeace, founded in Vancouver in 1970, and Earth First!, founded in Albuquerque in 1979, drew many of their volunteers from California's ecology movement.

The environmental sensitivity of the Bay Area inspired the planning of Sea Ranch in the mid-1960s, one of the earliest settlements designed with specific ecological criteria. Lawrence Halprin (b. 1916) prepared the site plan for the 5,000-acre vacation spot north of San Francisco on the windswept cliffs of the Mendocino coast. He gathered the units into dense clusters near thickets of trees to conserve as much of the open landscapes and beach lands as possible. The principal architect, Charles Moore (1925–1995) and his colleagues of Moore, Turnbull, Lyndon, and Whitaker (MTLW), borrowed from local vernacular barns, using single-pitched roofs and simple stave cladding.

The success of Sea Ranch influenced Christopher Alexander (b. 1936), a professor at the University of California at Berkeley. After 1968, Alexander rejected the highly mechanistic 'systems' theory to embrace the charm and wisdom of vernacular builders. His treatise, *A Pattern Language: Towns, Buildings, Construction* (1977), written with several colleagues, proposes 256 patterns, based on vernacular solutions from throughout the world. The scale ranges from the urban region to the window seat. The patterns are meant to be linked as sequences to create a cohesive environment. His 'timeless way' is holistic, derived from the ecological notion that everything is related to everything else. While reticent of bureaucratic codes, Alexander's *Pattern Language* leads to a series of its own codes from the scale of a building, to the placement of windows, to material choices, in the effort to reduce architecture's damage to the environment (Alexander et al. 1977).

A more direct approach to ecology came from Sim Van der Ryn (b. 1934), another professor at UC Berkeley, who in the 1970s became the California State Architect under Governor Jerry Brown. This led to a mandate for six energy-efficient state office buildings to be used as models. The 1977 Bateson Building in Sacramento remains the finest product of this programme, grouping the offices around an internal court served by a series of passive cooling devices. Van der Ryn also founded the Farallones Institute, an organization dedicated to promoting more ecological lifestyles. In 1974 the organization converted a typical single-family house on a standard lot in west Berkeley into the 'Integral Urban House', creating an exhibition to demonstrate how a normal family could live in greater harmony with natural elements and become relatively independent for food and energy (Van der Ryn, 1979).

The 1970s ecology movement generated a wide variety of eccentric design approaches such as Michael Reynolds' 'Earthships', desert houses made mostly from recycled tires, bottles, and adobe, or Steve Baer's

'Zomes', houses made from folded polyhedrons based on Buckminster Fuller's geodesic domes. Utopian groups formed in California and in Northern Europe. The Findhorn Commune in Scotland pursued a spiritual approach similar to Rudolph Steiner's, resulting in an Ecovillage for 400 residents. The artist Friedrichreich Hundertwasser (1928–2000) convinced the municipality of Vienna in the late 1970s to let him build a public housing project using an alternative biological-architecture, with trees planted in the walls and vibrant colours and neo-primitive decorations.

Occasionally non-Western experiments, such as the founding of Auroville on the east coast of India in 1968, provided alternatives. The slower development of India already made it one of the places in the world with the lowest per capita ecological footprint – less than a tenth of the typical American. The utopian followers of the guru Sri Aurobindi, the majority of whom were Westerners, pursued ecological premises in structuring their community. In this regard one should not forget the precedent of Mahatma Gandhi's Sabarmati Ashram founded at Ahmedabad in 1917, for which he returned to the principles of Thoreau's quest for self-reliance. His community grew its own food and produced the fabric for their modest clothes, living in utmost simplicity: 'The essence of civilization', Gandhi wrote, 'consists not in the multiplication of wants but in their deliberate and voluntary renunciation' (Brown 2008).

The most meaningful example of ecological sensibility published during the 1970s came from a non-Western source, the Egyptian architect Hasan Fathy. In *Architecture for the Poor* he recounted his attempt to teach low-income villagers ancient mud construction techniques to give them skills and direct the building industry away from imported materials and technologies, such as reinforced concrete (Fathy 1973). While his efforts in Egypt ultimately failed, the beauty of the work and the logic of its investment in local resources appealed to the movement for Intermediate Technology (later renamed Appropriate Technology), founded by the economist E.F. Schumacher (1911–1977). In this one seeks to build in the most eco-efficient way, within the limits of a region. Fathy helped to shift the discourse of ecology in architecture away from primarily Western perspectives to include a broader range of cultural sources (Schumacher 1973).

The first wave of responses to the Ecology Question fostered reforms in building codes, the proliferation of unsightly solar panels, and numerous utopian fantasies. In some cases the emphasis on functional criteria confined the discussion of ecology to technical or scientific data, in others the righteousness or the spiritualism of enthusiasts became esoteric. Utopianism tended to penalize ecology in the discourses of architecture. Most ecological utopias contain a high proportion of authoritarian prescriptions and require radical sacrifices concerning the individual's free will that are difficult to apply on a mass level. The transition to a more sustainable lifestyle, in communities such as Findhorn, required a quasi-religious commitment that most people would not accept. The quest for sustainability, with its numerous prohibitions, put citizens' rights to the test. Only in the area of 'organic' food did consumer society begin to open up to alternatives. Ecology-conscious architecture during the energy crisis remained for the most part on the margins and was categorically ignored by intellectuals and academics.

THE GREEN APOCALYPSE AND THE ADVENT OF LAND ARCHITECTURE

Attitudes to ecology changed a decade later. Two disturbing events brought the Ecology Question to the centre of discussions in many fields: the verification of the ozone hole(s) over Antarctica in 1985 and the catastrophe at the nuclear power plant of Chernobyl in 1986. The news seemed apocalyptic and provoked a new level of alarmism in the discourses of environmentalism. Man-made substances, especially chlorofluorocarbons (CFCs), were identified as the chief causes of ozone depletion in the stratosphere, permitting the penetration of dangerous levels of ultraviolet light. The UN's Montreal Accords of 1987 swiftly moved to ban CFCs, demonstrating a rare, but important moment of international cooperation. At Chernobyl, a human error led to a malfunction that released radioactive contamination across most of Europe. The disaster inspired grassroots movements throughout Europe to call for a ban on nuclear power and seek alternative, renewable sources of energy. Ecology quickly became a major theme in local and international politics.

In the background lurked an even darker environmental threat in the green apocalypse: global warming. The theory was first published in 1896 by the Swedish physicist Svante Arrhenius (1859–1927), who instead of being frightened by his prediction believed that the change in climate would benefit northern countries (Christiansen 1999). The hypothesis that industrial society's production of CO_2 and methane during the last two centuries led to exponential increases in the planet's natural greenhouse gases began to find support in the 1980s. James Hansen, one of the leading scientists at NASA, endorsed the hypothesis in 1988. The consistently hot summers of the 1990s triggered international apprehension, leading to the Kyoto Accords of 1997, an international treaty prepared by the UN which attempted to limit the production of greenhouse gases to five to eight percent below their 1990 levels. The awareness of global warming has intensified international concern: seventeen of the last twenty years of the twentieth century have been the hottest on record. The evidence of ecological imbalances now implicated buildings and cities as the chief source of the accumulation of CO_2 and other gases in the planet's atmosphere causing the 'greenhouse' effect. Ecological design, which previously was the province of eccentrics, dreamers, and outsiders, has now become a central concern for many practitioners.

The discussion of ecology became more intense with the threat of the green apocalypse. On the one hand researchers identified critical environmental agendas that demanded policy decisions, on the other hand, ecological ideologies moved in different directions. Deep Ecology, Ecofeminism, Social Ecology, and High Tech entered the academic arena. James Lovelock (b. 1919) proposed in the Gaia Theory that the biosphere analysed by Darwin and others as a holistic ensemble of interrelated species was in fact a single living organism in which humans were an insignificant component (Lovelock 1988). The most radical subscribers to this debunking of anthropocentrism followed the principles of Deep Ecology, articulated in 1973 by the Norwegian philosopher Arne Naess (1912–2009) as 'biospherical egalitarianism' (Naess 1989). It led to an unwitting sort of elitism that proposed that the rights of all living organisms in nature supersede human priorities (Nash 1989). This position led the eco-guerillas of Earth First! to spike redwood trees in California to prevent their destruction. Activist groups such as Greenpeace work from a similar point of view, planning actions against nuclear power, and interventions in defense of species threatened by multinational consumerism, interrupting whaling operations and disturbing laboratories that produce genetically modified grains.

Ecofeminism leveled its critique at Western anthropocentrism as the mindset that has prolonged the oppression of both women and the environment. Vandana Shiva (b. 1952) from India argued that women should be respected as having a closer connection to nature than men do (Shiva 1989). The theory of Social Ecology, a term coined by Murray Bookchin, interpreted ecological imbalances as originating from social inequities that require social solutions. In his objection to hierarchical solutions Bookchin notes: 'Ecology is being used against an ecological sensibility, ecological forms of organization, and ecological practices to win large constituencies, not to educate them'. Information, participation, and interaction, he argued, create the most solid base for a socially responsible ecology consciousness (Bookchin 1982).

Other ecology activists took a more tolerant view of consumer society, proposing the biblical notion of human stewardship of the environment. The liberal approach to ecology has attempted to reform consumerism from within by popularizing recycling, alternative transportation, bio-architecture, and activities such as community gardens. The High Tech position forms a branch of this reformist ecology, promoting science and technology as the solutions that will repair ecological damage without interfering with consumerist lifestyles or worldviews. High Tech architecture, while it appears completely alienated from the natural world, purports to supply the highest performance in sustainability. It generally operates with the apparent contradiction of proposing high entropy solutions for lowering entropy.

The High Tech position derived from the thoughts of the American engineer R. Buckminster Fuller (1895–1983). According to Fuller, the problem was not entropy per se but the great waste of potential in materials and energy, which was due to technological inefficiencies. His metaphor for the planet as 'Spaceship Earth', became central to the environmental movement. His theories of a 'dymaxion' world, based on maximizing such techniques as geodesic domes and tensegrity structures had broad appeal, culminating in the US Pavilion at the 1967 Montreal expo, a vast, plastic-covered geodesic sphere. Fuller's first large commission came from this, but his models also appealed to hippies, and were used by the anarchic group of artists that built Drop City, Colorado, in 1968, as a series of geodesic domes made of abandoned automobile carcasses (Pawley 1990).

Fuller's most successful follower, Lord Norman Foster (b. 1935), established a niche in architectural culture for very costly High Tech structures with ecological pretensions. Foster produced the Greater London Authority municipal building in London on the south bank of the Thames (in 2002) as a bioclimatic structure. Like a glass-covered beehive, its spherical volume tilts up to shade the southern exposure, and has a central atrium with a convection shaft for natural ventilation. Foster surpassed it with a more harmonious conical tower for the Re insurance company in central London. Its spiraling structure alternates planted landings that provide natural filters for the forced air. Foster borrowed the bioclimatic high-rise typology from Malaysian architect Ken Yeang (b. 1948), who realized it first in the Menara Mesiniaga Building of 1992. Despite the efficiency in energy savings of High Tech buildings, a strong doubt lingers that the high cost of construction can be amortized by good energy performance (McDonough and Braungart 2002).

Most ecology-conscious architects distrust the embodied energy in High Tech solutions and seek something closer to Intermediate Technology. Some of the best seekers of sustainable design include Swedish-British Ralph Erskine, Australian Glenn Murcutt, German Thomas Herzog, and American Sam Mockbee. Ralph Erskine (1914–2005) proposed some of the first ecology-conscious designs in the 1950s for arctic settlements. His Byker Wall project (1973–1978) in the suburbs of Newcastle-upon-Tyne, UK, became the paragon of a new participatory architecture, while his university works in Stockholm during the 1980s, offered bioclimatic solutions to natural light and heating.

Glenn Murcutt (b. 1936) employs an architectural language inspired by the minimalism of Mies van der Rohe, with the difference that every aspect of design is calculated to assist solar energy, natural ventilation, and the recovery of rainwater. Murcutt has been particularly careful in his work to conserve resources, and not use more technology than necessary to achieve a comfortable and sustainable environment. He frequently resorts to a double roof solution to draw off excess heat. His Riversdale Art Centre, finished in 2005 on a rural site near Cambewarra, Australia, provided a foundation with a residence for seminars, a large open hall, studios, and a long structure for pairs of apartments. The project is anchored into a hill on a narrow concrete base, while each pair of units is made of wooden panels that have been slipped into the frame, cantilevering over the base like a drawer in an armoire. The complex needs neither air-conditioning nor heating, achieving optimal temperatures by adjusting the windows and shutters. Although Murcutt employs some specially designed features for the storage and heating of water, most of the sustainability of his work comes from common sense about orientation, construction, and patterns of dwelling. Thomas Herzog (b. 1941) designs in a similar manner attempting to exploit solar orientation and passive systems, seen in his Linz Design Center (1996).

Sam Mockbee (1944–2001) founded Rural Studio, engaging his students as volunteers to build self-help housing and community buildings in rural Alabama. Using unconventional cast-off materials, his team patched together several stunning works. They built one house using hay bales, and another with stacks of carpet samples for thermal mass. At the Mason's Bend Community Center, finished in 2000, they built the walls of rammed earth, rafters fashioned from trees on the site, and glazing from eighty recycled automobile windscreens on a budget of less than $20,000. The costs of Rural Studio's buildings are a fraction of market-rate buildings, due to the choice of recycled materials and the elimination of design and construction expenses. The users participate in the planning and construction, resulting in complete satisfaction.

One response among architects echoes the efforts of Land Art to respond to the environmental crisis. Land Architecture attempts to evoke land forms or integrate into them. The idea was popularized by Mexican architect Emilio Ambazs, in the early 1980s, leading to his San Antonio Botanical Gardens, Texas (1985). His most recent effort, the Federal Prefectural Hall tower in Fukuoka, Japan (2005), steps up twenty grades with luxuriantly planted terraces like a contemporary Hanging Gardens of Babylon.

Renzo Piano created one of the first extensive green roofs in Europe at the Schlumberger Headquarters Complex built on the edge of Paris in 1983. The parking structure sits inside an artificial hill, perhaps as an act of expiation, considering Schlumberger's role in oil drilling. In a later work, the 2003 Paul Klee Museum on the outskirts of Berne, Piano carefully slipped three differently sized hoods into the slope of a farming landscape to enhance the sense of rolling wheat fields. In the Netherlands, MVRDV created a similar effect in 1997 with the RVU Building for broadcasting in Hilversum, a long parallelepiped that rises obliquely from a slope, covered by a grass roof. For the Netherlands' pavilion at the 2000 Hannover Expo, they built a layered series of six different biotopes as a provocation that architecture could become the support of natural habitats.

A literally 'green' solution for buildings came from the French botanist Patrick Blanc (b. 1953), who in the late 1990s perfected a method of creating collages of plant materials as cladding. Using steel frames and PVC plastic supports with a base of felt, he weaves a spectacular variety of plants into a growing mosaic. His *murs végétals* now grace major museums and institutions, including the Quai Branly in Paris and the Caixa Forum in Madrid.

Land Architecture, either through digging into or rising out of the land, keeps a building from being seen on its own. It opens the possibility of reconciliation of the artificial environment of architecture with that of nature. While primarily an aesthetic response to the Ecology Question, the green roofs and the thermal mass of berms function well in conserving water and energy. The effort to confound architecture with natural topography can be interpreted as an ex-voto to the green apocalypse, a return to the land and a losing of oneself in mother earth. At the Roden Crater, from 1979 to 2006 the artist James

Turrell (b. 1943) built a demonstration of the quest to regain a lost cosmology in the waste lands of Arizona. His monumental piece sends the participant through a sequence of tunnels and roofless chambers, creating a special vision of the heavens. He frames the sky in such a way that one cannot perceive distances and feels absorbed into it. Turrell's observatory reestablishes the connection between human time and the natural universe. It becomes a ritual act of redemption from two centuries of advanced entropy (de Rosa 2007).

ECOLOGICAL CORRECTNESS. SUSTAINABILITY, AND QUANTIFICATION

Following the publication of the UN's Brundtland Commission report in 1987, 'sustainable development', emerged as the new term signifying the minimization of the use of non-renewable resources. While sustainable design was previously confined to environmental activists in more developed countries, it has become an economic and legal issue on a world scale. During the 1990s, the political goal of ecological accounting would lead to efficient design and development. A further incentive to create normative practices came from the 1997 Kyoto Protocol for reduction of greenhouse gases to eight percent below the levels of 1990. To date, one hundred and eighty countries have signed the treaty, which went into effect in 2005. The US, which emits more than twenty-five percent of the world's greenhouse gases, has not signed due to fear of its economic impact. Many American municipalities and private companies nonetheless have attempted to satisfy the reduction of greenhouse gases specified in the Kyoto Protocol, voluntarily making amends for America's well-known overindulgence with six percent of the world's population consuming thirty percent of its resources.

The green apocalypse helped the German Green Party in the late 1980s take eight percent of the national vote. The Green Party came to power in some cities such as Freiburg, which soon after sponsored the most progressive European 'green' policies. Freiburg declared itself a 'solar region' and has encouraged the development of solar industries and the widespread use of photovoltaic panels on the top of public structures like garages, schools, and sports halls. Photovoltaic cladding was used on a high-rise at the train station. Freiburg's Vauban district, built on the site of an abandoned military barracks, provides a clear model of changes both in building policies and lifestyles. The apartments were constructed with sophisticated insulation, natural materials, and a collective heating system based on the consumption of biomass fuel. Solar panels heat the water and provide most of the electricity. Residents receive tax incentives not to own automobiles, and forty percent comply, preferring to bicycle on the city's 100 km of bike paths or use the bus system, both of which are easier to manage than cars.

Most buildings would be more sustainable simply through correct solar orientation, better insulation, and minimizing volume. An integrated approach was offered in the NMB Bank (now ING Bank) in the Bijlmermeer suburb of Amsterdam. When completed in 1987, it became one of the first large projects in Europe to attract attention for its ecological advantages. The architect Ton Alberts (1927–1999), educated at a Waldorf School according to the principles of Rudolf Steiner, created an Expressionist composition of ten mid-rise towers as an homage to the primal ecologist. The right angle, which Steiner claimed does not exist in nature, has been studiously renounced. The towers rise on battered walls to pentagonal solar collectors crowning the roofs. Their star-shaped plans are interconnected at the two lower levels, arranged like a necklace in a jagged S-shape. Each tower has a hollow circulation court that allows air and daylight to penetrate the different levels. Fountains using recycled rainwater nurture plants growing inside and outside the structure. The offices follow a narrow open plan around the courts, leaving no desk more than a metre from daylight. The energy savings proved to be the best of any office building of the time, but what surprised the evaluators after the first year's use was the reduction of staff absenteeism, from five percent absences per day to 0.3 percent. The NMB complex made people feel comfortable at work and better adjusted as a community (Zeiher 1996).

Sustainable buildings do not need to look organic. Will Bruder (b. 1944) designed one of the most energy-efficient buildings of the late twentieth century, the 1995 Phoenix Central Library, as a great copper-clad hood. It deploys active and passive solar technologies assembled in layers of structure. The gently bulging flanks sheathed in perforated copper work as 'saddle bags' carrying the mechanicals, offices, bathrooms, and service stairs. A diaphanous membrane protects the inner concrete walls from direct exposure to the desert sun and allows the structure to exhale the heat gain of the building's services. The shorter elevations are completely glazed. On the south, computer driven fins, like gigantic Venetian blinds, open and close during the day according to the intensity of sunlight. The north is protected from wind and glare by twenty-eight vertical ribbons of white teflon fabric fastened to steel pegs in the twisted positions of tacking sails. The internal concrete columns that support the five-level structure terminate in tapered cones that stop short of the vaulted ceiling of the reading room. The columns are crowned with steel nozzles that hook into a Fuller-inspired tensegrity space frame supporting the roof. While most libraries are labyrinthine and sepulchral, with little relation to the outdoors, the Phoenix Library is remarkably open, offering easy access to the stacks and exhilarating vistas to the horizon.

The theories of the first generation of ecological architects did not lend themselves to the sort of quantification demanded by international diplomacy since Kyoto. Sim Van der Ryn (with co-author Stuart Cohen) mapped out a holistic approach of five principles of ecological design that, though it might lead designers toward correct practices, does not attempt to convert into figures a calculable effect. Using his Real Goods Solar Living Center in Hopland, California (1996) as the model his recommendations are: 1) to grow solutions from the place, 2) to inform design through ecological accounting, 3) to mimic nature to fit with nature, 4) to realize that everyone is a designer, 5) to make nature visible. Only the second recommendation approaches the bureaucratic concerns of energy budgets, but which, as stated, does not lead to net results (Van der Ryn and Cohen 1996).

Van der Ryn's recommendations conform with the programme for *Natural Capitalism*, an ecological plan for industry put forth by another key player in the first generation of the ecology movement, Amory Lovins. In 1982 he founded the Rocky Mountain Institute, one of the leading research centres for ecology in the world, that as a building serves as a model of zero carbon use. With his colleagues he proposes Natural Capitalism as a means of reforming the consumer society toward less wasteful, more ecological lifestyles by: 1) recognizing the benefits of the conservation of matter and energy and demanding 'resource productivity', 2) treating industries with a biological paradigm, or 'biomimicry', as if they were natural organisms, 3) converting consumer goods into services rather than private property, 4) investing in renewable sources of energy (Hawkin et al. 1999).

Biomimicry in architecture was an inherent goal of Wright, Steiner, Soleri, and many others with an environmentalist agenda. But until recently it led designers toward formal solutions that resembled nature, rather than technical processes that worked like nature. McDonough and Braungart maintain that designers need to keep separate the things that work biologically as ingredients of the biosphere and those that belong to the technosphere. While buildings can copy the natural processes of growth, breath, and photosynthesis they should also provide for the containment and reuse of their inorganic components (McDonough and Braungart 2002).

The principles of biomimicry are in fact much clearer in the design of natural landscapes than in the design of buildings, or as Kahn called them what 'nature cannot make'. The elementary concepts of 'patch, edge, and corridor' are mapped out in the treatise, *Landscape Ecology Principles* (Dramstad et al. 1996). If buildings were conceived more like landscapes, that is made biomimetically, perhaps such criteria would work for architecture as well.

While the green apocalypse triggered a moral imperative for sustainable design, conventional practitioners often have difficulty in relating to such theoretical notions as biomimicry. Not everyone understands how to 'grow' a building from the site. New bureaucratic approaches to sustainability propose pragmatic checklists for the design professions to quantify the construction and performance of buildings. HOK, one of the largest corporate architectural offices in the world, has produced a primer on ecological design. While HOK's work does not instantly summon images of sustainability, they have been the architects of choice for a number of ecology-conscious agencies, including the Nature Conservancy in Arlington, Virginia, and the US Environmental Protection Agency in North Carolina. Their corporate method of solving the Ecology Question involves endless checklists that keep track of seven categories: team formation, education, information, design optimization, documents and specification, bidding and construction, operations and maintenance (Mendler and Odell 2000). The corporate method does nothing to change the positivist logic that created the initial problem but merely adds sustainability to its tabulations.

HOK's study seems to have been inspired by the criteria for LEED qualification. In 1998 the non-profit US Green Building Council established the LEED (Leadership in Energy and Environmental Design) evaluation system based on six categories: sustainable sites, water efficiency, energy and atmosphere, materials and resources, indoor environment quality, innovation and design process. During the last decade, this set of standards for environmentally efficient buildings has been applied to 14,000 projects, which have been awarded different levels of certification based on a point system. Among the few buildings to gain LEED platinum grade, the highest evaluation, is Renzo Piano's California Academy of Sciences in San Francisco (2008). The client desired to make a 'green' statement, which led to a few contradictions. Piano, for instance, was hoping to use glu-lam beams, but since this would have given the building a lower BTU rating, he was asked to use a recycled concrete and metal structure, which makes the museum less inviting. He received extra points for innovations, such as the use of photovoltaic cells in mosaic patterns in the pergola fringe surrounding the building. One of the innovations, however, derived from flawed logic: the extensive planted roof covering seven bulging knolls initially had trouble adhering to the steep surfaces of the mounds. Special trays were invented to grow the plants off site, and were pieced together on the roof like a carpet. While Piano's building looks ecological, covered by its natural mantle, other buildings that have earned high grades do not. Richard Meier's aluminium-clad Getty Center in Los Angeles (1997), obtained a silver LEED certification in 2008. Some of its questionable claims to sustainability include the extensive use of aluminium, the scattering of the volumes around the site, and over-exposure to the sun, while the cladding of luxurious blocks of Italian travertine rustication implies a great deal of embodied energy through importation. The rebuilding of 7 World Trade Center by David Childs of SOM, resulted in a glass-covered skyscraper completed in 2006, that earned a gold rating. Neither of these buildings would live up to Van der Ryn's biomimicry criterion for ecological design, but they succeed in the budget of sustainable cost–benefits.

While important institutions can afford to explore alternatives, the normal process of making housing and offices needs practical models. One of the most convincing was designed by Bill Dunster as BedZED (Beddington Zero Emissions Development, 2001) in suburban west London. It serves as a sort of marketing model for optimizing the development of an urban block. Built on a brownfield site, the compact rows of nearly a hundred units and forty atelier spaces for work-live situations is nearly self-sufficient for energy, using a combination of good insulation, solar orientation, triple glazed windows, a biomass-fed furnace, wind pipes for ventilation, and planted roofs with recycled rainwater for non-drinking-water uses. Residents can enroll in car-sharing, to use the dozen electric cars in the complex's garage that are fuelled by photovoltaic sources. All of the materials for the construction of BedZED came from local sources no farther than 35 km away, reducing transportation and embodied energy in construction (Buchanan 2003).

Alternatives such as BedZED are becoming competitive with market-rate housing. They cut as much as eighty percent of an individual's energy use. In developing countries, however, such high end projects are economically prohibitive. A different model was developed in Tilonia, India at the Barefoot College, a village in an arid region of Rajastan founded by Bunker Roy in 1971. His community, which now includes more than 125,000 people, revived Gandhi's principles of economic justice, non-hierarchical management, and self-sufficiency. Modesty of means has been enforced so that no one is allowed to earn more than $100 per month. The community produces intermediate technologies, such as solar cells and rainwater conservation tanks to be used in rural areas that lack power and water. In 1989 the Barefoot College built a new campus for its library, workshops, and residences, constructing over one hundred and fifty geodesic domes to cover structures built of local materials. Like Drop City, the village blacksmiths covered the polyhedrons with panels taken from abandoned automobile hoods. The lesson of living well with less, and producing enough energy to be self-sufficient holds great promise for communities that are disabled by their dependency on outside aid.

CONCLUSION: GLOBALIZATION AGAINST GLOBAL WARMING

During the 1990s, as global warming became a nagging obsession, globalization, a term signifying the historical consolidation of the world's markets and culture, intensified. While the process of globalization might be redirected to fight global warming, it currently helps multiply greenhouse gases rather than curtail them. The digital tools that have permitted flexible means of production and capital accumulation also have the potential to establish universal environmental education and international economic equity. Instead, as catalogued by Joseph Stiglitz, a former vice-president at the World Bank, Globalization has increased poverty in developing nations, discouraged democratic practices, and led to the overall American model of consumer culture (Stiglitz 2006). The dangers of global warming, however, underlined by Hurricane Katrina, which devastated New Orleans in 2005, may eventually lead to policy changes.

Among the most controversial books addressing the Ecology Question remains, *The Skeptical Environmentalist: Measuring the Real State of the World*, by Bjørn Lomborg (2001), who attempted to discredit the myths of the green apocalypse. A Danish statistician, Lomborg methodically contested the projections of doom made by Worldwatch Institute, World Wide Fund For Nature, and Greenpeace, claiming that there are significant errors in their presentations of diminishing natural resources, health problems, reduced biodiversity, overpopulation, and poverty. Within the safety of the liberal tradition, Lomborg theorizes in cost–benefit terms that during the past century 'mankind's lot has actually improved in terms of practically every measurable indicator'. While he admits that global warming is occurring, he argues that 'it will be far more expensive to cut CO_2 emissions radically than to pay the costs of adaptation to the increased temperatures'. In this respect he caters to those interested in short-term benefits over long-term effects. While his reasoning has tended to support the do-nothing camp in the debate, his scepticism is well taken. The Ecology Question too frequently exploits the fear of catastrophe and the guilt of the consumer, leading to irrational, and often authoritarian conclusions. Ecologists are often struggling against a mythical green apocalypse rather than seeking to defend a goal of more equitably distributed well-being (Lomborg 2001).

The late British architectural critic Martin Pawley, once a pioneer in cataloguing ecological design, also questions the logic of many sustainable options in his essay, 'Sand-Heap Urbanism of the Twenty-First Century' (Pawley 2001). Going against the conventional ecological wisdom that traditional urban patterns hold the solution for a sustainable future, he asks, 'If all the problems are urban problems, why should we not expect the answers to be urban answers?' In a futurist vein, he reasons that mobile phones and the internet already have created the virtual city. While city centres have been struggling with antiquated transportation systems and have been unable to build a minimum of new urban spaces for contemporary needs, millions of square metres have been successfully produced along trade routes as 'abstract urbanism', carrying out most of the functions of cities on the nebulous outskirts of metropolitan districts. Pawley proposes a 'dematerialized metropolis, ephemeralized, entropic, evenly distributed' destiny for an affluent, technocratic society. The proliferation of digital technologies adds a new factor to the Ecology Question.

The computer helped the success of globalization. In less than two generations, digitalization has also changed the way architects work. From CAD software to more sophisticated programs, design has become a keyboard activity. Parametric analyses can be used to generate both energy-conserving and energy-producing structures, such as a blob-like design by Jan Kaplicky (1937–2009) of Future Systems, known as the ZED project of 1995. The program used the criteria for zero emissions furnished by Bill Dunster, which resulted in two aerodynamically shaped towers with a wind turbine in the gap and louvres fitted with photovoltaic cells in the cladding (Hagan 2008b). The bulbous forms of the towers appear like bloated kitchen appliances, beautiful on their own, but unsettling in an urban context. Eager to find technical solutions to self-sufficiency, the designers did not include the factor of contextuality, which is perhaps too arbitrary to work with binary systems.

Although the Ecology Question was raised due to the pollution of industrialized nations in the West, it is by now a global dilemma. The high-entropy patterns of development that began in Manchester, England, have created a negative patrimony for developing countries. As China and India enter into a higher economic bracket they risk repeating the same errors with over a third of the world's population. Despite a few window-dressing projects such as Dong Tang, a proposed carbon neutral new town near Shanghai that is currently on hold, China continues to use environmentally inefficient models.

There are rays of hope for resource conservation, for the respect of traditions, and for ecology-consciousness in many different contexts. But positive change for the global environment will only come from collective and cumulative actions like the Kyoto Accords. In some parts of the Third World designers have improved traditional technologies. Diébédo Francis Kéré (b. 1969), a native of Burkina Faso, who studied architecture in Berlin before returning to his own country to build, produced a fine alternative to concrete boxes in the Primary School in Gando, built in 2001. The three rectangular volumes for the classrooms were built of mud bricks, with tall narrow windows and adjustable louvres. A single roof spans the three volumes set on a spindly space frame made from thin metal rebars that carries the curved tin roof from a small gap on the south to two metres above the ceilings of the classrooms on the north. The air is forced naturally through the gap due to the difference in temperatures between the upper tin roof and the lower brick roof. But such a conscientious approach is a rare exception.

While global warming seems single-minded in its course, there need to be many answers to the Ecology Question. Different places offer different potentials. Architecture has always provided a second nature that was both useful and beautiful, but in the age of global warming the utility and beauty of the built environment hinge on how well architects manage to make amends to the seriously altered natural environment. John Bellamy Foster in *Marx's Ecology, Materialism, and Nature* traces the theoretical connections between Marx and Darwin. Marx wrote his thesis on Epicurus, the intellectual precursor of ecologism who advocated the study of how everything in nature is linked to everything else. 'Nothing comes from nothing' remains the Epicurean invitation to experience nature through materialism. Marx focused on the ancient idea of entropy, called *mors immortalis*, as the essence of the world process (Foster 2000). His awareness of Darwin and all of the consequences that the idea of entropy had on the theory of dialectical materialism may help to rehabilitate Marx's intellectual contribution to the new political circumstances in a world increasingly concerned with environmental issues. The emergence of a 'dialectical ecologist' capable of seeing through the causes of environmental problems while resisting the authoritarian scenarios for obtaining sustainability, seems more valuable than all of the good intentions that designers have directed toward the Ecology Question.

33

Beyond Sustainability: Architecture in the Renewable City[1]

Peter Droege

New concepts enter architecture, landscape and urban design. 'Mitigation', 'adaptation', 'zero-emissions', 'climate protection', 'low-carbon', 'carbon neutral' or 'post-fossil' design are to resuscitate meaning in that worn word, 'sustainability'. Even terms borrowed from psychology are rallied to the battle: 'resilience' denotes the presumed ability to brave the adversities of climate change, energy and economic risks. The deluge of words belies the fact that comprehension and action lag behind the pace of climate change. Atmospheric CO_2 concentrations exceed safe levels by more than one third (Schellnhuber 2009, Hansen et al. 2008). To refer to this enormous problem as a 'sustainability challenge' is to marginalize, even trivialize. Naked survival is at stake. Were serious activity to suddenly break out at a large scale, much of the environmental, social and economic costs of the fossil and nuclear energy regime could be limited. And by all indications, employment generation and wealth creation could be boosted across the socio-economic spectrum. What holds sustainability back?

A lack of focus is missing, for one. Many sustainability programmes, like emission trading, are aimed at proximate forces rather than root causes. Statements like 'one of the biggest challenges facing us today [is] rapid urbanisation' (UCL 2009) are typical remnants of twentieth century discourse: rapid urbanization can surely be a problem but nothing like its trigger: the world of cheap and abundant fossil fuels. Seen in this light, twentieth century architecture manifests the great fossil fuel age. It is one of the central cultural landmarks of the machine age's great natural resource extraction drive. The inexorable decline in non-renewable resource production capacity, too, casts a stark new light on architecture's role, and that of the building industry architecture it stands for. Yet despite or perhaps because of their overwhelming presence, the fundamental role fossil fuels play in the manufacture of our spatial and cultural world is not well understood. The cultural imprint left by the century-long firestorm of a worldwide carbon fuel combustion wave is deeply ingrained in cognitive and behavioural patterns. Vested industry interests, perennially focused on short-term profits prevail. As a consequence, while it is scientifically not difficult to grasp that a bold transformation of the global energy regime is needed and possible, there is still a painful level of resistance to change.

This is manifest in the language deployed, often in lieu of action. *Sustainability* is a bruised and feeble term, twisted in 'triple-bottom-line' and other open-ended interpretations. This includes the circular definition famously placed into circulation by Gro Harlem Brundtland, former Norwegian Prime Minister. The final report 'Our Common Future', released by the World Commission on Environment and Development she chaired from its inception in 1983 until its conclusion in 1987, states: 'Sustainable development is development that meets the needs of the present without compromising the ability of future generations to meet their own needs' (WCED 1987). The smooth two-liner quickly conquered the world – without clarifying how one could determine what future generations' needs might possibly entail.

In the ensuing fog, all and sundry became 'sustainable'. It was generally ignored that the word has a precise meaning: in order to be truly sustainable, actions or processes cannot be based on non-renewable resource flows and use patterns. 'Sustainable growth' while coal power prevails, or 'sustainable use of fossil fuels' are paradoxical propositions, each a textbook oxymoron. Yet this focused understanding existed throughout history, such as in early industrializing development in Europe. During the seventeenth and eighteenth centuries it had become clear that the excessive felling of trees for thermal energy production, agriculture expansion, early mining structures and fleet construction had emerged as a profound challenge to sustainability. It had resulted in widespread deforestation across the continent until the rise of coal – then regarded as a limitless and benign resource – ironically made it practical to issue calls for sustainable forestry, for example those made by Saxony court official Hans Carl von Carlowitz (1645–1714) in his *Sylvicultura oeconomica* (von Carlowitz 2000 [1713]). In charge of Saxon mines, von Carlowitz also oversaw the management of forests, the source of timber for construction and energy for expansive silver extraction operations. These were the base of the political ambitions, societal opulence and architectural grandeur projected by Augustus II the Strong, Elector of Saxony and King of Poland (1670–1733). Von Carlowitz's tree-management programme had been informed by Jean-Baptiste Colbert's (1619–1683) *Grande rêformation de forêts*, the 1669 *Grande ordonnance* to protect France's forestry reserves advanced by the country's powerful *contrôleur général* – finance minister. It was intended to ensure that a sustainable stream of timber was maintained for Louis XIV's epic shipbuilding campaign. Founded on such kindred concepts, von Carlowitz documented a comprehensive strategy of planting and management, also bringing back to life knowledge lost during the Thirty Years War (1618–1648). Sustainability was a clearer vision in those seemingly simpler times. It needs to be regained, if we are to move beyond the misty myths of sustainability that fog urban and architectural design discourse today.

ENERGY AND URBAN CIVILIZATION IN THE TWENTY-FIRST CENTURY

Human civilization has come to be seen as predominantly urban: the end of the twentieth century is often celebrated as an Age of Cities. Since 2007 United Nations population statistics have allocated more than half of the world's population to urbanized areas. This is taken as an indication of a planetary destiny – even if much of present growth occurs in the impoverished megacity slums throughout the structurally adjusted developing world

(Davis 2006). Urban centres emerged as the engines of the global economy: much of urban literature lionized cities as drivers of prosperity and the home of the creative classes, even when highlighting the great equity gaps emerging (Castells 2000; Florida 2002; Friedmann and Wulff 1976; Hall 1977; 1998; Jacobs 1985; Mazza 1988; Sassen 2000 [1994]; 1991). A worldwide urban marketing drive resulted in the process, yet little effort is devoted to understanding the most potent yet fleeting growth driver: cheap and abundant fossil fuel.

Among the most successful and articulate of urban analyses of the 1990s, Saskia Sassen's influential editions of *Cities in a World Economy* (Sassen 2000 [1994]) managed to describe the global urban system without reference to the underlying fossil energy economy, the very engine that also structures and propels the global financial industry, focus of her *The Global City: New York, London, Tokyo* (Sassen 1991). Sassen's work is not alone in exhibiting this deep cognitive break; it runs through the entire literature genre. It is akin to the gap between shadow and reality in Aristotle's Allegory of the Cave: the financial world and urban socio-economic structures represent what the shackled prisoners read in shadows before them on the cave wall, while the great fossil fuel frenzy powering it represents what was carried behind them, casting shadows. Financial activity is the 'froth on the churning, petroleum-rich global resource consumption and value-adding streams' (Droege 2006). It is associated with power, connoting both heroism and grand villainy. Many leading architects make their living stage-managing this reality, like Rem Koolhaas 'surfing' the froth in unapologetic ways. Great structures of the past come to mind, from New York's Rockefeller Plaza to Kuala Lumpur's Petronas Tower, from the entire Pudong skyline in Shanghai on to Beijing's CCTV headquarter, and, as *pièce de résistance*, Dubai's waterfront, most memorable mirage of a fading age.

Other examples of late-twentieth century urban literature are equally reluctant to focus on root forces of the contemporary explosion in urban growth. Peter Hall's grand work on Western urban history, *Cities in Civilisation* (Hall 1998), describes the electrification of Berlin as powering its cultural ascent early in the twentieth century, yet, too, misses the grand narrative of fossil fuel's profound impact on the rise of modern cities and contemporary urbanism. Kevin Lynch's posthumous release, *Wasting Away* (Lynch 1990), took a long look at refuse and discarding in nature and human civilization. Yet modern waste belching fossil energy systems figured in it secondarily if at all, let alone the wasteful and risky nuclear fuel cycles and their enormous costs. This omission is surprising because of his personal misgivings (Lynch, Lee and Droege 1995), the rising expressions of anxiety throughout society, and since one of his mentors, Lewis Mumford, had focused on that very nexus so clearly (Mumford 1961). Indeed, Lynch himself had not felt that the book had been ready for publication.

Others positioned along the more to less critical spectrum of a recent literature stream – from Manuel Castells, Edward Soja and Aihwa Ong to Katharyne Mitchell and Kris Olds – stayed clear of energy aspects, despite or perhaps precisely because of energy's overwhelming role in shaping social and cultural realities and the very organization of globalizing metropolitan systems. Mike Davis' acidic insights, too, ignored the smoking gun of fossil fuel dependence, even if his focus did scan nearby territory. In his *City of Quartz* (1992), gasoline could have emerged as one drug in the cocktail of cultural hallucinogens that explain the depth and breadth of urban paranoia. And the more recent *Planet of Slums* (2006), with its topical focus on the bulging of squatter settlements in the structurally adjusted developing world, set the stage for a blistering analysis of the fossil-fuel connection – but one that is yet to come. Even Davis' 1999 *Ecology of Fear*, so firmly focused on Los Angeles as a city at the brink of environmental cataclysm, missed the very root resource causes of eco-mayhem. David Harvey's *Justice, Nature and the Geography of Difference* (Harvey 1996) framed many relevant issues but also avoided the globalizing fossil and nuclear energy dependencies, and the effect these had on cities: both directly and by proxy.

Since then, a new critical genre of theoretical writing began to focus on environmental upheaval – for example on the profit-making opportunities of what Naomi Klein has termed 'disaster capitalism' (Klein 2007). Still, while her book examined climate hazard battered New Orleans and the pretext its 2005 drowning provided for the privatization of the local education system, or its role in boosting contract security forces, it does also not yet quite fully focus on the unfolding surge of profits to be made from battling climate change induced calamities or oil resource wars. Seen in a historical context, the emergence of a Kleinian disaster capitalist period can also be seen as an early stage of what Meadows has described as the period of civilization in overshoot, when the economic costs of correcting the effects of pollution, including that of excess greenhouse gas, begin to outstrip the gains to be made from ravaging the Earth's resource base (Meadows 1972; 2004).

Among those who have been regarded as both theorists and practitioners of architecture, MVRDV stands virtually alone in having at least taken up the challenge of confronting the emerging reality, epitomised in its eco-friendly 'club sandwich' Dutch Pavilion at the Year 2000 World Expo held in Hannover, Germany. After a series of speculative published works the firm has generated towards the end of the first decade of the millennium hybrid energy projects like the poetically named 'Logrono Montecorvo Carbon Neutral Eco City', located in the Rioja region of Spain (2009), developed with Spanish partner GRAS (MVRDV 2009). Yet from an urban planning and architectural theory viewpoint, these are rare exceptions, still regarded as marginal if obligatory oddities, a fact attested to by the very placement of this section in this Handbook. But perhaps this should come as no surprise as even *bona fide* and very substantial energy-focused works of the past tend to tinker at the edges.

Peter Newman and Jeff Kenworthy's fundamental early work in the 1980s, with its focus so squarely trained on transport energy consumption in cities, too, did not entirely address the fuel replacement challenge of the fossil dependency syndrome and the tasks this poses for policy, design and cultural therapy. Their powerful observations of the gasoline waste inherent in sprawl inspired the compact city policies of countless municipalities since 1980s, and expressed in the oeuvre of revered thinkers such as Peter Calthorpe, Sim van der Ryn and others subscribing to the virtues of dense city cores and transit-oriented development. Even when and where this actually proved successful, the approach was only based on the hope of curtailing, not actually replacing the use of non-renewable resources. And even here, the *rebound effect* meant that the lower cost or freed capacity brought about by journeys thus saved opened the way for increased demand – not even considering the general rising trend in car use (Herring and Cleveland 2008).

A VERY LATE SHIFT IN PERCEPTION

Despite the extent and tradition of the urban sustainability literature, it is still seen as obscure by mainstream theorists. It was not until late in the first decade of the new millennium that a shift in the urban policy and practice literature began to take hold, expressed and documented in *Renewable City* (Droege 2006) and *Resilient Cities* (Newman 2009). Practical studies such as 'Fossil CO_2^- Free Munich' (Lechtenböhmer et al. 2009) were issued with the assistance of Germany's venerable Wuppertal Institute – still not quite regarded as mainstream despite its twenty-year track record in sustainability studies. And scientists like Manfred Lenzen and Barney Foran have long argued – and were ignored for just as long, by mainstream urban theorists and sustainability experts alike – that while household transport energy use was indeed lowered in the dense and wealthy urban cores of, say, Australian cities, the overall household energy consumption – including the embodied energy use in goods and services consumed – soared to twice that of surrounding rural areas and even suburbs. Indeed the fossil energy and associated carbon emissions represented by the overall acquisition of food, alcohol, tobacco, consumer electronics, entertainment, travel, and myriad of other items makes up to seventy per cent of overall household energy budgets, dwarfing operational and transport energy (Lenzen et al. 2008).

Like Mathis Wackernagel and William Rees' landmark work on the ecological footprint (Wackernagel and Rees 1996) embodied – or lifestyle based – energy consumption garnered a great deal of understanding among activist groups and academic research teams alike – but so far has found considerable space in PowerPoint presentations, yet little if any expression in concrete, practically applied local policy. Given the all-powerful if unacknowledged force of fossil power in structuring urban culture and its literature – from the city lionizing to the urban agonizing – it is astonishing that contemporary urban thought has proven to be so energy blind. And, indeed, in the vast number of local governments and communities it triggered little more than exhortations for 'sustainability', 'a smaller ecological footprint' or 'greater energy efficiency'. There is a large literature on the politics, evils and economic force of oil, and its pending expiration as a viable energy source, or the historical power and destructiveness of coal – but so little of it deals with architecture, buildings or cities that we can safely skip the area, while decrying the paucity of connective work in this important domain.

A DAMPER ON URBAN POPULATION GROWTH

The pathologically rising obesity of cities has been a central focus of urban discourse – and graphically documented in the collection of spectacular satellite images in *One Planet Many People – Atlas of our Changing Environment* (UNEP 2005). Rampant urban expansion from Beijing to Bogotá over the past thirty years has been registered with nervous exhilaration and pride among many free-market urbanists, as if globalization, economic strength, trade liberalization and *sheer development* were the sole movers behind this change. A more critical community of urban observers decried its effects in resounding chorus, even if its causes remained shrouded in the half-truths, dogmas and convenient myths of 'globalization', 'trade relations' and 'structural reform'.

Illusions about both dynamics and virtues of urban growth hark back to the credos expounded in the milestone volume *Urban World/Global City* (Clark 1996). They epitomize the 1980s and 1990s when seeing 'the world as an urban place' and 'urbanization as a global phenomenon' was *de rigeur* among geographers, sociologists, avant-garde designers and city marketeers alike. Even today, many regard it still as axiomatic that urbanization will continue unchanged at the precipitous rates known since London's explosion in the eighteenth and especially the nineteenth century: from 1800 to 1900 the British capital's population expanded nearly sevenfold. But this is not a plausible scenario for this coming century. Irreversible shifts such as peak oil and mounting pressures to drastically lower carbon emissions cannot but put a damper on urbanization rates, encourage more autonomous urban-regional constructs and boost the rise of rural self-sufficiency models.

The Fossil City approaches its apex. The simultaneous concentration and expansion of cities over the past half-century was mobilized by massive investment in centralized infrastructure, and especially power systems, within a greatly subsidised and hence seemingly cheap fossil-fuel economy, now at its peak. As a result, the cities in the thirty members states of the elite Organisation for Economic Co-operation and Development (OECD) until recently accounted for between sixty and eighty per cent of their respective national energy consumption, including transport (OECD 1995). This highlights modern cities' powerful role in the worldwide anthropogenic greenhouse gas emissions conundrum: in 1998 fossil fuels, at seventy-five percent the main source of anthropogenic CO_2-equivalent emissions, supplied 85.8 percent of total global commercial energy consumed: forty percent from oil alone. Nuclear reactors provided 6.5 percent; and hydropower seven percent – the remaining fraction stemming from biomass conversion (USGS 2005). And while there is some evidence that peak oil – the apex of the global petroleum production capacity – has already been reached in 2006, with an annual decline of between three and five percent to be expected at full economic expansion (Schindler and Zittel 2008), the staggering abuse of petroleum continues unabated. For electricity generation, coal combustion mounts year after year at a considerable rate – while nuclear power's share is in decline, Uranium is a far scarcer non-renewable resource than fossil hydrocarbon.

RISE OF FOSSIL FUEL CITIES: FROM MINING CARBON GRAVES THROUGH THE THIRD INDUSTRIAL REVOLUTION

Coal, methane – 'natural gas' – and petroleum formed in powerful and enduring chemo-physical processes over hundreds of millions of years from biomass in geographically distinct locations, sequestering atmospheric carbon dioxide with it, and lowering its concentrations to relatively stable levels, peaking over the past 800,000 years in rising and falling cycles at 280 parts per million (ppm). This benign window of climatic stability formed the basis for human evolution. And the very short period since the end of the last Ice Age, the past 12,000 years that are referred to as the Holocene, provided the climate for advanced, eventually urban, human civilization. The vast but geographically localized underground or underwater fields and strata of sequestered atmospheric carbon feed the regional and global production networks and distribution chains that comprise the global fossil fuel industry. Coal and petroleum were known and used marginally for millennia. Natural gas leaks created the miraculous Chimaera, the eternal flame of Olympos, inspiring the worship of Hephaestos, known as Vulcan to the Romans. Mining as a technological and cultural driver rose from the Iron and Bronze Periods and through the Middle Ages. Its role was boosted greatly from the sixteenth and seventeenth through to the eighteenth and nineteenth, as the bright new science of modern geology rose comet-like especially in England, led by Francis Bacon (1581–1626), Lord Chancellor of England, also regarded as father of scientific inquiry.

The geological exploration of the subterranean rose from an ancient body of knowledge to a pinnacle of modern engineering science, and engendered many popular scientific heroes of the time. Tangible rewards came in many guises: minerals, crystals, salts, metals, ores – coal, and later, with the turn to the twentieth century, 'rock oil' or petroleum. The first Industrial Revolution is here defined as economic historian T.S. Ashton's 1760 to 1830 period (Ashton 1948), and encompasses the invention of the steam engine, numerous other technological and engineering breakthroughs, their socio-economic impacts and cultural articulations – including architecture. A second revolution can be distinguished, stretching through and beyond the middle of the twentieth century, associated with the rise of coal and later oil as central cultural forces. A third Industrial Revolution can be defined by a boost to these established dynamics by the spread of telecommunications and thinking machinery: the rising information age of which genetics emerged more recently as a related feature. The fourth Industrial Revolution can be seen as the transcendence of the fossil fuel age, and hopes for overcoming its dark dimensions. My postulation of a fourth Industrial Revolution resonates with Beck's notions of a 'second modernity' (Beck 1992), but differs from it in its focus on the overwhelming factor of energy.

RISE AND FALL OF FOSSIL CITY

Fossil City's rapid metastasis around the globe, mapped since Doxiades and Papaioannou's *Inevitable City of the Future* (1974), is an extraordinary historical phenomenon, fit for a paradoxical age of abundance-in-scarcity. The cities of the nineteenth and twentieth centuries – and the culture they manufactured – were a product of the rising combustion economy. The logic of the industries and technologies they have given rise to has established urban settings as increasingly automated, mechanized and monitored structures, with hydrocarbon or nuclear powered construction machinery, transport structures, industrial processes and manufacturing systems. Intensive local economies and labour markets cluster around globally networked city regions, anchored by heavy investment in infrastructure: energy, transport and communications. This evolution has boosted the primacy of cities over – and ultimately their detachment from – their agrarian hinterlands (Sassen 1991; Scheer 2002). And reliance on cheap fossil fuels engendered a great sameness in architecture unlike any other force, due to the nurturing of a global industrial-scientific manufacturing complex transcending climate and culture alike: the mass production of taste and desire, along with machine intelligence.

Well before the twentieth century, London and other English cities rapidly expanded, as the coal-based power and steam machinery emerged that made this unprecedented, global-trade boosted growth possible. Mumford described urban change in industrializing countries between 1820 and 1900 as the dawn of 'Coketown', the conjuring of a 'Paleotechnic Paradise' (Mumford 1961). Early twentieth-century urban concepts in the Soviet Union, Europe and the United States, and across Asia, Africa and South America since, were jolted into life by the electrifying new energy, material and production technologies. While many local differences were expressed in the way cities evolved locally in the first and early second stages of the Industrial Revolution, under culturally varied administrative and planning regimes, a great sameness evolved in its late second and third stages, given a broad alignment of energy technology regimes, financial arrangements, trade principles and planning procedures.

In the middle of the twentieth century, nuclear power manifested itself in the great urban atrocities of Hiroshima and Nagasaki. Its 'peaceful' sister application, power generation, seemed too good to be true: a new social vision of global suburbia, humming in an infinite supply of clean energy, allowing human civilization to finally evolve, free from ancient and primitive solar power systems, graduating to fossil combustion, and finding eternal redemption in the nirvana of atomic fission and fusion. The father of the peak oil warning, Shell geophysicist Marion King Hubbert, projected a 5,000-year supply of the miraculous source, uranium, in his unpublished but still seminal paper (Hubbert 1956). Hundreds of significant mishaps, the near-meltdown at Three Mile Island and the catastrophes of Chernobyl and Fukushima put an end to this beautiful fantasy. The ultimate and uninsurable meltdown risks all atomic reactors carry, inexorably rising fuel costs and electricity prices, long-term ore production limits, unsolvable disposal problems and the unnerving reality of weapons proliferation have long discredited nuclear power as all but a source of political power and financial profits for a few.

Yet, amazingly, this great hangover from the twentieth century is still promoted as promise of progress, lingering in the hearts and minds of many powerful players today, manifest in a rising and nostalgic call for a nuclear renaissance.

FOLLOWERS OF FASHION

The fossil machine age is born of earlier mechanical, proto-industrial practices, such as the use of waterpower for grain and, later, textile mills. Coal, electricity and scientific workflow analysis gave rise to Frederick Taylor (1856–1915) and Henry Ford's (1863–1947) innovations in industrial production (Gideon 1948). Waves of mechanization propelled by coal-fired steam, electricity and petroleum engines buoyed the rising supremacy of cities. They also stirred mechanical urban form visions. *Technopolitan* designs and manifestos proliferated, at once revolutionary political and industrial icons. Peter Kropotkin's (1842–1921) ideal communities were of the times, as were Sir Ebenezer Howard's (1850–1928) plans, and the birth of the Garden City movement. Howard's ideas especially expressed the great ambiguity of *fin de siècle* longings, a search for recapturing nature using the principles of the mechanized age: *The Garden in the Machine* – I am borrowing Scott MacDonald's book title to heighten Leo Marx's original phrase and book title *The Machine in the Garden*, his brilliant, still astonishingly fresh work on the pastoral dream in a technologically suffused America (MacDonald 2001, Marx 1967).

The great architectural leaders of the modern design movement also admired the industrial innovations as drivers of urban change. From the dawn of the twentieth century the new fossil civilization begat a string of ideologically driven and frequently socially motivated manifesto based schools: Italian *Futurism*, Russian *Constructivism*, Dutch *De Stijl* and the German *Bauhaus*; and the declarations of *the International Modern Architecture Congresses* (CIAM – Les Congrès Internationaux de I'Architecture Moderne, 1928–1956). The International Style established its rule across the industrialized landscape as a capitalist mutation of the more socially concerned Bauhaus school. 'Fossilism' would most accurately describe the key historical driver, and ought to supplement or even replace the ideologically loaded term modernism. Fossilism describes the very technological drivers of a historical shift, while modernism frames its visual and cultural effects.

Modern carbon-based civilization is epitomized in the work of many architectural design titans, from two migrants to the United States: German ex-Bauhaus leaders Mies van der Rohe and Walter Gropius to their numerous disciples, such as Australia-bound emigrant Harry Seidler. Building functions and forms were transformed with the advance of the new carbon fuels, and by the social, cultural and economic realities they helped bring about. Civic settings and built form changed radically in the new fossil age, breaking with all traditions. The modern movement styled the mushrooming of electric and petroleum powered machinery, air conditioning, industrial steel products, advancing glass technology, mass-produced curtain walls, prefabricated building systems and a plethora of other, voraciously energy-consuming innovations.

The International Style had expressed a new thinking about buildings, delivering visually rarefied, abstractly honest, skeletally stripped, overtly industrialized yet still frequently individually crafted corporate structures. The advanced fossil age dawned in cities around the world, advertising a new realm of the possible on the skylines of the industrial world – like on so many gargantuan billboards, amplified as stage sets in cinema and television for decades to come. Buildings became disconnected from their climatic and cultural context – a logical consequence of the end of local resource dependency. But this visual purity was a tantalizing lie: the air-conditioned skeletons concealed the buildings' messy mechanical systems, stashed into internal closets, squirreled away on roof-tops, or squeezed into cavernous basements. Berlin-based solar architect Astrid Schneider has powerfully documented Mies van der Rohe's New National Gallery of 1968 as a surface illusion of perfect clarity and structure – albeit profusely bleeding heat in winter and leaking cold air in summer – with massive air handling machine intestines churning into the mechanical spaces below (Schneider 1996). The building can be seen as the last of the innocently modernist structures: only a few years later, in 1971, youthful renegades Renzo Piano and Richard Rogers won the competition for the Pompidou Centre. Their Pop Art inspired postmodern design poked fun at the make-believe world of the New National Gallery, and did so with extroverted aplomb, seemingly liberating its mechanical and power system as colour coded externalized ducting – as 'oil refinery in the centre of the city', as Parisian critics instantly and aptly dubbed it – not quite realizing the deeper truth of energy dependency revealed – only before the first OPEC crisis, the October 17, 1973 oil embargo declaration.

Other mid-twentieth-century greats, too, produced tell-tale fossilist ideas. Under the influence of kerosene and dazzled by the shining new machine age, pioneering Swiss architect and *urbaniste par excellence* Le Corbusier (Charles-Édouard Jeanneret, 1887–1965) formulated beguiling ideas about the radical remake of traditional cities. His urban dreams were celebrated as formally brilliant yet rejected by many as cold and naïve. As a technological determinist he was alert to the dreams of a new age in industrial production and the cultural aspirations driving mass consumption. He advocated the City of Tomorrow as a clean slate – the razing of pre-fossil urban areas and their wholesale substitution with elegantly standardized, quasi-industrial patterns deployed in parkland settings or, practically speaking, parking lots (Le Corbusier 1947 [1929]). Le Corbusier's formula of social salvation prescribed the suburbanization of central cities, in keeping with what the new technologies could most easily deliver.

This thinking was exemplified in the tabula rasa of the *Plan Voisin; La Ville Radieuse*; or the automobile-inspired viaduct and speedway shaped city formations of his *Obus* planning schemes for Algiers, an obsession that was sparked in 1931 and stayed with him for almost a decade. It led to no planning or design approvals locally but helped him achieve worldwide publishing penetration and influence – a successful formula for some architectural leaders still today. The plan for the Alsatian town of St. Dié (1945) presented by the Ministry for Reconstruction, united the community across its divided classes and parties into roundly rejecting the scheme. His vision of the *City of Tomorrow* as a human stacking machinery came closest to implementation in the famed lone pilot mass-housing module, *Unité d'Habitation* (1946–1952). Le Corbusier's single built urban planning achievement is Chandigarh (1950–1962), his capital vision of modernity. It was named such in 1952 by Jawaharlal Nehru, India's first Prime Minister, to honour the goddess Chandi, also connoting *shakti*: power or energy.

This new capital of Indian Punjab is still a famed icon among the pioneering fossil fuel based urban innovations of the world. Chandigarh and another great new capital foundation of the time, Brasilia (1956–1964), caricature the fossil-fuel era and its dreams, perfect historical artefacts of a bygone era. Today, Niemayer and Costa's plane-shaped capital is a listed UNESCO World Heritage site, a memorial to High Fossilism. In these two capitals, one national, one regional, Brazil and India expensively acquired full-scale fossil-age stage sets, sacrificial altars to achieve instant advanced-development status. Not unlike Walt Disney's 1982 Experimental Prototype Community of Tomorrow (Epcot), one of four theme parks in Walt Disney World Resort in Orlando, Florida, they were to serve as model settings for modern life, and incubators for new cultural, political and economic development realities. Yet despite their ostentatious celebration of the new and liberating power systems in city form, Brasilia and Chandigarh contain some of the twentieth century's finest examples of climatic design expressions in modern architecture by Oscar Niemeyer and Le Corbusier. Both have left thermal architecture legacies as quaint local responsiveness expressed in memorable form – such as the *bris soleil*, covered walkways, water-cooled sunken areas and the like – as if to acknowledge the fossil fuel era's limits of being able to entirely correct climatic differences.

In his urban work, Jeanneret presented a set of bold and simple-minded doctrines with great wit and elegance, even if they did reek of petroleum. Unfortunately, others came to apply these principles, too. *Ersatz* Corbusian forms were deployed with great enthusiasm around the world. Most lacked the subtle sophistication and quirky humour of Le Corbusier's work. The quarters of the less powerful and the teeming, often neglected, pre-fossil urban shells they lived in were to be levelled and replaced by cookie-cutter Pruitt-Igoe type innovations. While US developers relished suburban rollout, post-war Europe preferred heroic new-town plans, suspended among the spreading webs of electrification that criss-crossed former farmlands. Because of the role of rail-based transport in European new town planning it proved a little less effective in enforcing gasoline sales than chaotic suburban sprawl; still, it assisted the automobile and liquid fossil fuel industries rather well in artificially creating distances through functional separation and satellite configurations boosting motorway construction.

Frank Lloyd Wright's (1869–1959) Broadacre City, described in his article *The Disappearing City* (Wright 1932), was not the only visionary effort to anticipate the urban mutations of the middle of the twentieth century driven by mechanized mobility. General Motors' Futurama exhibition ride at the 1939 'Century of Progress' World Exposition in New York, assembled by Norman Geddes in a pavilion designed by Albert Kahn, modelled in eerie likeness the automobile-bound future world that was only just emerging. A little help among good friends did not hurt in proving these car clairvoyants right. During the 1940s and 1950s industrial and government transport policies turned urban America and other hapless followers of fashion across the globe from rail-based modes to technologies designed to maximize petroleum, automobile and tyre use (Morris 1982). Suburban deserts spreading along expanding road and power networks soon epitomized today's nexus of vexing challenges in the management of the fossil fuel charged, bulging cities. Augmented by vast, monopolist retail oases – suburban shopping malls – and cognitively suffused with televised and later web-based content, expanding city regions emerged as rambling machines to replicate, dream, shop and be silently deprived in. While city cores did experience a renaissance, many of these outlands and middle landscapes (Rowe 1992) now threaten to implode under the combined onslaught of untenable funding arrangements, rising petroleum prices and intractable amenity and community problems built into dysfunctional urban regions – a trigger of the so-called financial crisis since 2008.

CITIES AND URBAN ARCHITECTURE: HOME OF THE FOURTH INDUSTRIAL REVOLUTION

A race is on to rid the world of fossil fuels. The dark poison propelled twenthieth-century civilization in a dizzying growth curve – with a spectre of collapse rising in the twenty-first century. Human settlements emerge as the most visible and tangible staging ground for this battle. It promises to beget a new revolution the fourth in the great industrialization waves following the coal-fired steam engine, petroleum expansion and information technology augmented stages.

Here, renewable energy technology, biological carbon sequestration efforts and emission avoidance projects promise to proliferate. Great barriers are to be overcome, but the mechanisms are clear. National and geo-regional efforts provide important support, most prominently the German *Energieein-speisegesetz* (EEG), the energy feed-in law supporting building-integrated photovoltaic systems, wind and other renewable energy systems replacing non-renewable power, introduced in nearly fifty countries (Mendonca 2009).

The major urban policy challenges of this century are positioned between the global nature of greenhouse gas effects and fuel depletion dynamics on the one hand, and the local reality that represents both original source and final impact of such global changes on the other. The World Bank, United Nations and bilateral development organizations also begin to slowly embrace renewable settlement policies, confronting the reactive and energy blind nature of contemporary planning practice, established lines of command, limited know-how and influence peddling endemic to the development and aid industries. At a local level, progress can be stymied by a lack of resources and expertise, anachronistic institutional frameworks, the technical complexities of emissions accounting techniques and the many vagaries of municipal policy development and plan making. Declarations of commitment have been plentiful but effective strategies have been scarce – a phenomenon identified by Nancy Carlisle of the National Renewable Energy Laboratory as the 'planning gap' (Carlisle 2009).

But reasons for slowness in action run deeper than inadequate planning: local needs are up against larger interests when the redistribution of wealth is at stake. Also, fears among some leaders run deep: that a change in energy infrastructure may risk the pace, direction and nature of development, despite much evidence that changes are widely beneficial. Dramatic asymmetries in the distribution of global wealth, and the attempts at incorporating poor nation-states into the project of global neo-liberalism represent systemic political-economic impediments to the local renewable development model, too. 'The market at work' is often unmasked as a state-sponsored project of affording protection for the powerful – here in the form of nuclear and fossil fuel subsidies and bail-outs even where these risk system-threatening failures.

Despite (such odds), the project of the fourth industrial revolution proceeds. The southern German city of Munich is one of the largest municipalities shown to be capable of becoming 'fossil-carbon emission free' (Lechtenböhmer et al. 2009), and only one of a growing number striving for energy autonomy. Communities in Amsterdam, Berlin or Cape Town understand that the transformation of mobility systems, human settlement patterns and land management practices are important but insufficient requisites for serious sustainability improvements. Renewable hardware and combustibles – stationary and transport power systems and fuels – are central to the urban re-engineering challenge. But the change required goes deeper still, involving resource autonomy, and investment in endogenous energy assets within the local and regional economy. A new framework emerges from the smog of Fossilist urban discourse, revealing a refreshingly practical perspective. It spans all aspects of the urban renewable energy revolution, delineating the cultural and economic shift to local and regional autonomy and sufficiency, manifest in land use and transport efficiency, finance, regulation, demand management and distributed renewable energy generation technology. And amidst it all arise the concept and the practice of energy autonomous architecture: the building as distributed, renewable power generator.

SUSTAINABILITY IN STYLE

While it seems logical to extend the language of modernist aesthetic cool in carbon-neutral technology this makes sense only conceptually. Miesian modernism had little time to waste on solar aspect, or bioclimatic ideas. A deep look at the very role of the building as an energetic engine emerges, in addition to it serving as a movement, security and comfort provider. It is a historical opportunity to discard or rethink fossil formalisms and modern mannerisms. The logic of high carbon architecture is so removed from thermally informed design that it has become unavoidable to rethink buildings in their respective climatic locales and conceptualize them as diurnally responsive structures, such as in Ken Yeang's early work, or drawing renewable energy from the sun through its skin, the ground, the air and regional renewable power networks. Overlayed over this set of choices remains the matter of tectonic taste, of style. Walter Sobek's inspired and wide-ranging and luxuriant 'Triple-Zero' work, unashamedly modernist in its stripped-down aesthetic, is a case in point. As a modern engineer he chose minimal Miesian idioms. It has helped reward him with a Mies van der Rohe Professorship at Illinois Institute of Technology (IIT 2008). To Sobek it is all coming together in a new modern, the functionality of the advanced, resource neutral lifesaver. But other architectural innovators may bring to life an entirely new and authentic aesthetic of climatically responsive buildings performing as autonomous renewable energy sources – the architecture of the fourth industrial revolution.

NOTE

1 This chapter contains limited modified extracts from Droege, P. (2006). *Renewable City – A Comprehensive Guide to an Urban Revolution.* London: Wiley.

34

Tropical Variants of Sustainable Architecture: A Postcolonial Perspective

Jiat-Hwee Chang

In recent years, architectural discourses have been increasingly dominated by issues pertaining to sustainability. The wide acceptance of these discourses of sustainable architecture has led some critics to fear that they will become the new hegemonic knowledge – setting agendas and silencing other critical positions – in architectural education and practice (Jarzombek 1999). In response, some scholars argue that sustainable architecture can be understood pluralistically as situated socio-cultural practices, each with its own history, geography, and politics (Guy and Moore 2008). Despite this emphasis on the varieties of approaches, most studies of sustainable architecture, unlike scholarship in environmental politics and history, have largely been confined to the Euro-American contexts. Although exemplars from the 'developing' countries are sometimes included to give the impression of a global discourse, these studies tend to be silent on the variegated, historical and contested nature of the sustainability debate in the 'developing' countries.[1] Instead, the inclusion of exemplars from 'developing' countries serves to demonstrate that sustainable architecture is a new monolithic global entity – one without history and differentiated only in terms of technoscientific configurations responding to 'natural' variations, such as climate and ecology, but entirely unaffected by socio-political forces.

I propose to contribute to the pluralistic understanding of sustainable architecture by examining a few particular variants of it – permutations of tropical architecture in relation to the social, cultural and political conditions of the postcolonial contexts. By tropical architecture, I refer to the architectural discourses and practices that appear to give primacy to tropical nature, mostly in terms of climatic and environmental conditions, as the prime determinant of architectural form. Tropical architecture could be regarded as a variant of sustainable architecture as there are many similarities between the current discourses of sustainable architecture and the prior discourses of tropical architecture in terms of their shared emphasis on minimizing resource usage and waste production, their common concern for social and cultural issues of a locality, and their association with the diverse issues of socio-economic development. Moreover, tropical architecture has recently been recast as sustainable architecture (Lauber et al. 2005).

As has been convincingly argued elsewhere, the practices of sustainable architecture are better understood through narratives that attend to the particularities of a place and its socio-historical contingencies than through abstract models or best practice lists (Moore 2007), this chapter draws primarily from a situated study of architecture and discourses on sustainability in South and Southeast Asia, particularly Singapore, Malaysia, Indonesia and Sri Lanka. The architecture and discourses to be examined centred around the discourses and practices of the Aga Khan Award for Architecture (AKAA) in these countries in the past two decades or so. Although primarily concerned with architectural excellence and socio-cultural development in Muslim societies around the world, AKAA activities have nonetheless wielded considerable influences over the trajectories that the discourses and practices of tropical sustainable architecture in South and Southeast Asia took (Chang 2007). Not only were the key protagonists of tropical sustainable architecture, such as Geoffrey Bawa and Ken Yeang, involved in AKAA's activities, its transnational network also enabled the coalescence of discrete discourses and practices from different nation-states into larger unitary regional ones. Moreover, AKAA's focus on the Islamic and non-Western world highlights the tensions behind North–South and East–West socio-cultural inequalities and differences, key aspects of the sustainability concept often ignored in Euro-American discourses on sustainable architecture.

There are three main sections in this chapter, each representing a particular recent strand of tropical architecture, each with its own theories of sustainability, politics of development and entanglements with prior colonial history. In the first section, I examine recent tropical sustainable architecture in relation to the notions of ecological modernization and green developmentalism, and I show how it is in many ways an extension of the post-World-War-II development regime and the modern tropical architecture created then. In the second section, I examine neo-traditional tropical architecture as an alternative path of development in relation to the perceived failure of the post-World-War-II development regime and the rejection of modern tropical architecture produced under that regime. I look at how the traditional is imbued with the ecological. I will also review criticisms of this 'invention' of tradition, especially its elitism and its reproduction of colonial notions of tropicality. In the final section, I examine the self-help tropical architecture of squatter settlements in Indonesia in relation to how they address the social dimensions of sustainability, and I also examine them in relation to the governmental rationality of the global neoliberal regime in capacity building and producing self-reliant subjects.

I. GREEN DEVELOPMENTALISM, ECOLOGICAL MODERNIZATION, AND TROPICAL SUSTAINABLE ARCHITECTURE

If one looks at the tenth award cycle, 2005–2007, of the AKAA, the winners from Singapore and Malaysia – the Moulmein Rise Residential Tower designed by WOHA Architects and University of Technology Petronas designed by Foster and Partners – give the impression that sustainable architecture in the tropics is merely an extension of that elsewhere, differentiated only by climatic variations. Both projects are not untypical of recent large-scale sustainable architecture elsewhere; the Moulmein Rise Residential Tower is a high-rise condominium development targeted at the high-end housing market segment while the University of Technology Petronas is a new university established by Malaysia's state petroleum company to help the nation produce technologists and engineers to drive the nation's economy forward.

The Moulmein Rise Residential Tower was primarily lauded by the jury for addressing 'the challenges of the tropical climates' by successfully adopting passive cooling strategies for the high-rise residential typology, while the University of Technology Petronas was applauded for its 'contemporary reinterpretation of the classic metaphor for tropical architecture – an umbrella that offers protection from the sun and rain'(AKAA 2007). These two projects appear to continue the trend started by Menara Mesiniaga, a project designed by Hamzah and Yeang, which was an AKAA winner of the sixth award cycle in 1995. Menara Mesiniga is an office tower designed as a 'showcase building' for the agent of IBM in Malaysia. The standard office tower typology was reinterpreted through the incorporation of bioclimatic architectural features, such as the spiralling terraced garden balconies, sun-shading devices, and naturally ventilated spaces (Menara Mesiniaga 1995).[2] Seen in the larger context of the Singapore and Malaysia governments' recent initiatives in encouraging sustainable architecture through the funding of research in green technologies, building high profile energy efficient buildings, and the use of sustainable building assessment methods, these AKAA projects appeared to be in line with these initiatives (Chang 2005; Yap 2007). They are exemplary components of Singapore and Malaysia's larger environmental movement, perhaps following the well-trodden paths taken in certain Euro-American societies, towards what Michael Bess (2003) describes as the global 'light-green society.'

Underlying the light-green society and these projects are the characteristics of what has been described as ecological modernization (Barry 2005). Unlike the radical environmental politics of the 1970s, ecological modernization does not reject the basic tenets of capitalist modernization. Those who embrace ecological modernization seek *more* and *better* modernization. They share the modernization programme's fundamental faith in science and technology, and they believe in technological fixes for environmental problems. Ecological modernization typically entails programmes that establish and fund research infrastructure to re-engineer or to produce better technological systems in order to, for example, utilize energy more efficiently or to exploit renewable energies. In architecture, that could mean that energy profligate International Style modern buildings should be modified with green gadgets, such as photovoltaic cells, efficient air-conditioning systems and 'intelligent' lighting systems, to reduce energy consumption and their ecological footprints. It could mean embracing alternative or even seemingly radical design philosophies and methodologies, such as biomimicry, ecological design and whole system engineering, to rethink standard building typologies like the ubiquitous hermetically sealed air-conditioned office tower, and re-engineer their energy management systems (see for example McDonough and Braungart 2002).

Ecological modernization typically works hand in hand with green capitalism and green developmentalism (McAfee 1999). Green capitalism purportedly transforms the old regime of capitalist development, which dominated and destroyed nature, and reconciles the former opposition between economic growth and environmental protection. One of the basic assumptions is that environmental problems could be rectified by market solutions based on neo-classical economics promoted by the global hegemonic regime of neoliberalism. Green capitalism entails the use of market-based instruments to evaluate and value nature with the implication that in order for nature to be protected, it must first be demonstrated as a 'resource' or a 'natural capital'. Hence, for example, the protection of a tropical rainforest from logging and deforestation, and the conservation of its biodiversity could only happen if it is financed by the sale of access to eco-tourism sites in the rainforest, or the granting of rights of bio-prospecting in the rainforest to multinational pharmaceutical companies (Escobar 2004).

In a related manner, sustainable architecture and green design have in recent years gained widespread acceptance among diverse large corporations because investments in sustainable architecture and green design are often rationalized economically in terms of an increase in workforce satisfaction and the concomitant increase in productivity, cost savings through reduced energy consumption, or increase in symbolic capital to boost the company's green credentials and increase green consumerism.

Because ecological modernization works hand in hand with green capitalism and its attendant green consumerism, it does not require structural changes to be made to the economy. Existing consumption patterns remain largely unchanged, with perhaps the exception of the increasing commodification of nature, and the existing measures of development remain unquestioned. Although ecological modernization and green developmentalism have been equated with the hegemony of the sustainable development paradigm, as outlined in the Brundtland Report (WCED 1987) and further articulated in *Agenda 21* (following the 1992 Rio Earth Summit) (Carruthurs 2005), one of the three Es of the Brundtland Report – equity, ecology, economy – is ignored in the discourses and practices of ecological modernization and green developmentalism (Campbell 1996). Equity, or distributional justice, the key principle of sustainable development that seeks to address uneven development and unequal distribution of wealth and resources between the northern (temperate) and southern (tropical) hemispheres, and the resultant North–South development conflict, is simply not addressed.

Post-war development and technoscientific power-knowledge

When the AKAA jury referred to tropical architecture in their citation of the University of Technolgy Petronas, they drew upon the discourses and practices of modern tropical architecture produced in the post-World-War-II era of decolonization under another development regime. Those schemes were devised either by international agencies primarily under the aegis of the United States or the various imperial French and British agencies. In the context of the decolonizing British Empire, modern tropical architecture was mostly built by British or British-trained architects, including key figures such as Maxwell Fry, Jane Drew and James Cubitt (Crinson 2003; Fry and Drew 1964; Le Roux 2003). Modern tropical architecture was mainly built as part of the social development programmes in the colonies funded by the Colonial Development and Welfare Act (CD&W) first passed in 1940, in the forms of schools, hospitals, mass housing and other welfare facilities (Atkinson 1953; Stockdale et al. 1948). Although post-war development in general and CD&W programmes in particular are in some ways different from the later green developmentalism under the global neoliberal regime described earlier, there are quite a few significant similarities.

Just as green developmentalism in the guise of sustainable development was formulated to address uneven development and poverty in the global South in the 1980s, the CD&W was devised to compensate for years of neglect in social development and widespread poverty in many of the British tropical possessions in the late 1930s. It was primarily aimed at quelling anti-colonial sentiments and other 'disturbances' linked to the socio-economic problems in many parts of the British tropical possessions, and it was also in response to criticisms, both in the metropole and in the colonies, of exploitative colonialism (Cooper and Packard 1997). Not only were the problems similar, the practices employed in addressing the problems were also analogous. Many scholars argue that the different post-war development practices, be they in agriculture, health, education or housing, employed a particular way of problematizing that linked the diagnoses with specific prescriptions, and anticipated certain techniques required to solve the problem. Such an approach of 'rendering technical' in which socio-political problems were turned into technical ones has the effect of depoliticizing social problems (Li 2007). For example, despite the initial recognition that post-war colonial housing problems were part of the larger structural problems of poverty, the Colonial Office framed the housing problem as a strictly specialized technical problem of building cheaper and 'better' (in terms of meeting comfort and sanitary standards) housing (Chang 2010a). In doing so, the larger structural conditions of poverty for most of the colonial native populations and their inability to afford better housing were suppressed. In a related way, green developmentalism framed the question of sustainability strictly in terms of neo-classical economics and technological change while largely ignoring the underlying questions of distributional justice and socio-economic relations.

Central to rendering a problem technical was a corresponding body of technoscientific knowledge, which as scholars in science and technology studies have noted, is produced by a technoscientific infrastructure of research and educational institutions, experts and other trained personnel, normative practices and standardized instruments (Latour 1987). In the case of modern tropical architecture, it was supported by conferences (The Natal Regional Research Committee 1957; Foyle 1953), educational institutions such as the Department of Tropical Architecture established at the Architectural Association (Wakely 1983), and an international network of building research stations coordinated by the Colonial Liaison Unit of the Building Research Station in Garston, England (Atkinson 1952; Lea 1971). Technoscientific knowledge was privileged because the prevailing ideology of post-war development programmes, as exemplified by American president Harry Truman's Point Four Program, was a fundamental faith in the transformative power of science and technology, especially in terms of how the application of technoscientific knowledge would enable development and provide for welfare (Escobar 1995; Sachs 1992). Green developmentalism and ecological modernization that underlay tropical sustainable architecture also share this faith in technoscience. In fact, tropical sustainable architecture often draws directly on the technoscientific knowledge created earlier. Similar strategies of passive cooling and even common parti diagrams and architectural language were often adopted, although their uses are now enhanced by more advanced technologies. Likewise, the building research institutions may have evolved but they still play key roles in producing the technoscientific knowledge in tropical sustainable architecture.

Following scholars who criticized the discourses and practices of post-war development for reducing a complex life-world into abstract technical knowledge, it could be argued that the technoscientific practices of modern tropical architecture have the similar effect of dissolving the historical, social, cultural and political differences between the different tropical colonies into the common denominator of climate. Moreover, modern tropical architecture facilitated the replacement of embodied knowledge of place with abstract technical knowledge of climatic conditions and thermal comfort conditions, thus enabling the knowledge of 'place' from a distance through meteorological data and thermal comfort charts (Chang 2010a). To be sure, the point here is not to present a (false) dichotomy between, what James Scott conceptualizes as, the localized, quotidian and embodied knowledge (or *mētis*) and the codified, standardized and technical knowledge (or *episteme*) (Scott 1998, 309–341). Rather, the point here is to attend to the creation of a modern power-knowledge regime through, what Bruno Latour (1987, 215–257) calls 'network building' and to foreground its effects. In the case of modern tropical architecture, network building entailed the arduous work of collecting and analyzing standardized climatic data of different localities at certain 'centres of calculation'.

These localities were then grouped into climatic zones and the climatic data were abstracted into graphical design aids such as sun-path diagrams and prevailing wind charts. Together with thermal comfort standards and the use of instruments like the heliodon, which could simulate the positions of the sun and thus test the effectiveness of sun-shading devices in different localities at different times of a year, these processes allowed an architect based in, say, London to 'know' different localities in the tropics and propose design for them without having to visit these localities or be personally acquainted with them. As such, modern tropical architecture could be understood as a power-knowledge configuration, in that the accumulation of knowledge of the tropics was also the accrual of power, specifically the power to act on these places from a distance.

The new technoscientific power-knowledge on modern tropical architecture, along with neo-colonial capitalist development, also contributed to the creation of new building norms in the decolonizing developing countries, in terms of modern building standards, specifications, materials, components and construction methods. Certain commentators noted that, not only did these new norms displace traditional constructional crafts and materials, they also created a dependency on imported construction materials, components and expertise from the industrialized countries in the tropical colonies (Jayewardene 1986; 1988). In view of these, some post-development scholars suggest that post-war development schemes like the CD&W and, in extension, the introduction of modern tropical architecture, were part of a new hegemonic regime of power-knowledge to contain and manage the decolonizing/developing world economically and culturally (Escobar 1995; Sachs 1992). This reliance on imported expertise, building materials and building components appears to continue into tropical sustainable architecture given the continued technological gap and inequalities in distribution of resources between the countries in the tropical south and those in the industrial north. It should, however, be noted that modern tropical architecture and the attendant processes of technicalization did not necessarily lead to neo-colonial dominance and dependency. In some cases, local postcolonial architects were able to produce influential built exemplars in modern tropical architecture through local improvizations and innovations (e.g. Tay 2001c). Furthermore, in and of themselves, technicalization processes and the production of immutable mobiles were not the sole monopoly of Britain and other developed countries. Although disadvantaged socio-economically, developing countries could potentially still develop the technical infrastructure and produce the technoscientific knowledge themselves.

Postcolonial contestation

Given that tropical sustainable architecture has been interpreted by some as an extension of the neo-colonial power-knowledge regime that contributed to the underdevelopment of postcolonial nations in the tropics, does it mean then that any postcolonial subject pursuing tropical sustainable architecture is suffering from what a postcolonial critic called 'epistemic conquest' (Chatterjee 2001 [1986]) in which the power-knowledge regime of development paralyses him? There are two main problems with this reading. Firstly, it assumes that the structure of power-knowledge is so overbearingly powerful that the postcolonial architect in the tropics could not but be a '"bearer" of structure' (Bourdieu et al. 1991). Secondly, it assumes that all the postcolonial nations are a homogeneous entity, similarly caught up in a postcolonial mire of poverty and dependency. But as Foucault (1980, 98) notes, '[p]ower must be analyzed as something which circulates … It is never localized here or there, never in anybody's hands'. In fact Foucauldian theory emphasizes that 'power is only power when addressed to individuals who are free to act in one way or another' (Gordon 1991, 5). Thus, in spite of their powerful technoscientific configurations, the neo-colonial power-knowledge on modern tropical architecture was appropriated and interrogated by postcolonial subjects. Technical expertise could be acquired by postcolonial subjects; furthermore, technoscientific knowledge circulated it could be infused with socio-cultural meanings and re-politicized. In the context of Singapore and Malaysia, which, unlike many other developing countries in the tropics, were not impoverished by neo-colonial capitalist development but enjoyed rapid economic growth in the past few decades during the Asia economic 'miracle', the pursuit of tropical sustainable architecture has to be situated and perhaps understood differently.

In the context of 1980s Singapore and Malaysia, more than a decade before sustainability was being incorporated into the state's agendas, Singapore architect Tay Kheng Soon and Malaysia architect Ken Yeang undertook pioneering work on tropical architecture and urbanism (Chang 2010b; Tay 1989; Yeang 1987). Tay and Yeang's works then were both related to some of key issues and debates raised at an AKAA seminar on architecture and identity held at Kuala Lumpur in 1983 (Powell 1983). It was in a context of booming Asia economies and prevailing Asia Pacific Century boosterism that both Tay and Yeang, along with other architects in the region, sought to articulate their visions of the 'tropical city' as a regional architectural identity, in what Abidin Kusno (2000, 201) describes as 'a cultural restructuring of late capitalist development'. Both Tay and Yeang proposed designs that do not really differ architecturally from the ecological modernization paradigm described earlier. Green features such as sun-shading devices, rain-water collectors, and photovoltaic cells were incorporated into the designs. Bio-mimetic design strategies, such as the lowering of the ambient temperature of the city environs through simulating the micro-climatic conditions of the tropical rainforest, were also an intrinsic part of the designs. However, they were not simply designs using technoscientific discourse in the service of green developmentalism or green capitalism. Rather, they were also eco-social visions that reject both the Malaysia government's 'visible politics',[3] i.e. their imposition of ethnic-based architectural identity through the use of ethnic symbols on new buildings, and the crass commercialism of architectural postmodernism that was then sweeping through Southeast Asia. Tay (1989), in particular, sought inspiration 'from the environment itself, which is specific to time and place ... as a generator of form and expression and to create a sense of cohesive identity which transcends ethnicity and culture'. Tay is acutely aware of the historical role that colonial cities in the tropics played in the global division of labour during the age of imperialism. Tay (2001b, 268) describes the eco-social inequality as such:

> Looked at from an ecological perspective, colonialism's exploitation of tropical resources in effect transferred the surplus value of crops produced by solar infusion in a flow northwards of commodities in exchange for cheap manufactured goods at prices preferential to the North and disadvantageous to the South. Colonial economy was, in effect, a systemic appropriation of solar energy, which acted as a pump in service of the northern economies during their industrial revolution.

Tay sees this eco-social inequality lingering into the postcolonial present in the form of a hierarchical global network of cities and economies. According to Tay, the top-tier cities in the northern hemisphere control not only the economic production, but also have an hegemony over the intellectual and artistic production of the tropical cities in the southern hemisphere. Tay's vision of the 'tropical city' represents a way out of this neo-colonial dependency by creating an urban environment that is conducive to innovation and provides the conditions of possibilities for people in the tropics to overcome the northern hegemony. If anything, this example perhaps illustrates that technoscientific knowledge and practices of tropical architecture that reinforce neo-colonial dependency in one socio-political context could be appropriated and deployed in another context, and re-imagined as an emancipatory identity that purportedly frees the postcolonial subject 'from the political and taste-dictates of [his] masters' (Tay 2001a).

II. DEVELOPMENT ALTERNATIVES, THE INVENTION OF TRADITION, AND NEO-TRADITIONAL TROPICAL ARCHITECTURE

Besides the works mentioned earlier, there is another group of AKAA-winning projects that arguably represent a much more influential form of sustainable architecture in Southeast Asia. This group includes: the Tanjong Jara Beach Hotel in Terengganu, Malaysia, designed by the Hawaiian architectural firm of Wimberley, Whisenand, Allison, Tong and Goo, and awarded in 1983 during the second three-year cycle; the Datai Resort in Langkawi, Malaysia, designed by Kerry Hill Architects and awarded in 2001 during the eighth cycle; and the Salinger Residence in Selangor, Malaysia, designed by CSL Associates and awarded in 1998 during the seventh cycle. Tanjong Jara Beach Hotel was hailed by the jury for reviving local traditional crafts and for producing 'an architecture that is in keeping with traditional values and aesthetics, and of an excellence that matches the best surviving examples'. (Cantacuzino 1985, 141). Datai Resort and Salinger Residence were similarly celebrated for their use of local materials, crafts and reinterpretation of traditional built form (AKAA 2001) and uncovering the 'deeper meanings of a vernacular architectural tradition' (AKAA 1998). In other words, this group of projects is unified by their neo-traditionalism, i.e. their adaptation of traditional building practices and built forms of Malaysia, at the very time when these traditions were disappearing. The neo-traditional architecture is also aligned with ecological approaches to building. Their building features, such as the deep overhanging roof and the porous wall, are said to facilitate passive cooling through sun-shading and natural ventilation. The timber used in the Salinger Residence was justified as a local renewable resource with low embodied energy (Alamuddin 1998). The designers of both the Datai and the Tanjong Jara Beach Hotel approached their ecologically sensitive sites, i.e. the tropical rainforest and the beachfront breeding ground of a rare breed of leatherback turtles respectively, in ways that minimized the disturbances to the fragile ecosystems (Cantacuzino 1985; Mehrotra 2001).

When compared to the AKAA-winning projects discussed in the previous section on ecological modernization, the difference in built form and construction techniques could not be more marked – low-rise pitched roof buildings in contrast with mid-to-high-rise flat roof buildings, the use of timber and stone instead of concrete and steel, and the (selective) reliance on pre-industrial low technology ways of building against the use of industrial cutting-edge high technology. Underlying the differences in built form and building practices are said to be fundamental differences in ideology and outlook. In contrast to the faith in modern science and technology central to the ecological modernization paradigm, this group of buildings appears to reject the technocentric approach and seek a return to pre-modern traditional practices. One of the key impetuses behind this impulse to return to tradition arose from the disillusionment with post-war development and modernization programmes, which were said to promise the postcolonial developing world emancipation from economic poverty and social backwardness, but instead produced economic dependency and cultural demise (Rahnema and Bawtree 1997).

Criticisms of development and modernization are an integral part of the discourses that AKAA produced. For example, in an AKAA seminar on regionalism held in Dhaka, Bangladesh, the prominent Indian writer and art critic Mulk Raj Anand (1985, 41) captured the overall sentiment when he remarked poignantly: 'We were gifted with the word liberty, but were made slaves'. Criticisms were largely targeted at International Style modern architecture and how the importation of its foreign building norms and expertise into the developing countries since the post-war years repressed indigenous building traditions (Mumtaz 1985). Criticisms were also directed at how the technical practices of International Style modern architecture purportedly brought about homogenization and the destruction of local socio-cultural diversities. Undoubtedly also influenced by the scholarship on traditional architecture which first emerged in the 1960s (see for example Oliver 1969; Rudofsky 1964) and became widely disseminated and prominent by the 1980s, many of these critics found the panacea for all the evils of modernization, development and International Style modern architecture in traditional buildings and traditional building practices, and became their advocates. Instead of the dependence on foreign capital, building expertise and building materials required in the production of International Style modern architecture, these advocates saw traditional buildings as promoting self-reliance because of their utilization of local knowledge, local labour and locally available materials. In place of the abrupt break with the past that modernization and development programmes brought about, these advocates believed that the return to tradition meant socio-cultural continuity with the past. In contrast to the purported conditions of homogenization and placelessness brought about by International Style modern architecture, these advocates felt that the revival of traditional building would contribute to the construction of regional and place-based identity (Powell 1985). Set against the energy and resource profligacy of the International Style modern architecture and the domination of nature by man in the industrial West, the traditional architecture supposedly evoked an ecological pre-industrial past in which the built and the natural environments were in harmony.

The discourse of AKAA both reflected the larger sympathies towards traditional architecture while also playing the active role of shaping those sympathies by 'championing indigenous architecture' (Serageldin 1989b, 26). This is evident when one examines the list of AKAA winners, in which approximately half of the ninety-two winners (until 2007) are either heritage conservation projects or projects related to the reinterpretation and continuation of traditional building typologies, crafts, and materials.[4] In addition, two of the three recipients of prestigious AKAA Chairman's award, presented to an individual architect in recognition of his lifetime achievement, were exponents of 'neo-traditional' architecture – Hassan Fathy (in 1980) and Geoffrey Bawa (in 2001). The extent of AKAA's reverence for tradition was such that it was accused by one of its jurors of having 'a romantic bias towards traditionalism, historicism and the vernacular' (Pamir 1989, 75).

In the context of tropical architecture in Southeast Asia, Bawa's work is said to be especially significant. Bawa's work was considered to have influenced many architects in what one writer called 'Monsoon Asia', specifically Singapore, Malaysia and Indonesia, especially in the design of luxurious neo-traditional houses and resorts for the super-rich (Robson 2007). His work at the Batujimbar Estate in Bali for Australian artist Donald Friend is an important precedent that established a particular model of luxurious tropical 'Balinese Resort' that is purportedly sensitive to the cultural and ecological contexts of a place (Goad 2000). This model of luxurious tropical resort, although initially produced by the confluence of tourism, transnational capital, international artists and architects in Bali, subsequently proliferated transnationally beyond the confines of Bali and even Southeast Asia and became what a critic described as a 'non-specific Asian style' (Sudjic 2000). Two of the aforementioned AKAA winners, Tanjong Jara

Beach Hotel and especially the Datai Resort, represent the exemplars of this new model of resorts. The other winner, the Salinger Residence, is exemplary of the luxury neo-traditional houses that were influenced by the 'Balinese resorts'.

Postcolonial traditional elitism

Tradition is of course not a timeless, eternal entity 'out there' or from the past to be recovered by some historical actors (Al Sayyad 2004). Rather, there is no tradition that pre-exists its social, cultural, political and economic construction or 'invention'. Thus, it is perhaps pertinent for one to ask who is mobilizing what kind of tradition in service of what kind of visions and agendas? Recent studies have shown that the production of neo-traditional architecture in different parts of the developing world was intimately connected with social, cultural and political elitism (see for example Mitchell 2002, 179–205). Many of the key producers of neo-traditional architecture in different parts of developing world, such as Hassan Fathy and Geoffrey Bawa, were from the land-owning class. For these cosmopolitan professionally trained architects, their selective interpretations of the traditional architecture tended towards romantic idealization, made possible through their aloofness from the actual living traditions of the peasants. These supposed that 'architecture without architects' in fact had to be anointed through the cultural authority of the elite architect. Besides that, these interpretations of traditional architecture frequently draw from prior colonial construction. Historians of colonial societies argue that European scholars sought to study, classify and order the traditions and customs in these societies as these knowledges help to legitimize the colonizers' power and rule over the colonial societies (Metcalf 2002 [1989]). As such, many of the 'traditional' architectural forms that we often take for granted are in fact recent colonial 'inventions'. In the context of Sri Lanka, it is argued that Bawa's neo-traditional architecture reproduces the colonial gaze and the associated value system (Pieris 2007). Moreover, as mentioned, these neo-traditional architectures are often luxury houses and resorts, produced for an elite clientele that comes from the same privileged socio-economic stratum as the architects, i.e. those who could afford to share the cultural distinction as the architects themselves; not the poor or even the middle class. These neo-traditional architectures tended to rely heavily on a labour-intensive craft-based construction process, which was premised upon the availability of pools of cheap labour. Given that the return of tradition was often attributed to the failure of the modernization and development to liberate the developing world from poverty and backwardness, the elitism associated with neo-traditional architecture is paradoxical and its exploitation of the poorer class is, to say the least, ironic.

Landscape and tropicality

The history of the bungalow could be instructive for understanding of neo-traditional tropical architecture. Not only were there spatial similarities between neo-traditional tropical architecture and the Anglo-Indian bungalow in terms of features such as the verandah, large and lofty rooms, and large landscaped compound; neo-traditional tropical architecture is also akin to bungalows in British seaside resorts, in that they are both purpose-built holiday dwellings linked to the (post) colonial world economy. As the aforementioned building features of a bungalow contribute to a cool, shady interior environment and a picturesque landscape, neo-traditional tropical architecture was often considered by its advocates and other architecture connoisseurs to be in harmony with the tropical 'nature'. However, Anthony D. King (1995 [1984]) points out that the built form of the bungalow was inextricably connected to the colonial capitalist economy. For example, the plantation bungalow, one of the most common forms of bungalow, was an intrinsic part of the colonial tropical mode of production, i.e. that of the plantation system supplying raw material for industrial production in temperate Europe and America. Environmental historians argue that each mode of production also entails a specific mode of resource use (Gadgil and Guha 1992). In the case of the plantation in the tropics, it entails the conversion of 'useless', i.e. unproductive in the capitalist sense, 'virgin' tropical rainforest into plantations. In the early twentieth century, pestilential tropical nature, teeming with millions of parasites and pathogens that threatened the health of the white man and the plantation labourers, had to be transformed into a safe, romanticized Edenic tropical landscape through the pioneering anti-malarial and rural sanitary work by heroic figures such as Malcolm Watson and Ronald Ross (Watson 1915). From this perspective, far from being in harmony with some primal tropical nature, tropical architecture was in fact part of the resultant landscape produced through the colonial capital's transformation of tropical nature.

The colonial plantation bungalow in the tropics was also linked to the bungalow in the British seaside resorts in the nineteenth century through the colonial world economy, which facilitated not only the metropole's extraction of economic surpluses from the colonies but also the circulation and exchange of people, commodities and, especially in this case, building types. King notes that one of the effects of the accumulation of surplus capital through the colonial world economy, and the attendant social segmentation and spatial differentiation, in Victorian Britain was the production of new spaces of consumption and recreation. In addition, the use of the sea, specifically the breathing of its air and bathing in its water, with curative powers in the nineteenth century medical discourse and the romantic idealization of the Anglo-Indian bungalow in the travel literature of nineteenth century Britain helped to bring about the emergence of the seaside resort with its holiday bungalows (King 1995 [1984]). With the emergence of the seaside resorts, uneconomic stretches of the cliffs and beaches on the British coastline were converted into valuable real estate. Similar forces could be said to be at work in the neo-traditional resorts. With the rapid growth of international tourism in Southeast Asia from the 1960s onwards and the pursuit of tourism development by the Malaysian government in the economically less developed parts of the country in the 1970s and 1980s, resorts such as the Datai and Tanjong Jara were built in areas with pristine but 'unproductive' nature, such as the tropical rainforest in the case of the former and sandy beaches in the latter. At these resorts, the pristine nature was incorporated into the neo-traditional architecture and staged as part of the tourists' experience there. Unlike the earlier colonial moment, when pristine nature was of little value under the agricultural economy, the experience of pristine nature is key to value-creation in, what some business school gurus describe as, the 'experience economy' of the tourist resorts (Pine and Gilmore 1999).

Such a commodification of tropical nature draws on prior colonial constructions. Along the line of Saidian orientalism, scholars of colonial environmentalism argue that the colonial tropical landscape could be understood as an imaginative geography constructed as an alterity against the perceived normality of the temperate lands. It represented a way of seeing the tropics that entangled nature with socio-political notions such as race, civilization and gender, rendering tropical nature variously as the exotic, Edenic, pestilential or backward other (Anderson 2006; Arnold 1996; Stepan 2001). Not only did the imaginative geography shape the material landscape at different levels – from how tropical 'natural' landscape was moulded in the creation of gardens and plantations, to how architectural urban types such as bungalow, hill station and 'garden city' were planned in the tropics – these scholars also argue that the discursive construction of categories such as the Orient and the tropics in colonial knowledge helped to produce socio-political norms and shape subjectivities that underwrote the power structure of colonial rule.

III. GRASSROOT DEVELOPMENT, KAMPUNG IMPROVEMENT, AND SELF-HELP TROPICAL ARCHITECTURE

The final group of AKAA-winning projects to be examined represents the only projects in this chapter that attempted to address the social equity dimension of sustainability ignored by the previous two strands of tropical architecture. They are the Kampung Improvement Program (KIP) in Jakarta awarded in 1980 during the first three year cycle, Kampung Kebalen Improvement in Surabaya awarded in 1986 during the third cycle, and Kampung Kali Cho-de in Yogyakarta awarded in 1992 during the fifth cycle. These Indonesian projects, though fairly varied, do share quite a few similar characteristics. These projects dealt with not the elite socio-economic minority but the impoverished masses of the society and they sought to address the most rudimentary issues of housing these people. The KIP in Jakarta is an initiative that was first started in 1969 to improve the city's kampungs, which were the overcrowded and insanitary squatter settlements occupied by a large portion of Jakarta's population that could not afford better housing. These kampung dwellers built their own houses out of cheap local and cast-off building materials. As these houses squat on undeveloped land, they typically did not have proper electricity and water supplies, and sewerage systems. As a result, these kampung dwellers had to rely on polluted sources for water, and the problems with rubbish disposal and drainage led to frequent flooding during the rainy seasons and, consequently, major health problems (Holod and Rastorfer 1983). Kampung Kebalen was an exemplar for the KIP in Surabaya, which was also initiated in 1969 to deal with largely the same problems as those in the case of Jakarta (Serageldin 1989a; Silas 1992). In the case of Kampung Kali Cho-de, it was about helping a group of people who were not only very poor and disadvantaged but also stigmatized. This group of people, many of whom were ex-criminals or prostitutes, was considered *sampah masyarakat* or 'the dregs and outcasts of society'. They lived in 'miserable huts' made of cartons and plastic sheets, which disintegrated each time there was a heavy rain, erected on a site that was literally a refuse dump by the bank of the Cho-de river (Al-Radi and Moore 1992; Mangunwijaya 1992).

Unlike the neo-traditional tropical architecture, the environmental problems in these squatter settlements were not about the preservation of some pristine external nature through the use of certain exalted traditions; neither was it like the tropical sustainable architecture in which concerns were focused on energy and environmental resource profligacy that have to be reined in and modified. Instead, with limited funds from the local governments and international development institutions such as the World Bank, the improvements proposed for these squatter settlements were basic, aimed at improving fundamental environmental, and the attendant social, problems. The KIPs in Jakarta and Kebalen sought to address the problems of access, sanitation, health and certain aspects of social improvement. They entailed what is called a 'site and service' approach in which basic site infrastructure such as water supply, electricity supply, sewerage, drainage, roads and pavements were provided or improved. Furthermore, washing and toilet facilities, clinics and schools were also added.

The case of Kampung Kali Cho-de, however, was more complex. While the KIPs in Jakarta and Surabaya were sanctioned by the Indonesian state as part of a national development strategy, the inhabitants of Kampung Kali Cho-de were considered such undesirable members of the society that their wretched existence at the site might not even be tolerated by the authorities and they faced the likelihood of eviction. The strategy adopted by Y.B. Mangunwijaya, a Catholic priest-architect-social activist (Lindsay 1999), and Willi Prasetya, the social chief of the area, was to organize the inhabitants into a cooperative community to improve themselves and their built environment, so as to demonstrate that they were improvable subjects and thus worthy members of the society who deserved the state's recognition. With funds drawn from donations by the local newspapers, Mangunwijaya himself and his friends, the site was improved and the provisional huts were converted into permanent buildings. Unlike the KIPs, the focus was not on building services and site utilities; it was instead placed on creating an appealing appearance and making a good impression. The community was organized to keep the kampung compound and the adjoining riverbank clean and tidy. With the help of art student volunteers, the inhabitants painted their dwellings in colourful patterns. The transformation of the kampung from a ramshackle plot into an orderly, well-maintained and appealing place helped it gain the local authorities' acceptance. From the initial fear of being evicted, Kampung Kali Cho-de was 'benevolently tolerated' by the authorities after its improvement and subsequently it was even informally recognized by being permitted to be connected to the city's electricity system (Mangunwijaya 1992).

Another characteristic that unifies the different projects is their reliance on not only the professional architects, contractors and other usual members of the construction industry, but on the participation of the kampung inhabitants themselves and the help of volunteers and social activists from non-governmental organizations. Even though both KIPs were initiated by state agencies and adopted more or less top-down approaches to design decision-making, they sought help from non-governmental organizations and the design process frequently involved consulting the kampung inhabitants. For example, the Kampung Kebalen project enlisted the help of the professors and students from the local university's faculty of architecture to survey the site and conduct other preparatory planning work. These consultants emphasized that the kampung inhabitants were consulted and involved in their design and planning process (Serageldin 1989a). Similarly, in the Jakarta KIP, the kampung headmen and inhabitants were, to varying degrees, consulted in the planning process, and organized in the maintenance of the amenities built. As noted earlier, this sense of community participation and self-improvement was the most important aspect behind the strategy for the inhabitants of Kampung Kali Cho-de to gain acceptance by the local government and their officials.

Behind these projects was an important shift in the attitude towards squatter settlements and the urban poor who built and lived in them. Kampung improvement in Indonesia has a long history that could be traced to the Dutch colonial practices at the turn of the twentieth century. KIP was used by the Dutch colonial government as a political strategy of pacification, and these colonial practices of managing the native population no doubt shaped postcolonial kampung improvement practices (Kusno 2000, 120–143). However, the recognition bestowed upon KIP by transnational organizations such as AKAA, the funding of KIP by international development agencies such as the World Bank and the subsequent development of the KIP into, what a World Bank representative considered as, the 'best and richest model' (Darrundono and Tirtamadja 2000, 2–3) in the 1990s that others were emulating should be understood in relation to the influential international theories and practices of self-help housing drawn primarily from the Latin American exemplars. John Turner's seminal *Housing by People* (1976) and the first Habitat conference in Vancouver in 1976, marked this important shift towards recognizing the ability of the poor and the value of the self-help housing they built (Berner and Phillips 2005). These ideas were also accepted by the World Bank and incorporated into its loan assistance programme for urban projects in the developing countries at around the same time. Indonesia's post-independence KIPs started receiving World Bank loan assistance from 1976 onwards.

Behind this shift was a group of advocates who regarded the informal self-help housing as being better suited to local conditions and needs than the modern housing provided by either the state or the formal market. Rather than seeing the urban poor who engaged in self-help housing as a group of ignorant and marginalized people trapped in a 'culture of poverty', the advocates regarded them as resourceful individuals. They pushed for the recognition and the legalization of self-help housing and squatter settlements, along with their informal economic activities (De Soto 1989). They argued that the state should not demolish the squatter settlements; instead, it should facilitate and encourage the growth and improvement of the squatter settlements through schemes such as the provision of 'sites and services' and through providing security of tenure and financial aid. Like the other variants of tropical architectures discussed earlier, the shift of attitude towards self-help housing could also be attributed to the perceived failure of standard modernization and urbanization programmes, particularly the urban renewal, slum clearance and public housing programmes in the developing countries during the post-World-War-II decades. However, unlike the cases of tropical sustainable architecture and neo-traditional tropical architecture, there was no need for better modernization, nor was there a need to return to past traditions; the advocates for self-help housing saw the solution in recognizing what was already there – the squatter settlements and development from below.

Self-help housing initiatives received a further boost with the emergence of the global neoliberalism regime in the 1980s. The neoliberal institutions and policy-makers see self-help housing as the only feasible solution to developing countries' housing problems (Davis 2006). Encouraging and facilitating self-help housing is not just a cost efficient way of dealing with the severe housing problems and a justification for the fiscal austerity measures and the withdrawal of state housing subsidies that frequently accompanied the neoliberal economic restructuring in these developing countries. It is also a new technology of government that entails specific practices of identifying the targets to be governed, i.e. the urban poor, directing their conduct by supposedly empowering and optimizing their capacities for improvement, and thus producing self-reliant subjects (Dean 1999; Foucault 1991). As the consultants for Kampung Kebalen put it, the KIP was organized in a manner that would 'stimulate the community in the priority setting of the project components, upgrade their own private domain, and complement the result of the KIP in a process in order to enhance… their own life style' (AKAA 1986). Through an economy of means, in financial outlay, in the extent of construction, and also in terms of minimum intervention and exertion of power from the consultants and the government, the dwellers of squatter settlements would purportedly become self-reliant, entrepreneurial subjects. Moreover, these kampung dwellers were deemed to be producing climatically responsive 'tropical architecture'. One of the technical reviewers noted that the upgrades by the kampung dwellers enhanced the natural lighting and the ventilation in their houses and improved the microclimate in the kampung through their planting of trees, flowers and shrubs (AKAA 1986). The climatically-responsive architecture was seen as another demonstration of the ingenuity of the urban poor, of their ability to use limited resources in both an efficient and effective manner.

CONCLUSION

In this chapter, I review three different broad categories in the postcolonial tropical variants of sustainable architecture. I draw from a range of interdisciplinary scholarship to critique these variants of sustainable architecture. I started the chapter by arguing that each of three broad categories represents a specific configuration of theory of sustainability, politics of development and entanglements with prior colonial history. I will conclude by looking at the commonalities between the three categories, sieving out and summarizing four key themes and related theoretical insights.

The first theme is the need to historicize ideas and practices of sustainability. It has been noted that environmentalism, of which sustainability is a part, tended to be presented as something relatively new and thus without much of a history. As a result, much of the contemporary scholarship on environmentalism has been silent on how certain ideas in environmentalism have been part of longer and deeper historical and ideological debates. This inattention to the history of environmental ideas and practices is even more unfortunate in the case of the postcolonial nation-states. As scholars in postcolonial studies note, colonial knowledge and practices, and the attendant relations of power and difference, not only linger on after the formal end of colonialism but are continually being reactivated in the contemporary world. In my study of tropical sustainable architecture, I show that it draws significantly on the mid-twentieth-century knowledge and practices of colonial development and modern tropical architecture. Furthermore, in my review of neo-traditional tropical architecture, I argue that, in turning away from the modernization and development doctrine, the advocates of neo-traditional architecture returned to not so much a vaunted pre-modern tradition as to a colonial invented tradition and the colonial notions of tropicality.

The second theme concerns power-knowledge. Foucault (1995 [1977], 27) notes that 'power and knowledge directly imply one another, that there is no power relation without the correlative constitution of a field of knowledge, nor any knowledge that does not presuppose and constitute at the same time power relations'. The same could be said for the different knowledge of sustainable architecture. This is not simply innocuous knowledge as suggested by the anodyne phrase. Rather, the knowledge of sustainable architecture has been mobilized to augment different configurations of power relations. As my review of modern tropical architecture shows, the apparently objective and value-free technoscientific knowledge on climatic design was used to facilitate action at a distance and thus enabled the creation of 'centres of calculation'. Moreover, the practices of 'rendering technical' which produced the technoscientific knowledge not only reduced controversial social, cultural and political problems into abstract technical questions, they also led to larger structural conditions behind the problems to be glossed over. In my review of neo-traditional tropical architecture, I mention how it relied on previous colonial knowledge of the natives' traditions and customs that were used to legitimize colonial rule. Power-knowledge is also linked to the technologies of government under the regime of neoliberalism. As I note in my review of the KIPs in Indonesia, knowledge of the urban poor made their conduct amenable to intervention. It is, however, important to note that the very concept of power-knowledge implies that any knowledge is itself is a field of contestation. As I argue in the case of tropical architecture in Singapore and Malaysia during the 1980s, the technicalized colonial knowledge in tropical architecture was appropriated by postcolonial architects and re-invested with socio-cultural meanings.

Hybridity forms the third theme. This conception of hybridity comes, not from postcolonial studies but, from Bruno Latour's argument that distinct categories and especially dichotomies, such as humans versus non-humans and nature versus social as produced by the modern work of purification, fail to account for the complex reality (Latour 1993). Latour proposes that the artificial distinctions should be discarded and they should instead be understood as hybrid assemblies that gather and interconnect heterogeneous elements through networks and translations. Extending such a view, I argue that sustainability should be treated as a hybrid assembly that has to be understood in terms of how the three Es of economy, ecology and equity are interconnected. My critique of the three different broad categories of tropical architecture, especially the first two, lies also in how each category operates through privileging a particular narrow dimension of sustainability and isolating it from the other dimensions of the hybrid assembly of sustainability.

The fourth and final theme is on local–global interactions. I argue at the beginning of the chapter that any understanding of sustainability has to depend on local specificities. I also note that the local and global do not form a dichotomy. Rather, the local and global are linked in a complex network. The historical moments of the various variants of sustainable architecture in the tropics should be understood in the various larger global context, from the colonial world system in the nineteenth and early twentieth century, to the post-World-War-II regime of international development and modernization in the mid-twentieth century, to finally the neoliberal globalization from the late twentieth century onwards. Further complicating these is the regional discourse of AKAA, a unique model of transnational Islamic network. Thus, while I insist on situating this chapter in relation to local specificities, I am sure these particular variants of sustainable architecture that I study have wider resonances beyond the South and Southeast Asian contexts.

NOTES

1 For discussions on the differences between the environmentalism in the 'developed' and 'developing' countries, see, for example Greenough and Tsing (2003); Guha and Martâinez Alier (1998).

2 The bioclimatic approach was first advocated by the Olgyay brothers in the 1960s and Yeang has been further refining the approach for high rise buildings since the early 1980s, see Olgyay and Olgyay (1963); Powell (1989).

3 Sibel Bozdoğan's term in another context. She was describing how the Turkish state used architectural design as symbols of official nationalism (Bozdoğan 2001).

4 A large proportion of the rest of the projects are public housing and infrastructure related projects, including self-help housing improvement and the renowned Grameen Bank Housing Programme. Only a very small number of projects awarded could be considered 'modern', at least aesthetically. For a recent overview of the projects awarded under AKAA, see Özkan (2001).

Section 7 Bibliography

Abley, Ian (2001) 'Introduction', in Ian Abley and James Heartfield (eds) *Sustaining Architecture in the Anti-Machine Age*. London: Wiley-Academy, 6–21.

Adams, David (1992) 'Rudolf Steiner's first goetheanum as an illustration of organic functionalism', *Journal of the Society of Architectural Historians* 51: 182–204.

Aitken, Donald W. (1992) 'The solar hemicycle revisited: It's still showing the way', *Wisconsin Academic Review* 39(1): 33.

AKAA (1986) 'AKAA Kampung Kebalen Improvement Project Architects' Record', www.archnet.org, accessed December 15, 2007.

—— (1998) 'Technical Review Summary of Salinger Residence', www.archnet.org, accessed December 27, 2008.

—— (2001) 'Statement of the award master jury', in K. Frampton, C. Correa and D. Robson (eds) *Modernity and Community*. London: Thames & Hudson.

—— (2007) Aga Khan Award for Architecture: The Tenth Cycle Award, 2005–2007, www.akdn.org/agency/aktc_akaa.html, accessed December 14, 2007.

Alexander, Christopher (1979) *The Timeless Way of Building*. New York: Oxford University Press.

Alexander, Christopher, Sara Ishikawa and Murray Silverstein (1977) *A Pattern Language: Towns, Buildings, Construction*. New York: Oxford University Press.

Alamuddin, Hana (1998) 'AKAA 1998 Technical Review Summary of Salinger Residence', www.archnet.org, accessed December 27, 2008.

Al-Radi, Selma and Charles Moore (1992) 'Kampung Kali Cho-de', in J. Steele (ed.) *Architecture for a Changing World*. London: Academy Editions.

AlSayyad, Nezar (ed.) (2004) *The End of Tradition?* London: Routledge.

Anand, Mulk Raj (1985) 'Background', in R. Powell (ed.) *Regionalism in Architecture*. Singapore: Concept Media.

Anderson, Warwick (2006) *Colonial Pathologies*. Durham: Duke University Press.

Arnold, David (1996) *The Problem of Nature*. Oxford: Blackwell.

Southcliffe Ashton, Thomas (1948) 'The Industrial Revolution 1760–1830'. Retrieved from Online Edition http://www.questia.com/PM.qst?a=o&d=77198080 on 24 April 2011.

Atkinson, George Anthony (1952) 'The work of the colonial liaison building officer and building in the tropics', *The Quarterly Journal of the Institute of Architects of Malaya* 2(1): 35–43.

—— (1953) 'British architects in the tropics', *Architectural Association Journal* 69: 7–21.

Audacity (2009) Audacity website, www.audacity.org, accessed December 30, 2009.

Barry, John (2005) 'Ecological modernisation', in J.S. Dryzek and D. Schlosberg (eds) *Debating the Earth*. Oxford: Oxford University Press.

Beck, Ulrich (1992) *Risk Society: Towards a New Modernity*. London: Sage.

Berner, Erhard and Benedict Phillips (2005) 'Left to their own devices?', *Community Development Journal* 40(1): 17–29.

Bess, Michael (2003) *The Light-Green Society*. Chicago: University of Chicago Press.

Bevan, Richard (2009) 'The carbon casino', *Architectural Design* 79(5): 50–55.

Bookchin, Murray (1982) *The Ecology of Freedom, The Emergence and Dissolution of Hierarchy*. Edinburgh: AK Press.

Bourdieu, Pierre, Jean-Claude Chamboredon and Jean-Claude Passeron (1991) *The Craft of Sociology*. Translated by R. Nice. New York: Walter de Gruyter.

Bozdoğan, Sibel (2001) *Modernism and Nation Building*. Seattle: University of Washington Press.

Bramwell, Anna (1989) *Ecology in the 20th century: A History*. New Haven: Yale University Press.

Braun, Bruce and Noel Castree (2001) 'Preface', in Noel Castree and Bruce Braun (eds) *Social Nature: Theory, Practice, and Politics*. Oxford: Blackwell, xi–xiv.

Brown, Judith (ed.) (2008) *Mahatma Gandhi. The Essential Writings*. Oxford: Oxford University Press.

Buchanan, Peter (2003) *Ten Shades of Green, Architecture and the Natural World*. New York: Architecture League of New York.

Burchell, Graham, Colin Gordon and Peter Miller (eds) (1991) *The Foucault Effect*. Chicago: University of Chicago Press.

Butti, Ken and John Perlin (1980) *A Golden Thread: 2500 Years of Solar Architecture and Technology*. Palo Alto: Cheshire Books.

Campbell, Scott (1996) 'Green cities, growing cities, just cities?', *Journal of the American Planning Association* 62(3): 296–312.

Cantacuzino, Sherban (1985) 'Tanjong Jara Beach Hotel and Rantau Abang Visitor Centre', in S. Cantacuzino (ed.) *Architecture in Continuity*. New York: Aperture.

Carlisle, N. and Bush B. (2009) 'Closing the planning gap: moving to renewable communities' in Peter Droege (ed.) *100% Renewable Energy Autonomy in Action*. UK and USA: Earthscan.

Carruthurs, David (2005) 'From opposition to orthodoxy', in J.S. Dryzek and D. Schlosberg (eds) *Debating the Earth*. Oxford: Oxford University Press.

Castells, Manuel (2000) *The Rise of the Network Society*. Oxford: Blackwell.

Castree, Noel (2005) *Nature*. London: Routledge.

Chang, Jiat-Hwee (2005) 'Green (re)visions', *Singapore Architect* 228.

—— (2007) '"Natural" traditions', *Explorations* 7(1): 1–22.

—— (2010a) 'Building a (Post)colonial technoscientific network', in Duanfang. Lu (ed.) *Third World Modernism*. London: Routledge, 211–235.

—— (2010b) 'Deviating discourse', *Journal of Architectural Education* 63(2): 153–158.

Charlick, Pamela and Natasha Nicholson (2001) 'Ecological frequencies and hybrid natures', in Ian Abley and James Heartfield (eds) *Sustaining Architecture in the Anti-Machine Age*. London: Wiley-Academy, 64–71.

Chatterjee, Partha (2001 [1986]) *Nationalist Thought and the Colonial World*. Minneapolis: University of Minnesota Press.

Choay, Françoise (1997) *The Rule and the Model: On the Theory of Architecture and Urbanism*. Cambridge, MA: MIT Press.

Christianson, Gale E. (1999) *Greenhouse: The 200-Year Story of Global Warming*. Vancouver: Greystone Books.

Clark, David (1996) *Urban World/Global City*. London and New York: Sage.

Cooper, Frederick and Randall M. Packard (1997) 'Introduction', in F. Cooper and R.M. Packard (eds) *International Development and the Social Sciences*. Berkeley: University of California Press.

Crinson, Mark (2003) *Modern Architecture and the End of Empire*. Aldershot: Ashgate.

Darrundono, Danang A. and Baron A. Tirtamadja (eds) (2000) *Kampung Improvement Program III*. Jakarta: The Provincial Government of Jakarta and World Bank.

Davis, Mike (1992) *City of Quartz*. London: Vintage.

—— (1999) *Ecology of Fear*. London: Vintage.

—— (2006) *Planet of Slums*. London: Verso.

De Rosa, Agostino (2007) *James Turrell: Geometrie di luce. Roden Crater Project*. Milan: Electa.

De Soto, Hernando (1989) *The Other Path*. Translated by J. Abbott. New York: Harper and Row.

Dean, Mitchell (1999) *Governmentality: Power and Rule in Modern Society*. London: Sage.

Diamond, Jared (2005) *Collapse, How Societies Choose to Fail or Succeed*. London: Penguin Books.

Djalali, Amir and Piet Vollaard (2008) 'The complex history of sustainability', *Volume* 18: 33–41.

Doxiadis, Konstantinos A. and J.G. Papaioannou (1974) *Ecumenopolis: The Inevitable City of the Future*. Athens: Athens Center of Ekistics.

Dramstad, Wenche E., James D. Olson and Richard T. Forman (1996) *Landscape Ecology Principles in Landscape Architecture and Land-Use Planning*. Washington, DC: Island Press.

Droege, Peter (2006) *Renewable City – A Comprehensive Guide to an Urban Revolution*. New York: Wiley.

Edwards, Brian (2001) Guest edited issue on green architecture, *Architectural Design* 71(4): 4–93.

Edwards, Brian and Paul Hyett (2001) *Rough Guide to Sustainability*. London: RIBA Publications.

Engels, Frederich (1935 [1872]) *The Housing Question*. New York: International Publishers.

Escobar, Arturo (1995) *Encountering Development*. Princeton: Princeton University Press.

—— (2004) 'Constructing nature', in R. Peet and M. Watts (eds) *Liberation Ecologies*. London: Routledge.

Farmer, John (1996) *Green Shift: Towards a Green Sensibility in Architecture*. Oxford: Butterworth-Heinemann.

Fathy, Hasan (1973) *Architecture for the Poor: An Experiment in Rural Egypt*. Chicago: University of Chicago Press.

Fishman, Robert (1982) *Urban Utopias in the Twentieth Century: Ebenezer Howard, Frank Lloyd Wright, and Le Corbusier*. Cambridge, MA: MIT Press.

Florida, Richard (2002) *The Rise of the Creative Class: and How It's Transforming Work, Leisure, Community and Everyday Life*. New York: Basic Books.

Foster, John Bellamy (2000) *Marx's Ecology, Materialism and Nature*. New York: Monthly Review Press.

Foucault, Michel (1980) 'Two lectures', in C. Gordon (ed.) *Power/Knowledge*. New York: Pantheon Books, 78–108.

—— (1991) 'Governmentality', in M. Foucault, G. Burchell, C. Gordon and P. Miller (eds) *The Foucault Effect*. Chicago: University of Chicago Press, 87–104.

—— (1995 [1977]) *Discipline and Punish*. Translated by A. Sheridan. New York: Vintage Books.

Foyle, Arthur (ed.) (1953) *Conference on Tropical Architecture 1953*. London: University College London.

Frampton, Kenneth (2001) 'Technoscience and environmental culture: a provisional critique', *Journal of Architectural Education* 54(3): 123–129.

Friedmann, John and Robert Wulff (1976) *The Urban Transition: Comparative Studies of Newly Industrializing Societies*. London: Edward Arnold.

Fry, Maxwell and Jane Drew (1964) *Tropical Architecture in the Dry and Humid Zones*. London: Batsford.

Future Cities (2010) 'Review: *Sustainable Architectures: Cultures and Natures in Europe and North America*', Future Cities Project website, www.futurecities.org.uk, accessed January 17, 2010.

Gadgil, Madhav and Ramachandra Guha (1992) *This Fissured Land*. Delhi: Oxford University Press.

Geller, Howard (2002) *Energy Revolution: Policies for a Sustainable Future*. Washington, DC: Island Press.

Giddens, Anthony (2009) *The Politics of Climate Change*. Cambridge: Polity Press.

Giedion, Sigfried (1948) *Mechanization Takes Command: A Contribution to Anonymous History*. New York, NY: Oxford University Press.

Gissen, David (ed.) (2003) *Big and Green: Toward Sustainable Architecture in the 21st Century*. New York: Princeton Architectural Press.

Goad, Philip (2000) *Architecture Bali*. Sydney: Pesaro Publishing.

Gordon, Colin (1991) 'Governmental rationality: an introduction', in M. Foucault, G. Burchell, C. Gordon and P. Miller (eds) *The Foucault Effect*. Chicago: University of Chicago Press, 1–52.

Greenough, Paul R., and Anna Lowenhaupt Tsing, eds. (2003). *Nature in the Global South: Environmental Projects in South and Southeast Asia*. Durham: Duke University Press.

Guha, Ramachandra and Juan Martâinez Alier (1998) *Varieties of Environmentalism*. Delhi: Oxford University Press.

Guy, Simon and Graham Farmer (2001) 'Re-interpreting sustainable architecture: the place of technology', *Journal of Architectural Education* 54(3): 140–148.

Guy, Simon and Steven A. Moore (eds) (2005) *Sustainable Architectures: Cultures and Natures in Europe and North America*. New York: Spon.

—— (2008) 'Sustainable architecture and the pluralist imagination', *Journal of Architectural Education* 60(4): 15–23.

Haeckel, Ernst (1899–1904) *Kunstformen de Natur: 100 Illustrationstafeln mit beschreibenden Text*. Leipzig: Verlag des Bibliographischen Instituts.

Hagan, Susannah (2001) *Taking Shape: A New Contract Between Architecture and Nature*. Oxford: Architectural Press.

—— (2008a) 'Five reasons to adopt environmental design', in William S. Saunders (ed.) *Nature, Landscape, and Building for Sustainability: A Harvard Design Magazine Reader*. Minneapolis: University of Minnesota Press, 100–113.

—— (2008b) *Digitalia, Architecture and the Digital, the Environmental and the Avant-garde*. London: Routledge.

Hajer, Maarten (1995) *The Politics of Environmental Discourse: Ecological Modernization and the Policy Process*. Oxford: Oxford University Press.

Hall, Peter G. (1977) *The World Cities*. London: Weidenfeld & Nicolson.

—— (1998) *Cities in Civilization: Culture, Innovation and Urban Order*. London: Weidenfeld & Nicolson.

Hannigan, John A. (1995) *Environmental Sociology: A Social Constructionist Perspective*. London: Routledge.

Hansen, James et al. (2008) *Target Atmospheric CO_2: Where Should Humanity Aim?* NASA/Goddard Institute for Space Studies, www.columbia.edu/~jeh1/2008/TargetCO2_20080407.pdf.

Harvey, David (1996) *Justice, Nature and the Geography of Difference*. Oxford: Blackwell.

Hawkes, Dean (2001) *The Environmental Tradition: Studies in the Architecture of Environment*. London: Spon.

Hawkin, Paul, Amory Lovins and L. Hunter Lovins (1999) *Natural Capitalism. Creating the Next Industrial Revolution*. Boston: Little Brown and Company.

Herring, Horace (Lead Author) and Cutler Cleveland (Topic Editor). 'Rebound effect'. In *Encyclopedia of Earth*. Washington, D.C.: Environmental Information

Coalition, National Council for Science and the Environment. [First published in the *Encyclopedia of Earth* November 18, 2008; Retrieved April 23, 2011 <http://www.eoearth.org/article/Rebound_effect>]

Hillel, Daniel (1990) *Out of the Earth: Civilization and the Life of the Soil.* New York: Free Press.

Hinchliffe, Steve (2007) *Geographies of Nature: Societies, Environments, Ecologies.* London: Sage.

Hinchliffe, Steve and Sarah Whatmore (2006) 'Living cities: towards a politics of conviviality', *Science as Culture* 15(2): 123–138.

Holm, Michael Juul (2009) 'R&Sie(n) – interview with François Roche', in Michael Juul Holm and Kjeld Kjeldsen (eds) *Frontiers of Architecture II: Green Architecture for the Future.* Humlebæk, Denmark: Louisiana Museum of Modern Art, 132–135.

Holm, Michael Juul and Kjeld Kjeldsen (eds) (2009) *Frontiers of Architecture II: Green Architecture for the Future.* Humlebæk, Denmark: Louisiana Museum of Modern Art.

Holod, Renata and Darl Rastorfer (1983) 'Kampung Improvement programme', in R. Holodand and D. Rastorfer (eds) *Architecture and Community.* Millerton, New York: Aperture.

Hubbert, M. King (1956) *Nuclear Energy and the Fossil Fuels.* Shell Development Company.

IIT (Illinois Institute of Technology) (2008) 'Architect/ Structural Engineer Werner Sobek Joins IIT as Mies van der Rohe Studio Professor', IIT Media Room. www.iit.edu/departments/pr/mediaroom/ index.php

Jacobs, Jane (1985) *Cities and the Wealth of Nations: Principles of Economic Life.* New York: Vintage.

Jamison, Andrew (2001) *The Making of Green Knowledge: Environmental Politics and Cultural Transformation.* Cambridge: Cambridge University Press.

Jarzombek, Mark (1999) 'Money, molecules and design', *Thresholds* 18: 32–38.

Jayewardene, Shanti (1986) 'Bawa', *Mimar* 19: 47–49.

—— (1988) 'Reflections on design in the context of development', *Mimar* 27: 70–75.

Jodidio, Philip (2006) *Architecture: Nature.* Munich: Prestel.

Jørgensen, Kasper Guldager (2009) 'The material future', in Michael Juul Holm and Kjeld Kjeldsen (eds) *Frontiers of Architecture II: Green Architecture for the Future.* Humlebæk, Denmark: Louisiana Museum of Modern Art, 122–126.

King, Anthony D. (1995 [1984]) *The Bungalow.* New York: Oxford University Press.

Kirk, Andrew G. (2007) *Countercultural Green: The Whole Earth Catalogue and American Environmentalism.* Lawrence: University of Kansas.

Kjeldsen, Kjeld and Poul Erik Tøjner (2009) 'Foreword', in Michael Juul Holm and Kjeld Kjeldsen (eds) *Frontiers of Architecture II: Green Architecture for the Future.* Humlebæk, Denmark: Louisiana Museum of Modern Art, 5–7.

Klein, Naomi. (2007) *The Shock Doctrine.* Metropolitan Books.

Koenigsberger, Otto H., T.G. Ingersoll, Alan Mayhew and S.V. Szokolay (1974) *Manual of Tropical Housing and Building.* London: Longman.

Kusno, Abidin (2000) *Behind the Postcolonial.* New York: Routledge.

Latour, Alessandra (1991) *Louis I. Kahn: Writings, Lectures, Interviews.* New York: Rizzoli.

Latour, Bruno (1987) *Science in Action.* Cambridge, MA: Harvard University Press.

—— (1993) *We Have Never Been Modern.* Cambridge, MA: Harvard University Press.

—— (2003) 'The promises of constructivism', in Don Ihde and Evan Selinger (eds) *Chasing Technoscience: Matrix for Materiality.* Bloomington: Indiana University Press, 27–46.

—— (2004a) *The Politics of Nature: How to Bring Sciences into Democracy.* Cambridge, MA: Harvard University Press.

—— (2004b) 'Why has critique run out of steam? From matters of fact to matters of concern', *Critical Inquiry* 30(2): 225–248.

—— (2009) 'Spheres and networks: two ways to reinterpret globalization', *Harvard Design Magazine* 30: 138–144.

Lauber, Wolfgang, Peter Cheret, Klaus Ferstl and Eckhart Ribbeck (2005) *Tropical Architecture.* New York: Prestel.

Le Corbusier (1947 [1929]) *The City of Tomorrow and Its Planning* (*Urbanisme*). London: Architectural Press.

le Roux, Hannah (2003) 'The networks of tropical architecture', *The Journal of Architecture* 8: 337–354.

Lea, Frederick M. (1971) *Science and Building.* London: HMSO.

Lechtenböhmer, Stefan et al. (2009) 'Paths to a fossil CO_2-free Munich', in Peter Droege (ed.) *One Hundred Per Cent Renewable – Energy Autonomy in Action.* London: Earthscan.

Lenzen, M. et al. (2008) 'Direct versus embodied energy – the need for urban lifestyle transitions', in Peter Droege (ed.) *Urban Energy Transition.* Oxford: Elsevier.

Li, Tania Murray (2007) *The Will to Improve.* Durham: Duke University Press.

Lindsay, Jennifer (1999) 'Y.B. Mangunwijaya: 1929–1999', *Indonesia* 67: 201–203.

Lippsmeier, Georg, Walter Kluska and Carol Gray Edrich (1969) *Tropenbau/Building in the Tropics.* Munchen: Callwey.

Lomborg, Bjørn (2001) *The Skeptical Environmentalist: Measuring the Real State of the World.* Cambridge: Cambridge University Press.

Lovelock, James (1988) *The Ages of Gaia: A Biography of Our Living Earth.* New York: Bantam Books.

Lynch, Kevin (1990) *Wasting Away.* San Francisco: Sierra Club.

Lynch, Kevin, Tunney Lee and Peter Droege. (1995 [1984]) 'What Will Happen To Us?', in K. Lynch, T. Banerjee and M. Southworth (eds.) *City sense and city design: writings and projects of Kevin Lynch.* Cambridge, Massachusetts: MIT Press.

MacDonald, Scott (2001) *The Garden in the Machine: A Field Guide to Independent Films about Place.* Berkeley: University of Calfornia Press.

Mangunwijaya, Y.B. (1992) 'AKAA Kampung Kali Cho-de architects' record', www.archnet.org, accessed December 27, 2008.

Marcus, Steven (1974) *Engels, Manchester, and the Working Class.* New York: Random House.

Markus, Thomas A. and Deborah Cameron (2002) *The Words Between the Spaces: Buildings and Language.* London: Routledge.

Marx, Leo (1967) *The Machine in the Garden: Technology and the Pastoral Ideal in America.* Oxford: Oxford University Press.

Masdar City (2009) Masdar City website, www.masdarcity.ae, accessed December 30, 2009.

Mazza, Luigi (1988) *World Cities and the Future of the Metropoles.* Milan: Electa.

McAfee, Kathleen (1999) 'Selling nature to save it?', *Environment and Planning D: Society and Space* 17: 133–154.

McDonough, William and Michael Braungart (2002) *Cradle to Cradle, Remaking the Way We Make Things.* New York: North Point Press.

Meadows, D.H., Meadows, D.L. and J. Randers (1972) *The Limits to Growth.* US: Universe Books.

Meadows, D.H., Meadows, D.L. and J. Randers (2004). *Limits to Growth: The 30-Year Update.* US: Chelsea Green Publishing Company.

Mehrotra, Rahul (2001) 'AKAA technical review summary of the Datai resort', www.archnet.org, accessed July 15, 2008.

"Menara Mesiniaga" in C. C. Davidson (ed.) *Architecture Beyond Architecture.* London: Academy Editions.

Mendler, Sandra F. and William Odell (2000) *The HOK Guidebook to Sustainable Design.* New York: John Wiley and Sons.

Mendonça, Miguel and Girardet, Herbert (2009) *A Renewable World: Energy, Ecology, Equality: A Report for the World Future Council.*

Merchant, Caroline (1980) *The Death of Nature: Nature, Women, Ecology, and the Scientific Revolution.* San Francisco: Harper and Row.

Metcalf, Thomas R. (2002 [1989]) *An Imperial Vision.* New Delhi: Oxford University Press.

Mills, E. (2005) 'Insurance in a climate of change,' *Science* 309(5737): 1040–1044

Mitchell, Timothy (2002) *Rule of Experts.* Berkeley: University of California Press.

Moore, Steven A. (2007) 'Models, lists, and the evolution of sustainable architecture', in K. Tanzer and R. Longoria (eds) *The Green Braid.* New York: Routledge.

Morris, David (1982) *Self-reliant Cities: Energy and the Transformation of Urban America.* Washington, DC: Institute for Local Self-Reliance.

Mumford, Lewis (1961) *The City in History.* New York: Harcourt.

Mumtaz, Kamil Khan (1985) 'A case for indigenous development', in R. Powell (ed.) *Regionalism in Architecture.* Singapore: Concept Media.

MVRDV (2009) www.mvrdv.nl.

Myerson, George (2001) *Ecology and the End of Postmodernity.* Cambridge: Icon Books.

Naess, Arne (1989) *Ecology, Community and Lifestyle.* Cambridge: Cambridge University Press.

Nash, Roderick Frazier (1989) *The Rights of Nature. A History of Environmental Ethics.* Madison: University of Wisconsin Press.

Natal Regional Research Committee (1957) *Symposium on Design for Tropical Living.* Durban: The University of California.

Neutra, Richard (1954) *Survival through Design.* New York: Oxford University Press.

Newman, P., Went, A., and James, W. (2009) '100% Renewable Transport', in Peter Droege (ed.) *100% Renewable Energy Autonomy in Action.* UK and USA: Earthscan.

OECD – Organisation for Economic Co-operation and Development (1995) *Urban Energy Handbook.* Paris: Organisation for Economic Co-operation and Development (OECD).

Olgyay, Victor and Aladar Olgyay (1963) *Design with Climate.* Princeton: Princeton University Press.

Oliver, Paul (1969) *Shelter and Society.* London: Barrie & Rockliff/Cresset Press.

Oosterman, Arjen (2008) 'Editorial', *Volume* 18: 2–3.

Özkan, Suha (2001) 'Cultivating architecture', in K. Frampton, C. Correa and D. Robson (eds) *Modernity and Community.* London: Thames & Hudson.

Pamir, Mehmet Douruk (1989) 'Dissenting reports', in I. Serageldin (ed.) *Space for Freedom.* London: Butterworth Architecture.

Papenak, Victor (1995) *The Green Imperative: Ecology and Ethics in Design and Architecture*. London: Thames & Hudson.

Pawley, Martin (1990) *Buckminster Fuller*. London: Trefoil.

—— (2001) 'Sand-heap urbanism of the 21st Century', in Ian Abley and James Heartfield (eds) *Sustaining Architecture in the Anti-Machine Age*. Chichester: Wiley-Academy.

Pieris, Anoma (2007) *Imagining Modernity*. Colombo: Social Scientists' Association.

Pine, Joseph II and James H. Gilmore (1999) *The Experience Economy*. Boston: Harvard Business School Press.

Potsdam Institute for Climate Impact Ressearch (2009) 'Schellnhuber briefs UN on Tipping Elements and Budget Approach', www.pik-potsdam.de/news/in-short/schellnhuber-briefs-un-on-tippingelements-and-budget-approach.

Powell, Robert (ed.) (1983) *Architecture and Identity*. Singapore: Concept Media.

—— (ed.) (1985) *Regionalism in Architecture*. Singapore: Concept Media.

—— (1989) *Ken Yeang: Rethinking the Environmental Filter*. Singapore: Landmark Books.

Pyla, Panayiota (2008) 'Counter-histories of sustainability', *Volume* 18: 14–17.

Rahnema, Majid and Victoria Bawtree (1997) *The Post-Development Reader*. London: Zed Books.

Rees, William and Mathis Wackernagel (1996) 'Urban ecological footprints: Why cities cannot be sustainable – and why they are a key to sustainability', *Environmental Impact Assessment Review* 16: 223–248.

Rifkin, Jeremy and Ted Howard (1989) *Entropy: Into the Greenhouse World*. New York: Bantam Books.

Robson, David (2007) *Beyond Bawa*. London: Thames & Hudson.

Ross, Andrew (1992) *The Chicago Gangster Theory of Life: Nature's Debt to Society*. London: Verso.

Rowe, P.G. (1992) *Making a Middle Landscape*. Cambridge, MA: MIT Press.

Rudofsky, Bernard (1964) *Architecture Without Architects*. New York: Doubleday.

Sachs, Wolfgang (ed.) (1992) *The Development Dictionary*. London: Zed Books.

Saieh, Nico (2008) 'Eco boulevard in Valecas/Ecosistema Urbano', Arch Daily website, www.archdaily.com, September 17, 2008, last accessed January 16, 2010.

Sassen, Saskia (1991) *The Global City: New York, London, Tokyo*. Princeton: Princeton University Press.

—— (2000 [1994]) *Cities in a World Economy*. Thousand Oaks: Pine Forge Press.

—— (ed.) (2002) *Global Networks, Linked Cities*. London: Routledge.

Sattrup, Peter Andres (2009a) 'Ecosistema Urbano – Interview with José Luis Vallejo and Belinda Tato', in Michael Juul Holm and Kjeld Kjeldsen (eds) *Frontiers of Architecture II: Green Architecture for the Future*. Humlebæk, Denmark: Louisiana Museum of Modern Art, 13–17.

—— (2009b) 'Foster and Partners – interview with Stefan Behling and Gerard Evenden', in Michael Juul Holm and Kjeld Kjeldsen (eds) *Frontiers of Architecture II: Green Architecture for the Future*. Humlebæk, Denmark: Louisiana Museum of Modern Art, 49–55.

—— (2009c) 'Philippe Rahm Architects – interview with Philippe Rahm', in Michael Juul Holm and Kjeld Kjeldsen (eds) *Frontiers of Architecture II: Green Architecture for the Future*. Humlebæk, Denmark: Louisiana Museum of Modern Art, 88–93.

Saunders, William S (ed.) (2008) *Nature, Landscape and Building for Sustainability*. Minneapolis: University of Minnesota Press.

Scheer, Hermann (2002) *The Solar Economy. Renewable Energy for a Sustainable Global Future*. London: Earthscan.

Schellnhuber, H.J. (2009) quoted in www.pik-potsdam.de/news/in-short/schellnhuber-briefs-un-on-tipping-elements-and-budget-approach.

Schindler, Jörg and Zittel, Werner (2008) *Zukunft der weltweiten Erdölversorgung*. Berlin: Energy Watch Group/Ludwig-Bölkow-Stiftung.

Schlosberg, David (1999) *Environmental Justice and the New Pluralism: The Challenge of Difference in Environmentalism*. Oxford: Oxford University Press.

Schneider, Astrid (1996) *Solar Architektur für Europa*. Birkhäuser.

Schumacher, E.F. (1973) *Small is Beautiful: A Study of Economics as if People Mattered*. New York: Harper & Row.

Scott, James C. (1998) *Seeing Like a State*. New Haven: Yale University Press.

Serageldin, Ismail (1989a) 'The improvement of Kampung Kebalen', in I. Serageldin (ed.) *Space for Freedom*. London: Butterworth Architecture.

—— (ed.) (1989b) *Space for Freedom*. London: Butterworth Architecture.

Shiva, Vandana (1989) *Staying Alive: Women, Ecology and Development*. London: Zed Books.

Silas, Johan (1992) 'Government-community partnerships in Kampung improvement programmes in Surabaya', *Environment and Urbanization* 4(2): 33–41.

Slessor, Catherine (2001) *Eco-Tech: Sustainable Architecture and High Technology*. London: Thames & Hudson.

Smith, Maf, John Whitelegg and Nick Williams (1998) *Greening the Built Environment*. London: Earthscan.

Smith, Peter (2001) *Architecture in a Climate of Change: A Guide to Sustainable Design*. London: Architectural Press.

Soleri, Paolo (1969) *Arcology: The City in the Image of Man*. Cambridge, MA: MIT Press.

Soper, Kate (1995) *What is Nature? Culture, Politics and the Non-Human*. Oxford: Blackwell.

Steele, James (2005) *Ecological Architecture: A Critical History*. London: Thames & Hudson.

Stein, Richard (1978) *Architecture and Energy*. New York: Anchor Books.

Stepan, Nancy Leys (2001) *Picturing Tropical Nature*. Ithaca: Cornell University Press.

Stiglitz, Joseph (2006) *Making Globalization Work*. London: Penguin Books.

Stockdale, Frank, Robert Gardner-Medwin and S.M. de Syllas (1948) 'Recent planning developments in the colonies', *RIBA Journal* 55: 140–148.

Sudjic, Dejan (2000) 'Is that room service? Where am I?', *The Observer*, August 20.

Tay, Kheng Soon (1989) *Mega-Cities in the Tropics*. Singapore: Institute of Southeast Asian Studies.

—— (2001a) 'Neo-tropicality or neo-colonialism?', *Singapore Architect* 211: 21.

—— (2001b) 'Rethinking the city in the tropics', in A. Tzonis, B. Stagno and L. Lefaivre (eds) *Tropical Architecture*. Chichester: Wiley-Academic.

—— (2001c) 'Trade Union House and Singapore Conference Hall at Shenton Way', *Singapore Architect* 212.

Thayer, Robert L., Jr. (2008) 'Introduction', in William S. Saunders (ed.) *Nature, Landscape and Building for Sustainability*. Minneapolis: University of Minnesota Press, vii–xv.

Thoreau, Henry David (1962) *The Variorum Walden*. New York: Twayne Publishers.

Thyssen, Ole (2009) 'Nature is silent', in Michael Juul Holm and Kjeld Kjeldsen (eds) *Frontiers of Architecture II: Green Architecture for the Future*. Humlebæk, Denmark: Louisiana Museum of Modern Art, 56–62.

United States Geological Survey (2005) *Central Region Energy Resources Team: worldwide web information on United States Energy and World:* Energy Production and Consumption Statistics.

UCL (2009) Quoted in www.bartlett.ucl.ac.uk/planning/programmes/msc_dp/sust_u.htm

UNEP (2005) One Planet, Many People: Atlas of Our Changing Environment 2005 http://www.unep.org/publications/search/pub_details_s.asp?ID=3629

Vale, Brenda and Robert Vale (1991) *Green Architecture: Design for a Sustainable Future*. London: Thames & Hudson.

Van der Ryn, Sim (1979) *Integral Urban House: Self-Reliant Living in the City*. San Francisco: Sierra Club Books.

Van der Ryn, Sim and Stuart Cohen (1996) *Ecological Design*. Washington, DC: Island Press.

von Carlowitz, Hans Carl (2000 [1713]) *Sylvicultura oeconomica: Anweisung zur wilden Baum-Zucht*, Klaus Irmer and Angela Kießling (eds). Freiberg: TU Bergakademie/Akademische Buchhandlung.

Wackernagel, Mathias and William Rees (1996) *Our Ecological Footprint: Reducing Human Impact on the Earth*. Gabriola Island, Canada: New Society Publishers.

Wakely, Patrick I. (1983) 'The development of a school', *Habitat International* 7(5–6): 337–346.

Watson, Malcolm (1915) *Rural Sanitation in the Tropics*. London: J. Murray.

WCED (World Commission on Environment and Development) (1987) *Our Common Future*. Oxford: Oxford University Press.

White, Damien and Chris Wilbert (2006) 'Introduction: technonatural time-spaces', *Science as Culture* 14(2): 95–104.

Wigley, Mark (1999) 'Recycling, recycling', in Amerigo Marras (ed.) *Eco-Tec: Architecture of the Inbetween*. New York: Princeton Architectural Press, 38–49.

Williams, Austin (2001) 'Zen and the art of life-cycle maintenance', in Ian Abley and James Heartfield (eds) *Sustaining Architecture in the Anti-Machine Age*. London: Wiley-Academy, 42–51.

Williamson, Terry J, Anthony Radford and Helen Bennetts (2003) *Understanding Sustainable Architecture*. London: E&FN Spon.

Wines, James (2000) *Green Architecture: The Art of Architecture in the Age of Ecology*. London: Taschen.

Worster, Donald (1977) *Nature's Economy: A History of Ecological Ideas*. Cambridge: Cambridge University Press.

Wright, Frank Lloyd (1932) *The Disappearing City*. New York: William Farquhar Payson.

Yap, Yew Jin (2007) 'City & Country', *The Edge*; October 29.

Yeang, Ken (1987) *Tropical Urban Regionalism*. Singapore: Concept Media.

Zeiher, Laura C. (1996) *The Ecology of Architecture: A Complete Guide to Creating the Environmentally Conscious Building*. New York: Whitney Library of Design.

35

Landscapes

Kelly Shannon

The profound complexity inherent in landscapes – precisely because they embody culture and nature, art and science, the collective and the personal, the natural and the artificial, the static and the dynamic – has led to the use and abuse of the term (Berrizbeitia 2001). In an era when the city is progressively built by an ad-hoc project modus, the widespread (re)emergence of landscape is indicative of a paradigmatic shift. Indeed, over the course of the twentieth century, there has been a change from landscape as a

Figure 35.1 (Below) Investigation site at Fresh Kills Landfill, Staten Island, New York, looking South with empty debris barges at lower right. (Cryptome)

negotiated condition between 'natural' and 'artificial,' towards landscape as a richer term, embracing urbanism, infrastructure, strategic planning, architecture and speculative ideas. Landscape discourse has shifted from landscape-as-picture (and its historical associations to painting) to landscape-as-process (and thus the contemporary meta-narrative of biology) (Somol 2001, 128); landscape has evolved from the pictorial to the instrumental, strategic and operational.

This chapter will document and critically analyse a global spectrum of changing development conditions and the way landscape engages with them. It will focus on projects that exemplify what has become known as 'landscape urbanism', a mode of landscape architecture and urbanism that goes beyond conventional park and garden design on the one hand, and avant-garde topographical landscape manipulations on the other. Landscape urbanism emerged as a new term in the United States in the 1990s (Corner 1999); it became part of European theory a few years later (Marot 2003; Mostafavi and Najle 2003). It was introduced as a saviour to the discipline of urbanism and the more conventional and static tools of land-use and master-planning. Landscape urbanism cuts across numerous disciplines (landscape, urbanism, architecture) and approaches (design and engineering), and is an attempt to re-emphasize the importance of particular sites and the ecological/artificial processes they encompass. Landscape urbanism claims to benefit from the longstanding lineage of regional environmental planning – from Patrick Geddes through Lewis Mumford to Ian McHarg – yet remains distinct from that tradition (Waldheim 2006). As a whole, the field addresses sites in relation to the broader ecological/environmental, infrastructural and social/

Figure 35.2 (Below) Field Operations phase diagram for Fresh Kills Park. (Field Operations)

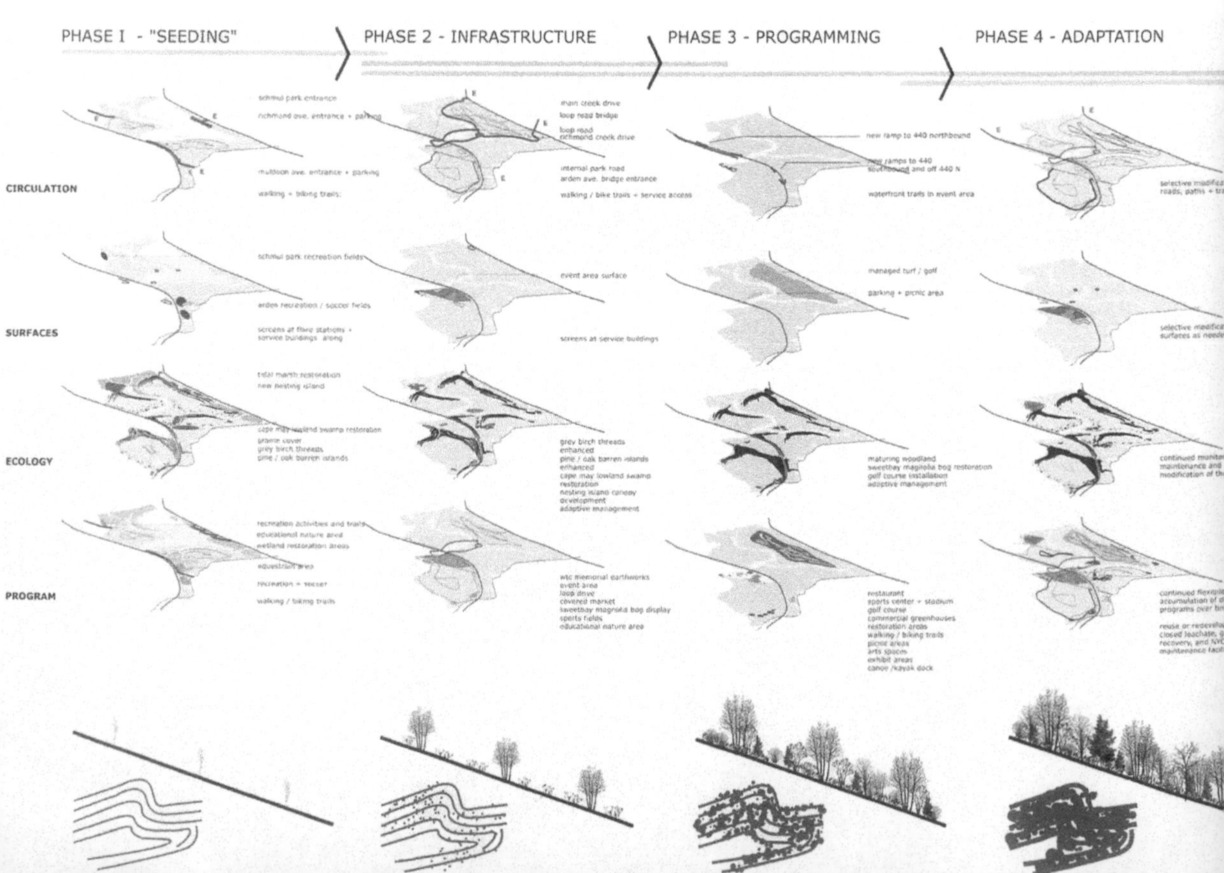

cultural processes and systems that constitute them. Much of the discourse on landscape urbanism – and the projects aligned with this emerging field – focus upon the challenges posed by post-industrial urban voids and concerns that are congruent with the politically correct, ecological biases and priorities of the developed, Western world. The recovery of brownfield sites and the reintroduction of natural processes and habitats are key issues linked to landscape urbanism.

The discipline is not yet widely known beyond the American-European context, but it can be argued that perhaps the rapidly urbanizing, developing world is indeed where landscape urbanism can have significant agency. Landscapes are seen as potential receptors of new economic development, sites of transformation and areas to be reclaimed. At the same time, they also have the potential to become an operative tool to actively resist the globalizing and homogenizing tendencies of built environments (Frampton 1995; Shannon 2004). In the developing, urbanizing world, landscape urbanism can be understood as structuring landscapes to guide their occupation, use and urbanization – an integral system of urbanization which is tied to the logics of landscapes.

Meanwhile, much of the developed world is engaged in the restructuring of territories – terrain 'vague', interstitial spaces, urban peripheries, zones of disturbance, obsolete areas and urban voids. Reclamation of post-industrial sites has resulted in innovative landscape projects concerning design approaches and the larger management and transformation of sites and regions. Not only must fundamental ecological issues be dealt with, but also new aesthetic and symbolic

Figure 35.3 (Below right) and 35.4 (Below left) French Gulch/Wellington Oro project. (Alan Berger & P-Rex)

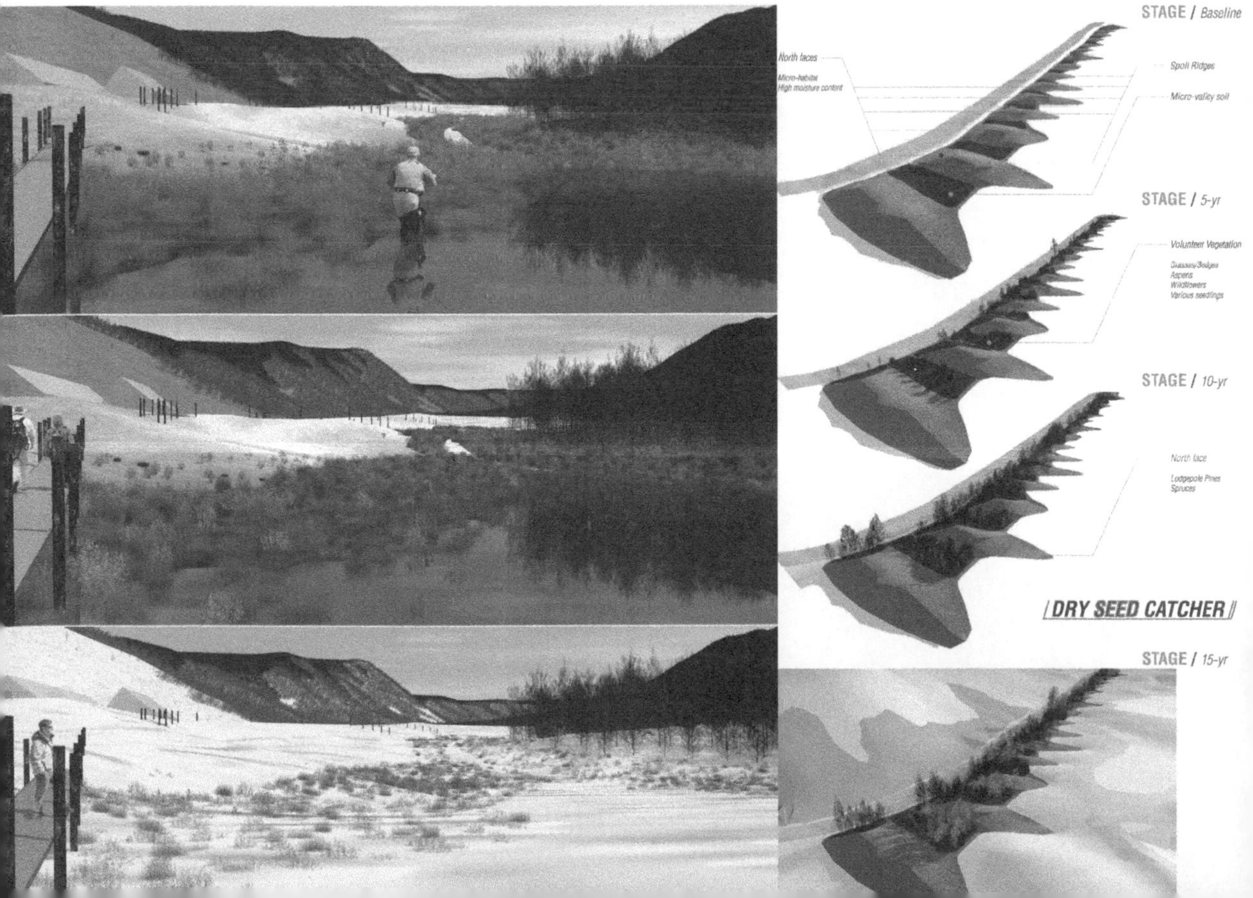

forms are appropriated. A project that is becoming increasingly influential is one developed for the 890 ha Fresh Kills Landfill site on the western coast of Staten Island, New York. It is emblematic of a huge twenty-first century reclamation project – where healing the Earth and reconstituted ecologies are to result from an interaction between human, natural and technological systems. It is also characteristic of a design approach in which a rhetorical and metaphorical cloud floats above projects that have embraced the instrumentalities of process. Field Operations, the firm headed by James Corner and which won the international design competition, is among a school of landscape architects and urbanists who claim to have abandoned complete and determined designs in lieu of an intricate layering of multiple flows through sites. The flows take their clues from larger territorial modes of production and result in continual change on site. The fifty-year working history of the site, its consequential pollution and recovery and reprogramming as a public landscape was the challenge. Fresh Kills opened in 1947 as a temporary landfill; it officially closed in mid-2001 but was reopened months later to receive the ruins of the World Trade Center catastrophe. The four large mounds (25–70 m high) of landfill (primarily household waste) leach toxic chemicals and heavy metals into the soil and methane gas into the air. Yet, as part of New York City's largest drive to create parks since the 1930s, the site is to become a recreational area and undisturbed natural habitat – three times the size of Central Park. The four mounds are to be capped and transformed into different landscapes and the site will host a broad range of activities not typically available in New York City

Figure 35.5 (Below left and right) French Gulch/Wellington Oro project. (Alan Berger & P-Rex Associates)

parks – including waterways for kayaking, an Olympic-level mountain-bike course and 64 km of trails and paths. Redevelopment of the landfill site was deliberately phased over thirty years which involves fixing permanent structures and setting up long term processes. Phase 1, 'seeding', is the initial implementation of securing public access into safe areas of the Reserve, beginning the restoration of native habitat and creating some landscapes of recreational amenity for the immediate neighbourhoods. Phase 2, 'infrastructure', is to occur after closure and stabilization of the landfill and installs new roadways, utilities, plantings and structures necessary to prepare the site for a wide range of programmes. Phase 3, 'programming', conveys the dynamic and flexible way in which the landscape will be occupied (ranging from suggestions of golf courses, to education to greenhouses). The landscape infrastructure is designed as open and flexible, able to accommodate any number or combination of programmes as needs and desires may demand. Phase 4, 'adaptation', is an extension of Phase 3, the 'free-form modification' of the landscape and its programmes over time as communities and public agencies negotiate changes in response to needs and circumstances.

As is evident, the emerging discourse is replete with terminology of change, dynamics and indeterminancy in contrast with permanence, reserve and long-term regeneration. However, it must be recognized that this project, and others following a similar trajectory, are defining form, fixing permanent structures and setting up long-term processes. They are designed landscapes even though they provide little programmatic guidance. Instead, they extend the conceptualization of ecology to include 'precise openness' – the potential change that, according to Anita Berrizbeitia, is entirely different from 'generic openness' that often passes for flexibility (Berrizbeitia 2001). Spatial configuration of the landscape

is precisely designed; however, there remains flexibility in the possible programmes that may appropriate the determined form. Field Operations embraces change vis-à-vis strategically framed rules of organization and variables for the recolonization of the site. They also develop an 'operations ecology' – plans for administering the parks. Their notion of colonization implies the power to appropriate space, sometimes against the will of those who already occupy or control it; they address the reality that the 'public' is not always consensual or even necessarily well-ordered, but rather contestory and perhaps even violent (Mitchell and Van Deusen 2001, 112). Field Operations' projects articulate the relationship of physical design not only to the complexity of geological, hydrological and biological processes, but also to administration and operations of the inherently contradictory nature of public space.

In another landscape reclamation project – this time in the western United States – the French Gulch/Wellington Oro project by Alan Berger reconfigures a site of extensive 'Gold Rush' placer mining (active from 1890–1960) into a speculative housing development with constructed wetland parks and topographical manipulations that creatively re-use dredge rock (waste gravel tailings). The Wellington Oro neighbourhood, of four hundred new homes in the 3400 m alpine setting of Colorado's Rocky Mountains, is to be built on a polluted site where subsurface water contamination and lead/arsenic soil poisoning are the primary concerns. Large parts of the territory are to be capped with a soil cover and vegetated to eliminate direct contact and prevent erosion of contaminated soil while daylight, air, vegetation

Figure 35.6 (Below) Expansion and protection of the public realm in Rio de Janeiro's Favela Bairro project.

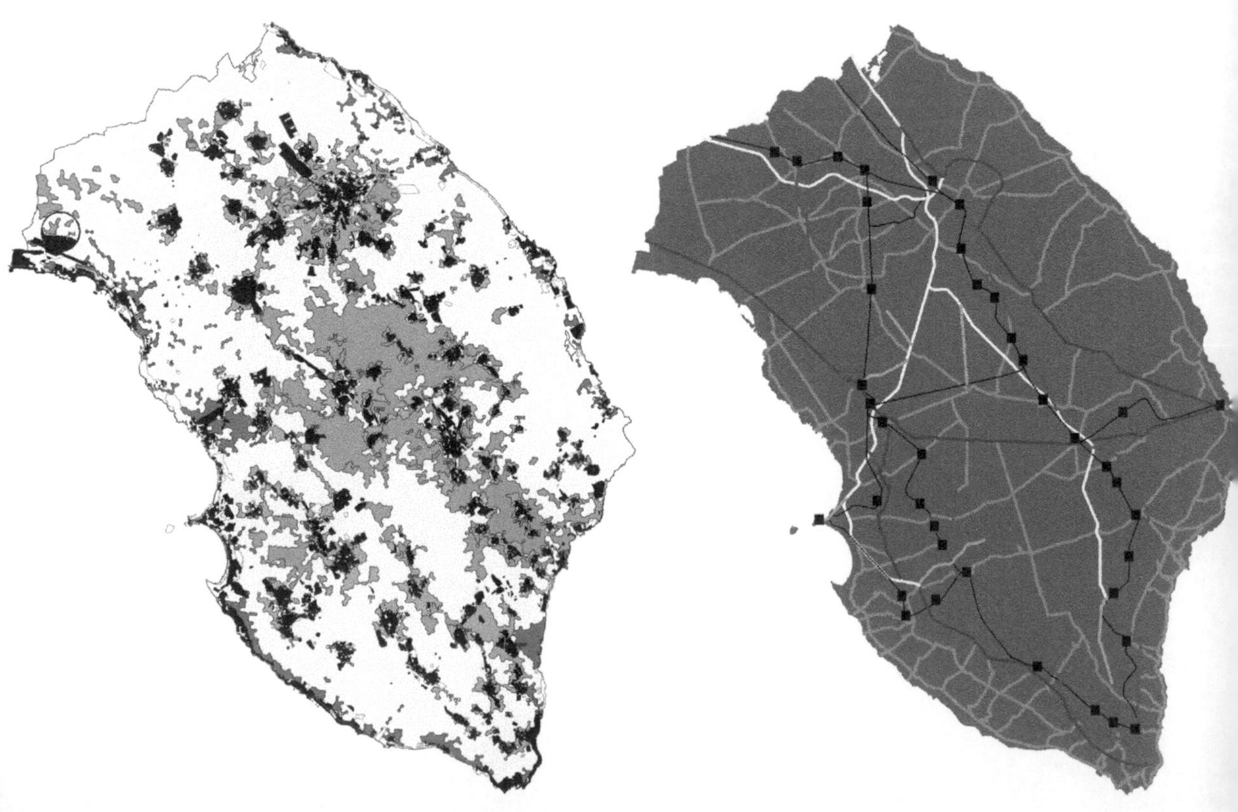

(phytoremediation) and the site's natural topographic gradients are utilized as tools of water purification. The polluted water (dissolved metals) is largely in a complex network of tunnels and shafts, buried by the massive amounts of dredge rock that fill the valley floor. In order for it to be cleansed, it requires exposure to air and therefore demands extensive rock moving – some of which is crushed and sold as gravel creating a budgetary surplus for construction. Other portions of the non-polluted rock are crushed and used as a surface treatment for the high access trail areas or as earthworks along the access road to the development – framing views and providing privacy to housing areas. The landscape infrastructure simultaneously reclaims the stream corridor, revitalizes the processes that allow ecological regimes to resume activity, broadens the public realm through the creation of recreational/didactic constructed wetlands and creates platforms for reprogramming – including parking areas near the back-country open-space trail system and staging locations for the stockpiling of soil-making materials, for site-maintenance sheds, and for greenhouses and incubation beds for re-vegetation.

In Europe, there are numerous exemplary projects of post-industrial landscape recovery projects, ranging from the well-known Emscher Park in Germany (by Peter Latz and others) to the Lyon Confluence project in France (by Michel Desvignes) to scenarios for mining sites and 'shrinking cities' of Eastern Europe (by Florian Beigel and others) – to name but a few. The structuring capacity of landscape and infrastructure is also an operative strategy in the revitalization of agricultural territories and restructuring of dispersed urbanity.

Figure 35.7 (Below) Urbanism framing a dynamic wetland landscape, Cayenne, French Guyana. (Agence Ter)

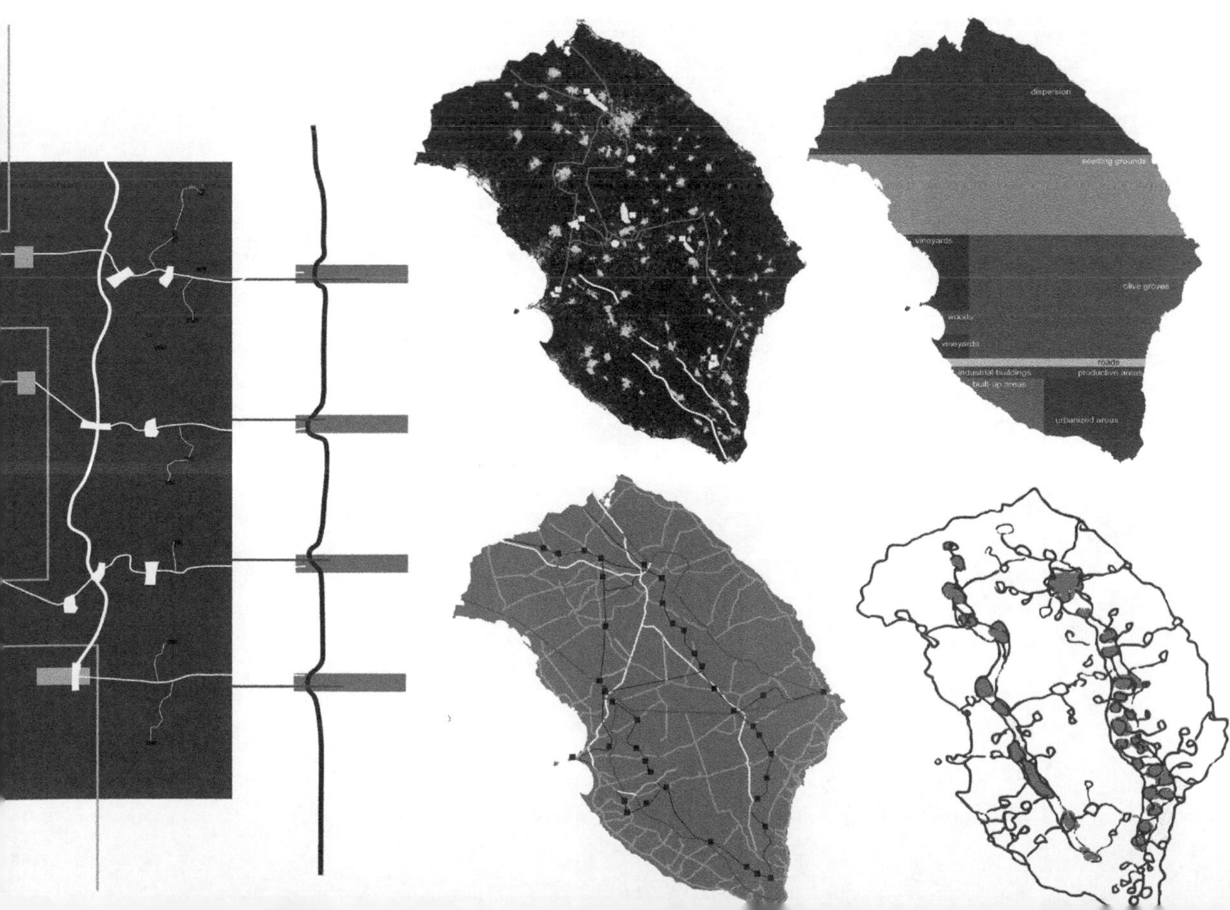

Paola Viganò, who has been working over the past years in partnership with Bernardo Secchi, has developed a landscape urbanism strategy for the Salento region in Italy's Province of Lecce. The region – 1800 square kilometres, of which 865 is covered with olive trees and vineyards – has a population of 800,000 and is visited by 2.2 million tourists annually. In many aspects it is representative of *città diffusa,* but, at the same time, it differs in that its modernization has been remote from mainstream western development; as a part of Italy's poorer southern area, the territory of the Salento region has widely been regarded as marginal. In the proposal, the territory has been conceived of as a park – an extensive, articulated and complex habitat. 'The term "park" is used in a contemporary sense and not only alludes to a place of leisure, but is to be understood as a group of environmental situations in the broadest sense, whose essential combination will go towards encouraging the development of some or all the main social activities as affairs .... Contrary to current opinion the porous character of the diffused city presents a great opportunity for paving the way for a correct development of biodiversity and expansion of nature, in order to construct landscape and an environment that will interpret the values of contemporary society' (Viganò 2001, 17, 65). For Viganò, the larger, existing landscape infrastructures form the basis for later urbanization. The project includes a series of scenarios for the region's future development which

Figure 35.8 (Below) Phasing of urban platforms, Cayenne, French Guyana. (Agence Ter)

Figure 35.9 (Below right) Shenyang Architectural University, northeast China. (Turenscape)

Figure 35.10 (Opposite top) Cayenne, French Guyana. (Agence Ter)

includes alternative energy and environment policies, requalification of coastal areas and new conceptions of tourism, expanded productive landscapes, increased infrastructure, concentrations of future urbanization and collective services. The strategy uses few fragments of existing nature and proposes their expansion, defines the conditions in which new elements of the natural countryside can be created and mitigates the effects of climate change by expanding wooded areas. The development counters a radial-centric and concentric model with an open ‘ladder’ model whereby settlement, production and recreation linked through a wide-mesh network is utilized as a series of ‘narrative itineraries’. Dispersed urbanism is not denied, but reorganized to achieve higher inhabitation standards and a more articulated distribution of facilities throughout the territory. In 2007, the project became the legal frame for the Province of Lecce and a number of policy implications are being developed. It was the first urban plan in Italy to have environmental and landscape concerns at its core. The Salento project is particularly relevant for contexts in which the productive landscape is extensive and has led to dispersed infrastructure systems – even if they are under-developed.

As the developed world is embroiled in the recovery of brownfields and re-qualification of under-utilized greenfields – a by-product of its modernization legacy – the developing South is in the midst of up-grading and creating new spatial patterns of colonization. Although 'landscape' is not often part of the present-day dialogue in the South, conditions are ripe for interventions which simultaneously aim to enlarge the public realm, delimit urban sprawl from fragile, natural environments and mediate between local communities and the pressures of global tourism. Landscapes once revered for their symbolic meaning and productive capacities are being transformed into urban agglomerations at an unprecedented speed and scale. At the same time, a number of Asian cities have consciously been developing the image of their landscapes in parallel with urban development. In semi-sedentary cultures of Africa the relationship of the built to the natural environment continues to produce unique cultural landscapes, and throughout much of Latin America, the mythical figure and influence of Roberto Burle-Marx looms.

Rio de Janeiro (the adopted home of Burle-Marx) – a mega-city in which nature and urbanity are powerfully confronted – is the site of one of the most acclaimed and revolutionary urban up-grading projects in recent years. The Favela Barrio Project in Rio de Janeiro, Brazil convincingly employed urban design as a tool for social reform and transformed marginalized slums/urban

Figure 35.11 (Below) Shenyang Architectural University, northeast China. (Turenscape)

Figure 35.12 (Below right) Shenyang Architectural University, northeast China. (Turenscape)

ghettoes within vulnerable landscapes into thriving, safe and well-provisioned communities. Part-and-parcel of the city's development process, Rio's slums come in a variety of morphologic patterns and inhabit diverse – yet always fragile (steep slopes, marshlands, valley crevices) – landscapes which are exposed to the extremes of sun, rain and wind. The Favela Barrio Project did what its name implies – turned favelas (slums) into barrios (neighbourhoods). The innovative project accepted slums as a new form of urban morphology that should not be destroyed but rather changed, improved and converted into a modest, liveable neighbourhood. Such a policy is radical departure from slum clearance and relocation programmes, and the notion of inclusion as opposed to exclusion is pursued though reurbanizing, regularizing, restoring, renovating and revitalizing favelas (informal settlements which house approximately twenty percent of the city's population). Under the programme, the municipal government and the Inter-American Development Bank (IDB) committed more than $600 million, the bulk of which was spent on public works in some 120 of the city's 600 'social pockmarks'.

The relation of landscape to urbanization was 'regularized' by improving inner accessways and providing appropriate services though the widening of roads, environmental initiatives, provision of sanitation, and a focusing on the pedestrian flow. The investments provided the favelas with basic urban services (potable water, garbage removal, lighting, sewers, telephones), social welfare equipment (well-designed public areas, schools, sports arenas, markets and daycare, training/employment and health care centres), a proper access system (well paved streets, buses and cable cars). New construction of community equipment was underpinned by technical or organizational support for home refurbishing on an individual or

self-help basis, with necessary legal provisions. As has been insightfully commented '... the language of architecture used for the favelas project is not especially sophisticated; it works more like a series of bandages that aid in survival, both functionally and psychologically. Bright yellow handrails along a hillside now signal the path leading to the community ... elsewhere, a bridge with a high-tech look spans an otherwise impassable valley full of garbage' (Mori 2003: 55). New landscape elements – vegetation – were also part of the strategy in order to provide slope stabilization, to enhance spatial experiences and to provide much-needed shade. Through what Rodolfo Machado has termed 'iconographic pragmatism' (Machado 2003, 15), the Favela Barrio Project has erased the opposition of the formal and informal city through hygienic betterment, engineering improvements and site specific interventions. The project realized an interconnected landscape arising from the provision of a new infrastructure of public facilities, public health and safety (water and waste management).

Finally, there are two projects that use landscape as the main structuring element to strategically guide new urbanization. In French Guyana, the landscape firm Agence Ter from Paris made a careful reading of the site which confirmed not only the geographical wealth of the island, but also revealed that traditional rural and urban habitats had ingenious ways of deals with topography and rainy season floods. The significance of water in the landscape was clearly evident – ranging from rivers and marshes (important in the overall regulating system of absorption of heavy rains and water excesses due to high tides) to man-made devices (canals, gutters and channels). Further research made evident that the La Crique Fouillée swamp that bisects the island was a former inlet which silted-up over time from erosion. The present-day inner-communal borderland was thus discovered as the eighteenth century hydrologic origin of the island and provided the impetus for future development and territorial unity. The area, exposed to enormous hydrological fluctuations because of tides and heavy tropical rainfall, is simultaneously being turned into a protected ecological zone and the site for new urban areas. A large green, floodable plain contains new canals for water discharge and links to a series of water retention ponds, which in turn are controlled by a series of sluices. Between the system of ponds, and at the foothills of the surrounding mountain peaks, are new centres for urbanization. Strong Cartesian geometries structure the buildable areas, while the limits of the natural reserve follow those of the topography. The floodable area was viewed as a 'green river' and settlement was located on the anchored piedmonts of the riverbank. The growth and evolution of the landscape and new tropical towns are simultaneously guided; geo-morphological and urban structures work as a total system, and larger environmental concerns – such as keeping development away from the fragile coastline – are addressed. Agence Ter has stressed that in this project, they sought 'geographic urbanization.'

Across the globe, the landscape design of the 80 ha suburban campus of Shenyang Architectural University in northeast China connects students to parts of Chinese society that they might otherwise shun. Rice fields are the main organizing design element for the campus plan – but they are not merely didactic and ornamental. The built 3 ha phase of the project is structured by highly productive landscapes, building on Shenyang's reputation as the source of high-quality short-grain rice. Elements of the traditional agricultural environment serve as tangible symbols and reminders of the historical and contemporary role of agriculture in China. The site was indeed a former paddy field and its irrigation system was still intact. The geometric layout, reminiscent of the earlier field parcellation, is interspersed with study platforms, accessed by narrow concrete pathways lined by no-maintenance native plants and shaded by popular trees. Other native crops, such as buckwheat grow in rotation across the campus annually and sheep are raised in the fields. A new vernacular underlines the beauty (and affordability) of rice and demonstrates how productive agricultural landscapes can become – through careful design and management – modern, usable space. The rice produced on the campus is harvested and distributed as 'Golden Rice', serving both as a keepsake for visitors and as a source of identity for the suburban campus. The project combines tradition and modernity – roughness and elegance – in a hybrid landscape designed to raise awareness of land and farming amongst college students who are leaving the land to become city dwellers. Faculty and students participate in the management, planting and harvesting of the paddy fields – hopefully sensitizing future architects to the possibilities of reinterpreting tradition.

The re-thinking and re-defining, through theory and projects, of the agency of landscape holds tremendous potentials for the re-shaping of urbanizing territories. Landscape urbanism is a paradigm shift – as it can be considered to inherently have the capacity to bring together different experts and stakeholders from urban, landscape, engineering and even management sectors; it is a coalition builder in innovative regional development. A descriptive landscape urbanism is particularly relevant for contexts of rapid urbanization and in places where the effects of climate change predictions are the most severe. Landscape urbanism projects can evolve from the careful reading of layered contested territories and design-based investigation of potentials. The existing logics of landscapes (including their historical layers and ad-hoc daily appropriations) can be reorganized at different scales and connected to new (infra)structures. Specific logics from the 'junkyard' of existing landscapes can be stressed and new interventions with structural capacities could reformulate reality. Landscape urbanism strategies can become powerful tools for negotiation between different actors and within the contested territories of twenty-first-century cities.

BIBLIOGRAPHY

Allen, Stan (2001) 'Mat Urbanism: The Thick 2-D', in Hashim Sarkis (ed.) *Case: Le Corbusier's Venice Hospital.* Cambridge: Harvard Graduate School of Design and Munich: Prestel 118–126.

Bava, Henri (2002) 'Landscape as a Foundation', *Topos* 40: 70–77.

Berrizbeitia, Anita (2001) 'Scales of Undecidability', in Julia Czerniak (ed.) *Downsview Park Toronto.* Cambridge: Harvard Design School and Munich: Prestel, 116–125.

Corner, James (1999) 'Introduction: Recovering Landscape as a Critical Cultural Practice', in *Recovering Landscape: Essays in Contemporary Landscape Architecture.* New York: Princeton Architectural Press, 1–28.

Corner, James and Stan, Allen (2002) 'Lifescape', *Praxis – Landscapes issue*, New Orleans, 20–27.

Frampton, Kenneth (1995) 'Toward an Urban Landscape,' *Columbia Documents*; New York: Columbia University, pp. 83–93.

Machado, Rodolfo (2003) 'Memoir of a Visit', in *The Favela Barrio Project: Jorge Mario Jáuregui Architects.* Cambridge: Harvard Graduate School of Design, 9–15.

Marot, Sébastian (2003) *Sub-urbanism and the Art of Memory.* London: AA Publications.

Mitchell, Don and Richard Van Deusen (2001) 'Downsview Park: Open Space or Public Space?' in Julia Czerniak (ed.) *Downsview Park Toronto.* Cambridge: Harvard Design School and Munich: Prestel, 102–115.

Mori, Toshiko (2003) 'Urbanism and Magical Realism', in Rodolfo Machado (ed.) *The Favela Barrio Project: Jorge Mario Jáuregui Architects.* Cambridge: Harvard Graduate School of Design, 48–59.

Mostafavi, Mohsen and Ciro Najle (eds) (2003) *Landscape Urbanism: A Manual for the Machinic Landscape.* London: Architectural Association.

Pollack, Linda (2002) 'Sublime Matters: Fresh Kills', *Praxis – Landscapes issue*, New Orleans, 58–63.

Shane, Grahame (2004) 'The Emergence of "Landscape Urbanism": Reflections on *Stalking Detroit*', *Harvard Design Magazine* 20, Spring/Summer.

Shannon, Kelly (2004) *Rhethorics & Realities, Addressing Landscape Urbanism, Three Cities in Vietnam*, unpublished doctoral dissertation, University of Leuven.

Somol, R.E. (2001) 'All Systems GO!: The Terminal Nature of Contemporary Urbanism', in Julia Czerniak (ed.) *Downsview Park Toronto*. Cambridge: Harvard Design School and Munich: Prestel, 126–147.

Swaffield, Simon (ed) (2002) *Theory in Landscape Architecture: A Reader*. Philadelphia: University of Pennsylvania Press.

Viganò, Paola (ed.) (2001) *Territories of a New Modernity*. Napoli: Electa Napoli.

Waldheim, Charles (ed.) (2006) *The Landscape Urbanism Reader*. New York: Princeton Architectural Press.

Yu, Kongjian and Mary, Padua (eds) (2006) *The Art of Survival: Recovering Landscape Architecture*. Mulgrove: The Images Publishing Group.

SECTION 8

City/Metropolis/Territory

36

Introduction: Metropolis, Megalopolis and Metacity

Brian McGrath and Grahame Shane

INTRODUCTION

With much fanfare, the urban century has arrived at the very moment that the definitions and meanings of the terms city, metropolis and territory seem to be exhausted. Manuel Castells (1999) pinpointed the dilemma when he said that more and more we live in an urban society without cities. Even within this Handbook's brief thirty-year time frame, architectural theories of the city have continually readjusted the meaning of these terms in response to huge shifts in the geopolitical landscape: the first oil shock and challenge to American hegemony in the 1970s, the rise of deregulated neo-liberal globalization and the fall of the Berlin Wall in the 1980s, the emergence of the internet's irrational exuberance and the promise of a transnational global village in the 1990s, and the shattering of this utopian moment on 9/11 with the resulting endless US War on Terror dominating the first decade of the twenty-first century. And now, the very metabolism of urbanization needs to be fundamentally transformed to ensure the survival of life on this planet and equitable access to its limited resources. We have witnessed the complete reversal of fortunes of cities – once seen as shrinking, dead, shattered or bursting at the seams, cities now can be seen as the crucial spaces of hope for the majority of the world's poor and the place in which the environmental and social crises of our times must be immediately addressed.

For us, the greatest evidence of the dramatic changes over the last thirty years has been the proliferation of competing models of urban form, each with its own formal order, metabolism and role for architecture in shaping the city. The imperial *metropolis*, symbolic centre of a controlled colonial world order at the beginning of the twentieth century gave way to the sprawling global *megalopolis* and its result the imploding megacity (see Chapter 38), the monstrous twin products of the 'open' neo-liberal world (dis)order at the beginning of the twenty-first. In this chapter, we will present this extraordinary and unprecedented reversal of the city/territory as a context for the necessary changes which lie ahead for architectural theory and practice. Therefore, we put forward a third city model as a synthesis of the dialectical opposition and social stratification of the metropolis, megalopolis and megacity: the networked multi-form *metacity*. This third urban model will lay the foundation for a theorization of architecture to take on a more expansive and less hierarchical role of critical participation in imagining the vast structural, social and metabolic urban transformations required in the decades ahead.

These three simultaneous and overlapping city models – metropolis, megalopolis and metacity – will be examined as competing theories of symbolic form, social order and environmental metabolism, each with a specific role for architecture to imagine, represent and shape. At the mid point of the twentieth century, following the collapse of the colonial world order, the imperial European metropole gave way to a dominant new urban form and way of life – the American Cold War megalopolis. The collapse of the colonial world system also resulted in the unexpected and uncontrolled growth of the informal implosion of the megacity as the flip side of the sprawling megalopolis. The three theoretical models coexist concurrently in the contemporary world, even as they emerged during three distinct historical periods and constitute distinct arenas for architectural practice and cultural theory. To illustrate the three models, Figures 36.1–36.3 represent their simultaneous coincidence in contemporary Bangkok.

We argue here that a more recent shift, which began with innovations in electronic communication and financial liberalizations in the 1980s, produced a radical reassembling of both the fragmented metropolis, the sprawling megalopolis and the imploding megacity. This has led to an unprecedented increase in the scale and interconnection of urbanization worldwide, a miniaturization of its metabolism, as well as a geopolitical shift away from European and North American hegemony. The metropolis, megalopolis and megacity are currently being shattered, dismantled, removed and reassembled at this moment of crisis following the end of the oil-based American century. Our last urban model – the *metacity* – calls for a re-assemblage of the social and natural ordering of metropolis, megalopolis and megacity in the new symbolic form and metabolic processes through new close-up and remote technologies and sensibilities (McGrath and Shane 2005).

Our three city theories represent very different formal, symbolic and social models of the city. While the metropolis is legible, controlled, contained, centralized and radiates out to zoned residential suburbs, satellite cities, agricultural land and forests, the megalopolis reverses the codes of the metropolis and is an unbounded, multi-nodal network of centres for work, living and pleasure interspersed with patches of farms and wilderness, strung together by landscaped highways. The megacity prefigures the emerging synthetic model of the metacity as it freely mixes urban and rural types in archipelagos of strange clusters through which people, information and materials constantly flow. These forms and flows are continually monitored by remote satellites and embedded sensors on the ground, and interlinked by the social and logistical webs of mobile phones and the internet. All three of our urban models currently coexist and interact in the contemporary urban landscape but rarely in the designer's imagination, as they become distinct territories of both theory and practice.

The emergence of the metropolitan and megalopolitan model both represented radical shifts in the metabolism of the city, as the biomass feudal city was supplanted by the coal, steam and railroad based industrial metropolis, which in turn has transformed into the decentralized oil-based automobile city linked by telephone lines and television broadcasting. While the rural migrants to the megacity frugally conserve, recycle and reuse, the necessary metabolic shift to the metacity can only occur now with the advent of internet and wireless technologies, which provide the monitoring, communication, social network and feedback tools to facilitate the creations of a global city based on equitable access to renewable natural resources and energy, sun, wind and geothermal power.

These three urban models also represent distinct arenas for architects in the shaping, imagining, representing and modelling of the city. The metropolitan architect alone commands the symbolic spatial ordering of the imperial capital, while the org-man, the corporate architecture firm of the Cold War megalopolis collaborates with large teams of landscape architects, planners and multiple consultants at the new scale and complexity of global practice while the megacity and its slums have attracted widespread attention from social scientists, non-governmental organizations and global institutions. While both the metropolitan figure of the signature architect and the anonymous corporate firm continue to dominate the practice of architecture, the architect-imagineer, tasked with branding the thematic identity of a city through spectacular formal expression, has also recently emerged (see also Chapter 14). Meanwhile, the vast majority of city building is without the help of professionals. Rarely does the self-built megacity or the anonymous sprawl of the 'junk space' of contemporary building production pass through the professional gaze of the architect. More recently, the symbolic order of the emerging metacity is continually inputted, updated and commented on by millions of digital citizens through blogs, tweets, text messages and web cams, creating a collectively imagined and constantly changing urban image.

The vast scalar disparities between the close-up and remote systems of sensing, information gathering, mapping, representation and communication within the contemporary metacity brings into question the rich archive of representational forms architects have brought to the metropolis, megalopolis and megacity: the figure-ground and typo-morphological mapping systems that attend to the historical continuities of urban form versus the cubist layering of transparent space that attests to urban mobility, transformation and change. The role of modelling and design has shifted again in the metacity, now that embedded information from mobile phones and internet activity leaves traces of climatic, social and biotic activity that can be mapped in real time through geographical information systems. These maps borrow from choreographic notation or Situationist maps that chart the movement of matter, individuals or crowds and which register the flow of life and events within particular sectors of the city.

Cinemetric digital video analyses enrich morphological conditions with on-the-ground visual information (McGrath and Gardner 2007), while temporal diagrams add another dimension to 3D modelling simultaneously providing time formations: the confluence of spatial and temporal information (McGrath 2008). Such representations underpin the speculative tradition in architecture that seeks to imagine, model and project alternative – utopian, dystopian, heterotopian, simultopian – futures for cities. They are further enriched by representations developed in other fields, such as ethnography, biology and economics. The conclusion of this chapter seeks to investigate how these different perspectives might be combined in order to better understand, imagine and remake the metacity everywhere here and now.

THE METROPOLIS

The metropolis as a model, symbol and rule for ordering the city was surprisingly revived thirty years ago with the publication of *Delirious New York* (1978) by architect Rem Koolhaas and the founding of the Office of Metropolitan Architecture (OMA) with Madelon Vriesendorp, Elia and Zoe Zhengelis (1978). During the economic crisis which followed the first oil shock in the 1970s, *Delirious New York* provided epic tales of a vibrant pre-World-War-II metropolitan architecture reviving the architect's deflated urban imagination. Koolhaas' 'retroactive manifesto' was crystallized in OMA's (including Zaha Hadid) winning proposal for the new Parliament building in The Hague. Although unbuilt, this project proposed a radically modernist post-Cold-War building – a hybrid of Russian revolutionary constructivism and Manhattan's

Figure 36.1 (Above) MahaNakhon, under construction, will be the tallest building in Bangkok when completed, designed by Ole Scheeren, partner of OMA, Beijing. The promotional material for the building mistranslated *mahanakhon,* part of the royal name for Bangkok, as 'metropolis'. In fact the term signifies the capital of Siam as an exalted space within a Buddhist cosmology. Scheeren describes the tower as a modernist slab which is cracked to allow the messy vibrancy of the Asian megacity to spiral up from the crowded streets.

metropolitan congestion – in the heart of a historical European city. This project can be seen as a continuation of the reconstructivist impulse of inserting strikingly modern buildings within older metropolitan centres, which had declined in importance relative to the Cold War suburban sprawl. This impulse was especially acute, where state reinvestment in older metropolitan centres was seen as a front against the assault of American popular cultural intrusions.

A symbolically renewed metropolis revitalized through new heroic architectural icons has become ubiquitous through the world, reaching an ironic culmination in OMA's monument for China's state broadcast company, the CCTV Tower in Beijing. Here, state planners have remodelled the centre of the city as in Paris' Grand Projects of the 1970s through to the 1990s or Barcelona's Olympic transformation in the 1980s. The Imperial city of the Ming Dynasty, transformed by Mao to a socialist industrial city, has been reborn as a monstrous mutation of Ebenezer Howard's metropolitan ideal, the *Garden Cities of Tomorrow* (1902). Spectacular architectural icons like CCTV, the 2008 Beijing National Stadium and the new Opera House give legibility to a vast metropolis with six ring roads, green belts and numerous satellite cities, planned to house a population capped at eighteen million people.

This section will examine the political, social and environmental dimensions of the revival of the metropolis at this particular moment in time. While the nineteenth century metropolis emerged as a way to make spatially coherent the hierarchical colonial world system, the peculiarly post-modern phenomenon of its revival through the agency of architecture represents a new era. As Foucault has shown, disciplinary authority is dispersed in the micro-politics of desire and the technologies of the self (see Chapter 39). At the end of the twentieth century, the architect was revived as the image maker, with multiple tools of print and digital communication, who can make the promise of the metropolis spectacularly seductive again.

Francoise Choay in *The Rule and the Model* (1997) sees the nineteenth century metropolitan order of Ildefons Cerdà's

Barcelona and Baron Haussmann's Paris, as combining two architectural theories of the city: first utopian texts that proscribe an ideal fixed model and second, general systems of rules that describe a relatively open generative system for urban design, analogous to an urban language. A new hybrid between model and rule forms the legible 'Rationalist' system of the nineteenth century European metropolis, clearly ordered yet dynamic and open to change. Choay traces these two theoretical approaches from Plato and Aristotle through to the Italian Renaissance, contrasting Alberti's generative system to Thomas More's perfect, frozen model of Utopia. The metropolitan order is a clear social diagram of power relations, and Haussmann's radiating boulevards connecting national monuments, cultural institutions and rail gateways continue to fix the image of Paris. The balance between rule and model can temper the stasis or dynamism of metropolitan order. For example, the 1811 grid plan of Manhattan is a generative pattern whose rules are constantly readjusted through new building technologies, corporate demands, zoning and community input as well as new forms of social life.

The nineteenth-century metropolitan hybrid model overlaid a progressive ideal of efficient, hygienic and easy to police urban streets with generative rules to create a diverse array of housing blocks and economic activities masked behind uniform façades. Le Corbusier transformed this ideal by reversing the building fabric/street code, creating his Ville Radieuse of free-standing slab blocks set in an idealized parkland in the 1930s (Rowe and Koetter 1978). While in *Good City Form* (1981), Kevin Lynch admires the legibility of the Baroque urban model favoured in the European metropolis, James C. Scott in *Seeing Like a State* forcefully demonstrates how an authoritative state's attempt to use spatial legibility and simplification for authoritative control undermines city life (1998). This becomes especially relevant in the postcolonial world of new nations asserting state control in the absence of European metropolitan order. Scott mentions Chandigarh and Brasilia in particular, but he also names the countless internationally funded 'schemes to improve the human condition' that have routinely failed. Architectural theorists like Le Corbusier and Koolhaas favoured the metropolitan model because of its top-down structure which gave the architect the illusion of control as the advisor to powerful urban actors, whether military dictators or freedom fighters devoted to modernizing their country.

The work of the new metropolitan architects must be situated in the re-articulation of the social context of architecture that emerged in the Venice, Berlin, London, New York theoretical axis which existed in the 1970s – a period of much architectural theorization and 'paper architecture' as building production itself collapsed in the shadow of the first oil shock (see Chapter 37). Aldo Rossi's *L'architettura della Città* (1982 [1966]) was translated and widely distributed through the Institute for Architecture and Urban Studies (IAUS), a think tank directed by Peter Eisenman. The IAUS served as the clearing house for European architects in New York, and Koolhaas was able to conduct his research on the fantastic metropolitan architecture of Coney Island and Rockefeller Center at the Institute.

Rossi sought collective, psychological archetypes to remain constant in the flux of urban change. He highlighted large urban institutions that acted as communal mnemonic devices and large fragments that constituted the collective imagination of the city, while the smaller scale urban fabric around these cities-within-cities changed within coded, typo-morphologic parameters. German Rationalists, like O.M. Ungers and the Krier brothers in the 1970s also adopted this binary pattern of fabric and icon and adapted early American grid plans to their purposes. In the US, Colin Rowe and the Contextualist School at Cornell in the 1960s pursued a parallel generative and figure-ground pattern research, leading to built projects such as Cooper and Eckstadt's Battery Park City design.

However, New York in the 1970s was a fragmented metropolis in deep distress, with much of the regional economic activity dispersed to the edge cities along the Boston–Washington corridor that Jean Gottman identified as the megalopolis (1961).

William Cronon's *Nature's Metropolis: Chicago and the Great West* (1992) challenged this presumption of generative autonomy. Cronon radically shifts the understanding of the metropolis as a rational and centralized artefact to a regional-global system which exploits natural resources according to economic and transportation logics at a continental scale. Chicago, a nineteenth century boom town on the frontier of America, is situated where the farms of the Midwest and the forests of the north meet the junction of the shipping infrastructure of the Great Lakes at the hub of the continental railway system. This confluence of history and geography produced an agglomeration of resources and demand at this pivotal hub between the resources of the west and the industrial urban east. In the case of Chicago, the opening up of the Great Plains by the railway companies and mechanized farming created a new breadbasket for the continent and world. This cornucopia was funnelled through Chicago and the Great Lakes, rapidly creating enormous wealth and a new boom town metropolis.

Cronon's portrait of *Nature's Metropolis* can be extrapolated at a global scale as the world, according to World Systems Theory, was divided into centres, semi-peripheries and peripheries (Wallerstein 2004). At the centre of the metropolitan system there are relatively few large 'mother cities' like London, Paris, Vienna, Berlin, Rome, Moscow, New York and Tokyo. On the periphery are millions of peasants, tied to the land, whether under a rigid regime of passes, like the former apartheid regime in South Africa, or under similar Stalinist pass-book systems in Russia or under Mao's strict huoku system of residency permits. In all these cases the majority of the population was detained as labour on the land away from the cities, as it was also in the colonial regimes of the European powers. Within the metropolitan and colonial system, rulers wanted to keep people on the land to supply the cities and industries with the raw material they required.

These imperial capitals or global trading centres stood at the heart of large colonial networks which fed down through a tree-like hierarchy of colonial towns, Canberra, New Delhi, Ottawa, Johannesburg, Hong Kong and Singapore, etc., in the case of the British Empire, to colonial territories and plantations. Earlier trading networks, like the Silk and Spice Routes from China to Europe, were subsumed within this system, with its classic 'choke points' of vulnerability, the Dardanelles at Istanbul, Gibraltar, the Suez Canal, the Gulf of Homuz, the straits of malacca and the Panama Canal. Metropolitan theorists highlighted the railways, electricity and coal-fired plants that still provided the bulk of the energy and transport in the 1950s.

The metabolism of the metropolis propelled the West to temporarily dominate the globe and provide a top-down rationalist social order to the streets. However, a century of carbon emissions, two world wars, and countless examples of social strife, revolution and unrest have demonstrated how vulnerable and unsustainable this urban model is as a global system. It can only support a relatively few urban centres in a world relegated to subsistence farming, low wages, and the exportation of natural resources to support the fortunate few metropolitan elite. In the next section, the social and spatial dimensions of the metropolis will be seen as reversed in the emergence of the post-war megalopolis, which reduced much of the social conflict of the top-down metropolis with its open, individualized social system, yet worsened the environmental impacts on the city, created fragmented social factions within the city and created new dimensions of class segregation. As we shall see, the megalopolis also produced a crisis for the role of the architect as the controller of the symbolic order and design imagination of the city.

THE MEGALOPOLIS

In *Megalopolis: The Urbanized Northeastern Seaboard of the United States* (1961) French geographer Jean Gottmann exhaustively maps the string of cities from Boston to Washington not as distinct metropolitan centres, but as a linked urban system. Gottmann, whose research ended just before the American civil unrest in the 1960s, celebrated the wealth and productivity of this new urban system, which housed the most prosperous, well educated and serviced social group – a population of over thirty million – that the world had ever seen. Gottmann asked his readers to 'abandon the idea of the city as a tightly settled and organized unit in which people, activities, and riches are crowded into a very small area clearly separated form its non-urban surroundings' – in other words, Gottmann asks us to abandon the limited image and anachronistic idea of the traditional metropolis, but unwittingly he also asks us to ignore the emerging underclass trapped in the soon to disappear industrial city.

Gottmann took the term megalopolis from Spengler, the author of *The Decline of the West* (1937), who like Georg Simmel saw psychological and social dangers in the giant metropolis of his time (1903). For Gottmann, Americans appeared to have solved these problems and moved on to another level of spatial organization based on an image of freedom, mobility and interconnectivity through broadcast media and telephone communication. Entire city systems appeared as megalopolitan constellations in this analysis, whose low-rise landscape built on Geddes' 'Biopolis' concept with its healthy 'Valley Section' described in his *Cities in Evolution* (1915). Reyner Banham saw Los Angeles as a geographically differentiated open ended urban megaform stretching across a huge agricultural basin between mountains and seaside in his *Los Angeles: The Architecture of Four Ecologies* (1971). Banham also acknowledged 'The Art of the Enclave' in the creation of attractors in this new symbolic landscape, like Disneyland or the many malls which constitute his cities-within-city. He drew on Ian McHarg's *Design with Nature* (1969) that provided a method for handling huge regional landscapes through a layered geographical mapping analysis. Landscape and highway design provided the green veil as a new symbolic order for the sprawling megalopolis.

In *Megalopolis Revisited: 25 Years Later,* Gottmann points to Japan as the location of the earliest and most enthusiastic adaptation of the concept (1987). Tokaido, the Tokyo-Osaka megalopolis, led the way in the 1960s, connected primarily by high-speed bullet trains. Similar interest was shown in the Benelux region and more recently in Italy (see Chapter 37). However, the metropolitan imagination emanating from Paris prevented the French from agreeing to politically re-centring the European Community around megalopolitan systems. The megalopolis also seemed logical to corporate architects working in fast-growing Asian cities, fuelled by Middle Eastern oil in the 1960s, who speculated that urban growth might also take on a new, spectacular, megaform.

Gottmann's recognition of a new urban model that emerged following the end of World War II was embraced by both architectural theorists and new forms of corporate practice. The Metabolist Group following Tange and his megastructural Tokyo Bay project of 1960 created a new urban language for the megalopolis. Fumihiko Maki introduced the term megaform and megastructure in his 1965 article 'Some thoughts on collective form', which showed his scheme for a new urban node at Shinjuku. Paul Rudolph had similar megastructural fantasies for Robert Moses' New York. Reyner Banham's 1976 *Megastructures: Urban Futures of the Recent Past* featured Rudolph's scheme for a giant, mixed-use, housing A-frame over a sunken highway cutting across Soho and Tribeca in New York, leading to the twin octagonal towers of his World Trade Center with a huge, multi-storied mall in the base.

Theorists imagined such dense megaform structures as liberating the individual and providing freedom within new vast *interior* rather than traditional urban landscapes. Megaform theory also draws inspiration from the self-generative patterns and fine grained scale of the traditional city. In avant-garde circles this ideal combined with more libertarian social agendas as in the work of Dutch Situationist Constant Nieuwenhuys in his New Babylon project (1957–1974). Here a huge megaform structure on pilotis housed a network of small self-created social spaces floating over the bourgeois Benelux landscape. Cedric Price's Fun Palace (1962–1963) was also a social utopia that imagined a megaform performance space for self-made cultural events, constantly readjusted to new social desires. Archigram's work in London such as Peter Cook's Plug-in City (1964) dreamt of permanent cranes moving housing capsules, all over a buried highway network. Piano and Rogers' scheme for the Pompidou Centre in the old Marais district of Paris together with the demolition of the old markets to make way of the Forum Les Halles created a state sponsored high-tech, megastructural style for contemporary cultural and leisure space.

Such visions became reality as new commercial consumer paradises in oil-rich locations such as Los Angeles or Houston. Banham's 1976 *Megastructures* book also contained Guy Obata of HOK's design for the first American mega-mall with office towers and a hotel attached, above an Olympic size skating rink in the Galleria Houston (1967) five miles from the centre of town. Around 1990, a new round of cheap oil sponsored a megastructural revival in such schemes as Cesar Pelli's World Financial Center (1986–1988) in New York, SOM's Canary Wharf in London (1988–1991), Piano's Potsdam Platz (1990 onwards) in Berlin and Foster's Al Faisaliah Tower complex in Riyadh (1994–2000), all containing both malls and towers. Later, high oil prices brought a new crop of megastructures in oil rich locations, like the $12 billion Moscow City new CBD

Figure 36.2 (Below) This large expressway interchange constitutes the pulsing heart of contemporary Bangkok. It was designed by King Rama 9, in order to alleviate the chronic traffic congestion of the sprawling megalopolis.

with its Federation Tower outside central Moscow, or SOM's design for the Burj Tower Dubai (2008). Other examples include Foster's spectacular, pyramidal Palace of Peace and Reconciliation (2004–2006) and conical Khan Shatyry Entertainment Centre in Astana, Kazakhstan (2006–2008).

Gottmann in his 1961 study of the megalopolis had noted the sprawling nature of the new city, referring to its 'nebulous' urban form. Urban theorists such as David Appleyard, Kevin Lynch and John Myer in their *View from the Road* (1963) stressed the visual impact and cognitive mapping of the new highway networks in the megalopolis, giving rise to a new inner city and suburban mental geography. Robert Venturi, Denise Scott-Brown and Steven Izenour in *Learning from Las Vegas* (1972) found new urban patterns and symbolic language in the auto-based environment of parking lots, casinos and signage. These new patterns keyed the break down of the metropolis to the peripheral visual explosion of the megalopolis experienced at new scales and speeds. Joel Garreau's *Edge City: Life on the New Frontier* (1991) highlighted the unplanned conglomerations of retail, commercial and office uses in emerging peripheral centres on orbital highways, like Tysons Corners outside Washington, DC.

While the new political reality of the Cold War world system unleashed megalopolitan edge cities in the cities of the North, much of the post-colonial world experienced an implosion of uncontrolled urbanization in the global South. The first recognition of the vast self-built Latin American favelas was by Janice Perlman, author of *The Myth of Marginality: Urban Poverty and Politics in Rio de Janeiro* (1976), who coined the term 'megacity' and later founded the Mega City Institute to study these urban conglomerations in Asia, Africa and Latin America. The United Nations recognized these bottom-up new towns for the first time at the 1976 Habitat I in Vancouver, when self-help NGOs found an advocate in the work of the architect-theorist John Turner, author of *Housing By People* (1977). In Mexico City, for instance, the government laid out the main infrastructural grid for the vast informal settlement of Chalco or Nezahualcoyotl (1990) but then left associations and individuals to build the dwellings as best they could. The World Bank in this period also encouraged 'Sites and Services' developments of local infrastructure, like B.V. Dhoshi's self-build Aranya housing in Indore, India (1989), where families built their own houses within a service grid.

Such housing projects designed by architects often quickly became gentrified and middle class, and represent only a tiny fraction of the enormous migrations to cities which accompanied the collapse of the European empires. For every new megaform construction in the developing world (like the Parque Central complex, Caracas), there was a shadow group form construction of self built and temporary accommodations for the workers (the barrios climbing the mountains in the planned Caracas green belt.) The partition of the British Raj produced a huge displaced population in India and both east and west Pakistan, while the European power's creation of Israel fed Gaza and refugee camps in Lebanon and Jordan, intended as temporary but now sixty years old. Even in oil-rich states like Mexico and Venezuela, cities like Caracas and Mexico City quickly fell into housing crises despite the best efforts of modernist architects, sometimes working for military dictatorships, like Carlos Villaneuva in Caracas. Peasants moving to the city had to build their own houses as best they could in the 1950s, resulting in the emergence of huge informal barrios and favellas beside the formal city. Dharavi, in Mumbai is reputedly Asia's largest self-built settlement. In a long established, previously peripheral informal village, a high-density, low-rise, mixed-use, highly productive downtown cottage industry enclave now sits across from the new financial district on some of Mumbai's most valuable real estate.

The UN adopted the term 'megacity' in 1986 and used it to refer to any city with over ten million people rather than in the specific sense of overcrowded self-built group form extensions of fast-growing developing cities as coined by Perlman. This tends to conflate Tokyo and Cairo rather than see them as extremely different conurbations which have emerged coincidentally in the developed and developing world. While emerging in tandem, the megalopolis and megacity have considerably different ecological footprints. Dhavari recycles much of the city's solid waste and despite appearances is much 'greener' than the oil-based megalopolis with its lush maintained foliage.

The megalopolis, while an Eden of opportunity for corporate architecture, for the most part remained a dilemma for independent architects outside of corporate practice, as they no longer could command the formal order of the city as they did in the metropolis. The affluence and prosperity of the sprawling edge cities across North America, Europe, Australia and New Zealand can never be replicated worldwide, as it exhausts resources at a global rather than regional scale. The unchecked growth of the megalopolis with its design megastructures around the world is also shadowed by the sprawling group form of the megacities, which have grown exponentially with the loosening of the metropolitan colonial order. In the last section of this chapter, we will introduce the metacity as a new urban model, which represents the necessary transformation of the metropolis, megalopolis and megacity in the coming decades. The metacity radically shifts the role architects must take in creating the city of the future, based on a design imagination enriched by new methods and technologies of collaboration and communication.

THE METACITY

In his book *Manhattan Transcripts* (1981) architect Bernard Tschumi presented a radically different view the-twentieth-century metropolis than Koolhaas' *Delirious New York*. While Koolhaas nostalgically looked back to the spectacular architecture of the first half of the twentieth century in his retroactive manifesto, Tschumi closely examines the fragmented, crime-ridden and unrestricted hedonism of New York City at the moment of its deep economic distress, social unravelling and crisis of image. Following the Situationist's psychogeographic dérives which critiqued and undermined the Hausmanian metropolitan order of Paris, Tschumi transcribes fictional events in Manhattan's grid, Central Park and Times Square at the same time as Robert Moses' great megalopolitan infrastructure is beginning to fall apart.

One example of New York City's state of deterioration is the partial collapse of Manhattan's elevated West Side Highway in 1973. After its closure, the elevated structure, which ran parallel with the abandoned shipping warehouses which lined the Hudson River, became an informal linear elevated park. Pioneer plant species took root, the homeless camped out and adventurous joggers and dog walkers learned to enjoy the harbour breezes and river views from the top of the abandoned highway. While the West Side Highway and much of the pier buildings were demolished to make way for the emphatically megastructural, and unbuilt Westway project, a small parallel fragment of an elevated rail-line has been reborn as a park – the celebrated Highline design (selected September 2004) by Field Operations with Diller, Scofidio and Renfro. The collapse of the West Side Highway coincided with the rise of community activism in response to Moses' ambitious plans for a regionally interconnected Greater New York. In the 1960s, Jane Jacobs, the author of *Death and Life of Great American Cities* (1961) famously contributed to halting the Lower Manhattan Expressway which was planned to run through Soho and the ethnic neighbourhood of the South Village. In the 1980s, environmental activists stopped the massive Westway project in court based on evidence of fish spawning in the pilings of the old piers and set in motion the building of the Hudson River Park.

The metacity was born in the exhaustion of metropolitan and megalopolitan urban models, the rise of the demands of activism in civil rights and environmentalism and the emergence of new sensing, communication and imaging technologies. The revival of metropolitan architecture appealed to tourist circuits of global elites and for staging spectacular events such as the Beijing Olympics, but the controlled world order and legibility of the metropolis could never be fully resurrected. The megalopolis as well came to a severe crisis with the growing scarcity of oil, and the environmental consequences of burning fossil fuels finally acknowledged at the Kyoto Accords of 1998. The term 'metacity' appeared in a millennial anxiety about overpopulation and renewed fears of the limits of growth, and for UN-HABITAT it refers to cities with a population over twenty million (2006). But the size of a few extra large cities is not the important question of the metacity, and population predictions have been consistently overestimated. For us the metacity does not refer to an extra-large conurbation, but an urbanization of the entire planet – including what was thought of as 'village', 'rural' or 'remote' – through new models of mobility and communication. The metacity implies that which exists above and beyond the traditionally defined city, metropolis and territory, when urban form becomes unbounded, uncontrolled and at once urban and rural, and everywhere is both centre and periphery.

If the megalopolis and megacity were created by the political unbounding of the colonial world system, the metacity emerged according to the logic of late global capital and the new information and communication technology tools which allowed for new forms of both concentration and dispersal. Recent development has been led by aggressive speculation and profit-seeking during a time of deregulation of global financial systems. This new global city based on the

Figure 36.3 (Below) Modern Bangkok has engulfed hundreds of agricultural villages in its uncontained growth. Ban Krua, shown here, was given to the Muslim Cham community outside the walls of the royal city, but today stands in the way of a planned expressway to connect to the spectacular malls of the Siam Central Shopping District.

dynamic generation of urban form through credit, risk and capital speculation has occurred at a moment where nature itself has been reconceived in a more dynamic way. Contemporary theories of disturbance ecology give us an understanding of nature neither in balance nor equilibrium, but in a constant state of flux. The ecology of the metacity should be understood as a complex adaptive system in disequilibrium, and the social actors of the city are seen as an integral part rather than separated from nature.

Following on Saskia Sassen's work on global cities (2001 [1991]) and Peter J. Taylor's studies of the global networks, relationships, ranking and hierarchies of cities (1995), architects became aware of the differentiation of functions between cities and within cities. Urban geographers like Ed Soja, studying Los Angeles initially (1989), and later more global systems in *Postmetropolis* (2000), emphasized both the multiple nodes of the global system with its linked networks, and the differentiation of patches within cities, as each patch linked in to different urban systems that had different global links. Patch dynamics is an urban ecological framework that emerged at the same time for modelling urban ecosystems (McGrath et al. 2007).

Architectural theorists of the city were slow to spot the emergence of this new hybrid world because of their preoccupation with built form in contrast to nature and natural processes. The interval between two international competitions for the old slaughterhouse district of La Villette in Paris marks a turning point in the professional design imagination. The first competition was explicitly metropolitan in conception, and the scheme by Leon Krier, which received a special prize, imagines a reconstitution of the legible residential quarter of the nineteenth-century metropolis. His plan for housing development was never developed, and instead a new competition for a 'park of the twenty-first century' was commissioned. In both Bernard Tschumi's and OMA's projects there is evidence of a new form of architectural practice based in the open space of the city as a field of unpredictable events which radically undermined the carefully constructed nature of Paris' metropolitan parks. These projects linked back to Unger's City Archipelago projects (1977) for Berlin that set high density urban fragments into Berlin's low rise archipelago of islands, lakes and forests.

In the data rich social democracy of the Netherlands, architect Winny Maas together with MVRDV developed an exhibition and catalogue *Meta City/Data Town* (1999) and became the first architects to theorize the metacity. *Meta City/Data Town* examines the three-dimensional consequences of the increased urbanization at global, national and meta scales. Their data town is site-less, and is modelled directly from statistics on population trends, needs of water, food and natural resources, as well as social experimentation. MRDV used the 'metacity' term to describe a city that was primarily only a pile of statistics and data, recording the presence of hidden patterns inside a huge urban conurbation, housing masses of people. Their idea was that from a properly organized analysis of these data a cellular, fractal structure of flows would emerge, which could be tweaked just a little by the architect to create a new urban architecture of flows.

But the metacity thrives in all corners of the world where data, indoor plumbing and architectural statements are rare, but electricity, televisions and mobile phones are ubiquitous. Urban environmentalists were quick to question the megalopolitan cult of bigness, and had their own cult of 'small is beautiful' (Schumacher 1973), justified in part by the rapid miniaturization of electronic devices that altered energy supply possibilities (making miniaturized solar power and wind generation possible), beside facilitating communications between individuals in social networks (aiding bottom-up organization and NGOs). Environmentalists were also much more aware of the differentiation of patches in the city, as in John Seymour and Herbert

Giradet's *Blueprint for a Green Planet* (1987) that rigorously explored urban systems, their energy sources, their enclaves of production and consumption, their flow systems, intakes and exhausts. They emphasized the limits of the earth's carrying capacity and measured urban impacts on ecological systems in an open, visual and accessible way.

Girardet's *Cities, People, Planet* (2004) places a big emphasis on urban agriculture and shows how this emerging hybrid morphology extends from Beijing to Cuba to Russia, Europe and even North America. Informal economic systems, farmers' markets and cooperatives also are acknowledged, as are self-organizing NGO groups in barrios, favellas and ranchos in South America that both provide food and education and seek to improve housing. Terry G. McGee coined the term desakota (desa=village + kota–city) studies in the Indonesian archipelago, showing how different urban actors chose different mixes of urban and rural activities, responding to both local and global conditions, changing quickly and never well regulated by the authorities (McGee and Yeung 1977; McGee 1991). Stephen Cairns (2003) writes that this hybrid Indonesian archipelago functioned as an international entrepot based on indigenous cultural practices, mixing agriculture, urbanization and international trade without central regulation, creating a powerful, local-global 'sorting machine'.

This desakota/rur-urban mixture ranges from Japan's rice production areas to China's SEZs in the fertile Pearl River and Yangtze Deltas or Bangkok's industrialized Eastern seaboard, forming the fabric of many Asian megacities. The UN-HABITAT programme studied design approaches to this hybrid situation in a variety of Asian cities in its *Urban Trialogues*, undertaken with KU Leuven's Post Graduate Centre for Human Settlements (Loeckx et al. 2004). David Sattherthwaite at the IIES together with Shanty Dwellers International (SDI) has also attempted to publicize bottom-up strategies that can help in this rur-urban fabric in an up-grading approach, without destroying their hybrid and mixed nature.

While the European and North American metropolis ages, sprawls, fragments or shrinks, Asian, Latin American and African cities now dominate the urbanizing world. Only immigrants and their children are responsible for the continued population growth of New York, Toronto, Los Angeles or Vancouver. Japan, South Korea and Taiwan are at the cusp of a demographic decline similar to Europe. The global corporate trading system is currently being restructured to reflect this demographic shift, with a redistribution of functions from command and control systems and centres (London, New York, Tokyo, etc.) to a new fractal system of secondary cities and out-sourcing back offices (see also Chapter 22). Problems with the scarcity and environmental impact of oil demand new energy and natural resource management models that will greatly impact city life and form. New modes of distribution mean restructuring highways, trucking, container ports and airports.

Our theory of the metacity is qualitatively different than just an extra-large city or big architecture. It is not just a question of hybridity and heterogeneity, mixture versus mono-functional zoning. The difference is the agency and reflexivity empowered by new media. Distant people can measure the differences between mixtures in patches or islands of the archipelago and make informed choices about their desires, goals and movement paths. Bottom-up participants play an increased role in this new city archipelago, evaluating and trying new mixtures. The metropolis, megalopolis and megacity are reconfigured in the metacity as is the role of architecture in this new multi-form rather than mega-form environment. Architects find themselves now designing the relations between urban islands and monitoring new mixtures in the reverse archipelago rather than just focusing on the architecture of the fragments themselves as Rossi and Rowe advocated. Most of our metacity is locally generated or reorganized through bottom-up social organization, and it is the relations and management of these fragments and hybrid mixtures in heterotopias that is the new horizon for architecture (Foucault 2007 [1967]; Shane 2005; Dehaene and De Cauter 2008). New media and communications systems – both close-up and remote – provide tools for offering architectural services to a wider range of actors than the current client-based system of the metropolitan architect or the corporate designer of the megalopolis. Representation takes on a new role of persuasion and of altering cognitive images of the city, rather than in articulating specialized units of construction.

CONCLUSION

The metropolis, megalopolis and metacity models each constitute specific theories, representations, and speculations about the city as well as distinct ways of theorizing the role of the architect in shaping embodied urban experiences and imagination. Our three models represent world views as well as attempts to maintain cities as respectively controlled (metropolis), open (megalopolis), or complex adaptive systems (metacity). The metropolis was a primary instrument of modernization and the uneven redistribution of resources at a world scale. It emerged at the height of the European colonial world system and its metabolism was based on coal, steam and resource extrapolation based on a peasantry bound to the periphery.

Figure 36.4 (Below left and right) Photo collage of the raised plaza in front of Siam Paragon, one of the largest shopping centres in Southeast Asia. The mall fronts the central exchange station of the Bangkok Transit Systems Skytrain, and contains a giant aquarium in the lower levels.

It culminated in the architectural splendour of world capitals – London, Paris, Berlin, Moscow, Beijing, Mexico City and Buenos Aires, as well as major trading and industrial centres – New York, Hong Kong, Singapore, São Paolo, and Barcelona, but collapsed in the totalitarian military fascisms centred on Berlin, Rome and Tokyo.

The spatial imagination of designers in the metropolis, the symbolic centre for civic order, was restricted and controlled. While the old walls that defined the traditional city came down in Paris and Beijing during the construction of the modern metropolis, it is still a conceptually and legally bounded entity, whose form is strictly maintained by centralized planning and land use control. Zoning dictates where the city ends and the countryside begins, and regulates the relative importance of institutions and individuals in a strictly hierarchical social order. Residential, commercial, industrial and agricultural uses are ideally separated and coded according to status, and the city's growth is controlled by incremental change in the land use. The metropolis is top-down and modernist, a product of enlightenment thinking. It forms a legible and rational tree structure at a global scale, a centralized hierarchical colonial world system. The architect is both the master planner and master builder of the metropolis, and contemporary urban theorists and practitioners nostalgically embrace this patriarchal and heroic role. However, social theories of the metropolis after Simmel (1903) point to the psycho-social diversity which emerges within this hierarchical, closed system, that continually put its ordering systems in crisis and risk. Heterotopias remain the masked, cloaked or hyper spaces of change for those people and activities which are excluded, the metropolitan other.

Designers in the megalopolis sought to house the complex organizational spaces of the new socio-economic order of the network city, with its deregulation, capital accumulation,

individual freedom and mobility. But its metabolism is powered by burning oil and its Cold War politics are based on the continuous supply of natural resources, consumer products and credit. Both flows of oil and capital require strict global military management at great expense. Gottmann's brilliant re-conception of the metropolis as a city network imagined the northeast seaboard of the US as a new spatial model, the megalopolis, even before the interstate highway system legislated by President Eisenhower in 1956 had its imprint. Gottmann recognized Boston, New York, Philadelphia and Washington, DC – BosWash – as a polynucleated network rather than a centralized system, linked by telephone communication and television broadcast. The most successful practising architects of the megalopolis became the org-men who can command the corporate architectural firms that serve the commercial and institutional megastructures of the megalopolis, from Victor Gruen, Eliel Saarinen to Wallace Harrison and today's faceless alphabet soup of global mega-firms: SOM, HOK, NBBJ, etc. Large fragmentary heterotopias that had been the basis of change in the periphery of the megalopolis, malls, office parks and theme parks, began to mutate, proliferating everywhere across the city network, empowered by hand-held and desk-top informational devices.

The megacity grew in parallel with the megalopolis, its implosion of growth from deregulated rural migrations in the global South reversed the explosion of suburban sprawl in the global North. The fragmentation of metropolitan order and rise of the massive scale and logics of the networked megalopolis led to a new wired spatial imagination and theories of architectural resistance – from the PR savvy, radical neighbourhood movement and micro-economics of Jane Jacobs to the self-reflexive anarchitecture of Gordon Matta Clark. The metacity grows out of the limits of the fossil fuel logics of the metropolis and the megalopolis as well as their structural fragmentation and unbounding. The new figure of the metacity architect is the designer and communicator of the relationships between the anarchy of the fragments, adept at complex urban ecosystem thinking through new close-up and remote technologies. Now designers' skills must also include navigating the ecologies of our urban dreams and desires, and articulating these dreams as powerful images back in the collective mediated realm of the city as desirable public goals.

The following chapters address particular issues within the tension between these three concurrent city models. Paola Viganò describes in Chapter 37 the fragmentation and dispersal of the new megalopolitan archipelagos around the unbounded European metropolis; she articulates the morphological change from metropolis to megalopolis at the territorial scale which represents new relationships between city, power and nature that constitute the important urban project for contemporary architects in Europe. Vyjayanthi Rao in Chapter 38 critiques the discourse of the megacity slum as theory and instead points to the megacity as an archipelago of self generated local systems and sites of design research and practice. Deborah Natsios in Chapter 39 looks at the fragmented and dispersed metacity in a post-9/11 geopolitical context. She cautions on the psychological realm of the political landscape of security that accompanies the reorganization of the Cold War megalopolis in a period of America's endless War on Terror. She argues for a new 'open city' and a new civic commons aided by the same technologies that seek to reassert national sovereignty and municipal order. Together, these three chapters fill in our sketch of the co-situational emergence of the metropolis, megalopolis and metacity as a layered psycho-socio-natural system and provide both detailed substantiation and caution to the limitations of our models.

37

The Contemporary European Urban Project: Archipelago City, Diffuse City and Reverse City

Paola Viganò

INTRODUCTION

In their introductory chapter to this section, McGrath and Shane have defended the idea that the European metropolis persists in capturing the imagination of both global architects and citizens. However, European urbanism[1] has focused in the most recent years on the prevailing interpretation of space in terms of the juxtaposition of fragments. At times a place for articulating differences, personal and individual rhythms, at others simply the inherited, residual, *terrain vague*, or again a separate and protected enclave, the fragment has represented the concrete condition of contemporary design action, whether in the old metropolis or in the new territories of dispersion. This interpretation, and material condition, has nurtured design positions that are very distant from one another. Some have exalted the freedom of the patchwork; others have worked in opposition to it, often confusing an inevitably episodic and fragmented return to the various forms of the traditional city with the real possibility of negating the fundamental meanings of contemporary space and practices. In response to McGrath and Shane's formulation of the emergence of the metacity, this chapter outlines some elements of the contemporary urban project inside the conceptual frame of the fragmented urban space and critically discusses it.

Along with design and epistemological thinking, some important theoretical images[2] have located the fragment as the basis of a new urban-territorial form that might involve and absorb heterogeneous patches within new spatial relationships. The city-archipelago, the city-territory, the diffuse city are not only descriptions of new spatial models, phenomena or economies; they are also attempts at redefining the field in which the fragment might possibly be imagined as a design component, taking into account its still-important role in the construction of the collective imaginary. The issue of infrastructure, of multi-scale supports that connect with contemporary lifestyles, assumes, in this context, a renewed central role as designers face the different, and often layered and contradictory forms of rationality, structure and hierarchy present in the territory. The project[3] for the city-territory, a 'reverse city', first and foremost tackles this question. The concepts that insistently recur refer to connectivity, porosity, permeability, multifunctionality in reaction to the compact, the impermeable and the functional simplification of fragments in many parts of the territory.

This chapter is divided into three parts, each of which addresses distinct issues. The first part defines some characteristics of the framework that provides the main motivations and justifications underlying the contemporary spatial fragmentation. The second refers to a specific Italian discourse, the conceptualization of the city-territory, stressing a connective tissue of landscape and infrastructures. The third part seeks to utilize the categories and tools defined in the previous sections to provide a possible reading – selective and not necessarily comprehensive – of some of the characteristics of the contemporary Reverse City project. All three parts contain specific hypotheses. The first, 'Fragments', posits that the most interesting contributions coming to us from the second half of the twentieth century concerned interpretations of fragmentary and diffuse spatial conditions as a potential expression of the subject's 'autonomization' process. The second, 'City Territory', observes the debate in Italy that began in the 1950s, and continued over the following decades as a search for new interpretations and images that could absorb the fragment within a new territorial scale. The third, 'Reverse City', advances the hypothesis that the logic of fragmentation is also, and increasingly, a logic of power and that it should, today, be deconstructed and analyzed in depth to go beyond it. New forms of city-territory – from megacities to the territories of dispersion – provide us with an opportunity to position the fragment within a different logic and within a new system of relations.

FRAGMENTS

A space of fragments: Differential space and the metropolitan city-region

The process of Western modernization came about as separation along with the invention of new distances (Foucault 1982), producing fragmented and dispersed space and a new urban dimension. Today this logic is magnified in the Latin American megacities but also, in more implicit and hidden ways, in European and western territories. During the last part of the twentieth century, many scholars sought to reveal and relate the mechanisms through which this kind of space was produced by defining categories to understand and reinterpret it as a potential expression of the subject's 'autonomization'.

In *La production de l'espace* (Lefebvre 1991 [1974]), Henri Lefebvre proposes inverting the dominating trend of fragmentation, separation and pulverization carried out by knowledge in the name of power. Differential space (*espace différentiel*) can only emerge out of difference with respect to the abstract institutional space of global capitalism, which is not homogeneous but attempts to reduce difference, to separate, scatter and segregate. Translating difference and other-ness into explicitly spatial terms, Lefebvre supports the right to difference, in opposition to processes of homogenization, sectorialization and hierarchization. The sector, in particular, an organizational device, rather than form, of division and separation, has been widely used in the European and non-European city. It is largely responsible for the episodic and fragmented nature of contemporary space. A triumphant device for urbanization in the modernized city (Mangin 2004), implicit or explicit citation of Le Corbusier's and Colin Buchanan's theories (Buchanan 1963), the sector is an expedient for separation and exclusion, thematic spatial organization, functionalist regional zoning and ordered hierarchization of flows: '... homogenizing and fractured space is broken down in highly complex fashion into models of sectors' (Lefebvre 1991, 311). The urbanism of sectors, opposed to the urbanism of *tracés*, eradicated Team 10's attempts to redefine a new relationship between habitat and street, today it has provided a structure for the new and difficult relationships between enclaves and the rest of the territory, a change in scale involving means of transport and a variety of actors (Graham and Marvin 2001).

Lefebvre's differential space renders visible the contradictions between abstract space with its global aspiration and its local fragmentation and sectorialization. The controversial aspect of this position has to do with the fragment's ambiguous role (both social and spatial) that is simultaneously the expression of splinters of power (even if globalized) and the starting point for the appropriation of space by social forces and individuals excluded from the very same power mechanisms.

As opposed to the figure of continuity, the fragment leads to 'a topological conception of space, to the depth of difference and specificities of place' (Secchi 2000); to incremental and specific ways of constructing and defining space; to the irreducible difference between subjects; to the impossibility of achieving a broad overview or even a comprehensive reading. The fragment seems to facilitate an interpretation of the city after Western civilization's first modernity: as the rupture of an existing whole to which to refer; as the result of a logic of separation and distancing; but also as the expression of freedom of choice in terms of settlement and location. Each fragment can be studied independently as an autonomous and perfect entity and does not necessitate, or, in any case, inhibit a general overview.

A space of idiorrhythms

In the mid-1970s, Roland Barthes speculated about ways of living together (*vivre ensemble*) and particularly about idiorrhythmic configurations. His inspiration derived from the Mount Athos monasteries where each monk lived according to his own individual and unique rhythm within a small group. The search for a separate space to host one's personal rhythm is the subject of Barthes' thinking which, through such literary references as Gide's *La sequestrée de Poitiers*, refers to certain spatial devices like the room. The forms analysed are all expressions of the search for autonomy – of a small group in relation to society; of an individual in relation to a group, to society or to power; of the search for configurations that are not concentrated but rather dispersed.

Without opposing community to society, as in Tönnies' *Gemeinschaft und Gesellschaft* (1887), Barthes' is an attempt to understand in greater depth the possibility for the coexistence and the juxtaposition of different rhythms, for obtaining a space for individual expression within group configurations, or the possibility for the presence of differentiated rhythms within collective conglomerates having different characteristics and forms.[4]

At about the same time, Colin Rowe dedicated his thinking and teaching to the theme of the collage city which was to become the title of his most famous book a few years later (Rowe and Koetter 1978). Even in the collage city, in the city which the modern movement's grand project was unable to reconstruct, the concept of the fragment initially seemed to open up spaces of freedom. The fragment, as an element within an idiorrhythmic configuration and the associative mode of collage allowed – according to the authors – the coexistence of heterogeneity and freedom. To think about urban space as the result of collage, lying at the limits of casual combinations like those of a *plan game*[5] was a way of thinking about the different forms and spaces of individual freedom within a collective environment, or, again, about idiorrhythmic space and that which can be shared within individual habits, behaviours and spaces.

The fragment in *Collage City* allows the introduction of slivers of utopia instead of totalizing scenarios. It allows us to think about the city in parts – each endowed with specific form (Aymonino 1978) – rather than its general form. It allows us to avoid, or at least not explicitly treat, the issue of the structure eventually unifying the fragments which, as Constant Nieuwenhuys shows us in his collages of New Babylon, encompasses the leftover, *l'objet trouvé*, just as the Milton Keynes new town includes the picturesque and eclectic within its overall grid.

Archipelago space and the city archipelago

If the use of collage, in reference to Lévi-Strauss' *bricoleur,* provided a design technique that could modify and manipulate a region of fragments, but not its *raison d'être* or its necessity, the concept of the archipelago explores the relationships between the fragments, expression of multiplicity and of distance between things that are irreducibly different. It seeks to establish not only the spatial characteristics, but also the social ones, of an aggregation of fragments. 'The intelligence of the archipelago divides and separates' (Cacciari 1997) and places the fragments in relation to one another. It is the 'fatigue' of a theory that leaves the different individualities unchanged but which assembles them within a space – or sea – of coexistence and of absence – the unity which was lost or never attained – 'Imperceptible and Unreachable' and which philosophy indicates as 'good'. Islands forced into dialogue – 'thus archipelago space, due to its very nature, does not tolerate subordination and hierarchical succession' (Cacciari 1997, 19–20). It is a space without a centre in constant tension between the need for dialogue and its own individuality or core.

The archipelago is the distance between things but it is also their erasure, the opening to unpredictable voids, the shrinking of the city and its reduction as a result of events transforming its economy, demography and social makeup. In declining Berlin in the mid-1970s, Ungers took the process of creating voids as a possible construction of a different principle for urban space (Ungers et al. 1978), generated by projects that could be better interpreted as fragments or partial solutions to a specific site, transcending the logic of a comprehensive, rigid and inflexible plan (Ungers 1976). In Berlin, islands became cities within cities resulting from the cancellation of parts of the urban fabric that could not be 'rehabilitated' or reintroduced into the current urban dynamics.

Ungers was one of the first to give visibility to a condition that was different from the one originally faced and in which modern urbanism was formed – a context defined by progress and by the stimulation of growth. But the image of the green archipelago, today reintroduced in the research on the shrinking city phenomenon, or as a last defence against sprawl,[6] finds a range of precedents. Scharoun's plan for the reconstruction of Berlin (Sohn 2007) reorganized the city of stone described by Hegemann along the Spree valley, drastically reducing density and imagining dwelling units in a sea of urban agriculture and green space. Another precedent is the German *Stadtlandschaft* planning tradition (city landscape or cityscape, an expression coined by the geographer Siegfried Passarge, 1867–1958) which, beginning in the 1920s, produced diagrams of cells whose receptacle – the liquid in which the cells were contained – remained more or less indistinct. From the depths emerged services, routes and voids with different characteristics. Empty space, an integral part of the cell concept, is the connective fabric between cells, each of which is different and completely identifiable. Ungers freed the enclaves – the new recognizable and singular islands – leaving behind the 'anonymity of the city' (Ungers et al. 1978). Between each fragment, the 'green lagoon' hosted collective activities and functions, the space for important commercial and recreational activities. The city was transformed into a union of fragments, of cells which strongly recalled the organic metaphor and which did not define a unitary image but rather a 'living collage' (Ungers et al. 1978).

The terms cited above are but a few of the many which interpret the contemporary fragmentary, dispersed spatial conditions as the result of a modernization process in which individual, group and society must rethink the ways in which they coexist. If philosophical and sociological thought placed the construction of spatial devices and their relations with power at the heart of rethinking the fragment, the urban and regional project, often referring to these theories along with intense territorial description, has developed some images whose value lies in what they evoke or refer to. Images are a 'space of representation' (Lefebvre 1991 [1974]), a new conceptualization of reality which 'the imagination seeks to change and appropriate. It overlays physical space making symbolic use of its objects' (1991, 39). In this way the 'physical city' (Quaroni 1981) fostered new images that in turn, described and interpreted the city as a design object.

CITY TERRITORY: THE ITALIAN DEBATE AND ITS INTERNATIONAL CONTEXT

City region; The new urban dimension

The discussion regarding the new dimension of the city, which came to the fore in Italy during the 1950s and 1960s and later, played an important role in defining interpretations and images seeking to integrate the fragment within the new territorial dimension that was beginning to materialize. The recognition of sprawl as an enduring phenomenon was not instantaneous. The urgency was rather to understand the changes underway, described as original and recent, in order to be able to shape and modify the city's attributes. A new urban dimension, a new (design) scale and a new social constellation (with greater mobility than in the past) were the three aspects underlying much research at the end of the 1950s. Underlining the importance of the city's new scale not only in economic and geographic terms, the discussion also became important for architecture and urbanism. Among the consequences of this position was the necessity to develop design scales and tools for intervening and understanding the territory in order to respond adequately to the new conditions. Influenced by the Anglo-Saxon discourse of Mumford (1938) and Dickinson (1964), the dispute on the city-region and the city-territory produced great and fascinating ambiguities between description, interpretation and design. It was distinguished from others during that same period because of the continuity it established between architecture and urbanism, not only in the sense of conceiving a new planning-architectural dimension, as Gregotti, Rossi and Aymonino affirmed at the time, but also because of the centrality of thinking about form on many scales and the relation between various fields in terms of different morphologies (social, economic, infrastructural, naturalistic, etc.).

The image of the city-region came down from Geddes whose appellation *conurbation,* coined in 1915, described a new spatial entity – an urban federation, specific to England and representative of its lifestyle: a city-region or a community inhabiting a vast, and almost completely urbanized, poly-nuclear space. But this clear definition of a territory in which the city no longer played a fundamental generative role was quickly flanked by other meanings and attributes that would contradict the original locution. In the 1920s, Lewis Mumford and Thomas Adams discussed the term *regional city* in reference to New York. If they both agreed that the menace to be eliminated was the congested and polluted industrial city, they differed regarding contents that defined the image of the *city region* (Robic 1998). For Mumford, it expressed a communitarian ideology represented, in planning terms, by a network of satellite cities. For Adams, it was the expression of a logic reinforcing the role of the large city as the centre of a vast region. Communitarianism and metropolitanism, while using similar devices (such as expansion by means of the introduction of new urban units), differed profoundly. Giancarlo De Carlo referred to Geddes' and Mumford's images of the city-region and linked them to increased economic well-being, to the acceleration of social and territorial mobility and to the consequent multiplication of choice. Later, in the Milan inter-municipal plan, De Carlo (1966) used the image of the *urban continuum* for which, and within which, city planning needed to identify systems and structures. De Carlo was interested in the structure of urban form, especially the structure of a new form of dispersed and open urbanity. Over time, a fundamental ambiguity, also present in his writings, was introduced and took root in the image of the city-region.

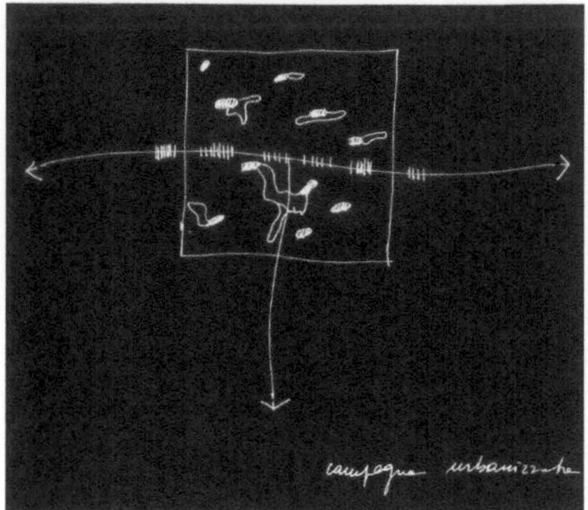

Figure 37.1 (Above) The 'urbanized countryside'. (Interpretation of Samonà's concept sketch by Paola Viganò)

The urbanized countryside

Samonà was a great promoter of images, which, in very intriguing ways, were located at the confines between interpretation and prediction. Samonà's images stimulated the designer's imagination and indicated a possible direction for the construction of a new kind of space. His 'urbanized countryside' was one of the most powerful images portraying the new territorial scale for design. It was born from the perception of the crisis of the countryside and the endangerment of traditional rural settlements throughout the Adige Valley in Trentino. It announced a territorial project inspired by this idea. The Trentino Plan, the result of work initiated in the early 1960s and exhibited in the XIII Milan Triennale (*Piano urbanistico del Trentino* 1968), faced the issues of the vast scale and territorial form and the creation of a project for it. At the time there was significant out-migration from rural areas. Rejecting the idea of urban concentration along the Adige River, the design hypothesis was summed up in the image of the 'urbanized countryside' – 'a kind of urbanization which reconstitutes an urban settlement in the countryside to offer an array of basic choices close to those that today characterize the traditional urban phenomenon' (1968, 50). The urbanized countryside was offered as a possible contemporary settlement form. Samonà entrusted to agriculture, and not only to industrial or infrastructural growth, the responsibility for producing urban development just as it had in the past. With the idea of the 'park facility' he attributed to agriculture, along with all other open space, the role of 'provocative element' for the integration of the archaic and rural world within the new urban condition.

The city-territory

Again in 1962, Piccinato, Quilici and Tafuri, representing the Roman office AUA (Associazione Urbanisti ed Architetti), introduced the image of the city-territory in the magazine *Casabella Continuità* into the broader Italian debate. This image indicated not only a change in scale, but a new point of view. The inability of planning and urbanism to read the new phenomena was, according to the authors, an ideological question as these disciplines were, at the time, involved in generating 'microcosms and neighbourhood units absolutely separated from its surrounding environment in every single aspect' (Piccinato et al. 1962, 16). Expressing strong criticism towards the intimate solutions of neo-empiricism, the authors, instead of facing the problem of searching for new instruments of intervention or inquiry, maintained that the problem lay in identifying issues and their relationships, something that required the definition of a new 'structural framework'.

Like De Carlo, the AUA group began from the consideration of increased well-being but introduced new attention to the issue of free time – the spread of *loisirs*, the emergence of the second home – and the progressive dispersion of industry that 'evaporated' into the territory abandoning its proximity to the urban centre. Insistence was on the acceleration of change, territorial dynamics, on the transformations in ways of living together. These positions were founded to counter the risk lying in the lack of understanding of the transformations underway, on the necessity of new techniques of enquiry, of new readings and surveys and the urgency of reformulating design tools. These were much graver questions than ones regarding obsolete institutional and legislative instruments.

A process-oriented idea of the project, which could no longer face the whole and in which the individual exercised his or her own freedom and autonomy, also took form around the image of the city-territory. 'The city territory moves its field of application from total city planning to the identification of elements to leverage ... but does not refute, however, a territorial scale plan' (Piccinato et al. 1962, 17). More extensive planning did not correspond to the dilation of the scale of the urban phenomenon but rather to the selection of the places underlying a broad-scale planning project. In those same years, Samonà began working on the Trentino Plan which was the first territorial and development plan in Italy to be drafted by architects and urbanists and not only by economists.

The territory that emerged at the time was both the result of, and stimulus for, important changes in society (Ardigò 1967). Starting from the phenomenon of decentralization of production, Arnaldo Bagnasco, an Italian sociologist at the University of Turin, established a connection between the diffused urbanization and the logic of dispersed localization of the small and medium enterprises, in particular in the north-east and in the centre of Italy (Bagnasco 1977). The problem was to provide a 'democratic direction' to the potential due to the ambition of the new affluent society 'to find, in all conditions, a variety of contacts and choices that the city has to offer' (Piccinato et al. 1962, 17). The idea of a movement in the direction of 'more evolved forms of territorial organization' was shared by many even if it was not clear if these forms were socially positive or not. As opposed to the modern movement which had proposed, and imposed, a progressive model of development on society, AUA underlined the impossibility of repeating or maintaining this ambition while focusing on the issue of the crisis in the constructivist position. They proposed transcending the rationalist approach in order to 'obtain, instead, a continuous process of rationalization' – the constant verification of the emergence of a new form of social life and a new way of coexisting.

Design tools and concepts for the diffuse city

Beginning in the mid-1960s and for almost twenty years, the production of images and the debate regarding the city-territory in Italy seemed to come to a halt until the second half of the 1980s when research on the new condition of urban sprawl and fragmentation documented the transformation that had come about (in the Anglo-American world this was the period of Kevin Lynch's *The View from the Road* (Appleyard et al. 1963),

Figure 37.2 (Above) Contemporary fragmentation and dispersion in Aarhus (Denmark). In white: built areas and roads. (GIS elaboration: N. Mathiesen, Aarhus School of Architecture)

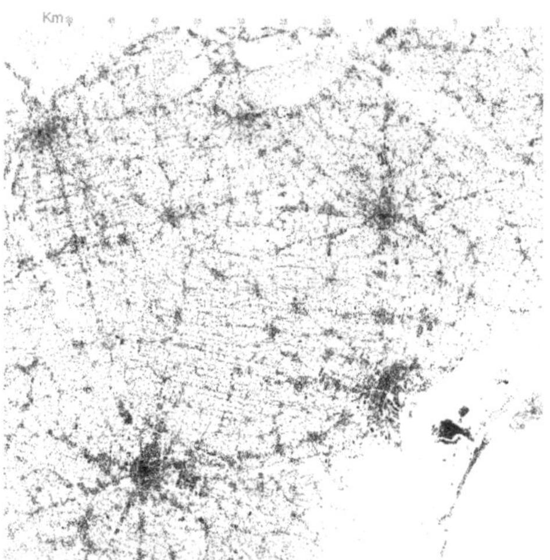

Figure 37.3 (Above) Contemporary dispersion in the Veneto region: built areas, Carta Tecnica Regionale – Veneto, 2000/2007 from: B. Secchi, P. Viganò, with L. Fabian, P. Pellegrini *Water and Asphalt, the project of Isotropy*, PRIN Research 2007–2008, Università Iuav di Venezia.

Iain McHarg's *Design With Nature* (1969), Reyner Banham's *Los Angeles; The Architecture of Four Ecologies* (1971) and the Venturi, Scott-Brown and Izenour group research *Learning from Las Vegas* (1972)). As mentioned above, criticism regarding the fragment and Archipelago City sought to utilize the concept of the fragment and transform it into 'differential space' (Lefebvre), 'idiorrhythm' (Barthes), locating them within a 'collage' (Rowe), or belonging to an 'archipelago' (Cacciari), all with an emphasis on context and connection. These interpretations fostered discussion and debate regarding the city-territory and its project.

In many Italian regions a 'diffuse city' – a term introduced by Francesco Indovina and Bernardo Secchi in 1990 and preceded by a series of studies on northeast and central Italy (Piccinato and De Luca 1983; Sartore 1988) – had already been formed. The diffuse city is a term describing a kind of hybrid megalopolitan spatial organization characterized by the presence of certain urban characteristics in the absence of others. It is the consequence of the dispersion of not only residential functions but also of other urban activities. It is the result of both spontaneous actions as well as policy positions. A first wave – due to the improvement in living conditions for the agricultural populations who passed over to the secondary services sector – was followed by a second one tied to the out-migration from the city by a part of its residents (middle classes, dissatisfied with the quality of urban life) driven by lower housing costs and by the possibility of living in a different way.

The diffuse city is an interpretative concept allowing us to face the issue of individual and collective freedom – a crucial point for Indovina – and for passing judgement on this new phenomenon. Different from a traditional metropolitan area characterized by vertical connections and intense hierarchy, the diffuse city is interwoven with horizontal relationships and distinguished by weaker hierarchical ones. Within this horizontal territory, which Secchi began to describe on a European scale, filaments, platforms, accumulations, still unstable areas of density, voids awaiting content – a 'world of objects' – could be recognized (Secchi 1991). Citing Banham, Secchi suggested a new ecology – in reality, many ecologies – tied, in fact, to the different histories of the urban phenomenon in Europe, awaiting description and design within a general framework recognizing the significant issues. If the term *città diffusa* soon became international – along with the armature of a new local political conscience and affirmation of territorial identity – in the rest of Europe other research was being carried out which only partially provided true occasions for comparison but which, in any case, contributed to revealing the important epochal change that had come about in the European territory.[7]

THE PROJECT FOR A REVERSE CITY

To what degree are the categories and images discussed in the preceding paragraphs involved in today's discussion on the project for the city-territory and metacity? Contemporary space has inverted the traditional code of urbanity; there is a new scale; there are new and original proportions between solid and void; agriculture and natural elements are contained within urban space. If we look at the thinking in the twentieth century that began to study the characteristics of diffusion and consider them in design work, we find some precursors (H.G. Wells' descriptions in *Anticipations*, 1901); diagrams illustrating the process of the construction of the new settlement forms and the centrality of thinking about space (from Wright's *Broadacre City* to Gutkind's centreless region); descriptions evoking new lifestyles and ways of using the territory (in Gottmann's *Megalopolis*, 1961). What emerges is parallel thinking about the city conceptualizing it in an inverse way with respect to traditional thinking – a 'reverse city' of discontinuity and distances with a void at its centre.

The Reverse City (Viganò 1999) is the space of the deconstruction of traditional urban relationships, an 'elementary city' in which innovation becomes the combination and juxtaposition of known elements and the invention of new materials. It is an inverse city because it negates traditional meanings of urban space – its continuities and discontinuities – and transforms them into new forms of urbanity within a territorial context.

Since all of the positions previously illustrated insist on the possibility of individuals to express themselves in a newly conceived space, the city of fragments might seem paradoxical if we do not also refer critically to its role as technique and as a new dispersed form of power. This is one of the reasons why today a new attempt at conceptualization has become necessary, beyond just analytically describing this fragmented and dispersed space. So the question that arises is the following: in what sense is the process of individualization – which characterized the contemporary era – represented by or in this space?

The European territorial project; new tools; 'urban grain' research

The research on the phenomenon of urban dispersion in Europe over the last twenty years can be grouped around some common issues and hypotheses: the modernization process as a producer of dispersion; urban diffusion as an ancient phenomenon rather than a more recent one – the result of an explicit political project in some cases, as in Flanders, and in others implicit, but clearly identifiable (in some Italian, Swiss and Portuguese regions this is more clearly manifested); the presence of a widespread infrastructure network creating the possibility for the extensive use of, and settlement in, the territory. Research also demonstrates that the great mobility infrastructure does not seem to have a direct link of necessity and inevitability with economic and urban

Figure 37.4 (Above) Hydrology network in the Veneto region, Carta Tecnica Regionale – Veneto, 2007 + Humid areas Clc 2000 from: B. Secchi, P. Viganò, with L. Fabian, P. Pellegrini *Water and Asphalt, the project of Isotropy*, PRIN Research 2007–2008, Università Iuav di Venezia.

Figures 37.5 (Below) and 37.6 (Below right) The Ruhr and the Veneto region: a comparison on a square of 10 km. In white: open spaces. (Elaboration: F. Volpiana and S. Rasia)

development, although in many cases it is associated with it; many territories of dispersion have a great underlying density of road, water and agricultural land use networks. However, beyond the apparent similarities – which are clear in some zenithal views and in certain uses of the territory – lie long histories that profoundly differ from one another.

Differences emerge in the 'grains' of dispersion, such as the coarse grain of the French territory in which the process of separation defines a contemporary geography of centralities. In France, the areas outside of urban centres are often the principal place of commerce managed by large groups who design their own very identifiable space. The lack of social and functional mix appears increasingly marked – from logistics platforms to activity zones, from office parks to shopping malls. Mono-functionality attracts investment and projects because of its ease of realization, lack of conflict and ostensible lower costs, but it does not take into account the longer term effects, deterioration, decline, social costs and control of underutilized portions of the territory.

Again, the coarse grain appears in some German regions like the Ruhr area where a long history of territorial-scale industrialization and heavy infrastructure projects progressively cut up and subdivided territorial space. There are many histories, only

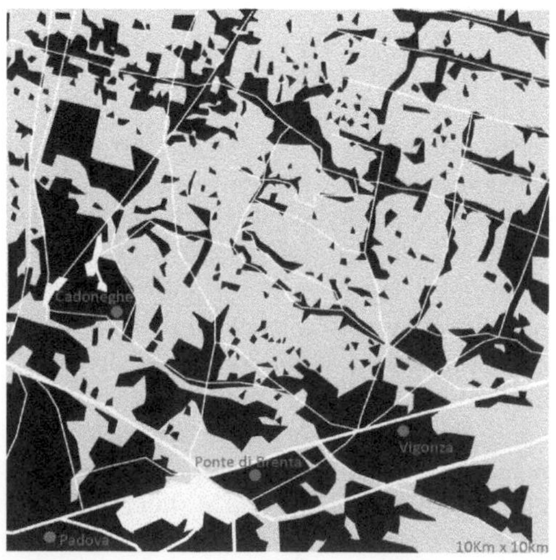

apparently similar, which, when examined separately, tell the story of the formation of the city-territory and the resistance of differences rooted in the land and in space along with episodes of homologation. The fine grain emerges in regions like Veneto, Flanders or Portugal where extensive water and road networks sustained individual initiative in the construction of places in which to live and work.

The new dimension of the European city equates the urban phenomenon with the great world megacities (Sieverts 2003 [1997]) not only due to their dimensions and growing density but also because of increasing immigration, and social and functional segregation. Separations, edges and confines limiting individual and collective liberties are ever more frequently organized around fragments. Forms of power are not static. They adapt to fragments and idiorrhythms, born against, and outside of, centralized power. The crises and paradoxes in the dispersed and fragmentary city are tied together because today it has become a technique and new form of power.

The common element in the research briefly described here is the centrality of the idea of territory not only as a place of change, but as a place in which to imagine the future. In other words, the territory emerges as one of the most important contexts in which to rethink the modern project and the project for the contemporary city – the place for the formation of a new imaginary.

New tools; images as 'connectors'

The importance of images emerges as a constant in territorial design and research.

Figure 37.7 (Below) View of the 'città diffusa', the plain in the metropolitan region of Venice. (Viganò)

These synthetic representations unite the different glances upon, and knowledge of, a territory, and interact among themselves. They are sufficiently fuzzy and vague to be considered pre-mature and so can guide more in-depth research that might confirm or falsify them.

Images play a key role in design, occupying a hybrid space between description and project. They can unify the heterogeneous points of view of the diverse disciplines involved in territorial thought and provide a 'vanishing point' for the different trajectories that they describe. Again, what unifies the different images is an attempt to overturn the traditional sequence of constructing a territorial project in order to propose original sequences of urban spaces and materials, to attempt to describe what they are and what they might become, establishing a more-or-less tense and conflicting, but dense, relationship between collective imagination and the disciplinary one. The images of the city-archipelago, the collage city or the patchwork metropolis have exercised enormous influence in constructing a different view of the contemporary city. These images are based upon the fragment; they adhere to it without distancing themselves from it. However, the Reverse City, the city which has radically modified its very form and dimensions, requires the production of new structural hypotheses without denying the fragment, a new idea of continuity and relations that is different from the past. It requires images that do not stop at the fragment – but integrate movements and dynamics in a new frame.

New tools; multiple models and supports

Today the project for the Reverse City is a fundamental place for redefining the domain of architecture and urbanism. It could not exist without open spaces and agriculture, along with economies and landscape. On the territorial scale, different types of projects emerge which, as a group, have formed the contemporary space: individual and informal projects, along with collective and institutional ones tied to the idea of decentralization and rebalancing. If we examine them in detail, some threads emerge. The first concerns the understanding and improvement of 'spontaneous' models of territorial construction. The second refers to the study of the innovations needed to connect different situations and eliminate their contradictions. In the Reverse City, different settlement modalities alternate and follow one another, each using specific materials and supports and each capable of being designed correctly and coherently with regard to specific natural and climatic conditions. The domain of the design project returns as a reflection upon models of spatial organization and their different supports.

The new form of the city pushes us to think more deeply about the limits of the traditional infrastructure system that has been perfected over the last two centuries and that was almost always conceived for compact and dense urban conditions. The territorial project deals first and foremost with the design of different infrastructural layers, thinking about what today constitutes necessary support for the reproduction of the social process and the welfare and risk that need to be redistributed.

Infrastructure is not synonymous with collective investment even if it cannot be completely detached from it. The territories of urban dispersion provide an excellent laboratory from this point of view. They are at the same time rich in infrastructure, especially in Europe, but having grave deficiencies in some aspects that are not always called to public attention (large parts of the population not connected to public sewage systems, for example, or lack of water purification systems and not just highways and airports). From the territory emerges an infrastructure model, a diffuse model which adapts and is modified over time. It is decentralized and not hierarchical, extensive and extendable. The contemporary territorial project studies the necessary technologies and attempts to give form to a different kind of rationality that is coherent with diffuse settlement patterns – sun and wind energy, energy programmes tied to cycles of water and waste management, local facilities plants, weakly connected networks. It is a project that is at the same time technological, territorial and environmental, as well as being economically and politically relevant (Sieverts 2003 [1997]; Viganò 2001).

This important programme requires rethinking the small-scale construction of the territory and not only its most important episodes – from the project for the diffusion of nature which requires space and time to come about without great investment; to the project for aquifer protection and recharging; to the project for natural water purification – differently conceived for areas of dispersion or for urban centres; to the improvement of microclimatic conditions; to interventions that counter the rapidly spreading desertification processes accelerated by climate change, or risk of flooding; to the project for the production of renewable energy sources; to the project for mobility which takes advantage of the 'sponge' of existing minor road and rail routes and their capacity to connect entire regions in a capillary manner. These and other projects are not innovative except for their broad, regional scale to which they refer and which gives them their importance. It is on the territorial scale that a project of minute rules can produce new landscapes, introduce new geographies and forms of rationality that are different from the past, or can rediscover an integrated and systemic logic rather than a fragmentary one.

CONCLUSIONS; A NEW MODERNITY; A 'MULTIFORM' URBAN CONDITION

The project for territorial supports transcends the sectoral logic of the metropolitan construction of the city. From this point of view, a project for a territorial architecture must recover its ability to interact with the disparate set of projects that crowd and fragment it. Some transversal sequences emerge from the study of strategies of coexistence, multifunctionality, re-use, reinterpretation. The city's new dimension and the increasingly intense processes of fragmentation, place the territorial scale with its different expressions and opportunities at the centre of discussion – from inverted relationships between solid and void, to the design of urban sprawl, to the vast dimensions of the transformations currently underway.

The Reverse City is a sphere in which to investigate new spaces such as under-utilized industrial areas which can become equipped platforms crossed by concentrations of nature to serve the creation of new businesses; streets which become narrative itineraries, dense spatial stories not only of the past but of present relations. Land forms are territorial forms which relate episodes and fragments, local and territorial scales, the institutional and the informal. They are elements of mediation between the situated project and the large scale; they transcend sectoral policy and administrative boundaries. If most of today's images and projects based on the logic of the fragment seek to absorb and avoid conflict, the project for territorial supports inevitably negates the intensification of the fragment and necessitates the discussion of differences.

Some years ago, Giuseppe De Matteis identified, in the cultural passage of the 1970s, the emergence of the 'subjective', of the qualitative and the specific in geographic studies, in opposition to the generalizing, quantitative and functionalist current that characterized human geography in the 1950s and 1960s. This conflict, or crisis, in geographic studies was not perceived as negative by De Matteis who considered it as 'something which allows it to represent the world as a dialectic interaction between homologating global tendencies and active resistance based on local specificity' (De Matteis 1992).

The condition of the project for the Reverse City is just this – to constitute, as De Matteis did for human geography, the right place to observe one of today's central issues 'in its multiform manifestations'. If geographic description revealed, through the production of images and interpretative categories, latent structures, settlement principles 'as responses of local subjects and environments to stimuli, impulses, decisions, etc. arriving from the global network of flows' (De Matteis 1992), the territorial project is the place in which discussion takes on an explicit form and refers to the future. The terms of resistance and identity are not adequate for resolving the question. The response of the 'local' often becomes aggressive especially in its immobility. A new spatial policy requires deep rethinking of our idea of individual and collective well-being, the transcendence of the limiting local–global, individual-society counterpoint and fresh inquiry into the necessity of a project for the territory, its goals, its sustainability and ecological rationality, its proposal of a new multi-form and diffuse modernity.

NOTES

1 While urbanism in the US most often refers to 'the ways of life of urban dwellers' as defined by sociologist William Wirth in the Chicago School of urban studies, here it refers to the European sense of a specific field of study in architecture of the form of cities, which in the Anglo-American context is usually treated as separate disciplines: urban design, city planning, regional design.

2 Here image is used in the sense of Bergson as more than a representation and less than matter. It has a mental reality in the sense that Kevin Lynch describes as cognitive mapping in *The Image of the City*, and the production of new images is one of the primary roles of urbanism. See also Secchi and Viganò 2009.

3 Project here, is used in the sense of projection, again a primary task of architecture as Robin Evans has described in *The Projective Cast* (1995).

4 The relationships between group ideology and the small group explored in the countercultural communes in the US and Europe in the 1960s cannot be ignored in this regard.

5 Sylvain Malfroy (2002), introduction to the new edition of *Collage City*, Folio Editions, Switzerland.

6 See for example, today's use, in France, of the figure of the archipelago (Veltz 1996) and its use as a metaphor for the construction of regional-scale plans (Chapuis 2003).

7 In 1993 Boeri, Lanzani and Marini, in *Il Territorio Che Cambia* attempt to group together the different dimensions of change revealed by the crisis in traditional and natural morphogenetic elements in the search for a new geographic image. Attention to the persistence and values of the street and road system is accompanied by an attempt to describe the different ways of modifying the territory, observing the practices which are not disconnected by the different urban spaces. See also the Italian national research project *Itaten*, in Clementi et al. (1996); Munarin and Tosi (2001); Viganò (2001; 2004); Bianchetti (2004).

In this context it is impossible to refer to all of the texts and authors in an exhaustive way. It is important to recall at least the research work of N. Portas on dispersion in Portugal, of A. Font on Barcelona's metropolitan area, of T. Sieverts on the Ruhr region, of M. Smets, B. De Meulder and M. Dehaene on Flanders.

38

Slum as Theory: Mega-Cities and Urban Models

Vyjayanthi Rao

In their book, *Cities: Reimagining the Urban* Ash Amin and Nigel Thrift (2002) offer what they characterize as a 'provisional diagram of how to understand the city'. They recognize, however, that this attempt is limited in several respects, but especially constrained by the specific geopolitics of inherited urban models. For models are precisely those forms that inform theory by positing normative conditions, either as representations that are extrapolated from extant reality or as propositions that might inform future developments.[1] Amin and Thrift usefully remind us of the role that models play in framing normative outcomes and desires in relation to cities. By concluding that their work is limited vis-à-vis 'gender, race and the environment' as well as constrained geographically only to account for transformations of the 'cities of the North', they invite us to think through what architect and urbanist Teddy Cruz (2005) has referred to as a 'political equator' – an imaginary line that divides the world into the 'functioning core' and the 'non-integrating gap' – using the Pentagon's rhetoric to describe the post-9/11 world.

The mega-cities of the global South are most easily located in this 'non-integrating gap'. Their distinct, post-colonial relationship to the project of modernity invites a theorization of the *kampungs*, *favelas*, *barrios* and *zhopadpattis* of these cities as responses to modernity's pressures to innovate and to capitalism's creative destruction.[2] Yet their material and experiential forms raise inevitable questions about the norms of urban development, in particular questions about whether or not these forms might in fact provide the codes for rearticulating urban norms in a global age. These questions invite a reflection not only on the material aspects and processes involved in the production of what Mike Davis has provocatively called the 'Planet of Slums' (2007 [2006]) but also on the epistemological and ethical underpinnings of urban theory today. The focus on residence and rights, rather than on the scales and economies produced by globalizing forces, as well as ecologies of habitational and livelihood practices leads to a peculiar situation in which the idea of the slum has become a theoretical as well as empirical shorthand for understanding postcolonial urbanisms and contemporary mega-cities. This chapter explores the emergence of such an approach and traces its limits in relation to both urban research and design practice.[3]

URBAN MODELS AND THE MEGACITY: THEORIZING SLUMS AND SLUM AS THEORY

As McGrath and Shane remind us (Chapter 36), there are at least two dominant models for imagining and representing contemporary urban conditions – the metropolis and the megalopolis. Although historically specific in terms of the conditions in which these models emerged, these models would coexist and overlap in any diagnosis of urban conditions around the globe in the contemporary moment. Further, they correctly point out that the megacity is a phenomenon that should be considered as existing in a shadowy relation to these dominant urban models. On the one hand, megacity forms – specifically modelled by the urban forms of cities of the global South – can be seen as a sub-set of the megalopolis model. Their emergence and continued growth can be understood as a symptom of the systemic international division of labour and investment, insofar as they harbour the conditions of possibility and the support systems for the megalopolitan urban forms of the global North. Thus they can be viewed in relational terms, as the necessary and enabling conditions of possibility for the global capitalist political system, as nodes within that system.

On the other hand, these forms are also being seen, more recently, as representing a kind of vanguard in the study of twenty-first-century urbanism. This view is increasingly held by numerous practising architects and theorists.[4] For architectural practices based in the North, the realization that much of the built environment of the world today bypasses the architect altogether constitutes a poignant revelation about the relevance of expertise. Yet, the megacity as it stands today – in concept and in material forms – also constitutes, for some, an invitation to rethink urbanism and architectural practice. It is the disorder that challenges normative thinking both in terms of expectations and outcomes. But this view reflects a universalist gaze that draws on the metropolis and the megalopolis as normative models. As McGrath and Shane point out, these models are themselves being challenged by the processes and crisis of globalization that have rendered it necessary to reconsider the usefulness of certain urban models.

In connecting the developed and developing world through a system of urbanisms where specific cities are nodes and patches of dynamic interconnection, they draw attention to the untenable relationship between a 'universally attractive, flatter social landscape and casual suburban style in the developed nations' and the development of megacity slums. They show how the transition from a system of distinct metropolitan centres, serviced by their regional and colonial peripheries to a linked and open-ended urban system anchored by megaforms and mega-structures, yielded the shadow world of the Southern megacity as a hybrid form, that visually represents the sprawling megalopolitan urban system of post-war Euro-America whilst ideologically reproducing a colonial metropolitan structure.[5]

In his essay 'The Aesthetics of Superfluity,' Achille Mbembe (2004) makes this transition visible and palpable through his history of Johannesburg's metropolitan character. On his reading, Johannesburg's ambiguous position as a node in the colonial metropolitan–periphery relationship haunts efforts like those of the Johannesburg Development Authority (JDA), a public–private partnership, to re-centre Johannesburg as a critical node in the contemporary flows of global capital. The ruptures and continuities revealed by such a haunting are specifically visible in the built landscape, as new developments reflect colonial, metropolitan fantasies within a proliferating landscape of informal development and abject poverty in the surrounding sprawl of former apartheid townships, as labour continues to be superfluous, the currency whose reckless and lavish expenditure sustains urban growth and neo-colonial wealth. This analysis is significant both for its particular reading of Johannesburg as well as its general applicability to other postcolonial cities, and connects with McGrath and Shane's analyses of interlocking urban forms and models in the contemporary city.

Some of the vibrant debate surrounding the mega-city precisely concerns its shadowy presence as a 'patch' between the strategies of the metropolitan architect and the tactics of architects, planners, policy-makers and ordinary urban residents in their attempts to substantiate the presence of the vast majorities of urban residents excluded from full citizenship.[6] Specifically, the questions that the megacity raises, as form, are questions about social composition and inclusion, questions concerning the nature of 'majorities' and their political status in relation to forms of governance, power and the equitable distribution of resources and outcomes. Not only do these urban situations of distress and breakdown invite reflection on these larger normative and ethical questions, but the processes by which residents of these cities survive in these extreme situations are increasingly also being seen as models for the kind of flexible, just-in-time urbanism that processes of globalization are likely to impose universally in the very near future, transcending the developed–developing world divide. Modelling the megacity as a 'patch' between the global North and the global South thus raises the possibility that these debates can serve as platforms for a more universal and inclusive understanding of urban systems. But before we can proceed to do that, it is necessary to unpack the dynamics of the universal and the particular in postcolonial understandings of modernity and their impact on urban theory and practice.

MODERNITY: GLOBAL, NATIONAL, URBAN

Whereas the experience of secular modernity in the West is explicitly associated with the development of the modern city, in the post-colonial contexts of Asia, Africa and Latin America liberal modernity with its associated promises of freedom and equality was often associated with the political form of the nation (see Chapters 11 and 12). Even a cursory survey of the literature on cities of the global South shows how closely their representations are tied to various forms of anxieties about their 'incomplete' or messy relation to the urban imaginaries of metropolitan modernity. In a recent article, the Mexican anthropologist Néstor García Canclini (2008) writes about a 'tension between *cultural* and *urban planning* imaginaries' that has rendered Mexico City a 'more disorderly than baroque' place, in which different imaginaries are nevertheless shared. This tension arises from the implicit differences between cultural or particular imaginaries and the more universal posturing of urban planning imaginaries. In regard to South Asia, numerous recent articles have pointed to a void in research about urban conditions and attribute this void specifically to the ideological relationship between nation-building and the promotion of village society as its ideal developmental space (see Khilnani 1998; Prakash 2002) The most well-known proponents of rural development as the site of national progress are, of course, Gandhi and Mao.

In the postcolonial nationalist imaginary therefore, there was an inevitable contest between a more positive apprehension of the city as an engine of modernity, modernization and development, and a more negative one connecting urban growth merely to the failures and exigencies of rural development, rather than having its own organic growth dynamic as a centre of trade, commerce and industry. By and large, the dominant historicist narrative of postcolonial ideologues described the unfolding of modern development within a nationalist and rural frame, rejecting the specificity of urban formations as modern social and political spaces.[7] For example, in his book *The Politics of the Governed*, Partha Chatterjee (2006) suggests that there was never an 'organic' imagination of the desired, modern Indian city of the future. He interprets India's first Prime Minister, Jawaharlal Nehru's invitation to Le Corbusier to design and build Chandigarh as a sign of desperation and exhaustion on the part of the nationalist imagination as far as modernism/modernity in the city form was concerned. We must address this problem of imagining the city as a vehicle for modern culture because it plays a critical role in the material investments that have been made into urban development in many parts of the global South. A straightforward materialist account of corruption, developmental lapses and bad governance fails to explain the conditions that prevail in many of the cities of the global South today. The problem of the disorderly and the dystopic metropolis is both a matter of theoretical imaginary as well as of brute material facts.

These 'failures' must also be situated against normative models of urban form and the ethico-political difficulties of postcolonial imaginaries with these universalizing visions. These are not failures of postcolonial nationalist imaginaries, rather they are ethico-political dilemmas faced by these nations in shaping their futures to be different from those of their colonizers while at the same time being recognizably modern. The literature on this subject is vast, especially in anthropology and history.[8] However, twentieth-century processes of globalization on the one hand, and specifically the urban or, more broadly, the spatial turn in social sciences on the other hand, have done a great deal to question and problematize this division of regions and concepts of multiple and distinct modernities in seeking to produce normative and generative models for historical speculation.[9]

As evidence for this claim, we point to the intensification of a particular kind of interest in these postcolonial cities after globalization. While scholars, activists and theorists have considerable interest in foregrounding the location of these cities as being part of a new geopolitical and spatial formation – the global South – characterized by extreme conditions of inequality, poverty and breakdown, there is also a growing literature that seeks to understand these cities as aspiring 'global cities' or at least as gateway cities or nodes in the global circulation of finance and manufacturing capital.[10] These two sets of nominations – 'cities of the global South' and 'global cities of the South' – are closely related but also distinct in terms of their political implications. I have argued elsewhere that the literature on the 'global cities of the South' can be read as shorthand for theoretical formulations that take the South as their point of departure en route to a theory of globalization (Rao 2006). In other words, for these works, the megacity rather than the megalopolis – to use McGrath and Shane's history (Chapter 36) – forms the frame for generating a new urban model capable of addressing globalization, thereby reversing the customary 'West to the Rest' framing, or universal to particular framing, for generating *normative* models.

GLOBALIZATION AND URBANIZATION: MEGACITY AS META-MODEL

In their introductory text (Chapter 36), McGrath and Shane point to an older, institutional interest in these urban conditions by drawing on the history of the UN Habitat conferences and other international and multilateral institutions, including the World Bank, as they began to register alarm over patterns of urban growth in the South. Mike Davis's provocative book *Planet of Slums* also takes up this particular history as a point of departure for an influential analysis of contemporary megacities (2007 [2006]). The book follows on from a path-breaking and provocative essay of the same name, published in *The New Left Review*, which is an extended reading of UN Habitat's 2003 report, *The Challenge of Slums: Global Report on Human Settlements 2003*. This report argued that slums constitute a crucial ingredient in the recent explosion of urbanization across the planet, but especially in the global South. Davis' own reading focuses on the emergence of a 'surplus humanity', consisting of the people cut out of the formal world economy and driven into urban slums due to the decoupling of urbanization and capital from industrialization and development per se, as dictated by more than a decade of IMF-led structural adjustment programmes. These cities of the South, rather than being engines of growth, are instead dumping grounds for this 'surplus humanity'.

According to Davis, the slum represents the only 'fully franchised solution to the problem of warehousing the twenty-first century's surplus humanity' (Davis 2004, 28). In this view, globalization has rendered cities of the South into 'gigantic concentrations of poverty' whose formal manifestation is the slum. For Davis, the slum is both a territorial and a demographic form, for it is the physical evidence for the claim of the emergence of an informal proletariat from a decade of structural adjustments.[11] However, the slum is not, of course, only a passive manifestation of the existence of a 'surplus humanity' but also a sign of things to come, historically speaking. Both the article and the book end by positioning the 'slum poor' as critical actors in the future of the 'War on Terror' which is envisaged to be turning into a war between the American empire and the slum poor. As historical subjects, Davis predicts that the 'slum poor' will inevitably tap into cultural and historical traditions of resistance. Thus, for example, he writes, '[e]verywhere the Moslem slums constitute seemingly inexhaustible reservoirs of highly disciplined desperation'. 'But', he emphasizes that 'in the last instance – and this is our principal claim – this is not a war of civilizations but an oblique clash between the American imperium and the labor-power it has expelled from the formal world economy' (Davis 2004, 14).

This passage from slum as population and terrain, to slum as theory or ground for disciplined philosophical speculation about historical process and the futures of mankind, happens within a particular, historicist narrative that centralizes empire as the subject and object, and within which the 'global' appears as an analytic category. But this is a history that rests upon the Southern megacity as its proxy subject. For Davis, a new understanding of the global emerges by situating the spaces of these cities at the epicentre of the catastrophic appetite of global capital flows and turning those spaces into a new territorial principle of order.

A different theorization of the future of modernity is found in Rem Koolhaas' work on non-Western cities, which envisions them as 'incubators of the future prospect of the global city' (Enwezor 2003, 113). Koolhaas' published work on non-Western cities has focused on the new cities of China and on Lagos. Focusing on Lagos, Koolhaas works out a theory of dysfunction as an incubator for the future. Instead of the impossibility of a future, we are offered an alternative way of reading the future and thereby redeeming the history of modernity in its terminal stages through urban design strategies. Davis' position, also redemptive, suggests that cultural or civilizational depth rather than aesthetic and topographic arrangements will enable the cultivation of modernity's future.[12] Koolhaas refers to Lagos as an 'icon of West African urbanity … [that] inverts every essential characteristic of the so-called modern city' (quoted in Enwezor 2003, 113). Yet, because Lagos seems to 'work', Koolhaas suggests that studying the city from the point of view of traditional urban systems is likely to lead only to 'anguish over its shortcomings'. Instead, he sees that the reasons for the continued functionality of Lagos and other megacities of the South should form the cause for revising our existing theories and models of urban systems.

Koolhaas suggests that rather than viewing the conditions of dysfunctionality as *African* ways of becoming modern, it is possible to argue that 'Lagos represents a developed, extreme paradigmatic case-study of *a city at the forefront of globalizing modernity*. This is to say that Lagos is not catching up with us. Rather we may be catching up with Lagos'. This hyperbolic gesture, as Okwui Enwezor points out, might be, and indeed has been, interpreted as a 'celebration of the pathological … the unstable and the culture of the make-do' (Enwezor 2003, 116). But Koolhaas goes further by situating these pathologies and excesses as evidence for the 'exorbitant values of modernity and modernization' in its globalizing moment, but always within a larger project interested in the dialectic between 'decline and return', between the 'phantasmic and the destructive', which runs through modernity. All locations of the urban world are joined together as evidence for this dialectic, with the 'radiological landscapes' of the African city functioning as a counterpoint to the advanced development of the 'culture of congestion' as represented by the emergent Asian city. In other words, these global cities of the South function as particular points in a spatialized narrative history of modernity.

Both these accounts, though based on the material realities of particular cities, strive to persuade readers of their generalized accounts of modern history and its ends. While empire is the subject of Davis's history, design is similarly Koolhaas' subject or protagonist. The Southern megacity becomes, in each account, a subject by proxy for a particular history of modernity and its terminal conditions, its excesses and its redemptive possibilities. However, as Matthew Gandy has pointed out in his essay 'Learning from Lagos', Lagos' urban form is the end result of a particular historical trajectory rather than a signifier of the steady, or terminal state indicative of the end of modernity. For, as he puts it:

> if Koolhaas and his colleagues, soaring over the city, can claim that the sight of the traders crammed beneath the Oshodi flyover is 'proof and evidence' that Lagos urbanism is 'one that works,' the conclusion is inescapable: in their perspective, it is the city's ability to sustain a market that is the sole signifier of its health. (Gandy 2005, 52)

In 'The Megacity: Decoding the Chaos of Lagos', the journalist George Packard also poses a useful counterpoint to Koolhaas' claim that Lagos is not 'a kind of backward situation' but, rather, 'an announcement of the future'. Packard writes: 'As a picture of the urban future, Lagos is fascinating only if you're able to leave it. After just a few days in the city's slum, it is hard to maintain Koolhaas' intellectual excitement. What he calls "self-organization" is simply collective adaptation to extreme hardship' (Packard 2006). Packard's account, like that of many scholars writing broadly within a policy framework, steers firmly away from historical generalizations and instead examines urban conditions inductively, attempting to move towards new understandings of politics.

Others have turned to examining these conditions for different reasons. For Teddy Cruz (2005), for example, the most 'contested and critical thresholds of the current global socio-political geography' can be found at the edges and borders dividing the world into the 'functioning core' and the 'non-integrating gap'. He writes: 'It is at critical junctures such as these that the shifting socio-cultural and economic dynamics around the world can be reflected and anticipated, potentially transforming our notions of housing, city, and territory'. His work on the 'urbanisms that have emerged from this zero set back condition of the border zone' amplifies the relational and networked nature of urbanism over one that favours the distinctiveness of the conditions of the global South. But for Cruz, these border conditions are critical because they can point to ways to a different urban future at the global level – both North and

South – by providing the opportunity to extract speculative models for urban processes from border transactions and juxtapositions and thus serving the goal of social transformation.

For the South African planner, Edgar Pieterse (2009) on the other hand, it is necessary to conceptually pin down what cities are, 'especially' as he writes, 'if one wants to bring to life more liberating and just futures'. The predominantly informal nature of economic and settlement practices, in which large sections of the city are off the grid in terms of services and a large number of residents are excluded from regular, salaried employment, are factors of special concern in discovering new 'conceptual coordinates' for thinking about and acting on/in/through cities. The model of the megacity, according to him, is nourished by the idea of the city as a bounded entity with municipal and historical limits, within which measurements of poverty, inequality and justice can take place. This is also the model within which multilateral institutions have operated since the Vancouver meeting of UN Habitat in 1976, which noted the substantial numbers of disenfranchised residents in these cities and began work toward substantiating their presence. The following section will detail some of the concrete steps taken by urban and multilateral institutions in dealing with these issues, including the theories of informal economy and informal settlement that inform these efforts. But here we will return to conceptualizations of the 'global cities of the South' and to the 'southern turn' in theorizing the contemporary city, which we alluded to at the beginning of this section in order to foreground the role of globalization in theorizing the contemporary city and in seeking ideas for its future.

URBAN INFORMALITY: OFFICIAL POLICIES

As should be clear from the preceding review, the material and experiential conditions of the Southern megacity have provided an enormously fertile ground for contemporary theorizations of space, capital and modernity. I stress the theoretical aspects of the debates that these conditions have engendered specifically to highlight the ethical implications of urban research. The idea of the slum, as much as the slum as a physical spatial manifestation of certain social, economic and cultural conditions, has generated questions about citizenship, rights and belonging, as well as theories of history and predictions about modernity. As David Satterthwaite summarizes them, the policy and political options with regard to low-income populations living in such situations are limited to just four types of policies, which have been used sequentially or simultaneously in numerous cities across the global South. These options are 'removing them (i.e. bulldozing), upgrading them, preventing them or ignoring them (Sattherthwaite 2008).[13] Satterthwaite writes 'in reality, most city governments implement a mixture of these – although few have policies with the *foresight and scale* to prevent them' (emphasis added). In addition, one might observe the recursive relationship between the policies and the populations that they call forth, often labeled the 'urban poor', which disregards the enormous heterogeneity, both in terms of class and in terms of strategies through which these citizens substantiate their presence in the city.

As Satterthwaite further points out, in every city there is a mismatch between the demand for affordable housing of fair quality and its supply. 'But,' he writes, 'the proportions of the city's population that has this problem varies from less than 1 percent to over 50 percent'. Similarly, he also points out that historically, 'in large part, "slums" came to exist and to be measured because governments introduced official standards against which to judge buildings or particular groups of buildings or neighbourhoods'. 'Much of the housing stock in cities prior to the industrial revolutions', he writes, 'would have been designated "slums" if these same official standards had been applied then'. These standards include both qualitative markers, such as building maintenance, provision of infrastructure and services, density and building quality, as well as legal markers, such as contraventions of designated land use or building regulations. Thus 'urban informality' is bound to cover a range of situations in which building stock, design, layout and aspects of occupation contravene aspects of regulation.[14]

Yet, these contraventions are both enabling and generative, especially in economic terms, serving to create territories that provide locationally competitive access to income-generating opportunities. These insights about demand and supply of housing stock, its quality and strategies of access, are of course important indicators of the history of urbanization and the explosive growth of urban economies across the world in the post-World-War-II period. As McGrath and Shane show (Chapter 36), the megalopolitan model emerges in this period, particularly in the United States. Across the Atlantic, European post-war modernism was being supported by a variety of initiatives including the Marshall Plan. Simultaneously, similar forms of urban expansion, albeit less acknowledged, were occurring across the postcolonial, post-imperial world in the wake of the collapse of European colonial empires. The linkages between these historical moments of urban expansion provides the meta-context for the twinning of the megalopolitan urban model with the reality of the megacity.[15]

Situations of urban expansion were replicated across newly independent nations. For example, the vast movement of refugees rendered homeless across British India at the time of independence and partition contributed to a fracturing of burgeoning urban landscapes in the new nations of South Asia, which could not be encompassed by projects and imaginaries of nation-building at that historical moment. The legacy of these failures is further reflected in what appear to be continuous policy attempts to grapple with these fractured urban landscapes, in the form of urban renewal projects, initially directed by multilateral interventions, and more recently directed by public–private partnerships in making cities more competitive for attracting global capital investment.

These discourses of urban renewal, and specifically policies concerning the occupation of urban space by various groups as well as questions of stability and mobility in residential patterns, are also predicated on the value added by urban economies to national and global organizations. As this value has steadily increased into the present – particularly through rent-maximization – we see the emergence of different strategies for dealing with urban occupation, and strategies of producing economically viable space. Various policies and technologies for dealing with urban informality – that productive and generative contravention of standards that are at once desired and called forth in their very formulation – also reflect these strategies of spatial occupation. To take the case of India, which the author is most familiar with, there have been various attempts, historically, on the part of the state to mitigate the increase in informal growth, as much out of a desire for policing and control as from a desire for development.

Thus, for example, the fracturing of the modernist narrative of development and progress reflected early on in the landscapes of post-war, postcolonial cities was met, sometimes even enthusiastically, by government-funded public housing programmes. However, as urbanization picked up speed, such programmes were no longer adequate, but clearly indifference was not a viable solution either. As a prominent civil servant in charge of one of the largest contemporary slum redevelopment projects – the Dharavi Redevelopment Project – put it in a recent interview, the state's inability to meet the housing needs of the growing population of Mumbai led to the emergence of various policies of accommodation, including issuing photo-passes to residents of various informal settlements as a symbolic form of tenure, and the adoption of the World Bank's vision of slum upgrading programmes at different scales.[16] These policy decisions were, however, neither consistent nor entirely successful, and especially in a populist, democratic situation, such schemes were continuously being revised, as well as interspersed with regular interludes of brutal evictions and demolitions. As David Satterthwaite puts it, 'in many cities, upgrading has become "the norm" with many "slums" no longer being "slums"'. The main effect of these programmes has been to officially recognize urban territories occupied and developed in productive and generative contravention of the dominant norms, forms and regulations of urban development.

The most recent policy shifts focus onto the reclamation of urban territories developed informally through the resettlement and relocation of populations, and the redevelopment of these territories in efforts to maximize rents and attract international firms and investment. Contemporary Mumbai serves as an extreme example of this rent-maximization process, as the entire city has been turned into a vast redevelopment and construction site through various public–private partnerships. These mega-projects have already set into motion the resettlement and displacement of tens of thousands of people across the city from districts that they have occupied and developed – for over half a century in some cases. Most of the arguments offered against this form of mega-development, most prominently but certainly not limited to Asian cities (especially the cities of India and China) centre around the injustice of the displacement of long-term residents, especially the poor, the dissolution of urban heritage and the increased fracturing of urban space (see also Porteous and Smith 2001). These arguments, in other words, are arguments for greater inclusivity, though not necessarily for the tolerance of heterogeneous forms of urban occupation – whether these are built forms or forms of economic and political action.

URBAN INFORMALITY: THE VIEW FROM WITHIN

While analyses of urban policy reveal various problems with approaches of mitigation, a question remains about the homogenizing assumptions of policy-makers whose practices produce equivalences between a wide variety of forms of urban settlement and economy. Throughout this chapter, we have stressed the emergence of the slum as the paradigmatic conceptual and material form through which such equivalence is effected. In this section, we will consider two sets of literature around these questions in specific relation to the Indian megacity in the era of global finance capital. In both these literatures, the slum and, by extension, urban informality is mobilized as the theoretic grounding for arguments about politics. This literature emerges, as it were, from the perspective of the 'cities of the global South' rather than from the externalized perspective of global history or global design.

The first set of arguments is exemplified by the recent work of anthropologist Arjun Appadurai and historian Partha Chatterjee, which takes the slum – as demographic, legal and territorial construct – as a central point of departure. In this work, the relation between dysfunction and the future of modernity under conditions of globalization is treated specifically in relation to the practices of democracy. Despite the obvious differences in the conceptualizations of their respective projects, Appadurai and Chatterjee's work can be read together through the lens of governmentality. Each author seeks to chart the emergence of geographies of governance within which groups of marginalized citizens seek to make claims upon the state. The slum is at the epicentre of each account, both as material and conceptual construct signaling disenfranchisement.

For Chatterjee (2006), these claims of the marginalized are fundamentally different from the claims of full citizens or those whose 'political fraternity' is theoretically affirmed as one and indivisible through the mediation of the nation. According to him, the claims of the marginalized are advanced through their participation in patently illegal activities, violating the rules upon which civil society is founded, including the transgression of property laws and so on. Illegality and informality thus tug at the normative roots of the state, leading to an arena charged with the violence of and toward the governed. These forms of violence are staged around the paternalistic welfare policies of the state designed to placate and manage populations whose civic, political and social rights are patently out of sync. Chatterjee understands the new landscapes of violence and conflict as emerging from what he calls the 'embourgeoisement' of the Indian city in the era of global capital, with a return of civil society groups to the active arena of politics, making claims as fully enfranchised citizens upon the public spaces of the city. Thus the city is a battleground where the battle is now a three-way fight for control, involving the state, bourgeois civil society groups and disenfranchised groups who fall outside the sphere of the bourgeois civil society of fully empowered citizens.

Appadurai's recent work, published in a series of essays in the journal *Public Culture* (2000; 2002) takes the rhetoric and practices of a Mumbai-based but globally linked urban activist movement of slum-dwellers and their supporters as its point of departure. The movement comprises an alliance of three distinct activist groups, including the National Slum Dwellers Federation (a powerful, grassroots organization), a women's collective called Mahila Milan, and a non-profit support and resource group called SPARC. This alliance is principally concerned with 'gaining secure tenure of land, adequate and durable housing, and access to elements of urban infrastructure, notably to electricity, transport, sanitation and allied services' (Appadurai 2002, 23). On Appadurai's reading, the claims made by this group of organized urban poor derive their efficacy from their ability to turn their life experiences and strategies of survival – which are viewed as 'illegal' from the point of view of the state and elite, empowered groups – into *legitimate* knowledge about surviving poverty. Furthermore, they are also interested in marketing that knowledge to the state and other agencies concerned with the amelioration of their situation as *precedents* in the elimination of poverty.

It is important to note that Appadurai's analysis is centred on the strategies of such groups to turn illicit and illegitimate occupational situations into legitimate grounds for making claims of citizenship. This is analytically distinct from the arguments of theorists like John Turner who base their recommendations to states about slum upgrading on the economic value of the slum as urban territories. Like Chatterjee, Appadurai is concerned with the slum as a space from which new strategies of governance and self-governance are emerging for disempowered citizens all over the world, rather than as a space to be managed by the state through the gradual provision of incentives. Specifically, Appadurai's analysis is based on three theoretical assumptions – first, concerning the emergence of 'new forms of globally organized power and expertise with the "skin" or "casing" of existing nation-states'; second, concerning a 'crisis of redundancy' afflicting the nation-state, as different dimensions of governance are outsourced to various agencies, both intra- and transnational; third, concerning the 'explosive growth of non-governmental organizations of all scales and varieties'. Appadurai carefully charts the empirical landscape of Mumbai of the 1990s (when liberalization policies were officially adopted by the Indian government). Within this landscape, the crisis of housing holds a very special place since it is precisely the point around which much of Mumbai's psychic life is organized (Appadurai 2000).

Taken together, these theoretical points of entry push Appadurai to read the actions of such globally linked urban activist groups as the practice of 'deep democracy'. Both Chatterjee and Appadurai are concerned with the political participation of the urban poor, who stand as the demographic and territorial sign of the Indian city. Extrapolating from this example, we might say that preoccupation with the tension between the city and nation as antagonistic sites of modernity in the global South has given way to attempts at understanding the new states of social and spatial emergency as a result of the crisis of governance in the era of globalization.[17] Both authors chart the emergence of new mechanisms of political participation in self-governance, but they do so assuming the inevitability of urban transformation driven specifically by the interests of global capital.

However, as Ananya Roy shows in a recent essay, the concern with inclusion and participation does not fundamentally challenge the grounds upon which such urban renewal or transformation projects – in most cases driven by public private partnerships – are based (Roy 2009). This landscape is what Solomon Benjamin refers to as the landscape of the 'mega' – the megaproject or megacity if one likes (Benjamin 2007). 'Mega', then, is the meta-sign of the contemporary city of the global South and a political landscape that is engulfing most megacities of the global South as they attempt to compete for global capital investments. Roy and Benjamin's work pushes the conceptual boundaries for the consideration of urban informality by questioning the very bases on which projects of participation and inclusion are formulated.

Much of the recent work of the Alliance that Appadurai writes about is concerned with fair and just resettlement of the communities being displaced by the construction of these megaprojects, rather than with questioning the codes upon which transformation is based. Thus the politics of participation is primarily a politics that is concerned with adequate representation and restitution for the poor in the processes of urban transformation, without questioning the design parameters of such transformation. Accounts like those of Appadurai and Chatterjee, in other words, are less concerned with how the urban territories that are being transformed, specifically *informal* urban territories, are constituted in the first place, and more with the fairness of the costs and sacrifices to be borne by their occupants in the process of urban renewal.

CONCLUSION: MEGACITY AS URBAN MODEL

From the viewpoint of design research, the historical question of how informal urban territories are constituted, as well as how they are *imagined*, is of particular interest, for it might yield new codes for renewal and justice at the urban scale, beyond and outside the ambit of the hegemonic policy and project landscapes of today – whether these are projects of mega developers or megaprojects of the state, including welfare projects. Here too, the particular understanding of slum as theory or as imaginary, rather than merely as empirical object, is critical for properly locating the 'meta' character of the megacity, or for positioning the megacity of the global South as a 'patch' that can yield inclusive insights about contemporary global urbanism. Solomon Benjamin's ethnographic work on urban economies and territories and AbdouMaliq Simone's recent work on what he calls 'majority' districts in Jakarta raise crucial questions about the constitution of informality, and its implications for the design of the future city and its relation to planning (Benjamin 2007; 2008; Simone 2009). Both Benjamin and Simone, as well as scholars like Pieterse, stress, in different ways, that the problem with much contemporary urban theory lies in its inevitable framing from the point of view of planning. By enshrining the plan as normative, they argue, urbanists miss out the range of everyday practices of place-making, and the different scales of economic activity that substantiate the presence of different groups and communities in the city.[18]

With the exception of places like Mumbai, where the majority does reside in officially deemed slums, in most cities of the global South, the numerical majority and their heterogeneous forms of urban occupation become invisible as they come to be absorbed into the aggrandizing logics of urban space by large-scale property developments. They also become invisible as the imaginary of the slum takes over the horizon of planning and policy. These majority districts exhibit patterns of what Solomon Benjamin calls 'occupancy urbanism', or practices of settlement in which the intersection of diverse income groups, built environments, histories and local economies allow these territories to constitute production systems in and of themselves. Benjamin's project on 'occupancy urbanism' is concerned with ethnographically charting the transformative potential of material views of 'localism' and locality, and the development of localities as economic terrains through the creative play with regulative structures and authorities.[19] It is not accidental that Benjamin's chosen method is ethnography or close grained observation at different scales. Benjamin asserts that 'occupancy urbanism shows how *incrementally developing land around diverse tenures forms the basis for a substantive economy*' (2007, 549, emphasis added).

By carefully studying the methods by which these informal and illicit forms of urban occupancy gain substance rather than simply legitimacy, Benjamin's work challenges the forms of urban futures that are imagined by projects at the 'mega' scale. Megacity planning – with its particular scales of property and infrastructure development – is contrasted with 'occupancy urbanism', which imagines the city as an interlocking set of scalar economic and territorial forms rather than as a singular, 'mega' entity, anchored by mega-structures, including the vertical mega-blocks that are imagined to be the solution to the crisis of informal settlements in various cities of the global South.

These new urban ethnographies rearticulate the questions of politics, participation and expertise in ways that are somewhat distinct from the preceding work reviewed in this chapter. Focusing on the substantive dimensions of occupation and the formation of urban territories that leverage scalar differences in plugging into larger urban economic networks, these more recent works open up new spaces of interest to both social scientists and designers. In so doing, they attempt to overcome a critical divide between the social science and design professions. This divide, we suggest, has implications for how we view different actors in the process of rethinking what constitutes urban community.

Whereas an earlier generation of urban ethnography leveraged the imaginary of the slum to generate insights about politics and participation, there was little attention to the design dimension of the rearticulated city. Design and questions of planning are treated as tools of intervention after the fact of securing adequate representation and rights to the city through a strategic politics of inclusion. More recent calls for 'participatory design' also follow the logic of this understanding of politics, because they are focused either on the maintenance and upgrading of the existing heritage or the development of more just and inclusive forms of urban residency.[20] What these approaches miss is a critical understanding of the relationship between theories of the urban and their framing from the point of view of planning.[21] These approaches implicitly view planning as a tool for intervention, which itself is deemed necessary and inevitable. Design actions, whether invoking 'participatory approaches' or not, are undertaken by assuming the normative outcome, *a priori*.[22] At the theoretic level, the focus on abstract processes of securing rights to the city and participation itself as the overarching political and policy goal has succeeded in giving a certain currency to the megacity as a model of urbanism. For participation itself, in the ways it has been extracted from struggles within the cities of the global South by scholars like Appadurai and Chatterjee, has become the normative condition worth aspiring toward.

The imaginary of the slum thus produces a model or a representation of self-conscious building extrapolated from existing conditions, and posits this representation as a proposition that might inform future developments.

Yet, as we revealed, a new generation of urban theory and modelling is beginning to realize the critical necessity of addressing the problem of participation outside of the normative horizons of planning. These works begin by questioning the assumptions of norms and horizons *a priori*, and instead begin investigations from the perspective of substantive forms on the ground. Thus, research itself begins from designs for living on the ground rather than viewed from the air, as does Koolhaas in his work on Lagos, or viewed as precedent setting forms of suffering and vulnerability in Appadurai's interpretation of the work of the Alliance. Theories of 'occupancy urbanism' for example eschew this *a priori* understanding of normativity. Instead, these thinkers seem to stress a different approach to normativity, which, following the French philosopher of science Georges Canguilhem, stresses the continual generation of new forms and states of normativity through the constant debate between life and its milieux.

Since design actions depend fundamentally upon such a continual articulation of life and its milieux, and therefore on the generation and regeneration of forms and states of normativity, these new theoretical endeavours might formally begin to address the relationship between the social sciences and the design professions. In particular, the emphasis that this new generation of urban theory places on the role of the imaginary; the narrative and rhetorical forms connected with the imaginary and regulatory complexity rejects the operating classificatory schemes that insist on dividing urban landscapes into formal and informal, and legal and illegal. Indeed it casts new light on the vocabulary of rights and claims, as it becomes clearer that 'urban residents are … concerned about what kinds of games, instruments, languages, sight lines, constructions and objects can be put into play in order to anticipate new alignments of social initiatives and resources and thus capacity' (Simone 2004).

Within the social sciences, the peculiarity of the urban as research context lies in the constant blurring of lines between research and design, or between the production of knowledge and its translation into acts of renovation and repair. Research itself, in other words, becomes a part of the circuit of breakdown, repair and renovation that characterizes the city. Megacity research in particular has become particularly entwined with policy-making, and therefore the boundaries between observation and participation, between critical distance and ethical expertise, are constantly breaking down. In such a context, scholarship that thinks through the relationship between participation and expertise is critical, particularly because the imaginary of participation is a key component in the emergence of the megacity as a valid, ethical model, or even a prototype of urban futures.

The problem with this understanding of the megacity, however, is that the theoretical landscape of the slum has rendered invisible other forms of participation in the urban economy and community. Correspondingly, the role of design has been reduced to a tool of intervention rather than one of innovation – even of disruptive innovation – drawing on the potential to be diagnostic and speculative. Both within academic and policy frameworks, the urban context of the global South has been largely thought through particular, normative hypotheses about what cities should generate – the good life, conviviality, friendship, citizenship and political belonging – in short, through developmentalism with its ideologies of a productive citizenry. Increasingly, even progressive academia and activism accept the inevitability of the marriage of these goals with global economic integration. The triad of development, productive citizenship and urban design and planning within the ambit of global capital seems to lock urban collectivities into particular visions of urban futures, ones that are resolutely modernist.

But there is a different understanding of knowledge production, one that reverses the relationship between research and design, breaking down the existing link between research and design by positing design itself as research method, as a method for probing the provisional, and for discerning, as well as producing emergent states and forms of normativity from the careful ethnographic study of the contestation between life and its milieu that characterizes the contemporary urban world. In this regard, forms of representative thinking – such as those exemplified by surveys and statistical methods – must be supplemented by representational thinking, for which techniques for visualizing data become critical. Such visualization exercises, like ethnography, are necessarily partial, open-ended and speculative.

Teddy Cruz's practice, with which we opened this chapter is but one example of this kind of critical work, moreover one that involves learning and interchange across the 'political equator' of the global North and the global South. Solomon Benjamin's studies of localities through the rubric of 'occupancy urbanism' is another example. Numerous student research projects have begun to build tools for 'remote ethnography' using the design capabilities of new media technologies to build new arguments for intervention, rather than constituting interventions in and of themselves. These examples are an invitation to think the megacity beyond the 'slum problem'. For to remain within the theoretical paradigms of the 'planet of slums' is to remain within the realm of design as a universal solvent in the modernist sense, and therefore to reproduce the problems of modernist urban planning. New methods for understanding the city increasingly position the city as an interactive diagram which has the potential to be acted on by multiple actors simultaneously. This means that we must pay attention to the speculative, innovative and productive potentialities of emergent collectivities, rather than assuming what such collectivities desire as outcomes.

NOTES

1 I use the term normative to signal the moral underpinnings of much of urban planning theory and practice. The idea of normativity as a basis for social order, as well as for knowledge about it, has been investigated in depth by the French theorist, George Canguilhem in his book, *The Normal and Pathological* (1991). Canguilhem shows how questions of the normative underlie not only the empirical conditions studied by social scientists but also how they inform the production of knowledge in the social sciences. Normative conditions and outcomes are also, of course, assumed by planners and architects whose practice involves the invocation of ideal conditions and ethical constraints that inform their practice (see, for example, Shane 2005). Throughout this text I therefore use the term normative as a term that crosses over, and is meaningful both to architects and social scientists.

2 See Berman (1982) for an elaboration of this understanding of modernity as a maelstrom of destruction in the pursuit of innovation and 'progress'. Berman also shows how this seemingly universal understanding of modernity as innovative pressure plays out differently in diverse urban contexts with particular political histories, such as New York, Paris and St. Petersburg.

3 Throughout this essay I use 'design', 'design actions' and 'design practice' in a very broad way, going beyond both the urban scale as well as the professional expert. I am concerned with practices of making, building and inhabiting urban spaces as works of design.

4 In addition to Teddy Cruz's work reflecting on the relation between research on informal urban conditions and architectural practice, Koolhaas' Project on the City series (2001) is also significant and has drawn both praise and criticism for its reach in connecting research and design questions.

5 The third model that they propose, that of the metacity, is an elaboration of the emergent urban region, most easily visible in the apparently messy coexistence of agriculture, industry and digital networks in global city regions around the world, including both developing and developed countries.

6 This distinction between strategies and tactics as forms of actions available from different positions vis-à-vis institutions of power is famously made by Michel de Certeau (1984) in the essays collected in *The Practice of Everyday Life*.

7 Historian Gyan Prakash (2002) has described the political and analytic consequences of this position in relation to India in his essay 'The Urban Turn'.

8 See Chakrabarty (2000), Spivak (1987), Stoler (1995), Thongchai (1994) among others for an elaboration.

9 On the urban turn in the social sciences, see specifically Soja (1989) following on a revival of interest in the Marxist philosopher Henri Lefebvre's writings on the production of space. Arjun Appadurai (1996) and Achille Mbembe (2001), have challenged notions of multiple modernities in very different ways. Appadurai, for example posits that modernity is 'at large', a project that is shaped differently in different historical, social and cultural circumstances, while Mbembe posits the spatio-temporal concept of the 'post-colony' as a complex space in which colonial relations of dominance remain immanent and emergent rather than transcended in space and time, implying a degree of continuity between colonial and de-colonized societies in regard to forms of governance and sociality. In so doing, he questions a division between colonizer and colonized over power and its abuse, thus theorizing modernity through the lens of the historical singularity of colonialism rather than regional and cultural difference. See also Chapters 1 and 3.

10 See Sassen (2001 [1991]) for the development of the global city concept.

11 Of course this view of the slum as evidence solely for the existence of an 'informal proletariat' has been contested both by well-meaning critics and activists who point to the enormous diversity amongst slum-dwellers around the world with regard to occupation and marks of identity, as well as by others who are concerned with the problem of consciousness in the building of these communities, and who raise questions about what it means to suggest that the slum might be the outcome, not simply of spontaneous and make-shift arrangements for living, but in fact an outcome of design processes that are more or less self-conscious.

12 Although this is not the occasion for it, it would be interesting to position the Marxian, liberationist teleology of modernity that Davis articulates in contrast with the understanding of modernity that Koolhaas operates with. Best articulated in his *Delirious New York* (1978), Koolhaas' understanding of modernity does not offer a modernist understanding of historical redemption, but rather foregrounds the oscillation between states of coherence and states of delirium as an ongoing process without any redemptive finale.

13 The section editors wish to thank David Satterthwaite for the multiple conversations in 2008 and correspondence, which this section refers to and quotes.

14 Of course, it should be pointed out that much of this policy literature concentrates on this demand/supply mismatch, and on the urban built forms that emerge in that gap contravening planning regulations. There is typically less attention to the heterogeneous forms of urban economy that such forms of settlement and occupation generate. Thus much of the literature in this tradition typically focuses on the politics of housing or on violent claims to citizenship and belonging made by residents of these districts.

15 It is critical to remember, however, that modernism is mirrored and fractured simultaneously in imperial centres and colonialized terrains as Filip De Boeck and Marie-Françoise Plissart point out in their seminal work on Kinshasa (2005).

16 Satterthwaite, among others, has emphasized the critical role played by John Turner's writings in facilitating the World Bank's vision of slum upgrading rather than outright removal. Based on his evaluation of the positive economic contribution of slum territories and slum dwellers to overall economic growth, right from his early studies in Latin America, Turner recommended the development of several interlocking, scale-sensitive and cumulative policies – both 'hard' (e.g. transport, sanitation and water infrastructures) and 'soft' (e.g. right of occupation and de facto security of tenure) for delivering services and extracting value from these urban territories (Turner 1977).

17 For examples of similar work outside of South Asia see Ferguson (1999), De Boeck and Plissart (2005), Simone (2004), McGrath et al. (2007), AlSayyad, N and A. Roy (2004).

18 Normative planning is usually a large-scale, top-down operation whether undertaken by the state, large landwowners, corporations or community. Modernist planning presumed the total control and design of all urban and industrial systems by either the state or commercial interests. This has proved impossible on a global scale or even on the scale of the metropolis or megalopolis, leading to the proliferation of economies at different scales and forms of occupation that are illicit though not considered entirely illegitimate because they are seen to be fulfilling a crucial need.

19 Benjamin defines occupancy urbanism in the following way: 'I propose the concept of Occupancy Urbanism as a way to read the everyday city and its spaces of politics. The city is understood as an intense dynamic that is being built incrementally via multiple contestations of land and location. This concept poses the urban "frontier" as an oppositional site rather than accepting it as a definitive edge to Capital. This site, built around land, economy and complex local politics, is shaped by multi-dimensional historicities embedded in daily practice'.

20 See, for example 'participatory design' workshops such as the urban typhoon workshop (http://www.urbantyphoon.com) and related calls

for participatory design cells to support 'user generated cities'.

21 Among others, Grahame Shane has argued that the difference between urban planning and urban design can be characterized as scalar. According to Shane, urban design emerges after World War II in response to the failure of top-down planning that sought to control all urban systems through centralization. Urban design provides a method for planning large fragments rather than controlling the entire system (see Shane 2005).

22 As mentioned earlier, I am using the term 'design actions' in a loose way, distinct from urban design as a professional practice, to include building and other actions related to infrastructure use, ecology and urban habitation in general. This is to acknowledge the role of non-expert actors in the production as well as inhabitation of the built environment.

39

Common Lines of Flight Towards the Open City

Deborah Natsios

An open city, by the law of land warfare, is a city that cannot be defended or attacked.

US Army Field Manual FM 3–06.11, Combined Arms Operations In Urban Terrain

PROLOGUE

Evolving theories of defence and securitization have underwritten the territorializations and deterritorializations of the city, shaping transformations of metropolis, megalopolis and metacity explored in this section (see Chapter 36). In the post-9/11 era, the distributed architectures of the twenty-first century metacity are being mediated by new infrastructures that enable overt and covert systems of discipline, control, regulation and resistance. This essay tracks such networked assemblages as they intersect in the hybrid spaces of the commons, spectacle, camp, museum, checkpoint and watchtower – way stations of a pilgrimage which can never return to the idealizations of the imperial metropolis captured by the locution 'White City'. Embodied in the monochrome exceptionalism of Chicago's World's Columbian Exposition of 1893, the White City of the global North would be contested in the post-Cold War metacity, no less so than by the variegated urbanisms that infiltrated the complex topographies of Amman, Jordan, a self-named White City of the global South.

The urbanizing assemblages of the metacity invoke the conditions of a new *città aperta* – the Open City – a state of exception posited by the codes of land warfare during the twentieth century, in which military practices of defence and attack were provisionally suspended. A new era of catastrophic aerial bombardment had produced treaties which acknowledged the privileged status of cultural patrimony and sought to spare urban landmarks from destruction. Articulated within the scripts of conventional warfare, the proposed Open City addressed threats to the historiographic narrative, calling for urban preservation through a demilitarized interregnum to be declared in anticipation of imminent occupation of the city by the enemy (see also Chapter 18). At the same time, the demilitarized hiatus opened up new terrains of resistance for insurgents who infiltrated urban space from which protocols of military attack and defence had been prohibited.

The twenty-first century's urban securitizations recall the *città aperta*'s ambiguities. Embedded among the metacity's legacy infrastructures, militarized new technologies and practices – both overt and covert – are being effectively demilitarized through a process of coercive normalization. Always anticipating imminent occupation by the enemy, the new Open City hovers in the lacunae between attack and defence, as insurgencies mobilize in the destabilized milieu to reclaim the prerogatives of civil society.

Bentham's prison had 'turned utopia inside out' (Ellin 1997, 16), improving modernity's individual deviant through confinement and a 'panoptic structuring of visibility' (Bogard 2006, 110). Haussman's metropolitan boulevards projected discipline beyond prison walls into the city of emergent capital flows, enabling the surveillance and militarized control of the metropolis and its dangerous classes (Harvey 2006, 21). Civil defence tropes that warned of 'the enemy within' enlisted suburban compliance throughout the regional-scale diffusions and accelerating flows of the Cold War megalopolis (Farish 2007; Colomina 2007; May 1999). Following the attacks of 9/11, preemptive risk management deployed surveillant assemblages to produce data used to calculate actuarial statistics relating to risk (Lyon 2005, 34), effectively indicting suspect groups before crimes had been committed.

In the post-disciplinary metacity, where global urban systems are bypassing the national (Sassen 2001 [1991]), venerable

Figure 39.1 (Below) CHOKEPOINT: An archaeology of urban defence and policing is exposed at The Narrows, the maritime chokepoint into New York harbor.

discourses on urban policing, criminology, penology and the architectures of defensible urban design – the disciplinary codes of the local – are being superseded by theories of transnational risk 'that operate within a negative logic that focuses on fear and the social distribution of "bads" more than on progress and social distribution of "goods"' (Ericson and Haggerty 1997, 6). The information age's policemen and private security services are 'knowledge workers' who traffic in risk data. Database-policing is transacted not through visibility, but rather, an invisibility which covertly segments territory and pariah populations into 'dystopias of exclusion' (Young 1999, 19). Intertwined itineraries of risk and resistance flowing through global networks of production and consumption are being constituted in the dispersed assemblages of the commons, spectacle, camp, museum, checkpoint, watchtower and White City.

COMMONS

A newspaper story tracked an unemployed, 23-year-old programmer in Amman, Jordan as he left his family's middle-class apartment for a nearby space where – notwithstanding his dream of someday achieving fame as a Microsoft programmer – he felt 'most free to express his anti-American views' (Davidson 2003). His destination was a small pizzeria where, instead of writing code for a software hegemon, he could articulate his desire to encode erasure through the discourse and practices of the *shaheed* – the martyred suicide bomber. A Jordanian sociologist quoted in the article traced the origins of such radical politicizations to the country's refugee camps, settled after the mobilization of the Palestinian diaspora in 1948. Such political sentiments had since migrated from the camps to all of Jordanian society, infiltrating class and ethnic boundaries.

'Bay Ridge is beautiful!' the pizzeria owner assured his disaffected young patron. The restaurant's iconic backdrop of red and white tiled walls was a checkerboard homage to its design prototype, a pizza parlour located some seven time zones to the west, in New York City's immigrant neighbourhood of Bay Ridge, Brooklyn. Repatriated to his native streets after a diasporic interlude spent rolling dough in Bay Ridge, the pizza man touted his pies as the equal of any in New York. Firing up his oven, he professed his dream of committing jihad against America, citing the omniscience of Jordan's ruthless secret police, the Mukhabarat, as one obstacle obstructing his jihadi path.

Mediated by global North reportage, this account of the global South pizzeria's contradictions situates its architecture as a staging zone among way stations of resistance, intervening within global capitalism's circuits of cultural, economic and political production and consumption. Flows of political speech percolating throughout Amman's diffuse flash points are lines of flight which evade hegemony's censors – collapsing the time, distance and spectacles separating remote Bay Ridge and Amman.

Cross-boundary flows of capital, technologies, goods and diasporas have introduced unexpected political performances to the pizza parlour's architecture. A single service counter and two round tables provide an ad

Figure 39.2 (Above) COMMONS: Instant communications constitute an urban commons networked at transnational scale.

hoc stage in support of a self-regulating urban commons (Hardt and Negri 2004, 204). These modest props enable monologues, dialogues, negotiations and feedbacks, which reproduce global effects, promoting the constitution and articulation of political identities and a new theory of the networked metacity linked by global communications.

The Ammani pizza parlour's networked site of contestatory discourse and practice is inscribing the contours of the metacity's counter-geopolitical cartographies. The politicization of this unremarkable space conforms with Hardt and Negri's assertion that – as a consequence of the new form of sovereignty which characterizes emerging logics and structures of global rule – 'there is no more outside' (Hardt and Negri 2001, 186). Western liberal political theory had produced an outside which was 'the proper place of politics, where the action of the individual is exposed in the presence of others and there seeks recognition' (Hardt and Negri 2001, 195). New logics forging the passage from modern to postmodern have degraded distinctions between the two spheres: 'public space has been privatized to such an extent that it no longer makes sense to understand social organization in terms of a dialectic between private and public spaces, between inside and outside' (Hardt and Negri 2001, 188).

Neither inside nor outside, the networked pizzeria's politicized space is a displaced legatee of the enclosive architecture of prison, factory and school – which, Foucault argued, structured the production of modern subjectivity in eighteenth- and nineteenth-century disciplinary society (Foucault 1995). Both the restaurateur's fear of the Mukhabarat (Jordan's secret police), and his grudging compliance with state prohibitions, corroborated post-panoptical mechanics, posited by Foucault as the internalization of the authoritarian gaze of a state power which is visible but unverifiable (Foucault 1995, 201). Deleuze has theorized a postmodern transition from disciplinary society to the society of control (Deleuze 1992) in which: 'The society of control might thus be characterized by an intensification and generalization of the normalizing apparatuses of disciplinarity that internally animate our common and daily practices, but in contrast to discipline, this control extends well outside the structured sites of social institutions through flexible and fluctuating networks' (Hardt and Negri 2001, 23).

SPECTACLE

Globalization logics of continuous control and instant communications help constitute a new commons within networked pizzeria space – a commonality which binds the Ammani parlour to its Bay Ridge prototype, and links both to a radicalized pizzeria 70 km west of Amman, located on the busy corner of Jerusalem's Jaffa Road and King George Street. One of the American Sbarro chain of one thousand franchises distributed across forty countries, the Jerusalem pizzeria was legitimized by marketing science's simulated sovereignties, which – despite the corporation's globalized dispersions – promised to deliver 'authentic Italian dishes and flavors' (Sbarro 2007).

Just as the Ammani pizzeria had been modelled after a Bay Ridge prototype, its patron was reproducing the inverted architectural codes of a remote template, established by the son of a Palestinian restaurateur who targeted Jerusalem's Sbarro's in 2001 in a suicide bomb attack which destroyed the pizzeria, killing fifteen and wounding 130. The incident had provoked a multiplicity of scenographic reproductions. A month after the attack, a student art project recreated the bombing at a Palestinian university on the West Bank, a mock-up which celebrated the *shadeed* by displaying 'not only gnawed pizza crusts but bloody plastic body parts suspended from the ceiling as if they were blasting through the air' (Fisher 2001). The *détournement* – which co-opted consumer culture's penchant for the spectacular

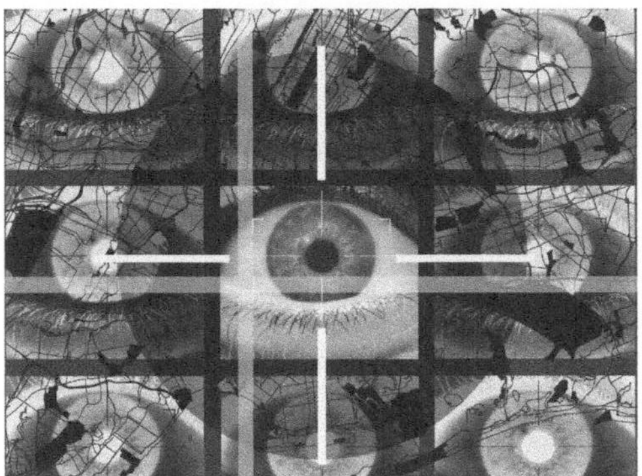

Figure 39.3 (Above) SPECTACLE: Debord's theory of the spectacle anticipates the scenographics of 21st century security theater.

Figure 39.4 (Above) CAMP: Corporate jets transport denationalized subjects across a matrix of extra-juridical detention camps.

mise-en-scènes of the theme park – nonetheless disappointed a visiting architecture student, a young Palestinian woman who criticized the representation's victims as too few in number (Fisher 2001). The same spectacular images of human and architectural carnage were recycled in a video montage posted online on YouTube's media-saturated space on the sixth anniversary of the attack. The video memorialized the bombing victims and condemned *shaheedi* discourses and practices, with a title declaring 'six years ago, Jerusalem saw EVIL ...' (Jewee 2007).

The urban commons mapped between the politicized space of the Ammani pizzeria and the radical representations of Sbarro's dismantled architectonics support Debord's analysis of the spectacle as the *non-place* of politics: 'The spectacle is at once unified and diffuse in such a way that it is impossible to distinguish any inside from outside – the natural from the social, the private from the public' (Hardt and Negri 2001, 188; see also Chapter 14 of this book). Giorgio Agamben asks 'Confronted with phenomena such as the power of the society of the spectacle that is everywhere transforming the political realm today, is it legitimate or even possible to hold subjective technologies and political techniques apart?' (Agamben 1998, 6).

CAMP

Propelled by globalization's accelerating *momenta*, the punitive self-disciplines of the pizza man's quotidian locale may be recalibrated within transnational carceral formations which are reinforcing the architectures of cross-border security networks. Just as the Americana of a Bay Ridge pizzeria provided the archetype for its shifting Ammani reflection, so too, the US Central Intelligence Agency's (CIA) geopolitical templates helped design its historical ally's secret police, Jordan's Mukhabarat, as an agent of the Cold War's bipolar worldmap (Kaplan and Ozernoy 2003) and regulator of the period's contentious decolonization processes.

Following coordinated attacks against the US on 9/11, the Mukhabarat, or General Intelligence Department (GID), reciprocated its American patron's largesse, providing services as proxy jailer for the CIA to support the George W. Bush administration's practice of 'extraordinary rendition'. A decentred policing technique foundational to control society, rendition consigned the detainee not to the juridical interiority of disciplinary society's sovereign prison, but to the so-called 'black site', an encrypted camp, wherein legal frameworks are suspended. Like the refugee camp, the black site is a spatial manifestation of the extrajuridical state of exception – in Agamben's words, a 'dislocating localization' or 'zone of indistinction between outside and inside' (Agamben 1998, 175, 170).

Transfers of US detainees to foreign custody permitted harsher interrogations than would be allowed under US law or the UN Convention on Torture (Priest 2004; HRW 2008). Political, economic and military reach assure US dominance in extraterritoriality, culminating a century-long legal trend of loosening geographic restraints to assert domestic law beyond sovereign borders (Raustiala 2006, 219, 248).

Exposed by journalistic reportage, the Ammani pizza man and his disaffected patron risked being conscripted among ghost detainees who populate the networked pizzeria's spatial doppelgänger, Jordan's black site matrix. The black site network's custodial practices are transforming existing carceral taxonomies. Handcuffs and leg-irons coerce the eighteenth century's disciplinary submissions; hoods censor the autobiographies and subjectivities of modernity's ghosts; anal plugs regulate the postmodern effluvia of quarantined bodies of denationalized Pakistanis, Georgians, Yemenis, Algerians, Saudis, Mauritanians, Syrians, Tunisians, Chechens, Libyans, Iraqis, Kuwaitis, Egyptians and Emirati (HRW 2008).

Transiting through a decentred urban matrix of networked legal lacunae – the non-places of civilian airport, military airbase and private airstrip – the disappearing subject sheds traces of encoded geodemographics as she is conveyed by elite globalization's aircraft of choice, the Gulfstream turbojet coveted by CEOs and celebrities (Priest 2004). Cruising under power of Rolls-Royce engines, the craft's enciphered vapour trails contaminate the jet streams of cross-border airline routes. The ghost detainee, no longer immobilized by the disciplinary city, is coerced into a forced migration across clandestine archipelagoes of the US's penal diaspora, recapitulating the black stages of exile along the lower stratosphere of counterterrorism's covert flyways. Agamben argues that extra-legal gulags and the states of exception they represent have become the twenty-first century's dominant political and spatial paradigm: 'The birth of the camp in our time appears as an event that decisively signals the political space of modernity itself' (Agamben 1998, 174).

The CIA and its proxy jailers collaborated in the production of black intelligence at one maximum-security enclave isolated in the barren landscapes of Jordan's remote, southern desert region: the GID's notorious Al Jafr Prison (Kaplan and Ozernoy 2003), built during the Cold War as a frequent destination of decolonization's dissidents. Satellite imagery reveals the site as an inscrutable glyph embedded in dun-coloured desert typography, mute colophon signalling a half-century's worth of untranscribable wails.

The Mukhabarat headquarters in Wadi Al-Sir conceals other urban metastases, grafted onto the periphery where the Western edge of Amman bleeds into dry riverbeds and a landscape of sanguine hills. The four-story detention centre's isolation cells sort ghost detainees by categorical branding, not due process of law (HRW 2008). These damaged goods are warehoused just blocks from the branded home decor stores and franchised food courts of fashionable Mecca Mall, where consumer desire is nourished by McDonald's, Pizza Hut, Starbucks and KFC (Al-Kurdi 2008). One mall tenant, the Body Shop, a worldwide chain of 2,200 toiletries stores, touts human and civil rights, and eschews animal testing during the distilling of its 'Milk Body Lotion' and 'Pink Grapefruit Body Butter' (Body Shop 2008). Minutes away from the fragrant emporium's lubricated patrons, biometrics which encode control society's docile body are being tested in an altogether dystopian body shop secreted in the GID detention centre's subterranean level. The Body Shop's signature 'Peppermint Cooling Foot Rescue Treatment' will provide no balm for victims of *falaqa* whippings, a form of torture targeting the soles of the feet while the immobilized subject is hung upside down in underground oubliettes, the forgotten spaces of inverted justice.

Like offsite plants that treat urban effluents, black sites provide a displaced infrastructure for regulation of the blackwater byproducts of urban securitization flows. Global cities investing in security architectures previously restricted to the inter-state scale are implicated in extrajuridical processing. Knowledge-based urban managers collude in the proxy interrogation of the ghost suspect, inflicting ordeals and pointed questions – when, where, how and by whom will the city be targeted? – whose distressed responses will be indicted by the discourses of urban database, geographic information systems (GIS) and watchlist.

Security discourses and practices constructed at the scale of national-state have been re-scaled for local policing among micro-processes which Saskia Sassen notes have begun to 'denationalize what had been constructed as national' (Sassen 2006, 223). After the 9/11 attacks, David Cohen, a former senior official of the CIA who had overseen its worldwide operations, was appointed as the New York Police Department's first Deputy Commissioner for Intelligence, tasked with 'enabling the NYPD to conduct its increasingly global law enforcement operations more effectively' (NYC 2002). The NYPD Intelligence and Counter Terror Divisions recruited officers with 'military, intelligence and diplomatic background' (Finnegan 2005), a trend consistent with Hardt and Negri's assertion that in control society, 'war is reduced to the status of police action' (Hardt and Negri 2001, p. 12).

The conventional limits of municipal jurisdiction have been exceeded by NYPD intelligence officers assigned to 'key international cities' – including Tel Aviv, London, Singapore, Santo Domingo, Toronto, Montreal, Paris, Lyons, Madrid and Amman – for information-sharing and coordination of counter-terror activities with host countries' police and intelligence agencies (NYC 2008). Utterances produced by the Mukhabarat's ghost sites will be decrypted by the Arabic-speaking NYPD sergeant assigned to Amman, and reconstituted in the NYPD Intelligence Division's maps of New York City neighbourhoods, which have redlined 'Significant Concentrations of Palestinians' – among other suspect enclaves (Finnegan 2005).

Linked through threatscape layers of geographic information systems, reconnaissance squads scope out the suspicious synchronicity of red and white tiles that link pizzerias in Bay Ridge and Amman. Captured in crosshairs of coordinated surveillance apparatuses, the pizza man dreaming of jihad and his *shaheedi* patron may soon be inducted into the watchlist – the database's discourse of 'pure writing' which, Mark Poster argues, 'reconfigures the constitution of the subject' (Poster 1996, 85).

MUSEUM

Only after displaying valid ID – being duly authenticated and purged of the threatening anonymity of modernity's observing subject – will a visitor be guided towards the barrel-vaulted galleries of New York City's Harbor

Figure 39.5 (Above) MUSEUM: The US Army Center of Military History valorizes the nation through exhibits of the Harbor Defense Museum at Fort Hamilton, the last active military base in New York City.

Defense Museum. Sequestered in a nineteenth-century fortress beneath the massive concrete anchorage of the Verrazano-Narrows Bridge, the small museum articulates its theories of state power at the southern margins of a paradigmatic urban sign of undisciplined mobility – Brooklyn's immigrant neighborhood of Bay Ridge.

Buffeted by salt sprays that gust off Lower New York Bay, the museum visitor thus legitimated is escorted to her destination by military police outfitted in the US Army Combat Uniform, whose digitized camouflage palette references next-generation warfare's operational environments: the green of woodlands, the grey of urban milieux and the desert's sand brown. Military police are deployed as gatekeepers of the Harbor Defense Museum's institutional sponsor, Fort Hamilton, which, as encoded uniforms, checkpointing procedures and onsite memorializations of state-sponsored violence suggest, is an active army base – the only such enclave remaining in metropolitan New York City.

The museum's information warfare of Hobbesian scripts, cartographies and militaria are housed in Fort Hamilton's granite caponier, a rare American example of a defensive structure, which spanned the historic fort's dry moat, linking the idealized geometries of its inner and outer works. Completed in 1831, the caponier was designed under supervision of a French military engineer trained in the tradition of Vauban, France's seventeenth-century theorist of fortifications. A specialist in the strategic hardening of cities and frontiers, Vauban engineered defences for the emerging system of sovereign national-states. A popular dictum held that a city fortified by Vauban was an impregnable city (Bornecque 1984, 13).

Fort Hamilton had prosecuted Vaubanian territoriality through strongpoint dominance during the nineteenth century, exploiting geographic control of the emblematic straits known as the Narrows, the strategic gateway to New York City's harbor. A mile-wide chokepoint at Fort Hamilton's edge, the Narrows delimited the complex tides and currents of Upper New York Bay's inner harbour from the Lower Bay, the outer harbour which flowed into the Atlantic shipping channels of the New York Bight and into the portolan charts of world trade beyond.

Maritime hues of azure and ultramarine are notably absent from the visual codes of Fort Hamilton's military police uniform, signalling the obsolescence of coastal forms of warfare commemorated in Harbor Defense Museum securitization discourses, which describe a port city at once threatened and enabled by the violence of premodern naval power. The defence of the Narrows had once privileged the site as a militarized gateway within the entrenched system of disciplinary enclosures that circumscribed urbanism's historic conception of the ordered city, a schema originating in the act of inclusion and exclusion which, Diken and Laustsen note (2002), distinguished the city's inside and sovereign subjects from its outside. Disciplinary enclosure was the 'sovereign act' which delimited urban order from exurban chaos and the domain of the outlaw beyond.

But, while Fort Hamilton's hardened chokepoint enforced sovereignty – nomadic fleets and the port city's maritime mobilities contested disciplinary enclosures and the rational authority of any urban masterplan. Overlaid feedback systems of ebbs, flows and infiltrations penetrated the coast's amphibious national frontier, an aqueous border ecology within which the city had evolved as a frontier town bridging imperial trade's aquatic and terrestrial networks. Fluid cosmopolitanisms percolated through the harbour city's fissured disciplinary walls, shaping Bay Ridge's working-class enclaves of one- and two-family rowhouses. In the twenty-first century, supply chain security and immigration controls are among interdictory regulators of the Port Authority of New York and New Jersey's jurisdictional zone of over 720 piers, three airports and the nation's most active bus terminal. The scope of the Port Authority's control over the special trade zone and intermodal nexus is circumscribed by the geometry of a 25-mile radius centred on the Upper Harbor's illuminated icon of the benevolent national-state, that presumptive enabler of global labour flows, the copper-sheathed beacon of the Statue of Liberty.

The nineteenth-century granite fort which houses Fort Hamilton's Harbor Defense Museum has been preserved as an historical artifact within the twentieth-century fort's suburbanized field of emerald lawns, whose low-rise structures service the garrison's programmatic needs of housing, administration and recruitment, as well as its support of expeditionary operations. The suburbanized fort's inverted figure-ground diagram reversed the taboos of military history's impenetrable city walls, which as David Grahame Shane reminds us, delimited urbanism's classic distinction between city and country (Shane 2005, 19).

Fort Hamilton's suburban inversions reflect the evolution of defence paradigms which abandoned naval technologies for World War II's anti-aircraft batteries and the Cold War's Nike missile emplacements. The twenty-first-century inversions of the fort's generic camp typology extend to its lightweight, industrial perimeter of translucent chain link fencing, whose ostensible transparency is effectively denied by overhead crenellations of looping razor wire, which invoke the primitive ordeals of flailed flesh and the modern concentration camp's conditions of bare life.

ID verification protocols negotiated by Fort Hamilton's military police at the monumental base of the Verrazano-Narrows Bridge help regulate flows within the modern fort's diagram of suburban diffusion, interdictions linked to the more extreme spatial displacements of its expeditionary operations on foreign soil, which include processing troops deploying to Iraq. Sanctioned by state-centric security discourses which sacralize the politics of 'national ethnos' (Appadurai 2006, 8), renewed tests of citizenship confirm the identification of citizenship with residence in territorial space as the national-state's central fact of political identity (Agnew and Corbridge 1995, 85).

CHECKPOINT

Checkpointing technologies challenge the cosmopolitan city's irrational nomads, whose mobilities destabilize the national-state's sovereign correlation between state borders, national boundaries and citizen loyalties (Schultz 2003; Nakashima 2008). New statistical tools and informational processes are 'anti-nomadic techniques' (Foucault 1995, 218) which supersede the percussive apparatus of disciplinary baton and riot shield – mobilizing the watchlist as new warden of the wall-less detention centre. Authenticated by password, algorithm and biometric detail – statistical instruments and information infrastructures reinforce the checkpoint's confrontational strategies, rendering the inspected body increasingly docile (Deleuze 1992; Lyon 2005, 52).

ID verifications are among flow regulating technologies wired within the US military's interoperable architecture for command, control, communications, computers, intelligence, surveillance and reconnaissance capabilities (C4ISR) (US DoD 1998). The consolidation of multiple systems into an interoperable whole produces the 'surveillant assemblage' (Haggerty and Ericson 2000), a visualizing device which will provide full-spectrum dominance of globalization's dispersed postmodern battlespace. Stephen Graham has

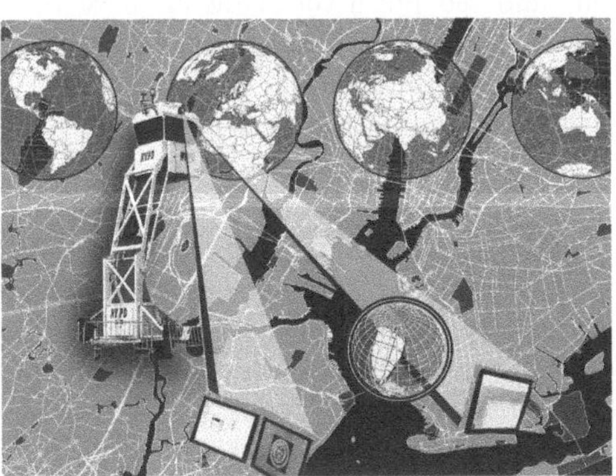

Figure 39.6 (Above) CHECKPOINT: Urban checkpoints deploy new information architectures to render the inspected body increasingly docile.

noted that such militarized technologies and practices have infiltrated civil policing: 'As part of the growth of neoliberal policy, many states have been militarizing their systems of criminal justice, law enforcement, and public space regulation, bringing the weapons, doctrines, and technologies of war to the streets of cities and the borders of nations' (Graham 2007, 17). These transfers conform with Hardt and Negri's assertion that: 'In addition to being a political power against all external political powers, a state against all other states, sovereignty is also a police power' (Hardt and Negri 2001, 87). Facilitated by new technologies and practices refined in the militarized context of expeditionary operations, the NYPD's 68th Precinct in Bay Ridge asserts its global awareness, obliquely announcing on its public website that 'over recent years there has been a significant influx of people of Middle-Eastern and Asian descent into the area' (NYC 2009).

The surveillant assemblage of command and control architectures provides a militarized prototype for urban policing in the era of global flow, interrogating citizenship to assess deviance along harbour-front streets of one of the networked city's key diasporic enclaves – Bay Ridge's long-established Arab neighbourhoods. Middle Eastern bakeries, halal butchers, Egyptian restaurants, storefront mosques, Islamic bookstores and sheesha cafés furnished with gold hookahs and red plush-velvet divans have been inserted into existing structures of Brooklyn's low-rise street armature, articulating hybrid patches of immigrant desire within a post-colonial assemblage of Palestinian, Lebanese, Syrian, Egyptian and Yemeni immigrants and asylum seekers. Street walls compress new data into archeological strata that document pre-existing ethnicity – including the façades of Gino's, Nino's, Rocco's and Vesuvio – pizzerias whose memorial signage recalls earlier generations of immigrant inflow and artisanal recipes, long-since legitimized through naturalization and franchising.

Numbered streets and avenues capture the neighbourhood's subordination to the grid. Instead of the densely verticalized development of the Manhattan's iconic skyscrapers, the Verrazano-Narrows Suspension Bridge, the nation's longest, provides a monumental sign of horizontal mobility, a corridor which promises expansive opportunities linking the working and middle class neighbourhood of two- and three-storey wood-frame and masonry units with the diffused suburban landscapes of Staten Island and the northeastern megalopolis which lies beyond.

Militarized policing refines boundary maintenance processes (Barth 1969, 38) which target immigrants who continue to settle in Bay Ridge just beyond Fort Hamilton's hardened perimeter. Bounded to its west by the harbour's vagaries of world trade, Bay Ridge is sheared off from the rest of Brooklyn to the east by the thrumming concrete ribbons of Robert Moses' masterplanned Gowanus Expressway, incorporated into the Interstate highway system as I-278. Bay Ridge has been carved by successive waves of urbanization into an arrowhead-shaped fragment whose fine-grained, local insularity is pierced by immigrant journeys. Home first to Scandinavian sailors, then successions of immigrant Irish, Italian, Greek, Russian and Chinese, its population includes New York City's largest Arab community, both Muslim and Christian, one of the oldest in the US (Bayoumi 2008, 8), helping make Brooklyn the country's largest Muslim enclave (Sheikh 2004; Al-Oraibi 2005).

Deterritorialized attachments to estranged homelands cycle through checkpoints, borders, jurisdictions and horizons that separate Bay Ridge's pizzerias from those of faraway Amman, Sanaa and Ramallah – global connectivities sustained by communications technologies, new media and low-cost international phone-cards, which promote reconciliation with the rapidly urbanizing global periphery. Nearby international airports promise two-way travel flows. They reverse the one-way directionality of earlier immigrant trajectories, which decanted from the tenements of New York's centric metropolis into the suburbs of the American dream, exfiltrating through the heroic portals of the Verrazano-Narrows Bridge into the dispersed postwar urbanized continuum that unfolds between Boston and Washington, DC.

Validated by Harbor Defense Museum narratives, ID checkpoints attempt to denaturalize the persistent ancestral voices of Gaza, Damascus, Cairo and Amman, which, having bypassed the coercions of mandate, protectorate, national border and city wall, have infiltrated translocal processes and identities, inscribing new homeland geographies within fractured postcolonial imaginaries. Pizzeria culture evades hegemony's foot soldiers, who enforce interdictory architectures of checkpoint and watchlist, suppressing the fluid cartographies of refugee camp, diaspora and jihad – the dispersals denoted by *al-shatat*, the absent homeland invoked by *al-ghurba*, the metaphysics of return and *al awda*, the spaces of peace and war delimited by *dar el Salam* and *dar el Harb* (Schultz 2003, 20).

That the disciplines of New York City's Vaubanized defences had been superseded by the efficiencies of globalization's inexorable mobilities was confirmed the morning of September 11, 2001, when air traffic controllers at nearby Newark Airport reported an aircraft had breached the Narrows – overflying the straits and the Verrazano-Narrows Bridge to penetrate vulnerable airspace of the Upper Bay (Brokaw 2006).

The nineteenth century's iron ship-barrier chains would not have restrained these cross-boundary raiders. Propelled with a ballistic momentum of 545 miles per hour, the commandeered craft would be crashed into the eightieth floor of the South Tower of the Port Authority's flagship property, Manhattan's World Trade Center, triggering the explosive incineration of 10,000 gallons

Figure 39.7 (Below) WATCHTOWER: Brooklyn's Metropolitan Detention Center enforces cross-border watch lists.

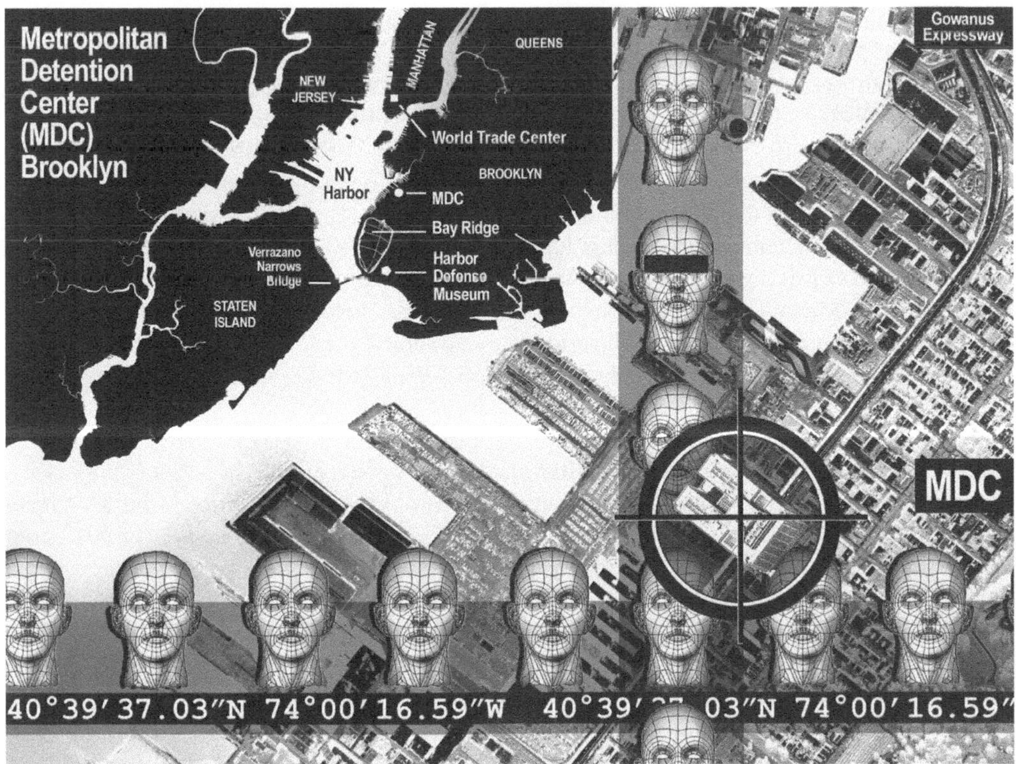

of jet fuel, a massive fireball which helped precipitate the collapse of the harbour's emblematic colossus, followed by that of its doomed twin. The concussive events, communicated to a global audience in mediated televisual real-time and celebrated by cross-border insurgent chatter, were witnessed in stunned, polyglot silence by Bay Ridge's recreational fishermen – South Asians, Russians, Latinos and Orthodox Jews angling for snapper, fluke, porgies and bluefish from the end of the pier which projects 69th Street out into the harbour from the northern magins of the neighbourhood's shore-front esplanade.

Inside the Harbour Defense Museum galleries, a single colour photograph documents the day – immobilizing a brief nanosecond within the slow-motion calculus of the de-architectonic process. The glossy photo provides a vanishing backdrop for gritty testimony retrieved from the attack site: the display case's votive relic – a cannonball-sized, cementitious mass of crushed grey debris, whose unidentifiable aggregates are shaped something like shards of shattered human bone.

WATCHTOWER

The breaching of the port city's disciplinary defences, registered in the destruction of the Port Authority's monumental obelisks, had targeted their hieroglyphic discourses and practices of neo-liberal trade. Following the insurgent sabotage, state power, invested in the flowing goods and bads of the neo-liberal system, mobilized control society's interdictory architectures. One such interdiction machine, Brooklyn's Metropolitan Detention Center (MDC), was activated in the ageing industrial waterfront just beyond Bay Ridge's northern margin. A vaguely corporate, thirteen-storey fortress of grey cast-in-place concrete built in 1996, the structure housed a 1,000-bed facility of the US Department of Justice's Federal Bureau of Prisons. Squeezed between the pier system to its west, and the arterial flows of Interstate-278's Gowanus Expressway to its east, the MDC overlooked lanes of south-bound traffic that were minutes from surging across the double decks of the Verrazano-Narrows Bridge into regional-scale transportation networks.

Paralleling New York Harbor's Gowanus Bay and the navigable forty-foot depth of its Bay Ridge Channel, the intermodal coastal zone of loft buildings, storage warehouses, rotting piers and railway tracks had almost been abandoned along with waterfront jobs lost in the 1960s and 1970s (Chait 2007, 32). But Bay Ridge's northern neighbour had perservered as an immigrant gateway with roots in the maritime working class of stevedore, longshoreman and stowaway, whose processing of cargo linked it to the dispersed geography of global trade's world labour markets.

A façade of vertical slit windows confirmed the carceral role of the Metropolitan Detention Center's harbour-front fortress on 29th Street, promoting a coerced visibility which recalled the panopticisms of the vestigial waterfront's manufactory floors. The MDC was a waterfront warehouse displaced from the heroic civic architecture of downtown Brooklyn's courthouse complex. In the months following 9/11, the MDC would exceed the carceral functions established by the traditions of penal law, which had produced both Brooklyn's courthouse enclave and modernity's disciplinary city.

In coordination with securitization infrastructures which enabled the neo-liberal restructuring of its failing waterfront, the post-9/11 MDC would be transformed from warehouse into a machine for extra-juridical sorting. Authorized by control society's exceptional regulatory practices, the Brooklyn MDC trafficked in the human byproducts of neo-liberalism's harbour-front processes. The detention centre negotiated human cargo flows, demanding custody of the mobile alien whose cross-border breaches were being reclassified as a risk to sovereignty's enclosures. Underwritten by the juridical exceptions of the George W. Bush administration's declaration of a post-9/11 state of emergency, the sorting of ghost nomads consigned to the waterfront detention centre transformed its disciplinary architecture into a provisional black site and urban analogue of the refugee internment camp.

Such securitizations were intended to mitigate urban vulnerabilites which, Timothy Luke points out, are integral to liberal capitalist democracies, economies and societies, where a 'culture of *liberal amicality* underpins codices of governmentality, and their structuring of population, territoriality, and sovereignty' (Luke 2007, 124). Interdictions and internments interrupt the inimical exploitation of an amicality built into spatial practices that mobilize material for economic production, as interdictory machines interrupt the bodies, machines and goods that flow through the ensembles of big systems and urban technostructures.

Building upon Cold War era discourses profiling the decolonizing Third World as an inimical region of political instability, the MDC's interdictory processes were supported by tropes that would condemn neighbouring Bay Ridge's hybrid urbanism as a malign example of 'the South within the North', echoing the indictment of the global South expressed through the rhetoric of the clash of civilizations (Taylor and Jasparo 2004, 220). The global South was 'disconnected' (Barnett 2004, 8), 'a worldwide zone of revolution' (Hobsbawm 1996, 434), a zone of feral, failed cities (Davis 2007 [2006], 205). Stephen Graham has reported that the US Army's new 'Revolution in Military Affairs'(RMA), in particular, has problematized global South urbanization (Graham 2006, 247). This problematization confirms the North–South rift anticipated by the maps of neighbouring Bay Ridge's Harbor Defense Museum, which tracked a premodern world system that privileged European empire and metropolis – within whose bounded cores could be discerned spectral reflections of the invisible cities of the punished colonial margin.

Like Jordan's extraterritorial black sites at Al Jafr and Wadi Al-Sir – the Brooklyn MDC produced extrajuridical space to validate state power's declaration of emergency. A Bay Ridge family of Syrian descent was rousted during the night in February 2002 by a squad of fifteen armed law-enforcement officers, detained in the MDC for months, but never charged (Bayoumi 2008, 21). The family was among MDC detainees culled from over 1,200 South Asian and Arab individuals arrested in mass sweeps throughout the US in the months following 9/11, some turned in by neighbours. Of 762 non-citizens retained on the custody list, sixty percent were from the New York City area (US DoJ 2003). Almost all would be expelled to their home countries (Sachs 2002). Some 82,000 Arab and Muslim men obligingly came forward in 2003 to register at the urging of immigration authorities. More than 13,000 went on to face deportation (Swarns 2003).

Sweeps, detentions, deportations and renditions are seminal practices of political displacement within the extraterritorial geographies inscribed in both Brooklyn and Amman – emerging logistics of control society's transnational carceral apparatus. Like ghost detainees of Jordan's black sites, the identities of so-called 'September 11 Detainees' – non-citizens deemed 'persons of high interest' held without charges at Brooklyn's MDC – were kept secret, citing the state of emergency's 'special factors' (Bernstein 2006). An Egyptian detainee testified: 'Worse than physical or verbal abuse was the feeling that we are being hidden from the outside world, and nobody knows in the outside world that we are arrested and in this place' (Bernstein 2006).

With basic rights suspended, detainees were confined to maximum security isolation cells twenty-three hours a day in a special unit with 'the highest level of restrictive detention' (Goodman 2005). Handcuffs and leg-irons linked by a restrictively short length of heavy Martin chain restrained individuals during interviews conducted within an interior architecture of reinforced iron grillwork, chainlink fencing and clear partitions (US DoJ 2003). Regulations exceeded the merely disciplinary, as surveillant apparatuses optimized statistical tools to produce docile bodies. Stationary security cameras recorded detainees within cells, while hand-held video cameras documented their movement without, when they were escorted through the premises in the grip of the required 'four-man hold restraint'.

One so-named 'multipurpose room' illuminated by standard fluorescent ceiling fixtures and furnished with a reclining medical exam chair sheathed in disposable sanitary paper, was used for 'medical examinations, strip searches, recreation, and individual meetings' (US DoJ 2003). Leisure society's recreational gambits provided an unlikely programmatic addendum to routine strip searches and invasive body cavity inspections, which stripped the value of the MDC's abandoned subjects, reducing them to the exclusions Agamben has referred to as 'bare life' – the condition symptomatic of the modern camp (Agamben 1998, 7).

Responding to detainee lawsuits subsequently filed by civil liberties activists, a US Justice Department investigation found in 2003 'systemic problems with immigrant detentions and widespread abuse' at the MDC. Acknowledging the constitutional contradictions inherent in the state of exception, the Justice Department's Inspector General issued recommendations to prevent 'unnecessary detentions and abuses of noncitizens in the event of a new national emergency' (US DoJ 2003; Bernstein 2006).

The MDC offers a compressed example of regulatory architectures whose logics of exception are being diffused throughout the fabric of the unbounded city through the deployment of deterritorialized assemblages. David Lyon asserts that the city's dense web of information networks – including those generated by city planning, marketing or community policing – makes it a crucial surveillance site (Lyon 2005, 49). Surveillant systems shape risk society's actuarial justice, intervening against norms for social and spatial justice, reproducing the space of the camp within the postmodern city. William Bogard notes that 'post-panoptic surveillance assemblages have evolved deterritorialized controls that radically subvert the movement to free societies' (Bogard 2006, 101).

The boundaries of the camp city will be inscribed through databasing algorithms which structure defensive urbanism throughout the de-bounded risks of 'world risk society' (Beck 2002, 39) – superseding architectural designs for the twentieth century's city of defensible space (Newman 1972). The camp city's census will be annotated through codes and passwords of databases which comingle categories of local, national and transnational – producing a new typology of state-managed, differentiated urban population which will be targeted for intervention through the watchlist. Docile bodies which populate the watchlist will be abstracted from the territorial setting of command cities and their peripheries into 'data-double' flows which fragment personal histories into disembodied biometric identifiers (Bigo 2006; Bogard 2006; Lyon 2006; Haggerty and Ericson 2000). Fingerprints, palm prints, iris prints and voice prints map a disjunctive choreography of bodily absence and loss. Reconstituted through the forensic interventions of passport, visa, ID card and residence permit, fractured identities emerge as new urban fictions.

Such post-panoptic effects are internalized through the immanence of the undercover informant, control society's deterritorialized enforcer, who inspires the 'familiar fear' that links Bay Ridge's residents to the totalitarianism of their countries of origin 'where informers for the security services were common and political freedoms curtailed' (Elliott 2006). A police informant of Egyptian descent frequented the Islamic Bookstore of Bay Ridge over a six-month period in 2004, inducing the young bookstore clerk, an illegal immigrant from Pakistan, into acts of political speech and planning that resulted in his arrest on terrorism charges and a thirty-year prison sentence (US DoJ 2007). Control society's paradigmatic self-regulation is in effect. A restaurateur reports 'After September 11, everyone stopped talking' (Rappleye 2008). The local Arab-American

Figure 39.8 (Above) WHITE CITY: Diasporic desire links Jordan's urban refugee camps with New York City's immigrant enclaves.

newspaper documents an 'endemic mistrust of the police and fears of reprisals' (Millard and Faisal 2008). The internalization of the sovereign gaze produces urban effects, transforming the public sphere, collapsing inside and outside: 'Some people stopped attending the neighborhood's two major mosques, preferring to pray at home. Others no longer idle on the street after work' (Elliott 2006).

Watchlisting the diaspora generates a regulatory architecture for the urban camp, inscribing the first narrative of the new extraterritorial, whose extrajuridical algorithms refine thresholds between inside and outside, between norm and exception, marking boundaries between normal and abnormal populations. Neo-liberal reductions and privatization of public space and the public sphere have found their ultimate antipodal state in the security city's camp, where the agora is being sucked into the black hole of its own negation – an inverted, extrajuridical black site of data-doubles and inaccessible public space modelled and encrypted by the state.

WHITE CITY

Incandescent white limestone clads Amman's architectural façades, linking Jordan's capital city to a regional geology whose tectonics, at the boundary of migrating African and Arabian plates, have also produced the Dead Sea rift. Detritus of long-evaporated seas, white sedimentary stone is embedded with shells of once-mobile marine life, calcified amidst disseminations of flint, silt and desert sand. Great blocks are quarried in seismic zones of Ma'an, 'Ajlun, Irbid and al-Azraq – only to be further split, sawed, chiseled, hammered, sand-blasted, flamed or polished to reveal their pelagic legacy – yielding textures and patterns which will be integrated into the capital city's masonry austerity (Shaer 2000). White veneers mask turbulent geologic origins just as they camouflage the political fault lines which have splintered Amman's urbanization since its emergence in 1920 as capital of Transjordania.

Built upon a distinctive topography of hills – *jabals* – and the deeply incised *wadis* of interstitial dry riverbeds, Amman's limestone clad equanimity earned it the sobriquet 'The White City'. The idealization provided continuity and a city theory to the layered archeology of Roman, Byzantine, Islamic and Ottoman masonry fragments until 1948, when the historic city of dressed stone was suddenly infiltrated by modernist settlements of wind-swept, utilitarian fabric. These were not the ecologically integrated tents of black goat-hair crafted by the region's mobile, desert-dwelling Bedu. Rather, the prefabricated structures of industrial canvas had been stitched together to shelter involuntary nomads of a postcolonial migration – the *al-Nakba*, or 'catastrophe', of 1948, when an estimated 100,000 Palestinians flowed into Jordan after being displaced from ancestral lands, followed by an additional 380,000 after the 1967 War (UNRWA 2008).

As the conflict-generated diaspora became seemingly irreversible, the transitional canvas shelters of tent cities were supplanted by the refugee camp's ad hoc urbanism of galvanized steel, aluminium, asbestos and cement – all linked by a pilgrim's peripatetic syntax of interconnected staircases built into steep hillsides, recalling Zygmunt Bauman's acknowledgement that the stateless refugee's journey is never completed (2007, 32).

The twenty-first century's urban camps are almost indistinguishable from low-income quarters of the city (McDonough 2003). But although Amman's urbanization has been driven by processes of refugee influx and resettlement (Gilen et al. 1994), camps have not become fully integrated into the White City of iconic stone. No explicit walls demarcate the city from Jabal al-Hussein camp, which crowns one of Amman's three original hills. But its exclusion from the architectural lingua franca of white limestone reflects the political ambiguities of placeless diaspora and the 'included exclusions' Agamben cites as immanent to modernity (Agamben 1998, 7).

Jordan granted Palestinian refugees citizenship in the 1950s – the only Arab country to do so. Many have left the camps and been assimilated into Jordanian society. But nominal citizenship has not insured loyalty to the state or rescinded refugee status (Al Abed 2004). Neighbourhoods grouped according to the inhabitants' Palestinian village of origin continue to provide a mnemonic armature for the internal organization of camps (Bokae'e 2003, 7). While this segregation for a time prevented political action under a unified identity (Talhami 2003), the fragmented urban geography served to construct a compensatory cartography of ancestral homeland, the names of whose abandoned villages had long since been erased from modern maps (Newman 2006, 20).

Failure to settle the Palestine question after 1967 had radicalized the camps as strongholds of stateless insurgency. By 1970, a guerrilla urbanism of proprietary visa controls, customs checks and checkpoints was installed, as the archipelago of politicized camps challenged what was perceived as a repressive territorial state. Guerrillas would be expelled from the kingdom by early 1971, but not before the violence of Black September 1970, which left thousands dead in Amman and its urban camps (Raab 2007, 168).

Unresolved urban pathologies and chronic unemployment would drive many of Jordan's Palestinians into the new economic diasporas of global labour flows, as they relocated from refugee camps to foreign worker enclaves in the Gulf States, Europe and the US (BADIL 2008) – including diasporic neighbourhoods like Bay Ridge, Brooklyn – from where earnings could be remitted to families left behind. Frequently assessed as a security risk, Palestinians have been rejected in favour of more compliant foreign workers (McDonough 2003; Feiler 1994; ArabicNews 2005). Terrence Lyons has noted that 'diaspora remittances are key resources to a conflict and often sustain parties engaged in civil war' (Lyons 2006, 111). Some 200,000 Jordanians and 150,000 Palestinians were expelled from states of the Gulf Cooperation Council during the second Gulf War (ArabicNews 2005). In New York City, the NYPD Intelligence Division has red-lined the Palestinian presence on its neighbourhood maps.

CITTÀ APERTA

The pizza man had left Amman for Bay Ridge only to return years later bearing the culinary and architectural codes of the pizza-making commons. It is not clear whether his return to Amman had been voluntary. Had he been detained at the Metropolitan Detention Center after 9/11 among other Bay Ridge residents, and deported in a forced migration from Brooklyn's black site to the White City's exclusions? The would-be jihadi risked being displaced once again, propelled into the clandestine flows of Jordan's own extra-territorial gulags, recapitulating his itinerary through the architecture of the commons, spectacle, camp, museum, checkpoint, watch-tower and White City.

The Mukhabarat's surveillant assemblages had been mobilized in November 2005 after three of Amman's luxury hotels were targeted by deadly suicide bombings – attacks perpetrated by Iraqis linked to Al-Qaeda in Mesopotamia who had infiltrated Jordan using counterfeit passports. The attacks were symptoms of profound urban impacts experienced throughout the White City after up to a million displaced Iraqis flowed into Jordan, escaping violent consequences of the US invasion of 2003 (Shahbazi 2007; AI 2008; Beehner 2007). The settlement patterns of Iraqi exiles diverged from those that followed population displacements in 1948 and 1967, when refugee camps were established to absorb Palestinians who became Jordan's majority population. Iraqis infiltrated existing fabric throughout the stratified city, producing a more diffuse enclaving of vaguely defined exilic boundaries and socio-economic mixings, a debounding of risk which provoked control society's regulatory infrastructures, reproducing the conditions of the refugee camp within the city of incandescent stone.

Sequestered in the networked pizzeria which is neither inside nor outside, the diasporic restaurateur and his disaffected patron are negotiating new political performances. Their audiences will participate from myriad sites of the dispersed global commons. Apprentice pizza men include Chinese Muslims from the Uighur ethnic minority released from the US black site at Guantanamo, Cuba, after four and a half years of unwarranted internment. Granted political asylum by Albania, the Uighurs are receiving government-sponsored vocational training as pizza-makers. Television news has shown the released detainees behind the counter of a halal takeout shop in Tirana, kneading dough and baking pizza (*European Journal* 2009).

Meanwhile, clandestine informants continue to infiltrate the networked spaces of the global commons, preparing classified reviews of political performances. They order pizza as they annotate their watchlists, encrypting the passenger manifests which will be tracking one-way transit from diaspora to black site. Escaping the detritus of imperial metropolis and Cold War megalopolis, the nomadic architect responds, plotting common lines of flight past spectacle, camp, museum, checkpoint and watchtower. Navigating the *città aperta*'s provisional interregnum, the architect charts a new geography of the open city.

Section 8 Bibliography

Agamben, Giorgio (1998) *Homo Sacer: Sovereign Power and Bare Life*. Stanford: Stanford University Press.

Agnew, John and Stuart Corbridge (1995) *Mastering Space: Hegemony, Territory and International Political Economy*. London: Routledge.

AI (2008) *Iraq – Rhetoric and Reality: The Iraqi Refugee Crisis*. Report by Amnesty International, June 15. www.amnesty.org/en/library/. Accessed June 29, 2008.

Al Abed, Oroub (2004) *Palestinian Refugees in Jordan*, Report by Forced Migration Online, February. www.forcedmigration.org/guides/fmo025/. Accessed June 25, 2008.

Al-Kurdi (2008) *About Mecca Mall*. Al Kurdi Real-Estate Group website. www.meccamall.jo/about-mecca-mall. Accessed June 29, 2008.

AlSayyad, Nezar and Ananya Roy (eds.) (2004) *Urban Informality: Perspectives from the Middle East, Latin America and South Asia*. Lanham and London: Lexington Books.

Al-Oraibi, Mina (2005) 'The recovery of New York's muslim community from 9/11', *Asharq Alawsat*, December 17. http://aawsat.com/english/news.asp?section=3&id=3083. Accessed May 17, 2008.

Amin, Ash and Nigel Thrift (2002) *Cities: Reimagining the Urban*. Cambridge: Polity Press.

Appadurai, Arjun (1996) *Modernity at Large: Cultural Dimensions of Globalization*. Minneapolis: University of Minnesota Press.

—— (2000) 'Spectral housing and urban cleansing: notes on millennial Mumbai', *Public Culture* 12(3): 627–651.

—— (2002) 'Urban governmentality and the horizon of politics', *Public Culture* 14(1): 21–47.

—— (2006) *Fear of Small Numbers: An Essay on the Geography of Anger*. Durham: Duke University Press.

Appleyard, David, Kevin Lynch and John R. Myer, (1963) *The View from the Road*. Cambridge, MA: MIT Press.

ArabicNews (2005) '$30 billion in remittance annually by foreign workers in the Gulf states', *Arabicnews.com*. September 23. www.arabicnews.com/ansub/daily/day/050923/2005092321.html. Accessed July 3, 2008.

Ardigò, Achille (1967) *La Diffusione Urbana*. Roma: Ave-An Veritas Ed.

Aymonino, Carlo (1964) 'La Città Territorio', in AAVV, *La Città Territorio*. Bari: Leonardo A Vinci Editore.

—— (1978) *Origini e Sviluppo della Città Moderna*. Venezia: Marsilio.

BADIL (2008) *Statistics: Population*. BADIL Resource Center For Palestinian Residency & Refugee Rights. www.badil.org/statistics/statistics.htm. Accessed July 5, 2008.

Bagnasco, Arnaldo (1977) *Tre Italie. La Problematica Territoriale Dello Sviluppo Urbano*. Bologna: Il Mulino.

Banham, Reyner (1971) *Los Angeles: The Architecture Of Four Ecologies*. London: Penguin.

—— (1976) *Megastructures: Urban Futures of the Recent Past*. New York: Harper & Row.

Barattucci, Chiara (2004) *Urbanizzazioni Disperse. Interpretazioni e Azioni in Francia e in Italia, 1950–2000*. Roma: Officina Edizioni.

Barnett, Thomas P. (2004) *The Pentagon's New Map*. New York: G.P. Putnam's Sons.

Barth, Frederik (1969) *Ethnic Groups and Boundaries: The Social Organization of Culture Difference*. Boston: Little, Brown.

Barthes, Roland (2002) *Comment vivre ensemble. Simulations romanesques de quelques espaces quotidiens*. Notes de cours et de seminaries au Collège de France, 1976–1977. Paris: Seuil IMEC.

Bauman, Zygmunt (2007) 'Archipelago of exceptions', *Urbanitats* 18: 23–58.

Bayoumi, Moustafa (2008) *How Does It Feel to Be a Problem? Being Young and Arab in America*. New York: Penguin.

Beck, Ulrich (2002) 'The terrorist threat: World risk society revisited', *Theory, Culture And Society* 19(4): 39–55.

Beehner, Lionel (2007) 'Iraq's refugees in waiting', CFR.Org, Council On Foreign Relations, 2 April. www.cfr.org/publication/12967/iraqs_refugees_in_waiting.html. Accessed 29 June, 2008.

Benjamin, Solomon (2005) 'Touts, pirates and ghosts', Sarai Reader 05: 'Bare acts', www.sarai.net/publications/readers/05-bare-acts/. Accessed March 20, 2009.

—— (2007) 'Occupancy Urbanism: Ten Theses' In *Sarai* Reader 2007: Frontiers, 538–563.

—— (2008) 'Occupancy urbanism: ten theses', Sarai Reader 07: 'Frontiers' 538, www.sarai.net/publications/readers/07-frontiers/. Accessed March 20, 2009.

Berman, Marshall (1982) *All that Is Solid Melts into Air: The Experience of Modernity*. New York: Simon & Schuster.

Bernstein, Nina (2006). 'Held in 9/11 net, muslims return to accuse US', *The New York Times*, January 23.

Bianchetti, Cristina (ed.) (2004) *Territori Sempre Più Simili, Piano Progetto Città* 22–23.

—— (2008) *Urbanistica e Sfera Pubblica*. Roma: Donzelli Editore.

Bigo, Didier (2006) 'Security, exception, ban and surveillance', in D. Lyon (ed.) *Theorizing Surveillance: The Panopticon and Beyond*. Cullompton: Willan Publishing.

Body Shop (2008) *About Us*. Body Shop website. www.thebodyshop.com. Accessed August 6, 2008.

Boeri, Stefano, Arturo Lanzani and Edoardo Marini (1993) *Il Territorio Che Cambia*. Milano: Editrice Abitare Segesta.

Bogard, William (2006) 'Surveillance assemblages and lines of flight', in D.Lyon (ed.) *Theorizing Surveillance: The Panopticon and Beyond*. Cullompton: Willan Publishing.

Bokae'e, Nihad (2003) 'Palestinian internally displaced persons inside Israel: challenging the solid structures', Bethlehem: BADIL Resource Center for Palestinian Residency and Refugee Rights,www.badil.org/publications/monographs/palestinian.IDPs.pdf. Accessed July 10, 2008.

Bornecque, Robert (1984) *La France de Vauban*. Paris: Arthaud.

Brokaw, Tom (2006) 'The skies over America: the air traffic controllers on 9/11 saw the nightmare coming', NBCNews.Com, September 9. www.msnbc.msn.com/id/14754701/. Accessed June 17, 2008.

Buchanan, Colin (1963) *Traffic in Towns. A Study of the Long Term Problems of Traffic in Urban Areas*. Reports of the Steering Group and Working Group Appointed by the Minister of Transport, Her Majesty's Stationery Office, London.

Cacciari, Massimo (1997) *L'arcipelago*. Milano: Adelphi.

Cairns, Stephen (ed) (2003) *Drifting: Architecture and Migrancy*. London: Routledge.

Canclini, Néstor García (2008) 'Mexico City 2010: improvising globalization', in Andreas Huyssen (ed.) *Other Cities, Other Worlds: Urban Imaginaries in a Globalizing Age*. Durham: Duke University Press.

Canguilhem, George (1991) *The Normal and Pathological*. New York: Zone Books.

Castells, Manuel (1999) *The Culture of Cities in the Information Age*, Lecture at the Buell Center for American Architecture, Columbia University Graduate School of Architecture, Planning and Preservation.

Chait, Jocelyne (2007) *New Connections/New Opportunities: Sunset Park 197-A Plan*. Report by Brooklyn Community Board 7, June. www.lostinbrooklyn.com/bklyncb7/197a/pdf/bklyncb7_197a_entire.pdf. Accessed August 1, 2008.

Chakrabarty, Dipesh (2000) *Provincializing Europe: Postcolonial Thought and Historical Difference*. Princeton: Princeton University Press.

Chapuis, Jean Yves (2003) 'De la ville historique à la ville archipel', *Etudes Foncières* 105(September–October).

Chatterjee, Partha (2006) *The Politics of the Governed: Reflections on Popular Politics in Most of the World*. New York: Columbia University Press.

Choay, Francoise (1997 [1980]) *The Rule and the Model: On the Theory of Architecture and Urbanism*. Cambridge, MA: MIT Press. (Translation of *La règle et le modèle*.)

Clementi, Alberto, Giuseppe De Matteis and Pier Carlo Palermo (eds) (1996) *Le Forme Del Territorio Italiano*. Bari: Laterza.

Colomina, Beatriz (2007) *Domesticity at War*. Cambridge, MA: MIT Press.

Corboz, André (1997) *Ordine sparso*. Milano: Franco Angeli.

Cronon, William (1992) *Nature's Metropolis: Chicago and the Great West*. New York: W.W. Norton.

Cruz, Teddy (2005) Stirling Memorial Lecture 'Border postcards: chronicles from the edge', www.cca.qc.ca/en/education-and-events/259-teddy-cruz-border-postcards-chronicles-from-the-edge. Accessed December 13, 2008.

Davidson, Adam (2003) 'Loves Microsoft, hates America'. *The New York Times*, 9 March.

Davis, Mike (2007 [2006]) *Planet of Slums*. London: Verso.

De Boeck, Filip and Marie-Françoise Plissart (2005) *Kinshasa: Tales of the Invisible City*. Ghent: Ludion.

De Carlo, Giancarlo (ed.) (1966) *La Pianificazione Territoriale e Urbanistica Nell'area Milanese*. Padova: Marsilio.

de Certeau, Michel (1984 [1980]) *The Practice of Everyday Life*. Berkeley: University of California Press. (Translation of *Arts de faire*.)

Dehaene, Michiel and Lieven De Cauter (eds) (2008) *Heterotopia and the City: Public Space in a Post Civil Society*. London: Routledge.

Deleuze, Gilles (1992) 'Postscript on the societies of control', *October* 59 (Winter).

De Matteis, Giuseppe (ed.) (1992) *Il Fenomeno Urbano in Italia: Interpretazioni, Prospettive e Politiche*. Milano: Franco Angeli.

Dickinson, Robert (1964) *City and Region*. London: Routledge & Kegan Paul Ltd.

Diken, Bülent and Carsten B. Laustsen (2002) 'Zones of indistinction: security, terror, and bare life', *Space and Culture* 5(3): 290–307.

Ellin, Nan (1997) *Architecture of Fear*. New York: Princeton Architectural Press.

Elliott, Andrea (2006) 'Undercover work deepens police–muslim tensions', *The New York Times*, May 27, A1.

Enwezor, Okwui (2003) 'Terminal modernity: Rem Koolhaas' discourse on entropy', in V. Patteeuw (ed.) *What is OMA: Considering Rem Koolhaas and the Office for Metropolitan Architecture*. Rotterdam: NAi Publishers.

Ericson, Richard V. and Kevin D. Haggerty (1997) *Policing the Risk Society*. Toronto: University of Toronto Press.

Escobar, Arturo (1995) *Encountering Development: The Making and Unmaking of the Third World*. Princeton: Princeton University Press.

European Journal (2009) 'Albania: asylum for former Guantanamo inmates', Television broadcast *Deutsche Welle European Journal*, February 12. www.dwworld.de/dw/article/0,,3959733,00.html. Accessed January 25, 2009.

Evans, Robin (1995) *The Projective Cast*. Cambridge, MA: MIT Press.

Farish, Matthew (2007) 'Another anxious urbanism: simulating defense and disaster in Cold War America', in S. Graham (ed.) *Cities, War, and Terrorism: Towards an Urban Geopolitics* Malden: Blackwell Publishing, 93–109.

Feiler, Gil (1994) 'Creating jobs for the Palestinians', *Palestine–Israel Journal* 1(1) www.pij.org/details.php?id=1099. Accessed July 3, 2008.

Ferguson, James (1999) *Expectations of Modernity: Myths and Meanings of Urban Life on the Zambian Copperbelt*. Berkeley: University of California Press.

Finnegan, William (2005) 'The terrorism beat: how is the NYPD defending the city?', *The New Yorker*, July 25.

Fisher, Ian (2001) 'An exhibit on campus celebrates grisly deed', *The New York Times*, 26 September.

Foucault, Michel (1982) 'Space. Knowledge and Power'. *Skyline*, March.

—— (1995 [1975]) *Discipline & Punish: The Birth of the Prison*. New York: Vintage Books. (Translation of *Surveiller et punir: Naissance de la prison*.)

—— (2007 [1967]) 'Of other spaces', in Michiel Dehaene and Lieven De Cauter (eds) *Heterotopia and the City: Public Space in a Post Civil Society*. London: Routledge, 13–30.

Gandy, Matthew (2005) 'Learning from Lagos', *New Left Review* 33: 36–52.

Garreau, Joel (1991) *Edge City: Life on the New Frontier*. New York: Doubleday.

Geddes, Patrick (1915) *Cities in Evolution. An Introduction to the Town Planning Movement*. London: Williams and Norgate.

Gilen, Signe et al. (1994) *Finding Ways: Palestinian Coping Strategies in Changing Environments*, Fafo-Report 177, Oslo: Fafo Research Foundation. www.fafo.no/pub/177.htm. Accessed June 28, 2008.

Girardet, Herbert (2004) *Cities, People, Planet: Liveable Cities for a Sustainable World*. Hoboken: John Wiley & Sons.

Goodman, Amy (2005) 'Brooklyn's Abu Ghraib: detainees in post 9/11 sweep allege abuse in New York detention center', *Democracy Now*, March 1. www.democracynow.org/2005/3/1/brooklyns_abu_ghraib_detainees_in_post. Accessed August 11, 2008.

Gottmann, Jean (1961) *Megalopolis: The Urbanised Northeastern Seaboard of the United States*. New York: The Twentieth Century Fund.

—— (1987) *Megalopolis Revisited: 25 Years Later*, Institute for Urban Studies Mondograph Series. College Park: University of Maryland.

Graham, Stephen (2006) 'Surveillance, urbanization, and the US "revolution" in military affairs', in D. Lyon (ed.) *Theorizing Surveillance: The Panopticon and Beyond.* Cullompton: Willan Publishers, 247–269.

—— (2007) 'Cities, warfare and states of emergency', in *Cities, War and Terrorism: Towards an Urban Geopolitics.* Malden: Blackwell, 1–25.

Graham, Stephen and Simon Marvin (2001) *Splintering Urbanism.* New York: Routledge.

Gregotti, Vittorio (1963) *La Forma Del Territorio,* Monographic Issue of *Edilizia Moderna*, No. 87–88.

—— (1966) *Il Territorio Dell'architettura.* Milano: Feltrinelli.

Gutkind, Erwin Anton (1962) *The Twilight of Cities.* New York: Macmillan.

Haggerty, Kevin D. and Richard V. Ericson (2000) 'The surveillant assemblage', *British Journal of Sociology* 51(4): 605–622.

Hardt, Michael and Antonio Negri (2001) *Empire.* Cambridge, MA: Harvard University Press.

—— (2004) *Multitude: War and Democracy in the Age of Empire.* New York: Penguin.

Harvey, David (2006) 'The political economy of public space', in S. Low and N. Smith (eds) *The Politics of Public Space.* New York: Routledge.

Hobsbawm, Eric (1996) *The Age of Extremes: A History of the World, 1914–1991.* New York: Vintage.

Howard, Ebenezer (1905) *Garden Cities of Tomorrow.* London: Swann and Sonnenschein.

HRW (2008) 'Double jeopardy: CIA renditions to Jordan', *Human Rights Watch*, April 7. www.hrw.org/en/reports/2008/04/07/double-jeopardy-0ilses. Accessed August 7, 2008.

ILSES, Istituto Lombardo di Scienze Economiche e Sociali (1962), Relazioni del seminario *La nuova dimensione della città, la città-regione*, Proceeedings of the Symposium held in Stresa, Milan.

Indovina, Francesco (1990) *La Città Diffusa.* Dipartimento di Analisi Economica e Sociale del Territorio, Istituto Universitario di Architettura, Venezia.

Jacobs, Jane (1961) *Death and Life of Great American Cities.* New York: Modern Library.

Jewee (2007) 'Six years later', *YouTube*, 6 April. www.youtube.com/watch?v=jo09wnqrtpo. Accessed January 7, 2009.

Kaplan, David E. and Ilana Ozernoy (2003) 'Al Qaeda's Desert Inn. Hard time', *US News And World Report*, June 2.

Khilnani, Sunil (1998) *The Idea of India.* New York: Farrar, Strauss, and Giroux.

Koolhaas, Rem (1978) *Delirious New York.* London/New York: Oxford University Press.

Koolhaas, Rem, Sefano Boeri and Sanford Kwinter (2001) *Mutations.* Barcelona/New York: Actar.

Laquian, Aprodicio A. (2005) *Beyond Metropolis: The Planning and Governance of Asia's Mega-Urban Regions.* Baltimore: Johns Hopkins University Press.

Lefebvre, Henri (1991 [1974]) *The Production of Space.* Oxford: Blackwell. (Translation of *La production de l'espace.*)

Lévi-Strauss, Claude (1962) *La pensée sauvage.* Paris: Plon.

Lobsinger, Mary Lou (2006) 'The new urban scale in Italy', *Journal Of Architectural Education* No. 59.

Loeckx, André et al. (2004) (eds) *Urban Trialogues: Visions, Projects, Co-productions.* Nairobi: UN Habitat.

Luke, Timothy W. (2007) 'Everyday technics as extraordinary threats: urban technostructures and non-places in terrorist actions', in S. Graham (ed.) *Cities, War And Terrorism: Towards An Urban Geopolitics.* Malden: Blackwell, 120–140.

Lynch, Kevin (1981) *Good City Form.* Cambridge, MA: MIT Press.

Lyon, David (2005) *Surveillance Society: Monitoring Everyday Life.* Buckingham: Open University Press.

—— (2006) (ed.) *Theorizing Surveillance: The Panopticon and Beyond.* Cullompton: Willan Publishers.

Lyons, Terrence (2006) 'Diasporas and homeland conflict', in M. Kahler and B.F. Walter (eds) *Territoriality and Conflict in an Era of Globalization.* Cambridge: Cambridge University Press, 111–129.

Malfroy Sylvain (2002) '*Introduction to Colin Rowe, Fred Koetter French edition of Collage City'.* Switzerland: Infolio.

Maki, Fumihiko (1965) 'Some thoughts on collective form', in G. Kepes (ed.) *Structure in Art and Science.* New York: Braziller.

Mangin, David (2004) *La Ville Franchisée. Formes et Structures de la Ville Contemporaine.* Paris: Éditions de la Villette.

May, Elaine T. (1999) *Homeward Bound: American Families in the Cold War Era.* New York: Basic Books.

Mbembe, Achille (2001) *On the Postcolony.* Berkeley: University of California Press.

—— (2004) 'The aesthetics of superfluity', in A. Mbembe and S. Nuttall (eds) *Johannesburg: The Elusive Metropolis.* Durham: Duke University Press.

McDonough, Challiss (2003) 'Refugees: Palestinians in Jordan', *Voice Of America News Report,* June 19.

www.globalsecurity.org/military/library/news/2003/06/mil-030620-33e4ce93.htm. Accessed June 25, 2008.

McGee, Terry G. (1991) 'The emergence of *Desakota* regions in Asia: expanding a hypothesis', in Norton Ginsburg, Bruce Koppel and Terry G. McGee (eds) *The Extended Metropolis: Settlement Transition in Asia*. Honolulu: University of Hawaii Press.

McGee, Terry G and Y.M. Yeung, (1977) *Hawkers in Southeast Asian Cities: Planning for the Bazaar Economy*. Ottawa: International Development Research Centre.

McGrath, Brian (2007) 'Bangkok: the architecture of three ecologies', in Kanu Agrawal, Melanie Domino, Edward Richardson and Brad M. Walters (eds) *Reurbanism: Transforming Captials*. New Haven: Perspecta 29, The Yale Architctural Journal.

—— (2008) *Digital Modelling for Urban Design*. London: John Wiley & Sons.

McGrath, Brian and Jean Gardner (2007) *Cinemetrics: Architectural Drawing Today*. London: John Wiley & Sons.

McGrath, Brian and David Grahame Shane (2005) *Sensing the 21st Century City: Close-up and Remote*. London: John Wiley & Sons.

McGrath, Brian, Victorial Marshall, M.L. Cadenasso, J.Morgan Grove, S.T.A. Pickett, Richard Plunz and Joel Towers (2007) *Designing Patch Dynamics*. New York: Columbia University Graduate School of Architecture, Planning and Preservation.

McHarg, Ian (1969) *Design with Nature*. New York: The Natural History Press.

Millard, Rachel and Antoine Faisal (2008) 'NYPD's highest ranking Arab American talks to Aramica', *Aramica* 6(126): 14–15.

Mumford, Lewis (1938) *The Culture of Cities*. New York: Harcourt Brace.

Munarin, Stefano and Maria Chiara Tosi (2001) *Tracce di Città*. Milano: Franco Angeli.

MVRDV (1999) *Meta City/Data Town*. Rotterdam: 010 Publishers.

Nakashima, Ellen (2008) 'US is tracking citizens at border checkpoints: data from checkpoints to be kept for 15 years', *The Washington Post*, August 20, A01.

Newman, David (2006) 'The resilience of territorial conflict in an era of globalization', in M. Kahler and B. F. Walter (eds) *Territoriality and Conflict in an Era of Globalization*. Cambridge: Cambridge University Press, 85–110.

Newman, Oscar (1972) *Defensible Space: Crime Prevention through Urban Design*. New York: Macmillan.

NYC (2002) 'Appointment of NYPD Deputy Commissioner of Intelligence', New York City Press Release-02-02, NYC.gov, January 24. www.nyc.gov/html/nypd/html/administration/intelligence_co.shtml. Accessed May 17, 2008.

NYC (2008) 'NYPD and Madrid police sign counter-terrorism policing agreement', New York City Press Release #PH02, NYC.gov, February 26. http://home2.nyc.gov/html/nypd/html/pr/pr_photo_2008_002.shtml. Accessed August 7, 2008.

NYC (2009) '68th Precinct profile', NYC.gov, www.nyc.gov/html/nypd/html/precincts/precinct_068.shtml. Accessed August 7, 2008.

Packard, George (2006) 'The megacity: Decoding the chaos of Lagos', *The New Yorker*, November 13. www.newyorker.com/archive/2006/11/13/061113fa_fact_packer. Accessed August 13, 2008.

Perlman, Janice (1976) *The Myth of Marginality: Urban Poverty and Politics in Rio de Janeiro*. Berkeley: University of California Press.

Piano Urbanistico del Trentino (1968) Padova: Marsilio.

Piccinato, Giorgio and Giuseppe De Luca (1983) 'Verso Una Nuova Città? Analisi Dei Processi di Diffusione Urbana', *Oltre Il Ponte* 2.

Piccinato, Giorgio, Vieri Quilici and Manfredo Tafuri (1962) 'La città territorio, verso una nuova dimensione', *Casabella Continuità* 270.

Pieterse, E. (2009) 'Deciphering city futures'. www.cluster.eu/v2/themes/pieterse/. Accessed March 20, 2009.

Porteous, J. Douglas and Sandra E. Smith (2001) *Domicide: The Global Destruction of Home*. Montreal: McGill-Queen's University Press.

Poster, Mark (1996) 'Database as discourse, or electronic interpellations', in P. Heelas, S. Lash and P. Morris (eds) *Detraditionalization*. Cambridge, MA: Blackwell, 277–293.

Prakash, Gyan (2002) 'The urban turn', Sarai Reader 02, 'The cities of everyday life', www.sarai.net/publications/readers/02-the-cities-of-everyday-life. Accessed March 20, 2009.

Priest, Dana (2004) 'Jet is an open secret in terror war', *The Washington Post*, December 27, A01.

Quaroni, Ludovico (1981) *La Città Fisica*. Roma-Bari: Laterza.

Raab, David (2007) *Terror in Black September*. New York: Palgrave Macmillan.

Rao, Vyjayanthi (2006) 'Slum as theory: The South-Asian city and globalization', *International Journal of Urban and Regional Research*. 30(1): 225–232.

Rappleye, Hannah (2008) 'Brooklyn's little Middle-East: Food and politics mix in Bay Ridge',

New School Free Press, April 30. Thenewcampus.org. Accessed August 7, 2008.

Raustiala, Kal (2006) 'The evolution of territoriality: international relations and American law', in M. Kahler and B.F. Walter (eds) *Territoriality and Conflict in an Era of Globalization*. Cambridge: Cambridge University Press, 219–250.

Robic, Maire-Claire (1998) 'Ville et région dans les échanges transatlantiques entre géographes de la première moitié du XX siècle: Convergences et Diversité des Expériences', *Finisterra* 33 (65).

Rossi, Aldo (1982 [1966]) *The Architecture of the City*. Cambridge, MA: MIT Press. (Translation of *L'architettura della Città*.)

Rowe, Colin and Fred Koetter (1978) *Collage City*. Cambridge, MA: MIT Press.

Roy, Ananya (2009) 'Civic governmentality: the politics of inclusion in Beirut and Mumbai', *Antipode* 41(1): 159–179.

Sachs, Susan (2002) 'Traces of terror: The detainees; US deports most of those arrested in sweeps after 9/11', *The New York Times*, 11 July.

Samonà, Giuseppe (1959 [1971 Second Edition]) *L'urbanistica e l'avvenire della Città Negli Stati Europei*. Bari: Laterza.

Sartore, Mariano (1988) 'Forme e processi di urbanizzazione diffusa. Un'analisi della morfologia insediativa in un'area rurale del veneto centrale', *Archivio Di Studi Urbani E Regionali* 32.

Sassen, Saskia (2000) *Cities in a World Economy*. Thousand Oaks: Pine Forge Press.

—— (2001 [1991]) *The Global City: New York, London, Tokyo*. Princeton: Princeton University Press.

—— (2006) *Territory, Authority, Rights: From Medieval To Global Assemblages*. Princeton: Princeton University Press.

Sattherwaite, David (2008) unpublished correspondence with section editors.

Sbarro (2007) *About Us*. Sbarro website. www.sbarro.com/aboutus/aboutus.php. Accessed 31 December 2008.

Schultz, Helena L. (2003) *The Palestinian Diaspora: Formation of Identities and Politics of Homeland*. New York: Routledge.

Schumacher, Ernst Friedrich (1973) *Small Is Beautiful: Economics as if People Mattered*. New York: Harper & Row.

Scott, James C. (1998) *Seeing Like a State*. New Haven: Yale University Press.

Secchi, Bernardo (1991) 'La Periferia', *Casabella* 583.

—— (2000) *Prima Lezione Di Urbanistica*. Bari-Roma: Laterza.

—— (2005) *La Città Del XX Secolo*. Bari-Roma: Laterza.

Secchi, Bernardo and Paola Viganò (2009) *Antwerp – Territory of a New Modernity*, Amsterdam: SUN.

Seymour, John and Herbert Giradet (1987) *Blueprint for a Green Planet: Your Practical Guide to Restoring the World's Environment*. New York: Prentice Hall.

Shaer, May (2000) 'The Use of Stone In Amman', unpublished paper, Conservation and Restoration Center in Petra (CARCIP). Archnet.org/library/documents/one-document.jsp?document_id=2585. Accessed June 26, 2008.

Shahbazi, Rudabeh (2007) 'The plight of Iraq's refugees', *Frontline/World*, WGBH Boston, September 14. www.pbs.org/frontlineworld/blog/2007/09/jordans_iraqi_r.html. Accessed June 28, 2008.

Shane, David G. (2005) *Recombinant Urbanism: Conceptual Modelling in Architecture, Urban Design, and City Theory*. Chichester: John Wiley & Sons.

Sheikh, Shahid (2004) 'New York City muslim families face increased risk of homelessness', *New America Media*, June 14. http://news.ncmonline.com/news/view_article.html?article_id=8d97fc54b4d71e3d9a15b011379ed304. Accessed May 17, 2008.

Sieverts, Thomas (2003 [1997]) *Cities Without Cities. An Interpretation of the Zwischenstadt*. London: Spon Press and New York: Routledge. (Translation of *Zwischenstadt*.)

Simmel, Georg (1903) 'The metropolis and mental life', reprinted in *The Blackwell City Reader*. London: Wiley-Blackwell (2002), 11–19.

Simone, AbdouMaliq (2004) *For the City Yet to Come: Changing African Life in Four Cities*. Durham: Duke University Press.

—— (2007) 'At the frontier of the urban periphery'. Sarai Reader 07: 'Frontiers', www.sarai.net/publications/readers/07-frontiers/. Accessed March 20, 2009.

—— (2009) *City Life from Jakarta to Dakar: Movements at the Crossroads*. New York & London: Routledge.

Smets, Marcel (1987) 'La Belgique ou la Banlieue Radieuse', in *Paysage d'Architectures*, Exhibition Catalogue, Fondation de l'Architecture, Brussels.

Sohn, Elke (2007) 'Organicist concepts of city landscape in German planning after the Second World War', *Landscape Research* 32(4): 499–523.

Soja, Edward W. (1989) *Postmodern Geographies: The Reassertion of Space in Critical Social Theory*. London/New York: Verso.

—— (2000) *Postmetropolis: Critcal Studies of Cities and Regions*. Malden: Blackwell Publishers.

Spengler, Oswald (1937) *The Decline of the West*. New York: A.A. Knopf. (Translation of *Der Untergang des Abendlandes*, 1918–1922.)

Spivak, Gayatri Chakravorty (1987) *In Other Worlds: Essays in Cultural Politics*. New York: Routledge.

Stoler, Ann Laura (1995) *Race and the Education of Desire: Foucault's History of Sexuality and the Colonial Order of Things*. Durham: Duke University Press.

Swarns, Rachel L. (2003). 'Thousands of Arabs and muslims could be deported, officials say', *The New York Times* June 7.

Talhami, Ghada H. (2003) *Palestinian Refugees: Pawns to Political Actors*. New York: Nova Science Publishers, Inc.

Taylor, Peter (1995) *Geographies of Global Change: Mapping the World in the Late Twentieth Century*. Oxford: Blackwell.

Taylor, Jonathan and Chris Jasparo (2004) 'Editorials and geopolitical explanations for 11 September', in S.D. Brunn (ed.) *11 September and Its Aftermath: The Geopolitics of Terror*. London: Frank Cass, 217–252.

Tongchai, Winichakul (1994) *Siam Mapped: A History of the Geo-body of a Nation*. Honolulu: University of Hawaii Press.

Tönnies, Ferdinand (1887) *Gemeinschaft und Gesellschaft*. Leipzig: O.R. Reislad.

Tschumi, Bernard (1981) *Manhattan Transcripts*. London: Academy Editions.

Turner, John (1977) *Housing by People: Towards Autonomy in Building Environments*. New York: Pantheon Books.

Ungers, Oswald Mathias (1976) 'Planning criteria', *Lotus International* 11.

Ungers, Oswald Mathias et al. (1978) 'Die Stadt in der Stadt. Berlin Das Grüne Stadtarchipel', *Lotus International* 19.

UN Habitat, H. Peter Oberlander (ed.) (2006) *Initiatives, 1976–2006: Turning Ideas into Action: The World Urban Forum*. Vancouver: Centre for Human Settlements, University of British Columbia.

UNRWA (2008) 'Jordan refugee camp profile'. Website of United Nations Relief and Works Agency. www.un.org/unrwa/refugees/jordan.html. Accessed June 28, 2008.

US DoD (1998) *C4isr Architecture Working Group Final Report*. Washington, DC: US Department of Defense. www.fas.org/irp/program/core/fnlrprt.pdf. Accessed May 15, 2008.

US DoJ (2003) *The September 11 Detainees: A Review of the Treatment of Aliens Held on Immigration Charges in Connection with the Investigation of the September 11 Attacks*. Washington, DC: US Department of Justice Office of the Inspector General. www.usdoj.gov/oig/special/0306/index.htm. Accessed August 11, 2008.

—— (2007) *Shahawar Matin Siraj Sentenced to Thirty Years of Imprisonment for Conspiring to Place Explosives at the 34th Street Subway Station in New York*. Washington, DC: US Department of Justice. www.doj.gov/siraj_pr.pdf. Accessed April 16, 2008.

Veltz, Pierre (1996) *Mondialisation, Villes et Territoires: Une Économie d'Archipel*. Paris: PUF.

Venturi, Robert, Denise Scott-Brown and Steven Izenour (1972) *Learning from Las Vegas*. Cambridge, MA: MIT Press.

Viganò, Paola (1999) *La Città Elementare*. Milano: Skira.

—— (2001) 'Un Projetto per Il Territorio'/'A Territorial Project', in *Territori Della Nuova Modernità/ Territories of a New Modenity*. Napoli: Electa.

—— (ed.) (2004) *New Territories, Q2*. Roma: Officina.

—— (2010) *I territori dell'urbanistica. Il Progetto Come Produttore di Conoscenza*. Roma: Officina.

Wallerstein, Immanuel (2004) *World-Systems Analysis: An Introduction*. Durham: Duke University Press.

Wells, Herbert George (1901) *Anticipations of the Reaction of Mechanical and Scientific Progress upon Human Life and Thought*. London: Chapman & Hall.

Young, Jock (1999) *The Exclusive Society: Social Exclusion, Crime And Difference In Late Modernity*. London: Sage.

40

Housing

Iain Low

The twenty-first century has realised the urbanization of fifty percent of the world's population, of whom almost half live in so-called 'informal settlements'. This substantial proportion of the world's population is essentially 'homeless', being marginalized from formal economic systems and excluded from the fundamental transactions that enable an everyday life of a standard that might be expected in a modern, globalizing world. Seldom capable of breaking from their

Figure 40.1 (Below) San Miguel de la Vega, Caracas, Venezuela (1998–2001). View from upgraded neighbourhood to Caracas. (Mateo and Matias Pinto D'Lacoste)

socio-economic situation, they build on land that is occupied illegally and use found materials for their dwellings. They have little choice. Many have migrated to the city looking for opportunities for work.

Such informal settlements are often located on the urban periphery, on the 'badlands' of the poorest neighbourhoods, on wastelands adjacent to industry, or on other marginal areas such as wetlands or railway reserves. Informal settlements are generally high density, low-rise buildings in a disorderly sprawl. They characteristically comprise almost entirely residential constructions and most economic activity is 'incidental' and predominantly home-based. Informal settlements are limited in every aspect. Their communities have no land title, little access to basic urban infrastructures (sanitation, power), supportive services (such as education or health facilities), or satisfactory employment. These settlements are outside of everything that constitutes normal life in modern civil society. The inhabitants of such settlements are often young, usually unemployed,

Figure 40.2 (Below left and right – drawing) San Miguel de la Vega, Caracas. Plan. (Mateo and Matias Pinto D'Lacoste)

Figure 40.3 (Below left and right – photographs) San Miguel de la Vega, Caracas. Pedestrian traffic along main thoroughfare. (Mateo and Matias Pinto D'Lacoste)

Figure 40.4 (Opposite top) San Miguel de la Vega, Caracas. Infrastructure diagram. (Mateo and Matias Pinto D'Lacoste)

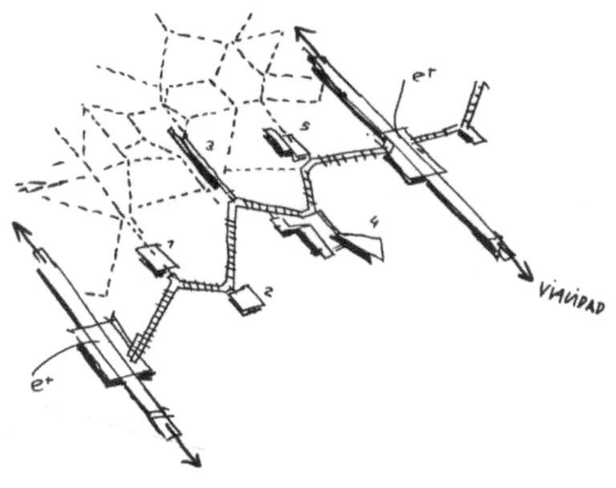

and have slender chances of ever entering the formal economy. They dwell qualitatively and quantitatively below the breadline. The result is a people locked in a cycle of poverty, whose circumstance compounds with each new generation and daily in-migration. Furthermore, these living conditions are full of uncertainty and instability. This is a mode of urban living that is associated with the highest levels of social and economic risk.

Local community responses to these conditions has given rise to innovative building strategies of various kinds, ranging from vertical extensions, the adding of backyard rooms for extended families and/or rental, and the construction of frontyard shops. Under such conditions, where every piece of open ground is under pressure to be used or built upon, public collective space becomes a luxury. With such intensive informal use these settlements are under continuous threat of disaster in the form of fire, disease and crime, including gangsterism. Such living conditions mean these

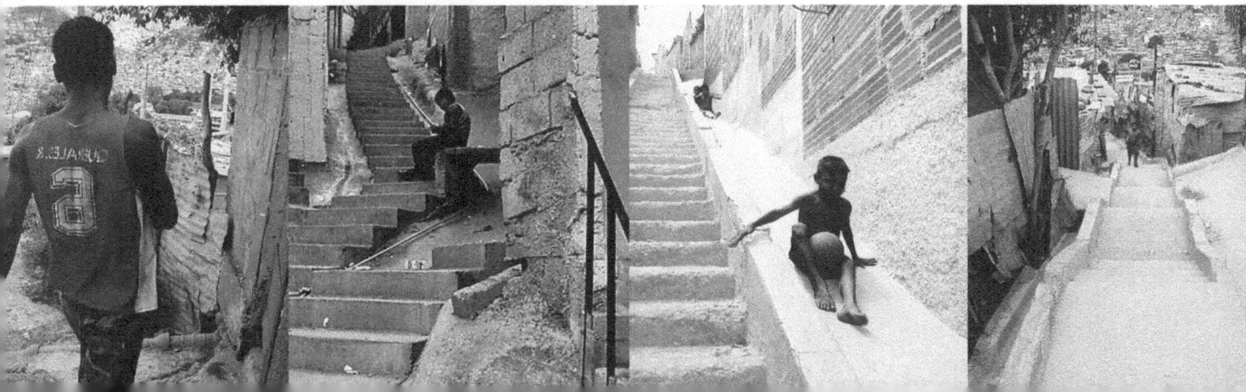

settlements and their populations are vulnerable to political and other exploitation. And the unpredictability experienced in all aspects of life is unconducive to the development of a sense of community and the associated vital urban culture that is supportive of civil society. The imaginative resolution of this phenomenon is a challenge that faces governments and civil society agencies in most developing countries. What follows are the outlines of three architectural interventions that engage with this kind of challenge (Low, 2005).

SAN MIGUEL DE LA VEGA, CARACAS, VENEZUELA (1998–2001)

Conceptualised by the Ministry of Urban Development, the Caracas Slum-Upgrading Project (CAMEBA) was intended to identify contiguous settlement areas for consolidation.

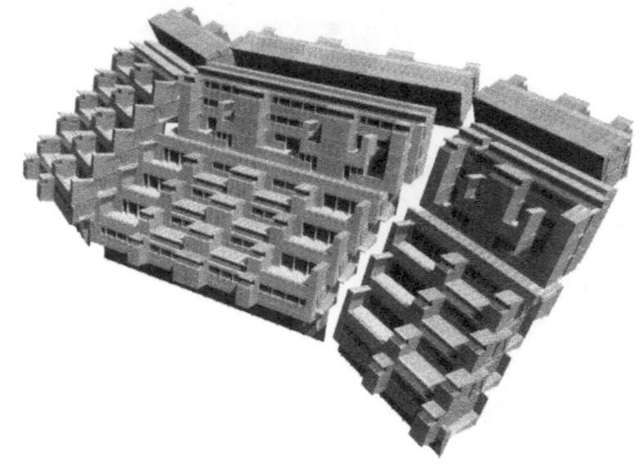

A government-sponsored Sectorial Plan comprised guidelines for neighbourhood scale renewal in order to: (1) effect infrastructure upgrade to the barrios; (2) support local institutional development; and (3) fund financing for home improvements.

The Project was commissioned jointly by the National Housing Institute in Venezuela (CONAVI) and Hidrocapital, the local water commission. It was funded, in part, through a loan from the World Bank. The pilot schemes at La Vega presented the Pinto brothers' architectural team with the opportunity of intelligent experimentation. The upgrading strategy proposed a shift from previous 'slum-clearance' toward an in-situ, bottom-up, people-centred process. By being in-situ it mitigated against the costs associated with upgrading that entails the resettlement of entire communities. Being in-situ also guarded against the concomitant loss of social communality that can accompany relocation. This Urban Pilot Project involves upgrading in-situ as a way of integrating an informal component into the larger order of Caracas (Pinto D'Lacoste M & M, 2003).

Figure 40.5 (Opposite left) San Miguel de la Vega, Caracas. Computer model for terraced structure. (Mateo and Matias Pinto D'Lacoste)

Figure 40.6 (Below left) San Miguel de la Vega, Caracas. New infrastructure. (Mateo and Matias Pinto D'Lacoste)

Figure 40.7 (Below) Mansel Road, Durban, KwaZulu-Natal, South Africa (1993–1995). (Harber Masson Associates)

One issue faced in the upgrade at La Vega was the unique topographic conditions. The barrio is on a steep slope and one problem was linking its upper and lower reaches. The overall upgrade comprised a number of building projects that were linked by a vertical access system. This was realized through intervention in the existing interior pedestrian systems that organize the settlement. Difficulty in accessing individual dwellings, severe problems with rainwater run-off, poor light penetration, ventilation and visibility, and the absence of collective social space, have been creatively addressed through these interventions.

Working directly with the community afforded a means for careful urban renewal and resulted in an urban intervention that

synthesized engineering with architectural work. The interventions also created new inventive relationships between infrastructure and culture. For example, the interventions made pedestrian access within the barrio easier and therefore afforded new opportunities for chance encounters between residents. The creation of multiple extended platforms enabled contiguous land parcels to be assembled, which could then be used for collective services such as a children's playground. The strategic placement of these platforms meant that they overlapped with movement routes, generally encouraging social interaction.

Budget constraints meant that the upgrade followed a limited formal palette. However, its successful in-situ application adds credence to the suitability of a stripped-down-to-essentials architecture in such contexts. For example, the casting of simple concrete platforms, steps, retaining walls and water channels, have evolved an integrated membrane capable of serving the community in multiple ways.

Similar ingenuity has been applied in the design and implementation of 'Casa Comunal', the La Vega Community Centre. Maximizing opportunity within the constraints of limited available open space, this project is strategically sited at the topographical 'base' of the La Vega barrio. Being located in this way allows the building to establish a threshold between the informal settlement and the local industrial area and act simultaneously as 'bridge and gateway' between the community and the wider urban metropolis. Housing a major sports court on its upper level, the building is supported by two levels of practice areas, with meeting rooms below. Together with the ancillary services and ablutions, this ambitious community facility has integrated well with difficult surroundings (Verna, 2003).

A third intervention in this upgrading involved the construction of an extended

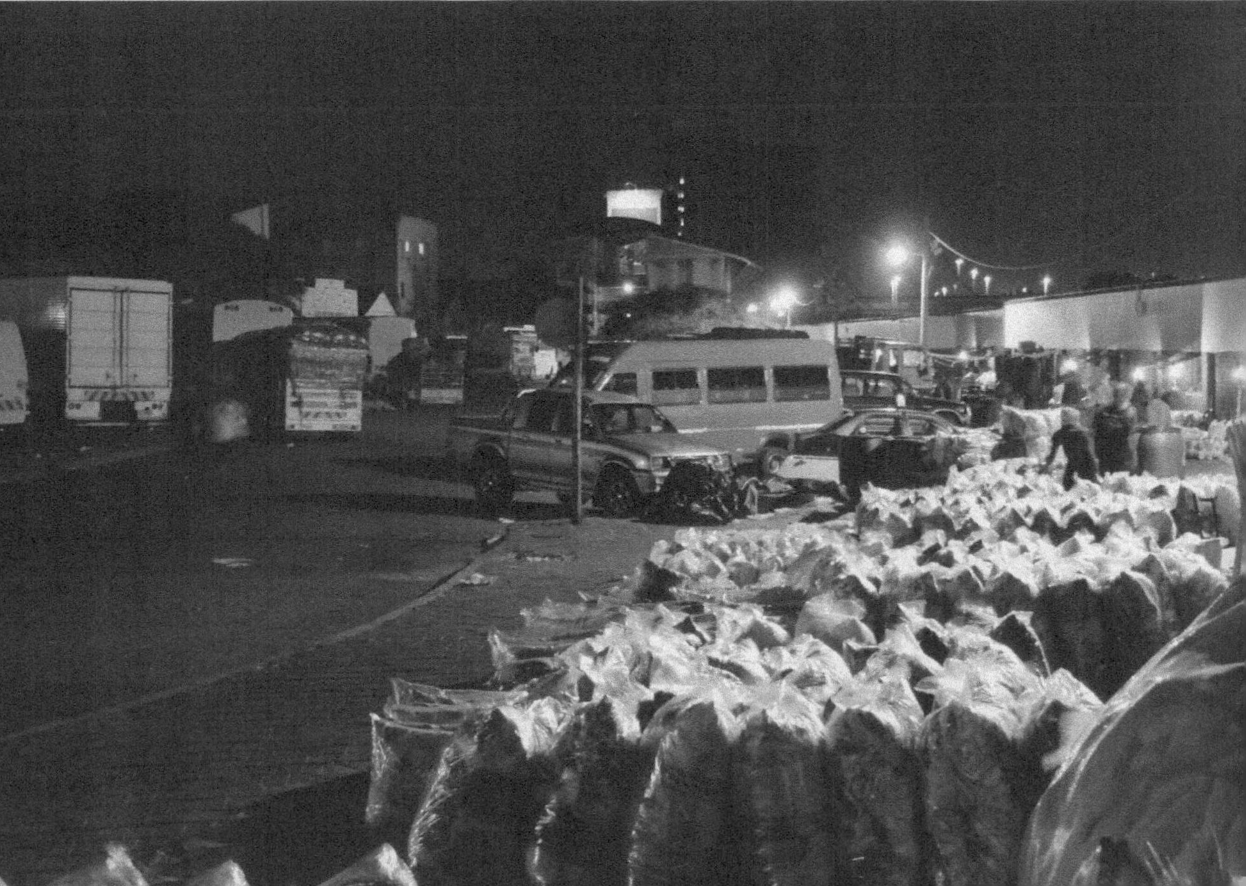

landscape to accommodate the needs of the barrio community to expand. Based on a re-interpretation of the complex occupational patterns, a re-configured ground has been produced. This builds upon an interpretation of the barrio as vertical access system and through it the inhabitants are presented with an extended or thickened groundplane. An innovative 3D structure is capable of accommodating and ordering complex occupational patterns. Through a simple sectional strategy, a series of platforms, supported by a steel frame, begin to describe a system of spaces whose potential lies in their capacity for multiple infill options.

This is an architectural intervention that mediates between specificity and indeterminacy. The outcome was intended to produce a living organism that hovers between the irregular logics of the barrio and the rationality of the tower in the park. It has sought to offer new ways to meet the flexible needs of barrio families. The approach is conclusively resolved in the 2001 La Ladera Block Housing Solution project designed by atelier Pinto for the San Miguel de La Vega barrio.

Figures 40.8 (Below left) and 40.9 (Below) Mansel Road, Durban, KwaZulu Natal, South Africa (1993–1995). (Harber Masson Associates)

MANSEL ROAD, DURBAN, KWAZULU-NATAL, SOUTH AFRICA (1993–1995)

Mansel Road is a feeder road adjacent to railway sidings on the outskirts of Durban's central business district. It leads to Block AK, a portion of land remaining following the demolition of a residential area, previously occupied mainly by Indians. It was demolished by the government of the

previous Afrikaner Nationalist Party under their 'forced removal' strategy to sanitise the built environment for 'whites only'.

Durban, the port and trading capital of the KwaZulu-Natal province in South Africa, is home to the largest Indian community outside of India. Their ancestors were indentured under colonial rule to work the sugarfields. Durban is also a highly desirable shopping destination for rural communities. Since the early 1980s, chartered buses have regularly ferried rural women from the hinterlands surrounding Durban to shop in the city. Elected by their village communities, these women are entrusted with considerable savings to purchase essential supplies in bulk. Purchases include durable plastic watertanks, cast iron pots and galvanized containers.

Typically such journeys take place over a weekend with buses arriving in the city close to midnight. Exhausted drivers have claimed Block AK as their resting place, sleeping aboard their buses until called upon to return the following afternoon. The frequency

Figure 40.10 (Above) Iquique, Chile. Aravena, Tomas Cortese, Equipo Arquitectura. Unoccuplied completed housing units. (Victor Oddo)

Figures 40.11 (Below) and 40.12 (Below right) Iquique, Chile. Aravena, Tomas Cortese, Equipo Arquitectura. Participatory design session. (Victor Oddo)

of these shopping visits and the demands by bus drivers looking for a rest stop, has led traders in the vicinity of Block AK to move to the sidewalk adjacent to the bus station. Covering their drum merchandise with tarpaulins, this area of 'temp' dwellings has now become a permanent settlement. This informal settlement posed a health and safety risk to residents and traders alike. Consequently, in 1993, the city commissioned South African practice Harber, Masson and Associates to 'solve the problem' of what had come to be known as the 'drum ladies'.

The first task was to understand the situation as infrastructure. A detailed measured 1:50 drawing identified forty-four units, one tap and two chemical toilets. This initial survey work enabled the architects to get closer to the community and better comprehend the situation. It revealed to them, and the city agencies, that a vibrant and cohesive community of women traders had established itself in and around these shopping trips. It was determined that a conventional design that sought to formalize what existed in-situ would have been inappropriate. Relocating the bus station would be the only way to relocate these women, and in so doing re-establish the community on a firmer footing.

The City of Durban has a long tradition of experimentation with urban renewal. Unlike other local metropolitan councils in South Africa, its Architectural Branch appears to have benefited from a more enlightened approach to positive collaboration. The Planning, Economic Development and Building branches seem to operate within a developmental framework, seeking constructive alliances, rather than preserving individual departmental autonomies. This form of collaboration is necessary to effect change for the marginalised.

The design phase included a series of 'in-loco' workshops. Out of this came a

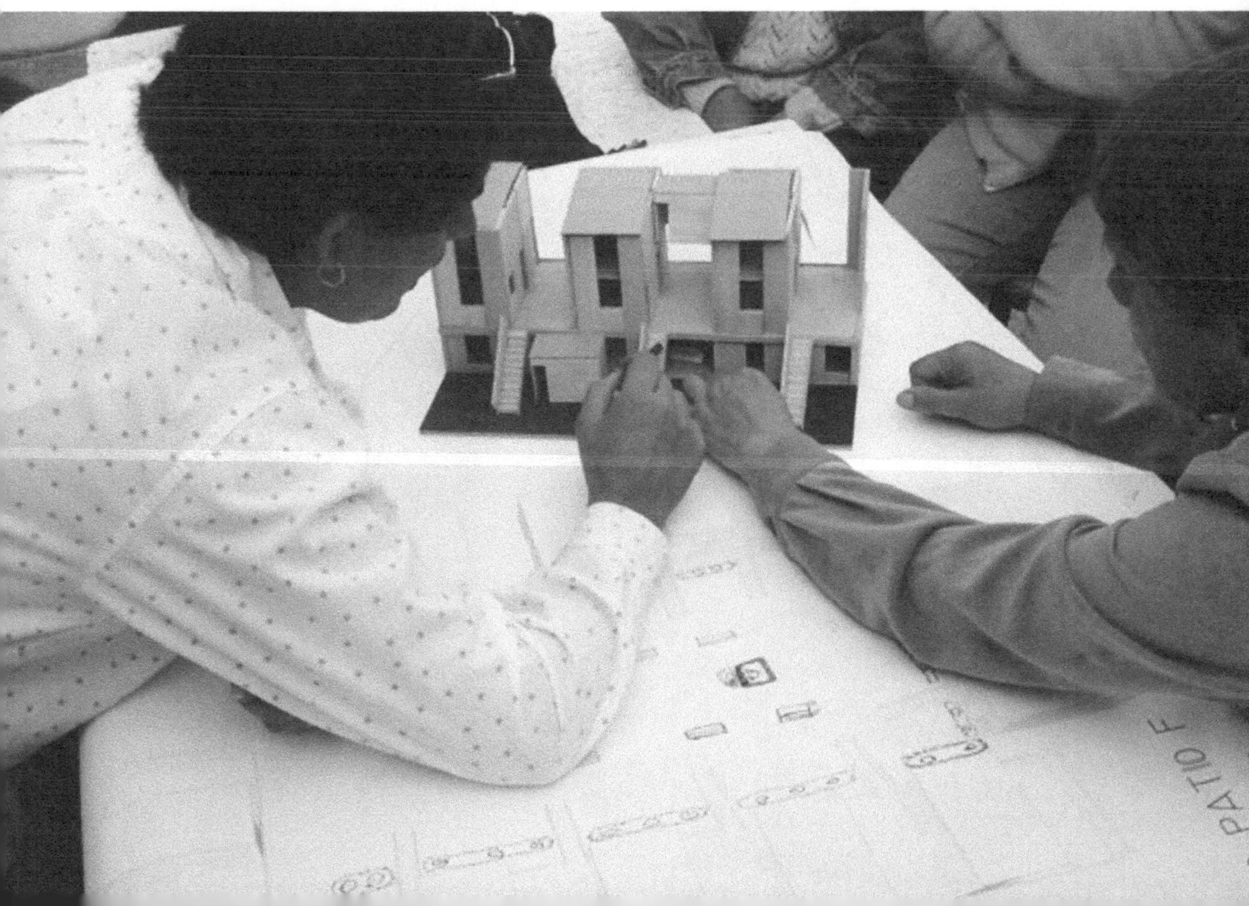

compromise of urban facility and unit layouts. The scheme incorporated not simply dwelling units, but a set of components that acted as a first phase for a unique new inner-city settlement. Catering to diverse users, the scheme also included a convenience store, the equivalent of the 'corner store', public toilets and showers and a communal bathhouse. These facilities support what the designers conceived of as 'crossings'. Firstly, these facilities are centrally sited. A tower marks a fork in the settlement and identifies the 'convenience store' where social exchange occurs. Uniquely, the store proprietor pays the city rent, but is then cleverly contractually obligated to manage and administer the public ablution facility. Entry to the showers is by means of coupons that operate hot water supplied from roof solar panels, which is subsequently recycled to flush custom built toilets.

Adjacent to this central feature is a row of live/work dwelling units, designed to replace the 'drum ladies' sidewalk shelters. Negotiating public/private life, they are staggered, comprising a retail shop outlet at the front, and a rear residential unit, mediated by an open courtyard in-between. The front unit contains a small internal ablution block, serving both enclosed spaces. The resultant ensemble provides one of the most provocative responses to an interpretation of traditional rural life within the emerging globalising city. At the front, a wide sidewalk enables trade spill-over into the public domain whilst the flat roof suggests ease of future vertical extension.

Other functional components of this development include an extensive covered terrain prepared for carboot-salespeople, in order to

Figures 40.13 (Below) and 40.14 (Below right) Iquique, Chile. Occupied housing units. (Victor Oddo)

relocate and incorporate further groups of informal traders. Operating out of pick-ups and private vehicles, they successfully exploit the transient nature of marginality. This component offers another commercial element and assists in the longer term establishment of a mini agora, and provides economic opportunity for disempowered people, relieving the growing need for welfare assistance in urban areas. A transitional overnight housing unit serves the bus drivers and itinerant traders (Harber, Undated notes).

QUINTA MONROY, IQUIQUE, CHILE (2002–2004)

The project 'Elemental Chile' represents an amplified form of agency which demonstrates a viable and meaningful alternative way to engage with the predicament of urban marginality. It showcases Design Build Research (DBR) as a tool for the investigation of housing solutions with meaningful socio-economic outcomes. Elemental Chile grew out of a desire to find innovative ways to address the growing housing crisis in Chile. It offers a contemporary update on the historic relationship between avant-garde architectural design and low-income housing solutions. For example, drawing from predecessor examples such as Germany's Weissenhofsiedlung of 1927 and Peru's Previ-Lima initiative of 1967, Elemental Chile sought to offer a third proposition. With support from the Chilean government, the proposal was to initiate a new movement of avant-garde housing design, and to do so by way of an international architectural competition. With the aim of soliciting the best architecture and urban design, seven architects would design and implement seven exemplary housing projects, each of a couple of hundred units, on seven sites throughout Chile. The challenge was to conceive of

low- cost, innovative technologies that could offer design solutions to the structural security of poor housing. The schemes should also adhere to principles of community participation and assume collaboration with families during pre- and post-implementation phases. Showcasing top quality design married with technological innovation and progressive developmental practices, these schemes demonstrate genuine alternatives to questions of housing the poor in developing contexts.

By way of demonstration, Elemental Chile brought together a unique collaboration of different participants to solve the situation of local residents at one of the sites in Quinta Monroy, Iquique, in Northern Chile. Collaborators included academic practitioners from the Harvard GSD and the Schools of Architecture and Engineering, Harvard's David Rockefeller Centre of Latin American Studies, as well as the Program of Public Policies at the Universidad Catolica de Chile. It also included government agencies such as the Housing Ministry of Chile (MINVU), together with leading Chilean construction companies (Pizarreno Companies, Cements Bio-Bio and Sodimac). Finally it brought on board various other social institutions such as Techos para Chile and Habita para la Humanidad. It was supported by Fondef/ CONICYT of the Chilean government. This collaboration constituted an amended form of design, implementation and delivery through the creation of an integrating agency. Based as it was on university-linked collaboration, the programme had the unique capacity to interrogate design through research speculation. A horizontal organizational structure maximized networks across all possible interfaces, particularly with respect to the empowerment of community.

Elemental Chile architect, Alejandro Aravena, reflected on how the brief issued by the Chilean government for the project in the desert city of Iquique was expressed through a clear quantitative pragmatism. The government conceptualized the problem thus: to re-settle one hundred families on the same 5,000 m^2 site that they had illegally occupied for the last thirty years. This had to be achieved by working within the framework of the current housing policy and utilizing the US$7,500 subsidy which had to pay for the land, infrastructure and architecture. Despite the site's expensive price the aim was to re-settle the families in the same site, instead of displacing them to the periphery.

Chilean architects face similar spatial and typological demands. The autonomy of the one-house/one-site model has predominated in people's perception of what formal housing should be. If, in addressing this question, one starts assuming one house=one family= one plot, one would have been only able to accommodate about thirty families on this site. The problem of individual houses is that autonomy incurs severe inefficiencies in terms of land use, infrastructure provision and socialization. This is one of the primary reasons that social housing projects are forced to look for land that costs so little and, because of that, are inevitably located far from the urban areas that offer opportunities of employment, education, recreation, transportation and health care. A universal consequence of this is that most social housing schemes are located in marginal and impoverished urban areas. The result is a zoning of mono-functional sprawl that constructs realms of resentment, characterized by social conflict and inequity wherein community is constantly in a state of struggle.

Elemental's first initiative was to conceive of the problem differently. They shifted the mindset from the logic of the quantitative (Aravena aims for the best possible US$7,500 object to be multiplied a hundred times over) to the logic of the qualitative (the best possible US$750,000 building capable of accommodating one hundred families and their long-term expansion and needs). They conceived of the house not as a completed object but as a start for user-based growth. For example, they specified a new typology of space, this being the 'in-between': on the one hand the space between units (horizontal adjacency) and the space between ground level and top floor (vertical adjacency). Designing a start-up building that had just a partial ground and top floor, Elemental Chile envisioned social housing as an ongoing investment and not as a one-off expense. The devised system utilizes the initial subsidy to provide a basis for the adding of value over time.

It is estimated that about fifty percent of each unit's eventual volume will be self-built. As such, the building has to be porous, enabling expansion within the envelope of the structure. The initial building needed to provide a supporting, rather than a constraining framework, in order to avoid any negative effects of self-build on the urban environment over time, whilst facilitating the process of orderly expansion.

In designing like this, the architects managed to identify a housing solution by which a unit can increase its value over time, well within the value constraints of the start-up government subsidy. Also by achieving a sufficient density, without overcrowding, it was possible to use a more costly, centrally located site that was better able to hold and increase in value over time.

Related to this longer-term viability, is the provision of a physical space for the 'extended family'. As is known in poorer contexts, the well-being and sustainability of households often depends on the economic and social benefits of the extended family. For example, in between the private and public space exists a collective space (a common property with restricted access) which supports the formation of an intermediate level of association between the households and others. Finally, instead of designing a tight and contained 30 m^2 house, Elemental provided the domestic infrastructure that could cope with the larger, 'middle-income' 72 m^2 house anticipated.

Of course, when funding is enough for just a part of a house as was the case here, a key question becomes which part does one construct first? Elemental chose to design and built the portion of the domestic dwelling that a family individually would never be able to achieve on their own. This offers an inspirational model for how designers might reconceive of their contribution toward non-architectural questions such as overcoming poverty. What Elemental Chile has brought to the question of housing is multi-dimensional. There are clear and direct lessons for others to reflect upon. Elemental Chile might be a site/country specific experiment, but it posits a template for how to approach housing design in any number of contexts. These approaches might be set out under the following three headings: (1) Design as Agency. Innovation occurs best under supportive conditions. In the case of Iquique, conventional models of delivery were reconfigured. A cross-disciplinary, inter-departmental design-led collaboration enabled the integration of the various concerns (professional, community, government, contractor) in the housing development process. (2) Design as Mediator. Elemental has identified that innovation requires spatial re-configuration; the physical fabric has a direct effect in empowering community. (3) Design as Capacitator. Community is a product of the co-dependency between the physical and social dimensions of settlement. The assimilation and development of existing human capacity is fundamental, and becomes the single most important foundation for successful work (Aravena, 2004).

CONCLUSION

The projects highlighted here remind us of the necessity for the design imagination in social housing provision to extend into questions of agency, innovation, inquiry and practice. The global imperative to upgrade squatter settlements and enfold 'slums' into the formal sector presents an opportunity for such imaginative thinking. Any move toward creatively engaging with such informal settlements needs to move away from the strictures of scientific/

governmental rationality. To do so requires a radical but complementary change in method. This is probably one of the most challenging aspects in architecture's efforts to evolve resilient urban housing forms for human sustainability.

ACKNOWLEDGEMENTS

I thank Mateo Pinto, Alejandro Aravena and Rodney Harber and their colleagues for the generous hospitality and open sharing of information, images and texts, upon which this article is reliant.

BIBLIOGRAPHY

Aravenas, A (2004) 'On Public Service'; *Harvard Design Magazine* Fall 2004/Winter 2005: 21.

Harber, R, Architect's notes on Mansel Road.

Low, Iain (2005) 'Space and Transformation: 10 Years 10 Buildings; in Space and Transformation 10 years of Democracy', *Digest of South African Architecture* 9: 5.

Pinto D'Lacoste, Mateo and Matias Pinto D'Lacoste (2003) 'Casa Comunal – Urban Upgrading: A new community center in the barrios of Caracas', *Praxis* 5: 72–77.

—— (2005) 'Casa Comunal + Gimnas Vertical [Community Centre + Vertical Gymnasium]', *Quaderns* 248: 64–68.

—— (2007) Personal Portfolio and summary of design projects and built works.

Verna, Inna (2003) 'Urban upgrading: A new community center in the barrios of Carracas: Matias and Mateo Pinto', *Praxis* 5: 72–77.

Index

Introductory Note

References such as "178–9" indicate (not necessarily continuous) discussion of a topic across a range of pages. Wherever possible in the case of topics with many references, these have either been divided into sub-topics or only the most significant discussions of the topic are listed. Because the entire work is about 'architecture' the use of this term (and certain others which occur constantly throughout the book) as an entry point has been minimized. Information will be found under the corresponding detailed topics.